INVESTMENTS: Analysis and Management

7TH EDITION

INVESTMENTS

Analysis and Management

Charles P. Jones

North Carolina State University

John Wiley & Sons, Inc.

NEW YORK CHICHESTER WEINHEIM BRISBANE TORONTO SINGAPORE

EDITOR	Marissa Ryan
DIRECTOR OF MARKETING	Steve Kraham
COVER DESIGN	Harry Nolan
COVER ILLUSTRATION	Norm Christiansen
INTERIOR DESIGN	Meryl Levavi/Digitext
ILLUSTRATION COORDINATOR	Anna Melhorn
OUTSIDE PRODUCTION MANAGEMENT	UG / GGS Information Services, Inc.

This book was set in Berkeley by UG / GGS Information Services, Inc. and printed and bound by RR Donnelley/ Willard. The cover was printed by Lehigh Press.

Recognizing the importance of preserving what has been written, it is a policy of John Wiley & Sons, Inc. to have books of enduring value published in the United States printed on acid-free paper, and we exert our best efforts to that end.

The paper in this book was manufactured by a mill whose forest management programs include sustained yield harvesting of its timberlands. Sustained yield harvesting principles ensure that the numbers of trees cut each year does not exceed the amount of new growth.

Library of Congress Cataloging in Publication Data:

Jones, Charles Parker, 1943–
Investments analysis and management / c Charles P. Jones—7th ed.
p. cm.
Includes bibliographical references and index.
ISBN 0-471-33114-7
1. Investments. 2. Investment analysis. I. Title.
HG4521.J663 1999
332.6 21—dc21 99-046667
CIP

Printed in the United States of America

10 9 8 7 6 5 4 3 2 1

DEDICATION

To Kay and Kathryn,

for making every year special

Preface

Why should you care about investing? Just consider the large annual stock returns since 1995 as well as the accelerating trend to self-directed retirement programs with more and more workers deciding which assets to hold in their retirement accounts. To succeed in this environment, you need to understand the fundamentals of investing.

Investors are being deluged with information, and they must learn how to sift through and evaluate this information overload. Today more than 10,000 web sites are devoted to investing information and their number grows daily. Bad advice abounds, the Internet is unregulated, and scammers are on the phone constantly trying to lure unsophisticated investors. You can protect yourself by learning essential investing facts.

We live in a fast-changing world. While terminology and trading mechanisms may change, learning to carefully analyze and evaluate investment opportunities will pay off under any circumstances. You can become a smart investor with reasonable efforts because this text covers the basic terminology and techniques and shows you how to evaluate investment opportunities in a concise, readable, and efficient manner.

GOALS OF THE TEXT

Investments: Analysis and Management is designed to provide a firm understanding of the field of investments while stimulating interest in this fascinating subject. My goals in writing this text are to help you

(1) to understand what the investment opportunities are
(2) to make good investment decisions
(3) to recognize where investment problems and controversies arise and to know how to deal with them.

Also, this text specifically focuses on Internet investing, highlighting the important resources on the Internet and allowing readers to become comfortable with using the Internet as an integral part of their investment activities.

This text is self-contained and designed for readers with varying backgrounds. It assumes the standard prerequisite courses generally in statistics, basic accounting, economics, financial management. However, I have sought to minimize formulas and to simplify difficult material in a presentation that is consistent with current ideas and practices. Relevant, state-of-the-art material has been simplified and structured specifically for the reader's benefit.

The emphasis in this text is on readability—making investments material more readily accessible, as well as interesting and thoughtful to the beginner. *What is most important for you to gain from this text is the desire and ability to make good investing decisions!*

ORGANIZATION OF THE TEXT

This edition is built around the approach that you don't cover something until you need to, and you cover only what is critical to understand the important issues. Unnecessary detail, and advanced topics, are left for a later day. The text is divided into eight parts for organizational purposes—organized around background, returns and basic portfolio theory, the analysis of different types of securities (four parts), modern investment theory, and portfolio management.

Part One provides the background everyone needs before delving into the specifics of security analysis and portfolio management. The goal of this introductory set of chapters is to familiarize beginners with an overview of what investing is all about. After a general discussion of the subject in Chapter 1, the next four chapters describe the variety of securities available when investing directly, investing indirectly (investment companies), the markets in which they are traded, and the mechanics of securities trading.

Part Two is concerned with an analysis of returns and risk, along with the basics of portfolio theory and capital market theory. Chapter 6 contains a careful and complete analysis of the important concepts of risk and return that dominate any discussion of investments. Chapter 7 contains a complete discussion of expected return and risk for both individual securities and portfolios. The primary emphasis is on the essentials of Markowitz portfolio theory. Furthermore, beta, systematic and nonsystematic risk, and the CAPM are introduced in Chapter 7 in order that these important concepts (which are all you really need) can be used throughout the course.

Parts Three and Four focus on the basics of valuation (and therefore the fundamentals of security analysis) by presenting "how-to" tools and techniques for bonds and stocks respectively. Part Three examines the analysis, valuation, and management of bonds, a logical starting point in learning how to value securities. Part Four builds on these concepts in discussing the analysis, valuation, and management of common stocks. Chapter 12 explains the Efficient Market Hypothesis and provides some insights into the controversy surrounding this topic.

Part Five is, like Part Four, devoted to common stocks, a reasonable allocation given investor interest in common stocks. ***Part Five covers fundamental analysis, the heart of security analysis.*** Because of its scope and complexity, three chapters are required to adequately cover the fundamental approach based on the top-down approach. Technical analysis is also covered.

Part Six discusses the other major securities available to investors, derivative securities. Chapter 17 analyzes options (puts and calls), a popular investment alternative in recent years. Stock index options also are covered. Chapter 18 is devoted to financial futures, an important topic in investments. Investors can use these securities to hedge their positions and reduce the risk of investing.

Part Seven contains additional details covering portfolio theory and capital market theory. Chapter 19 continues the discussion of portfolio concepts by concentrating on portfolio selection, based on the concept of efficient portfolios. The separation theorem and systematic and nonsystematic risk are discussed. Chapter 20 discusses capital market theory, a natural extension of portfolio theory. This discussion is divided between the Capital Asset Pricing Model and Arbitrage Pricing Theory.

Finally, ***Part Eight concludes the text with a discussion of portfolio management and the issue of evaluating portfolio performance.*** Chapter 21 is structured around the Association for Investment Management and Research's approach to portfolio management as a process. Chapter 22 is a logical conclusion to the entire book because all investors are keenly interested in how well their investments have performed. Mutual funds are used as examples of how to apply these portfolio performance measures and how to interpret the results.

SPECIAL FEATURES

This text offers several important features, some of which are unique. These features will help you learn how to invest more quickly and easily.

FLEXIBLE CHAPTER SEQUENCE

The sequence of chapters has been carefully restructured and streamlined in the seventh edition. Most of the material on portfolio theory and capital market theory has been moved to Part Seven, although the basics of Markowitz and the CAPM are covered in Chapter 7. Therefore, *you can use the critical elements of portfolio theory and capital market theory throughout most of the course without getting involved in all of the details of capital market theory early on, which tend to be difficult.* Furthermore, this allows you to get to the material on bonds and stocks earlier in the semester, where the real action is.

I have diligently sought to ensure that the text length is reasonably manageable for a one semester course. You will benefit greatly from reading the entire text, but reading various combinations of chapters can also be very beneficial.

PRACTICAL PEDAGOGY

The pedagogy is specifically designed to help the reader understand and apply the basic concepts of investing.

- **Learning objectives** begin each chapter, which will aid the reader in determining what is to be accomplished with a particular chapter.

- **Key words** in boldface, are carefully defined as marginal definitions; they also are included in the glossary. Other important words are italicized.

- **Boxed inserts** continue to provide timely and interesting material from the popular press, enabling the reader to see the real-world side of issues and concepts discussed in the text.

- **"Investments Intuition" sections** set off from the regular text for easy identification, are designed to help the reader quickly grasp the intuitive logic of, and therefore better understand, particular investing issues.

- **"Some Practical Advice"** *sections* offer the reader useful suggestions and cautions.

- **"Using the Internet" sections** throughout the text, contain web addresses dealing with a particular topic being discussed in the text.

- **A detailed summary** at the end of each chapter contains a "bulleted" list of important points for quick and precise reading.

- **Numbered examples** an extensive set in each chapter, are designed to clearly illustrate key concepts.

- **End-of-chapter questions** keyed to specific concepts, are designed to thoroughly review the material in each chapter.

- **Separate problem sets** are designed to illustrate the quantitative material in many chapters. Some of these problems can be solved in the traditional manner; and some are best solved with appropriate software.

- **Demonstration problems** are included with some problem sets to show the reader how to solve the most important types of problems.

- **Chartered Financial Analysts (CFA) exam questions and problems** are included in many chapters. These allow students to see that the concepts and problem-solving processes they are studying in class are exactly the same as those asked on professional examinations for people in the money-management business.

CHANGES IN THE SEVENTH EDITION

The seventh edition has been thoroughly updated using the latest data and numbers available. At the time of publication, most data reflect the most current information. The most important content changes in the seventh edition include:

- Part One has been streamlined to include five chapters, rather than six. Part Two consists of two chapters, with Chapter 6 covering historical returns, and Chapter 7 covering expected returns. This format allows students to concentrate solely on the issue of returns, both historical and prospective, immediately following the introductory background chapters. It also breaks up the material into more manageable parts.
- Chapter 7 in Part Two covers basic portfolio theory and the CAPM, giving students only the essentials of portfolio theory and capital market theory necessary to use the important topics throughout most of the course. The remainder of the portfolio theory and capital market theory material has been moved to Part Seven, where it can be treated as a stand-alone section. Although capital market theory is important, covering all the details early in Part Two (as in the sixth edition) resulted in a significant part of the semester being used up before students get to the important topics of bonds and stocks. This material is also difficult, and may cause students to become frustrated from their study of investments. Finally, the simple truth in many cases is that beginning students do not need so much detail about capital market theory—they simply are not likely to utilize concepts like the capital market line, the separation theorem, and arbitrage pricing theory in a beginning course.

Note that as a result of this reorganization of Part Two, the chapter on market efficiency, now Chapter 12, concludes Part Four on the analysis and management of common stocks.

Everyone needs to consider the Efficient Market Hypothesis to analyze and manage common stocks.

- More questions from previous Chartered Financial Analyst (CFA) examinations are included as part of the end-of-chapter questions and problems.

SUPPLEMENTS

The seventh edition includes a complete set of supplements:

- **Instructor's Manual.** For each chapter, chapter objectives, lecture notes, notes on the use of transparency masters, and additional material relevant to the particular chapter are included. Answers to all questions and problems in the text are provided. The Instructor 's Manual was carefully prepared by the author.
- **Testbank.** The testbank includes numerous multiple choice and true—false questions for each chapter as well as short discussion questions and problems. Most of these have been extensively tested in class and are carefully checked. The Testbank is also available in a computerized format.
- **Internet Exercises.** Developed by P. V. Viswanath of Pace University, this set of exercises presents practical investing situations that use internet resources. The importance of the Internet dictates that students utilize these resources, and this package has exercises to accompany each chapter of the text.
- **PowerPoint.** PowerPoint presentation materials are available.
- **Transparency Masters.** These include selected text art, selected items from other sources, and solutions to selected end-of-chapter problems in the text. These transparencies are held over from the fifth edition for the benefit of those wishing to continue using them.
- **Software.** *The Investment Portfolio,* v. 2.5, a Windows-based software package produced by John Wiley, is available for special packaging with the text. It contains modules on portfolio management, equilibrium, statistics, valuation models, bonds, options, futures and evaluation, and includes data for use with all modules. Users may also enter their own data in spreadsheet or ASCII format. This software is available with extensive documentation as well as a workbook.
- **Website.** John Wiley makes available a website that allows adopters of the text to obtain additional materials.
- **Data Disk.** A file containing returns on financial assets from 1871 is available *to adopters.* These definitive data have been developed over many years by Charles Jones and Jack Wilson at North Carolina State University. Please contact John Wiley.
- **Videos.** A set of NBR videos is available free to adopters. These videos include such topics as "How Wall Street Works."

ACKNOWLEDGMENTS

A number of individuals have contributed to this project. I particularly thank Jack W. Wilson, North Carolina State University, a highly valued friend and colleague who has offered many useful comments, provided material for some of the tables, figures and appendices, and worked out many of the problems (including the extended problems) for the text. He has continued his valuable assistance by supplying data, graphs, suggestions, and insights. Some of the material used in this book and the accompanying supplements is based on Jack's pathbreaking work in the area of asset returns and has generously been made available by him, for which I am very grateful.

A text does not reach its seventh edition unless it has met the needs of a large number of instructors who find it to be a useful tool in assisting their teaching. The earlier editions of this text benefited substantially from the reviews of many instructors whose suggestions for improvements are found on many pages of this text. I owe a debt of gratitude to these teachers and colleagues who helped on past editions.

In developing the sixth edition, I benefited greatly from instructors teaching this course, including: Bala Arshanapalli, *Indiana University Northwest*; Christopher Blake, *Fordham University*; Vincent Deni, *Oakland Community College*; Clark Hawkins, *New Mexico State University*; Cheryl McGaughey, *Angelo State University*; Frederick Puritz, *State University of New York at Oneonta*; David L. Scott, *Valdosta State University*; Howard Van Auken, *Iowa State University*; Richard Voth, *Pacific Union College*; Stephen Avard, *Texas A&M University*; Richard B. Carter, *Iowa State University*; James F. Gatti, *The University of Vermont*; Carl Hubbard, *Trinity University*; Bruce McManis, *Nicholls State University*; Maury Randall, *Rider University*; Milan P. Sigetich, *Southern Oregon State College*; Glenn Wood, *California State University—Bakersfield*; and Dennis Zocco, *University of San Diego*.

The seventh edition has benefited from reviews by: Joseph Volk, *UC Berkeley Extension*; Howard Van Auken, *Iowa State University*; Dean Kiefer, *Northern Kentucky University*; Dennis Mahoney, *University of Pennsylvania*; Suresh Srivastava, *University of Alaska at Anchorage*; Mustafa Gultekin, *University of North Carolina at Chapel Hill*; James Gatti, *University of Vermont*; Halina Orlowski, *Sacred Heart University*; Bong-Soo Lee, *University of Houston*; and Philip Young, *Southern Missouri State University*.

I would also like to thank my former editors at Wiley, Rich Esposito, Joe Dougherty, John Woods, and Whitney Blake. My current editor, Marissa Ryan, has been most helpful in developing new supplements and dealing with the fast-changing world of Investments as it affects the total instructional package. The other Wiley professionals with whom I have worked on this project have been excellent, including Jennifer LiMarzi and Cynthia Rhoads.

Finally, I would like to thank my family, who continue to put up with the interruptions caused by writing a book. Without their support, a project such as this is difficult at best. I thank in particular my wife, Kay, who has helped me tremendously in the preparation of various editions of this text. My daughter Kathryn has played a larger role in the seventh edition and been helpful in developing internet-related aspects of this material. Kay and Kathryn make a difficult job bearable, and worth doing.

Charles P. Jones
North Carolina State University

Brief Contents

Contents

PART ONE BACKGROUND

Chapter 1: Understanding Investments 1

Chapter 2: Investment Alternatives 23

Chapter 9: Bonds: Analysis and Strategy 224

PART FOUR COMMON STOCKS: ANALYSIS, VALUATION, AND MANAGEMENT

Chapter 10: Common Stock Valuation 250

Chapter 11: Common Stocks: Analysis and Strategy 287

Chapter 12: Market Efficiency 310

PART FIVE SECURITY ANALYSIS

PART SEVEN MODERN INVESTMENT THEORY

Chapter 19: Portfolio Selection 510

Chapter 20: Capital Market Theory 531

PART EIGHT INVESTMENT MANAGEMENT

Chapter 21: Portfolio Management 557

INVESTMENTS: Analysis and Management

chapter 1

UNDERSTANDING INVESTMENTS

Chapter 1 provides the foundation for the study of Investments by analyzing what investing is all about. The critically important trade-off between expected return and risk is explained and important considerations that every investor must deal with in making investment decisions are analyzed. An organizational structure for the entire text is provided.

After reading this chapter you will be able to:

- **Understand why return and risk are the two critical components of all investing decisions.**
- **Appreciate the scope of investment decisions and the operating environment in which they are made.**
- **Follow the organization of the investment decision process as we progress through the text.**

In the late summer of 1998, the Dow Jones Industrial Average dropped almost 20 percent. With volatility like this, should most investors avoid common stocks, particularly for their retirement plans?

In one recent year the Asia Pacific Fund gained 109 percent, and the Turkish Investment Fund gained 152 percent. Should U.S. investors be participating in "emerging" stock markets? If so, how? Should most investors invest some part of their funds in international assets?

In the early 1990s, 75 percent of all company employees with self-directed retirement plans had none of their funds invested in stocks, although over the years stocks have significantly outperformed the alternative assets they did hold. Is this smart?

For a recent 10-year period, only one-third of professionally managed stock portfolios were able to outperform the overall stock market. Why?

One stock returned 57,000 percent in less than eight years during the period 1990–1998? What is the chance an individual investor could have recognized this company and gotten in on the ride?

Is it possible to have earned 40 percent or more investing in default-free Treasury bonds in a single year?

How can futures contracts, with a reputation for being extremely risky, be used to reduce an investor's risk?

What is the historical average annual rate of return on common stocks? What can an investor reasonably expect to earn from stocks in the future?

The objective of this text is to help you understand the investments field as it is currently understood, discussed, and practiced so that you can intelligently answer questions such as the preceding and make sound investment decisions that will enhance your economic welfare. To accomplish this objective, key concepts are presented to provide an appreciation of the theory and practice of investments.

Both descriptive and quantitative materials on investing are readily available. Some of this material is very enlightening; much of it is entertaining but debatable because of the many controversies in investments; and some of it is worthless. This text seeks to cover what is particularly useful and relevant for today's investment climate. It offers some ideas about what you can reasonably expect to accomplish by using what you learn, and therefore what you can realistically expect to achieve as an investor in today's investment world. Many investors have unrealistic expectations, and this will ultimately lead to disappointments in results achieved, or worse.

Learning to avoid the many pitfalls awaiting you as an investor by clearly understanding what you can reasonably expect from investing your money may be the single most important benefit to be derived from this text. For example, would you entrust your money to someone offering 36 percent annual return on riskless Treasury securities? Some 600 investors did and lost some $10 million to a former Sunday school teacher. Intelligent investors learn to say no and to avoid many of the mistakes that can be prevented by simply knowing when to say no.

THE NATURE OF INVESTMENTS

SOME DEFINITIONS

The term *investing* can cover a wide range of activities. It often refers to investing money in certificates of deposit, bonds, common stocks, or mutual funds. More knowledgeable investors would include other "paper" assets, such as warrants, puts and calls, futures contracts, and convertible securities, as well as tangible assets, such as gold, real estate, and collectibles. Investing encompasses very conservative positions as well as aggressive speculation. Whether your perspective is that of a college graduate starting out in the workplace or that of a senior citizen concerned with how to live after retirement, investing decisions can be very important to you.

Investment The commitment of funds to one or more assets that will be held over some future time period

Investments The study of the investment process

An **investment** can be defined as the commitment of funds to one or more assets that will be held over some future time period. The field of **investments**, therefore, involves the study of the investment process. Investments is concerned with the management of an investor's *wealth*, which is the sum of current income and the present value of all future income. (This is why present value and compound interest concepts have an important role in the investment process.) Although the field of investments encompasses many aspects, as the title of this text suggests, it can be thought of in terms of two primary functions: analysis and management.

Financial Assets Pieces of paper evidencing a claim on some issuer

Real Assets Physical assets, such as gold or real estate

Marketable Securities Financial assets that are easily and cheaply traded in organized markets

In this text, the term investments refers in general to financial assets and in particular to marketable securities. **Financial assets** are paper (or electronic) claims on some issuer, such as the federal government or a corporation; on the other hand, **real assets** are tangible assets such as gold, silver, diamonds, art, and real estate. **Marketable securities** are financial assets that are easily and cheaply tradable in organized markets. Technically, investments include both financial and real assets, and both marketable and nonmarketable assets. Because of the vast scope of investment opportunities available to investors, our primary emphasis is on marketable securities; however, the basic principles and techniques discussed in this text are applicable to real assets.

Even when we limit our discussion primarily to financial assets, it is difficult to keep up with the proliferation of new products. Two such assets that did not exist a few years ago are SPDRs (Standard & Poor's Depository Receipts) and WEBS (World Equity Benchmark Shares), both of which are discussed in a later chapter.

A PERSPECTIVE ON INVESTING IN FINANCIAL ASSETS

The investment of funds in various assets is only part of the overall financial decision making and planning that most individuals must do. Before investing, each individual should develop an overall financial plan. Such a plan should include the decision on whether to purchase a house, which for most individuals represents a major investment. In addition, decisions must be made about insurance of various types—life, health, disability, and protection of business and property. Finally, the plan should provide for emergency reserve funds.[1]

Portfolio The securities held by an investor taken as a unit

This text assumes that investors have established their overall financial plan and are now interested in managing and enhancing their wealth by investing in an optimal combination of financial assets. The idea of an "optimal combination" is important because our wealth, which we hold in the form of various assets, should be evaluated and managed as a unified whole. Wealth should be evaluated and managed within the context of a **portfolio**, which consists of the asset holdings of an investor. For example, if you own four stocks and three mutual funds, that is your portfolio. If your parents own 23 stocks, some municipal bonds, and some CDs, that is their portfolio of financial assets.

WHY DO WE INVEST?

We invest to make money! Although everyone would agree with this statement, we need to be more precise. (After all, this is a college textbook and those paying for your education expect more.) We invest to improve our welfare, which for our purposes can be defined as

[1] Personal finance decisions of this type are discussed in personal finance texts.

monetary wealth, both current and future. We assume that investors are interested only in the monetary benefits to be obtained from investing, as opposed to such factors as the psychic income to be derived from impressing one's friends with one's financial prowess.

Funds to be invested come from assets already owned, borrowed money, and savings or foregone consumption. By foregoing consumption today and investing the savings, investors expect to enhance their future consumption possibilities by increasing their wealth. Don't underestimate the amount of money many individuals can accumulate. By the mid-1990s there were approximately 3 million households that qualify as "millionaires," and the number of individuals with $1 million portfolios had tripled over the past 12 years.

Investors also seek to manage their wealth effectively, obtaining the most from it while protecting it from inflation, taxes, and other factors. To accomplish both objectives, people invest.

THE IMPORTANCE OF STUDYING INVESTMENTS

THE PERSONAL ASPECTS

It is important to remember that all individuals have wealth of some kind; if nothing else, this wealth may consist of the value of their services in the marketplace. Most individuals must make investment decisions sometime in their lives. Some people may wish to improve the return from their "savings account" funds by investing in alternatives to insured savings accounts. Many employees can decide whether their retirement funds are to be invested in stocks or bonds.

EXAMPLE 1-1

A good example of the investing decisions facing a typical individual, and the critical importance of making good investment decisions, is the Individual Retirement Account (IRA). Up to $2,000 annually can be fully deducted by some working taxpayers, and anyone can contribute up to $2,000 to a nondeductible IRA. In either case, the earnings on the contributions are not taxed until they are withdrawn. Furthermore, for 1997 and later years, joint filers may be able to deduct IRA contributions up to $2,000 for each spouse, a significant improvement in the tax law that favors savers.

IRA funds can be invested in a wide range of assets, from the very safe to the quite speculative. IRA owners are allowed to have self-directed brokerage accounts, which offer a wide array of investment opportunities. Since these funds may be invested for as long as 40 or more years, good investment decisions are critical, as shown by the examples in Table 1-1 for both one individual contributing $2,000, and each spouse contributing $2,000,

TABLE 1-1 POSSIBLE PAYOFFS FROM LONG-TERM INVESTING

		Final Wealth if Funds Are Invested at		
Amount Invested per Year ($)	Number of Years	5%	10%	15%
2000	20	$ 66,132	$ 114,550	$ 204,880
2000	30	132,878	328,980	869,480
2000	40	241,600	885,180	3,558,000
4000	20	132,264	229,100	409,760
4000	30	265,756	657,960	1,738,960
4000	40	483,200	1,770,360	7,116,000

annually. Over many years of investing, the differences in results that investors realize, owing solely to the investment returns earned, can be staggering. Note that in the case of a $4,000 annual contribution for 40 years, the payoff at an earnings rate of 15 percent is over $7,000,000, whereas at an earnings rate of 10 percent the payoff is $1,770,360, a great retirement fund but significantly less than $7 million.

Some Practical Advice

IT'S YOUR MONEY, AND YOUR DECISIONS A major revolution in personal finance in the 1990s is to provide employees with self-directed retirement plans (defined contribution plans rather than defined benefit plans) for which they must make investment decisions. The best example of this is a *401(k) plan* offered by many employers, whereby employees contribute a percentage of salary to a tax-deferred plan, and the employer often matches part of the contribution. By the beginning of 1999, these plans had $1 trillion in assets (a doubling in four years).

Whereas traditional defined-benefit retirement plans guarantee retirees an amount of money each month, the new emphasis on self-directed retirement plans means that you will have to choose among stock funds, bond funds, guaranteed investment contracts, and other alternatives. Your choices are many—many 401(k) participants can choose from thousands of mutual funds. Your success, or lack thereof, will directly affect your retirement benefits. Therefore, while employees in the past typically did not have to concern themselves much with investing decisions relative to their company's retirement plan, future employees will have to do so. This is a very important personal reason for studying the subject of investments!

USING THE INTERNET Investors can find many websites with so-called retirement calculators. For example, www.quicken.com offers a popular format. You input your age, salary, and current savings, make some assumptions about the rate of return you will earn and the inflation rate, indicate likely pension income and Social Security payments, and Quicken's *Retirement Planner* produces an estimate of terminal wealth at retirement, shortfalls, and amounts needed to be saved. Vanguard, the giant mutual fund company, offers extensive information on retirement planning at www.vanguard.com. Vanguard's *Pre-Retirement Savings Modeler* allows the user to enter personal and financial information and determine how long savings will last during retirement. At www.bloomberg.com, users can find (in the *Tools* section) a simplified retirement calculator that allows the user to calculate the annual contribution required to reach a goal, or the final amount that occurs from an annual contribution, given the number of years and an earnings rate.

The study of investments is more important than ever in the 1990s. After being net sellers of stocks from 1968 through 1990, individual investors have swarmed into the financial markets, either by force (becoming part of a self-directed retirement plan) or by choice (seeking higher returns than those available from financial institutions). Over $500 billion flowed out of certificates of deposit (CDs) as their rates tumbled in the early 1990s, and this money had to be invested elsewhere. In one recent year, 3 percent of households with $1 million or more sold a business while 15 percent of the same group received a lump-sum distribution from a retirement plan and, once again, this money had to be invested somewhere.

Individual investor interest in the stock market in the 1990s is best expressed by the power of mutual funds (explained in Chapter 3), a favorite investment vehicle of small investors in the 1990s. Mutual funds are now the driving force in the marketplace. With so much individual investor money flowing into mutual funds, and with individual investors owning a large percentage of all stocks outstanding, the study of investments is as important as ever, or more so.

In the final analysis, we study investments in the hope of earning better returns in relation to the risk we assume when we invest. A careful study of investment analysis and portfolio management principles can provide a sound framework for both managing and increasing wealth. Furthermore, a sound study of this subject matter will allow you to obtain maximum value from the many articles on investing that appear daily in newspapers and magazines, which in turn will increase your chances of reaching your financial goals.

Box 1-1, taken from *The Wall Street Journal*, discusses how important it can be to raise the return earned on one's investment, clearly an important topic. However, this one article implicitly or explicitly discusses all of the following topics, which many readers of the article will be unaware of, and which have implications and/or assumptions connected to them that most readers will fail to appreciate. All of these issues are covered in the text, and learning about them will make you a much smarter investor:

1. Financial assets available to investors
2. Total rate of return vs. yield
3. Compounding effects and terminal wealth
4. Realized returns vs. expected returns
5. How to compare taxable bonds to municipal (tax-exempt) bonds
6. Index funds and mutual fund expenses
7. How diversification works to reduce risk
8. The asset allocation decision
9. The significance of market efficiency to investors

INVESTMENTS AS A PROFESSION

In addition to the above reasons for the importance of studying investments, the world of investments offers several rewarding careers, both professionally and financially. A study of investments is an essential part of becoming a professional in this field.

Investment bankers, who arrange the sale of new securities as well as assist in mergers and acquisitions, enjoyed phenomenal financial rewards in the booming 1980s. Although there is less activity of this type in the 1990s relative to the 1980s, an experienced *merger and acquisition specialist* still can earn compensation in the $1 million range. Even someone with limited experience of a few years can earn $200,000 to $400,000 in this area.

Top *traders* and *salespeople* seem to do best on Wall Street. A junior bond trader on Wall Street can earn $300,000 to $400,000 or more, while an experienced bond trader can earn in the neighborhood of $750,000. A bond salesperson who sells to institutional investors can earn $200,000 or more if relatively inexperienced and $600,000 to $700,000 if experienced.

EXAMPLE 1-2

In the mid-1990s the demand for traders and salespersons in the junk bond (lower-quality debt issues) market exploded, with the result that individuals who were earning $500,000 were doubling that amount, many with multiyear contracts. Relative newcomers were able to command 50 percent more than one year earlier, and pay of $1.5 to $2 million was not unusual among experienced people.

For those interested in doing research, which is less glamorous and less profitable for the firms involved, the good jobs on Wall Street still pay well. A *security analyst* on Wall Street

BOX 1-1

For Retirement Savings, Modest Boosts In Annual Returns Make Big Difference

When saving for retirement, little things can mean a lot.

If you want your nest egg to fatten faster, it would be nice if you happened to own the next highflying growth stock or the next superstar mutual fund. But it sure isn't necessary.

Instead, to make a big difference in your eventual retirement income, all you need is a modest increase in your portfolio's annual return. For proof, consider some numbers put together by Robert Bingham, a San Francisco investment adviser.

Mr. Bingham looked at a 40-year-old investor with $80,000 in retirement savings who socked away $6,000 a year until age 65 and then used those savings to pay for a retirement that lasts 25 years. Mr. Bingham assumed that inflation ran at 3 percent throughout the period and that our hypothetical investor boosted the amount he or she saved each year along with inflation.

Result? If our investor earned 7 percent a year, annual retirement income would be $27,665, figured in today's dollars. You want more? Suppose our investor earned 7½ percent instead. That would produce $31,719 a year, or 15 percent more. What about 8 percent? That raises retirement income to $36,347, an extra 31 percent. How about 8½ percent? That gets the investor up to $41,626, or more than 50 percent more.

Not bad. You earn an extra 1.5 percentage points a year and you get 50 percent more retirement income. But how? Here are a few simple steps that should crank up your returns:

Boost Your Stock Holdings Mr. Bingham calculates that, after figuring in investment costs, you probably need a mix of 40 percent stocks and 60 percent bonds to earn 7 percent a year in a period of 3 percent inflation. Looking for 8 percent instead? Mr. Bingham suggests switching to 60 percent stocks and 40 percent bonds.

Snatch the Match In pursuit of higher returns, make full use of your employer's 401(k) or 403(b) retirement-savings plan. Your contributions are probably tax-deductible, your money will grow tax-deferred and your employer may match your contribution, throwing in maybe 50 cents for every $1 you contribute. Thanks to a combination of tax savings, investment gains and the employer match, your contributions could garner a first-year return of 80 percent or 90 percent.

Flee the Bank When buying cash investments, steer clear of bank products, such as savings accounts, short-term certificates of deposit and money-market accounts. Instead, consider a money-market mutual fund, which should offer a much better yield.

Trim Investment Costs If you skimp on brokerage commissions, trade infrequently and stick with low-expense mutual funds, you should bolster your annual returns. This is true for all investments, including stocks and stock-mutual funds.

But the impact is especially clear with bond and cash investments. Low-expense bond and money-market funds, for instance, almost always outperform higher-cost funds that buy similar securities.

Act Your Tax Bracket If you are in the 28 percent tax bracket or above and you want to buy high-quality U.S. bonds for your taxable account, go for tax-exempt municipals. The tax savings will more than compensate for the municipals' lower yield. On the other hand, if you are in the 15 percent bracket, seek the higher yields offered by taxable government and corporate bonds. Even after paying the tax involved, you will still be better off.

Straightforward, right? It seems not. Many folks own the wrong sort of bonds, according to an analysis of Internal Revenue Service data by Chicago municipal-bond experts John Nuveen & Co.

Nuveen found that taxpayers in the 15 percent bracket receive a surprisingly large amount of tax-exempt interest. Meanwhile, only a fifth of the tax returns showing adjusted gross income between $100,000 and $200,000 reported any municipal-bond income.

Exercise Sloth Less stock-market trading is better than more. But that's doubly true if you invest in a taxable account. If you trade a lot, not only do you enrich your broker, but also you enrich the IRS, because you realize your gains quickly and thus trigger a tax bill.

To keep Uncle Sam at bay and thereby boost your returns, consider buying and holding stocks in your taxable account. A good way to do that is with index funds, which simply purchase the stocks that constitute a market index in an effort to match the index's performance. Index funds have the added virtue of outperforming most actively managed funds.

Stay the Course If you are going to earn decent returns over time, you need to settle on an appropriate mix of stocks, bonds and cash investments. Also make sure you diversify broadly, keep down investment costs and save regularly. Thereafter, it's a matter of sticking with it. Don't be swayed by market turmoil or over-hyped investment opportunities.

"You don't need to do anything extraordinary to get returns that will set you up well for later life," Mr. Bingham argues. "You don't need to put 30 percent of your portfolio in a risky real-estate deal. You don't need to put half of your U.S. stocks in one high-tech start-up company. If you're lucky, you can look great. But if you're not, you can end up wiping out years of investment gains."

SOURCE: Jonathan Clements, "For Retirement Savings, Modest Boosts In Annual Returns Make Big Differences," *The Wall Street Journal*, December 17, 1996, p. C1. Reprinted by permission of *The Wall Street Journal*,

with a few years of experience can earn $200,000 or more, while one with 10 years of experience can earn up to $500,000.

A range of financial institutions—including brokerage firms and investment bankers as well as banks and insurance companies—need the services of investment analysts. Brokerage houses need them to support their registered representatives who in turn serve the public—for example, preparing the research reports provided to customers. Investment bankers need analysts to assist in the sale of new securities and in the valuation of firms as possible merger or acquisition candidates. Banks and insurance companies own portfolios of securities that must be evaluated in order to be managed. Mutual funds need analysts to evaluate securities for possible purchase or sale.

All the financial firms mentioned above need *portfolio managers* to manage the portfolios of securities handled by these organizations. Portfolio managers are responsible for making the actual portfolio buy and sell decisions—what to buy and sell, when to buy and sell, and so forth. Portfolio performance is calculated for these managers, and their jobs may depend on their performance relative to other managed portfolios and to market averages.

What about the 80,000 *registered representatives* (stockbrokers) employed in cities across the country? A few superbrokers earn $1 million or more per year. The average broker in the early 1990s earned almost $100,000 per year, although the median compensation (half above, half below) was $63,000.

Finally, the number of *financial planners* continues to grow. Because no standard credentials for financial planners exist, anyone can claim to be a financial planner. Although most planners must register with the Securities and Exchange Commission as a *Registered Investment Advisor (RIA)*, this involves only the filling out of a form providing information on education and background and the payment of a $150 registration fee. Otherwise, financial planners are bound only by the job requirements of professional organizations to which they belong, and individuals seeking a financial planner may wish to contact these organizations.[2]

Designations that do connote training in the financial planning field include: *Certified Financial Planner (CFP)*, awarded by the Certified Financial Planning Board of Standards, an industry group, requires course work and a five-part examination; *Chartered Financial Consultant (ChFC)* requires a comprehensive examination; and *Personal Financial Specialist*, awarded by the American Institute of Certified Public accountants, requires experience in personal financial planning and a comprehensive examination. All three designations require continuing education.

[2] These include the National Association of Personal Financial Advisors (800-366-2732); the International Association for Financial Planning (800-945-4237); and the Institute of Certified Financial Planners (800-282-7526).

Financial planners are compensated by three methods: fee-based, commission-based, or fee-and-commission based, which is the most common form of compensation. Planners indicate that they average about $100 an hour regardless of method of compensation. According to one survey, planners gross a little over $100,000 per year, primarily from selling products for commissions and from managing clients' assets for a percentage of the assets under management.

Chartered Financial Analyst (CFA) A professional designation for people in the investments field

Individuals interested in careers in the investments field, as opposed to financial planning, should consider studying to become a **Chartered Financial Analyst (CFA)**. This is a professional designation for people in the investments area, not unlike the CPA designation for accountants. The CFA designation is widely recognized in the investments industry today. It serves as an indication that areas of knowledge relevant to investing have been studied and that high ethical and professional standards have been recognized and accepted. Details of the CFA program are included in Appendix 1-A. Throughout this text we will use relevant parts of the CFA curriculum, procedures, and philosophy because it directly relates to a study of investments.

UNDERSTANDING THE INVESTMENT DECISION PROCESS

An organized view of the investment process involves analyzing the basic nature of investment decisions and organizing the activities in the decision process.

Common stocks have produced, on average, significantly larger returns over the years than savings accounts or bonds. Should not all investors invest in common stocks and realize these larger returns? The answer to this question is—*to pursue higher returns investors must assume larger risks*. Underlying all investment decisions is the trade-off between expected return and risk. Therefore, we first consider these two basic parameters that are of critical importance to all investors and the trade-off that exists between expected return and risk.

Given the foundation for making investment decisions—the trade-off between expected return and risk—we next consider the decision process in investments as it is typically practiced today. Although numerous separate decisions must be made, for organizational purposes this decision process has traditionally been divided into a two-step process: security analysis and portfolio management. Security analysis involves the valuation of securities, whereas portfolio management involves the management of an investor's investment selections as a portfolio (package of assets), with its own unique characteristics.

THE BASIS OF INVESTMENT DECISIONS

Return Why invest? Stated in simplest terms, investors wish to earn a return on their money. Cash has an opportunity cost: By holding cash, you forego the opportunity to earn a return on that cash. Furthermore, in an inflationary environment, the purchasing power of cash diminishes, with high rates of inflation (such as that in the early 1980s) bringing a relatively rapid decline in purchasing power.

INVESTMENTS INTUITION Investors buy, hold, and sell financial assets to earn returns on them. Within the spectrum of financial assets, why do some people buy common stocks instead of safely depositing their money in an insured savings account or a U.S. savings bond with a guaranteed minimum return? The answer is that they are trying to earn returns larger than those available from such safer (and lower yielding) assets. They know they are taking a greater risk of losing some of their money by buying common stocks, but they expect to earn a greater return.

Expected Return The ex ante return expected by investors over some future holding period

Realized Return Actual return on an investment for some previous period of time

In investments it is critical to distinguish between an **expected return** (the anticipated return for some future period) and a **realized return** (the actual return over some past period). Investors invest for the future—for the returns they expect to earn—but when the investing period is over, they are left with their realized returns. What investors actually earn from their holdings may turn out to be more or less than what they expected to earn when they initiated the investment. This point is the essence of the investments process: Investors must always consider the risk involved in investing.

Risk Investors would like their returns to be as large as possible; however, this objective is subject to constraints, primarily risk.[3] The stock market had four great years during 1995–1998, with total returns each year in excess of 20 percent on a broad cross-section of common stocks. Nevertheless, several professionally managed funds performed poorly relative to the market, and some managed to lose money in one or more of those years. As this example shows, marketable securities offering variable returns across time are risky. The investment decision, therefore, must always be considered in terms of both risk and return. The two are inseparable.

Risk The chance that the actual return on an investment will be different from the expected return

There are different types, and therefore different definitions, of risk. **Risk** is defined here as the chance that the actual return on an investment will be different from its expected return.[4] Using the term risk in this manner, we find that the nominal (current dollar) return on a Treasury bill has no practical risk because there is no reasonable chance that the U.S. government will fail to redeem these obligations as they mature in 13 or 26 weeks. On the other hand, there is some risk, however small, that Exxon or General Electric will be unable to redeem an issue of 30-year bonds when they mature. And there is a very substantial risk of not realizing the expected return on any particular common stock over some future holding period, such as a year, six months, one month, or even one day.

Risk-Averse Investor An investor who will not assume a given level of risk unless there is an expectation of adequate compensation for having done so

It is easy to say that investors dislike risk, but more precisely, we should say that investors are risk averse.[5] A **risk-averse investor** is one who will not assume risk simply for its own sake and will not incur any given level of risk unless there is an expectation of adequate compensation for having done so. Note carefully that it is not irrational to assume risk, even very large risk, as long as we expect to be compensated for it. In fact, investors cannot reasonably expect to earn larger returns without assuming larger risks.

Investors deal with risk by choosing (implicitly or explicitly) the amount of risk they are willing to incur. Some investors choose to incur high levels of risk with the expectation of high levels of return. Other investors are unwilling to assume much risk, and they should not expect to earn large returns.

We have said that investors would like to maximize their returns. Can we also say that investors, in general, will choose to minimize their risks? No! The reason is that there are costs to minimizing the risk, specifically a lower expected return. Taken to its logical conclusion, the minimization of risk would result in everyone holding risk-free assets such as savings accounts and Treasury bills. Thus, we need to think in terms of the expected return-risk trade-off that results from the direct relationship between the risk and the expected return of an investment.

The Expected Risk-Return Trade-off Within the realm of financial assets, investors can achieve virtually any position on an expected return-risk spectrum such as that

[3] Although risk is the most important constraint on investors, other constraints clearly exist. Taxes and transaction costs are often viewed as constraints. Some investors may face legal constraints on the types of securities they can purchase or the amount they can hold.

[4] As we shall see in Chapter 7, expected return is a precise statistical term, not simply the return the investor expects. As indicated in our definition, risk involves chances, or probabilities, which will also be discussed in Chapter 7 along with measures of the dispersion in the expected return.

[5] Do investors dislike risk? In economics in general, and investments in particular, the standard assumption is that investors are rational. Rational investors prefer certainty to uncertainty.

FIGURE 1-1

The expected return-risk trade-off available to investors.

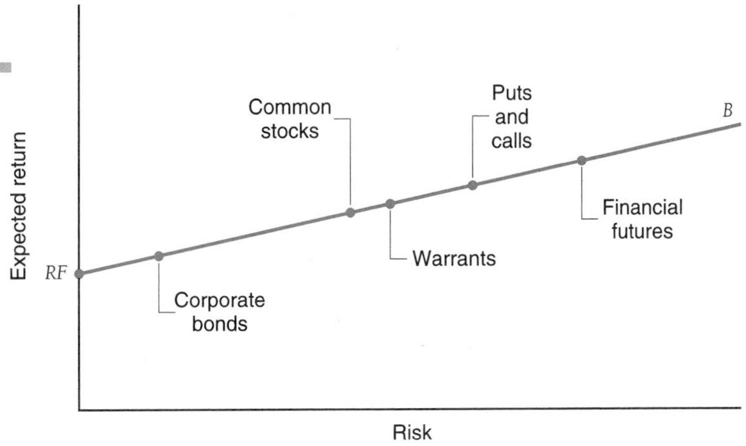

depicted in Figure 1-1. The line RF to B is the assumed trade-off between expected return and risk that exists for all investors interested in financial assets. This trade-off always slopes upward, because the vertical axis is expected return, and rational investors will not assume more risk unless they expect to be compensated for doing so. The expected return should be large enough to compensate for taking the additional risk; however, there is no guarantee that the additional returns will be realized.

RF in Figure 1-1 is the return on a riskless asset such as Treasury bills. This position has zero risk and an expected return equal to the current rate of return available on riskless assets such as Treasury bills. This **risk-free rate of return**, which is available to all investors, will be designated as RF throughout the text.

Risk-Free Rate of Return
The return on a riskless asset, often proxied by the rate of return on Treasury securities

Figure 1-1 shows approximate relative positions for some of the financial assets that will be discussed in Chapter 2. As we move from riskless Treasury securities to more risky corporate bonds, equities, and so forth, we assume more risk in the expectation of earning a larger return. Common stocks are quite risky, in relation to bonds, but they are not as risky as an unhedged purchase of options (puts and calls) or futures contracts. (All of these terms are defined in Chapter 2.)

Obviously, Figure 1-1 depicts broad categories. Within a particular category, such as common stocks, a wide range of expected return and risk opportunities exists at any time.

The important point in Figure 1-1 is the trade-off between expected return and risk that should prevail in a rational environment. Investors unwilling to assume risk must be satisfied with the risk-free rate of return, RF. If they wish to try to earn a larger rate of return, they must be willing to assume a larger risk as represented by moving up the expected return-risk trade-off into the wide range of financial assets available to investors. In effect, investors have different limits on the amount of risk they are willing to assume and, therefore, the amount of return that can realistically be expected.[6]

Always remember that the risk-return trade-off depicted in Figure 1-1 is *ex ante*, meaning "before the fact." That is, before the investment is actually made, the investor expects higher returns from assets that have a higher risk. This is the only sensible expectation for risk-averse investors, who are assumed to constitute the majority of all investors. *Ex post* (meaning "after the fact" or when it is known what has occurred), for a given period of time,

[6] In economic terms, the explanation for these differences in preferences is that rational investors strive to maximize their utility, the perception of which varies among investors. Utility theory is a complex subject; however, for our purposes we can equate maximization of utility with maximization of welfare. Because welfare is a function of present and future wealth, and wealth in turn is a function of current and future income discounted (reduced) for the amount of risk involved, in effect, investors maximize their welfare by optimizing the expected return-risk trade-off. In the final analysis, expected return and risk constitute the foundation of all investment decisions.

such as a month or a year or even longer, the trade-off may turn out to be flat or even negative. Such is the nature of risky investments!

STRUCTURING THE DECISION PROCESS

Investors can choose from a wide range of securities in their attempt to maximize the expected returns from these opportunities. They face constraints, however, the most pervasive of which is risk. Traditionally, investors have analyzed and managed securities using a broad two-step process: security analysis and portfolio management.

Security Analysis The first part of the investment decision process, involving the valuation and analysis of individual securities

Security Analysis The first part of the investment decision process involves the valuation and analysis of individual securities, which is referred to as **security analysis**. Professional security analysts are usually employed by institutional investors. Of course, there are also millions of amateur security analysts in the form of individual investors.

The valuation of securities is a time-consuming and difficult job. First of all, it is necessary to understand the characteristics of the various securities and the factors that affect them. Second, a valuation model is applied to these securities to estimate their price, or value. Value is a function of the expected future returns on a security and the risk attached. Both of these parameters must be estimated and then brought together in a model.

The valuation process is difficult for common stocks. The investor must deal with the overall economy, the industry, and the individual company. Both the expected return and the risk of common stocks must be estimated. In addition, investors must consider the possibility that securities markets, particularly the equity markets, are efficient. In an efficient market, the prices of securities do not depart for any length of time from the justified economic values that investors calculate for them. Economic values for securities are determined by investor expectations about earnings, risks, and so on, as investors grapple with the uncertain future. If the market price of a security does depart from its estimated economic value, investors act to bring the two values together. Thus, as new information arrives in an efficient marketplace, causing a revision in the estimated economic value of a security, its price adjusts to this information quickly and, on balance, correctly. In other words, securities are efficiently priced on a continuous basis. We discuss the full implications of this statement in Chapter 12.

Despite the difficulties, some type of analysis is performed by most investors serious about their portfolios. Unless this is done, one has to rely on personal hunches, suggestions from friends, and recommendations from brokers—all dangerous to one's financial health, or one chooses to follow a passive approach as explained below.

Portfolio Management The second step in the investment decision process, involving the management of a group of assets (i.e., a portfolio) as a unit

Passive Investment Strategy A strategy that determines initial investment proportions and assets and makes few changes over time

Portfolio Management The second major component of the decision process is **portfolio management**. After securities have been evaluated, a portfolio should be selected. Concepts on why and how to build a portfolio are well known. Much of the work in this area is in the form of mathematical and statistical models, which have had a profound effect on the study of investments in this country in the last 30 years.

Having built a portfolio, the astute investor must consider how and when to revise it. This raises a number of important questions. Portfolios must be managed, regardless of whether an investor is active or passive:

- A **passive investment strategy** involves determining the desired investment proportions and assets in a portfolio and maintaining these proportions and assets, making few changes. Even if investors follow a passive strategy, questions to be considered include taxes, transaction costs, maintenance of the desired risk level, and so on.

Active Investment Strategy A strategy that seeks to change investment proportions and/or assets in the belief that profits can be made

- An **active investment strategy** involves specific decisions to change the investment proportions chosen, or the assets in a particular category, based on the belief that an investor can profit by doing so. If the investor pursues an active strategy, the issue of market efficiency must be considered. If prices reflect information quickly and fully, investors should consider how this will affect their buy and sell decisions.

Efficient Market Hypothesis (EMH) The proposition that securities markets are efficient, with the prices of securities reflecting their economic value

The possibility that the stock market is efficient, as discussed above, has significant implications for investors. In fact, one's knowledge of and belief in this idea, known as the **Efficient Market Hypothesis (EMH)**, will directly affect how one views the investment process and makes investment decisions. Strong believers in the EMH may adopt, to varying degrees, a passive investment strategy, because of the likelihood that they will not be able to find underpriced securities. These investors will seek to minimize transaction costs and taxes, as well as the time and resources devoted to analyzing securities, which, if the EMH is correct, should be correctly priced to begin with.

Investors who do not accept the EMH, or have serious doubts, pursue active investment strategies, believing that they can identify undervalued securities and that lags exist in the market's adjustment of these securities' prices to new (better) information. These investors generate more search costs (both in time and money) and more transaction costs, but they believe that the marginal benefit outweighs the marginal costs incurred.

Finally, all investors are interested in how well their portfolio performs. This is the bottom line of the investment process. Measuring portfolio performance is an inexact procedure, even today, and needs to be carefully considered.

IMPORTANT CONSIDERATIONS IN THE INVESTMENT DECISION PROCESS FOR TODAY'S INVESTORS

Intelligent investors should be aware of the fact that the investment decision process as just described can be lengthy and involved. Regardless of individual actions, however, certain factors in the investment environment affect all investors. These factors should constantly be kept in mind as investors work through the investment decision process.

THE GREAT UNKNOWN

The first, and paramount, factor that all investors must come to grips with is uncertainty. Investors buy various financial assets, expecting to earn various returns over some future holding period. These returns, with few exceptions, may never be realized. The simple fact that dominates investing, although many investors never seem to appreciate it fully, is that *the realized return on an asset with any risk attached to it may be different from what was expected—sometimes, quite different.*

At best, estimates are imprecise; at worst, they are completely wrong. Some investors try to handle uncertainty by building elaborate quantitative models, and others simply keep it in the back of their mind. All investors, however, are affected by it, and the best they can do is make the most informed return and risk estimates they can, act on them, and be prepared for shifting circumstances. Regardless of how careful and informed investors are, the future is uncertain, and mistakes will be made.

As an illustration of how commonplace are the mistakes in judgments and estimates concerning the investments arena—indeed, they are inevitable—consider Box 1-2. *Smart Money*, an excellent monthly magazine designed for individual investors, publishes a "Reality Check" in each issue. These comments, which are representative of the total stream of com-

Box 1-2

Reality Check

"Someday, no doubt . . . the bull market will return, and a great day that will be. But it's not likely to come any time soon."

—JOSEPH NOCERA, *FORTUNE*, SEPT. 28, 1998

That's not likely to be remembered as one of the author's best predictions. The market, in fact, recovered from last fall's correction within weeks and has since gained 38 percent.

"We believe payrolls will increase by 200,000 in March."

—MERRILL LYNCH REPORT, MAR. 26, 1999

Oops, Payrolls rose by just 46,000 in March. But you can't blame Merrill for trying: Its January employment forecast went too far in the opposite direction, underestimating payrolls by 120,000.

"We expect the international trade deficit to widen by $1 billion in January [to $14.8 billion]."

—WARBURG DILLON READ REPORT, MAR. 12, 1999

Not-so-great expectations. Warburg should have nearly tripled its forecast, as the trade gap expanded by $2.94 billion in January to a whopping $16.8 billion.

"Next week will mark the one-year anniversary that an ex-girlfriend hacked into the MSDW computer system and published the '100 Reasons to Buy Gold' report with my name on it."

—MORGAN STANLEY DEAN WITTER REPORT "GOLD: 100 REASONS TO BUY . . . OH, NEVER MIND," MAR. 31, 1999

Analyst Douglas Cohen's own Reality Check for his bullish call on gold a year before prices dropped 10 percent.

SOURCE: *SmartMoney*, June 1999, p. 36.

ments on financial markets that appear regularly, illustrate how easily one's predictions and estimates can turn out to be incorrect. It is important to understand that the people making these comments are no more prone to error than anyone else. *All market participants, individual investors as well as the professionals, make errors.*

Investors may, and very often do, use past data to make their estimates. They frequently modify these data to incorporate what they believe is most likely to happen. What is important to remember is that basing investment decisions solely on the past is going to lead to errors. A 10 percent average return on all stocks for the last 10 years in no way guarantees a 10 percent return for the next year, or even an average 10 percent return for the next 10 years.

Someone can always tell you what you should have bought or sold in the past. No one, however, can guarantee you a successful portfolio for next year or any other specified period of time because no one can consistently forecast what will happen in the financial markets, including the professionals who are paid to make recommendations. Unanticipated events will affect the financial markets.

Investment decisions are both an art and a science. To succeed in investing, we must think in terms of what is expected to happen. We know what has happened, but the past may or may not repeat itself. Although the future is uncertain, it is manageable, and a thorough understanding of the basic principles of investing will allow investors to cope intelligently.[7]

THE GLOBAL INVESTMENTS ARENA

Now more than ever, investors must think of investments in a global context. Although foreign investments have been possible for a number of years, and some investors bought and sold

[7] In addition, some new tools and techniques are now being used that may help investors to make better decisions. These new techniques include neural networks, genetic algorithms, chaos theory, and expert systems.

on an international basis, most investors did not, particularly U.S. investors. Today, however, an international perspective is very important to all investors.

A global marketplace of round-the-clock investing opportunities is emerging, and the astute investor no longer thinks only of domestic investment alternatives. Why restrict yourself only to U.S. investment opportunities if you can increase your returns, or reduce your risk, or both, by investing on an international basis?

Foreign markets have grown rapidly, and several are now large by any measure. The Japanese market is well known, having reached very high levels followed by very low levels. Western European markets are well developed and offer investors numerous alternatives in what some observers feel will be the premier economic power of the future.

A significant event occurred on January 1, 1999 with the launch of European economic and monetary union, or EMU, along with the euro, Europe's common currency. The euro is the official currency of 11 countries, to be used for commercial transactions, with euro notes and coins due in 2002. This marks a significant change for Europe and European financial markets. For example, beginning in 1999, *The Wall Street Journal* quotes shares from markets in these countries in euros rather than in local currencies, and investors had to adjust their thinking accordingly. Perhaps in anticipation of this event, most European stock markets were up 20 to 30 percent in 1998.

Emerging Markets Markets of less developed countries, characterized by high risks and potentially large returns

A hot investment concept of the 1990s was that of **emerging markets**.[8] Several Asian markets, such as Singapore, Indonesia, and Thailand, are rapidly emerging. South American countries are coming on strong, and in the early 1990s Mexico's stock market had several stocks that were very popular with U.S. investors. Investors in emerging markets earned an average return of almost 70 percent in one recent year. Nevertheless, consistent with our discussion of the uncertainty involved in financial markets as well as the return-risk trade-off that underlies all investment decision, emerging markets peaked in 1994 and suffered a disastrous collapse in the mid-1990s. Notable disasters included Brazil, Russia, and many of the Asian countries.

Why should investors be so concerned with international investing? First, many U.S. companies now derive a very large percentage of their revenues from abroad; Coca-Cola and Merck Pharmaceuticals are examples. The average company in the S&P 500 Composite Stock Index (an important measure of large U.S. companies) now derives in excess of 25 percent of its sales from abroad. This trend can be expected to continue.

Thus, U.S. investors investing in what traditionally are thought of as classic American companies are vitally affected by what happens abroad. A downturn in some key foreign companies, or an adverse movement in exchange rates, can have unhappy consequences for U.S. investors holding what they believe are solid U.S. companies. For example, when the dollar is strong, multinational producers are affected because foreign currency revenues and operating profits are translated into fewer U.S. dollars when results are reported on the U.S. parent's financial statements.

Second, U.S. investors should be aware of capital flows from abroad into domestic financial markets. By 1998 foreign governments and investors owned $1.5 trillion of Treasury bonds, approximately one-third of all those outstanding at the time. Of course, this dependence on foreign capital inflows could be a problem if these buyers sold their U.S. bonds, depressing bond prices and driving up yields.

Third, the rates of return available in foreign securities have often been larger than those available from U.S. markets. For example, for several years in a row the average compound rate of return for eight major Asian markets was approximately double that of the primary measure of U.S. stocks. In one year alone, the typical international investor enjoyed returns of roughly 40 percent, and the downside was *plus* 20 percent. Thus, by ignoring foreign

[8] The World Bank classifies a stock market as "emerging" if its country's economy had less than $7,910 in U.S. dollars in per capita gross domestic product (GDP) in 1991.

investment opportunities, U.S. investors forego potentially larger returns relative to domestic returns only.

Fourth, adding foreign securities allows the investor to achieve beneficial risk reduction inasmuch as some foreign markets move differently than do U.S. markets. For example, when U.S. stocks are doing poorly, some foreign stocks may be doing well, which would help offset the poor U.S. performance. This risk reduction in a portfolio is a result of diversification. The simple point is that if domestic diversification in a portfolio reduces an investor's risk, which it clearly does, foreign diversification should provide even more risk reduction—and it does!

Given that international investing has now been going on for a number of years, it is not surprising that a recent analysis of international equity investing for the last 20 years concludes that "global portfolio diversification is no longer a *new* route to higher returns and lower risks, as it was two decades ago." Nevertheless, evidence for the past 20 years "indicates that thoughtful international equity diversification can improve the risk/return characteristics of investors' portfolios."[9]

Thus, we should consider foreign markets as well as the U.S. financial environment. We will do so throughout this text as an integral part of the discussion, rather than as a separate chapter. Although the technical details may vary, the principles of investing are applicable to financial assets and financial markets wherever they exist.

Does a consideration of foreign investing ensure our success as investors? No, because of the first issue we discussed—the great unknown. As in any other area of investing, the experts are often wrong. Consider the following quote from an article in *The Wall Street Journal*: "As we entered the 1990s, many investment advisers, market pundits and well-meaning journalists were betting that the U.S. stock market was in for lackluster returns, but that foreign stocks might take up the slack. We couldn't have been more wrong."[10]

THE RISE OF THE INTERNET

Any discussion of the investment decision process today must include the role of the Internet, which in a short time has significantly changed the investments environment. Now, all investors can access a wealth of information about investing, trade cheaply and quickly in their brokerage accounts, obtain real-time quotes throughout the day, and track their portfolios.

This is a true revolution—the Internet has democratized the flow of investment information. Any investor, at home, at work, or on vacation, can download an incredible array of information, trade comments with other investors, do security analysis, manage portfolios, check company filings with government agencies, and carry out numerous other activities not thought possible for a small investor only a few years ago. While some of these information sources and/or services carry a fee, most of it is free.

By late 1998 approximately 100 on-line discount brokers were competing intensely for investor business. One large discount brokerage firm, Charles Schwab, had 2 million on-line accounts. Ten percent of all daily U.S. trading was being done on-line. Commissions for web trades had dropped 70 percent in two years, and averaged about $16, with some firms offering much cheaper rates (in contrast, full-service brokerage firms were charging several hundred dollars for many trades).

Institutional Investors Pension funds, investment companies, bank trust departments, life insurance companies, and so forth, all of whom manage large portfolios of securities

INSTITUTIONAL INVESTORS

There are two broad categories of investors: individual investors and **institutional investors**. The latter group, consisting of bank trust departments, pension funds, mutual funds, insur-

[9] Both quotes are from Richard O. Michaud, Gary L. Bergstrom, Ronald D. Frashure, and Brian K. Wolahan. "Twenty Years of International Equity Investing," *The Journal of Portfolio Management*, Fall 1996, p. 20.

[10] See Jonathan Clements, "Foreign Funk: Our '90s Advice Is Wrong So Far," *The Wall Street Journal*, October 1, 1996, p. C1.

ance companies, and so forth, includes the professional money managers, who are often publicized in the popular press. The amount of money managed by these institutions is staggering. For example, in one recent year, Goldman, Sachs & Company managed some $16 billion in money market and bond funds. Two months after deciding to again manage stock portfolios (Goldman had abandoned this function some years earlier), wealthy individuals offered the company some $200 million to manage before it actually began accepting funds.

Given the figures for individual companies, it is not hard to see why, by the beginning of the 1990s, institutional investors in the United States held almost $6 trillion in assets. However, these institutional investors do not constitute a monolithic bloc of investors. Instead, they are made up of thousands of different organizations, most of which have multiple money managers.

The first issue to note about institutional investors is that their relative importance has changed. For 30 or more years up to the 1990s, it was the pension funds and corporate raiders who had the big impact on Wall Street. Although pension funds remain the primary institutional owner of common stocks, with about one-quarter of all stock, their importance has declined because many plans have either been terminated or converted into self-directed plans. The private pension plans bought all of the *net* equities available in the 1960s and 1970s, while in the 1980s corporate restructurings—mergers, acquisitions, and stock buybacks—took one-half trillion dollars of equity out of the market. In the 1990s, however, it is the mutual funds that are the primary buying force in the stock market. We will analyze mutual funds in detail in Chapter 3.

The second issue to note about institutional investors is their dual relationship to individual investors. On the one hand, individuals are the indirect beneficiaries of institutional investor actions, because they own or benefit from these institutions' portfolios. On a daily basis, however, they are "competing" with these institutions in the sense that both are managing portfolios of securities and attempting to do well financially by buying and selling securities.

Institutional investors are indeed the "professional" investors, with vast resources at their command. Quite frankly, they are often treated differently from individual investors because some companies disclose important information selectively to some institutional investors. According to a survey by the National Investor Relations Institute, an association for investor-relations professionals, perhaps one-third of public companies disclose sensitive information concerning their stock that may disadvantage individual investors.[11]

EXAMPLE 1-3

Bank of New York Co. announced to 92 analysts and institutional investors in a 2 P.M. conference call that it would set aside $350 million to cover expected losses. It did not announce this to the public until after the market closed that day, and the share price had fallen by that time.

Another advantage that institutional investors have is that they can trade in the "aftermarket" (negotiated trades conducted electronically among institutions) following exchange closings at 4 P.M. Eastern time. By the time a stock opens the next morning, the price may have adjusted significantly.

EXAMPLE 1-4

On one day Intel closed at $70, and then announced better than expected earnings. The stock opened the next morning at $74. Individuals were generally unable to participate in this movement.

[11] This discussion and the following two examples are based on Toddi Gutner, "How To Keep The Little Guy In The Loop," *Business Week*, July 24, 1996, p. 32.

Does the average investor, then, have a reasonable chance in the market? Yes—in the sense that he or she can generally expect to earn a fair return for the risk taken. *On average*, the individual investor will probably do just as well as the big institutional investors, because markets are usually quite efficient and securities fairly priced.

Some individual investors do even better either by superior skill and insight, or luck. Furthermore, some opportunities can more easily be exploited by individual investors than by institutional investors.

EXAMPLE 1-5

Individual investors can exploit a *spin-off* (defined as a division of a company that is turned into a separate publicly held company), better than institutional investors in some cases.[12] Some institutional investors will not purchase the new companies because they often pay no dividends immediately after spin-off, and they may be too small to be held by some institutions. Also, these companies often look unattractive at the time of spin-off because they had problems as a division. However, these problems tend to be solved by a new, proactive management, and these companies become attractive as take-over candidates.

A study of 150 spin-offs found that the average three-year total return was about 75 percent, 30 percentage points higher than a comparable group of companies. Investors are advised to defer purchases of spin-offs until they have been trading for a few weeks because some institutions may sell the shares they received in the spin-off, and prices are often lower weeks later than at the time trading begins in the new companies.

Relative to our discussion above about the Internet, individual investors are now on a more competitive basis with institutional investors, given the information they can access. Furthermore, we would expect the market to become more efficient, because information is even more quickly and freely available.

The question of how well individual investors do relative to institutional investors raises the issue of market efficiency, which we consider in Chapter 12. All intelligent investors who seek to do well when investing must ultimately come to grips with the issue of market efficiency.

ORGANIZING THE TEXT

The following chapters are organized around the two major components of the investment decision process: asset valuation (security analysis) and portfolio management. The investments business has traditionally been divided into these two broad areas, each of which encompasses a wide spectrum of activities.

Four chapters of background material follow this introductory chapter to form Part I, which covers background. The financial assets available to investors—both from direct investing and indirect investing—are examined in separate chapters, followed by a discussion of the securities markets in which they trade. This, in turn, is followed by an analysis of how securities are actually traded.

Part II deals with the important issues of return and risk, which underlie all investment decisions. Chapter 6 covers returns that investors have earned in the financial markets in the past, along with the risk involved, because investors must have an understanding of the results of investing in major assets such as stocks and bonds if they are to make intelligent estimates of the future. Chapter 7, in turn, deals with the estimation of return and risk, which all investors must do as they choose portfolios of securities to hold for the future.

Nine chapters of the text, involving Parts III, IV, and V, are devoted to evaluating

[12] See "Personal Investing," *Fortune*, April 18, 1994, pp. 31–32.

alternative investment opportunities and explaining the basics of asset valuation. We begin with a study of bonds in Part III because the valuation process can be learned most quickly by studying bonds. Common stocks are analyzed in Part IV. For both bonds and stocks, valuation techniques are discussed in the first of the two chapters, and analysis and management in the second. For stocks, a chapter on market efficiency is included because this important concept affects the strategies followed in selecting and managing stocks.

Because of the complexity of common stocks, four additional chapters are needed to describe the basics of security analysis, the most popular method for analyzing stocks. Part V is purposefully sequenced from market to industry to company analysis, followed by a discussion of technical analysis.

Part VI contains a complete basic analysis of alternative investment opportunities involving derivative securities. Separate chapters cover options and futures.

Part VII of the text is concerned with portfolio concepts and capital market theory. We discuss portfolio selection in Chapter 19, following up on the basic Markowitz principles learned in Chapter 7. In Chapter 20 we consider asset pricing models and market equilibrium.

Part VIII contains two chapters involving the portfolio management process. Chapter 21 describes the process that investors or managers should follow in managing portfolios. The text concludes with the logical capstone to a study of investments, the measurement of portfolio performance, in Chapter 22.

SUMMARY

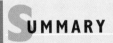

- An investment is the commitment of funds to one or more assets that will be held over some future period. The field of investments involves the study of the investment process.
- The investment opportunities considered in this text consist primarily of a wide array of financial assets (primarily marketable securities), which are financial claims on some issuer.
- The basic element of all investment decisions is the trade-off between expected return and risk. Financial assets are arrayed along an upward sloping expected return-risk trade-off, with the risk-free rate of return as the vertical axis intercept.
- Expected return and risk are directly related; the greater (smaller) the expected return, the greater (smaller) the risk.
- Investors seek to maximize expected returns subject to constraints, primarily risk.
- Risk is defined as the chance that the actual return on an investment will differ from its expected return.
- Rational investors are risk averse, meaning that they are unwilling to assume risk unless they expect to be adequately compensated.
- For organizational purposes, the investment decision process has traditionally been divided into two broad steps: security analysis and portfolio management.
- Security analysis is concerned with the valuation of securities. Valuation, in turn, is a function of expected return and risk.
- Portfolio management encompasses building an optimal portfolio for an investor. Considerations include initial portfolio construction, revision, and the evaluation of portfolio performance.
- Major factors affecting the decision process include uncertainty in investment decisions, the global nature of investing, institutional investors, and the efficiency of the market. As they study investments, evaluate information and claims, and make decisions, investors should consider these factors carefully.

KEY WORDS

Active investment strategy
Chartered Financial Analyst (CFA)
Efficient Market Hypothesis (EMH)
Emerging markets
Expected return
Financial assets
Institutional investors
Investment
Investments
Marketable securities
Passive investment strategy
Portfolio
Portfolio management
Real assets
Realized return
Risk
Risk-averse investor
Risk-free rate of return
Security analysis

QUESTIONS

1-1. Define the term *investments.*

1-2. Describe the broad two-step process involved in making investment decisions.

1-3. Is the study of investments really important to most individuals?

1-4. Distinguish between a financial asset and a real asset.

1-5. Carefully describe the risk-return trade-off faced by all investors.

1-6. In terms of Figure 1-1, when would an investor expect to earn the risk-free rate of return?

1-7. "A risk-averse investor will not assume risk." Do you agree or disagree with this statement?

1-8. Summarize the basic nature of the investment decision in one sentence.

1-9. Distinguish between expected return and realized return.

1-10. Define risk. How many specific types can you think of?

1-11. What other constraints besides risk do investors face?

1-12. Are all rational investors risk averse? Do they all have the same degree of risk aversion?

1-13. What external factors affect the decision process? Which do you think is the most important?

1-14. What are institutional investors? How are individual investors likely to be affected by institutional investors?

1-15. What is meant by the expression *efficient market*?

1-16. Of what significance is an efficient market to investors?

1-17. Why should the required rate of return be different for a corporate bond and a Treasury bond?

1-18. Discuss some reasons why U.S. investors should be concerned with international investing? Do you think the exchange rate value of the dollar will have any effect on the decision to invest internationally?

SELECTED REFERENCES

A strongly recommended book for the 1990s investor that is very enlightening, as well as highly entertaining, is:

Malkiel, Burton G. *A Random Walk Down Wall Street.* New York: W. W. Norton & Company, 1995.

A very popular book on investing by a former mutual fund manager who achieved great success and notoriety is:

Lynch, Peter. *One Up on Wall Street.* New York: Penguin Books, 1989.

A book many consider to be one of the important stock market books of the 1990s, involving the well-known investor Warren Buffet, is:

Hagstrom, Robert G. Jr. *The Warren Buffet Way*. New York: John Wiley & Sons, 1994.

www.wiley.com/college/jones7
This chapter is an introduction to the subject of Investments. The exercises for this chapter will introduce some of the websites that provide information that is useful for investors.

APPENDIX 1-A

THE CHARTERED FINANCIAL ANALYST PROGRAM

The Association for Investment Management and Research (AIMR) is a nonprofit professional organization of investment practitioners and academics formed in 1990 from a merger of the Financial Analysts Federation and the Institute of Chartered Financial Analysts (ICFA). AIMR, an autonomous, self-regulatory organization, seeks to maintain a professional organization with high ethical, professional, and educational standards for the investment community, broadly defined. More than 35,000 members make up this global nonprofit organization, and another 60,000 plus are registered to take the examinations.

Since 1963 the ICFA has offered a study and examination program, the CFA program, involving a body of knowledge that encompasses a range of topics important to those in the investment business. This program is designed for investment professionals or those who wish to become investment professionals. Candidates enrolled in the CFA program must show that they have mastered important material in Economics, Quantitative Analysis, Ethical and Professional Standards, Financial Accounting, Fixed Income Securities, Equity Securities Analysis, and Portfolio Management. Candidates must successfully complete three examinations, referred to as Level I, Level II, and Level III, in order to be awarded a CFA designation.

The basis of the CFA Study and Examination Program is a Body of Knowledge (BOK). The BOK is organized along functional rather than topical lines and is structured around the investment decision-making process. The BOK functional areas are Ethics and Professional Standards, Investment Tools, Asset Valuation, and Portfolio Management.

For each level of the exam, the curriculum is organized around a functional area:

Level I study program—emphasizes tools and inputs
Level II study program—emphasizes asset valuation
Level III study program—emphasizes portfolio management

Ethical and Professional Standards are considered an integral part of all three functional areas and are covered at all levels of the curriculum.

These six-hour examinations are given throughout the United States and around the world once a year, approximately on June 1, and must be completed sequentially. Because a candidate may sit for only one exam each year, completion of the CFA program requires a minimum of three years.

As of 1997, more than 200,000 examinations had been administered to candidates during the 35-year history of the program from 1963 through 1997, and more than 27,000 charters had been awarded. A substantial percentage of the CFA candidates currently are from outside North America, which indicates the global nature of investments and the distinctions to be earned within the investment profession. Over 20 percent of CFA candidates are female, and more than 40 percent of all candidates are from outside the United States.

What does it mean to be awarded the CFA charter? Increasingly, employers are recognizing the value of this designation and the potential benefits that an employee with this designation can offer to a company. The CFA charter represents a combination of academic achievement and professional experience along with a commitment to a stringent code of professional and ethical standards. CFAs must annually renew their pledge to abide by the code, and violations of the code can carry severe sanctions.

The investments profession, like many others, involves life-long learning. After receiving the CFA designation, investment professionals can participate in the CFA Accreditation Program in order to remain current on investment issues. This program allows them to earn continuing education credits through a variety of means, including workshops, seminars, and reading on their own.

AIMR has done an outstanding job of fostering a professional environment for investment practitioners and academics and is *the* professional organization for investment professionals. Similarly, the CFA professional designation is the designation for serious investment professionals committed to the highest standards of professionalism in investing activities and to the highest possible standards of ethical and professional conduct. All individuals interested in a serious career in the investments field should investigate the possibility of being awarded a CFA charter.

Complete information about AIMR and its programs, as well as the CFA program, can be found at the AIMR website, www.aimr.org.

chapter 2

Investment Alternatives

Chapter 2 explains the most important investment alternatives available to investors, ranging from money market securities to capital market securities—primarily, bonds and stocks—to derivative securities. The emphasis is on the basic features of these securities, providing the reader with the necessary knowledge to understand the investment opportunities of interest to most investors. Recent trends such as securitization are considered, as is international investing.

After reading this chapter you will be able to:

- **Identify money market and capital market securities and understand the important features of these securities.**
- **Recognize key terms such as asset-backed securities, stock splits, bond ratings, and ADRs.**
- **Understand the basics of two derivative securities, options and futures, and how they fit into the investor's choice set.**

This chapter's purpose is to organize the types of financial assets available in the money and capital markets and provide the reader with a good understanding of the securities that are of primary interest to most investors, particularly bonds and stocks.

Although our discussion is as up to date as possible, changes in the securities field occur so rapidly that investors are regularly confronted with new developments. Investors in the 1990s have a wide variety of investment alternatives available, and it is reasonable to expect that this variety will only increase. However, if investors understand the basic characteristics of the major existing securities, they will likely be able to understand new securities as they appear.

ORGANIZING FINANCIAL ASSETS

The emphasis in this chapter (and in the text in general) is on *financial assets*, which, as explained in Chapter 1, are financial claims on the issuers of the *securities*, which are claims that are negotiable, or saleable, in various marketplaces, as discussed in Chapter 4.

Direct Investing Investors buy and sell securities themselves, typically through brokerage accounts

Indirect Investing The buying and selling of the shares of investment companies, which, in turn, hold portfolios of securities

This chapter concentrates on investment alternatives available through **direct investing**, which involves securities that investors buy and sell themselves (typically, using their brokerage accounts), primarily capital market securities and derivative securities. In Chapter 3 we examine **indirect investing**. Rather than invest directly in securities, investors can invest in a portfolio of securities by purchasing the shares of a financial intermediary that invests in various types of securities on behalf of its shareowners. Indirect investing is a very important alternative for all investors to consider, and has become tremendously popular in the last few years with individual investors.

Investors who invest directly in financial markets, either using a broker or by other means, have a wide variety of assets from which to choose. Nonmarketable investment opportunities, such as savings accounts at thrift institutions, are discussed briefly at the beginning of the chapter since investors often own, or have owned, these assets and are familiar with them. Henceforth, we will consider only marketable securities, which may be classified into one of three categories: the money market, the capital market, and the derivatives market.

Investors should understand money market securities, particularly Treasury bills, but they typically will not own these securities directly, choosing instead to own them through the money market funds explained in Chapter 3. Within the capital market, securities can be classified as either fixed-income or equity securities. Finally, investors may choose to use derivative securities in their portfolios. The market value of these securities is derived from an underlying security such as common stock.

Figure 2-1 organizes the types of financial assets to be analyzed in this chapter and in Chapter 3 using the above classifications. Although for expositional purposes we cover direct investing and indirect investing in separate chapters, it is important to understand that investors can do both, and often do, investing directly through the use of a brokerage account and investing indirectly in one or more investment companies. Furthermore, brokerage accounts that accommodate the ownership of investment company shares are becoming increasingly popular, thereby combining direct and indirect investing into one account.

AN INTERNATIONAL PERSPECTIVE

As noted in Chapter 1, investors should adopt an international perspective in making their investment decisions. The investment alternatives analyzed in this chapter, in particular some

FIGURE 2-1

Major types of financial assets.

	DIRECT INVESTING
Nonmarketable	• Savings deposits • Certificates of deposit • Money market deposit accounts • U.S. savings bonds
Money market	• Treasury bills • Negotiable certificates of deposit • Commercial paper • Eurodollars • Repurchase agreements • Banker's acceptances
Capital market	• *Fixed income* Treasuries Agencies Municipals Corporates • *Equities* Preferred stock Common stock
Derivatives market	• Options • Future contracts
	INDIRECT INVESTING
Investment companies	• Unit investment trust • *Open end* Money market mutual fund Stock, bond, and income funds • Closed end

money market assets, bonds, and stocks, are available from many foreign markets to U.S. investors. Thus, the characteristics of these basic securities are relevant whether investors limit themselves to domestic or foreign stocks, or both. Furthermore, assets that have traditionally been thought of as U.S. assets are, in reality, heavily influenced by global events. Investors should understand that in many instances they own securities heavily influenced by international events.

EXAMPLE 2-1

Coca-Cola is justifiably famous for its management, and its marketing skills. Its success, however, is heavily dependent upon what happens in the foreign markets it has increasingly penetrated. If foreign economies slow, Coke's sales may be hurt. Furthermore, Coke must be able to convert its foreign earnings into dollars at favorable rates and repatriate them. Therefore, investing in Coke involves betting on a variety of foreign events.

U.S. investors typically invest internationally by investing indirectly through investment company shares. Most U.S. investors invest internationally by turning funds over to a professional investment organization, the investment company, which makes all decisions on behalf of investors who own shares of the company. We will discuss details of doing this in Chapter 3.

NONMARKETABLE FINANCIAL ASSETS

We begin our discussion of investment alternatives by mentioning those that are nonmarketable simply because most individuals will own one or more of these assets regardless of what else they do in the investing arena. For example, approximately 15 percent of total financial assets of U.S. households is in the form of deposits, including checkable deposits and currency, and time and savings deposits. Furthermore, these assets represent useful contrasts to the marketable securities we will concentrate on throughout the text.

A distinguishing characteristic of these assets is that they represent personal transactions between the owner and the issuer. That is, you as the owner of a savings account at a bank must open the account personally, and you must deal with the bank in maintaining the

TABLE 2-1 IMPORTANT NONMARKETABLE FINANCIAL ASSETS

1. *Savings accounts.* Undoubtedly the best-known type of investment in the United States, savings accounts are held at commercial banks or at "thrift" institutions such as savings and loan associations and credit unions. Savings accounts in insured institutions (and your money should not be in a noninsured institution) offer a high degree of safety on both the principal and the return on that principal. Liquidity is taken for granted and, together with the safety feature, probably accounts substantially for the popularity of savings accounts. Historically, the rate of interest paid on these accounts has been regulated by various government agencies. As of April 1, 1986, the interest rate ceiling on all deposit accounts was removed.
2. *Nonnegotiable certificates of deposit.* Commercial banks and other institutions offer a variety of savings certificates known as certificates of deposit (CDs). These certificates are available for various maturities, with higher rates offered as maturity increases. (Larger deposits may also command higher rates, holding maturity constant.) In effect, institutions are free to set their own rates and terms on most CDs. Because of competition for funds, the terms on CDs have been liberalized. Although some CD issuers have now reduced the stated penalties for early withdrawal, and even waived them, penalties for early withdrawal of funds can be, and often are, imposed.
3. *Money market deposit accounts (MMDAs).* Financial institutions offer money market deposit accounts (MMDAs) with no interest rate ceilings. Money market "investment" accounts, with a required minimum deposit to open, pay competitive money market rates and are insured up to $100,000 by the Federal Deposit Insurance Corporation (FDIC), if the bank is insured. Six pre-authorized or automatic transfers are allowed each month, up to three of which can be by check. As many withdrawals as desired can be made in person or through automated teller machines (ATMs), and there are no limitations on the number of deposits.

   Financial institutions also offer NOW (Negotiable Order of Withdrawal) accounts, checking accounts that pay interest at the so-called NOW interest rate. NOW accounts pay a relatively low rate of interest while permitting unlimited check-writing privileges. A "Super NOW account" combines unlimited check-writing privileges with money market rates of interest (which typically will be higher than rates paid in a regular NOW account).
4. *U.S. government savings bonds.* The nontraded debt of the U.S. government, savings bonds, are nonmarketable, nontransferable, and nonnegotiable, and cannot be used for collateral. They are purchased from the Treasury, most often through banks and savings institutions. Series EE bonds are sold at 50 percent of face value, with denominations of $50, $75, $100, $200, $500, $1,000, $5,000, and $10,000. Investors receive interest on Series EE bonds in a lump sum only at redemption, which can occur anytime beginning six months from the issue date. When held for at least five years, an investor will receive the higher of a market-based rate or a guaranteed minimum rate (4 percent since March 1993). The market-based rate of interest is calculated as 85 percent of the average return during that time on Treasury securities with a five-year maturity.

   Rates on savings bonds are reset every six months; therefore, depending on how long the bond is held and the prevailing interest rates, investors receive more or less than the face amount at redemption. Based on a 4 percent interest rate, savings bonds would reach their face value in 18 years. They can continue to earn interest for 30 years, and federal tax can be deferred until the bond is redeemed. The interest is exempt from state and local taxes.

account or in closing it. In contrast, marketable securities trade in impersonal markets—the buyer (seller) does not know who the seller (buyer) is, and does not care.

Liquidity The ease with which an asset can be bought or sold quickly with relatively small price changes

These are "safe" investments, occurring at (typically) insured financial institutions or issued by the U.S. government. At least some of these assets offer the ultimate in **liquidity**, which can be defined as the ease with which an asset can be converted to cash. An asset is liquid if it can be disposed of quickly, with, at most, small price changes, assuming no new information in the marketplace. Thus, we know we can get all of our money back from a savings account, or a money market deposit account, very quickly.

Table 2-1 describes the four primary nonmarketable assets held by investors. Note that new innovations are occurring in this area. For example, the Treasury now offers *I bonds*, or inflation-indexed savings bonds. The yield on these bonds is a combination of a fixed rate of return and a semiannual inflation rate.[1]

MONEY MARKET SECURITIES

Money Market The market for short-term, highly liquid, low-risk assets such as Treasury bills and negotiable CDs

Money markets include short-term, highly liquid, relatively low-risk debt instruments sold by governments, financial institutions, and corporations to investors with temporary excess funds to invest. This market is dominated by financial institutions, particularly banks, and governments. The size of the transactions in the money market typically is large ($100,000 or more). The maturities of money market instruments range from one day to one year and are often less than 90 days.

Some of these instruments are negotiable and actively traded, and some are not. Investors may invest directly in some of these securities, but more often they do so indirectly through money market mutual funds, which are investment companies organized to own and manage a portfolio of securities and which in turn are owned by investors. Thus, many individual investors own shares in money market funds that, in turn, own one or more of these money market certificates.

Treasury Bill A short-term money market instrument sold at discount by the U.S. government

Another reason a knowledge of these securities is important is the use of the **Treasury bill** (T-bill) as a benchmark asset. Although in some pure sense there is no such thing as a risk-free financial asset, on a practical basis the Treasury bill is risk free. There is no practical risk of default by the U.S. government. The Treasury bill rate, denoted RF, is used throughout the text as a proxy for the nominal (today's dollars) *risk-free rate of return* available to investors (e.g., the RF shown and discussed in Figure 1-1).

In summary, money market instruments are characterized as short-term, highly marketable investments, with an extremely low probability of default. Because the minimum investment is generally large, money market securities are typically owned by individual investors indirectly in the form of investment companies known as money market mutual funds, or, as they are usually called, money market funds.

Money market rates tend to move together, and most rates are very close to each other for the same maturity. Treasury bill rates are less than the rates available on other money market securities, approximately one-third of a percentage point, because of their risk-free nature.

Table 2-2 describes the major money market securities of most interest to individual investors. (Other money market securities exist, such as federal funds, but most individual investors will never encounter them.)

---

[1] *I bonds* are purchased at face value. Earnings grow inflation-protected for maturities up to 30 years. Face values range from $50 to $10,000. Federal taxes on earnings are deferred until redemption.

TABLE 2-2 IMPORTANT MONEY MARKET SECURITIES

1. *Treasury bills.* The premier money market instrument, a fully guaranteed, very liquid IOU from the U.S. Treasury. They are sold on an auction basis every week at a discount from face value in denominations of $10,000 to $1 million; therefore, the discount determines the yield. The greater the discount at time of purchase, the higher the return earned by investors. Typical maturities are 13 and 26 weeks. New bills can be purchased by investors on a competitive or noncompetitive bid basis. Outstanding (i.e., already issued) bills can be purchased and sold in the secondary market, an extremely efficient market where government securities dealers stand ready to buy and sell these securities.
2. *Negotiable certificates of deposit* (CDs). Issued in exchange for a deposit of funds by most American banks, the CD is a marketable deposit liability of the issuer, who usually stands ready to sell new CDs on demand. The deposit is maintained in the bank until maturity, at which time the holder receives the deposit plus interest. However, these CDs are negotiable, meaning that they can be sold in the open market before maturity. Dealers make a market in these unmatured CDs. Maturities typically range from 14 days (the minimum maturity permitted) to one year. The minimum deposit is $100,000.
3. *Commercial paper.* A short-term, unsecured promissory note issued by large, well-known, and financially strong corporations (including finance companies). Denominations start at $100,000, with a maturity of 270 days or less. Commercial paper is usually sold at a discount either directly by the issuer or indirectly through a dealer, with rates comparable to CDs. Although a secondary market exists for commercial paper, it is weak and most of it is held to maturity. Commercial paper is rated by a rating service as to quality (relative probability of default by the issuer).
4. *Eurodollars.* Dollar-denominated deposits held in foreign banks or in offices of U.S. banks located abroad. Although this market originally developed in Europe, dollar-denominated deposits can now be made in many countries, such as those of Asia. Eurodollar deposits consist of both time deposits and CDs, with the latter constituting the largest component of the eurodollar market. Maturities are mostly short term, often less than six months. The eurodollar market is primarily a wholesale market, with large deposits and large loans. Major international banks transact among themselves with other participants including multinational corporations and governments. Although relatively safe, eurodollar yields exceed those of other money market assets because of the lesser regulation for eurodollar banks.
5. *Repurchase agreement* (RPs). An agreement between a borrower and a lender (typically institutions) to sell and repurchase U.S. government securities. The borrower initiates an RP by contracting to sell securities to a lender and agreeing to repurchase these securities at a prespecified price on a stated date. The effective interest rate is given by the difference between the purchase price and the sale price. The maturity of RPs is generally very short, from three to 14 days, and sometimes overnight. The minimum denomination is typically $100,000.
6. *Banker's acceptance.* A time draft drawn on a bank by a customer, whereby the bank agrees to pay a particular amount at a specified future date. Banker's acceptances are negotiable instruments because the holder can sell them for less than face value (i.e., discount them) in the money market. They are normally used in international trade. Banker's acceptances are traded on a discount basis, with a minimum denomination of $100,000. Maturities typically range from 30 to 180 days, with 90 days being the most common.

FIXED-INCOME SECURITIES

Capital Market The market for long-term securities such as bonds and stocks

Fixed-Income Securities Securities with specified payment dates and amounts, primarily bonds

Capital markets encompass fixed-income and equity securities with maturities greater than one year. Risk is generally much higher than in the money market because of the time to maturity and the very nature of the securities sold in the capital markets. Marketability is poorer in some cases. The capital market includes both debt and equity securities, with equity securities having no maturity date.

We begin our review of the principal types of capital market securities typically owned directly by individual investors with **fixed-income securities**. All of these securities have a specified payment schedule. In most cases, such as with a traditional bond, the amount and date of each payment are known in advance. Some of these securities deviate from the traditional-bond format, but all fixed-income securities have a specified payment or repayment schedule—they must mature at some future date.

Bonds Long-term debt instruments representing the issuer's contractual obligation

BONDS

Bonds can be described simply as long-term debt instruments representing the issuer's contractual obligation, or IOU. The buyer of a newly issued coupon bond is lending money to the issuer who, in turn, agrees to pay interest on this loan and repay the principal at a stated maturity date.

Bonds are *fixed-income securities* because the interest payments (if any) and the principal repayment for a typical bond are specified at the time the bond is issued and fixed for the life of the bond. At the time of purchase, the bond buyer knows the future stream of *cash flows* to be received from buying and holding the bond to maturity. Barring default by the issuer, these payments will be received at specified intervals until maturity, at which time the principal will be repaid. However, if the buyer decides to sell the bond before maturity, the price received will depend on the level of interest rates at that time.

USING THE INTERNET Detailed information on bonds can be found at http://quote.yahoo.com. This site contains current information on the bond market, information on various segments, including governments, corporates, and municipals, and a tutorial entitled "The Bond Professor." At http://bloomberg.com, investors can obtain a wide array of market information from one of the major providers of financial information. Treasury and municipal interest rates are available on separate screens.

Par Value (Face Value) The redemption value of a bond paid at maturity, typically $1,000

Bond Characteristics The **par value (face value)** of most bonds is $1,000, and we will use this number as the amount to be repaid at maturity.[2] The typical bond matures (terminates) on a specified date and is technically known as a *term bond*.[3] Most bonds are coupon bonds, where *coupon* refers to the periodic interest that the issuer pays to the holder of the bonds.[4] Interest on bonds is typically paid semiannually.

EXAMPLE 2-2

A 10-year, 10 percent coupon bond has a dollar coupon of $100 (10 percent of $1,000); therefore, knowing the percentage coupon rate is the same as knowing the coupon payment in dollars.[5] This bond would pay interest (the coupons) of $50 on a specified date every six months. The $1,000 principal would be repaid 10 years hence on a date specified at the time the bond is issued.

Zero Coupon Bond A bond sold with no coupons at a discount and redeemed for face value at maturity

A radical innovation in the format of traditional bonds is the **zero coupon bond**, which is issued with no coupons, or interest, to be paid during the life of the bond. The purchaser pays less than par value for zero coupons and receives par value at maturity. The difference in these two amounts generates an effective interest rate, or rate of return. As in the case of Treasury bills, which are sold at discount, the lower the price paid for the coupon bond, the higher the effective return.

Issuers of zero coupon bonds include corporations, municipalities, government agencies, and the U.S. Treasury. In 1985 the Treasury created its STRIPS, or Separate Trading of Registered Interest and Principal of Securities. Under this program, all new Treasury bonds

[2] The par value is almost never less than $1,000, although it easily can be more.

[3] The phrase *term-to-maturity* denotes how much longer the bond will be in existence. In contrast, a serial bond has a series of maturity dates. One issue of *serial bonds* may mature in specified amounts year after year, and each specified amount could carry a different coupon.

[4] The terms *interest income* and *coupon income* are interchangeable.

[5] The coupon rate on a traditional, standard bond is fixed at the bond's issuance and cannot vary.

and notes with maturities greater than 10 years are eligible to be "stripped" to create zero coupon Treasury securities that are direct obligations of the Treasury.

Bond prices are quoted as a percentage of par value. By convention, corporations and Treasuries use 100 as par rather than 1,000. Therefore, a price of 90 represents $900, and a price of 55 represents $550 using the normal assumption of a par value of $1,000. Each "point," or a change of "1," represents 1 percent of $1,000, or $10. The easiest way to convert quoted bond prices to actual prices is to remember that they are quoted in percentages, with the common assumption of a $1,000 par value.

EXAMPLE 2-3

A closing price of 101 3/8 on a particular day for an IBM bond represents 101.375 percent of $1,000, or $1013.75.

Example 2-3 suggests that an investor could purchase the IBM bond for $1,013.75 on that day. Actually, bonds trade on an *accrued interest* basis. That is, the bond buyer must pay the bond seller the price of the bond as well as the interest that has been earned (accrued) on the bond since the last semiannual interest payment. This allows an investor to sell a bond any time without losing the interest that has accrued. Bond buyers should remember this additional "cost" when buying a bond because prices are quoted in the paper without the accrued interest.[6]

The price of the IBM bond is above 100 (i.e., $1,000) because market yields on bonds of this type declined after this bond was issued. The coupon on this particular bond became more than competitive with the going market interest rate for comparable newly issued bonds, and the price increased to reflect this fact. At any point in time some bonds are selling at *premiums* (prices above par value), reflecting a decline in market rates after that particular bond was sold. Others are selling at *discounts* (prices below par value of $1,000), because the stated coupons are less than the prevailing interest rate on a comparable new issue.

Call Provision Gives the issuer the right to call in a security and retire it by paying off the obligation

The **call provision** gives the issuer the right to "call in" the bonds, thereby depriving investors of that particular fixed-income security.[7] Exercising the call provision becomes attractive to the issuer when market interest rates drop sufficiently below the coupon rate on the outstanding bonds for the issuer to save money.[8] Costs are incurred to call the bonds, such as a "call premium" and administrative expenses. However, issuers expect to sell new bonds at a lower interest cost, thereby replacing existing higher interest-cost bonds with new, lower interest-cost bonds.[9]

[6] The *invoice price*, or the price the bond buyer must pay, will include the accrued interest.

[7] Unlike the call provision, the *sinking fund* provides for the orderly retirement of the bond issue during its life. The provisions of a sinking fund vary widely. For example, it can be stated as a fixed or variable amount and as a percentage of the particular issue outstanding or the total debt of the issuer outstanding. Any part or all of the bond issue may be retired through the sinking fund by the maturity date. One procedure for carrying out the sinking fund requirement is simply to buy the required amount of bonds on the open market each year. A second alternative is to call the bonds randomly. Again, investors should be aware of such provisions for their protection.

[8] There are different types of call features. Some bonds can be called any time during their life, given a short notice of 30 or 60 days. Many callable bonds have a "deferred call" feature, meaning that a certain time period after issuance must expire before the bonds can be called. Popular time periods in this regard are 5 and 10 years.

[9] The call premium often equals one year's interest if the bond is called within a year; after the first year, it usually declines at a constant rate.

INVESTMENTS INTUITION The call feature is a disadvantage to investors who must give up the higher yielding bonds. The wise bond investor will note the bond issue's provisions concerning the call, carefully determining the earliest date at which the bond can be called and the bond's yield if it is called at the earliest date possible. (This calculation is shown in Chapter 8.) Some investors have purchased bonds at prices above face value and suffered a loss when the bonds were unexpectedly called in and paid off at face value.[10]

Some bonds are not callable. Most Treasury bonds cannot be called, although some older Treasury bonds can be called within five years of the maturity date.[11]

A bond has certain legal ramifications. Failure to pay either interest or principal on a bond constitutes default for that obligation. Default, unless quickly remedied by payment or a voluntary agreement with the creditor, leads to bankruptcy. A filing of bankruptcy by a corporation initiates litigation and involvement by a court, which works with all parties concerned.

TYPES OF BONDS

There are four major types of bonds in the United States based on the issuer involved (U.S. government, federal agency, municipal, and corporate bonds), and variations exist within each major type.

Federal Government Securities The U.S. government, in the course of financing its operations through the Treasury Department, issues numerous notes and bonds with maturities greater than one year.[12] The U.S. government is considered the safest credit risk because of its power to print money; therefore, *for practical purposes investors do not consider the possibility of risk of default for these securities.* An investor purchases these securities with the expectation of earning a steady stream of interest payments and with full assurance of receiving the par value of the bonds when they mature.

Treasury Bond Long-term bonds sold by the U.S. government

Treasury bonds generally have maturities of 10 to 30 years, although a bond can be issued with any maturity.[13] Like Treasury bills, they are sold at competitive auctions; unlike bills, they are sold at face value, with investors submitting bids on yields. Interest payments (coupons) are paid semiannually. Face value denominations are $1,000, $5,000, $10,000, $100,000, $500,000, and $1 million.

Government Agency Securities Since the 1920s, the federal government has created various federal agencies designed to help certain sectors of the economy, through either direct loans or guarantee of private loans. These various credit agencies compete for funds in the marketplace by selling **government agency securities**.

Government Agency Securities Securities issued by federal credit agencies (fully guaranteed) or by government-sponsored agencies (not guaranteed)

There are two types of federal credit agencies: federal agencies and federally sponsored credit agencies. Legally, federal agencies are part of the federal government and their securities are fully guaranteed by the Treasury. The most important "agency" for investors is the Government National Mortgage Association (often referred to as "Ginnie Mae").

[10] A bond listed as "nonrefundable" for a specified period can still be called in and paid off with cash in hand. It cannot be refunded through the sale of a new issue carrying a lower coupon.

[11] Treasury bonds issued after February 1985 cannot be called.

[12] Through 1982, Treasury securities were sold in bearer form, meaning they belong to the bearer (whoever possesses them). Most federal, state and local, and corporate bonds issued after January 1, 1983, must be registered in the owner's name (unless the maturity is one year or less).

[13] U.S. securities with maturities greater than 1 year and less than 10 years technically are referred to as Treasury notes.

In contrast to federal agencies that are officially a part of the government, federally sponsored credit agencies are privately owned institutions that sell their own securities in the marketplace in order to raise funds for their specific purposes. Although these agencies have the right to draw on Treasury funds up to some approved amount, their securities are not guaranteed by the government as to principal or interest. Nevertheless, the rapidly growing agency market is dominated by these federally sponsored credit agencies, which include the Federal National Mortgage Association, the Federal Home Loan Mortgage Corporation, the Federal Home Loan Bank, the Farm Credit System, and the Student Loan Marketing Association.

EXAMPLE 2-4

Perhaps the best known of these federally sponsored agencies is the Federal National Mortgage Association (FNMA, typically referred to as "Fannie Mae"), which is designed to help the mortgage markets. Although government sponsored, it is now a privately owned corporation, and its securities are not a direct obligation of the U.S. government. A variety of Fannie Mae issues are available, with maturities ranging from short term to long term.

The Federal National Mortgage Association, the Government National Mortgage Association, and the Federal Home Loan Mortgage Corporation (Freddie Mac) issue and guarantee securities backed by conventional mortgages bought from lenders. These securities are part of the rapidly growing market of fixed-income securities known as asset-backed securities, which are discussed separately below.

INVESTMENTS INTUITION

Federal agency securities can be thought of as an alternative to U.S. Treasury securities from the investor's standpoint. The feeling in the marketplace seems to be that the Treasury would not stand by and permit a government-sponsored agency to default; however, they have to be viewed as having slightly greater default risk. Also, longer term issues may trade less frequently than comparable Treasury bonds. Together, these two factors cause these securities to carry slightly higher yields than Treasury securities of comparable maturity.

Municipal Securities Bonds sold by states, counties, cities, and other political entities (e.g., airport authorities, school districts) other than the federal government and its agencies are called **municipal bonds**. There are roughly 50,000 different issuers with roughly 1.5 million different issues outstanding and credit ratings ranging from very good to very suspect. Thus, risk varies widely, as does marketability. Overall, however, the default rate on municipal bonds has been quite favorable compared to corporate bonds.

Municipal Bonds Securities issued by political entities other than the federal government and its agencies, such as states and cities

Two basic types of municipals are *general obligation bonds*, which are backed by the "full faith and credit" of the issuer, and *revenue bonds*, which are repaid from the revenues generated by the project they were sold to finance (e.g., a toll road or airport improvement).[14] In the case of general obligation bonds, the issuer can tax residents to pay for the bond interest and principal. In the case of revenue bonds, the project must generate enough revenue to service the issue.

Most long-term municipals are sold as *serial bonds*, which means that a specified number of the original issue matures each year until the final maturity date. For example, a 10-year serial issue might have 10 percent of the issue maturing each year for the next 10 years.

[14] Municipalities also issue short-term obligations. Some of these qualify for money market investments because they are short term and of high quality.

The distinguishing feature of most municipals is their exemption from federal taxes. Because of this feature, the stated rate on these bonds will be lower than that on comparable nonexempt bonds. The higher an investor's tax bracket, the more attractive municipals become. To make the return on these bonds comparable to those of taxable bonds, the *taxable equivalent yield* (TEY) can be calculated. The TEY shows the interest rate on taxable bonds necessary to provide an after-tax return equal to that of municipals. The TEY for any municipal bond return and any marginal tax bracket can be calculated using the following formula:

$$\text{Taxable equivalent yield} = \frac{\text{Tax-exempt municipal yield}}{1 - \text{Marginal tax rate}} \qquad (2\text{-}1)$$

EXAMPLE 2-5

An investor in the 28 percent marginal tax bracket who invests in a 5 percent municipal bond would have to receive

$$0.05/(1 - 0.28) = 6.94\%$$

from a comparable taxable bond to be as well off.[15]

In some cases, the municipal bondholder can also escape state and/or local taxes. For example, a North Carolina resident purchasing a bond issued by the state of North Carolina would escape all taxes on the interest received. To calculate the TEY in these cases, first determine the *effective state rate*:

$$\text{effective state rate} = \text{marginal state tax rate} \times (1 - \text{Federal marginal rate})$$

Then, calculate the *combined effective federal/state tax rate* as:

$$\text{combined tax rate} = \text{effective state rate} + \text{federal rate}$$

Use Equation 2-1 to calculate the combined TEY, substituting the combined effective tax rate for the federal marginal tax rate shown in Equation 2-1.

Corporate Bonds Long-term debt securities of various types sold by corporations

Senior Securities Securities, typically debt securities, ahead of common stock in terms of payment or in case of liquidation

Debenture An unsecured bond backed by the general worthiness of the firm

Convertible Bonds Bonds that are convertible, at the holder's option, into shares of common stock of the same corporation

Corporates Most of the larger corporations, several thousand in total, issue **corporate bonds** to help finance their operations. Many of these firms have more than one issue outstanding. AT&T, for example, has several different issues of bonds listed on the New York Exchange Bonds page of *The Wall Street Journal*. Although an investor can find a wide range of maturities, coupons, and special features available from corporates, the typical corporate bond matures in 20 to 40 years, pays semiannual interest, is callable, carries a sinking fund, and is sold originally at a price close to par value, which is almost always $1,000.

Corporate bonds are **senior securities**. That is, they are senior to any preferred stock and to the common stock of a corporation in terms of priority of payment and in case of bankruptcy and liquidation. However, within the bond category itself there are various degrees of security. The most common type of unsecured bond is the **debenture**, a bond backed only by the issuer's overall financial soundness.[16] Debentures can be subordinated, resulting in a claim on income that stands below (subordinate to) the claim of the other debentures.

Convertible bonds have a built-in conversion feature. The holders of these bonds have the option to convert whenever they choose. Typically, the bonds are turned in to the cor-

[15] As a result of tax reform, municipal bonds used to finance nonessential government functions are now taxable—specifically, private-purpose municipal bonds issued after August 7, 1986. Some of these bonds are fully taxable to all investors, while others are taxable only to investors subject to the alternative minimum tax.

[16] Bonds that are "secured" by a legal claim to specific assets of the issuer in case of liquidation are called *mortgage bonds*.

FIGURE 2-2

Standard & Poor's debt-rating definitions.

AAA	Extremely strong capacity to pay interest and repay principal.
AA	Strong capacity to pay interest and repay principal.
A	Strong capacity to pay interest and repay principal but more vulnerable to an adverse change in conditions than in the case of AA.
BBB	Adequate capacity to pay interest and repay principal. Even more vulnerable to adverse change in conditions than A-rated bonds.
	Debt rated BB and below is regarded as having predominantly speculative characteristics.
BB	Less near-term risk of default than lower rated issues. These bonds are exposed to large ongoing uncertainties or adverse change in conditions.
B	A larger vulnerability to default than BB but with the current capacity to pay interest and repay principal.
CCC	A currently identifiable vulnerability to default and dependent on favorable conditions to pay interest and repay principal.
CC	Applied to debt subordinated to senior debt rated CCC.
C	Same as CC.
D	A debt that is in default.
+ or −	may be used to show relative standings within a category.

poration in exchange for a specified number of common shares, with no cash payment required. Convertible bonds are two securities simultaneously: a fixed-income security paying a specified interest payment and a claim on the common stock that will become increasingly valuable as the price of the underlying common stock rises. Thus, the prices of convertibles may fluctuate over a fairly wide range, depending on whether they currently are trading like other fixed-income securities or are trading to reflect the price of the underlying common stock.

INVESTMENTS INTUITION Investors should not expect to receive the conversion option free. The issuer sells convertible bonds at a lower interest rate than would otherwise be paid, resulting in a lower interest return to investors.

Bond Ratings Letters assigned to bonds by rating agencies to express the relative probability of default

Corporate bonds, unlike Treasury securities, carry the risk of default by the issuer. Two rating agencies, Standard & Poor's (S&P) Corporation and Moody's Investors Service Inc., provide investors with **bond ratings**, that is, current opinions on the *relative* quality of most large corporate and municipal bonds, as well as commercial paper. As independent organizations with no vested interest in the issuers, they can render objective judgments on the relative merits of their securities. By carefully analyzing the issues in great detail, the rating firms, in effect, perform the *credit analysis* for the investor.

Standard & Poor's bond ratings consist of letters ranging from AAA, AA, A, BBB, and so on, to D. (Moody's corresponding letters are Aaa, Aa, A, Baa, etc., to D.) Plus or minus signs can be used to provide more detailed standings within a given category.[17] Figure 2-2

[17] Moody's uses numbers (i.e., 1, 2, and 3) to designate quality grades further. For example, bonds could be rated Aa1 or Aa2. Major rating categories for Moody's include: Aaa, Aa, A, Baa, Ba, B, Caa, Ca, and C.

shows Standard & Poor's rating definitions and provides a brief explanation of the considerations on which the ratings are based.

The first four categories, AAA through BBB, represent *investment grade* securities. AAA securities are judged to have very strong capacity to meet all obligations, whereas BBB securities are considered to have adequate capacity. Typically, institutional investors must confine themselves to bonds in these four categories. Other things being equal, bond ratings and bond coupon rates are inversely related.

Bonds rated BB, B, CCC, and CC are regarded as speculative securities in terms of the issuer's ability to meet its contractual obligations. These securities carry significant uncertainties, although they are not without positive factors. Bonds rated C are currently not paying interest, and bonds rated D are in default.

Of the large number of corporate bonds outstanding, traditionally more than 80 percent have been rated A or better (based on the value of bonds outstanding). Utilities and finance companies have the fewest low-rated bonds, and transportation companies the most (because of problems with bankrupt railroads).[18]

Despite their widespread acceptance and use, bond ratings have some limitations. The two agencies may disagree on their evaluations. Furthermore, because most bonds are in the top four categories, it seems safe to argue that not all issues in a single category (such as A) can be equally risky. Finally, it is extremely important to remember that *bond ratings are a reflection of the relative probability of default*, which says little or nothing about the absolute probability of default.

ASSET-BACKED SECURITIES

The money and capital markets are constantly adapting to meet new requirements and conditions. This has given rise to new types of securities that were not previously available.

Asset-Backed Securities (ABS) Securities issued against some type of asset-linked debts bundled together, such as credit card receivables or mortgages

Securitization refers to the transformation of illiquid, risky individual loans into more liquid, less risky securities referred to as **asset-backed securities (ABS)**. The best example of this process, the *mortgage-backed securities* issued by the federal agencies mentioned above, such as Ginnie Mae, are securities representing an investment in an underlying pool of mortgages.[19]

The federal agencies discussed earlier purchase mortgages from banks and thrift institutions, repackage them in the form of securities, and sell them to investors as mortgage pools. Investors in mortgage-backed securities are, in effect, purchasing a piece of a mortgage pool, taking into consideration such factors as maturity and the spread between the yield on the mortgage security and the yield on 10-year Treasuries (considered a benchmark in this market). Investors in mortgage-backed securities assume little default risk because most mortgages are guaranteed by one of the government agencies. However, these securities present investors with uncertainty because they can receive varying amounts of monthly payments depending

[18] Less is known about the ratings of state and local government bonds, but the majority apparently are rated in the top three categories based on value. We do know that approximately 70 percent of newly issued *insured* municipal bonds carry a rating of A or better, and that less than 1 percent of all outstanding insured municipals have ratings that have declined below investment grade.

[19] In the area of mortgage-backed securities, **collateralized mortgage obligations (CMOs)** have been created to offer investors an alternative mortgage security. CMOs are bonds backed by a trust created to hold Ginnie Mae and other government-guaranteed mortgages. They are issued by brokerage firms. Shorter maturities are typically purchased by institutions, while individual investors often purchase the longer term issues known as "companion" CMOs. One advantage of CMOs is their lower minimum investment of $1,000, compared to $25,000 for Ginnie Maes. Yields are higher than for Ginnie Maes, perhaps one-half percentage point, presumably because of their lower liquidity. CMOs can be redeemed by random calls by the trust as the principal accumulates in a redemption fund. Like Ginnie Maes, investors in CMOs face the risk of early redemption as a result of mortgage refinancings.

on how quickly homeowners pay off their mortgages. Although the stated maturity can be as long as 40 years, the average life of these securities to date has been much shorter.

Ginnie Mae issues are well known to investors. This wholly owned government agency issues fully backed securities (i.e., they are full faith and credit obligations of the U.S. government) in support of the mortgage market. The GNMA *pass-through securities* have attracted considerable attention in recent years because the principal and interest payments on the underlying mortgages used to collateralize them are "passed through" to the bondholder monthly as the mortgages are repaid.[20]

As a result of the trend to securitization, asset-backed securities have proliferated as financial institutions have rushed to securitize various types of loans. After issuing $75 billion of ABS in 1994 and $108 billion in 1995, corporations issued roughly $140 billion in 1996. ABSs are created when an underwriter, such as a bank, bundles some type of asset-linked debt (typically consumer oriented) and sells to investors the right to receive payments made on that debt.

EXAMPLE 2-6

Citicorp, a large bank, has a large Visa operation. It regularly takes the cash flows from the monthly payments that customers make on their Visa accounts, securitizes them, and sells the resulting bonds to investors.

Marketable securities have been backed by car loans, credit-card receivables, railcar leases, small-business loans, photocopier leases, aircraft leases, and so forth. The assets that can be securitized seem to be limited only by the imagination of the packagers, as evidenced by the fact that by 1996 new asset types included royalty streams from films, student loans, mutual fund fees, tax liens, monthly electric utility bills, and delinquent child support payments.

Why do investors like these asset-backed securities? The attractions are relatively high yields and relatively short maturities (often, five years) combined with investment-grade credit ratings, typically the highest two ratings available.[21] Investors are often protected by a bond insurer. Institutional investors such as pension funds and life insurance companies have become increasingly attracted to ABS because of the higher yields, and foreign investors are now buying these securities more often.

As for risks, securitization works best when packaged loans are homogeneous, so that income streams and risks are more predictable. This is clearly the case for home mortgages, for example, which must adhere to strict guidelines. This is not the case for some of the newer loans being considered for packaging, such as loans for boats and motorcycles; the smaller amount of information results in a larger risk from unanticipated factors.

Rates on Fixed-Income Securities Interest rates on fixed-income securities fluctuate widely over the years as inflationary expectations change as well as demand and supply conditions for long-term funds. As we would expect on the basis of the return-risk trade-off explained in Chapter 1, corporate bond rates exceed Treasury rates because of the possible risk of default, and lower-rated corporates yield more than do higher-rated bonds. The mu-

[20] A related mortgage-backed security is "Freddie Mac," issued by the Federal Home Loan Mortgage Corporation. This is a *participation certificate* paying a monthly return. Unlike Ginnie Mae, Freddie Mac is not guaranteed by the U.S. government itself. Fannie Mae also issues pass-throughs called mortgage-backed securities. These also are not guaranteed by the U.S. government; however, payment of interest and principal is guaranteed by Fannie Mae.

[21] To date, some 75 percent of ABS have been rated AAA.

nicipal bond rate as reported is below all other rates, but we must remember that this is an after-tax rate. To make it comparable, municipal bond yields should be adjusted to a taxable equivalent yield using Equation 2-1. When this is done, the rate will be much closer to the taxable rates. Investors can obtain daily information on the rates available on fixed-income securities in the "Credit Markets" section of *The Wall Street Journal.*

EQUITY SECURITIES

Unlike fixed-income securities, equity securities represent an ownership interest in a corporation. These securities provide a residual claim—after payment of all obligations to fixed-income claims—on the income and assets of a corporation. There are two forms of equities, preferred stock and common stock. Investors are primarily interested in common stocks.

PREFERRED STOCK

Preferred Stock An equity security with an intermediate claim (between the bondholders and the stockholders) on a firm's assets and earnings

Although technically an equity security, **preferred stock** is known as a hybrid security because it resembles both equity and fixed-income instruments. As an equity security, preferred stock has an infinite life and pays dividends. Preferred stock resembles fixed-income securities in that the dividend is fixed in amount and known in advance, providing a stream of income very similar to that of a bond. The difference is that the stream continues forever, unless the issue is called or otherwise retired (most preferred is callable). The price fluctuations in preferreds often exceed those in bonds.[22]

Preferred stockholders are paid after the bondholders but before the common stockholders in terms of priority of payment of income and in case the corporation is liquidated. However, preferred stock dividends are not legally binding but must be voted on each period by a corporation's board of directors. If the issuer fails to pay the dividend in any year, the unpaid dividend(s) will have to be paid in the future before common stock dividends can be paid if the issue is cumulative. (If noncumulative, dividends in arrears do not have to be paid.)[23]

More than one-third of the preferred stock sold in recent years is convertible into common stock at the owner's option. A large amount of the total outstanding is variable-rate preferred; that is, the dividend rate is tied to current market interest rates. New trends in preferred stocks include auction-rate preferred, a type of floating-rate preferred where the dividend is established by auction every 49 days.

A new trend in this area is a hybrid security combining features of preferred stock and corporate bonds. These hybrid securities are available from brokerage houses under various acronyms, such as MIPS and QUIPS (*monthly income preferred securities* and *quarterly income preferred securities*), issued by Goldman Sachs, and TOPrS, or *trust originated preferred security*, originated by Merrill Lynch. For individual investors, these securities are an alternative to corporate bonds and traditional preferred stocks.

Most are traded on the NYSE, offer fixed monthly or quarterly dividends considerably higher than investment-grade corporate bond yields, are rated as to credit risk, and have

[22] Corporations are the largest buyer of preferreds because of a unique tax advantage: 70 percent of the dividends are not taxed, resulting in an effective tax rate of only 10.2 percent (assuming the maximum marginal corporate tax rate of 34 percent).

[23] In the event of omitted dividends, preferred stock owners may be allowed to vote for the directors of the corporation.

maturities in the 30–49-year range. Hybrids are sensitive to interest rate changes and can be called, although a fixed dividend is paid for five years.[24]

COMMON STOCK

Common Stock An equity security representing the ownership interest in a corporation

Common stock represents the ownership interest of corporations, or the equity of the stockholders, and we can use the term *equity securities* interchangeably. If a firm's shares are held by only a few individuals, the firm is said to be "closely held." Most companies choose to "go public"; that is, they sell common stock to the general public. This action is taken primarily to enable the company to raise additional capital more easily. If a corporation meets certain requirements, it may, if it chooses to, be listed on one or more exchanges. Otherwise, it will be listed in the over-the-counter market (this process is discussed in Chapter 4).

As a purchaser of 100 shares of common stock, an investor owns 100/*n* percent of the corporation (where *n* is the number of shares of common stock outstanding). As the residual claimants of the corporation, stockholders are entitled to income remaining after the fixed-income claimants (including preferred stockholders) have been paid; also, in case of liquidation of the corporation, they are entitled to the remaining assets after all other claims (including preferred stock) are satisfied.[25]

As owners, the holders of common stock are entitled to elect the directors of the corporation and vote on major issues.[26] Each owner is usually allowed to cast votes equal to the number of shares owned for each director being elected. Such votes occur at the annual meeting of the corporation, which each shareholder is allowed to attend.[27] Most stockholders vote by *proxy*, meaning that the stockholder authorizes someone else (typically management) to vote his or her shares. Sometimes proxy battles occur, whereby one or more groups unhappy with corporate policies seek to bring about changes.

Stockholders also have *limited liability*, meaning that they cannot lose more than their investment in the corporation. In the event of financial difficulties, creditors have recourse only to the assets of the corporation, leaving the stockholders protected. This is perhaps the greatest advantage of the corporation and the reason why it has been so successful.

Like other types of financial assets, new financial assets are created in the equity area.

SPDRs Tradable securities representing a claim on a market index

SPDRs (pronounced "spiders") combine the performance of an equity index (one for large stocks and one for mid-cap stocks) with the trading advantages of a stock. SPDRs, traded on the American Stock Exchange, are fully backed by shares held in a trust and pay quarterly dividends. Like any equity, the price is continually changing because the market underlying these securities is continually moving up and down.

Characteristics of Common Stocks The *par value* (stated or face value) for a common stock, unlike a bond or preferred stock, is generally not a significant economic variable. Corporations can make the par value any number they choose—for example, the par value

[24] Unlike a traditional preferred stock, hybrids can suspend dividend payments no longer than five years.

[25] The *preemptive right* in a corporation's charter grants existing stockholders the first right to purchase any new common stock sold by the corporation. The "right" is a piece of paper giving each stockholder the option to buy a specified number of new shares, usually at a discount, during a specified short period of time. Because of this, rights are valuable and can be sold in the market.

[26] The *voting rights* of the stockholders give them legal control of the corporation. In theory, the board of directors controls the management of the corporation, but in many cases the effective result is the opposite. Stockholders can regain control if they are sufficiently dissatisfied.

[27] Most shareholders do not attend, often allowing management to vote their proxy. Therefore, although technically more than 50 percent of the outstanding shares are needed for control of a firm, effective control can often be exercised with considerably less because not all of the shares are voted.

of Coca-Cola is $0.25 per share. An often-used par value is $1. Some corporations issue no-par stock. New stock is usually sold for more than par value, with the difference recorded on the balance sheet as "capital in excess of par value."

Book Value The accounting value of the equity as shown on the balance sheet

The **book value** of a corporation is the accounting value of the equity as shown on the books (i.e., balance sheet). It is the sum of common stock outstanding, capital in excess of par value, and retained earnings. Dividing this sum, or total book value, by the number of common shares outstanding produces the *book value per share*. In effect, book value is the accounting value of the stockholders' equity. Although book value per share plays a role in making investment decisions, market value per share is the critical item of interest to investors.

EXAMPLE 2-7

The Coca-Cola Company, an international soft drink company, reported $8.403 billion as total stockholders' equity for fiscal year-end 1998. This is the book value of the equity. Based on average shares outstanding of 2.496 billion for that year (a figure typically obtained for a company from its annual report), the book value per share was $3.37.

The market value (i.e., price) of the equity is the variable of concern to investors. The *aggregate market value* for a corporation, calculated by multiplying the market price per share of the stock by the number of shares outstanding, represents the total value of the firm as determined in the marketplace. The market value of one share of stock, of course, is simply the observed current market price. At the time the observation for Coca-Cola's book value was recorded, the market price was in the $60 range.

Dividends Cash payments declared and paid quarterly by corporations to stockholders

Dividends are the only cash payments regularly made by corporations to their stockholders. They are decided upon and declared by the board of directors and can range from zero to virtually any amount the corporation can afford to pay (typically, up to 100 percent of present and past net earnings). Although roughly three-fourths of the companies listed on the NYSE pay dividends, *the common stockholder has no specific promises to receive any cash from the corporation since the stock never matures, and dividends do not have to be paid.* Therefore, common stocks involve substantial risk because the dividend is at the company's discretion and stock prices typically fluctuate sharply, which means that the value of investors' claims may rise and fall rapidly over relatively short periods of time.

The following two dividend terms are important:

Dividend Yield Dividends divided by current stock price

Payout Ratio Dividends divided by earnings

- The **dividend yield** is the income component of a stock's return stated on a percentage basis. It is one of the two components of total return, which is discussed in Chapter 6. Dividend yield typically is calculated as the most recent 12-month dividend divided by the current market price.
- The **payout ratio** is the ratio of dividends to earnings. It indicates the percentage of a firm's earnings paid out in cash to its stockholders. The complement of the payout ratio, or (1.0 − payout ratio), is the *retention ratio*, and it indicates the percentage of a firm's current earnings retained by it for reinvestment purposes.

EXAMPLE 2-8

Coca-Cola's 1998 earnings were $1.42 per share, and it paid an annual dividend per share that year of $0.60. Assuming a price for Coca-Cola of $67, the dividend yield would be 0.9 percent. The payout ratio was $0.60/$1.42, or 42 percent.

Dividends are declared and paid quarterly. To receive a declared dividend, an investor must be a *holder of record* on the specified date that a company closes its stock transfer books and compiles the list of stockholders to be paid. However, to avoid problems the brokerage industry has established a procedure of declaring that the right to the dividend remains with the stock until four days before the holder-of-record date. On this fourth day, the right to the dividend leaves the stock; for that reason this date is called the *ex-dividend* date.

EXAMPLE 2-9

Assume that the board of directors of Coca-Cola meets on May 24 and declares a quarterly dividend, payable on July 2. May 24 is called the *declaration date*. The board will declare a *holder-of-record date*—say, June 7. The books close on this date, but Coke goes *ex-dividend* on June 5. To receive this dividend, an investor must purchase the stock by June 4. The dividend will be mailed to the stockholders of record on the *payment date*, July 2.

Stock Dividend A payment by the corporation in shares of stock rather than cash

Stock Split The issuance by a corporation of shares of common stock in proportion to the existing shares outstanding

Stock dividends and stock splits attract considerable investor attention. A **stock dividend** is a payment by the corporation in shares of stock instead of cash. A **stock split** involves the issuance of a larger number of shares in proportion to the existing shares outstanding. With a stock split, the book value and par value of the equity are changed; for example, each would be cut in half with a 2-for-1 split. However, on a practical basis, there is little difference between a stock dividend and a stock split.

EXAMPLE 2-10

A 5 percent stock dividend would entitle an owner of 100 shares of a particular stock to an additional five shares. A 2-for-1 stock split would double the number of shares of the stock outstanding, double an individual owner's number of shares (e.g., from 100 shares to 200 shares), and cut the price in half at the time of the split.

The New York Stock Exchange reported 246 stock distributions in 1998, consisting of 80 stock dividends and 166 stock splits (almost all of which were 2-for-1 to 2 and 1/2 for 1). The total number of such distributions ranged from a high of 260 in 1997 to a low of 104 in 1988.

Stock data, as reported to investors in most investment information sources and in the company's reports to stockholders, typically are adjusted for all stock dividends and stock splits. Obviously, such adjustments must be made when stock splits or stock dividends occur in order for legitimate comparisons to be made for the data.

The important question to investors is the value of the distribution, whether a dividend or a split. It is clear that the recipient has more shares (i.e., more pieces of paper), but has anything of real value been received? Other things being equal, these additional shares do not represent additional value because proportional ownership has not changed. Quite simply, the pieces of paper, stock certificates, have been repackaged. For example, if you own 1,000 shares of a corporation that has 100,000 shares of stock outstanding, your proportional ownership is 1 percent; with a 2-for-1 stock split, your proportional ownership is still 1 percent, because you now own 2,000 shares out of a total of 200,000 shares outstanding. If you were to sell your newly distributed shares, however, your proportional ownership would be cut in half.

Regardless of the above, some evidence does suggest that the stock price receives a boost following a split. For example, David Ikenberry finds that such stocks tend to outperform the market in the first year following a split by an average eight percentage points and that the effect continues for some three years following the split. According to S&P data, split shares tend to outperform the market for some 18 months following the split. One S&P study of 359 NYSE stocks with 2-for-1 or more stock splits for the period 1995–1997 found that these stocks did four times as well as the S&P Index on the day of the split, and even better in the 20 days prior to the execution dates; however, this particular study found that these stocks trailed in the Index in the next 12 months. In contrast, a study by Merrill Lynch found for a 12-year period that each year the group that split enjoyed superior performance over the next 12 months.[28]

Typically, the dividend is raised at the time of the split, which would have a positive effect by itself. If the above findings are indeed correct, it suggests that management signals with splits and dividends that they are confident about future prospects, which in turn should boost investor confidence.

P/E Ratio (Earnings Multiplier) The ratio of stock price to earnings, using historical, current or estimated data

The **P/E ratio**, also referred to as the *earnings multiplier*, is typically calculated as the ratio of the current market price to the firm's earnings. It is an indication of how much the market as a whole is willing to pay per dollar of earnings.

It is standard investing practice to refer to stocks as selling at, say, 10 times earnings, or 15 times earnings. Investors have traditionally used such a classification to categorize stocks. Growth stocks, for example, have typically sold at high multiples, compared to the average stock, because of their expected higher earnings growth.

The P/E ratio is a widely reported variable, appearing in daily newspapers carrying stock information, in brokerage reports covering particular stocks, in magazine articles recommending various companies, and so forth. As reported daily in newspapers, and in most other sources, it is an *identity* because it is calculated simply by dividing the current price by the latest 12-month earnings. However, variations of this ratio are often used in the valuation of common stocks. In fact, the P/E ratio in its various forms is one of the best-known and most often cited variables in security analysis and is familiar to almost all investors.[29]

Investing Internationally in Equities Foreign firms can also arrange to have their shares traded on an exchange or a market in another country. In the United States, two alternatives are available for trading internationally listed foreign securities. One is for the shares to be traded directly, exactly like a U.S. company.

American Depository Receipts (ADRs) Securities representing an ownership interest in the equities of foreign companies

The second alternative is via **American Depository Receipts (ADRs)**, which have existed since 1927. ADRs represent indirect ownership of a specified number of shares of a foreign company.[30] These shares are held on deposit in a bank in the issuing company's home country, and the ADRs are issued by U.S. banks called depositories. Examples of well-known companies that trade as ADRs include De Beers Consolidated, Toyota, Volvo, Sony, and Glaxo. The prices of ADRs are quoted in dollars, and dividends are paid in dollars.

In effect, ADRs are tradable receipts issued by depositories that have physical possession of the foreign securities through their foreign correspondent banks or custodian.[31] The securities are to be held on deposit as long as the ADRs are outstanding. The bank (or its correspondent) holding the securities collects the dividends, pays any applicable foreign withholding taxes, converts the remaining funds into dollars, and pays this amount to the ADR

[28] See Michelle DeBlasi, "Go Forth and Multiply," *Bloomberg Personal Finance*, March 1999, pp. 18–19.

[29] In calculating P/E ratios, on the basis of either the latest reported earnings or the expected earnings, problems can arise when comparing P/E ratios among companies if some of them are experiencing, or are expected to experience, abnormally high or low earnings. To avoid this problem, some market participants calculate a *normalized* earnings estimate. Normalized earnings are intended to reflect the "normal" level of a company's earnings; that is, transitory effects are presumably excluded, thus providing the user with a more accurate estimate of "true" earnings.

[30] It is not unusual for an ADR issue to represent several of the foreign issuer's underlying shares. Therefore, it is important to know the terms attached.

[31] ADRs are initiated by the depository bank, assuming the corporation does not object.

holders. Holders can choose to convert their ADRs into the specified number of foreign shares represented by paying a fee.

ADRs are an effective way for an American investor to invest in specific foreign stocks without having to worry about currency problems. The only realistic alternative for many Americans is to purchase investment companies (mutual funds or closed-end funds) specializing in foreign securities as discussed in the next section.

DERIVATIVE SECURITIES

Derivative Securities Securities that derive their value in whole or in part by having a claim on some underlying security

Warrant A corporate-created option to purchase a stated number of common shares at a specified price within a specified time (typically several years)

We will focus our attention here on the two types of derivative securities that are of interest to most investors. Options and futures contracts are **derivative securities**, so named because their value is derived from their connected underlying security. Numerous types of options and futures are traded in world markets. Furthermore, there are different types of options other than the puts and calls discussed here. For example, a **warrant** is a corporate-created long-term option on the underlying common stock of the company. It gives the holder the right to buy the stock from the company at a stated price within a stated period of time, typically several years.

Options and futures contracts share some common characteristics. Both have standardized features that allow them to be traded quickly and cheaply on organized exchanges. In addition to facilitating the trading of these securities, the exchange guarantees the performance of these contracts and its clearinghouse allows an investor to reverse his or her original position before maturity. For example, a seller of a futures contract can buy the contract and cancel the obligation that the contract carries. The exchanges and associated clearinghouses for both options and futures contracts have worked extremely well.

Options and futures contracts are important to investors because they provide a way for investors to manage portfolio risk. For example, investors may incur the risk of adverse currency fluctuations if they invest in foreign securities, or they may incur the risk that interest rates will adversely affect their fixed-income securities. Options and futures contracts can be used to limit some, or all, of these risks, thereby providing risk-control possibilities.

Options Rights to buy or sell a stated number of shares of stock within a specified period at a specified price

Options and futures contracts have important differences in their trading, the assets they can affect, their riskiness, and so forth. Perhaps the biggest difference to note now is that a futures contract is an obligation to buy or sell, but an options contract is only the right to do so, as opposed to an obligation. The buyer of an option has limited liability, but the buyer of a futures contract does not.

OPTIONS

Put An option to sell a specified number of shares of stock at a stated price within a specified period

Call An option to buy a specified number of shares of stock at a stated price within a specified period

LEAPS Puts and calls with longer maturity dates, up to two years

In today's investing world, the word **options** refers to **puts** and **calls**. Options are created not by corporations but by investors seeking to trade in claims on a particular common stock. A call (put) option gives the buyer the right to purchase (sell) 100 shares of a particular stock at a specified price (called the exercise price) within a specified time. The maturities on most new puts and calls are available up to several months away, although a new form of puts and calls called **LEAPs** has maturity dates up to a couple of years. Several exercise prices are created for each underlying common stock, giving investors a choice in both the maturity and the price they will pay or receive.

Buyers of calls are betting that the price of the underlying common stock will rise, making the call option more valuable. Put buyers are betting that the price of the underlying common stock will decline, making the put option more valuable. Both put and call options are written (created) by other investors who are betting the opposite of their respective purchasers. The sellers (writers) receive an option premium for selling each new contract while the buyer pays this option premium.

Once the option is created and the writer receives the premium from the buyer, it can be traded repeatedly in the secondary market. The premium is simply the market price of the contract as determined by investors. The price will fluctuate constantly, just as the price of the underlying common stock changes. This makes sense, because the option is affected directly by the price of the stock that gives it value. In addition, the option's value is affected by the time remaining to maturity, current interest rates, the volatility of the stock, and the price at which the option can be exercised.

Puts and calls allow both buyers and sellers (writers) to speculate on the short-term movements of certain common stocks. Buyers obtain an option on the common stock for a small, known premium, which is the maximum that the buyer can lose. If the buyer is correct about the price movements on the common, gains are magnified in relation to having bought (or sold short) the common because a smaller investment is required. However, the buyer has only a short time in which to be correct. Writers (sellers) earn the premium as income, based on their beliefs about a stock. They win or lose, depending on whether their beliefs are correct or incorrect.

Options can be used in a variety of strategies, giving investors opportunities to manage their portfolios in ways that would be unavailable in the absence of such instruments. For example, since the most a buyer of a put or call can lose is the cost of the option, the buyer is able to truncate the distribution of potential returns. That is, after a certain point, no matter how much the underlying stock price changes, the buyer's position does not change.

FUTURES CONTRACTS

Futures contracts have been available on commodities such as corn and wheat for a long time. Recently, they have also become available on several financial instruments, including stock market indexes, currencies, Treasury bills, Treasury bonds, bank certificates of deposit, and GNMAs.

Futures Contract Agreement providing for the future exchange of a particular asset at a currently determined market price

A **futures contract** is an agreement that provides for the future exchange of a particular asset between a buyer and a seller. The seller contracts to deliver the asset at a specified delivery date in exchange for a specified amount of cash from the buyer. Although the cash is not required until the delivery date, a "good faith deposit," called the margin, is required to reduce the chance of default by either party. The margin is small compared to the value of the contract.

Most futures contracts are not exercised. Instead, they are "offset" by taking a position opposite to the one initially undertaken. For example, a purchaser of a May Treasury bill futures contract can close out the position by selling an identical May contract before the delivery date, while a seller can close out the same position by purchasing that contract.

Most participants in futures are either hedgers or speculators. Hedgers seek to reduce price uncertainty over some future period. For example, by purchasing a futures contract, a hedger can lock in a specific price for the asset and be protected from adverse price movements. Similarly, sellers can protect themselves from downward price movements. Speculators, on the other hand, seek to profit from the uncertainty that will occur in the future. If prices are expected to rise (fall), contracts will be purchased (sold). Correct anticipations can result in very large profits because only a small margin is required.

One of the newest innovations in financial markets is options on futures. Calls on futures give the buyer the right, but not the obligation, to assume the futures position.

SUMMARY

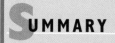

- Important investment alternatives for investors include nonmarketable assets, money market instruments, capital market securities (divided into fixed-income and equity securities), derivative securities, and indirect investments in the form of investment company shares.
- Nonmarketable financial assets, widely owned by investors, include savings deposits, nonnegotiable certificates of deposit, money market deposit accounts, and U.S. savings bonds.
- Money market investments, characterized as short-term, highly liquid, very safe investments, include (but are not limited to) Treasury bills, negotiable certificates of deposit (CDs), commercial paper, eurodollars, repurchase agreements, and banker's acceptances. The first three are obligations (IOUs) of the federal government, banks, and corporations, respectively.
- Capital market investments have maturities in excess of one year.
- Fixed-income securities, one of the two principal types of capital market securities, have a specified payment and/or repayment schedule. They include four types of bonds: U.S. government, federal agency, municipal, and corporate bonds.
- Equity securities include preferred stock and common stock.
- Preferred stock, while technically an equity security, is often regarded by investors as a fixed-income type of security because of its stated (and fixed) dividend. Preferred has no maturity date but may be retired by call or other means.
- Common stock (equity) represents the ownership of the corporation. The stockholder is the residual claimant in terms of both income and assets.
- Derivative securities include options and futures.
- Options allow both buyers and sellers (writers) to speculate on and/or hedge the price movements of stocks for which these claims are available. Calls (puts) are multiple-month rights to purchase (sell) a common stock at a specified price.
- Futures contracts provide for the future exchange of a particular asset between a buyer and a seller. A recent innovation is options on futures.

KEY WORDS

American Depository Receipts (ADRs)
Asset-backed securities (ABS)
Bonds
Bond ratings
Book value
Calls
Call provision
Capital market
Collateralized mortgage obligations (CMOs)
Common stock
Convertible bonds
Corporate bonds
Debenture
Derivative securities
Direct investing
Dividends
Dividend yield
Government agency securities
Fixed-income securities
Futures contract
Indirect investing
LEAPs
Liquidity
Money markets
Municipal bonds
Options
Par value (face value)
Payout ratio
P/E ratio
Preferred stock
Puts

Senior securities
Stock dividend
Stock split
Treasury bill
Treasury bond
Warrant
Zero coupon bond

QUESTIONS

2-1. Outline the classification scheme for marketable securities used in the chapter. Explain each of the terms involved.

2-2. What is the difference between a savings deposit and a certificate of deposit?

2-3. How do money market deposit accounts at banks and thrifts differ from the other investment opportunities they offer investors?

2-4. What does it mean for Treasury bills to be sold at a discount?

2-5. Distinguish between a negotiable certificate of deposit and the certificate of deposit discussed in the section "Nonmarketable Securities."

2-6. Name the four issuers of bonds discussed in this chapter. Which do you think would be most risky as a general proposition?

2-7. From an issuer standpoint, what is the distinction between Fannie Mae and Ginnie Mae?

2-8. Name and explain the difference between the two types of municipal securities.

2-9. What does it mean to say that investors in Ginnie Maes face the risk of early redemption?

2-10. What are the advantages and disadvantages of Treasury bonds?

2-11. Is there any relationship between a savings bond and a U.S. Treasury bond?

2-12. Why is preferred stock referred to as a "hybrid" security?

2-13. Why is the common stockholder referred to as a "residual claimant"?

2-14. Do all common stocks pay dividends? Who decides?

2-15. What is meant by the term *derivative security*?

2-16. What is meant by the term *securitization*?

2-17. Give at least two examples of asset-backed securities.

2-18. Distinguish between a serial bond and a term bond.

2-19. What is meant by "indirect" investing?

2-20. Why should we expect six-month Treasury bill rates to be less than six month CD rates or six-month commercial paper rates?

2-21. Why is the call provision on a bond generally a disadvantage to the bondholder?

2-22. Is a typical investor more likely to hold zero coupon bonds in a taxable account or a nontaxable account? Why?

2-23. What are the potential advantages to investors of MIPS and TOPrS as compared to conventional bonds?

2-24. What is an ADR? What advantages do they offer investors?

2-25. Of what value to investors are stock dividends and splits?

2-26. What are the advantages and disadvantages of being a holder of the common stock of IBM as opposed to being a bondholder?

2-27. Assume that a company in whose stock you are interested will pay regular quarterly dividends soon. Looking in *The Wall Street Journal*, you see a dividend figure of \$3.20 listed for this stock. The board of directors has declared the dividend payable on September 1, with a holder-of-record date of August 15. When must you buy the stock to receive this dividend, and how much will you receive if you buy 150 shares?

PROBLEMS

2-1. Assuming an investor is in the 15 percent tax bracket, what taxable equivalent must be earned on a security to equal a municipal bond yield of 9.5 percent?

2-2. Assume an investor is in the 36 percent tax bracket? Other things equal, after taxes are paid would this investor prefer a corporate bond paying 12.4 percent or a municipal bond paying 8 percent?

2-3. Assume an investor is in the 31 percent federal tax bracket and faces a 7 percent marginal state tax rate. What is the combined TEY for a municipal bond paying 6 percent?

SELECTED REFERENCES

The best sources of information about the financial assets available to investors, changes in their characteristics, and new financial assets that become available are the financial press, including:

The Wall Street Journal
Business Week
Financial World
Forbes
Fortune
Kiplinger's Personal Finance Magazine
Money
Smart Money
Worth

www.wiley.com/college/jones7

This chapter explains the important investment alternatives available to investors, and explores some recent trends in investing, such as international investment and securitization. The website exercises will present specific securities and allow the student to explore some of their distinctive characteristics.

APPENDIX 2-A

TAXES AND INVESTING

There are now five marginal tax rates for IRS purposes: 15, 28, 31, 36, and 39.6 percent. Any state (or city) income taxes also must be considered and could easily raise the effective marginal tax rate several percentage points.

Capital assets include property of all types. Gains can be unrealized (the asset has not been sold) or realized (the asset has been sold). Until an actual sale occurs, the gain or loss is not "realized," and therefore no tax is due.

The basis is the actual cost of an asset purchased. The capital gain or loss realized when an asset is sold is the difference between the value received and the asset's basis. Special rules on basis apply when the asset is received as a gift or from an inheritance.

Investors must distinguish between short-term and long-term capital gains. The holding period to become a long-term capital gain or loss is one year or more. A special lower rate now applies to holding periods of five years or more. Investors first aggregate all short-term gains and losses together to obtain either a net short-term gain or loss. They do the same with long-term gains and losses.

Long-term capital gains can be offset with long-term capital losses on a dollar-for-dollar basis, and the same is also true for short-term gains and losses. Finally, offsetting net long-term gains with net short-term losses produces the net capital gains referred to above. Up to $3,000 of net capital loss can be used for the current tax year to offset ordinary income, and the balance can be carried forward.

Aggregate short-term gains for assets held less than one year are taxed at the investor's ordinary income rate (one of the five brackets above). If the holding period is 12 months or more, the aggregate gain is taxed at a rate of 20 percent. If the holding period is five years or more, the capital gain is taxed at 18 percent. In both cases, if the investor is in the 15 percent tax bracket, the rate is less—10 percent and 8 percent, respectively.

Dividend income and interest income are taxed at ordinary rates. Municipal bond interest is generally exempt from federal taxes but may be subject to state taxes. Treasury securities are exempt from state taxes but are subject to federal income taxes.

Most investment income will be subject to taxes at some time, although various procedures such as tax-deferred retirement plans can delay that date for a long time. Investors do have the ability to control the realization of capital gains and losses by choosing when to sell the asset.

Taxes have a significant impact on investor returns and should be carefully considered in making investment decisions. For example, the 10 largest equity mutual funds returned an average annualized total return of 14.9 percent for the five years ending in 1993. After taxes, the return was 10.8 percent, a 28 percent difference (assuming reinvestment of distributions after taxes were paid at the highest federal rates in effect at the time, and the sale of shares and payment of capital gains taxes at the end of the period).

In recognition of this situation, the Vanguard Group of investment companies now offers *Vanguard Tax-Managed Fund*, the first series of no-load portfolios specifically designed to minimize the impact of taxes on investment returns. To do this, the Fund seeks to minimize portfolio turnover (which limits capital gains distributions), uses a disciplined sell selection method that sells securities with the highest original cost and realizes capital losses, and expressly encourages long-term investors through the use of a redemption fee. Three different portfolios are available: Growth and Income, Capital Appreciation, and Balanced.

chapter 3

INVESTMENT COMPANIES

Chapter 3 discusses the very important alternative of indirect investing used by many investors—primarily, buying and selling mutual funds. All types of investment companies are considered, with primary emphasis on mutual funds where both money market funds and bond and stock funds are analyzed. Mutual fund performance is also considered.

After reading this chapter you will be able to:

- **Appreciate the importance of indirect investing (the use of investment companies) to individual investors.**
- **Distinguish between unit investment trusts, closed-end funds, and mutual funds.**
- **Understand key features of mutual funds, such as the sales charge, the management fee, and the net asset value.**

NYSE survey data indicate that tens of millions of individual investors now own stocks either directly or indirectly—one of every four adult Americans.[1] Nevertheless, according to Federal Reserve data, individual investors were net sellers of stocks (purchases of stocks less sales, including equity mutual funds) since the early 1980s. For example, during the 1980s individual investors sold $800 billion of stocks, and from 1990 to 1997, U.S. households sold (net) $1.2 trillion of equity holdings from sources other than mutual funds. In mid-1992, for the first time in U.S. financial history, individuals no longer *directly* held a majority of all publicly traded U.S. stocks. The percentage of stocks held declined to 49 percent, compared to 84 percent in 1965 and 71 percent as late as 1980.[2]

Are individuals really bailing out of stocks? The answer is NO! U.S. households own several trillion dollars of stocks directly, and when we add in mutual fund assets representing *indirect ownership* of stocks, individuals account for ownership of more than 50 percent of all outstanding stocks.[3] Basically, households have three choices with regard to savings options:

1. Hold the liabilities of traditional intermediaries, such as banks, thrifts, and insurance companies. This means holding savings accounts, MMDAs, NOW accounts (all discussed in Chapter 2), and so forth.
2. Hold securities directly, such as stocks and bonds, purchased directly through brokers and other intermediaries.
3. Hold securities indirectly, through mutual funds and pension funds.

A pronounced shift has occurred in these alternatives since World War II. Households have increasingly turned away from the direct holding of securities and of the liabilities of traditional intermediaries and toward indirect holdings of assets through pension funds and mutual funds.

Households own an increasingly large amount of pension fund reserves, and they are actively involved in the allocation decisions of more than $1 trillion of pension funds through 401(k) plans and other defined contribution plans. Most of this amount is being invested by pension funds, on behalf of households, in equity and fixed-income securities that, as we noted in Chapter 2, are the primary securities of interest to most individual investors. Pension funds (both public and private) are the largest single institutional owner of common stocks, accounting for roughly 25 percent of corporate equity holdings.

The assets of mutual funds, the most popular type of investment company, grew tenfold in the 1980s to $1 trillion, and by June 1999, approximated $6.0 trillion. Mutual funds had the highest growth rate of any financial intermediary over the period 1985–1995. The dramatic growth in mutual fund assets, clearly demonstrated in Figure 3-1, is perhaps the most important trend in the 1990s affecting the average household with regard to their investing activities and programs.

Mutual funds owned almost 19 percent of all U.S. stocks by the beginning of 1999, and since they are simply intermediaries between households and equities, this represents a significant household investment in equities.

Investors now rely heavily on indirect investing. The 401(k) plan has become the most popular type of defined-contribution plan, and mutual funds at the end of 1998 had 42 percent of the 401(k) market. With some 50 million mutual fund IRA accounts at the end of

[1] Out of the total population, adults and nonadults, the incidence of ownership was 20 percent. This type of data can be found in the annual *Fact Book* issued by the New York Stock Exchange.

[2] Numbers such as these are available from the Securities Industry Association.

[3] Furthermore, some newer evidence indicates that households were not so much active sellers of stock as simply beneficiaries of the retirement of stocks by mergers and buybacks.

FIGURE 3-1

Assets of mutual funds (billions of dollars)

SOURCE: Federal Reserve and other data.

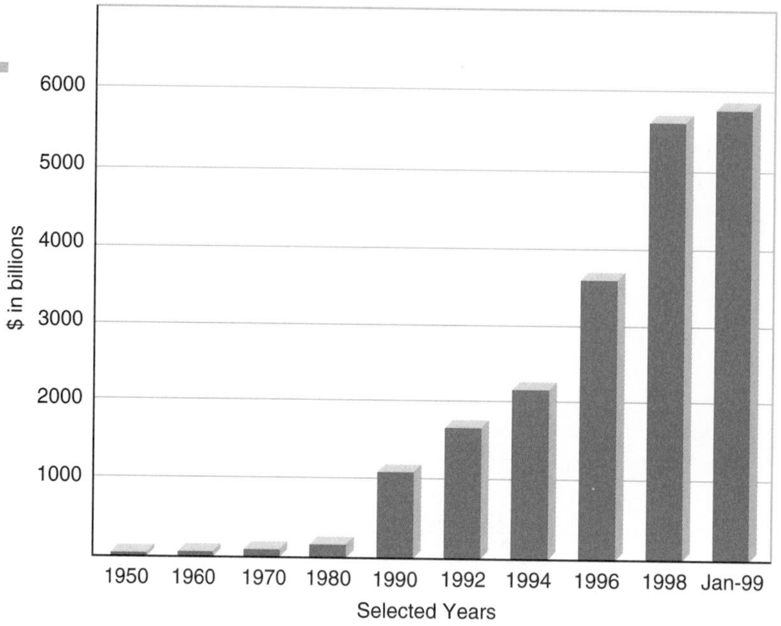

1998, mutual funds held 44 percent of the IRA market. Clearly, indirect investing through mutual funds deserves careful attention.

INVESTING INDIRECTLY THROUGH INVESTMENT COMPANIES

An investment company such as a mutual fund is a clear alternative for an investor seeking to own stocks and bonds. Rather than purchase securities and manage a portfolio, investors can, in effect, indirectly invest by turning their money over to an investment company and allow it to do all the work and make all the decisions (for a fee, of course).

Indirect investing in this discussion refers to the buying and selling of the shares of investment companies that, in turn, hold portfolios of securities. Investors who purchase shares of a particular portfolio managed by an investment company are purchasing an ownership interest in that portfolio of securities and are entitled to a pro rata share of the dividends, interest, and capital gains generated. Shareholders must also pay a pro rata share of the company's expenses and its management fee, which will be deducted from the portfolio's earnings as it flows back to the shareholders.

The contrast between direct and indirect investing is illustrated in Figure 3-2, which shows that indirect investing essentially accomplishes the same thing as direct investing. The essential difference is that the investment company stands between the investors and the portfolio of securities. Although technical qualifications exist, the point about indirect investing is that investors gain and lose through the investment company's activities in the same manner that they would gain and lose from holding a portfolio directly. The differences are the costs (any sales charges plus the management fee) and the additional services gained from the investment company, such as record-keeping and check-writing privileges.

The decision of whether to invest directly or indirectly is an important one that all investors should think about carefully. Because each alternative has possible advantages and disadvantages, it is not necessarily easy to choose one over the other. Investors can be active investors, investing directly, or passive investors, investing indirectly. Of course, they can do both at the same time, and many individuals do exactly that!

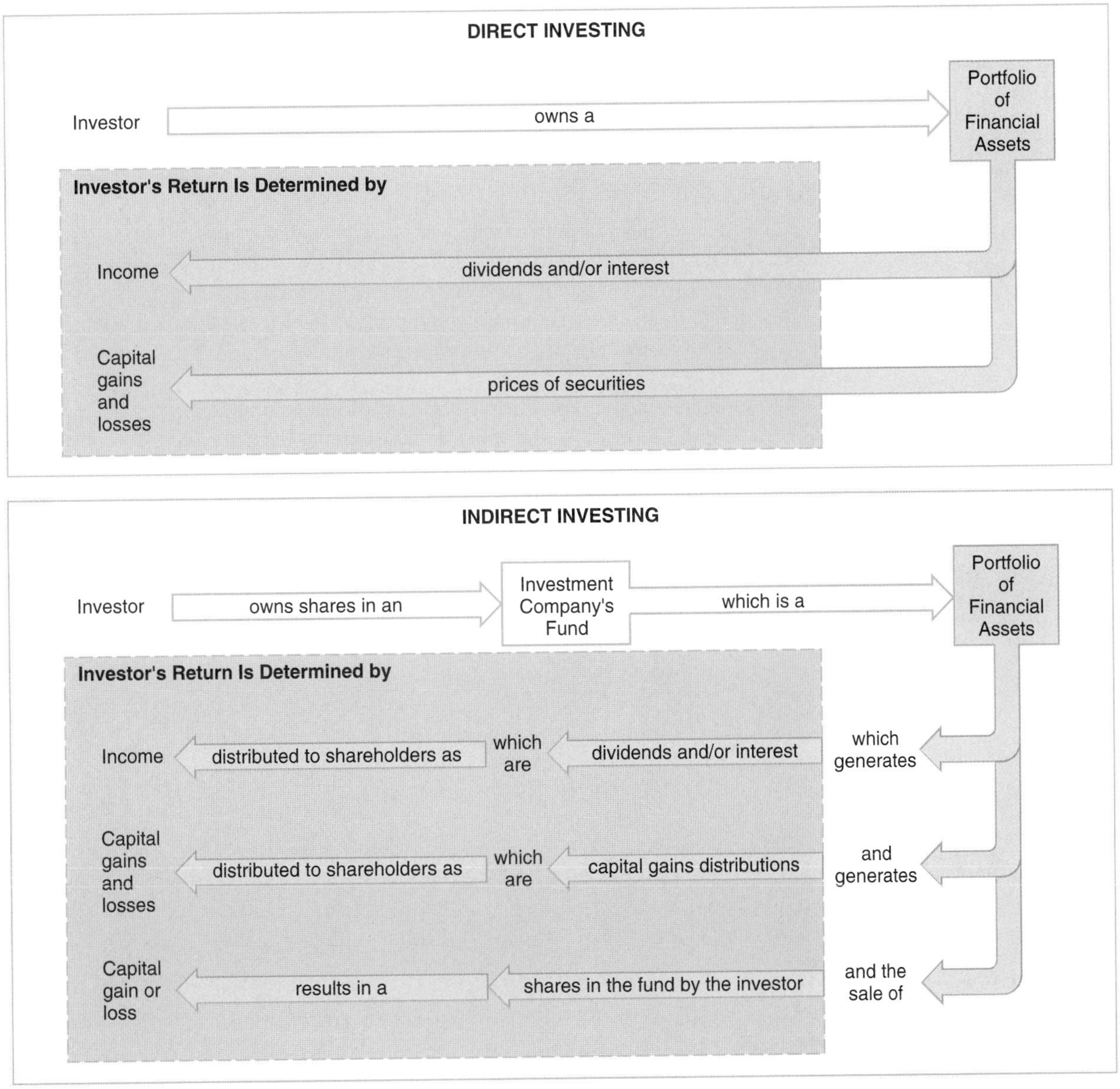

FIGURE 3-2

Direct vs. indirect investing

The line between direct and indirect investing is becoming blurred. For example, investors can invest indirectly by investing directly—through their brokerage accounts—at no additional expense. This is explained at the end of the chapter when we discuss fund "supermarkets."

WHAT IS AN INVESTMENT COMPANY?

Investment Company A financial company that sells shares in itself to the public and uses these funds to invest in a portfolio of securities

An **investment company** is a financial service organization that sells shares in itself to the public and uses the funds it raises to invest in a portfolio of securities such as money market instruments or stocks and bonds. By pooling the funds of thousands of investors, a widely diversified portfolio of financial assets can be purchased and the investment company can offer its owners (shareholders) a variety of services.

EXAMPLE 3-1

Fidelity Investments is the largest mutual fund company in the United States, offering over 100 equity funds and over 100 bond and money market funds to investors. Fidelity manages among its 200+ funds the Equity-Income Fund, and we will use this fund throughout the chapter to illustrate mutual funds (the major type of investment company).

A regulated investment company can elect to pay no federal taxes on any distribution of dividends, interest, and realized capital gains to its shareholders. The investment company acts as a conduit, "flowing through" these distributions to stockholders who pay their own marginal tax rates on them. In effect, fund shareholders are treated as if they held the securities in the fund's portfolio. Shareholders should pay the same taxes they would pay if they owned the shares directly.[4]

Fund taxation is unique, with income taxed only once when it is received by its shareholders. A fund's short-term gains and other earnings are taxed to shareholders as ordinary income, while its long-term capital gains are taxed to shareholders as long-term capital gains. Tax-exempt income received by a fund is generally tax exempt to the shareholder.

Investment companies are required by the Investment Company Act of 1940 to register with the Securities and Exchange Commission (SEC).[5] This detailed regulatory statute contains numerous provisions designed to protect shareholders.[6] (The SEC and the Investment Company Act of 1940 are discussed in Chapter 5.) Both federal and state laws require appropriate disclosures to investors.[7] It is important to note that investment companies are not insured or guaranteed by any government agency, or by any financial institution from which an investor may obtain shares. These are risky investments, losses can and do occur, and investment companies' promotional materials state this clearly.

EXAMPLE 3-2

Fidelity states on the cover of its prospectus for Equity-Income Fund: "Mutual fund shares are not deposits or obligations of, or guaranteed by, any depository institution. Shares are not insured by the FDIC, Federal Reserve Board, or any other agency, and are subject to investment risks, including possible loss of principal account invested."

TYPES OF INVESTMENT COMPANIES

All investment companies begin by selling shares in themselves to the public. Most investment companies are managed companies, offering professional management of the portfolio as one of the benefits. One less well-known type of investment company is unmanaged. We begin here with the unmanaged type and then discuss the two types of managed investment com-

[4] To qualify as a regulated investment company, a fund must earn at least 90 percent of all income from security transactions and distribute at least 90 percent of its investment company taxable income each year. Furthermore, the fund must diversify its assets. For at least 50 percent of the portfolio, no more than 5 percent of the fund's assets can be invested in the securities of any one issuer, and a position in any one security cannot exceed 25 percent of the fund's assets.

[5] The 1940 act was amended in 1970. These amendments, among other things, prohibited the charging of excessive commissions to share purchasers and the payment of excessive fees to investment company advisors.

[6] Investment companies are also regulated under the Securities Acts of 1933, the Securities Exchange Act of 1934, and the Investment Advisers Act of 1940. These acts are discussed in Chapter 5.

[7] Most states also regulate investment companies selling shares within the state.

panies. After we consider each of the three, we focus on mutual funds, the most popular type of investment company for the typical individual investor.

UNIT INVESTMENT TRUSTS

Unit Investment Trust An unmanaged form of investment company, typically holding fixed-income securities, offering investors diversification and minimum operating costs

An alternative form of investment company that deviates from the normal managed type is the **unit investment trust**, which typically is an unmanaged, fixed-income security portfolio put together by a sponsor and handled by an independent trustee. Redeemable trust certificates representing claims against the assets of the trust are sold to investors at net asset value plus a small commission. All interest (or dividends) and principal repayments are distributed to the holders of the certificates. Most unit investment trusts hold tax-exempt securities.[8] The assets are almost always kept unchanged and the trust ceases to exist when the bonds mature, although it is possible to redeem units of the trust.[9]

In general, unit investment trusts are *passive investments*. They are designed to be bought and held, with capital preservation as a major objective. They enable investors to gain diversification, provide professional management that takes care of all the details, permit the purchase of securities by the trust at a cheaper price than if purchased individually, and ensure minimum operating costs. If conditions change, however, investors lose the ability to make rapid, inexpensive, or costless changes in their positions.

CLOSED-END INVESTMENT COMPANIES

Closed-End Investment Company An investment company with a fixed capitalization whose shares trade on exchanges and Nasdaq

One of the two types of *managed* investment companies, the **closed-end investment company**, usually sells no additional shares of its own stock after the initial public offering. Therefore, their capitalizations are fixed unless a new public offering is made. The shares of a closed-end fund trade in the secondary markets (e.g., on the exchanges) exactly like any other stock.[10] To buy and sell, investors use their brokers, paying (receiving) the current price at which the shares are selling plus (less) brokerage commissions. Figure 3-3 shows an example of typical closed-end data. Such data appear every Monday in *The Wall Street Journal*. Shown here is only one classification, "General Equity Funds." Other classifications shown in the weekly compilations include specialized equity funds, world equity funds, investment grade bond funds, national municipal bond funds, single state municipal bond funds, and several others. The information shown in Figure 3-3 also includes the stock exchange where traded, the NAV, and the market price (price and NAV data are hypothetical).

Because shares of closed-end funds trade on stock exchanges, their prices are determined by the forces of supply and demand. Interestingly, however, the market price is seldom equal to the actual per-share value of the closed-end shares. We examine the issue of closed-end discounts and premiums later in the chapter. These discounts and premiums can be seen in Figure 3-3.

Closed-end funds have been around for a long time; in fact, they were a popular investment before the great crash of 1929. After the crash, they lost favor and were relatively unimportant until they started to attract significant investor interest again following the crash of 1987. Although the number of closed-end funds grew fourfold in recent years, only a few hundred closed-end funds exist. Furthermore, only a handful of new closed-end funds of any

---

[8] An innovation in the 1990s is the *stock trust* designed for small investors. Typical initial investment is $1,000, and a typical projected holding period is one to five years. Like a bond trust, these trusts intend to keep their positions basically unchanged, selling an individual stock only in the event of major problems with the company.

[9] The sponsor makes a market in these certificates for those who wish to sell, with the units generally being sold back at the net asset value. It is also possible to find secondary markets for unit trusts among brokers and dealers.

[10] A special type of closed-end fund is the dual-purpose fund, which has a limited life and sells two classes of shares to investors.

FIGURE 3-3

Example of the data available weekly for closed-end funds.

Closed-End Funds
NAV and Price Data
(Traded on the NYSE (N), ASE (A), Nasdaq (O), Chicago (C) and Toronto (T) Exchanges)

Selected General Equity Funds	Exchange	NAV	Mk. Price	Dis/Prem %
Adams Express	N	31.80	27.75	−12.7
Engex	A	11.05	10.25	− 7.2
Gabelli Equity	N	11.65	11.75	+ 0.1
MFS Special Value	N	14.32	16.5	+15.2
Royce Micro Cap	O	9.95	8.625	−13.3
Tri-Continental	N	34.75	29.75	−14.4

NAV = net asset value of the fund
Mk. Price = current market price
Dis/Prem % = (NAV − Mk. Price)/NAV

type are currently launched in a given year, which has led a number of observers to say that closed-end funds have outlived their usefulness.

OPEN-END INVESTMENT COMPANIES (MUTUAL FUNDS)

Open-End Investment Company An investment company whose capitalization constantly changes as new shares are sold and outstanding shares are redeemed

Mutual Funds The popular name for open-end investment companies

Open-end investment companies, the most familiar type of managed company, are popularly referred to as **mutual funds** and continue to sell shares to investors after the initial sale of shares that starts the fund. The capitalization of an open-end investment company is continually changing—that is, it is open-ended—as new investors buy additional shares and some existing shareholders cash in by selling their shares back to the company.

Mutual funds typically are purchased either:

1. Directly, from a fund company, using mail, telephone, or at office locations;
2. Indirectly, from a sales agent, including securities firms, banks, life insurance companies, and financial planners.

Mutual funds may be affiliated with an "underwriter," which usually has an exclusive right to distribute shares to investors. Most underwriters distribute shares through broker/dealer firms.

Mutual funds are corporations typically formed by an investment advisory firm that selects the board of trustees (directors) for the company. The trustees, in turn, hire a separate management company, normally the investment advisory firm, to manage the fund. The management company is contracted by the investment company to perform necessary research and to manage the portfolio, as well as to handle the administrative chores, for which it receives a fee.

EXAMPLE 3-3

As stated in its prospectus (which is designed to describe a particular fund's objectives, policies, operations, and fees), "Equity-Income is a mutual fund: an investment that pools shareholders' money and invests it toward a specified goal. . . . The fund is governed by a Board of Trustees, which is responsible for protecting the interests of shareholders. . . . The fund is managed by FMR, which chooses the fund's investments and handles its business affairs."

FIGURE 3-4

Minimum investment requirements for mutual funds

SOURCE: Reprinted by permission of the Investment Company Institute, *1996 Mutual Fund Fact Book*, p. 38.

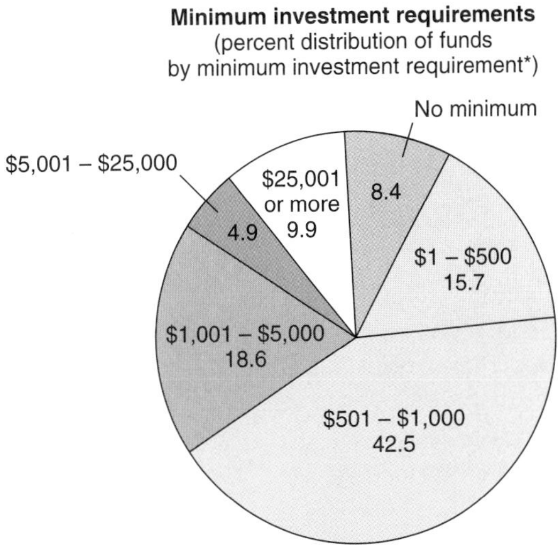

*Many mutual funds offer lower investment minimums for Individual Retirement Accounts and automatic investment plans.

Given the economies of scale in managing portfolios, expenses rise as assets under management increase, but not at the same rate as revenues. Because investment managers can oversee various amounts of money with few additional costs, management companies seek to increase the size of the fund(s) being managed. Many operate several different funds simultaneously. Investors can now choose from more than 400 mutual *fund complexes* (a fund complex is a group of funds under substantially common management).

Mutual funds are the most popular form of investment company for the typical investor. One reason is that the minimum investment requirements for most funds are small, as Figure 3-4 shows. Two-thirds of all funds require $1,000 or less for investors to get started, and 85 percent require $5,000 or less. For IRA and other retirement accounts, the minimum required is often lower.

EXAMPLE 3-4

$2,500 is required to open an account in the Equity-Income Fund (only $500 for Fidelity retirement accounts). Minimum balances are $2,000. Minimums to add to the account are $250 in either case, or $100 through an automatic investment plan.

Net Asset Value (NAV) The total market value of the securities in an investment company's portfolio divided by the number of investment company fund shares currently outstanding

Owners of fund shares can sell them back to the company (redeem them) any time they choose; the mutual fund is legally obligated to redeem them. Investors purchase new shares and redeem their existing shares at the **net asset value (NAV)**, which for any investment company share is computed daily by calculating the total market value of the securities in the portfolio, subtracting any trade payables, and dividing by the number of investment company fund shares currently outstanding.[11]

[11] Total market value of the portfolio is equal to the product of each security's current market price multiplied by the number of shares of that security owned by the fund.

EXAMPLE 3-5

Using Equity-Income Fund numbers for the year 1998, the NAV was calculated as:[12]

NAV, year-end 1998		**$44.47**
Income from investment operations		
net investment income	$ .94	
net realized and unrealized gain	9.79	
Total from investment operations	$10.73	
Less Distributions		
from net investment income	(.96)	
from net realized gain	(2.04)	
Total distribution	(3.00)	
NAV, end of period		**$52.20**

As this example shows, the net asset value is the per share value of the portfolio of securities held by the investment company. It changes during the year as the value of the securities held changes, and as income from the securities held is received.

MAJOR TYPES OF MUTUAL FUNDS

There are two major types of mutual funds:

- Money market mutual funds (short-term funds)
- Stock funds and bond & income funds (long-term funds)

These types of funds parallel our discussion in Chapter 2 of money markets and capital markets. Money market funds concentrate on short-term investing by holding portfolios of money market assets, whereas stock funds and bond & income funds concentrate on longer term investing by holding mostly capital market assets. We will discuss each of these two types of mutual funds in turn.

MONEY MARKET FUNDS

Money Market Fund (MMF) A mutual fund that invests in money market instruments

A major innovation in the investment company industry has been the creation, and subsequent phenomenal growth, of **money market funds (MMFs)**, which are open-end investment companies whose portfolios consist of money market instruments. Created in 1974, when interest rates were at record-high levels, MMFs grew rapidly as investors sought to earn these high short-term rates. However, with the deregulation of the thrift institutions, competition has increased dramatically for investors' short-term savings. Money market deposit accounts (MMDAs) (as discussed in Chapter 2) pay competitive money market rates and are insured and have attracted large amounts of funds. Nevertheless, in February 1999, retail money market mutual funds had total assets of $862 billion, with another $594 billion in institutional money market funds, for an aggregate of $1.46 trillion.

Money market funds can be divided into taxable funds and tax-exempt funds. At the

[12] Equity-Income data is based on January 31 as the year end. Therefore, 1998 covers February 1997 through January 1998.

Stock Funds

Aggressive Growth Funds seek maximum capital growth; current income is not a significant factor. These funds invest in stocks out of the mainstream, such as new companies, companies fallen on hard times, or industries temporarily out of favor. They may use investment techniques involving greater than average risk.

Growth Funds seek capital growth; dividend income is not a significant factor. They invest in the common stock of well-established companies.

Growth and Income Funds seek to combine long-term capital growth and current income. These funds invest in the common stock of companies whose share value has increased and that have displayed a solid record of paying dividends.

Precious Metals/Gold Funds seek capital growth. Their portfolios are invested primarily in securities associated with gold and other precious metals.

International Funds seek growth in the value of their investments. Their portfolios are invested primarily in stocks of companies located outside the U.S.

Global Equity Funds seek growth in the value of their investments. They invest in stocks traded worldwide, including those in the U.S.

Income-Equity Funds seek a high level of income by investing primarily in stocks of companies with good dividend-paying records.

Bond and Income Funds

Flexible Portfolio Funds allow their money managers to anticipate or respond to changing market conditions by investing in stocks *or* bonds *or* money market instruments, depending on economic changes.

Balanced Funds generally seek to conserve investors' principal, pay current income, and achieve long-term growth of principal and income. Their portfolios are a mix of bonds, preferred stocks, and common stocks.

Income-Mixed Funds seek a high level of income. These funds invest in income-producing securities, including stocks and bonds.

Income-Bond Funds seek a high level of current income. These funds invest in a mix of corporate and government bonds.

U.S. Government Income Funds seek current income. They invest in a variety of government securities, including U.S. Treasury bonds, federally guaranteed mortgage-backed securities, and other government notes.

GNMA (Ginnie Mae) Funds seek a high level of income. The majority of their portfolios is invested in mortgage securities backed by the Government National Mortgage Association (GNMA).

Global Bond Funds seek a high level of income. These funds invest in debt securities of companies and countries worldwide, including those in the U.S.

Corporate Bond Funds seek a high level of income. The majority of their portfolios is invested in corporate bonds, with the balance in U.S. Treasury bonds or bonds issued by a federal agency.

High-yield Bond Funds seek a very high yield, but carry a greater degree of risk than corporate bond funds. The majority of their portfolios is invested in lower-rated corporate bonds.

National Municipal Bond Funds-Long-term seek income that is not taxed by the federal government. They invest in bonds issued by states and municipalities to finance schools, highways, hospitals, bridges, and other municipal works.

State Municipal Bond Funds-Long-term seek income that is exempt from both federal tax and state tax for residents of that state. They invest in bonds issued by a single state.

Money Market Funds

Taxable Money Market Funds seek to maintain a stable net asset value. These funds invest in the short-term, high-grade securities sold in the money market, such as U.S. Treasury bills, certificates of deposit of large banks, and commercial paper. The average maturity of their portfolios is limited to 90 days or less.

Tax-exempt Money Market Funds-National seek income that is not taxed by the federal government with minimum risk. They invest in municipal securities with relatively short maturities.

Tax-exempt Money Market Funds-State seek income that is exempt from federal tax and state tax for residents of that state. They invest in municipal securities with relatively short maturities issued by a single state.

FIGURE 3-5

Major investment objectives of mutual funds

SOURCE: Reprinted by permission of the Investment Company Institute, *1997 Mutual Fund Fact Book*, pp. 24-25.

beginning of 1999, the assets of the taxable funds approximated $1.26 trillion, while the assets of tax-exempt funds totaled about $201 billion. Investors in higher tax brackets should carefully compare the taxable equivalent yield on tax-exempt money market funds (see Chapter 2) with that available on taxable funds because the tax-exempt funds often provide an edge.

Taxable MMFs hold assets such as Treasury bills, negotiable CDs, and prime commercial paper. Some funds hold only bills, whereas others hold various mixtures. Commercial paper typically accounts for 40 to 50 percent of the total assets held by these funds, with Treasury bills, government agency securities, domestic and foreign bank obligations, and repurchase agreements rounding out the portfolios. The average maturity of money market portfolios ranges from approximately one month to two months. SEC regulations limit the maximum average maturity of money funds to 90 days.

Tax-exempt money market funds consist of *national funds*, which invest in short-term municipal securities of various issuers, and *state tax-exempt money market funds*, which invest only in the issues of a single state, thereby providing additional tax benefits. These classifications are explained in Figure 3-5 and discussed below.

Investors in money market funds pay neither a sales charge nor a redemption charge, but they do pay a management fee. Interest is earned and credited daily. The shares can be redeemed at any time by phone or wire. Many funds offer check-writing privileges for checks of $500 or more, with the investor earning interest until the check clears.[13]

[13] Shareholders have made only limited use of the check-writing privilege, however, indicating that they regard money market funds primarily as a way to save.

Money market funds (MMFs) provide investors with a chance to earn the going rates in the money market while enjoying broad diversification and great liquidity. The rates have varied as market conditions changed. The important point is that their yields corresponded to current market conditions. Although investors may assume little risk because of the diversification and quality of these instruments, money market funds are not insured. Banks and thrift institutions have emphasized this point in competing with money market funds for the savings of investors.

EQUITY AND BOND & INCOME FUNDS

The board of directors (trustees) of an investment company must specify the objective that the company will pursue in its investment policy. The companies try to follow a consistent investment policy, according to their specified objective. Investors purchase mutual funds on the basis of their objectives.

EXAMPLE 3-6

"Equity-Income seeks reasonable income by investing mainly in income-producing equity securities. In selecting investments, the fund also considers the potential for capital appreciation."

The Investment Company Institute, a well-known organization that represents the investment company industry, uses 21 major categories of investment objectives, 18 of which are for equity and bond & income funds (the other three are for money market funds as previously explained). These are identified and explained in Figure 3-5.

As Figure 3-5 shows, investors in equity and bond & income funds have a wide range of investment objectives from which to choose. Traditionally, investors often opted for *growth funds*, which seek capital appreciation, or *balanced funds*, which seek both income and capital appreciation. Now investors can choose from *global funds*, either bonds or stocks, *precious metal funds*, *municipal bond funds*, and so forth. In terms of number of funds available, long-term municipal bond funds rank first, followed by growth funds.

These types of categories based on investment objectives such as "growth" and "growth and income" may change in the future. Some believe it is more important to describe a fund's *investment style* and actual portfolio holdings rather than state that the fund is seeking "growth of capital," which could be accomplished in several different ways. As part of this new trend, Morningstar, Inc., a Chicago mutual fund research firm discussed in Appendix 3-A, decided at the end of 1996 to use only nine categories for U.S. stock funds. These categories, such as "large cap," "mid cap," "small cap," "value," and "growth," are intended to describe investment styles.[14]

Figure 3-6 shows the investment style for Equity-Income Fund as shown in their prospectus, and as supplied by Morningstar. This fund concentrates on large-cap stocks using a value approach.

Lipper Inc., a well-known tracker of mutual funds since 1973, announced a new classification system for U.S. diversified equity mutual funds, effective mid-1999, to replace its "General Equity Investment Objectives." Funds are assigned to one of five investment objectives: aggressive equity, growth equity, general equity, value equity, and income equity. The market capitalization of the funds is also recognized—for example, large-cap funds—and a

[14] "Cap" refers to capitalization, or market value for a company, calculated as the price of the stock times the total number of shares outstanding. A mutual fund that invests in stocks with a median market cap of $5 billion or more would be considered to be a large-cap fund, while a small-cap fund is one with a median market cap of $1 billion or less.

FIGURE 3-6

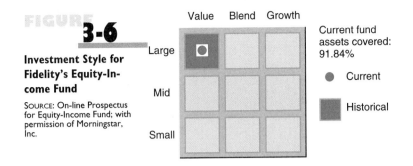

Investment Style for Fidelity's Equity-Income Fund

SOURCE: On-line Prospectus for Equity-Income Fund; with permission of Morningstar, Inc.

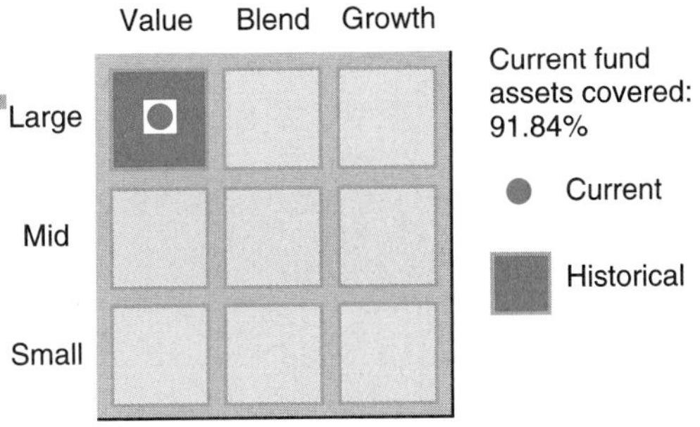

special size category, flexible-cap range, was created for the roughly 1,500 funds that do not fit regularly into size categories. Lipper indexes for mutual fund categories are carried daily in *The Wall Street Journal*.

Most stock funds can be divided into two categories based on their approach to selecting stocks, *value funds* and *growth funds*. A value fund generally seeks to find stocks that are cheap on the basis of standard fundamental analysis yardsticks, such as earnings, book value, and dividend yield. Growth funds, on the other hand, seek to find companies that are expected to show rapid future growth in earnings, even if current earnings are poor or, possibly, nonexistent.

Value funds and growth funds tend to perform well at different times. Therefore, fund investors should distinguish between the two types, which is not always easy to do.[15] A more risk-averse investor worrying about a market decline may wish to emphasize value funds, while more aggressive investors seeking good performance in an expected market rise would probably favor growth funds. Given the evidence on efficient markets, the best strategy is probably to buy both types of funds.

An analysis of the portfolio composition of the stock funds and bond & income funds indicates that equities (both common and preferred) represented almost 60 percent of total net assets for these funds at the beginning of 1996. Municipal bonds and U.S. government securities constituted about 12 and 14 percent, respectively, of total assets.

THE GROWTH IN MUTUAL FUNDS

As stated earlier, the growth in mutual funds and their assets has been one of the important stories in recent years. The number of mutual funds has grown rapidly in recent years. In 1980, there were 564 funds; at the beginning of 1997, there were approximately 7,000 funds, and in January, 1999, there were more than 12,000 domestic funds (more than 40,000 worldwide).

Quite dramatic is the change in the distribution of assets held by type of fund. In the 1950s and 1960s, mutual funds were generally thought of in terms of equity investments, with some bond holdings as a stabilizer. During the mid-1980s, however, money market funds accounted for about 40 percent of total assets as a result of relatively high, and rising, interest rates, and relatively low stock prices. Equity funds accounted for only about 20 percent of total assets. By the beginning of 1999, the situation had changed significantly. Equity funds accounted for 54 percent of total assets, and bond & income funds another 21 percent, for a total of roughly 75 percent. Figure 3-7 shows the distribution of total net assets by type of fund.

[15] Some well-known mutual fund groups that tend to emphasize value investing include Gabelli, Lindner, Merrill Lynch, Neuberger & Berman, and Templeton. Some well-known fund groups that tend to emphasize growth stocks include Janus, Kemper, IDS, Phoenix, and Twentieth Century Investors.

FIGURE 3-7

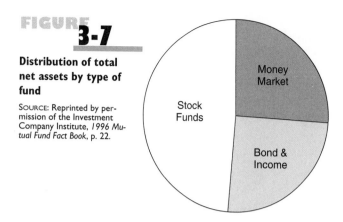

Distribution of total net assets by type of fund

SOURCE: Reprinted by permission of the Investment Company Institute, *1996 Mutual Fund Fact Book*, p. 22.

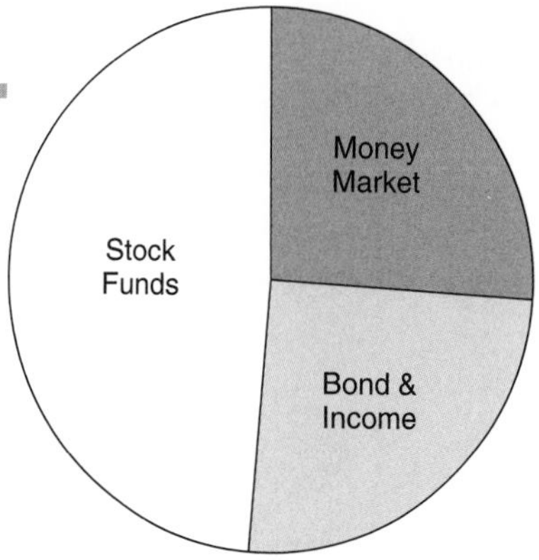

THE MECHANICS OF INVESTING INDIRECTLY

Investors transact indirectly via investment companies by buying, holding, and selling shares of closed-end funds and mutual fund shares (as well as unit investment trusts). In this section, we analyze some of the details involved in these transactions.

CLOSED-END FUNDS

Historically, the market prices of closed-ends have varied widely from their net asset values (NAVs). A *discount* refers to the situation in which the closed-end fund is selling for less than the NAV. If the market price of the fund exceeds the NAV, as it sometimes does for some closed-end funds, the fund is said to be selling at a *premium*. That is,

If NAV > market price, the fund is selling at a discount.
If NAV < market price, the fund is selling at a premium.

Although several studies have addressed the question of why these funds sell at discounts and premiums, no totally satisfactory explanation has been widely accepted by all market observers. Some explanations that have been cited to explain discounts in various closed-end funds include illiquidity, either for the fund's holdings or in the fund's shares themselves, high expenses, poor performance, and unrealized capital gains. Another of these explanations—anti-takeover provisions—would prevent investors from taking over the fund and liquidating it in order to realize the full NAV.

By purchasing a fund at a discount, an investor is actually buying shares in a portfolio of securities at a price below their market value. Therefore, even if the value of the portfolio remains unchanged, an investor can gain or lose if the discount narrows or widens over time. That is, a difference exists between the portfolio's return, based on net asset values, and the shareholder's return, based on closing prices.

Funds trade at premiums as well as discounts across time, and the variance between funds is great. In one recent year while such well-known closed-end funds as Adams Express and Tri-Continental were trading at discounts of approximately 11 percent and 16 percent, respectively, the Korea Fund was trading at an astounding premium of approximately 87 percent, an increase from the previous year's premium of 63 percent. In other words, investors buying the shares of Korea Fund were willing to pay about 87 percent more than the net asset value of the fund to obtain the shares.

Some Practical Advice

Initial public offerings of closed-end funds have been fast and furious because of investor demand for stocks and bonds. Such new offerings typically involve brokerage commissions of 6 or 7 percent. Brokers often support the price in the aftermarket temporarily, but then the price drops to NAV, or below. Many small investors would do well not to purchase the IPOs of closed-end funds.

MUTUAL FUNDS

Some mutual funds use a sales force to reach investors, with shares available from brokers, insurance agents, and financial planners. In an alternative form of distribution called direct marketing, the company uses advertising and direct mailing to appeal to investors. About 60 percent of all stock, bond, and income fund sales are made by funds using a sales force.

Mutual funds can be subdivided into:

- Load funds (those that charge a sales fee)
- No-load funds (those that do not charge a sales fee)

Load funds charge investors a sales fee for the costs involved in selling the fund. This sales fee, added to the fund's NAV, currently ranges up to about 6 percent. On a $1,000 purchase of a load mutual fund, with a 6 percent load fee, an investor would pay $60 "commission," acquiring only $940 in shares. Many load funds now charge less than the maximum they could charge because of market conditions or competition.

The load or sales charge goes to the marketing organization selling the shares, which could be the investment company itself or brokers. The fee is split between the salesperson and the company employing that person. The load fee percentage usually declines with the size of the purchase. The old adage in the investment company business is that "mutual fund shares are sold, not bought," meaning that the sales force aggressively sells the shares to investors. However, the percentage of stock and bond funds with the full 8.5 percent sales fee declined from almost one-third of all such funds in 1980 to only about 5 percent of all such funds by the beginning of 1990.

EXAMPLE 3-7

American Funds is one of the largest mutual fund organizations. Rather than advertise extensively as does Fidelity, the no-load and low-load giant, American sells funds through brokers at a sales charge (load charge) of 5.75 percent, a decrease in 1988 from the 8.5 percent charged previously. Despite the sales charges, American's funds, such as Investment Company of America and Washington Mutual Investors Fund, have attracted large amounts of money from investors.

Typically, no redemption fee (or "back-end" load) is imposed when the shares are redeemed, although in the early 1980s some funds began charging redemption fees in the 1 to 3 percent range. A relatively recent fee is an annual fee known as the *12b-1 fee*, named after the Securities and Exchange Commission ruling allowing such a fee to be charged.

The 12b-1 fee is of more importance to investors because roughly half of all mutual funds now impose it. It is a "distribution fee," covering a fund's cost of distribution, marketing, and advertising. The rationale for imposing it is that existing shareholders should benefit by paying such a fee that helps to attract new shareholders, thereby spreading the overhead. This fee is a fraction of a percent of the fund's average assets, and for some funds it has ranged as high as 1.00 percent.

In the 1990s, brokers began to emphasize a new trend in mutual fund sales whereby they offer two or three classes of shares of a fund, each with a different combination of front-end load (sales charge), annual or 12b-1 fee, and redemption fee. The idea is that if investors are reluctant to pay higher sales charges, for example, the brokers can do as well by charging less up front and more in annual and redemption fees. All fees must be stated in the prospectus. Investors should carefully read a fund's prospectus before investing.

EXAMPLE 3-8

Equity-Income Fund has no sales charge on purchases, no deferred sales charge on redemptions, no exchange fee, and no 12b-1 fee.

In contrast to the load funds, *no-load funds* are bought at net asset value directly from the fund itself. No sales fee is charged because there is no sales force to compensate. Investors must seek out these funds by responding to advertisements in the financial press, and purchase and redeem shares by mail, wire, or telephone. Perhaps this explains why even in the 1990s approximately 60 percent of all mutual funds were still sold through brokers with load fees.

Some of the giants of the mutual fund industry, such as Fidelity, Vanguard, and T. Rowe Price, advertise no-load funds aggressively in the major financial publications such as *The Wall Street Journal*.

EXAMPLE 3-9

The Vanguard Group operates a well-known family of mutual funds, all of which are no-load. Vanguard advertises some of its funds virtually each day in *The Wall Street Journal*. Investors interested in no-load funds such as these can send in the coupon provided in the paper, or call 24 hours a day. Vanguard also has a web site.

USING THE INTERNET Investors can access many websites for information about investment companies. For example, www.morningstar.net provides investors with extensive information about both the market and various funds. It includes a free section as well as a premium section. Www.quicken.com has a separate section for mutual funds, offering quotes on funds, screening criteria for fund selection, and more. Investors can search a database of more than 8,000 funds at www.bloomberg.com. Investors can find extensive information on mutual funds at CBS's MarketWatch— http://cbs.marketwatch.com.

Quite a few funds are said to be "low-load" funds, with sales charges of 2 to 3 percent. A single investment company—for example, Fidelity Investments—may simultaneously offer both no-load and low-load funds.

EXAMPLE 3-10

Fidelity offers numerous no-load funds, such as its High Yield bond fund and its Balanced stock fund as well as the Equity-Income Fund discussed throughout the chapter. It also offers numerous low-load funds, such as its Blue Chip stock fund (with a 3 percent load charge) and its Growth and Income stock fund (with a 2 percent sales charge).

A question that is often asked is, "If the no-load funds charge no sales fee, how is the investment company compensated?" The answer is that all funds, open-end and closed-end, load funds and no-load funds, charge the shareholders an expense fee for operating expenses.

This fee is paid out of the fund's income, derived from the dividends, interest, and capital gains earned during the year and is typically stated as a percentage of average net assets. The annual expense fee consists of management fees, overhead, and 12b-1 fees, if any.

Typical annual management fees begin at 0.5 percent of the fund's total market value (in other words, 50 cents per year per $100 of assets under management). The average operating expense for all mutual funds is around 1.25 percent of assets, whereas the average for stock funds is approximately 1.5 percent of assets. The median expense ratio for bond funds is 1.04 percent, for growth and income stock funds, 1.11 percent, and for capital appreciation funds, 1.42 percent.

EXAMPLE 3-11

The Equity-Income Fund has an operating expense of 0.68 percent, consisting of a management fee of 0.44 percent and other expenses of 0.24 percent. The Fund calculates that if the annual return is 5 percent and its operating expenses are 0.68 percent, for every $1,000 invested an investor would pay $7, $22, $38, and $85 after 1, 3, 5, and 10 years, respectively.

INVESTMENT COMPANY PERFORMANCE

Few topics in investments are as well reported on a regular basis as is the performance of investment companies, and in particular mutual funds. *Business Week*, *Forbes*, *Money Magazine*, *U.S. News & World Report*, and *The Wall Street Journal*, among other popular press publications, regularly cover the performance of mutual funds, emphasizing their returns and risks. Appendix 3-A has a more detailed discussion of the major sources of information on mutual fund performance available to investors in both the popular press and specialized services.

We will discuss the calculation of investment returns in much more detail in Chapter 6, but the primary focus in that chapter is on individual securities and indices of securities and the actual mechanics involved. Furthermore, we will discuss in detail the evaluation of portfolio performance in Chapter 22, and therefore we do not consider the evaluation of mutual performance in detail now. Nevertheless, it is instructive at this point to consider some of the basic points about mutual fund returns.

Throughout this text we will use *total return* (explained in detail in Chapter 6) to measure the return from any financial asset, including a mutual fund. Total return for a mutual fund includes reinvested dividends and capital gains, and therefore includes all of the ways investors make money from financial assets. It is stated as a percentage or a decimal, and can cover any time period—one month, one year, or multiple years.

A *cumulative total return* measures the actual cumulative performance over a stated period of time, such as the past 3, 5 or 10 years. This allows the investor to assess total performance over some stated period of time.

EXAMPLE 3-12

For fiscal periods ended January 31, 1999, the cumulative total returns for the Equity-Income Fund as well as the S&P 500, a well-known measure of equity returns, were:

	Past 1 Year	Past 5 Years	Past 10 Years
Equity Income Fund	12.79%	224.54%	403.15%
S&P 500	32.49	296.13	562.80

This means that an investor who invested \$10,000 in Equity-Income Fund on January 31, 1989 would have \$40,315 on January 31, 1999, found by converting to a decimal, 4.0315, and multiplying by \$10,000. Note this total consists of the cumulative total return earned on the \$10,000 plus the original \$10,000 investment.

Standard practice in the mutual fund industry is to calculate and present the **average annual return**, a hypothetical rate of return that, if achieved annually, would have produced the same cumulative total return if performance had been constant over the entire period. The average annual return is a geometric mean (discussed in Chapter 6) and reflects the compound rate of growth at which money grew over time. As noted in the Equity-Income prospectus, "Average annual total returns smooth out variations in performance; they are not the same as actual year-by-year results."

EXAMPLE 3-13

The average annual total returns for the Equity-Income Fund and the S&P 500 Index for fiscal periods ended January 31, 1999 were:

	Past 1 Year	Past 3 Years	Past 5 Years	Past 10 Years
Equity-Income Fund	12.79%	19.63%	17.56%	14.96%
S&P 500 Index	32.49	28.55	24.25	18.86

Therefore, investing \$10,000 in the Equity-Income Fund and compounding at the rate of 14.96 percent each year for 10 years would produce a final wealth of \$40,315, which corresponds to the \$40,315 number in Example 3-12 (this total includes the \$10,000 starting investment).

Average annual total returns allow investors to make direct comparisons among funds as to their performance, assuming they do so legitimately, as explained in Chapter 22 when we discuss the evaluation of performance. This means that the risk of the funds being compared should be equivalent, and the funds should have the same general objectives. We expect, on average, for equity funds to outperform bond funds and money market funds.

BENCHMARKS

Investors need to relate the performance of a mutual fund to some benchmark in order to judge relative performance with (hopefully) a comparable investment alternative. Fidelity's Equity-Income Fund, presented above, was compared to the S&P 500 Composite Index. Other firms make different comparisons and claims, as one will quickly discover by looking at their ads. For example, T. Rowe Price notes that its Dividend Growth Fund has a 5-star Morningstar rating for overall risk-adjusted performance, and compares its fund to the Lipper Growth & Income Funds Average. As mentioned earlier, Lipper Inc. is a well-known provider of fund rankings and performance. The Kaufmann Fund, on the other hand, a well-known small company aggressive growth fund, compares its performance to the Russell 2000, an index of small companies, and (in one ad) only for a 10 year period.

HOW IMPORTANT ARE EXPENSES?

An important issue for all fund investors is that of expenses. Should they be overly concerned about the load charges, given the large number of no-load funds? What about annual operating expenses?

Consider the following evidence. *Mutual Funds*, a leading magazine covering mutual funds, reported in early 1999 that over the previous five years, the 25 top-performing domestic diversified growth funds returned 207 percent, while averaging only 1.09 percent in operating expenses. In contrast, the 25 worst-performing funds appreciated only 26 percent over that period, and averaged 3.25 percent in operating costs. According to this source, "Inefficient portfolio management and inefficient cost management are highly correlated."[16]

CONSISTENCY OF PERFORMANCE

Given the returns numbers above, widely available for mutual funds, can they help investors choose this year's, or next year's, winner? The consistency of performance of mutual funds has long been a controversy, and this continues to be true. Earlier studies tended to find a lack of consistency of fund performance, while some recent studies find some persistence in fund performance. For example, in the 1990s, Grinblatt and Titman found persistence in differences between funds over time, and more recently Elton, Gruber, and Blake and Gruber found evidence that performance differences persist.[17]

Malkiel has also found such evidence, although he found period effects, with differences persisting in the 1970s but not in the 1980s.[18] Malkiel, famous for many years as a strong believer in market efficiency, would have a difficult time saying past performance matters in selecting a fund. However, Box 3-1, an interview with Malkiel on this subject, suggests that investors may gain when selecting funds by relying on recent good performance. As the article notes, there are no guarantees when investing, but a possible advantage is to be appreciated.

Before you get your hopes up on selecting funds based on their records, consider some recent work by Droms and Walker, who examined the 151 funds in existence for the entire 20 years ended in 1990. Only 40 of these funds beat a well-known market index in more than 10 of these 20 years, and no funds beat the market index in all four of the five-year subperiods of the 20-year stretch. Funds that did well in the first 10 years were no more likely than other funds to do well in the next 10 years.[19]

Results such as these led a number of years ago to **index funds**, which are funds designed to replicate a market index such as the Standard & Poor's 500 Composite Index. Index funds have become quite popular—the second largest mutual fund in terms of assets is Vanguard's S&P Index 500, with about $70 billion in assets at the end of 1998. Index funds have lower expenses because they are "unmanaged" funds seeking only to duplicate the chosen index. While the typical equity fund has operating expenses of almost 1.5 percent of assets annually, the typical index fund has expenses of only 0.56 percent, and Vanguard's Index 500 has an amazing low expense rate of 0.18 percent.

---

[16] See "Fund World: Expensive Funds Aren't Worth It," *Mutual Funds*, March 1999, p. 20.

[17] See Mark Grinblatt and Sheridan Titman, "The Persistence of Mutual Fund Performance," *The Journal of Finance*, December 1992, pp. 1977–1984; Edwin Elton, Martin J. Gruber, and Christopher Blake, "The Persistence of Risk-Adjusted Mutual Fund Performance," *Journal of Business*, April 1996, pp. 133–157; and Martin J. Gruber, "Another Puzzle: The Growth in Actively Managed Mutual Funds," *The Journal of Finance*, July 1996, pp. 783–809.

[18] Burton G. Malkiel, "Returns From Investing in Equity Mutual Funds: 1971 to 1991," *The Journal of Finance*, June 1995, pp. 549–572.

[19] See Jonathan Clements, "By the Numbers: What the Researchers Are Digging Up on Fund Performance," *The Wall Street Journal*, December 24, 1996, p. C1.

Box 3-1

DOES PAST PERFORMANCE REALLY MATTER?

You see the disclaimer in most mutual fund ads: Past performance is not a guarantee of future results. Yet you want to believe that the portfolio managers with proven track records—the "hot hands"—will continue to provide their shareholders with spectacular gains in the coming years.

A new study by Princeton University professor Burton G. Malkiel indicates that hot hands play an important part in a fund's continued success—despite Malkiel's waffling on the subject (more on that later).

The study, which examined all diversified domestic stock funds from 1973 through 1991, reveals that the top ten funds of one year returned, on average, 15.6 percent the following year. In contrast, the popular mutual fund benchmark, the S&P 500, averaged 11.5 percent per annum. Result: A $10,000 investment in the benchmark grew to $79,100 in this period, while the same investment in the top 10 funds nearly doubled that, reaching $157,100. A similar success pattern held true for the top 20 and top 40 funds.

Interestingly, if you ask Malkiel if he has proved that past performance does, indeed, matter, he'll deny it. Yes, he admits, the hot hands approach "shows just a remarkable amount of persistency in the '70s, no question about it." But, he adds, "there wasn't any in the 1980s."

Malkiel bases his argument on results in four subperiods of the study. Between 1973 and 1977, the top 10 funds easily beat the S&P 500, averaging a 4 percent annual return versus a loss of 0.2 percent for the S&P. Between 1978 and 1981, the top ten averaged a whopping 27 percent per year versus only 12 percent for the S&P. The advantage for the top ten shrank between 1982 and 1986, 20 percent to 19.8 percent. And between 1987 and 1991, the top ten slightly underperformed the S&P, 14.6 percent to 15.3 percent.

We asked the professor if these weren't precisely the kinds of turns most investors hoped for—beating the market handily in good periods without losing to it in the poor ones.

After much hedging, he answered: "If you want to put the best face on it that you possibly could, you could argue that the funds that have done particularly well in some periods continued to do well, and when you did lose by that strategy, you didn't lose by very much.

"So I guess if you pushed me to the wall and said, 'Look, I've got some no-load funds here with low expense ratios and you're a betting man, what would you do, would you buy the ones with the best performance?' I'd say, 'Sure, I probably would.' But if you asked me, 'Can you count on that to produce first-rate returns in the future?' I'd say, 'Absolutely not.' If you're counting on that, that's the will of the wisp."

Of course, investors know that they can never *count* on anything; they're just looking for an advantage based on probabilities. And Malkiel's study shows that following the hot hands does just that. Still, Malkiel would rather place his bet on an unmanaged index fund with very low expenses. He also subscribes to the strategy of buying closed-end funds that are trading at steep discounts below their net asset values.

Though he stubbornly clings to the notion that "there is no evidence of consistent hot-handedness," his figures seem to prove otherwise. "There's no question about the fact that there are a few funds with 20-year records that have outperformed the market," he says. "There's no doubt about that. The problem is, could you have identified them 20 years ago?"

Fortunately, Malkiel's study shows you only need to identify the hot hands one year at a time.

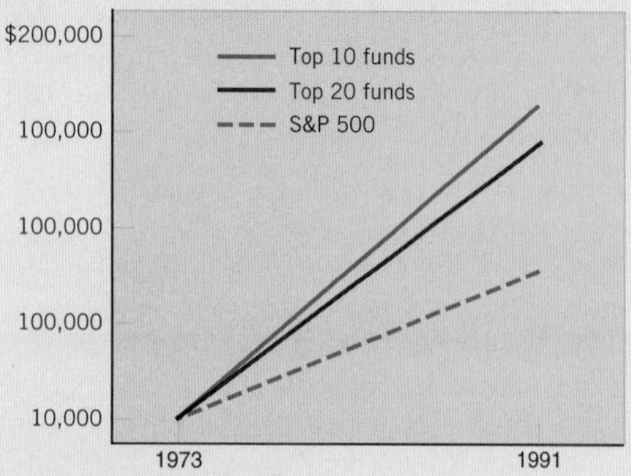

Hotter is Better A study by Princeton professor Burton Malkiel found that "hot hands" usually stay hot. An investor who owned the prior year's top ten funds in the following year would have nearly doubled the S&P 500's performance over the course of the study, which ran from 1973 through 1991.

SOURCE: "Does Past Performance Really Matter?" *Mutual Funds*, November 1995, pp. 97–98. Reprinted by permission.

How have index funds fared in recent years? Over the 10 year period ending in 1998, index funds outperformed 80 percent of the actively managed funds on a compound return basis. In 1998, index funds outperformed 73 percent of active funds, and in 1997 88 percent.

INVESTING INTERNATIONALLY THROUGH INVESTMENT COMPANIES

The mutual fund industry has become a global industry. Open-end funds around the world have grown rapidly, including emerging market economies. Worldwide assets at the end of 1997 were about $7 trillion, with $2 trillion of this non-U.S. and $5 trillion the assets of U.S. funds. One estimate for 10 years later (2007) by Lipper Analytical Services is $30 trillion, equally divided between the United States and the rest of the world.

Aggregate mutual fund assets in Europe amount to about one-third of the world total. In Latin America roughly one out of every 200 people owns a mutual fund (compared to one in three in the United States). In Japan, mutual fund assets approximate one-half trillion dollars. In early 1999, there were more than 41,000 funds worldwide.

U.S. investors can invest internationally by buying and selling both mutual funds or closed-end funds whose shares are traded on exchanges. Funds that specialize in international securities have become both numerous and well known in recent years.

International Funds Mutual funds that concentrate primarily on international stocks

Global Funds Mutual funds that keep a minimum of 25 percent of their assets in U.S. securities

Single-Country Fund Investment companies, primarily closed-end funds, concentrating on the securities of a single country

- So-called **international funds** tend to concentrate primarily on international stocks. In one recent year Fidelity Overseas Fund was roughly one-third invested in Europe and one-third in the Pacific Basin, whereas Kemper International had roughly one-sixth of its assets in each of three areas, the United Kingdom, Germany, and Japan.
- **Global funds** tend to keep a minimum of 25 percent of their assets in the United States. For example, in one recent year Templeton World Fund had over 60 percent of its assets in the United States, and small positions in Australia and Canada.
- Most mutual funds that offer "international" investing invest primarily in non-U.S. stocks, thereby exposing investors to foreign markets, which may behave differently from U.S. markets. However, investors may also be exposed to currency risks. An alternative approach to international investing is to seek international exposure by investing in U.S. companies with strong earnings abroad, which is a natural extension of the globalization concept. Based on a belief that the best-managed global companies tend to be based in the United States, this is a safer strategy. The Papp America-Abroad Fund is an example of this strategy.
- Another alternative in indirect investing, the **single-country funds**, concentrates on the securities of a single country. These funds traditionally have been closed-end, with a fixed number of shares outstanding. Like their domestic counterparts, international closed-end funds typically sell at either a discount or a premium to their net asset value as do their domestic counterparts. For example, during one recent year the Brazil Fund sold at a discount of more than 40 percent, whereas the Spain Fund sold at a premium of more than 120 percent.

U.S. fund managers are now expanding globally by setting up foreign funds for sale in foreign markets. Such funds are tailored to meet the needs of the particular country. These separate foreign management subsidiaries both sponsor and advise foreign funds.

NEW DEVELOPMENTS IN INTERNATIONAL INVESTING

The most important new trend in international investing via investment companies is *passively managed country funds* geared to match a major stock index of a particular country. Each of these offerings will typically be almost fully invested, have little turnover, and offer significantly reduced expenses to shareholders.

Morgan Stanley has created *World Equity Benchmark Shares (WEBS)*, which track a predesignated index (one of Morgan Stanley's international capital indices) for each of 17 countries. These are closed-end funds and trade on the AMEX.

Deutsche Morgan Grenfell has created *CountryBaskets*, designed to replicate the Financial Times/Standard & Poor's Actuaries World Indices. These are available for each of nine countries. Unlike WEBS, which attempt to match the performance of a particular index without owning all of the stocks in the index, CountryBaskets own every stock in the index for that country.

THE FUTURE OF INDIRECT INVESTING

One of the hottest new movements concerning indirect investing is the mutual fund "supermarket" whereby investors can buy the funds of various mutual fund families through one source, such as a brokerage firm. "Supermarket" refers to the fact that an investor has hundreds of choices available through one source, and does not have to go to other sources to obtain his or her choices. The mutual funds participating in the supermarket pay the firms offering the funds distribution fees (typically, 0.25 percent to 0.40 percent of assets per year).[20]

The discount brokerages of Schwab, Fidelity, and Jack White have been pioneers in making hundreds of funds available to investors through brokerage accounts offered by them. By mid-1998 Schwab's OneSource program had $71 billion in assets, and accounted for about one-fifth of fund sales in 1997 (available as OneSource Online at www.schwab.com).

The Internet will have a substantial impact on investors who buy and sell mutual funds. Already, the major investment companies such as Fidelity and Vanguard offer extensive websites with much information. One estimate is that by the year 2000, individuals will be managing $30 billion in mutual fund assets on-line.

SUMMARY

- As an alternative to purchasing financial assets themselves, all investors can invest indirectly, which involves the purchase of shares of an investment company.
- Investment companies are financial intermediaries that hold a portfolio of securities on behalf of their shareholders.
- Investment companies are classified as either open-end or closed-end, depending on whether their own capitalization (number of shares outstanding) is constantly changing or fixed.
- Open-end investment companies, commonly called mutual funds, can be divided into two categories, money market funds and stock, bond, and income funds.
- Money market mutual funds concentrate on portfolios of money market securities, providing investors with a way to own these high face value securities indirectly.
- Stock, bond, and income funds own portfolios of stocks and/or bonds, allowing investors to participate in these markets without having to purchase these securities directly.
- Investors transacting indirectly in closed-end funds encounter discounts and premiums, meaning that the price of these funds is unequal to their net asset values.
- Mutual funds can be load funds or no-load funds, where the load is a sales charge.

[20] Participating mutual funds do not know the names of the new shareholders and cannot communicate with them directly because the supermarkets keep client lists secret.

- All investment companies charge a management fee.
- Total return for a mutual fund includes reinvested dividends and capital gains. A cumulative total return measures the actual performance over a stated period of time, such as the past 3, 5, or 10 years. The average annual return is a hypothetical rate of return that, if achieved annually, would have produced the same cumulative total return if performance had been constant over the entire period.
- International funds tend to concentrate primarily on international stocks while global funds tend to keep a minimum of 25 percent of their assets in the United States.
- Single-country funds, which traditionally have been closed-end funds, concentrate on the securities of a single country.

KEY WORDS

Average annual return
Closed-end investment company
Global funds
Index funds
International funds
Investment company
Money market funds (MMFs)
Mutual funds
Net asset value (NAV)
Open-end investment companies
Single-country funds
Unit investment trust

QUESTIONS

3-1. What is meant by "indirect" investing?

3-2. What is an investment company? Distinguish between an open-end and a closed-end company.

3-3. What is a money market fund? Why would it appeal to investors?

3-4. It has been said that many closed-end funds are "worth more dead than alive." What is meant by this expression?

3-5. What does it mean for an investment company to be regulated?

3-6. List the benefits of a money market fund for investors? List the disadvantages. What alternative investment is a close substitute?

3-7. What is meant by an investment company's "objective"? What are some of the objectives pursued by equity, bond, and income fund?

3-8. How does a unit investment trust holding municipal bonds differ from a mutual fund holding municipal bonds?

3-9. How is the net asset value for a mutual fund calculated?

3-10. What is meant by the term *pure intermediary*?

3-11. List some reasons an investor might prefer a closed-end fund to an open-end fund.

3-12. Distinguish between a global fund and an international fund.

3-13. What is the difference between the average annual return for a fund and the cumulative total return?

3-14. Distinguish between a value fund and a growth fund.

3-15. Why are unit investment trusts considered to be passive investments?

3-16. Distinguish between the direct and indirect methods by which mutual fund shares are typically purchased.

3-17. How would the owner of some shares of Fidelity's Equity-Income Fund "cash out" when he or she was ready to sell the shares?

3-18. How have investor preferences with regard to mutual fund investing changed over time?

3-19 Who owns a mutual fund? Who determines investment policies and objectives?

3-20. What does it mean when someone says "Mutual funds involve investment risk"?

3-21. What is the difference between a load fund and a no-load fund? What is a low-load fund?

3-22. What are passively managed country funds? Give an example.

3-23. What is meant by the exchange privilege within a "family of funds"?

SELECTED REFERENCES

One of the best sources of information about mutual funds has been written by the chairman of the Vanguard Group of Investment Companies:

Bogle, John C. *Bogle on Mutual Funds*. Homewood, Ill.: Richard D. Irwin, 1994.

Another good source of information on mutual funds is:

Mutual Funds, a monthly magazine.

www.wiley.com/college/jones7

This chapter discusses an indirect investment strategy—the use of mutual funds. The exercises will take you to the websites of some of the larger mutual funds, and help you to work through the advantages and disadvantages of mutual funds.

APPENDIX 3-A

OBTAINING INFORMATION ON INVESTMENT COMPANIES

Because of their popularity and prominence in the investments world, and the fact that they are heavily regulated under the Investment Company Act of 1940, considerable information is available on investment companies. This information originates with the companies themselves, the popular press, and specialized services devoted to funds and/or carrying specialized information on investment companies as part of their overall coverage.

DAILY AND WEEKLY PRICE AND PERFORMANCE INFORMATION

For daily printed results on investment companies, investors usually consult *The Wall Street Journal*, which carries daily quotations at the end of "Section C" on most open-end funds as well as a weekly listing on Monday of closed-end funds. Daily information on closed-end funds would be found on the exchange where such funds are traded. For example, daily information on the Germany Fund would be found on the page for "New York Stock Exchange Composite Transactions." As noted, this paper carries a weekly listing of all closed-end funds on Monday.

Barron's, a weekly financial newspaper, carries a comprehensive list of quotations, including yield and capital gains for the previous 12 months. *Barron's* also carries a list of closed-end funds with both the net asset value and the current market price (and therefore the discount or premium), including quotes on dual-purpose funds.

OBTAINING INFORMATION ABOUT INVESTMENT COMPANIES

Investment companies must file a registration statement with the SEC disclosing their investment policies, practices, and so on. In addition, they must make available to stockholders a prospectus that outlines in detail the fund's operations. Complete information about operations is supplied to shareholders at least twice a year; most companies supply it four times a year.

The Wall Street Journal now provides a monthly supplement on mutual funds, summarizing performance and providing other information.

Forbes, a biweekly investment magazine, provides an annual rating of investment company performance in its early September issue. Both risk and return aspects are considered, and performance is related to up and down periods for the overall market. Letter ratings are assigned for both market conditions, ranging from A to D in an up market and A to F in a down market.[21] This gives investors some guidance in choosing a fund. If a market rise is expected, for example, the investor might select a fund that has done extremely well during such periods, regardless of its performance in a declining market. On the other hand, a risk-averse investor might prefer a fund that has performed reasonably well in both good and bad markets.

Money magazine devotes articles to mutual funds and also provides its own annual rankings of funds in the February issue. Total returns over four time periods and peer-group rankings for three years are provided, along with down-market performance.

Business Week also rates mutual funds in an issue around the end of January, providing very complete data. Its *Mutual Fund Scoreboard* categorizes each fund as to its level of risk (very high, high, average, low, and very low) based on five-year risk-adjusted performance, relative to the S&P 500. Funds are given an overall performance rating from A to F. One, 3, 5, and 10 year average annual total returns are shown, on both a pre-tax and after-tax basis.

A relatively new source of mutual fund data has become very popular and is regarded by many observers as the best source of data available on mutual funds. *Morningstar Mutual Funds* covers over 1,200 funds, including both load and no-load funds and both equity and fixed-income funds. Morningstar provides information concerning current happenings at the fund, holdings of the fund, rankings against other funds, and performance data. It also provides a five-star rating system measuring both return and risk.

Subsequent to Morningstar, the publisher of *The Value Line Investment Survey* began publishing *The Value Line Mutual Fund Survey*. Similar in format to the stock service, Value Line covers some 2,000 mutual funds, providing analyses, ratings, and reports. Included are a bull versus bear comparison and a matching of each fund with others of the same type and with the S&P 500 Index.

A new magazine on mutual funds is *Mutual Funds Magazine*. This is a very good source

[21] In up markets, 5 percent of the funds rated by *Forbes* receive a rating of A+; the next 15 percent receive an A; the next 25 percent, a B; the next 25 percent, a C; the next 25 percent, a D; the bottom 5 percent, an F. In down markets, a similar distribution is used, with ratings ranging from A to F.

of information, with interesting articles. By the end of January it reports complete results for the prior year on many funds.

A rapidly expanding source of information and investment advice is provided by the mutual fund newsletters sold by individuals and companies to mutual fund shareholders. Some newsletters specialize in the funds for one company; for example, at least four cover only the funds of Fidelity. By the beginning of 1990 some 40 newsletters were being sold.

An important source of information for closed-end funds is Thomas J. Herzfeld Advisors, a pioneer in closed-end investing. This firm invests clients' money in promising closed-end funds and publishes "The Investor's Guide to Closed-End Funds."

A newer source of readily available information is *Morningstar Closed-End Funds*, offering a full page of coverage on more than 300 closed-end funds. Published every two weeks, this service rates, evaluates, and tracks the most actively traded closed-end funds, including emerging-market funds and municipal bond funds as well as the more traditional equity and bond funds.

Of course, the rapid expansion of the Internet has made available a considerable amount of information about investing in general, and mutual funds in particular. Most of the major mutual fund families, such as Fidelity, Janus, and Vanguard, have extensive websites. Many of the popular press magazines can be accessed on-line, and they cover mutual funds. Some major sites are:

www.vanguard.com
www.fidelity.com
www.troweprice.com

chapter 4

SECURITIES MARKETS

Chapter 4 outlines the structure of the markets where investors buy and sell securities. Although primary markets, including the role of investment bankers, are considered, the emphasis is on secondary markets. Bond markets, equity markets, and derivative markets are covered, with emphasis on secondary markets where most investors are active. Changes in the securities markets are considered, including the globalization that is occurring.

After reading this chapter you will be able to:

- **Distinguish between primary and secondary markets.**
- **Describe where the three types of securities discussed in Chapter 2—bonds, equities, and derivatives—are traded.**
- **Understand how the equity markets, where stocks are traded, are organized, how they operate, and how they differ from each other.**
- **Recognize the various stock market indexes typically encountered by investors.**
- **Follow changes that are occurring in the financial markets based on your understanding of what has happened in the past.**

This chapter outlines the structure of the securities markets, with primary emphasis on markets in the United States because they will be of most interest to U.S. investors. However, global market issues are increasingly important and are also covered here. We focus mainly on stocks, and to a lesser extent on bonds and derivative securities, because these are the securities investors most often buy and sell. The factors involving other securities are discussed in the chapters dealing specifically with each security.

The structure and operating mechanisms of the securities markets in the United States have changed drastically in the last 20 years. Accordingly, this chapter concludes with a look at some of these changes and what the future may hold.

THE IMPORTANCE OF FINANCIAL MARKETS

In order to finance their operations as well as expand, business firms must invest capital in amounts that are beyond their capacity to save in any reasonable period of time. Similarly, governments must borrow large amounts of money to provide the goods and services that the people demand of them. The financial markets permit both business and government to raise the needed funds by selling securities. Simultaneously, investors with excess funds are able to invest and earn a return, enhancing their welfare.

Financial markets are absolutely vital for the proper functioning of capitalistic economies, since they serve to channel funds from savers to borrowers. Furthermore, they provide an important allocative function by channeling the funds to those who can make the best use of them—presumably, the most productive. In fact, the chief function of a capital market is to allocate resources optimally.[1]

The existence of well-functioning secondary markets, where investors come together to trade existing securities, assures the purchasers of primary securities that they can quickly sell their securities if the need arises. Of course, such sales may involve a loss, because there are no guarantees in the financial markets. A loss, however, may be much preferred to having no cash at all if the securities cannot be sold readily.

In summary, in the United States secondary markets are indispensable to the proper functioning of the primary markets. The primary markets, in turn, are indispensable to the proper functioning of the economy.

THE PRIMARY MARKETS

Primary Market The market for new issues of securities, typically involving investment bankers

Initial Public Offering (IPO) Common stock shares of a company being sold for the first time

A **primary market** is one in which a borrower issues new securities in exchange for cash from an investor (buyer). New sales of Treasury bills, or IBM stock, or North Carolina bonds all take place in the primary markets. The issuers of these securities—the U.S. government, IBM, and the state of North Carolina, respectively—receive cash from the buyers of these new securities, who in turn receive financial claims that previously did not exist.

Note that in all three of these examples, some amount of these securities is outstanding before the new sales occur. Sales of common stock of a publicly traded company are called *seasoned new issues*.

If the issuer is selling securities for the first time, these are referred to as **initial public offerings (IPOs)**. Once the original purchasers sell the securities, they trade in secondary

[1] A securities market with this characteristic is said to be *allocationally efficient*. An *operationally efficient* market, on the other hand, is one with the lowest possible prices for transactions services.

markets. New securities may trade repeatedly in the secondary market, but the original issuers will be unaffected in the sense that they receive no additional cash from these transactions.

In the five years through 1996, more than 2,500 companies raised in excess of $150 billion, with 1996 alone generating $46 billion for approximately 700 companies (compared to $28 billion raised by 463 new offerings in 1995). The market for IPOs was very heated in 1995–1996, generating a lot of attention as investors scrambled to try and buy "hot" issues at the offering price, which often doubled or more on opening day. In 1995, Standard & Poor's New Issues Index was up 96.5 percent, although individual results varied widely.

EXAMPLE 4-1

Among IPOs in early 1999, the best performers were, not surprisingly, Internet stocks. MarketWatch.com, in its first two hours of trading, went from $17 (the offering price) to $130 before falling back to $97.50. This first-day gain of 474 percent was second, all time, to another Internet stock, theglobe.com, which rose over 600 percent on its opening day.

THE INVESTMENT BANKER

Investment Banker Firm specializing in the sale of new securities to the public, typically by underwriting the issue

In the course of selling new securities, issuers often rely on an **investment banker** for the necessary expertise as well as the ability to reach widely dispersed suppliers of capital. Along with performing activities such as helping corporations in mergers and acquisitions, *investment banking firms* specialize in the design and sale of securities in the primary market while operating simultaneously in the secondary markets. For example, Merrill Lynch offers investment banking services while operating a large retail brokerage operation throughout the country.

Investment bankers act as intermediaries between issuers and investors. The issuer sells its securities to investment bankers, who in turn sell the securities to investors. For firms seeking to raise long-term funds, the investment banker can provide important advice to their clients during the planning stage preceding the issuance of new securities. This advice includes providing information about the type of security to be sold, the features to be offered with the security, the price, and the timing of the sale.

Underwriting The process by which investment bankers purchase an issue of securities from a firm and resell it to the public

Investment bankers often **underwrite** new issues by purchasing the securities (once the details of the issue have been negotiated) and assuming the risk of reselling them to investors. Investment bankers provide a valuable service to the issuers at this stage. The issuer receives its check and can spend the proceeds for the purposes for which the funds are being raised. The investment bankers own the securities until they are resold. Although many issues are sold out quickly (e.g., the first day they are offered to the public), others may not be sold for days or even weeks. Investment bankers are compensated by a spread, which is the difference between what they pay the issuer for the securities and what they sell them for to the public (i.e., the securities are purchased from the issuer at a discount).

In addition to having expertise in these matters and closely scrutinizing any potential issue of securities, investment bankers can protect themselves by forming a *syndicate*, or group of investment bankers. This allows them to diversify their risk. One investment banker acts as the managing underwriter, overseeing the underwriting syndicate. This syndicate becomes part of a larger group that sells the securities.

Prospectus Provides information about an initial public offering of securities to potential buyers

Figure 4-1 illustrates a primary offering of securities through investment bankers, a process referred to as a syndicated offering. The issuer (seller) of the securities works with the originating investment banker in designing the specific details of the sale.[2] A **prospectus**,

[2] All documents are prepared to satisfy federal laws. In particular, the issuer files a registration statement, which contains financial and other information about the company, with the appropriate government agency.

FIGURE 4-1

A primary offering of securities

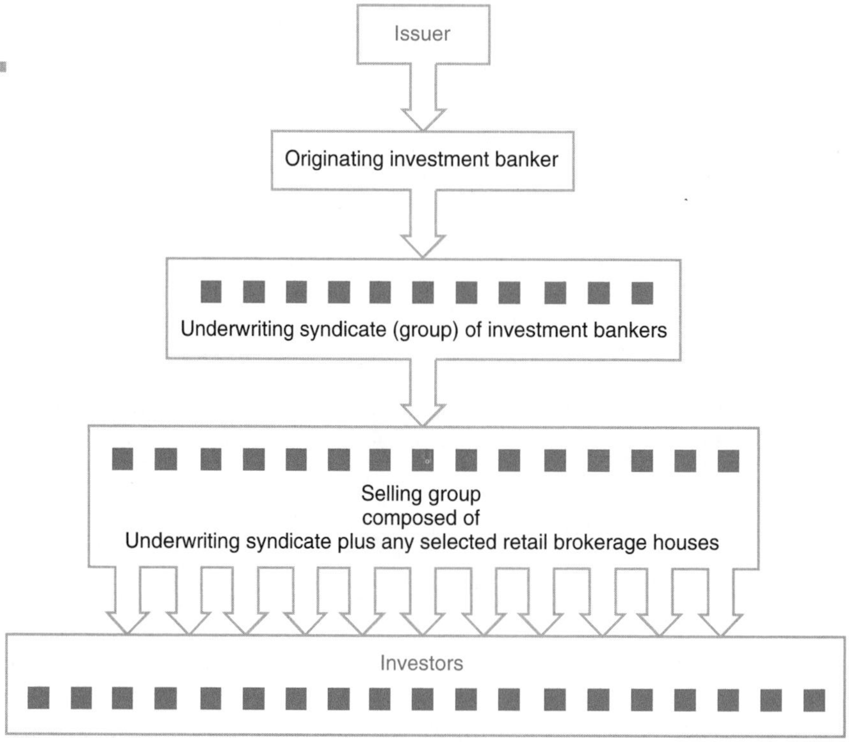

which summarizes this information, offers the securities for sale officially.[3] The underwriter forms a syndicate of underwriters who are willing to undertake the sale of these securities once the legal requirements are met.[4] The selling group consists of the syndicate members and, if necessary, other firms affiliated with the syndicate. The issue may be fully subscribed (sold out) quickly, or several days (or longer) may be required to sell it.[5]

Shelf Rule Permits qualified companies to file a short form registration and "place on the shelf" securities to be sold over time under favorable conditions

Securities and Exchange Rule 415 (the **shelf rule**), effective in 1982, permits qualified companies to file a "short form registration" and to "place on the shelf" securities to be sold. The issuing company can sell the new securities over time by auctioning pieces of the issue to the lowest cost bidder, providing flexibility and savings.

A recent change has occurred among many newly public companies seeking additional financing. Rather than using the underwriter involved in their initial IPO, young companies selling additional stock often switch to an underwriter with "star" stock-research analysts who can tout the stock.

GLOBAL INVESTMENT BANKING

The global perspective now in place allows companies in various countries to raise new capital in amounts that would have been impossible only a few years earlier because these companies

[3] However, the selling group can send out a preliminary prospectus to investors describing the new issue. No offering date or price is shown, and the prospectus is identified clearly as an informational sheet and not a solicitation to sell the securities. For this reason, the preliminary prospectus is often referred to as a "red herring."

[4] New issues must be registered with the SEC at least 20 days before being publicly offered. Upon approval from the SEC, the selling group begins selling the securities to the public.

[5] During this time, the underwriting manager can legally elect to stabilize the market by placing purchase orders for the security at a fixed price. Underwriters believe that such stabilization is sometimes needed to provide for an orderly sale (thereby helping the issuer) and reduce their risk (thereby helping themselves).

often were limited to selling new securities in their own domestic markets. The global equity offering has changed all that. An important new development in investment banking is the emphasis on managing the global offerings of securities. A lead investment banker can act as a "global coordinator," linking separate underwriting syndicates throughout the world in selling equity issues.

As of 1999, U.S. firms are now selling bonds in the new euro market. Although the dollar accounts for one-third to one-half of all new bond issues, more companies are selling bonds in Europe, and the euro market expects to challenge the U.S. bond market. The appeal for U.S. firms is that bond yields in the new euro market are lower than in the United States by as much as 40 percent. U.S. firms with foreign operations can also raise foreign currency in the form of euros by directing selling bonds in that market, thereby saving the costs of converting dollars to euros.

PRIVATE PLACEMENTS

In recent years an increasing number of corporations have executed *private placements*, whereby new securities issues (typically, debt securities) are sold directly to financial institutions, such as life insurance companies and pension funds, bypassing the open market. One advantage is that the firm does not have to register the issue with the SEC, thereby saving both time and money.[6] Investment bankers' fees also are saved because they are not typically used in private placements, and even if they are used, the underwriting spread is saved. The disadvantages of private placements include a higher interest cost, because the financial institutions usually charge more than would be offered in a public subscription, and possible restrictive provisions on the borrower's activities.[7]

THE SECONDARY MARKETS

Once new securities have been sold in the primary market, an efficient mechanism must exist for their resale if investors are to view securities as attractive opportunities. **Secondary markets** give investors the means to trade existing securities.

Secondary Markets Markets where existing securities are traded among investors

Secondary markets exist for the trading of common and preferred stock, warrants, bonds, and puts and calls. Figure 4-2 diagrams the structure of the secondary markets, which is discussed below in the following order: equities, bonds, and derivative securities.

Auction Market A securities market with a physical location, such as the New York Stock Exchange, where the prices of securities are determined by the actions of buyers and sellers

Broker An intermediary who represents buyers and sellers in securities transactions and receives a commission

EQUITY SECURITIES—AUCTION MARKETS

Common stocks, preferred stocks, and warrants are traded in the equity markets. Some secondary equity markets are **auction markets**, involving an auction (bidding) process in a specific physical location. Investors are represented by **brokers**, intermediaries who represent both buyers and sellers and attempt to obtain the best price possible for either party in a transaction. Brokers collect commissions for their efforts and generally have no vested interest in whether a customer places a buy order or a sell order, or, in most cases, in what is bought or sold (holding constant the value of the transaction).

The U.S. auction markets include the New York Stock Exchange, the American Stock Exchange, and the regional exchanges. Negotiated markets involve the over-the-counter market. We consider both auction and negotiated markets in turn.

[6] The savings in time can sometimes be important, for market conditions can change rapidly between the time an issue is registered and sold.

[7] In addition, a lack of marketability exits, because the issue is unregistered. Therefore, the buyer may demand additional compensation from the lender in the form of a higher yield.

FIGURE 4-2

Structure of the secondary markets

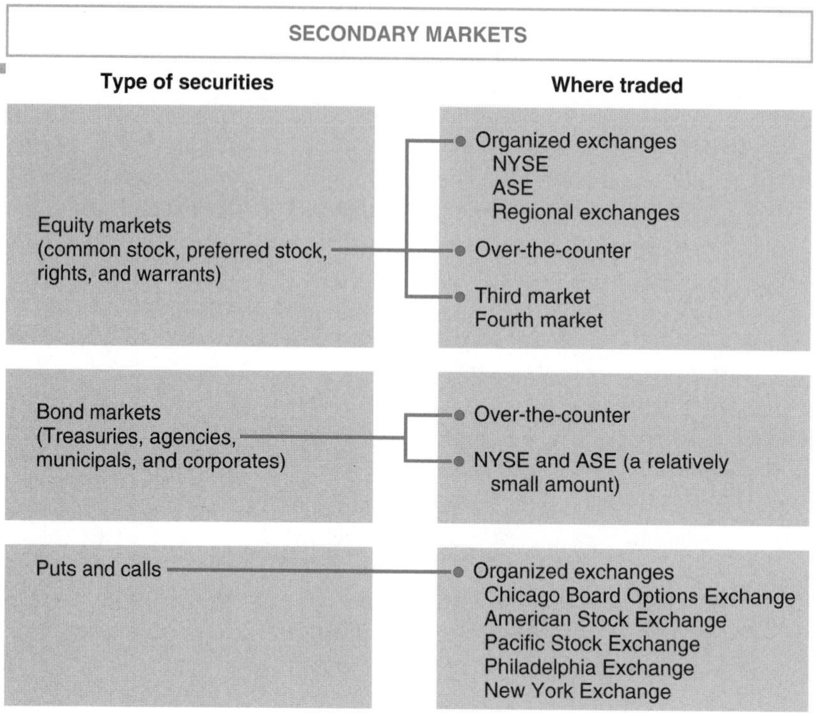

New York Stock Exchange (NYSE) The major secondary market for the trading of equity securities

New York Stock Exchange Founded in 1792, the **New York Stock Exchange (NYSE)** is the oldest and most prominent secondary market in the United States. By 1992 it had regained its traditional place as the world's largest secondary market, following the decline of the Tokyo Stock Exchange. The NYSE typically is regarded as the best regulated exchange in the world and has proven its ability to function in crisis. For example, on Black Monday in October 1987, this exchange handled some 600 million shares when other marketplaces discussed below were experiencing significant problems.

The NYSE is a not-for-profit corporation with 1,421 members, 1,366 of whom own a seat.[8] Most of the members are partners or directors of stockbrokerage houses.[9] Members may transfer seats, by sale or lease, subject to the approval of the exchange. The price of a seat has varied sharply over the years, ranging from less than $100,000 in the mid-1970s to a peak in February, 1998 of $2,000,000. At the beginning of 1999, a seat was going for $1.2 million, possibly reflecting the changing securities markets as technology diminished the role of traditional financial exchanges.

Members of the exchange can combine with others to operate as a member organization and do business with the public. In early 1999, 289 NYSE member firms, out of a total of 426 member organizations, were doing business with the public (both numbers have declined in recent years).

Specialist A member of an organized exchange who is charged with maintaining an orderly market in one or more stocks by buying or selling for his or her own account

Specialists, who own roughly 33 percent of all the seats on the NYSE, are assigned to each trading post on the floor of the NYSE, where they handle one or more of the stocks traded at that post. Some specialists firms are part of well-known brokerage operations, while many others are virtually unknown to the public.

[8] The other 55 individuals paid an annual fee to have access to the trading floor. The number of seats has remained constant since 1953.

[9] For example, Merrill Lynch, the largest retail stockbrokerage firm, owns over 20 seats.

EXAMPLE **4-2**

Specialists of well-known institutions include Merrill Lynch Specialists, which handles the trading in Coca-Cola and Johnson & Johnson, and Bear Stearns Hunter Specialists, which handles Texas Instruments and Alcoa. Examples of specialists firms not known to the public include the largest specialist firm, Spear, Leeds & Kellogg, which handles more than 200 stocks, including IBM and Mobil, or the second largest firm, JJC Specialists, which handles Sears and General Electric, among other companies.

The New York Stock Exchange has specific listing requirements that companies must meet in order to be listed (i.e., accepted for trading). In considering an application to be listed, the NYSE pays particular attention to the degree of national interest in the company, its relative position and stability in the industry, and its prospects for maintaining its relative position. Requirements include specified amounts of earning power and net tangible assets, $40,000,000 market value of publicly traded shares, and a total of 1,100,000 common shares publicly held. New companies are added each year. In early 1999, 3,107 companies had stock (common and preferred) listed on the NYSE. This represented about 250 billion shares worth some $10.5 trillion available for trading on the exchange.

In 1998 the NYSE had an aggregate share volume of over 171 billion shares, compared to 1994 volume of 73.4 billion shares. The dollar value of trading was $7.4 trillion. Daily trading volume averaged 674 million shares in 1998, involving over a half million transactions.

Blocks Transactions involving at least 10,000 shares

Institutional investors often trade in large **blocks**, which are defined as transactions involving at least 10,000 shares. The average size of a trade on the NYSE has grown sharply over the years, as has institutional participation by block volume on both the NYSE and the Nasdaq National Market. A record 3.52 million block transactions were traded on the NYSE in 1998, accounting for almost 83 billion shares, or 49 percent of NYSE volume.

Program Trading Involves the use of computer-generated orders to buy and sell securities based on arbitrage opportunities between common stocks and index futures and options

A new trend of potential significance that is often discussed in the popular press is **program trading**, which the NYSE defines as the purchase or sale of a basket of 15 stocks or more and valued at $1 million or more. It is used to accomplish certain trading strategies, such as arbitrage against futures contracts and portfolio accumulation and liquidation strategies. By the beginning of 1999, program trading volume accounted for approximately 17 percent of total NYSE volume and averaged some 88 million shares daily.

American Stock Exchange The American Stock Exchange (AMEX) is the only other national organized exchange. Its organization and procedures resemble those of the NYSE, most notably in being a specialist-based system. Relative to the NYSE, the AMEX is smaller (approximately 650 seats) and fewer companies are listed there (approximately 770 at the beginning of 1999). The listing requirements are less stringent for stocks on the AMEX than for stocks on the NYSE.

Although equity trading volume increased 18 percent in 1998 from a year earlier, it amounted to only 7 billion shares, a very small percentage of total share volume in 1998. Typically, the NYSE does more trading in the first hour than the AMEX does during the entire day. However, the AMEX does a large business in options and derivative securities, with almost 30 percent of the market in stock-option trading. Its SPDRs and Diamonds, a form of investment trust (which was explained in Chapter 3), have proven to be quite popular. In fact, the most active issue on the AMEX in 1998 was SPDRs, which traded 1.8 billion shares. Diamonds^{SM}, launched in 1998, were the most successful launch of any AMEX product in history.

Regardless of volume, some companies choose to be listed on the AMEX.

EXAMPLE 4-3

Metromedia International, following its restructuring, chose to be listed on the AMEX, citing lower listing costs and the right to choose its own specialist, which the AMEX allows firms to do.

In November, 1998, the NASD (explained below) and the AMEX completed their announced merger, thereby creating the first financial marketplace to combine the central auction specialist and multiple market maker systems. Nasdaq (explained below) and AMEX will operate as separate markets under the management of the Nasdaq-AMEX Market Group. Nasdaq-AMEX intends to build a globally linked marketplace that provides investment choices to all investors worldwide.

Regional Exchanges The United States has several regional exchanges patterned after the NYSE, although their listing requirements are considerably more lenient.[10] Regional exchanges list small companies that may have limited geographic interest. In addition, they engage in dual listing; that is, they list securities that are also listed on the NYSE and the AMEX.[11] This allows local brokerage firms that are not members of a national exchange to purchase a seat on a regional exchange and trade in dual-listed securities. Regional exchanges accounted for approximately 9 percent of share volume in early 1999.

In the 1990s, institutional investors aggressively sought lower trading costs. One way for Wall Street firms to accommodate these demands by their institutional clients was to take some trades to the regional exchanges where commissions are often lower. The NYSE continues to have an advantage in handling big block trades, which traders call liquidity.

Over-the-Counter (OTC) Market A network of securities dealers linked together to make markets in securities

Negotiated Market A market involving dealers, such as the OTC

Dealer An individual (firm) who makes a market in a stock by buying from and selling to investors

Nasdaq Stock Market (Nasdaq) The automated quotation system for the OTC market, showing current bid-ask prices for thousands of stocks

National Association of Securities Dealers (NASD) A self-regulating body of brokers and dealers overseeing OTC practices

EQUITY SECURITIES—NEGOTIATED MARKETS

In contrast to auction markets, the **over-the-counter (OTC) market** is a **negotiated market** consisting of a network of **dealers** who make a market by standing ready to buy and sell securities at specified prices. Unlike brokers, dealers have a vested interest in the transaction because the securities are bought from them and sold to them, and they earn a profit in these trades by the spread, or difference, between the two prices.

Transactions not handled on an organized exchange are handled in this market; that is, this market essentially handles unlisted securities, or securities not listed on a stock exchange, although some listed securities are now traded in this market. Thousands of stocks trade in the aggregate OTC market, roughly 35,000, many of which are small, thinly traded stocks that do not generate much interest. However, most of the actively traded OTC stocks are part of the **Nasdaq Stock Market**^{SM}, or **Nasdaq**. Figure 4-3 shows a comparison of Nasdaq companies with NYSE and AMEX companies. As we can see, there are roughly 3,000 NYSE companies and more than 5,000 Nasdaq companies.

Formally, Nasdaq is a national and international stock market consisting of communications networks for the trading of thousands of stocks. Technically, Nasdaq has insisted for several years that its market is not synonymous with the OTC market.[12] This market is a wholly owned subsidiary of the **National Association of Security Dealers (NASD)**, a self-

[10] Examples include the Midwest Stock Exchange, the Pacific Stock Exchange, the Boston Stock Exchange, the Philadelphia Stock Exchange, and the Cincinnati Stock Exchange. The combined Nasdaq-AMEX is now acquiring the Philadelphia Stock Exchange.

[11] In fact, most of the securities traded on the regional exchanges are also traded on the NYSE or the AMEX.

[12] Nasdaq traditionally was the acronym for the National Association of Securities Dealers Automated Quotation system. Nasdaq now states that the word is not an acronym.

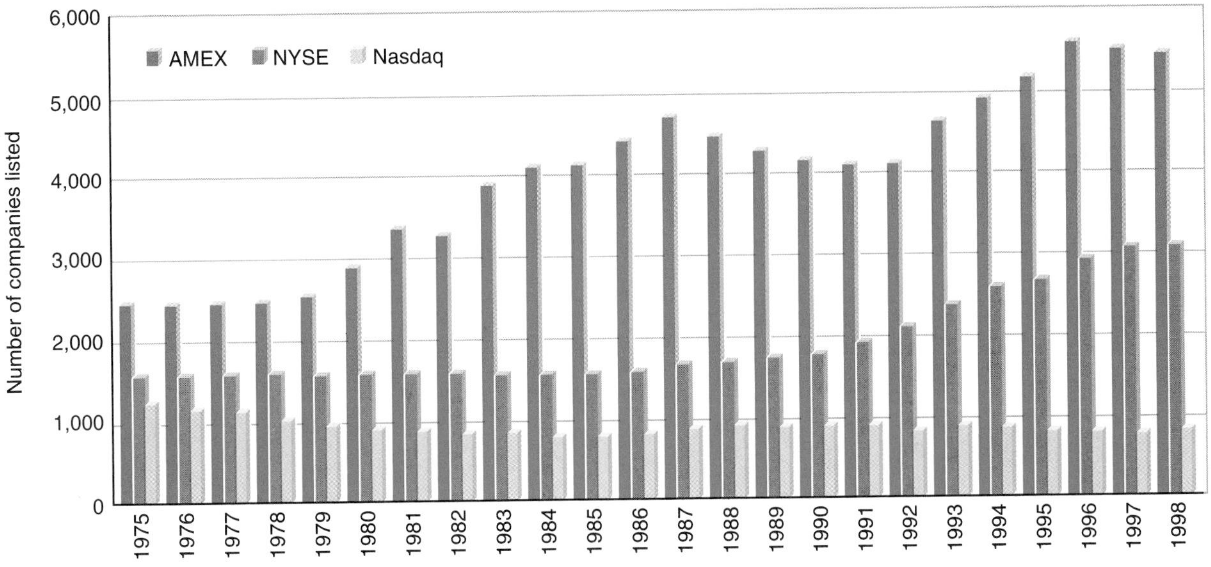

FIGURE 4-3

A comparison of number of companies traded for NYSE, AMEX, and Nasdaq, 1975 through 1998

SOURCE: Nasdaq Market Data, www.nasd.com.

regulating body of brokers and dealers that oversees OTC practices, much as the NYSE does for its members. The NASD:

1. Licenses brokers when they successfully complete a qualifying examination.
2. Provides for on-site compliance examinations of member firms. Violation of the fair practices prescribed by the NASD are grounds for censure, fine, suspension, or expulsion for both firms and principals in the firms. This self-regulating function of the NASD serves to protect the public as well as the interest of its members.
3. Provides automated market surveillance.
4. Reviews member advertising and underwriting arrangements.
5. Provides a mechanism for the arbitration of disputes between member firms and investors.

Market Maker A broker/dealer who is registered to trade in a given security on the Nasdaq

Unlike the NYSE, the Nasdaq Stock Market does not have a specific location. Rather, it is a way of doing business. It consists of a network of **market makers** or *dealers* linked together by communications devices who compete freely with each other through an electronic network of terminals, rather than on the floor of an exchange. These dealers conduct transactions directly with each other and with customers. Each Nasdaq company has a number of competing dealers who make a market in the stock, with a minimum of two and an average of 11. (Some large Nasdaq companies have 40 or more dealers.)

Nasdaq National Market System (Nasdaq/NMS) A combination of the competing market markers in OTC stocks and the up-to-the-minute reporting of trades using data almost identical to that shown for the NYSE and AMEX

Nasdaq features an electronic trading system as the centerpiece of its operations. This system provides instantaneous transactions as Nasdaq market makers compete for investor orders. An investor who places an order with his or her broker for a Nasdaq security will have this order executed in one of two ways: (1) If the broker's firm makes a market in the security, the order will be executed internally at a price equal to or better than the best price quoted by all competing market makers; or (2) if the broker's firm is not a market maker in this security, the firm will buy from or sell to a market maker at another firm. *SelectNet*[SM] is a screen-based negotiation service that member firms use to quickly obtain efficient execution of orders in Nasdaq securities.

The **Nasdaq National Market System (Nasdaq/NMS)**, a component of the Nasdaq market, is a combination of the competing market makers in OTC stocks and the up-to-

FIGURE 4-4

Distribution of holdings of Nasdaq/NMS Common Stocks, 1998

SOURCE: *The Nasdaq Stock Market: 1998 Fact Book*, National Association of Securities Dealers, Inc., Washington, D.C., 1999, p. 29. Reprinted by permission.

Market Value of Holdings

	dollar amount (billions)	percentage of total
Institutional	$902.8	48.0%
Individual	$534.4	28.4%
Other	$442.5	23.5%
Total	**$1,879.7**	**100.0%**

Shares Held

	shares held (billions)	percentage of total
Institutional	27.5	40.0%
Individual	22.9	33.3%
Other	18.3	26.6%
Total	**64.7**	**100.0%**

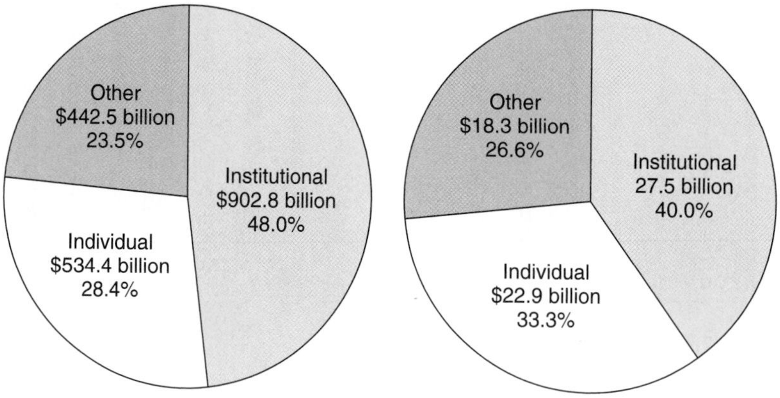

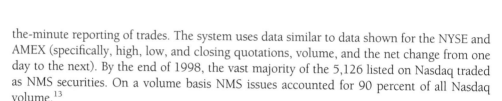

the-minute reporting of trades. The system uses data similar to data shown for the NYSE and AMEX (specifically, high, low, and closing quotations, volume, and the net change from one day to the next). By the end of 1998, the vast majority of the 5,126 listed on Nasdaq traded as NMS securities. On a volume basis NMS issues accounted for 90 percent of all Nasdaq volume.[13]

The Nasdaq Stock Market has become a major player in the securities markets and in all likelihood will continue to gain in importance. Consider the following facts about the Nasdaq Stock Market:

1. Slightly more than half of all equity shares traded in the United States daily are traded on the Nasdaq Stock Market.
2. Share volume in 1998 amounted to 202 billion shares, and dollar volume amounted to $5.8 trillion (both of these numbers represent a doubling since 1995).
3. The 273 IPOs on Nasdaq in 1998 amounted to $14 billion.
4. Twelve non-U.S. companies were listed on Nasdaq in 1998, bringing the total foreign-based companies traded to 440. Nasdaq is the primary U.S. market for trading shares of non-U.S.-based companies.

An important trend in the OTC market is the emergence of institutional investors as dominant players. Traditionally, the OTC market has been known as the market for mostly small and less well-known companies, where individual investors trade. Since 1982, the institutions have assumed an increasingly larger role and by year-end 1993 were the largest single group, a position they have maintained.

Figure 4-4 shows the distribution of holdings of Nasdaq/NMS common stocks, divided among individuals, institutions, and others (officers, directors, and beneficial owners of 10 percent or more). At year-end 1997 institutions accounted for 40 percent of the shares held

[13] This discussion is based on the *NASDAQ Fact Book* for the appropriate year (Washington, D.C.: National Association of Securities Dealers, Inc.).

and for 48 percent of the market value of the holdings, surpassing individual investors in both categories. Investment firms and mutual firms account for about three-fourths of both shares held and the market value of holdings.

In summary, the common stock issues traded in the OTC market vary widely in size, price, quality, and trading activity. Many are small, struggling, speculative companies that are often not far removed from having obtained public financing in a primary offering. Others are comparable to NYSE stocks and could, if they chose, be listed there. A number of Nasdaq companies have chosen to remain Nasdaq companies rather than move on to the AMEX or NYSE.

As noted above, in November 1998 Nasdaq and the AMEX merged to offer competing market and auction specialists markets. The intent is to offer investors more efficient pricing, faster trade execution, and reduced transaction costs.[14]

USING THE INTERNET Information, primarily factual, on the NYSE can be obtained at www.nyse.com. This site has extensive historical data as well as information about the NYSE and its companies. Information on the AMEX and Nasdaq can be obtained at www.nasdaq-amex.com, which offers quotes, news, market activity, and portfolio tracking. The Nasdaq-AMEX Newsroom℠ at www.nasdaq-amexnews.com offers numerous press releases and key reports. By going to http://www.nasdaqnews.com and accessing "Nasdaq© Backgrounder," an interested individual can call up numerous reports on how this market functions, the companies traded, Nasdaq indexes, listing standards, and so forth.

ELECTRONIC COMMUNICATIONS NETWORKS (ECNs)

Electronic Communications Network (ECNs) A computerized trading network for institutions and large traders

Increasingly, the traditional financial markets are being changed by new advances in electronic trading. Electronic Communications Networks (ECNs) are taking business away from Nasdaq in particular, and to a lesser extent the NYSE. In early 1999 eight ECNs were functioning.

An ECN is a computerized trading network that matches buy and sell orders electronically entered by customers. If no match is currently possible, the ECN acts sort of like a broker, posting its best bid and ask offer (under its own name) on Nasdaq's trading screen. Another party who sees these prices and wants to transact would enter the appropriate buy or sell order. Trading is limited to members only, which means institutional investors or large traders. ECNs offer automation, lower costs, and anonymity as to who is doing the buying or selling.

Instinet An electronic trading network, one of the ECNs

Instinet (Institutional Network), owned by Reuters, is the original electronic trading network, started in 1969 long before the term ECN, which is a recent innovation. It is a system offering equity transactions and research services only for brokers, dealers, exchange specialists, institutional fund managers, and plan sponsors who pay commissions of about one cent a share and also receive free proprietary terminals. Instinet is always open for trading stocks on any of the exchanges worldwide to which Instinet belongs.

Instinet offers anonymous trading, allowing large traders to bypass brokers with their often attendant leaks on who is transacting. Trades are often less than 10,000 shares each, and an institution can do multiple trades to get into or out of a position in a stock without others knowing.

[14] The new website, nasdaq-amex.com, offers fundamental stock information on all publicly traded companies. Enhanced information is available both for Nasdaq and AMEX companies, including analyst and stock reports, SEC filings, website links, and more.

FIGURE 4-5

How stocks are traded

SOURCE: Greg Ip, "Big Board Gets Feedback on Nasdaq Concept," *The Wall Street Journal*, March 1, 1999, p. C1. Reprinted by permission of *The Wall Street Journal* © 1999, Dow Jones & Company, Inc. All Rights Reserved Worldwide. Permission conveyed through Copyright Clearance Center, Inc.

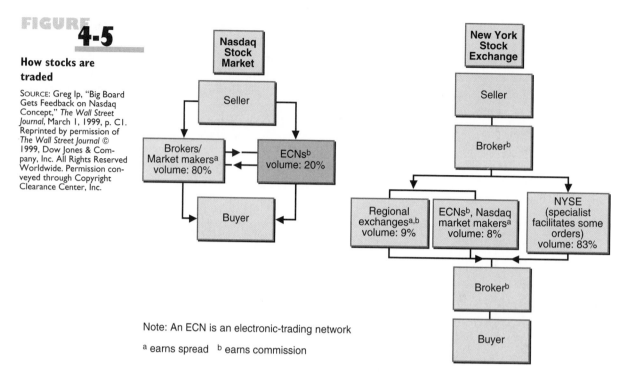

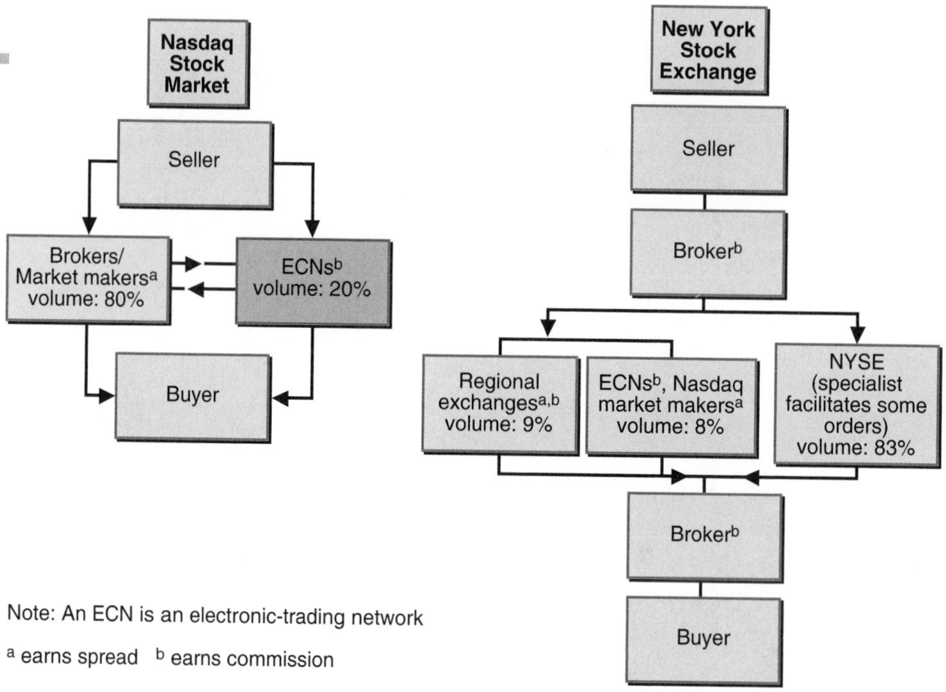

EXAMPLE 4-4

In a famous episode of the market knowing what traders are doing, Jeff Vinik, then the manager of Magellan Fund, starting sell semiconductor stocks, and in particular Micron Technology when supposedly he was bullish on the stock. Word got out, and others followed suit. Trading on Instinet could prevent this.

New ECNs attracting attention include Island (owned by Datek Online Holdings) and Brass Utility (known as Brut). The prospect is for these electronic networks to grow because of institutional trader frustration with the ability of the exchanges to handle large blocks of securities. As of April 1999, ECNs are allowed to register as exchanges under Securities and Exchange Commission rules.

The NYSE has been frustrated by its inability to attract the hot Internet and technology companies, such as Cisco, Dell, Intel, and Microsoft. Because the ECNs are getting some of the business for these companies, the NYSE is exploring how it might link up with them. It could buy an ECN, or arrange a partnership with one. As of early 1999, the NYSE did not trade Nasdaq stocks, but Nasdaq handles some trades in NYSE-listed stocks, as Figure 4-5 shows.

Figure 4-5 shows the current status of stock trading in the United States. Note that two other groups account for roughly 17 percent of NYSE trading, while ECNs are accounting for 20 percent of Nasdaq trading.

In-House Trading Along with the electronic networks, a new trend that has significant implications for the NYSE is the internal trading, or *in-house trading*, by fund managers without the use of a broker or an exchange. At a large institution with several funds or accounts, traders agree to buy and sell in-house, or cross-trade, perhaps at the next closing price. For example, at a large bank with several pension fund accounts, the manager of Account A might wish to buy IBM at the same time that the manager of Account B is selling a position in IBM.

EXAMPLE 4-5

Fidelity Investments, the largest mutual fund organization, operates an in-house trading system for its own funds because of the tremendous amount of buying and selling it does every day. In addition, it has set up the *Investor Liquidity Network*, which is now used by other brokerage firms and institutional clients. This electronic routing system is said to handle 5 percent of the NYSE's volume, and Fidelity's in-house trading accounts for at least that much more.

FOREIGN MARKETS

As noted, investors have become increasingly interested in equity markets around the world because the United States now accounts for only about one-third of the world's stock market capitalization. Many equity markets exist. Examples in the developed countries include the United Kingdom, France, Germany, Italy, Switzerland, Japan, Hong Kong, and Canada. Investors are also interested in *emerging markets* such as Mexico, Brazil, and Indonesia.[15] Because of the large number and variety of foreign markets, we will consider only a few highlights here.

Western Europe has several mature markets, including in addition to those mentioned above Belgium, Finland, Spain, and Sweden. U.S. investors sent more money to Britain in the last few years than any other country in the world. The London Stock Exchange (LSE) is an important equity market, handling both listed equities and bonds as well as unlisted securities. Germany has continental Europe's largest stock market. Switzerland is home to some of the largest global companies in the world, including Nestle (food and beverage) and Hoffman La Roche (drug manufacturer).

Interestingly, analysts now refer to Europe's emerging markets. These include the Czech Republic, Hungary, and Poland where potential profits are large, but risks are also large: illiquidity is great, corporate information is difficult to obtain, and political risk of a type unknown to U.S. investors still exists. Turkey is another example of an emerging market.

The Far East is the fastest growing region in the world, with growth rates twice that of the United States; U.S. investors have been particularly active in the Far Eastern markets. These markets also have been very volatile, with large gains and losses because of illiquidity (a scarcity of buyers at times) as well as currency risks and political risks.

Japan, the dominant Asian economic power, has one of the largest stock markets in the world, although the Japanese markets have been severely battered in the mid and late 1990s. Although Japan has eight stock exchanges, the Tokyo Stock Exchange (TSE) dominates that country's equity markets even more than the NYSE dominates the U.S. markets. Both domestic and foreign stocks are listed on the TSE, and among domestic issues a relatively few are traded on the floor of the exchange; the rest (as well as foreign stocks) are handled by computer.

Other Asian markets include Hong Kong, which next to Japan is the largest Asian market in terms of market capitalization, India, Indonesia, Japan, South Korea, Malaysia, Pakistan, the Philippines, Singapore, Sri Lanka, Taiwan, and Thailand. Of course, some of these markets are quite small. The "Four Dragons"—Hong Kong, Singapore, South Korea, and Taiwan—dominate these markets when Japan is excluded.

The big unknown in Asian markets is, of course, China, an emerging economy of potentially great importance. China is booming as an economy but with great risks, for politics strongly affects investments in China. Its financial markets are still tiny by other countries'

[15] There is no precise definition of an *emerging market*, but generally it involves a stable political system, fewer regulations, and less standardization in trading activity.

FIGURE 4-6

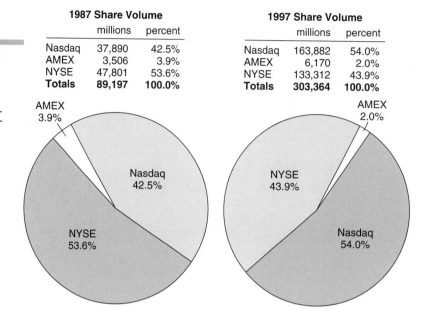

Comparison of share volume: Nasdaq, NYSE, and AMEX

SOURCE: *The Nasdaq Stock Market: 1998 Fact Book*, National Association of Securities Dealers, Inc., Washington, D.C., 1999, p. 9. Reprinted by permission.

1987 Share Volume

	millions	percent
Nasdaq	37,890	42.5%
AMEX	3,506	3.9%
NYSE	47,801	53.6%
Totals	**89,197**	**100.0%**

1997 Share Volume

	millions	percent
Nasdaq	163,882	54.0%
AMEX	6,170	2.0%
NYSE	133,312	43.9%
Totals	**303,364**	**100.0%**

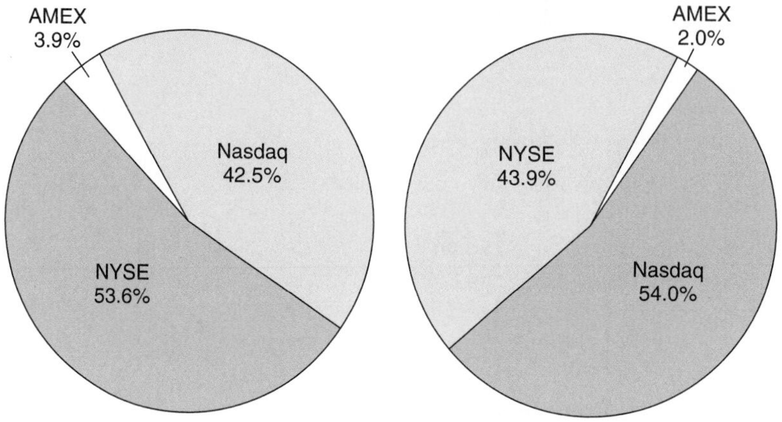

standards. Chinese companies do trade on the Hong Kong exchange as well as on exchanges in China such as Shanghai.

Latin America is the remaining emerging marketplace that has been of great interest to investors recently. The markets in Latin America include Argentina, Brazil, Chile, Colombia, Mexico, Peru, and Venezuela. Mexico's market is the largest, followed by Brazil, with the others small by comparison in terms of market capitalization. As we would expect in emerging markets, profit potentials are large, but so are risks—volatile prices, liquidity problems, and political risks such as the assassination of Mexico's leading presidential candidate in 1994. In early 1999, Brazil suffered a severe financial crisis.

COMPARISONS OF EQUITY MARKETS

Figure 4-6 shows annual share volume comparisons for the major domestic markets for one recent year. Significantly, in 1998 Nasdaq accounted for 53 percent of total volume compared to 45 percent for the NYSE.

Figure 4-7 shows the *dollar* volume of equity trading in major world markets for the year 1997. As we can see, by this measure New York dominated, followed by Nasdaq, London, and so forth, with the AMEX last. Based on *dollar volume*, the NYSE remains a major player in the United States, with 50 percent of the dollar volume in 1998 compared to 48 percent for Nasdaq.

STOCK MARKET INDICATORS

The most popular question asked about stock markets is probably, "What did the market do today?" To answer this question, we need a composite report on market performance, which is what stock market averages and indices are designed to provide. Because of the large number of equity markets, both domestic and foreign, there are numerous stock market indicators. In this section, we outline only some basic information on these averages and indices, with subsequent chapters containing more analysis and discussion as needed. Ap-

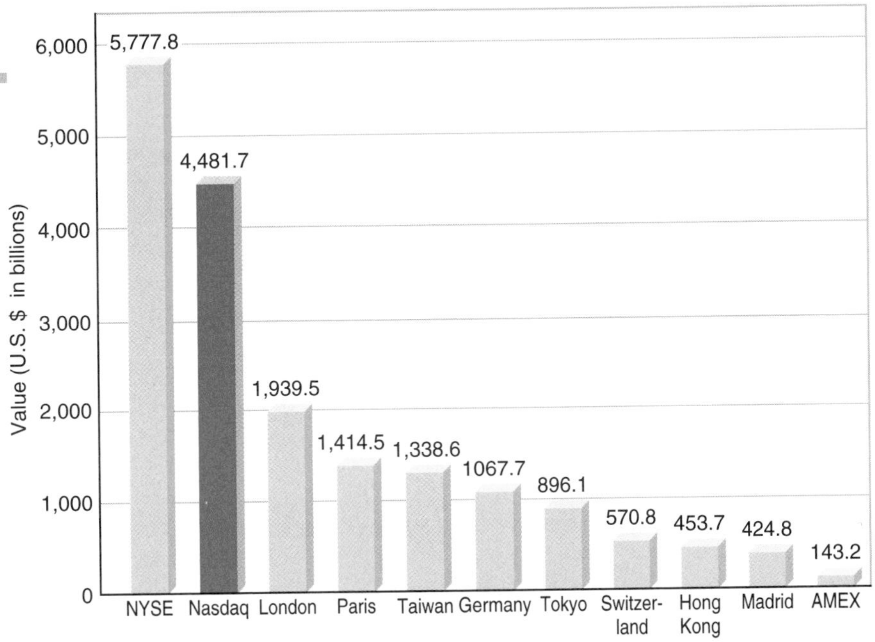

FIGURE 4-7

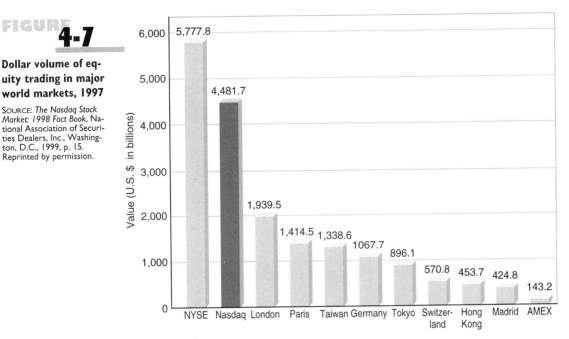

Dollar volume of equity trading in major world markets, 1997

SOURCE: *The Nasdaq Stock Market: 1998 Fact Book*, National Association of Securities Dealers, Inc., Washington, D.C., 1999, p. 15. Reprinted by permission.

pendix 4-A provides additional details on these indicators, including composition and construction details.

Dow Jones Industrial Average (DJIA) A price-weighted series of 30 leading industrial stocks, used as a measure of stock market activity

Blue-Chip Stocks Stocks with long records of earnings and dividends—well-known, stable, mature companies

The Dow Jones Averages The best known average in the United States is the **Dow Jones Industrial Average (DJIA)**, probably because it is carried by *The Wall Street Journal*.[16] It is the oldest market measure, originating in 1896 and modified over the years.[17] The DJIA is computed from 30 leading industrial stocks whose composition changes slowly over time to reflect changes in the economy. This average is said to be composed of **blue-chip stocks**, meaning large, well-established, and well-known companies. Dow Jones & Company also computes, and the *Journal* publishes, a transportation average and a public utility average. It is important to note that the DJIA is a price-weighted series. Although it gives equal weight to equal dollar changes, high-priced stocks carry more weight than low-priced stocks. A 1 percent change in the price of stock A at $200 will have a much different impact on the DJIA from that of a 1 percent change in stock B at $20. This also means that as high-priced stocks split and their prices decline, they lose relative importance in the calculation of the average, whereas nonsplit stocks increase in relative importance. This bias against growth stocks, which are the most likely stocks to split, can result in a downward bias in the DJIA. Like any index, its level reflects the decisions that have been made on which stocks to include in the index. Changes in the composition of the DJIA have occurred only infrequently.

The DJIA has been criticized because of its use of only 30 stocks, because it is price weighted (rather than value weighted), and because the divisor is not adjusted for stock dividends of less than 10 percent.[18] Nevertheless, it is the oldest continuous measure of the

[16] There are three other Dow-Jones Averages: the transportation, the public utility, and the composite. The first two encompass 20 and 15 stocks, respectively, and the composite consists of these two groups plus the DJIA (i.e., 65 stocks). Each average is calculated similarly to the DJIA, with changes made in the divisor to adjust for splits and other factors. Daily information on these averages can be found in *The Wall Street Journal* and other newspapers.

[17] The first average of U.S. stocks appeared in 1884 and consisted of 11 stocks, mostly railroads.

[18] Perhaps in part as a result of such criticisms, there now is a capitalization-weighted Dow Jones Equity Market Index. It consists of 700 stocks covering approximately 80 percent of the U.S. equity market.

stock market, and it remains the prominent measure of market activity for many investors. Furthermore, the DJIA does fulfill its role as a measure of market activity for stocks such as those on the New York Stock Exchange.

It is important to note that because of the adjustments in the divisor of the DJIA over time, to account for stock splits and stock dividends, one point on the Dow is not equal to $1. In early 1999 the divisor was 0.24275; therefore, a change in the DJIA, given a one-point change in only one stock in the index, amounted to 1/.24275, or 4.12 points. Furthermore, a movement of 30 points in the DJIA results in an average movement of the component stocks of only $.24.

EXAMPLE 4-6

On January 22, 1999, the DJIA fell 143.41 points, which most people would consider a large decline. However, IBM, one of the 30 Dow stocks, declined $17.31, which accounted for 4.12(17.31) or 71.32 points of the Dow's decline, almost exactly half.

Standard & Poor's Stock Price Indexes Standard & Poor's Corporation, which publishes financial data for investors, also publishes five market indices, including a 400-stock Industrial Average, a 40-stock Utility Average, a 20-stock Transportation Average, a 40-stock Financial Average, and, finally, all of these combined into a 500-stock Composite Index.[19] The Composite Index is carried in the popular press such as *The Wall Street Journal*, and investors often refer to it as a "good" measure of what the overall market is doing, at least for large NYSE stocks.

S&P 500 Composite Index (S&P 500) Market value index of stock market activity covering 500 stocks

Unlike the Dow Jones Industrial Average, the **Standard & Poor's 500 Composite Index (S&P 500)** is a market value index. It is expressed in relative numbers with a base period set to 10 (1941–1943). All stock splits and dividends are automatically accounted for in calculating the value of the index because the number of shares currently outstanding (i.e., after the split or dividend) and the new price are used in the calculation. Unlike the Dow Jones Average, each stock's importance is based on relative total market value instead of relative per-share price.

The S&P 500 is obviously a much broader measure than the Dow, and it should be more representative of the general market. However, it consists primarily of NYSE stocks, and it is clearly dominated by the largest corporations.[20] Nevertheless, the S&P 500 is typically the measure of the market preferred by institutional investors. They most often compare their performance to this market index instead of the DJIA. Like any index, the S&P 500 is affected by the performance of the individual stocks in the index.

Nasdaq Indexes The National Association of Security Dealers produces several indexes. Eight Nasdaq indexes cover industrials, banks, insurance, other finance, transportation, telecommunications, computers, and biotechnology. All of these together comprise the Composite Index. The base period January 1971 is assigned a value of 100 for the Composite Index and the Industrial Index, and monthly data is available from January 1971.

In addition to these, the Nasdaq/NMS Industrial Index and the Nasdaq/NMS Composite Index were begun on July 10, 1984, with an initial value for each of 100. The Nasdaq-100 and Nasdaq-Financial 100 were begun on February 1, 1985, with an initial value of 250. Each consists of the 100 largest market-capitalized firms in their respective categories.

[19] Standard & Poor's also publishes indices for various groupings of stocks, covering specific industries, low-priced stocks, high-grade stocks, and so on.

[20] The S&P 500 contains some bank and insurance company stocks traded in the OTC market.

Relationships Between Domestic Stock Indexes As the previous discussion indicates, numerous measures of the "market," ranging from the DJIA to the broadest measure of the market, the Wilshire Index (discussed in Appendix 4-A), are available. It is obvious that the overall market is measured and reported on in several different ways.

The following observations about the various market measures can be made:

1. Although the DJIA contains only 30 stocks and has often been criticized because of this small number and the manner in which the average is computed, it parallels the movements of the broader market-value-weighted indexes involving NYSE stocks—specifically, the NYSE Composite Index (discussed in Appendix 4-A) and the S&P 500 Composite Index. The correlation between the price changes for the three indexes (S&P, NYSE, and DJIA) traditionally has been very high, on the order of 0.90.
2. Regardless of the close relationship noted in 1, the DJIA will show significantly different percentage changes over shorter intervals of time, such as a year. This arises in recent years because the DJIA does not contain the hot technology stocks, such as Dell or Cisco.

EXAMPLE 4-7

In 1995, the DJIA showed a total return of 36.53 percent and the S&P 500 showed a very similar return, 37.11 percent. However, for 1998, the Dow showed a return of 18.01 percent while the S&P 500 showed a return of 28.34 percent. The same was true for 1997, 24.75 percent for the Dow and 33.10 percent for the S&P 500.

3. The greatest divergence in market indexes often occurs when comparisons are made between those indexes that involve only NYSE stocks and those that cover other exchanges, or NYSE stocks plus stocks from other exchanges. The AMEX Index (described in Appendix 4-A) and the Nasdaq Composite can perform quite differently in certain years relative to indexes such as the S&P 500.

EXAMPLE 4-8

For the 12 months ending November 30, 1998, the S&P 500 Index gained 23.7 percent, while the Russell 2000, a small stock index, lost 6.6 percent. For the five year period ending on that date, the S&P index almost exactly doubled the Russell index on an average annualized return basis.

Regardless of divergences, over time the major market indexes also tend to show strong similarities, as Figure 4-8 shows. Ups and downs generally occur about the same time.

Foreign Stock Market Indicators Stock market indices are available for most foreign markets, but the composition, weighting, and computational procedures vary widely from index to index. This makes it difficult to make comparisons. To deal with these problems, some organizations have constructed their own set of indices on a consistent basis. Certain international indices also are regularly computed.

EAFE Index The Europe, Australia, and Far East Index, a value-weighted index of the equity performance of major foreign markets

A well-known index of foreign stocks is the **EAFE Index**, or the Europe, Australia, and Far East Index. This index, compiled by Morgan Stanley Capital International, is, in effect, a non-American world index.

The Dow Jones World Stock Index covers the Pacific Region, Europe, Canada, Mexico, and the United States. It is designed to be a comprehensive measure, and represents approx-

FIGURE 4-8

Major market measures over time

SOURCE: Standard & Poor's *The Outlook*, September 2, 1998, vol. 70, no 33, p. 1. Reprinted by permission of Standard & Poor's, a division of the McGraw-Hill Co.

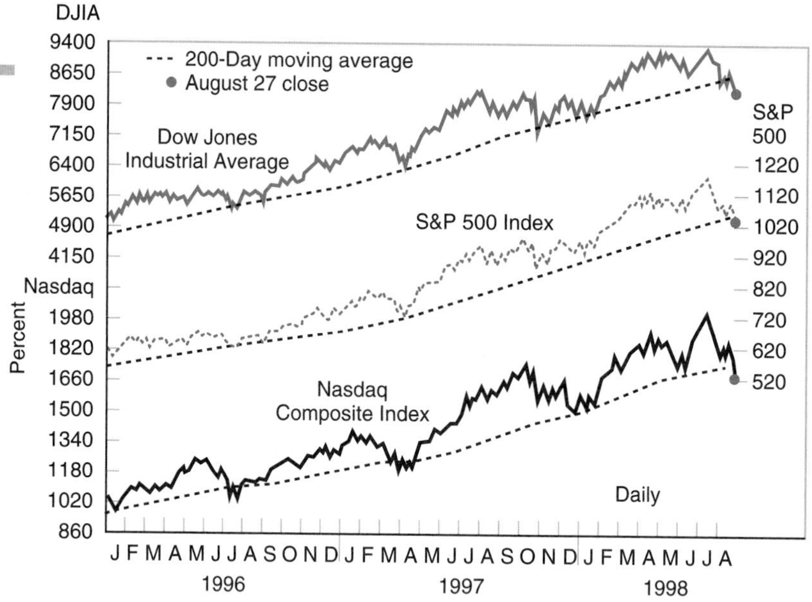

imately 80 percent of the world's stock markets. Unlike the DJIA, the World Stock Index is a capitalization-weighted index. *The Wall Street Journal* calculates and reports the DJ World Stock Index as part of its "Dow Jones Global Indexes" carried daily in the *Journal*. Stock market indexes for all of the major foreign markets are also shown on this page in the *Journal*.

BOND MARKETS

Just as stockholders need good secondary markets to be able to trade stocks and thus preserve their flexibility, bondholders need a viable market in order to sell before maturity. Otherwise, many investors would be reluctant to tie up their funds for up to 30 years. At the very least, they would demand higher initial yields on bonds, which would hinder raising funds by those who wish to invest productively.

Investors can purchase either new bonds being issued in the primary market or existing bonds outstanding in the secondary market. Yields for the two must be in equilibrium. If IBM's bonds are trading in the secondary market to yield 12 percent over a 20-year period, for example, comparable new IBM bonds will be sold with approximately the same yield.

A few thousand bonds are traded on the NYSE and a very few on the AMEX; the prices of many of these bonds can be seen daily in *The Wall Street Journal*. The reported bond volume (par value) for 1998 on the NYSE was approximately $3.8 billion, with average daily volume of $15 million.

The NYSE has the largest centralized bond market of any exchange. This order-driven bond market features an *Automated Bond System (ABS)*, a fully automated trading system that allows subscribing firms to directly enter and execute bond orders from their own terminals. Approximately 85 percent of NYSE bond volume is in nonconvertible debt and is processed through ABS.

Despite the 2,100 bond issues traded on the NYSE and its impressive ABS, *the secondary bond market is primarily an OTC market*, with a large network of dealers making markets in the various bonds. The volume of bond trading in the OTC market dwarfs that of all the exchanges combined.

Investors can buy and sell bonds through their brokers, who in turn trade with bond dealers. Certain features of the bond markets should be noted.

Treasury Bonds U.S. Treasury notes and bonds are widely purchased, held, and traded. The Federal Reserve conducts open-market operations with Treasury securities, resulting in a broad and deep market, with a volume of transactions exceeding that of any other security.[21] Many large banks act as dealers (make markets) in particular issues. Although larger investors can transact directly with these dealers, most investors use their banks and brokers and pay commissions on the order of $30 to $50 per purchase or sale.

Agency Bonds Federal agency securities trade in good secondary markets, with basically the same dealer market and procedures used as in the case of Treasury securities. Larger issues are more easily traded than smaller issues, and recently issued securities are usually more actively traded than those that have been in existence for some time.

Municipal Bonds Despite the fact that the municipal bond market is a $1 trillion plus market in size, municipal securities often have a relatively thin market, with only moderate activity in the secondary market. This is because most bonds are held to maturity and therefore are traded infrequently. Probably fewer than 5 percent of all securities firms maintain an active municipal bond operation.

When individual investors are ready to sell, it may be difficult to find a buyer for just a few bonds unless significant price concessions are made. Investors with less than $50,000 to put into municipals are sometimes advised to buy a unit investment trust, an indirect investing method.[22]

Corporate Bonds Although a substantial number of corporate bonds are listed on the exchanges, exchange trading in corporate bonds is only a very small part of this market.[23] Liquidity is not always good for these small transactions, with delays occurring in the trade, and price concessions often have to be made. Investors should be careful in trading small amounts of corporate bonds and be prepared for delays and costs. The price that appears in newspapers for these exchange-traded bonds may vary significantly from the actual price at which the bond trades.

Most corporate bonds are traded off the exchanges by institutions dealing in round lots of at least 250 bonds and often larger amounts. This institutional market behaves independently of the bond trading on the exchanges, where a computer collects bids to buy and offers to sell from around the country and executes a trade when a match is made. At times, prices between the two markets can differ by several points.

USING THE INTERNET By the end of 1998, approximately 30 firms were offering electronic bond trading or were planning to do so. However, most of these systems catered to institutional investors, with individual investors, as well as broker-dealers, resisting the use of the Internet for trading bonds. With no bond exchange to speak of, and many more bonds than stocks, investors are overwhelmed in the bond market. And except for Treasuries, no accurate way has existed to check prices. This is now changing, as explained in Chapter 9. Check out E*Trade's Bond Center at www.etrade.com.

---

[21] The Treasury bond market consists of selected market makers who trade with the open-market desk of the Federal Reserve Bank of New York. These large dealers include the bond departments of several banks.

[22] These are fixed, diversified portfolios of bonds sold in multiples of $1,000 each (with a sales charge of about 4 percent) which pay interest monthly. They are discussed in Chapter 3.

[23] For example, on a typical day some two-thirds of the issues on the NYSE's bond board do not trade at all, and a typical trade is less than 15 bonds.

DERIVATIVES MARKETS

We discuss the details of derivatives markets in their respective chapters. At this point, however, we can note that options trade on the floor of exchanges, such as the Chicago Board Options Exchange, using a system of market makers. A bid and asked price is quoted by the market maker, and floor brokers can trade with the market maker or with other floor brokers.

In contrast, futures contracts are traded on exchanges in designated "pits," using as a trading mechanism an open-outcry process. Under this system, the pit trader offers to buy or sell contracts at an offered price and other pit traders are free to transact if they wish. This open-outcry system is unique in securities trading. There are few sights in the financial system that can rival frenzied trading activity in a futures market pit.

THE CHANGING SECURITIES MARKETS

For the last 15 to 20 years the securities markets have been changing rapidly, with many more changes expected over the coming years. At least two factors explain why markets underwent such rapid changes. First, institutional investors have different requirements and often different views from individual investors, and their emergence as the dominant force in the market necessitated significant changes in market structure and operation. Large-block activity on the NYSE is an indicator of institutional participation.

One indication of the impact of institutional investors on trading power can be seen by examining only one institutional investor, mutual funds. In 1985 mutual fund trading was the equivalent of about 15 percent of NYSE volume on a dollar basis. For the last several years, mutual funds have accounted for about 45 percent of the dollar volume traded on the NYSE.

The second factor stimulating a change in our markets, the passage of the Securities Acts Amendments in 1975, represents the most far-reaching securities legislation since the 1930s. This act seeks to promote a fully competitive national system of securities trading. Specifically, it called for a **national market system (NMS)**, but it left its final form undefined. The result was the evolution toward some type of national market, but its final form is not mandated and remains undetermined.

National Market System (NMS) The market system for U.S. securities called for, but left undefined, by the Securities Acts Amendments of 1975

One aspect of a national market, a central order routing system, is designed to help investors obtain the best executions possible. This objective is accomplished by electronically routing orders to whatever market is offering the best price to a buyer or a seller. Such a system promotes competition and should lower spreads, because the dealers with the most attractive prices would automatically receive the orders. Brokerage houses, in particular Merrill Lynch, now have electronic systems that search out the best market for a customer's order and send the order to that market quickly.

One alternative to a routing system is the **Intermarket Trading System (ITS)**, a central order system for shares registered on the NYSE. This network of electronic terminals links together nine markets.[24] The ITS allows brokers—as well as specialists and market makers trading for their own accounts—on any one of the nine markets to interact with their counterparts on any of the other exchanges. These participants can use the nationwide composite quotation system to check for a better price. However, the ITS system does not guarantee that the orders will be routed because NYSE brokers can ignore better quotes on other exchanges. It is the system favored by the NYSE.

Intermarket Trading System (ITS) A form of a central routing system, consisting of a network of terminals linking together several stock exchanges

[24] The nine markets are the New York, American, Boston, Chicago, Cincinnati, Pacific, and Philadelphia exchanges, the Chicago Board Options Exchange, and the NASD.

Like other recent developments in the marketplace, ITS started slowly but has grown rapidly. Starting with 11 stocks on two exchanges in April 1978, it had expanded to 4,844 issues, with record volume of 4.6 billion shares, by year-end 1998.

Where do we go from here? More changes will occur, but the final structure of the securities market cannot yet be predicted. An important development that could influence the direction and form of securities markets in the future is the emerging Nasdaq National Market System (NMS) discussed earlier. This system of trading OTC stocks with competitive multiple market makers reporting last-sale data continuously (i.e., real-time trade reporting) has made a significant impact in the relatively short time it has existed. Both individual and institutional investors are attracted by the increased visibility of the securities traded in this manner. ECNs likely will have a big impact on investor trading.

An important issue that remains controversial is the role of the NYSE, the dominant secondary market in the United States. Of special concern to many is the nearly 200-year-old specialist system, which the NYSE continues to defend and justify, while others criticize it as a system that is not attuned to the needs of the modern market. The NYSE defends the specialist system vigorously, citing such evidence as the 1987 market crash, when the specialists stayed at their posts to handle orders while many over-the-counter dealers refused to answer the phone.

THE GLOBALIZATION OF SECURITIES MARKETS

As the 1990s began, the move toward around-the-clock trading—which many expected to be the wave of the future—continued, though slowly. The Nasdaq International Market started in 1991, trading OTC stocks early in the morning during regular trading hours in London. Evening sessions for futures trading were started on the Chicago Board of Trade. In mid-1991 the NYSE began two after-hour "crossing sessions," which last from 4:15 P.M. to 5:30 P.M. One session is for individual stocks, and the other is for baskets of stocks, and by early 1999 the NYSE was seriously considering expanding its trading hours significantly.

Instinet, mentioned earlier in the chapter, is an electronic trading mechanism allowing large investors (primarily institutions) to trade with each other electronically at any hour.[25] This system offers such investors privacy—traders' transactions involve much less disclosure—and low trading costs because regular brokerage fees do not have to be paid. In addition, institutions are able to negotiate prices electronically with each other.

Through such sources as Instinet, stock prices can change quickly although the exchanges themselves are closed. The after-hours trading is particularly important when significant news events occur, or when an institutional investor simply is anxious to trade a position. Such activity could, in a few years, lead to the 24-hour trading for stocks such as that which already exists for currencies.

What about bonds? In today's world, bonds increasingly are being traded at all hours around the globe, more so than stocks. The emergence of global offerings means that bonds are traded around the clock, and around the world. The U.S. Treasury securities market in particular has become a 24-hour a day marketplace. The result of this global trading in bonds is that bond dealers and investors are having to adopt to the new demands of the marketplace, being available to react and trade at all hours of the day and night. This includes new employees in various locales, expanded hours, and computer terminals in the home.

Foreign markets are changing rapidly. Stockmarkets in London, Frankfurt, and elswhere

[25] Instinet also offers the Crossing Network, which allows large investors to trade blocks of stock at daily closing prices.

in Europe have formed alliances. This is being done to reduce costs and attract business because electronic trading costs are lower than those on an exchange. The British and French stock markets are almost totally computerized, and other countries are moving in that direction.

The NYSE's Role in the Global Marketplace The NYSE's role in the global marketplace of the future will depend on several events. For example, it could redesign its after-hours trading sessions so that traders could negotiate prices electronically. However, the NYSE has been reluctant to do this because it would be the start of an electronic exchange, and its position traditionally has been that investors need, and benefit from, a public auction market.

Another important variable in the NYSE's future role is the listing of big foreign stocks, which the NYSE wants to do but which the SEC has been reluctant to allow. The conflict arises from the lesser financial disclosures of many foreign firms—in particular, German firms which use a very different accounting system—as compared to the disclosure rules for the NYSE. Although the NYSE has already traded foreign stocks, it would like to trade hundreds more in order not to become a "regional exchange" in a global marketplace. The SEC argues that it is protecting U.S. investors from the risk that might arise from foreign firms that are not required to disclose as much information as U.S. firms.

For years, the SEC imposed roadblocks for electronic trading networks in terms of registering as exchanges. Now, the SEC is encouraging electronic exchanges. The Internet clearly is having a major impact here.

The NYSE has shown itself to be very resilient, and tends to act to meet the competition. It is a good bet that this institution will adapt to changing conditions, and continue to be one of the most important components of U.S. securities markets. For example, in 1999 the NYSE planned to introduce *Institutional Xpress*, which allows investors to bypass the floor completely in executing some large orders. This system is designed to appeal to institutional traders. When this system is used, floor brokers will not be able to trade with an order of 10,000 shares or more unless they can provide a better price within seconds.

SUMMARY

- Financial markets include primary markets, where new securities are sold, and secondary markets, where existing securities are traded.
- Primary markets involve investment bankers who specialize in selling new securities. They offer the issuer several functions, including advisory, underwriting, and marketing services.
- Alternatives to the traditional public placements include private placements.
- Secondary markets consist of equity markets, bond markets, and derivative markets.
- The equity markets consist of auction markets (exchanges) and negotiated markets (over-the-counter, or OTC, markets). Brokers act as intermediaries, representing both buyers and sellers; dealers make markets in securities, buying and selling for their own account.
- On the New York Stock Exchange (NYSE), which is still the premier secondary market, specialists act to provide a continuous market for NYSE stocks.
- The AMEX, on which fewer and generally smaller stocks trade, resembles the NYSE in its operations. Finally, several regional exchanges around the country list small companies of limited interest as well as securities traded on the NYSE and AMEX.
- The OTC market is a network of dealers making markets in unlisted securities. The National Association of Security Dealers (NASD) oversees OTC practices.

- The Nasdaq Stock Market is an electronic network of terminals linking together hundreds of market makers who compete for investor orders by buying and selling for their own account.
- The Nasdaq National Market System (NMS) offers multiple market makers and up-to-the-minute price information in a format similar to that on the organized exchanges.
- Instinet, a network for trading among institutions and brokers, has become the largest computerized brokerage in the world. It offers anonymous trading on any of 16 exchanges worldwide for commissions of about one cent per share.
- A new trend that has significant implications for the NYSE is internal trading at large institutions with several funds or accounts without the services of a broker.
- Investors have become increasingly interested in equity markets around the world because the United States now accounts for only about one-third of the world's stock market capitalization. Many equity markets exist.
- The best known stock market indicator in the United States is the Dow Jones Industrial Average (DJIA), computed from 30 leading industrial stocks. Standard & Poor's 500-stock Composite Index is carried in the popular press, and investors often refer to it as a "good" measure of what the overall market is doing, at least for large NYSE stocks. The National Association of Security Dealers produces 11 indexes in total.
- Although some bonds are traded on the NYSE (and to a lesser extent on the AMEX), most bond trading occurs in the OTC market.
- Although Treasury bonds and federal agency bonds enjoy broad markets, the markets for municipal bonds and corporate bonds are often less liquid.
- Derivatives markets involve options and futures contracts. Puts and calls are traded on option exchanges using market makers, while futures contracts are traded in pits using an open-outcry system.
- The securities markets are changing rapidly, stimulated by the demands of institutional investors and by the mandate of the Securities Acts Amendments of 1975 to create a national market system (NMS).
- Although the exact form NMS might take remains unknown, changes in the securities markets will continue.
- Securities markets increasingly are linked globally.

KEY WORDS

Auction markets
Blocks
Blue-chip stocks
Brokers
Dealers
Dow Jones Industrial Average (DJIA)
EAFE Index
Initial public offerings (IPOs)
Instinet (Institutional Network)
Intermarket Trading System (ITS)
Investment banker
Market makers
Nasdaq Stock Market℠ (Nasdaq)
Nasdaq National Market System (Nasdaq/NMS)
National Association of Security Dealers (NASD)
National market system (NMS)
Negotiated market
New York Stock Exchange (NYSE)
Over-the-counter (OTC) market
Primary market
Program trading

Prospectus
Secondary market
Shelf rule
Specialist
Standard & Poor's 500 Composite Index (S&P 500)
Underwrite

QUESTIONS

4-1. Discuss the importance of the financial markets to the U.S. economy. Can primary markets exist without secondary markets?

4-2. Discuss the functions of an investment banker.

4-3. Outline the process for a primary offering of securities involving investment bankers.

4-4. Outline the structure of equity markets in the United States. Distinguish between auction markets and negotiated markets.

4-5. In what way is an investment banker similar to a commission broker?

4-6. Explain the role of the specialists, describing the two roles they perform. How do they act to maintain an orderly market?

4-7. Do you think that specialists should be closely monitored and regulated because of their limit books?

4-8. Is there any similarity between an over-the-counter dealer and a specialist on an exchange?

4-9. Explain the difference between NASD and Nasdaq.

4-10. Distinguish between the third market and the fourth market.

4-11. What are two primary factors accounting for the rapid changes in U.S. securities markets?

4-12. Why do you think the New York Stock Exchange favors the Intermarket Trading System (ITS)?

4-13 Outline recent international developments that relate to U.S. financial markets.

4-14. How does the Nasdaq/NMS differ from the conventional OTC market? What are its implications for the future?

4-15. What is the Dow Jones Industrial Average? How does it differ from the S&P 500 Composite Index?

4-16. What is meant by the term *blue-chip stocks*? Cite three examples.

4-17. What is the EAFE Index?

4-18. What is meant by block activity on the NYSE? How important is it on the NYSE?

4-19. What is the NYSE's current situation in terms of global trading?

4-20. What is Instinet? How does it affect the over-the-counter market?

4-21. What is meant by in-house trading? Who is likely to benefit from this activity?

4-22. What is meant by the statement, "The bond market is primarily an OTC market?"

4-23. How is the DJIA biased against growth stocks?

4-24. How has the role of institutional investors as participants in the Nasdaq market changed?

4-25. What does it mean to say an IPO has been underwritten by Merrill Lynch?

SELECTED REFERENCES

Factual information concerning major secondary markets can be found in:

NASD Fact Book. Annual. Washington, D.C.: National Association of Securities Dealers, Inc.

New York Stock Exchange, Fact Book. Annual. New York: New York Stock Exchange, Inc.

www.wiley.com/college/jones7

This chapter discusses the structure of various securities markets. The exercises will take you to the websites of some of the stock exchanges. The exercises will familiarize you with the major stock indices and their construction.

APPENDIX 4-A

STOCK MARKET INDEXES

Several issues must be dealt with in the construction of a stock market index or average. The most important involve the composition of the index or average, the weighting procedure used, and the method of calculation.

What is the composition of the market measure? Is a subsample of one exchange to be used, or a subsample from the major exchanges? Furthermore, should a subsample from the over-the-counter (OTC) market be included? Alternatively, should every stock on an exchange, or exchanges, be used, and if so, how should OTC stocks be handled (e.g., every active OTC stock or every OTC stock for which daily quotes are available)?

If investors need a broad measure of stock performance, several markets (NYSE, AMEX, and OTC) need to be included. If investors want to know the performance of the "largest" stocks, a measure of NYSE performance may be sufficient. Some market measures use subsamples of one or more markets, whereas others use every stock on one or more markets. It is important to be aware of compositional differences among the various market measures.

A second issue involves the weighting procedure used in constructing the index or average. Does each stock receive equal weight, or is each weighted by its market value (i.e., market price multiplied by shares outstanding)? Alternatively, the measure could be price weighted, resulting in higher priced stocks carrying more weight than lower priced stocks.

The third issue is the calculation procedures used. The primary question here is whether an index or an average is being used. A market average is an arithmetic average of the prices for the sample of securities being used. It shows the arithmetic mean behavior of the prices at a given time.

A market index measures the current price behavior of the sample in relation to a base period established for a previous time. Indexes, therefore, are expressed in relative numbers, whereas averages are simply arithmetic means (weighted or unweighted). The use of an index allows for more meaningful comparisons over long periods of time because current values can be related to established base period values.

The Dow Jones Averages are arithmetic averages, but virtually all the other market measures are indices.

THE DOW-JONES INDUSTRIAL AVERAGE

In principle, calculation of the DJIA involves adding up the prices of the 30 stocks and dividing by 30 to obtain the average. This is not done because of stock splits and dividends. Instead, the divisor is adjusted to reflect the stock splits and dividends that have occurred and today is much less than 1.0. As a result, a one-point change in the DJIA does not represent a change of $1 in the value of an average share; rather, the change amounts to only a few cents. You should keep this in mind the next time someone gets excited about a 50- or 60-point rise in one day in the DJIA.

The DJIA is calculated as:

$$\text{DJIA}_t = P_{it}/n^* \tag{4A-1}$$

where P is the price of a stock i at time t and n^* indicates an adjusted divisor.

STANDARD & POOR'S STOCK PRICE INDEXES

To calculate the index, the market value of all firms is calculated (current market price times number of shares), and this total value is divided by the market value of the 500 securities for the base period. This relative value is multiplied by 10, representing the base period.[26] In equation form, the S&P 500 is calculated as:

$$\text{S\&P}_{500} = \frac{P_{it}Q_{it}}{P_{ib}Q_{ib}}(k) \tag{4A-2}$$

where

P = the price of a stock i at time t
Q = number of shares of stock i at time t
b = the base period
k = the base number

A current value of 200 for the S&P 500 would indicate that the average price of the 500 stocks in the index has increased by a factor of 20 in relation to the base period. If IBM had a market value that was 10 times as great as that of Apple Computer, a 1 percent change in IBM's price would have more than 10 times the impact of a 1 percent change in Apple's price.

Despite the well-known methodology for calculating the S&P 500 Index, slightly different values often are reported for this index. For example, for one recent year the S&P's performance varied by more than half a percentage point, depending on the firm doing the calculations. The reasons for the variations lie in such factors as when the dividends included in the total return calculation are considered to be received—on the declaration date or the payment date.[27]

Does such a difference matter? Yes! In the world of professional money management, managers often are compensated on the basis of how well they perform relative to the S&P 500. Since success often is measured in hundredths of a percentage point, such differences are significant.

Which is the correct figure? No one knows for certain, because Standard & Poor's has been unable to establish its figure as the official one after failing to pay attention to the issue for many years.

NEW YORK STOCK EXCHANGE INDEX

The NYSE Composite Index is broader still, covering all stocks listed on the NYSE. It is similar to the S&P indexes in that it is a total-market-value-weighted index. The base index value is 50 (as of year-end 1965).[28]

[26] Before multiplying by 10, the S&P 500 at any point in time can be thought of as the price, in relation to the beginning price of $1, of all stocks in the index weighted by their proportionate total market values.

[27] The information in this discussion is based on James A. White, "Will the Real S&P 500 Please Stand up?" *The Wall Street Journal*, January 26, 1989, p. C1.

[28] Subindexes are available and include Industrial, Utility, Transportation, and Financial.

The NYSE Composite Index, although comparable to the S&P indexes, is a true reflection of what is happening on the NYSE, because it covers all stocks listed.[29] Thus, an investor who purchases a variety of NYSE stocks may find this index to be a better reflection of average performance against which to measure the performance of his or her securities.

AMERICAN STOCK EXCHANGE INDEX

The American Stock Exchange introduced a new index in 1973, replacing the previous index based on price changes. The base period, August 31, 1973, was assigned an index number of 100. This index is similar to the S&P and NYSE indices in that it is based on market values. All common stocks, warrants, and American Depository Receipts (ADRs) listed on the AMEX are covered in this index.

THE WILSHIRE INDEX

The broadest of all indicators is the so-called Wilshire 5000 Index, which actually contains more than 7,000 stocks representing the dollar market value of all NYSE and AMEX stocks, as well as all actively traded OTC stocks. In effect, it is the total price for stocks for which daily quotations can be obtained.[30] It is quoted in billions of dollars, with a base of $1.404 billion set to December 31, 1980.

VALUE LINE INDEX

The Value Line Investment Survey, perhaps the best known investment advisory service in the United States, publishes several indexes of stock prices.[31] Since the Value Line company is a well-known investment advisory service, its indexes receive attention. Investors, however, should be aware of how these unique indexes differ from the others.

The Value Line Composite Index is unique in that it is an equally weighted geometric average of stock prices. It is based on the roughly 1,700 companies in the 90-plus industries that Value Line chooses to cover in its reports. June 1961 is assigned the base index of 100.

Since a daily net percentage change in price is computed for the stocks, each stock in the index has the same percentage weight. Therefore, a 20 percent movement in a stock's price has the same impact on the index, whether 10 million or 100 million shares are outstanding. Neither a stock's market value nor its price level will impact the index. The small, low-priced stocks covered by Value Line will have the same impact as the larger stocks.

In effect, the Value Line Composite is an unweighted index covering a broad cross-section of stocks. Some market observers feel that because it is unweighted, it is more reflective of general market trends.

In March 1988, Value Line introduced a new index, the Value Line Arithmetic Index (VLA). The change in this arithmetically averaged index is the sum of the price changes for all stocks in the index divided by the number of stocks. Value Line sees this index as a good estimate of the price performance of an equal dollar portfolio of stocks, whereas changes in the geometric index provide a good estimate of the median price changes of the stocks covered.

[29] This is the only available index limited solely to the NYSE but covering all the stocks on it.

[30] This index typically is referred to as the Wilshire 5000. Since it currently contains more than 6,000 stocks, *Forbes* is now referring to it as the Wilshire index.

[31] Specifically, Value Line publishes an Industrial, Rail, Utility, and Composite Index. More than 80 percent of these stocks are listed on the NYSE.

chapter 5

How Securities Are Traded

Chapter 5 discusses the mechanics of trading securities, critical information for every investor. Brokerage firms and their activities are analyzed, as are the types of orders to buy and sell securities, and the handling of these orders. The regulation of the securities markets is discussed. Finally, the various aspects of trading securities that investors often encounter are considered.

After reading this chapter you will be able to:

- **Explain brokers' roles and how brokerage firms operate.**
- **Appreciate the changing nature of the securities business.**
- **Understand how orders to buy and sell securities work in the various marketplaces.**
- **Assess the role of regulation in the securities markets.**
- **Understand how margin trading and short selling contribute to investor opportunities.**

In Chapter 4 we considered how securities markets are organized. In this chapter we learn the mechanics of trading securities which investors must know in order to operate successfully in the marketplace. The details of trading, like the organization of securities markets, continue to evolve, although the basic procedures remain the same.

BROKERAGE TRANSACTIONS

BROKERAGE FIRMS

In general, it is quite easy for any responsible person to open a brokerage account. An investor selects a broker or brokerage house by personal contact, referral, reputation, and so forth. Member firms of the NYSE are supposed to learn certain basic facts about potential customers, but only minimal information is normally required. Actually, personal contact between broker and customer seldom occurs, with transactions carried out by telephone or by computer.

Customers can choose the type of broker they wish to use. They can be classified according to the services offered and fees charged.

Full-Service Brokers Traditionally, brokerage firms offered a variety of services to investors, particularly information and advice. Today, investors can still obtain a wide variety of information on the economy, particular industries, individual companies, and the bond market from **full-service brokers**, including Merrill Lynch, Paine Webber, Morgan Stanley Dean Witter, Salomon Smith Barney, and Prudential. These large retail brokerage firms execute their customers' orders, provide advice, and send them publications about individual stocks, industries, bonds, and so forth.

Full-Service Broker A brokerage firm offering a full range of services, including information and advice

Today's full-service stockbrokers go by different titles, such as financial consultants or investment executives (or simply registered representatives). This change in title reflects the significant changes that have occurred in the industry. Full-service brokerage firms now derive only a small percentage of their revenues from commissions paid by individual investors, a significant change from the past. And the typical full-service stockbroker, whatever he or she is called, now derives less than 50 percent of his or her income from customer commissions. This is why firms such as Merrill Lynch are trying to encourage their brokers to become more like fee-based professionals and less like salespeople.

How do brokers earn the rest of their income? One alternative is to sell mutual funds owned by their own firms. These funds carry a load or sales charge, and the broker selling shares in these funds earns part of this sales charge.

Another alternative involves "principal transactions," or brokerage firms trading for their own accounts. When these firms end up owning shares they really do not want, brokers are often encouraged to sell these securities to their customers, with some additional financial incentives provided. Smart investors, when given a recommendation to buy a security by their broker, ask if the firm has issued a public buy recommendation or if the broker is being compensated to sell this security.

Yet another source of income is the sale of new issues of securities (IPOs), discussed in Chapter 4. Underwriting new issues is a profitable activity for brokerage firms, and brokers may have an incentive to steer their customers into the new issues.

Other sources of revenue today that were nonexistent or much smaller in the past include administrative fees resulting from imposing charges on customer accounts. For example, inactive-account, transfer, and maintenance fees may be imposed on customers. By one estimate, Merrill Lynch now earns over $100 million a year in handling fees.

Commissions on products sold by brokers will vary depending on the product. Treasury securities carry a commission of less than 1 percent, whereas a complicated limited partnership carries a commission of 8 percent or more. In some cases, the commission is "transparent" to the investor. For example, with many bonds the commission is built in, and as a result the investor does not realize that the commission is included.

EXAMPLE 5-1

A $10,000 purchase of bonds may require an even $10,000 payment by the customer; however, a "spread" of perhaps 2 percent is built into this transaction. The result is that a sale of the same security immediately would net only $9,800.

How much does a typical full-service stockbroker earn? Obviously, annual compensation varies depending on market conditions that lead to more trading or less trading. For example, in one recent year the average pay was about $117,000, which was actually a drop of 9 percent from the previous year for the approximately 93,000 active brokers. However, this average can be misleading because of the small number of superbrokers who earn $1 million or more. The median brokerage income in the same year, representing the point at which half are above and half are below, was $72,600, a decline of some 19 percent from the previous year. Because of Internet trading, the future may be very different.

Discount Brokers Investors can choose to use a discount broker who will provide virtually all of the same services except advice and publications and will charge less for the execution of trades.[1] Smart investors choose the alternative that is best for them in terms of their own needs. Some investors need and want personal attention and research publications, and are willing to pay in the form of higher brokerage commissions. Others, however, prefer to do their own research and to pay only for order execution.

Discount Broker Brokerage firms offering execution services at prices typically significantly less than full-line brokerage firms

In contrast to the full-service brokers, **discount brokers** concentrate on executing orders and are able to charge less than the full-service brokers. Most offer services frequently used by investors in a manner similar to the full-service brokers, but many provide little, if any, investing information and no discount broker offers advice. Thus, investors pay less and receive less. Prominent discount brokers include Charles Schwab, Quick & Reilly, and Fidelity Investments.[2]

As of early 1999, there were more than 100 discount brokers. Approximately one-fourth of these were primarily on-line brokers. Most discount brokers, however, offer access to trading by phone and Internet, and the Internet portion of the business is growing rapidly (as recently as 1995, Schwab had no exposure to the Internet, and now it is the largest Internet brokerage firm).

EXAMPLE 5-2

Fidelity Investments is one of the largest discount brokers. By the beginning of 1999, it had 3 million on-line accounts, and 70 percent of commissionable trades were being made via the web (compared to 7 percent in January 1997). Fidelity's *Personal Investing* assets exceeded $128 billion before the end of 1998.

[1] Some discount brokers do provide research information. This includes standard information supplied to the brokerage from outside sources and customized information generated in-house.

[2] Although a large discount broker such as Schwab has a sizable branch network, access to live brokers over the phone, and offers multiple services, by most people's definition it is not a full-service broker because Schwab does not offer its own stock research, having no analysts and no list of favorite stocks (furthermore, it does not assign a designated representative for each individual account).

TYPES OF BROKERAGE ACCOUNTS

Cash Account The most common type of brokerage account in which a customer may make only cash transactions

Margin Account An account that permits margin trading, requiring $2,000 to open

Asset Management Account Brokerage accounts involving various services for investors, such as investment of cash balances and check-writing privileges

The most basic type of account is the **cash account**, whereby the customer pays the brokerage house the full price for any securities purchased. Many customers open a **margin account**, which allows the customer to borrow from the brokerage firm to purchase securities. (Margin is explained in some detail later in this chapter.) The NYSE requires a minimum margin deposit of $2,000 to open this type of account (regardless of the transaction contemplated).

Asset management accounts require a minimum balance to open (from $1,000 to $25,000) and the payment of an annual fee, from zero in the case of a discount brokerage such as Schwab to $100 or more in the case of some of the full-service brokerage firms. All offer automatic reinvestment of the account holders' free credit balances in shares of a money market fund (taxable or nontaxable) or other fund, such as a government securities fund. Money is typically swept daily into such funds, although a minimum balance of $500 or $1,000 may be required.

Account holders are issued bank checks and a bank card. Checks can be written against the account's assets, and the checking account is no minimum, no fee. In addition, instant loans based on the marginable securities in the account can be obtained for virtually any purpose, not just securities transactions, at the current broker's call money rate plus 0.75 to 2.25 percent. For example, if you write a check for $10,000 against your account and your money market fund contains only $5,000, you will automatically borrow the other $5,000. Each month the customer receives a comprehensive summary statement.

Wrap Account A new type of brokerage account where all costs are wrapped in one fee

Wrap Accounts In an important development in brokerage accounts, brokers now act as middlemen, matching clients with independent money managers.[3] Using the broker as a consultant, the client chooses an outside money manager from a list provided by the broker. Under this **wrap account**, all costs—the cost of the broker-consultant and money manager, all transactions costs, custody fees, and the cost of detailed performance reports—are wrapped in one fee. For stocks, a typical fee is 3 percent (maximum) of the assets managed, dropping to 2 percent or less for multimillion dollar accounts.[4]

Large brokerage houses such as Merrill Lynch pioneered wrap accounts for investors with a minimum of $100,000 to commit. Because of their popularity, other financial companies have begun offering these accounts.

COMMISSIONS

For most of its long history, the New York Stock Exchange required its members to charge fixed (and minimum) commissions.[5] Although this requirement was a source of bitter contention and gave rise to the third market, or off-the-market trading, little changed until 1975, when Congress, as part of the Securities Acts Amendments of 1975, eliminated all fixed commissions. Fees are supposed to be negotiated, with each firm free to act independently.

Investors can attempt to negotiate with their brokers, and different brokers charge different commissions. In practice, the larger full-service brokerage houses have specified commission rates for the typical small investor. However, the overall competition in the industry has an effect on the rates that are set. Customers are free to shop around, and smart ones do so because according to a survey by the National Council of Individual Investors, the difference in commissions among major firms can exceed 600 percent.

[3] This discussion is based on James A. White, "Stockbrokers Turning into 'Consultants,'" *The Wall Street Journal*, March 1, 1990, p. C1.

[4] Fees are lower for bond portfolios or combinations of stocks and bonds.

[5] Technically, this is price fixing and therefore illegal, but the NYSE was exempted from prosecution under the antitrust laws.

In contrast, negotiated rates are the norm for institutional customers, who deal in large blocks of stock. The rates charged institutional investors have declined drastically, from an average of 25 cents a share in 1975 to an average of only a few cents a share for exchange-listed stocks. Institutional investors also receive a better deal when trading in OTC stocks.

Investors now have three choices when executing trades:

1. Full-service brokers—example, Merrill Lynch
2. Large discount brokers—example, Charles Schwab
3. Small discount brokers—example, Jack White & Company

Brokerage costs have changed rapidly because of competition and the rise of the Internet. Commissions charged by discount brokers vary widely, depending on the method used to calculate them. The following example is only one illustration because generalized comparisons are impossible. Investors need to check out various brokers themselves for both brokerage costs, other costs, and the services provided.

EXAMPLE 5-3

For a phone transaction, one full-service broker charges $319 for the purchase of 800 shares of a $20 stock, a well-known discount broker charges $130 for the same transaction, and one smaller discount firm charges $15 to $20 for the same transaction. However, even within categories, rates can vary widely. Looking at discount brokers, the well-known discount broker charged $29 for the same transaction via the web, while the smaller discount broker charged the same $15 to $20.

The large discount brokers such as Charles Schwab, Quick & Reilly, and Fidelity Brokerage Services advertise aggressively, have offices scattered around the country, and are very familiar to many investors. Of course, full-service brokers such as Merrill Lynch are well known, provide investors with numerous publications and services, and have the most offices for those customers seeking personal contacts. Merrill Lynch also offers Internet trading.

ELECTRONIC TRADING AND THE INTERNET

Obviously, we are now in the age of electronic trading. In addition to contacting brokerage firms the traditional way by phone, many investors now use their personal computer. In 1992, E*Trade became the first brokerage service to offer on-line trading, and by 1996 this company featured brokerage rates as low as $14.95. As we would expect, other firms rushed to offer their services on the Internet. For example, Fidelity Investments offers Internet trading for its customers to obtain quotes, place orders, and update their accounts, when they choose and as often as they choose. Charles Schwab offers complete Internet trading.

While many discount brokerages offer on-line trading over the Internet, full-service firms were slow to offer this service because of their staff of registered representatives. Such firms do not want to give up their higher commissions, nor break the direct link between broker and client that currently exists. Full-service brokers claim that regardless of the information investors can obtain on the Internet, "Technology can't replace advice." However, widespread investor use of the Internet has forced changes, and by late 1998 even Merrill Lynch, which had previously declared it would not do so, planned to offer Internet trading to its clients.

USING THE INTERNET Investors can access a wide range of brokerage firms on the Internet. Fidelity Investments, the giant mutual fund company, offers extensive brokerage services at www.fidelity.com. Schwab advertises extensively and can be reached at www.schwab.com, and E*Trade can be reached at www.etrade.com. An annual survey of discount brokers and the services they offer, as well as net addresses and phone numbers, can be found in the January issue of *AAII Journal*, a very useful publication intended for average individual investors. See http://www.aaii.org.

INVESTING WITHOUT A BROKER

Dividend Reinvestment Plan (DRIPs) A plan offered by a company whereby stockholders can reinvest dividends in additional shares of stock at no cost

At the beginning of 1999, some 1,600 companies offered **dividend reinvestment plans (DRIPs)**. For investors enrolled in these plans, the company uses the dividends paid on shares owned to purchase additional shares, either full or fractional. Typically, no brokerage or administrative fees are involved. The advantages of such plans include dollar cost averaging, whereby more shares are purchased when the stock price is low than when it is high.

In order to be in a company's dividend reinvestment plan, investors often buy the stock through their brokers, although some companies sell directly to individuals. On becoming stockholders, investors can join the dividend reinvestment program and invest additional cash at specified intervals.

DRIPs are starting to resemble brokerage accounts. Investors can purchase additional shares by having money withdrawn from bank accounts periodically, and shares can even be redeemed by phone at many companies.

It is possible to invest in the market without a stockbroker or a brokerage account in the traditional sense. As an outgrowth of their dividend reinvestment plans, a number of companies now offer *direct stock purchase programs* (DSPs) to first-time investors.

EXAMPLE 5-4

Exxon now permits investors to buy up to $8,000 a month worth of Exxon stock from the company itself, with no commissions. Investors can open a direct-purchase account with Exxon with as small an investment in Exxon stock as $250. Other companies that offer similar plans include Texaco, Mobil, Kroger, Sears, Procter & Gamble, and Home Depot.

Investors make their initial purchase of stock directly from the company for purchase fees ranging from zero to about 7 cents a share. The price paid typically is based on the closing price of the stock on designated dates, and no limit orders are allowed. The companies selling stock by this method view it as a way to raise capital without underwriting fees and as a way to build goodwill with investors.

Treasury bond buyers can also avoid brokers by using the *Treasury Direct Program*. Investors can buy or sell Treasuries by phone or Internet, and check account balances, reinvest Treasuries as they mature, and get the forms necessary to sell Treasuries. Investors eliminate brokerage commissions, but some fees are involved ($34 per security sold, and in some cases a $25 account fee).[6]

[6] Treasury Direct can be reached at 800-943-6864 or www.publicdebt.treas.gov.

USING THE INTERNET See www.dripcentral.com for complete information on DRIP plans and the companies offering them. Also see www.netstockdirect.com for specifics on companies offering plans. The Motley Fool also has information on DRIPs.

HOW ORDERS WORK

ORDERS ON THE ORGANIZED EXCHANGES

The NYSE is often called an agency auction market. That is, agents represent the public at an auction where the interactions of buyers and sellers determine the price of stocks traded on the NYSE.

Traditionally, a typical order from an investor for 100 shares of IBM might be handled as follows. The investor phones his or her broker, or registered representative, and asks how IBM is doing. The broker can punch a few buttons on an electronic console and immediately see the last trade for IBM, as well as other information, such as the high and low for the day and the number of shares traded. Assuming that the investor is willing to pay the last trade price for IBM, or a price close to that, the broker can be instructed to buy, say, 100 shares of IBM "at the market." This order will be transmitted to the broker's New York office and then to the member partner on the exchange floor (or the broker may work through some other exchange member). The representative on the floor will go to the trading post for IBM, where the specialist handling IBM is located, and ask, "How's IBM?"

The specialist is charged with maintaining a fair and orderly market in IBM. The specialist knows the current quotes for IBM because he or she keeps a record of all limit orders for the stock. Assuming no other member partner has come to the post to sell IBM, the specialist will quote a current bid and the asked price for 100 shares. The partner then indicates that there is a purchase order to be filled (at the asking price). A confirmation is relayed back to the investor's broker, who notifies the investor.

The trade will appear on the NYSE consolidated tape, which prints transactions for all NYSE-listed securities on participating markets. This involves several stock exchanges (in addition to the NYSE), the over-the-counter market, and Instinet. Daily papers such as *The Wall Street Journal* report the high and low prices for each stock wherever they occur.[7]

The role of the specialist is critical on an auction market such as the NYSE. Also referred to as NYSE-assigned dealers by the NYSE and representing a system nearly 200 years old on the NYSE, specialists are expected to maintain a fair and orderly market in those stocks assigned to them. They act as both brokers and dealers.

- As brokers, specialists maintain the limit book, which records all limit orders, or orders that investors have placed to buy or sell a security at a specific price (or better) and that will not be executed until that price is reached. The commission brokers leave the limit orders with the specialist to be filled when possible; therefore, the specialist receives part of the broker's fee.
- As dealers, specialists buy and sell shares of their assigned stock(s) to maintain an orderly market. The stock exchanges function essentially as a continuous market, assuring investors that they can almost always buy and sell a particular security at some price. Assuming that public orders do not arrive at the same time, so that they can be

[7] An investor needs to realize that a limit order placed to sell a stock at, say, 101½ may not have been executed, although the quotes from yesterday's trading in today's paper show a price of 101½ as the high. This will happen if the investor's broker placed the order on the NYSE, but the stock's high was reached on the Pacific Stock Exchange, for example.

matched, the specialist will buy from commission brokers with orders to sell and will sell to those with orders to buy, hoping to profit by a favorable spread between the two sides.

Since specialists are charged by the NYSE with maintaining a continuous, orderly market in their assigned stocks, they often must go "against the market," which requires adequate capital. The NYSE demands that specialists be able to assume a position of 5,000 shares in their assigned stocks.[8] However, the NYSE does not require specialists to fund all the liquidity for the market at a particular time, and these stabilization trades are only a small part of total trading.

Most of the NYSE volume results from public orders interacting directly with other public orders. Using NYSE data, in 1998 specialist participation, measured as the total shares bought and sold by specialists divided by twice total volume accounted for about 13 percent of the share volume traded. This implies that 87 percent of share volume resulted from public and member firm orders meeting directly in the NYSE market.[9] It is important to note that specialists are not on both sides of any trade.

How well does the system work? According to NYSE figures, in one recent year some 98.2 percent of all transactions occurred with no change in price or within the minimum change permissible on the NYSE—one-eighth of a point. The quotation spread between bid and asked prices was one-fourth of a point or less in 93 percent of NYSE quotes. As an indication of market depth, for volume of 3,000 shares or more, the average stock price showed no change, or one-eighth point change, 91 percent of the time.[10]

Automation of the NYSE In actuality, the NYSE has become highly automated.[11] About 93 percent of orders and almost half of the volume is handled electronically. An electronic system matches buy and sell orders entered before the market opens, setting the opening price of a stock. The NYSE has **SuperDot**, an electronic order routing system for NYSE-listed securities. Member firms send orders directly to the specialist post where the securities are traded, and confirmation of trading is returned directly to the member firm over the same system. The system's peak capacity has been increased to an order processing capability of 2 billion shares per day.

SuperDOT An electronic order-routing system for NYSE-listed securities

As part of SuperDot, the *Opening Automated Report Service (OARS)* automatically and continuously scans the member firms' preopening buy and sell orders, pairing buy and sell orders and presenting the imbalance to the specialist up to the opening of a stock. This helps the specialist to determine the opening price. OARS handles preopening market orders up to 30,099 shares.

SuperDot also includes a postopening market order system designed to accept post-opening market orders of up to 2,099 shares. These market orders are executed and reported back to the member firm sending the order within 25 seconds, on average.

The specialist's volume-handling and volume-processing capabilities have been enhanced electronically by creating the Specialist's Electronic Book, which is yet another part

[8] Specialists must be approved by the Board of Governors of the NYSE and must have experience, ability as dealers, and specified minimum capital.

[9] According to the *NYSE Fact Book*, no more than 45 percent of NYSE volume involved a member firm as principal in one recent year.

[10] A recent study suggests that NYSE specialists regularly choose not to inform traders on the exchange about the highest bids and lowest offers that have been received. According to a study by Robert Wood and Thomas McInish of Memphis State University, approximately half of the time specialists opted not to announce this information on the consolidated tape, which is relied on by traders of the NYSE. Specialists are not required to announce the best bids and offers on the tape. Because traders on the floor of the NYSE can learn this additional information by talking with the specialists, some believe that traders on the regional exchanges and other outsiders are at a disadvantage. See Robert Steiner and Kevin G. Salwen, "Stock Specialists Often Keep Best Quotes to Themselves," *The Wall Street Journal*, May 8, 1992, p. C1.

[11] The same is true for the AMEX.

of the SuperDot system. This database system assists in recording and reporting limit and market orders. Not only does it help to eliminate paperwork and processing errors, but also it now handles about 98 percent of all SuperDot orders.[12]

The NYSE now allows large institutional investors to avoid trading on the floor of the exchange under certain conditions. For years institutions could arrange big block trades "upstairs," meaning off the exchange floor, but such trades had to take into account floor orders.[13] Often, the broker simply routed these orders to a regional exchange, thereby bypassing the NYSE altogether. The new "clean-cross" rule permits brokers to arrange trades of 25,000 shares or more between customers without considering orders at the same price from other investors on the NYSE floor. However, orders at a better price would have to be accepted. As explained in Chapter 4, in 1999 the NYSE expects to launch Institutional Xpress, allowing institutions to bypass floor brokers in many cases with orders of 10,000 shares or more.

ORDERS IN THE OVER-THE-COUNTER MARKET

Traditionally, market makers (dealers) in the OTC market arrive at the prices of securities by both negotiating with customers specifically and by making competitive bids. They match the forces of supply and demand, with each market maker making a market in certain securities. They do this by standing ready to buy a particular security from a seller or to sell it to a buyer. Dealers quote bid and asked prices for each security; the **bid price** is the highest price offered by the dealer, and the **asked price** is the lowest price at which the dealer is willing to sell. The dealer profits from the spread between these two prices.

Bid Price The price at which the specialist or dealer offers to buy shares

Asked Price The price at which the specialist or dealer offers to sell shares

Assume you place an order for a Nasdaq stock. The brokerage firm will forward it to one of several market maker firms for that stock (Nasdaq averages about 11 market makers per security). These market makers are constantly buying and selling shares and keeping the spread, the compensation for acting as a middleman. In effect, they are being paid to make the market. While market makers are expected to execute each order at the best available market price, they are not required to do so.[14]

TYPES OF ORDERS

Market Order An order to buy or sell at the best price when the order reaches the trading floor

Limit Order An order to buy or sell at a specified (or better) price

Stop Order An order specifying a certain price at which a market order takes effect

Investors use three basic types of orders: **market orders**, **limit orders**, and **stop orders**. Each of these orders is explained in Table 5-1. Today investors are often advised to enter limit orders whenever possible in order to avoid the range of prices that may result from a market order.

Investors can enter limit orders as day orders, which are effective for only one day, or as good-until-canceled orders or open orders, which remain in effect for six months unless canceled or renewed.[15] There is no guarantee that all orders will be filled at a particular price limit when that price is reached because orders are filled in a sequence determined by the rules of the various exchanges. Limit orders for more than one share can be filled in whole or in part until completed (involving more than one trading day) unless the order is specified as *all or none* (fill the whole order or no part of it), *immediate or cancel* (fill the whole order or any part immediately, canceling the balance), or *fill or kill* (fill the entire order immediately or cancel it).

[12] This information is based on various *NYSE Fact Books* (New York: New York Stock Exchange).
[13] Thus, floor traders could attempt to participate in any big block "crosses."
[14] Market makers often share some of the profits from the spread with brokerage firms supplying the orders. This is called "payment for order flow."
[15] A market order remains in effect only for the day.

TABLE 5-1 TYPES OF ORDERS USED BY INVESTORS

1. *Market orders*, the most common type of order, instruct the broker to buy or sell the securities immediately at the best price available. As a representative of the buyer or seller, it is incumbent upon the broker to obtain the best price possible. A market order ensures that the transaction will be carried out, but the exact price at which it will occur is not known until its execution and subsequent confirmation to the customer.
2. *Limit orders* specify a particular price to be met or bettered. They may result in the customer obtaining a better price than with a market order or in no purchase or sale occurring because the market price never reaches the specified limit. The purchase or sale will occur only if the broker obtains that price, or betters it (lower for a purchase, higher for a sale). Limit orders can be tried immediately or left with the broker for a specific time or indefinitely. In turn, the broker leaves the order with the specialist who enters it in the limit book.

EXAMPLE: Assume the current market price of a stock is $50. An investor might enter a buy limit order at $47; if the stock declines in price to $47, this limit order, which is on the specialist's book, will be executed at $47 or less. Similarly, another investor might enter a sell limit order for this stock at $55; if the price of this stock rises to $55, this investor's shares will be sold.

3. *Stop orders* specify a certain price at which a market order takes effect. For example, a stop order to sell at $50 becomes a market order to sell as soon as the market price reaches (declines to) $50. However, the order may not be filled exactly at $50 because the closest price at which the stock trades may be $49⅞. The exact price specified in the stop order is therefore not guaranteed and may not be realized.

EXAMPLE 1: A sell stop order can be used to protect a profit in the case of a price decline. Assume, for example, that a stock bought at $32 currently trades at $50. The investor does not want to limit additional gains, but may wish to protect against a price decline. To lock in most of the profit, a sell stop order could be placed at $47.

EXAMPLE 2: A buy stop order could be used to protect a profit from a short sale. Assume an investor sold short at $50, and the current market price of the stock is $32. A buy stop order placed at, say, $36 would protect most of the profit from the short sale.

Stop orders are used to buy and sell after a stock reaches a certain price level. A buy stop order is placed above the current market price, while a sell stop order is placed below the current price. A stop limit order automatically becomes a limit order when the stop limit price is reached.

A standard order is a round lot, which is 100 shares or a multiple of 100; an odd lot is any number of shares between 1 and 99. Odd lots are now executed by the NYSE directly by computer. Total odd-lot volume on the NYSE was only 1.4 billion shares in 1998, with sales slightly exceeding purchases. Some large brokerage firms now handle their own odd lots, and most investors who transact in odd lots are actually transacting with a dealer.

CLEARING PROCEDURES

Most securities are sold on a regular way basis, meaning the settlement date is three business days (as of June 1995) after the trade date. On the settlement date the customer becomes the legal owner of any securities bought, or gives them up if sold, and must settle with the brokerage firm by that time. Most customers allow their brokerage firm to keep their securities in a **street name**, that is, the name of the brokerage firm. The customer receives a monthly statement showing his or her position as to cash, securities held, any funds borrowed from the broker, and so on.

Street Name When customers' securities are held by a brokerage firm in its name

Use of stock certificates as part of the settlement is dying out in the United States. The Depository Trust Company (DTC) has helped to eliminate their use by placing these transactions on computers. Members (brokers and dealers) who own certificates (in street name) deposit them in an account and can then deliver securities to each other in the form of a bookkeeping entry. This book-entry system, as opposed to the actual physical possession of securities in either registered or "bearer" form, is essential to minimize the tremendous amount of paperwork that would otherwise occur with stock certificates. Such a system may help in other ways also; in one recent year some $2.6 billion in securities were lost, missing, or stolen.

INVESTOR PROTECTION IN THE SECURITIES MARKETS

Investors should be concerned that securities markets are properly regulated for their protection. Our financial system depends heavily on confidence in that system. In the late nineteenth and early twentieth centuries, significant abuses in securities trading did occur; at the same time there was a lack of information disclosure, and trading procedures were not always sound. The market crash in 1929 and the Great Depression served as catalysts for reforms, which effectively began in the 1930s.

Investor protection can be divided into government regulation, primarily federal, and self-regulation by the industry. Although states also regulate securities transactions, the primary emphasis is on federal regulation, and so we will concentrate on that.

GOVERNMENT REGULATION

Federal Legislation Much of the legislation governing the securities markets and industry was enacted during the Great Depression. Many fraudulent and undesirable practices occurred in the 1920s, and the markets as a whole were shattered in the crash of 1929. Congress subsequently sought to improve the stability and viability of the securities markets, enacting the basis of all securities regulation in the 1930s. Additional acts have been legislated over the last 50 years. Table 5-2 contains a brief description of the major legislation affecting securities markets.

The Justice Department can investigate alleged abuses in the financial markets. For example, an important development occurred in late 1994 concerning bid and asked prices on Nasdaq. Two professors discovered that actively traded Nasdaq stock spreads were typically quoted in quarters rather than eighths. This finding caused quite an uproar, with the Justice Department looking into the issue of alleged price fixing among brokerage firms on the Nasdaq market. Settlements of such cases vary widely.

TABLE 5-2 MAJOR LEGISLATION REGULATING THE SECURITIES MARKETS

1. The Securities Act of 1933 (the Securities Act) deals primarily with new issues of securities. The intent was to protect potential investors in new securities by requiring issuers to register an issue with full disclosure of information. False information is subject to criminal penalties and lawsuits by purchasers to recover lost funds.
2. The Securities Exchange Act of 1934 (SEA) extended the disclosure requirements to the secondary market and established the SEC to oversee registration and disclosure requirements. Organized exchanges are required to register with the SEC and agree to be governed by existing legislation.
3. The Maloney Act of 1936 extended SEC control to the OTC market. It provides for the self-regulation of OTC dealers through the National Association of Securities Dealers (NASD), which licenses and regulates members of OTC firms. The SEC has authority over the NASD, which must report all its rules to the SEC.
4. The Investment Company Act of 1940 requires investment companies to register with the SEC and provides a regulatory framework within which they must operate. Investment companies are required to disclose considerable information and to follow procedures designed to protect their shareholders. This industry is heavily regulated.
5. The Investment Advisors Act of 1940 requires individuals or firms who sell advice about investments to register with the SEC. Registration connotes only compliance with the law. Almost anyone can become an investment advisor because the SEC cannot deny anyone the right to sell investment advice unless it can demonstrate dishonesty or fraud.
6. The Securities Investor Protection Act of 1970 established the Securities Investor Protection Corporation (SIPC) to act as an insurance company in protecting investors from brokerage firms that fail. Assessments are made against brokerage firms to provide the funds with backup government support available.
7. The Securities Act Amendments of 1975 was a far-reaching piece of legislation, calling for the SEC to move toward the establishment of a national market. This act abolished fixed brokerage commissions.

EXAMPLE 5-5

In July 1996, the Justice Department settled a civil agreement whereby the 24 firms involved did not have to admit any violations but did have to agree to obey the law in the future and establish trade-monitoring systems at a cost of $100 million. The Justice Department claims that spreads have narrowed on many of the most actively traded Nasdaq stocks.

Securities and Exchange Commission (SEC) A federal government agency established by the Securities Exchange Act of 1934 to protect investors

The Securities and Exchange Commission In 1934 Congress created the **Securities and Exchange Commission (SEC)** as an independent, quasi-judicial agency of the U.S. government. Its mission is to administer laws in the securities field and to protect investors and the public in securities transactions. The commission consists of five members appointed by the president for five-year terms. Its staff consists of lawyers, accountants, security analysts, and others divided into divisions and offices (including nine regional offices). The SEC has approximately 200 examiners.

In general, the SEC administers all securities laws. Thus, under the Securities Act of 1933, the SEC ensures that new securities being offered for public sale are registered with the commission, and under the 1934 act it does the same for securities trading on national exchanges. The registration of securities in no way ensures that investors purchasing them will not lose money. Registration means only that the issuer has made adequate disclosure. In fact, the SEC has no power to disapprove securities for lack of merit.

Under the two acts of 1940—the Investment Company Act and the Investment Advisors Act—investment companies and investment advisors must register with the SEC and disclose certain information. The SEC ensures that these two groups will meet the requirements of the laws affecting them. One problem, however, is that the number of registered investment advisors increased fourfold in the 1980s to over 16,000, and the number of investment companies increased to some 3,500. The SEC has a staff of only a few hundred to deal with these two groups.

The SEC is required to investigate complaints or indications of violations in securities transactions. As mentioned above, the Justice Department began an antitrust investigation of the Nasdaq Stock Market. The focus was particularly on the spreads—the difference between what buyers pay for a stock and what they sell it for. The SEC launched its own investigation of this and related issues. It forced the NASD into significant reforms, such as becoming a holding company with two units, the Nasdaq market itself and a separate unit for regulation called NASD Regulation Inc. SEC actions are designed to help investors.

EXAMPLE 5-6

In August 1996, the SEC instituted some new procedures to better protect investors trading in the Nasdaq market. The new rules require dealers to give customers the better prices quoted on such electronic markets as Instinet, discussed in Chapter 4, and to ensure that all investors are fully informed of the best prices offered by market makers.

A well-known illustration of SEC activity involves "insider trading," which has been a primary enforcement emphasis of the SEC. "Insiders" (officers and directors of corporations) are prohibited from misusing (i.e., trading on) corporate information that is not generally available to the public and are required to file reports with the SEC showing their equity holdings.

Several major insider-trading "scandals" have been reported in recent years. In the 1980s, Dennis Levine, a key member of the mergers and acquisitions department of Drexel Burnham Lambert, Inc., was charged with insider trading in a major case with many repercussions. Also, a well-known arbitrageur, Ivan Boesky, was fined $100 million by the SEC in

Box 5-1

HOW A ROUND OF GOLF COST $1 MILLION

A real estate developer was puzzled by his golfing buddies. They'd been friends almost all their lives, attending the same high school. They knocked off early nearly every Friday to golf together. But on the afternoon of March 7, 1986, they kept snickering about something they wouldn't share with the developer.

Only in the clubhouse after the round did one of the group who was the hub of this chatter finally tell the developer what he'd already told some of the others: Buy the stock of Revco Drug Stores. It hadn't been announced yet, but the big Ohio-based chain was going to be taken over by its management. "I know the guy doing the deal," the friend confided.

The discloser figured he was doing his friends a favor when he passed along his big secret. When they thought about it at all, they considered the hot tip and their subsequent trading in Revco nothing more than a pleasant and profitable diversion, hardly something they needed to worry about. Nearly two years later, one of the golfers got a phone call from someone who said he was a Securities and Exchange Commission investigator.

Not funny But in the eyes of the SEC, the businessmen were in a crucial respect indistinguishable from the notorious Wall Street arbitrager and securities felon. Two months ago, both of the individuals, two other friends and their stockbroker were charged by the SEC with insider trading. They have paid about $1 million in penalties and legal fees to settle the case. They have lain awake at night before giving testimony about—and in some cases, against—their oldest friends.

SOURCE: Adapted from Thomas E. Richs, "How 4 Pals Who Mixed Golf and Stock Tips Landed in the Rough," *The Wall Street Journal*, July 21, 1989, p. A1. Reprinted by permission of *The Wall Street Journal*, © 1990 Dow Jones & Company, Inc. All Rights Reserved Worldwide. Permission conveyed through Copyright Clearance Center, Inc.

a highly publicized insider-trading case. Although questions remain about exactly what constitutes insider trading, even small investors can be charged with possessing "material, nonpublic information," as Box 5-1 illustrates.

Smaller insider-trading cases occur regularly, primarily as a result of mergers and takeovers. The individuals involved are charged with the use of inside information to trade the stock of a company about to be acquired.

EXAMPLE 5-7

In 1996 the SEC accused four individuals of gaining illegal profits by trading on inside information in early 1995.[16] The case involved Affymax NV, which at that time was involved in a secret proposed acquisition by Glaxo PLC. One of the accused was the legal assistant to the general counsel of the company, and the others were acquaintances or family. Following a typical pattern, at the time of the report one of the individuals had agreed to settle the charges without admission of guilt by repaying profits plus interest.

USING THE INTERNET The SEC maintains a well-known database called "EDGAR" (electronic data gathering and retrieval). The SEC requires all filings made by public domestic companies as of May 6, 1996, to be placed in EDGAR, and the SEC posts filings within 24 hours of receipt. Investors can search for companies in multiple ways (by ticker symbol, type of business, SIC code, etc.) at www.sec.gov/edgarhp.htm.

[16] "See Californians Accused of Insider Trading in Purchase of Affymax," *The Wall Street Journal*, September 16, 1996, p. B7.

SELF-REGULATION

Regulation of the Stock Exchange Stock exchanges regulate and monitor trading for the benefit of investors and the protection of the financial system. The NYSE in particular has a stringent set of self-regulations and declares that it "provides the most meaningful market regulation in the world." The NYSE regulates itself as part of a combined effort involving the SEC (already discussed) itself and member firms (discussed below). Together, this triad enforces federal legislation and self-regulation for the benefit of the investing public.

During a typical trading day, the NYSE continuously monitors all market participants. It also closely monitors the performance of specialists in their responsibility for maintaining a fair and orderly market in their assigned stocks. NYSE rules and regulations are self-imposed and approved by the SEC.

In response to the market crash in 1987 and a smaller decline in 1989, the NYSE has instituted several measures to reduce market volatility and serve the investors' best interests. Because of the strong rise of the market in 1995 and 1996, the NYSE agreed in late 1996 to revise the trigger points. These safeguards are referred to as "circuit-breakers" and include:

- Trading Halts. Trading halts occur based on trigger levels of 10, 20, and 30 percent of the DJIA using average closing values for the prior month. The halts vary according to conditions, and range from 30 minutes to the remainder of the day.
- Sidecar. A five-minute "sidecar" period occurs when the S&P 500 futures contract declines 12 points from the previous day's close. All program trading market orders are sent to a separate file for five minutes, after which buy and sell orders are paired off and are eligible for execution. Trading in a stock is halted if orderly trading cannot resume. The sidecar rule does not apply in the last 35 minutes of trading.
- Rule 80A. If the Dow Jones Industrial Average moves 50 points or more from the previous day's close, index arbitrage orders in stocks comprising the Standard & Poor 500 Index are subject to a tick test. In down- (up-) markets sell (buy) orders can be executed only on a plus or zero-plus (minus or zero-minus) tick which was revised in 1999.

The National Association of Securities Dealers (NASD) The National Association of Securities Dealers (NASD) is a trade association established to enhance the self-regulation of the securities industry.[17] Virtually all securities firms are members. The NASD regulates brokers and dealers, thereby protecting investors. All brokers must register with the NASD in order to trade securities, and the NASD keeps records of disciplinary actions taken against stockbrokers and securities firms.[18]

What exactly can the NASD do to members who are suspected of dubious dealings? First, it can bar the individual from association with any NASD member, although having done so, the NASD has no jurisdiction over the individual. Second, the NASD can fine an individual; in one case involving penny stocks in 1991, one person was fined almost $2 million. However, these penalties can be appealed to the SEC, which suspends the monetary penalties until resolution.

OTHER INVESTOR PROTECTIONS

Insured Brokerage Accounts The Securities Investor Protection Corporation (SIPC), a nonprofit, membership corporation, insures each customer account of member

[17] The SEC can revoke the NASD's registration, giving the SEC power over this organization comparable to its powers over exchanges.

[18] Some examples of such actions against both firms and individuals include failing to honor arbitration awards and to maintain minimum required net capital, conducting trades at excessive markups and markdowns, receiving funds from investors without depositing them in an escrow account, and engaging in stock manipulation schemes.

brokers against brokerage firm failure. Each account is covered for as much as $500,000. (Coverage of cash is limited to $100,000.)[19] From 1970 to 1990 SIPC paid out in excess of $180 million in helping some 200,000 investors recover over $1 billion from failed brokers with SIPC insurance. (Would you want a broker without such insurance?)

What happens when you are unhappy with your broker, feeling perhaps that you were given bad advice? Since 1987, most investors, in order to open an account, must sign away their right to sue their broker or financial advisor. However, investors can seek damages from independent arbitration panels. And lawsuits are still possible: one individual in 1991 received an award of almost $600,000 from a financial planner.

Arbitration Investors who have disputes with their brokers generally cannot seek relief in court. Instead, they must rely on binding arbitration before the NASD. Many feel that this has worked to the advantage of the brokerage industry and to the disadvantage of investors. Any damages awarded usually amount to recovery of monies lost, plus interest. Punitive damages are rare—for example, in 1995 less than 15 percent of the total damage awards was for punitive damages, although it does happen. In 1996, one large brokerage firm was ordered to pay more than $1 million in damages to a former client, including $750,000 in punitive damages.

In 1996 the NASD proposed new changes that simplify the process, particularly document disclosure, and give investors more of a say in the selection of arbitrators. Furthermore, the six-year time limit for filing a claim was to be suspended.

ONE EXAMPLE OF REGULATION—THE CASE OF PENNY STOCKS

One ongoing problem for small investors involves so-called penny stocks, which are the common stocks of very small companies selling for pennies per share. Typically, "boiler-room operations" are set up whereby several people "cold call" hundreds of prospects a day to sell them penny stocks without the individuals seeing any information about the company. These operations often involve stock manipulation schemes that could work in the following manner: after the initial public offering, for example, at one cent per share, another broker working with the manipulator, whose firm makes a market in these shares, will purchase much of the offering at a slightly higher price, say 1.5 cents per share. These shares are then sold back to accounts controlled by the manipulator at, say, 2 cents per share. They may then be sold to the public at several cents per share.

Because of widespread abuses in the 1980s, state and federal regulators cracked down hard on the major abusers, effectively shutting them down. The SEC even passed rules in 1990 governing the sale of stocks trading at less than $5 per share. Nevertheless, new firms opened to replace those that had been closed down, and in many cases the people involved in the old firms moved to the new firms. In a typical year many enforcement cases involve penny stocks. One brokerage firm encouraged its brokers to act like "phone terrorists." A disturbing new trend by the penny-stock dealers is the sale of foreign stocks to U.S. investors, making it even more difficult for regulators to investigate.

MARGIN

As previously noted, investor accounts at brokerage houses can be either cash accounts or margin accounts. Opening a margin account requires some deposit of cash or marginable

[19] In addition, many brokerage firms carry additional insurance, often for several million dollars, to provide even more protection for customers.

securities. The NYSE requires that member firms establish a minimum deposit of $2,000 or its equivalent in securities for customers opening a margin account, but individual firms may require more. For example, Fidelity Investments requires a customer to have a minimum equity of $5,000 in cash or marginable securities.

With a margin account, the customer can pay part of the total amount due and borrow the remainder from the broker, who in turn typically borrows from a bank to finance customers. The bank charges the broker the "broker call rate," and the broker in turn charges the customer a "margin interest rate," which is the broker call rate plus a percentage added on by the brokerage firm.[20]

A margin account can be used to:

1. Purchase additional securities by leveraging the value of the eligible shares to buy more.[21]
2. Borrow money from a brokerage account for personal purposes. The margin interest rate is comparable to a bank's prime rate.
3. Provide overdraft protection in amounts up to the loan value of the marginable securities for checks written (or debit card purchases).

INVESTMENTS INTUITION The traditional appeal of margin trading to investors is that it magnifies any gains on a transaction by the reciprocal of the margin requirement (i.e., 1/margin percentage; for example, with a margin of 40 percent, the magnification is 1/0.4 = 2.50). Unfortunately, the use of margin also magnifies any losses. Regardless of what happens, the margin trader must pay the interest costs on the margin account. An investor considering a margined stock purchase should remember that the stock price can go up, remain the same, or go down. In two of these three cases, the investor loses. Even if the stock rises, the breakeven point is higher by the amount of the interest charges.

Margin The part of a transaction's value that a customer has as equity in the transaction

Initial Margin That part of a transaction's value that a customer must pay to initiate the transaction, with the other part being borrowed from the broker

Margin is that part of a transaction's value that a customer has as equity in the transaction; that is, it is that part of the total value of the transaction that is not borrowed from the broker. Cash has 100 percent loan value, and stock securities have 50 percent loan value. Other securities have differing amounts.

The Board of Governors of the Federal Reserve System (Fed), using Regulation T, has the authority to specify the **initial margin**, which is used as a policy device to influence the economy. Historically, the initial margin for stocks has ranged between 40 and 100 percent, with a current level of 50 percent since 1974.[22] The initial margin can be defined as:

$$\text{Initial margin} = \frac{\text{Amount investor puts up}}{\text{Value of the transaction}}$$

EXAMPLE 5-8

If the initial margin requirement is 50 percent on a $10,000 transaction (100 shares at $100 per share), the customer must put up $5,000, borrowing $5,000 from the broker.[23] The customer could put up $5,000 in cash or by depositing $10,000 in marginable securities.

[20] One large discount brokerage firm adds 2 percent for margin loans up to $10,000, 1.5 percent for loans up to $25,000, 1 percent for loans up to $50,000, and 0.50 percent for loans above $50,000.

[21] Starting in 1990, brokers can extend credit on certain foreign equity and corporate debt securities.

[22] Exchanges and brokerage houses can require more initial margin than that set by the Fed if they choose.

[23] With a 60 percent requirement, the customer must initially put up $6,000.

Maintenance Margin The percentage of a security's value that must be on hand as equity

All exchanges and brokers require a **maintenance margin** below which the actual margin cannot go. The NYSE requires an investor to maintain an equity of 25 percent of the market value of any securities held (and in practice brokers usually require 30 percent or more) on long positions.

As the stock price changes, the investor's equity changes. This is calculated as the market value of the collateral stock minus the amount borrowed. The market value of the stock is equal to the current market price multiplied by the number of shares.

If the investor's equity exceeds the initial margin, the excess margin can be withdrawn from the account, or more stock can be purchased without additional cash. Conversely, if the investor's equity declines below the initial margin, problems can arise, depending on the amount of the decline. It is at this point that the maintenance margin must be considered.

EXAMPLE 5-9

Assume that the maintenance margin is 30 percent, with a 50 percent initial margin, and that the price of the stock declines from \$100 to \$90 per share. Equation 5-1 is used to calculate actual margin.[24]

$$\text{Actual margin} = \frac{\text{Current value of securities} - \text{Amount borrowed}}{\text{Current value of securities}}$$

$$44.44\% = (\$9{,}000 - \$5{,}000)/\$9{,}000$$

The actual margin is now between the initial margin of 50 percent and the maintenance margin of 30 percent. This could result in a restricted account, meaning that additional margin purchases are prohibited, although the customer does not have to put additional equity (cash) into the account.

Brokerage houses calculate the actual margin in their customers' accounts daily to determine whether a margin call is required. This is known as having the brokerage accounts marked to market.

Margin Call A demand from the broker for additional cash or securities as a result of the actual margin declining below the maintenance margin

A **margin call** (maintenance call or "house call") occurs when the market value of the margined securities less the debit balance (amount owed) of the margin account declines below the maintenance requirement set by the brokerage house (typically 30 percent on stocks). This type of call is payable on demand, and the brokerage house may reserve the right to take action without notice if market conditions are deteriorating badly enough.

EXAMPLE 5-10

Assume in the previous example that the maintenance margin is 30 percent. If the price of the stock drops to \$80, the actual margin will be 37.5 percent [(\$8,000 − \$5,000) / \$8,000]. Because this is above the maintenance margin, there is no margin call. However, if the price of the stock declines to \$66.66, the actual margin will be 25 percent [(\$6,666 − \$5,000) / \$6,666]. This results in a maintenance call to restore the investor's equity to the minimum maintenance margin.

The price at which a margin call will be issued can be calculated as:

$$\text{MC price} = \frac{\text{Amount borrowed}}{\text{Number of shares } (1 - \text{maintenance margin percentage})}$$

where MC price equals the price of the stock that triggers a margin call.

[24] The difference between the market value of the securities and the amount borrowed is the investor's equity.

EXAMPLE 5-11

Using the above data, for 100 shares, $5,000 borrowed, and a maintenance margin of 30 percent, a margin call will be issued when the price is:

$$\text{MC price} = \frac{\$5{,}000}{100\ (1 - .30)}$$
$$= \$71.43$$

Although the initial margin requirement for common stocks and convertible bonds is 50 percent, it is only 30 percent (or less) of market value for "acceptable" municipal and corporate bonds.[25] U.S. government securities and GNMAs require an initial margin of only 8 to 15 percent, whereas Treasury bills may require only 1 percent of market value.

While the initial margin requirement for common stocks is 50 percent, and that is how virtually all investors think of it, the margin option does not have to be fully employed. That is, investors could limit their borrowing to one-third of their account, in which case the value of the account could decline 50 percent before a margin call was issued. With borrowing limited to 20 percent of the account, the value of the account could decline 70 percent before a margin call occurred. Particularly in the latter situation, an investor would have an extremely low probability of ever encountering a margin call.

SHORT SALES

The purchase of a security technically results in the investor being "long" the security.

- Normal transaction (long the position)—A security is bought, and owned, because the investor believes the price is likely to rise. Eventually, the security is sold and the position is closed out.
- Reverse the transaction (short the position)—What if the investor thinks that the price of a security will decline? If he or she owns it, it might be wise to sell. If the security is not owned, the investor wishing to profit from the expected decline in price can sell the security short. **Short sales** are a normal part of market transactions. Eventually, the investor buys the security back and the position is closed.

Short Sale The sale of a stock not owned in order to take advantage of an expected decline in the price of the stock

How can an investor sell short, which is to say sell something he or she does not own? Not owning the security to begin with, the investor will have to borrow from a third party. The broker, on being instructed to sell short, will make these arrangements for this investor by borrowing the security from those held in street-name margin accounts and, in effect, lending it to the short seller.[26]

The short seller's broker sells the borrowed security in the open market, exactly like any other sale, to some investor who wishes to own it. The short seller expects the price of the security to decline. Assume that it does. The short seller instructs the broker to repurchase the security at the currently lower price and cancel the short position (by replacing the

[25] This may also be stated as a percentage of principal—for example, 10 percent for nonconvertible corporates and 15 percent for municipals.

[26] The securities could be borrowed from another broker. If the lending firm calls back the stock loan, the broker may be forced to close the short position. Also, individuals sometimes agree to lend securities to short sellers in exchange for interest-free loans equal to the collateral value of the securities sold short. Collateral value equals the amount of funds borrowed in a margin transaction.

TABLE 5-3 THE DETAILS OF SHORT SELLING

1. Dividends declared on any stock sold short must be covered by the short seller. After all, the person from whom the shares were borrowed still owns the stock and expects all dividends paid on it.
2. Short sellers must have a margin account to sell short and must put up margin as if they had gone long. The margin can consist of cash or any restricted securities held long.
3. The net proceeds from a short sale, plus the required margin, are held by the broker; thus, no funds are immediately received by the short seller. The lender must be fully protected. To do this, the account is marked-to-the-market (as mentioned earlier in connection with margin accounts). If the price of the stock declines as expected by the short seller, he or she can withdraw the difference between the sale price and the current market price. If the price of the stock rises, however, the short seller will have to put up more funds.
4. There is no time limit on a short sale. Short sellers can remain short indefinitely. The only protection arises when the lender of the securities wants them back. In most cases the broker can borrow elsewhere, but in some situations, such as a thinly capitalized stock, this may not be possible.
5. Short sales are permitted only on rising prices, or an uptick. A short seller can sell short at the last trade price only if that price exceeded the last different price before it. Otherwise, they must wait for an uptick. Although the order to the broker can be placed at any time, it will not be executed until an uptick occurs.

borrowed security). The investor profits by the difference between the price at which the borrowed stock was sold and the price at which it was repurchased.

EXAMPLE 5-12

Assume an investor named Helen believes that the price of General Motors (GM) will decline over the next few months and wants to profit if her assessment is correct. She calls her broker with instructions to sell 100 shares of GM short (she does not own GM) at its current market price of $50 per share. The broker borrows 100 shares of GM from Kellie, who has a brokerage account with the firm and currently owns GM ("long"). The broker sells the borrowed 100 shares at $50 per share, crediting the $5,000 proceeds (less commissions, which we will ignore for this example) to Helen's account.[27] Six months later the price of GM has declined, as Helen predicted, and is now $38 per share. Satisfied with this drop in the price of GM, she instructs the broker to purchase 100 shares of GM and close out the short position. Her profit is $5,000 − $3,800, or $1,200 (again, ignoring commissions). The broker replaces Kellie's missing stock with the just-purchased 100 shares, and the transaction is complete.[28]

Several technicalities are involved in a short sale; these are outlined in Table 5-3. Keep in mind that to sell short an investor must be approved for a margin account because short positions involve the potential for margin calls. Using our earlier example of Fidelity Investments, we see that the initial minimum equity to open a margin account would be $5,000, the initial margin requirement would be 50 percent of the short sale, and the maintenance margin would be 30 percent of market value.

How popular are short sales? In 1998 roughly 18 billion shares (in round lots) were sold short on the NYSE, which was about 10 percent of all reported volume. NYSE members accounted for about two-thirds of short sales on the NYSE, and the public accounted for the

[27] Note that Kellie knows nothing about this transaction, nor is she really affected. Kellie receives a monthly statement from the broker showing ownership of 100 shares of GM. Should Kellie wish to sell the GM stock while Helen is short, the broker will simply borrow 100 shares from Elizabeth, a third investor who deals with this firm and owns GM stock, to cover the sale. It is important to note that all of these transactions are book entries and do not typically involve the actual stock certificates.

[28] Notice that two trades are required to complete a transaction, or "round trip." Investors who purchase securities plan to sell them eventually. Investors who sell short plan to buy back eventually; they have simply reversed the normal buy-sell procedure by selling and then buying.

remainder. Specialists, who often sell short to meet public buy orders, accounted for about 40 percent of the members' total. Specialists, in their role of maintaining an orderly market, must often sell short to meet an inflow of buy orders. Although individual investors have often bypassed short selling in the OTC market, this is changing as short selling has become more accessible to them.

If you are interested in selling stocks short, how do you go about obtaining short-sale recommendations? Investors can do their own analysis or use investment advisory services. As in other areas of investing, the results of those who provide recommendations vary over a wide range.

SUMMARY

- Brokerage firms consist of full-service brokers, discount brokers, and deep-discount brokers.
- Full-service stockbrokers earn their incomes from a variety of sources including individuals' trades, in-house mutual fund sales, principal transactions, new issues, and fees.
- With a cash brokerage account, the customer pays in full on the settlement date, whereas with a margin account money can be borrowed from the broker to finance purchases.
- Asset management accounts offering a variety of services are commonplace, and wrap accounts, where all costs are wrapped in one fee, are increasingly popular.
- Brokerage commissions are negotiable. Full-line brokerage houses charge more than discount brokers but offer recommendations. Some Internet-only discount brokers charge the least.
- Investors can invest without a broker through dividend reinvestment plans. Some companies sell shares directly to investors.
- Most orders sent to the exchanges involve a specialist and are highly automated. Specialists on the NYSE are charged with maintaining a continuous, orderly market in their assigned stocks.
- The NYSE is highly automated, with its SuperDot electronic order routing system handling much of the routine trading.
- Market orders are executed at the best price available, whereas limit orders specify a particular price to be met or bettered.
- Stop orders specify a certain price at which a market order is to take over.
- Investor protection includes government regulation, primarily federal, and self-regulation by the industry. The Securities and Exchange Commission administers the securities laws.
- The NYSE has a stringent set of self-regulations. The National Association of Securities Dealers regulates brokers and dealers and has significantly improved the functioning of the OTC market.
- Margin is the equity an investor has in a transaction. The Federal Reserve sets an initial margin, but all exchanges and brokers require a maintenance margin. The appeal of margin to investors is that it can magnify any gains on a transaction, but it can also magnify losses.
- An investor sells short if a security's price is expected to decline. The investor borrows the securities sold short from the broker, hoping to replace them through a later purchase at a lower price.

KEY WORDS

Asked price
Asset management account
Bid price
Cash account
Discount broker
Dividend reinvestment plan (DRIPs)
Full-service broker
Initial margin
Limit order
Maintenance margin
Margin
Margin account
Margin call
Market order
Securities and Exchange Commission (SEC)
Short sale
Stop order
Street name
SuperDot
Wrap account

QUESTIONS

5-1. Discuss the advantages and disadvantages of a limit order versus a market order. How does a stop order differ from a limit order?

5-2. What is meant by selling securities on a "regular way" basis?

5-3. What are the advantages and disadvantages of using a street name?

5-4. Explain the margin process, distinguishing between initial margin and maintenance margin. Who sets these margins?

5-5. What conditions result in an account being "restricted"? What prompts a margin call?

5-6. How can an investor sell a security that is not currently owned?

5-7. What conditions must be met for an investor to sell short?

5-8. Explain the difference, relative to the current market price of a stock, between the following types of orders: sell limit, buy limit, buy stop, and sell stop.

5-9. What is the margin requirement for U.S. government securities?

5-10. What is a wrap account? How does it involve a change in the traditional role of the broker?

5-11. Distinguish between a large discount broker such as Fidelity and an Internet-only discount broker.

5-12. How can investors invest without a broker?

5-13. Explain the role of a specialist on the NYSE. How can specialists act as both brokers and dealers?

5-14. What is the role of SuperDot on the NYSE?

5-15. What is the difference between a day order and an open order?

5-16. What is the role of the SEC in the regulation of securities markets?

5-17. Who regulates brokers and dealers? What types of actions can be taken against firms and individuals?

5-18. Why are investors interested in having margin accounts? What risk do such accounts involve?

5-19. How popular are short sales relative to all reported sales?

5-20. Explain the basis of regulation of mutual funds. How successful has this regulation been?

5-21. What assurances does the Investment Advisors Act of 1940 provide investors in dealing with people who offer investment advice?

5-22. How could a "circuit-breaker" lead to a trading halt on the NYSE?

5-23. Given the lower brokerage costs charged by discount brokers and deep-discount brokers, why might an investor choose to use a full-service broker?

5-24. What assurances as to the success of a company does the SEC provide investors when an IPO is marketed?

5-25. Contrast the specialist system used on the NYSE and AMEX with the dealer system associated with the OTC market.

PROBLEMS

5-1. a. Consider an investor who purchased a stock at $100 per share. The current market price is $125. At what price would a limit order be placed to assure a profit of $30 per share?

b. What type of stop order would be placed to ensure a profit of at least $20 per share?

5-2. Assume an investor sells short 200 shares of stock at $75 per share. At what price must the investor cover the short sale in order to realize a gross profit of $5,000? $1,000?

5-3. Assume that an investor buys 100 shares of stock at $50 per share and the stock rises to $60 per share. What is the gross profit, assuming an initial margin requirement of 50 percent? 40 percent? 60 percent?

5-4. Assume an initial margin requirement of 50 percent and a maintenance margin of 30 percent. An investor buys 100 shares of stock on margin at $60 per share. The price of the stock subsequently drops to $50.

a. What is the actual margin at $50?

b. The price now rises to $55. Is the account restricted?

c. If the price declines to $49, is there a margin call?

d. Assume that the price declines to $45. What is the amount of the margin call? At $35?

5-5. You open a margin account at Charles Pigeon, a discount broker. You subsequently short Exciting.com at $286, believing it to be overpriced. This transaction is done on margin, which has an annual interest rate cost of 9 percent. Exactly one year later Exciting has declined to $54 a share, at which point you cover your short position. You pay brokerage costs of $20 on each transaction you make.

a. Assume the margin requirement is 55 percent. Calculate your dollar gain or loss on this position, taking into account both the margin interest and the transaction costs.

b. Calculate the percentage return on your investment (the amount of money you put up initially, counting the brokerage costs to buy).

5-6. Using your same brokerage account as in Problem 5-5 (same margin rate and transaction costs), assume you buy IBM at $156 a share, on 60 percent margin. During the year IBM pays a dividend of $1.30 per share. One year later you sell the position at $233.

a. Calculate the dollar gain or loss on this position.

b. Calculate the percentage return on your investment.

SELECTED REFERENCES

Information on the mechanics of trading appears in most popular press magazines and newspapers, including:

Barron's

Business Week

Forbes
Fortune
Money Magazine
Smart Money
The Wall Street Journal
Worth

www.wiley.com/college/jones7

This chapter discusses the mechanics of trading securities and the regulation of securities. Accordingly, the web exercises will engage you in exercises related to issues such as short-selling and trading on margin, as well as the role of the regulator.

chapter 6

The Returns and Risks from Investing

Chapter 6 analyzes the returns and risks from investing. We learn how well investors have done in the past investing in the major financial assets. Investors must have a good understanding of the returns and risk that have been experienced to date before attempting to estimate returns and risk, which they must do as they build and hold portfolios for the future.

After reading this chapter you will be able to:

- **Calculate the return and risk for financial assets, using the formulation appropriate for the task.**
- **Use key terms involved with return and risk, including geometric mean, cumulative wealth index, inflation-adjusted returns, and currency-adjusted returns.**
- **Discuss the historical returns on major financial assets.**
- **Understand clearly the returns and risk investors have experienced in the past, an important step in estimating future returns and risk.**

The field of investments traditionally has been divided into security analysis and portfolio management. Parts III, IV, and V discuss security analysis for fixed-income and equity securities. The heart of security analysis is the valuation of financial assets. Value, in turn, is a function of return and risk. These two concepts are, therefore, very important in the study of investments. In fact, they are the foundation of investment decisions.

Return and risk are described, measured, and estimated throughout the text. Particular forms of these concepts will be used when needed, but before beginning an analysis of the various securities, it is extremely valuable to obtain a working knowledge of return and risk. Therefore, we must consider these concepts and learn how to analyze and measure them. In this chapter we concentrate on the measurement of *realized* return and risk, while in Chapter 7 we consider *expected* return and risk.

As we learned in Chapter 1, *realized return* is what the term implies; it is ex post (after the fact) return, or return that was or could have been earned. Realized return has occurred and can be measured with the proper data. *Expected return*, on the other hand, is the estimated return from an asset that investors anticipate (expect) they will earn over some future period. As an estimated return, it is subject to uncertainty and may or may not occur.

As explained in Chapter 1, the investment decision can be described as a trade-off between risk and expected return. We will consider this trade-off, which describes the future, in detail in subsequent chapters. Before doing so, however, it is very important to have a perspective on realized returns and risks from investing. How would investors have fared, on average, over the past by investing in the major marketable securities? What are the returns and risk from investing, based on the historical record? We answer questions such as these in this chapter.

Although there is no guarantee that the future will be exactly like the past, a knowledge of historical risk-return relationships is a necessary first step for investors in making investment decisions for the future. Furthermore, there is no reason to assume that *relative* relationships will differ significantly in the future. Thus, if stocks have returned more than bonds, and Treasury bonds more than Treasury bills, over the entire financial history available, there is every reason to assume that such relationships will continue over the long-run future. Therefore, it is very important for investors to understand what has occurred in the past.

RETURN

As noted in Chapter 1, the objective of investors is to maximize expected returns, although they are subject to constraints, primarily risk. Return is the motivating force in the investment process. It is the reward for undertaking the investment.

Returns from investing are crucial to investors; they are what the game of investments is all about. The measurement of realized (historical) returns is necessary for investors to assess how well they have done or how well investment managers have done on their behalf. Furthermore, the historical return plays a large part in estimating future, unknown returns.

THE COMPONENTS OF RETURN

Return on a typical investment consists of two components:

- **Yield:** The basic component that usually comes to mind when discussing investing returns is the periodic cash flows (or income) on the investment, either interest or dividends. The distinguishing feature of these payments is that the issuer makes the

Yield The income component of a security's return

Capital Gain (Loss) The change in price on a security over some period of time

payments in cash to the holder of the asset. **Yield** measures relate these cash flows to a price for the security, such as the purchase price or the current market price.

- **Capital gain (loss):** The second component is also important, particularly for common stocks but also for long-term bonds and other fixed-income securities. This component is the appreciation (or depreciation) in the price of the asset, commonly called the **capital gain (loss)**. We will refer to it simply as the price change. In the case of a long position, it is the difference between the purchase price and the price at which the asset can be, or is, sold; for a short position, it is the difference between the sale price and the subsequent price at which the short position is closed out. In either case, a gain or a loss can occur.[1]

Given the two components of a security's return, we need to add them together (algebraically) to form the total return, which for any security is defined as:

$$\text{Total return} = \text{Yield} + \text{Price change} \qquad (6\text{-}1)$$

where: the yield component can be 0 or +
 the price change component can be 0, +, or −

Equation 6-1 is a conceptual statement for the total return for any security. The important point here is that a security's total return consists of the sum of two components, yield and price change. Investors' returns from assets can come only from these two components—an income component (the yield) and/or a price change component, regardless of the asset.

EXAMPLE 6-1

A bond purchased at par ($1,000) and held to maturity provides a yield in the form of a stream of cash flows or interest payments, but no price change. A bond purchased for $800 and held to maturity provides both a yield (the interest payments) and a price change. The purchase of a nondividend-paying stock, such as Dell Computer, that is sold six months later produces either a capital gain or a capital loss but no income. A dividend-paying stock, such as IBM, produces both a yield component and a price change component (a realized or unrealized capital gain or loss).

RISK

It is not sensible to talk about investment returns without talking about risk because investment decisions involve a trade-off between the two—*return and risk are opposite sides of the same coin*. Investors must constantly be aware of the risk they are assuming, know what it can do to their investment decisions, and be prepared for the consequences.

Risk was defined in Chapter 1 as the chance that the actual outcome from an investment will differ from the expected outcome. Specifically, most investors are concerned that the actual outcome will be less than the expected outcome. The more variable the possible outcomes that can occur (i.e., the broader the range of possible outcomes), the greater the risk.

Investors should be willing to purchase a particular asset if the expected return is adequate to compensate for the risk, but they must understand that their expectation about

[1] This component involves only the difference between the beginning price and the ending price in the transaction. An investor can purchase or short an asset and close out the position one day, one hour, or one minute later for a capital gain or loss. Furthermore, gains can be realized or unrealized. See Appendix 2-A for more discussion on capital gains and losses and their taxation.

the asset's return may not materialize. If not, the realized return will differ from the expected return. In fact, realized returns on securities show considerable variability. Although investors may receive their expected returns on risky securities on a long-run average basis, they often fail to do so on a short-run basis.

INVESTMENTS INTUITION It is important to remember how risk and return go together when investing. An investor cannot reasonably *expect* larger returns without being willing to assume larger risks. Consider the investor who wishes to avoid any practical risk on a nominal basis. Such an investor can deposit money in an insured savings account, thereby earning a guaranteed return of a known amount. However, this return will be fixed, and the investor cannot earn more than this rate. Although risk is effectively eliminated, the chance of earning a larger return is also removed. To have the opportunity to earn a larger return than the savings account provides, investors must be willing to assume risks—and when they do so, they may gain a larger return, but they may also lose money.

SOURCES OF RISK

What makes a financial asset risky? Traditionally, investors have talked about several sources of total risk, such as interest rate risk and market risk, which are explained below because these terms are used so widely. Following this discussion, we will define the modern portfolio sources of risk, which will be used later when we discuss portfolio and capital market theory.

Interest Rate Risk The variability in a security's returns resulting from changes in interest rates

Interest Rate Risk The variability in a security's return resulting from changes in the level of interest rates is referred to as **interest rate risk**. Such changes generally affect securities inversely; that is, other things being equal, security prices move inversely to interest rates.[2] Interest rate risk affects bonds more directly than common stocks, but it affects both and is a very important consideration for most investors.

Market Risk The variability in a security's returns resulting from fluctuations in the aggregate market

Market Risk The variability in returns resulting from fluctuations in the overall market—that is, the aggregate stock market—is referred to as **market risk**. All securities are exposed to market risk, although it affects primarily common stocks.

Market risk includes a wide range of factors exogenous to securities themselves, including recessions, wars, structural changes in the economy, and changes in consumer preferences.

Inflation Risk A factor affecting all securities is purchasing power risk, or the chance that the purchasing power of invested dollars will decline. With uncertain inflation, the real (inflation-adjusted) return involves risk even if the nominal return is safe (e.g., a Treasury bond). This risk is related to interest rate risk, since interest rates generally rise as inflation increases, because lenders demand additional inflation premiums to compensate for the loss of purchasing power.

Business Risk The risk of doing business in a particular industry or environment is called business risk. For example, AT&T, the traditional telephone powerhouse, faces major changes today in the rapidly changing telecommunications industry.

[2] The reason for this movement is tied up with the valuation of securities and will be explained in later chapters.

Financial Risk Financial risk is associated with the use of debt financing by companies. The larger the proportion of assets financed by debt (as opposed to equity), the larger the variability in the returns, other things being equal. Financial risk involves the concept of financial leverage, explained in managerial finance courses.

Liquidity Risk Liquidity risk is the risk associated with the particular secondary market in which a security trades. An investment that can be bought or sold quickly and without significant price concession is considered liquid. The more uncertainty about the time element and the price concession, the greater the liquidity risk. A Treasury bill has little or no liquidity risk, whereas a small OTC stock may have substantial liquidity risk.

EXAMPLE 6-2

A good illustration of liquidity risk is limited partnerships, which have highly illiquid secondary markets. Limited partnerships have been established to invest in commercial real estate or oil and gas, and enjoy some tax benefits not available to corporations, such as passing tax write-offs through to investors (thereby constituting a "tax shelter"). Of the over 3,000 public limited partnerships in existence, less than 1,000 trade each year and only 200 to 300 trade with any frequency.

Exchange Rate Risk All investors who invest internationally in today's increasingly global investment arena face the prospect of uncertainty in the returns after they convert the foreign gains back to their own currency. Unlike the past when most U.S. investors ignored international investing alternatives, investors today must recognize and understand **exchange rate risk**, which can be defined as the variability in returns on securities caused by currency fluctuations. Exchange rate risk is sometimes called *currency risk*.

Exchange Rate Risk The variability in returns on securities caused by currency fluctuations

For example, a U.S. investor who buys a German stock denominated in marks must ultimately convert the returns from this stock back to dollars. If the exchange rate has moved against the investor, losses from these exchange rate movements can partially or totally negate the original return earned.

Obviously, U.S. investors who invest only in U.S. stocks on U.S. markets do not face this risk, but in today's global environment where investors increasingly consider alternatives from other countries, this factor has become important. Currency risk affects international mutual funds, global mutual funds, closed-end single-country funds, American Depository Receipts, foreign stocks, and foreign bonds.

Country Risk Country risk, also referred to as political risk, is an important risk for investors today. With more investors investing internationally, both directly and indirectly, the political, and therefore economic, stability and viability of a country's economy need to be considered. The United States has the lowest country risk, and other countries can be judged on a relative basis using the United States as a benchmark. Examples of countries that needed careful monitoring in the 1990s because of country risk included the former Soviet Union and Yugoslavia, China, Hong Kong, and South Africa.

TYPES OF RISK

Thus far, our discussion has concerned the total risk of an asset, which is one important consideration in investment analysis. However, modern investment analysis categorizes the traditional sources of risk identified previously as causing variability in returns into two general types: those that are pervasive in nature, such as market risk or interest rate risk, and those that are specific to a particular security issue, such as business or financial risk. Therefore, we must consider these two categories of total risk. The following discussion introduces these terms. We discuss these two sources of risk in more detail in other chapters.

Dividing total risk into its two components, a general (market) component and a specific (issuer) component, we have systematic risk and nonsystematic risk, which are additive:

$$\begin{aligned} \text{Total risk} &= \text{General risk} + \text{Specific risk} \\ &= \text{Market risk} + \text{Issuer risk} \\ &= \text{Systematic risk} + \text{Nonsystematic risk} \end{aligned} \tag{6-2}$$

Systematic Risk As shown in later chapters, an investor can construct a diversified portfolio and eliminate part of the total risk, the diversifiable or nonmarket part. What is left is the nondiversifiable portion or the market risk. Variability in a security's total returns that is directly associated with overall movements in the general market or economy is called **systematic (market) risk**.

Systematic (Market) Risk Risk attributable to broad macro factors affecting all securities

Virtually all securities have some systematic risk, whether bonds or stocks, because systematic risk directly encompasses interest rate, market, and inflation risks. The investor cannot escape this part of the risk because no matter how well he or she diversifies, the risk of the overall market cannot be avoided. If the stock market declines sharply, most stocks will be adversely affected; if it rises strongly, as in the last few months of 1982, most stocks will appreciate in value. These movements occur regardless of what any single investor does. Clearly, market risk is critical to all investors.

Nonsystematic Risk The variability in a security's total returns not related to overall market variability is called the **nonsystematic (nonmarket) risk**. This risk is unique to a particular security and is associated with such factors as business and financial risk as well as liquidity risk. Although all securities tend to have some nonsystematic risk, it is generally connected with common stocks.

Nonsystematic (Nonmarket) Risk Risk attributable to factors unique to a security

MEASURING RETURNS

TOTAL RETURN

A correct returns measure must incorporate the two components of return, yield and price change, as discussed earlier. Returns across time or from different securities can be measured and compared using the total return concept. Formally, the **total return (TR)** for a given holding period is a decimal (or percentage) number relating all the cash flows received by an investor during any designated time period to the purchase price of the asset. Total return is defined as

Total Return Percentage measure relating all cash flows on a security for a given time period to its purchase price

$$\text{TR} = \frac{\text{Any cash payments received} + \text{Price changes over the period}}{\text{Price at which the asset is purchased}} \tag{6-3}$$

All the items in Equation 6-3 are measured in dollars. The dollar price change over the period, defined as the difference between the beginning (or purchase) price and the ending (or sale) price, can be either positive (sales price exceeds purchase price), negative (purchase price exceeds sales price) or zero. The cash payments can be either positive or zero. Netting the two items in the numerator together and dividing by the purchase price results in a decimal return figure that can easily be converted into percentage form. Note that in using the TR, the two components of return, yield and price change, have been measured.[3]

The general equation for calculating TR is

$$TR = \frac{CF_t + (P_E - P_B)}{P_B} = \frac{CF_t + PC}{P_B} \tag{6-4}$$

where

CF_t = cash flows during the measurement period t
P_E = price at the end of period t or sale price
P_B = purchase price of the asset or price at the beginning of the period
PC = change in price during the period, or P_E minus P_B

The cash flow for a bond comes from the interest payments received, and that for a stock comes from the dividends received. For some assets, such as a warrant or a stock that pays no dividends, there is only a price change. Part A of Exhibit 6-1 illustrates the calculation of TR for a bond, a common stock, and a warrant. Although one year is often used for convenience, the TR calculation can be applied to periods of any length.

In summary, the total return concept is valuable as a measure of return because it is all-inclusive, measuring the total return per dollar of original investment. It facilitates the comparison of asset returns over a specified period, whether the comparison is of different assets, such as stocks versus bonds, or different securities within the same type, such as several common stocks. Remember that using this concept does not mean that the securities have to be sold and the gains or losses actually realized—that is, the calculation applies to unrealized gains, or realized gains (see Appendix 2-A).

Table 6-1 shows corrected estimates of the Standard & Poor's (S&P) 500 Stock Composite Index for the years 1920 through 1998. Included in the table are end-of-year values for the index, from which capital gains and losses can be computed, and dividends on the index, which constitute the income component.[4]

EXAMPLE 6-3

The TRs for each year as shown in Table 6-1 can be calculated as shown in Equation 6-4. As a demonstration of these calculations, the TR for 1990 (the last year a loss was recorded on the S&P 500 through 1998) is −3.135 percent, calculated as:

$$[330.22 - 353.40 + 12.10]/353.40 = -3.135$$

In contrast, in 1995 the same market index showed a TR of 37.113 percent, calculated as:

$$([615.93 - 459.27 + 13.79]/459.27) = .3711 \text{ or } 37.11\%$$

RETURN RELATIVE

It is often necessary to measure returns on a slightly different basis than total returns. This is particularly true when calculating either a cumulative wealth index or a geometric mean, both

[3] This can be seen more easily by rewriting Equation 6-2 to show specifically its income and price change components.

$$TR = \frac{\text{Cash payments received}}{\text{Purchase price}} + \frac{\text{Price change over the period}}{\text{Purchase price}}$$

The first term is a yield component, whereas the second term measures the price change.

[4] Note that these are simple end-of-year values. When we analyze total returns later in the chapter, we assume monthly reinvestment of dividends.

Exhibit 6-1

EXAMPLES OF TOTAL RETURN AND PRICE RELATIVE CALCULATIONS

A. TOTAL RETURN (TR) CALCULATIONS

I. Bond TR

$$\text{Bond TR} = \frac{I_t + (P_E - P_B)}{P_B} = \frac{I_t + PC}{P_B}$$

I_t = the interest payment(s) received during the period
P_B and P_E = the beginning and ending prices, respectively
PC = the change in price during the period

EXAMPLE

Assume the purchase of a 10 percent-coupon Treasury bond at a price of \$960, held one year, and sold for \$1,020. The TR is

$$\text{Bond TR} = \frac{100 + (1020 - 960)}{960} = \frac{100 + 60}{960} = 0.1667 \text{ or } 16.67\%$$

II. Stock TR

$$\text{Stock TR} = \frac{D_t + (P_E - P_B)}{P_B} = \frac{D_t + PC}{P_B}$$

D_t = the dividend(s) paid during the period

EXAMPLE

100 shares of DataShield are purchased at \$30 per share and sold one year later at \$26 per share. A dividend of \$2 per share is paid.

$$\text{Stock TR} = \frac{2 + (26 - 30)}{30} = \frac{2 + (-4)}{30} = -0.0667 \text{ or } -6.67\%$$

III. Warrant TR

$$\text{Warrant TR} = \frac{C_t + (P_E - P_B)}{P_B} = \frac{C_t + PC}{P_B} = \frac{PC}{P_B}$$

where C_t = any cash payment received by the warrant holder during the period. Because warrants pay no dividends, the only return to an investor from owning a warrant is the change in price during the period.

EXAMPLE

Assume the purchase of warrants of DataShield at \$3 per share, a holding period of six months, and the sale at \$3.75 per share.

$$\text{Warrant TR} = \frac{0 + (3.75 - 3.00)}{3.00} = \frac{0.75}{3.00} = 0.25, \text{ or } 25\%$$

B. RETURN RELATIVE CALCULATIONS

The return relative for the preceding bond example shown is

$$\text{Bond return relative} = \frac{100 + 1020}{960} = 1.1667$$

The return relative for the stock example is

$$\text{Stock return relative} = \frac{2 + 26}{30} = 0.9333$$

The return relative for the warrant example is

$$\text{Warrant return relative} = \frac{3.75}{3.00} = 1.25$$

To convert from a return relative to a TR, subtract 1.0 from the return relative.

TABLE 6-1 Historical Composite Stock Price Index (1941–43 = 10), Based on Standard & Poor's Estimates, Dividends in Index Form, and Total Returns (TRs), 1919–1998. Values are end-of-year.

Year	Index Value	Div.	TR%	Year	Index Value	Div.	TR%
1919	10.35	—	—				
1920	7.99	0.56	−17.382	1960	58.11	1.95	0.284
1921	8.36	0.51	10.990	1961	71.55	2.02	26.605
1922	10.31	0.56	30.038	1962	63.10	2.13	−8.833
1923	10.00	0.58	2.633	1963	75.02	2.28	22.504
1924	11.98	0.61	25.971	1964	84.75	2.50	16.302
1925	14.60	0.67	27.415	1965	92.43	2.72	12.271
1926	15.05	0.75	8.195	1966	80.33	2.87	−9.986
1927	19.16	0.81	32.763	1967	96.47	2.92	23.727
1928	25.63	0.84	38.136	1968	103.86	3.07	10.843
1929	22.07	0.95	−10.185	1969	92.06	3.16	−8.319
1930	14.92	0.90	−28.311	1970	92.15	3.14	3.509
1931	7.90	0.76	−41.958	1971	102.09	3.07	14.118
1932	6.80	0.46	−8.012	1972	118.05	3.15	18.719
1933	10.20	0.37	55.341	1973	97.55	3.38	−14.502
1934	10.11	0.40	2.998	1974	68.56	3.60	−26.028
1935	13.93	0.41	41.788	1975	90.19	3.68	36.917
1936	17.61	0.68	31.384	1976	107.46	4.05	23.639
1937	11.15	0.78	−32.290	1977	95.10	4.67	−7.156
1938	13.61	0.52	26.698	1978	96.11	5.07	6.393
1939	13.20	0.59	1.312	1979	107.94	5.65	18.187
1940	11.52	0.67	−7.631	1980	135.76	6.16	31.480
1941	9.59	0.74	−10.335	1981	122.55	6.63	−4.847
1942	10.45	0.64	15.627	1982	140.64	6.87	20.367
1943	12.61	0.64	26.726	1983	164.93	7.09	22.312
1944	14.34	0.68	19.173	1984	167.24	7.53	5.966
1945	18.89	0.68	36.483	1985	211.28	7.90	31.057
1946	17.10	0.77	−5.432	1986	242.17	8.28	18.539
1947	16.76	0.92	3.429	1987	247.08	8.81	5.665
1948	16.12	1.05	2.434	1988	277.72	9.73	16.339
1949	18.12	1.13	19.452	1989	353.40	11.05	31.229
1950	21.96	1.40	28.931	1990	330.22	12.10	−3.135
1951	25.00	1.36	20.026	1991	417.09	12.20	30.001
1952	26.96	1.38	13.350	1992	435.71	12.38	7.432
1953	25.87	1.41	1.182	1993	466.45	12.58	9.942
1954	36.76	1.51	47.928	1994	459.27	13.18	1.286
1955	44.55	1.69	25.787	1995	615.93	13.79	37.113
1956	46.35	1.82	8.124	1996	740.74	14.90	22.683
1957	39.99	1.87	−9.675	1997	970.43	15.50	33.101
1958	55.21	1.75	42.443	1998	1229.23	16.20	28.338
1959	59.89	1.83	11.791	1999	na		

SOURCES: Data from 1919 through 1957 are based on estimates by Jack Wilson and Charles Jones from the discontinued Standard & Poor's Weekly Composite Index, as used by Alfred Cowles, *Common Stock Indexes*, Second Edition, (Bloomington, Indiana: Principia Press, Inc., 1938), and Cowles updates through 1940. From 1958 through 1998 the data are from Standard & Poor's Statistical Service. Total returns are based on annual reinvestment of dividends. The S&P data are reprinted by permission of Standard & Poor's Corporation, a division of McGraw-Hill.

NOTE: Standard & Poor's sometimes revises the data; furthermore, because of differences in data and calculations, the TRs shown here will not agree with the TRs reported by Ibbotson Associates, and therefore means and cumulative wealths could vary between these data and those for Ibbotson Associates.

of which are explained below, because negative returns cannot be used in the calculation. The **return relative** solves this problem by adding 1.0 to the total return. Although return relatives may be less than 1.0, they will be greater than zero, thereby eliminating negative numbers.

Return Relative The total return for an investment for a given time period stated on the basis of 1.0

EXAMPLE 6-4

A TR of 0.10 for some holding period is equivalent to a return relative of 1.10, and a TR of −3.135, as calculated in Example 6-3, is equivalent to a return relative of 0.96865.

Equation 6-4 can be modified to calculate return relatives directly by using the price at the end of the holding period in the numerator, rather than the change in price, as in Equation 6-5.

$$\text{Return relative} = \text{RR} = \frac{\text{CF}_t + \text{P}_\text{E}}{\text{P}_\text{B}} \tag{6-5}$$

Examples of return relative calculations for the same three assets as the preceding are shown in Part B of Exhibit 6-1.

EXAMPLE 6-5

The return relative for 1995 (Example 6-3) is

$$(615.93 + 13.79)/459.27 = 1.3711$$

CUMULATIVE WEALTH INDEX

Return measures such as TRs measure changes in the level of wealth. At times, however, it is more desirable to measure levels of wealth (or prices) rather than changes. In other words, we measure the cumulative effect of returns over time given some stated beginning amount, typically \$1. To capture the *cumulative* effect of returns, we use index values, which simply means we have a specified beginning value. The value of the **cumulative wealth index**, CWI_n, is computed as:

Cumulative Wealth Index Cumulative wealth over time, given an initial wealth and a series of returns on some asset

$$\text{CWI}_n = \text{WI}_0\,(1 + \text{TR}_1)(1 + \text{TR}_2)\cdots(1 + \text{TR}_n) \tag{6-6}$$

where

CWI_n = the cumulative wealth index as of the end of period n
WI_0 = the beginning index value, typically \$1
$\text{TR}_{1,n}$ = the periodic TRs in decimal form (when added to 1.0 in Equation 6-6, they become return relatives)

EXAMPLE 6-6

For the S&P total returns in Table 6-1, the cumulative wealth index for the period 1990–1998 would be, using return relatives:

$$\begin{aligned}\text{CWI}_{90-98} &= 1.00(0.9687)(1.30001)(1.07432)(1.09942)(1.01286)\\&\quad(1.37113)(1.22683)(1.33101)(1.28338)\\&= 4.3289\end{aligned}$$

Thus, \$1 (the beginning index value arbitrarily chosen) invested at the end of 1989 (the beginning of 1990) would have been worth \$4.3289 by the end of 1998. Obviously, any beginning wealth value can be used to calculate cumulative wealth. Thus, \$10,000 invested under the same conditions would have been worth \$43,289 at the end of 1998.

Note that the values for the cumulative wealth index can be used to calculate the rate of return for a given period, using Equation 6-7.

$$TR_n = \frac{CWI_n}{CWI_{n-1}} - 1 \tag{6-7}$$

where

TR_n = the total return for period n
CWI = the cumulative wealth index

EXAMPLE 6-7

Using the total returns illustrated above for the years 1990–1998, we can make the following calculations.

$$CWI_{90-98} = 1.00\ (0.9687)(1.30001)(1.07432)(1.09942)(1.01286)(1.37113)(1.22683)(1.33101)(1.28338)$$
$$= 4.3289$$
$$CWI_{90-97} = 1.00\ (0.9687)(1.30001)(1.07432)(1.09942)(1.01286)(1.37113)(1.22683)(1.33101)$$
$$= 3.3731$$
$$TR_{1998} = (4.3289/3.3731) - 1$$
$$= .2834 \text{ (rounded) or } 28.34\%$$

Thus, the total return for 1998 was 28.34 percent (rounded), which agrees with Table 6-1.

INTERNATIONAL RETURNS

When investors buy and sell assets in other countries, they must consider exchange rate risk. This risk can convert a gain from an investment into a loss or a loss from an investment into a gain. An investment denominated in an appreciating currency relative to the investor's domestic currency will experience a gain from the currency movement, while an investment denominated in a depreciating currency relative to the investor's domestic currency will experience a decrease in the return because of the currency movement.

To calculate the return from an investment in a foreign country, we use Equation 6-8. The foreign currency is stated in domestic terms; that is, the amount of domestic currency necessary to purchase one unit of the foreign currency.

$$\text{Total return in domestic terms} = \left[\text{RR} \times \frac{\text{Ending value of foreign currency}}{\text{Beginning value of foreign currency}}\right] - 1.0 \tag{6-8}$$

EXAMPLE 6-8

Consider a U.S. investor who invests in WalMex at 175.86 pesos when the value of the peso stated in dollars is $0.29. One year later WalMex is at 195.24 pesos, and the stock did not pay a dividend. The peso is now at $0.27, which means that the dollar appreciated against the peso.

Return relative for WalMex = 195.24/175.86 = 1.11

Total return to the U.S. investor *after currency adjustment* is

$$\text{TR denominated in \$} = \left[1.11 \times \frac{\$0.27}{\$0.29}\right] - 1.0$$
$$= [1.11 \times 0.931] - 1.0$$
$$= 1.0334 - 1.0$$
$$= .0334 \text{ or } 3.34\%$$

In this example, the U.S. investor earned an 11 percent total return denominated in Mexican currency, but only 3.34 percent denominated in dollars because the peso declined in value against the U.S. dollar. With the strengthening of the dollar, the pesos from the investment in WalMex buy less U.S. dollars when the investment is converted back from pesos, pushing down the 11 percent return a Mexican investor would earn to only 3.34 percent for a U.S. investor.

SUMMARY STATISTICS FOR RETURNS

The total return, return relative, and wealth index are useful measures of return for a specified period of time. Also needed in investment analysis are statistics to describe a series of returns. For example, investing in a particular stock for 10 years or a different stock in each of 10 years could result in 10 TRs, which must be described by one or more statistics. Two such measures used with returns data are described below.

Arithmetic Mean The best known statistic to most people is the arithmetic mean. Therefore, when someone refers to the *mean return* they usually are referring to the arithmetic mean unless otherwise specified. The arithmetic mean, customarily designated by the symbol $\overline{X}$ (X-bar), of a set of values is

$$\overline{X} = \frac{\Sigma X}{n} \tag{6-9}$$

or the sum of each of the values being considered divided by the total number of values n.

EXAMPLE 6-9

Based on data from Table 6-1 for the 9 years of the 1990s ending in 1998, the arithmetic mean is calculated in Table 6-2.

$$\overline{X} = [-3.135 + 30.001 + \cdots + 28.338]/9$$
$$= 166.761/9$$
$$= 18.529\%$$

Geometric Mean The arithmetic mean return is an appropriate measure of the central tendency of a distribution consisting of returns calculated for a particular time period, such as 10 years. However, when percentage changes in value over time are involved, as a result of compounding, the arithmetic mean of these changes can be misleading. A different mean, the geometric mean, is needed to describe accurately the "true" average rate of return over multiple periods.

TABLE 6-2 Calculation of the Arithmetic and Geometric Mean for the Years 1990–1998 for the S&P 500 Stock Composite Index

Year	S&P 500 TRs (%)	S&P 500 Return Relative
1990	−3.135	0.9687
1991	30.001	1.30001
1992	7.432	1.07432
1993	9.942	1.09942
1994	1.286	1.01286
1995	37.113	1.37113
1996	22.683	1.22683
1997	33.101	1.33101
1998	28.338	1.28338

Arithmetic Mean $= [-3.135 + 30.001 + \cdots + 28.338]/9$
$= 18.529\%$

Geometric Mean $= [(0.9687)(1.30001)(1.07432)(1.09942)(1.01286)$
$(1.37113)(1.22683)(1.33101)(1.28338)]^{1/9} - 1$
$= 1.1768 - 1$
$= .1768$, or 17.68%

The geometric mean return measures the compound rate of growth over time. It is often used in investments and finance to reflect the steady *growth rate* of invested funds over some past period; that is, the uniform rate at which money actually grew over time, per period. Therefore, it allows us to measure the realized change in wealth over multiple periods.

Geometric Mean The compound rate of return over time

The **geometric mean** is defined as the *n*th root of the product resulting from multiplying a series of return relatives together, as in Equation 6-10.[5]

$$G = [(1 + TR_1)(1 + TR_2) \cdots (1 + TR_n)]^{1/n} - 1 \quad (6\text{-}10)$$

where TR is a series of total returns in decimal form. Note that adding 1.0 to each total return produces a return relative. Return relatives are used in calculating geometric mean returns, because TRs, which can be negative, cannot be used.[6]

EXAMPLE 6-10

Continuing the example from Table 6-2, consisting of the 9 years of data ending in 1998 for the S&P 500, we find that the geometric mean would be as shown in Table 6-2:

$$G = [(0.9687)(1.30001)(1.07432)(1.09942)(1.01286)(1.37113)(1.22683)(1.33101)(1.28338)]^{1/9} - 1$$
$$= 1.1768 - 1 = .1768, \text{ or } 17.68\%$$

The geometric mean reflects compound, cumulative returns over more than one period. Thus, $1 invested in the S&P 500 Composite Index would have compounded at an average annual rate of 17.68 percent over the period January 1, 1990 through December 31, 1998

[5] Obviously, in most situations a calculator or computer is needed to calculate the geometric mean. Calculators with power functions can be used to calculate roots.

[6] An alternative method of calculating the geometric mean is to find the log of each return relative, sum them, divide by *n*, and take the antilog.

(nine years), producing a cumulative ending wealth of \$4.3284. Notice that this geometric average rate of return is lower than the arithmetic average rate of return of 18.529 percent because it reflects the variability of the returns.

The geometric mean will always be less than the arithmetic mean unless the values being considered are identical. The spread between the two depends on the dispersion of the distribution: the greater the dispersion, the greater the spread between the two means.

Arithmetic Mean Versus Geometric Mean When should we use the arithmetic mean and when should we use the geometric mean to describe the returns from financial assets? The answer depends on the investor's objective:

- The arithmetic mean is a better measure of average (typical) performance over single periods. It is the best estimate of the expected return for next period.
- The geometric mean is a better measure of the change in wealth over time (multiple periods). It measures the realized compound rate of return at which money grew over a specified period.

EXAMPLE 6-11

As an illustration of how the arithmetic mean can be misleading in describing returns over multiple periods, consider the data in Table 6-3, which show the movements in price for two stocks over two successive holding periods. Both stocks have a beginning price of \$10. Stock A rises to \$20 in period 1 and then declines to \$10 in period 2. Stock B falls to \$8 in period 1 and then rises 50 percent to \$12 in period 2. For stock A, the indicated annual average arithmetic rate of change in price is 25 percent. This is clearly not sensible, because the price of stock A at the end of period 2 is \$10, the same as the beginning price. The geometric mean calculation gives the correct annual average rate of change in price of 0 percent per year.

For stock B, the arithmetic average of the annual percentage changes in price is 15 percent. However, if the price actually increased 15 percent each period, the ending price in period 2 would be \$10 (1.15) (1.15) = \$13.23. We know that this is not correct, because the price at the end of period 2 is \$12. The annual geometric rate of return, 9.54 percent, produces the correct price at the end of period 2: \$10 (1.0954)(1.0954) = \$12.

As this simple example demonstrates, over multiple periods the geometric mean shows the true average compound rate of growth that actually occurred—that is, the rate at which an invested dollar has grown. On the other hand, we should use the arithmetic mean to represent the likely or typical performance for a single period. Consider the TR data for the S&P Index for the years 1990–1998 as described earlier. Our best representation of any one year's performance would be the arithmetic mean of 18.529 percent because it was necessary to average this rate of return for a particular year, given the wide spread in the yearly numbers, in order to realize an actual growth rate of 17.68 percent after the fact.

TABLE 6-3 Contrasting the Arithmetic and Geometric Means

Stock	Period 1	Period 2	Annual Arithmetic Rate of Return	Annual Geometric Rate of Return
A	\$20	\$10	[100% + (−50%)]/2 = 25%	$[2.0(0.5)]^{1/2} - 1 = 0\%$
B	\$ 8	\$12	[−20% + (50%)]/2 = 15%	$[.8(1.5)]^{1/2} - 1 = 9.54\%$

EXAMPLE 6-12

Assume that the returns for two consecutive years for a particular stock were 16.76 percent and −2.0 percent. The arithmetic mean return for these two years would be exactly 7.38 percent; however, $1 invested at these rates of return would have grown to $1 × 1.1676 × 0.98 = $1.1442, a geometric mean rate of return of only 6.97 percent. Based only on these two observations, our best estimate of the average return for next year would be 7.38 percent, not 6.97 percent.

INFLATION-ADJUSTED RETURNS

All of the returns discussed above are *nominal returns*, or money returns. They measure dollar amounts or changes but say nothing about the purchasing power of these dollars. To capture this dimension, we need to consider *real returns*, or inflation-adjusted returns.

To calculate inflation-adjusted returns, we divide 1 + nominal total return by 1 + the inflation rate as shown in Equation 6-11. This calculation is sometimes simplified by subtracting rather than dividing, producing a close approximation.

$$TR_{IA} = \frac{(1 + TR)}{(1 + IF)} - 1 \qquad (6\text{-}11)$$

where

TR_{IA} = the inflation-adjusted total return
IF = the rate of inflation

This equation applies to both individual years and average total returns.

EXAMPLE 6-13

The total return for the S&P 500 Composite in 1998 was 28.5731 percent (assuming monthly reinvestment of dividends). The rate of inflation was 1.6119 percent. Therefore, the real (inflation-adjusted) total return for large common stocks in 1998 was:

1.285731/1.016119 = 1.265335

1.265335 − 1.0 = .265335 or 26.5335%

Now consider the entire period 1920–1998. The geometric mean for the S&P 500 Composite for the entire period was 10.98 percent, and for inflation, 2.62 percent. Therefore, the real (inflation-adjusted) geometric mean rate of return for large common stocks for the period 1920–1998 was:

1.1098/1.0262 = 1.0815

1.0815 − 1.0 = .0815 or 8.15%

The Consumer Price Index (CPI) typically is used as the measure of inflation. The resulting total returns are in real or constant purchasing-power terms.

The compound annual rate of inflation over the period 1920–1998 was 2.6154 percent. This means that a basket of consumer goods purchased at the beginning of 1920 would cost approximately $7.6876 at year-end 1998. This is calculated as $(1.026154)^{79}$ because there are 79 years from December 1919 (the beginning of 1920) and the end of 1998.[7]

[7] To determine the number of years in a series such as this, subtract the beginning year from the ending year and add 1.0. For example, 1998 − 1920 = 78, and we add 1.0 to account for the fact that 1920 is a full year of data.

MEASURING RISK

Risk is often associated with the dispersion in the likely outcomes. Dispersion refers to variability. Risk is assumed to arise out of variability, which is consistent with our definition of risk as the chance that the actual outcome of an investment will differ from the expected outcome. If an asset's return has no variability, in effect it has no risk. Thus, a one-year Treasury bill purchased to yield 10 percent and held to maturity will, in fact, yield (a nominal) 10 percent. No other outcome is possible, barring default by the U.S. government, which is not considered a reasonable possibility.

Consider an investor analyzing a series of returns (TRs) for the major types of financial assets over some period of years. Knowing the mean of this series is not enough; the investor also needs to know something about the variability in the returns. Relative to the other assets, common stocks show the largest variability (dispersion) in returns, with small common stocks showing even greater variability. Corporate bonds have a much smaller variability and therefore a more compact distribution of returns. Of course, Treasury bills are the least risky. The dispersion of annual returns for bills is compact.

In order to appreciate the range of outcomes for major financial asset classes, consider Figure 6-1. It shows the range of outcomes, and the mean (given by the circle) for each of the following asset classes for the period December 1919 through December 1998, in order from left to right: large common stocks (S&P 500 Composite Index), smaller common stocks (bottom 20 percent of NYSE), Treasury bonds, Aaa corporate bonds, Treasury bills, and inflation.

As we can see from Figure 6-1, stocks have a much wider range of outcomes than do bonds and bills. Smaller common stocks have a wider range of outcomes than do large common stocks. Given this variability, investors must be able to measure it as a proxy for risk. They often do so using the standard deviation.

STANDARD DEVIATION

Standard Deviation A measure of the dispersion in outcomes around the expected value

The risk of distributions can be measured with an absolute measure of dispersion, or variability. The most commonly used measure of dispersion over some period of years is the **standard deviation**, which measures the deviation of each observation from the arithmetic mean of the observations and is a reliable measure of variability because all the information in a sample is used.[8]

FIGURE 6-1

Graph of spread in returns over the period 1920–1998 for major asset classes

SOURCE: Based on data calculated by Jack Wilson and Charles P. Jones, North Carolina State University.

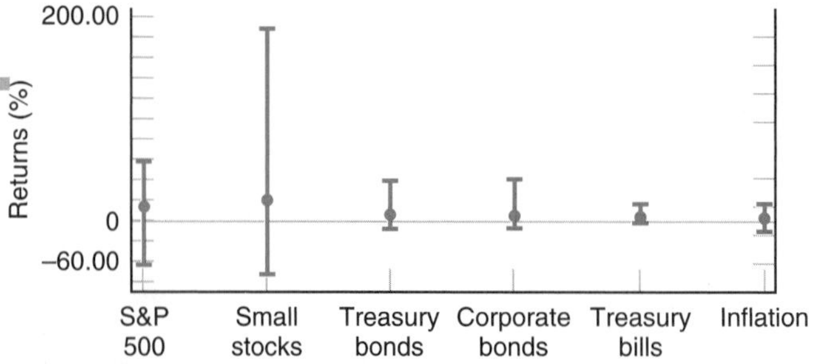

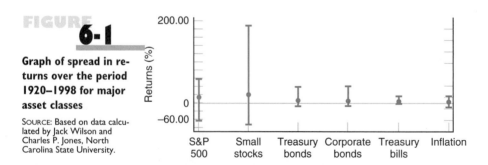

[8] The variance is the standard deviation squared. The variance and the standard deviation are similar and can be used for the same purposes; specifically, in investment analysis, both are used as measures of risk. The standard deviation, however, is used more often.

The standard deviation is a measure of the total risk of an asset or a portfolio. It captures the total variability in the asset's or portfolio's return, whatever the source(s) of that variability. The standard deviation can be calculated from the variance, which is calculated as:

$$\sigma^2 = \frac{\sum_{i=1}^{n}(X - \overline{X})^2}{n - 1} \tag{6-12}$$

where

σ^2 = the variance of a set of values
X = each value in the set
$\overline{X}$ = the mean of the observations
n = the number of returns in the sample
σ = $(\sigma^2)^{1/2}$ = standard deviation

Knowing the returns from the sample, we can calculate the standard deviation fairly easily.

EXAMPLE 6-14

The standard deviation of the 10 TRs for the decade of the 1970s, 1970–1979, for the Standard & Poor's 500 Index can be calculated as shown in Table 6-4.

In summary, the standard deviation of return measures the total risk of one security or the total risk of a portfolio of securities. The historical standard deviation can be calculated for individual securities or portfolios of securities using TRs for some specified period of time. This *ex post* value is useful in evaluating the total risk for a particular historical period and in estimating the total risk that is expected to prevail over some future period.

The standard deviation, combined with the normal distribution, can provide some useful information about the dispersion or variation in returns. For a *normal distribution*, the probability that a particular outcome will be above (or below) a specified value can be determined. With one standard deviation on either side of the arithmetic mean of the distribution,

TABLE 6-4 Calculating the Historical Standard Deviation for the Period 1970–1979

Year	TR (%), X	$X - \overline{X}$	$(X - \overline{X})^2$
1970	3.51	− 3.87	14.98
1971	14.12	6.74	45.43
1972	18.72	11.34	128.6
1973	−14.50	−21.88	478.73
1974	−26.03	33.41	1116.23
1975	36.92	29.54	872.61
1976	23.64	16.26	264.39
1977	− 7.16	14.54	211.41
1978	6.39	− .99	.98
1979	18.19	10.81	116.86
	$\overline{X}$ = 7.38	$\Sigma(X - \overline{X})^2$ =	3250.22

$$\sigma^2 = \frac{3250.22}{9} = 361.14$$

$$\sigma = (361.14)^{1/2} = 19.00\%$$

68.3 percent of the outcomes will be encompassed; that is, there is a 68.3 percent probability that the actual outcome will be within one (plus or minus) standard deviation of the arithmetic mean. The probabilities are 95 percent and 99 percent that the actual outcome will be within two or three standard deviations, respectively, of the arithmetic mean.

RISK PREMIUMS

Risk Premium The additional compensation for assuming risk

Equity Risk Premium The difference between stocks and the risk-free rate

A **risk premium** is the additional return investors expect to receive, or did receive, by taking on increasing amounts of risk. It measures the payoff for taking various types of risk. Such premiums can be calculated between any two classes of securities.

An often-discussed risk premium is the **equity risk premium**, defined as the difference between stocks and a risk-free rate (proxied by the return on Treasury bills). In order to maintain consistency with our other series, risk premiums are measured as the geometric differences between pairs of return series. Therefore:

$$ERP = \frac{(1 + TR_{CS})}{(1 + RF)} - 1 \tag{6-13}$$

where

ERP = the equity risk premium

TR_{CS} = the total return on stocks

RF = the risk-free rate (the Treasury bill rate)

Other risk premiums can also be calculated. For example, the *bond default premium* is measured by the difference between the return on long-term corporate bonds and the return on long-term government bonds. This premium reflects the additional compensation for investing in risky corporate bonds, which have some probability of default, rather than government bonds, which do not.

REALIZED RETURNS AND RISKS FROM INVESTING

We are now in a position to examine the returns and risks from investing in major financial assets that have occurred in the United States. We also will see how the preceding return and risk measures are typically used in presenting realized return and risk data of interest to virtually all financial market participants.

Table 6-5 shows the average annual geometric and arithmetic returns, as well as standard deviations, for major financial assets for the period December 1919–December 1998 (79 years). Included are both nominal returns and real returns.

These data are comparable to those produced and distributed by Ibbotson Associates on a regular basis. The Ibbotson data are widely known, used, and quoted. We report these data because:

- We have good data going back earlier than the starting point for Ibbotson Associates, which is 1926.
- We think that the S&P 500 Composite can be calculated more accurately between 1920 and 1957 than is typically done based on a painstaking reconstruction of the data.
- We have an improved series for inflation rates.

TABLE 6-5 Summary Statistics of Annual Total Returns for Major Financial Assets, December 1919 through December 1998, Nominal and Inflation-Adjusted

Nominal Returns	Arithmetic Mean	Geometric Mean	Standard Deviation
S&P Composite	12.8173%	10.9758%	20.7143%
Small Stocks*	18.8794	12.7711	39.5357
Aaa Corporates	6.2699	5.9456	8.0742
Treasury Bonds	5.6040	5.4636	8.1427
Treasury Bills	4.0772	4.0260	3.1929
Inflation	2.7179	2.6154	4.6179
Inflation-Adjusted Returns	**Arithmetic Mean**	**Geometric Mean**	**Standard Deviation**
S&P Composite	9.9852%	8.1473%	20.8192%
Small Stocks	15.4582	9.5466	39.3171
Aaa Corporates	3.7114	3.2454	9.9575
Treasury Bonds	3.0578	2.5907	9.9618
Treasury Bills	1.4840	1.3746	4.7907

*Small Stocks are for the period 1926–1998, and show capital appreciation only. There is no reliable dividend series available for small stocks.

SOURCE: Jack W. Wilson and Charles P. Jones, North Carolina State University.

The Ibbotson Associates data is a very fine compilation of asset returns that most investors use. This is simply an alternative series reconstructed by Jack Wilson and Charles Jones that provides basically the same information for a slightly longer time period.

TOTAL RETURNS AND STANDARD DEVIATIONS

Table 6-5 indicates that common stocks, as measured by the well-known Standard & Poor's 500 Composite Index, had a geometric mean annual return over this 79-year period of 10.98 percent (rounded). Hence, $1 invested in the market index at the beginning of 1920 would have grown at an average annual compound rate of 10.98 percent over this very long period. In contrast, the arithmetic mean annual return for stocks was 12.82 percent. The best estimate of the "average" return for stocks in any one year, using only this information, would be 12.82 percent, not the 10.98 percent geometric mean return.

The difference between these two means is related to the variability of the stock return series. Given the data in Table 6-5, the linkage between the geometric mean and the arithmetic mean is approximated by Equation 6-14:

$$(1 + G)^2 \approx (1 + A.M.)^2 - (S.D.)^2 \tag{6-14}$$

where

G = the geometric mean of a series of asset returns
A.M. = the arithmetic mean of a series of asset returns
S.D. = the standard deviation of the arithmetic series of returns

EXAMPLE 6-15

Using the data in Table 6-5 for common stocks:

$$(1.1098)^2 \approx (1.1282)^2 - (0.207)^2$$
$$1.2317 \approx 1.2728 - 0.0428$$
$$1.2317 \approx 1.2300$$

Thus, if we know the arithmetic mean of a series of asset returns and the standard deviation of the series, we can approximate the geometric mean for this series. As the standard deviation of the series increases, holding the arithmetic mean constant, the geometric mean decreases.

Table 6-5 also shows that small company stocks (primarily, the smallest 20 percent of NYSE stocks according to market value) had a geometric mean return of 12.77 percent and an arithmetic mean of 18.88 percent, the highest numbers recorded in this data set (for the years 1926–1998). The spread between these two numbers reflects the even greater variability of this series—with such a large standard deviation, the geometric mean will be significantly smaller than the arithmetic mean.

Corporate and Treasury bonds had geometric means that were roughly half that of the S&P 500 Composite Index, but the risk was considerably smaller. Standard deviations for the bond series were only about 40 percent as large as that for the S&P 500 Composite.[9]

Finally, as we would expect, Treasury bills had the smallest returns of any of the major assets shown in Table 6-5, as well as the smallest risk (as measured used annual returns).

The deviations for each of the major financial assets in Table 6-5 reflect the dispersion of the returns over the 79-year period covered in the data. The standard deviations clearly show the wide dispersion in the returns from common stocks compared with bonds and Treasury bills. Furthermore, smaller common stocks can logically be expected to be riskier than the S&P 500 stocks, and the standard deviation indicates a much wider dispersion.

CUMULATIVE WEALTH INDEXES

Figure 6-2 shows the cumulative wealth indexes for the major financial assets and the corresponding index number for inflation from the data in Table 6-5. The series starts at the end

FIGURE 6-2

Wealth indices of investments in U.S. stocks, bonds, bills, and inflation: 1920–1998

SOURCE: Based on data calculated by Jack Wilson and Charles P. Jones, North Carolina State University.

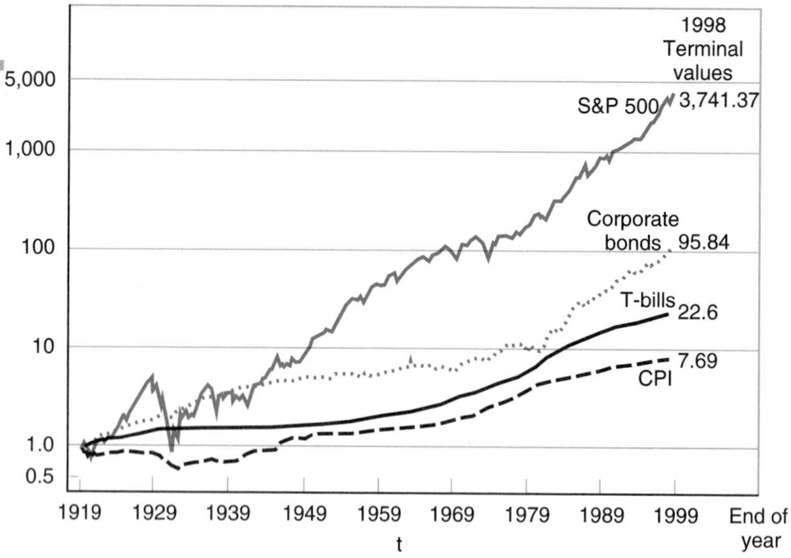

[9] The reason for the distribution of Treasury bonds and Treasury bills, which have no practical risk of default, is that this is a distribution of annual returns, where negative numbers are possible. Thus, a Treasury bond purchased at $1,000 on January 1 could decline to, say, $900 by December 31, resulting in a negative TR.

[10] A logarithmic scale greatly facilitates comparisons of different series across time because the same vertical distance represents the same percentage change in a particular series return. The logarithmic scale allows the user to concentrate on rates of return and ignore the dollar amounts involved.

of 1919 and shows the cumulative results of starting with $1 in each of these series and going through the end of 1998. Note that the vertical axis of Figure 6-2 is a log scale.[10]

As Figure 6-2 shows, the cumulative wealth on stocks, as measured by the S&P 500 Composite Index, completely dominated the returns on corporate bonds over this period—$3,741.37 versus $95.84. Note that we use the geometric mean from Table 6-5 to calculate cumulative ending wealth for each of the series shown in Figure 6-2.

EXAMPLE 6-16

The ending wealth value of $3,741.37 for common stocks in Figure 6-2 is the result of compounding at 10.9758 percent for 79 years, or

$$CWI_{1998} = WI_0(1.109758)^{79} = \$1.00(3{,}741.40) = \$3{,}741.40$$

(difference caused by rounding error)

The large cumulative wealth index value for stocks as shown in Figure 6-2 speaks for itself. Remember, however, that the variability of this series is considerably larger, as shown by the standard deviations in Table 6-5.

Inflation-Adjusted Cumulative Wealth On an inflation-adjusted basis, the cumulative ending wealth for any of the series can be calculated as

$$CWI_{IA} = \frac{CWI}{CI_{INF}} \tag{6-15}$$

where

CWI_{IA} = the cumulative wealth index value for any asset on inflation-adjusted basis
CWI = the cumulative wealth index value for any asset on a nominal basis
CI_{INF} = the ending index value for inflation, calculated as (1 + geometric rate of inflation)^n, where n is the number of periods considered

EXAMPLE 6-17

For the period 1920–1998 the cumulative wealth index for the S&P 500 Composite was $3,741.40. Inflation had a total index value of 7.6876. Therefore, the real cumulative wealth index, or inflation-adjusted cumulative wealth for the period 1920–1998, was:

$$\$3{,}741.40/7.6876 = \$486.68$$

Alternatively, we can calculate real cumulative wealth by raising the geometric mean for inflation-adjusted returns to the appropriate power:

$$(1.081473)^{79} = \$486.67$$

The Components of Cumulative Wealth The cumulative wealth index is equivalent to a cumulative total return index and, as such, can be decomposed into the two components of total return, the yield component and the price change component. Because the

CWI is a multiplicative relationship, these two components are multiplicative. To solve for either one, we divide the CWI by the other, as in Equation 6-16.

$$\text{CPC} = \frac{\text{CWI}}{\text{CYI}} \tag{6-16}$$

$$\text{CYI} = \frac{\text{CWI}}{\text{CPC}} \tag{6-17}$$

where

CPC = the cumulative price change component of total return on an index number basis
CWI = the cumulative wealth index or total return index for a series
CYI = the cumulative yield component of total return on an index number basis

EXAMPLE 6-18

The CWI for common stocks (S&P 500) for 1920–1998 was $3,741.37. The cumulative price change index for common stocks was $118.77, which represents a geometric average annual return of

$$(\$118.77)^{1/79} - 1.0 = 1.0623$$
$$= 0.0623 \text{ or } 6.23\%$$

The CYI for common stocks, therefore, is

$$\text{CYI} = \$3741.37/\$118.77$$
$$= \$31.50$$

The compound annual average rate of return for the yield component of total return is

$$(\$31.50)^{1/79} - 1.0 = 1.0446 - 1.0$$
$$= 4.446\%$$

Note that the annual average geometric mean return relative for common stocks is the product of the corresponding geometric mean return relatives for the two components:

$$\begin{aligned} G_{TR} &= G_{CY} \times G_{PC} \\ 1.10975 &= (1.0623)(1.0446) \end{aligned} \tag{6-18}$$

Compounding and Discounting Of course, the single most striking feature of Figure 6-2 is the tremendous difference in ending wealth between stocks and bonds. This difference reflects the impact of compounding substantially different mean returns over long periods of time, which produces almost unbelievable results. The use of compounding points out the importance of this concept and of its complement, discounting. Both are important in investment analysis and are used often. *Compounding* involves future value resulting from compound interest—earning interest on interest. As we saw, the calculation of wealth indexes involves compounding at the geometric mean return over some historical period.

Present value (discounting) is the value today of a dollar to be received in the future. Such dollars are not comparable, because of the time value of money. In order to be comparable, they must be discounted back to the present. Present value concepts are used extensively in Chapters 8 and 10 and in other chapters as needed.

Tables are readily available for both compounding and discounting, and calculators and computers make these calculations a simple matter. These tables are available at the end of this text.

SUMMARY

- Return and risk go together in investments; indeed, these two parameters are the underlying basis of the subject. Everything an investor does, or is concerned with, is tied directly or indirectly to return and risk.
- The term *return* can be used in different ways. It is important to distinguish between realized (ex post, or historical) return and expected (ex ante, or anticipated) return.
- The two components of return are yield and price change (capital gain or loss).
- The total return is a percentage return concept that can be used to correctly measure the return for any security.
- The return relative, which adds 1.0 to the total return, is used when calculating the geometric mean of a series of returns.
- The cumulative wealth index (total return index) is used to measure the cumulative wealth over time given some initial starting wealth—typically, $1—and a series of returns for some asset.
- Return relatives, along with the beginning and ending values of the foreign currency, can be used to convert the return on a foreign investment into a domestic return.
- The geometric mean measures the compound rate of return over time. The arithmetic mean, on the other hand, is simply the average return for a series and is used to measure the typical performance for a single period.
- Inflation-adjusted returns can be calculated by dividing 1 + the nominal return by 1 + the inflation rate as measured by the CPI.
- Risk is the other side of the coin: risk and expected return should always be considered together. An investor cannot reasonably expect to earn large returns without assuming greater risks.
- The general components of risk have traditionally been categorized into interest rate, market, inflation, business, financial, and liquidity risks. Investors today must also consider exchange rate risk and country risk. Each security has its own sources of risk, which we will discuss when we discuss the security itself.
- Historical returns can be described in terms of a frequency distribution and their variability measured by use of the standard deviation.
- The standard deviation provides useful information about the distribution of returns and aids investors in assessing the possible outcomes of an investment.
- Common stocks over the period 1920–1998 had an annualized geometric mean total return of 10.98 percent, compared to roughly half that for long-term bonds.
- Over the period 1920–1998, common stocks had a standard deviation of returns of 20.7 percent, about two and one-half times that of long-term government and corporate bonds and over six times that of Treasury bills.

KEY WORDS

Capital gain (loss)
Cumulative wealth index
Equity risk premium
Exchange rate risk
Geometric mean
Interest rate risk
Market risk
Nonsystematic (nonmarket) risk
Return relative
Risk premium
Standard deviation
Systematic (market) risk
Total return (TR)
Yield

QUESTIONS

6-1. Distinguish between historical return and expected return.

6-2. How long must an asset be held to calculate a TR?

6-3. Define the components of total return. Can any of these components be negative?

6-4. Distinguish between TR and holding period return.

6-5. When should the geometric mean return be used to measure returns? Why will it always be less than the arithmetic mean (unless the numbers are identical)?

6-6. When should the arithmetic mean be used in talking about stock returns?

6-7. What is the mathematical linkage between the arithmetic mean and the geometric mean for a set of security returns?

6-8. What is an equity risk premium?

6-9. According to Table 6-5, common stocks have generally returned more than bonds. How, then, can they be considered more risky?

6-10. Distinguish between market risk and business risk. How is interest rate risk related to inflation risk?

6-11. Classify the traditional sources of risk as to whether they are general sources of risk or specific sources of risk.

6-12. Explain what is meant by country risk. How would you evaluate the country risk of Canada and Mexico?

6-13. Assume that you purchase a stock on a Japanese market, denominated in yen. During the period you hold the stock, the yen weakens relative to the dollar. Assume you sell at a profit on the Japanese market. How will your return, when converted to dollars, be affected?

6-14. Define risk. How does use of the standard deviation as a measure of risk relate to this definition of risk?

6-15. Explain verbally the relationship between the geometric mean and a cumulative wealth index.

6-16. As Table 6-5 shows, the geometric mean return for stocks over a 79-year period has been around 11 percent. The returns on corporate bonds for some recent years have averaged approximately this rate, leading some to recommend that investors avoid stocks and purchase bonds because the returns are similar (or even better on bonds) and the risk is far less. Critique this argument.

6-17. Explain how the geometric mean annual average inflation rate can be used to calculate inflation-adjusted stock returns over the period December 1919–December 1998.

6-18. Explain the two components of the cumulative wealth index for common stocks. If we know one of these components on a cumulative wealth basis, how can the other be calculated?

6-19. Common stocks have returned slightly less than twice the compound annual rate of return for corporate bonds. Does this mean that common stocks are about twice as risky as corporates?

6-20. What does it mean if the cumulative wealth index for government bonds over a long period is 0.85?

The following question was asked on the 1990 CFA Level I examination:

6-21. Fundamental to investing is the control of investment risk while maximizing total investment return. **Identify** *four* primary *sources* of risk faced by investors, and **explain** the possible impact on investment returns.

DEMONSTRATION PROBLEMS

6-1. CALCULATION OF ARITHMETIC MEAN AND GEOMETRIC MEAN:

IBM DATA

Year(t)	(1) End-of-Year Price (P_t)	(2) Calendar-Year Dividends (D_t)	TR%
19X0	$ 74.60	$2.88	—
19X1	64.30	3.44	− 9.2%
19X2	67.70	3.44	10.6
19X3	56.70	3.44	−11.2
19X4	96.25	3.44	75.8
19X5	122.00	3.71	30.6

The arithmetic mean of the total returns for IBM, 19X1–19X5:

$$\frac{\Sigma(\text{TR\%})}{n} = \frac{96.6}{5} = 19.32\%$$

The *geometric* mean in this example is the fifth root of the product of the $(1 + r)$ version of the TR percent. We formed the TR percent by multiplying the decimal by 100 to get r percent. Now back up to the $(1 + r)$:

Year	TR% = r%	r	$(1 + r)$
19X1	− 9.2%	−0.092	0.908
19X2	10.6	0.106	1.106
19X3	−11.2	−0.112	0.888
19X4	75.8	0.758	1.758
19X5	−30.6	0.306	1.306

The geometric mean is $\text{GM} = [(1 + r_1)(1 + r_2) \cdots (1 + r_n)]^{1/n} - 1$. Therefore, take the fifth root of the product

$(0.908)(1.106)(0.888)(1.758)(1.306) = 2.047462654$, and

$(2.047462654)^{1/5} = 1.1541 = (1 + r)$, $r = 0.1541$, $r\% = 100r = 15.41\%$

6-2. **THE EFFECTS OF REINVESTING RETURNS:** The difference in meaning of the arithmetic and geometric mean, holding IBM stock over the period January 1, 19X1 through December 31, 19X5 for two different investment strategies, is as follows:

Strategy A—keep a fixed amount (say, \$1,000) invested and do *not* reinvest returns.
Strategy B—reinvest returns and allow compounding.

First, take IBM's TRs and convert them to decimal form (r) for Strategy A, and then to $(1 + r)$ form for Strategy B.

Strategy A				Strategy B			
Jan. 1 Year	Amount Invested	× r_i	= Return	Jan. 1 Year	Amt. Inv.	× $(1 + r_t)$	= Terminal Amt.
19X1	\$1000	−0.092	−\$92.00	19X1	\$1000	0.908	\$908.00
19X2	1000	0.106	106.00	19X2	908.00	1.106	1004.25
19X3	1000	−0.112	−112.00	19X3	1004.25	0.888	891.77
19X4	1000	0.758	758.00	19X4	891.77	1.758	1567.74
19X5	1000	0.306	306.00	19X5	1567.74	1.306	2047.46
19X6	1000			19X6	2047.46		

Using Strategy A, keeping \$1,000 invested at the beginning of the year, total returns for the years 19X1–19X5 were \$966, or \$193.20 per year average (\$966/5), which on a \$1,000 investment is \$193.20/1000 = 0.1932, or 19.32 percent per year—the same value as the arithmetic mean in Demonstration Problem 6-1 earlier.

Using Strategy B, compounding gains and losses, total return was \$1,047.46 (the terminal amount \$2,047.46 minus the initial \$1,000). The average annual rate of return in this situation can be found by taking the nth root of the terminal/initial amount:

$$[2047.46/1000]^{1/5} = (2.04746)^{1/5} = 1.1541 = (1 + r),\ r\% = 15.41\%$$

which is exactly the set of values we ended up with in Demonstration Problem 6-1 when calculating the geometric mean.

6-3. **CALCULATING THE STANDARD DEVIATION:** Using the TR values for IBM for the five years 19X1–19X5, we can illustrate the deviation of the values from the mean ($\bar{Y}$) graphically:

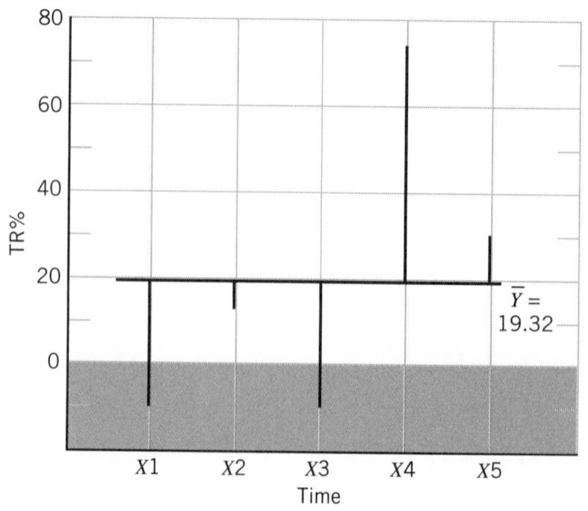

The numerator for the formula for the variance of these Y_t values is $\Sigma(Y_t - \bar{Y})^2$ which we will call SS_y, the sum of the squared deviations of the Y_t around $\bar{Y}$. Algebraically, there is a simpler alternative formula.

$$SS_y = \Sigma(Y_t - \bar{Y})^2 = \Sigma Y_t^2 - \frac{(\Sigma Y_t)^2}{n}$$

Using IBM's annual total returns, we will calculate the SS_y both ways.

Year	Y_t = TR	$(Y_t - \bar{Y})$	$(Y_t - \bar{Y})^2$	Y_t^2
19X1	− 9.2%	28.52	813.3904	84.64
19X2	10.6	− 8.72	76.0384	112.36
19X3	−11.2	−30.52	931.4704	125.44
19X4	75.8	56.48	3189.9904	5745.64
19X5	30.6	11.28	127.2384	936.36
Sum	96.6	-0-	5138.1280	7004.44

$\bar{Y} = 19.32\%$

$SS_y = \Sigma(Y_t - \bar{Y})^2 = 5138.128$, and also

$$SS_y = \Sigma Y^2 - \frac{(\Sigma Y)^2}{n} = 7004.44 - \frac{(96.6)^2}{5} = 5138.128$$

The variance is the "average" squared deviation from the mean:

$$s^2 = \frac{SS_y}{(n-1)} = \frac{5138.128}{4} = 1284.532 \text{ "squared percent"}$$

The standard deviation is the square root of the variance:

$$s = (s^2)^{1/2} = (1284.532)^{1/2} = 35.84\%$$

The standard deviation is in the same units of measurement as the original observations, as is the arithmetic mean.

6-4. **CALCULATION OF CUMULATIVE WEALTH INDEX AND GEOMETRIC MEAN:** By using the geometric mean annual average rate of return for a particular financial asset, the cumulative wealth index can be found by converting the TR on a geometric mean basis to a return relative by adding 1.0, and raising this return relative to the power representing the number of years involved. Consider the geometric mean of 12.8 percent for small common stocks for the period December 1925–December 1998. The cumulative wealth index, using a starting index value of \$1, is

$$\$1(1.128)^{73} = \$6585.13$$

Conversely, if we know the cumulative wealth index value, we can solve for the geometric mean by taking the nth root and subtracting out 1.0.

$$(\$6585.13)^{1/73} - 1.0 = 1.128 - 1.0 = 12.8\%$$

6-5. **CALCULATION OF INFLATION-ADJUSTED RETURNS:** Knowing the geometric mean for inflation for some time period, we can add 1.0 and raise it to the nth power. We then divide the cumulative wealth index on a nominal basis by the ending value for inflation to obtain inflation-adjusted returns. For example, given a cumulative wealth index of \$3,741.37 for common stocks for December 1919–December 1998, and a geometric mean inflation rate of 2.62 percent, the inflation-adjusted cumulative wealth index for this 79-year period is calculated as

$$\$3741.37/(1.0262)^{79} = \$3741.37/7.715 = \$484.95$$

6-6. **ANALYZING THE COMPONENTS OF A CUMULATIVE WEALTH INDEX:** Assume that we know that for the period December 1919–December 1998 the yield component for common stocks was 4.46 percent, and that the cumulative wealth index was \$3,741.37. The cumulative wealth index value for the yield component was

$$(1.0446)^{79} = 31.50$$

The cumulative wealth index value for the price change component was

$$\$3,741.37/31.50 = 118.77$$

The geometric mean annual average rate of return for the price change component for common stocks was

$$(118.77)^{1/79} = 1.0623$$

The geometric mean for common stocks is linked to its components by the following

$$1.0446\ (1.0623) = 1.1097$$

The cumulative wealth index can be found by multiplying together the individual component cumulative wealth indexes

$$\$118.77\ (\$31.50) = \$3,741.37$$

PROBLEMS

6-1. Using the data for IBM from Demonstration Problem 6-1, calculate the capital gain (loss) and total return for the years 19X1–19X5 and confirm the 19X3 and 19X4 TRs.

6-2. Assume that an investor in a 28 percent marginal tax bracket buys 100 shares of a stock for \$40, holds it for five months, and sells it at \$50. What tax, in dollars, will be paid on the gain?

6-3. Calculate the TR and the return relative for the following assets:

a. A preferred stock bought for \$70 per share, held one year during which \$5 per share dividends are collected, and sold for \$63.

b. A warrant bought for \$11 and sold three months later for \$13.

c. A 12 percent bond bought for \$870, held two years during which interest is collected, and sold for \$930.

6-4. Calculate the future value of \$100 at the end of 5, 10, 20, and 30 years, given an interest rate of 12 percent. Calculate the present value of \$1 to be received at the end of those same periods, given the same interest rate.

6-5. Calculate, using a calculator, the arithmetic and geometric mean rate of return for the Standard & Poor 500 Composite Index (Table 6-1) for the years 1980–1985.

6-6. Calculate, using a calculator, the standard deviation of TRs (from Table 6-1) for the years 1980 through 1985.

6-7. Calculate the index value for the S&P 500 (Table 6-1) assuming a \$1 investment at the beginning of 1980 and extending through the end of 1989. Using only these index values, calculate the geometric mean for these years.

6-8. Calculate cumulative wealth for common stocks for the period December 1919 through December 1998, assuming the geometric mean was 10.98 percent.

6-9. Calculate cumulative wealth for corporate bonds for the period 1920–1998, using data in Table 6-5 (79 years).

6-10. Calculate the cumulative wealth index for government bonds for the period 1926–1993, assuming a geometric mean annual average rate of return of 5 percent.

6-11. Given a cumulative wealth index for corporate bonds of $95.84 for the period 1920–1998, calculate the geometric mean annual average rate of return.

6-12. Given an inflation rate of 3.00 percent over the period 1926–1998 (geometric mean annual average), calculate the inflation-adjusted cumulative wealth index for "small" common stocks as of year-end 1998, assuming that the nominal cumulative wealth index for this asset class was $13,293.14.

6-13. If a basket of consumer goods cost $1 at the end of 1925 and $9 at the end of 1999, calculate the geometric mean annual average rate of inflation over this period.

6-14. Assume that over the period December 1919–December 1998 the yield index component of common stocks had a geometric mean annual average of 1.0446. Calculate the cumulative wealth index for this component as of year-end 1998. Using this value, calculate the cumulative wealth index for the price change component of common stocks using information in Figure 6-2.

6-15. Assume that the yield component of the total return for small common stocks was 1 percent (geometric mean) for the period December 1919–December 1998. Also assume that the cumulative wealth index for the price change component for this series was $6056.65. Calculate the cumulative wealth index for small common stocks for this period.

6-16. Assume that over the period December 1919–December 1998 the geometric mean annual average rate of return for government bonds was 5.46 percent. The corresponding number for the rate of inflation was 2.62 percent. Calculate, two different ways, the cumulative wealth index for government bonds for 1998, on an inflation-adjusted basis.

6-17. Using the TRs for the years 1926–1931 from Table 6-1, determine the geometric mean for this period. Show how the same result can be obtained from the ending wealth index value for 1931 of 0.79591.

6-18. Using data for three periods, construct a set of TRs that will produce a geometric mean equal to the arithmetic mean.

6-19. According to Table 6-5, the standard deviation for all common stocks for the period 1920–1998 was 20.71 percent. Using data from Table 6-1, calculate the standard deviation for the years 1981–1991 and compare your results.

6-20. Verify that the standard deviation calculated in Table 6-4 is correct. Change the 1975 TR from 36.92 to 26.92 and recalculate the standard deviation. What happened, and why?

Questions 6-21 through 6-32 are part of a comprehensive problem set using the information on rates of return for the period December, 1919 through December 1998 as given below:

	Geometric Mean	Arithmetic Mean	Std. Dev.
Common stocks	11 %	12.8%	20.7%
Small company stocks	12.8	18.9	39.5
Long-term corporates	5.9	6.3	8.1
Long-term governments	5.5	5.6	8.1
Treasury bills	4.0	4.1	3.2
Inflation	2.6	2.7	4.6

6-21. Calculate the cumulative wealth index from an investment of $1 in common stocks at the end of 1919. There are 79 years involved.

6-22. Compare this with the corresponding ending wealth for long-term corporates.

6-23. Calculate the cumulative wealth index from an investment of $1 in small common stocks at the end of 1925. How do you explain the large difference in ending wealth between common stocks (the S&P 500) and small common stocks given only the roughly 2 percentage point difference in the geometric means?

6-24. According to the data, the capital appreciation index for common stocks amounted to 118.78 by the end of 1998. Explain what this number means relative to
a. the beginning point at the end of 1919.
b. the cumulative index for common stocks of 3741.37.

6-25. Given the cumulative wealth index of 3741.37 and the capital appreciation index of 118.78:
a. What is the other component of total return for common stocks?
b. Calculate both the ending wealth index and the geometric mean annual rate of return for this component.
c. What do the two components of total return on an annual average basis imply about the relative importance of each?

6-26. Assume that the wealth index for common stocks was 675.592 for 1991 and 517.449 for 1990. What was the annual rate of return for common stocks for 1991?

6-27. Assume that for long-term governments, the capital appreciation index was 0.87 for the entire period.
a. Calculate the cumulative wealth index for long-term governments based on the table above.
b. Calculate the geometric mean annual average rate of return for the capital appreciation component.
c. What does this say about the income component of total return for long-term governments?

6-28. Calculate the ending index number for inflation as of 1998. How can this value be interpreted?

6-29. Now consider real returns—that is, inflation-adjusted returns. Based on the previous numbers given for the cumulative wealth index for common stocks and the ending index number for inflation, calculate the real (inflation-adjusted) cumulative wealth index for common stocks at the end of 1998.

6-30. Calculate the geometric mean annual average real return for stocks.

6-31. Given a geometric mean inflation-adjusted corporate bond annual return of 3.2 percent, calculate the cumulative wealth index for corporate bonds and compare this number to that of stocks.

6-32. Compare the arithmetic and geometric means in the table above. What factor(s) do you think account for the difference between the two for any given asset, such as for stocks or government bonds? Assume you could invest in a new category of high-risk common stocks with an expected arithmetic mean annual return over the December 1995–1998 period of 15 percent, with a standard deviation of 50 percent. Estimate the geometric mean rate of return for this new category of stocks.

Questions 6-33 through 6-38 are part of a comprehensive problem set using the information on closed-end funds as given below:

Consider total return data for some closed-end investment companies (discussed in Chapter 3). Exactly like mutual funds, various types of closed-end funds invest in portfolios of securities on behalf of their own shareholders. Some invest in stocks (domestic, foreign, or both) and some in bonds (taxable, nontaxable, foreign, and so forth). The following data are available from a variety of sources:

INA Investment Securities, classified as a general corporate bond fund. This fund seeks income, with capital appreciation a secondary objective; 90 percent of funds must be invested in debt and preferred stock of issuers within the highest four debt ratings. (See Chapter 2 for a discussion of bond ratings.)

Adams Express, classified as a domestic equity fund. One of the oldest closed-end funds, Adams Express has as its major objective the preservation of capital, with income and capital appreciation secondary objectives. It holds no bonds, but it may have a small percentage of assets in convertibles.

Bergstrom Capital—classified as a domestic equity fund. However, unlike Adams Express, this fund has as its objective long-term capital appreciation. There are no limits on the types of securities it can invest in.

The following **total returns** are available for 1980–1992:

	INA Investment Securities	Adams Express	Bergstrom Capital	S&P 500 Index
1980	−2.18%	42.51	62.44	31.48
1981	− 0.48	5.97	− 7.83	− 4.85
1982	28.24	34.46	40.79	20.37
1983	10.25	14.48	22.16	22.31
1984	15.28	4.39	25.42	5.97
1985	24.61	30.09	42.61	31.06
1986	13.55	23.14	15.74	18.54
1987	− 2.26	− 4.72	− 10.75	5.67
1988	10.26	11.39	16.54	16.34
1989	10.66	20.30	50.75	31.23
1990	− 3.79	5.41	− 1.32	− 3.13
1991	29.94	40.76	107.32	30.00
1992	5.43	14.08	10.68	7.48

6-33. Based on the discussion of return and risk in general, and on the stated objective of each of these funds, rank these funds from highest (1) to lowest (3) on the basis of both the return and risk (standard deviation) that would typically be expected from these types of funds over time.

6-34. Without doing any calculations, and using 1992 as the last year, rank the funds in the table below on the basis of likely performance with regard to arithmetic mean total return for the last 3, 5, and 10 years. The 1-year ranking for 1992 is shown in the table.

	INA Investment	Adams Express	Bergstrom Capital
1 year perf.	3	1	2
3 year avg.			
5 year avg.			
10 year avg.			

6-35. Using a spreadsheet or appropriate tools, calculate the arithmetic mean return, standard deviation, and geometric mean for these funds and for the S&P 500 for the years 1980–1992.

6-36. Is the S&P 500 the correct benchmark to use for INA Investment? Which of the two stock funds would you expect to be more closely related to the return on the S&P 500?

6-37. Determine the cumulative wealth index over the period 1980–1992 from investing $1 in each of the three funds.

6-38. Compare the geometric mean annual return for the two stock funds for this period to the S&P 500 for the same period and to the S&P 500 for the overall period 1926–1992. What conclusions can you draw from this analysis?

SELECTED REFERENCE

The best known source for the returns and risk of major financial assets is:

Ibbotson Associates, Inc. *Stocks, Bonds, Bills and Inflation: Yearbook*. Annual. Chicago: Ibbotson Associates.

www.wiley.com/college/jones7

This chapter analyzes the returns and risks from investing. Obviously, a first step is measuring these quantities. The web exercises will address the measurement of returns, and of risk.

chapter 7

EXPECTED RETURN AND RISK

Chapter 7 analyzes *expected* return and risk, the two key components needed to construct portfolios. The critically important principle of Markowitz diversification is explored, focusing primarily on the concepts of the correlation coefficient and covariance as applied to security returns. The Capital Asset Pricing Model, which gives investors a way to calculate the required rate of return for a stock and links return and risk together, is also considered.

After reading this chapter you will be able to:

- **Understand the expected return and risk calculations for individual securities.**
- **Understand portfolio return and risk measures as formulated by Markowitz.**
- **Utilize two measures of risk, standard deviation and beta.**
- **Estimate the required rate of return for a security using the Capital Asset Pricing Model.**

As stated in Chapter 1, this text is concerned primarily with investing in marketable securities. An investment in financial assets represents the current commitment of an investor's funds (wealth) for a future period of time in order to earn a flow of funds that compensates for two factors: the time the funds are committed, and the risk involved. In effect, investors are trading a known present value (the purchase price of the asset) for some *expected* future value—that is, one not known with certainty.

When we invest, we defer current consumption in order to increase our future consumption. We are concerned with the increase in wealth from our investments, and this increase is typically measured as a rate of return in order to adjust for differing dollar amounts of investment.

As noted in Chapter 1, risk is the chance that the actual return from an investment will differ from its expected return. In an uncertain world, risk is the opposite side of the coin from return. Investors are concerned primarily with how to achieve the highest possible returns without bearing unacceptable risk.

In this chapter, we outline the nature of risk and return as it applies to investment decisions. Unlike Chapter 6, we are talking about the future—which involves *expected returns*, and not the past—which involves *realized returns*. Investors must estimate and manage the returns and risk from their investments. They reduce risk to the extent possible without affecting returns by building diversified portfolios. Therefore, we must be concerned with the investor's total portfolio and analyze investment risk accordingly. As we shall see, diversification is the key to effective risk management.

At the conclusion of this analysis, we will be able to understand the two key characteristics of every investment decision—its expected return and risk—on both an individual security basis and, more importantly, on a portfolio basis. We will also understand the basic principles of Markowitz portfolio theory, a very well-known investments concept.

DEALING WITH UNCERTAINTY

In Chapter 6 we discussed the average returns, both arithmetic and geometric, that investors have experienced over the years from investing in the major financial assets available to them. We also considered the risk of these asset returns as measured by the standard deviation. Analysts often refer to the realized returns for a security, or class of securities, over time using these measures as well as other measures such as the cumulative wealth index.

Realized returns are important for several reasons. For example, investors need to know how their portfolios have performed. Realized returns also can be particularly important in helping investors to form expectations about future returns because investors must concern themselves with their best estimate of return over the next year, or six months, or whatever. How do we go about estimating returns, which is what investors must actually do in managing their portfolios?

First of all, note that we will use the return and risk measures developed in Chapter 6. The total return measure, TR, is applicable whether one is measuring realized returns or estimating future (expected) returns. Because it includes everything the investor can expect to receive over any specified future period, the TR is useful in conceptualizing the estimated returns from securities.

Similarly, the variance, or its square root, the standard deviation, is an accepted measure of variability for both realized returns and expected returns. We will calculate both the variance and the standard deviation below and use them interchangeably as the situation dictates.

Sometimes it is preferable to use one, and sometimes the other. We will also consider another measure of risk, beta, which relates to the systematic risk of an asset.

To estimate the returns from various securities, investors must estimate the cash flows these securities are likely to provide. The basis for doing so for bonds and stocks will be covered in their respective chapters. For now it is sufficient to remind ourselves of the uncertainty of estimates of the future, a problem emphasized at the outset of Chapter 1.

USING PROBABILITY DISTRIBUTIONS

The return an investor will earn from investing is not known; it must be estimated. Future return is an *expected* return and may or may not actually be realized. An investor may expect the TR on a particular security to be 0.10 for the coming year, but in truth this is only a "point estimate." Risk, or the chance that some unfavorable event will occur, is involved when investment decisions are made. Investors are often overly optimistic about expected returns, as Box 7-1 points out.

Probability Distributions To deal with the uncertainty of returns, investors need to think explicitly about a security's distribution of probable TRs. In other words, investors need to keep in mind that, although they may expect a security to return 10 percent, for example, this is only a one-point estimate of the entire range of possibilities. Given that investors must deal with the uncertain future, a number of possible returns can, and will, occur.

In the case of a Treasury bond paying a fixed rate of interest, the interest payment will be made with 100 percent certainty barring a financial collapse of the economy. The probability of occurrence is 1.0, because no other outcome is possible.

With the possibility of two or more outcomes, which is the norm for common stocks, each possible likely outcome must be considered and a probability of its occurrence assessed. The probability for a particular outcome is simply the chance that the specified outcome will occur. The result of considering these outcomes and their probabilities together is a *probability distribution* consisting of the specification of the likely outcomes that may occur and the probabilities associated with these likely outcomes.

Probabilities represent the likelihood of various outcomes and are typically expressed as a decimal. (Sometimes fractions are used.) The sum of the probabilities of all possible outcomes must be 1.0, because they must completely describe all the (perceived) likely occurrences.

How are these probabilities and associated outcomes obtained? In the final analysis, investing for some future period involves uncertainty, and therefore subjective estimates. Although past occurrences (frequencies) may be relied on heavily to estimate the probabilities, the past must be modified for any changes expected in the future.

Probability distributions can be either discrete or continuous. With a discrete probability distribution, a probability is assigned to each possible outcome. In Figure 7-1*a*, five possible TRs are assumed for a stock for next year. Each of these five possible outcomes has an associated probability, with the sum of the probabilities equal to 1.0.

With a continuous probability distribution, as shown in Figure 7-1*b*, an infinite number of possible outcomes exist. Because probability is now measured as the area under the curve in Figure 7-1*b*, the emphasis is on the probability that a particular outcome is within some range of values.

The most familiar continuous distribution is the normal distribution depicted in Figure 7-1*b*. This is the well-known bell-shaped curve often used in statistics. It is a two-parameter distribution in that the mean and the variance fully describe it.

Box 7-1

THE PERILS OF GREAT EXPECTATIONS

Lulled into complacency by more than a decade of exceptional returns in stocks and bonds, many investors seeking future riches have built castles in the air. Stock market gains of 15 percent to 20 percent a year have now become expected. High investment earnings have become today's sure thing.

Hate to spoil the party, but you know what they say about sure things. Let the others celebrate their rip-roaring returns. Smart investors—those with a sense of history about the markets—will take this time to do a reality check.

The facts: Over the past 12 years, returns in stocks, bonds, even Treasury bills have been anything but normal. Blue-chip stocks have returned an average of more than 16 percent per year since this great bull market took off in late 1982. Bond investors have earned double-digit returns during these years as well. Long-term government bonds, for example, have gained an average just shy of 15 percent per year since late 1982. Even the most conservative investors who parked their capital in Treasury bills got rich during the period. Treasury bills returned an average 7 percent annually, handily beating the inflation rate.

The fiction: Such rates will continue.

Investors have grown accustomed to these extraordinary rates. That's natural. But to count on them continuing is to court big trouble. Whenever investment returns stray above or below their long-run averages for a prolonged period, they tend to reverse for an extended period as well. Therefore, it's exceedingly likely that both blue-chip stocks and long-term bonds will provide returns far below their long-run averages for the remainder of the decade.

There are a couple of exceptions to this admittedly gloomy outlook. Small-cap stocks, for example, which underperformed for most of the 1980s, will likely be overachievers. The same is probably true of gold and silver. However, these are guesses, not sure bets. The bottom line is, no one should expect to keep earning the high figures that a broad spectrum of financial assets has provided during the last decade or so. And don't believe anyone who says otherwise.

Hordes of people out there are, of course, eager to tell you otherwise. And why not take advantage of investors with unreasonable expectations? Securities regulators say that investors are much more likely to be defrauded by financial scamsters in roaring markets than in dismal ones.

Whose mailbox hasn't been crammed with letters sent by investment gurus promising fabulous wealth? Lately, the tone of these pitches has become mighty shrill. The quieter ones promise "safe" returns of 15 to 20 percent per year. Others go further. William M. Seay, editor of *The Dynamic Investor*, claims that his "system" produces returns of 30 percent or more. *The Cabot Market Letter* exceeds even that outrageous number: Its stock-picking method can "turn $5,000 into $20,000, even $50,000 or more." The last figure would be a 900 percent gain.

These returns are being touted for a reason. Direct-mail experts say that customers are unlikely to respond to marketing campaigns unless promised annual gains of 20 percent or more.

This hasn't been that hard to do recently. So some of these folks' claims are probably accurate. After all, the S&P 500 index has returned an average of 16.7 percent since 1985. During the past five years, 84 mutual funds have posted gains of 20 percent and higher. That's about 1 out of every 20 funds that have been around that long.

The numbers like these are anything but easy to achieve in the long run. Check out the table below, which lists historical returns and risks of a variety of investments going back to 1945. One thing that's immediately apparent: No category of investment has returned an average of 20 percent annually during that period. Emerging-market stocks, the top-performing asset category, returned an average of 16 percent per year. But, mark this: The asset categories that produced the higher returns carried the highest risks. Finally, note that Treasury bills, the lowest-risk asset category, have barely produced any meaningful return at all; after adjusting for inflation, T-bill rates fall to a meager 0.3 percent annually.

Remember, too, that these returns are higher than what we mortals can achieve, even if we pick the right investments. That's because the returns found in the table have come out of hypothetical portfolios and thus have not been adjusted for either transaction costs or income taxes. When you adjust for both of these items, returns are reduced.

Consider the portfolio of large-capitalization,

blue-chip stocks represented by the S&P stock index. If you are an active trader and turn over your portfolio once a year, paying 1 percent in brokerage commissions to buy and another 1 percent to sell, your true annual return falls from 11.7 percent to 9.7 percent. Apply a 28 percent tax rate to these profits, and your net gain falls to 7 percent a year. Deduct the annual rate of inflation and you get a 2.5 percent real return. At this rate, it would take 18 years for a $10,000 investment to grow to $1 million. Doesn't sound much like the promises you see in mutual fund advertisements today, does it?

History and financial theory will tell you that anyone promising a safe but high—say, 30 percent—average annual return is lying. If you want to believe in such fibs, you are an investment victim waiting to happen. Of the 150 investment newsletters tracked by Mark Hulbert, editor of *The Hulbert Financial Digest* the top performer, *Value Line Investment Survey's* portfolio of number-one-ranked stocks, has returned 18.5 percent annually during the 13 years that Hulbert has been ranking newsletters. Take a hint from history. If high-risk equities return an average of 10 percent per year, the only way you're going to earn more is to assume even greater risks. And if you do, you are upping the odds that your hard-earned bankroll will disappear.

With all the hype and hoopla that has accompanied the bull market in stocks and bonds, there is no doubt that many investors are at this moment being led, like lemmings, into some very risky portfolios. This is particularly true now that declining interest rates have driven many savers out of bank CDs and money market funds and into dicier venues like bond and stock funds.

Take the numbers in this table to heart. Don't allow yourself to be victimized by investment gurus preying on your too-great expectations. See real and reachable hope for your portfolio's return based on historical averages. Then, adjust the hypothetical returns to reflect transaction costs, taxes and inflation. If you plan properly for the lower rates of return that are almost certainly ahead, you may ironically enough, wind up with more money in your pocket.

SOURCE: Gerald Perrit, "The Perils of Great Expectations," *Worth*, March 1994, pp. 49–50. Reprinted with permission.

ANNUAL RATES OF RETURN, 1945–1992

	Return	Inflation-Adjusted Return	Risk Index
Emerging-market equities	16%	11.5%	29.6
Venture capital	15.9	11.4	35.4
Japanese stocks	15.9	11.4	29.2
Emerging growth stocks	13.7	9.2	27.1
Small-cap stocks	13.5	9.0	25.7
Europe/Asia stock index	12.7	8.2	26.5
S&P 500 index	11.7	7.2	16.5
U.S. farmland	9.9	5.4	7.4
Art	8.5	4.0	15.0
Real estate (commercial)	7.6	3.1	5.7
Real estate (residential)	7.3	2.8	4.0
Corporate bonds	5.4	0.9	6.2
Long-term government bonds	4.9	0.4	9.7
Gold	4.9	0.4	26.0
Treasury bills	4.8	0.3	3.2
Silver	4.2	−0.3	56.2
Inflation	4.5		

SOURCE: Morgan Stanley Capital International

FIGURE 7-1

(*a*) A discrete probability distribution.
(*b*) A continuous probability distribution.

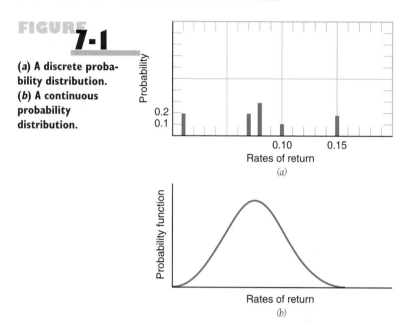

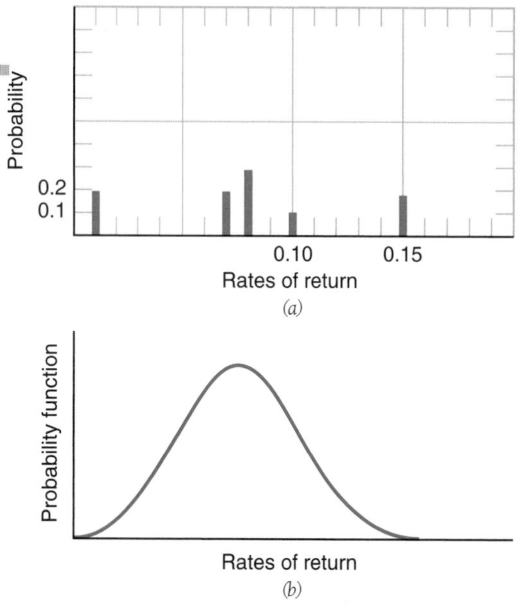

CALCULATING EXPECTED RETURN

Expected Return The ex ante return expected by investors over some future holding period

To describe the single most likely outcome from a particular probability distribution, it is necessary to calculate its *expected value*. The expected value is the weighted average of all possible return outcomes, where each outcome is weighted by its respective probability of occurrence. Since investors are interested in returns, we will call this expected value the *expected rate of return*, or simply **expected return**, and for any security, it is calculated as

$$E(R) = \sum_{i=1}^{m} R_i pr_i \qquad (7\text{-}1)$$

where

$E(R)$ = the expected return on a security
R_i = the *i*th possible return
pr_i = the probability of the *i*th return R_i
m = the number of possible returns

EXAMPLE 7-1

The expected return for the discrete probability distribution in Figure 7-1*a* is 0.08.

CALCULATING RISK

Investors must be able to quantify and measure risk. To calculate the total risk associated with the expected return, the variance or standard deviation is used. As we know from Chapter 6, the variance and its square root, standard deviation, are measures of the spread or dispersion in the probability distribution; that is, they measure the dispersion of a random variable around its mean. The larger this dispersion, the larger the variance or standard deviation.

To calculate the variance or standard deviation from the probability distribution, first calculate the expected return of the distribution using Equation 7-1. Essentially, the same

TABLE 7-1 CALCULATING THE STANDARD DEVIATION USING EXPECTED DATA

(1) Possible Return	(2) Probability	(3) (1) × (2)	(4) $R_i - EV$	(5) $(R_i - EV)^2$	(6) $(R_i - EV)^2P(R_i)$
0.01	0.2	0.002	−0.070	0.0049	0.00098
0.07	0.2	0.014	−0.010	0.0001	0.00002
0.08	0.3	0.024	0.000	0.0000	0.00000
0.10	0.1	0.010	0.020	0.0004	0.00004
0.15	0.2	0.030	0.070	0.0049	0.00098
	1.0	0.080 = EV			0.00202

$s = (0.00202)^{1/2} = 0.0449 = 4.49\%$

procedure used in Chapter 6 to measure risk applies here, but now the probabilities associated with the outcomes must be included, as in Equation 7-2.

$$\text{the variance of returns} = \sigma^2 = \sum_{i=1}^{m} [R_i - E(R)]^2 \, pr_i \tag{7-2}$$

and

$$\text{the standard deviation of returns} = \sigma = (\sigma^2)^{1/2} \tag{7-3}$$

where all terms are as defined previously.

EXAMPLE 7-2

The variance and standard deviation for the hypothetical stock shown in Figure 7-1*a* are calculated in Table 7-1.

Calculating a standard deviation using probability distributions involves making subjective estimates of the probabilities and the likely returns. However, we cannot avoid such estimates because future returns are uncertain. The prices of securities are based on investors' expectations about the future. The relevant standard deviation in this situation is the *ex ante* standard deviation and not the *ex post* based on realized returns.

Although standard deviations based on realized returns are often used as proxies for *ex ante* standard deviations, investors should be careful to remember that the past cannot always be extrapolated into the future without modifications. *Ex post* standard deviations may be convenient, but they are subject to errors when used as estimates of the future.

One important point about the estimation of standard deviation is the distinction between individual securities and portfolios. Standard deviations for well-diversified portfolios are reasonably steady across time, and therefore historical calculations may be fairly reliable in projecting the future. Moving from well-diversified portfolios to individual securities, however, makes historical calculations much less reliable. Fortunately, the number one rule of portfolio management is to diversify and hold a portfolio of securities, and investors should diversify in order to deal with the uncertainty involved when investing. Therefore, we need to consider the expected return and risk for a portfolio.

PORTFOLIO RETURN AND RISK

When we analyze investment returns and risks, we must be concerned with the total portfolio held by an investor. Individual security returns and risks are important, but it is the return and risk to the investor's total portfolio that ultimately matters because investment opportunities can be enhanced by packaging them together to form portfolios. As we learned in Chapter 1, an investor's portfolio is his or her combination of assets.

As we will see, portfolio risk is a unique characteristic and not simply the sum of individual security risks. A security may have a large risk if it is held by itself but much less risk when held in a portfolio of securities. Since the investor is concerned primarily with the risk to his or her total wealth, as represented by his or her portfolio, individual stocks are risky only to the extent that they add risk to the total portfolio.

PORTFOLIO EXPECTED RETURN

Portfolio Weights Percentages of portfolio funds invested in each security, summing to 1.0

The expected return on any portfolio is easily calculated as a weighted average of the individual securities' expected returns. The percentages of a portfolio's total value that are invested in each portfolio asset are referred to as **portfolio weights**, which we will denote by w. The combined portfolio weights are assumed to sum to 100 percent of total investable funds, or 1.0, indicating that all portfolio funds are invested. That is,

$$w_1 + w_2 + \cdots + w_n = \sum_{i=1}^{n} w_i = 1.0 \tag{7-4}$$

EXAMPLE 7-3

With equal dollar amounts in three securities, the portfolio weights are 0.333, 0.333, and 0.333. Under the same conditions with a portfolio of five securities, each security would have a portfolio weight of 0.20. Of course, dollar amounts do not have to be equal. A five-stock portfolio might have weights of .40, .10, .15, .25, and .10, or .18, .33, .11, .22, and .16.

The expected return on any portfolio p can be calculated as

$$E(R_p) = \sum_{i=1}^{n} w_i\, E(R_i) \tag{7-5}$$

where

$E(R_p)$ = the expected return on the portfolio
w_i = the portfolio weight for the ith security
Σw_i = 1.0
$E(R_i)$ = the expected return on the ith security
n = the number of different securities in the portfolio

EXAMPLE 7-4

Consider a three-stock portfolio consisting of stocks G, H, and I with expected returns of 12 percent, 20 percent, and 17 percent, respectively. Assume that 50 percent of investable funds is invested in security G, 30 percent in H, and 20 percent in I. The expected return on this portfolio is:

$$E(R_p) = 0.5(12\%) + 0.3(20\%) + 0.2(17\%) = 15.4\%$$

Regardless of the number of assets held in a portfolio, or the proportion of total investable funds placed in each asset, the expected return on the portfolio is always a weighted average of the expected returns for individual assets in the portfolio. This is a very important principle that should always be kept in mind.

INVESTMENTS INTUITION The expected return for a portfolio must fall between the highest and lowest expected returns for the individual securities making up the portfolio. Exactly where it falls is determined by the percentages of investable funds placed in each of the individual securities in the portfolio.

PORTFOLIO RISK

The remaining computation in investment analysis is that of the risk of the portfolio. Risk is measured by the variance (or standard deviation) of the portfolio's return, exactly as in the case of each individual security.

It is at this point that the basis of modern portfolio theory emerges, which can be stated as follows: Although the expected return of a portfolio is a weighted average of its expected returns, portfolio risk (as measured by the variance or standard deviation) is *not* a weighted average of the risk of the individual securities in the portfolio. Symbolically,

$$E(R_p) = \sum_{i=1}^{n} w_i \, E(R_i) \tag{7-6}$$

But

$$\sigma_p^2 \neq \sum_{i=1}^{n} w_i \sigma_i^2 \tag{7-7}$$

Precisely because Equation 7-7 is an inequality, investors can reduce the risk of a portfolio beyond what it would be if risk were, in fact, simply a weighted average of the individual securities' risk. In order to see how this risk reduction can be accomplished, we must analyze portfolio risk in detail.

ANALYZING PORTFOLIO RISK

RISK REDUCTION—THE INSURANCE PRINCIPLE

To begin our analysis of how a portfolio of assets can reduce risk, assume that all risk sources in a portfolio of securities are independent. As we add securities to this portfolio, the exposure to any particular source of risk becomes small. According to the *Law of Large Numbers*, the larger the sample size, the more likely it is that the sample mean will be close to the population expected value. Risk reduction in the case of independent risk sources can be thought of as the *insurance principle*, named for the idea that an insurance company reduces its risk by writing many policies against many independent sources of risk.

We are assuming here that rates of return on individual securities are statistically independent such that any one security's rate of return is unaffected by another's rate of return. In this situation, the standard deviation of the portfolio is given by

$$\sigma_p = \frac{\sigma_i}{n^{1/2}} \tag{7-8}$$

As Figure 7-2 shows, the risk of the portfolio will quickly decline as more securities are added. Notice that no decision is to be made about which security to add because all have identical properties. The only issue is how many securities are added.

FIGURE 7-2

Risk reduction when returns are independent.

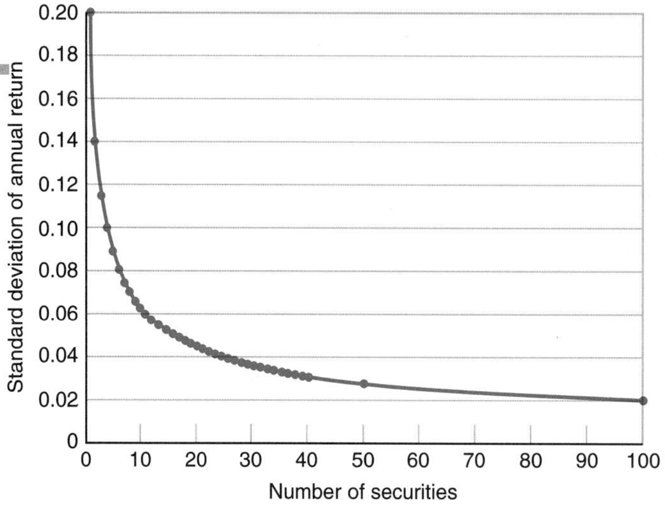

EXAMPLE 7-5

Figure 7-2 shows how risk declines given that the risk of each security is 0.20. The risk of the portfolio will quickly decline as more and more of these securities are added. Equation 7-7 indicates that for the case of 100 securities the risk of the portfolio is reduced to 0.02:

$$\sigma_p = \frac{0.20}{100^{1/2}}$$
$$= 0.02$$

Figure 7-2 illustrates the case of independent risk sources. As applied to investing, all risk is firm-specific. Therefore, the total risk in this situation can continue to be reduced. Unfortunately, the assumption of statistically independent returns on stocks is unrealistic in the real world. Going back to the definition of market risk in Chapter 6, we find that most stocks are positively correlated with each other; that is, the movements in their returns are related. Most stocks have a significant level of comovement with the overall market of stocks, as measured by such indexes as the S&P 500 Composite Index. While risk can be reduced, it cannot be eliminated because common sources of risk affect all firms. For example, a rise in interest rates will affect most firms adversely because most firms borrow funds to finance part of their operations.

DIVERSIFICATION

The insurance principle illustrates the concept of attempting to diversify the risk involved in a portfolio of assets (or liabilities). In fact, diversification is the key to the management of portfolio risk because it allows investors to significantly lower portfolio risk without adversely affecting return. Throughout our discussion in both this chapter and the next, we will be focusing on the diversification principle. We begin with random diversification and move to efficient diversification.

Random Diversification *Random or naive diversification* refers to the act of randomly diversifying without regard to relevant investment characteristics such as expected return and industry classification. An investor simply selects a relatively large number of securities randomly—the proverbial "throwing a dart at *The Wall Street Journal* page showing stock quotes." For simplicity, we assume equal dollar amounts are invested in each stock.

Table 7-2 uses actual data for domestic stocks to illustrate naive diversification. As we

TABLE 7-2 EXPECTED STANDARD DEVIATIONS OF ANNUAL PORTFOLIO RETURNS

Number of Stocks in Portfolio	Expected Standard Deviation of Annual Portfolio Returns	Ratio of Portfolio Standard Deviation to Standard Deviation of a Single Stock
1	49.236	1.00
2	37.358	0.76
4	29.687	0.60
6	26.643	0.54
8	24.983	0.51
10	23.932	0.49
12	23.204	0.47
14	22.670	0.46
16	22.261	0.45
18	21.939	0.45
20	21.677	0.44
25	21.196	0.43
30	20.870	0.42
35	20.634	0.42
40	20.456	0.42
45	20.316	0.41
50	20.203	0.41
75	19.860	0.40
100	19.686	0.40
200	19.423	0.39
300	19.336	0.39
400	19.292	0.39
450	19.277	0.39
500	19.265	0.39
600	19.247	0.39
700	19.233	0.39
800	19.224	0.39
900	19.217	0.39
1000	19.211	0.39
Infinity	19.158	0.39

SOURCE: Meir Statman, "How Many Stocks Make a Diversified Portfolio?" *Journal of Financial and Quantitative Analysis* (September 1987), p. 355.

can see, for randomly selected portfolios average portfolio risk can be reduced to approximately 19 percent. As we add securities to the portfolio, the total risk associated with the portfolio of stocks declines rapidly. The first few stocks cause a large decrease in portfolio risk. Based on these actual data, 51 percent of portfolio standard deviation is eliminated as we go from 1 to 10 securities.

Unfortunately, the benefits of random diversification do not continue as we add more securities. As subsequent stocks are added, the marginal risk reduction is small. Nevertheless, adding one more stock to the portfolio will continue to reduce the risk, although the amount of the reduction becomes smaller and smaller.

EXAMPLE 7-6

Based on the data in Table 7-2, going from 10 to 20 securities eliminates an additional 5 percentage points of the portfolio standard deviation, while going from 20 to 30 securities eliminates only an additional 2 percentage points of the standard deviation.

A large number of securities are not required to achieve substantial diversification benefits. On the other hand, note that the risk of the portfolio in Table 7-2 levels out at approximately 19 percent. Therefore, no matter how many securities we add to this portfolio beyond this point, the risk will not decline any significant amount. (The decline has to be measured in thousandths of a percent.)

International Diversification Our discussion above assumed random diversification in domestic securities such as stocks traded on the NYSE. However, we have learned about the importance of taking a global approach to investing. What effect would this have on our diversification analysis?

Considering only the potential for risk reduction and ignoring the additional risks of foreign investing, such as currency risk, we could reasonably conclude that if domestic diversification is good, international diversification must be better. Figure 7-3 illustrates the benefits of international diversification in reducing portfolio risk. Throughout the entire range of portfolio sizes, the risk is reduced when international investing is compared to U.S. stocks, and the difference is dramatic—about one-third less.

Markowitz Diversification Now that we understand how random diversification works, we need to be more sophisticated and take advantage of information that we can calculate, such as the expected return and risk for individual securities and measures of how stock returns move together. This will allow us to understand the true nature of portfolio risk and why Equation 7-7 is an inequality. It will also allow us to optimize our diversification, achieving the maximum portfolio risk reduction possible in a given situation.

In the 1950s, Harry Markowitz, considered the father of modern portfolio theory, originated the basic portfolio model that underlies modern portfolio theory. Before Markowitz, investors dealt loosely with the concepts of return and risk. Investors have known intuitively for many years that it is smart to diversify, that is, not to "put all of your eggs in one basket." Markowitz, however, was the first to develop the concept of portfolio diversification in a formal way. He showed quantitatively why, and how, portfolio diversification works to reduce the risk of a portfolio to an investor.

Markowitz sought to organize the existing thoughts and practices into a more formal framework and to answer a basic question: Is the risk of a portfolio equal to the sum of the risks of the individual securities comprising it? Markowitz was the first to develop a specific measure of portfolio risk and to derive the expected return and risk for a portfolio based on covariance relationships. We consider covariances in detail in the discussion below.

FIGURE 7-3

Domestic vs. international diversification in reducing portfolio risk.

SOURCE: Bruno Solnik, "Why Not Diversify Internationally Rather Than Domestically," *Financial Analysts Journal*, July 1974. Reprinted by permission.

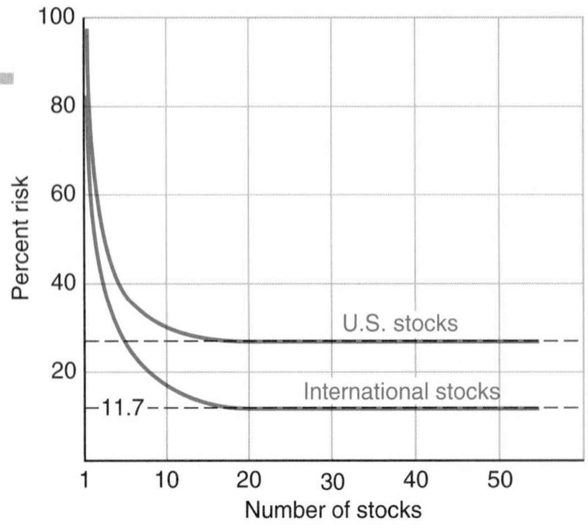

As noted above, portfolio risk is *not* simply a weighted average of the individual security risks. Rather, as Markowitz first showed, we must account for the interrelationships among security returns in order to calculate portfolio risk, and in order to reduce portfolio risk to its minimum level for any given level of return. Therefore, we now consider how to measure these interrelationships, or comovements, among security returns.

MEASURING COMOVEMENTS IN SECURITY RETURNS

In order to remove the inequality sign from Equation 7-7 and develop an equation that will calculate the risk of a portfolio as measured by the variance or standard deviation, we must account for two factors:

1. Weighted individual security risks (i.e., the variance of each individual security, weighted by the percentage of investable funds placed in each individual security).
2. Weighted comovements between securities' returns (i.e., the covariance between the securities' returns, again weighted by the percentage of investable funds placed in each security).

As explained below, covariance is an absolute measure of the comovements between security returns used in the calculation of portfolio risk. We need the actual covariance between securities in a portfolio in order to calculate portfolio variance or standard deviation. Before considering covariance, however, we can easily illustrate how security returns move together by considering the correlation coefficient, a relative measure of association learned in statistics.

Correlation Coefficient A statistical measure of the extent to which two variables are associated

The Correlation Coefficient As used in portfolio theory, the **correlation coefficient** (ρ_{ij}, pronounced "rho") is a statistical measure of the *relative* comovements between security returns. It measures the extent to which the returns on any two securities are related; however, it denotes only association, not causation. It is a relative measure of association that is bounded by +1.0 and −1.0, with

$$\rho_{ij} = +1.0$$
$$= \text{perfect positive correlation}$$
$$\rho_{ij} = -1.0$$
$$= \text{perfect negative (inverse) correlation}$$
$$\rho_{ij} = 0.0$$
$$= \text{zero correlation}$$

With perfect positive correlation, the returns have a perfect direct linear relationship. Knowing what the return on one security will do allows an investor to forecast perfectly what the other will do. In Figure 7-4, stocks A and B have identical return patterns over the six-year period 1993–1998. When stock A's return goes up, stock B's does also. When stock A's return goes down, stock B's does also.

Consider the return and standard deviation information in Figure 7-4. Notice that a portfolio combining stocks A and B, with 50 percent invested in each, has exactly the same return as does either stock by itself, since the returns are identical. The risk of the portfolio, as measured by the standard deviation, is identical to the standard deviation of either stock by itself. There is no variation in this return series.

With perfect negative correlation, the securities' returns have a perfect inverse linear relationship to each other. Therefore, knowing the return on one security provides full knowl-

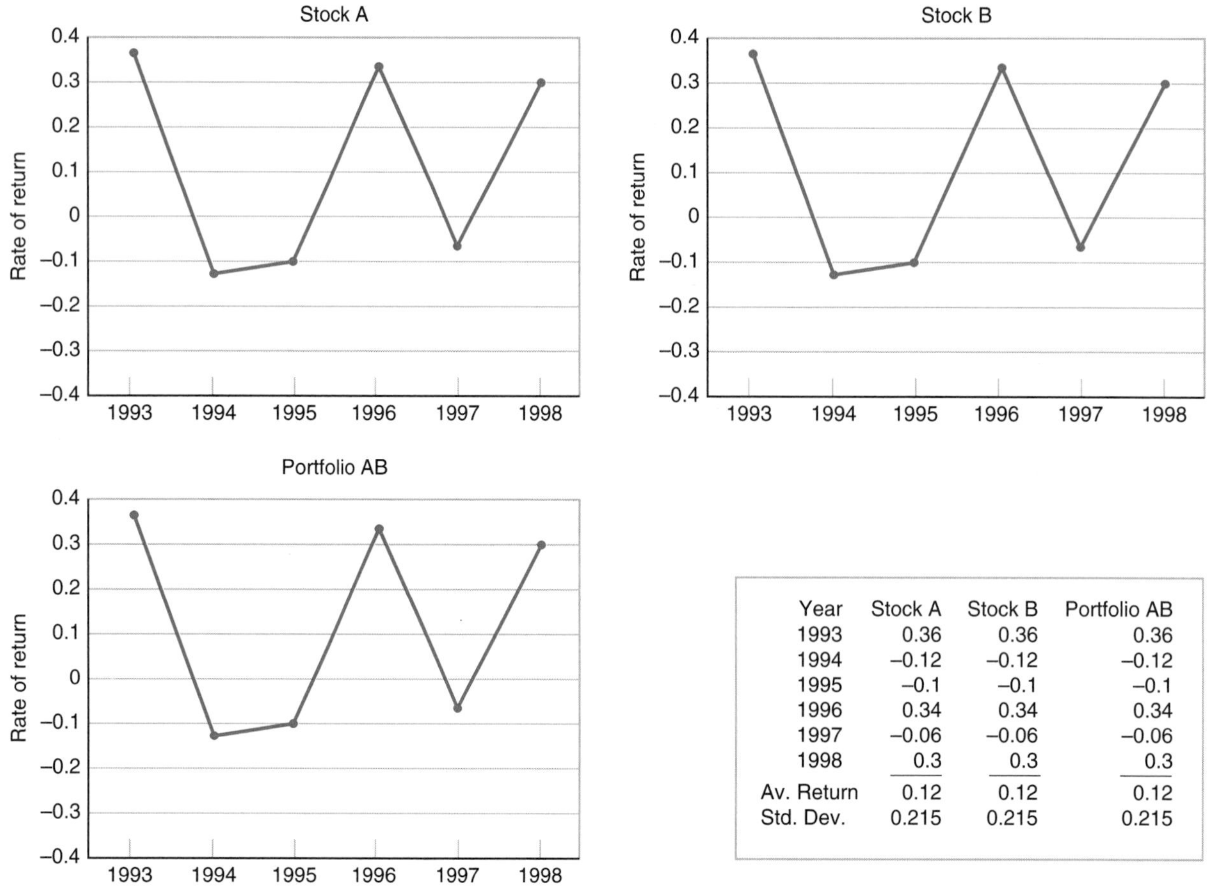

Year	Stock A	Stock B	Portfolio AB
1993	0.36	0.36	0.36
1994	−0.12	−0.12	−0.12
1995	−0.1	−0.1	−0.1
1996	0.34	0.34	0.34
1997	−0.06	−0.06	−0.06
1998	0.3	0.3	0.3
Av. Return	0.12	0.12	0.12
Std. Dev.	0.215	0.215	0.215

FIGURE 7-4

Returns for the years 1993–1998 on two stocks, A and B, and a portfolio consisting of 50% A and 50% B, when the correlation coefficient is +1.0.

edge about the return on the second security. When one security's return is high, the other is low.

In Figure 7-5, stocks A and C are perfectly negatively correlated with each other. Notice that the information given for these two stocks states that each stock has exactly the same return and standard deviation. When combined, however, the deviations in the returns on these stocks around their average return of 12 percent cancel out, resulting in a portfolio return of 12 percent. This portfolio has no risk. It will earn 12 percent each year over the period measured, and the average return will be 12 percent.

With zero correlation, there is no relationship between the returns on the two securities. Knowledge of the return on one security is of no value in predicting the return of the second security.

When does diversification pay?

1. Combining securities with perfect positive correlation with each other provides no reduction in portfolio risk. The risk of the resulting portfolio is simply a weighted average of the individual risks of the securities. As more securities are added under the condition of perfect positive correlation, portfolio risk remains a weighted average. There is no risk reduction.
2. Combining two securities with zero correlation (statistical independence) with each other reduces the risk of the portfolio. If more securities with uncorrelated returns are added to the portfolio, significant risk reduction can be achieved. However, portfolio risk cannot be eliminated in this case.

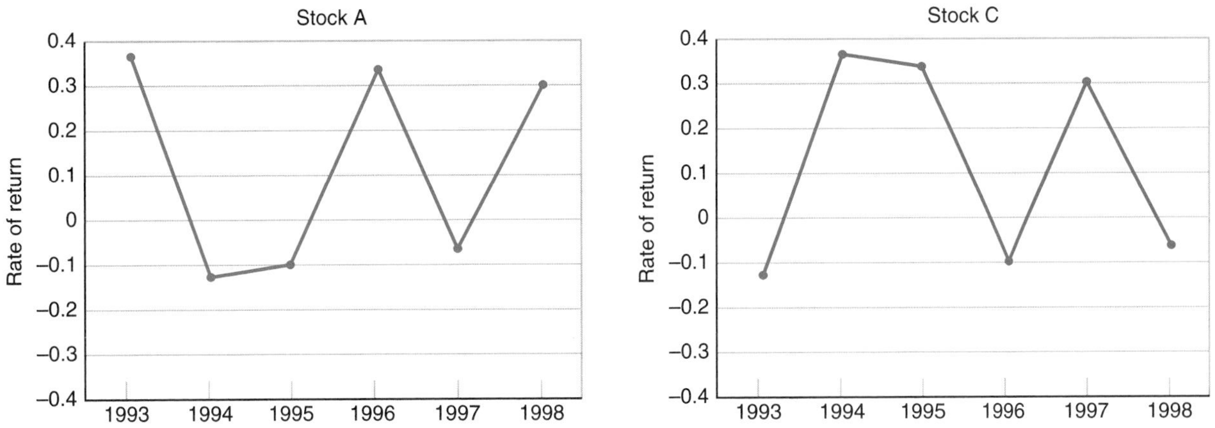

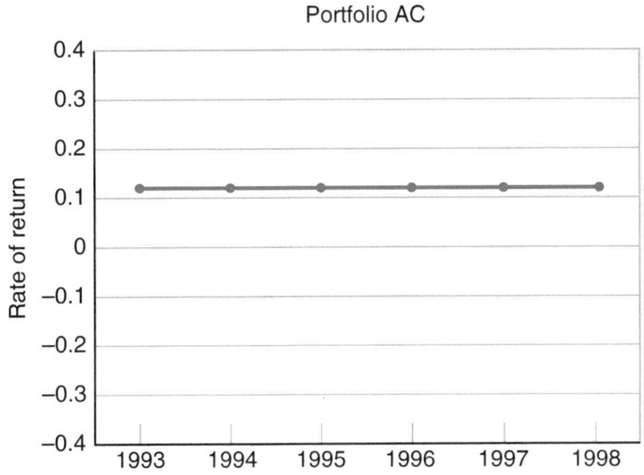

Year	Stock A	Stock C	Portfolio AC
1993	0.36	−0.12	0.12
1994	−0.12	0.36	0.12
1995	−0.1	0.34	0.12
1996	0.34	−0.1	0.12
1997	−0.06	0.3	0.12
1998	0.3	−0.06	0.12
Av. Return	0.12	0.12	0.12
Std. Dev.	0.215	0.215	0.000

FIGURE 7-5

Returns for the years 1993–1998 on two stocks, A and B, and a portfolio consisting of 50% A and 50% B, when the correlation coefficient is −1.0.

3. Combining two securities with perfect negative correlation with each other could eliminate risk altogether. This is the principle behind hedging strategies, some of which are discussed in Chapter 18.
4. Finally, we must understand that in the real world, these extreme correlations are rare. Rather, securities typically have some positive correlation with each other. Thus, although risk can be reduced, it usually cannot be eliminated. Other things being equal, investors wish to find securities with the least positive correlation possible. Ideally, they would like securities with negative correlation or low positive correlation, but they generally will be faced with positively correlated security returns.

Figure 7-6 illustrates the more normal case of stocks A and D positively correlated with each other at a level of $\rho = +0.55$. This is approximately the typical correlation of NYSE stocks with each other, thereby representing a "normal" situation encountered by investors. Note that the standard deviation of each security is still .215, with an average return of .12, but when combined with equal weights of .50 into the portfolio *AD* the average return remains the same, but the risk is somewhat reduced, to a level of .18. Any reduction in risk that does not adversely affect return has to be considered beneficial.

Covariance Given the significant amount of correlation among security returns, we must measure the amount of comovement and incorporate it into any measure of portfolio risk because such comovements affect the portfolio's variance (or standard deviation).

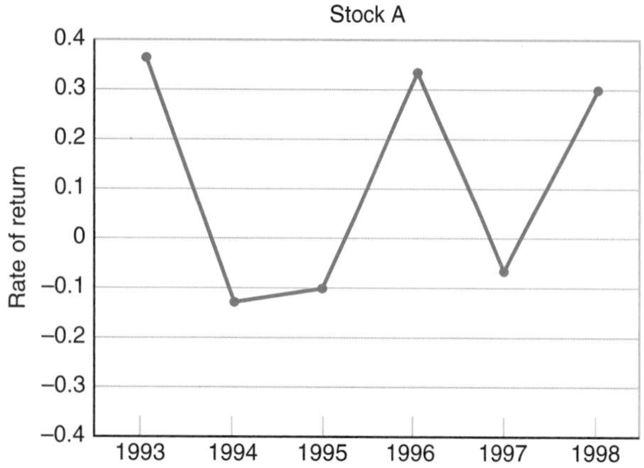

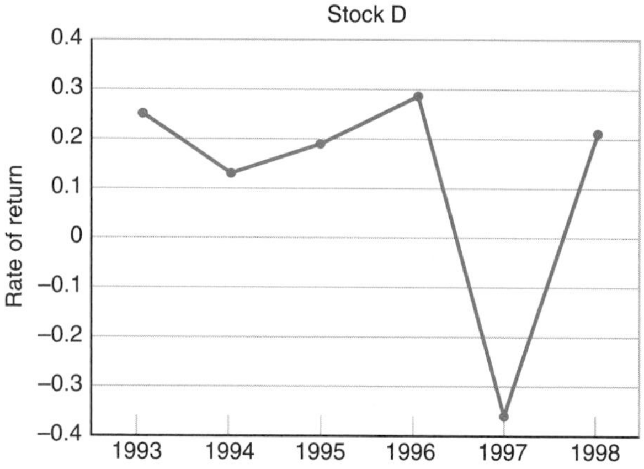

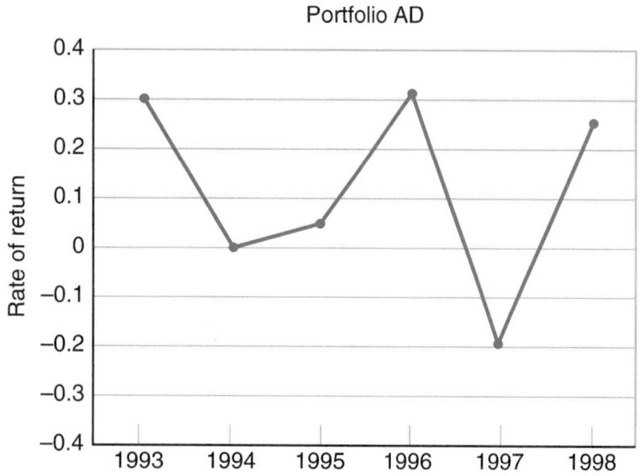

Year	Stock A	Stock D	Portfolio AD
1993	0.36	0.25	0.305
1994	−0.12	0.13	0.005
1995	−0.1	0.19	0.045
1996	0.34	0.28	0.31
1997	−0.06	−0.35	−0.205
1998	0.3	0.22	0.26
Av. Return	0.12	0.12	0.12
Std. Dev.	0.215	0.215	0.180

FIGURE 7-6

Returns for the years 1993–1998 on two stocks, A and B, and a portfolio consisting of 50% A and 50% B, when the correlation coefficient is +0.55.

The covariance is an absolute measure of the degree of association between the returns for a pair of securities. **Covariance** is defined as the extent to which two random variables covary (move together) over time. As is true throughout our discussion, the variables in question are the returns (TRs) on two securities. As in the case of the correlation coefficient, the covariance can be

Covariance An absolute measure of the extent to which two variables tend to covary, or move together

1. Positive, indicating that the returns on the two securities tend to move in the same direction at the same time; when one increases (decreases), the other tends to do the same. When the covariance is positive, the correlation coefficient will also be positive.
2. Negative, indicating that the returns on the two securities tend to move inversely; when one increases (decreases), the other tends to decrease (increase). When the covariance is negative, the correlation coefficient will also be negative.
3. Zero, indicating that the returns on two securities are independent and have no tendency to move in the same or opposite directions together.

The formula for calculating covariance is

$$\sigma_{AB} = \sum_{i=1}^{m} [R_{A,i} - E(R_A)][R_{B,i} - E(R_B)]\, pr_i \qquad (7\text{-}9)$$

where

σ_{AB} = the covariance between securities A and B
R_A = one possible return on security A
$E(R_A)$ = the expected value of the return on security A
m = the number of likely outcomes for a security for the period

Equation 7-8 indicates that covariance is the expected value of the product of deviations from the mean. The size of the covariance measure depends upon the units of the variables involved and usually changes when these units are changed. Therefore, the covariance primarily provides information about whether the association between variables is positive, negative, or zero because simply observing the number itself is not very useful.

Relating the Correlation Coefficient and the Covariance The covariance and the correlation coefficient can be related in the following manner:

$$\rho_{AB} = \frac{\sigma_{AB}}{\sigma_A \sigma_B} \tag{7-10}$$

This equation shows that the correlation coefficient is simply the covariance standardized by dividing by the product of the two standard deviations of returns.

Given this definition of the correlation coefficient, the covariance can be written as

$$\sigma_{AB} = \rho_{AB}\sigma_A\sigma_B \tag{7-11}$$

Therefore, knowing the correlation coefficient, we can calculate the covariance because the standard deviations of the assets' rates of return will already be available. Knowing the covariance, we can easily calculate the correlation coefficient.

CALCULATING PORTFOLIO RISK

Now that we understand how to measure the covariances that account for the comovements in security returns, we are ready to calculate portfolio risk. First, we will consider the simplest possible case, that of two securities, in order to see what is happening in the portfolio risk equation. We will then consider the case of many securities, where the calculations soon become too large and complex to analyze with any means other than a computer.

THE TWO-SECURITY CASE

The risk of a portfolio, as measured by the standard deviation of returns, for the case of two securities, 1 and 2, is

$$\sigma_p = [w_1^2\sigma_1^2 + w_2^2\sigma_2^2 + 2(w_1)(w_2)(\rho_{1,2})\sigma_1\sigma_2]^{1/2} \tag{7-12}$$

Equation 7-11 shows us that the risk for a portfolio encompasses not only the individual security risks but also the covariance between these two securities and that three factors, not two, determine portfolio risk:

- The variance of each security
- The covariances between securities
- The portfolio weights for each security

The standard deviation of the portfolio will be directly affected by the correlation between the two stocks. Portfolio risk will be reduced as the correlation coefficient moves from +1.0 downward.

EXAMPLE 7-7

Assume we have some data for two companies, EG&G and GF, and that the estimated TRs are 26.3 percent and 11.6 percent, respectively, with standard deviations of 37.3 percent and 23.3 percent. The correlation coefficient between their returns is +0.15. To see the effects of changing the correlation coefficient, assume weights of 0.5 each—50 percent of investable funds is to be placed in each security. Summarizing the data in this example,

$$\sigma_{EG\&G} = .373$$
$$\sigma_{GF} = .233$$
$$w_{EG\&G} = 0.5$$
$$w_{GF} = 0.5$$
$$\rho_{EG\&G,GF} = 0.15$$

With these data, the standard deviation, or risk, for this portfolio, σ_p, is

$$\sigma_p = [(0.5)^2(0.373)^2 + (0.5)^2(0.233)^2 + 2(0.5)(0.5)(0.373)(0.233)\ \rho_{EG\&G,GF}]^{1/2}$$
$$= [0.0348 + 0.0136 + 0.0435\ \rho_{EG\&G,GF}]^{1/2}$$

since 2(0.5)(0.5)(0.373)(0.233) = 0.0435.

The risk of this portfolio clearly depends heavily on the value of the third term, which in turn depends on the correlation coefficient between the returns for EG&G and GF. To assess the potential impact of the correlation, consider the following cases: a ρ of +1, +0.5, +0.15, 0, −0.5, and −1.0. Calculating portfolio risk under each of these scenarios produces the following portfolio risks:

If $\rho = +1.0$: $\sigma_p = [0.0348 + 0.0136 + 0.0435(1)]^{1/2} = 30.3\%$
If $\rho = +0.5$: $\sigma_p = [0.0348 + 0.0136 + 0.0435(0.5)]^{1/2} = 26.5\%$
If $\rho = +0.15$: $\sigma_p = [0.0348 + 0.0136 + 0.0435(0.15)]^{1/2} = 23.4\%$
If $\rho = 0.0$: $\sigma_p = [0.0348 + 0.0136]^{1/2} = 22.0\%$
If $\rho = -0.5$: $\sigma_p = [0.0348 + 0.0136 + 0.0435(-0.5)]^{1/2} = 16.0\%$
If $\rho = -1.0$: $\sigma_p = [0.0348 + 0.0136 + 0.0435(-1.0)]^{1/2} = 7.0\%$

These calculations clearly show the impact that combining securities with less than perfect positive correlation will have on portfolio risk. The risk of the portfolio steadily decreases from 30.3 percent to 7 percent as the correlation coefficient declines from +1.0 to −1.0. Note, however, that the risk has declined from 30.3 percent to only 22 percent as the correlation coefficient drops from +1 to 0, and it has only been cut in half (approximately) by the time ρ drops to −0.5.

We must also recognize the importance of the portfolio weights in the calculation of portfolio risk. The size of the portfolio weights placed in one security as opposed to another has an effect on portfolio risk. In order to minimize portfolio risk, we must find the minimum variance combination given a level of expected return.

FIGURE 7-7

The effects of portfolio weights on the standard deviation of the portfolio.

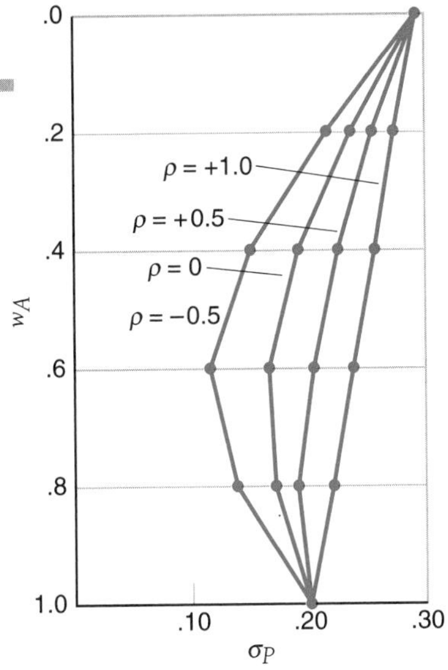

EXAMPLE 7-8

Assume we have two stocks A and B with the same expected returns. The standard deviation of A is .20, and that for B, .30. Figure 7-7 shows the effects of portfolio weights on the standard deviation of the portfolio for four different correlations of the pattern of returns over time. If ρ is 1.0, the minimum variance is achieved with 100 percent of funds placed in A. If ρ is -0.5, the minimum variance is achieved with a portfolio weight for A of .6, and the same is true if ρ is 0.0. On the other hand, if ρ is 0.5, the minimum variance combination involves a portfolio weight for A of .80. Clearly, the minimum variance, or lowest portfolio risk, depends upon the weights selected.

THE *n*-SECURITY CASE

The two-security case can be generalized to the *n*-security case. Portfolio risk can be reduced by combining assets with less than perfect positive correlation. Furthermore, the smaller the positive correlation, the better.

Portfolio risk is a function of each individual security's risk and the covariances between the returns on the individual securities. Stated in terms of variance, portfolio risk is

$$\sigma_p^2 = \sum_{i=1}^{n} w_i^2\sigma_i^2 + \sum_{i=1}^{n}\sum_{\substack{j=1 \\ i\neq j}}^{n} w_i w_j \sigma_{ij} \tag{7-13}$$

where

σ_p^2 = the variance of the return on the portfolio
σ_i^2 = the variance of return for security *i*
σ_{ij} = the covariance between the returns for securities *i* and *j*
w_i = the portfolio weights or percentage of investable funds invested in security *i*
$\sum_{i=1}^{n}\sum_{j=1}^{n}$ = a double summation sign indicating that n^2 numbers are to be added together (i.e., all possible pairs of values for *i* and *j*)

TABLE 7-3 THE VARIANCE-COVARIANCE MATRIX INVOLVED IN CALCULATING THE STANDARD DEVIATION OF A PORTFOLIO

Two securities:				
	$\sigma_{1,1}$	$\sigma_{1,2}$		
	$\sigma_{2,1}$	$\sigma_{2,2}$		
Four securities:				
	$\sigma_{1,1}$	$\sigma_{1,2}$	$\sigma_{1,3}$	$\sigma_{1,4}$
	$\sigma_{2,1}$	$\sigma_{2,2}$	$\sigma_{2,3}$	$\sigma_{2,4}$
	$\sigma_{3,1}$	$\sigma_{3,2}$	$\sigma_{3,3}$	$\sigma_{3,4}$
	$\sigma_{4,1}$	$\sigma_{4,2}$	$\sigma_{4,3}$	$\sigma_{4,4}$

Equation 7-13 illustrates the problem associated with the calculation of portfolio risk using the Markowitz mean-variance analysis. In the case of two securities, there are two covariances, and we multiply the weighted covariance term in Equation 7-12 by two since the covariance of A with B is the same as the covariance of B with A. In the case of three securities, there are six covariances; with four securities, 12 covariances; and so forth. The number of covariances grows quickly based on the calculation of $n(n - 1)$, where n is the number of securities involved. Because the covariance of A with B is the same as the covariance of B with A, there are $[n(n - 1)]/2$ unique covariances.

Table 7-3 illustrates the variance-covariance matrix associated with these calculations. For the case of two securities, there are four terms in the matrix—two variances and two covariances. For the case of four securities, there are 16 terms in the matrix—four variances and 12 covariances. The variance terms are on the diagonal of the matrix and, in effect, represent the covariance of a security with itself.

One of Markowitz's real contributions to portfolio theory is his insight about the relative importance of the variances and covariances. As the number of securities held in a portfolio increases, the importance of each individual security's risk (variance) decreases, while the importance of the covariance relationships increases. In a portfolio of 500 securities, for example, the contribution of each security's own risk to the total portfolio risk will be extremely small; portfolio risk will consist almost entirely of the covariance risk between securities.[1]

We can rewrite Equation 7-13 into a shorter format:

$$\sigma_p^2 = \sum_{i=1}^{n} \sum_{j=1}^{n} w_i w_j \sigma_{ij} \tag{7-14}$$

or

$$\sigma_p^2 = \sum_{i=1}^{n} \sum_{j=1}^{n} w_i w_j \rho_{ij} \sigma_i \sigma_j \tag{7-15}$$

[1] To see this, consider the first term in Equation 7-13:

$$\sum_{i=1}^{n} w_i^2 \sigma_i^2$$

Assume equal amounts are invested in each security. The proportions, or weights, will be $1/n$. Rewriting this term produces

$$\sum_{i=1}^{n} [(1/n)^2]\, \sigma_i^2 = \frac{1}{n} \sum_{i=1}^{n} \sigma_i^2/n$$

The term in brackets represents an average variance for the stocks in the portfolio. As n becomes larger, this average variance becomes smaller, approaching zero for large values of n. Therefore, the risk of a well-diversified portfolio will be largely attributable to the impact of the second term in Equation 7-13 representing the covariance relationships.

These equations account for both the variance and the covariances because when $i = j$, the variance is calculated; when $i \neq j$, the covariance is calculated.

To calculate portfolio risk using either Equation 7-14 or Equation 7-15, we need estimates of the variance for each security and estimates of the correlation coefficients or covariances. Both variances and correlation coefficients can be (and are) calculated using either *ex post* or *ex ante* data. If an analyst uses *ex post* data to calculate the correlation coefficient or the covariance and then uses these estimates in the Markowitz model, the implicit assumption is that the relationship that existed in the past will continue into the future. The same is true of the variances for individual securities. If the historical variance is thought to be the best estimate of the expected variance, it should be used. However, it must be remembered that an individual security's variance and the correlation coefficient between securities can change over time (and does).

SIMPLIFYING THE MARKOWITZ CALCULATIONS

The Markowitz model explained earlier allows us to calculate portfolio expected return and risk, and it generates the correct solution to the portfolio selection problem. It does so, however, at considerable cost. The major problem with the Markowitz full-covariance model is its complexity. It requires a full set of covariances between the returns of all securities being considered in order to calculate portfolio variance. There are $[n(n-1)]/2$ unique covariances for a set of n securities.[2]

EXAMPLE 7-9

An analyst considering 100 securities must estimate $[100(99)]/2 = 4{,}950$ unique covariances. For 250 securities, the number is $[250(249)]/2 = 31{,}125$ unique covariances.

Obviously, estimating large numbers of covariances quickly becomes a major problem for model users. Since many institutional investors follow as many as 250 or 300 securities, the number of inputs required may become an impossibility. In fact, until the basic Markowitz model was simplified in terms of the covariance inputs, it remained primarily of academic interest.

On a practical basis, analysts are unlikely to be able to directly estimate the large number of correlations necessary for a complete Markowitz analysis. In his original work, Markowitz suggested using an index to which securities are related as a means of generating covariances.

The Single Index Model is considered in Chapter 19.

USING THE INTERNET An interesting demonstration of estimating portfolio return and risk through simulation can be observed on a demonstration basis at www.financialengines.com. Select "The Service" and "Demonstration." You can choose several mutual funds, beginning investment amounts, and time horizon. The program will go through many simulations and report some final data on likely investment results. This website is being developed by William Sharpe, Nobel prize winner in Economics whose work is mentioned several times in this text.

[2] Although for n securities there are $n(n-1)$ total covariances, $\sigma_{ij} = \sigma_{ji}$; therefore, there are only one-half as many unique covariances.

EFFICIENT PORTFOLIOS

Efficient Portfolio A portfolio with the highest level of expected return for a given level of risk or a portfolio with the lowest risk for a given level of expected return

Markowitz's approach to portfolio selection is that an investor should evaluate portfolios on the basis of their expected returns and risk as measured by the standard deviation. He was the first to derive the concept of an **efficient portfolio**, defined as one that has the smallest portfolio risk for a given level of expected return or the largest expected return for a given level of risk. Investors can identify efficient portfolios by specifying an expected portfolio return and minimizing the portfolio risk at this level of return. Alternatively, they can specify a portfolio risk level they are willing to assume and maximize the expected return on the portfolio for this level of risk. Rational investors will seek efficient portfolios because these portfolios are optimized on the two dimensions of most importance to investors, expected return and risk.

To begin our analysis, we must first determine the risk-return opportunities available to an investor from a given set of securities. Figure 7-8 illustrates the opportunities available from a given set of securities. A large number of possible portfolios exist when we realize that varying percentages of an investor's wealth can be invested in each of the assets under consideration. Is it necessary to evaluate all of the possible portfolios illustrated in Figure 7-8? Fortunately, the answer is no because investors should be interested in only that subset of the available portfolios known as the efficient set.

The assets in Figure 7-8 generate the *attainable set* of portfolios, or the opportunity set. The attainable set is the entire set of all portfolios that could be found from a group of n securities. However, risk-averse investors should be interested only in those portfolios with the lowest possible risk for any given level of return. All other portfolios in the attainable set are *dominated*.

Using the inputs described earlier—expected returns, variances, and covariances—we can calculate the portfolio with the smallest variance, or risk, for a given level of expected return based on these inputs.[3] Given the minimum-variance portfolios, we can plot the *minimum-variance frontier* as shown in Figure 7-8. Point A represents the *global minimum-variance portfolio* because no other minimum-variance portfolio has a smaller risk. The bottom segment of the minimum-variance frontier, AC, is dominated by portfolios on the upper segment, AB. For example, since portfolio X has a larger return than portfolio Y for the same level of risk, investors would not want to own portfolio Y.

FIGURE 7-8

The attainable set and the efficient set of portfolios.

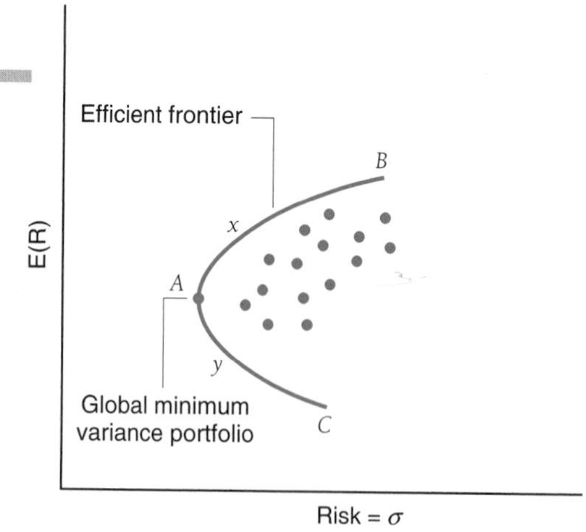

[3] Each investor doing this may use a different set of inputs, and therefore the outputs will differ.

The segment of the minimum-variance frontier above the global minimum-variance portfolio, AB, offers the best risk-return combinations available to investors from this particular set of inputs. This segment is referred to as the **efficient set** or efficient frontier of portfolios. This efficient set is determined by the principle of dominance—portfolio X dominates portfolio Y if it has the same level of risk but a larger expected return, or the same expected return but a lower risk.

The solution to the Markowitz model revolves around the portfolio weights, or percentages of investable funds to be invested in each security.[4] Because the expected returns, standard deviations, and correlation coefficients for the securities being considered are inputs in the Markowitz analysis, the portfolio weights are the only variable that can be manipulated to solve the portfolio problem of determining efficient portfolios.

Think of efficient portfolios as being derived in the following manner. The inputs are obtained and a level of desired expected return for a portfolio is specified, for example, 10 percent. Then all combinations of securities that can be combined to form a portfolio with an expected return of 10 percent are determined, and the one with the smallest variance of return is selected as the efficient portfolio. Next, a new level of portfolio expected return is specified—for example, 11 percent—and the process is repeated. This continues until the feasible range of expected returns is processed. Of course, the problem could be solved by specifying levels of portfolio risk and choosing that portfolio with the largest expected return for the specified level of risk.

DIVERSIFIABLE RISK VERSUS NONDIVERSIFIABLE RISK

Diversifiable Risk Specific risk related to a particular security that can be diversified away; nonsystematic risk

Nondiversifiable Risk Variability in a security's total returns directly associated with overall movements in the general market or economy; systematic risk

As we saw earlier, the riskiness of the portfolio generally declines as more stocks are added. This is because we are eliminating the **diversifiable risk**, or nonsystematic risk. This is unique risk related to a particular company. However, the extent of the risk reduction depends upon the degree of correlation among the stocks. As a general rule, correlations among stocks, at least domestic stocks and particularly large domestic stocks, are positive, although less than 1.0. Adding more stocks will reduce risk at first, but no matter how many partially correlated stocks we add to the portfolio, we cannot eliminate all of the risk.

Variability in a security's total returns that is directly associated with overall movements in the general market or economy is called market risk or **nondiversifiable risk** or systematic risk. Virtually all securities have some systematic risk, whether bonds or stocks, because systematic risk directly encompasses interest rate risk, market risk, and inflation risk. We defined nonsystematic and systematic risk in Chapter 6.

After the nonsystematic risk is eliminated, what is left is the nondiversifiable portion, or the market risk (systematic part). This part of the risk is inescapable because no matter how well an investor diversifies, the risk of the overall market cannot be avoided. If the stock market declines sharply, as in the summer of 1998, most stocks will be adversely affected; if it rises strongly, as in much of 1999, most stocks will appreciate in value. These movements occur regardless of what any single investor does.

Investors can construct a diversified portfolio and eliminate part of the total risk, the diversifiable or nonmarket part (nonsystematic part). Figure 7-9 illustrates this concept of declining nonsystematic risk in a portfolio of securities. As more securities are added, the nonsystematic risk becomes smaller and smaller, and the total risk for the portfolio approaches its systematic risk. Since diversification cannot reduce systematic risk, total portfolio risk can be reduced no lower than the total risk of the market portfolio.

How many securities does it take to eliminate most or all of the nonsystematic risk? It has become commonplace to say that approximately 10 to 15 securities will provide a diver-

[4] Technically, the basic Markowitz model is solved by a complex technique called quadratic programming.

FIGURE 7-9

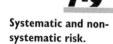

Systematic and non-systematic risk.

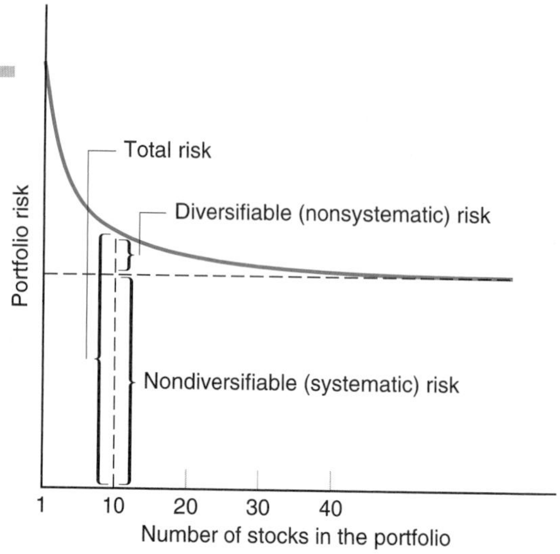

sified portfolio.[5] However, newer evidence suggests that at the very least 30 stocks, and perhaps more, are needed for a well-diversified portfolio.[6] Unfortunately, this study also suggests that individuals do not hold portfolios that are well diversified.

Diversification can substantially reduce the unique risk of a portfolio. However, Figure 7-9 indicates that no matter how much we diversify, we cannot eliminate systematic risk. The declining total risk curve in that figure levels off and becomes asymptotic to the systematic risk. Clearly, market risk is critical to all investors. It plays a central role in asset pricing because it is the risk that investors can expect to be rewarded for taking.

We know that the basic premise of investing is that investors demand a premium for bearing risk. However, we now know the importance of selecting portfolios of financial assets rather than holding individual securities. The relevant risk of an individual stock is its contribution to the riskiness of a well-diversified portfolio. The return that should be expected on the basis of this contribution can be estimated by the capital asset pricing model.

THE CAPITAL ASSET PRICING MODEL

Investors should expect a risk premium for buying a risky asset such as a stock. The greater the riskiness of that stock, the higher the risk premium should be. If investors hold well-diversified portfolios, they should be interested in portfolio risk rather than individual security risk. Different stocks will affect a well-diversified portfolio differently. The relevant risk for an individual stock is its contribution to the riskiness of a well-diversified portfolio. And the risk of a well-diversified portfolio is market risk, or nondiversifiable risk.

BETA

Beta A measure of volatility, or relative systematic risk

Beta is a measure of the systematic risk of a security that cannot be avoided through diversification. Beta is a *relative measure* of risk—the risk of an individual stock relative to the

[5] See J. Evans and S. Archer, "Diversification and the Reduction of Dispersion: An Empirical Analysis," *Journal of Finance* 23 (December 1968), pp. 761–767.

[6] See Meir Statman, "How Many Stocks Make a Diversified Portfolio?" *Journal of Financial and Quantitative Analysis* (September 1987), pp. 353–363.

FIGURE 7-10

Illustrative betas of 1.5(A), 1.0(B), and 0.6(C).

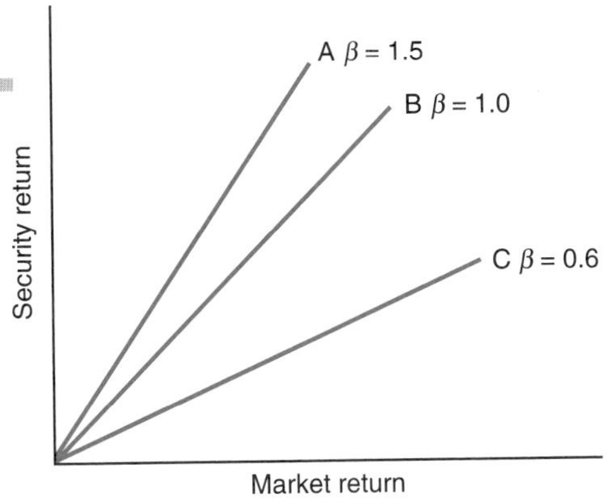

market portfolio of all stocks. If the security's returns move more (less) than the market's returns as the latter changes, the security's returns have more (less) volatility (fluctuations in price) than those of the market. For example, a security whose returns rise or fall on average 15 percent when the market return rises or falls 10 percent is said to be an aggressive, or volatile, security.

Securities with different slopes have different sensitivities to the returns of the market index. If the slope of this relationship for a particular security is a 45-degree angle, as shown for security B in Figure 7-10, the beta is 1.0. This means that for every 1 percent change in the market's return, *on average* this security's returns change 1 percent. The market portfolio has a beta of 1.0.

EXAMPLE 7-10

In Figure 7-10 Security A's beta of 1.5 indicates that, *on average*, security returns are 1.5 times as volatile as market returns, both up and down. A security whose returns rise or fall on average 15 percent when the market return rises or falls 10 percent is said to be an aggressive, or volatile, security. If the line is less steep than the 45-degree line, beta is less than 1.0; this indicates that, on average, a stock's returns have less volatility than the market as a whole. For example, security C's beta of 0.6 indicates that stock returns move up or down, on average, only 60 percent as much as the market as a whole.

In summary, the aggregate market has a beta of 1.0. More volatile (risky) stocks have betas larger than 1.0, and less volatile (risky) stocks have betas smaller than 1.0. As a relative measure of risk, beta is very convenient. Beta is useful for comparing the relative systematic risk of different stocks and, in practice, is used by investors to judge a stock's riskiness. Stocks can be ranked by their betas. Because the variance of the market is a constant across all securities for a particular period, ranking stocks by beta is the same as ranking them by their absolute systematic risk.[7] Stocks with high (low) betas are said to be high (low) risk securities.

The Capital Asset Pricing Model (APM) A model relating the expected (required) rate of return for a security or portfolio to its systematic risk

THE CAPM'S EXPECTED RETURN—BETA RELATIONSHIP

The **Capital Asset Pricing Model (CAPM)** formally relates the expected rate of return for any security or portfolio with the relevant risk measure. The CAPM's expected return—beta relationship is the most-often cited form of the relationship. Beta is the relevant measure of

[7] The absolute systematic risk for a stock is the product of the stock's beta squared and the variance of the return for the overall market.

risk that cannot be diversified away in a portfolio of securities and, as such, is the measure that investors should consider in their portfolio management decision process.

The CAPM in its expected return—beta relationship form is a simple but elegant statement. It says that the expected rate of return on an asset is a function of the two components of the **required rate of return**—the risk-free rate and the risk premium. Thus,

Required Rate of Return The minimum expected rate of return on an asset required by an investor to invest in that asset

$$k_i = \text{Risk-free rate} + \text{Risk premium}$$
$$= RF + \beta_i[E(R_M) - RF] \quad (7\text{-}16)$$

where

k_i = the required rate of return on asset i
$E(R_M)$ = the expected rate of return on the market portfolio
β_i = the beta coefficient for asset i

This relationship provides an explicit measure of the risk premium. It is the product of the beta for a particular security i and the **market risk premium**, $E(R_M) - RF$. Thus,

Market Risk Premium The difference between the expected return for the equities market and the risk-free rate of return

Risk premium for security i

$$= \beta_i(\text{market risk premium})$$
$$= \beta_i[E(R_M) - RF]$$

INVESTMENTS INTUITION Equation 7-16 indicates that securities with betas greater than the market beta of 1.0 should have larger risk premiums than that of the average stock and therefore, when added to RF, larger required rates of return. This is exactly what investors should expect, since beta is a measure of risk, and greater risk should be accompanied by greater return. Conversely, securities with betas less than that of the market are less risky and should have required rates of return lower than that for the market as a whole. This will be the indicated result from the CAPM, because the risk premium for the security will be less than the market risk premium and, when added to RF, will produce a lower required rate of return for the security.[8]

The CAPM's expected return–beta relationship is a simple but elegant statement about expected (required) return and risk for any security or portfolio. It formalizes the basis of investments, which is that the greater the risk assumed, the greater the expected (required) return should be. This relationship states that an investor requires (expects) a return on a risky asset equal to the return on a risk-free asset plus a risk premium, and the greater the risk assumed, the greater the risk premium.

EXAMPLE 7-11 Assume that the beta for IBM is 1.15. Also assume that RF is 0.05 and that the expected return on the market is 0.12. The required return for IBM can be calculated as

$$k_{IBM} = 0.05 + 1.15(0.12 - 0.05)$$
$$= 13.05\%$$

The required (or expected) return for IBM is, as it should be, larger than that of the market because IBM's beta is larger—once again, the greater the risk assumed, the larger the required return.

[8] The risk premium on the security will be less than the market risk premium, because we are multiplying by a beta less than 1.0.

FIGURE 7-11

The security market line (SML).

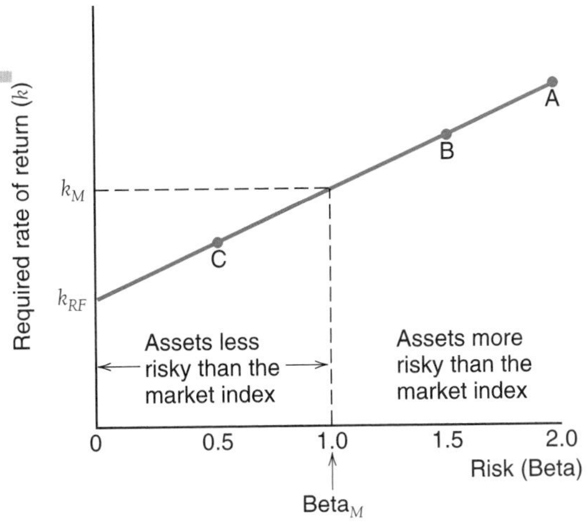

The Security Market Line (SML) The graphical depiction of the CAPM

The Security Market Line Equation 7-16 is the CAPM specification of how risk and required rate of return are related. This theory posits a linear relationship between an asset's risk and its required rate of return. This linear relationship, called the **Security Market Line (SML)**, is shown in Figure 7-11. Required rate of return is on the vertical axis and beta, the measure of risk, is on the horizontal return. The slope of the line is the difference between the required rate of return on the market index and RF, the risk-free rate.

It is worthwhile to note that the SML shows the required return and risk at a particular point in time. The SML can, and does, change over time as a result of:

1. Changes in the risk-free rate
2. Changes in the risk premium, which reflects investor beliefs

SUMMARY

- The expected return from a security must be estimated and may not be realized.
- Probability distributions are involved in the calculation of expected return.
- The standard deviation or variance of expected return for a security is a measure of the risk involved in the expected return; therefore, it also incorporates probabilities.
- The expected return for a portfolio is the weighted average of the individual security expected returns.
- Portfolio weights, designated w_i, are the percentages of a portfolio's total funds that are invested in each security, where the weights sum to 1.0.
- Portfolio risk is not a weighted average of the individual security risks. To calculate portfolio risk, we must take account of the relationships between the securities' returns.
- The correlation coefficient is a relative measure of the association between security returns. It is bounded by +1.0 and −1.0, with zero representing no association.
- The covariance is an absolute measure of association between security returns and is used in the calculation of portfolio risk.
- Portfolio risk is a function of security variances, covariances, and portfolio weights.
- The covariance term captures the correlations between security returns and determines how much portfolio risk can be reduced through diversification.
- The risk of a well-diversified portfolio is largely attributable to the impact of the covariances.

- The major problem with the Markowitz model is that it requires a full set of covariances between the returns of all securities being considered in order to calculate portfolio variance.
- Investors need to focus on that part of portfolio risk that cannot be eliminated by diversification because this is the risk that should be priced in financial markets.
- Total risk can be divided into systematic risk and nonsystematic risk. Nonsystematic risk, also called diversifiable risk, can be eliminated by diversification.
- Market risk cannot be eliminated by diversification and is the relevant risk for the pricing of financial assets in the market.
- Based on the separation of risk into its systematic and nonsystematic components, the Capital Asset Pricing Model (CAPM) can be constructed for individual securities (and portfolios). What is important is each security's contribution to the total risk of the portfolio, as measured by beta.
- Using beta as the measure of risk, the SML graphically depicts the trade-off between required return and risk for securities. The SML is a graph of the CAPM.
- Beta is a relative measure of risk. It indicates the volatility of a stock.

KEY WORDS

Beta
Capital Asset Pricing Model (CAPM)
Characteristic Line
Correlation coefficient
Covariance
Diversifiable risk
Efficient portfolio
Efficient set
Expected return
Market risk premium
Nondiversifiable risk
Portfolio weights
Required rate of return
Security market line (SML)
Systematic risk

QUESTIONS

7-1. Distinguish between historical return and expected return.

7-2. How is expected return for one security determined? For a portfolio?

7-3. Evaluate this statement: With regard to portfolio risk, the whole is not equal to the sum of the parts.

7-4. How many, and which, factors determine portfolio risk?

7-5. The Markowitz approach is often referred to as a mean-variance approach. Why?

7-6. When, if ever, would a stock with a large risk (standard deviation) be desirable in building a portfolio?

7-7. What is the relationship between the correlation coefficient and the covariance, both qualitatively and quantitatively?

7-8. Many investors have known for years that they should not "put all of their eggs in one basket." How does the Markowitz analysis shed light on this old principle?

7-9. How would the expected return for a portfolio of 500 securities be calculated?

7-10. What does it mean to say that portfolio weights sum to 1.0 or 100 percent?

7-11. What are the boundaries for the expected return of a portfolio?

7-12. What is meant by naive diversification?

7-13. How many covariance terms would exist for a portfolio of 10 securities? How many unique covariances?

7-14. How many terms would exist in the variance-covariance matrix for a portfolio of 30 securities? How many of these are variances, and how many covariances?

7-15. What type of risk tells us that the assumption of statistically independent returns on stocks is unrealistic?

7-16. In explaining diversification concepts and the analysis of risk, why is the correlation coefficient more useful than the covariance?

7-17. Should investors expect positive correlations between stocks and bonds? Bonds and bills? Stocks and real estate? Stocks and gold?

7-18. Calculate the number of covariances needed for an evaluation of 500 securities using the Markowitz model. Also, calculate the total number of pieces of information needed.

The following questions were asked on the 1991 CFA Level I examination:

CFA
7-19. Given the following:

Stock A standard deviation = 0.45
Stock B standard deviation = 0.32

If stock A and stock B have perfect positive correlation, which portfolio combination represents the minimum-variance portfolio?

a. 100% stock A
b. 50% stock A/50% stock B
c. 100% stock B
d. 30% stock A/70% stock B

CFA
7-20. Stocks A, B, and C each have the same expected return and standard deviation. Given the following correlations, which portfolio constructed from these stocks has the lowest risk?

Correlation Matrix

Stock	A	B	C
A	+1.0		
B	+0.9	+1.0	
C	+0.1	−0.4	+1.0

a. A portfolio equally invested in stocks A and B
b. A portfolio equally invested in stocks A and C
c. A portfolio equally invested in stocks B and C
d. A portfolio totally invested in stock C

CFA

7-21. Which statement about portfolio diversification is correct?

a. Proper diversification can reduce or eliminate systematic risk.

b. The risk-reducing benefits of diversification do not occur meaningfully until at least 10–15 individual securities have been purchased.

c. Because diversification reduces a portfolio's total risk, it necessarily reduces the portfolio's expected return.

d. Typically, as more securities are added to a portfolio, total risk is expected to fall at a decreasing rate.

CFA

7-22. For a two-stock portfolio, what would be the preferred correlation coefficient between the two stocks?

a. +1.00

b. +0.50

c. 0

d. −1.00

CFA

7-23. The unsystematic risk of a specific security

a. is likely to be higher in a rising market.

b. results from its own unique factors.

c. depends on market volatility.

d. cannot be diversified away.

7-24. Consider the following information for Exxon and Merck:

Expected return for each stock is 15 percent.
Standard deviation for each stock is 22 percent.
Covariances with other securities vary.

Everything else being equal, would the prices of these two stocks be expected to be the same? Why or why not?

7-25. Select the true statement from among the following:

a. The risk for a portfolio is a weighted average of individual security risks.

b. Two factors determine portfolio risk.

c. Having established the portfolio weights, the calculation of the expected return on the portfolio is independent of the calculation of portfolio risk.

d. When adding a security to a portfolio, the average covariance between it and the other securities in the portfolio is less important than the security's own risk.

7-26. Select the correct statement from among the following:

a. The risk of a portfolio of two securities, as measured by the standard deviation, would consist of two terms.

b. The expected return on a portfolio is usually a weighted average of the expected returns of the individual assets in the portfolio.

c. The risk of a portfolio of four securities, as measured by the standard deviation, would consist of 16 covariances and four variances.

d. Combining two securities with perfect negative correlation could eliminate risk altogether.

7-27. Select the false statement from among the following:

a. Under the Markowitz formulation, a portfolio of 30 securities would have 870 covariances.
b. Under the Sharpe formulation, a portfolio of 30 securities would require 92 pieces of data to implement.
c. Under the Markowitz formulation, a portfolio of 30 securities would have 870 terms in the variance-covariance matrix.
d. Under the Markowitz formulation, a portfolio of 30 securities would require 435 unique covariances to calculate portfolio risk.

7-28. Concerning the riskiness of a portfolio of two securities using the Markowitz model, select the true statements from among the following set:

a. The riskiness depends on the variability of the securities in the portfolio.
b. The riskiness depends on the percentage of portfolio assets invested in each security.
c. The riskiness depends on the expected return of each security.
d. The riskiness depends on the amount of correlation among the security returns.
e. The riskiness depends on the beta of each security.

7-29. Select the correct statement from the following statements regarding the Markowitz model:

a. As the number of securities held in a portfolio increases, the importance of each individual security's risk also increases.
b. As the number of securities held in a portfolio increases, the importance of the covariance relationships increases.
c. In a large portfolio, portfolio risk will consist almost entirely of each security's own risk contribution to the total portfolio risk.
d. In a large portfolio, the covariance term can be driven almost to zero.

PROBLEMS

7-1. Calculate the expected return and risk (standard deviation) for General Foods for 1999, given the following information:

Probabilities:	0.15	0.20	0.40	0.10	0.15
Expected returns:	0.20	0.16	0.12	0.05	−0.05

7-2. Four securities have the following expected returns:

$$A = 15\%, B = 12\%, C = 30\%, \text{and } D = 22\%$$

Calculate the expected returns for a portfolio consisting of all four securities under the following conditions:

a. The portfolio weights are 25 percent each.
b. The portfolio weights are 10 percent in A, with the remainder equally divided among the other three stocks.
c. The portfolio weights are 10 percent each in A and B, and 40 percent each in C and D.

7-3. Assume the additional information provided below for the four stocks in Problem 7-2.

	ρ (%)	Correlations with A	B	C	D
A	10	1.0			
B	8	0.6	1.0		
C	20	0.2	−1.0	1.0	
D	16	0.5	0.3	0.8	1.0

a. Assuming equal weights for each stock, what are the standard deviations for the following portfolios?
   A, B, and C
   B and C
   B and D
   C and D

b. Calculate the standard deviation for a portfolio consisting of stocks B and C, assuming the following weights: (1) 40 percent in B and 60 percent in C; (2) 60 percent in C and 40 percent in B.

c. In part a, which portfolio(s) would an investor prefer?

The following data apply to Problems 7-4 through 7-7.

Assume expected returns and standard deviations as follows:

	EG&G	GF
Return (%)	25	23
Standard deviation (%)	30	25
Covariance (%)	112.5	

The correlation coefficient, ρ, is +.15.

Proportion in EG&G w_i	GF $w_j = (1 - w_i)$	(1) Portfolio Expected Returns (%)	(2) Variance (%)	(3) Standard Deviation
1.0	0.0	25.0	900	30.0
0.8	0.2	24.6	637	25.2
0.6	0.4	24.2	478	21.9
0.2	0.8	23.4	472	21.7
0.0	1.0	23.0	625	25.0

7-4. Confirm the expected portfolio returns in column 1.

7-5. Confirm the expected portfolio variances in column 2.

7-6. Confirm the expected standard deviations in column 3.

7-7. On the basis of these data, determine the lowest risk portfolio.

The following questions were asked on the 1991 CFA Level I examination:

Use the following expectations on stocks X and Y to answer questions 7-8 through 7-10. (Round to the nearest percent.)

	Bear Market	Normal Market	Bull Market
Probability	0.2	0.5	0.3
Stock X	−20%	18%	50%
Stock Y	−15%	20%	10%

CFA
7-8. What is the expected return for stocks X and Y?

	Stock X	Stock Y
a.	18%	5%
b.	18%	12%
c.	20%	11%
d.	20%	10%

CFA
7-9. What is the standard deviation for returns on stocks X and Y?

	Stock X	Stock Y
a.	15%	26%
b.	20%	4%
c.	24%	13%
d.	28%	8%

CFA
7-10. Assume you invest your $10,000 portfolio into $9,000 in stock X and $1,000 in stock Y. What is the expected return on your portfolio?

a. 18%
b. 19%
c. 20%
d. 23%

The following questions were asked on the 1992 CFA Level I examination:

CFA
7-11. Given $100,000 to invest, what is the expected risk premium in dollars of investing in equities versus risk-free T-bills (U.S. Treasury bills) based on the following table?

Action	Probability	Expected Return
Invest in equities	.6	$50,000
	.4	−$30,000
Invest in risk-free T-bill	1.0	$ 5,000

a. $13,000
b. $15,000
c. $18,000
d. $20,000

CFA

7-12. Based on the scenarios below, what is the expected return for a portfolio with the following return profile?

	Market Condition		
	Bear	Normal	Bull
Probability	.2	.3	.5
Rate of return	−25%	10%	24%

a. 4%
b. 10%
c. 20%
d. 25%

7-13. Given the following information:
Expected return for the market, 12%
Standard deviation of market return, 21%
Risk-free rate, 8%
Correlation coefficient between
Stock A and the market, 0.8
Stock B and the market, 0.6
Standard deviation for stock A, 25%
Standard deviation for stock B, 30%

a. Calculate the beta for stock A and stock B.
b. Calculate the required return for each stock.

7-14. Assume that RF is 7 percent, the estimated return on the market is 12 percent, and the standard deviation of the market's expected return is 21 percent. Calculate the expected return and risk (standard deviation) for the following portfolios:
a. 60 percent of investable wealth in riskless assets, 40 percent in the market portfolio
b. 150 percent of investable wealth in the market portfolio
c. 100 percent of investable wealth in the market portfolio

7-15. Assume that the risk-free rate is 7 percent and the expected market return is 13 percent. Show that the security market line is

$$E(R_i) = 7.0 + 6.0\beta$$

Assume that an investor has estimated the following values for six different corporations:

Corporation	β_i	R_i(%)
GF	0.8	12
PepsiCo	0.9	13
IBM	1.0	14
NCNB	1.2	11
EG&G	1.2	21
EAL	1.5	10

Calculate the ER_i for each corporation using the SML, and evaluate which securities are overvalued and which are undervalued.

7-16. Assume that Exxon is priced in equilibrium. Its expected return next year is 14%, and its beta is 1.1. The risk-free rate is 6%.

a. Calculate the slope of the SML.
b. Calculate the expected return on the market.

The following question was asked on the 1993 CFA Level I examination.

CFA
7-17. Within the context of the Capital Asset Pricing Model (CAPM), assume:

- Expected return on the market = 15%
- Risk free rate = 8%
- Expected rate of return on XYZ security = 17%
- Beta of XYZ security = 1.25

Which *one* of the following is *correct*?

a. XYZ is overpriced.
b. XYZ is fairly priced.
c. XYZ's alpha is −0.25%.
d. XYZ's alpha is 0.25%.

www.wiley.com/college/jones7

In previous chapters of this text, you have been introduced to different kinds of instruments, and how they have performed over time. This chapter set us off on the road to understanding portfolio construction by introducing expected return and risk, the two key components necessary for this purpose. The corresponding exercises for Chapter Seven on the Jones Investments website address the following topics:

- Why stock prices change over time;
- Stock return and asset return distributions; and
- Domestic and International Diversification.

chapter 8

BOND YIELDS AND PRICES

Chapter 8 provides the analysis of bond yields and prices, including the valuation of bonds. An important part of this analysis is a consideration of how interest rates affect bond investors, which in turn helps us to understand how bond prices change over time. This chapter discusses the important concepts in bond analysis, such as yield to maturity and duration and covers the mechanics of bond calculations, an important part of an investor's toolkit.

After reading this chapter you will be able to:

- **Understand and calculate various bond yield measures, most importantly the yield to maturity.**
- **Calculate the price of a bond as a result of understanding how to value financial assets.**
- **Determine how bond prices change as the interest rate changes.**
- **Understand, calculate, and use the concept of duration.**

This chapter builds on the background developed in Part I and the return concepts discussed in Part II. Having discussed the characteristics of bonds in Chapter 2, we now focus on the basic principles governing bond yields and prices. A thorough understanding of these principles is essential to an investor's success in bond investing.

In addition to the total return concept considered in Chapter 6, which is applicable to any security, bond investors must also understand specific measures of bond yields. It is traditional in the bond markets to use various yield measures and to quote potential returns to investors on the basis of these measures. However, these measures can mislead unwary investors who fail to understand the basis on which they are constructed. Investors must understand that bond yields shown daily in sources such as *The Wall Street Journal* do not indicate the "true" yield an investor is promised when he or she buys bonds in the marketplace and holds them to maturity. On the other hand, "correct" yield quotes from your broker may lead you to expect a very different return from what you will actually earn.

How is the price of a bond determined? This question introduces the subject of valuation, a critical topic in any study of investments. The basic valuation principles we learn here are very important and will be used when considering other investing alternatives, particularly common stocks. In addition to calculating the price of a bond, we will learn why bond prices change and why some bonds are more sensitive to a change in market rates than are other bonds. As part of this analysis we will consider the important concept of duration, now widely recognized and used by bond investors.

BOND YIELDS

Bond yields and interest rates are the same concept. Therefore, we begin our discussion of bond yields with a brief consideration of interest rates.

Interest rates measure the price paid by a borrower to a lender for the use of resources over some time period—that is, interest rates are the price for loanable funds. The price differs from case to case, based on the demand and supply for these funds, resulting in a wide variety of interest rates. The spread between the lowest and highest rates at any point in time could be as much 10 to 15 percentage points. In bond parlance, this would be equivalent to 1,000 to 1,500 basis points since one percentage point of a bond yield consists of 100 **basis points**.

Basis Points 100 basis points is equal to one percentage point

It is convenient to focus on the one interest rate that provides the foundation for other rates. This rate is referred to as the short-term riskless rate (designated RF in this text) and is typically proxied by the rate on Treasury bills. All other rates differ from RF because of two factors: (1) maturity differentials, and (2) risk premiums.

THE BASIC COMPONENTS OF INTEREST RATES

Explaining interest rates is a complex task that involves substantial economics reasoning and study. Such a task is not feasible in this text.[1] However, we can analyze the basic determinants of nominal (current) interest rates with an eye toward recognizing the factors that affect such rates and cause them to fluctuate. The bond investor who understands the foundations of market rates can then rely on expert help for more details and be in a better position to interpret and evaluate such help.

[1] Most money and banking texts, as well as texts on financial markets, contain a good, concise discussion of interest rates.

Real Risk-Free Rate of Interest The opportunity cost of foregoing consumption, given no inflation

The basic foundation of market interest rates is the opportunity cost of foregoing consumption, representing the rate that must be offered to individuals to persuade them to save rather than consume. This rate is sometimes called the **real risk-free rate of interest**, because it is not affected by price changes or risk factors.[2] We will refer to it simply as the *real rate* and designate it RR in this discussion.

Nominal interest rates on Treasury bills consist of the RR plus an adjustment for *expected inflation*. A lender who lends \$100 for a year at 10 percent will be repaid \$110. But if inflation is 12 percent a year, the \$110 that the lender receives upon repayment of the loan is worth only (1/1.12) (\$110), or \$98.21. Lenders therefore expect to be compensated for the *expected* rate of price change in order to leave the real purchasing power of wealth unchanged. *As an approximation for discussion purposes*, this inflation adjustment can be added to the real risk-free rate of interest. Unlike RR, which is often assumed by market participants to be reasonably stable with time, adjustments for *expected* inflation vary widely over time.

Thus, for short-term risk-free securities, such as three-month Treasury bills, the nominal interest rate is a function of the real rate of interest and the *expected* inflationary premium. This is expressed as Equation 8-1, which is an approximation:[3]

$$RF \approx RR + EI \tag{8-1}$$

where

RF = short-term Treasury bill rate
RR = the real risk-free rate of interest
EI = the expected rate of inflation over the term of the instrument

Equation 8-1 is known as the *Fisher hypothesis* (named after Irving Fisher). It implies that the nominal rate on short-term risk-free securities rises point-for-point with anticipated inflation, with the real rate of interest remaining unaffected.[4] Turning Equation 8-1 around, estimates of the real risk-free rate of interest can be *approximated* by subtracting the *expected* inflation rate from the observed nominal interest rate.[5]

One of the best sources of expected inflation data is the survey of consumers conducted by the University of Michigan. Participants are asked to predict how much prices will change over a horizon of five to 10 years.

All market interest rates are affected by a *time factor* which leads to maturity differentials. That is, although long-term Treasury bonds are free from default risk in the same manner as Treasury bills, Treasury bonds typically yield more than Treasury notes, which typically yield more than Treasury bills. This typical relationship between bond maturity and yield applies to all types of bonds, whether Treasuries, corporates, or municipals. The *term structure of interest rates*, discussed in Chapter 9, accounts for the relationship between time and yield—that is, the maturity differentials.

Market interest rates other than those for riskless Treasury securities are also affected by a third factor, a *risk premium*, which lenders require as compensation for the risk involved. This risk premium is associated with the issuer's own particular situation or with a particular

---

[2] The real rate of interest cannot be measured directly. It is often estimated by dividing (1.0 + MIR) by (1.0 + EI), where MIR is the market interest rate and EI is expected inflation. This result can be approximated by subtracting estimates of inflation from nominal (market) interest rates (on either a realized or expected basis).

[3] The correct procedure is to multiply (1 + the real rate) by (1 + the expected rate of inflation), and subtract 1.0. For purposes of our discussion, the additive relationship is satisfactory.

[4] Fisher believed that inflation expectations were based on past observations as well as information about the future and that inflation expectations were slow to develop and slow to disappear.

[5] While estimates of the real federal funds rate can be made by subtracting actual inflation for the same quarter because federal funds are of very short duration, estimates of real rates on instruments with longer maturities require measures of expected inflation over the term of the instrument.

market factor. The risk premium is often referred to as the *yield spread* or yield differential. Yield spreads are discussed in Chapter 9.

MEASURING BOND YIELDS

Several measures of the yield on a bond are used by investors. It is very important for bond investors to understand which yield measure is being discussed, and what the underlying assumptions of any particular measure are.

Current Yield A bond's annual coupon divided by the current market price

Current Yield

Current yield is defined as the ratio of the coupon interest to the current market price and is the measure reported daily in *The Wall Street Journal* for those corporate bonds shown under the sections "New York Exchange Bonds" and "AMEX Bonds." The current yield is clearly superior to simply citing the coupon rate on a bond because it uses the current market price as opposed to the face amount of a bond (almost always, \$1,000). However, current yield is not a true measure of the return to a bond purchaser because it does not account for the difference between the bond's purchase price and its eventual redemption at par value.

Yield to Maturity The promised compounded rate of return on a bond purchased as the current market price and held to maturity

Yield to Maturity

The rate of return on bonds most often quoted for investors is the **yield to maturity (YTM)**, which is the bond's expected rate of return assuming no default and assuming the bond is held to maturity. It is the compound rate of return an investor will receive from a bond purchased at the current market price and held to maturity. If purchased at par, the YTM consists solely of interest income. If purchased for a price other than par, the YTM captures the coupon income to be received on the bond as well as any capital gains and losses realized by purchasing the bond for a price different from face value and holding to maturity.

The yield to maturity is the periodic interest rate that equates the present value of the expected future cash flows (both coupons and maturity value) to be received on the bond to the initial investment in the bond, which is its current price. To calculate the yield to maturity, we use Equation 8-2 where the market price, the coupon, the number of years to maturity, and the face value of the bond are known, and the discount rate or yield to maturity is the variable to be determined.

$$P = \sum_{t=1}^{2n} \frac{C_t/2}{(1 + YTM/2)^t} + \frac{MV}{(1 + YTM/2)^{2n}} \qquad (8\text{-}2)$$

where

P = the market price of the bond, which is known
n = the number of years to maturity
YTM = the yield to maturity to be solved for
C = the coupon in dollars
MV = the maturity value (or face value or par value)

Since both the left-hand side of Equation 8-2 and the numerator values (cash flows) on the right side are known, the equation can be solved for YTM. Because of the semiannual nature of interest payments, the coupon is divided in half and the number of periods is doubled. What remains (conceptually) is a trial-and-error process to find a discount rate (YTM) that equates the inflows from the bond (coupons plus maturity value) with its current price (cost). Different rates are tried until the left-hand and right-hand sides are equal. In reality, financial calculators or personal computers are set up to solve YTM problems.

For purposes of providing an *intuitive understanding* of the YTM, we illustrate the trial-and-error (iteration) process involved in this calculation by referring to the present value tables at the end of the text. The purpose is simply to demonstrate conceptually how to calculate the YTM. Investors will normally use a calculator or computer to do computations such as these.

EXAMPLE 8-1

A 10 percent coupon bond has 10 years remaining to maturity. Assume that the bond is selling at a discount with a current market price of \$885.30. *A bond is selling at a discount if the coupon rate is less than the current yield.* Because of the inverse relation between bond prices and market yields, it is clear that yields have risen since the bond was originally issued, because the price is less than \$1,000. Using Equation 8-2 to solve for yield to maturity,[6]

$$\$885.30 = \sum_{t=1}^{20} \frac{\$50}{(1 + \text{YTM}/2)^t} + \frac{\$1{,}000}{(1 + \text{YTM}/2)^{20}}$$

$$\$885.30 = \$50 \text{ (present value of an annuity, 6\% for 20 periods)} + \$1{,}000 \text{ (present value factor, 6\% for 20 periods)}$$

$$\$885.30 = \$50(11.4699) + \$1{,}000(0.3118)$$

$$\$885.30 = \$885.30$$

$$6\% = \text{semiannual YTM}$$

$$2 \times 6\% = \text{annual YTM}$$

In this example, the solution is 6 percent on a semiannual basis, which by convention is doubled to obtain the annual YTM of 12 percent. A YTM calculated by annualizing in this manner is referred to as the **bond-equivalent yield**.

Bond-Equivalent Yield Yield on annual basis, derived by doubling the semiannual yield

The YTM calculation for a zero-coupon bond is based on the same process expressed in Equation 8-2—equating the current price to the future cash flows. Because there are no coupons, the process reduces to Equation 8-3, with all terms as previously defined:

$$\text{YTM} = [\text{MV/P}]^{1/2n} - 1 \quad (8\text{-}3)$$

EXAMPLE 8-2

A zero-coupon bond has 12 years to maturity and is sold for \$300. Given the 24 semiannual periods, the power to be used in raising the ratio of \$1,000/\$300, or 3.333, is 0.04167 (calculated as 1/(2 × 12). Using a calculator with a power function produces a value of 1.0514. Subtracting the 1.0 and multiplying by 100 leaves a semiannual yield of 5.145 percent. Because YTM numbers typically are stated on an annual basis, the yield as calculated from Equation 8-3 must be doubled, which produces in this case an annual yield of 10.29 percent (the bond equivalent yield).

An investor who purchases a bond and holds it to maturity will earn the YTM as calculated on the purchase date (barring default or failure to receive the cash flows in a timely manner). Nevertheless, the bond's price, and its YTM, change daily, because interest rates fluctuate constantly.

[6] The present value of an annuity factor for 6 percent for 20 periods, 11.4699, is taken from Table A-4 at the end of the text; 0.3118, the present value of \$1 for 6 percent for 20 periods, is taken from Table A-2.

Yield to Call The promised return on a bond from the present to the date that the bond is likely to be called

Yield to Call Most corporate bonds, as well as some government bonds, are callable by the issuers, typically after some deferred call period. For bonds likely to be called, the yield-to-maturity calculation is unrealistic. A better calculation is the **yield to call**. The end of the deferred call period, when a bond can first be called, is often used for the yield-to-call calculation. This is particularly appropriate for bonds selling at a premium (i.e., high-coupon bonds with market prices above par value).[7]

To calculate the yield to first call, the YTM formula (Equation 8-2) is used, but with the number of periods until the first call date substituted for the number of periods until maturity and the call price substituted for face value. These changes are shown in Equation 8-4.

$$P = \sum_{t=1}^{2c} \frac{C_t/2}{(1 + YTC/2)^t} + \frac{CP}{(1 + YTC/2)^{2c}} \qquad (8\text{-}4)$$

where

c = the number of years until the first call date
YTC = the yield to first call
CP = the call price to be paid if the bond is called

Bond prices are calculated on the basis of the lowest yield measure. Therefore, for premium bonds selling above a certain level, yield to call replaces yield to maturity, because it produces the lowest measure of yield.

Realized Compound Yield (RCY) Yield earned based on actual reinvestment rates

Realized Compound Yield After the investment period for a bond is over, an investor can calculate the **realized compound yield (RCY)**. This rate reflects the compound yield on the bond investment assuming that all coupons are reinvested during the life of the bond. This is appropriate for an investor interested in accumulating a future sum of money from the bond investment, similar to investing a given amount and allowing it to compound over time. Note again that RCY cannot be calculated until after the investment period is over.

EXAMPLE 8-3

Assume an investor has $1,000 to invest for 20 years. This investor finds an investment (for example, a high-yield guaranteed CD) that will pay 10 percent annually, compounded semi-annually at the rate of 5 percent. Therefore, at the end of 20 years the investor would expect to have

$$\$1,000(1.05)^{40} = \$1,000(7.0400) = \$7,040$$

which includes the initial investment of $1,000 (in other words, the investor will earn $6,040 on the $1,000, given the compounding over time). What YTM would the investor have to earn on a bond investment of $1,000 to achieve the same result, which is to have a RCY of 10 percent over a 20 year period by earning $6,040 on the $1,000 bond investment?

The investor in Example 8-3 would have to earn a YTM of 10 percent over the life of the bond. However, the YTM on a bond will equal the RCY on the same bond only if all coupons are reinvested at an interest rate equal to the bond's YTM. If all coupons are reinvested at the calculated yield to maturity, the YTM will equal the realized compound yield after the investment period ends. If the coupons are reinvested at different rates, however,

[7] That is, bonds with high coupons (and high yields) are prime candidates to be called.

this will not be true. This highlights the importance of reinvestment rates to investors, and, therefore, reinvestment rate risk.

Interest on Interest The process by which bond coupons are reinvested to earn interest

Reinvestment Rate Risk That part of interest rate risk resulting from uncertainty about the rate at which future interest coupons can be reinvested

Reinvestment Risk When we consider the accumulation of wealth over some future period, using the YTM as the expected return measure, the YTM calculation assumes that the investor reinvests all coupons received from a bond at a rate equal to the computed YTM on that bond, thereby earning **interest on interest** over the life of the bond *at the computed YTM rate*. In effect, this calculation assumes that the reinvestment rate on all cash flows during the life of the bond is the calculated yield to maturity.

If the investor spends the coupons, or reinvests them at a rate different from the assumed reinvestment rate, the realized compound yield that will actually be earned at the termination of the investment in the bond will differ from the calculated YTM. And, in fact, coupons almost always will be reinvested at rates higher or lower than the computed YTM. This gives rise to **reinvestment rate risk**.

INVESTMENTS INTUITION Consider what happens when investors purchase bonds at high YTMs, such as 18 percent, when interest rates reached record levels in the summer of 1982. Those investors expecting to compound their money at, say, 18 percent were disappointed unless they reinvested the coupons at these YTMs; that is, investors did not actually achieve a realized compound yield equal to the calculated YTM. For the expected YTM to become a realized compound yield, coupons had to be reinvested over time at the record rates existing at the purchase date of the bond, an unlikely situation for a high-YTM bond with a long maturity. The subsequent decline in interest rates during the fall of 1982 illustrates the fallacy of believing that one has "locked up" record yields during a relatively brief period of very high interest rates. Investors in this situation are sometimes said to be subject to *yield illusion*.

This interest-on-interest concept significantly affects the potential total dollar return on a bond investment. The exact impact is a function of coupon and time to maturity, with reinvestment becoming more important as either coupon or time to maturity, or both, rises. Specifically:

1. Holding everything else constant, the longer the maturity of a bond, the greater the reinvestment risk.
2. Holding everything else constant, the higher the coupon rate, the greater the dependence of the total dollar return from the bond on the reinvestment of the coupon payments.

To illustrate the importance of interest on interest in YTM calculations involving future wealth accumulation, Table 8-1 shows the realized compound yields under different assumed reinvestment rates for a 10 percent noncallable 20-year bond purchased at face value, which compares directly to the alternative described in Example 8-3. If the reinvestment rate exactly equals the YTM of 10 percent, the investor actually earns a 10 percent realized compound yield when the bond is held to maturity, with $4,040 of the total dollar return from the bond attributable to interest on interest. At a 12 percent reinvestment rate, the investor will achieve a 11.14 percent realized compound yield, with almost 75 percent of the total return coming from interest on interest ($5,738/$7,738). With no reinvestment of coupons (spending them as received), the investor will achieve only a 5.57 percent realized compound yield.

Clearly, the reinvestment portion of the YTM concept is critical in these calculations. In fact, for long-term bonds, when coupons are reinvested, the interest-on-interest component of the realized compound yield achieved may account for more than three-fourths of the bond's total dollar return.

TABLE 8-1 REALIZED YIELDS, USING DIFFERENT REINVESTMENT RATE ASSUMPTIONS, FOR A 10 PERCENT 20-YEAR BOND PURCHASED AT FACE VALUE

(1) Coupon Income[a] ($)	(2) Assumed Reinvestment Rate (%)	(3) Total Return[b] ($)	(4) Amount Attributable to Reinvestment[c] ($)	(5) Realized Yields[d] (%)
2000	0	2000	0	5.57
2000	5	3370	1370	7.51
2000	8	4751	2751	8.94
2000	9	5352	3352	9.46
2000	10	6040	4040	10.00
2000	11	6830	4830	10.56
2000	12	7738	5738	11.14

[a]Coupon income = total dollars received from coupons over 20 years (40 semiannual periods) = $50 coupon received *semiannually* × 40 periods. 10 percent coupon bond generates $100 income annually.

[b]Total return = all coupons received plus all income earned from reinvesting the coupons over the life of the bond = sum of an annuity for 40 periods, $50 semiannual coupons
Example: at 10 percent reinvestment rate, $50 × 120.80 (120. 80 is the 5 percent, 40 period sum of an annuity factor) = $6,040.

[c]Amount attributable to reinvestment of coupons = total return minus coupon income. This is also known as the interest on interest. Notice that in each case it is $2,000 (the amount of the coupons) less than the Total Return.

[d]Realized yield = [Future Value per Dollar Invested]$^{1/N}$ − 1, where future value per dollar invested = (total return + the cost of bond)/cost of the bond.
Example: at a 10 percent reinvestment rate, future value per dollar invested is $6,040 + $1,000 (the cost of the bond)/ cost of the bond = $7,040/$1,000 = 7.04.
Next, raise 7.04 to the 1/40 or .025 power: $7.04^{.025} = 1.05$; 1.05 − 1.0 = .05 on a semiannual basis; {Note: 7.04 is the same value one would obtain by raising the semiannual rate of .05 to the 40th power (which reflects semiannual compounding for 20 years)—that is, $1.05^{40} = 7.04$.}
The result of this calculation is the realized yield on a semiannual basis. To put this on an annual basis, this figure must be doubled. This has been done for the yields in Table 8-1.

The realized compound yields shown in Table 8-1 can be calculated using the following formula:

$$\text{RCY} = \left[\frac{\text{Total dollars received}}{\text{Purchase price of bond}}\right]^{1/2n} - 1.0 \qquad (8\text{-}5)$$

EXAMPLE 8-4

For the bond calculations shown in Table 8-1, consider the realized compound yield an investor would achieve at an assumed reinvestment rate of 12 percent. The total dollars received equals the total dollar return shown in Table 8-1, $7,738, plus the cost of the bond, $1,000, or $8,738. Therefore,

$$\begin{aligned}\text{RCY} &= [\$8{,}738/1{,}000]^{1/40} - 1.0\\ &= [8.738]^{.025} - 1.0\\ &= 1.05569 - 1.0\\ &= 0.05569, \text{ or } 5.569\% \text{ on a semiannual basis}\end{aligned}$$

Once again, to place this on an annual basis, multiply by 2. The annual RCY is 5.569 percent × 2 = 11.14 percent.

One advantage of a zero-coupon bond is the elimination of reinvestment rate risk because there are no coupons to be reinvested. At the time of purchase investors know the YTM that will be realized when the bond is held to maturity.

Horizon Return Bond investors today often make specific assumptions about future reinvestment rates in order to cope with the reinvestment rate problem illustrated earlier.

Horizon Return Bond returns to be earned based on assumptions about reinvestment rates

This is sometimes referred to as *horizon analysis*. Given their explicit assumption about the reinvestment rate, investors can calculate the **horizon return** to be earned if that assumption turns out to be accurate.

The investor makes an assumption about the reinvestment rate expected to prevail over the planned investment horizon. The investor may also make an assumption about the yield to maturity expected to prevail at the end of the planned investment horizon, which in turn is used to estimate the price of the bond at that time. Based on these assumptions, the total future dollars expected to be available at the end of the planned investment horizon can be determined. The horizon return is then calculated as the interest rate that equates the total future dollars to the purchase price of the bond.

USING THE INTERNET The "Calculator" Section can be used at www.wallstreetcity.com to make a variety of bond calculations, including yield to maturity. A section on yield to call is also included.

BOND PRICES

THE VALUATION PRINCIPLE

What determines the price of a security? The answer is *estimated* value! A security's estimated value determines the price that investors place on it in the open market.

Intrinsic Value The estimated value of a security

A security's **intrinsic value**, or estimated value, is the present value of the expected cash flows from that asset. Any security purchased is expected to provide one or more cash flows some time in the future. These cash flows could be periodic, such as interest or dividends, or simply a terminal price or redemption value, or a combination of these. Since these cash flows occur in the future, they must be discounted at an appropriate rate to determine their present value. The sum of these discounted cash flows is the estimated intrinsic value of the asset. Calculating intrinsic value, therefore, requires the use of present value techniques. Equation 8-6 expresses the concept:

$$\text{Value}_{t=0} = \sum_{t=1}^{n} \frac{\text{Cash flows}}{(1 + k)^t} \tag{8-6}$$

where

$\text{Value}_{t=0}$ = the value of the asset now (time period 0)
Cash flows = the future cash flows resulting from ownership of the asset
k = the appropriate discount rate or rate of return required by an investor for an investment of this type
n = number of periods over which the cash flows are expected

To solve Equation 8-6 and derive the intrinsic value of a security, it is necessary to determine the following:

1. The expected *cash flows* from the security. This includes the size and type of cash flows, such as dividends, interest, face value *expected* to be received at maturity, or the *expected* price of the security at some point in the future.
2. The *timing* of the expected cash flows. Since the returns to be generated from a security occur at various times in the future, they must be properly documented for discounting back to time period 0 (today). Money has a time value, and the timing of future cash flows significantly affects the value of the asset today.

3. The *discount rate*, or required rate of return demanded by investors. The discount rate used will reflect the time value of the money and the risk of the security. It is an *opportunity cost*, representing the rate foregone by an investor in the next best alternative with comparable risk.

BOND VALUATION

The intrinsic value of a bond should equal the present value of its expected cash flows.[8] The coupons and the principal repayment are known, and the fundamental value is determined by discounting these future payments from the issuer at an appropriate required yield, r, for the issue. Equation 8-7 is used to solve for the value of a coupon bond.[9]

$$P = \sum_{t=1}^{2n} \frac{C_t/2}{(1 + r/2)^t} + \frac{MV}{(1 + r/2)^{2n}} \tag{8-7}$$

where

P = the present value of the bond today (time period 0)
C = the annual coupons or interest payments
MV = the maturity value (or par value) of the bond
n = the number of years to maturity of the bond
r = the appropriate discount rate or market yield

In order to conform with the existing payment practice on bonds of paying interest semiannually rather than annually, the discount rate being used (r) and the coupon (C_t) on the bond must be divided by 2, and the number of periods must be doubled. Equation 8-7 is the equation that underlies published bond quotes and standard bond practices.

For expositional purposes, we will illustrate the calculation of bond prices by referring to the present value tables at the end of the text; in actuality, a calculator or computer is used. The present value process for a typical coupon-bearing bond involves three steps, given the dollar coupon on the bond, the face value, and the current market yield applicable to a particular bond:

1. Using the *present value of an annuity* table (Table A-4 in the appendix), determine the present value of the coupons (interest payments).
2. Using the *present value* table (Table A-2 in the appendix), determine the present value of the maturity (par) value of the bond; for our purposes, the maturity value will always be $1,000.
3. Add the present values determined in steps 1 and 2 together.

EXAMPLE 8-5

Consider newly issued bond A with a three-year maturity, sold at par with a 10 percent coupon rate. Assuming semiannual interest payments of $50 per year for each of the next three years, the price of bond A, based on Equation 8-7, is:

$$P(A) = \sum_{t=1}^{6} \frac{\$50}{(1 + 0.05)^t} + \frac{\$1{,}000}{(1 + 0.05)^6} = \$50(5.0757) + \$1{,}000(0.7462)$$
$$= \$999.99, \text{ or } \$1{,}000$$

which, of course, agrees with our immediate recognition that the bond's price should be $1,000 since it has just been sold at par.

[8] An investor purchasing a bond must also pay to the seller the accrued interest on that bond.
[9] This formulation is nothing new; John Burr Williams stated it in a book in 1938. See John Burr Williams, *The Theory of Investment Value* (Cambridge, Mass.: Harvard University Press, 1938.)

Now consider bond B, with characteristics identical to A's, issued five years ago when the interest rate demanded for such a bond was 7 percent. Assume that the current discount rate or required yield on bonds of this type is 10 percent and that the bond has three years left to maturity. Investors certainly will not pay \$1,000 for bond B and receive the dollar coupon of \$70 per year, or \$35 semiannually, when they can purchase bond A and receive \$100 per year. However, they should be willing to pay a price determined by the use of Equation 8-7.

$$\begin{aligned} P(B) &= \sum_{t=1}^{6} \frac{\$35}{(1 + 0.05)^t} + \frac{\$1{,}000}{(1 + 0.05)^6} = \$35(5.0757) + \$1{,}000(0.7462) \\ &= \$923.85 \end{aligned}$$

Thus, bond B is valued, as is any other asset, on the basis of its future stream of benefits (cash flows), using an appropriate market yield. Since the numerator is always specified for coupon-bearing bonds at time of issuance, the only problem in valuing a typical bond is to determine the denominator or discount rate. The appropriate discount rate is the bond's required yield.

The *required yield*, *r*, in Equation 8-7 is specific for each particular bond. It is the current market rate being earned by investors on comparable bonds with the same maturity and the same credit quality. (In other words, it is an opportunity cost.) Thus, market interest rates are incorporated directly into the discount rate used to solve for the fundamental value of a bond.

Since market interest rates fluctuate constantly, required yields do also. When solving for a bond price it is customary to use the yield to maturity. If the YTM is used, we can, for convenience, restate Equation 8-7 in terms of price and YTM, as in Equation 8-8.

$$P = \sum_{t=1}^{2n} \frac{C_t/2}{(1 + YTM/2)^t} + \frac{MV}{(1 + YTM/2)^{2n}} \tag{8-8}$$

INVESTMENTS CALCULATION Solving for the price of a bond is an easy procedure in today's financial world using either a financial calculator or personal computer. For example, by using a basic financial calculator such as the HP-10B, price can be solved for after entering the cash flows and required yield.

BOND PRICE CHANGES

BOND PRICE CHANGES OVER TIME

We now know how to calculate the price of a bond, using the cash flows to be received and the YTM as the discount rate. Assume that we calculate the price of a 20-year bond issued five years ago and determine that it is \$910. The bond still has 15 years to maturity. What can we say about its price over the next 15 years?

When everything else is held constant, including market interest rates, any bond prices that differ from the bond's face value (assumed to be \$1,000) must change over time. Why? On a bond's specified maturity date, it must be worth its face value or maturity value. Therefore, over time, holding all other factors constant, a bond's price must converge to \$1,000 on the maturity date.

After bonds are issued they sell at discounts (prices less than \$1,000) and premiums (prices greater than \$1,000) during their lifetimes. Therefore, a bond selling at a discount will experience a rise in price over time, holding all other factors constant, and a bond selling at a premium will experience a decline in price over time, holding all other factors constant, as the bond's remaining life approaches the maturity date.

FIGURE 8-1

Bond price movements over time assuming constant yields for a 10 percent coupon, 15-year bond.

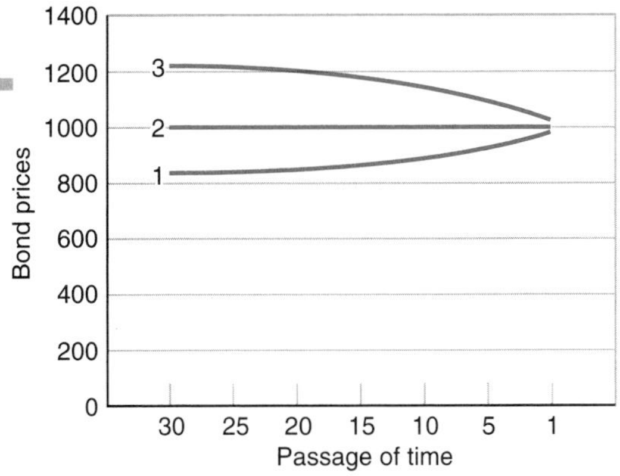

Figure 8-1 illustrates bond price movements over time assuming constant yields. Bond 2 in Figure 8-1 illustrates a 10 percent coupon, 30-year bond assuming that yields remain constant at 10 percent. The price of this bond does not change, beginning at $1,000 and ending at $1,000. Bond 1, on the other hand, illustrates an 8 percent coupon, 30-year bond assuming that required yields start, and remain constant, at 10 percent. The price starts below $1,000 because bond 1 is selling at a discount as a result of its coupon of 8 percent being less than the required yield of 10 percent. Bond 3 illustrates a 12 percent coupon, 30-year bond assuming that required yields start, and remain constant, at 10 percent. The price of bond 3 begins above $1,000 because it is selling at a premium (its coupon of 12 percent is greater than the required yield of 10 percent).

If all other factors are held constant, the price of all three bonds must converge to $1,000 on the maturity date. In actuality, however, other factors do not remain constant, in particular interest rates or yields to maturity. As interest rates change, and they do constantly, bond prices change. Furthermore, the sensitivity of the price change is a function of certain variables, especially coupon and maturity. We now examine these variables.

BOND PRICE CHANGES AS A RESULT OF INTEREST RATE CHANGES

Bond prices change because interest rates and required yields change. Understanding how bond prices change given a change in interest rates is critical to successful bond management. The basics of bond price movements as a result of interest rate changes have been known for many years. For example, over 30 years ago Burton Malkiel derived five theorems about the relationship between bond prices and yields.[10] Using the bond valuation model, he showed the changes that occur in the price of a bond (i.e., its volatility), given a change in yields, as a result of bond variables such as time to maturity and coupon. We will use Malkiel's bond theorems to illustrate how bond prices change as a result of changes in interest rates.

Bond Prices Move Inversely to Interest Rates Investors must always keep in mind a fundamental fact about the relationship between bond prices and bond yields: *Bond prices move inversely to market yields.* When the level of required yields demanded by investors on new issue changes, the required yields on all bonds already outstanding will also change. For these yields to change, the prices of these bonds must change. This inverse relationship is the basis for understanding, valuing, and managing bonds.

[10] Burton G. Malkiel, "Expectations, Bond Prices, and the Term Structure of Interest Rates," *Quarterly Journal of Economics*, May 1962, pp. 197–218.

TABLE 8-2 BOND PRICE AND MARKET YIELDS FOR A 10 PERCENT COUPON BOND

Time to Maturity	Bond Prices at Different Market Yields and Maturities				
	6%	8%	10%	12%	14%
1	$1,038.27	$1,018.86	$1000	$981.67	$963.84
5	1,170.60	1,081.11	1000	926.40	859.53
10	1,297.55	1,135.90	1000	885.30	788.12
15	1,392.01	1,172.92	1000	862.35	751.82
20	1,462.30	1,197.93	1000	849.54	733.37
25	1,514.60	1,214.82	1000	842.38	723.99
30	1,553.51	1,226.23	1000	838.39	719.22

EXAMPLE 8-6

Table 8-2 shows prices for a 10 percent coupon bond for market yields from 6 to 14 percent and for maturity dates from 1 to 30 years. For any given maturity, the price of the bond declines as the required yield increases and increases as the required yield declines from the 10 percent level. Figure 8-2 shows this relationship using data from Table 8-2.

An interesting corollary of the inverse relationship between bond prices and interest rates is as follows: *Holding maturity constant, a decrease in rates will raise bond prices on a percentage basis more than a corresponding increase in rates will lower bond prices.*

EXAMPLE 8-7

Table 8-2 shows that for the 15-year 10 percent coupon bond, the price would be $1,172.92 if market rates were to decline from 10 percent to 8 percent, resulting in a price appreciation of 17.29 percent. On the other hand, a rise of two percentage points in market rates from 10 percent to 12 percent results in a change in price to $862.35, a price decline of only 13.77 percent.

Obviously, bond price volatility can work for, as well as against, investors. Money can be made, and lost, in risk-free Treasury securities as well as more risky corporate bonds.

Although the inverse relationship between bond prices and interest rates is the basis of all bond analysis, a complete understanding of bond price changes as a result of interest rate changes requires additional information. An increase in interest rates will cause bond prices

FIGURE 8-2

The relationship between bond prices and market yields.

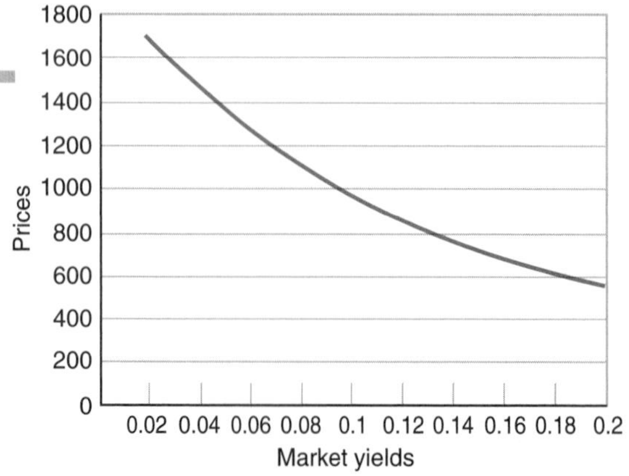

to decline, but the exact amount of decline will depend on important variables unique to each bond such as time to maturity and coupon. We will examine each of these in turn.

The Effects of Maturity The effect of a change in yields on bond prices depends on the maturity of the bond. An important principle is that *for a given change in market yields, changes in bond prices are directly related to time to maturity*. Therefore, as interest rates change, the prices of longer term bonds will change more than the prices of shorter term bonds, everything else being equal.

EXAMPLE 8-8

Given two 10 percent coupon bonds and a drop in market yields from 10 percent to 8 percent, we can see from Table 8-2 that the price of the 15-year bond will be $1,172.92, while the price of the 30-year bond will be $1,226.23.

The principle illustrated here is simple but important. Other things being equal, bond price volatility is a function of maturity. Long-term bond prices fluctuate more than do short-term bond prices.

A related principle regarding maturity is as follows: *The percentage price change that occurs as a result of the direct relationship between a bond's maturity and its price volatility increases at a diminishing rate as the time to maturity increases.*

EXAMPLE 8-9

As we saw above, a two percentage point drop in market yields from 10 percent to 8 percent increased the price of the 15-year bond to $1,172.92, a 17.29 percent change, while the price of the 30-year bond changed to $1,226.23, a 26.23 percent change.

This example shows that the percentage of price change resulting from an increase in time to maturity increases, but at a decreasing rate. Put simply, a doubling of the time to maturity will not result in a doubling of the percentage price change resulting from a change in market yields.

The Effects of Coupon In addition to the maturity effect, the change in the price of a bond as a result of a change in interest rates depends on the coupon rate of the bond. We can state this principle as (other things equal): *Bond price fluctuations (volatility) and bond coupon rates are inversely related*. Note that we are talking about percentage price fluctuations; this relationship does not necessarily hold if we measure volatility in terms of dollar price changes rather than percentage price changes.

The Implications of Malkiel's Theorems for Investors Malkiel's derivations for bond investors lead to a practical conclusion: the two bond variables of major importance in assessing the change in the price of a bond, given a change in interest rates, are its coupon and its maturity. This conclusion can be summarized as follows: A decline (rise) in interest rates will cause a rise (decline) in bond prices, with the most volatility in bond prices occurring in longer maturity bonds and bonds with low coupons. Therefore:

1. A bond buyer, in order to receive the maximum price impact of an expected change in interest rates, should purchase low-coupon, long-maturity bonds.
2. If an increase in interest rates is expected (or feared), an investor contemplating his or her purchase should consider those bonds with large coupons or short maturities, or both.

These relationships provide useful information for bond investors by demonstrating how the price of a bond changes as interest rates change. Although investors have no control over the change and direction in market rates, they can exercise control over the coupon and maturity, both of which have significant effects on bond price changes. Nevertheless, it is cumbersome to calculate various possible price changes on the basis of these theorems. Furthermore, maturity is an inadequate measure of the sensitivity of a bond's price change to changes in yields because it ignores the coupon payments and the principal repayment.

Investors managing bond portfolios need a measure of time designed to more accurately portray a bond's "average" life, taking into account all of the bond's cash flows, including both coupons and the return of principal at maturity. Such a measure, called duration, is available and is widely used today.

MEASURING BOND PRICE VOLATILITY: DURATION

In managing a bond portfolio, perhaps the most important consideration is the effects of yield changes on the prices and rates of return for different bonds. The problem is that a given change in interest rates can result in very different percentage price changes for the various bonds that investors hold. We saw earlier that both maturity and coupon affect bond price changes for a given change in yields.

Although maturity is the traditional measure of a bond's lifetime, it is inadequate, because it focuses only on the return of principal at the maturity date. Two 20-year bonds, one with an 8 percent coupon and the other with a 15 percent coupon, do not have identical *economic* lifetimes. An investor will recover the original purchase price much sooner with the 15 percent coupon bond. Therefore, a measure is needed that accounts for the entire pattern (both size and timing) of the cash flows over the life of the bond—the *effective maturity of the bond*. Such a concept, called duration, was conceived over 50 years ago by Frederick Macaulay. Duration is very useful for bond management purposes because it combines the properties of maturity and coupon.

Duration A measure of a bond's lifetime that accounts for the entire pattern of cash flows over the life of the bond

Duration Defined **Duration** measures the weighted average maturity of a (noncallable) bond's cash flows on a present value basis; that is, the present values of the cash flows are used as the weights in calculating the weighted average maturity.[11]

Figure 8-3 illustrates the concepts of both time to maturity and duration for a bond with five years to maturity, a 10 percent coupon, and selling for $1,000. As the figure indicates, the stream of cash flows generated by this bond over the term to maturity consists of $50 every six months, or $100 per year, plus the return of principal of $1,000 at the end of the five years. The last cash flow combines the interest payment of $50 with the principal repayment of $1,000 which occurs at the maturity date.

Although the term to maturity for the bond illustrated in Figure 8-3 is five years, its duration is only 4.055 years as indicated by the arrow. This means that the time-value-of-money weighted average number of years needed to recover the cost of this bond is 4.055. It is important that we understand how this duration value is calculated so that we can appreciate the purpose of duration, which is as a measure of the interest-rate sensitivity of a bond.

Calculating Duration To calculate duration, it is necessary to calculate a weighted time period. The time periods at which the cash flows are received are expressed in terms of years and denoted by t in this discussion. When all of these t's have been weighted and summed, the result is the duration, stated in years.

[11] This discussion applies only to option-free bonds.

FIGURE 8-3

Illustration of the cash flow pattern of a 10 percent-coupon, five-year maturity bond paying interest semiannually and returning the principal of $1,000 at maturity.

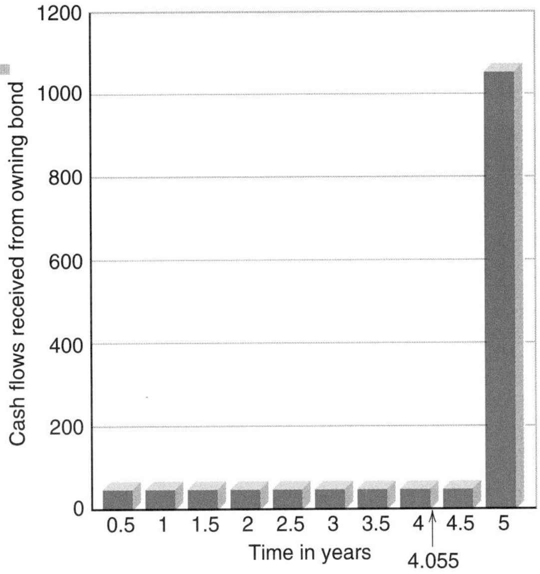

The present values of the cash flows serve as the weighting factors to apply to the time periods. Each weighting factor shows the relative importance of each cash flow to the bond's total present value, which is simply its current market price. The sum of the weighting factors will be 1.0, indicating that all cash flows have been accounted for. The sum of all the discounted cash flows from the bond will equal the bond's price. Putting this all together gives us the equation for duration, Equation 8-9:

$$\text{Macaulay Duration} = D = \sum_{t=1}^{n} \frac{\text{PV}(\text{CF}_t)}{\text{Market price}} \times t \tag{8-9}$$

where

- t = the time period at which the cash flow is expected to be received
- n = the number of periods to maturity
- $\text{PV}(\text{CF}_t)$ = present value of the cash flow in period t discounted at the yield-to-maturity
- Market price = the bond's current price or present value of all the cash flows

As Equation 8-9 shows, duration is obtained by multiplying each period's weighted cash receipt (weighted by the price of the bond) by the number of periods when each is to be received, and summing. Note that *duration is measured in years.*

EXAMPLE 8-10

Table 8-3 provides an example of calculating the duration for a bond, using the same bond as shown in Figure 8-3. This is a 10 percent coupon bond with five years remaining to maturity. The bond is priced at $1,000 for ease of exposition, and the YTM is 10 percent.[12]

[12] A shortcut formula can be used for coupon bonds selling at face value:

$$\text{Duration} = \frac{1 + \text{YTM}}{\text{YTM}} [1 - (1/(1 + \text{YTM})^n)]$$

Using the semiannual rate and doubling the number of periods, we must divide the answer by 2.0 to put it on an annual basis.

TABLE 8-3 AN EXAMPLE OF CALCULATING THE DURATION OF A BOND USING A 10 PERCENT COUPON, FIVE-YEAR MATURITY BOND PRICED AT $1,000

Coupon rate = 10% Period (t)	Term = 5 yrs. Cash Flow	Price = $1,000 PV Factor 5%	Yield = 10% PV of CF	t × PVCF
1	50	0.952	47.6	47.6
2	50	0.907	45.35	90.7
3	50	0.864	43.2	129.6
4	50	0.823	41.15	164.6
5	50	0.784	39.2	196
6	50	0.746	37.3	223.8
7	50	0.711	35.55	248.85
8	50	0.677	33.85	270.8
9	50	0.645	32.25	290.25
10	1050	0.614	644.7	6447
Total			1000.15	8109.2

Macaulay Duration in half years = 8109.20/1000 = 8.109

Macaulay Duration in years = 8.109/2 = 4.055

The cash flows consist of ten $50 coupons (the annual coupon is $100) plus the return of principal at the end of the fifth year. Notice that the final cash flow of $1,050 ($50 coupon plus $1,000 return of principal) accounts for 64.5 percent of the value of the bond. Because we do the calculation using semiannual periods, we must divide the result as calculated by 2 to convert to years, as shown in Table 8-3. The duration of 4.055 years is almost one year less than the term to maturity of five years. As we will see, duration will always be less than time to maturity for bonds that pay coupons.

Understanding Duration How is duration related to the key bond variables previously analyzed? An examination of Equation 8-9 shows that the calculation of duration depends on three factors:[13]

- The final maturity of the bond
- The coupon payments
- The yield to maturity

1. *Duration expands with time to maturity but at a decreasing rate* (holding the size of coupon payments and the yield to maturity constant, particularly beyond 15 years time to maturity). Even between 5 and 10 years time to maturity, duration is expanding at a significantly lower rate than in the case of a time to maturity of up to 5 years, where it expands rapidly.[14] Note that for all coupon-paying bonds, duration is always less than maturity. For a zero-coupon bond, duration is equal to time to maturity.[15]

[13] The duration of a bond can change significantly if there is a sinking fund or a call feature.

[14] The duration of a perpetuity is (1 + YTM)/YTM. This indicates that maturity and duration can differ greatly since the maturity of a perpetuity is infinite, but duration is not. That is, perpetuities have an infinite maturity but a finite duration.

[15] Deep discount bonds are an exception to the general rule. Their duration first increases with time to maturity, up to some distant point, and then decreases in duration beyond this point. This is because deep discount bonds with very long maturities behave like perpetuities.

2. *Yield to maturity is inversely related to duration* (holding coupon payments and maturity constant).
3. *Coupon is inversely related to duration* (holding maturity and yield to maturity constant). This is logical because higher coupons lead to quicker recovery of the bond's value, resulting in a shorter duration, relative to lower coupons.

Why is duration important in bond analysis and management? First, it tells us the difference between the effective lives of alternative bonds. Bonds A and B, with the same duration but different years to maturity, have more in common than bonds C and D with the same maturity but different durations. For any particular bond, as maturity increases the duration increases at a decreasing rate.

EXAMPLE 8-11

Given the 10 percent coupon bond discussed above with a yield to maturity of 10 percent and a five-year life, we saw that the duration was 4.055 years. If the maturity of this bond was 10 years, it would have an effective life (duration) of 6.76 years, and with a 20-year maturity it would have an effective life of 9.36 years—quite a different perspective. Furthermore, under these conditions, a 50-year maturity for this bond would change the effective life to only 10.91 years. The reason for the sharp differences between the term to maturity and the duration is that cash receipts received in the distant future have very small present values and therefore add little to a bond's value.

Second, the duration concept is used in certain bond management strategies, particularly immunization, as explained in Chapter 9.

Third, and most importantly for bond investors, duration is a measure of bond price sensitivity to interest rate movements; that is, it is a direct measure of interest rate risk. Malkiel's bond price theorems are inadequate to examine all aspects of bond price sensitivity. This issue is considered in some detail below because of its potential importance to bond investors.

Estimating Price Changes Using Duration The real value of the duration measure to bond investors is that it combines coupon and maturity, the two key variables that investors must consider in response to expected changes in interest rates. As noted earlier, duration is positively related to maturity and negatively related to coupon. However, bond price changes are directly related to duration; that is, the percentage change in a bond's price, given a change in interest rates, is proportional to its duration. Therefore, duration can be used to measure interest rate exposure.

Modified Duration Duration divided by 1 + yield to maturity

The term **modified duration** refers to Macaulay's duration in Equation 8-9 divided by $(1 + r)$, using annual interest, or $(1 + r/2)$, using semiannual interest.

$$\text{Modified duration} = D^* = D/(1 + r/2) \tag{8-10}$$

where

D^* = Modified duration
r = the bond's yield to maturity

and using semiannual interest to calculate duration.

EXAMPLE 8-12

Using the duration of 4.055 years calculated earlier and the YTM of 10 percent, the modified duration based on semiannual interest would be

$$D^* = 4.055/(1 + 0.05) = 3.86$$

The modified duration can be used to calculate the percentage price change in a bond for a given change in the yield, or r; that is, for small changes in yield, the price movements of most bonds will vary proportionally with modified duration. This is shown by Equation 8-11 *which is an approximation.*[16]

$$\text{Percentage change in bond price} \approx \frac{-D}{(1 + r)} \times \text{Percentage point change in the } r \tag{8-11}$$

or

$$\Delta P/P \approx -D^* \, \Delta r \tag{8-12}$$

where

ΔP = change in price
P = the price of the bond
$-D^*$ = modified duration with a negative sign (the negative sign occurs because of the inverse relation between price changes and yield changes)
Δr = the instantaneous change in yield

EXAMPLE 8-13

Using our same bond with a modified duration of 3.86, assume an instantaneous yield change of 20 basis points (+0.0020) in the YTM, from 10 percent to 10.20 percent. The approximate change in price, based on Equation 8-12 would be:

$$\Delta P/P = -3.86 \times (+0.0020) \times 100 = -0.772\%$$

Given the original price of the bond of \$1,000, this percentage price change would result in an estimated bond price of \$992.28. For very small changes in yield, Equation 8-11 or 8-12 produces a good approximation.[17]

In summary, a bond's modified duration shows the bond's percentage change in price for a one percentage point change in its yield. It can be used to measure the price risk of a bond or a bond portfolio since the same holds true for a portfolio of bonds.

Convexity Although Equation 8-11 generally provides only an approximation, for very small changes in the required yield the approximation is quite close and at times could be exact. However, as the changes become larger the approximation becomes poorer. The problem is that modified duration produces symmetric percentage price change estimates using Equation 8-11 (if r had decreased 0.20 percent, the price change would have been +0.772 percent) when, in actuality, the price-yield relationship is not linear. This relationship is, in fact, curvilinear, as Figure 8-2 shows.

Convexity A measure of the degree to which the relationship between a bond's price and yield departs from a straight line

We refer to the curved nature of the price-yield relationship as the bond's convexity (the relationship is said to be convex because it opens upward). More formally, **convexity** is the term used to refer to the degree to which duration changes as the yield to maturity changes. The degree of convexity is not the same for all bonds. Calculations of price changes should

[16] This formula can provide an exact estimate of the percentage price change if the change in yield is very small and the security does not involve options.

[17] To prove this, we could solve for the price of this bond using a YTM of 10.20 percent. If we did, we would find that the price should decline to \$992.32, a percentage decline of .768 percent as compared to our estimate of .772 percent. For larger changes in yield, such as 100 or 200 basis points, the approximate percentage price change is less good.

FIGURE 8-4

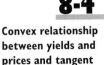

Convex relationship between yields and prices and tangent line representing modified duration for a 10 percent, 10-year bond.

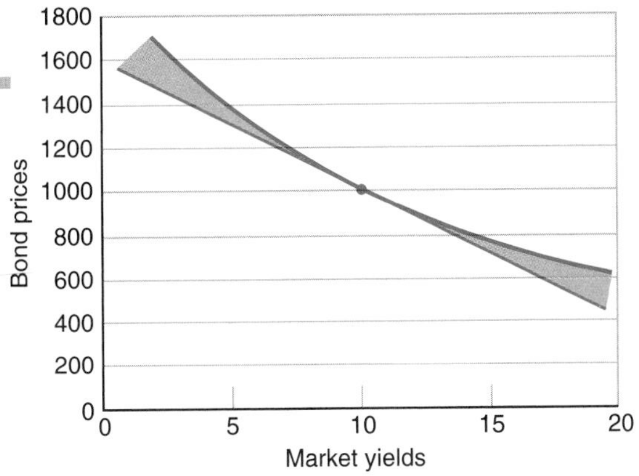

properly account for this convexity in order to improve the approximation of a bond's price change given some yield change.[18]

To understand the convexity issue, Figure 8-4 repeats the analysis from Figure 8-2 which shows a 10 percent coupon bond at different market yields and prices. We can think of duration graphically as the slope of a line that is tangent to the convex price-yield curve of Figure 8-4 at the current price and yield of the bond, which is assumed to be $1,000 and 10 percent.[19] In effect, we are using a tangent line to measure the slope of the curve that depicts bond prices as a function of market yields. For a very small change in yield, such as a few basis points, the slope of the line—the duration—provides a good approximation for the rate of change in price given a change in yield. As the change in yield increases, the error that results from using a straight line to estimate a bond's price behavior as given by a curve increases.[20]

As we move away from the point of tangency in Figure 8-4 in either direction, we underestimate the change in price of the bond using duration; that is, the price change is always more favorable than suggested by the duration. Notice that the shaded area in Figure 8-4 captures the convexity areas both above and below the starting point of 10 percent and $1,000. If yields decrease, prices increase, and the duration tangent line fails to indicate the true higher price, which is given by the curve. Conversely, when yields increase, prices decrease, but the duration tangent line overstates the amount of the price decrease relative to the true convex relationship. This helps to illustrate what is meant by the term *positive convexity*.

Convexity is largest for low coupon bonds, long-maturity bonds, and low yields to maturity. A zero-coupon, long-term bond would have a large amount of convexity. If convexity is large, large changes in duration are implied, with corresponding inaccuracies in forecasts of price changes.

Convexity calculations can be made similar to those with modified duration discussed earlier. These calculations produce an approximate percentage price change due to convexity which can be added to the approximate percentage price change based on duration discussed earlier. This *total percentage price change* is still an approximation, but it is considerably improved over that using only duration.

[18] An in-depth discussion of convexity is beyond the scope of this text. For a more detailed discussion, see Frank J. Fabozzi and T. Dessa Fabozzi, *The Handbook of Fixed Income Securities*. Fourth Edition. Irwin Professional Publishing, 1995.

[19] Technically, the slope of the tangent line in Figure 8-4 is equal to the negative of modified duration multiplied by the bond's current market price.

[20] As the yield changes, the tangency line and slope also change; that is, modified duration changes as yield changes.

Box 8-1

LENGTH DOES MATTER: MANAGE DURATION TO GET GOOD RETURNS FROM U.S. BONDS

Investors these days look to U.S. government bonds for more than security—they want good returns, too. How do you put together a bond portfolio that will help you meet your goals while keeping risk in check? The answer, according to Douglas Rogers, comanager of Heartland U.S. Government Securities Fund, may be to "add a little defense to [your] offense."

Rogers knows what he's talking about. In 1994, when six short-term-rate increases by the Federal Reserve drove the average short-term bond-fund return down to −1.27 percent, the Sit U.S. Government Securities Fund, which he then managed with Michael Brilley, gained 1.77 percent. The following year, Rogers moved to Heartland, where he and comanager Patrick Retzer have generated returns that in 1997 placed the fund into the top 10 percent of its peer group.

How do Rogers and Retzer meld defense and offense? They look for the maturity range that promises the best risk-adjusted returns and then buy and sell specific bonds within this group, practicing sector rotation and duration management.

Rogers and Retzer focus on intermediate-term bonds with three to 10 years to maturity. Heartland Funds studied the performance of U.S. Treasury securities during the 25 years from January 1971 through December 1995 and found that though the long maturities beat the intermediates in compound average annual return, 9.7 percent to 9 percent, they were also 80 percent more volatile. The long bonds had a Sharpe ratio—which measures return per unit of risk—of 0.2, compared with 29.4 for the intermediates.

Within the intermediate segment, the managers pick their purchases in much the same way as you might shop for a car: comparing models with the same performance and safety features, then buying the cheapest one. In the case of bonds, *cheap* translates into *relatively high yield.* (Prices fall when interest rates rise, so a 20-year bond that yields more than other long-term debt in the market is less expensive.)

"Say we're considering two mortgage-backed securities, and we estimate that they're both five-year investments," says Rogers. "But when we compare their historical yields, it appears that one is trading 90 basis points above the curve—and we think it should be at 75. So we buy the one paying an above-average yield. If we're right, the yield will drop back to a normal level, and the bond's price will increase more than similar issues. Then we sell." (Since a mortgage-backed bond's yield is based on a presumed level of prepayments by homeowners, Rogers also compares the expected cash flows of the securities he's considering.)

Rogers sets a target price for each bond he holds. When this price is reached, he cashes in and buys a new cheap bond. He calls this technique sector rotation—trading out of fully valued securities into undervalued ones. The potential for price appreciation protects his returns against small rate rises. To guard against *large* moves, however, he practices duration management.

Duration measures how sensitive a bond's price is to moves in interest rates—the longer the duration, the more the price will be affected by a change in rates. When Rogers thinks interest rates are going to fall (pushing up bond prices), he weights his portfolio toward bonds with longer durations; when he believes rates have bottomed out, he shortens the fund's overall duration.

If you want to practice this type of management, you can do so using index bond funds that target duration. By combining long-, intermediate-, and short-term funds (including money markets), you can fine-tune the duration of your portfolio just as professionals do.

To estimate your interest-rate risk, multiply the duration that each fund targets by the percentage of your portfolio it accounts for. For example, if 50 percent of your bond money is in a fund with a duration of 5 and the rest in one with a duration of 10, your overall duration is 7.5. To boost it to 8, rebalance so that 60 percent of your portfolio is in the longer fund and 40 percent in the shorter one. You can do this either by shifting money between the funds or by adding new money to the longer one.

But keep your duration bets small. Remember: Longer bonds offer only slightly more return for a lot more risk.

SOURCE: William Hester, "Length Does Matter," *Bloomberg Personal Finance,* July/August 1998, p. 21. Reprinted by permission.

Some Conclusions on Duration What does this analysis of price volatility mean to bond investors? The message is simple—to obtain the maximum (minimum) price volatility from a bond, investors should choose bonds with the longest (shortest) duration. If an investor already owns a portfolio of bonds, he or she can act to increase the average modified duration of the portfolio if a decline in interest rates is expected and the investor is attempting to achieve the largest price appreciation possible. Fortunately, duration is additive, which means that a bond portfolio's modified duration is a (market-value) weighted average of each individual bond's modified duration.

How popular is the duration concept in today's investment world? This concept has become widely known and referred to in the popular press. Investors can find duration numbers in a variety of sources, particularly with regard to bond funds. See Box 8-1 for a discussion of duration management.

Although duration is an important measure of bond risk, it is not necessarily always the most appropriate one. Duration measures volatility, which is important but is only one aspect of the risk in bonds. If an investor considers volatility an acceptable proxy for risk, duration is the measure of risk to use along with the correction for convexity. Duration may not be a complete measure of bond risk, but it does reflect some of the impact of changes in interest rates.

SUMMARY

- The level of market interest rates for short-term, risk-free securities is a function of the real rate of interest and inflationary expectations. Inflationary expectations are the primary variable in understanding changes in market rates for short-term, default-free securities.
- Other interest rates vary from the short-term riskless rate as a result of maturity differential and risk premiums.
- The yield to maturity is defined as the compound rate of return an investor will receive from a bond purchased at the current market price and held to maturity.
- The yield to call is the expected yield to the end of the deferred call period, when a bond first can be called.
- The horizon return is the total rate of return earned on a bond over some time period given a specified reinvestment rate of return.
- A security's intrinsic value is its estimated value, or the present value of the expected cash flows from that asset. To calculate intrinsic value, the expected cash flows, specified as to amounts and timing, and the discount rate or required rate of return are needed.
- Bonds are valued using a present value process. The cash flows for a bond—interest payments and principal repayments—are discounted at the bond's required yield.
- Bond prices change over time independent of other factors because they must be worth their face value (typically, $1,000) on the maturity date.
- Bond prices move inversely with interest rates, with price increasing (decreasing) as the required yield decreases (increases).
- Changes in bond prices are directly related to time to maturity and inversely related to bond coupons.
- The two bond variables of major importance in assessing the change in price of a bond, given a change in interest rates, are its coupon and its maturity.
- Duration, stated in years, is the weighted average time to recovery of all interest payments plus principal repayment.

- Duration expands with time to maturity but at a decreasing rate, and it is inversely related to coupon and yield to maturity.
- The modified duration can be used to calculate the percentage price change in a bond for a given change in the bond's yield to maturity.
- The bond price-yield relationship is not linear but convex, and precise calculations of price changes should properly account for this convexity.

KEY WORDS

Basis points
Bond-equivalent yield
Convexity
Current yield
Duration
Horizon return
Interest on interest
Intrinsic value
Modified duration
Realized compound yield (RCY)
Real risk-free rate of interest
Reinvestment rate risk
Yield to call
Yield to maturity (YTM)

QUESTIONS

8-1. Define YTM. How is YTM determined?

8-2 Why is YTM important?

8-3. What does it mean to say that YTM is an expected yield?

8-4. If YTM is merely a promised yield, why do investors not use some other measure of yield?

8-5. What is meant by interest on interest?

8-6. Which bond is more affected by interest-on-interest considerations?
a. Bond A—12 percent coupon, 20 years to maturity
b. Bond B—6 percent coupon, 25 years to maturity

8-7. Distinguish between YTM and RCY. How does interest on interest affect the RCY?

8-8. How can bond investors eliminate the reinvestment rate risk inherent in bonds?

8-9. How is the intrinsic value of any asset determined? How are intrinsic value and present value related?

8-10. How is the price of a bond determined? Why is this process relatively straightforward for a bond?

8-11. What effect does the use of semiannual discounting have on the value of a bond in relation to annual discounting?

8-12. What are the implications of Malkiel's bond price theorems to bond investors? Which two bond variables are of major importance in assessing bond price changes?

8-13. How does duration differ from time to maturity? What does duration tell you?

8-14. How is duration related to time to maturity? to coupon? Do the same relationships hold for a zero-coupon bond?

8-15. Assume that a bond investor wishes to maximize the potential price volatility from a portfolio of bonds about to be constructed. What should this investor seek in the way of coupon, maturity, and duration?

8-16. Is duration a complete measure of bond risk? Is it the best measure?

8-17. When is a bond selling at a discount, based on coupon rate and current yield? A premium?

8-18. What assumptions are involved in calculating the horizon return?

8-19. How is duration related to the final maturity of the bond? the coupon payments? the yield to maturity?

8-20. What is meant by convexity? Why should bond investors consider it?

8-21. Duration may be calculated by two widely used methods. Identify these two methods, and briefly discuss the primary differences between them.

DEMONSTRATION PROBLEMS

8-1. CALCULATE THE PRICE OF A BOND:

Consider a bond with the following characteristics:

C = an \$80 coupon = (0.08)(\$1,000)
par = \$1,000 face value
r = 0.10, the discount rate, the going market interest rate on similar securities
n = exactly three years—the time to maturity under two different conditions:

a. Annual coupon payments, \$80 is received at the end of each year.
b. Semiannual coupon payments, \$40 is received every six months.

Under either condition, the price of the bond is the present value of the discounted cash flows, as follows:

Future Date	Assumption A	Assumption B
6 months		$\$40/(1.05) = \$38.095$
1 year	$\$80/(1.10) = \$72.726$	$\$40/(1.05)^2 = 36.281$
1.5 years		$\$40/(1.05)^3 = 34.554$
2 years	$\$80/(1.10)^2 = 66.116$	$\$40/(1.05)^4 = 32.908$
2.5 years		$\$40/(1.05)^5 = 31.341$
3 years	$\$80/(1.10)^3 = 60.105$	$\$40/(1.05)^6 = 29.849$
3 years	$\$1000/(1.10)^3 = 751.315$	$\$1000/(1.05)^6 = 746.215$
Price	\$950.26	\$949.243

Since the discount rate (10 percent) exceeds the coupon rate (8 percent), the bond is selling at a discount. The prices differ because of the timing of the coupon payments.

8-2. CALCULATE THE PRICE OF A BOND, ALTERNATIVE FORMULA:

Here is an equivalent formula, used in bond tables, that appears more complex but actually is easier to calculate. For the bond described in Demonstration Problem 8-1, the value of the sum of the coupon payments can be calculated together with the discounted value of par. For the annual coupons (Assumption A):

$$P = \frac{C}{r}\left[1 - \frac{1}{(1+r)^t}\right] + \frac{\text{Par}}{(1+r)^t} = \frac{80}{0.10}\left[1 - \frac{1}{(1.10)^3}\right] + \frac{1{,}000}{(1.10)^3}$$

$$= 198.948 + 751.315 = \$950.26$$

Using semiannual coupons and discount rates (Assumption B):

$$P = \frac{C/2}{r/2}\left[1 - \frac{1}{(1 + r/2)^{2t}}\right] + \frac{\text{Par}}{(1 + r/2)^{2t}}$$

$$= \frac{40}{.05}\left[1 - \frac{1}{(1.05)^6}\right] + \frac{1{,}000}{(1.05)^6}$$

$$= \$203.028 + \$746.215 = \$949.24$$

8-3. THE CALCULATION OF DURATION ON A SEMIANNUAL BASIS:

C = an \$80 coupon = (0.08)(\$1,000)
par = \$1,000 face value
r = 0.10, the discount rate, the going market interest rate on similar securities
n = exactly three years—the time to maturity

(1) Future Date	(2) PV of Cash Flows	(3)/ 949.243	(4) Years	(3) × (4)
6 months	38.095	0.04013	0.5	0.02007
1 year	36.281	0.03822	1.0	0.03822
1.5 years	34.554	0.03640	1.5	0.05460
2 years	32.908	0.03467	2.0	0.06934
2.5 years	31.341	0.03302	2.5	0.08255
3 years	29.849	0.03145	3.0	0.09435
3 years	746.215	0.78612	3.0	2.35836
Sum	949.246	1.00120		2.71749
				Duration = 2.72 years

PROBLEMS

8-1. Using the information in Demonstration Problem 8-1, if the coupon rate for the bond is 10 percent and the discount rate is 8 percent, with the same three years to maturity, show that the price of the bond is \$1,051.54 with annual discounting and \$1,052.24 with semiannual discounting. Use a calculator to determine the discount factors.

What would be the price of this bond if both the coupon rate and the discount rate were 10 percent?

8-2. Using the information in Demonstration Problem 8-2, solve for the price of the bond in Problem 8-1 using both annual and semiannual discounting. Use a calculator to solve these problems.

8-3. With reference to Problem 8-2, what would be the price of the bond if the coupon were paid quarterly?

8-4. Calculate the price of a 10 percent coupon bond with eight years to maturity, given an appropriate discount rate of 12 percent, using both annual and semiannual discounting. Use the tables contained in the appendix at the end of the text.

8-5. Calculate the price of the bond in Problem 8-4 if the maturity is 20 years rather than eight years. Use semiannual discounting and the tables in the appendix. Which of Malkiel's principles are illustrated when comparing the price of this bond to the price determined in Problem 8-1?

8-6. The YTM on a 10 percent, 15-year bond is 12 percent. Calculate the price of the bond.

8-7. Calculate the YTM for a 10-year zero-coupon bond sold at \$400. Recalculate the YTM if the bond had been priced at \$300.

8-8. Calculate the realized compound yield for a 10 percent bond with 20 years to maturity and an expected reinvestment rate of 8 percent.

8-9. Consider a 12 percent 10-year bond purchased at face value. Based on Table 8-1 and assuming a reinvestment rate of 10 percent, calculate:

a. The interest on interest
b. The total return
c. The realized return

8-10. Consider a junk bond with a 12 percent coupon and 20 years to maturity. The current required rate of return for this bond is 15 percent. What is its price? What would its price be if the required yield rose to 17 percent? 20 percent?

8-11. A 12 percent coupon bond with 10 years to maturity is currently selling for \$913.50. Determine the modified duration for this bond.

8-12. Consider a 4 percent coupon bond with 15 years to maturity. Determine the YTM that would be necessary to drive the price of this bond to \$300.

8-13. Determine the point at which duration decreases with maturity for a 4 percent bond with an original maturity of 15 years. Use increments in maturity of five years. The market yield on this bond is 15 percent.

8-14. Calculate the yield to first call for a 10 percent, 10-year bond that is callable five years from now. The current market price is \$970, and the call price is \$1,050.

8-15. Calculate the YTM for the following bonds.

a. A 12 percent, 20-year bond with a current price of \$975
b. A 6 percent, 10-year bond with a current price of \$836
c. A 9 percent, 8-year bond with a current price of \$714

8-16. Ohio Oil's bonds, the 10s of 2014, are selling at 109 3/8. Exactly 14 years remain to maturity. Determine the

a. Current yield
b. Yield to maturity

8-17. Using Problem 8-16, assume that 28 years remain to maturity. How would the yield to maturity change? Does the current yield change?

8-18. Mittra Products' bonds, the 11s of 2015, sell to yield 12.5 percent. Exactly 15 years remain to maturity. Determine the current market price of the bonds. If the YTM had been 11.5 percent, what would the price of the bonds be? Explain why this difference occurs.

8-19. A 12 percent coupon bond has 20 years to maturity. It is currently selling for 20 percent less than face value. Determine its YTM.

8-20. Given a 10 percent, three-year bond with a price of \$1,052.24, where the market yield is 8 percent, calculate its duration using the format illustrated in Table 8-3.

8-21. Using the duration from Problem 8-20, determine:

a. The modified duration
b. The percentage change in the price of the bond if r changes 0.50 percent.

8-22. Calculate the duration of a 12 percent coupon bond with 10 years remaining to maturity and selling at par. Use annual interest rates.

8-23. Given the duration calculated in Problem 8-22, calculate the percentage change in bond price if the market discount rate for this bond declines by 0.75 percent.

The following question was asked on the 1984 CFA Level I examination:

CFA

8-24 Assume a \$10,000 par value zero coupon bond with a term-to-maturity at issue of 10 years and a market yield of 8 percent.

1. Determine the duration of the bond.
2. Calculate the initial issue price of the bond at a market yield of 8 percent, assuming semiannual compounding.
3. Twelve months after issue, this bond is selling to yield 12 percent. Calculate its then-current market price. Calculate your pre-tax rate of return assuming you owned this bond during the 12-month period.

Assume a 10 percent coupon bond with a Macaulay duration of 8 years, semiannual payments, and a market rate of 8 percent.

1. Determine the modified duration of the bond.
2. Calculate the percent change in price for the bond, assuming market rates decline by two percentage points (200 basis points).

The following question was asked on the 1988 CFA Level I examination:

CFA

8-25 You are asked to consider the following bond for possible inclusion in your company's fixed income portfolio:

Issuer	Coupon	Yield-to-Maturity	Maturity	Duration
Wiser Company	8%	8%	10 years	7.25 years

1. Explain why the Wiser bond's duration is less than its maturity.
2. Explain whether a bond's duration or its maturity is a better measure of the bond's sensitivity to changes in interest rates.

Briefly explain the impact on the duration of the Wiser Company bond under each of the following conditions:

I. The coupon is 4 percent rather than 8 percent
II. The yield-to-maturity is 4 percent rather than 8 percent
III. The maturity is seven years rather than 10 years

SELECTED REFERENCE

Detailed information on fixed-income securities, 62 chapters written by well-known authorities on fixed-income securities, can be found in:

Fabozzi, Frank J. Editor. *The Handbook of Fixed Income Securities*. Fifth Edition. Irwin Professional Publishing, 1997.

www.wiley.com/college/jones7

This chapter analyzes bond yields and prices. The web exercises will take you to sites that post bond prices and yields; you will get the opportunity to see how these numbers relate to each other. You will also see the relation between bond duration and bond price volatility.

APPENDIX 8A

CONVERTIBLE BONDS

Convertible Securities Bonds or preferred stock convertible into common stock

A form of equity-derivative securities is the convertible bond, which permits the owner to convert the security into common stock under specified conditions. **Convertible securities** or "convertibles," which also include convertible preferred stock, carry a claim on the common stock of the same issuer, which is *exercisable at the owner's initiative*.[21] If the option is never exercised, the convertible bond remains in existence until its maturity date, whereas a convertible preferred could remain in existence forever, since preferred stock has no maturity date.

Unlike puts and calls and warrants, convertible securities derive only part of their value from the option feature (i.e., the claim on the underlying common stock). These securities are valuable in their own right, as either bonds or preferred stock. Puts and calls and warrants, on the other hand, are only as valuable as the underlying common stock. They have no value beyond their claim on the common stock.

Convertibles have increased in popularity in recent years because they offer a unique combination of equity and bond characteristics.

TERMINOLOGY FOR CONVERTIBLE SECURITIES

Conversion Ratio The number of shares of common stock that the owner of a convertible security receives upon conversion

Conversion Price Par value divided by the conversation ratio

Conversion Value A convertible security's value based on the current price of the common stock

Convertible securities, whether bonds or preferred stock, have a certain terminology.

1. The **conversion ratio** is the number of shares of common stock that a convertible holder receives on conversion, which is the process of tendering the convertible security to the corporation in exchange for common stock.[22]
2. The **conversion price** is the par value of the bond or preferred divided by the conversion ratio.[23]

$$\text{Conversion price} = \text{Par value/Conversion ratio} \tag{8A-1}$$

3. The **conversion value** is the convertible's value based on the current price of the common stock. It is defined as

$$\text{Conversion value} = \begin{array}{c}\text{Conversion ratio} \\ \times \text{ Current price of common}\end{array} \tag{8A-2}$$

[21] Many convertible bonds cannot be converted for an initial period of 6–24 months.
[22] Forced conversion results when the issuer initiates conversion by calling the bonds.
[23] It is obvious that the conversion privilege attached to a convertible can be expressed in either conversion ratio or conversion price terms. Both the conversion price and the conversion ratio are almost always protected against stock splits and dividends.

Conversion Premium With convertible securities, the dollar difference between the market price of the security and its conversion value

4. The **conversion premium** is the dollar difference between the market price of the security and its conversion value.

$$\text{Conversion premium} = \begin{array}{l}\text{Market price of convertible} \\ \quad - \text{Conversion value}\end{array} \tag{8A-3}$$

Convertible securities are, by construction, hybrid securities. They have some characteristics of debt or preferred stock and some characteristics of the common stock on which they represent an option. However, to value them one must consider them in both contexts.

THE BASICS OF CONVERTIBLE BONDS

Convertible bonds are issued by corporations as part of their capital-raising activities. Similar to a warrant, a convertible feature can be attached to a bond as a sweetener, thereby allowing the issuer to obtain a lower interest cost by offering investors a chance for future gains from the common stock. Convertibles are sometimes sold as temporary financing instruments with the expectation that over a period of months (or years) the bonds will be converted into common stock. The bonds are a cheaper source of financing to the issuer than the common stock, and their gradual conversion places less price pressure on the common stock. Finally, convertibles offer a corporation the opportunity to sell common stock at a higher price than the current market price. If the issuer feels that the stock price is temporarily depressed, convertible bonds can be sold at a 15 percent to 20 percent premium. The result of this premium is that the price of the stock must rise by that amount before conversion is warranted.

Most bonds, whether convertible or not, are callable by the issuer. This results in additional concerns for the convertible bondholder.

Convertible bonds are typically issued as debentures. They are often subordinated to straight (nonconvertible) debentures, increasing their risk. Using S&P and Moody's bond ratings, most convertible bonds are one class below a straight debenture issue. Nevertheless, convertible bonds enjoy good marketability. Large issues on the New York Stock Exchange are often actively traded, in contrast to many nonconvertible issues of the same quality.

ANALYZING CONVERTIBLE BONDS

A convertible bond offers the purchaser a stream of interest payments and a return of principal at maturity. It also offers a promise of capital gains if the price of the stock rises sufficiently. To value a convertible bond, it is necessary to account for all of these elements. The convertible bond model is illustrated graphically to provide a framework for analysis. We shall then illustrate the components of value individually.

GRAPHIC ANALYSIS OF CONVERTIBLE BONDS

Figure 8A-1 shows the components of the convertible bond model. This diagram depicts the expected relationships for a typical convertible bond. The horizontal line from PV (par value) on the left to the maturity value (MV) on the right provides a reference point; any bond sold at par value would start out at PV, and all bonds will mature at their maturity value. If such a bond is callable, the call price will be above the par value in the early years because of the call premium; by maturity this price would converge to the maturity value.

Each convertible bond has an investment value (IV) or straight-debt value, which is the

FIGURE 8A-1

Conceptual model for understanding convertible bonds.

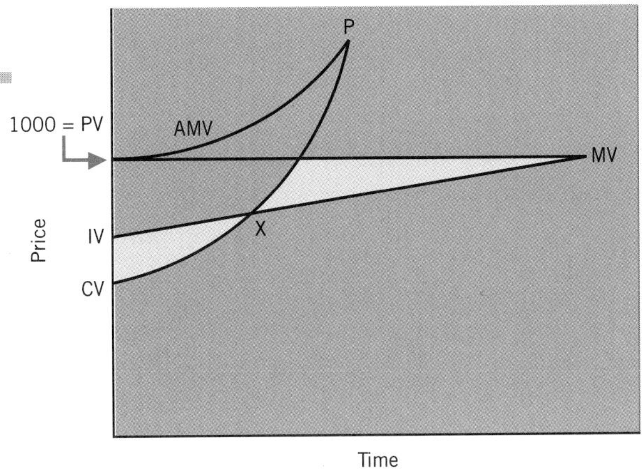

price at which a convertible would sell to equal the yield on a comparable nonconvertible. In other words, the investment value is the convertible's estimated value as a straight bond. By evaluating the coupons and the maturity value of the convertible at the going required rate of return for a comparable straight bond, the beginning investment value can be determined. Remember that the straight (i.e., nonconvertible) bond has a higher market yield because it does not offer a speculative play on the common stock. The investment value is represented in Figure 8A-1 by the line from IV to MV.

Each convertible has a conversion value at any point in time. The original conversion value (point CV) is established by multiplying together the conversion ratio and the price of the common stock at the time the convertible is issued. The conversion value curve in Figure 8A-1 is then drawn on the assumption that the price of the stock will grow at a constant rate, g; that is,

$$P_1 = P_0(1 + g)$$
$$P_2 = P_1(1 + g)$$

and so forth. Obviously, this is an expected relationship and may not occur in this manner. Using this assumption, the conversion value rises above the par value as the price of the stock rises, tracing out the curve CV-P in Figure 8A-1.

Finally, because the convertible often sells at a premium, it is necessary to draw an actual market value (AMV) curve, which is shown in Figure 8A-1 as AMV-P. This curve eventually approaches the conversion value curve as the conversion value increases. This is attributable primarily to the fact that the convertible may be called, forcing conversion. If this occurs, the convertible holder can receive only the conversion value. Therefore, investors are not likely to pay more than this for the convertible.

The shaded area in Figure 8A-1 is the premium over conversion value, which declines as the market price of the convertible rises. This reflects the fact that the bond is callable.

BOND VALUE

Every convertible bond has an investment value or straight debt value, which is the price at which the bond would sell with no conversion option. This price is given by the present value calculations for a bond, as explained in Chapter 8.

$$IV = \sum_{t=1}^{2n} \frac{C_t/2}{(1 + r/2)^t} + \frac{MV}{(1 + r/2)^{2n}} \qquad (8A\text{-}4)$$

where

IV = intrinsic value or present value of the bond
C = the interest payments (coupons)
PV = par value of the bond
n = number of years to maturity
r = appropriate required rate of return

EXAMPLE 8A-1

Consider the 8.5s of 2008 convertible debenture of Hartmarx Corporation (formerly, Hart, Schaffner & Marx), a NYSE-listed manufacturer of men's clothing. This bond, issued in late 1982, was convertible into 34.095 common shares, which is its conversion ratio. The conversion price at that time was \$29.33, or \$1,000/34.095.[24] At one observation point after its issuance, the common stock of Hartmarx was selling at 35 1/4 while this debenture was selling at \$1,210. The conversion value of Hartmarx at that observation point was therefore 34.095 × \$35.125 = \$1,197.59.

In the case of the Hartmarx bond, the expiration date was set at January 15, 2008. Valuing this bond at the observation point just used (after the July 15 interest payment) meant that 24.5 years remained to maturity, or 49 semiannual interest payments. Based on *The Value Line Convertible Survey's* assigned investment grade value of 0 for this issue and the market rates in effect at that time, 12.2 percent was chosen as the applicable discount rate for a bond of this risk category.[25] Therefore, the bond or investment value for this Hartmarx convertible debenture was[26]

$$\begin{aligned} BV &= \sum_{t=1}^{49} \frac{\$42.75}{(1 + 0.061)^t} + \frac{\$1{,}000}{(1 + 0.061)^{49}} \\ &= \$717.23 \end{aligned}$$

Of course, the bond value fluctuates over time as market interest rates change.

BOND VALUE

Every convertible bond has a conversion value, or the value of the common stock received upon conversion. At the time of issuance, a convertible bond has a conversion value equal to the market price of the common stock multiplied by the number of shares of stock that can be received by converting. As noted, the conversion price is usually set 15–20 percent above the current market price of the common, so that conversion would not be worthwhile. Over time, if the price of the common stock grows, the conversion value should also grow at the same rate. This happened for the Hartmarx bond, which, as noted, had a conversion value of \$1,197.59.

MINIMUM (FACE) VALUE

Every convertible bond has a *floor value*, or minimum value. A convertible will always sell *for no less than* the larger of (1) its bond (investment) value or (2) its conversion value.

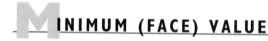

[24] Many convertible bonds have a conversion price that increases over time.
[25] This information is available in each weekly issue.
[26] To solve this equation, the present value of the annuity must be found using the formula $1/[(1 - (1 + r)^n)/r]$. The present value factor for 49 periods can be found as $1/(1.061)^{49}$.

Even if the value of the conversion feature is zero, with virtually no prospect of a change in this value, a convertible bond would have a minimum price of its investment or straight bond value (i.e., its value as a nonconvertible debt instrument). If the price were to decline below this value, bond investors would buy it because its yield would be greater than alternative comparable bonds. The bond value for the Hartmarx debenture as of the valuation date was $717.23, the absolute minimum price for this bond as of that time.

INVESTMENTS INTUITION In a similar manner, a convertible bond cannot sell below its conversion value. If it did, arbitragers would buy the bond, convert it into common stock, and sell the shares, or simply establish an equity position at a cost lower than would otherwise be possible. Since the Hartmarx conversion value of $1,197.59 was higher than its bond value, this was its minimum, or floor, value at the time of these calculations.

In Figure 8A-1, the line IV-X-P represents the minimum market value for the convertible bond. This minimum market value is made up of part of the investment value line (IV to X) and part of the conversion value curve (X to P). We can call this the effective market value floor.

ACTUAL BOND VALUE (PRICE)

Convertible bonds usually sell at prices above their minimum value, which, as we have seen, is the higher of the bond value or the conversion value. This difference between the actual bond value and the effective market value floor is the premium.

EXAMPLE 8A-2 The Hartmarx bond was selling at $1,210 at the observation point with a conversion value of $1,197.59. The dollar premium, therefore, was the difference, or $12.41.

The reasons convertibles sell at premiums include the following:

1. The conversion option has a positive value because the right to convert any time during the life of the bond is valuable and investors are willing to pay for it. In effect, this is equivalent to owning a call on the stock, and calls command positive premiums.
2. A convertible bond offers investors downside protection, thereby decreasing their risk. If the price of the common declines sharply, resulting in a sharp decline in the conversion value, the convertible will still sell as a bond and will have a bond value determined by the present value of interest payments and principal. This dual minimum-price feature of convertibles reduces investors' risk and commands a premium in doing so.

In evaluating convertible bonds, certain details should be kept in mind in addition to the preceding factors. When a convertible bond is converted, the holder loses the accrued interest from the last interest payment date. Furthermore, if a holder converts after the ex dividend date, the common stock dividend on the newly received common shares could be lost. Since the issuer can call the bonds and force conversion, these factors can be important. It is not unusual for issuers to choose a time favorable to themselves.

A bond is subject to call if the market price exceeds the call price. Investors who pay a premium over the conversion value in these circumstances run a risk of having the bond called as the company forces conversion.

USING THE INTERNET Convertible bond quotes are available at www.convertbond.com. To make some calculations, a web calculator can be used at www.numa.com/derivs/ref/calculat/cb/calc-cba.htm.

RISK AND RETURN ON CONVERTIBLE BONDS

Some detailed studies have been done on convertible bonds. One such study that provides such detail is by Edward Altman. He analyzed convertible bond behavior during the 1980s and drew the following conclusions:[27]

1. Convertible issues, which typically are unsecured and subordinated, tend to be small, with a median issue size in 1987 of about $35 million.
2. Both investment grade and noninvestment grade convertibles had a lower average yield to maturity than comparable straight debt.
3. For the period 1983–1987, the average total returns on convertibles was less than that for high-yield straight debt, government bonds, the NYSE Index, and the S&P 500 Index using as a sample all convertible bonds covered by *Value Line*.
4. High-yield straight debt was significantly less volatile than either the convertible bond sample or the stock market indexes.
5. There was a high correlation between convertible bonds and stock market returns, which suggests that convertible performance is heavily dependent on stock market activity.
6. On the basis of mutual fund data for convertible bond funds, government bond funds, and high-yield straight debt funds, convertible security funds did not do particularly well over a three-year period and a five-year period. However, the convertible funds had almost twice the total return over a 10-year period, apparently reflecting the strong performance of the stock market during that time.
7. The default loss on convertibles exceeded that of straight debt for every year examined.

SHOULD INVESTORS BUY CONVERTIBLE BONDS?

Why should investors consider convertible bonds? Are there disadvantages?

As for advantages, convertible bonds offer investors a unique combination of an income stream from a fixed-income security and a chance to participate in the price appreciation of the common stock. Convertibles offer downside protection in relation to owning the common stock, because regardless of what happens to the price of the common, the convertible bond will not decline below its value as a straight bond. On average, a convertible suffers only half the loss of the underlying common when prices decline. They offer upside potential, because a convertible bond must always be worth at least its conversion as the price of the common

[27] These findings are taken from Edward I. Altman, "The Convertible Debt Market: Are Returns Worth the Risk?" *Financial Analysts Journal*, July–August 1989, pp. 23–31.

stock rises. On average, convertibles tend to rise two-thirds of the increase in the underlying common.

The yield on a convertible bond usually exceeds that of the common stock, and interest payments have first order of priority.[28] Compared to common stock owners, convertible bond holders enjoy a yield advantage while awaiting appreciation in the stock price.

As for disadvantages, convertible bonds typically (but not always) yield less than do straight bonds of similar risk and maturity. Investors must give up some yield to receive the conversion feature. Convertibles are callable, and in many cases the issuer can and will force conversion. When a convertible bond is called, the holder will choose the better alternative—accept the call price or convert into common stock. If a corporation calls a bond at, say, \$1,100 (face value of \$1,000 plus one year's interest of \$100 for a call premium), and the conversion value is, say, \$1,200, the bondholders in effect are forced to convert. They give up their fixed-income security and the chance for future capital gains from the common stock.

[28] In the case of Hartmarx, the yields at the observation point were 7 percent and 2.7 percent, respectively, a 4.3 percent yield advantage for the convertible.

chapter 9

BONDS: ANALYSIS AND STRATEGY

Chapter 9 concludes Part III on fixed-income securities by discussing issues in the management of a bond portfolio. We consider why investors buy bonds as well as the issues an investor should consider in managing a bond portfolio. The basic strategies available to a bond investor are organized along the lines of passive versus active strategies, an important distinction that also applies to stock investors.

After reading this chapter you will be able to:

- **Analyze the reasons why investors buy bonds.**
- **Recognize important considerations in managing a bond portfolio, including the term structure of interest rates and yield spreads.**
- **Differentiate between the passive and active strategies for managing a bond portfolio.**
- **Consider how both conservative investors and aggressive investors go about building a fixed-income portfolio.**

In the previous chapter we studied the calculation of bond prices and yields as well as their relationships. From that analysis we know the importance of interest rate changes as well as the impact of coupon and time to maturity on bond prices, given a change in yields. The call feature also can affect the price and yield on a bond, as can a variety of other issuer-unique factors such as the credit rating, the collateral, sinking fund provisions, and any conversion feature that may exist.

A consideration of bond analysis and strategies is a natural capstone to our discussion of bond yields and prices. In the final analysis, bond investors construct and manage portfolios of securities, whether bonds only or combinations of bonds and other securities such as common stocks. In doing so, they may very well employ concepts we have previously studied, such as duration. They must also grapple with the overall strategy issue facing investors of whether to be active or passive in their investment approach.

WHY BUY BONDS?

As noted in Chapter 6, the total return on bonds can be separated into two components, which helps to explain why bonds appeal to both conservative investors seeking steady income and aggressive investors seeking capital gains. A wide range of investors participate in the fixed-income securities marketplace, ranging from individuals who own a few government or corporate bonds to large institutional investors who own billions of dollars of bonds. Most of these investors are presumably seeking the basic *steady return-low risk* characteristics that most bonds offer; however, quite different overall objectives can be accomplished by purchasing bonds. It is worthwhile to consider these points.

As fixed-income securities, bonds are desirable to many investors because they offer a steady stream of interest income over the life of the obligation and a return of principal at maturity. The promised yield on a bond held to maturity is known at the time of purchase. Barring default by the issuer, the buyers will have the bond principal returned to them at maturity. By holding to maturity, investors can escape the risk that interest rates will rise, thereby driving down the price of the bonds, although other risks may not be eliminated.

As an illustration of the return and risk situation for this type of investor, who is seeking steady returns, consider long-term Treasury securities for the period 1857–1995.[1] There is no practical risk of default. At the end of 1995, investors in these government bonds would have earned an average compound growth rate of 4.8 percent. Over the earlier subperiod from 1857 through 1925, the average annual compound return was 4.55 percent, while for the later subperiod 1926–1995 it was 5.07 percent. The point is that government bonds, as well as corporate bonds, offer a stream of steady returns over long periods of time, with small risks, as measured by the standard deviation.

Some investors are interested in bonds exactly because bond prices will change as interest rates change. If interest rates rise (fall), bond prices will fall (rise). These investors are interested not in holding the bonds to maturity but rather in earning the capital gains that are possible if they correctly anticipate movements in interest rates. Because bonds can be purchased on margin, large potential gains are possible from speculating on interest rates over relatively short periods. (Of course, large losses are also possible.)

To obtain some idea of the changes in returns that can result from changes in interest rates, consider again Treasury bonds. Some of the total annual returns were very large, far

[1] These data, and the returns below on Treasuries, are taken from Jack W. Wilson and Charles P. Jones, "Long-Term Returns and Risk for Bonds," *The Journal of Portfolio Management*, Vol. 23, No. 3, Spring 1997, pp. 15–28, updated for recent years.

beyond the yield component alone. In 1982, for example, the total return was almost 42 percent, in 1985 it was 32 percent, and in 1995 it was 31 percent. Clearly, successful bond speculation in each of those years resulted in very large returns.

Speculation has been heavy in the bond markets in recent years. In the past, bonds were viewed as very stable instruments whose prices fluctuated very little in the short run. This situation changed drastically in the 1980s, however, with the bond markets becoming quite volatile. Interest rates in the early 1980s reached record levels, causing large changes in bond prices.

Bond speculators encompass a wide range of participants, from financial institutions to individual investors. All are trying to take advantage of an expected movement in interest rates. Thus, investors seeking the income component from bonds as well as investors attempting to speculate with bonds are keenly interested in the level of interest rates and any likely changes in the level. A key part of any bond analysis, therefore, must involve these interest rate considerations.

BUYING FOREIGN BONDS

Why do U.S. investors consider foreign bonds for inclusion in their portfolios? One obvious reason is that foreign bonds may offer higher returns at a given point in time than alternative domestic bonds. Such a situation occurred in mid-1992 when European interest rates were quite high relative to U.S. interest rates. In some cases, European government bonds offered twice the yield of U.S. Treasuries. Thus, it would seem that investors could make a case for buying foreign bonds on the basis of potentially attractive returns.

A second important reason for buying foreign bonds is the diversification aspect. Diversification is extremely important, both in a stock portfolio and a bond portfolio. Bond prices in some foreign countries may be rising at the same time that U.S. bond prices are declining.

Individual investors have found it difficult to invest directly in European bonds. Some brokerage firms do not offer foreign bonds to individual investors, while others require a minimum investment of at least $10,000, and often much more. Selling foreign bonds that are directly owned also can be a problem. Secondary markets in Europe are not comparable to the huge U.S. Treasury markets. This means that individual investors selling small amounts of foreign bonds abroad will typically incur significant price concessions.

What About the Euro? Investors who are considering direct investment in foreign bonds face the additional issue of transaction costs. Dollars must be converted into the foreign currency to make purchases, and receipts from the foreign bonds must be converted back into dollars. On small transactions, these costs can significantly impact returns. However, this situation may improve significantly with the introduction of the European Economic and Monetary Union (EMU) of 11 countries. The euro represents an important new change in the traditional situation.

Finally, investors in foreign bonds must deal with exchange rate risk. An adverse movement in the dollar can result in an American investor's return being lower than the return on the asset, or even negative. If the euro weakens instead of strengthens, an investor's dollar-denominated return suffers.

IMPORTANT CONSIDERATIONS IN MANAGING A BOND PORTFOLIO

UNDERSTANDING THE BOND MARKET

The first consideration for any investor is to understand the basic nature of the bond market. It has been commonplace to talk about the bond market benefiting from a weak economy. If

FIGURE 9-1

Real gross domestic product growth rates, consumer price index growth rates, and yields on 10-year treasuries, 1962–1992.

SOURCE: David C. Wheelock, "What Drives the Bond Market," *Monetary Trends*, The Federal Reserve Bank of St. Louis, October 1994, p. 1

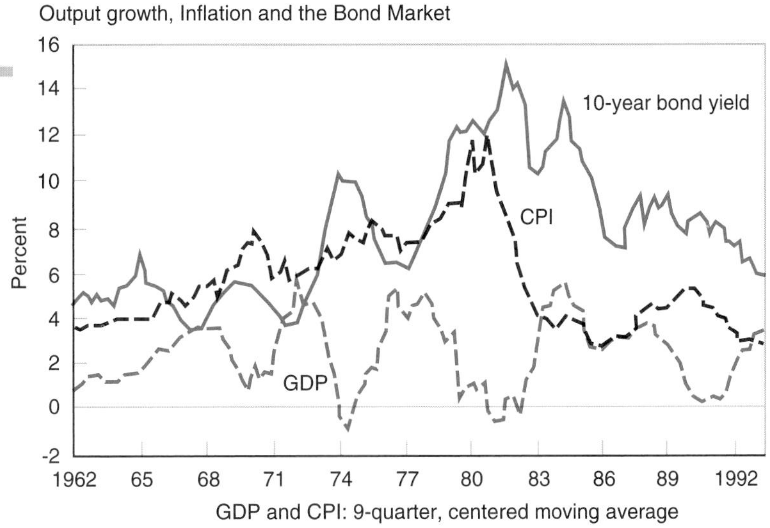

the economy is growing slowly, interest rates may decline, and bond prices rise. In effect, a decline in economic growth may lead to fewer investment opportunities, leading savers to increase their demand for bonds, which pushes bond prices up and bond yields down. Talk of a rapidly growing economy is thought to frighten bond investors.

The relationship that really matters in this view is between bond yields and inflation, not between economic growth and bond yields. As we know from Chapter 8, interest rates reflect expected inflation. If investors expect a rise in inflation, they demand more from a bond to compensate for the expected decline in the purchasing power of their cash flows from the bond investment. Therefore, an increase in expected inflation will tend to depress bond prices and increase yields.

Figure 9-1 shows a plot of the yield on 10-year Treasuries, moving averages of real Gross Domestic Product (GDP), and the growth rate of the Consumer Price Index over the period 1962–1992.[2] Note that real GDP growth had no trend over the 30 year period while bond yields had an upward trend for approximately the first 20 years, and a downward trend thereafter. The CPI growth rate behaved in a similar manner. Inflation tended to move counter to GDP growth over business cycles and more than offset any increased demand for bonds resulting from a weakening economy.

Consider the more recent period from 1981, which stands out in Figure 9-1. While it appears that bond yields declined with declining GDP growth, the linkage with the growth in the CPI is clearer. Bond yields declined, and bond prices rose, as inflation growth declined. What makes this analysis tricky is that bond yields can continue to rise after inflation has peaked because investors are reacting to *expectations* of future inflation rather than actual current inflation.

Therefore, while the bond market appears to like a weak economy, *the bond market clearly dislikes inflation*. Bond investors fear inflation because of its negative effect on fixed-income securities, and they favor Fed actions that temper economic growth and reduce inflation. Investors may react quite favorably to a tightening of monetary policy because this helps to calm inflation fears.

Leverage has become a big factor in the bond markets, and this leverage has magnified the swings in bond prices. According to some sources, leveraged speculation resulted in the bond rally of 1993, and a major debacle in 1994. *Fortune* magazine estimated that as of mid-

[2] This discussion draws heavily on David C. Wheelock, "What Drives the Bond Market," *Monetary Trends*, The Federal Reserve Bank of St. Louis, October 1994, p. 1.

September, 1994, the rise in rates on the 30-year Treasury bond (about one and one-half percentage points) resulted in a $600 billion loss on U.S. bonds, and a possible $1.5 trillion loss worldwide.[3] Is it any wonder that *Fortune* titled this article "The Great Bond Market Massacre"?

Global Factors and the Bond Markets The bond market may also respond favorably to a strengthening of the dollar. A stronger dollar increases the value of dollar-denominated assets to foreign investors.

Other events of a global nature affect the bond market. When the Brazilian crisis erupted around the end of 1998, there was a flight to safety in the form of purchases of Treasuries. As the crisis diminished, this demand for Treasuries decreased. On the other hand, with Japanese interest rates on the rise, bond investors feared that Japanese investors would liquidate their holdings of Treasuries in order to buy their own government bonds. Such a movement decreases the demand for Treasuries and hence their prices.

THE TERM STRUCTURE OF INTEREST RATES

Term Structure of Interest Rates The relationship between time to maturity and yields for a particular category of bonds

The **term structure of interest rates** refers to the relationship between time to maturity and yields for a particular category of bonds at a particular point in time. Ideally, other factors are held constant, particularly the risk of default. The easiest way to do this is to examine U.S. Treasury securities, which have no practical risk of default, have no sinking fund, and are taxable. By eliminating those that are callable and those that may have some special feature, a quite homogeneous sample of bonds is obtained for analysis.

Yield Curve A graphical depiction of the relationship between yields and time for bonds that are identical except for maturity

Yield Curves The term structure is usually plotted in the form of a **yield curve**, which is a graphical depiction of the relationship between yields and time for bonds that are identical except for maturity. The horizontal axis represents time to maturity, whereas the vertical axis represents yield to maturity.

Figure 9-2*a* shows yield curves for certain periods in 1988 and 1989 for Treasury securities. The upward-sloping curve in October 1988 is considered typical; that is, interest rates that rise with maturity are considered the "normal" pattern. Notice that by spring of 1989 the yield curves were "humped," peaking in this case at the two-year note.

Figure 9-2*b* shows additional yield curves for Treasuries in 1989. Note the downward-sloping curves for June and July, with short rates above long rates. These "inverted" yield curves are unusual, and some market participants believe they indicate that short-term rates will fall. In fact, interest rates did decline in the early 1990s, reaching modern lows in 1993 before turning up again.

Figure 9-2*c* shows some additional shapes for yield curves in 1996. Notice the difference between the January yield curve and those late in the year, which are steeper and straighter.

Most observations about yield curves involve tendencies and not exact relationships. For example, there generally is a negative relationship between short rates and the yield spread. A higher short rate typically is associated with a flatter yield curve because long rates do not increase by quite as much. However, this relationship does not always hold.

Expectations Theory States that the long-term rate of interest is equal to an average of the short-term rates that are expected to prevail over the long-term period

Term Structure Theories A theory of the term structure of interest rates is needed to explain the shape and slope of the yield curve and why it shifts over time. Theories traditionally advanced are the expectations theory, the liquidity premium theory, the preferred habitat theory, and the market segmentation theory.

The *pure or "unbiased"* **expectations theory** of the term structure of interest rates asserts

[3] See Al Ehrbar, "The Great Bond Market Massacre," *Fortune*, October 17, 1994, pp. 77–92.

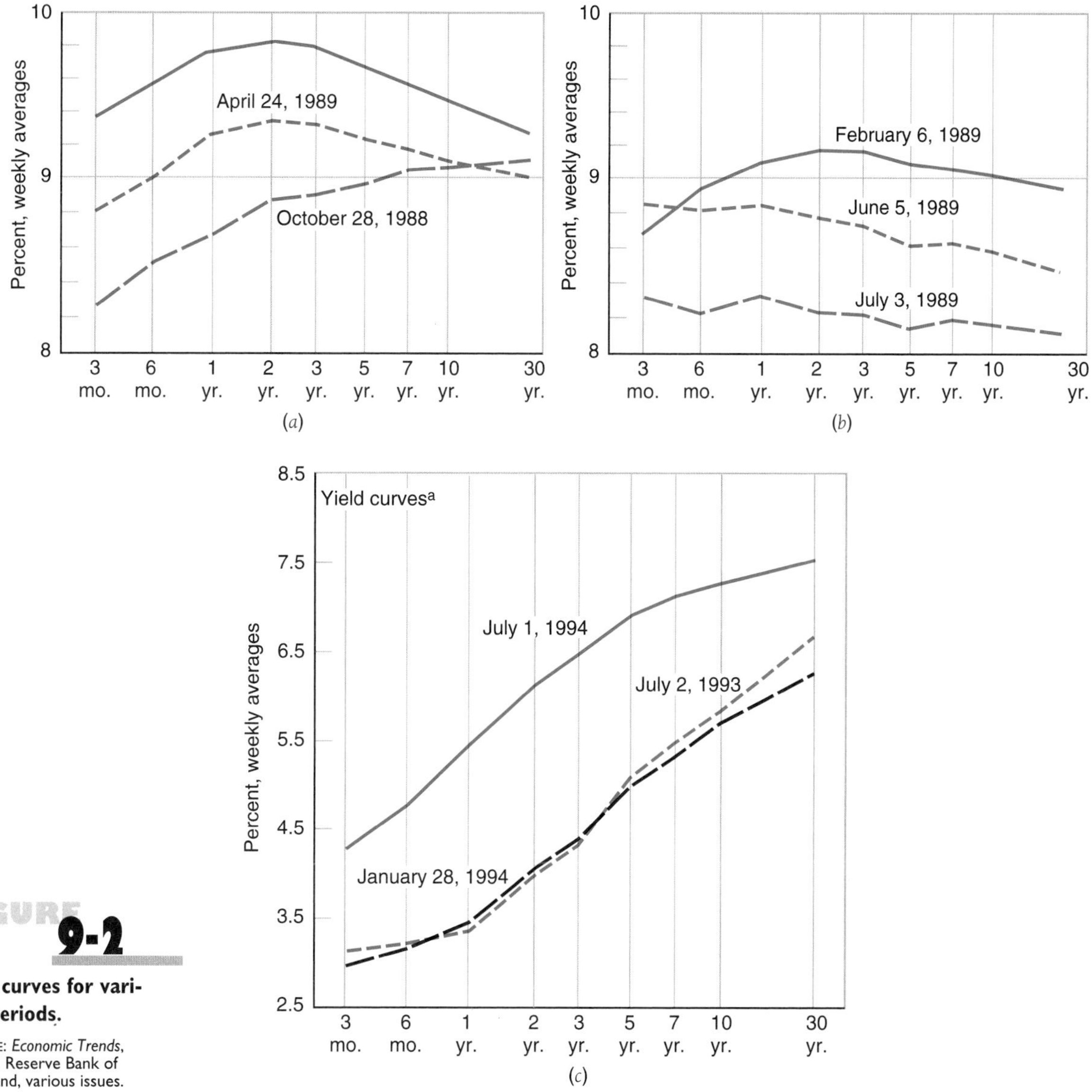

FIGURE 9-2

Yield curves for various periods.

SOURCE: *Economic Trends*, Federal Reserve Bank of Cleveland, various issues.

that financial market participants determine security yields such that the return from holding an *n*-period security equals the average return expected from holding a series of one-year securities over the same *n* periods. In other words, the long-term rate of interest is equal to an average of the present yield on short-term securities plus the expected future yields on short-term securities that are expected to prevail over the long-term period. For each period, the total rate of return is expected to be the same on all securities regardless of time to maturity.

Forward Rates Unobservable rates expected to prevail in the future

In effect, the term structure consists of a set of forward rates and a current known rate. **Forward rates** are rates that are expected to prevail in the future; that is, they are unobservable but anticipated future rates.

Under the expectations theory, long rates must be an average of the present and future short-term rates. For example, a three-year bond would carry an interest rate that is an average of the current rate for one year and the expected forward rates for the next two years. The same principle holds for any number of periods; therefore, the market rate for any period to maturity can be expressed as an average of the current rate and the applicable forward rates. Technically, the average involved is a geometric rather than an arithmetic average.

For expositional purposes:

$_{t}R_{n}$ = the current known yield (i.e., at time t), on a security with n periods to maturity

$_{t+1}r_{n}$ = the yield expected to prevail one year from today (at time $t + 1$) for n periods—these are forward rates

The rate for the three-year bond referred to above must be a geometric average of the current one-year rate ($_{t}R_{1}$) and the expected forward rates for the subsequent two years.

Therefore, in equation form

$$(1 + {}_{t}R_{3}) = [(1 + {}_{t}R_{1})(1 + {}_{t+1}r_{1})(1 + {}_{t+2}r_{1})]^{1/3} - 1.0 \quad (9\text{-}1)$$

where

$(1 + {}_{t}R_{3})$ = the rate on a three-year bond
$(1 + {}_{t}R_{1})$ = the current known rate on a one-year bond
$(1 + {}_{t+1}r_{1})$ = the expected rate on a bond with one year to maturity beginning one year from now
$(1 + {}_{t+2}r_{1})$ = the expected rate on a bond with one year to maturity beginning two years from now

EXAMPLE 9-1

Assume the current one-year bond rate ($_{t}R_{1}$) is 0.07, and the two forward rates are 0.075 ($_{t+1}r_{1}$) and 0.082 ($_{t+2}r_{1}$). The rate for a three-year bond, $(1 + {}_{t}R_{3})$, would be

$$\begin{aligned}(1 + {}_{t}R_{3}) &= [(1.\ 07)(1.075)(1.082)]^{1/3} - 1.0\\ &= 1.07566 - 1.0\\ &= 0.07566 \text{ or } 7.566\%\end{aligned}$$

The same principle applies for any number of periods. Any long-term rate is a geometric average of consecutive one-period rates.

Forward rates cannot be easily measured, but they can be inferred for any one-year future period. The expectations theory, however, does not say that these future expected rates will be correct; it simply says that there is a relationship between rates today and rates expected in the future.

Under this hypothesis, investors can expect the same return regardless of the choice of investment. Any combination of securities for a specified period will have the same expected return. For example, a five-year bond will have the same expected return as a two-year bond held to maturity plus a three-year bond bought at the beginning of the third year. The assumption under this hypothesis is that expected future rates are equal to computed forward rates. Profit-seeking individuals will exploit any differences between forward rates and expected rates, ensuring that they equilibrate.

Liquidity Preference Theory States that interest rates reflect the sum of current and expected short rates, as in the expectations theory, plus liquidity (risk) premiums

The second theory, the **liquidity preference theory**, states that interest rates reflect the sum of current and expected short rates, as in the expectations theory, plus liquidity (risk) premiums. Because uncertainty increases with time, investors prefer to lend for the short run. Borrowers, however, prefer to borrow for the long run in order to be assured of funds. Investors receive a liquidity premium to induce them to lend long term, while paying a price premium (in the form of lower yields) for investing short term. The implication of this theory is that longer-term bonds should offer higher yields.

The difference between the liquidity preference theory and the expectations theory is the recognition that interest rate expectations are uncertain. Risk-averse investors seek to be compensated for this uncertainty. Forward rates and estimated future rates are not the same; they differ by the amount of the liquidity premiums.

Market Segmentation Theory States that investors confine their activities to specific maturity sectors and are unwilling to shift from one sector to another to take advantage of opportunities

Preferred Habitat Theory States that investors have preferred maturity sectors in which they seek to invest but are willing to shift to other maturities if they can expect to be adequately compensated

The third hypothesis for explaining the term structure of interest rates is the **market segmentation theory**. This theory states that various institutional investors, having different maturity needs dictated by the nature of their liabilities, confine themselves to specific maturity segments. Investors are not willing to shift from one maturity sector to another to take advantage of any opportunities that may arise. Under the market segmentation theory, the shape of the yield curve is determined by the supply and demand conditions for securities within each of the multiple maturity sectors.

The **preferred habitat theory** is similar to, but not identical with, the market segmentation theory. Under this hypothesis, investors have preferred maturity sectors, or habitats. For example, a thrift institution with many five-year CDs to pay off will not wish to take the reinvestment rate risk that would result from investing in one-year Treasury bills.

What if imbalances arise in a given maturity range between the demand and supply of funds? *The preferred habitat theory states that borrowers and lenders can be induced to shift maturities if they are adequately compensated by an appropriate risk premium*, which distinguished this theory from the market segmentation theory. The implication of this theory for the term structure is that both expectations concerning future interest rates and risk premiums play a role, and the yield curve can take any shape.[4]

The preferred habitat theory is related to, but not identical with the market segmentation theory. This theory states that the various institutional investors, having different maturity needs dictated by the nature of their liabilities, confine themselves to specific maturity segments. Investors are not willing to shift from one maturity sector to another to take advantage of any opportunities that may arise. Under segmentation theory, the shape of the yield curve is determined by the supply and demand conditions for securities within each of the multiple maturity sectors.

Which of these theories is correct? The issue of the term structure has not been resolved; although many empirical studies have been done, the results are at least partially conflicting. Therefore, definitive statements cannot be made. The empirical evidence on the expectations hypothesis is equivocal at best. The evidence on the liquidity premium hypothesis is the most unequivocal. Substantial evidence suggest that risk premia exist, but their behavior over time is subject to debate.

In actual bond practice, market observers and participants do not tend to be strict adherents to a particular theory. Rather, they accept the reasonable implications of all three and try to use any available information in assessing the shape of the yield curve. For example, many market participants will focus on expectations but allow for liquidity premiums.

Since the 1930s, upward-sloping yield curves have been the norm, as would be predicted by the liquidity preference theory. This theory is more compatible than the other two with the study of investments, which emphasizes the risk-return trade-off that exists. The liquidity preference theory stresses the idea that because of larger risks, longer maturity securities require larger returns or compensation.[5]

[4] See Frank Fabozzi and Franco Modigliana, *Capital Markets: Institutions and Instruments*, Prentice-Hall, 1992, pp. 387–389. This book has good discussions of several important investment topics.

[5] The expectations theory categorizes investors as return maximizers, whereas the preferred habitat theory categorizes investors as risk minimizers.

Regardless of which of the above theories is correct, it seems reasonable to assert that investors demand a premium from long-term bonds, because of their additional risk. After all, uncertainty increases with time, and as we shall learn long-term bonds are more sensitive to interest rate fluctuations than are short-term bonds. Furthermore, the typical shape of the yield curve is upward sloping, which indicates that investors are more averse to the risk of long bonds than to short-term securities.

Using the Yield Curve Investors should use yield curves for the right reasons, and understand their limitations. We consider both sides of the issue.

The yield curve should not be used to price a bond. Rather, a bond should be viewed as a package of zero-coupon instruments, and the price of a bond should equal the value of all these zero-coupon instruments. To value each zero-coupon instrument, we need to know the spot rates, or yields on zero-coupon Treasuries with the same maturity. It is possible to derive a **theoretical spot rate curve**, and apply these spot rates to price a bond.

Theoretical Spot Rate Curve A graph depicting the relationship between spot rates and maturities, based on theoretical considerations

Investors use yield curves as clues to the future. One study showed that the slope of the yield curve is a good predictor of changes in activity 12 to 18 months out.[6] All six recessions identified were preceded by a flattening or inverted yield curve (however, one inverted yield curve was not followed by a recession). A recent paper by a Federal Reserve bank found the slope of the yield curve to be the best predictor of economic growth. It also found a negative slope typically preceding a recession. Therefore, investors should be quite concerned when yield curves become inverted.

EXAMPLE 9-2

Brazil, having already experienced a crisis, faced inverted yield curves in January 1999. Apparently, bond buyers felt there was more risk of being repaid in the short run than in the long run. They may have been influenced by the situation in Russia, where the yield curve inverted before Russia defaulted on its obligations.

THE RISK STRUCTURE OF INTEREST RATES—YIELD SPREADS

Assume that market interest rates on risk-free securities are determined as explained above. If the expected rate of inflation rises, the level of rates also rises. Similarly, if the real rate of interest were to decline, market interest rates would decline; that is, the level of rates would decrease. Furthermore, as seen in the term structure analysis, yields vary over time for issues that are otherwise homogeneous. The question that remains is, "why do rates differ between different bond issues or segments of the bond market?"

The answer to this question lies in what bond analysts call the risk structure of interest rates, or simply yield spreads. **Yield spreads** refer to the relationships between bond yields and the particular issuer and issue characteristics and constitute the risk premiums mentioned earlier. Yield spreads are often calculated among different bonds holding maturity constant. They are a result of the following factors:

Yield Spreads The relationship between bond yields and the particular features on various bonds such as quality, callability, and taxes

1. Differences in quality, or risk of default. Clearly, other things being equal, a bond rated BAA will offer a higher yield than a similar bond rated AAA because of the difference in default risk.
2. Differences in call features. Bonds that are callable have higher YTMs than otherwise identical noncallable bonds. If the bond is called, bondholders must give it up, and

[6] See Arturo Estrella and Gikas Hardouvelis, "The Term Structure as a Predictor of Real Economic Activity," *The Journal of Finance*, June 1991.

they could replace it only with a bond carrying a lower YTM. Therefore, investors expect to be compensated for this risk.

3. Differences in coupon rates. Bonds with low coupons have a larger part of their YTM in the form of capital gains.
4. Differences in marketability. Some bonds are more marketable than others, meaning that their liquidity is better. They can be sold either more quickly or with less of a price concession, or both. The less marketable a bond, the higher the YTM.
5. Differences in tax treatments.
6. Differences between countries.

Junk Bonds Bonds that carry ratings of BB or lower, with correspondingly higher yields

EXAMPLE **9-3**

Junk bonds are high-risk, high-yield bonds that carry ratings of BB (S&P) or Ba (Moody's) or lower, with correspondingly higher yields.[7] An alternative, and more reassuring, name used to describe this area of the bond market is the *high-yield debt market*.[8] Between 1987 and 1992, junk bond returns showed only a 51 percent correlation with stocks (27 percent with Treasury bonds), providing good diversification benefits for investor portfolios.

One yield spread of interest to some investors is the difference between the yields on investment grade bonds, or Treasuries, and junk bonds. This spread can change for a number of reasons. In February, 1995, the spread between Treasuries and B-rated junk bonds was about 490 basis points (4.9 percent). By August, 1995, the spread was 600 basis points, making the junk bonds relatively more attractive (the default rate for these bonds historically is around 2 percent). On the other hand, the spread between junk bonds rated BB and Treasuries remained at 367 basis points on each of those dates.

Other Factors Affecting Yield Spreads Clearly, yield spreads are a function of the variables connected with a particular issue or issuer. Investors expect to be compensated for the risk of a particular issue, and this compensation is reflected in the risk premium. However, investors are not the only determining factor in yield spreads. The actions of borrowers also affect them. Heavy Treasury financing, for example, may cause the yield spreads between governments and corporates to narrow as the large increase in the supply of Treasury securities pushes up the yields on Treasuries.

The level of interest rates also plays a role in explaining yield spreads. As a general proposition, risk premiums tend to be high when the level of interest rates is high.

Yield Spreads over Time Yield spreads among alternative bonds may be positive or negative at any time. Furthermore, the size of the yield spread changes over time. Whenever the differences in yield become smaller, the yield spread is said to "narrow", as the differences increase, it "widens."

As one example of how yield spreads change over time, consider one of the most prominent spreads, that between different categories of corporate bonds. Figure 9-3 shows the difference between Baa corporates (medium-grade bonds) and Aaa corporates (high-grade bonds). This risk premium has averaged 1.15 percentage points since 1970, 0.95 since 1984,

[7] Bonds rated BB or below are regarded as being speculative with respect to capacity to pay interest and repay principal.

[8] Junk bonds are issued in connection with:

1. Mergers
2. Leveraged buyouts
3. Companies with heavy debts to repay—such as bank loans
4. Stock buybacks by corporations

FIGURE 9-3

An illustration of corporate yield spreads: the difference between Baa corporates and Aaa corporates.

SOURCE: Federal Reserve Bank of St. Louis, *Monetary Trends*, November 1998, p. 1.

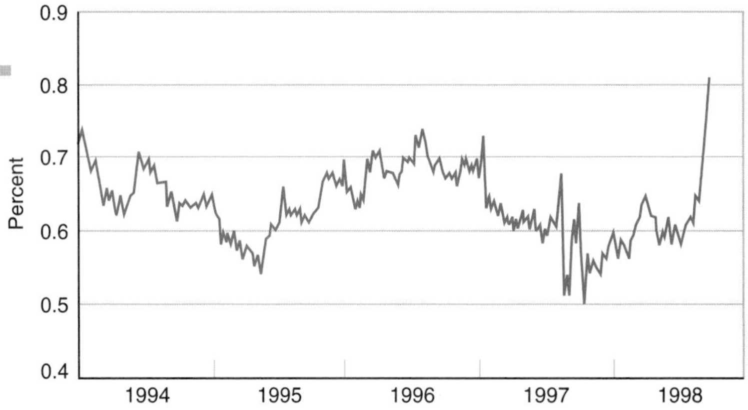

and only 0.64 since the beginning of 1994 (perhaps because of fewer recessions, and overall general prosperity, relative to the longer run history). Following Russia's default on debt in August 1998, the risk premium rose by 20 basis points, as Figure 9-3 shows, as yields on Baa corporates rose. This was true despite bond yields declining since August 1998, as investors rushed to quality issues in the face of the uncertainty. Treasury yields fell even more as investors rushed to quality. Thus, the emerging markets crisis caused a change in the yield spreads, and investors trying to determine which bonds to hold have to be prepared for such shifts.[9]

It seems reasonable to assume that yield spreads widen during recessions, when investors become more risk-averse, and narrow during times of economic prosperity. Since the probability of default is greater during a recession, investors demand more of a premium. Yield spreads were at their widest during the early 1930s when the Depression was at its worst. In contrast, yield spreads narrow during boom periods because even financially weak companies have a good chance of surviving and paying their debt obligations. Some historical evidence supports these trends; thus, we can state that the yield spread varies inversely to the business cycle.

BOND STRATEGIES

We now consider the basic approaches that bond investors can use in managing their bond portfolios, or the bond portion of their overall portfolio. An understanding of these strategies requires more than an understanding of the basic factors affecting the valuation and analysis of bonds.

Bond investing has become increasingly popular, no doubt as a result of record interest rates in recent years. Unfortunately, the theoretical framework for bond portfolio management has not developed to the same extent as that for common stocks. In some ways common stocks have been more "glamorous," and more attention has been devoted to them. Furthermore, more data exist for common stocks, undoubtedly because the most prominent stocks trade on the New York Stock Exchange where daily prices can be collected and analyzed. The same is not true for bonds. Even today investors may have difficulty obtaining instantaneous, current quotes on many bonds.

Despite the incomplete theory of bond portfolio management, investors must manage

[9] This discussion is based on "Risk Premiums among Corporate Bonds," *Monetary Trends*, November 1998, p. 1. This free publication of the Federal Reserve Bank of St. Louis is a good source of information on monetary matters and financial market events. See www.stls.frb.org.

their bond portfolios and make investment decisions. Different bond investors have adopted different strategies, depending on their risk preferences, knowledge of the bond market, and investment objectives.

For organizational purposes, and because this scheme corresponds to the two broad strategies that any investor can follow with any type of portfolio, we will concentrate primarily on passive and active management of bond portfolios while discussing a hybrid approach. Active and passive approaches can be distinguished by the types of inputs needed. Active management depends upon expectations data, while passive strategies do not.

PASSIVE MANAGEMENT STRATEGIES

Passive Management Strategy A strategy whereby investors do not actively seek out trading possibilities in an attempt to outperform the market

As we will learn in Chapter 12, which deals with efficient markets, many investors agree that securities are fairly priced in the sense that the expected return is commensurate with the risk taken. This belief can justify a **passive management strategy**, meaning that the investor does not actively seek out trading possibilities in an attempt to outperform the market. Passive bond strategies are based on the proposition that bond prices are fairly determined, leaving risk as the portfolio variable to control. In effect, passive management strategies are based on inputs that are known at the time, rather than expectations. These strategies have a lower expected return and risk than do active strategies.

A *passive investment strategy does not mean that investors do nothing*. They must still monitor the status of their portfolios in order to match their holdings with their risk preferences and objectives. Conditions in the financial markets change quickly, and investors must also make fast changes when necessary. Passive management does not mean that investors accept changes in market conditions, securities, and so on, if these changes cause undesirable modifications in the securities they hold.

The passive approach is supported by evidence for various periods of years showing that the performance of bond managers during the years examined failed to equal that of a market index. For example, reporting on a five year period when the managers of fixed-income portfolios had an annualized total return of 14.4 percent compared to 14.5 percent for a bond index (and this was before fees) *Forbes* magazine noted that "The average pension fund would have done better with its bond money in a passive index fund."[10]

A recent comprehensive study examining the performance of bond mutual funds, using two samples of bond funds, found that such funds underperformed relevant indexes from the fixed-income area.[11] The results were robust across a wide choice of models. For the most part, this underperformance approximated the average management fees; therefore, before expenses, funds performed about as well as the indexes. There was no evidence of predictability using past performance to predict future performance.

A good case for passive bond investing was made by Mark Hulbert, a columnist for *Forbes* magazine who publishes a report on the performance of investment advisors.[12] His analysis, based on the results achieved by investment advisors, makes a strong argument for passive bond investing, at least as regards attempts to time swings in the bond market. As Hulbert concludes, "Timing the bond market is just about impossible. My advice is: Resist the temptation to try."[13]

Strategies for investors following a passive bond management approach include buy and hold and indexing.

[10] Taken from Steve Kichen, "The *Forbes*/TUCS Institutional Portfolio Report," *Forbes*, August 21, 1989, p. 112.

[11] See Christopher Blake, Edwin Elton, and Martin Gruber, "The Performance of Bond Mutual Funds," *The Journal of Business*, July 1993, pp. 371–403.

[12] Hulbert publishes the *Hulbert Financial Digest*, which has become a well-known source of information on the performance of financial newsletters that are sold to investors.

[13] See Mark Hulbert, "A Fool's Game," *Forbes*, August 8, 1991, p. 119.

Buy and Hold An obvious strategy for any investor interested in nonactive trading policies is simply to buy and hold. This investor carefully chooses a portfolio of bonds and does not attempt to trade them in a search for higher returns. An important part of this strategy is to choose the most promising bonds that meet the investor's requirements. Making this selection requires some knowledge of bonds and markets. Simply because an investor is following a basic buy-and-hold strategy does not mean that the initial selection is unimportant.

The buy-and-hold investor must have knowledge of the yield advantages of various bonds (for example, agency securities over U.S. Treasuries), the default risk, call risk, the marketability of a bond, any current income requirements, and taxes.

One alternative for the buy-and-hold investor is to try to duplicate the overall bond market by purchasing a broad cross section of bonds. Another is to selectively build a portfolio of bonds based on characteristics that match those that the investor is seeking, whether a high level of safety, an intermediate maturity, large coupons, and so forth. Regardless of the bonds sought, individual investors have traditionally faced a very difficult job because the bond market caters to institutional investors, using real-time data bases not available to individuals. Therefore, individual investors could not determine current prices. As of the beginning of 1999, however, this situation was changing dramatically.

USING THE INTERNET An important development occurred in early 1999 when a new firm, Bond Exchange, created a platform that securities firms can use to sell bonds to investors. Investors can see a demo at www.bond-exchange.com. Investors can search by type, rating, coupon, industry, and more. Prices (and markups) are generally very favorable compared to the past. E*Trade and Vanguard Brokerage Services now use this platform. This is the first real breakthrough for individual investors interested in bonds, allowing them to build a bond portfolio by buying and selling at fair prices.

Investors interested in municipal bonds should check www.investinginbonds.com. This site contains previous day's prices for approximately 1,000 actively traded municipals, and it allows you to search a database of bonds by state. Note that this is a reference site, and prices do not represent actual trading prices.

Still another variation for bond investors who do not wish to be active in the market but instead protect themselves from some risk is the *ladder approach*. Under a laddering approach, investors protect themselves to some degree against rises in interest rates by purchasing bonds with different maturity dates. The investor chooses dates that mesh with his or her own situation. For example, with $100,000 to invest, an investor could put approximately $20,000 in each of five bonds, with the first bond maturing two years from now, the second one maturing three years from now, and so forth. Thus, if interest rates rise, the investor will have some principal returned periodically which can be reinvested in new bonds with a higher yield. If interest rates decline, some of the previous higher yields are locked up until those bonds mature. Any type of bond can be used in a laddering strategy.

Index Funds Mutual funds holding a bond or stock portfolio designed to match a particular market index

Indexing If investors decide that they are unlikely to outperform a market index, they may opt to buy a portfolio that will match the performance of a well-known bond index such as the Shearson Lehman Index or Salomon Brothers Index.[14] Mutual funds designed to match the performance of some index are known as **index funds**, and such funds are available for both bonds and stocks (stock index funds are discussed in Chapter 11). While the typical

[14] In practice, it is not feasible to exactly replicate a broad bond index. For example, the Lehman Brothers Aggregate Bond Index covers more than 6,000 securities. Most bond-index funds use a sampling approach to replicate the index as much as possible.

actively managed bond fund has an expense ratio of almost 1 percent, the average expense ratio of bond-index funds is half that, and some are less.

EXAMPLE 9-4

The *Vanguard Total Bond Market Index* is the largest bond index fund at $10 billion in assets in early 1999. Its expense ratio is a mere 0.2 percent. This fund outperformed 89 percent of actively managed bond funds over the period 1996–1998.

How important are expense ratios for bond funds? Very important! In early 1999, with high-grade corporates yielding approximately 5.5 percent and Treasuries even less, the impact of a 0.2 percent expense ratio subtracted from these returns versus about one percent subtracted from these returns is obvious.

How popular has bond indexing become? Not very, despite outperforming active funds. At the beginning of 1999, about 30 bond index funds were in operation, accounting for only 2 percent of overall assets in bond funds.

IMMUNIZATION—A STRUCTURED PORTFOLIO STRATEGY

Because interest rates change over time, investors face uncertainty about the realized returns from bonds. This, of course, is the nature of interest rate risk. The strategy of immunizing (protecting) a portfolio against interest rate risk (i.e., changes in the general level of interest rates) is called **immunization**. This is one form of a structured portfolio strategy, which aims to have a portfolio achieve the performance of a benchmark that has been specified beforehand.

Immunization The strategy of immunizing (protecting) a portfolio against interest rate risk by canceling out its two components, price risk and reinvestment rate risk

To see how such a strategy works, think of interest rate risk as being composed of two parts:

1. The *price risk*, resulting from the inverse relationship between bond prices and required rates of return.
2. The *reinvestment rate risk*, resulting from the uncertainty about the rate at which future coupon income can be reinvested. As discussed in Chapter 8, the YTM calculation assumes that future coupons from a given bond investment will be reinvested at the calculated yield to maturity. If interest rates change so that this assumption is no longer operable, the bond's realized YTM will differ from the calculated (expected) YTM.

Notice that these two components of interest rate risk move in opposite directions:

- If interest rates rise, reinvestment rates (and therefore income) rise, whereas the price of the bond declines.
- If interest rates decline, reinvestment rates (and therefore income) decline, whereas the price of the bond rises.

In effect, the favorable results on one side can be used to offset the unfavorable results on the other. This is what immunization is all about, protecting a bond portfolio against interest rate risk by canceling out the two components of interest rate risk, reinvestment rate risk and price risk.

The duration concept discussed earlier is the basis for immunization theory. Specifically, a portfolio is said to be immunized (the effects of interest rate risk are neutralized) if the duration of the portfolio is made equal to a preselected investment horizon for the portfolio. Note carefully what this statement says. An investor with, say, a 10-year horizon does not

TABLE 9-1 ENDING WEALTH FOR A BOND FOLLOWING A CHANGE IN MARKET YIELDS WITH AND WITHOUT IMMUNIZATION

Bond A: Purchased for $1,000, five-year maturity, 7.9% coupon, 7.9% yield to maturity.
Bond B: Purchased for $1,000, six-year maturity, 7.9% coupon, 7.9% yield to maturity, duration = 5.00 years

Part A: Ending Wealth for Bond A If Market Yields Remain Constant at 7.9%

Years	Cash Flow	Reinvestment Rate (pct.)	Ending Wealth
1	$ 79	—	$ 79.00
2	79	7.9	164.24
3	79	7.9	256.22
4	79	7.9	355.46
5	79	7.9	462.54
5	1000	—	1462.54

Part B: Ending Wealth for Bond A If Market Yields Decline to 6% in Year 3

Years	Cash Flow	Reinvestment Rate (pct.)	Ending Wealth
1	$ 79	—	$ 79.00
2	79	7.9	164.24
3	79	6.0	253.10
4	79	6.0	347.29
5	79	6.0	477.13
5	1000	—	1447.13

Part C: Ending Wealth for Bond B If Market Yields Decline to 6% in Year 3 (Bond B has a duration of five years.)

Years	Cash Flow	Reinvestment Rate (pct.)	Ending Wealth
1	$ 79	—	$ 79.00
2	79	7.9	164.24
3	79	6.0	253.10
4	79	6.0	347.29
5	79	6.0	477.13
5	1017.92[a]	—	1465.05

[a]The price of bond B with one year left to maturity and a market yield of 6% is $1,017.92.

choose bonds with 10 years to maturity but bonds with a duration of 10 years—quite a different statement. The duration strategy will usually require holding bonds with maturities in excess of the investment horizon.[15]

For an example of the immunization concept, consider Table 9-1 which illustrates for a portfolio consisting of one bond what ideally could happen with a portfolio of several bonds. Assume an investor has a five-year investment horizon after which she wishes to liquidate her bond portfolio and spend the proceeds. The current yield to maturity for AAA-rated bonds, the only investment grade our investor is willing to consider, is 7.9 percent for both five-year and six-year bonds because of the flatness of the yield curve. In order to simplify the calculations, we will assume that interest is paid annually so that we can concentrate on the immunization principle.

Because the YTM is 7.9 percent, our investor, understanding the reinvestment rate

[15] For additional information on reinvestment rate risk, see R. W. McEnally, "How to Neutralize Reinvestment Rate Risk," *The Journal of Portfolio Management*, Spring 1980. Also, see William L. Nemerever, "Managing Bond Portfolios Through Immunization Strategies," reprinted in *The Revolution in Techniques for Managing Bond Portfolios* (Charlottesville, Va.: Institute of Chartered Financial Analysts, 1983).

implications of bonds, expects that her investment should yield, after five years, an ending wealth ratio of $(1.079)^5$, or 1.46254, or \$1.46254 per dollar invested today. That is, if she invests \$1,000 in a bond today and the intermediate coupons are reinvested at 7.9 percent each, as the YTM calculation assumes, the ending wealth for this investment in a bond that can be purchased for face value should be \$1,000 $(1.079)^5$, or \$1,462.54.

Our investor can purchase bond A, with a 7.9 percent coupon and a five-year maturity, or bond B, with a 7.9 percent coupon, a six-year maturity, and a duration of five years. The top panel of Table 9-1 illustrates what happens if bond A is purchased and market yields remain constant for our investor's five-year investment horizon. Because the intermediate cash flows are reinvested at exactly 7.9 percent each year, the ending amounts cumulate toward the final ending wealth of \$1,462.54, or a wealth ratio of 1.46254. Notice in these examples that we separate year five from the other four because of the return of principal (\$1,000) at the end of year five; obviously, no compound interest is earned on the return of this \$1,000 at the end of the year. In a similar manner, no interest is earned on the first year's cash flow of \$79, which is assumed to occur at the end of the year.

Now consider what would happen if our investor bought bond A and in the third year of its five-year life market yields for this and comparable bonds declined to 6 percent and remained at that level for the remainder of the five-year period. As a result, the intermediate cash flows in the last three years of the bond's life would be reinvested at 6 percent rather than at 7.9 percent. Therefore, the reinvestment rate risk present in bond investments has a negative impact on this particular bond investment.

The results of a drop in the reinvestment rate are shown in the middle panel of Table 9-1, using the same format as previously. As this panel shows, at the end of year five the ending amount of wealth for bond A now is only \$1,447.13, representing a shortfall for the investor's ending-wealth objective. This result occurred because she did not immunize her bond portfolio against interest rate risk, but instead purchased a bond based on matching the maturity of the bond with her investment horizon. As explained above, to protect against this interest rate risk it is necessary to purchase a bond whose duration is equal to the investor's investment horizon.

Assume that a \$1,000 bond with a coupon rate of 7.9 percent and a six-year maturity could have been purchased at the same time. The duration of this bond, which we call bond B, is exactly five years, matching the investor's investment horizon. In this case, the bond would be immunized against interest rate risk because any shortfall arising from a declining reinvestment rate would be offset by a higher price for the bond at the end of the investment horizon because the drop in interest rates produces an increase in the price of the bond. Note that at the end of five years, which is our investor's investment horizon, bond B has one year left to maturity and could be sold in the market.

The bottom panel of Table 9-1 illustrates the same process as before for bond B. Notice that the ending cash flows are the same for the first four years as they were for the previous situation with the five-year bond. At the end of year five, the bond still has one year to go to maturity. Its price has risen because of the drop in interest rates. As the analysis in Table 9-1 demonstrates, the ending wealth is more than enough to meet the investor's objective of \$1,462.54 per \$1,000 invested.

Thus, the example in Table 9-1 illustrates the basic concept of immunization. By choosing a bond or a portfolio of bonds with a duration equal to a predetermined investment horizon, it is possible, in principle, to immunize the portfolio against interest rate risk.

Immunization is only one of the structured portfolio strategies. These strategies occupy a position between passive strategies and active strategies. Although the classical immunization discussed here could possibly be thought of as a passive strategy, we must be aware of the real-world problems involved in implementing such a strategy. In truth, this strategy is not easy to implement, and it is not a passive strategy in application. To achieve immunization as discussed here requires frequent rebalancing because duration should always be equal to the investment horizon. An investor simply cannot set duration equal to investment horizon at the beginning of the process and ignore the bond, or portfolio, thereafter.[16]

ACTIVE MANAGEMENT STRATEGIES

Active Management Strategy A strategy designed to provide additional returns by trading activities

Although bonds are often purchased to be held to maturity, frequently they are not. Many bond investors use **active management strategies**. Such strategies have traditionally sought to profit from active management of bonds by either:

1. Forecasting changes in interest rates, because we know that bond prices will change as well; or
2. Identifying relative mispricing between various fixed-income securities.

Notice that, unlike the passive strategy, the key inputs are not known at the time of the analysis. Instead, investors have expectations about interest rate changes and mispricings among securities.

We will consider each of these alternatives in turn. We will also examine briefly some of the newer techniques for actively managing a bond portfolio.

Forecasting Changes in Interest Rates Changes in interest rates are the chief factor affecting bond prices because of the inverse relationship between changes in bond prices and changes in interest rates. When investors project interest rate declines, they should take action to invest in bonds, and the right bonds, for price appreciation opportunities. When interest rates are expected to rise, the objective is to minimize losses by not holding bonds or holding bonds with short maturities.

How does an investor forecast interest rates? Not very well, on a consistent and accurate basis, because interest rate forecasting is a notoriously difficult proposition. Nevertheless, reasonable forecasts can be made about the likely growth rate of the economy and the prospects for inflation, both of which affect interest rates and, therefore, bond investors. Assuming that an investor has a forecast of interest rates, what strategy can be used? The basic strategy is to change the maturity of the portfolio. Specifically, an investor should lengthen (shorten) the maturity of a bond portfolio when interest rates are expected to decline (rise).

Duration plays an important role in active strategies involving interest rate forecasting. If interest rates are expected to fall, the duration of the portfolio would be increased; duration would be reduced if interest rates are expected to rise. A portfolio's duration may be changed by swapping bonds to achieve a new target duration, or using interest-rate futures contracts.

It is important to be aware of the trade-offs in strategies involving maturity.

1. Short maturities sacrifice price appreciation opportunities and usually offer lower coupons (income), but serve to protect the investor when rates are expected to rise.
2. Longer maturities have greater price fluctuations; therefore, the chance for bigger gains (and bigger losses) is magnified. However, longer maturities may be less liquid than Treasury bills.

An important component in forecasting interest rates is the yield curve, discussed earlier in connection with the term structure of interest rates. The shape of the yield curve at any

[16] There are several variations of the basic immunization strategy. The most popular variation is called *horizon-matching*, or combination matching. This involves a portfolio that is duration-matched and also cash-matched in the first few years.

An alternative variation is *contingent* immunization, which involves active management plus a lower floor return that is ensured for the horizon period. The portfolio manager must act to earn the floor return by immunizing the portfolio if necessary. Otherwise, the manager can actively manage the portfolio or some portion thereof.

point in time contains potentially valuable information about the future course of interest rates. Bond market participants in particular, and investors in general, pay close attention to yield curves as an aid in forecasting interest rates and as part of deciding what segments of the bond market to invest in.

EXAMPLE 9-5

Consider the situation in mid-1992. The yield curve for Treasury securities had a range of rates that represented a historic high. The difference between three-month bills and 30-year bonds was approximately 4½ percent (450 basis points), an incredible difference by historic standards. The normal difference between longs and shorts is less than 2 percent (200 basis points). Many observers at the time predicted that long rates would decrease, thereby making the yield curve more "normal."

One form of interest rate forecasting, *horizon analysis*, involves the projection of bond performance over a planned investment horizon. The investor evaluates bonds that are being considered for purchase over a selected holding period in order to determine which will perform the best. To do this, the investor must make assumptions about reinvestment rates and future market rates and calculate the *horizon returns* for the bonds being considered based on that set of assumptions. Note that this concept is different from the yield-to-maturity concept, which does not require expectations to be integrated into the analysis. Horizon analysis requires users to make assumptions about reinvestment rates and future yields but allows them to consider how different scenarios will affect the performance of the bonds being considered. Horizon analysis was discussed in Chapter 8.

Bond Swaps An active bond management strategy involving the purchase and sale of bonds in an attempt to improve the rate of return on the bond portfolio

Identifying Mispricings Among Securities Managers of bond portfolios attempt to adjust to the constantly changing environment for bonds (and all securities) by engaging in what are called **bond swaps**. The term usually refers to the purchase and sale of bonds in an attempt to improve the rate of return on the bond portfolio by identifying temporary mispricings in the bond market. These are relative mispricings among different types of bonds.

EXAMPLE 9-6

In late 1998, the convertibles of HealthSouth were yielding the same as its straight debt, possibly because hedge funds sold unusual amounts of convertibles to raise cash, thereby depressing prices.

Box 9-1 illustrates the possibility of exploiting another potential mispricing. In late 1998, the yield on municipals exceeded the yield on comparable-maturity Treasuries, and that was before the taxable equivalent yield was calculated. In other words, based on the past, municipals appeared to be mispriced and appeared to be a great buy for investors. This article also discusses the issue of investing in municipals indirectly using bond funds.

USING THE INTERNET Investors can obtain information on global events, including U.S. interest rates and bond markets, from Morgan Stanley Dean Witter's website at www.ms.com. Access the "Global Strategy Bulletin" for a list of headline stories.

Use of Newer Techniques The bond markets have changed rapidly in recent years because numerous structural changes and record interest rates have occurred. These changes

Box 9-1

REVVING UP

For years, investing in municipal bonds has bestowed few bragging rights at cocktail parties. "It goes along with 'I just bought a new Buick,'" says John Smith, a Rowayton, Connecticut, resident and muni investor.

Now, for the first time in 12 years, Smith and others have something to boast about. Muni bonds—debt issued by cities, towns, schools, and public agencies—are paying interest rates higher than those on taxable U.S. Treasury bonds. In the beginning of October, 30-year insured issues yielded 4.85 percent, as measured by the Bond Market Association and Bloomberg, compared with 4.74 percent for 30-year Treasuries. And that's before factoring in the real gravy: munis' state, local, and federal tax exemptions, which, for investors in the 36 percent tax bracket, would bring the taxable-equivalent yield on the 30-year insured index to 7.58 percent.

"High-grade munis are an absolute screaming buy," says David Kotok, who manages about $400 million for individual investors at Cumberland Advisors in Vineland, New Jersey. "Any investor who doesn't want to accept a gift is silly."

Muni bonds outyielding Treasuries is an anomaly not seen since 1986, when Sen. Bob Packwood proposed reforms that would reduce the munis' tax advantage. Now the tax exemption appears secure, but munis are again relatively cheap. Why? Non-U.S. investors, who don't benefit from munis' special tax status, have snubbed these bonds while snapping up Treasuries. So though yields for both fell from May to September, those of T-bonds tumbled about 1 percentage point, versus a mere 30 basis points for insured 30-year muni revenue bonds.

Domestic demand is beginning to pick up the slack. This may be a reaction to the stock market's recent stumble, in which the Dow Jones fell about 2 percent from January to October 1998. During the same period, the Lehman Brothers Long Insured Muni Index rose 6.83 percent.

Financial advisers recommend munis to investors seeking less volatile portfolios of equities and fixed-income investments. Munis are normally safe, with less than 1 percent of the approximately $1.4 trillion bonds outstanding going into default. About half those sold in 1998 were insured, meaning their interest and principal payments are guaranteed and giving them the highest rating possible: triple A. Moreover, experts say, local governments and states are now better prepared than ever to weather the effects of global economic turmoil. In fact, securities-rating service Standard & Poor's handed out more than twice as many upgrades as downgrades in the third quarter of 1998, the 12th straight in which raised ratings outnumbered lowered ones.

How can you reap munis' benefits? Individual issues pose problems. They often sell in multiples of $5,000, making it difficult to construct a diversified portfolio. And although the market has been pushing for more transparency, many of the more than 5,000 tradable municipal issues may go days without a single buy or sell. "If you buy muni bonds on your own, you should try to get two to three offerings on the same bonds and compare the pricing," say Sylvan Feldstein, research analyst at Guardian Life Insurance Co. of America, which runs about $1.5 billion in bonds. "But if you don't know the municipal market, you may want to be in a fund."

Funds have lower minimum invesments and offer diversification benefits, spreading your risk geographically or among different entities, should you choose to hold debt issued in one state. For instance, if you live in New York or California, you might want a state-specific fund that exempts you from the high state as well as federal taxes. Another consideration is the management fee, which can reduce your returns significantly. Opt for a fund with an expense ratio lower than category average, 1.04 percent according to Morningstar.

And review the holdings: "If you see names you can't pronounce," warns Feldstein, "you know they are small credits, and that may present a problem." Bonds backed by state or major-city obligations that guarantee their full faith and credit are generally considered the most sound.

Still dislike munis' low yields, despite their security and relative cheapness? Well, today's yields may soon look good. "'Sticker shock' has occurred at 6, 7, and 8 percent yields," say Kotok. "Now it's occurring at 5 percent. But we're headed for 4 percent. If you have sticker shock now, you are really going to have it then."

SOURCE: Thomas Cahill, "Revving Up," *Bloomberg Personal Finance*, December 1998, P. 34. Reprinted by permission.

have been accompanied by new techniques for the active management of fixed-income portfolios.

The distinction between the bond market and the mortgage market is now blurred, with mortgage instruments competing in the capital markets in the same manner as bonds. The mortgage has been transformed into a security, and the mortgage market has become more uniform and standardized. These securities are alternatives to bonds, especially corporate bonds, and can be used in the portfolio as substitutes.

Financial futures are now a well-known part of the investor's alternatives. Their use has grown tremendously, in particular to hedge positions and to speculate on the future course of interest rates. Futures will be discussed in more detail in Chapter 18.

BUILDING A FIXED-INCOME PORTFOLIO

Having reviewed some active and passive strategies for managing a bond portfolio, we will now consider how to build a fixed-income portfolio. The first consideration, which is true throughout the range of investment decisions, is to decide on the risk-return tradeoff that all investors face. If investors seek higher expected returns, they must be prepared to accept greater risk. In building a fixed-income portfolio, it is useful to think of the two broad approaches an investor can take, a conservative or an aggressive approach. We will use these two broad strategies below to organize the discussion.

CONSERVATIVE INVESTORS

Conservative investors view bonds as fixed-income securities that will pay them a steady stream of income. In most cases the risk is small, and Treasury issues have practically no risk of default. These investors tend to use a buy-and-hold approach.

Investors following this strategy seek to maximize their current income subject to the risk (quality of issue) they are willing to assume: corporates should return more than Treasury issues, BAA should return more than A or AA or AAA, longer maturities should return more than short maturities, and so on.

Even conservative investors in bonds must consider a number of factors. Assume that an investor wishes to purchase only Treasury issues, thereby avoiding the possible risk of default. Careful consideration should be given to the maturity of the issue, since the range is from Treasury bills of a few months' duration to bonds maturing in the twenty-first century. Reinvestment rate risk must be considered, as must call risk for a few Treasury issues. For investors who may need their funds back before the bonds mature, interest rate risk is relevant.

The investor's choice will depend to a large extent on interest rate forecasts. Even conservative buy-and-hold investors should probably avoid long-term issues if interest rates are expected to rise over an extended period of time. Finally, these investors may wish to consider the differences in coupons between issues. Previous discussion has shown that the lower the coupon on a bond, the higher the price volatility. Although many investors in this group may plan to hold to maturity, conditions can change, and they may need to sell some of these bonds before maturity.

EXAMPLE 9-7

As an example of what can happen to conservative investors when they are buying and holding a bond portfolio, consider the situation facing municipal bond investors in mid-1992. Most municipal bonds can be called after 10 years. Many investors bought municipals in 1982 when interest rates were at record highs. On July 1, 1992, several billion dollars of municipals were redeemed, with more calls expected in the future on the typical call dates, January 1 and July 1. Investors were forced to give up high-yielding municipals at a time when interest rates were quite low. Moreover, in trying to replace the income stream, they had to consider alternatives with lower quality (and therefore greater risk) and/or longer maturity (and therefore subject to interest rate risk as rates rose), or simply resign themselves to a bond portfolio with a new, lower return.

Indirect investing is another possibility. In addition to the bond funds holding Treasuries, municipals, and corporates, or mixtures of any of these, with a wide range of maturities, investors can consider *flexible-income funds*. These funds invest in bonds of all types, convertible securities, and stocks. The emphasis on these funds tends to be on income, but their investment strategies vary greatly. The annual yields on these funds may be only a percentage point or so below long-term Treasury yields, and their total returns tend to be much higher. Examples include Vanguard Wellsley Income, USAA Income, and Berwyn Income.

AGGRESSIVE INVESTORS

Aggressive investors are interested in capital gains that arise from a change in interest rates. There is a substantial range of aggressiveness, from the really short-term speculator to the somewhat less aggressive investor who is willing to realize capital gains over a longer period while possibly earning high yields.

The short-term speculator studies interest rates carefully and moves into and out of securities on the basis of interest rate expectations. If rates are expected to fall, this investor can buy long-term, low-coupon issues and achieve maximum capital gains if the interest rate forecast is correct. Treasury bonds can be bought on margin to further magnify gains (or losses). Treasury securities, for example, can be purchased on 10 percent margin. The speculator often uses Treasury issues (the highest quality bond available) or high-grade corporates in doing this kind of bond trading. It is not necessary to resort to low-quality bonds.

Another form of aggressive behavior involves seeking the highest total return, whether from interest income or capital gains. Investors who follow this strategy plan on a long horizon in terms of holding a portfolio of bonds but engage in active trading during certain periods when such actions seem particularly appropriate. One such period was 1982, when bonds were offering record yields to maturity and interest rates were widely expected to decline. Even mildly aggressive investors could purchase Treasury bonds yielding high-coupon income and have a reasonable expectation of capital gains. The downside risk in this strategy at this time was small. These investors still needed to consider maturity and coupon questions, however, because no interest rate decline can be assumed with certainty.

THE INTERNATIONAL PERSPECTIVE

When investors build bond portfolios, they should consider the opportunities available in the international bond markets. Investors can invest directly or indirectly in foreign bonds by making their own decisions and using their broker or by purchasing shares in an investment company holding foreign bonds.

EXAMPLE 9-8

Assume that you were a bond speculator in the spring of 1992. Large amounts of money had already been made in U.S. bonds by speculators borrowing at rates lower than the rates being paid on the short-term Treasuries they bought. When interest rates declined, they made large capital gains. Assuming U.S. opportunities had been mostly exploited, what about foreign opportunities?

Investors looking at foreign bonds observed that a five-year French government bond could be bought with a yield more than two percentage points greater than a five-year U.S. Treasury bond.[17] Thus, investors willing to switch to a bond denominated in French francs could pick up a substantial increase in yield. Furthermore, since the French yield curve was inverted (sloped downward), there was a good chance of earning a capital gain on the French bond as rates returned to more normal relationships.

As we know by now, larger returns are associated with larger risks. In the case of foreign bonds such as the French example, investors were implicitly betting on the future direction of interest rates in these foreign countries, which in turn reflected bets on their economies. A slowdown would favor the odds of lower interest rates and higher bond prices. Furthermore, investors in foreign bonds face exchange rate or currency risk. Adverse currency fluctuations could significantly reduce the returns to a cash bond investor and wipe out an investor on margin. Therefore, the investors had to decide whether to hedge the position against adverse currency movements. Investors who were bullish on the foreign currency, such as the French franc, could take unhedged positions, while investors who were bearish would probably choose to hedge their positions.

In Chapter 2 we noted that investors always have an alternative to direct investing. They can invest indirectly by purchasing shares of investment companies that, in turn, invest in the securities in which they are interested. In the case of European bonds, the practical way for investors to invest is through mutual funds. Among the foreign bond funds, short-term world multimarket income funds have been popular. Such funds were recently emphasizing short-term European securities because of their relatively high returns. They differ from money market mutual funds in that their prices can fluctuate, whereas money market fund prices typically are maintained at a constant value of $1 per share.

Investors interested in foreign bonds can also purchase world bond funds which invest in long-term bonds. Such funds invariably are betting on the future course of interest rates because of the inverse relation between bond prices and interest rates. Investors can also invest in a few funds that buy the short-term debt securities of only one country. For example, Fidelity, the largest mutual fund company, has separate funds that specialize in German securities and British securities.

Investment companies with funds specializing in foreign government bonds include Fidelity, T. Rowe Price, Putnam, Scudder, and Templeton. Some of these funds hedge European currencies. Alliance Capital, for example, with both a money market and a short-term bond fund, hedges the European currencies, thereby minimizing currency risk.

How does the U.S. dollar affect the foreign bond investor? If the U.S. economy improves, the dollar will probably rise. If the dollar rises against the currencies involved in the foreign bonds, their returns to U.S. investors are impacted.

SUMMARY

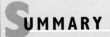

- A wide range of investors are interested in bonds, ranging from those who seek a steady stream of interest income and return of principal to those seeking capital gains by speculating on future interest rate movements.
- In understanding what drives the bond market, fears of inflation play a key role.

[17] This information, as well as the analysis below, is based on Robert Lenzner "How to Play Foreign Yields," *Forbes*, March 16, 1992, p. 71.

- The term structure of interest rates denotes the relationship between market yields and time to maturity. A yield curve graphically depicts this relationship with upward-sloping curves being the norm.
- None of the prevalent theories proposed to explain term structure—the expectations theory, the liquidity preference theory, the preferred habitat theory, and the market segmentation theory—is dominant.
- Yield spreads are the relationship between bond yields and particular bond features such as quality and callability. Differences in type, quality, and coupon account for most of the yield spreads.
- Bond investment strategies can be divided into passive and active strategies.
- Passive bond strategies, whereby the investor does not actively seek out trading possibilities in an attempt to outperform the market, include buy and hold and indexing.
- Immunization is the strategy of protecting (immunizing) a portfolio against interest rate risk by attempting to have the two components of interest rate risk, reinvestment rate risk and price risk, cancel each other out.
- Active management strategies can be broadly divided into forecasting changes in interest rates and identifying relative mispricing between various fixed-income securities. New techniques include the use of mortgage instruments and strategies with financial futures.
- Interest rate swaps are now a significant item in the management of bond portfolios by institutions.
- In building a bond portfolio, investors must make a decision on the risk-return trade-off faced by all investors. Conservative investors will probably consider some issues that are different from those considered by aggressive investors.

KEY WORDS

Active management strategy
Bond swaps
Expectations theory
Forward rates
Immunization
Junk bonds
Liquidity preference theory
Market segmentation theory
Passive management strategy
Preferred habitat theory
Term structure of interest rates
Theoretical spot rate curve
Yield curve
Yield spreads

QUESTIONS

9-1. Describe two different types of investors interested in bonds as an investment.

9-2. List some of the problems involved for U.S. investors in purchasing and selling foreign bonds.

9-3. What is the key factor in analyzing bonds? Why?

9-4. Identify and explain at least two passive bond management strategies.

9-5. Explain the concept of immunization. What role, if any, does duration play in this concept?

9-6. Identify and explain two specific active bond management strategies. Are the two related?

9-7. Assume you have correctly forecast that interest rates will soon decline sharply. Also assume that you will invest only in fixed-income securities and that your time horizon is one year; how would you construct a portfolio?

9-8. When would investors find bonds with long maturities, selling at large discounts, particularly unattractive as investment opportunities?

9-9. What is meant by the term "bond swaps?"

9-10. How can horizon analysis be used to manage a bond portfolio?

9-11. Assume that you are interested in some British government bonds that are currently yielding three percentage points more than comparable Treasury securities. If you think the British economy will slow down, is this favorable or unfavorable for your decision to purchase British bonds? If you are also bullish on the British pound, does this suggest a hedged or unhedged position when you buy the bonds?

The following questions were asked on the 1992 CFA Level I examination:

CFA
9-12. If a bond manager swaps a bond for one that is identical in terms of coupon rate, maturity, and credit quality but offers a higher yield-to-maturity, the swap is:

a. a substitution swap
b. an interest rate anticipation swap
c. a tax swap
d. an intermarket spread swap

CFA
9-13. The concepts of spot and forward rates are most closely associated with which one of the following explanations of the term structure of interest rates?

a. Expectations hypothesis
b. Liquidity premium theory
c. Preferred habitat hypothesis
d. Segmented market theory

CFA
9-14. The interest rate risk of a bond normally is:

a. greater for shorter maturities
b. lower for longer duration
c. lower for higher coupons
d. none of the above

The following question was asked on the 1990 CFA Level I examination:

CFA
9-15. Robert Devlin and Neil Parish are portfolio managers at the Broward Investment Group. At their regular Monday strategy meeting, the topic of adding international bonds to one of their portfolios came up. The portfolio, an ERISA-qualified pension account for a U.S. client, was currently 90 percent invested in U.S. Treasury bonds, and 10 percent invested in 10-year Canadian government bonds.

Devlin suggested buying a position in 10-year West German government bonds, while Parish argued for a position in 10-year Australian government bonds.

a. Briefly discuss the three major issues that Devlin and Parish should address in their analysis of the return prospects for German and Australian bonds relative to those of U.S. bonds.

Having made no changes to the original portfolio, Devlin and Parish hold a subsequent strategy meeting and decide to add positions in the government bonds of Japan, United Kingdom, France, West Germany, and Australia.

b. Identify and discuss two reasons for adding a broader mix of international bonds to the pension portfolio.

PROBLEMS

The following question was asked on the 1992 CFA Level I examination:

CFA 9-1. The table below shows selected data on a German government bond (payable in deutsche marks) and a U.S. government bond. Identify the components of return and calculate the total return in U.S. dollars for *both* of these bonds for the year 1991. Show the calculations for *each* component. (Ignore interest on interest in view of the short time period.)

	Coupon	Market Yield 1/1/91	Market Yield 1/1/92	Modified Duration	Exchange Rate (DM/$U.S.) 1/1/91	Exchange Rate (DM/$U.S.) 1/1/92
German government bond	8.50%	8.50%	8.00%	7.0	1.55	1.50
U.S. government bond	8.00%	8.00%	6.75%	6.5	—	—

The following question was asked on the 1991 CFA Level I examination:

CFA 9-2. Bill Peters is the investment officer of a $60 million pension fund. He has become concerned about the big price swings that have occurred lately in the fund's fixed-income securities. Peters has been told that such price behavior is only natural given the recent behavior of market yields. To deal with the problem, the pension fund's fixed-income money manager keeps track of exposure to price volatility by closely monitoring bond duration. The money manager believes that price volatility can be kept to a reasonable level as long as portfolio duration is maintained at approximately seven to eight years.

a. Discuss the concepts of duration and convexity and explain how each fits into the price/yield relationship. In the situation described above, explain why the money manager should have used both duration and convexity to monitor the bond portfolio's exposure to price volatility.

b. One of the bonds held in the portfolio is a 15-year, 8 percent U.S. Treasury bond with a modified duration of 8.0 years and a convexity of 94.36. It has been suggested that the fund swap out of the 15-year bond and into a barbell position made up of the following two U.S. Treasury issues:

Bond	Coupon	Maturity	Modified Duration	Convexity
1	8%	5 years	3.97 years	19.58
2	8%	30 years	9.73 years	167.56

Construct a barbell position from these two bonds that results in a modified duration of 8.0 years. Compare the price volatility of the barbell position to the bond currently held under each of the following interest rate environments:

i. market rates drop by 50 basis points (e.g., from 9 percent to 8.50 percent), and
ii. market rates drop by 250 basis points (e.g., from 9 percent to 6.50 percent).

The following question was asked on the 1989 CFA Level I examination:

CFA 9-3. On June 1, 1989, a bond portfolio manager is evaluating the following data concerning three bonds held in his portfolio.

Bond	Bond Rating	Coupon	Maturity	Call Price (Date)	Market Price	Yield-to-Maturity	Modified Duration	Change In Market Price*
X	AA	0%	8/14/94	Non-callable	59.44	10.25%	5.2 years	+5.1%
Y	AA	14.00	3/30/98	Non-callable	116.60	11.00	5.2	+5.5
Z	AA	10.25	7/15/97	100 6/1/90	98.63	10.50	5.2	+2.4

*Following a 100-basis-point decline in rates

It is noted that all three bonds have the same modified duration and thus are expected to rise in price by 5.20 percent for a 100-basis-point decline in interest rates. However, the data show that a different change in price occurs for each bond.

Discuss three reasons for the discrepancy between the expectations and the actual change in market price for the bonds.

SELECTED REFERENCES

Bond return strategies for investors are discussed in:

Fong, H. Gifford, and Fabozzi, Frank J. "How to Enhance Bond Returns with Naive Strategies." *The Journal of Portfolio Management*, Summer 1985, pp. 58–60.

A good discussion of duration and reinvestment rate risk can be found in:

McEnally, Richard W. "Duration as a Practical Tool for Bond Management." *The Journal of Portfolio Management*, Summer 1977, pp. 53–57.

McEnally, Richard W. "How to Neutralize Reinvestment Rate Risk." *The Journal of Portfolio Management*, Spring 1980, pp. 59–63.

Interest rate risk and related concepts are discussed in:

Maloney, Kevin J., and Yawitz, Jess B. "Interest Rate Risk, Immunization, and Duration." *The Journal of Portfolio Management*, Spring 1986, pp. 41–48.

www.wiley.com/college/jones7

This chapter discusses passive and active bond portfolio management strategies. The web exercises will enable you to understand the term structure of interest rates and their roles in the forecasting of interest rates. You will also work on exercises that examine the relative superiority of passive versus active strategies.

chapter 10

COMMON STOCK VALUATION

Chapter 10 concentrates on the valuation of common stocks. The dividend discount model is covered in detail, as is an alternative valuation model, the P/E ratio model. Both of these models are used by investors to assess the intrinsic value of stocks and their likely prospects for the future. Every serious investor should be comfortable with the principles of common stock valuation as presented in this chapter.

After reading this chapter you will be able to:

- **Understand the foundation of valuation for common stocks, and how this process differs from that used in valuing bonds.**
- **Use the Dividend Discount Model to estimate the prices of stocks.**
- **Analyze stocks on the basis of the P/E ratio and understand the determinants of the P/E ratio.**
- **Recognize other valuation models sometimes used by investors.**

What determines the value of a common stock? What approaches are commonly used by investors interested in valuing and selecting stocks? These questions are answered in the next few chapters. Because of the complexity of common stocks and the related questions that are raised in their analysis, several chapters are needed to describe adequately the most frequently used analysis and selection processes.

Two basic approaches to valuing common stocks using fundamental security analysis are:

1. The present value approach (capitalization of income method)
2. The P/E ratio (multiple of earnings) approach

- The present value analysis is similar to the discounting process used for bonds in Chapter 8. The future stream of cash flows to be received from a common stock is discounted back to the present at an appropriate discount rate (that is, the investor's required rate of return).
- The P/E ratio approach is probably more widely used by practicing security analysts. A stock is said to be worth some multiple of its future earnings. In effect, investors determine a stock's value by deciding how many dollars (the multiple) they are willing to pay for every dollar of estimated earnings.

THE PRESENT VALUE APPROACH

The classic method of calculating intrinsic (estimated or formula) value involves the use of present value analysis, which is often referred to as the *capitalization of income method*. As explained in Chapter 8, the value of a security can be estimated by a present value process involving the capitalization (discounting) of expected future cash flows. That is, the *intrinsic value* or estimated value of a security is equal to the discounted (present) value of the future stream of cash flows that an investor expects to receive from the asset. Repeating from Chapter 8,

$$\text{Estimated value of security} = \sum_{t=1}^{n} \frac{\text{Cash flows}}{(1 + k)^t} \qquad (10\text{-}1)$$

where

k = the appropriate discount rate or required rate of return[1]

To use such a model, an investor must

1. Estimate an appropriate required rate of return.
2. Estimate the amount and timing of the future stream of cash flows.
3. Use these two components in a present value model to estimate the value of the security, which is then compared to the current market price of the security.

Figure 10-1 summarizes the present value process used in *fundamental analysis*. It emphasizes the factors that go into valuing common stocks. The exact nature of the present

[1] This concept is explained in more detail in Chapter 11.

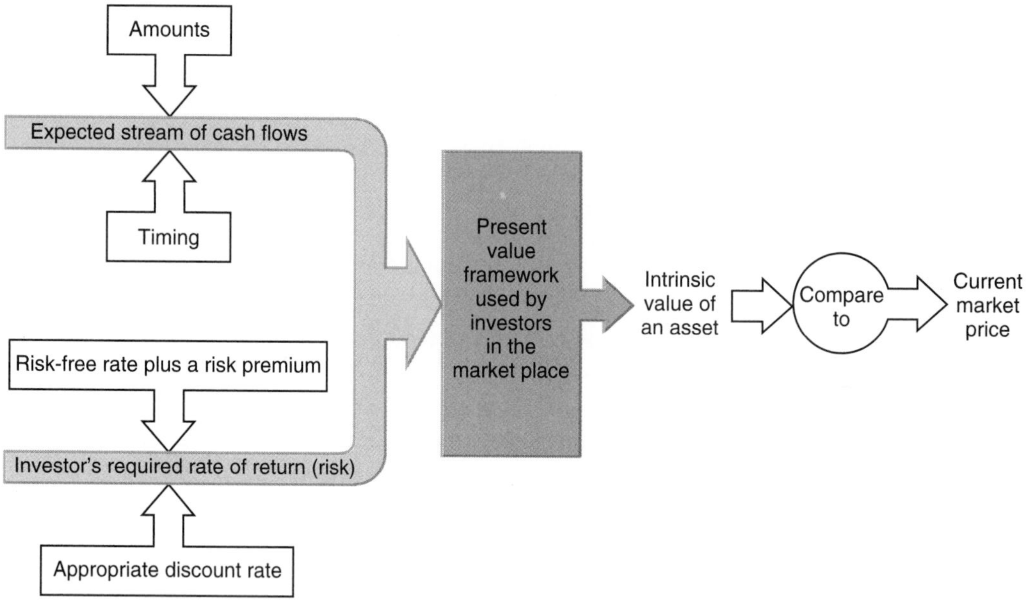

FIGURE 10-1

The present value approach to valuation.

value process used by investors in the marketplace depends upon assumptions made about the growth rate in the expected stream of cash flows, as explained later in this chapter.

THE REQUIRED RATE OF RETURN

An investor who is considering the purchase of a common stock must assess its risk and, given its risk, the *minimum expected rate of return* that will be required to induce the investor to make the purchase. This minimum expected return, or *required rate of return*, is an opportunity cost. It is the same concept as the required yield used in Chapter 8 to value bonds.

The *required rate of return*, *capitalization rate*, and *discount rate* are interchangeable terms in valuation analysis. Regardless of which term is used, it is challenging to determine the numerical value to use for a particular stock. While in theory we know what this variable is, in practice it is not easy to determine a precise discount rate. Because of this complexity, we will generally assume that we know the capitalization rate and concentrate on the other issues involved in valuation, which are difficult enough. In the next chapter, we consider the required rate of return in more detail.

THE EXPECTED CASH FLOWS

The other component that goes into the present value framework is the expected stream of cash flows. Just as the value of a bond is the present value of any interest payments plus the present value of the bond's face value that will be received at maturity, the value of a common stock is the present value of all the cash flows to be received from the issuer (corporation). The questions that arise are:

1. What are the cash flows to use in valuing a stock?
2. What are the expected amounts of the cash flows?
3. When will the expected cash flows be received?

INVESTMENTS INTUITION To find which cash flows are appropriate in the valuation of a common stock, ask yourself the following question: If I buy a particular common stock and place it in a special trust fund for the perpetual benefit of myself and my heirs, what cash flows will be received? The answer is *dividends*, because this is the only *cash* distribution that a corporation actually makes to its stockholders. Although a firm's earnings per share in any year belong to the stockholders, corporations generally do not pay out all their earnings to their stockholders.

Stockholders may plan to sell their shares sometime in the future, resulting in a cash flow from the sales price. As shown later, however, even if investors think of the total cash flows from common stocks as a combination of dividends and a future price at which the stock can be sold, this is equivalent to using the stream of all dividends to be received on the stock.

What about earnings? Are they important? Can they be used in valuing a stock? The answer to both questions is yes. Dividends are paid out of earnings, so earnings are clearly important. And the second approach to fundamental analysis, to be considered later, uses the earnings and a P/E ratio to determine intrinsic value. Therefore, earnings are an important part of fundamental analysis; in fact, earnings receive more attention from investors than any other single variable when they are analyzing and considering stocks to buy and sell.

If all earnings are paid out as dividends, they will be accounted for as dividends. If earnings are retained by the corporation, they presumably will be reinvested, thereby enhancing future earnings and, ultimately, dividends. The present value analysis should not count the earnings reinvested currently and also paid later as dividends. If properly defined and separated, these two variables produce the same results. This means that more than one present value model is possible.[2] However, it is always correct to use dividends in the present value analysis, and this is what is almost always done when investors use the present value approach to common stock valuation.

Because dividends are the only cash flow stream to be received directly by investors under normal conditions, it is appropriate to have a valuation model based on dividends. We now consider such a model, the dividend discount model, which is the basis for understanding the fundamental valuation of common stocks.

THE DIVIDEND DISCOUNT MODEL

Since dividends are the only cash payment a stockholder receives directly from a firm, *they are the foundation of valuation for common stocks*. In adapting Equation 10-1 specifically to value common stocks, the cash flows are the dividends *expected* to be paid in each future period. An investor or analyst using this approach carefully studies the future prospects for a company and estimates the likely dividends to be paid. In addition, the analyst estimates an appropriate required rate of return or discount rate based on the risk foreseen in the dividends and given the alternatives available. Finally, he or she would discount to the present the entire stream of estimated future dividends, properly identified as to amount and timing.

The present value approach to calculating the value of a common stock is conceptually no different from the approach used in Chapter 8 to value bonds, or in Appendix 10-A to value preferred stock. Specifically, Equation 10-1 adapted for common stocks, where divi-

[2] In addition to dividends and earnings, the variable referred to as "cash flow" (earnings after tax plus depreciation) has been suggested for these models.

Dividend Discount Model (DDM) A model for determining the estimated price of a stock by discounting all future dividends

dends are the cash flows, results in Equation 10-2. This equation, known as the **dividend discount model (DDM)**, states that the value of a stock today is the discounted value of all future dividends:

$$\begin{aligned} P_{cs} &= \frac{D_1}{(1+k_{cs})} + \frac{D_2}{(1+k_{cs})^2} + \frac{D_3}{(1+k_{cs})^3} + \cdots + \frac{D_\infty}{(1+k_{cs})^\infty} \\ &= \sum_{t=1}^{\infty} \frac{D_t}{(1+k_{cs})^t} \qquad (10\text{-}2) \\ &= \text{Dividend discount model} \end{aligned}$$

where

P_{cs} = intrinsic value or estimated value of a common stock today based on the model user's estimates of the future dividends and the required rate of return

$D_1, D_2, \ldots$ = the dividends expected to be received in each future period

k_{cs} = the required rate of return for this stock, which is the discount rate applicable for an investment with this degree of riskiness (again, the opportunity cost of a comparable risk alternative)

Two immediate problems with Equation 10-2:

1. The last term in Equation 10-2 indicates that investors are dealing with infinity. They must value a stream of dividends that may be paid forever, since common stock has no maturity date.
2. The dividend stream is uncertain:
   a. There are no specified number of dividends, if in fact any are paid at all. Dividends must be declared periodically by the firm's board of directors. (Technically, they are declared quarterly but conventional valuation analysis uses annual dividends.)
   b. The dividends for most firms are expected to grow over time; therefore, investors usually cannot simplify Equation 10-2 to a **perpetuity** as in the case of a preferred stock.[3] Only if dividends are not expected to grow can such a simplification be made. Although such a possibility exists, and is covered below, it is unusual.

Perpetuity A security without a maturity date

How are these problems resolved? The first problem, that Equation 10-2 involves an infinite number of periods and dividends, will be resolved when we deal with the second problem, specifying the expected stream of dividends. However, from a practical standpoint the infinity problem is not as troublesome as it first appears. At reasonably high discount rates, such as 12 percent, 14 percent, or 16 percent, dividends received 40 or 50 years in the future are worth very little today, so that investors need not worry about them. For example, the present value of \$1 to be received 50 years from now, if the discount rate is 15 percent, is 0.0009.

The conventional solution to the second problem, that the dollar amount of the dividend is expected to grow over time, is to make some assumptions about the *expected growth rate* of dividends. That is, the investor or analyst estimates or models the expected *percentage* rate of growth in the future stream of dividends. To do this, he or she classifies each stock to be valued into one of three categories based on the *expected growth rate in dividends*. In summary: *The dividend discount model is operationalized by estimating the expected growth rate(s) in the dividend stream.*

[3] Refer to Appendix 10-A for the valuation of preferred stock.

A time line will be used to represent the three alternative growth rate versions of the dividend discount model. All stocks that pay a dividend, or that are expected to pay dividends sometime in the future, can be modeled using this approach. It is critical to remember in using the DDM that an investor must account for all dividends from now to infinity by modeling the growth rate(s). As shown below, the mechanics of this process are such that we don't actually see all of these dividends because the formulas reduce to a simplified form, but nevertheless we are accounting for all future dividends when we use the DDM.

It is necessary in using the DDM to remember that the dividend currently being paid on a stock (or the most recent dividend paid) is designated as D_0 and is, of course, known. Specifically, D_0 designates the current dividend being paid, or the most recent dividend paid. Investors must estimate the future dividends to be paid, starting with D_1, the dividend expected to be paid in the next period.

The three *growth rate models* for dividends are:

1. A dividend stream with a zero growth rate resulting from a fixed dollar dividend equal to the current dividend, D_0, being paid every year from now to infinity. This is typically referred to as the no-growth rate or zero-growth rate model:

D_0	D_0	D_0	D_0	$+ \cdots +$	D_0	Dividend stream
0	1	2	3	$+ \cdots +$	∞	Time period

2. A dividend stream that is growing at a constant rate g, starting with D_0. This is typically referred to as the constant or normal growth version of the dividend discount model:

D_0	$D_0(1+g)^1$	$D_0(1+g)^2$	$D_0(1+g)^3$	$+ \cdots. +$	$D_0(1+g)^\infty$	Dividend stream
0	1	2	3	$+ \cdots. +$	∞	Time period

3. A dividend stream that is growing at variable rates, for example, g_1 for the first four years and g_2 thereafter. This is referred to as the multiple-growth version of the dividend discount model:

D_0	$D_1 = D_0(1+g_1)$	$D_2 = D_1(1+g_1)$	$D_3 = D_2(1+g_1)$	$D_4 = D_3(1+g_1)$
0	1	2	3	4

$D_5 = D_4(1+g_2)$	$+ \cdots +$	$D_\infty = D_{\infty-1}(1+g_2)$	Dividend stream
5	$+ \cdots +$	∞	Time period

The Zero-Growth Model The *fixed dollar* dividend model reduces to a perpetuity. Assuming a constant *dollar* dividend, Equation 10-2 simplifies to the *no-growth model* shown as Equation 10-3.

$$P_0 = \frac{D_0}{k_{cs}} = \text{Zero-growth version of the dividend discount model} \tag{10-3}$$

where D_0 is the constant dollar dividend expected for all future time periods and k_{cs} is the opportunity cost or required rate of return for this particular common stock.

The no-growth case is equivalent to the valuation process for a preferred stock because, exactly like a preferred stock, the dividend (numerator of Equation 10-3) remains unchanged. Therefore, a zero growth rate common stock is a perpetuity and is easily valued once k_{cs} is determined.

It is extremely important in understanding the valuation of common stocks using the DDM to recognize that in all cases an investor is discounting the future stream of dividends from now to infinity. This fact tends to be overlooked when using the perpetuity formula involved with the zero growth rate case because the discounting process is not visible. Nevertheless, we are accounting for all dividends from now to infinity in this case, as in all other cases. It is simply a mathematical fact that dividing a constant dollar amount by the discount rate, k, produces a result equivalent to discounting each dividend from now to infinity separately and summing all of the present values.

The Constant Growth Model The other two versions of the DDM indicate that to establish the cash flow stream of expected dividends, which is to be subsequently discounted, it is first necessary to compound some beginning dividend into the future. Obviously, the higher the growth rate used, the greater the future amount; furthermore, the longer the time period, the greater the future amount.

A well-known scenario in valuation is the case in which dividends are expected to grow at a constant rate over time. This *constant-* or *normal-growth model* is shown as Equation 10-4.

$$P_0 = \frac{D_0(1+g)}{(1+k_{cs})} + \frac{D_0(1+g)^2}{(1+k_{cs})^2} + \frac{D_0(1+g)^3}{(1+k_{cs})^3} + \cdots + \frac{D_0(1+g)^\infty}{(1+k_{cs})^\infty} \qquad (10\text{-}4)$$

where D_0 is the current dividend being paid and growing at the constant rate g, and k_{cs} is the appropriate discount rate.

Equation 10-4 can be simplified to the following equation:[4]

$$P_0 = \frac{D_1}{k-g} = \text{Constant-growth version of the dividend discount model} \qquad (10\text{-}5)$$

where D_1 is the dividend expected to be received at the end of Year 1.

Equation 10-5 is used whenever the *growth rate* of future dividends is estimated to be a constant. In actual practice, it is used quite often because of its simplicity and because it is the best description of the actual behavior of a large number of companies and, in many instances, the market as a whole.

EXAMPLE 10-1

Assume Summa Corporation is currently paying $1 per share in dividends and investors expect dividends to grow at the rate of 7 percent a year for the foreseeable future. For investments at this risk level, investors require a return of 15 percent a year. The estimated price of Summa is:

$$P_0 = \frac{D_1}{k-g}$$

$$= \frac{\$1.00\,(1.07)}{0.15 - 0.07} = \$13.38$$

Note that a current dividend (D_0) must be compounded one period because *the constant-growth version of the DDM specifies the numerator as the dividend expected to be received one period from now, which is D_1*. In valuation terminology, D_0 represents the dividend currently

[4] Note that k must be greater than g, or nonsensical results are produced. Equation 10-4 collapses to Equation 10-5 as the number of periods involved approaches infinity.

being paid, and D_1 represents the dividend expected to be paid in the next period. If D_0 is known, D_1 can always be determined:[5]

$$D_0 = \text{Current dividend}$$
$$D_1 = D_0(1 + g)$$

where g is the expected growth rate of dividends.

To completely understand the constant-growth model, which is widely used in valuation analysis, it is instructive to think about the process that occurs under constant growth. Table 10-1 illustrates the case of Summa's growth stock with a current dividend of \$1 per share (D_0), an expected constant-growth rate of 7 percent, and a required rate of return, k, of 15 percent.

As Table 10-1 shows, the expected dollar dividend for each period in the future grows by 7 percent. Therefore, D_1 = \$1.07, D_2 = \$1.14, D_{10} = \$1.97, and so forth. Only the first 60 years of growth are shown, at the end of which time the dollar dividend is \$57.95. The last column of Table 10-1 shows the discounted value of each of the first 60 years of dividends. Thus, the present value of the dividend for Period 1, discounted at 15 percent, is \$0.93, while the present value of the actual dollar dividend in Year 60, \$57.95, is only \$0.01 today. Obviously, dividends received far in the future, assuming normal discount rates, are worth very little today.

Figure 10-2 shows this growth in the dollar dividend for only the first 30 years in order to provide some scale to the process. Because k is greater than g, the present value of each future dividend is declining—for example, the present value of D_1 = \$0.93, the present value of D_2 = \$0.87, and the present value of D_{10} = \$0.49. Therefore, the present-value-of-dividends curve at the bottom of Figure 10-2 is declining more rapidly than the growth-in-dividends-over-time curve above it is growing.

The estimated price of Summa, as illustrated in Table 10-1 and Figure 10-2, is the sum of the present values of each of the future dividends. Adding each of these present values together from now to infinity would produce the correct estimated value of the stock. Note from Table 10-1 that adding the present values of the first 60 years of dividends together produces an estimated value of \$13.20. The correct answer, as obtained from adding all years from now to infinity, or using Equation 10-5, is:

$$P_0 = \text{Estimated price} = \frac{\$1.07}{0.15 - 0.07} = \$13.38$$

Thus, years beyond 40 to 50 typically add very little to the estimated value of a stock. Adding all of the discounted dividends together for the first 60 years produces a present value, or estimated value for the stock, of \$13.20, which is only \$0.18 different from using Equation 10-5. Therefore, years 61 to infinity add a total value of \$0.18 to the stock price.

Table 10-1 illustrates the very important point about these valuation models that was explained earlier. The constant-growth version of the DDM—Equation 10-5—takes account of all future cash flows from now to infinity, although this is not apparent from simply looking at the equation itself. Although Equation 10-5 has no summation or infinity sign, the results produced by this equation are equivalent to those that would be obtained if the dividend for each future period is determined and then discounted back to the present. Again, the mathematics of the process involving a constant-growth rate to infinity reduces to a very simple expression, masking the fact that all dividends from now to infinity are being accounted for.

To fully understand the constant-growth rate version of the DDM, it is also important to realize that the model implies that the stock price for any one period is estimated to grow at the same rate as the dividends, which is g. This means that the growth rate in price plus the growth rate in dividends will equal k, the required rate of return.

[5] D_2 can be determined in the constant-growth model as $D_0(1 + g)^2$ or $D_1(1 + g)$.

TABLE 10-1 PRESENT VALUE OF 60 YEARS OF DIVIDENDS (Current Dividend = $1 $g = 7\%$ $k = 15\%$)

Period	Dollar Dividend	PV Factor	PV of Dollar Dividend
1	1.07	0.8696	0.93
2	1.14	0.7561	0.87
3	1.23	0.6576	0.81
4	1.31	0.5718	0.75
5	1.40	0.4972	0.70
6	1.50	0.4323	0.65
7	1.61	0.3759	0.60
8	1.72	0.3269	0.56
9	1.84	0.2843	0.52
10	1.97	0.2472	0.49
11	2.10	0.2149	0.45
12	2.25	0.1869	0.42
13	2.41	0.1625	0.39
14	2.58	0.1412	0.36
15	2.76	0.1229	0.34
16	2.95	0.1069	0.32
17	3.16	0.0929	0.29
18	3.38	0.0808	0.27
19	3.62	0.0703	0.25
20	3.87	0.0611	0.24
21	4.14	0.0531	0.22
22	4.43	0.0462	0.20
23	4.74	0.0402	0.19
24	5.07	0.0349	0.18
25	5.43	0.0304	0.16
26	5.81	0.0264	0.15
27	6.21	0.0230	0.14
28	6.65	0.0200	0.13
29	7.11	0.0174	0.12
30	7.61	0.0151	0.11
31	8.15	0.0131	0.11
32	8.72	0.0114	0.10
33	9.33	0.0099	0.09
34	9.98	0.0086	0.09
35	10.68	0.0075	0.08
36	11.42	0.0065	0.07
37	12.22	0.0057	0.07
38	13.08	0.0049	0.06
39	13.99	0.0043	0.06
40	14.97	0.0037	0.06
41	16.02	0.0032	0.05
42	17.14	0.0028	0.05
43	18.34	0.0025	0.05
44	19.63	0.0021	0.04
45	21.00	0.0019	0.04
46	22.47	0.0016	0.04
47	24.05	0.0014	0.03
48	25.73	0.0012	0.03
49	27.53	0.0011	0.03
50	29.46	0.0009	0.03

TABLE 10-1 (continued)

Period	Dollar Dividend	PV Factor	PV of Dollar Dividend
51	31.52	0.0008	0.03
52	33.73	0.0007	0.02
53	36.09	0.0006	0.02
54	38.61	0.0005	0.02
55	41.32	0.0005	0.02
56	44.21	0.0004	0.02
57	47.30	0.0003	0.02
58	50.61	0.0003	0.02
59	54.16	0.0003	0.01
60	57.95	0.0002	0.01
	Sum of dividends = $870.47		
		Sum of 1st 60 years of discounted dividends = $13.20	

EXAMPLE 10-2

For Summa, the estimated price today is $13.38 and for the end of Period 1, using D_2 in the numerator of Equation 10-5, it is:

$$P_1 = \frac{(\$1.07)(1.07)}{0.15 - 0.07}$$
$$= \$14.31$$

This estimated price at the end of Period 1 is 7 percent higher than the estimated price today of $13.38, or (rounding causes slight differences)

$$\text{Price change} = \frac{\text{Ending price} - \text{Beginning price}}{\text{Beginning price}}$$
$$= (\$14.31 - \$13.38)/\$13.38 = 7\%$$

FIGURE 10-2

The constant growth model: $g = 7\%$; $k = 15\%$.

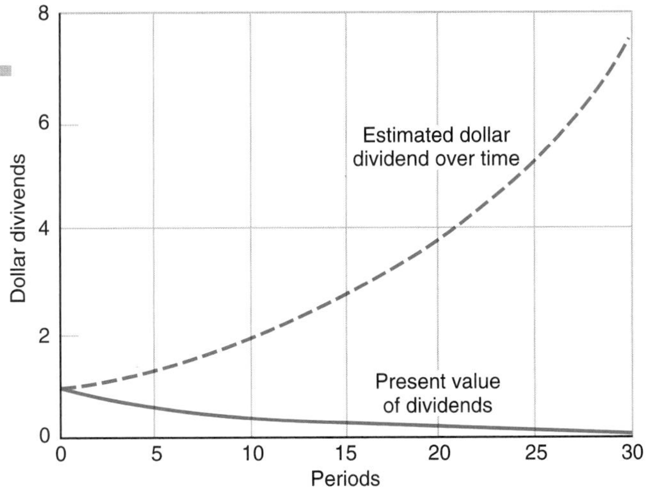

An examination of Equation 10-5 quickly demonstrates the factors affecting the price of a common stock, assuming the constant-growth version of the dividend discount model to be the applicable valuation approach:

1. If the market lowers the required rate of return for a stock, price will rise (other things being equal).
2. If investors decide that the expected growth in dividends will be higher as the result of some favorable development for the firm, price will also rise (other things being equal). Of course, the converse for these two situations also holds—a rise in the discount rate or a reduction in the expected growth rate of dividends will lower price.

The present value or intrinsic value calculated from Equation 10-5 is quite sensitive to the estimates used by the investor in the equation. Relatively small variations in the inputs can change the estimated price by large percentage amounts.

EXAMPLE 10-3

For Summa, assume the discount rate used, *k*, is 16 percent instead of 15 percent, with other variables held constant:

$$P = \frac{\$1(1.07)}{0.16 - 0.07} = \$11.89$$

In this example, a 1-percentage-point rise in *k* results in an 11.14 percent decrease in price, from $13.38 to $11.89.

EXAMPLE 10-4

Assume that for Summa the growth rate, *g*, is 6 percent instead of 7 percent, with other variables held constant:

$$P = \frac{\$1(1.06)}{0.15 - 0.06} = \$11.77$$

In this example, a 1-percentage-point decline in g results in a 12 percent decrease in price, from $13.38 to $11.77.

EXAMPLE 10-5

Assume that for Summa the discount rate rises to 16 percent, and the growth rate declines to 4 percent:

$$P = \frac{\$1(1.04)}{0.16 - 0.04} = \$8.67$$

In this example, the price declines from $13.38 to $8.67, a 35 percent change.

These differences suggest why stock prices constantly fluctuate as investors make their buy and sell decisions. Even if all investors use the constant-growth version of the dividend discount model to value a particular common stock, many different estimates of value will be obtained because of the following:

1. Each investor has his or her own required rate of return, resulting in a relatively wide range of values of *k*.

2. Each investor has his or her own estimate of the expected growth rate in dividends. Although this range may be reasonably narrow in most valuation situations, small differences in g can produce significant differences in price, everything else held constant.

Thus, at any point in time for a particular stock, some investors are willing to buy, whereas others wish to sell, depending on their evaluation of the stock's prospects. This helps to make markets active and liquid.

THE MULTIPLE-GROWTH CASE

Many firms grow at a rapid rate (or rates) for a number of years and then slow down to an "average" growth rate. Other companies pay no dividends for a period of years, often during their early growth period. The constant-growth model discussed earlier is unable to deal with these situations; therefore, a model is needed that can. Such a variation of the DDM is the *multiple-growth model.*

Multiple growth is defined as a situation in which the expected future growth in dividends must be described using two or more growth rates. Although any number of growth rates is possible, most stocks can be described using two or possibly three. It is important to remember that at least two different growth rates are involved; *this is the distinguishing characteristic of multiple-growth situations.*

A number of companies have experienced rapid growth that could not be sustained forever. During part of their lives their growth exceeded that of the average company in the economy, but later the growth rate slowed. Examples from the past include McDonald's, Disney, Polaroid, Xerox, and IBM.

To capture the expected growth in dividends under this scenario, it is necessary to model the dividend stream during each period of different growth. It is reasonable to assume that at some point the company's growth will slow down to that of the economy as a whole. At this time the company's growth can be described by the constant-growth model (Equation 10-5). What remains, therefore, is to model the exact dividend stream up to the point at which dividends slow to a normal-growth rate and to find the present value of all the components.

A well-known multiple-growth rates model is the two-stage growth rate model. This model assumes near-term growth at a rapid rate for some period (typically, 2 to 10 years) followed by a steady long-term growth rate that is sustainable (i.e., a constant-growth rate as discussed earlier). This can be described in equation form as

$$\mathrm{P}_0 = \sum_{t=1}^{n} \frac{\mathrm{D}_0(1 + g_1)^t}{(1 + k)^t} + \frac{\mathrm{D}_n(1 + g_c)}{k - g} \frac{1}{(1 + k)^n} \tag{10-6}$$

where

P_0 = the intrinsic or estimated value of the stock today
D_0 = the current dividend
g_1 = the supernormal (or subnormal) growth rate for dividends
g_c = the constant-growth rate for dividends
k = required rate of return
n = the number of periods of supernormal (or subnormal) growth
D_n = the dividend at the end of the abnormal growth period

Notice in Equation 10-6 that the first term on the right side defines a dividend stream covering n periods, growing at a high (or low) growth rate of g_1 and discounted at the required rate of return, k. This term covers the period of supernormal (or subnormal) growth, at which time the dividend is expected to grow at a constant rate forever. The second term on the right-hand side is the constant-growth version discussed earlier, which takes the dividend expected for the next period, $n + 1$, and divides by the difference between k and g.[6] Notice, however, that the value obtained from this calculation is the value of the stock at the beginning of period $n + 1$ (or the end of period n), and it must be discounted back to time period zero by multiplying by the appropriate discount (present value) factor. Conceptually, the valuation process being illustrated here is:

P_0 = Discounted value of all dividends through the unusual growth period n + the discounted value of the constant-growth model which covers the period $n + 1$ to ∞

Think about the second term in Equation 10-6 as representing a P_n, or the expected price of the stock derived from the constant-growth model as of the end of period n. The constant-growth version of the dividend discount model is used to solve for expected price at the end of period n, which is the beginning of period $n + 1$. Therefore,

$$P_n = \frac{D_{n+1}}{k - g_c}$$

Because P_n is the expected price of the stock at the end of period n, it must be discounted back to the present. When added to the value of the discounted dividends from the first term, the intrinsic value of the stock today (P_0) is produced.

EXAMPLE 10-6

Figure 10-3 illustrates the concept of valuing a multiple-growth rate company. In this example, the current dividend is \$1 and is expected to grow at the higher rate (g_1) of 12 percent a year for five years, at the end of which time the new growth rate (g_c) is expected to be a constant 6 percent a year. The required rate of return is 10 percent.

The first step in the valuation process illustrated in Figure 10-3 is to determine the dollar dividends in each year of supernormal growth. This is done by compounding the beginning dividend, \$1, at 12 percent for each of five years, producing the following:

$$D_0 = \$1.00$$
$$D_1 = \$1.00(1.12) = \$1.12$$
$$D_2 = \$1.00(1.12)^2 = \$1.25$$
$$D_3 = \$1.00(1.12)^3 = \$1.40$$
$$D_4 = \$1.00(1.12)^4 = \$1.57$$
$$D_5 = \$1.00(1.12)^5 = \$1.76$$

Once the stream of dividends over the supergrowth period has been determined, they must be discounted to the present using the required rate of return of 10 percent. Thus,

$$\$1.12(0.909) = \$1.02$$
$$\$1.25(0.826) = \$1.03$$
$$\$1.40(0.751) = \$1.05$$
$$\$1.57(0.683) = \$1.07$$
$$\$1.76(0.621) = \underline{\$1.09}$$
$$\$5.26$$

[6] The dividend at period $n + 1$ is equal to the dividend paid in period n compounded up by the new growth rate, g_c. The designation $n + 1$ refers to the first period after the years of abnormal growth.

Summing the five discounted dividends produces the value of the stock for its first five years only, which is \$5.26. To evaluate Years 6 on, when constant growth is expected, the constant growth model is used.

$$\begin{aligned} P_n &= \frac{D_{n+1}}{(k - g_2)} \\ &= \frac{D_6}{(k - g_2)} \\ &= \frac{D_5(1.06)}{(k - g_2)} \\ &= \frac{1.76(1.06)}{0.10 - 0.06} \\ &= \$46.64 \end{aligned}$$

Thus, \$46.64 is the expected price of the stock at the beginning of Year 6 (end of Year 5). It must be discounted back to the present, using the present value factor for five years and 10 percent, 0.621. Therefore,

$$\begin{aligned} P_n \text{ discounted to today} &= P_n \text{ (PV factor for 5 years, 10\%)} \\ &= \$46.64(0.621) \\ &= \$28.96 \end{aligned}$$

The last step is to add the two present values together:

\$ 5.26	=	present value of the first five years of dividends
28.96	=	present value of the price at the end of Year 5, representing the discounted value of dividends from Year 6 to ∞
\$34.22	=	P_0, the present value of this multiple growth rate stock

FIGURE 10-3

Valuing a multiple-growth company.

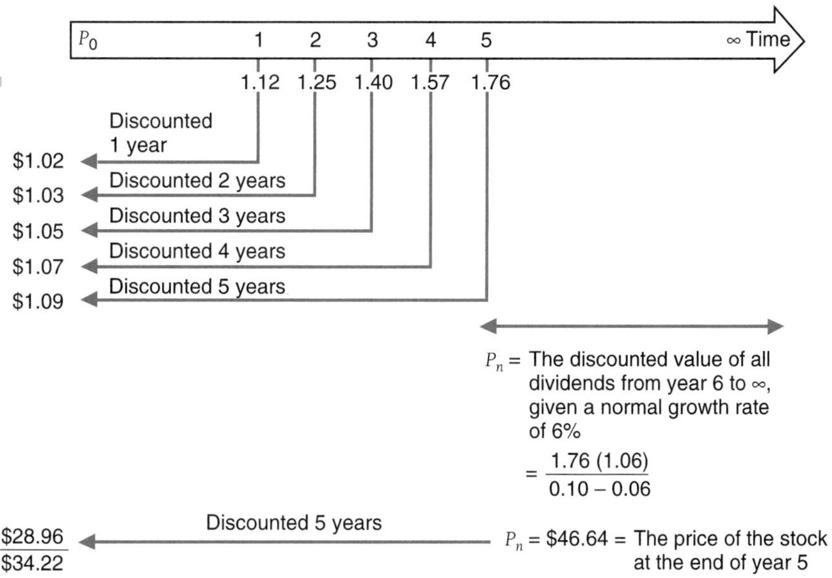

DIVIDENDS, DIVIDENDS—WHAT ABOUT CAPITAL GAINS?

In their initial study of valuation concepts, investors often are bothered by the fact that the dividend discount model contains only dividends, and an infinite stream of dividends at that. Although this is true, many investors are sure that (1) they will not be here forever and (2) they really want capital gains. Dividends may be nice, but buying low and selling high is wonderful! Since so many investors are interested in capital gains, which by definition involves the difference between the price paid for a security and the price at which this security is later sold, a valuation model should seemingly contain a stock price somewhere. Thus, in computing present value for a stock, investors are interested in the present value of the expected price two years from now, or six months from now, or whatever the expected, and finite, holding period is. How can price be incorporated into the valuation—or should it be?

In truth, the only cash flows that an investor needs to be concerned with are dividends. Expected price in the future is built into the dividend discount model given by Equation 10-2—it is simply not visible. To see this, ask yourself at what price you can expect to sell a common stock that you have bought. Assume, for example, that you purchase today and plan to hold for three years. The price you receive three years from now will reflect the buyer's expectations of dividends from that point forward (at the end of years 4, 5, etc.). The estimated price today of the stock is equal to

$$P_0 = \frac{D_1}{(1 + k_{cs})} + \frac{D_2}{(1 + k_{cs})^2} + \frac{D_3}{(1 + k_{cs})^3} + \frac{P_3}{(1 + k_{cs})^3} \tag{10-7}$$

But P_3 (the estimated price of the stock at the end of Year 3), is, in turn, equal to the discounted value of all future dividends from Year 4 to infinity. That is,

$$P_3 = \frac{D_4}{(1 + k_{cs})^4} + \frac{D_5}{(1 + k_{cs})^5} + \cdots + \frac{D_\infty}{(1 + k_{cs})^\infty} \tag{10-8}$$

Substituting Equation 10-8 into 10-7 produces Equation 10-2, the basic dividend discount model. Thus, the result is the same whether investors discount only a stream of dividends or a combination of dividends and price. Since price at any point in the future is a function of the dividends to be received after that time, the price today for a common stock is best thought of as the discounted value of all future dividends.

INTRINSIC VALUE

After making careful estimates of the expected stream of benefits and the required rate of return for a common stock, the intrinsic value of the stock is obtained through the present value analysis—that is, the dividend discount model. This is the objective of fundamental analysis. What does intrinsic value imply? Traditionally, investors and analysts specify a relationship between the intrinsic value (IV) of an asset and its current market price (CMP). Specifically:

If IV > CMP, the asset is undervalued and should be purchased or held if already owned.
If IV < CMP, the asset is overvalued and should be avoided, sold if held, or possibly sold short.
If IV = CMP, this implies an equilibrium in that the asset is correctly valued.

An important question to ask at this point is, "What do you really have when you value an asset by determining its intrinsic value?" The intrinsic value of an asset is that value that exists when the asset is correctly valued—its "true" value based on the capitalization of income process. Intrinsic value is simply the present value concept used in a financial context.

INVESTMENTS INTUITION A problem with intrinsic value is that it is derived from a present value process involving estimates of uncertain (future) benefits and use of (varying) discount rates by different investors. Therefore, the same asset may have many intrinsic values—it depends on who, and how many, are doing the valuing. This is why, for a particular asset on a particular day, some investors are willing to buy and some to sell. Because future benefits are uncertain and investors have differing required rates of return, the use of fundamental valuation models will result in varying estimates of the intrinsic value of an asset. The market price of an asset at any point in time is, in this sense, the consensus intrinsic value of that asset for the market.

Does the problem of varying estimates of value render valuation models useless? No, because individual investors cannot make intelligent investment decisions without having an intelligent estimate of the value of an asset. If General Motors is currently priced at $55 a share, is it a good buy for you? It may or may not be, depending on your own required rate of return (discount rate), your estimate of the future benefit stream to be derived from owning GM, and certain other factors.

EXAMPLE 10-7

Assume that you require 18 percent to invest in GM; that is, your opportunity cost for alternative investment opportunities of similar risk is 18 percent. Also assume that the current dividend is $6.25 and is expected to grow at the rate of 6 percent a year for the indefinite future. Based on these figures and using the constant-growth dividend discount model, the intrinsic value (justified price) of GM to you would be estimated at approximately $52 per share. Based on the intrinsic value principle, GM is overvalued and should not be purchased if the current market price of GM is more than $52 per share, which it is in our example.

Notice that this valuation process tells you that if you can pay $52 per share for GM, you will earn your required rate of return of 18 percent, *if* the assumed dividend growth rate is correct. You can, therefore, pay $50 per share, or $45, or $48, and earn more than the required rate of return.

Other investors with different opinions about k and g may be on the margin valuing this security, only slightly higher or slightly lower than $55. They are potential traders if the price moves slightly or if a news event causes even slight variations in their k or their g.

INVESTMENTS INTUITION The valuation process can establish justified prices for assets or indicate whether or not you can *expect* to earn your required rate of return on a prospective asset. Remember, however, that you are not assured of earning your required rate of return. Investment decisions always involve a forward-looking process. Estimates are made under uncertainty, based on the best information available. But even the best estimates may not be realized. As discussed in Chapter 1, uncertainty will always be the dominant feature of the environment in which investment decisions are made. Furthermore, other factors are at play, including the psychology of the market. And with the rise of the internet, and investors interacting with each other there, information, including false or misleading information, can be spread quickly, and prices affected accordingly.

THE DIVIDEND DISCOUNT MODEL IN PRACTICE

Many money managers and investment services firms, including a number of large Wall Street firms, use the DDM in various ways to estimate the intrinsic values of stocks. Regardless of who uses the model, and how it is used, estimates will always be involved. Investors should always remember this in using, or evaluating, output from these models. However, this also applies to any other valuation model that is used. All involve judgments and estimates because all valuation models are dealing with the uncertain future.

THE P/E RATIO APPROACH

Earnings Multiplier The P/E ratio for a stock

An alternative fundamental analysis method of valuation often used by practicing security analysts is the P/E ratio or **earnings multiplier** approach. The P/E ratio is the number of times investors value earnings as expressed in the stock price. For example, a stock priced at \$100, with earnings of \$5, is selling for a multiple of \$20.

Practicing security analysts probably use some variant of this method more often than the formal dividend discount models, although DDMs command more and more attention and are now quite commonly discussed by investors, the popular press, and investment publications. Because the P/E ratio model appears easier to use than the DDM, its very simplicity causes investors to forget that estimation of the uncertain future is also involved here. This is an important point to reemphasize.

❑ *Every valuation model and approach, properly done, requires estimates of the uncertain future.*

The conceptual framework for the P/E model is not as solidly based on economic theory as the DDM. However, it is derived from an identity this is unquestionably correct. For example, the P/E ratio as reported daily in such sources as *The Wall Street Journal* is simply an identity calculated by dividing the current market price of the stock by the latest 12-month earnings. As such, it tells investors the price being paid for each \$1 of earnings.

EXAMPLE 10-8

In March, 1999 investors were willing to pay 38 times (the most recent 12-month) earnings for General Electric but only 12 times earnings for Ford. Burlington Industries was selling at only four times earnings.

These P/E ratios provide the foundation for valuing stocks, or at least making investment recommendations about stocks, by showing the underlying identity on which the P/E valuation model is based: This identity is

$$P_0 = \text{Current market price} = E_0 \times P_0/E_0 \tag{10-9}$$

It is worth emphasizing.

❑ Stock price is the product of two variables:

1. EPS
2. The P/E multiple

To implement the earnings multiplier model as a valuation model that goes beyond the basic identity, investors could use the P/E model to make estimates of intrinsic value, or fair price.

One alternative is to estimate the justified P/E ratio, and multiply by the current earnings to obtain an estimate of intrinsic value.

EXAMPLE 10-9

If Dell Computers is currently earning \$0.70 a share and investors believe that a P/E ratio of 60 is justified because of Dell's great growth prospects, then Dell would be valued today at

$$\begin{aligned} P_0 &= E_0 \times \text{justified P/E} \\ &= \$0.70 \times 60 \\ &= \$42 \end{aligned}$$

USING THE INTERNET One valuation model that calculates a "fair value" price using a P/E ratio model can be found at http://www.pathfinder.com/money/value. The model will calculate an estimate of fair value for any stock for which the ticker symbol is inputted by multiplying an estimate of P/E by this year's earnings. The worksheet allows users to vary the inputs and make some adjustments for their own estimates of expected inflation, interest rates and the volatility of the stock. The model's estimate of fair value is then compared to the current market price of the stock to determine if the stock is undervalued or overvalued. Users of this model will quickly discover that large differences can occur between the model's estimates of fair price and current market prices, particularly for supergrowth firms.

USING THE P/E RATIO METHOD IN PRACTICE

In actual practice, because of the problems inherent in trying to estimate intrinsic value using the P/E ratio model, investors and analysts tend to use the multiplier model more informally than in the case of the DDM, a model that leads directly to an estimate of intrinsic value.

A typical P/E formulation uses estimated earnings for the next 12 months. The basic equation then becomes

$$\begin{aligned} P_0 &= \text{estimated earnings} \times \text{estimated P/E ratio} \\ &= E_1 \times P_0/E_1 \end{aligned} \tag{10-10}$$

EXAMPLE 10-10

In late January, 1999, S&P Corporation was estimating WalMart's 1999 earnings at \$2.19. The estimated P/E based on these earnings was 36.5, calculated by dividing price by the estimated earnings. Therefore, WalMart's then-current price of \$80 was a function of

$$\$80 = \$2.19 \times 36.5$$

Analysts and investment advisory services often recommend stocks on the basis of the P/E itself. For example, they calculate the P/E ratio using estimated earnings and then decide if this P/E is lower than is justified by the stock's prospects—if so, the stock is undervalued, and if it is higher than is justified by the prospects, it is overvalued.

Exhibit 10-1 shows a detailed recommendation by S&P's weekly publication, *The Outlook*. Shown at the bottom are per share data, including earnings and P/E ratios. Notice that the high and low stock price for each year shown is a product of the current earnings and the high and low P/E ratio—that is, we are using Equation 10-9, the identity. In the upper left of the Exhibit, earnings are estimated for 1999 and 2000, and the P/E ratio for 2000 is

Exhibit 10-1

A STOCK RECOMMENDATION BASED ON P/E RATIOS AND EARNINGS

This company's recent agreement to open 1,500 full-line General Nutrition stores within Rite Aid drugstores over the next three years enhances long-term prospects. With an approximate 14% share of the domestic vitamin market, General Nutrition is the nation's dominant specialty retailer of vitamin and mineral supplements, sports nutrition items and various other health-related products.

The company has more than 3,900 retail stores operating primarily under the General Nutrition Centers and GNC Live Well names in all 50 states and Puerto Rico and is in 23 international markets. The Rite Aid alliance will increase General Nutrition's store locations by 40%. While the company has recently stumbled due to competitive pricing pressures, the fast-growing nutritional supplement industry and the Rite Aid joint venture agreement should enable it to regain its growth momentum.

Despite the pricing pressures, retail supplement industry sales are expected to climb to $12 billion by 2001 from $7 billion in 1997. Growth should be driven by increased consumer acceptance of supplements, as well as by an aging population that continues to increase its use of nutritional supplements. Some 73% of vitamin users are over 35 years of age, and this segment is estimated to climb from 134 million in 1997 to 150 million by 2005. Meanwhile, acceptance of these products appears to be growing as vitamin usage increased from 36% of the population in 1993 to 43% in 1997.

In addition to the store openings, the agreement with Rite Aid calls for the two companies to develop an exclusive brand of vitamins and supplements, called

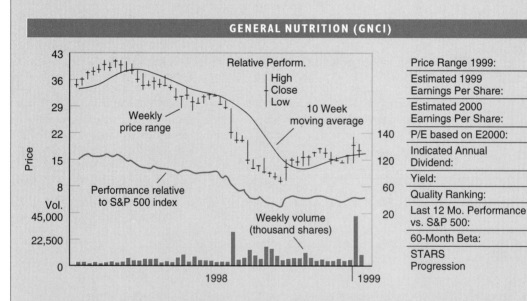

GENERAL NUTRITION (GNCI)

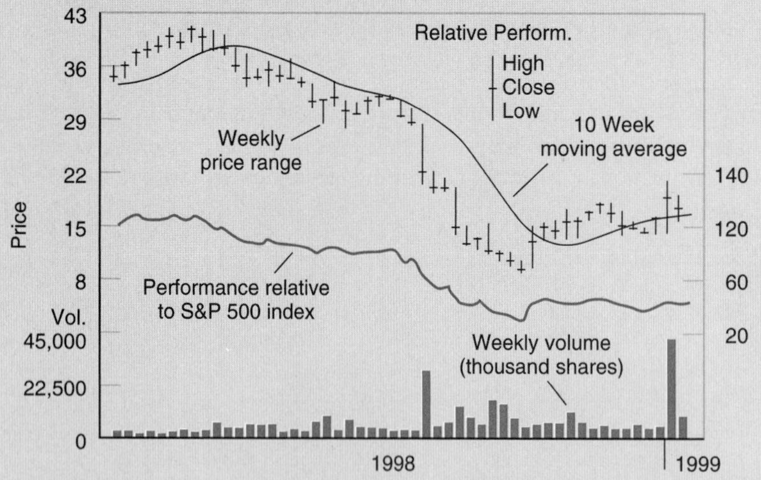

Price Range 1999:	21–14¼
Estimated 1999 Earnings Per Share:	$1.38
Estimated 2000 Earnings Per Share:	$1.60
P/E based on E2000:	10.6
Indicated Annual Dividend:	None
Yield:	Nil
Quality Ranking:	NR
Last 12 Mo. Performance vs. S&P 500:	0.38 to 1.00
60-Month Beta:	1.61
STARS Progression	10/27/98: 2 8/4/98: 3 1/7/99: 5

PER SHARE DATA ($)

	-Stock Price- High		Low	[2]Earnings	[1]Cash Flow	P/E Ratio High		Low	Divd. Paid	Book Value
1998	41¼	-	9	E1.38	1.92	30	-	7	None	N.M.
1997	35	-	16½	1.24	1.77	28	-	13	None	0.53
1996	26	-	13¼	0.05	0.52		N.M.		None	N.M.
1995	26½	-	11¼	0.78	1.18	34	-	14	None	0.32

Based on net income plus depreciation/amortization, E-Estimated, N.M.-Not meaningful.

[2]Year ending January of following year.

PharmAssure, and for GNC to become the sole manufacturer of all of Rite Aid's private label nutritional supplements. The PharmAssure brand could prove to be highly successful in that the products will be developed and endorsed by pharmacists, adding to their credibility with consumers. The brand will be supported by $30 million in marketing that will by funded by savings from GNC's manufacture of Rite Aid's private label supplements.

Rite Aid and General Nutrition also will develop a joint internet site for vitamin and supplement sales. While the Internet site is not likely to be profitable in the first two years, it should help boost brand awareness and consumer knowledge about nutritional supplements.

GNC units within Rite Aid stores will measure 400, 700, or 1000 square feet and be expensed by Rite Aid. The Rite Aid GNC units should help General Nutrition boost revenues by breaking into the $2 billion mass merchant segment for nutritional supplements, as well as add to GNC credibility because of Rite Aid's strong brand association. We estimate profits will advance to $1.38 a share in fiscal 1999 (ending January) from $1.24 in fiscal 1998. For fiscal 2000, $1,60 is likely, and in fiscal 2001, we look for $1.95.

The shares (GNCI, 17, Nasdaq ★★★★★; Quality ranking: NR), which are sharply below their 1998 high, are undervalued at less than 11 times our fiscal 2000 earnings estimate in view of expected profit growth of more than 15% over the next three to five years.

SOURCE: "General Nutrition Has Appeal for Appreciation," Standard & Poor's *The Outlook*, January 27, 1999, p. 16. Reprinted by permission. of Standard & Poor's, a division of the McGraw-Hill Co.

estimated. The conclusion is: "The shares, which are sharply below their 1998 high, are undervalued at less than 11 times our fiscal 2000 earnings estimate in view of expected profit growth of more than 15 percent over the next three to five years." Thus, S&P is recommending General Nutrition on the basis of a lower-than-justified P/E ratio without determining a current "fair price" for the stock which could be compared to the current market price.

DETERMINANTS OF THE P/E RATIO

What determines a P/E ratio? To shed some light on this question, the P/E ratio can be derived from the dividend discount model, which, as we have seen, is the foundation of valuation for common stocks. Note, however, that this process directly applies only for the case of constant growth. If a multiple-period growth model is applicable to the stock being considered, a different formulation from the one presented here will be needed. In fact, using the P/E ratio for supergrowth companies can be misleading and should be done with care.

Start with Equation 10-5, the estimated price of a stock using the constant-growth version of the model.

$$P_0 = \frac{D_1}{k - g} \tag{10-5}$$

Dividing both sides of Equation 10-5 by expected earnings, E_1,

$$P_0/E_1 = \frac{D_1/E_1}{k - g} \tag{10-11}$$

Equation 10-11 indicates those factors that affect the estimated P/E ratio.

1. The dividend payout ratio, D/E
2. The required rate of return
3. The expected growth rate of dividends

The following relationships should hold, other things being equal:

1. The higher the payout ratio, the higher the P/E.
2. The higher the expected growth rate, g, the higher the P/E.
3. The higher the required rate of return, k, the lower the P/E.

It is important to remember the phrase "other things being equal" because usually other things are not equal and the preceding relationships do not hold by themselves. It is quite obvious, upon reflection, that if a firm could increase its estimated P/E ratio, and therefore its market price, by simply raising its payout ratio, it would be very tempted to do so. However, such an action would in all likelihood reduce future growth prospects, lowering g, and thereby defeating the increase in the payout. Similarly, trying to increase g by taking on particularly risky investment projects would cause investors to demand a higher required rate of return, thereby raising k. Again, this would work to offset the positive effects of the increase in g.

Variables 2 and 3 are typically the most important factors in the preceding determination of the P/E ratio because a small change in either can have a large effect on the P/E ratio.

EXAMPLE 10-11

Assume that the payout ratio is 60 percent. By varying k and g, and therefore changing the difference between the two (the denominator in Equation 10-12), investors can assess the effect on the P/E ratio as follows:

Assume $k = 0.15$ and $g = 0.07$

$$P/E = \frac{D_1/E_1}{k - g}$$

$$P/E = \frac{0.60}{0.15 - 0.07}$$

$$= \frac{0.60}{0.08} = 7.5$$

Now assume $k = 0.16$ and $g = 0.06$

$$P/E = \frac{0.60}{0.10} = 6$$

or that $k = 0.14$ and $g = 0.08$

$$P/E = \frac{0.60}{0.06} = 10$$

Think about each of these P/E ratios being used as a multiplier with an expected earnings for stock i for next year of \$3. The possible prices for stock i would be \$22.50, \$18, and \$30, respectively, which is quite a range, given the small changes in k and g that were made.

UNDERSTANDING THE P/E RATIO

Most investors intuitively realize that the P/E ratio should be higher for companies whose earnings are expected to grow rapidly. However, how much higher is not an easy question to answer. The market will assess the degree of risk involved in the expected future growth of earnings—if the higher growth rate carries a high level of risk, the P/E ratio will be affected accordingly. Furthermore, the high growth rate may be attributable to several different factors, some of which are more desirable than others. For example, rapid growth in unit sales owing to strong demand for a firm's products is preferable to favorable tax situations, which may change, or liberal accounting procedures, which one day may cause a reversal in the firm's situation.

FIGURE 10-4

Stock market capitalizations and P/E ratios.

SOURCE: Standard & Poor's *The Outlook*, January 27, 1999, p. 1. Reprinted by permission of Standard & Poor's, a division of The McGraw-Hill Companiess.

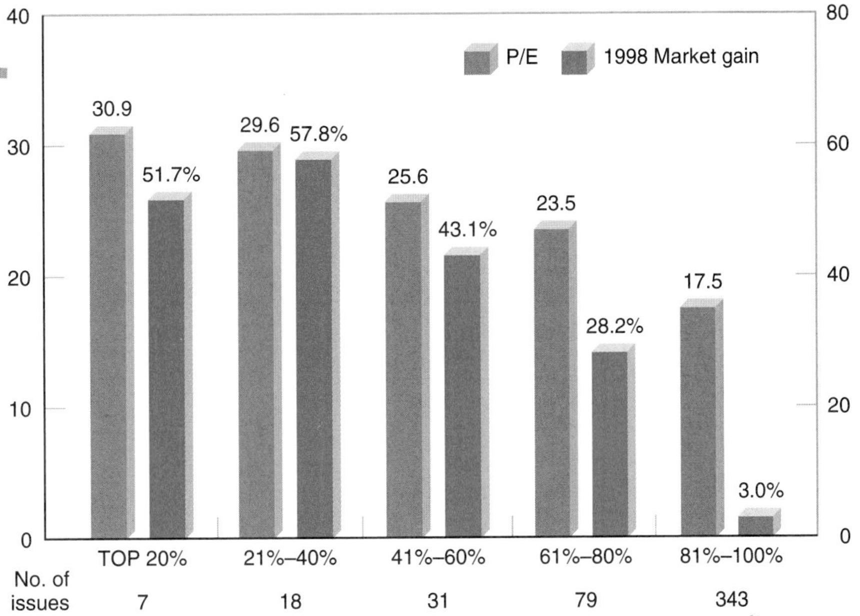

P/E ratios reflect investors' expectations about the growth potential of a stock and the risk involved. These two factors can offset each other. Other things equal, the greater the risk of a stock, the lower the P/E ratio; however, growth prospects may offset the risk and lead to a higher P/E ratio. The Internet companies that were so popular in the late 1990s were clearly very risky, but investors valued their potential very highly, and were willing to pay very high prices for these companies.

At first glance, some stocks may not appear to warrant the high P/E ratios they have. Consider Figure 10-4 which shows that at the end of 1998 the largest stocks commanded the highest P/E ratios, and had the largest market gains in 1998. Why would the largest capitalization stocks warrant such high P/E ratios?

From 1994 through much of 1999, investors favored large cap stocks. In 1998, for example, the largest 25 stocks in the S&P 500 accounted for almost two-thirds of the gain in the S&P 500 for the year. The popularity of the large stocks occurred for two reasons: they were perceived as less risky, as economists forecasted a slowdown in the economy, and they showed strong earnings growth. One estimate was that the average earnings growth rate of the 30 largest companies over the five years ending in 1998 was almost twice that of the 11.6 percent for all companies in the S&P 500 Index.[7] This demonstrates that investors are paying (with high P/Es) for earnings growth.

P/E RATIOS AND INTEREST RATES

The P/E ratio reflects investor optimism and pessimism. It is related to the required rate of return. As the required rate of return increases, other things being equal, the P/E ratio decreases, as can be seen from Equation 10-11.

The required rate of return, in turn, is related to interest rates, which are the required returns on bonds. As interest rates increase, required rates of return on all securities, including stocks, also generally increase. As interest rates increase, bonds become more attractive compared to stocks on a current return basis.

[7] See "Big Cap, Big Edge," *Business Week*, March 1, 1999, p. 94.

TABLE 10-2 THE RELATIONSHIP BETWEEN YIELDS AND P/E RATIOS, 1976–1999

	Yields				
Year	AAA Industrial	Long-Term Treasuries	Municipals	Preferred Stock	P/E Ratio
1999	N/A	N/A	N/A	N/A	N/A
1998	6.22	5.69	4.98	N/A	32.0
1997	6.77	6.67	5.19	N/A	24.43
1996	7.38	6.80	5.52	7.02	19.13
1995	7.59	6.93	5.95	7.21	18.14
1994	7.97	7.41	6.18	7.58	15.3
1993	7.22	6.45	5.60	6.89	21.3
1992	8.14	7.52	6.45	7.46	22.81
1991	8.77	8.16	6.90	8.17	26.12
1990	9.32	8.74	7.31	8.96	15.47
1989	9.26	8.45	7.00	8.75	14.69
1988	9.71	8.94	7.36	9.23	11.68
1987	9.38	8.64	7.14	8.37	14.12
1986	9.02	8.14	6.95	8.76	16.52
1985	11.37	10.75	8.60	10.49	14.15
1984	12.71	11.99	9.61	11.59	9.95
1983	12.04	10.84	8.80	11.02	11.67
1982	13.79	12.23	10.86	12.53	11.13
1981	14.17	12.87	10.43	12.36	7.98
1980	11.94	10.81	7.85	10.57	9.16
1979	9.63	8.74	5.92	9.07	7.31
1978	8.73	7.89	5.52	8.25	7.79
1977	8.02	7.06	5.20	7.60	8.73
1976	8.43	6.78	5.66	7.97	10.84

SOURCE: Federal Reserve *Bulletins*. The P/E ratios for the Standard & Poor's 500 Stock Index are based on calendar-year earnings and end-of-year prices from Standard & Poor's Statistical Service, *Security Price Index Record*. Reprinted by permission of Standard & Poor's, a division of The McGraw-Hill Companies.

Based on these relationships, an inverse relationship between P/E ratios and interest rates is to be expected. As interest rates rise (decline), other things being equal, P/E ratios should decline (rise). Table 10-2 shows interest rates (yields) on corporate, federal, and municipal bonds, yields on preferred stocks, and P/E ratios for the Standard & Poor's 500 Composite Index for recent years. Although the interest rate data are based on averages of monthly data during the year, whereas the P/E ratio data are based on year-end figures, the inverse relationship between the two can be seen clearly. As interest rates rose from 1976 through 1981, the P/E ratio on the S&P 500 Composite Index declined. Conversely, as interest rates declined from 1982 through 1986, the P/E ratio on the stock composite rose. Interest rates rose in 1987 and 1988, and the P/E ratio declined in each year relative to 1986. Other examples can also be seen in the table.

INVESTMENTS INTUITION Notice in Table 10-2 how the yields on preferred stocks tend to track the yields on bonds. Preferred stock, although technically an equity security, should behave like a fixed-income security because of the fixed dividend payment. Preferred stocks are substitutes for bonds in the eyes of many investors interested in obtaining a fixed, steady stream of payments.

WHICH APPROACH TO USE?

We have described the two most often used approaches in fundamental analysis—the dividend discount model and the P/E ratio (multiplier) model. Which should be used?

In theory, the dividend discount model is a correct, logical, and sound position. The best estimate of the current value of a company's common stock is probably the present value of the (estimated) dividends to be paid by that company to its stockholders. However, some analysts and investors feel that this model is unrealistic. After all, they argue, no one can forecast dividends into the distant future with very much accuracy. Technically, the model calls for an estimate of all dividends from now to infinity, which is an impossible task. Finally, many investors want capital gains and not dividends, so for some investors focusing solely on dividends is not desirable.

The previous discussion dealt with these objections that some raise about the dividend discount model. Can you respond to these objections based on this discussion?

Possibly because of the objections to the dividend discount model cited here, or possibly because it is easier to use, the earnings multiplier or P/E model remains a popular approach to valuation. It is a less sophisticated, less formal, and more intuitive model. In fact, understanding the P/E model can help investors to understand the dividend discount model. Because dividends are paid out of earnings, investors must estimate the growth in earnings before they can estimate the growth in dividends or dividends themselves.

Rather than view these approaches as competing alternatives, however, it is better to view them as complements. Each is useful, and together they provide analysts with a better chance of valuing common stocks. There are several reasons for viewing them as complementary:

1. The P/E model can be derived from the constant growth version of the dividend discount model. They are, in fact, alternative methods of looking at value. In the dividend discount model, the future stream of benefits is discounted. In the P/E model, an estimate of expected earnings is multiplied by a P/E ratio or multiplier.
2. Dividends are paid out of earnings. To use the dividend discount model, it is necessary to estimate the future growth of earnings. The dividends used in the dividend discount model are a function of the earnings for the firm, an estimate of which is used in the earnings multiplier model.
3. Neither model can be used in all situations. It is difficult to use the DDM when a company pays no dividends, although expected future dividends can be discounted. On the other hand, the P/E ratio model cannot be used with negative earnings, and for supergrowth companies must be used very carefully.
4. Finally, investors must always keep in mind that valuation is no less an art than a science, and estimates of the future earnings and dividends are subject to error. In some cases it may be desirable to use one or the other method, and in other cases both methods can be used as a check on each other. The more procedures investors have to value common stocks, the more likely they are to obtain reasonable results.

Regardless of which approach is used, it is important to remember that valuation employing fundamental analysis, or any other approach, is always subject to error. This is because we are dealing with the uncertain future. *No matter who does the analysis, or how it is done, mistakes will be made.*

In the first three chapters of Part V, we extensively utilize the overall logic of the fundamental valuation approach—namely, that the intrinsic value of a common stock, or the aggregate market, is a function of its expected returns and accompanying risk, as proxied by the required rate of return. The dividend discount model and the P/E ratio model are used interchangeably to illustrate the fundamental valuation process.

OTHER VALUATION TECHNIQUES

Investors use other valuation techniques, based on fundamental analysis concepts. Two that are often mentioned are price to book value and price/sales ratio.

Book value, the accounting value of the firm as reflected in its financial statements, measures the actual values recorded under accounting conventions. As such, book values have the advantages and disadvantages of accounting numbers.

PRICE TO BOOK VALUE

Price to Book Value The ratio of stock price to per share stockholders' equity

Price to book value is calculated as the ratio of price to stockholders' equity as measured on the balance sheet (and explained in Chapter 15). It is sometimes used to value companies, particularly financial companies. Banks have often been evaluated using this ratio because the assets of banks have book values and market values that are similar. If the value of this ratio is 1.0, the market price is equal to the accounting (book) value. It is also used in merger and acquisition analysis.

Values of the price to book value ratio for a broad index of industrial stocks have ranges from about 2.0 in the early 1970s to about 1.3 by the beginning of the 1980s, increasing to around 3.0 by the market crash in 1987, and then a decline in the late 1980s to around 2.3. Several analysts recommend as a decision rule stocks with low price to book value ratios. To use this measure of relative value, comparisons should be made to the firm's own ratio over time as well as to its industry ratio and that of the market as a whole.

The price to book value ratio (or, as it is commonly stated, the book value to price [or market equity] ratio) has received support in empirical tests. For example, a study by Rosenberg et al. found that stocks with low price to book values significantly outperformed the average stock.[8] This variable got a significant boost in 1992 with the publication of an article by Eugene Fama and Kenneth French, which found that two basic variables, size (market value of equity, or ME) and book to market equity (BV/ME), effectively combined to capture the cross-sectional variation in average stock returns during the period 1963–1990. Furthermore, the book to market equity ratio had a consistently stronger role in average returns.[9]

PRICE/SALES RATIO (PRS)

Price/Sales Ratio A company's total market value divided by its sales

A valuation technique that has received increased attention recently is the **price/sales ratio (PSR)**. This ratio is calculated as a company's total market value (price times number of shares) divided by its sales. In effect, it indicates what the market is willing to pay for a firm's revenues.

[8] See Barr Rosenberg, Kenneth Reid, and Ronald Lanstein, "Persuasive Evidence of Market Inefficiency," *The Journal of Portfolio Management* 11 (Spring 1985): pp. 9–17.

[9] See Eugene Fama and Kenneth French, "The Cross-Section of Expected Stock Returns," *The Journal of Finance* 47 (June 1992): pp. 427–465.

EXAMPLE 10-12 In one recent year General Mills had sales of $5,179 million. Based on an average of the high and low price for the year of $51, and 87 million shares outstanding, the total market value was $443.7 million. The PSR ratio, therefore, was 0.86. Thus, General Mills was selling at 86 percent of its annual sales.

A 1996 book, *What Works on Wall Street*, by James O'Shaugnessy, gives new emphasis to the price/sales ratio. Using Compustat data back to 1951, he analyzed all of the basic investment strategies used to select common stock, such as book value, cash flow, P/E, ROE, yield and so forth. O'Shaugnessy found that the 50 stocks with the lowest PSRs, based on an annual rebalancing of the portfolio, performed at an annual rate of 15.42 percent over the 40 years since 1954 through 1994, compared to 12.45 percent annually for his universe of stocks. Stocks with the highest PSRs earned only 4.15 percent annually. Furthermore, combining low PSR stocks (generally, a PSR of 1.0 or lower) with stocks showing *momentum* (the best 12-month price performance) produced results of 18.14 percent annually over the full 40 year period.

ECONOMIC VALUE ADDED

Economic Value Added (EVA) A technique for focusing on a firm's return on capital in order to determine if stockholders are being rewarded

A new technique for evaluating stocks is to calculate the **economic value added**, or EVA.[10] In effect, EVA is the difference between operating profits and a company's true cost of capital for both debt and equity and reflects an emphasis on return on capital. If this difference is positive, the company has added value. Some studies have shown that stock price is more responsive to changes to EVA than to changes in earnings, the traditional variable of importance.[11]

Some mutual funds are now using EVA analysis as the primary tool for selecting stocks for the fund to hold. One recommendation for investors interested in this approach is to search for companies with a return on capital in excess of 20 percent because this will in all likelihood exceed the cost of capital and, therefore, the company is adding value.

SOME FINAL THOUGHTS ON VALUATION

Valuing stocks is difficult under the best of circumstances. Judgments must be made, and variables estimated. No one knows with precision which valuation model should be used for any particular stock. It is almost impossible to prove that an investor's calculations for a valuation model are correct, or incorrect (although many calculations could be judged by most people to be "reasonable"or not "reasonable)."

In the final analysis, stocks are worth what investors pay for them. Valuations may appear out of line, but market prices prevail. See Box 10-1 for a thoughtful discussion about valuation.

[10] This term has been trademarked by Stern Stewart, a consulting firm that pioneered the use of this concept.

[11] This discussion is based on Maggie Topkis, "A New Way to Find Bargains," *Fortune*, December 6, 1996, pp. 265–266.

Box 10-1

ABOUT THOSE VALUATIONS

Please! Not another article on the market's "excessive" valuation. We heard it in 1995 and the S&P 500 Index jumped 38%; again in '96 as the S&P rose 23%; still again in '97 when the S&P thundered up another 33%; yadah, yadah, yadah in 1998 and another 29% gain for the blue chip average. Do we really need another essay on this?

I think so. In the long run, value does count for something, and value is really missing in this market. For now, let's leave the Internet madness aside. The "irrational exuberance" there, to use Federal Research Chairman Alan Greenspan's phrase, is probably reason enough to expect a bear market. But even though there are thousands of stocks in the market, a comparative handful of large-capitalization issues favored by mutual funds are really responsible for the market's advance.

Let's start with General Electric, which until a couple of months ago was the largest stock, by market value, in the world. GE's $300-billion-plus valuation is the market's assessment of the worth of a company with $53 billion of sales and $9 billion of profits that grew earnings all of 14% last year, and will grow something less than that this year by Wall Street estimates. There was a time when a big multinational blue-chip like GE was worth 10, maybe 15, times earnings. Only the highest of high flyers fetched more than 30 times. In today's market, GE gets 34. Its business isn't growing much; rather, aggressive, management techniques have enabled it to double its profit margins over the last ten years. But as evidenced by the slow earnings growth, that's reaching practical limits.

By investor's assessment, the company that replaces GE as the largest company in the world is Microsoft, which is now worth $400 billion. Bill Gates' company is a phenomenal success story. But look at the numbers. Microsoft's sales in the last twelve months were $16 billion, giving it a price/sales (not price/earnings) ratio of 25. The Redmond, Washington, wonder earns what amounts to monopolistic profit margins, so about $5 billion of that came down to the bottom line, giving the stock a P/E of 68. As we discuss in one of our internet features this issue, most people need a new computer to surf the Internet in comfort, and Microsoft will make an operating system royalty on nearly every PC sold. Earnings grew a nice, but not earth-shaking, 35% last year, and will increase perhaps 30% this year. Is Microsoft worth 68 times earnings? Maybe.

Speaking of PCs, take a look at PC maker Dell, one of the fastest-moving stocks in the market. This company netted $1.2 billion last year. The market thinks the company is worth $120 billion, about 100 times as much. Last year, earnings grew 64%. This year, *The Value Line Investment Survey* says maybe only 38%. Think Dell is a high-tech flyer deserving of such a rich valuation? Do yourself a favor. Take a screwdriver and open up your PC. We did. Although we really didn't understand what was going on in the printed circuit board (Dell doesn't make that) or in the floppy, CD-ROM, or hard drives (Dell doesn't make those either), to us, the inside of a toaster looks more complicated. The mystique about the top PC makers is that they are high tech par excellence. The truth is they are little more than component bundlers and great marketers. Anybody can bundle, and anybody can hire good marketers. Is Dell worth 100 times earnings?

Finally, there's EMC. You probably haven't heard about that one—yet. EMC makes data-storage products for large computers manufactured by IBM and Unisys. A nice business, and one expected to mushroom over the next few years. The company is valued at a heady 11 times sales and 65 times earnings. It may be the buy of the year. At a February investment conference at which we spoke, five of the six members of a technology fund panel volunteered that this was one of their favorite stocks. We were instantly reminded of the theory of contrary opinion: When everybody is already bullish, who's left to buy?

Okay. Lecture's over. Let's go out now and put down our entire bull market fortunes on the funds that love these stocks.

SOURCE: Norman Fosback, "Yawn . . . About Those Valuations," *Mutual Funds*, April 1999, p. 108. Reprinted by permission.

SUMMARY

- Two primary approaches for analyzing and selecting common stocks are fundamental analysis and technical analysis. Efficient market considerations should be taken into account.
- Fundamental analysis seeks to estimate the intrinsic value of a stock, which is a function of its expected returns and risk. Two fundamental approaches to determining value are the present value approach and the earnings multiplier (P/E ratio) approach.
- The present value approach for common stocks is similar to that used with bonds. A required (minimum) expected rate of return must be determined, based on the risk-free rate and a risk premium.
- As for expected returns, since dividends are the only cash flows directly paid by a corporation, they are the logical choice for a present value model.
- According to the dividend discount model, the value of a stock today is the discounted value of all future dividends. To account for an infinite stream of dividends, stocks to be valued are classified by their expected growth rate in dividends.
- If no growth is expected, the dividend discount model reduces to a perpetuity. If two or more growth rates are expected, a multiple-growth model must be used in which the future stream of dividends is identified before being discounted.
- The constant-growth version of the dividend discount model is used most often; it reduces to the ratio of the dividend expected next period to the difference between the required rate of return and the expected growth rate in dividends.
- The dividend discount model is sensitive to the estimates of the variables used in it; therefore, investors will calculate different prices for the same stock while using an identical model. This model implicitly accounts for the terminal price of a stock.
- The multiplier or P/E ratio approach is based on the identity that a stock's current price is the product of its actual earnings per share and the P/E ratio. It follows that the P/E ratio can be calculated by dividing the current price by the actual earnings per share.
- To implement the P/E ratio approach to estimate the value of a stock, we must estimate the earnings and the P/E ratio for next period.
- The P/E ratio itself is a function of the dividend payout ratio, the required rate of return, and the expected growth rate of dividends.
- Also, P/E ratios are inversely related to interest rates because interest rates are directly related to required rates of return.

KEY WORDS

Dividend discount model (DDM)
Earnings multiplier
Economic Value Added (EVA)
Perpetuity
Price to book value
Price/sales ratio

QUESTIONS

10-1. What is meant by "intrinsic value"? How is it determined?

10-2. Why is the required rate of return for a stock the discount rate to be used in valuation analysis?

10-3. Why can earnings not be used as readily as dividends in the present value approach?

10-4. What is the dividend discount model? Write this model in equation form.

10-5. What problems are encountered in using the dividend discount model?

10-6. Describe the three possibilities for dividend growth. Which is the most likely to apply to the typical company?

10-7. Since dividends are paid to infinity, how is this problem handled in the present value analysis?

10-8. Demonstrate how the dividend discount model is the same as a method that includes a specified number of dividends and a terminal price.

10-9. Assume that two investors are valuing General Foods Company and have agreed to use the constant-growth version of the dividend valuation model. Both use $3 a share as the expected dividend for the coming year. Are these two investors likely to derive different prices? Why or why not?

10-10. Once an investor calculates intrinsic value for a particular stock, how does he or she decide whether or not to buy it?

10-11. How valuable are the P/E ratios shown daily in *The Wall Street Journal*?

10-12. What factors affect the P/E ratio? How sensitive is it to these factors?

10-13. Some investors prefer the P/E ratio model to the present value analysis on the grounds that the latter is more difficult to use. State these alleged difficulties and respond to them.

10-14. Indicate the likely direction of change in a stock's P/E ratio if

a. The dividend payout decreases.
b. The required rate of return rises.
c. The expected growth rate of dividends rises.
d. The riskless rate of return decreases.

The following question was given on the 1993 CFA Level I Examination

CFA

10-15. Using book value to measure profitability and to value a company's stock has limitations. **Discuss** *five* such limitations from an accounting perspective. Be specific.

Reprinted, with permission, from the Level I 1994 *CFA Study Guide*.

DEMONSTRATION PROBLEMS

10-1. Puglisi Pharmaceuticals is currently paying a dividend of $2 per share, which is not expected to change. Investors require a rate of return of 20 percent to invest in a stock with the riskiness of Puglisi. Calculate the intrinsic value of the stock.

Solution: The first step to solving a common stock valuation problem is to identify the type of growth involved in the dividend stream. The second step is to determine whether the dividend given in the problem is D_0 or is it D_1.

In this problem it is clear that the growth rate is zero and that we must solve a zero-growth valuation problem (Equation 10-3). The second step is not relevant here because all of the dividends are the same.

$$P_0 = \frac{D_0}{k}$$

$$= \frac{\$2.00}{0.20}$$

$$= \$10.00$$

10-2. Richter Construction Company is currently paying a dividend of $2 per share, which is expected to grow at a constant rate of 7 percent per year. Investors require a rate of return of 16 percent to invest in stocks with this degree of riskiness. Calculate the implied price of Richter.

Solution: Since dividends are expected to grow at a constant rate, we use the constant-growth version of the dividend discount model (Equation 10-5). Note carefully that this equation calls for D_1 in the numerator and that the dividend given in this problem is the current dividend being paid, D_0. Therefore, we must compound this dividend up one period to obtain D_1 before solving the problem.

$$\begin{aligned} D_1 &= D_0(1 + g) \\ &= \$2.00(1.07) \\ &= \$2.14 \end{aligned}$$

and

$$\begin{aligned} P &= \frac{D_1}{k - g} \\ &= \frac{\$2.14}{.16 - .07} \\ &= \$23.78 \end{aligned}$$

10-3. Baddour Legal Services is currently selling for $60 per share and is expected to pay a dividend of $3. The expected growth rate in dividends is 8 percent for the foreseeable future. Calculate the required rate of return for this stock.

Solution: To solve this problem, note first that this is a constant-growth model problem. Second, note that the dividend given in the problem is D_1 because it is stated as the dividend to be paid in the next period. To solve this problem for k, the required rate of return, we simply rearrange Equation 10-5:

$$\begin{aligned} k &= \frac{D_1}{P_0} + g \\ &= \frac{\$3.00}{\$60} + 0.08 \\ &= .13 \end{aligned}$$

Note that we could also solve for g by rearranging Equation 10-5 to solve for g rather than k.

10-4. O. M. Joy Golf Tours has been undergoing rapid growth for the last few years. The current dividend of $2 per share is expected to continue to grow at the rapid rate of 20 percent a year for the next three years. After that time Joy is expected to slow down, with the dividend growing at a more normal rate of 7 percent a year for the indefinite future. Because of the risk involved in such rapid growth, the required rate of return on this stock is 22 percent. Calculate the implied price for Joy Golf Tours.

Solution: We can recognize at once that this is a multiple-growth case of valuation because more than one growth rate is given. To solve for the value of this stock, it is necessary to identify the entire stream of future dividends from Year 1 to infinity, and discount the entire stream back to time period zero. After the third year a constant growth model can be used which accounts for all dividends from the beginning of Year 4 to infinity.

We first calculate the dividends for each individual year of the abnormal growth period, and we discount each of these dividends at the required rate of return.

$$D_1 = \$2.00(1 + 0.20) = \$2.40$$

$$D_2 = \$2.00(1 + 0.20)^2 = \$2.88$$

$$D_3 = \$2.00(1 + 0.20)^3 = \$3.46$$

$$\$2.40(0.820) = \text{present value of } D_1 = \$1.97$$

$$2.88(0.672) = \text{present value of } D_2 = \$1.94$$

$$3.46(0.551) = \text{present value of } D_3 = \underline{\$1.91}$$

Present value of the first three years of dividends = \$5.82

$$P_3 = \frac{\$3.46(1.07)}{0.22 - 0.07} = \$24.68, \text{ which is the}$$

Present value of the stock at the end of Year 3

$$P_0 = \$24.68(0.551) = \$13.60, \text{ which is the}$$

Present value of P_3 at time period zero

$$\hat{P}_0 = \$5.82 + \$13.60 = \$19.42, \text{ which is the}$$

Present value of the stock at time period zero

Note that the price derived from the constant model is the price of the stock at the end of Year 3, which is equivalent to the price of the stock at the beginning of Year 4. Therefore, we discount it back three periods to time period zero. Adding this value to the present value of all dividends to be received during the abnormal growth period produces the intrinsic value of this multiple-growth period stock.

PROBLEMS

10-1. Billingsley Products is currently selling for \$45 a share with an expected dividend in the coming year of \$2 per share. If the growth rate in dividends expected by investors is 9 percent, what is the required rate of return for this stock?

10-2. Assume that Chance Industries is expected by investors to have a dividend growth rate over the foreseeable future of 8 percent a year and that the required rate of return for this stock is 13 percent. The current dividend being paid (D_0) is \$2.25. What is the price of the stock?

10-3. Mittra Motors is currently selling for \$50 per share and pays \$3 in dividends (D_0). Investors require 15 percent return on this stock. What is the expected growth rate of dividends?

10-4. Howe Poultry pays \$1.50 a year in dividends, which is expected to remain unchanged. Investors require a 15 percent rate of return on this stock. What is its price?

10-5. a. Given a preferred stock with an annual dividend of \$3 per share and a price of \$40, what is the required rate of return?

b. Assume now that interest rates rise, leading investors to demand a required rate of return of 9 percent. What will the new price of this preferred stock be?

10-6. An investor purchases the common stock of a well-known house builder, DeMong Construction Company, for \$25 per share. The expected dividend for the next year is \$3 per share, and the investor is confident that the stock can be sold one year from now for \$30. What is the implied required rate of return?

10-7. a. The current risk-free rate (RF) is 10 percent, and the expected return on the market for the coming year is 15 percent. Calculate the required rate of return for (1) stock A, with a beta of 1.0, (2) stock B, with a beta of 1.7, and (3) stock C, with a beta of 0.8.

b. How would your answers change if RF in part (a) were to increase to 12 percent, with the other variables unchanged?

c. How would your answers change if the expected return on the market changed to 17 percent, with the other variables unchanged?

10-8. Rader Chocolate Company is currently selling for \$60 and is paying a \$3 dividend.

a. If investors expect dividends to double in 12 years, what is the required rate of return for this stock?

b. If investors had expected dividends to approximately triple in six years, what would the required rate of return be?

10-9. Wingler Company is currently selling for \$36, paying \$1.80 in dividends, and investors expect dividends to grow at a constant rate of 8 percent a year.

a. If an investor requires a rate of return of 14 percent for a stock with the riskiness of Wingler Company, is it a good buy for this investor?

b. What is the maximum an investor with a 14 percent required return should pay for Wingler Company? What is the maximum if the required return is 15 percent?

10-10. The Hall Dental Supply Company sells at \$32 per share, and Randy Hall, the CEO of this well-known Research Triangle firm, estimates the latest 12-month earnings are \$4 per share with a dividend payout of 50 percent. Dr. Hall's earnings estimates are very accurate.

a. What is Hall's current P/E ratio?

b. If an investor expects earnings to grow by 10 percent a year, what is the projected price for next year if the P/E ratio remains unchanged?

c. Ray Parker, President of Hall Dental Supply, analyzes the data and estimates that the payout ratio will remain the same. Assume the expected growth rate of dividends is 10 percent, and an investor has a required rate of return of 16 percent, would this stock be a good buy? Why or why not?

d. If interest rates are expected to decline, what is the likely effect on Hall's P/E ratio?

10-11. The required rate of return for Agravel Industries is 15.75 percent. The stock pays a current dividend of \$1.30, and the expected growth rate is 11 percent. Calculate the formula price.

10-12. In Problem 10-11, assume that the growth rate is 16 percent. Calculate the formula price for this stock.

10-13. McEnally Motorcycles is a rapidly growing firm. Dividends are expected to grow at the rate of 18 percent annually for the next 10 years. The growth rate after the first 10 years is expected to be 7 percent annually. The current dividend is \$1.82. Investors require a rate of return of 19 percent on this stock. Calculate the intrinsic value of this stock.

10-14. Avera Software Products is currently paying a dividend of \$1.20. This dividend is expected to grow at the rate of 30 percent a year for the next five years, followed by a growth rate of 20 percent a year for the following five years. After 10 years the dividend is expected to grow at the rate of 6 percent a year. The required rate of return for this stock is 21 percent. What is its intrinsic value?

10-15. In Problem 10-14, assume that the growth rate for the first five years is 25 percent rather than 30 percent. How would you expect the value calculated in Problem 10-14 to change? Confirm your answer by calculating the new intrinsic value.

10-16. Wansley Corporation is currently paying a dividend of \$1.60 per year, and this dividend is expected to grow at a constant rate of 8 percent a year. Investors require a 16 percent rate of return on Wansley. What is its estimated price?

10-17. Johnson and Johnson Pharmaceuticals is expected to earn \$2 per share next year. Johnson has a payout ratio of 40 percent. Earnings and dividends have been growing at a constant rate of 10 percent per year, but analysts are estimating that the growth rate will be 7 percent a year for the indefinite future. Investors require a 15 percent rate of return on Johnson and Johnson. What is its estimated price?

10-18. General Foundries is expected to pay a dividend of \$0.60 next year, \$1.10 the following year, and \$1.25 each year thereafter. The required rate of return on this stock is 18 percent. How much should investors be willing to pay for this stock?

10-19. Rocky Mountain Power and Gas is currently paying a dividend of \$1.80. This dividend is expected to grow at a rate of 6 percent in the future. Rocky Mountain Power is 10 percent less risky than the market as a whole. The market risk premium is 7 percent, and the risk-free rate is 5 percent. What is the estimated price of this stock?

10-20. Wilson Industries is currently paying a dividend of \$1 per share, which is not expected to change in the future. The current price of this stock is \$12. What is the expected rate of return on this stock?

10-21. Cascade Gas is currently selling for \$40. It's current dividend is \$2, and this dividend is expected to grow at a rate of 7 percent a year. What is the expected rate of return for this stock?

10-22. Morris Company is not expected to pay a dividend until five years have elapsed. At the beginning of Year 6, investors expect the dividend to be \$3 per share and to remain that amount forever. If an investor has a 25 percent required rate of return for this stock, what should he or she be willing to pay for Morris?

10-23. General Foods is currently selling for \$50. It is expected to pay a dividend of \$2 next period. If the required rate of return is 10 percent, what is the expected growth rate?

10-24. Poindexter Industries is expected to pay a dividend of \$10 per year for 10 years and then increase the dividend to \$15 per share for every year thereafter. The required rate of return on this stock is 20 percent. What is the estimated stock price for Crandall?

10-25. Roenfeldt Components recently paid a dividend of \$1 per share. This dividend is expected to grow at a rate of 25 percent a year for the next five years, after which it is expected to grow at a rate of 7 percent a year. The required rate of return for this stock is 18 percent. What is the estimated price of the stock?

10-26. Rendleman Software is expected to enjoy a very rapid growth rate in dividends of 30 percent a year for the next three years. This growth rate is then expected to slow to 20 percent a year for the next five years. After that time, the growth rate is expected to be 6 percent a year. D_0 is \$2. The required rate of return is 20 percent. What is the estimated price of the stock?

10-27. Peterson Corporation makes advanced computer components. It pays no dividends currently, but it expects to begin paying \$1 a share four years from now. The expected dividends in subsequent years are also \$1 a share. The required rate of return is 14 percent. What is the estimated price for Peterson?

The following question was given on the 1991 CFA Level I Examination.

CFA

10-28. As a firm operating in a mature industry, Arbot Industries is expected to maintain a constant dividend payout ratio and constant growth rate of earnings for the foreseeable future. Earnings were \$4.50 per share in the recently completed fiscal year. The dividend payout ratio has been a constant 55 percent in recent years and is expected to remain so. Arbot's return on equity (ROE) is expected to remain at 10 percent in the future, and you require an 11 percent return on the stock.

a. Using the constant-growth dividend discount model, calculate the current value of Arbot common stock. Show your calculations.

After an aggressive acquisition and marketing program, it now appears that Arbot's earnings per share and ROE will grow rapidly over the next two years. You are aware that the dividend discount model can be useful in estimating the value of common stock even when the assumption of constant growth does not apply.

b. Calculate the current value of Arbot's common stock using the dividend discount model, assuming Arbot's dividend will grow at a 15 percent rate for the next two years, return in the third year to the historical growth rate, and continue to grow at the historical rate for the foreseeable future. Show your calculations.

The following question was given on the 1990 CFA Level I Examination.

CFA

10-29. The constant-growth dividend discount model can be used both for the valuation of companies and for the estimation of the long-term total return of a stock.

Assume: $20 = the price of a stock today
8% = the expected growth rate of dividends
$0.60 = the annual dividend one year forward

a. Using *only* the above data, **compute** the expected long-term total return on the stock using the constant-growth dividend discount model. **Show** calculations.
b. **Briefly discuss** *three* disadvantages of the constant-growth dividend discount model in its application to investment analysis.
c. **Identify** *three* alternative methods to the dividend discount model for the valuation of companies.

The following question was given on the 1992 CFA Level I Examination.

CFA

10-30. Mulroney recalled from her CFA studies that the constant-growth discounted dividend model (DDM) was one way to arrive at a valuation for a company's common stock. She collected current dividend and stock price data for Eastover and Southampton, shown in Table 4.

a. Using 11 percent as the required rate of return (i.e., discount rate) and a projected growth rate of 8 percent, **compute** a constant-growth DDM value for Eastover's stock and **compare** the computed value for Eastover to its stock price indicated in Table 4. **Show** calculations.

Mulroney's supervisor commented that a two-stage DDM may be more appropriate for companies such as Eastover and Southampton. Mulroney believes that Eastover and Southampton could grow more rapidly over the next three years and then settle in at a lower but sustainable rate of growth beyond 1994. Her estimates are indicated in Table 5.

b. Using 11 percent as the required rate of return, **compute** the two-stage DDM value of Eastover's stock and **compare** that value to its stock price indicated in Table 4. **Show** calculations.
c. **Discuss** *two* advantages and *three* disadvantages of using a constant-growth DDM. **Briefly discuss** how the two-stage DDM improves upon the constant-growth DDM.

TABLE 4 CURRENT INFORMATION

	Current Share Price	Current Dividends Per Share	1992 EPS Estimate	Current Book Value Per Share
Eastover (EO)	$ 28	$ 1.20	$ 1.60	$ 17.32
Southampton (SHC)	48	1.08	3.00	32.21
S&P 500	415	12.00	20.54	159.83

TABLE 5 PROJECTED GROWTH RATES

	Next 3 Years (1992, 1993, 1994)	Growth Beyond 1994
Eastover (EO)	12%	8%
Southampton (SHC)	13%	7%

SELECTED REFERENCES

A discussion of the price/earnings ratio can be found in:

Beaver, William, and Morse, Dale. "What Determines Price-Earnings Ratios?" *Financial Analysts Journal* (July-August 1978): 65–76.

The dividend discount model is discussed in:

Farrell, James L. "The Dividend Discount Model: A Primer." *Financial Analysts Journal* (November-(December 1985): 16–25.

Nagorniak, John J. "Thoughts on Using Dividend Discount Models." *Financial Analysts Journal* (November-December 1985): 13–15.

A new book that examines 40 years of stock market data using various selection criteria:

O'Shaughnessy, James. *What Works on Wall Street*. McGraw-Hill, 1996.

www.wiley.com/college/jones7
This chapter presents the basic structure for the valuation of stocks. We will look at the market prices of stocks on the Internet and work on exercises that bring P/E ratios and models such as the dividend discount model to life.

APPENDIX 10-A

THE ANALYSIS AND VALUATION OF PREFERRED STOCK

In Chapter 2 preferred stock was classified for investment analysis purposes as a fixed-income security, although technically it is an equity security. It is best described as a hybrid security, having some characteristics similar to fixed-income securities (i.e., bonds) and some similar to common stocks.

ANALYSIS

Preferred stock can be described as a perpetuity, or perpetual security, since it has no maturity date and will pay the indicated dividend forever. Although perpetual, many preferred stock issues carry a sinking fund, which provides for the retirement of the issue, usually over a period of many years. Furthermore, many preferred stocks are callable by the issuer, which also potentially limits the life of preferreds. Finally, roughly half of all preferred stocks issued in recent years are convertible into common stock. Therefore, although preferred stock is perpetual by definition, in reality many of the issues will not remain in existence in perpetuity.

Preferred stock dividends, unlike common stock dividends, are fixed when the stock is issued and do not change. These dividends are specified as an annual dollar amount (although paid quarterly) or as a percentage of par value, which is often either $25 or $100. The issuer can forgo paying the preferred dividend if earnings are insufficient. Although this dividend is specified, failure to pay it does not result in default of the obligation, as is the case with bonds. Most preferred issues have a cumulative feature, which requires that all unpaid preferred dividends must be paid before common stock dividends can be paid.

Investors regard preferred stock as less risky than common stock because the dividend is specified and must be paid before a common stock dividend can be paid. They regard preferreds as more risky than bonds, however, because bondholders have priority in being paid and in case of liquidation. Investors should, therefore, require higher rates of return on preferred stock than on bonds of the same issuer, but a smaller required return than on common stocks. A complicating factor in this scenario, however, is that 70 percent of dividends received by one corporation from another are excludable from corporate income taxes, making preferred stock an attractive investment for corporations. As a result of this tax feature, preferred stocks often carry slightly lower yields than bonds of comparable quality.

VALUATION

The value of any perpetuity can be calculated as follows:

$$V_p = \frac{C}{(1 + k_p)} + \frac{C}{(1 + k_p)^2} + \cdots \qquad (10A\text{-}1)$$
$$= \frac{C}{k_p}$$

where

V_p = the value of a perpetuity today
C = the constant annual payment to be received
k_p = the required rate of return appropriate for this perpetuity

Because preferred stock is a perpetuity, Equation 10A-1 is applicable in its valuation. We simply substitute the preferred dividend (D) for C and the appropriate required return (k_{ps}) for k_p, resulting in Equation 10A-2.

$$V_{ps} = \frac{D}{k_{ps}} \qquad (10A\text{-}2)$$

A preferred stock, or any perpetuity, is easy to value because the numerator of Equation 10A-2 is known and fixed, forever. No present value calculations are needed for a perpetuity, which simplifies the valuation process considerably. If any two of the values in 10A-2 are known, the third can easily be found.

As an example of the valuation analysis, consider the $1.59 preferred stock of Duke Energy. This $1.59 annual dividend is fixed. To value this preferred, investors need to estimate the required rate of return appropriate for a preferred stock with the degree of riskiness of Duke. Suppose the k, or required rate of return, is 10 percent. The value of this preferred would be

$$V_{\text{Duke}} = \frac{\$1.59}{0.10}$$
$$= \$15.90$$

On the other hand, a required rate of return of 11 percent would result in a value of $11.80.

If the current price for this preferred, as observed in the marketplace, is used in Equation 10A-2, the yield can be solved by using Equation 10A-3.

$$k_{ps} = \frac{D}{P_{ps}} \tag{10A-3}$$

In the case of Duke Energy, the price at mid-March 1999 was about \$27.50, indicating a yield, or required rate of return, of about 5.8 percent.

Notice from Equation 10A-2 that as the required rate of return rises, the price of the preferred stock declines; obviously, the converse is also true. Because the numerator is fixed, the value (price) of a preferred stock changes as the required rate of return changes. At the time of the price observation for Duke, the range for the preceding 52 weeks was \$26 3/4 to \$29. Clearly, investors' required rates of return fluctuate across time as interest rates and other factors change. As rates fluctuate, so do preferred stock prices.

chapter 11

Common Stocks: Analysis and Strategy

Chapter 11 covers the analysis and strategy for selecting and holding common stocks. Similar to the passive approach to bonds, investors can follow a buy-and-hold strategy, or buy index funds that mimic some market index. Under the active approach, we analyze the primary alternatives of stock selection, sector rotation, and market timing and consider the implications of the efficient market hypothesis. A framework for fundamental analysis is outlined, which forms the organization for Part V.

After reading this chapter you will be able to:

- **Recognize the overall impact of the market on stocks, and understand the importance of the required rate of return.**
- **Analyze the pros and cons of a passive approach to building a stock portfolio.**
- **Evaluate critically the well-known active strategies for stocks used by investors.**
- **Differentiate between technical analysis and fundamental analysis, and understand the framework used in doing fundamental analysis.**

In this chapter we consider how investors should go about analyzing some important issues involving common stocks as well as the most common strategies available for selecting stocks. We begin by reviewing a key part of any analysis of common stocks, the impact of the overall stock market. Because of its importance in the analysis of common stocks, we analyze in some detail the required rate of return used in the valuation process.

Much as we did in our discussion of analysis and strategy for bonds, we divide stock strategies into two categories, passive and active. Common stock investors need to carefully consider whether they will follow an active approach, a passive approach, or a combination of the two. Within the active approach, they must decide what activity to concentrate on—selecting stocks, timing the market, and so forth.

We conclude by considering the two basic approaches typically used in security analysis. The fundamental approach, which ties in closely with the analysis of the previous chapter, is described first, followed by a brief description of technical analysis. We also analyze a framework for fundamental analysis. This discussion provides the reader with an overall view of security analysis and sets the stage for Part V, which covers security analysis in detail with a complete discussion of both fundamental analysis and technical analysis.

ANALYZING SOME IMPORTANT ISSUES INVOLVING COMMON STOCKS

In Chapter 9 we analyzed bonds in terms of interest rates because of the fundamental relationship between interest rates and bond prices. In a similar manner we now consider the impact of market risk on common stock investors. The impact of the market on every investor in common stocks is pervasive and dominant, and must be fully appreciated by investors if they are to be successful.

We also consider the required rate of return in detail. This variable is important in any analysis of common stocks. As we saw in Chapter 10, the required rate of return is a very important component of the valuation process using the dividend discount model.

THE IMPACT OF THE OVERALL MARKET ON INDIVIDUAL STOCKS

Market risk is the single most important risk affecting the price movements of common stocks.

Aggregate market movements remain the largest single factor explaining fluctuations in both individual stock prices and portfolios of stocks.

This is particularly true for a diversified portfolio of stocks. As we now know, the basic tenet of portfolio theory is to diversify into a number of securities (properly chosen). For adequately diversified portfolios, market effects often account for 90 percent and more of the variability in the portfolio's return. In other words, for a well-diversified portfolio, which each investor should hold, the market is the dominant factor affecting the variability of its return. Although any given portfolio may clearly outperform the market, it will usually be significantly influenced by what happens on an overall basis.

EXAMPLE 11-1

Consider the performance of Twentieth Century Heritage Investors Fund over a recent six-year period, as shown in Figure 11-1. This fund, part of the well-known Twentieth Century Investors' family of funds, invests exclusively in dividend-paying companies. Notice that, although this fund outperformed the aggregate market as measured by the S&P 500

FIGURE 11-1

Returns for a well-diversified portfolio and the S&P 500 Index.

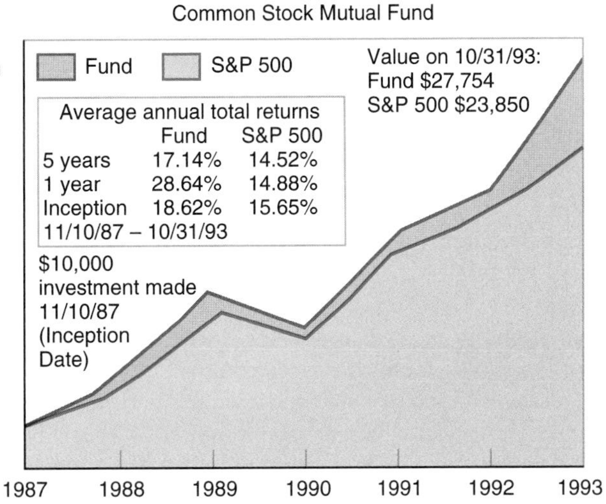

Index by approximately three percentage points annually since inception, its movements roughly paralleled those of the market, peaking in 1989, declining in 1990, and rising thereafter.

The International Perspective U.S. investors buying foreign stocks face the same issues when it comes to market risk. Some of these markets have performed very well, and some have performed poorly over specified periods of time. The investor fortunate enough to have invested in the Brazilian stock market in the first half of 1994 experienced an average gain of 25 percent, whereas the Hong Kong market declined about 21 percent during the same period.

Perhaps the best foreign example of the impact of the overall market on investors is Japan, clearly an economic superpower in recent years. In the 1980s Japan seemed invincible in its economic performance, and its stock market, as measured by the Nikkei stock index, reflected Japan's success with seemingly unending rises in stock prices. The Nikkei stock index peaked at the end of 1989 at a level of almost 39,000. By mid-1992, the index had declined below the 15,000 level, representing a staggering decline of some 60 percent. As one well-known magazine put it, this was the "biggest erasure of wealth in history." As of the beginning of 1999, the Japanese stock market was still in a slump at around 13,000. Such is the impact of the overall market on investor wealth.

THE REQUIRED RATE OF RETURN

The required rate of return was used in the previous chapter as the discount rate for valuing common stocks and in Chapter 8 to determine the price of a bond.

Required Rate of Return The minimum expected rate of return necessary to induce an investor to purchase a security

The **required rate of return** for a common stock, or any security, is defined as the minimum expected rate of return needed to induce an investor to purchase it. That is, given its risk, a security must offer some minimum expected return before a particular investor can be persuaded to buy it.

This discussion is directly related to the CAPM discussion in Chapter 7. The CAPM provides investors with a method of actually calculating a required (expected) rate of return for a stock, an industry, or the market as a whole. Our interest here is to think of the required rate of return on an overall basis as it affects the strategies that investors employ and the management of their portfolios.

What do investors require (expect) when they invest? First of all, investors can earn a riskless rate of return by investing in riskless assets such as Treasury bills. This nominal risk-free rate of return has been designated RF throughout this text. It consists of a real risk-free rate of interest and an inflation premium.[1] In summary, as an approximation:[2]

$$\text{Risk-free rate of return} = \text{Real rate of return} + \text{Inflation premium} \tag{11-1}$$

In addition to the risk-free rate of return available from riskless assets, rational risk-averse investors purchasing a risky asset expect to be compensated for this additional risk. Therefore, risky assets must offer **risk premiums** above and beyond the riskless rate of return. And the greater the risk of the asset, the greater the promised risk premium must be.

Risk Premium That part of a security's return above the risk-free rate of return

The risk premium must reflect all the uncertainty involved in the asset. Thinking of risk in terms of its traditional sources, such components as the business risk and the financial risk of a corporation would certainly contribute to the risk premium demanded by investors for purchasing the common stock of the corporation. After all, the risk to the investor is that the expected income (return) will not be realized because of unforeseen events.

The particular business that a company is in will significantly affect the risk to the investor. One has only to look at the automobile and steel industries in the last few years to see this. And the financial decisions that a firm makes (or fails to make) will also affect the riskiness of the stock.

Understanding the Required Rate of Return The required rate of return for any investment opportunity can be expressed as Equation 11-2. This is, in effect, the CAPM discussed in Chapter 7.

$$\text{Required rate of return} = \text{Risk-free rate} + \text{Risk premium} \tag{11-2}$$

It is important to note that there are many financial assets and therefore many different required rates of return. The average required rate of return on bonds is different from the average required rate of return on preferred stocks, and both are different from that generally required from common stocks, warrants, or puts and calls. Furthermore, within a particular asset category such as common stocks, there are many required rates of return. Common stocks cover a relatively wide range of risk, from conservative utility stocks to small, risky high-technology stocks.

It is also important to be aware that the level of required rates of return changes over time. For example, required rates of return change as inflationary expectations change, because the inflation premium is a component of the risk-free rate of return, which in turn is a component of the required rate of return. The level also changes as the risk premiums change. Investor pessimism will increase the risk premium and the required rate; investor optimism lowers both.

Risk and Required Rate of Return We know from Chapter 7 that the tradeoff between the required rate of return and risk is linear and upward sloping, as shown in Figure 11-2; that is, the required rate of return increases as the risk, measured by beta, increases. The stock market taken as a whole has a beta of 1.0, indicated by point M in the diagram. The required rate of return for all stocks is therefore k_M. A stock with a beta lower than 1.0 has a required rate of return below k_M because its risk (beta) is less than that of the market.

[1] The real risk-free rate of interest (i.e., the real time value of money) is the basic exchange rate in the economy, or the price necessary to induce someone to forego consumption and save in order to consume more in the next period. It is defined within a context of no uncertainty and no inflation.

[2] The actual calculation involves adding 1.0 to both the pure rate and the inflation premium, multiplying the two together, and subtracting the 1.0 from the product. In the example given, $[(1 + 0.02)(1 + 0.05)] - 1.0 = 0.071$, or 7.1 percent.

FIGURE 11-2

The trade-off between required rate of return and risk for common stocks.

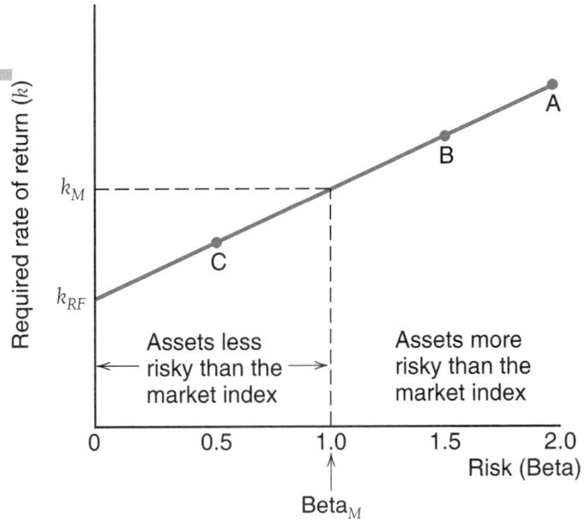

On the other hand, a stock with a beta greater than 1.0 has a required rate of return greater than that of the market.

BUILDING STOCK PORTFOLIOS

We now consider how investors go about selecting stocks to be held in portfolios. Individual investors often consider the investment decision as consisting of two steps:

1. Asset allocation
2. Security selection

We will assume that the asset allocation decision—what percentage of portfolio funds to allocate to each asset class such as stocks, bonds, and bills—has been made so that our focus is only on common stocks. The common stock portion could constitute 100 percent of the total portfolio or any other percentage an investor chooses.

Recall that in our discussion of bond strategies we considered the passive and active approaches. The same approaches are applicable to investors as they select and manage common stock portfolios, or select investment company managers who will manage such portfolios on their behalf. Which of these to pursue will depend on a number of factors, including the investor's expertise, time, and temperament, and, importantly, what an investor believes about the efficiency of the market, as discussed in Chapter 12. We will consider each of these two strategies in turn.

THE PASSIVE STRATEGY

A natural outcome of a belief in efficient markets is to employ some type of passive strategy in owning and managing common stocks. If the market is totally efficient, no active strategy should be able to beat the market on a risk-adjusted basis. The efficient market hypothesis has implications for fundamental analysis and technical analysis, both of which are active strategies for selecting common stocks. That is why we consider it in Chapter 12.

Passive strategies do not seek to outperform the market but simply to do as well as the market. The emphasis is on minimizing transaction costs and time spent in managing the portfolio because any expected benefits from active trading or analysis are likely to be less than the costs. Passive investors act as if the market is efficient and accept the consensus estimates of return and risk, accepting current market price as the best estimate of a security's value.

Paralleling our discussion of passive approaches to bond management, an investor can simply follow a buy-and-hold strategy for whatever portfolio of stocks is owned. Alternatively, a very effective way to employ a passive strategy with common stocks is to invest in an indexed portfolio. We will consider each of these strategies in turn.

BUY-AND-HOLD STRATEGY

A buy-and-hold strategy means exactly that—an investor buys stocks and basically holds them until some future time in order to meet some objective. The emphasis is on avoiding transaction costs, additional search costs, and so forth. The investor believes that such a strategy will, over some period of time, produce results as good as alternatives that require active management whereby some securities are deemed not satisfactory, sold, and replaced with other securities. These alternatives incur transaction costs and involve inevitable mistakes.

Evidence to support this view comes from a study by Odean and Barber, who examined 60,000 investors. They found the average investor earned 15.3 percent over the period 1991–1996 while the most active traders (turning over about 10 percent of their holdings each month) averaged only 10 percent.

Notice that a buy-and-hold strategy is applicable to the investor's portfolio, whatever its composition. It may be large or small, and it may emphasize various types of stocks. Also note that an important initial selection must be made to implement the strategy. The investor must decide to buy stocks A, B, and C and not X, Y, and Z.

Note that the investor will, in fact, have to perform certain functions while the buy-and-hold strategy is in existence. For example, any income generated by the portfolio may be reinvested in other securities. Alternatively, a few stocks may do so well that they dominate the total market value of the portfolio and reduce its diversification. If the portfolio changes in such a way that it is no longer compatible with the investor's risk tolerance, adjustments may be required. The point is simply that even under such a strategy investors must still take certain actions.

An interesting variant of this strategy that has been widely popularized is to buy-and-hold the 10 highest dividend-yielding stocks among the DJIA at the beginning of the year, hold for a year, and replace any stocks, if necessary, at the beginning of the next year with the newest highest-yielding stocks in the DJIA. This strategy does not require stock selection since it is based only on using the easily-calculated dividend yield for 30 identified stocks, and making substitutions when necessary. This strategy is said to have produced amazing results over the years and has gained considerable attention. However, like many other proposed strategies for investing, the popularity of this one sees to have rendered it much less effective in recent periods.

INDEX FUNDS

An increasing amount of mutual fund and pensions fund assets can be described as passive equity investments. Using **index funds,** these asset pools are designed to duplicate as precisely as possible the performance of some market index, similar to bond index funds discussed in Chapter 9.

A stock-index fund may consist of all the stocks in a well-known market average such as the Standard & Poor 500 Composite Stock Index. No attempt is made to forecast market movements and act accordingly, or to select under- or overvalued securities. Expenses are kept to a minimum, including research costs (security analysis), portfolio managers' fees, and brokerage commissions. Index funds can be run efficiently by a small staff.

EXAMPLE 11-2

The Vanguard Group of Investment Companies offers its Vanguard Index Trust portfolios, the largest selection of index funds in the industry, to allow investors to duplicate the broad market of all common stocks at a low cost. Investors can choose from among several portfolios in the trust.

1. *The Index Trust 500 Portfolio* consists of stocks selected to duplicate the S&P 500 and emphasizes large-capitalization stocks.
2. *The Extended Market Portfolio* consists of a statistically selected sample of the Wilshire 4500 Index, and of medium- and small-capitalization stocks.
3. The *Total Stock Market Portfolio* seeks to match the performance of all (approximately 7000) publicly traded U.S. stocks.
4. The *Small Capitalization Stock Portfolio* seeks to match the performance of the Russell 2000 Small Stock Index, consisting of 2000 small-capitalization stocks.
5. The *Value Portfolio* seeks to match the investment performance of the S&P/BARRA Value Index, which consists of stocks selected from the S&P 500 Index with lower than average ratios of market price to book value.
6. The *Growth Portfolio* seeks to match the investment performance of the S&P 500/BARRA Growth Index, which consists of stocks selected from the S&P 500 Index with higher than average ratios of market price to book value.
7. The Total International Portfolio covers 31 countries across Europe, the Pacific, and emerging markets, and holds over 1500 stocks. The European Portfolio invests in Europe's 14 largest markets, while the Pacific Portfolio invests in the six most developed countries in the Pacific region. The Emerging Markets Portfolio invests in 14 of the most accessible markets in the less developed countries.

There are no sales charges or exit charges of any kind. Total operating expenses for several of these funds is about 0.20 percent annually, which is extremely low.

INVESTMENTS INTUITION

Index funds arose in response to the large body of evidence concerning the efficiency of the market, and they have grown as evidence of the inability of mutual funds to consistently, or even very often, outperform the market continues to accumulate. If the market is efficient, many of the activities normally engaged in by funds are suspect; that is, the benefits are not likely to exceed the costs. The available evidence indicates that many investment companies have failed to match the performance of broad market indexes. For example, for the period 1986–1995, 78 percent of general equity mutual funds were outperformed by the S&P 500 Index, and 68 percent of international stock funds were outperformed by their comparative index.

How important are equity index funds into today's investing world? Vanguard's Index Trust 500 fund had approximately $75 billion in assets by the beginning of 1999, making it the second largest mutual fund in the United States. And Vanguard Group is the second largest fund group in the United States, based primarily on the amount of money in its index funds. Fidelity Investments, which remains the largest fund family, traditionally based its prowess on actively managed equity funds. It has now doubled its index offerings to six funds after publicly declaring some years ago it would not run index funds.

One of the strongest cases for index funds has been made by Burton Malkiel, an Economics Professor at Princeton and author of the new book, *Earn More, Sleep Better: The Index Fund Solution.* According to Malkiel, "On average, the typical actively managed fund underperforms the index by about two percentage points a year. And that calculation ignores the sales charges that are imposed by some actively managed funds and the extra taxes an investor pays on funds that turn over their portfolios rapidly."[3]

According to Malkiel, there are four reasons why indexing works:

1. Securities markets are extremely efficient in digesting information.
2. Indexing is cost efficient, with expenses much lower than actively managed funds.
3. Funds incur heavy trading expenses. Trading costs can amount to 0.5 percent to 1.0 percent per year.
4. Indexing has a tax advantage, deferring the realization of capital gains while earlier realization of capital gains reduces net returns significantly.

THE ACTIVE STRATEGY

Most of the techniques discussed in this text involve an active approach to investing. In the area of common stocks the use of valuation models to value and select stocks indicates that investors are analyzing and valuing stocks in an attempt to improve their performance relative to some benchmark such as a market index. They assume or expect the benefits to be greater than the costs.

Pursuit of an active strategy assumes that investors possess some advantage relative to other market participants. Such advantages could include superior analytical or judgment skills, superior information, or the ability or willingness to do what other investors, particularly institutions, are unable to do. For example, many large institutional investors cannot take positions in very small companies, leaving this field for individual investors. Furthermore, individuals are not required to own diversified portfolios and are typically not prohibited from short sales or margin trading as are some institutions.

Most investors still favor an active approach to common stock selection and management, despite the accumulating evidence from efficient market studies and the published performance results of institutional investors. The reason for this is obvious—the potential rewards are very large, and many investors feel confident that they can achieve such awards even if other investors cannot.

There are numerous active strategies involving common stocks. We consider the most prominent ones below. Because of its importance, we then consider the implications of market efficiency for these strategies.

SECURITY SELECTION

The most traditional and popular form of active stock strategies is the selection of individual stocks identified as offering superior return-risk characteristics. Such stocks typically are se-

[3] See Burton Malkiel, "The Case for Index Funds," *Mutual Funds Magazine,* February 1999, p. 72. This entire discussion involving Malkiel is based on this article, pp. 72–75.

lected using fundamental security analysis, but technical analysis is also used, and sometimes a combination of the two. Many investors have always believed, and continue to believe despite evidence to the contrary from the EMH, that they possess the requisite skill, patience, and ability to identify undervalued stocks.

We know from Chapter 1 that a key feature of the investments environment is the uncertainty that always surrounds investing decisions. Most stock pickers recognize the pervasiveness of this uncertainty and protect themselves accordingly by diversifying. Therefore, the standard assumption of rational, intelligent investors who select stocks to buy and sell is that such selections will be part of a diversified portfolio.

The Importance of Stock Selection How important is stock selection in the overall investment process? Most active investors, individuals or institutions, are, to various degrees, stock selectors. The majority of investment advice and investment advisory services is geared to the selection of stocks thought to be attractive candidates at the time. *The Value Line Investment Survey* (discussed in Chapter 15), the largest investment advisory service in terms of number of subscribers, is a good example of stock selection advice offered to the investing public.

To gain some appreciation of the importance of stock selection, consider the cross-sectional variation in common stock returns. Latane', Tuttle, and Jones were the first to point out the widely differing performances of stocks in a given year using the interquartile range.[4] Examining data through 1972, they found a remarkable constancy from year to year in the spread between the performance of stocks in the upper quartile and the performance of stocks in the lower quartile.[5]

A subsequent study by McEnally and Todd for the period 1946–1989 found that investors who successfully confined stock selection to the stocks in the highest quartile would have largely avoided losing years, and even the bad years showed only modest losses.[6] Conversely, for the bottom quarter, results were negative about 55 percent of the time, and about 25 percent of the time even the best stocks would have lost money despite generally favorable market conditions. The implication of these results is that "For those who do attempt to pick stocks, the rewards can be very high, but the risk and negative consequences of poor selection are substantial."[7] An additional finding of this study is that cross-sectional variation of returns has been increasing steadily over the decades, making stock selection even more important in recent years.

The importance of stock selection cannot be overemphasized. Although we outline an approach to security analysis below that logically places company analysis last, its importance is obvious. As Peter Lynch, one of the most celebrated portfolio managers of recent years as former head of Fidelity's Magellan Fund, states: "If it's a choice between investing in a good company in a great industry, or a great company in a lousy industry, I'll take the great company in the lousy industry any day."[8] Lynch goes on to discuss what we can learn from the top 100 winners over the past decade. The basic lesson is that small stocks make big moves—the trick is identifying them. But as Lynch notes, "What do the great successes of the past 20 years tell us? It's the company, stupid."

---

[4] See H. Latane', D. Tuttle, and C. Jones, *Security Analysis and Portfolio Management,* 2nd ed. (New York: Ronald Press, 1975), pp. 192–193.

[5] In an ordered set of numbers, the interquartile range is the difference between the value that cuts off the top quarter of these numbers and the value that cuts off the bottom quarter of these numbers. The interquartile range is an alternative measure of dispersion.

[6] See Richard McEnally and Rebecca Todd, "Cross-Sectional Variation in Common Stock Returns," *Financial Analysts Journal* (May/June 1992): 59–63.

[7] McEnally and Todd, p. 61.

[8] See Peter Lynch, "The Stock Market Hit Parade," *Worth,* July/August 1994, p. 32.

USING THE INTERNET Screening stocks for possible selection, based on a set of criteria, is where a computer can really aid investors in making decisions. By going to www.financialweb.com, and selecting "Rapid Research," investors can use either a Basic Screen, with about six criteria, or an Advanced Screening, allowing about 27 criteria. In either case screening can be done by exchange and by industry. Www.quicken.com also has a stock screening section (go to Investments, and then Stock Search). A large number of criteria can be specified, based on ranges for the values or minimum and maximum values. Www.aol.com also provides stock screening for its subscribers, allowing up to 12 variables. StockTools Super Stock Screener, www.stocktools.com, offers both fundamental and technical screening. Investors can specify a number of technical criteria, such as historic trading price ranges and 52-week highs and lows as well as fundamental criteria such as growth rates, yield, and so forth. At www.marketguide.com, investors can obtain price and earnings information and download StockQuest, which allows you to screen stocks using more than 50 variables.

The Role of the Security Analyst Stocks are, of course, selected by both individual investors and institutional investors. Rather than do their own security analysis, individual investors may choose to rely on the recommendations of the professionals. An important part of the institutional side of stock selection and recommendation is the role of the security analyst (also called equity analyst, or, simply, analyst) in the investment process. There are perhaps 5,000 analysts on Wall Street covering, to various degrees, some 9,000 actively traded stocks in the United States.

The security analyst typically works for an institution concerned with stocks and other financial assets, but the analysts' product is often available to the individual investor in the form of brokerage reports (primarily, full-service brokerage firms) and newsletters, reports from Standard & Poor's and other recommendation services, and so forth. Therefore, when considering stock selection investors must understand the role of the analyst.

A typical analyst report contains a description of the company's business, how the analyst expects the company to perform, earnings estimates, prices estimates or price targets for the year ahead, and recommendations as to buy, hold, or sell. Investors should be wary of any analyst report in which the analyst cannot satisfactorily explain what a company does. Analysts should do more than simply recommend companies expected to grow rapidly.

The central focus of the analysts' job is to attempt to forecast a specific company's return. Alternatively, it can involve the inputs to a valuation model such as those we considered in the previous chapter. Investors interested in stock selection use valuation models, and for inputs they can utilize their own estimates or, in some cases, use those provided by analysts.[9] The most important part of what the analyst produces in this regard is the estimate of a company's earnings.

What sources of information do analysts use in evaluating common stocks for possible selection or selling? The major sources of information are presentations from the top management of the companies being considered, annual reports, and Form 10-K reports that must be filed by the companies with the SEC. According to surveys of analysts, they consistently emphasize the long term over the short term. Variables of major importance in their analysis include expected changes in earnings per share, expected return on equity (ROE), and industry outlook. The important point to note here is that the security analysis process used by financial analysts—in terms of information sources and processes—is the same one that we will learn in Part V.

One of the most important responsibilities of an analyst is to forecast earnings per share for particular companies because of the widely perceived linkage between expected earnings

[9] In Chapter 15 we will consider company analysis in detail, and this discussion will be organized around the two valuation models we studied in the previous chapter—the dividend discount model and the P/E ratio model.

and stock returns. Earnings are critical in determining stock prices, and what matters is *expected* earnings (what is referred to on Wall Street as earnings estimates). Therefore, the primary emphasis in fundamental security analysis is on expected earnings, and analysts spend much of their time forecasting earnings. Regardless of the effort expended by analysts, investors should be cautious in accepting analysts' forecasts of EPS. Errors can be large, and occur often. See Box 11-1 for a good insight into how analysts operate in terms of herd behavior.

Box 11-1

WHAT ANALYSTS AND CATTLE HAVE IN COMMON

Risk taking is often associated with youth—one reason, for instance, that teenagers pay so much for auto insurance. But when it comes to Wall Street, it turns out that the youngest and least experienced securities analysts tend to be the most risk averse. That's according to a recent report by three economists who studied "sell side" analysis. They found that the longer an analyst spends in the business, the more his forecasts deviate from those of others covering the same company. More experienced analysts are also more likely to publish their forecasts first, and once they do, they're less likely to change them. In short, as analysts age, they become more willing to stick their necks out.

Stock analysts as a group appear to engage in herd behavior in part because they're constantly evaluated against their peers, says Harrison Hong, one of the report's authors. When forecasting earnings, young analysts figure it's better to fit in with the crowd—even if the crowd is wrong—than to risk being off on their own. That's because a few notable failures can crush reputations. Later, when analysts are more established, they can stray from the pack without risking as much. Herd behavior is prominent in almost all work settings, says Bengt Holmstrom of MIT, who pioneered the theory of reputation-based behavior. But stock analysts make particularly good subjects for study because they produce uniform, quantifiable outputs, like earnings forecasts.

What makes Hong's study interesting is that it could have turned out quite differently. Common sense suggests that there should be some herd impulse among analysts, just as there should be among any group of people competing. But it's not clear whether the effects should diminish or intensify with age. For instance, one might argue that older analysts should be more cautious than their more callow counterparts, since they have a lot more to lose. Similarly, younger analysts might intentionally stray further from the herd, since they can gain celebrity status by taking a risky position that turns out to be correct, Hong says.

Sure, it's obvious to Wall Street watchers that analysts tend to behave like cattle—when one analyst switches a recommendation on a stock, others often follow. However, that might happen simply because the analysts are all working from the same data. For instance, when housing starts decline, real estate analysts will trim their forecasts. That's not "herd behavior"—that's just being smart.

But by focusing on how analysts' behavior changes with age, the study factored out this type of clustering, concentrating on behavior that occurs when analysts stick to a consensus for the sake of blending in. Goldman Sachs' David Fleischer, one of the top-ranked natural-gas and pipeline analysts, says that Hong's "older is bolder" interpretation makes sense to him. In 1991 he was the only analyst on Wall Street to publish a buy recommendation on Columbia Gas—an apparently curious decision, given that the firm was in the middle of a Chapter 11 bankruptcy proceeding. Why did he do it? "It was because I understood the industry," says Fleischer, 50. "It wouldn't have ruined my career if I was wrong. . . . If a new kid was wrong on something like that, they'd say, 'How could you be so stupid, to recommend a company in bankruptcy?' " (Turned out Fleischer was right. The stock has since risen from $12 to $56.)

Having convincingly demonstrated the correlation between herding and age, Hong now plans to slice the data again to see exactly which analysts cleave most closely to the herd—those at mainstream investment banks or those at boutiques. Whatever the results, one lesson for individual investors is sure to survive: Use analysts' reports as sources of insight and raw data, but take the earnings forecasts with more than a grain of salt. Young analysts looking out for their careers will always tend to herd. Investors need to make sure they don't get trampled.

SOURCE: Matt Siegel, "What Analysts and Cattle Have in Common," *Fortune*, August 17, 1998, p. 230. Reprinted by permission.

Empirical studies indicate that current expectations of earnings, as represented by the average of the analysts' forecasts, are incorporated into current stock prices. Perhaps more importantly, revisions in the average forecast for year-ahead earnings may have predictive ability concerning future stock returns. We will consider the related issues of consensus earnings estimates, "guidance" of forthcoming earnings by company management, pre-announcements of earnings, whispers about earnings, and earnings surprises in Chapter 15.

In doing their job of estimating expected returns, analysts supposedly present their recommendations in the form of "Buy," "Hold," and "Sell." However, investors who receive brokerage reports typically will see recommendations for specific companies as either "buy" or "hold" or "speculative hold" or other words such as these. Analysts are under great pressure to avoid the word "sell" from the companies they follow. For example, according to one story, when Boston Chicken held a meeting for analysts, one was banned because he had issued a "sell" recommendation on the stock. One study reported that two-thirds of analysts surveyed felt that a negative recommendation on a company would severely impact their access to the company's management.

Analysts are also under pressure from their own firms which are seeking to be the underwriter on lucrative stock and bond underwritings. Analysts lose their objectivity by being at least partly rewarded on the basis of investment banking business. Another story holds that Nations Bank stopped all stock and bond trading for its trust accounts with Kidder Peabody because one of its analysts had issued a "sell" recommendation on Nations Bank. Supposedly, reprisals by companies against brokerage firms, in terms of cutting off investment banking business, is widespread.

Perhaps because of their rarity, sell recommendations have a pronounced effect. According to one study, sell recommendations result in an average two-day decline of almost 5 percent, and an additional 9 percent decline in the next six months. The six-month decline was confirmed by another study, but this one found a turnaround in such stocks whereby they subsequently beat the market.

USING THE INTERNET Consensus earnings estimates as well as brokerage recommendations can be found at www.zacks.com and at First Call, www.firstcall.com.

SECTOR ROTATION

An active strategy that is similar to stock selection is group or sector rotation. This strategy involves shifting sector weights in the portfolio in order to take advantage of those sectors that are expected to do relatively better, and avoid or deemphasize those sectors that are expected to do relatively worse. Investors employing this strategy are betting that particular sectors will repeat their price performance relative to the current phase of the business and credit cycle.

An investor could think of larger groups as the relevant sectors, shifting between cyclicals, growth stocks, and value stocks. It is quite standard in sector analysis to divide common stocks into four broad sectors: interest-sensitive stocks, consumer durable stocks, capital goods stocks, and defensive stocks. Each of these sectors is expected to perform differently during the various phases of the business and credit cycles. For example, interest-sensitive stocks would be expected to be adversely impacted during periods of high interest rates, and such periods tend to occur at the latter stages of the business cycle. As interest rates decline, the earnings of the companies in this sector—banks, finance companies, savings and loans, utilities, and residential construction firms—should improve.

Defensive stocks deserve some explanation. Included here are companies in such businesses as food production, soft drinks, beer, pharmaceuticals, and so forth that often are not hurt as badly during the down side of the business cycle as are other companies because people will still purchase bread, milk, soft drinks, and so forth. As the economy worsens and more problems are foreseen, investors may move into these stocks for investment protection. These stocks often do well during the late phases of a business cycle.

Investors may view industries as sectors and act accordingly. For example, if interest rates are expected to drop significantly, increased emphasis could be placed on the interest-sensitive industries such as housing, banking, and the savings and loans. The defense industry is a good example of an industry in recent years that has experienced wide swings in performance over multiyear periods. The defense buildup that occurred under the Reagan administration was followed by a deemphasis of defense following the dramatic end of the cold war and the dissolution of the Soviet Union in the early 1990s.

It is clear that effective strategies involving sector rotation depend heavily on an accurate assessment of current economic conditions. A knowledge and understanding of the phases of the business cycle are important, as is an understanding of political environments, international linkages among economies, and credit conditions both domestic and international.

Indirect Investing in Sectors Investors can pursue the sector investing approach using mutual funds. For example, Invesco, a large mutual fund company, has offered sector funds for more than 12 years. Its sector funds now include worldwide communications, energy, financial services, technology, worldwide capital goods, environmental services, gold, health sciences, leisure, and utilities. Each sector fund contains 40 to 70 stocks, providing strong diversification within that sector. Invesco's Technology Sector Fund recorded an annualized 10-year average total return of 25.19 percent over the period 1990–1999.

There are now roughly 500 sector funds, with assets in excess of $100 billion. Real estate, utilities, and health care are three prominent sectors for funds. Sector funds are particularly popular with momentum traders. Morningstar, a provider of mutual fund information, has increased its coverage of sector listings.

Sector funds have performed well. For recent five-year performance rankings of all mutual funds, eight of the top 10 were sector funds. However, the bottom 10 performers were also sector funds—all precious metal funds.

Sector investing in mutual funds offers the potential of large returns, but the risks are also large.

USING THE INTERNET Sector performance can be found at www.smartmoney.com, using their "sector tracker." Different time periods can be specified.

MARKET TIMING

Market timers attempt to earn excess returns by varying the percentage of portfolio assets in equity securities. One has only to observe a chart of stock prices over time to appreciate the profit potential of being in the stock market at the right times and being out of the stock market at the bad times.

When equities are expected to do well, timers shift from cash equivalents such as money market funds to common stocks. When equities are expected to do poorly, the opposite occurs. Alternatively, timers could increase the betas of their portfolios when the market is expected to rise and carry most stocks up, or decrease the betas of their portfolio when the market is expected to go down. One important factor affecting the success of a market timing strategy is the amount of brokerage commissions and taxes paid with such a strategy as opposed to those paid with a buy-and-hold strategy.

Mark Hulbert, publisher of a service that monitors the performance of investment advisory letters called the *Hulbert Financial Digest,* believes that the popularity of market timing follows a cycle of its own.[10] If the market is strongly up, market timing falls into disrepute, and buying and holding is the popular strategy. Following a secular market decline, however, market timing comes into vogue, and the buy and hold strategy is not popular.

Like many issues in the investing arena, the subject of market timing is controversial. Can some investors regularly time the market effectively enough to provide excess returns on a risk-adjusted basis? The only way to attempt to answer this question is to consider the available evidence on the subject, keeping in mind that market timing is a broad topic and that it is difficult to summarize all viewpoints.

Much of the empirical evidence on market timing comes from studies of mutual funds. A basic issue is whether fund managers increase the beta of their portfolios when they anticipate a rising market and reduce the beta when they anticipate a declining market. Several studies found no evidence that funds were able to time market changes and change their risk levels in response. Veit and Cheney, for example, found in a study of 74 mutual funds that they were not able to successfully change their risk levels based on their timing strategies.[11]

Chang and Lewellen examined the performance of mutual funds and found little evidence of any market timing ability. Furthermore, the average estimated down-market beta turned out to be slightly higher than the average estimated up-market beta.[12] Overall, this study supported the conclusion that mutual funds do not outperform a passive investment strategy. This conclusion was also supported by Henriksson in a study of 116 mutual funds using monthly data.[13] He found that mutual fund managers are not able to successfully employ strategies involving market timing. Moreover, these managers were not successful with market timing involving only large changes in the market.

Considerable research now suggests that the biggest risk of market timing is that investors will not be in the market at critical times, thereby significantly reducing their overall returns. Investors who miss only a few key months may suffer significantly. For example, over a recent 40-year period, investors who missed the 34 best months for stocks would have seen an initial $1,000 investment grow to only $4,492 instead of $86,650. Even Treasury bills would have been a better alternative in this situation.[14]

If you are still considering market timing as a strategy suitable for the average individual investor, think again, particularly after considering the following information. For the period 1986–1995, inclusive, returns on the S&P 500 Composite Index were:

Fully invested—annualized rate of return	= 14.8 percent
Take out the 10 best days	= 10.2 percent
Take out the 20 best days	= 7.3 percent
Take out the 30 best days	= 4.8 percent
Take out the 40 best days	= 2.5 percent

EFFICIENT MARKETS AND ACTIVE STRATEGIES

One of the most significant developments in recent years is the proposition that securities markets are efficient. This idea has generated considerable controversy concerning the analysis

[10] See Mark Hulbert, "New tool for contrarians," *Forbes,* November 18, 1996, p. 298.

[11] See E. Theodore Veit and John M. Cheney, "Are Mutual Funds Market Timers?" *The Journal of Portfolio Management,* 8, no. 2 (Winter 1982): 35–42.

[12] Eric Chang and Wilbur Lewellen, "Market Timing and Mutual Fund Investment Performance," *Journal of Business,* 57, no. 1, part 1 (January 1984): 57–72.

[13] Roy D. Henriksson, "Market Timing and Mutual Fund Performance: An Empirical Investigation," *Journal of Business,* 57, no. 1, part 1 (January 1984): 73–96.

[14] See Jonathan D. Pond, "The Harsh Reality of Market Timing," *Worth,* May 1994, pp. 117–118.

and valuation of securities because of its significant implications for investors. Regardless of how much (or how little) an investor learns about investments, and regardless of whether an investor ends up being convinced by the efficient markets literature, it is prudent to learn something about this idea early in one's study of investments.

Much evidence exists to support the basic concepts of the EMH, and it cannot be ignored simply because one is uncomfortable with the idea or because it sounds too improbable. It is appropriate to consider this concept with any discussion of active strategies designed to produce excess returns—that is, returns in excess of those commensurate with the risk being taken. After all, if the evidence suggests that active strategies are unlikely to be successful over time after all costs have been assessed, the case for a passive strategy becomes much more important.

As we will see in Chapter 12, the efficient market hypothesis is concerned with the assessment of information by investors. Security prices are determined by expectations about the future. Investors use the information available to them in forming their expectations. If security prices fully reflect all the relevant information that is available and usable, a securities market is said to be efficient.

If the stock market is efficient, prices reflect their fair economic value as estimated by investors. Even if this is not strictly true, prices may reflect their approximate fair value after transaction costs are taken into account, a condition known as economic efficiency. In such a market, where prices of stocks depart only slightly from their fair economic value, investors should not employ trading strategies designed to "beat the market" by identifying undervalued stocks. Nor should they attempt to time the market in the belief that an advantage can be gained. Sector rotation also will be unsuccessful in a highly efficient market.

The implications of an efficient market are extremely important for investors. They include one's beliefs about how to value securities in terms of the two approaches to selecting common stocks discussed below—the fundamental and the technical approach. This, in turn, encompasses questions about the time and effort to be devoted to these two approaches. Other implications include the management of a portfolio of securities. Again, in terms of the above discussion, should management be active or passive? Efficient market proponents often argue that less time should be devoted to the analysis of securities for possible inclusion in a portfolio and more to such considerations as reducing taxes and transaction costs and maintaining the chosen risk level of a portfolio over time.

Suffice it to say that an intelligent investor must be aware of this issue and form some judgment about its implications if he or she is to formulate a reasonable investment strategy. A person's beliefs about market efficiency will have a significant impact on the type of stock strategy implemented. The efficiency of the market, and how investors should act in selecting portfolios of stocks, remains controversial.

Investors are constantly being bombarded with reports of techniques and procedures that appear to offer above-average returns, thereby contradicting the idea that the market is so efficient that they should not attempt to outperform it. Intelligent investors examine such claims and strategies carefully before using them.

APPROACHES FOR ANALYZING AND SELECTING STOCKS

The two traditional and well-known approaches to analyzing and/or selecting common stocks are fundamental analysis and technical analysis. However, the significant amount of research in recent years on the concept of efficient markets has widespread implications for the analysis and valuation of common stock. Therefore, our discussion of common stocks is built around these approaches and any implications from the efficient markets literature.

Traditionally, fundamental analysis has occupied the majority of resources devoted to the analysis of common stocks. All investors should understand the logic of, and rationale for, fundamental analysis. It deserves, and receives, careful consideration in Part V, which is devoted to security analysis. The other approach to security analysis, technical analysis, is also analyzed in Part V. The efficient market concept has implications for both approaches as well as for portfolio management.

The two basic approaches, technical and fundamental analysis, are described briefly here, followed by a consideration of efficient market concepts and implications. The fundamental approach is then developed in some detail in the remainder of this chapter, thereby setting the stage for the next three chapters, which analyze the fundamental approach in a specific, recommended order.

TECHNICAL ANALYSIS

One of the two traditional strategies long available to investors is technical analysis, which is examined in detail in Chapter 16. In fact, technical analysis is the oldest strategy and can be traced back to at least the late nineteenth century.

Technical Analysis The search for identifiable and recurring stock price patterns

The term **technical analysis** refers to the methodology of forecasting fluctuations in securities prices. This methodology can be applied either to individual securities or to the market as a whole (i.e., forecasting a market index such as the Dow Jones Industrial Average).

The rationale behind technical analysis is that the value of a stock is primarily a function of supply and demand conditions. These conditions, in turn, are determined by a range of factors, from scientific to opinions and guesses. The market uses all of these factors in determining the changes in prices. These prices will move in trends that may persist, with changes in trends resulting from changes in supply and demand conditions. Technicians seek to detect, and act upon, changes in the direction of stock prices.

In its purest sense, technical analysis is not concerned with the underlying economic variables that affect a company or the market; therefore, the causes of demand and supply shifts are not important. The basic question to be asked can be stated as follows: Does excess demand or supply exist for a stock, and can such a condition be detected by studying either the patterns of past price fluctuations or the movements of certain technical indicators or rules? Technicians study the market using graphical charting of price changes, volume of trading over time, and a number of technical indicators.

Momentum Investing Investing on the basis of recent movements in the price of a stock

Momentum Strategies One of the most popular investing strategies relies heavily on price trends. **Momentum investing** involves buying companies whose earnings or stock prices are rising, with heavy emphasis on price momentum. The basic premise of momentum investing is that if a stock has outperformed the market over some recent period, it is likely to continue to do so. Momentum investing is a short-run approach. For example, stocks that are strong for the prior six months tend to outperform the market only over the next 6 to 12 months.

In today's market, managers have varied the technique to include buying (selling) companies with positive (negative) earnings surprises and earnings estimate revisions as part of a momentum strategy (and they may not use the term "momentum)."

EXAMPLE 11-3 Rite-Aid Corp. was a momentum stock, rising from \$15 in 1996 to \$50 in early 1999. At \$37, in March 1999, Rite-Aid sold for a P/E of 48 (using trailing earnings). When Rite-Aid warned that its fourth quarter fiscal earnings would be significantly lower, it declined to \$22.5 in one day. The momentum ride was over, and investors bailed out.

According to a survey done by Merrill Lynch on fund managers' styles that covers a decade, momentum (in various forms) was the most popular style, with more than half the managers using estimate revision and earnings surprises forms, and 40 percent using earnings momentum. Only 25 percent used price-to-book value.[15]

The Value Line Investment Survey, the largest investment advisory service available to investors (and discussed in Chapter 15), ranks stocks on the basis of both price and earnings momentum, and *Value Line* has the best 15-year ranking in the *Hulbert Financial Digest*. According to Hulbert, the best performing investment advisory letters over the last 10 and 5 years respectively rely heavily on price momentum.[16]

According to Hulbert, such an approach also seems to work with mutual funds. Investors should buy those funds showing the strongest relative strength or momentum. Hulbert notes that investment advisory letters that recommend those mutual funds with the greatest momentum have performed better than the market as a whole.

FUNDAMENTAL ANALYSIS

Fundamental Analysis The study of a stock's value using basic data such as its earnings, sales, risk, and so forth

Fundamental analysis is based on the premise that any security (and the market as a whole) has an intrinsic value, or the true value as estimated by an investor. This value is a function of the firm's underlying variables, which combine to produce an expected return and an accompanying risk. By assessing these fundamental determinants of the value of a security, an estimate of its intrinsic value can be determined. This estimated intrinsic value can then be compared to the current market price of the security. Similar to the decision rules used for bonds in Chapter 11, decision rules are employed for common stocks when fundamental analysis is used to calculate intrinsic value.

In equilibrium, the current market price of a security reflects the average of the intrinsic value estimates made by investors. An investor whose intrinsic value estimate differs from the market price is, in effect, differing with the market consensus as to the estimate of either expected return or risk, or both. Investors who can perform good fundamental analysis and spot discrepancies should be able to profit by acting before the market consensus reflects the correct information.

BEHAVIORAL FINANCE IMPLICATIONS

Given the widespread discussion of market efficiency, investors sometimes overlook the issue of psychology in financial markets—that is, the role that emotions play. Particularly in the short run, investors' emotions affect stock prices, and markets, and those making investment decisions need to be aware of this.

Behavorial Finance The study of investment behavior, based on the belief that investors may act irrationally

Behavioral finance is a hot topic in investing today. While traditional economics is built on the proposition that investors act rationally on the basis of utility theory, behavioral finance recognizes that investors can, and do, behave irrationally. Markets overreact, both up and down. Investors are motivated by numerous "irrational" forces, such as overconfidence, regrets about decisions, aversion to losses, and so forth. Unfortunately, despite several promising research findings, behavioral finance currently does not have a unifying theory that ties everything together.

David Dreman, a money manager and columnist for *Forbes*, has been a leading proponent of behavioral finance. He particularly espouses the "investor overreaction hypothesis,"

[15] Information about Rite-Aid and the survey is based on Greg Ip, "Market Mass Times Velocity = Momentum," *The Wall Street Journal*, March 15, 1999, p. C1.

[16] See Mark Hulbert, "Mutual momentum," *Forbes*, June 3, 1996, p. 178. This discussion of momentum investing is indebted to that article.

which states that investors overreact to events in a predictable manner, overvaluing the best alternatives and undervaluing the worst. Premiums and discounts are the result, and eventually these situations reverse as assets regress toward the mean, or average valuation. This behavior has led Dreman to his "contrarian" philosophy, which involves taking positions that are currently out of favor. For example, in 1998 growth investing was much more profitable than value investing (both concepts are explained below), but Dreman continued to recommend stocks that looked promising on a value basis on the assumption that value stocks would once again excel.[17]

A FRAMEWORK FOR FUNDAMENTAL ANALYSIS

Under either of these fundamental approaches an investor will obviously have to work with individual company data. Does this mean that the investor should plunge into a study of company data first and then consider other factors such as the industry within which a particular company operates or the state of the economy, or should the reverse procedure be followed? In fact, each of these approaches are used by investors and security analysts when doing fundamental analysis. These approaches are referred to as the "top-down" approach and the "bottom-up" approach.

BOTTOM-UP APPROACH TO FUNDAMENTAL ANALYSIS

Bottom-Up Approach Approach to fundamental analysis that focuses directly on a company's fundamentals

With the **"bottom-up" approach,** investors focus directly on a company's basics, or fundamentals. Analysis of such information as the company's products, its competitive position, and its financial status leads to an estimate of the company's earnings potential, and, ultimately, its value in the market.

Considerable time and effort is required to produce the type of detailed financial analysis needed to understand even relatively small companies. The emphasis in this approach is on finding companies with good long-term growth prospects, and making accurate earnings estimates. To organize this effort, bottom-up fundamental research is often broken into two categories, growth investing and value investing.

Value versus Growth Growth stocks carry investor expectations of above-average future growth in earnings and above-average valuations as a result of high price/earnings ratios. Investors expect these stocks to perform well in the future, and they are willing to pay high multiples for this expected growth. Recent examples include Microsoft, Cisco Systems, and Intel.

Value stocks, on the other hand, feature cheap assets and strong balance sheets. Value investing can be traced back to the value-investing principles laid out by the well-known Benjamin Graham, who wrote a famous book on security analysis that has been the foundation for many subsequent security analysts.

Growth stocks and value stocks tend to be in vogue over different periods, and the advocates of each camp prosper and suffer accordingly. For example, value investing dominated from 1981 through 1988, but lagged for the next three years through 1991 as growth stock investing returned to favor. Much of 1992, however, saw rough going for growth stocks. On the other hand, growth stock investing dominated value investing in 1998. In fact, 1998 was the worst year for value investing in many years.

[17] Dreman has published a new book called *Contrarian Investment Strategies: The Next Generation,* by Simon and Schuster. He also is starting a new journal, *The Journal of Psychology and Financial Markets.*

In many cases bottom-up investing does not attempt to make a clear distinction between growth and value. Many companies feature strong earnings prospects and a strong financial base or asset value, and therefore have characteristics associated with both categories.

TOP-DOWN APPROACH TO FUNDAMENTAL ANALYSIS

Top-Down Approach Approach to fundamental analysis that proceeds from market/economy to industry to company

The **top-down approach** is the opposite to the bottom-up approach. Investors begin with the economy and the overall market, considering such important factors as interest rates and inflation. They next consider likely industry prospects, or sectors of the economy that are likely to do particularly well (or particularly poorly). Finally, having decided that macro factors are favorable to investing, and having determined which parts of the overall economy are likely to perform well, individual companies are analyzed.

There is no "right" answer to which of these two approaches to follow. However, fundamental analysis can be overwhelming in its detail, and a structure is needed. This text takes the position that the better way to proceed in fundamental analysis is the top-down approach: First, analyze the overall economy and securities markets to determine if now is a good time to commit additional funds to equities; second, analyze industries and sectors to determine which have the best prospects for the future; and finally, analyze individual companies. Using this structure, the valuation models presented in Chapter 10 can be applied successively at each of the three levels.

Thus, the preferred order for fundamental security analysis used here is (1) the economy and market, (2) the industry, and (3) the company. This approach is used in Part V, which explains fundamental security analysis in detail. Here we consider only the justification for this approach.

Economy/Market Analysis It is very important to assess the state of the economy and the outlook for primary variables such as corporate profits and interest rates. Investors are heavily influenced by these variables in making their everyday investment decisions. If a recession is likely, or under way, stock prices will be heavily affected at certain times during the contraction. Conversely, if a strong economic expansion is under way, stock prices will be heavily affected, again at particular times during the expansion. Thus, the status of economic activity has a major impact on overall stock prices. It is, therefore, very important for investors to assess the state of the economy and its implications for the stock market.

In turn, the stock market impacts each individual investor. Investors cannot very well go against market trends. If the market goes up (or down) strongly, most stocks are carried along. Company analysis is likely to be of limited benefit in a year such as 1974, when the stock market was down 25 percent. Conversely, almost all investors did well in 1995 regardless of their specific company analysis, because the market was up about 37 percent as measured by the S&P 500.

Another indication of the importance of the economy/market on common stocks is the impact on the earnings for a particular company. Available evidence suggests that from one-fourth to one-half of the variability in a company's annual earnings is attributable to the overall economy (plus some industry effect).

The economy also significantly affects what happens to various industries. One has only to think of the effects of import quotas, record high interest rates, and so forth, to see why this is so. Therefore, economy analysis must precede industry analysis.

Industry Analysis After completing an analysis of the economy and the overall market, an investor can decide if it is a favorable time to invest in common stocks. If it is, the next step should be industry analysis. King identified an industry factor as the second component (after overall market movements) affecting the variability in stock returns.

Individual companies and industries tend to respond to general market movements, but the degree of response can vary significantly. Industries undergo significant movements over both relatively short and relatively long periods. Industries will be affected to various degrees by recessions and expansions. For example, the heavy goods industries will be severely affected in a recession. (Examples include the auto and steel industries in the 1981–1982 recession.) Consumer goods will probably be much less affected during such a contractionary period. During a severe inflationary period such as the late 1970s and very early 1980s, regulated industries such as utilities were severely hurt by their inability to pass along all price increases. Finally, new "hot" industries emerge from time to time and enjoy spectacular (if short-lived) growth. Examples include synthetic fuels and genetic engineering.

Company Analysis Although the first two steps are important and should be done in the indicated order, great attention and emphasis should be placed on company analysis. Security analysts are typically organized along industry lines, but the reports that they issue usually deal with one (or more) specific companies.

The bottom line for companies, as far as most investors are concerned, is earnings per share. There is a very close relationship between earnings and stock prices, and for this reason

FIGURE 11-3

A framework for fundamental security analysis.

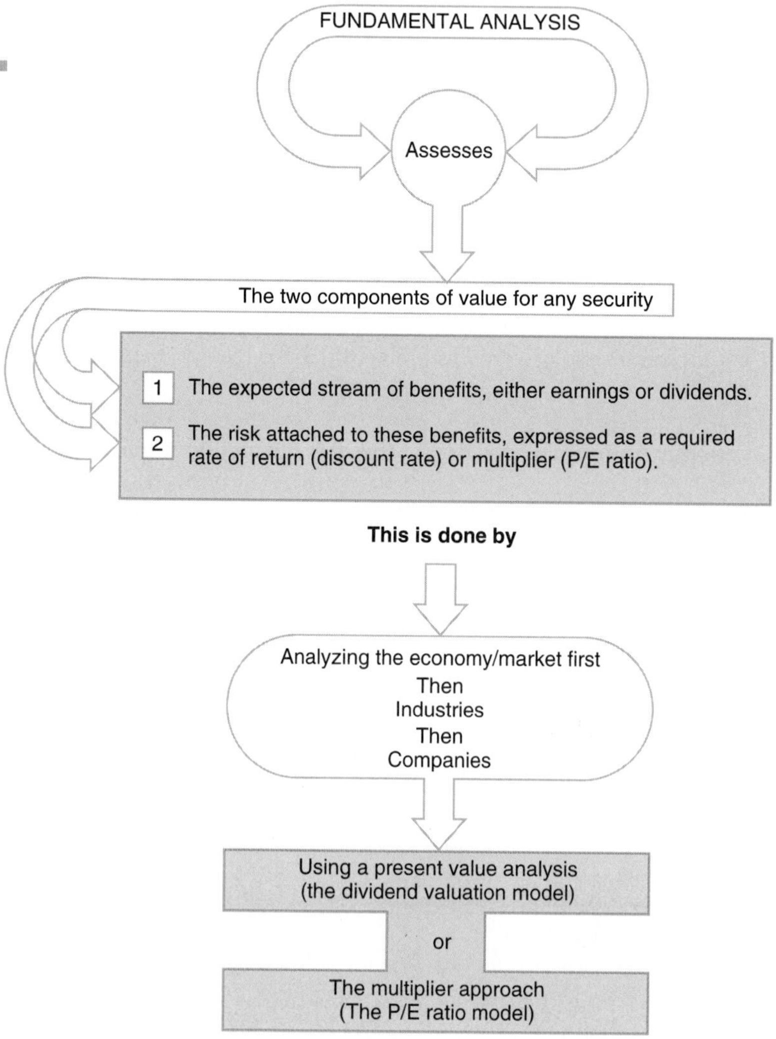

most attention is paid to earnings. Dividends, after all, are paid out of earnings. The dividends paid by companies are closely tied to earnings, but not necessarily the current quarterly (or even annual) earnings.

A number of factors are important in analyzing a company. However, because investors tend to focus on earnings and dividends, we need to understand the relationship between these two variables, and between them and other variables. We also need to consider the possibilities of forecasting earnings and dividends.

Because dividends are paid out of earnings, we will concentrate on earnings in our discussion of company analysis in Chapter 15. Earnings are the real key to the fundamental analysis of a common stock. A good understanding of earnings is vital if an investor is to understand, and perform, fundamental analysis.

THE FRAMEWORK FOR FUNDAMENTAL ANALYSIS IN PERSPECTIVE

It is useful to summarize the framework for fundamental analysis we are using because the following three chapters are based on this framework.

Figure 11-3 depicts the fundamental valuation process. We should examine the economy and market first, then industries, and finally individual companies. Fundamental valuation is usually done within the context of a present value model, primarily the dividend discount model, or a multiplier (P/E ratio) model. In either case, the two components of the value of any security being examined are (1) the expected stream of benefits, either earnings or dividends, and (2) the required rate of return (discount rate)—alternatively, the multiplier or P/E ratio. Investors should concentrate on these two factors as they systematically proceed through the three levels of analysis: economy/market, industry, and company.

SUMMARY

- Market risk is the single most important risk affecting the price movements of common stocks.
- For well-diversified portfolios, market effects account for 90 percent and more of the variability in the portfolio's return.
- The required rate of return for a common stock, or any security, is defined as the minimum expected rate of return needed to induce an investor to purchase the stock.
- The required rate of return for any investment opportunity can be expressed as the sum of the risk-free rate of return and a risk premium.
- The trade-off between the required rate of return and risk is linear and upward sloping, which means that the required rate of return increases as the risk, measured by beta, increases.
- If the market is totally efficient, no active strategy should be able to beat the market on a risk-adjusted basis, and, therefore, a passive strategy may be superior.
- Passive strategies include buy-and-hold and the use of index funds.
- Pursuit of an active strategy assumes that investors possess some advantage relative to other market participants.
- Active strategies include stock selection, sector rotation, and market timing.
- The efficient market hypothesis, which states that current stock prices reflect information quickly and without bias, has implications for all stock investors.
- There are two traditional and well-known approaches to analyzing and/or selecting common stocks: fundamental analysis and technical analysis.

- The rationale behind technical analysis is that stock prices will move in trends that may persist and that these changes can be detected by analyzing the action of the market price itself.
- Fundamental analysis is based on the premise that any security (and the market as a whole) has an intrinsic value that is a function of the firm's underlying variables. This estimated intrinsic value can then be compared to the current market price of the security.
- Fundamental security analysis can be done following a bottom-up approach or a top-down approach.
- The approach used in Part V, the top-down approach, considers, in order: (1) the economy/market, (2) the industry, and (3) the company.

KEY WORDS

Behavioral finance
Bottom-up approach
Fundamental analysis
Momentum investing
Required rate of return
Risk premium
Technical analysis
Top-down approach

QUESTIONS

11-1. What impact does the market have on well-diversified portfolios? What does this suggest about the performance of mutual funds?

11-2. How does an investor in common stocks reconcile the large variability in stock returns, and the big drops that have occurred, with taking a prudent position in owning a portfolio of financial assets?

11-3. Given the drastic—some would say unprecedented—drop in the prices of Japanese stocks, how can U.S. investors justify owning foreign stocks?

11-4. What is meant by the required rate of return? Explain your answer in the context of an investor considering the purchase of IBM shares.

11-5. What are the two components of the required rate of return?

11-6. Is there one required rate of return? If not, how many are there?

11-7. What is the shape of the trade-off between the required rate of return for a stock and its risk? Must this shape always prevail?

11-8. What is the required rate of return on the overall market?

11-9. Outline the rationale for passive strategies.

11-10. Describe three active strategies involving common stocks.

11-11. What are the major sources of information used by security analysts in evaluating common stocks?

11-12. How does the cross-sectional variation in common stock returns relate to the issue of stock selection?

11-13. What is meant by sector rotation? What is the key input in implementing effective strategies in sector rotation?

11-14. What does the evidence cited on market timing suggest about the likelihood of success in this area?

11-15. What is the basic idea behind the efficient market hypothesis?

11-16. What are the implications of the efficient market hypothesis to both stock selectors and market timers?

11-17. Identify and differentiate the two traditional approaches to analyzing and selecting common stocks.

11-18. What is the recommended framework for fundamental analysis? Is this a "top-down" or "bottom-up" approach?

11-19. How does this recommended framework relate to the discussion about the impact of the market on investors?

11-20. What is the relationship between fundamental analysis and intrinsic value?

SELECTED REFERENCES

Burton Malkiel's new book on index investing is a good source of information about an important strategy available to all investors.

Richard Evans and Burton Malkiel, *Earn More, Sleep Better: The Index Fund Solution,* 1999, Simon & Schuster.

For those investors interested in behavioral finance from a practical level, and contrarian stragegies:

David Dreman, *Contrarian Investment Strategies: The Next Generation,* 1998, Simon and Schuster.

www.wiley.com/college/jones7

This chapter considers different approaches to building an equity portfolio. The web exercises will help you evaluate the pros and cons of these different approaches, using actual stock prices off the Internet.

chapter 12

MARKET EFFICIENCY

Chapter 12 considers the question of how quickly and accurately information about securities is disseminated in financial markets. The efficient market hypothesis is considered in detail, including various tests of market efficiency. The implications of market efficiency to investors are analyzed. Chapter 12 concludes with a careful consideration of the well-known anomalies that constitute exceptions to market efficiency.

After reading this chapter you will be able to:

- **Analyze the efficient market hypothesis (EMH) and recognize its impact on all aspects of investing.**
- **Discuss the EMH in each of its three forms: weak, semistrong, and strong.**
- **Understand how the EMH is tested, and what the evidence has shown.**
- **Recognize the anomalies (exceptions to market efficiency) that have been put forward, and be in a position to know when and how you might use this evidence in your own investment strategies.**

Should you as an investor care if the market is efficient? In an informationally efficient market, many traditional investing activities are suspect at best and useless at worst. Why? Because in a truly efficient market it should be impossible to discriminate between a profitable investment and an unprofitable one given currently available information. Therefore, you need to carefully consider your investing activities, particularly with regard to how active or passive you are as an investor. Furthermore, if you are interested in a job in the securities business you need to consider what a truly efficient market would mean. Your expected probability of "beating" the market as a portfolio manager is small, while the value of the product of a typical security analyst may be close to zero.

The idea of an efficient market has generated tremendous controversy, which continues today, and a number of participants refuse to accept it. This is not surprising in view of the enormous implications that an efficient market has for everyone concerned with securities. Some market participants' jobs and reputations are at stake, and they are not going to accept this concept readily.

Because of its significant impact and implications, the idea that markets are efficient deserves careful thought and study. Beginning investors should approach it with an open mind. The fact that some well-known market observers and participants reject or disparage this idea does not reduce its validity. Furthermore, the argument that the stock market is efficient is not going to disappear, because too much evidence exists to support this argument regardless of the counterarguments and exceptions to market efficiency that apparently continue to remain unexplained. The intelligent approach for investors, therefore, is to learn about it and from it.

First, we consider what an efficient market is. Although the concept of market efficiency applies to all financial markets, we concentrate on the equities market. Next, we will sample the evidence that has accumulated in support of the concept of market efficiency, as well as some evidence of possible market anomalies (i.e., inefficiencies). We also consider the implications of efficient markets for investors because, after all, that is the bottom line.

THE CONCEPT OF AN EFFICIENT MARKET

WHAT IS AN EFFICIENT MARKET?

Investors determine stock prices on the basis of the expected cash flows to be received from a stock and the risk involved. Rational investors should use all the information they have available or can reasonably obtain. This information set consists of both known information and beliefs about the future (i.e., information that can reasonably be inferred). Regardless of its form, *information is the key to the determination of stock prices and therefore is the central issue of the efficient markets concept.*

Efficient Market A market in which prices of securities quickly and fully reflect all available information

An **efficient market (EM)** is defined as one in which the prices of all securities quickly and fully reflect all available information about the assets. This concept postulates that investors will assimilate all relevant information into prices in making their buy and sell decisions. Therefore, the current price of a stock reflects:

1. All known information, including:
   - past information (e.g., last year's or last quarter's earnings)
   - current information as well as events that have been announced but are still forthcoming (such as a stock split).

FIGURE 12-1

The adjustment of stock prices to information: (*a*) if the market is efficient; (*b*) one possibility if the market is inefficient.

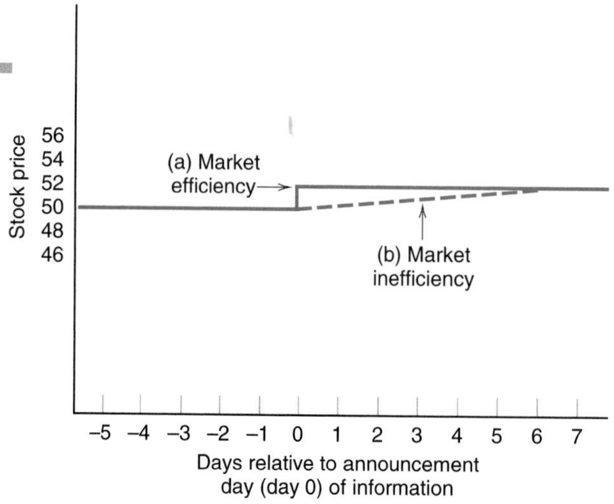

2. Information that can reasonably be inferred; for example, if many investors believe that interest rates will decline soon, prices will reflect this belief before the actual decline occurs.

To summarize, a market is efficient relative to any information set if investors are unable to earn abnormal profits by using that information set in their investing decisions.

The early literature on market efficiency made the assumption that market prices incorporated new information instantaneously. The modern version of this concept does not require that the adjustment be literally instantaneous, only that it occur very quickly as information becomes known. Given the extremely rapid dissemination of information in the United States through electronic communications equipment, which virtually all brokerage houses and institutional investors have, information is spread very quickly, almost instantaneously, to market participants with access to these sources. For individual investors without this access, important information can be received daily on radio and television (including specialized cable TV programs) or, at the latest, the following day in such sources as *The Wall Street Journal*.

The widespread use of the Internet in today's investing world means that investors have quick and cheap access to information on a continual basis. Numerous websites offer updated information during the day about the economy, the financial markets, and individual companies.

The concept that markets are efficient does not claim, or require, a perfect adjustment in price following the new information. Rather, the correct statement involved with this concept is that the adjustment in prices resulting from information is "unbiased."[1] The new price does not have to be the new equilibrium price, but only an unbiased estimate of the final equilibrium price that will be established after investors have fully assessed the input of the information.

Figure 12-1 illustrates the concept of market efficiency for one company for which a significant event occurs that has an effect on its expected profitability. The stock is trading at \$50 on the announcement date of the significant event—Date 0 in Figure 12-1 is the an-

[1] This means that the expected value of the adjustment error is zero—sometimes too large and at other times too small, but on average balancing out and correct.

nouncement date for the event. If the market is fully efficient, the price of a stock always reflects all available information. Investors will very quickly adjust a stock's price to its intrinsic (fair) value. Assume that the new fair value for the stock is $52. In an efficient market, an immediate increase in the price of the stock to $52 will occur, as represented by the solid line in Figure 12-1. Since, in our example, no additional new information occurs, the price of the stock will continue at $52.

If the market adjustment process is inefficient, a lag in the adjustment of the stock prices to the new information will occur and is represented by the dotted line. The price eventually adjusts to the new fair value of $52 as brokerage houses disseminate the new information and investors revise their estimates of the stock's fair value. Note that the time it would take for the price to adjust is not known ahead of time—the dotted line is only illustrative.

WHY THE MARKET CAN BE EXPECTED TO BE EFFICIENT

If the type of market adjustment described above seems too much to expect, consider the situation from the following standpoint. It can be shown that an efficient market can exist if the following events occur:

1. A large number of rational, profit-maximizing investors exist who actively participate in the market by analyzing, valuing, and trading stocks. These investors are price takers; that is, one participant alone cannot affect the price of a security.
2. Information is costless and widely available to market participants at approximately the same time.
3. Information is generated in a random fashion such that announcements are basically independent of one another.
4. Investors react quickly and fully to the new information, causing stock prices to adjust accordingly.

These conditions may seem strict, and in some sense they are. Nevertheless, consider how closely they parallel the actual investments environment. There is no question that a large number of investors are constantly "playing the game." Both individuals and institutions follow the market closely on a daily basis, standing ready to buy or sell when they think it is appropriate. The total amount of money at their disposal at any one time is more than enough to adjust prices at the margin.

Although the production of information is not costless, for institutions in the investments business, generating various types of information is a necessary cost of business, and many participants receive it "free" (obviously, investors pay for such items indirectly in their brokerage costs and other fees). It is widely available to many participants at approximately the same time as information is reported on radio, television, and specialized communications devices now available to any investor willing to pay for such services.

Information is largely generated in a random fashion in the sense that most investors cannot predict when companies will announce significant new developments, when wars will break out, when strikes will occur, when currencies will be devalued, when important leaders will suddenly suffer a heart attack, and so forth. Although there is some dependence in information events over time, by and large announcements are independent and occur more or less randomly.

If these conditions are generally met in practice, the result is a market in which investors adjust security prices very quickly to reflect random information coming into the market. Prices reflect fully all available information. Furthermore, price changes are independent of one another and move in a random fashion. Today's price change is independent of the one

FIGURE 12-2

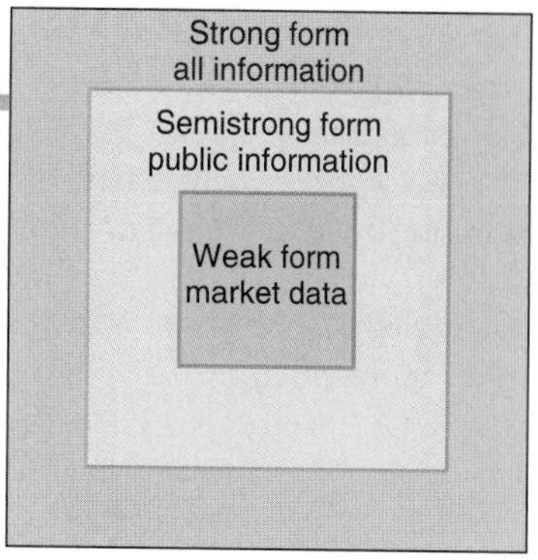

Cumulative levels of market efficiency and the information associated with each.

yesterday because it is based on investors' reactions to new, independent information coming into the market today.

FORMS OF MARKET EFFICIENCY

If, as discussed, the conditions necessary to produce market efficiency exist, exactly how efficient is the market and what does this imply for investors? We have defined an efficient market as one in which all information is reflected in stock prices quickly and fully. Thus, the key to assessing market efficiency is information. In a perfectly efficient market, security prices always reflect immediately all available information, and investors are not able to use available information to earn abnormal returns because it already is impounded in prices. In such a market, every security's price is equal to its intrinsic (investment) value, which reflects all information about that security's prospects.

If some types of information are not fully reflected in prices or lags exist in the impoundment of information into prices, the market is less than perfectly efficient. In fact, the market is not perfectly efficient, and it is certainly not perfectly inefficient, so it is a question of degree. Therefore, we can think of market efficiency with respect to specific sets of information and ask if investors, on average, can earn abnormal returns using a set of information to buy and sell securities—in other words, exactly how efficient is the market?

Efficient Market Hypothesis The idea that securities markets are efficient, with the prices of securities reflecting their economic value

Standard practice since 1970 is to discuss the EM concept in the form of the **efficient market hypothesis (EMH),** which is simply the formal statement of market efficiency previously discussed.[2] The EMH is concerned with the extent to which security prices quickly and fully reflect the different types of available information, which can be divided into the three cumulative types illustrated in Figure 12-2.

Market Data Primarily stock price and volume information

Weak Form That part of the efficient market hypothesis stating that prices reflect all price and volume data

1. Weak Form: One of the most traditional types of information used in assessing security values is **market data,** which refers to all past price (and volume) information. If security prices are determined in a market that is **weak-form** efficient, historical price and volume data should already be reflected in current prices and should be of no value in predicting future price changes. Since price data are the basis of technical analysis, technical analysis that relies on the past history of price information is of little or no value.

Tests of the usefulness of price data are called weak-form tests of the EMH. If the weak form of the EMH is true, past price changes should be unrelated to future price changes. In

[2] See E. Fama, "Efficient Capital Markets: A Review of Theory and Empirical Work," *The Journal of Finance,* 25, no. 2 (May 1970): 383–417. In a sequel some 20 years later, entitled "Efficient Capital Markets: II," Fama refers to a "weaker and economically more sensible version of the efficiency hypothesis" which deals with prices reflecting information to the extent that it is not financially worthwhile to act on any information. See Eugene F. Fama, "Efficient Capital Markets: II," *The Journal of Finance,* 46 (December 1991): 1575–1617.

other words, a market can be said to be weakly efficient if the current price reflects all past market data. The correct implication of a weak-form efficient market is that the past history of price information is of no value in assessing future changes in price.[3]

Semistrong Form That part of the efficient market hypothesis stating that prices reflect all publicly available information

2. Semistrong Form: A more comprehensive level of market efficiency involves not only known and publicly available market data, but all publicly known and available data, such as earnings, dividends, stock split announcements, new product developments, financing difficulties, and accounting changes. A market that quickly incorporates all such information into prices is said to show **semistrong-form** efficiency. Thus, a market can be said to be "efficient in the semistrong sense" if current prices reflect all available information. Note that a semistrong efficient market encompasses the weak form of the hypothesis because market data are part of the larger set of all publicly available information.

Tests of the semistrong EMH are tests of the speed of adjustment of stock prices to announcements of new information. A semistrong efficient market implies that investors cannot act on new public information after its announcement and expect to earn above-average risk-adjusted returns. If lags exist in the adjustment of stock prices to certain announcements, and investors can exploit these lags and earn abnormal returns, the market is not fully efficient in the semistrong sense.

Strong Form That part of the efficient market hypothesis stating that prices reflect all information, public and private

3. Strong Form: The most stringent form of market efficiency is the **strong form,** which asserts that stock prices fully reflect all information, public and nonpublic. If the market is strong-form efficient, no group of investors should be able to earn, over a reasonable period of time, abnormal rates of return by using publicly available information in a superior manner. This applies in particular to all nonpublic information, including information that may be restricted to certain groups such as corporate insiders and specialists on the exchanges.

In effect, the strong form of the EMH refers to the successful use of a monopolistic access to information by certain market participants. Strong-form efficiency encompasses the weak and semistrong forms and represents the highest level of market efficiency.

EVIDENCE ON MARKET EFFICIENCY

Because of the significance of the efficient markets hypothesis to all investors, and because of the controversy that surrounds the EMH, we will examine some empirical evidence on market efficiency. Many studies have been done over the years and continue to be done. Obviously, we cannot begin to discuss them all, nor is it necessarily desirable to discuss several in detail. Our purpose here is to present an idea of how these tests are done, the scope of what has been done, and some results. The empirical evidence will be separated into tests of the three forms of market efficiency previously discussed.

The key to testing the validity of any of the three forms of market efficiency is the consistency with which investors can earn returns in excess of those commensurate with the risk involved. Short-lived inefficiencies appearing on a random basis do not constitute evidence of market inefficiencies, at least in an economic (as opposed to a statistical) sense. Therefore, it makes sense to talk about an economically efficient market, where assets are priced in such a manner that investors cannot exploit any discrepancies and earn unusual returns after consideration of all transaction costs. In such a market, some securities could be priced slightly above their intrinsic values and some slightly below, and lags can exist in the processing of information, but again not in such a way that the differences can be exploited.

[3] It is not correct to state, as is sometimes done, that the best estimate of price at time $t + 1$ is the current (time t) price, because this implies an expected return of zero. The efficient market in no way implies that the expected return on any security is zero.

What about the time period involved? In the short run, investors may earn unusual returns even if the market is efficient. After all, you could buy a stock today, and tomorrow a major discovery could be announced that would cause its stock price to increase significantly. Does this mean the market is inefficient? Obviously not; it means you are either very skillful or, more likely, very lucky. The question is, can you, and enough other investors, do this a sufficient number of times in the long run to earn abnormal profits? Even in the long run, some people will be lucky given the total number of investors.

WEAK-FORM EVIDENCE

As noted, weak-form efficiency means that price data are incorporated into current stock prices. If prices follow nonrandom trends, stock-price changes are dependent; otherwise, they are independent. Therefore, weak-form tests involve the question of whether all information contained in the sequence of past prices is fully reflected in the current price.

The weak-form EMH is related to, but not identical with, an idea from the 1960s called the *random walk hypothesis*. If prices follow a random walk, price changes over time are random (independent).[4] The price change for today is unrelated to the price change yesterday, or the day before, or any other day. This is a result of the scenario described at the outset of the chapter. If new information arrives randomly in the market and investors react to it immediately, changes in prices will also be random.

One way to test for weak-form efficiency is to statistically test the independence of stock-price changes. If the statistical tests suggest that price changes are independent, the implication is that knowing and using the past sequence of price information is of no value to an investor. In other words, trends in price changes do not exist.

INVESTMENTS INTUITION It should be apparent upon reflection that we are talking about price changes and not about the level of price itself. Obviously, a $60 stock has a price on any given day that will be related closely to its price tomorrow, since it is unlikely on a typical day to go much above or below $60. In addition, we are not concerned with whether the change in today's price, say +½, is related to the change in tomorrow's price, say −¼. Dollar price changes such as these are also related. The issue centers on percentage price changes over time—are they related or not?

A second way to test for weak-form efficiency, after testing the pure statistical nature of price changes, is to test specific trading rules that attempt to use past price data. If such tests legitimately produce risk-adjusted returns beyond that available from simply buying a portfolio of stocks and holding it until a common liquidation date, after deducting all costs, it would suggest that the market is not weak-form efficient.

Statistical Tests of Price Changes Stock-price changes in an efficient market should be independent. Two simple statistical tests of independence are the serial correlation test and the signs test. The serial correlation test involves measuring the correlation between price changes for various lags, such as one day, two days, and so on, whereas the signs test involves classifying each price change by its sign, which means whether it was +, 0, or − (regardless of amount). Then the "runs" in the series of signs can be counted and compared

[4] Technically, the random walk hypothesis is more restrictive than the weak-form EMH. Stock prices can conform to weak-form efficiency without meeting the conditions of a random walk.

to known information about a random series. If there are persistent price changes, the length of the runs will indicate it.

Fama studied the daily returns on the 30 Dow Jones Industrial stocks and found that only a very small percentage of any successive price change could be explained by a prior change.[5] Serial correlation tests by other researchers invariably reached the same conclusion.

The signs test also supports independence. Although some "runs" do occur, they fall within the limits of randomness, since a truly random series exhibits some runs (several + or − observations in succession).

Technical Trading Rules The statistical tests described above demonstrate that trends, other than those consistent with a random series, do not appear to exist in stock prices. However, technical analysts believe that such trends not only exist but can also be used successfully (technical analysis is discussed in Chapter 16). They argue that the statistical tests do not detect more sophisticated or realistic strategies. Because an almost unlimited number of possible technical trading rules exist, not all of them can be examined; however, if a sufficient number are examined and found to be ineffective, the burden of proof shifts to those who argue that such techniques have value. This is exactly the situation that prevails. Little evidence exists that a technical trading rule based solely on past price and volume data can, after all proper adjustments have been made, outperform a simple buy-and-hold strategy.

Again it is important to emphasize the difference between statistical dependence and economic dependence in stock-price changes. The statistical tests discussed earlier detected some small amount of dependence in price changes.[6] Not all of the series could be said to be completely independent statistically. However, they were economically independent in that one could not exploit the small statistical dependence that existed. After brokerage costs, excess returns disappear. After all, this is the bottom line for investors—can excess returns be earned with a technical trading rule after all costs are deducted?[7]

Weak-Form Contraevidence DeBondt and Thaler have tested an "overreaction hypothesis," which states that people overreact to unexpected and dramatic news events.[8] As applied to stock prices, the hypothesis states that, as a result of overreactions, "loser" portfolios outperform the market after their formation. DeBondt and Thaler found that over a half-century period, the loser portfolios of 35 stocks outperformed the market by an average of almost 20 percent for a 36-month period after portfolio formation. Winner portfolios earned about 5 percent less than the market. Interestingly, the overreaction seems to occur mostly during the second and third year of the test period. DeBondt and Thaler interpreted this evidence as indicative of irrational behavior by investors, or "overreaction."

This tendency for stocks that experience extreme returns to go through subsequent return reversals after portfolios are formed, and for the effect to be observed years after portfolio formation, has implications for market efficiency. Specifically, it indicates substantial weak-form inefficiencies, because DeBondt and Thaler are testing whether the overreaction hypothesis is predictive. In other words, according to their research, knowing past stock returns appears to help significantly in predicting future stock returns.

---

[5] E. Fama, "The Behavior of Stock Market Prices," *The Journal of Finance,* 38, no. 1 (January 1965): 34–105.

[6] Stock returns tend to exhibit a slight positive correlation.

[7] Some studies have indicated that trading rules can produce profits after making the necessary adjustments. For a study that argues that trading rules may not be so readily implemented under actual conditions, see Ray Ball, S. P. Kothari, and Charles Wasley, "Can We Implement Research on Stock Trading Rules?" *The Journal of Portfolio Management* (Winter 1995): 54–63.

[8] Werner F. M. DeBondt and Richard Thaler, "Does the Stock Market Overreact?" *The Journal of Finance* (July 1985): 793–805.

A recent study of the overreaction hypothesis, which adjusts for several potential problems, found an "economically important overreaction effect" even after adjusting for time variations in beta and for size effects.[9] Using five-year periods to form portfolios, the study revealed that extreme prior losers outperformed extreme prior winners by 5 to 10 percent per year over the following five years. The overreaction effect was considerably stronger for smaller firms (held predominantly by individuals) than for larger firms (held predominantly by institutions).

SEMISTRONG-FORM EVIDENCE

Weak-form tests, of both the statistical and the trading rule types, are numerous and almost unanimous in their findings (after necessary corrections and adjustments have been made). Semistrong tests, on the other hand, are also numerous but more diverse in their findings. Although most of these studies support the proposition that the market adjusts to new public information rapidly, some do not.

Semistrong-form tests are tests of the speed of price adjustments to publicly available information. The question is whether investors can use publicly available information to earn excess returns, after proper adjustments. As a benchmark, we can use a buy-and-hold strategy with equivalent risk, or perhaps the market as a whole.

Event Study An empirical analysis of stock price behavior surrounding a particular event

This empirical research often involves an **event study,** which means that a company's stock returns are examined to determine the impact of a particular event on the stock price.[10] This methodology uses an index model of stock returns. An index model states that security returns are determined by a market factor (index) and a unique company factor. The single-index model from Chapter 19 is an example.

Abnormal Return Return on a security beyond that expected on the basis of its risk

Company-unique returns are the residual error terms representing the difference between the security's actual return and that given by the index model. In other words, after adjusting for what the company's return should have been, given the index model, any remaining portion of the actual return is an **abnormal return** representing the impact of a particular event.

$$\text{Abnormal return} = AR_{it} = R_{it} - E(R_{it})$$

where

AR_{it} = the abnormal rate of return for security i during period t
R_{it} = the actual rate of return on security i during period t
$E(R_{it})$ = the expected rate of return for security i during period t, based on the market model relationship

Cumulative Abnormal Return (CAR) The sum of the individual abnormal returns over the time period under examination

The **cumulative abnormal return (CAR)** is the sum of the individual abnormal returns over the period of time under examination and is calculated as

$$CAR_i = \sum_{t=1}^{n} AR_{it}$$

where

CAR_i = the cumulative abnormal return for stock i

[9] See Navin Chopra, Josef Lakonishok, and Jay R. Ritter, "Measuring Abnormal Performance: Do Stocks Overact?" *The Journal of Financial Economics*, 31 (1992): 235–268.

[10] In his new survey of efficient capital markets, Fama uses the "now common title, event studies," instead of semistrong-form tests. See Fama, "Efficient Capital Markets."

Below we consider a sampling of often-cited studies of semistrong efficiency without developing them in detail. It is important to obtain a feel for the wide variety of information tested and the logic behind these tests. The methodology and a detailed discussion of the results are not essential for our purposes. At this point we consider evidence that tends to support semistrong efficiency.

1. Stock splits. An often cited study of the long-run effects of stock splits on returns was done by Fama, Fisher, Jensen, and Roll (FFJR) and was the first event study.[11] A stock split adds nothing of value to a company and, therefore, should have no effect on the company's total market value. FFJR found that, although the stocks they studied exhibited sharp increases in price prior to the split announcement, abnormal (i.e., risk-adjusted) returns after the split announcement were very stable. Thus, the split itself did not affect prices. The results indicate that any implications of a stock split appear to be reflected in price immediately following the announcement, and not the event itself, which supports the semistrong form of market efficiency.[12]

2. Accounting changes. Several studies have examined the effects stock prices have on announcements of accounting changes. The accounting changes include depreciation, the investment tax credit, inventory reporting (LIFO versus FIFO), and other items. Essentially, two different types of changes are involved:

a. The change may affect only the manner in which earnings are reported to stockholders, and therefore should not affect stock prices. The reason for this is that such changes do not affect the firm's cash flows and thus its real economic value.

b. The change may affect the firm's economic value by affecting its cash flows. This is a true change and should therefore generate a change in market prices. In an efficient market, stock prices should adjust quickly to the announcement of this type of change.

In general, the studies indicate that the market is able to distinguish the superficial changes described in the first type from the real changes described in the second type.

3. Initial public offerings. A company that goes public creates an initial public offering, or IPO. Given the risk the underwriters face in trying to sell a new issue where the true price is unknown, the underwriters may be underpricing the new issue to ensure its rapid sale. The investors who are able to buy the IPO as its offering price may be able to earn abnormal profits, but if prices adjust quickly investors buying the new issues shortly after their issuance should not benefit.

The evidence indicates that new issues purchased at their offering price yield abnormal returns to the fortunate investors who are allowed to buy the initial offering.[13] This is attributed to underpricing by the underwriters. Investors buying shortly after the initial offering, however, are not able to earn abnormal profits because prices adjust very quickly to the "true" values.

4. Reactions to announcements and news. Investors are constantly given a wide range of information concerning both large-scale events and items about particular companies. Each of these types of announcements has been examined for the effects on stock prices.

[11] E. Fama, L. Fisher, M. Jensen, and R. Roll, "The Adjustment of Stock Prices to New Information," *International Economics Review,* 10, no. 1 (February 1969): 2–21.

[12] A later study provided a very extensive analysis of a sample of stock splits in order to determine stock-price reactions. Effects such as dividend announcements and cash dividends were controlled for. The findings of this study suggest that the price reactions extend several days beyond the announcement date of the stock split or stock dividend. These results imply that there must be some information associated with such distributions. See Mark Grinblatt, Ronald Masulis, and Sheridan Titman, "The Valuation Effects of Stock Splits and Stock Dividends," *The Journal of Financial Economics,* 13 (December 1984): 461–490.

[13] For a review of this literature, see Roger Ibbotson, Jody Sindelar, and Jay Ritter, "Initial Public Offerings," *Journal of Applied Corporate Finance,* 1 (Summer 1988): 37–45.

One form of announcement involves economic news, such as money supply, real economic activity, inflation, and the Fed's discount rate. A study of these announcements found no impact on stock prices that lasted beyond the announcement day.[14] Even an analysis of hourly stock-price reactions to surprise announcements of money supply and industrial production found that any impact was accounted for within one hour.[15]

The "Heard in the Street" column in *The Wall Street Journal* is a daily feature highlighting particular companies and analysts' opinions on stocks. A recent study of public takeover rumors from the "Heard on the Street" column found that the market is efficient at responding to published takeover rumors.[16] Excess returns could not be earned on average by buying or selling rumored takeover targets at the time the rumor appeared. No significant excess returns occurred on the day the takeover rumor in *The Wall Street Journal* was published, although a positive cumulative excess return of approximately 7 percent occurs in the calendar month before the rumor appears in the "Heard on the Street" column.

STRONG-FORM EVIDENCE

The strong form of the EMH states that stock prices immediately adjust to and reflect all information, including private information.[17] Thus, no group of investors has information that allows them to earn abnormal profits consistently, even those investors with monopolistic access to information. Note that investors are prohibited not from possessing monopolistic information, but from profiting. This is an important point in light of the studies of insider trading reported below.

One way to test for strong-form efficiency is to examine the performance of groups presumed to have access to "true" nonpublic information. If such groups can consistently earn above-average risk-adjusted returns, the strong form will not be supported. We will consider corporate insiders, a group that presumably falls into the category of having monopolistic access to information.

Corporate Insiders A corporate insider is an officer, director, or major stockholder of a corporation who might be expected to have valuable inside information. The Securities and Exchange Commission (SEC) requires insiders (officers, directors, and owners of more than 10 percent of a company's stock) to report their monthly purchase or sale transactions to the SEC by the tenth of the next month. This information is made public in the SEC's monthly publication, *Official Summary of Security Transactions and Holdings (Official Summary).*

Insiders have access to privileged information and are able to act on it and profit before the information is made public. This is logical and not really surprising. Therefore, it is not surprising that several studies of corporate insiders found they consistently earned abnormal returns on their stock transactions.[18] Other studies, however, have found that insiders do only slightly better than chance alone in predicting the direction of a company's stock.

A recent study of insider trades by chairpersons, presidents, and other top officials of

[14] See Doug Pearce and Vance Roley, "Stock Prices and Economic News," *Journal of Business,* 59 (Summer 1985): 49–67.

[15] See Prom C. Jain, "Response of Hourly Stock Prices and Trading Volume to Economic News," *Journal of Business,* 61 (April 1988): 219–231.

[16] See John Pound and Richard Zeckhauser, "Clearly Heard on the Street: The Effect of Takeover Rumors on Stock Prices," *Journal of Business* (July 1990): 291–308.

[17] Fama, in his 1991 paper, refers to these tests as "tests for private information" instead of strong-form tests. See Fama, "Efficient Capital Markets."

[18] See, for example, J. Jaffe, "Special Information and Insider Trading," *Journal of Business,* 47 (July 1974): 410–428, and Ken Nunn, G. P. Madden, and Michael Gombola, "Are Some Investors More 'Inside' Than Others?" *Journal of Portfolio Management,* 9 (Spring 1983): 18–22.

firms over the period 1975–1989 found that these groups substantially outperformed the market when they made large trades. Trades by top executives of 1,000 shares or more were "abnormally profitable" for insiders.[19] On the other hand, most insiders did only slightly better than a coin toss.

An even more recent study covering the period 1975–1995, by Lakonishok and Lee, found that companies with a high incidence of insider buying outperform those where insiders have done a large amount of selling. The margin was almost 8 percentage points for the subsequent 12-month period. Interestingly, the largest differences occurred in companies with a market capitalization of less than $1 billion.

Profitable insider trading is a violation of strong-form efficiency, which requires a market in which no investor can consistently earn abnormal profits. Furthermore, successful use of this information by outsiders (the general public) would be a violation of semistrong efficiency. Investors without access to this private information can observe what the insiders are doing by studying the publicly available reports that appear in the Official Summary. Several investment information services compile this information and sell it to the public in the form of regularly issued reports, and it is available weekly in *Barron's* and *The Wall Street Journal*. Furthermore, such services as *The Value Line Investment Survey* report insider transactions for each company they cover.

In a recent study, Rozeff and Zaman used the typical abnormal return methodology of previous studies and found that outsiders can earn profits by acting on the publicly available information concerning insider transactions.[20] However, when they used an abnormal returns measure that takes into account size and earnings/price ratio effects, these profits decreased substantially and disappeared altogether when transactions cost of 2 percent are included. Furthermore, imposition of the 2 percent transactions cost on corporate insiders reduces their abnormal returns to an average of 3 to 3.5 percent per year. Therefore, this study reaffirms semistrong market efficiency with respect to insider trading and also suggests that corporate insiders do not earn substantial profits from directly using inside information, which in effect supports strong-form efficiency.

There are several reasons why insider transactions can be very misleading, or simply of no value as an indicator of where the stock price is likely to go. Selling shares acquired by option grants to key executives has become commonplace—they need the cash, and they sell shares acquired as part of their compensation. Similarly, acquiring shares through the exercise of options can simply represent an investment decision by the executive.

IMPLICATIONS OF THE EFFICIENT MARKET HYPOTHESIS

The nonexhaustive evidence on market efficiency presented here is impressive in its support of market efficiency. What are the implications to investors if this evidence is descriptive of the actual situation? How should investors analyze and select securities and manage their portfolios if the market is efficient?

FOR TECHNICAL ANALYSIS

As mentioned earlier, technical analysis and the EMH directly conflict with each other. Technicians believe that stock prices exhibit trends that persist across time, whereas the weak-

[19] See Alexandra Peers, "Insiders Reap Big Gains from Big Trades," *The Wall Street Journal*, September 23, 1992, pp. C1 and C12.

[20] See Michael S. Rozeff and Mir A. Zaman, "Market Efficiency and Insider Trading: New Evidence," *Journal of Business* (January 1988): 25–45.

form EMH states that price (and volume) data are already reflected in stock prices. EMH proponents believe that information is disseminated rapidly and that prices adjust rapidly to this new information. If prices fully reflect the available information, technical trading systems that rely on knowledge and use of past trading data cannot be of value.

Although technical analysis cannot be categorically refuted because of its many variations and interpretations, the evidence accumulated to date overwhelmingly favors the weak-form EMH and casts doubt on technical analysis. The evidence is such that the burden of proof has shifted to the proponents of technical analysis to demonstrate, using a properly designed test procedure (e.g., adjusting for transaction costs, risk, and any other factors necessary to make a fair comparison), that technical analysis outperforms a buy-and-hold strategy.

FOR FUNDAMENTAL ANALYSIS

The EMH also has implications for fundamental analysis, which seeks to estimate the intrinsic value of a security and provide buy or sell decisions depending on whether the current market price is less than or greater than the intrinsic value. If the semistrong form is true, no form of "standard" security analysis based on publicly available information will be useful. In this situation, since stock prices reflect all relevant publicly available information, gaining access to information others already have is of no value.

Given the evidence on market efficiency, clearly superior fundamental analysis becomes necessary. For example, an investor's estimates of future variables such as earnings must be better, or at least more consistent, than those of other investors. This investor must also derive more and better insights from information that is publicly available to all investors. There is no theoretical reason why an investor could not do a superior job of analysis and profit thereby. However, the EMH suggests that investors who use the same data and make the same interpretations as other investors will experience only average results.

FOR MONEY MANAGEMENT

What about money management activities? First, the evidence:[21]

- For the 16½ year period from August 1982 (start of the bull market) through 1998, the Vanguard 500 Index Fund had an annual average return of 19.7 percent, the average big-cap fund averaged 18.2 percent, and the average equity fund averaged 15.9 percent. Thus, the index fund clearly performed equity money managers.
- In 1998, the S&P 500 rose 28.6 percent. One-fifth of all U.S. equity funds lost money, and only 17 percent beat the index.
- Fewer than 5 percent of all U.S. equity funds beat the S&P 500 Index over the five year period ending in 1998.

Assume for a moment that the market is efficient. What would this mean to the money management process, that is, to professional money managers? The most important effect would be a reduction in the resources devoted to assessing individual securities. For the manager to act in this respect, he or she would have to believe that an analyst had come up with some superior insights. Passive strategies would become the norm. Nevertheless, the

[21] See "Who Needs a Money Manager," *Business Week*, February 22, 1999, p. 127.

portfolio manager would still have tasks to perform in this efficient market. These tasks would consist of at least the following:

1. Diversification: As we saw in Chapter 7, the basic tenet of good portfolio management is to diversify the portfolio. The manager would have to be certain that the correct amount of diversification had been achieved.
2. Portfolio risk: Depending on the type of portfolio being managed and its objectives, the manager must achieve a level of risk appropriate for that portfolio as well as maintain the desired risk level.
3. Taxes: Investors are interested in the amount of return they are allowed to keep after taxes. Accordingly, their tax situation should be kept in mind as investment alternatives are considered. Tax-exempt portfolios have their own needs and interests.
4. Transaction costs: Trading costs can have a significant impact on the final performance of the portfolio. Managers should seek to reduce these costs to the extent possible and practical. Index funds are one possibility.

Before deciding that these tasks may be all that is left to do in the portfolio management process in the face of an efficient market, we should examine some evidence that suggests possibilities for investors interested in selecting stocks. This evidence is in contrast with that discussed thus far and constitutes a good conclusion for this chapter by indicating that, regardless of how persuasive the case for market efficiency is, the final answer is not in and may never be.

EVIDENCE OF MARKET ANOMALIES

Market Anomalies Techniques or strategies that appear to be contrary to an efficient market

Having considered the type of evidence supporting market efficiency, we now can appropriately consider some **market anomalies.** By definition, an anomaly is an exception to a rule, or model. In other words, the results from these anomalies are in contrast to what would be expected in a totally efficient market, and they cannot easily be explained away.

We will examine several anomalies that have generated much attention and have yet to be satisfactorily explained. However, investors must be cautious in viewing any of these anomalies as a stock selection device guaranteed to outperform the market. There is no such guarantee because empirical tests of these anomalies may not approximate actual trading strategies that would be followed by investors. Furthermore, if anomalies exist and can be identified, investors should still hold a portfolio of stocks rather than concentrating on a few stocks identified by one of these methods. As we saw in Chapter 7, diversification is crucial for all investors.

EARNINGS ANNOUNCEMENTS

The adjustment of stock prices to earnings announcements has been studied in several papers, opening up some interesting questions and possibilities. The information found in such announcements should, and does, affect stock prices. The questions that need to be answered are as follows:

1. How much of the earnings announcement is new information and how much has been anticipated by the market. In other words, how much of the announcement is a "surprise"?
2. How quickly is the "surprise" portion of the announcement reflected in the price of the stock? Is it immediate, as would be expected in an efficient market, or is there

a lag in the adjustment process? If a lag occurs, investors have a chance to realize excess returns by quickly acting on the publicly available earnings announcements.

To assess the earnings announcement issue properly, we must separate a particular earnings announcement into an expected and an unexpected part. The expected part is that portion anticipated by investors by the time of announcement and that requires no adjustment in stock prices, whereas the unexpected part is unanticipated by investors and requires an adjustment in price.

Latane', Tuttle, and Jones studied quarterly earnings reports in 1968 and found them to be positively correlated with subsequent short-term price movements. This finding indicated a lag in the adjustment of stock prices to the information in these reports.[22] Following several papers that examined the value of quarterly earnings in stock selection, Henry Latane', Charles Jones, and Robert Rieke in 1974 developed the concept of **standardized unexpected earnings (SUE)** as a means of investigating the earnings surprises in quarterly data.[23] SUE is defined as

Standardized Unexpected Earnings (SUE) A variable used in the selection of common stocks, calculated as the ratio of unexpected earnings to a standardization factor

$$\begin{aligned} \text{SUE} &= \frac{\text{Actual quarterly earnings} - \text{Predicted quarterly earnings}}{\text{Standardization factor to adjust for size differences}} \\ &= \text{Unexpected earnings/Standard error of the estimate} \end{aligned}$$

The actual quarterly earnings are the earnings reported by the company and available on brokerage house wire services the same day as reported, or in *The Wall Street Journal* the following day. Predicted earnings for a particular company are estimated from historical earnings data before the earnings are reported. As each company's earnings are announced, the SUE can be calculated and acted on. Companies with high (low) unexpected earnings are expected to have a positive (negative) price response.

Latane' and Jones have documented the performance of SUE in a series of papers. SUE was shown to have a definite relationship with subsequent excess holding-period returns. In one paper the authors documented the precise response of stock prices to earnings announcements using a large sample of stocks (over 1,400) for the 36 quarters covering mid-1971 to mid-1980.[24] Daily returns were used, allowing the exact response of stock prices to quarterly earnings announcements to be analyzed before, on, and after the day the earnings were announced.

Figure 12-3 shows a similar analysis for an updated period involving a sample size ranging from about 1,700 companies per quarter to almost 2,000 companies. SUEs are separated into 10 categories based on the size and sign of the unexpected earnings. Category 10 contains all SUEs larger than 4.0, and category 1 contains all SUEs smaller than −4.0; categories 5 and 6 contain the smallest unexpected earnings.

Excess returns are calculated for each security as the difference between a security's return for each day and the market's return for that day. These excess returns are cumulated for the period beginning 63 days before the announcement date of earnings through 63 days following the announcement date. (There are approximately 63 trading days in a quarter.) As Figure 12-3 shows, the SUE categories follow a monotonic discrimination, with category 10 performing the best and category 1 the worst. Categories 5 and 6 show virtually no excess returns after the announcement date of earnings, as would be expected from the smallest unexpected earnings.

[22] See H. A. Latane', Donald L. Tuttle, and Charles P. Jones, "E/P Ratios vs. Changes in Earnings in Forecasting Future Price Changes," *Financial Analysts Journal* (January–February 1969): 117–120, 123.

[23] For a discussion of much of this literature, see O. Joy and C. Jones, "Earnings Reports and Market Efficiencies: An Analysis of Contrary Evidence," *Journal of Financial Research,* 2 (Spring 1979): 51–64.

[24] See Charles P. Jones, Richard J. Rendleman, and Henry A. Latane', "Stock Returns and SUEs during the 1970s," *Journal of Portfolio Management* (Winter 1984): 18–22.

FIGURE 12-3

Cumulative excess returns surrounding the announcement date of quarterly earnings for 10 SUE categories.

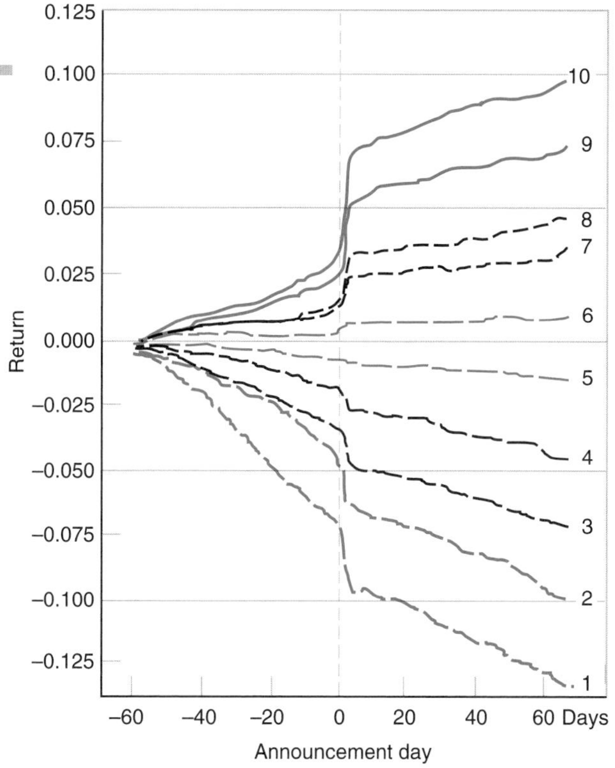

Figure 12-3 indicates that, although a substantial adjustment to the forthcoming earnings announcements occurs before the actual announcement, a substantial adjustment also occurs after the day of announcement. This is the unexplained part of the SUE puzzle. In an efficient market, prices should adjust quickly to earnings, rather than with a lag.

By the mid-1980s considerable evidence had been presented about the relationship between unexpected earnings and subsequent stock returns. Although such evidence is not in any way conclusive, it cannot be easily dismissed. Different researchers, using different samples and different techniques, have examined the unexpected earnings issue and have found similar results. It must be emphasized, however, that techniques such as SUE are not a guarantee of major success for investors. The relationships discussed are averages and do not necessarily reflect what any single investor would experience.

LOW P/E RATIOS

One of the more enduring concepts in investments concerns the price/earnings (P/E) ratio discussed earlier in the valuation chapters. A number of investors believe that low P/E stocks, on average, outperform high P/E stocks. The rationale for this concept is not explicit, but the belief persists.

Basu studied this issue by ranking stocks by their P/E ratios and comparing the results of the high P/E ratio group with those of the low P/E ratio group 12 months following purchase.[25] Since the P/E ratio is known information and presumably reflected in price, a

[25] S. Basu, "Investment Performance of Common Stocks in Relation to Their Price-Earnings Ratios: A Test of the Efficient Market Hypothesis," *The Journal of Finance,* 32, No. 2 (June 1977): 663–682.

relationship between the P/E ratio and subsequent returns should not exist if the market is efficient. The results of Basu's study indicated that the low P/E ratio stocks outperformed the high P/E ratio stocks. Furthermore, risk was not a factor. After various adjustments for risk, the low P/E stocks were still superior performers.

These results attracted considerable attention because of their implications for the concept of market efficiency and because the P/E ratio is an easy, well-known strategy to use in selecting stocks. Subsequently, questions about the validity of the P/E ratio were raised by other academic researchers in studies of the firm size effect, which is discussed later as another anomaly.

In response to the questions raised, Basu conducted a study to reexamine the relationship between the P/E ratio, the size effect, and returns on NYSE stocks for the period 1963–1980.[26] He found that the stocks of low P/E firms generally had higher risk-adjusted returns than firms with high P/E ratios. Furthermore, this P/E ratio effect was significant even after adjustments were made for differences in firm size. Controlling for differences in both risk and P/E ratios, Basu found that the size effect virtually disappeared.

In view of some research suggesting that the P/E effect is confined to low-beta-risk securities, a recent study examined the P/E anomaly with respect to both total risk and systematic risk.[27] The results indicate that the P/E effect is not confined to low-beta-risk securities. Regardless of the risk measure used, low P/E securities provided significant positive excess returns across all risk levels.

The P/E ratio anomaly appears to offer investors a potential strategy for investing that could produce returns superior to many alternatives they may be using. Some well-known commentators continue to advocate investing in low P/E stocks. For example, David Dreman (discussed in Chapter 11 in connection with contrarian analysis) recommends that investors ignore professional investment advice and select stocks with low P/E ratios. His hypothesis is that low P/E stocks may currently be unwanted, but if they have strong finances, high yields, and good earnings records, they almost always do well eventually.

According to Dreman, for the 20 year period through 1993, for a sample of 1,200 small stocks, low P/E stocks outperform high P/E stocks over long periods of time. The lowest P/E group returned 22.9 percent on an annual basis compared to 11.3 percent for the highest P/E group and 17.2 percent for the mean small-capitalization sample. Over the more recent 10 years, the smallest quintile outperformed the largest quintile by almost a three to one ratio.[28]

Investors need to be careful when following the low P/E strategy. Although a diversified portfolio, as always, is critical, rigid adherence to a low P/E strategy could result in an inadequately diversified portfolio. Dreman has indicated that he takes a minimum of 25 stocks in 15 to 18 industries and that "most [low-P/E stocks] have significant problems or very good reasons why you don't want to own them." Only about 1 in 10 candidates on the basis of low P/E passes his additional screens, such as dividend yields higher than average and accelerating earnings growth over the past. Dreman also suggests an emphasis on large stocks as opposed to small-company stocks.

According to some evidence, the low P/E strategy does well neither in turbulent markets nor in periods of slow economic growth. However, these stocks may perform well in a "full-blown" bear market because of their higher dividend yields. Overall, the low-P/E strategy should be viewed as a long-run strategy, to be pursued through both good and bad markets.

[26] S. Basu, "The Relationship Between Earnings' Yield, Market Value and Return for NYSE Common Stocks: Further Evidence," *Journal of Financial Economics*, 12 (June 1983): 129–156.

[27] See David Goodman and John Peavy, "The Risk Universal Nature of the P/E Effect," *The Journal of Portfolio Management* (Summer 1985): 14–17.

[28] See David Dreman, "Emotion Versus Logic," *Forbes*, November 7, 1994, p. 351.

THE SIZE EFFECT

Size Effect The observed tendency for smaller firms to have higher stock returns than large firms

A third anomaly is the firm **size effect,** referred to earlier. In a well-publicized study, Rolf Banz found that the stocks of small NYSE firms earned higher risk-adjusted returns than the stocks of large NYSE firms (on average).[29] This size effect appears to have persisted for many years. Mark Reinganum, using a sample of both NYSE and AMEX firms, also found abnormally large risk-adjusted returns for small firms.[30] Both of these researchers attributed the results to a misspecification of the CAPM rather than to a market inefficiency. That is, in the face of persistent abnormal returns attributed to the size effect, both Banz and Reinganum were unwilling to reject the idea that the market could have inefficiencies of this type.

Additional research on the size effect indicates that "small" firms with the largest abnormal returns tend to be those that have recently become small (or have recently declined in price), that either pay no dividend or have a high dividend yield, that have low prices, and that have low P/E ratios.[31] Donald Keim found that roughly 50 percent of the return difference reported by Reinganum is concentrated in January.[32]

It is easy today to get confused about the size effect, given all of the research findings and the various definitions of small caps. While many investors generally accept the notion that small caps outperform large caps, it is nevertheless true that from 1926 through 1979, small caps had a mean annualized return of 12.2 percent, while large caps showed 8.2 percent. From 1980 to 1996, small caps had a 13.3 percent return, while large caps showed 15.9 percent. Thus, by this measure, the small-cap "premium" has disappeared.

THE JANUARY EFFECT

Several studies in the past have suggested that seasonality exists in the stock market. Recent evidence of stock return seasonality has grown out of studies of the size anomaly explained in the previous section. Keim studied the month-to-month stability of the size effect for all NYSE and AMEX firms with data for 1963–1979.[33] His findings again supported the existence of a significant size effect (a 30.5 percent small-size premium). However, roughly half of this size effect occurred in January, and more than half of the excess January returns occurred during the first five trading days of that month. The first trading day of the year showed a high small-firm premium for every year of the period studied. The strong performance in January by small-company stocks has become known as the **January effect.**[34]

January Effect The observed tendency to be higher in January than in other months

Another paper by Keim further documented the abnormal returns for small firms in January. Keim also found a yield effect—the largest abnormal returns tended to accrue to firms either paying no dividends or having high dividend yields.[35]

---

[29] R. Banz, "The Relationship Between Returns and Market Value of Common Stocks," *Journal of Financial Economics,* 9 (March 1981): 3–18.

[30] M. Reinganum, "Misspecification of Capital Asset Pricing: Empirical Anomalies Based on Earnings Yield and Market Values," *Journal of Financial Economics,* 9 (March 1981): 19–46.

[31] See, for example, Donald B. Keim, "Dividend Yields and the January Effect," *Journal of Portfolio Management* (Winter 1986): 54–60. Keim finds that the largest abnormal returns accrue to smaller firms either paying no dividends or having high dividend yields.

[32] These results, as well as a discussion of most of the anomalies, can be found in Donald B. Keim, "The CAPM and Equity Return Regularities," *Financial Analysts Journal* (May–June 1986): 19–34.

[33] See Donald B. Keim, "Size-Related Anomalies and Stock Return Seasonality," *Journal of Financial Economics,* 12 (1983): 13–32.

[34] See Richard Roll, "Vas ist das? The Turn of the Year Effect and the Return Premium of Small Firms," *The Journal of Portfolio Management* (Winter 1983): 18–28. Roll also found a turn-of-the-year effect with abnormal returns for small firms on the last trading day in December.

[35] See Donald B. Keim, "Dividend Yields and the January Effect," *The Journal of Portfolio Management* (Winter 1986): 54–60.

Recent evidence on the January effect, as measured by the performance of the Nasdaq Composite Index for the month of January is:

1985	+12.7%	1993	+ 2.9%
1986	+ 3.3%	1994	+ 3.1%
1987	+12.4%	1995	+ 0.4%
1988	+ 4.3%	1996	+ 0.7%
1989	+ 5.2%	1997	+ 6.9%
1990	− 8.6%	1998	+ 3.1%
1991	+10.8%	1999	+14.28
1992	+ 5.8%	2000	NA

This simple evidence, which makes no comparisons or other judgments, suggests that the January effect has continued to exist in recent years, at least in the sense of a solid January performance for these stocks. As the data indicate, there was only one negative year during this 15-year period.

The information about a possible January effect has been available for years and has been widely discussed in the press. The question arises, therefore, as to why a January effect would persist and reoccur again and again. Nevertheless, Haugen and Jorion find no evidence that the January effect has disappeared for NYSE stocks.[36] They detect no significant change in the magnitude of the effect, nor trend that would suggest the January effect will disappear. As Haugen and Jorion indicate, "Because the anomaly can be inexpensively exploited, its persistence has implications for the theory of efficient markets and for the persistence of anomalies in general."[37]

Some Practical Advice

Abnormally high returns in January are most significant for micro caps, which have gained about 8.6 percent in January on average, compared to 1.9 percent for the market as a whole and 4.8 percent for small caps. For small-cap stocks overall, the January effect appears to be moving into December. Since 1980 the average return for small caps in December was 2.4 percent, and since 1990, 4.1 percent. For micro caps, these numbers reversed—4.8 percent since 1990 versus 5.7 percent since 1980.[38]

THE VALUE LINE RANKING SYSTEM

The Value Line Investment Survey is the largest, and perhaps best-known, investment advisory service in the country.[39] *Value Line* ranks each of the roughly 1,700 stocks it covers from 1 (best) to 5 (worst) as to its "timeliness"—probable relative price performance within the next 12 months. These timeliness ranks, updated weekly, have been available since 1965.

[36] See Robert A. Haugen and Phillipe Jorion, "The January Effect: Still There after All These Years," *Financial Analysts Journal* (January–February 1996): 27–31.

[37] A 1992 study of the January anomaly indicates that the previous studies of abnormal returns for small firms may be biased by incomplete consideration of a price effect and transaction costs. This study argues, on the basis of the years 1967–1986, that the January effect is a low-price phenomenon rather than a small-firm effect. Further tests indicated that, after adjusting for differential transaction costs, portfolios of lower price stocks almost always underperformed the market portfolio. Therefore, the large before-transaction-costs excess January returns observed on low-price stocks may be explainable by higher transaction costs and a bid-ask bias. The implication of this study is that the reported January anomaly is not persistent and is not likely to be exploitable by most investors. See Ravinder K. Bhardaj and Leroy D. Brooks, "The January Anomaly: Effects of Low Share Price, Transaction Costs, and Bid-Ask Bias," *The Journal of Finance,* 47 (June 1992): 553–575.

[38] See Daniel Coker, "Leap Into the New Year," *Bloomberg Personal Finance,* December 1998, p. 29.

[39] This investment advisory service is discussed in more detail in Chapter 15.

The performance of the five rankings categories has been spectacular, based on *Value Line*'s calculations. For example, the complete record of *Value Line* rankings for timeliness from 1965 shows that the ranking system clearly discriminates in a monotonic order. Without allowing for changes in ranks (equal amounts are invested in each stock in each grouping at the beginning of the year and held for 12 months without allowing for subsequent changes in ranking), Group 3 stocks performed in an average manner (using the average of the stocks covered by *Value Line*), whereas Groups 1 and 2 performed much better than either the average or the two market measures reported. On the other hand, shortselling Groups 4 and 5 would have been unsuccessful. Allowing for changes in ranks produced spectacular results. However, such a procedure would have resulted in a prohibitive portfolio turnover rate.

According to available evidence, for the period mid-1980 through 1993 Group 1 stocks showed an annualized return of 19.3 percent. According to Mark Hulbert, who tracks the performance of investment letters for his *Hulbert Financial Digest,* this made *Value Line* the best overall performer for this period of all the investment letters tracked.

The Value Line Investment Survey now regularly reports a comparison of the performance of its Group 1 stocks with four other strategies: low P/E, low cap (small size), low price/book value, and low price/sales. These results provide some information on two of the strategies discussed earlier, low P/E and the size effect, as well as two valuation techniques that are discussed in Chapter 10, price/book value and price/sales.

Several studies of the success of *Value Line*'s rankings have been made. It appears that the rankings, and changes in the rankings, do contain useful information. However, there is evidence that the market adjusts quickly to this information (one or two trading days following the Friday release) and that true transaction costs can negate much of the price changes that occur as a result of adjustments to this information.[40]

The Value Line Investment Survey is an important source of information for investors and is one of the most used investment advisory services available. We will refer to it again in Chapter 15. Box 12-1 discusses *Value Line*'s system, its performance, the use of momemtum as a stock selection criterion (momentum is discussed in Chapter 11), and the relation of *Value Line*'s performance to the efficient market hypothesis.

OTHER ANOMALIES

The above list of anomalies is not exhaustive. Others have been reported and discussed, including in particular several calendar anomalies such as the day of the week, turn-of-the-month, day preceding a holiday, and so forth. One anomaly of interest, because it is consistent with the commonsense notion that market efficiency is most likely applied to the larger, well-known stocks as opposed to all stocks, is the **neglected firm effect.** Neglect in this case means that few analysts follow the stock or that few institutions own the stock. The area of neglected stocks would appear to be a good opportunity for small investors interested in security analysis and stock selection.

USING THE INTERNET An excellent source of information about the anomalies can be found by choosing "Anomalies" at www.investorhome.com. Most of the anomalies are discussed, and each discussion has links to both the original research and recent articles on the subject.

[40] See Scott Stickel, "The Effect of Value Line Investment Survey Changes on Common Stock Prices," *Journal of Financial Economics,* 14 (March 1985): 121–143. A good review that attempts to reconcile the various findings about *Value Line* can be found in Gur Huberman and Shmuel Kandel, "Market Efficiency and Value Line's Record," *Journal of Business,* 63 (April 1990): 187–216.

Box 12-1

VALUE LINE VS. THE EFFICIENT MARKET HYPOTHESIS

You'd think that after three decades as a successful stock picker, Samuel Eisenstadt would have complete faith in his own system. Not quite. At age 76, the research chairman for Value Line, Inc.—and the coinventor of what may be the most famous stock-picking system in the world, the Value Line timeliness ranking—still has doubts.

These days Eisenstadt is skeptical of the high ratings that the system gives to Internet-related stocks like Yahoo and America Online. AOL was up about sevenfold last year and trades at 270 times trailing earnings. "I wouldn't buy it," Eisenstadt admits. But the Value Line rating system doesn't have any gut instincts, and it doesn't care that a stock's price/earnings ratio is higher than the market's. Rather, the system picks up on AOL's accelerating net income and share price, and the fact that the stock's P/E, however high, is not out of line with its growth rate.

Do you trust the man or his machine? Go with the machine, urges Eisenstadt, "I'm right once in a while. But over time the system will beat me," he says.

Subscribers to the *Value Line Investment Survey*, one of six newsletters on the 1999 Forbes/Hulbert Investment Letter Honor Roll, know Eisenstadt's work. Since 1980 Value Line's suggested portfolio has gained an average of 17.9% per year after trading costs, compared with 16.4% for the Wilshire 5000 index, according to the *Hulbert Financial Digest*. We don't have an independent evaluation of the *Value Line* system prior to 1980, but *Value Line* says that someone who hypothetically owned just the top-rated stocks for 32 years to 1997 would have made 20.8% annually before allowing for trading costs.

Eisenstadt, the son of an immigrant Brooklyn cabinetmaker, had little in his background to recommend a financial career. His only formal training was a statistics program at the City University of New York, where he earned a degree in 1943. After Army service as an artilleryman in France in World War II, he returned home and found a $2,000-a-year part-time job as a proofreader for *Value Line*.

Value Line's founder, Arnold Bernhard, had been searching for a scientific approach to picking stocks. With Eisenstadt's help, Bernhard tried, with only some success, to come up with formulas to explain the price movements of individual stocks. In 1965 Eisenstadt proposed a different approach: Compare stocks to each other, in an effort to predict which ones are most likely to outperform over the next 6 to 12 months. It was a breakthrough.

While the exact formulas are a secret, *Value Line* has told its subscribers a lot about what factors will put a stock high on the timeliness scale. The Eisenstadt formula relies heavily on momentum. The theory is that companies whose earnings and stock prices have risen the most lately will continue to do best for a while longer. Accelerating earnings gains and volatility also figure in, as do positive earnings surprises (reported earnings above analyst expectations).

Momentum is an old game on Wall Street, but Eisenstadt is rare if not unique in reducing the approach to a rigid formula. "Our objective was to squeeze as much science into investing as we could, even if it's a small advantage," recalls Eisenstadt.

That small advantage compounds over time, and it has helped puncture the theories of a generation of "random walk" fans who said that the stock market is too efficient to be beaten. The small statisical advantage also translates into a large advantage for *Value Line* in selling its data-packed weekly stock reports. *Value Line* gets $570 a year for its service, which covers 1,700 companies.

The statistical advantage has not translated into any great wealth for Eisenstadt, who owns no shares in the company he helped build and was paid a modest $215,000 last year. (He lives with his wife in a condo in Little Neck, N.Y.) But the statistics have made a lot of money for *Value Line's* subscribers over the years, and they made Bernhard wealthy.

At his death in 1987, control of the company passed to his daughter, Jean Bernhard Buttner. She holds a stake now worth $320 million.

SOURCE: John Gorham, "The Momentum Formula," *Forbes*, January 25, 1999, p. 114. Reprinted by permission of FORBES Magazine © Forbes Inc., 1999.

SOME CONCLUSIONS ABOUT MARKET EFFICIENCY

Given all of the evidence about market efficiency discussed previously—the studies supporting it as well as the anomalies evidence—what conclusions can be drawn? In truth, no definitive conclusion about market efficiency can be stated. The evidence in support of market efficiency is persuasive because of the large amount of research done over many years by numerous investigators. However, many technicians and fundamentalists are convinced that they can outperform the market, or at least provide more benefits than cost. Paradoxically, this belief helps to make the market efficient.

Box 12-2 is an interesting discussion of market efficiency as it relates to British markets and mutual funds, bringing together many of the points discussed in this chapter. The points made in this article apply equally well to the U.S. markets.

INVESTMENTS INTUITION The paradox of efficient markets and active investors is that investors, in an attempt to uncover and use important information about security prices, help to make the market efficient. In other words, in the course of searching out undervalued and overvalued stocks, investors discover information and act on it as quickly as possible. If the information is favorable, the discoverers will buy immediately, and if unfavorable, they will sell immediately. As investors scramble for information and attempt to be the first to act, they make the market more efficient. If enough of this activity occurs, all information will be reflected in prices. Thus, the fact that a number of investors do not believe in the EMH results in actions that help to make the market efficient.

The evidence on anomalies has yet to be explained satisfactorily. The earnings surprise evidence is particularly strong, and this technique is widely used. However, Eugene Fama, a long-time proponent of market efficiency, argues that the evidence on anomalies does not refute the EM proposition.[41] He believes that many of the studies showing anomalies contain statistical problems. He also believes that overreaction and underreaction are about equally likely to be found, which suggests that markets are efficient because this behavior can be attributable to chance. For example, the post-announcement earnings drift observed in the SUE studies and similar work suggest underreaction to information. The poor performance of IPOs over five years is evidence of overreaction.

Interestingly, even Fama, in making these arguments, recognizes the validity of the work that has been done documenting the post-announcement drift that occurs following quarterly earnings announcements. The SUE results, and similar analyses showing a delayed reaction to earnings announcements, have never been satisfactorily refuted and stand today as a documented anomaly. Thus, while Fama may be right in general, exceptions do seem to exist. And others, such as Dreman, continue to make a strong case for other anomalies such as low P/E ratio stocks.

In the final analysis, it is probably best to accept the idea that the market is quite efficient, but not totally. Most of the research done to date suggests that information is received and acted on quickly, and generally the correct adjustments are made. To outperform the market, fundamental analysis beyond the norm must be done. The fundamental analysis that is routinely done every day is already reflected in stock prices. The marginal value of one more investor performing the same calculations that have been done by other investors is

[41] See Eugene Fama, "Market Efficiency, Long-Term Returns, and Behavioral Finance," *Journal of Financial Economics* (September, 1998).

Box 12-2

FISHING FOR INEFFICIENCIES

"You can't justify fund managers unless they outperform the market," declares Jim Cox. And Mr. Cox knows how heavy that burden of proof can feel. He manages £2.5 billion of mutual-fund assets for Schroders, a British investment bank and has underperformed his benchmark by 16% over the past year. "It feels horrible," he admits. Then again, investors who bought Mr. Cox's British-equity fund in 1988, when it was launched, suffer no such pangs. Their investment—*annus horribilis* notwithstanding—is today worth 24% more than it would be had they simply invested in the wider British stockmarket through the FTSE index instead. With colleagues like Mr. Cox, "active" fund managers should find it easy enough to justify their existence.

Indeed, a look through the personal-finance press in most countries suggests that investing is all about which fund manager to choose, not *whether* to choose one. In America hacks fill page after page with glitzy profiles of the year's shooting, and fallen, stars. But the silly hype obscures a more fundamental debate: why do fund managers exist at all?

Investors have long had their doubts. For over a decade, while the bull market was in full swing, more and more have been deciding that active managers are not worth the money, opting instead for lower-cost, unmanaged, index funds that blindly track a market average. Fund managers were reduced to warning investors about the dangers of a downturn, when they would learn the hard way the risks of not putting their money in the hands of professionals.

Last August, when world stockmarkets turned down, should therefore have been the money-managers' moment of glory. It was not to be. For many active managers it was a bloodletting. The months that have followed have done little to assuage the cynics' doubts about the profession.

Those investors most disillusioned this year had probably fallen victim to the most pernicious myth of investment folklore: that professionals have crystal balls, telling them to switch into, say, cash just before a stockmarket dip. They don't, of course. Overall opinions on where the markets are heading and what share of a person's wealth should be in cash, bonds and shares are best taken individually and with advice, not by a manager switching into and out of asset classes for anonymous shareholders.

Serious fund-managers, in fact, do not bother with market-timing. Ask Anthony Bolton, a manager in London for Fidelity, the world's largest investment organisation, whether there is currently a bubble in world stockmarkets, and he shrugs: "There might be." So he is in cash? Not at all, he is nearly always fully invested. "I take stock picks not market-timing bets."

But what about stock-picking? Can one assume that some people are better at it than others? Messrs. Bolton and Cox, to name but two, are among those reputed to have such powers (although neither of them basks in, or even endorses, this reputation). Both of them have done dismally this year but brilliantly in the longer term.

Most people implicitly accept that the past is as good a guide to the future as anything else. A whole industry of performance measurers has sprung up to supply tomes of historical track records. Some, such as Morningstar in America, summarize past performance in star ratings, as if managers were restaurants. Funds with a five-star accolade (the best) gleefully smack it on their advertisements.

So much nonsense, according to Peter Jeffreys, who runs S&P Fund Research, a London fund-rating outfit. He has screened 4,800 funds, going back to 1982, to see if past winners repeat their success in the future. The probability of that, he found, comes down to "almost pure random chance." Using three-year rolling-average performance as a measure, he discovered that, of the funds that beat the average for six consecutive years, only just over half did so again the year after. Of the below-averages, just over half continued to underperform.

One quarter where this will evoke no surprise is academia. Ivory-tower types have always insisted that it is futile for anyone to try to beat the market. Barring flows of illegal inside information, all the facts about companies are there for all to see. Share and bond prices therefore adjust only when new information arrives—and it is the nature of news to be unpredictable. Outdoing the market consistently would require not only knowing more than somebody else at some point in time, but more than everybody else all the time.

But even diehard theorists have to concede that company directors trading in shares of their own companies tend to beat the market. Insider trading aside, this suggests that some people may indeed be more plugged in than others—in other words that markets are not perfectly efficient.

All fund managers, by necessity, work on that assumption. "If you don't think you can beat the market, what are you doing in it?", says Robert Shelton, who runs an equity fund for Newton, a British asset-management group. Most active managers believe they can spot pricing anomalies and make money out of them.

But by and large, the likelihood that the market badly misprices Microsoft, Lloyds TSB, British Telecom, or other giants is low. Armies of analysts at the world's top investment banks do nothing but follow large companies, and share prices at the top tend to be up-to-date. For smaller and more obscure companies, on the other hand, markets in their shares may be less efficient. Not surprisingly, it is smaller companies that Messrs. Cox and Bolton consider their most promising hunting grounds—at a price, though, in a year when fashion has favoured large companies (in America as in Britain).

At least in part, this seems to vindicate the existence of fund managers (and the fees they charge). It would clearly be wrong for investors to scour the glossies for the hottest names and hand over their money—they know best the risk they can live with and the asset allocation that goes with it. Nor, perhaps, would they be well-advised to hire expensive managers to run their blue-chip investments. But if they fancy some exotics on top, then it might be worth paying a bit extra for talent.

SOURCE: "Fishing for Inefficiencies," *The Economist*, December 12, 1998, pp. 74–75.

zero. Until more evidence to the contrary is forthcoming, technical analysis remains questionable at best.

Simon Keane has argued that investors must choose between a belief in operational efficiency and operational inefficiency.[42] In an operationally efficient market, some investors with the skill to detect a divergence between price and semistrong value earn economic rents. For the majority of investors, however, such opportunities are not available. An operationally inefficient market, on the other hand, contains inefficiencies that the average investor can spot. The evidence to date suggests that investors face an operationally efficient market.[43]

Some anomalies do seem to exist, and since the late 1970s the flow of research reporting on anomalies has accelerated. These anomalies require considerable work to document scientifically and do not represent a guarantee of investment riches. However, these anomalies appear to offer opportunities to astute investors. The reasons why these anomalies exist remain unsettled. The quantity and quality of the research in this area has undermined the extreme view that the market is so perfectly efficient that no opportunities for excess returns could possibly exist.

One difficult problem for those who believe in efficient markets is the crash of October 1987. The S&P 500 Index lost over 20 percent in one day. Is it really reasonable to argue that investors, efficiently discounting information, decided in one day that the market should be valued some 20 percent less? Not many people, including efficient market proponents, are comfortable making this argument.

In addition to the above challenges to the concept of market efficiency, mathematicians are helping a new kind of trader to justify the position that the market is not very efficient, using leading-edge ideas such as chaos theory, neural networks, and genetic algorithms.

The controversy about market efficiency remains. Every investor is still faced with the choice between an active and a passive investment strategy.

[42] See Simon Keane, "The Efficient Market Hypothesis on Trial," *Financial Analysts Journal* (March–April 1986): 58–63. This article presents an excellent discussion of the current debate on efficient markets.

[43] For evidence that the market is not perfectly efficient and therefore offers investors investment opportunities, see Robert F. Vandell and Robert Panino, "A Purposeful Stride Down Wall Street," *The Journal of Portfolio Management* (Winter 1986): 31–39.

SUMMARY

- Investors must consider the implications of efficient markets for investment decisions.
- An efficient market is defined as one in which the prices of securities fully reflect all known information quickly and accurately.
- The conditions that guarantee an efficient market can be shown to hold to a large extent: many investors are competing, information is widely available and generated more or less randomly, and investors react quickly to this information.
- To assess market efficiency, three cumulative forms (or degrees) of efficiency are discussed: the weak form, the semistrong form, and the strong form. The weak form involves market data, whereas the semistrong and strong form involve the assimilation of all public and private information, respectively.
- The weak-form evidence, whether statistical tests or trading rules, strongly supports the hypothesis.
- Many tests of semistrong efficiency have been conducted, including, among others, stock splits, money supply changes, accounting changes, dividend announcements, and reactions to other announcements. Although all the studies do not agree, the majority support semistrong efficiency.
- Strong-form evidence takes the form of tests of the performance of groups presumed to have "private" information and of the ability of professional managers to outperform the market. Insiders apparently are able to do well, although the decisions of the managers of mutual funds have not been found to add value.
- Most knowledgeable observers accept weak-form efficiency, reject strong-form efficiency, and feel that the market is, to a large degree, semistrong efficient. This casts doubt on the value of both technical analysis and conventional fundamental analysis.
- Although the EMH does not preclude investors from outperforming the market, it does suggest that this is quite difficult to accomplish and that the investor must do more than the norm.
- Even if the market is efficient, money managers still have activities to perform, including diversifying the portfolio, choosing and maintaining some degree of risk, and assessing taxes and transaction costs.
- Several major "anomalies" that have appeared over the last several years have yet to be satisfactorily explained. These anomalies, which would not be expected in a totally efficient market, include the following:
    1. Unexpected earnings, as represented by SUE: The market appears to adjust with a lag to the earnings surprises contained in quarterly earnings. SUE has been shown to be a monotonic discriminator of subsequent short-term (e.g., three-month) stock returns.
    2. P/E ratios: Low P/E stocks appear to outperform high P/E stocks over annual periods, even after adjustment for risk and size.
    3. The size effect: Evidence suggests that small firms have outperformed large firms, on a risk-adjusted basis, over a period of many years.
    4. The January effect: Much of the abnormal return for small firms occurs in the month of January, possibly because tax-induced sales in December temporarily depress prices, which then recover in January.
    5. *Value Line*'s performance: The *Value Line* rankings for timeliness have performed extremely well over the period 1965–1986 and appear to offer the average investor a chance to outperform the averages.

KEY WORDS

Abnormal return
Cumulative abnormal return (CAR)
Efficient market (EM)
Efficient market hypothesis (EMH)
Event study
January effect
Market anomalies
Market data
Semistrong form
Size effect
Standardized unexpected earnings (SUE)
Strong form
Weak form

QUESTIONS

12-1. What is meant by an efficient market?

12-2. Describe the three forms of market efficiency.

12-3. What are the conditions for an efficient market? How closely are they met in reality?

12-4. Why is a market that is weak-form efficient in direct opposition to technical analysis?

12-5. What do semistrong market efficiency tests attempt to test for?

12-6. Describe two different ways to test for weak-form efficiency.

12-7. Distinguish between economic significance and statistical significance.

12-8. If the EMH is true, what are the implications for investors?

12-9. Could the performance of mutual fund managers also be a test of semistrong efficiency?

12-10. Describe the money management activities of a portfolio manager who believes that the market is efficient.

12-11. What are market anomalies? Describe four.

12-12. If all investors believe that the market is efficient, could that eventually lead to less efficiency in the market?

12-13. What is the relationship between SUE and fundamental analysis?

12-14. What other types of events or information could be used in semistrong-form tests?

12-15. What are the benefits to society of an efficient market?

12-16. If the market moves in an upward trend over a period of years, would this be inconsistent with weak-form efficiency?

12-17. Do security analysts have a role in an efficient market?

12-18. Evaluate the following statement: "My mutual fund has outperformed the market for the last four years. How can the market be efficient?"

12-19. What are the necessary conditions for a scientific test of a trading rule?

12-20. Are filter rules related to timing strategies or stock selection strategies? What alternative should a filter rule be compared with?

12-21. Assume that you analyze the activities of specialists on the NYSE and find that they are able to realize consistently above-average rates of return? What form of the EMH are you testing?

12-22. What are some possible explanations for the size anomaly?

12-23. How can data on corporate insiders be used to test both the semistrong and the strong forms of the EMH?

12-24. How can data on the performance of mutual funds be used to test both the semistrong and the strong forms of the EMH?

12-25. Assume that the price of a stock remains constant from time period 0 to time period 1, at which time a significant piece of information about the stock becomes available. Draw a diagram that depicts the situation if (a) the market is semistrong efficient and (b) there is a lag in the adjustment of the price to this information.

12-26. How is the SUE concept related to technical analysis?

12-27. What is meant by an operationally efficient market?

The following question was asked on the 1992 CFA Level I examination:

CFA

12-28. a. **List** and **briefly define** the three forms of the Efficient Market Hypothesis.
b. **Discuss** the role of a portfolio manager in a perfectly efficient market.

The following questions were asked on the 1993 CFA Level I examination:

CFA

12-29. According to the efficient market hypothesis:

a. high-beta stocks are consistently overpriced.
b. low-beta stocks are consistently overpriced.
c. positive alphas on stocks will quickly disappear.
d. negative alpha stocks consistently yield low returns for arbitragers.

CFA

12-30. Assume that a company announces an unexpectedly large cash dividend to its shareholders. In an efficient market *without* information leakage, one might expect:

a. an abnormal price change at the announcement.
b. an abnormal price increase before the announcement.
c. an abnormal price decrease after the announcement.
d. no abnormal price change before or after the announcement.

CFA

12-31. Which *one* of the following would provide evidence *against* the semistrong form of the efficient market theory?

a. About 50 percent of pension funds outperform the market in any year.
b. All investors have learned to exploit signals about future performance.
c. Trend analysis is worthless in determining stock prices.
d. Low P/E stocks tend to have positive abnormal returns over the long-run.

The following question was asked on the 1992 CFA Level I examination:

CFA

12-32. The weak form of the efficient market hypothesis contradicts:

a. technical analysis, but supports fundamental analysis as valid.
b. fundamental analysis, but supports technical analysis as valid.
c. both fundamental and technical analysis.
d. technical analysis, but is silent on the possibility of successful fundamental analysis.

PROBLEM

CFA

12-1. Calculate the SUE for a stock with actual quarterly earnings of $0.50 per share and expected quarterly earnings of $0.30 per share. The standard error of estimate is 0.05. Is this a good buy?

SELECTED REFERENCES

An interesting discussion entitled "Are Stock Prices Predictable" forms Chapter 1 of Peter Bernstein's book entitled *Capital Ideas.*

Bernstein, Peter L. *Capital Ideas.* The Free Press (New York: 1992).

An alternative explanation of market anomalies can be found in:

Arbel, Avner. "Generic Stocks: The Key to Market Anomalies." *The Journal of Portfolio Management* (Summer 1985): 4–13.

One of the best articles available on efficient markets is:

Keane, Simon. "The Efficient Market Hypothesis on Trial." *Financial Analysts Journal* (March–April 1986): 58–63.

www.wiley.com/college/jones7

This chapter looks at how well market prices reflect relevant information. The web exercises will ask you to evaluate different trading strategies with a view to getting a more informed opinion on the informational efficiency of financial markets.

chapter 13

ECONOMY/MARKET ANALYSIS

Chapter 13 analyzes the market and the economy because of their importance in impacting stock returns. A key issue here is the relationship between the economy and the stock market since they do not move in lockstep.

After reading this chapter you will be able to:

- **Understand the relationship between the stock market and the economy.**
- **Analyze conceptually the determinants of the stock market.**
- **Make some basic forecasts of possible changes in the level of the market.**

As discussed in Chapter 11, our study of fundamental security analysis uses the "top-down approach," which analyzes the economy-stock market first, then industries, and finally individual companies. This chapter considers the first step, economy/market analysis.

Ultimately, investors must make intelligent judgments about the current state of the financial markets as well as changes that have a high probability of occurring in the future. Is the stock market at unusually high or low levels, and what is it likely to do in the next three months or year or five years?

A logical starting point in assessing the stock market is to analyze the economic factors that affect stock prices. Understanding the current and future state of the economy is the first step in understanding what is happening and what is likely to happen to the market.

Based on a knowledge of the economy-market relationship, we apply valuation concepts to the market using the same models we used in Chapter 10 to value individual securities. In this chapter we also consider how to make forecasts of changes in the stock market. Although *investors cannot possibly hope to be consistently correct in their forecasts of the stock market,* they can expect to make some intelligent inferences about major trends in the market. Because of the market's impact on investor success, investors should seriously consider the market's likely direction over some future period.

THE ECONOMY AND THE STOCK MARKET

The stock market is, of course, a significant and vital part of the overall economy. Clearly, a strong relationship exists between the two. If the economy is doing badly, most companies will also be performing poorly, as will the stock market. Conversely, if the economy is prospering, most companies will also be doing well, and the stock market will reflect this economic strength.

Business Cycle The recurring patterns of expansion, boom, contraction, and recession in the economy

For discussion purposes, think of the economy in terms of the **business cycle.** Investors are very concerned about whether the economy is experiencing an expansion or a contraction because stock prices will clearly be affected. This recurring pattern of expansion and contraction is referred to as the business cycle.

THE BUSINESS CYCLE

The business cycle reflects movements in economic activity as a whole, which is comprised of many diverse parts. The diversity of the parts ensures that business cycles are virtually unique, with no two parts identical. However, cycles do have a common framework, with a beginning (a trough), a peak, and an ending (a trough). Thus, economic activity starts in depressed conditions, builds up in the expansionary phase, and ends in a downturn, only to start again (perhaps because of government stimulus).

The typical business cycle in the United States seems to consist of an expansion averaging about 29 months if measured from 1854 through 1945, but almost 50 months if measured since the end of World War II. Contractions since the war average slightly less than one year. Obviously, however, these are only averages, and we cannot rely on them exclusively to interpret current or future situations. For example, the longest expansion on record covered 106 months from February 1961 through December 1969 (growth was prolonged by defense spending during the Vietnam War), and the March 1991 expansion became the longest peacetime expansion in August 1999 at 102 months (and still going). Business cycles cannot be neatly categorized as to length and turning points at the time they are occurring; only in hindsight can such nice distinctions be made.

To make good use of business cycle data, an investor needs to monitor indicators of the economy. A good source of help in this regard is the National Bureau of Economic Research (NBER), a private nonprofit organization, the official arbiter of economic turning points.

The NBER dates the business cycle when possible. The duration of the contraction and expansion is measured in addition to other pertinent data. In their examination process, the NBER attempts to identify those components of economic activity that move at different times from each other. Such variables can serve as indicators of the economy in general.

Composite Indexes of General Economic Activity Leading, coincident, and lagging indicators of economic activity

Current practice is to identify leading, coincident, and lagging **composite indexes of general economic activity.**[1] The NBER currently focuses on 10 leading indicators as representing the best combination of desirable characteristics.[2] An increase in the composite index of 10 leading economic indicators generally relates positively to an expansion over the following three to 12 months, while a decrease in this composite indicates the likelihood of an immediate downturn. The coincident and lagging indicators serve to confirm (or negate) the indications of the leading series. If the leading index signal is not confirmed first by the coincident index and then by the lagging index, investors should reconsider the signal.[3]

How useful is the index of leading indicators? Many feel it is not too accurate in the economy of the 1990s, having given a number of incorrect signals. This is perhaps due to the changing nature of a dynamic economy such as the U.S. economy. The leading indicators were developed in the 1960s, before the move to a global economy, downsizing, the large use of temporary employees, and the emphasis on technology. However, they are revised periodically in an attempt to be better attuned to the current and future state of the economy.

The Stock Market and the Business Cycle The relationship between the economy and the stock market is interesting—stock prices generally lead the economy. Historically, it is the most sensitive indicator of the business cycle. Therefore, we must deal with a complex relationship. The market and the economy are closely related, but stock prices tend to almost always turn before the economy.

EXAMPLE 13-1

This business cycle–stock-price relationship is illustrated by the 1982–1983 expansion and stock market boom. The recession worsened in late 1982, but the stock market soared, whereas in early 1983, when the economy showed signs of recovery, stock prices wavered for a time.

The 1982–1983 action was consistent with the previous 10 major business slumps since 1929. Measuring the Dow Jones Industrial Average from the low point in a slump to the point when the economy started to recover, the index rose an average of 27.8 percent. In the following 12 months, it rose an average of only 17 percent. In only three cases of the 10 did the index rise faster after business turned up than before.

[1] This information can be found in the *Survey of Current Business,* including the median lead or lag for each series in relation to the business cycle and several characteristics of each series.

[2] The November 1996 index reflected a change, with two of the previous components dropped, and a yield curve measuring the spread between the rate on 10-year Treasury notes and the federal funds rate added.

[3] The Bureau of Economic Analysis now publishes a "composite index of four roughly coincident indicators" to condense the information from the most important monthly indicators into a summary measure.

INVESTMENTS INTUITION Why is the market a leading indicator of the economy? Basically, investors are discounting future earnings, because, as the valuation analysis in Chapter 10 showed, stocks are worth today the discounted value of all future cash flows. Current stock prices reflect investor expectations of the future. Stock prices adjust quickly if investor expectations of corporate profits change. Of course, the market can misjudge corporate profits, resulting in a false signal about future movements in the economy.

An alternative explanation for stock prices leading the economy involves an investor change in the required rate of return, which again would result in an immediate change in stock prices. Note that the valuation model allows for a change in confidence (psychological elements) because a change in investor confidence changes the required rate of return (in the opposite direction). Psychological elements are sometimes used in explaining market movements.

How reliable is this relationship between the stock market and the business cycle? It is widely known that the market has given false signals about future economic activity, particularly with regard to recessions, and it is important to note that the market has registered an increased number of false alarms. However, the ability of the market to predict recoveries is much better than its ability with recessions.[4]

Has the Business Cycle Been Tamed? As of August 1999, the economy had been expanding for 102 months, and the bull market that began in the fall of 1990 had become the longest running bull market on record (the previous record was 1921–1929). Some observers were asking if the business cycle is dead. This is based in part on the belief by some that slumps are not inevitable but rather are caused by accidents that happen. Also, as one CEO noted, "We are in a global economy . . ." which "has changed the paradigm. . . . We don't see the cyclical events that characterized the past."[5]

The other side of the coin is that as the expansion continues, people tend to forget the lessons learned from prior recessions. As one researcher on business cycles noted, "Who can eliminate herding?," referring to the tendency of people getting collectively carried away. Expansions typically end for one of the following reasons: an overheating economy with rising inflation, forcing the Fed to raise interest rates; an external shock, such as a sharp rise in oil prices; or a financial crash following a break in a speculative **bubble** (when speculation pushes asset prices to unsustainable highs). For example, the Japanese economic expansion burst following a break in the speculative bubble that drove stock prices and land values to record levels.

Bubble When speculation pushes asset prices to unsustainable highs

It is easy for investors to forget that markets do decline, sometime sharply. Obviously, the Great Depression was a period of enormous declines, with the Dow Jones Average declining almost 90 percent in less than three years. The worst bear (down) market since the Great Depression occurred in 1973–1974, when the Dow lost 45 percent of its value in 21 months.

THE RELATIONSHIP BETWEEN THE BOND MARKET AND THE STOCK MARKET

Investors today hear much talk about the relationship between bond prices and stock prices. What is the relationship, if any, and how does it affect stock investors?[6]

[4] Jeremy J. Siegel, "Does It Pay Stock Investors to Forecast the Business Cycle," *Journal of Portfolio Management* (Fall 1991).

[5] This quote and discussion is based on Jacob M. Schlesinger, "The Business Cycle Is Tamed, Many Say, Alarming Some Others," *The Wall Street Journal*, November 15, 1996, p. A1 and p. A16.

[6] This discussion is indebted to Laszlo Birinyi Jr., "Coping with Volatility," *Forbes*, August 12, 1996, p. 164.

Despite some claims to the contrary, historically bond investors and stock investors paid little attention to each other. However, the nature of the bond market has changed dramatically over time with the introduction of mortgage-backed securities and derivative securities of various types, the explosion of the federal debt in the 1980s, and the sharp swings in the inflation rate since the 1970s. Volatility has become pronounced in the bond market.

Today, investors pay attention to the bond market because interest rates are available daily as an indicator of what is happening in the economy. Unlike stock data, which is available only quarterly, monthly, and weekly, the bond market can provide daily signals of what bond traders and investors think about the economy. Bond traders react to news of unemployment, or rising sales, or changes in the money supply, thereby affecting interest rates and bond prices on a daily basis.

Thus, rightly or wrongly, in today's world bond investors react to daily information about the economy, and the stock market, in turn, is affected.

MACROECONOMIC FORECASTS OF THE ECONOMY—ARE THEY ANY GOOD?

Good economic forecasts are of obvious significant value to investors. Since the economy and the market are closely related, good forecasts of macroeconomic variables would be very useful. How good are such forecasts, which are widely available?

According to McNees, macroeconomic forecasts have been more accurate in recent years than in the 1970s.[7] However, this tendency toward improvement may not continue, and, in any case, there is much room for improvement. Although the well-known forecasters tend to outperform statistical rules of thumb for macro variables, the margin of superiority is small.

McNees concludes that the forecasts of the prominent forecasters are very similar and that differences in accuracy are very small, suggesting that investors can use any of a number of such forecasts. Obviously, not all forecasters are equally accurate. The only good news is that forecast accuracy has increased.

As an illustration of the difficulty in forecasting economic activity, consider monetary activity. Because of its vital role in the economy, monetary policy was traditionally assumed to have an important effect on the economy, stock prices, and interest rate.

Does money forecast economic activity? Traditionally, most economists have believed that the quantity of money was useful in forecasting changes in national output.[8] Almost all theories of the macroeconomy postulate a relationship between money and future economic activity, with the relationship depending on whether changes in money stock can be attributed to shifts in money supply or money demand. For example, increases in money supply tend to increase economic activity, whereas increases in money demand tend to reduce economic activity.

Some recent research indicates that money remains a useful indicator of future economic activity. According to this research, when the period from the fourth quarter of 1979 through the fourth quarter of 1982 is omitted from the analysis, money still has usefulness in forecasting economic activity. This three-year period represented a change in operating procedures for the Federal Reserve, and after the Reserve abandoned this procedure in 1982 the relationship between money and economic activity was reestablished. Thus, according to this

[7] This discussion is based on Stephen J. McNees, "How Accurate Are Macroeconomic Forecasts?" *New England Economic Review* (July–August 1988).

[8] This discussion is based on Sean Beckett and Charles Morris, "Does Money Still Forecast Economic Activity?" *Economic Review* (Fourth Quarter 1992), pp. 65–77.

research, after excluding this period, "money's ability to forecast economic activity is undiminished."[9]

Furthermore, even more recent research indicates that an alternative measure of money called MZM has, over the last 20 years, exhibited a stable relationship with nominal GDP.[10] MZM is defined as M2, a well-known measure of money, plus savings deposits (including MMDAs), small time deposits, and retail money market mutual funds. This measure appears to be immune to the innovations in the mutual fund industry that caused M2, widely used to assess the relationship between money and economic activity, to lose its usefulness as an indicator.

When the Chairman Speaks Regardless of money's current role in forecasting economic activity, many investors keep an eye on the actions of the Federal Reserve because of its role in monetary policy and its impact on interest rates. When the chairman, Alan Greenspan, testifies before Congress or otherwise makes a public statement, the financial markets scrutinize every word for clues as to the future of the economy and financial markets.

Some evidence on the importance of Fed actions does exist. "The two tumbles and a jump" signal, formulated by Norman Fosback of the Institute for Econometric Research, holds that two cuts in either the discount rate, the banking reserve requirement or the margin requirement, following an increase, results in a market gain. This occurs quickly, within 20 days. Fosback states that within six months the average S&P gain is about 16 percent, and within one year, about 30 percent. He has found the signal correct in the sense of positive returns in 18 of 19 calls.

USING THE INTERNET Investors can access information about the economy from numerous sources. A detailed listing of busines cycle contraction and expansion dates can be found at www.nber.org. Go to www.smartmoney.com to find a set of nine important economic indicators, including data on sales, earnings, exports, prices, and jobs. Monthly statistics on the leading indicators as well as other indicators can be found at www.yardeni.com. The Federal Reserve Banks have numerous details on various aspects of economic activity and all of them can be accessed through any of the regional banks, such as www.frb.clev.org. A daily commentary on economic activity can be found in the "Research," "Economics," part of Lehman's website at www.lehman.com.

UNDERSTANDING THE STOCK MARKET

WHAT DO WE MEAN BY THE "MARKET"?

How often have you heard someone ask, "How did the market do today?" or "How did the market react to that announcement?" Virtually everyone investing in stocks wants a general idea of how the overall market for equity securities is performing, both to guide their actions and to act as a benchmark against which to judge the performance of their securities. Fur-

[9] Research by Friedman and Kuttner challenge the usefulness of money as an economic indicator. They find that money lost the ability to forecast economic activity after the 1970s. It is reasonable to argue that deregulation of the financial economy, along with financial innovation, created considerable havoc on the relationship between measures of money and the economy (as well as interest rates). Thus, their evidence suggests money is not a useful tool for policymakers to use when making decisions about future economic activity.

[10] See John B. Carlson and Benjamin D. Keen, "MZM: A Monetary Aggregate for the 1990s?" *Economic Review*, Federal Reserve Bank of Cleveland, 1996 Quarter 2, pp. 15–23.

thermore, several specific uses of market measures can be identified, as discussed in the next section.

When most investors refer to the "market," they mean the stock market in general as proxied by some market index or indicator as discussed in Chapter 4. Because the "market" is simply the aggregate of all security prices, it is most conveniently measured by some index or average of stock prices.

As we know from Chapter 4, most market indexes are designed to measure a particular market segment, such as blue-chip NYSE stocks (the Dow Jones Industrial Average), all stocks on the NYSE, over-the-counter stocks, and foreign stocks. When discussing the market, it is possible to use a broad market index, such as the Wilshire 5000 Index. Typically, however, most investors today, when they refer to the market, use as their indicator of the market either the Dow Jones Industrial Average (reported daily in *The Wall Street Journal* and on the nightly television news) or the Standard and Poor's 500 Composite Index (favored by most institutional investors and money managers). Therefore, when we discuss the market, we are referring to the market as measured by one of these two market indexes.

Uses of Market Measures Market measures tell investors how all stocks in general are doing at any time or give them a "feel" for the market. Many investors are encouraged to invest if stocks are moving upward, whereas downward trends may encourage some to liquidate their holdings and invest in money market assets or funds.

The historical records of market measures are useful for gauging where the market is in a particular cycle and possibly for shedding light on what will happen. Assume, for example, that the market has never fallen more than X percent, as measured by some index, in a six-month period. Although this information is no guarantee that such a decline will not occur, this type of knowledge aids investors in evaluating their potential downside risk over some period of time.

Market measures are useful to investors in quickly judging their overall portfolio performance. Because stocks tend to move up or down together, the rising or falling of the market will generally indicate to the investor how he or she is likely to do. Of course, to determine the exact performance, each investor's portfolio must be measured individually, a topic to be discussed in Chapter 22.

Technical analysts need to know the historical record of the market when they are seeking out patterns from the past that may repeat in the future. Detection of such patterns is the basis for forecasting the future direction of the market using technical analysis, which is discussed in Chapter 16.

Market indexes are also used to calculate betas, an important measure of risk discussed in earlier chapters. An individual security's returns are regressed on the market's returns in order to estimate the security's beta, or relative measure of systematic risk.

THE DETERMINANTS OF STOCK PRICES

How are stock prices determined? In Chapter 10, we established the determinants of stock prices using the dividend discount model—dividends and the required rate of return—and using the P/E ratio model—earnings and the P/E ratio. Although these are the ultimate determinants of stock prices, a more complete model of economic variables is desirable when we are attempting to understand the stock market. Such a model is shown in Figure 13-1, which is a flow diagram of stock-price determination described by a Federal Reserve economist several years ago. It indicates the variables that interact to determine stock prices. Although presented over 30 years ago, this classic model remains an accurate description of the conceptual nature of stock-price determination then, now, and for the future.

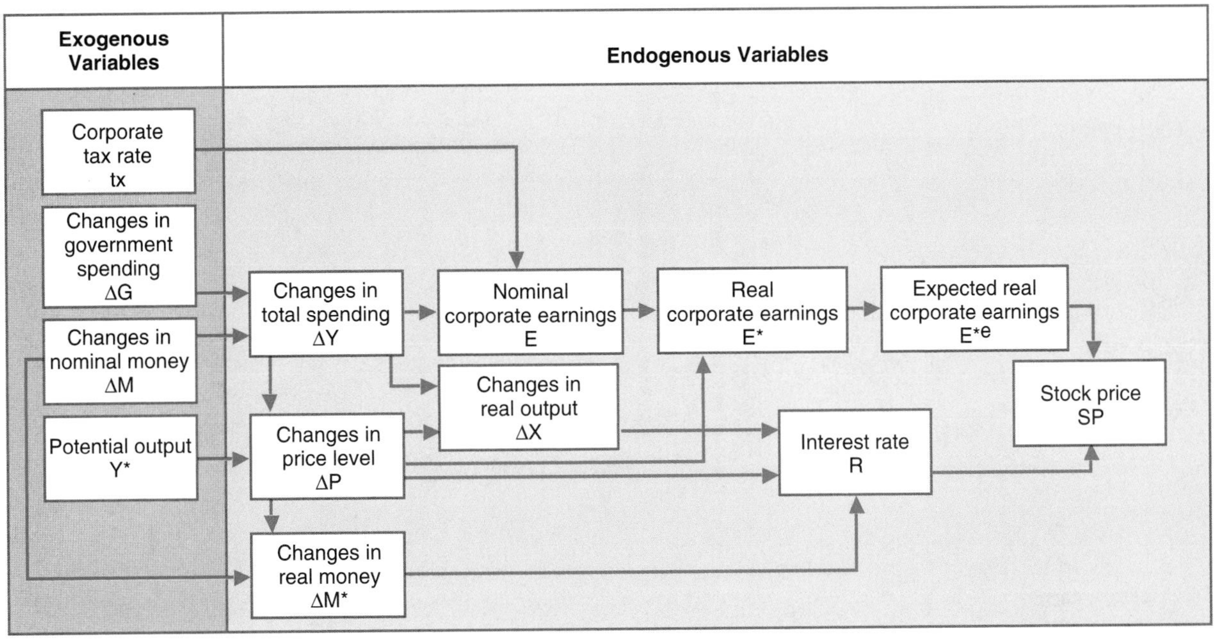

FIGURE 13-1

A flow diagram of stock price determination.

SOURCE: Michael W. Keran, "Expectations, Money and the Stock Market," *Review*, Federal Reserve Bank of St. Louis, January, 1971, p. 27.

Figure 13-1 shows four exogenous (independent) variables that ultimately affect stock prices: the potential output of the economy (Y*), which is a nonpolicy variable, and three policy variables (i.e., variables subject to government policy decisions)—the corporate tax rate (tx), changes in government spending or fiscal policy (G), and changes in nominal money (M). All variables to the right of the gray area are determined within the economy and are called endogenous variables.

The two primary exogenous policy variables, G and M, affect stock prices through two channels:

1. They affect total spending (Y), which, together with the tax rate (tx), affects corporate earnings.[11] Expected changes in (real) corporate earnings (E*) are positively related to changes in stock prices (SP).
2. They affect total spending, which, together with the economy's potential output (Y*) and past changes in prices, determine current changes in prices (P). Y and P determine current changes in real output (X). Changes in X and P generate expectations about inflation and real growth, which in turn influence the current interest rate (R). *Interest rates, a proxy for the discount rate in a valuation model, have a negative influence on stock prices (SP).*

The Keran model remains a classic description of stock-price determination because it indicates the major factors that determine stock prices. Thus, active policy variables such as:

1. fiscal policy (government spending)
2. monetary policy (money supply)
3. the corporate tax rate

[11] Technically, both the current level and lagged changes in Y affect corporate earnings.

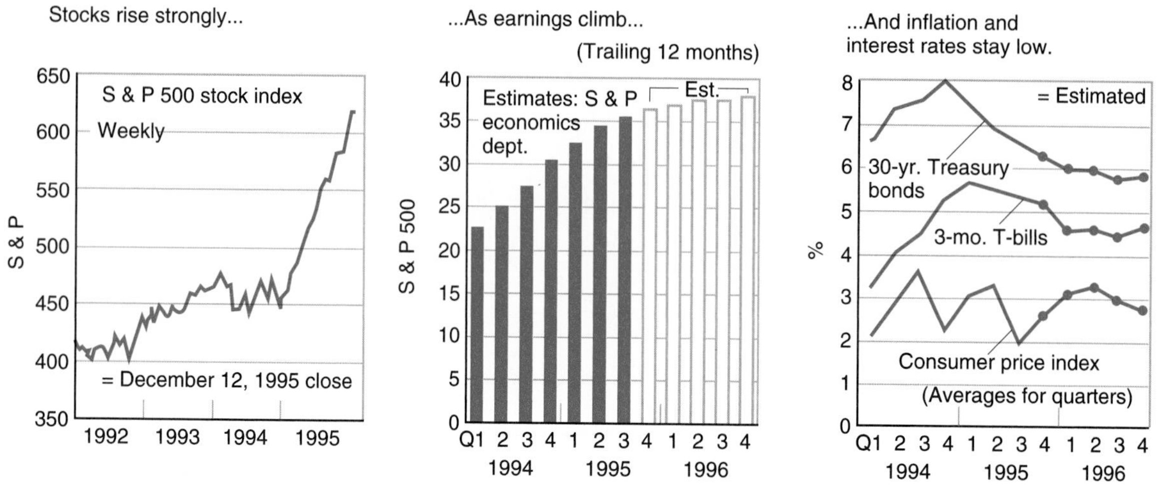

FIGURE 13-2

Stock prices, earnings, and interest rates.

SOURCE: Standard & Poor's Corporation, *The Outlook*, December 20, 1995, p. 3. Reprinted by permission of Standard & Poor's, a division of The Mc-Graw Hill Co.

And the potential output of the economy affect three changes in the economy:

1. total spending
2. price level
3. real money

These three changes ultimately affect:

1. corporate earnings
2. interest rates, which are inversely related to P/E ratios and, in turn, corporate earnings and P/E ratios determine stock prices.

Corporate Earnings, Interest Rates, and Stock Prices As shown in the Keran model in Figure 13-1, the ultimate determinants of stock prices are expected corporate earnings and interest rates (which serve as a proxy for investors' required rate of return). Empirical evidence supports this assertion. For example, Fama found that almost 60 percent of the variance in annual market returns for the period 1953–1987 was explained by changes in industrial production and interest rate factors.[12] Furthermore, while the Keran diagram was formulated many years ago, the modern explanation of stock prices remains the same. Figure 13-2 is taken from *The Outlook,* a publication of Standard & Poor's. It gives the same message—stocks rise strongly as earnings climb and interest rates stay low. In other words, investors must be concerned with earnings and interest rates as they assess the outlook for stocks.

It is logical to expect a relationship between corporate profits and stock prices. The valuation discussion in Chapter 10 showed that the estimated value for one stock or the market as a whole should be a function of the expected cash flows and the required rate of return demanded by investors. Therefore, if the economy is prospering, investors will expect corporate earnings and dividends to rise and, other things being equal, stock prices to rise.

Figure 13-3 shows corporate profits after taxes over the period since 1985. On a broad basis, the general trend for corporate profits in the late 1980s was mixed, and the late 1980s had a mixed performance in terms of total returns, generally good, but with a negative return in 1990. In the 1990s strong earnings performance has been associated, in general, with

[12] See Eugene Fama, "Stock Returns, Expected Returns, and Real Activity," *The Journal of Finance* (September 1990).

FIGURE 13-3

S&P 500 earnings and total returns on the S&P 500, 1985–1998.

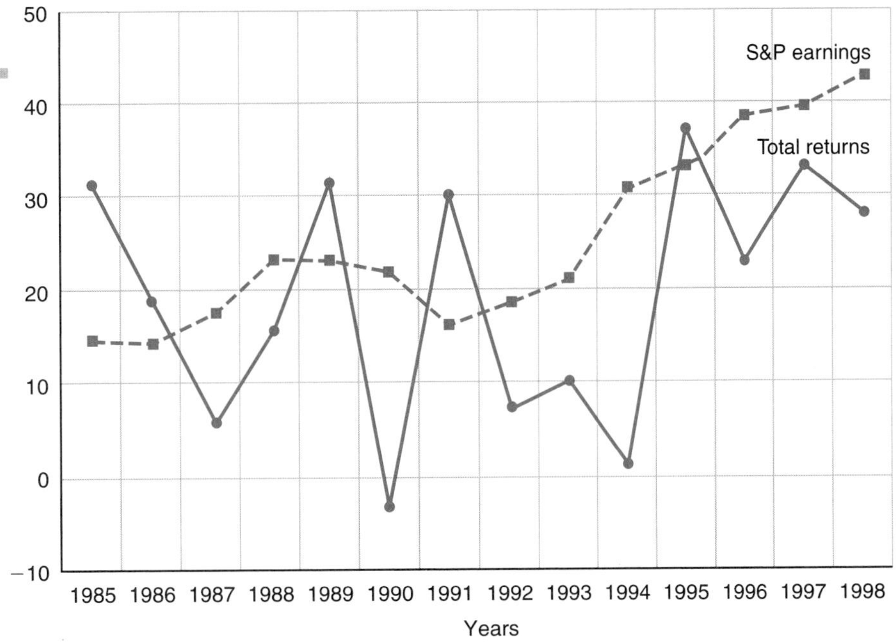

strong market performance. Earnings have gone up since 1991, and in each of the years since 1991 through 1998 the total return on the S&P 500 has been positive.

Interest rates, the other variable determining stock prices as shown in Figure 13-1, are a basic component of discount rates, with the two usually moving together. It is necessary, therefore, to consider the relationship between interest rates and stock prices.

There is clearly a relationship between interest rate movements and stock prices, just as there is with GNP and corporate profits. In this case, however, the relationship is inverse; that is, as interest rates rise (fall), stock prices fall (rise), other things being equal.

Figure 13-4 shows the corporate AAA bond rate and total returns for the S&P 500 Index. In 1989 interest rates declined, and the S&P return was 31.2 percent, while in 1990 interest rates rose, and the S&P return was −3.14 percent. The years 1991, 1992, and 1993 saw declining interest rates and S&P total returns of 30 percent, 7.4 percent, and 9.94 percent, respectively. On the other hand, interest rates rose in 1994, causing severe turmoil in both the stock market (which had a gain of 1.3 percent) and the bond market. Interest rates declined in 1995, a great year for stocks, and again in 1997 and 1998, both very good years for stocks. Note, however, that although interest rates rose in 1996, the S&P had a total return of 22.7 percent. This simply illustrates that these basic relationships do not always go in the expected direction.

Why is there an inverse relationship? Recall from Chapter 10 that the basic fundamental valuation model is given by the following equation (assuming the constant-growth version of the dividend valuation model):

$$P_0 = \frac{D_1}{k - g} \tag{13-1}$$

The k in Equation 13-1 is the required rate of return (discount rate) that investors use in discounting future cash flows. It is the rate of return that investors demand in order to invest in common stocks. This rate can be thought of as the sum of a riskless rate of interest plus a risk premium determined by the riskiness of the stock being valued. Most observers use the rate on Treasury securities as a proxy for the riskless rate of return, because Treasuries

FIGURE 13-4

Corporate AAA interest rates and total returns on the S&P 500, 1985–1998.

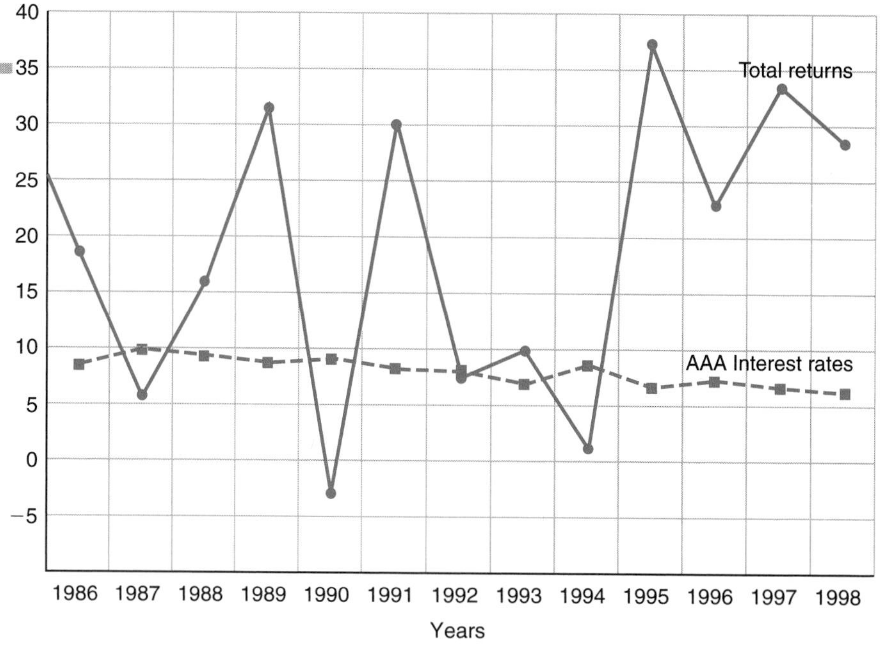

have no practical risk of default. Therefore, the discount rate k is intimately tied to interest rates. That is why the Keran model (or any other model) can use interest rates in discussing stock-price determination.

INVESTMENTS INTUITION

If interest rates rise, the riskless rate of return, RF, rises, because it is tied to interest rates, and other things being equal, the required rate of return (discount rate) rises because the riskless rate is one of its two components.

Alternatively, as we saw in Chapter 10, interest rates and P/E ratios are inversely related. When fixed-income securities are paying less return, investors are willing to pay more for stocks; therefore, P/E ratios are higher. The increase in P/E ratios in years like 1997 and 1998 was the driving factor in higher stock prices, and was attributable mostly to declining interest rates (for example, 30-year Treasury yields fell from 5.93 percent at the end of 1997 to 5.02 percent in December 1998).

Like most relationships involving investing, the relationship between interest rates and stock prices is not perfect. Nor do interest rates have a linear effect on stock prices. One estimate for the 1980s is that a 25 percent decline in interest rates resulted in a 64 percent rise in stock prices, assuming no other changes.[13] This represents a magnification of about 2.5 times of stock prices to interest rates.

Investors need to understand the role of changes in interest rates in affecting investor expectations. Investors pay close attention to announcements by the Federal Reserve that could possibly affect interest rates, as well as to any other factors that may play a role. In turn, the popular press reports possible changes in interest rates as they might affect the stock market.

[13] See John Peavy, "Stock Prices: Do Interest Rates and Earnings Really Matter?" *Financial Analysts Journal* (May–June 1992).

EXAMPLE 13-2

Consider the following headlines from *The Wall Street Journal* within a six-week period:
"Markets Fall on Absence of Rate Cut"
"Recent Rise in Long-Term Interest Rates May Mean Trouble for the Stock Market"
"As Interest Rates Rise, Will Stocks Fall?"
"Benchmark Treasury Yield Tops 8%; Stocks Fall"

VALUING THE MARKET

To value the market using the fundamental analysis approach explained in Chapter 10, we must use the primary variables used in fundamental analysis, as previously explained in Chapter 10—specifically, the expected cash flows (dividends) and the rate of return required by investors or, alternatively, as we will discuss here, a multiplier or P/E ratio. The following estimates are needed:

1. Dividends or earnings
2. The required rate of return or the earnings multiplier

These estimates are used in Equations 13-2, 13-3, and 13-4 and were explained in Chapter 10:

$$P_0 = \frac{D_1}{k - g} \tag{13-2}$$

$$P_0/E_1 = \frac{D_1/E_1}{k - g} \tag{13-3}$$

$$P_0 = P_0/E_1 \times E_1 \tag{13-4}$$

where

D_1 = expected dividends
E_1 = expected earnings
k = discount rate or required rate of return
g = expected growth rate in dividends or earnings

These equations apply equally to the aggregate market or an individual stock. Here we are concerned with an aggregate market index such as the S&P 500 Composite Index. Conceptually, the value of this index is the discounted value of all future cash flows to be paid (i.e., the index value of dividends). Alternatively, it is the estimated earnings on the S&P 500 Index multiplied by the estimated P/E ratio, or multiplier. In summary,

$$\text{Value of S\&P 500 today} = \frac{\text{Dividends to be paid on index next period}}{\text{Required rate of return} - \text{Expected growth rate in dividends}}$$

or

$$\text{Value of S\&P 500} = \text{Estimated earnings on the index} \times \text{Estimated P/E ratio}$$

Our discussion focuses on the multiplier approach.

THE EARNINGS STREAM

Estimating earnings for purposes of valuing the market is not easy. The item of interest is the earnings per share for a market index or, in general, corporate profits after taxes.

Corporate profits are related to GDP, the broadest measure of economic activity, and are derived from corporate sales, which in turn are related to GDP. A detailed, complete fundamental analysis would involve estimating each of these variables, starting with GDP, then corporate sales, working down to corporate earnings before taxes, and finally to corporate earnings after taxes. Each of these steps can involve various levels of difficulty.

USING THE INTERNET Edward Yardeni, chief economist and global investment strategist for Deutsche Bank Services in New York, has a website at www.yardeni.com. The section titled "Earnings Forecasts" has estimates for the S&P 500 from I/B/E/S, Yardeni, and other investment organizations showing forecasts and percentage changes for S&P 500 earnings per share for one and two years ahead (for example, in 1999 estimates were available for 2000 and 2001).

THE MULTIPLIER

The multiplier to be applied to the earnings estimate is as important as the earnings estimate and, sometimes, more so. Investors sometimes mistakenly ignore the multiplier and concentrate only on the earnings estimate. But earnings growth is not always the leading factor in significant price changes in the market. Instead, low interest rates may lead to high P/E ratios, which in turn may account for the majority of the price changes.

EXAMPLE 13-3 The S&P 500 Index increased about 150 percent between the end of 1994 and December 1998. Less than one-third of that increase was attributable to higher earnings, with the remainder attributable to an increase in the P/E ratio. At the end of 1997, the P/E based on current earnings was 21.5. In December 1998, it was 26. Over the period 1994–1998, corporate earnings rose about 40 percent and the P/E ratio doubled, thereby creating the sharp rise in the S&P 500.

The multiplier is more volatile than the earnings component and, therefore, is even more difficult to predict. Consider Figure 13-5, which shows the P/E ratio for the Standard & Poor's 500 Index since 1947. A trend line has been included to show the general upward swing of P/E ratios across time. Also, three different levels of P/Es are identified with the bars, showing that at different times (the 1960s and early 1970s, the late 1970s and early 1980s, and the late 1980s and early 1990s), P/Es tended to cluster together.

The P/E ratio began to rise in the early 1950s, reached a peak by 1960, and declined to the 16–18 area and remained around that level through 1972. As inflation heated up in 1973 and interest rates rose, the multiplier started to decline, and by 1974 it was around 7, less than half its previous level—a drastic cut for such a short time. Therefore, what was considered normal (about 17) in the 1960s and early 1970s was not the norm in the late 1970s and early 1980s. Most investors did not anticipate P/E ratios this low for this length of time.

The lesson from this analysis is obvious: Investors cannot simply extrapolate P/E ratios, because dramatic changes occur over time. Perhaps the most that can be said is that in the postwar period, P/E ratios of broadly based indices have ranged from an average of about 7 to an average of about 17. For the S&P 500 Composite Index, the average P/E for the period 1928–1995 was approximately 14, and for the period 1947–1998 it was 15.

P/E ratios tend to be high when inflation and interest rates are low, such as the period of the mid-to-late 1990s, when P/E ratios were at quite high levels by historical standards.

FIGURE 13-5

S&P 500 price/earnings ratios, 1947–1998.

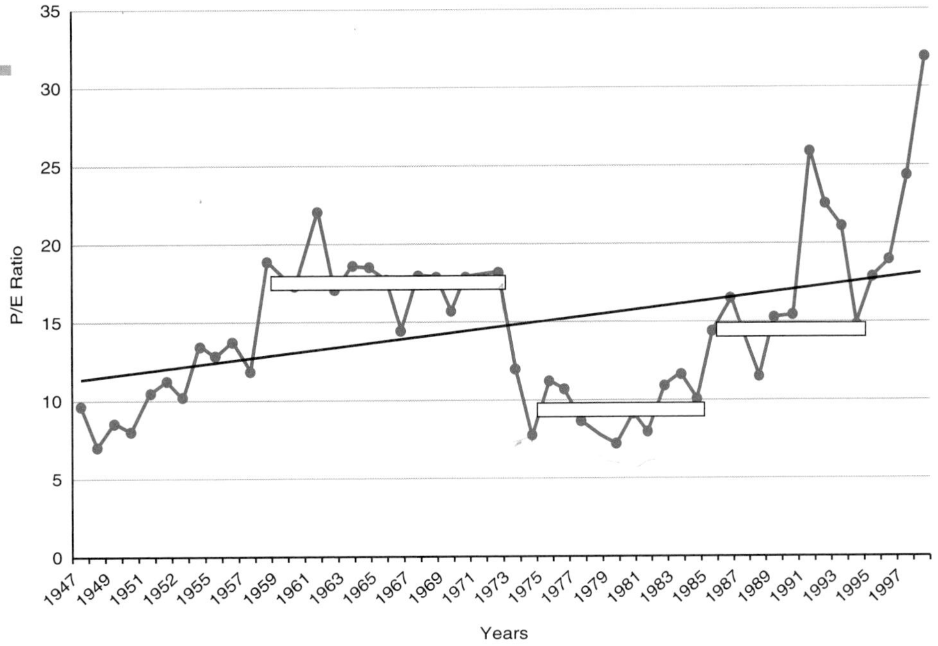

When earnings are growing and the upward profit trend appears sustainable, investors are willing to pay more for today's earnings.

Investors must be careful when using P/E ratios to place them in the proper context. P/E ratios can refer to historical data, an average for the year, or a prospective period such as the year ahead. Obviously, a significant difference can exist between P/E ratios calculated using these different definitions.

PUTTING THE TWO TOGETHER

Valuing the aggregate market is not easy, nor will it ever be, because it involves estimates of the uncertain future. If valuing the aggregate market were relatively easy, many investors would become wealthy by knowing when to buy and sell stocks.

As noted, it is difficult to analyze all the complicated details required to perform fundamental market analysis. A thorough analysis involves studying utilization rates, tax rates, depreciation, GNP, and other factors, as well as applying some sophisticated statistical techniques. It is instructive, however, to analyze some general results of our basic valuation techniques. Regardless of the difficulty in doing market analysis and the extent to which an analyst or investor goes, the methodology outlined above is the basis on which to proceed.

The years 1981 and 1982 offer a good contrast. Stock prices declined in 1981 and rose in 1982, whereas earnings rose in 1981 and declined in 1982. The multipliers must have been moving in the opposite direction. (Interest rates moved in opposite directions in these years.)

The year 1982 offers a good example for market valuation. A very strong bull market began in August 1982, which was widely attributed to a decline in interest rates and to investor belief that this decline would continue. Interest rates are closely related to discount rates (required rates of return). With a decline in the discount rate, other things being equal, the multiplier rose as did stock prices. Although earnings on the S&P declined for the year 1982, they rose sharply in 1983, and the stock market presumably was looking ahead.

The conclusion of this analysis is that to value the market, an investor must analyze both factors that determine value: earnings (or dividends) and multipliers (or required rates of return). More important, the investor must make some type of forecast of these variables in order to forecast the market.

FORECASTING CHANGES IN THE MARKET

Most investors want to forecast changes in financial markets. Not only do they want to know what these markets are doing currently and why, but also where they are likely to go in the future. As part of this process, as discussed earlier, they need to clearly analyze the overall economy.

Accurate forecasts of the stock market, particularly short-term forecasts, are impossible for anyone to do *consistently*. As discussed in Chapter 12, there is strong evidence that the market is efficient; this implies that changes in the market cannot be predicted on the basis of information about previous changes. Another implication is that even professional money managers cannot consistently forecast the market using available information, and the available evidence on the performance success of professional investors supports this proposition. Such implications are supported by a wealth of available data.

EXAMPLE 13-4

As a good example of the difficulties in forecasting the market consider a December 1996 issue of *Business Week* which noted that "Not even the best and brightest on Wall Street predicted that the Dow could move at such an astonishing pace. In fact, coming off 1995's 33.5 percent increase, many strategists began the year believing that the Dow would gain just 5 percent in 1996, well below its historical average of 10 percent or so a year."[14]

What we are seeking here are general clues as to the economy and the market's direction and the duration of a likely change. For example, to say that we are confident the market will go to 13,000 or 6,000 (as measured by the Dow Jones Industrial Average) one year from now is foolish. Similarly, a strong prediction that corporate earnings will rise next year by 10 percent is a virtually certain prescription for embarrassment.

EXAMPLE 13-5

Industry analysts are notoriously optimistic when forecasting market earnings, such as the growth for the S&P 500. In 1998 they forecast earnings growth of about 14 percent, while actual earnings declined about 1 percent. For 1999 they started out forecasting earnings growth of about 19 percent, on average. They then started cutting this number as more data became available.

Some Practical Advice

When investors look for forecasts of expected earnings, they should be very wary of industry analysts' forecasts, because they are almost always overly optimistic. A better source of information are market strategists who advise firms on investment policy. These strategists are not linked to particular companies and industries, and biased by these connections. Their projections for 1998 earnings were much closer to the final results than was true for analysts. Their projections for 1999 earnings (made in early 1999) called for an increase of only 4.6 percent.

[14] See "We're On Uncharted Ground," *Business Week*, December 9, 1996, p. 36.

In truth, most individual investors—indeed, most professional investors—cannot time the market consistently. What, then, should they do? The best approach for most investors is to recognize the futility of consistently timing the market successfully, but also recognize that periodically situations will develop that suggest strong action. An example is 1982 when interest rates reached record peaks. Either rates were going to decline, or the U.S. economy faced a crisis situation. They did decline, and so they launched one of the greatest bull markets in U.S. history.

Box 13-1 is an interesting analysis of why investors may simply choose to stand pat, and even buy, when the market appears to be ready to decline—or many people are claiming that it is. According to the evidence presented, investors lose more by missing a bull market than by dodging a bear market. The most important point, however, is the same as before—the impact of the overall market on an investor's portfolio is enormous.

USING THE BUSINESS CYCLE TO MAKE MARKET FORECASTS

Earlier we established the idea that certain composite indexes can be helpful in forecasting or ascertaining the position of the business cycle. However, stock prices are one of the leading indicators, tending to lead the economy's turning points, both peaks and troughs.

What is the investor who is trying to forecast the market to do? This leading relationship between stock prices and the economy must be taken into account in forecasting likely changes in stock prices. Stock prices generally decline in recessions, and the steeper the recession, the steeper the decline. However, investors need to think about the business cycle's turning points months before they occur in order to have a handle on the turning points in the stock market. If a business cycle downturn appears likely in the future, the market will also be likely to turn down some months ahead of the economic downturn.

We can be somewhat more precise about the leading role of stock prices. Because of this tendency to lead the economy, total return on stocks (on an annual basis) could be negative (positive) in years in which the business cycle peaks (bottoms). Stock prices have almost always risen as the business cycle is approaching a trough. These increases have been large, so that investors do well during these periods. Furthermore, stock prices often remain steady or even decline suddenly as the business cycle enters into the initial phase of recovery. After the previous sharp rise as the bottom is approached, a period of steady prices or even a decline typically occurs. The economy, of course, is still moving ahead.

Based on the above analysis:

1. If the investor can recognize the bottoming out of the economy before it occurs, a market rise can be predicted, at least based on past experience, before the bottom is hit.
2. As the economy recovers, stock prices may level off or even decline. Therefore, a second significant movement in the market may be predictable, again based on past experience.
3. Based on the last 10 economic slumps, the market P/E usually rises just before the end of the slump. It then remains roughly unchanged over the next year.

The importance of analyzing business cycle turning points as an aid to market timing cannot be overemphasized. Investors would have always increased their returns, over the entire sweep of U.S. economic history, by switching into cash before the business cycle peaks and into stocks before the cycle reaches its trough. It is particularly important to switch into stocks before business cycle troughs.

Box 13-1

OVERCOMING THE BEAR MARKET BLUES

For more than three years the stock market steadily marched to higher ground. Then, in February, the Federal Reserve Board, fearful of a return of inflation, began to curb monetary growth and raise interest rates. That set off the stock market's first significant downdraft since the Persian Gulf War started in 1991. Now nervous investors are wondering: Should I stay in stocks, or should I go?

During market declines, emotion tends to overtake reason and large numbers of investors make the biggest mistakes of their investment lives. The overpowering urge is to dump stocks or equity mutual funds and retreat to the safety of money market funds and bank accounts. These urges are understandable. However, investors who act on them often lock in losses and miss profit opportunities when stocks eventually rebound.

Instead of selling during market slumps, history suggests that investors should put their fears aside. If anything, it's a good time for an investor to start bargain hunting, with the intention of making an even bigger commitment to stocks. Riding out a bear market certainly can be painful. But the rewards of moving to safer ground—even when it's done with impeccable timing—are far less dramatic than is generally supposed. What's more, standing pat can be far less damaging to a portfolio than the cost of missing a major upward move in stock prices.

Want proof? Let's consider an imaginary investor with flawless timing skills, one who was able to switch his money from stocks to Treasury bills during each of the market's five worst years from 1940 through 1993. We're assuming this investor exited the market completely and then put 100 percent of his portfolio back into stocks the following year. This strategy, requiring perfect foresight, would certainly have beaten the performance of the Standard & Poor's 500 index. But not by much. For all his brilliance, our investor would have earned a compounded annual return of 13.9 percent, compared with an 11.7 percent return for the S&P 500.

Now let's look at what would have happened to an investor who missed the market's biggest upswings—switching his money out of stocks and into Treasury bills during each of the market's five *best* years. This unfortunate soul would have earned an average annual return of only 8.7 percent.

The lesson: There is more to lose by missing a bull market than there is to be gained by dodging a bear. And the easiest way to capture the profits provided by future bull markets is to remain fully invested in stocks over the long term. "Time cures a lot of things, including volatility," says Carl Gargula, managing director at Ibbotson Associates, a Chicago investment-consulting firm.

Still, the biggest fear investors have now is that if they were to buy stocks, they'd be plunging in at or near the top of the market. What could be worse than buying equities a day or two before the onset of a bear move?

Although it may seem counterintuitive, data show that buying at market tops is not as destructive to a portfolio's health as investors might think. Since 1940, the stock market has declined by 5 percent or more on 45 occasions. Thirteen of those declines exceeded 15 percent, and four exceeded 25 percent. In all, the stock market has spent 28 percent of that time in significant

INVESTING AT MARKET PEAKS

THE RESULTS OF INVESTING $5,000 PER YEAR IN THE S&P 500 INDEX AT THE PEAK OF THE MARKET THAT YEAR

Market Top	Cumulative Investment	Account Value at Year End
1/3/74	$5,000	$3,601
7/15/75	$10,000	$9,756
9/21/76	$15,000	$17,163
1/3/77	$20,000	$20,590
9/12/78	$25,000	$26,544
10/5/79	$30,000	$36,358
11/28/80	$35,000	$53,041
1/6/81	$40,000	$55,127
11/9/82	$45,000	$71,958
10/10/83	$50,000	$92,947
11/6/84	$55,000	$103,692
12/16/85	$60,000	$141,534
12/2/86	$65,000	$172,690
8/25/87	$70,000	$185,361
10/21/88	$75,000	$220,879
10/9/89	$80,000	$295,604
7/16/90	$85,000	$290,959
12/31/91	$90,000	$384,223
12/18/92	$95,000	$418,426
12/28/93	$100,000	$465,397

SOURCE: American Funds Group

retreat. These declines have typically lasted four months, with share prices tumbling an average of 12.5 percent.

Here's where it gets interesting: The folks at the American Funds Group, a mutual fund firm in Los Angeles, recently did a study that illustrates what would have happened had an investor bought at the peak of the market not once, but every year for the last two decades. The table shows what would have happened to an investor's portfolio if $5,000 was invested in the S&P 500 index during each of the last 20 years on the day the market peaked for that year. In other words, each investment lost money almost immediately after it was made as the market fell—the ultimate in a worried investor's nightmare.

The surprise is that after 20 years, this starcrossed investor's portfolio fared pretty darn well. Nobody's wrong all the time, but even our hopelessly unlucky investor would have earned a 13.7 percent compounded annual return. According to American Funds Group, the $100,000 this hypothetical investor would have put into the market over the 20 years would gradually have transformed itself into a portfolio valued at $465,397.

Given the astronomical odds against an investor buying at precisely the wrong moment 20 years in a row, you can bet that your own stock market performance would be even higher than this.

Of course, it's disturbing to see the value of a portfolio drop during a stock market correction. However, since stock market corrections are a fact of life, investors must learn to live with them. Avoid the urge to cut and run. It may seem like the safe thing to do at the time, but the long-term risks of missing an upturn are even more dangerous. Individuals who have the financial resources to do so should use stock market declines as opportunities to add to their portfolios, seeking out high-quality stocks for sale at discount prices. In the end, those who do will be much wealthier for their fortitude.

SOURCE: Gerald Perritt, "Overcoming the Bear Market Blues," *Worth*, July/August 1994, pp. 107–108. Used by permission.

USING KEY VARIABLES TO MAKE MARKET FORECASTS

A number of key market indicators and macro variables have been touted by both individuals and organizations as potential predictors of future movements in the economy and/or the market. Perhaps the best known market indicator is the price/earnings ratio. Over the last 30-plus years the P/E ratio for the S&P 500 Index has typically ranged from roughly 7 to 22. Many market observers are extremely nervous when the P/E reaches levels in the high 20s, as it did in the late 1990s.

A good example of a widely watched indicator of likely market movements is the dividend yield. Many market participants believe that when the dividend yield on the S&P 500 Index declines below 3 percent, the market is in for a downward correction. The logic is that with stock prices high enough to make the dividend yield so low (below 3 percent), investors will abandon equities in favor of higher returns on safe fixed-income securities. The resulting sale of equities will drive down equity prices and drive up the dividend yield, restoring a balance. Dividend yield supposedly has a higher correlation with future S&P 500 changes than any other indicator over the long run.

Dividend yields declined below 3 percent in late 1961 (total return on the S&P 500 was negative in 1962), in late 1965 (negative total return in 1966), in late 1968 (negative return in 1969), all of 1972 and early 1973 (negative returns in 1973 and 1974), and in the summer of 1987 (a large market drop occurred in October 1987).

The problem with key market indicators is deciding when they are signaling a change and how reliable the signal is. We can reasonably assume that the "normal" value of some of these indicators changes over time so that what is regarded as a low or high signal at one point in time does not have the same meaning at some other point in time. Still another problem is how quickly any change signaled by key market indicators and macro variables might occur. In the final analysis, this is an inexact process, subject to considerable interpretations as well as errors.

EXAMPLE 13-6

Consider some of the key indicators and macro variables in recent years. On October 1, 1987, prior to the great one-day crash of October 19, 1987, when the market declined some 22 percent, the P/E ratio was 20 compared to a P/E ratio in October 1992 of roughly 24. The 1992 level would be considered high by historical standards. However, the S&P 500 return for 1992 was 7.67 percent, and for 1993, 9.99 percent. In 1994 the return was only 1.31 percent. How helpful was the level of the P/E ratio during this time in predicting total returns?

A comparison of dividend yields shows that the dividend yield in early October 1987 was below 3 percent, and the market crashed on October 19, 1987. In early October 1992, the dividend yield was only slightly above 3 percent. The yield subsequently moved below 3 percent and flashed a sell signal for two years, even as the market advanced over 2000 points.

By early 1995, the dividend yield had been below 3 percent for well over two years, which is without precedent in market history. Some well-known forecasters expected a sharp market decline. In fall 1998, the Dow Jones Industrial Average broke the 9300 level, an all-time record, and by mid 1999 had hit new highs above 11,300. Meanwhile, the dividend yield was at its all-time low level.

Investors attempting to forecast the economy should pay attention to certain important variables. Interest rates are an obvious variable to watch, and a good bellweather is the Treasury's 30-year maturity bond as reported in *The Wall Street Journal*. The direction of commodity prices, as opposed to levels, is also important. Finally, unit labor costs are considered by many to be an important economic indicator, with anything above 3 percent signaling a potential problem.

Finally, as you consider the state of the market and whether you should invest now, you might ask if any particular month is riskier than others. Some believe that October is, and the historical evidence seems to support this idea: Six of the 10 biggest down days since 1926 have occurred in October. As Mark Twain said, "October is one of the peculiarly dangerous months to speculate in stocks." However, the rest of his quote goes as follows: "The others are: July, January, September, April, November, May, March, June, December, August, and February."

USING VALUATION MODELS TO MAKE MARKET FORECASTS

Based on the valuation models developed earlier, it is necessary to use one of two approaches.

1. Use D_1, k, and g, based on Equation 13-1, $P_0 = D_1/(k - g)$.
2. Use E_1 and P/E, based on Equation 13-2, $P_0 = (E_1)P_0/E_1$.

If we are to attempt some forecasts of the stock market, we must form some judgments about likely changes in these variables. As an example of trying to make some forecasts of the market, consider Figure 13-6, which shows *Value Line*'s Industrial Composite (IC) of about 740 industrial, retail, and transportation companies, accounting for about 75 percent of all income earned by nonfinancial corporations in the United States. Per-share figures are based on the total number of shares outstanding for all the companies in the composite. The data shown in Figure 13-6 include actual and forecasted earnings per share (EPS), dividends per share (DPS), growth rates for these and other variables, and several balance sheet and income statement items.

First, we can analyze two of the figures given at the top of Figure 13-6 as of January

FIGURE 13-6

***Value Line*'s Industrial Composite of industrial, retail and transportation companies.**

SOURCE: *The Value Line Investment Survey*, "Selection and Opinion," January 22, 1999, p. 5773. Copyright 1999 by Value Line Publishing Inc. Used by permission.

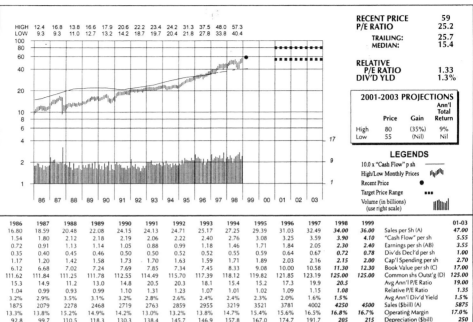

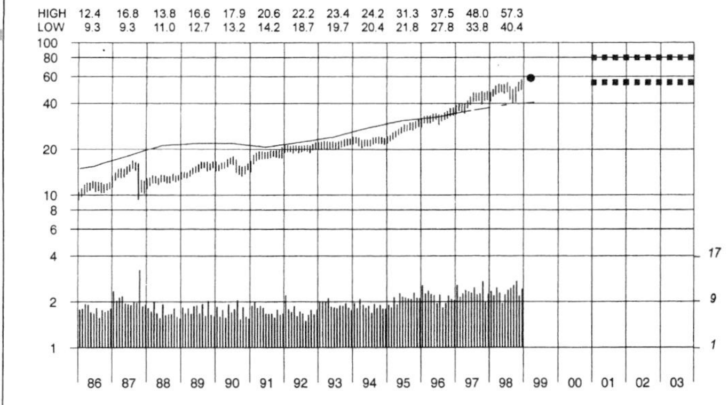

RECENT PRICE 59
P/E RATIO 25.2
TRAILING: 25.7
MEDIAN: 15.4

RELATIVE P/E RATIO 1.33
DIV'D YLD 1.3%

2001-2003 PROJECTIONS

	Price	Gain	Ann'l Total Return
High	80	(35%)	9%
Low	55	(Nil)	Nil

LEGENDS

10.0 x "Cash Flow" p sh
High/Low Monthly Prices
Recent Price
Target Price Range
Volume (in billions) (use right scale)

1986	1987	1988	1989	1990	1991	1992	1993	1994	1995	1996	1997	1998	1999		01-03
16.80	18.59	20.48	22.08	24.15	24.13	24.71	25.17	27.25	29.39	31.03	32.49	**34.00**	**36.00**	Sales per Sh (A)	**47.00**
1.54	1.80	2.12	2.18	2.19	2.06	2.22	2.40	2.76	3.08	3.25	3.59	**3.90**	**4.10**	"Cash Flow" per sh	**5.55**
0.72	0.91	1.13	1.14	1.05	0.88	0.99	1.18	1.46	1.71	1.84	2.05	**2.30**	**2.40**	Earnings per sh (AB)	**3.55**
0.35	0.40	0.45	0.46	0.50	0.50	0.52	0.52	0.55	0.59	0.64	0.67	**0.72**	**0.78**	Div'ds Decl'd per sh	**1.00**
1.17	1.20	1.42	1.58	1.73	1.70	1.63	1.59	1.71	1.89	2.03	2.16	**2.15**	**2.00**	Cap'l Spending per sh	**2.70**
6.12	6.68	7.02	7.24	7.69	7.85	7.34	7.45	8.33	9.08	10.00	10.58	**11.30**	**12.30**	Book Value per sh (C)	**17.00**
111.62	111.84	111.25	111.78	112.55	114.49	115.70	117.39	118.12	119.82	121.85	123.19	**125.00**	**125.00**	Common shs Outst'g (D)	**125.00**
15.3	14.9	11.2	13.0	14.8	20.5	20.3	18.1	15.4	15.2	17.3	19.9	**20.5**		Avg Ann'l P/E Ratio	**19.00**
1.04	0.99	0.93	0.99	1.10	1.31	1.23	1.07	1.01	1.02	1.09	1.15	**1.08**		Relative P/E Ratio	**1.35**
3.2%	2.9%	3.5%	3.1%	3.2%	2.8%	2.6%	2.4%	2.4%	2.3%	2.0%	1.6%	**1.5%**		Avg Ann'l Div'd Yield	**1.5%**
1875	2079	2278	2468	2719	2763	2859	2955	3219	3521	3781	4002	**4250**	**4500**	Sales ($bill) (A)	**5875**
13.3%	13.8%	15.2%	14.9%	14.2%	13.0%	13.2%	13.8%	14.7%	15.4%	15.6%	16.5%	**16.8%**	**16.7%**	Operating Margin	**17.0%**
92.8	99.7	110.5	118.3	130.3	138.4	145.7	146.9	157.8	167.0	174.7	191.7	**205**	**215**	Depreciation ($bill)	**250**
80.2	102.1	125.9	127.2	118.0	100.4	114.6	138.0	171.9	205.0	224.1	252.6	**285**	**305**	Net Profit	**445**
42.9%	40.3%	37.4%	37.2%	39.3%	38.3%	36.1%	34.9%	35.8%	35.4%	35.8%	35.3%	**35.0%**	**35.0%**	Income Tax Rate	**35.0%**
4.3%	4.9%	5.5%	5.2%	4.3%	3.6%	6.4%	4.7%	5.3%	5.8%	5.9%	6.3%	**6.8%**	**6.7%**	Net Profit Margin	**7.6%**
216.0	249.2	332.1	328.4	321.1	330.6	326.5	335.8	375.8	380.7	429.5	440.3	**450**	**470**	Working Cap'l ($bill)	**625**
324.3	342.6	415.7	520.5	553.1	579.4	585.6	587.2	622.8	667.4	712.3	770.3	**820**	**860**	Long-Term Debt ($bill)	**1010**
699.2	760.5	796.6	841.3	897.9	932.7	889.9	916.5	1024.3	1124.3	1258.3	1341.3	**1460**	**1580**	Shr. Equity ($bill)	**2170**
9.6%	11.0%	12.2%	11.4%	10.2%	8.5%	9.5%	10.7%	11.9%	12.9%	12.7%	13.3%	**14.0%**	**13.5%**	Return on Total Cap (E)	**15.0%**
11.5%	13.4%	15.8%	15.1%	13.1%	10.8%	12.9%	15.1%	16.8%	18.2%	17.8%	18.8%	**19.5%**	**19.0%**	Return on Shr. Equity	**20.5%**
5.8%	7.5%	9.6%	9.2%	6.9%	4.5%	6.0%	8.4%	10.5%	12.0%	11.8%	12.9%	**14.0%**	**13.0%**	Retained to Com Eq (F)	**15.0%**
51%	45%	40%	42%	49%	60%	55%	47%	40%	36%	36%	34%	**32%**	**33%**	All Div'ds to Net Prof	**29%**

ANNUAL RATES of change (per sh)	Past 10 Yrs.	Past 5 Yrs.	Est'd '95-'97 to '01-03
Sales	5.0%	5.0%	7.0%
"Cash Flow"	6.0%	9.0%	9.0%
Earnings	7.5%	14.0%	11.5%
Dividends	4.5%	4.5%	8.0%
Book Value	4.0%	5.5%	9.5%

QUARTERLY SALES ($bill.)

Fiscal Year Begins	Qtr. I	Qtr. II	Qtr. III	Qtr. IV	Full Fiscal Year
1995	837	891	881	912	3521
1996	903	958	965	955	3781
1997	963	1011	1004	1024	4002
1998	**1015**	**1075**	**1070**	**1090**	**4250**
1999	**1070**	**1135**	**1130**	**1145**	**4480**

EARNINGS PER SHARE

Fiscal Year Begins	Qtr. I	Qtr. II	Qtr. III	Qtr. IV	Full Fiscal Year
1995	0.41	0.44	0.40	0.46	1.71
1996	0.40	0.49	0.47	0.48	1.84
1997	0.47	0.53	0.49	0.56	2.05
1998	**0.53**	**0.60**	**0.56**	**0.61**	**2.30**
1999	**0.55**	**0.62**	**0.59**	**0.64**	**2.40**

QUARTERLY DIVIDENDS PAID

Cal. Year Begins	Qtr. I	Qtr. II	Qtr. III	Qtr. IV	Full Year
1995	0.14	0.15	0.15	0.15	0.59
1996	0.16	0.16	0.16	0.16	0.64
1997	0.16	0.17	0.17	0.17	0.67
1998	**0.18**	**0.18**	**0.18**	**0.18**	**0.72**
1999					

EXPLANATION

The Industrial Composite consists of 740 industrial, retail, and transportation companies. Financial data and stock market values for these companies have been pooled as if they belong to one giant conglomerate. The Composite includes about three-fourths of Value Line's 93 industries; excluded sectors are financial services (banks, thrifts, insurance, real estate, securities brokerage, and investment companies), utilities (electrics, natural gas distribution, and telecommunications services), and non-North American companies. Estimates for 1998 and 1999 and projections for 2001-2003 were prepared using Value Line's economic forecast, which was last updated in Selection & Opinion *on November 27, 1998. Except for earnings, all per-share figures were computed using the sum of shares outstanding at yearend for all included companies. In 1997, the integrated petroleum sector provided 12.8% of net profits (excluding nonrecurring and extraordinary items), compared with 13.3% in 1996.*

FOOTNOTES

(A) *Company fiscal years end between 7/1 of year shown and 6/30 of next year. Years for about 80% of companies end 12/31.* ***(B)*** *Primary earnings per share through 1997, diluted thereafter. Excludes non-recurring charges: '86, d$0.07; '87, d$0.01; '88, d$0.01; '89, d$0.02; '90, d$0.07; '91, d$0.20; '92, d$0.75; '93, d$0.41; '94, d$0.07; '95, d$0.18; '96, d$0.06; '97, d$0.13.* ***(C)*** *Includes intangibles. In '97: $3.02 per share.* ***(D)*** *In billions.* ***(E)*** *(Net profit + 1/2 Long-Term Interest)/(Long-Term Debt + Share Equity).* ***(F)*** *(Net Profit-All Div'd)/Common Equity.*

Bold figures are Value Line estimates.

1999: a recent price of 59 and a P/E ratio of 25.2. *Value Line*'s estimate of the Industrial Composite EPS for 1999 at this time (January 1999) was \$2.40, as shown in the third row of the data. Using the P/E ratio model of valuation explained in Chapter 10 based on the assumption of constant growth, we find that

$$P_0 = P_0/E_1 \times E_1$$
$$P_0 = 25.2 \times \$2.40$$
$$\approx \$60.5$$

Therefore, *Value Line*'s Industrial Composite was (approximately) a combination of a P/E of 25.2 and expected earnings of \$2.40.

Assuming a constant-growth dividend discount model for the market, we see that an estimate of the required rate of return for 1999 was as follows:[15]

$$k = D_1/P + g$$
$$= \$0.78/\$60.5 + 0.08$$
$$= 9.3\%$$

Solving Equation 13-2,

$$P_0/E_1 = \frac{D_1/E_1}{k - g}$$
$$= \frac{\$0.78/\$2.40}{0.093 - 0.08}$$
$$= 25$$

Thus, the models and variables discussed in Chapter 10 are internally consistent with these data.

Now what about forecasts, or at least likely possibilities?

EXAMPLE 13-7

Assume that the spread between k and g, 0.013, holds. Now assume you think earnings will be slightly less in 1999, say \$2.20, and that dividends will decline to \$0.70.

$$\text{Estimated P/E for 1999} = \frac{.70/2.20}{0.013}$$
$$= 24.48$$

In this scenario, if the spread between k and g remained constant, the P/E would be expected to decrease slightly because the payout ratio would decrease slightly.

EXAMPLE 13-8

Using the above information, the estimated price, P_E, would be

$$P_E \text{ for 1999} = \text{estimated P/E} \times \text{estimated earnings}$$
$$= 24.48 \times \$2.20$$
$$= \$53.86$$

Thus, one estimated price for the IC (as a proxy for the stock market) for 1999, \$53.86, is 8.7 percent lower than the recent price given in Figure 13-6 of \$59.

[15] The g value of 0.08 is taken from the estimates of growth for earnings in the bottom left panel under "Annual Rates." The dividend figure is taken from the fourth line of the data and is a preliminary estimate for 1999.

EXAMPLE 13-9

Assumptions could be made about a change in the spread between k and g, which would change the P/E ratio. What if the spread widens to 0.02, as a result of k increasing from 0.093 to .10? Assume estimated earnings of \$2.40.

$$\text{Previous} \quad k - g = 0.093 - 0.08 = 0.013$$

$$\text{New} \quad k - g = 0.10 - 0.08 = 0.02$$

$$\text{Estimated P/E} = \frac{0.325}{0.02}$$

$$= 16.25$$

$$P_E \text{ for 1999} = \text{estimated P/E} \times \text{estimated E}$$

$$= 16.25 \times \$2.40$$

$$= \$39$$

A small increase in k, leading to a wider spread between k and g, results in a substantially lower estimated price for the IC, from \$59 to \$39, or a 33.9 percent change.

On the other hand, assume that k declines slightly because of a decrease in either the riskless rate of return or the risk premium demanded by investors.

EXAMPLE 13-10

Estimated earnings continue to be \$2.40.

$$\text{Estimated P/E} = \frac{0.325}{0.09 - 0.08}$$

$$= 32.5$$

and

$$P_E \text{ for 1999} = \text{Estimated P/E} \times \text{Estimated E}$$

$$= 32.5 \times \$2.40$$

$$= \$78$$

Assuming no change in the estimated earnings, we note that these calculations suggest a higher estimated price for the IC of \$78, a 32 percent increase from the former level of \$59.

The foregoing examples illustrate the fundamental analysis approach to making some forecasts of the market using data readily available to investors. Such forecasts are not easy, at best, and are clearly subject to errors, some often substantial. Investors should count on the unexpected occurring. Nevertheless, the average investor can make some intelligent and useful forecasts of the market at certain times, at least as to direction. In 1981–1982, for example, when interest rates had reached record levels in the United States and the economy was in a recession, clearly significant events were likely to occur. Investors had only to convince themselves that some recovery would occur, thereby increasing earnings, or more important, that interest rates would decline, thereby lowering the required rate of return (i.e., raising the P/E ratio). This is exactly what happened, of course, launching the great bull market of mid-1982 to mid-1983.

Investors should consider the foregoing type of analysis when making forecasts for the stock market. Although it is not a perfect process by any means, useful forecasts of likely major market trends can be made.

USING THE INTERNET An interesting compilation of market opinions and forecasts can be found in the "Bulls and Bears" section of www.investorhome.com. This is said to be a "random collection of statistics, articles, and predictions by individuals that have publicly declared their bullish or bearish opinions on the U.S. stock market."

SUMMARY

- The recurring pattern of expansion and contraction in the economy is referred to as the business cycle. Stock prices are related to the phases of the business cycle.
- Leading, lagging, and coincident indicators are used to monitor the economy in terms of business cycle turning dates.
- It is important to remember that stock prices, one of the set of leading indicators, typically lead the economy. Therefore, although the market and the economy are clearly related, stock prices usually turn before the economy.
- Macroeconomic forecasts have become more accurate, but there is much room for improvement.
- Although money's effectiveness in forecasting the economy is controversial, investors should monitor the actions of the Federal Reserve.
- The "market" is the aggregate of all security prices and is conveniently measured by some average or, most commonly, by some index of stock prices.
- To understand the market (i.e., what determines stock prices), it is necessary to think in terms of a valuation model. The two determinants of aggregate stock prices are the expected benefits stream (earnings or dividends) and the required rate of return (alternatively, the P/E ratio).
- Keran's model is useful for visualizing the economic factors that combine to determine stock prices. In trying to understand the market in conceptual terms, it is appropriate to think of corporate earnings and interest rates as the determinants of stock prices.
- Corporate earnings are directly related to stock prices, whereas interest rates are inversely related.
- To value the market, investors should think in terms of corporate earnings and the P/E ratio. (Alternatively, the dividend valuation model could be used.)
- Forecasting market changes is difficult. The business cycle can be of help in understanding the status of the economy, and investors then need to relate the market, which typically leads, to the economy.
- Some intelligent estimates of possible changes in the market can be made by considering what is likely to happen to corporate profits and P/E ratios (or interest rates) over some future period, such as a year.
- An alternative approach to forecasting likely changes in the market is to apply the valuation model based on dividends or earnings to some aggregate data such as the *Value Line* Industrial Composite. It is important to think in terms of broad changes and not be concerned with trying to make precise market forecasts.

KEY WORDS

Bubble

Business cycle

Composite indexes of general economic activity

QUESTIONS

13-1. Why is market analysis so important?

13-2. What are the two determinants of stock prices? How are these two determinants related to a valuation model?

13-3. How can the Keran model use interest rates as one of the two determinants of stock prices when the interest rate does not appear in either the dividend valuation model or the earnings multiplier model?

13-4. In terms of the Keran model, how can the Federal Reserve affect stock prices?

13-5. What is the historical relationship between stock prices, corporate profits, and interest rates?

13-6. How can investors go about valuing the market?

13-7. What was the primary cause of the rise in stock prices in 1982?

13-8. What is the "typical" business cycle–stock-price relationship?

13-9. If an investor can determine when the bottoming out of the economy will occur, when should stocks be purchased—before, during, or after such a bottom? Would stock prices be expected to continue to rise as the economy recovers (based on historical experience)?

13-10. Can money supply changes forecast stock-price changes?

13-11. What is the historical relationship between the market's P/E ratio and recessions?

13-12. Based on Table 13-1, what is the likely explanation for the stock market's lackluster performance in the last half of the 1970s?

13-13. Suppose that you know with certainty that corporate earnings next year will rise 15 percent above this year's level of corporate earnings. Based on this information, should you buy stocks?

The following question was asked on the 1993 CFA Level II examination:

CFA

13-14. Universal Auto is a large multinational corporation headquartered in the United States. For segment reporting purposes, the company is engaged in two businesses: production of motor vehicles and information processing services.

The motor vehicle business is by far the larger of Universal's two segments. It consists mainly of domestic U.S. passenger car production, but also includes small truck manufacturing operations in the U.S. and passenger car production in other countries. This segment of universal has had weak operating results for the past several years, including a large loss in 1992. While the company does not break out the operating results of its domestic passenger car business, that part of Universal's business is generally believed to be primarily responsible for the weak performance of its motor vehicle segment.

Idata, the information processing services segment of Universal, was started by Universal about 15 years ago. This business has shown strong, steady growth which has been entirely internal; no acquisitions have been made.

Adam's research report continued as follows:

". . . With a business recovery already underway, the expected profit surge should lead to a much higher price for Universal Auto stock. We strongly recommend purchase."

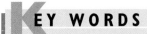

a. Discuss the business cycle approach to investment timing. (Your answer should describe actions to be taken on both stocks and bonds at different points over a typical business cycle.)
b. Assuming Adam's assertion is correct—that a business recovery is already underway, evaluate the timeliness of his recommendation to purchase Universal Auto, a cyclical stock, based on the business cycle approach to investment timing.

PROBLEMS

13-1. In the text the *Value Line* Industrial Composite is used in an example of market valuation. For this problem, the Standard & Poor's 400 Industrial Index and Equations 13-1, 13-2, and 13-3 are used. The annual data for the years 19X1 through 19X6 are provided:

Year	End-of-Year Price (P)	Earnings (E)	Dividends (D)	P/E	(D/E)100 (%)	(D/P)100 (%)
19X1	107.21	13.12	5.35	8.17	40.78	4.99
19X2	121.02	16.08	6.04	7.53	37.56	4.99
19X3	154.45	16.13	6.55	9.58	40.61	4.24
19X4	137.12	16.70	7.00	8.21	41.92	5.11
19X5	157.62	13.21	7.18	11.93	54.35	4.56
19X6	186.24	15.24	6.97			

The 19X6 values in italics are projected, like those of the Value Line Industrial Composite.
a. Calculate the 19X6 values for those columns left blank.
b. Why would you expect this index to differ from the *Value Line* Index?
c. On the assumption that $g = 0.095$, calculate k for 19X6 using the formula $k = (D/P) + g$ and show that $k = 0.132425$.
d. Using the 19X6 values in Equation 13-2, show that P/E = 12.22.
e. Assuming a projection that 19X7 earnings will be 25 percent greater than the 19X6 value, show that projected earnings for the S&P 400 are expected to be 19.05.
f. Assuming further that the dividend-payout ratio will be 0.40, show that projected dividends for 19X7 will be 7.62.
g. Using the projected earnings and dividends for 19X7, and the same k and g used in problem c, show that Equation 13-2 yields an expected P/E for 19X7 of 10.69.
h. Using these expected values for 19X7, evaluate Equation 13-3, and show that the expected price is 203.61.
i. Recalculate the values for 19X7 P/E and P, using the same $g = 0.095$, but with (1) $k = 0.14$; (2) $k = 0.13$, and (3) $k = 0.12$.

SELECTED REFERENCES

Stock market cycles are discussed in:

Renshaw, Edward F. "The Anatomy of Stock Market Cycles." *Journal of Portfolio Management* (Fall 1983), pp. 53–57.

A discussion of the theory of stock price movements can be found in:

Schiller, Robert J. "Theories of Aggregate Stock Price Movements." *Journal of Portfolio Management* (Winter 1984), pp. 28–37.

A good overall view of the economy can be found in:

United States Government Printing Office, *Economic Report of the President,* yearly.

www.wiley.com/college/jones7

This chapter analyzes the effect of market-wide and economy-wide events on stock returns. The web exercises will take you to sites that provide information on these macroeconomic events and help you look at how the information impacts on stock returns.

APPENDIX 13-A

PUBLISHED INFORMATION ABOUT THE ECONOMY—GOVERNMENT PUBLICATIONS

The federal government, through a variety of agencies and departments, provides much information about the economy, industries, and companies. Although this information is available to investors either free or for a small charge, many do not know of its existence or utilize it very often.

Government publications are a primary source for data concerning the state of the economy. A summary report of recent and prospective activity is contained in the *Economic Report of the President,* which the president sends to the Congress. The report includes over 200 pages covering such issues as monetary policy, inflation, tax policy, the international economy, and review and outlook. In addition, it contains over 100 pages of tables showing historical data for the gross national product (GNP), price indexes, savings, employment, production and business activity, corporate profits, agriculture, international statistics, and so forth.

The *Federal Reserve Bulletin,* a monthly publication of the Board of Governors of the Federal Reserve System, is a prime source for monetary data, money and credit data, and figures on GNP, labor force, output, and the international economy. It also contains data pertinent to the Federal Reserve System, including member-bank reserves and reserve requirements, and open-market transactions.

Most of the 12 Federal Reserve Banks also have their own publications, featuring data and analyses of economic activity. The Federal Reserve Bank of St. Louis produces several publications of special interest to economists and other economic observers. For example, *U.S. Financial Data* is a weekly analysis of money market conditions, and *National Economic Trends* is a monthly publication dealing with aggregate business.

Economic Indicators is a monthly publication of the Council of Economic Advisors. It contains data on income, spending, employment, prices, money and credit, and other factors on both a monthly and an annual basis.

Business Conditions Digest (BCD), published monthly by the Department of Commerce, contains data on indicators of the economy from the National Bureau of Economic Research. Some 90 indicators, and over 300 components, are included. These indicators are important in attempting to discern the economy's movements, which make BCD a valuable information source for those interested in forecasting economic activity. BCD contains the basic data for many of the economic activity charts often seen by investors.

A third monthly source of economic data is the Department of Commerce's *Survey of Current Business.* This source provides detailed information on the national income accounts, as well as data on such variables as industrial production, employment and wages, and interest rates. The Survey also reviews recent developments in the economy.

chapter 14

INDUSTRY ANALYSIS

Chapter 14 analyzes the industry issue, considering the importance of industry factors to company results. Over long periods some industries have greatly outperformed others.

After reading this chapter you will be able to:

- **Assess the significance of industry analysis in the top-down approach to security analysis.**
- **Recognize how industries are classified and the stages that industries go through over time.**
- **Understand the basic tenets of competitive strategy as it applies to industry analysis.**

The second step in the fundamental analysis of common stocks is industry analysis. An investor who is convinced that the economy and the market offer favorable conditions for investing should proceed to consider those industries that promise the most opportunities in the coming years. In the 1990s, for example, investors will not view some U.S. industries with the same enthusiasm they would have even 10 years earlier. On the other hand, it is obvious that the telecommunications and computer-related industries are changing the way most Americans live.

The actual security analysis of industries as performed by professional security analysts often is tedious. Numerous factors are involved, including multiple demand and supply factors, a detailed analysis of price factors, labor issues, government regulation, and so forth.

In this chapter we concentrate on the *conceptual issues* involved in industry analysis. The basic concepts of industry analysis are closely related to our previous discussion of valuation principles. Investors can apply these concepts in several ways, depending on the degree of rigor sought, the amount of information available, and the specific models used. What we seek to accomplish here is to learn to think analytically about industries.

The significance of industry analysis can be established by considering the performance of various industries over multiple year periods. This analysis will indicate the value to investors of selecting certain industries while avoiding others. We will also establish the need for investors to continue analyzing industries by showing the inconsistency of industry performance over consecutive yearly periods. Such a demonstration justifies an analysis of industries.

PERFORMANCE OF INDUSTRIES OVER TIME

THE IMPORTANCE OF INDUSTRY ANALYSIS OVER LONG PERIODS

Before embarking on industry analysis, we should consider its potential value. To establish the value of industry analysis, we can assess the performance of industry groups over long periods of time. Standard & Poor's calculates weekly and monthly stock price indexes for a variety of industries, with data available for a 50-year-plus period. Since the data are reported as index numbers, long-term comparisons of price performance can be made for any industry covered. Note that the base number for S&P data is 1941–1943 = 10; therefore, dividing the index number for any industry for a particular year by 10 indicates the number of times the index has increased over that period.

Table 14-1 shows the price performance of randomly selected industries for the years 1973, 1983, and 1995 (using 1941–1943 as the base).[1] The S&P 500 Composite Index in 1973 was almost 10 times (98/10) its 1941–1943 level, a continuously compounded average in excess of 8 percent annually over this 31-year period. However, this average growth rate consisted of widely varying performance over the industries covered by Standard & Poor's.

Over the 31-year period 1943–1973, the electrical equipment industry did well, rising to 28 times the base number, while the entertainment industry was only 3.4 times the base.

Over longer periods of time, as the last two columns at the top of Table 14-1 show, industries perform quite differently. The entertainment industry went on to outstanding per-

[1] All data are based on December closing index values.

TABLE 14-1 STANDARD & POOR'S WEEKLY STOCK PRICE INDEXES FOR SELECTED INDUSTRIES USING DATA FOR VARIOUS YEARS, ALL WITH A BASE OF 1941–1943 = 10

	1941–1943 = 10		
	1973	1983	1995
Automobiles	61	100	234
Aluminum	90	185	393
Beverages (alcoholic)	133	84	463
Beverages (soft drinks)	145	157	2343
Electrical equipment	280	522	1798
Entertainment	34	264	2431
Foods	59	134	1037
Health care (drugs)	218	259	2223
S&P 500 Index	98	165	616

	1941–1943 = 10				
	1982	1986	1989	1995	1998*
Broadcast media	889	2309	4980	9437	15856
Entertainment	307	577	1383	2431	3645
Health care (drugs)	248	540	949	2223	5686
Money center banks	65	66	111	233	365
Retail stores composite	104	159	375	321	616
S&P 500 Index	141	242	353	616	1017

*= end of September

SOURCE: Standard & Poor's *Statistical Service: Security Price Index Record,* various issues. Reprinted by permission.

formance by 1995 at 243 times the base, while the electrical equipment industry, which was significantly ahead of the entertainment industry in 1973, did well, but not as well as entertainment. Notice the dramatic difference in the Alcoholic Beverages industry and the Soft Drink Beverages industry over this period.[2]

The lower half of Table 14-1 shows selected and matched Standard & Poor's Industry Stock Price indexes for the years 1982, 1986, 1989, 1995, and 1998 (based on 1941–1943 = 10). This provides both a 50-year-plus picture of industry performance, which approximates the maximum investing lifetime of many individuals, and a look at how much change can occur in shorter periods of time such as three (1986–1989), four (1982–1986), seven (1982–1989), thirteen (1982–1995), and sixteen (1982–1998) years.

Tremendous differences exist for industries in the 1980s, and between periods in the 1980s and 1998. Notice how Money Center Banks did nothing between 1982 and 1986, but then almost doubled and redoubled through 1995. Broadcast Media performed in an incredibly strong manner over the entire period from 1982 to 1998, while Retail Stores, having declined from 1989 to 1995, almost doubled from 1995 to 1998.

The lesson to be learned from Table 14-1 is simple. Industry analysis pays because industries perform very differently over time—both shorter periods and longer periods—and

[2] Standard & Poor's has changed industry classifications over time because of changes in the economy. S&P introduced a new classification system effective July 1, 1996, which divided stocks into 11 economic sectors and 118 industry groups. However, the S&P 500 Index contains only 104 of these industry groups because some industries contain no large-capitalization companies (for example, independent power producers). The 11 economic sectors include transportation, utilities and financial, and the industrial sector divided into eight new sectors: basic materials, capital goods, communications services, consumer cyclicals, consumer staples, energy, health care, and technology.

investor performance will be significantly affected by the particular industries in which investors select stocks. Investors are seeking to identify the Broadcast Media and Health Care (Drugs) industries of the future, and avoid the Money Center Banks and Retail Stores industries.

CONSISTENCY OF INDUSTRY PERFORMANCE

The previous section established the value of industry analysis from a long-term perspective. Those investors who select the growth industries and maintain their positions will generally receive far better returns than those who have the misfortune to concentrate in industries that perform poorly over long periods of time.

Can relative industry performance be predicted reliably on the basis of past success, as measured by the previous price performance? To answer this question, consider Table 14-1 again. Assume that an investor calculated the top part of the table sometime in 1974, when the 1973 data were available. Should this investor count on past performance to carry him or her through the next several years—for example, through 1983? The answer is that such a procedure can be unreliable.

The Health Care (Drugs) industry, a strong performer through 1973, was only slightly higher by 1982. But an investor who gave up on this industry at that point would have missed the explosive growth that occurred thereafter. The same is true for the Soft Drink Beverage industry, which grew little between 1973 and 1983 but then exploded by 1995.

As the bottom of Table 14-1 shows, the Retail Stores Composite industry performed well between 1986 and 1989, declined by 1995, but then almost doubled by 1998 (while still performing less well than the market as a whole). Investors who thought that by 1989 the Broadcast Media industry had probably grown far beyond what could be reasonably expected would have missed a doubling once again by 1995, and continued strong performance into 1998.

What about industry performance over shorter periods of time? Should investors screen industries to find those that are currently performing well and are, therefore, likely to be the source of the most promising opportunities, from which company analysis will be done? Once again, such a procedure may produce some good results, but with wide variance. There are many examples of industries performing at opposite ends of the scale from one year to the next, while others continue to perform well for two or three years in a row.

Standard & Poor's reports the performance of industries for the previous year in an early January issue of *The Outlook,* a publication available in public libraries. Comparing the rankings of industries for two consecutive years shows that some industries continue to perform similarly for the following year, while others do not. The trucking industry, for example, finished in last place in both 1995 and 1996. On the other hand, the top two performing industries in 1995—Electronics: Defense (up 96 percent) and Health Care: Drugs (up 67 percent)—performed well in 1996, but only slightly above the market as a whole.

Even over very short periods, such as one month, industries can perform very differently. A dramatic example is the performance of industry groups around the great market crash of October 1987, when the S&P 500 Index declined some 22 percent in one month. All industries were adversely affected, but some industries showed only small losses (such as utilities) while others suffered losses of 40 percent or more in this one month period.

In summary, although industry analysis is clearly valuable over time, with some industries far outperforming others, industry rankings on some periodic basis (e.g., yearly or quarterly) are not consistent. Investors cannot simply choose those industries that have performed well recently and reliably expect them to continue to do so for the next several periods. While some continuation in performance certainly occurs, surprises do also.

Perhaps just as important, investors should not ignore industries simply because their recent performance has been poor. Their subsequent performance over relatively short periods of time may be, and often is, at the opposite extreme! It is necessary, therefore, to learn the basic concepts of industry analysis. First, however, let us consider exactly what an industry is.

WHAT IS AN INDUSTRY?

At first glance, the term *industry* may seem self-explanatory. After all, everyone is familiar with the auto industry, the drug industry, and the electric utility industry. But are these classifications as clear-cut as they seem? For example, a consumer can drink beer out of glass containers or aluminum cans or steel cans. Does this involve one industry, containers, or three—the glass, steel, and aluminum industries (or perhaps two: glass and metals).

The problem becomes even messier when companies in diversified lines of business are considered.

EXAMPLE 14-1

Harvey Group is an American Stock Exchange company that showed the following breakdown by sales for one year: retailing of professional and home audio and video equipment, 56 percent; food brokerage, 44 percent. However, by percentage of total profits the breakdowns are 32 percent and 68 percent, respectively. In what industry is Harvey Group? It is not easy to classify such a company, particularly in relation to Cascade Natural Gas, a New York Stock Exchange company whose only activity is the distribution of natural gas in 84 communities in Washington and Oregon.

There are complications in classifying even a seemingly "clear" example such as General Motors, the world's largest automobile manufacturer. In 1984 GM acquired EDS, a computer services firm, and in 1985 it acquired Hughes Aircraft.

The message is clear. Industries cannot casually be identified and classified, at least in many cases. It seems safe to assert that industries have been, and will continue to become, more mixed in their activities and less identifiable with one product or service.

CLASSIFYING INDUSTRIES

Standard Industrial Classification (SIC) System A classification of firms on the basis of what they produce using Census data

Regardless of the problems, analysts and investors need methods with which to classify industries. One well-known and widely used system is the **Standard Industrial Classification (SIC) system** based on Census data and developed to classify firms on the basis of what they produce.[3] SIC codes have 11 divisions, designated A through K. For example, agriculture-forestry-fishing is Industry Division A, mining is B, retail trade is G, and K, the last group, is nonclassifiable establishments. Within each of these divisions are several major industry groups, designated by a two-digit code. The primary metal industries, for example, are a part of Division D, manufacturing, and are assigned the two-digit code 33.

The major industry groups within each division are further subdivided into three-, four-, and five-digit SIC codes to provide more detailed classifications. A specific industry is

[3] See *Census of Manufacturers* (Washington, D.C.: U.S. Government Printing Office).

assigned a three-digit code, as are entire companies.[4] Plants carrying out specific functions (such as producing steel) are assigned four-digit SIC codes. A five-digit code indicates a specific product. Thus, the larger the number of digits in the SIC system, the more specific the breakdown.

SIC codes have aided significantly in bringing order to the industry classification problem by providing a consistent basis for describing industries and companies. Analysts using SIC codes can focus on economic activity in as broad, or as specific, a manner as desired.

Other Industry Classifications The SIC system of industry classification is probably the most consistent system available, and possibly the easiest to use. However, it is not the only industry designation in actual use. Standard & Poor's Corporation provides weekly stock indexes on roughly 110 industry groupings (or parts of industries). Many of the individual series go back 50 years or more.

The Value Line Investment Survey covers roughly 1700 companies, divided into approximately 90 industries, with a discussion of industry prospects preceding the company analysis. As discussed later, these industry classifications could be important, because *Value Line* ranks their expected performance (relatively) for the year ahead.

Other sources of information use different numbers of industries in presenting data. The important point to remember is that no one industry classification system is widely used in the standard investment publications.

ANALYZING INDUSTRIES

Industries, as well as the market and companies, are analyzed through the study of a wide range of data, including sales, earnings, dividends, capital structure, product lines, regulations, innovations, and so on. Such analysis requires considerable expertise and is usually performed by industry analysts employed by brokerage firms and other institutional investors.

A useful first step is to analyze industries in terms of their stage in the life cycle. The idea is to assess the general health and current position of the industry. A second step involves a qualitative analysis of industry characteristics designed to assist investors in assessing the future prospects for an industry. Each of these steps is examined in turn.

THE INDUSTRY LIFE CYCLE

Many observers believe that industries evolve through at least three stages: the pioneering stage, the expansion stage, and the stabilization stage. There is an obvious parallel in this idea to human development. The concept of an **industry life cycle** could apply to industries or product lines within industries. The industry life cycle concept is depicted in Figure 14-1, and each stage is discussed in the following section.

Industry Life Cycle The stages of an industry's evolution from pioneering to stabilization and decline

Pioneering Stage In the pioneering stage, rapid growth in demand occurs. Although a number of companies within a growing industry will fail at this stage because they will not survive the competitive pressures, most experience rapid growth in sales and earnings, possibly at an increasing rate. The opportunities available may attract a number of companies,

[4] Companies involved in several lines of activity are assigned multiple SIC codes.

FIGURE 14-1

The industry life cycle.

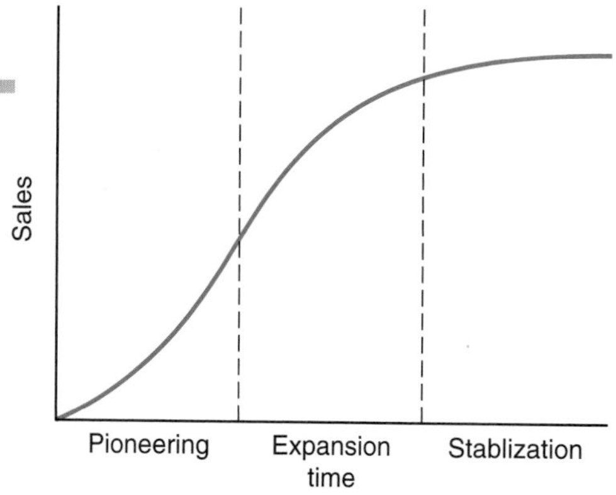

as well as venture capital. Considerable jockeying for position occurs as the companies battle each other for survival, with the weaker firms failing and dropping out. Investor risk in an unproven company is high, but so are expected returns if the company succeeds. At the pioneering stage of an industry, it can be difficult for security analysts to identify the likely survivors, just when the ability to identify the future strong performers is most valuable. By the time it becomes apparent who the real winners are, their prices may have been bid up considerably beyond what they were in the earlier stages of development.

In the early 1980s, the microcomputer business—both hardware and software—offered a good example of companies in the pioneering stage. Given the explosion in expected demand for these products, many new firms entered the business, hoping to capture some share of the total market. By 1983, there were an estimated 150 manufacturers of home computers, a clearly unsustainable number over the longer run.

Expansion Stage In the second stage of an industry's life cycle, the expansion stage, the survivors from the pioneering stage are identifiable. They continue to grow and to prosper, but the rate of growth is more moderate than before.

At the expansion stage of the cycle, industries are improving their products and perhaps lowering their prices. They are more stable and solid, and at this stage they often attract considerable investment funds. Investors are more willing to invest in these industries now that their potential has been demonstrated and the risk of failure has decreased.

Financial policies become firmly established at this stage. The capital base is widened and strengthened. Dividends often become payable, further enhancing the attractiveness of these companies to a number of investors.

Stabilization Stage Finally, industries evolve into the stabilization stage (sometimes referred to as the maturity stage), at which point the growth begins to moderate. Sales may still be increasing, but at a much slower rate than before. Products become more standardized and less innovative, the marketplace is full of competitors, and costs are stable rather than decreasing through efficiency moves, for example. Industries at this stage continue to move along but without significant growth. Stagnation may occur for considerable periods of time, or intermittently.

Assessing the Industry Life Cycle This three-part classification of industry evolvement helps investors to assess the growth potential of different companies in an industry. Based on the stage of the industry, they can better assess the potential of different companies within an industry. However, there are limitations to this type of analysis. First, it is only a generalization, and investors must be careful not to attempt to categorize every industry, or all companies within a particular industry, into neat categories that may not apply. Second, even the general framework may not apply to some industries that are not categorized by many small companies struggling for survival. Finally, the bottom line in security analysis is stock prices, a function of the expected stream of benefits and the risk involved.

The industrial life cycle tends to focus on sales and share of the market and investment in the industry. Although all of these factors are important to investors, they are not the final items of interest. Given these qualifications to industry life cycle analysis, what are the implications for investors?

The pioneering stage may offer the highest potential returns, but it also poses the greatest risk. Several companies in a particular industry will fail or do poorly. Such risk may be appropriate for some investors, but many will wish to avoid the risk inherent in this stage.

Investors interested primarily in capital gains should avoid the maturity stage. Companies at this stage may have relatively high dividend pay-outs because they have fewer growth prospects. These companies often offer stability in earnings and dividend growth.

Perhaps a fourth stage could be added to the analysis of the industrial life cycle—decline, on either a relative or an absolute basis. Clearly, investors should seek to spot industries in this stage and avoid them. For the year 2000 and beyond, with the United States in the era of information processing, certain industrial sectors will decline. (In some cases, this decline has already started.)

It is the second stage, expansion, that is probably of most interest to investors. Industries that have survived the pioneering stage often offer good opportunities, for the demand for their products and services is growing more rapidly than the economy as a whole. Growth is rapid but orderly, an appealing characteristic to investors.

QUALITATIVE ASPECTS OF INDUSTRY ANALYSIS

The analyst or investor should consider several important qualitative factors that can characterize an industry. Knowing about these factors will help investors to analyze a particular industry and will aid in assessing its future prospects.

The Historical Performance As we have learned, some industries perform well and others poorly over long periods of time. Although performance is not always consistent and predictable on the basis of the past, an industry's track record should not be ignored. In Table 14-1 we saw that the lead and zinc industry performed poorly in both 1950 and 1960 (in relation to the base of 1941–1943). It continued to do badly in 1973 and afterward. The broadcast media industry on the other hand, showed strength at each of the 1950 and 1960 checkpoints since 1982.

Investors should consider the historical record of sales and earnings growth and price performance. Although the past cannot simply be extrapolated into the future, it does provide some useful information.

Competition The nature of the competitive conditions existing in an industry can provide useful information in assessing its future. Is the industry protected from the entrance of new competitors as a result of control of raw materials, prohibitive cost of building plants, the level of production needed to operate profitably, and so forth?

Michael Porter has written extensively on the issue of competitive strategy, which involves the search for a competitive position in an industry. The intensity of competition in

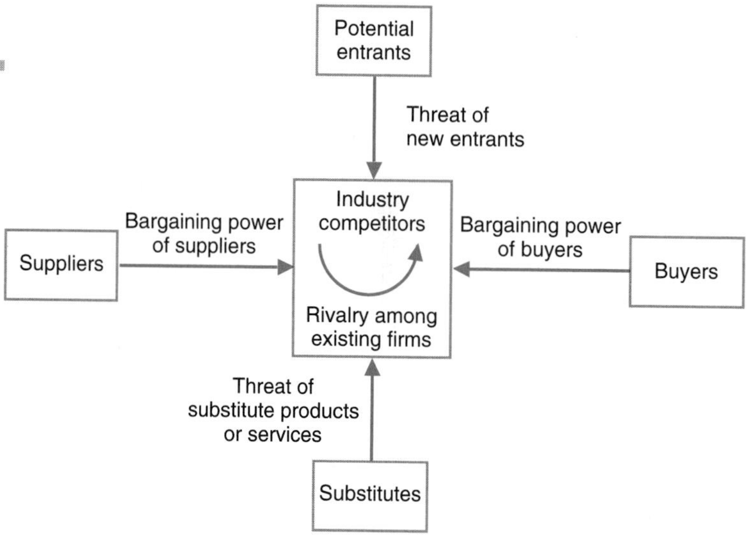

FIGURE 14-2

The five competitive forces that determine industry profitability.

SOURCE: Reprinted with the permission of the Free Press, a division of Simon & Schuster, Inc. from COMPETITIVE ADVANTAGE: Creating and Sustaining Superior Performance by Michael E. Porter. Copyright © 1985 by Michael E. Porter.

an industry determines that industry's ability to sustain above-average returns.[5] This intensity is not a matter of luck, but a reflection of underlying factors that determine the strength of five basic competitive factors:

1. Threat of new entrants
2. Bargaining power of buyers
3. Rivalry between existing competitors
4. Threat of substitute products or services
5. Bargaining power of suppliers

These five competitive forces are shown as a diagram in Figure 14-2. Because the strength of these five factors varies across industries (and can change over time), industries vary from the standpoint of inherent profitability.

The five competitive forces determine industry profitability because these influence the components of return on investment. The strength of each of these factors is a function of industry structure. The important elements of industry structure are shown in Figure 14-3. This figure shows all the elements of industry structure that affect competition within an industry.

The important point of the Porter analysis is that industry profitability is a function of industry structure. Investors must analyze industry structure to assess the strength of the five competitive forces, which in turn determine industry profitability.

Government Effects Government regulations and actions can have significant effects on industries. The investor must attempt to assess the results of these effects or, at the very least, be well aware that they exist and may continue.

Consider the breakup of AT&T as of January 1, 1984. This one action has changed the telecommunications industry permanently, and perhaps others as well. As a second example, the deregulating of the financial services industries resulted in banks and savings and loans

[5] See Michael E. Porter, "Industry Structure and Competitive Strategy: Keys to Profitability," *Financial Analysts Journal* (July–August 1980), pp. 30–41. See also Michael Porter, *Competitive Advantage: Creating and Sustaining Superior Performance* (New York: Free Press, 1985).

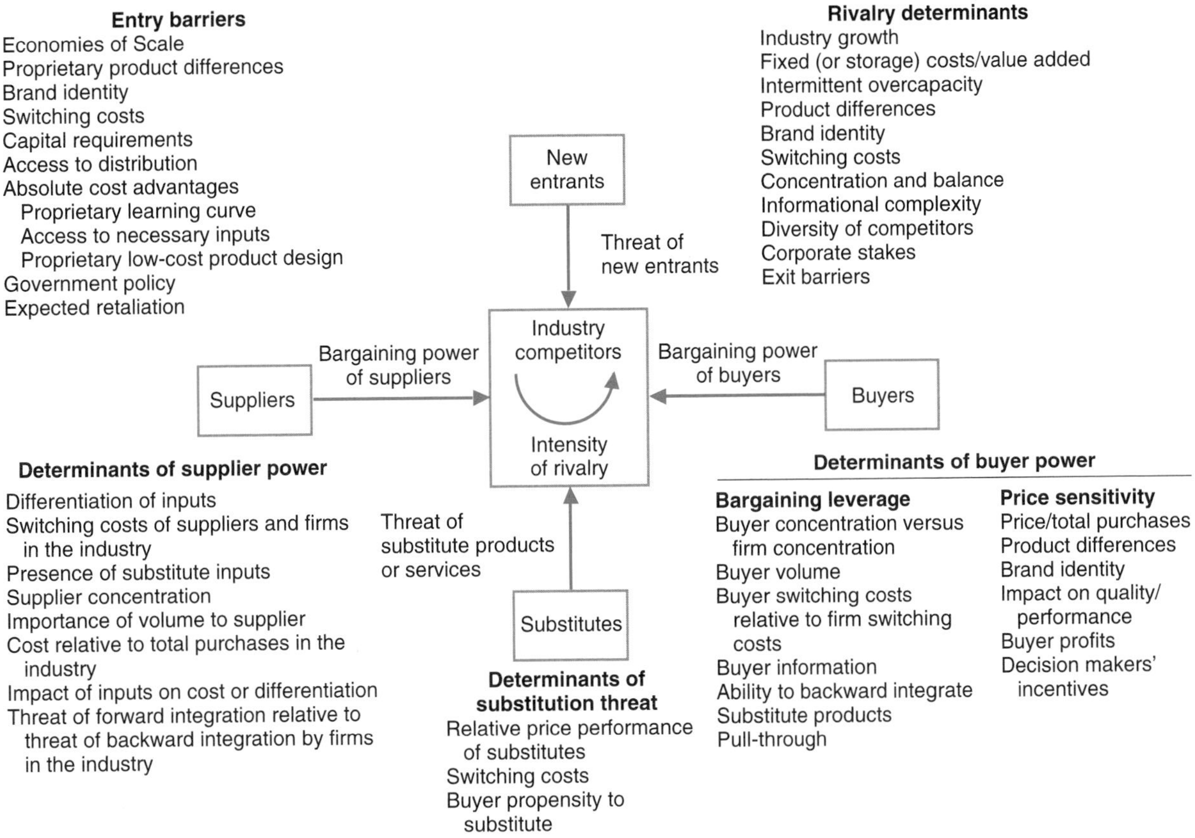

FIGURE 14-3

Elements of industry structure.

SOURCE: Reprinted with the permission of the Free Press, a Division of Simon & Schuster, Inc. from COMPETITIVE ADVANTAGE: Creating and Sustaining Superior Performance by Michael E. Porter. Copyright © 1985 by Michael E. Porter.

competing more directly with each other, offering consumers many of the same services. Such an action has to affect the relative performance of these two industries as well as some of their other competitors, such as the brokerage industry (which can now also offer similar services in many respects).

Structural Changes A fourth factor to consider is the structural changes that occur in the economy. As the United States continues to move from an industrial society to an information-communications society, major industries will be affected. New industries with tremendous potential are, and will be, emerging, whereas some traditional industries, such as steel, may never recover to their former positions.

Structural shifts can occur even within relatively new industries. For example, in the early 1980s the microcomputer industry was a young, dynamic industry with numerous competitors, some of whom enjoyed phenomenal success in a short time. The introduction of microcomputers by IBM in 1982, however, forever changed that industry. Other hardware manufacturers sought to be compatible with IBM's personal computer, and suppliers rushed to supply items such as software, printers, and additional memory boards. IBM's decision to enter this market significantly affected virtually every part of the industry.

EVALUATING FUTURE INDUSTRY PROSPECTS

Ultimately, investors are interested in expected performance in the future. They realize that such estimates are difficult and are likely to be somewhat in error, but they know that equity prices are a function of expected parameters, not past, known values. How, then, is an investor to proceed?

ASSESSING LONGER-TERM PROSPECTS

To forecast industry performance over the longer run, investors should ask the following questions:

1. Which industries are obvious candidates for growth and prosperity over, say, the next decade? (In the early 1980s, such industries as microcomputers, the software industry, telecommunications, and cellular telephones could have been identified; in the early 1990s, technology firms could be identified; what about in 2000?)
2. Which industries appear likely to have difficulties as the United States changes from an industrial to an information-collecting and -processing economy?

PICKING INDUSTRIES FOR NEXT YEAR

On a shorter-run basis, investors would like to value industries along the lines discussed in Chapter 13 for the market. They would like to be able to estimate the expected earnings for an industry and the expected multiplier and combine them to produce an estimate of value. However, this is not easy to do. It requires an understanding of several relationships and estimates of several variables. Fortunately, considerable information is readily available to help investors in their analysis of industries. Investors should be aware of the primary sources of information about industries and the nature of the information available. These issues are discussed in Appendix 14-A.

To determine industry performance for shorter periods of time (e.g., one year), investors should ask themselves the following question: Given the current and prospective economic situation, which industries are likely to show improving earnings? In many respects, this is the key question for industry security analysis. Investors can turn to *I/B/E/S,* which compiles institutional brokerage earnings estimates, for analysts estimates of earnings for various industries, which are revised during the year.

Given the importance of earnings, and the availability of earnings estimates for industries and companies, are investors able to make relatively easy investment choices? The answer is no, because earnings estimates are notoriously inaccurate. In one recent year, for example, Standard & Poor's was estimating that the banking industry's profits would increase 15 percent for the year, while IBES estimated 29 percent—obviously, a big difference.

Dreman reports on a study of 61 industries for a 17 year period. Three-fourths of all estimates within industries missed reported earnings by 30 percent or more, and 15 percent showed errors of 80 percent or more. The average forecast error grouped by industries was 50 percent (median error of 43 percent). Only 16 of the 61 industries over the 17 years showed forecast errors of 29 percent or less.[6]

Of course, investors must also consider the likely P/E ratios for industries. Which industries are likely to show improving P/E ratios? Dreman has also reported on the issue of whether, like companies, investors pay too much for favored companies in an industry. Buying the lowest 20 percent of P/Es in each of 44 industry groups over 25 years (based on the 1,500

[6] David Dreman, "Cloudy Crystal Balls," *Forbes,* October 10, 1994, p. 154.

largest companies on the Compustat database measured by market capitalization) produced an average annual return of 18 percent compared to 12.4 percent for the highest 20 percent P/E group. Dreman also found that buying the lowest P/E stocks across industries produced smaller losses when the market is down relative to the market as a whole and to the highest P/E group.[7]

Other questions to consider are the likely direction of interest rates and which industries would be most affected by a significant change in interest rates? A change in interest rates, other things being equal, leads to a change in the discount rate (and a change in the multiplier). Which industries are likely to be most affected by possible future political events, such as a new administration, renewed inflation, new technology, an increase in defense spending, and so on?

As with all security analysis, we can use several procedures in analyzing industries. Much of this process is common sense. For example, if you can reasonably forecast a declining number of competitors in an industry, it stands to reason that, other things being equal, the remaining firms will be more profitable.

USING THE INTERNET The "Research Library" portion of the www.lehman.com website has information organized by industries. At http://quote.yahoo.com, financial news is organized by industry. Investors can find a section on industry reports from *Individual Investor* at www.iionline.com. A large supplier of company information, Hoover's, has industry analysis also at www.hoover's.com.

Box 14-1 is an interesting discussion of a technique suggested by S&P in its publication, *The Outlook*. It indicates that picking industries on the basis of their prior year's performance relative to the S&P 500 Index can produce superior results.[8] What is interesting about this is that both last year's leaders and last year's laggards are recommended, as long as they are exhibiting upward momentum.

BUSINESS CYCLE ANALYSIS

A useful procedure for investors to assess industry prospects is to analyze industries by their operating ability in relation to the economy as a whole. That is, some industries perform poorly during a recession, whereas others are able to weather it reasonably well. Some industries move closely with the business cycle, outperforming the average industry in good times and under-performing it in bad times. Investors, in analyzing industries, should be aware of these relationships.

Growth Industries Industries with expected earnings growth significantly above the average of all industries

Most investors have heard of, and are usually seeking, growth companies. In **growth industries** earnings are expected to be significantly above the average of all industries, and such growth may occur regardless of setbacks in the economy. Growth industries in the 1980s included genetic engineering, microcomputers, and new medical devices. Current and future growth industries include robotics and cellular telephones. Clearly, one of the primary goals of fundamental security analysis is to identify the growth industries of the near and far future.

[7] See David Dreman, "A New Approach to Low-P/E Investing," *Forbes*, September 23, 1996, p. 241.
[8] Relative strength is discussed in more detail in Chapter 16.

Box 14-1

PICKING TOP INDUSTRIES FOR THE YEAR AHEAD

A study by Standard & Poor's shows that investing in industries based on their prior year's performance relative to the S&P 500 is a way to beat the market.

You can outperform the general market by buying both the strongest and weakest industries of the prior year, according to a new study by S&P. But last year's leaders and laggards must be turning the corner in terms of their own performance, as measured by their nine-month moving averages (an indicator that technical analysts find useful), to qualify for purchase.

First, at the end of November of each of the past 10 years, we determined which of the industry group indexes that make up the S&P 500 index did best over the prior 12 months relative to the S&P 500 index itself and which did worst relative to the "500." We then eliminated any of these leaders and laggards whose relative performances for the 12-month period were below their own nine-month moving averages of relative performance.

We found that industries that ranked highest in this regard and were bought at December 31 tended to do well in the following year, as did those that ranked lowest, although, again, both the best and worst had to be showing relative strength greater than the nine-month average of their relative strength, to indicate upward momentum. Rankings at the end of November determined which industries to buy on December 31 of each year and hold until December 31 one year later.

The table at right shows the performance of the leaders and laggards based on industries in the S&P 500 from 1987 through 1996. By investing in the five strongest industries at the end of each year, an investor would have beaten the market seven out of ten years and would have achieved a compound average annual return of 13.8 percent vs. the S&P 500's annual return of 11.8 percent (before dividends).

The results would have been even better had you bought the five industries with the lowest relative strength. Although many studies have determined that investors would have done poorly buying the previous year's laggards, by including one selection criterion (relative strength for the past 12 months must be above the nine-month average of relative strength), we found the opposite to be the case. The nine-month moving average helps to identify those industry groups that are depressed but may have turned the corner.

PERFORMANCE OF LEADING AND LAGGING GROUPS IN FOLLOWING YEARS

Year	S&P 500	Laggards	Leaders
1987	2.0%	30.1%	7.5%
1988	12.4	17.0	19.3
1989	27.3	28.2	28.6
1990	−6.6	−3.2	−11.1
1991	26.3	35.1	35.5
1992	4.5	8.1	−0.4
1993	7.1	11.6	23.1
1994	−1.5	12.6	−13.7
1995	34.1	28.3	35.3
1996	20.4	13.1	28.1
Compound Avg. Return	11.8	17.5	13.8
Times Beat Market	NA	8	7
Standard Deviation	13.0	11.4	17.4
†Relative Risk Rank	0.9	1.5	0.8

NA—Not available.
†Average return divided by standard deviation.

At the end of November 1996, the five industries with the strongest 12-month relative strength that were also above their nine-month moving averages were Oil & Gas Drilling & Equipment, Semiconductors, Computer Software & Services, Money Center Banks and Consumer Finance.

During the ten-year period, the laggards outperformed the market in eight years, or 80 percent of the time, and posted an average compound return of 17.5 percent. They thus not only beat the S&P 500's return of 11.8 percent for the 10 years, but they also topped the 13.8 percent average annual gain of the top five industry groups. And they did so with lower risk. The group's relative risk rank (calculated by dividing the average return by standard deviation, a common measure of price volatility) was considerably higher than both the S&P 500 and the leaders. This means the laggards offered a higher return with lower risk.

For the year through November 1996, the five industries with the lowest 12-month relative strength, but above their nine-month moving averages of relative strength, were Paper & Forest Products, Entertainment, Paper Containers, Waste Management and General Merchandise Retailers.

SOURCE: Sam Stovall, "Picking Top Industries for 1997 Using 'Relative Strength'," *The Outlook,* January 15, 1997, pp. 8–9. Reprinted by permission.

Growth stocks suffer much less during a recession, such as 1990, than do the cyclical stocks explained below. For example, growth stocks gained 2.5 percent in 1990 while cyclicals lost about 20 percent.

Defensive Industries Industries least affected by recessions and economic adversity

At the opposite end of the scale are the **defensive industries,** which are least affected by recessions and economic adversity. Food has long been considered such an industry. People must eat, and they continue to drink beer, eat frozen yogurt, and so on, regardless of the economy. Public utilities might also be considered a defensive industry.

Cyclical Industries Industries most affected, both up and down, by the business cycle

Cyclical industries are most volatile—they do unusually well when the economy prospers and are likely to be hurt more when the economy falters. Durable goods are a good example of the products involved in cyclical industries. Autos, refrigerators, and stereos, for example, may be avidly sought when times are good, but such purchases may be postponed during a recession, because consumers can often make do with the old units.

In the 1990 recession, cyclical stocks declined 20 percent, three times as much as the S&P 500. In 1994, General Motors, a prime example of a cyclical company, declined 40 percent. On the other hand, when the economy recovers, such as 1992–1993, cyclicals do very well.

Cyclicals are said to be "bought to be sold." When should investors pursue cyclical industries? When the prices of companies in the industry are low, relative to the historical record, and P/Es are high. This seems counterintuitive to many investors, but the rationale is that earnings are severely depressed in a recession and therefore the P/E is high, and this may occur shortly before earnings turn around.

Countercyclical industries also exist, actually moving opposite to the prevailing economic trend. The gold mining industry is known to follow this pattern.

Interest-Sensitive Industries Industries particularly sensitive to expectations about changes in interest rates

These three classifications of industries according to economic conditions do not constitute an exhaustive set. Additional classifications are possible and logical. For example, **interest-sensitive industries** are particularly sensitive to expectations about changes in interest rates. The financial services, banking, and real estate industries are obvious examples of interest-sensitive industries. Another is the building industry.

What are the implications of these classifications for investors? To predict the performance of an industry over shorter periods of time, investors should carefully analyze the stage of the business cycle and the likely movements in interest rates. If the economy is heading into a recession, cyclical industries are likely to be affected more than other industries, whereas defensive industries are the least likely to be affected. With such guidelines investors may make better buy or sell decisions. Similarly, an expected rise in interest rates will have negative implications for the savings and loan industry and the home building industry, whereas an expected drop in interest rates will have the opposite effect.

These statements reinforce the importance of market analysis. Not only do investors need to know the state of the economy and market before deciding to invest, but such knowledge is valuable in selecting, or avoiding, particular industries. Furthermore, investors need to consider the possibility of overcapacity as well as global competition.

As an example of applying business cycle considerations to industry analysis, consider the memory-chip industry. As shortages occurred in the early 1990s and prices rose, suppliers rushed to build new plants in order to cash in on the demand for chips. By the end of 1995, memory-chip production was growing in excess of 20 percent, but sales were slipping. A glut emerged, and in 1996 prices dropped more than 80 percent. The shell of a $2.5 billion chip plant owned by Micron Technology stands empty, waiting for the next rebound. The stock prices of chip makers suffered sharp drops in mid-1996 as the results of this activity became apparent.[9]

---

[9] This discussion is based on Jacob M. Schlesinger, "The Business Cycle Is Tamed, Many Say, Alarming Some Others," *The Wall Street Journal*, November 15, 1996, p. A1 and p. A16.

INVESTMENTS INTUITION Clearly, business cycle analysis for industries is a logical and worthwhile part of fundamental security analysis. Industries have varying sensitivities to the business conditions and interest rate expectations at any given time, and the smart investor will think carefully about these factors.

SUMMARY

- Industry analysis is the second of three steps in a top-down framework of fundamental security analysis, following economy/market analysis but preceding individual company analysis. The objective is to identify those industries that will perform best in the future in terms of returns to stockholders.
- Is industry analysis valuable? Yes, because over the long term some industries perform much better than others.
- Industry performance is not consistent; past price performance does not always predict future price performance. Particularly over shorter periods such as one or two years, industry performance rankings may completely reverse themselves.
- Although the term *industry* at first seems self-explanatory, industry definitions and classifications are not straightforward, and the trend toward diversification of activities over the years has blurred the lines even more.
- The Standard Industrial Classification system, a comprehensive scheme for classifying major industry groups, specific industries, specific functions, and specific products, brings some order to the problem.
- A number of investment information services, such as Standard & Poor's, Value Line, and Media General, use their own industry classifications.
- To analyze industries, a useful first step is to examine their stage in the life cycle, which in its simplest form consists of the pioneering, expansion, and maturity stages. Most investors will usually be interested in the expansion stage, in which growth is rapid and risk is tolerable.
- A second industry analysis approach is business cycle analysis. Industries perform differently at various stages in the business cycle.
- A third phase involves a qualitative analysis of important factors affecting industries.
- Investors interested in evaluating future industry prospects have a wide range of data available for their use. These data can be used for a detailed, in-depth analysis of industries using standard security analysis techniques for examining recent ratings of industry performance (e.g., the *Forbes* data) or for ranking likely industry performance (e.g., the Value Line industry rankings in Figure 14A-1).

KEY WORDS

Cyclical industries
Defensive industries
Growth industries
Industry life cycle
Interest-sensitive industries
Standard Industrial Classification (SIC) system

QUESTIONS

14-1. Why is it difficult to classify industries?

14-2. Why is industry analysis valuable?

14-3. Name some industries that you would expect to perform well in the next 5 years and in the next 10 to 15 years.

14-4. How consistent is year-to-year industry performance?

14-5. What are the stages in the life cycle for an industry? Can you think of other stages to add?

14-6. Name an industry that currently is in each of the three life cycle stages.

14-7. In which stage of the life cycle do investors face the highest risk of losing a substantial part of the investment?

14-8. Which industries are the most sensitive to the business cycle? the least sensitive?

14-9. Explain how aggregate market analysis can be important in analyzing industries in relation to the business cycle.

14-10. Explain the concept used in valuing industries.

14-11. What sources of information would be useful to an investor doing a detailed industry analysis?

14-12. Explain how Figure 14-1 might be useful to an investor doing industry analysis.

The following question was asked on the 1991 CFA Level II examination:

INTRODUCTION

The KCR Fund, a tax-exempt retirement plan, has owned shares of Merck & Co., Inc., a major international drug company, for many years. The investment in Merck has performed well due to rapid growth in sales and earnings.

Peter Higgens, CFA, an analyst employed by the investment manager of the DCR Fund, has been asked to recommend whether the investment in Merck should be replaced by one in Ford Motor Company.

Ford is an international manufacturer of motor vehicles, parts, and accessories, and derives 70 percent of its revenues from sales of these products in North America. Automotive and Financial Services operations have generated substantially all of Ford's earnings in the past five years. While Ford is the second largest North American auto manufacturer, it is the largest U.S. auto manufacturer overseas. The mature auto industry is sensitive to business cycles, and Japanese and European products have eroded the position of the three largest auto producers in North America.

Merck is one of the largest and "purest" of the major U.S. drug companies. It is a long-term leader in patent-protected drugs for two chronic diseases—hypertension and arthritis—and has recently captured a major position in intravenous antibiotics and anti-ulcer drugs. Merck's research and development effort is the largest in the industry. Imported drugs account for less than 5 percent of total industry sales in the United States.

The competitive environment faced by Ford is significantly different than that faced by Merck. Higgens suspects this is the major reason Merck has been more profitable than Ford, and that Merck would likely remain more profitable in the future.

CFA
14-13. Higgens is aware of three general strategies that companies may follow in seeking to create a strong competitive position:

- cost leadership
- product differentiation, and
- focus on market segments

Ford has been largely unsuccessful in exploiting these strategies. Merck, however, appears to have successfully implemented one or more of them.

Higgens is also aware of five competitive forces faced by companies. Explain how three of these competitive forces faced by Ford and Merck may have affected the relative ability of the two companies to utilize one or more of the general strategies listed above.

The following question was asked on the 1993 CFA Level II examination:

CFA
14-14. Universal Auto is a large multinational corporation headquartered in the United States. For segment reporting purposes, the company is engaged in two businesses: production of motor vehicles and information processing services.

The motor vehicle business is by far the larger of Universal's two segments. It consists mainly of domestic U.S. passenger car production, but also includes small truck manufacturing operations in the U.S. and passenger car production in other countries. This segment of Universal has had weak operating results for the past several years, including a large loss in 1992. While the company does not break out the operating results of its domestic passenger car business, that part of Universal's business is generally believed to be primarily responsible for the weak performance of its motor vehicle segment.

Idata, the information processing services segment of Universal, was started by Universal about 15 years ago. This business has shown strong, steady growth that has been entirely internal; no acquisitions have been made.

In another excerpt from the research report Adam states:

> Based on our assumption that Universal will be able to increase prices significantly on U.S. passenger cars in 1993, we project a multi-billion dollar profit improvement. . . .

A. Discuss the concept of an industrial life cycle by describing each of its four phases.
B. Identify where each of Universal's two primary businesses, passenger cars and information processing, is in such a cycle.
C. Discuss how product pricing should differ between Universal's two businesses, based on the location of each in the industrial life cycle.

SELECTED REFERENCES

One of the most detailed and well-known analyses of industries can be found in Michael Porter's work. See, as an example:

Porter, Michael E. "Industry Structure and Competitive Strategy: Keys to Profitability." *Financial Analysts Journal* (July–August 1980): 30–41.

Porter, Michael E. *Competitive Advantage: Creating and Sustaining Superior Performance*. New York: Free Press, 1985.

www.wiley.com/college/jones7

This chapter looks at the importance of industry factors in the performance of individual stocks. The website exercises will address topics such as:

- How to identify industry
- Similarities and dissimilarities between firms in the same industry.

APPENDIX 14-A SOURCES OF INDUSTRY INFORMATION

GENERAL INFORMATION

Several sources provide basic data on industries, including the following:

1. Standard & Poor's: (a) *The Annual Analysis Handbook* with monthly supplements provides per-share statistics for the industries covered. The data include sales, profit margin, income taxes, depreciation, earnings, dividends, capital expenditures, and so on. (b) The *Industry Survey* covers major industries with basic analysis revised annually and current analysis revised quarterly. (c) Standard & Poor's *Register* provides Standard Industrial Classification codes for all companies.[10]
2. *Robert Morris Associates Annual Studies* and *Dun & Bradstreet Key Business Ratios* provide ratios for a number of industries.

   The *Quarterly Financial Report for Manufacturing, Mining and Trade Corporations,* published jointly by the Federal Trade Commission and the Securities and Exchange Commission, provides timely information on individual industries. Included are data on sales, net profit, and so forth. Individual industries can be compared to groups of industries (e.g., all mining corporations) and to all manufacturing corporations.

   Forbes magazine has an annual rating of industry performance in their early January issue. Five-year figures on profitability and growth of sales and earnings are shown for a large number of industries and for individual companies within those industries.[11] Thus, this source provides investors with calculated information they can use to assess industries (and companies within those industries).

   The Value Line Investment Survey covers both individual companies and the industries that the covered companies comprise. Companies are organized by industry, with each weekly issue giving information on several industries at a time. A write up of industry developments, financial data, and trends introduces each group

[10] Using the four-digit code starting with industry 0111 and going through industry 9661, companies are listed under each code in alphabetical order.

[11] Additional information includes the debt/equity ratio, return on total capital, and the net profit margin.

Exhibit 14A-1

WEEKLY INDUSTRY RANKINGS IN ORDER OF TIMELINESS BY THE VALUE LINE INVESTMENT SURVEY.

INDUSTRIES, IN ORDER OF TIMELINESS*

Arrow (▲▼) before name indicates that a **significant change in Rank** has occurred since the preceding week

1	Internet	25	Recreation	49	Steel (Integrated)	73	Natural Gas(Diversified)
2	Retail Building Supply	26	Drug	50	Investment Co.	74	Copper
3	Advertising	27	Investment Co.(Foreign)	51	Entertainment	75	Chemical (Diversified)
4	Environmental	28	Cable TV	52	Machinery	76	R.E.I.T.
5	Semiconductor	29	Financial Services	53	Paper & Forest Products	77	Gold/Silver Mining
6	Semiconductor Cap Equip	30	Foreign Telecom	54	Oilfield Services/Equip.	78	Food Wholesalers
7	Telecom. Equipment	31	Railroad	55	Electrical Equipment	79	Food Processing
8	Furn./Home Furnishings	32	Thrift	56	Foreign Electron/Entertn	80	Packaging & Container
9	Toiletries/Cosmetics	33	Securities Brokerage	57▲	Auto Parts (OEM)	81	Canadian Energy
10	Trucking/Transp. Leasing	34	Bank (Midwest)	58	Manuf. Housing/Rec Ven	82	Chemical (Basic)
11	Retail (Special Lines)	35	Telecom. Services	59	Aerospace/Defense	83	Tobacco
12	Educational Services	36	Hotel/Gaming	60	Apparel	84	Natural Gas (Distrib.)
13	Homebuilding	37	Medical Supplies	61	Grocery	85	Water Utility
14	Computer & Peripherals	38	Beverage (Alcoholic)	62	Diversified Co.	86	Healthcare Information
15	Auto & Truck	39	Medical Services	63	Bank	87	Bank (Canadian)
16	Cement & Aggregates	40	Building Materials	64	Metal Fabricating	88	Electric Utility (East)
17	Home Appliance	41	Precision Instrument	65▼	Office Equip & Supplies	89	Petroleum (Integrated)
18	Computer Software & Svcs	42	Household Products	66▲	Steel (General)	90	Textile
19	Retail Store	43	Industrial Services	67	Maritime	91	Electric Util. (Central)
20	Tire & Rubber	44	Aluminum	68	Newspaper	92	Insurance(Prop/Casualty)
21	Air Transport	45	Auto Parts (Replacement)	69	Petroleum (Producing)	93	Beverage (Soft Drink)
22	Restaurant	46	Drugstore	70	Chemical (Specialty)	94	Electric Utility (West)
23	Shoe	47	Insurance (Life)	71	Insurance (Diversified)		
24	Electronics	48	Metals & Mining (Div.)	72	Publishing		

***Based on the Timeliness ranks of the stocks in the industry**

SOURCE: *The Value Line Investment Survey*, "Summary and Index," June 11, 1999, p. 24.

of companies (industry) covered by *Value Line*. Investors can obtain data on such variables as industry sales, operating margin, profit margin, tax rate, and capital structure.

Value Line estimates industry statistics both for the current year and the coming year. It also *ranks* all industries in terms of timeliness (probable performance over the next 12 months); therefore, investors have a unique and readily available short-term forecast. Exhibit 14A-1 shows a weekly ranking of all industries covered by *Value Line*.

Business Week carries an "Industry Outlook" for the new year in a January issue of the magazine available around the first of the year. This is a good source of information about the industries most investors are concerned with.

SPECIFIC INFORMATION

Many publications that contain specific industry information are available. Industry magazines are a good example, including such publications as *Chemical Week* and *Automotive News*. Another source of specific industry information is trade associations, which compile statistics for their particular industries. Examples include the American Banker's Association and the Iron and Steel Institute.

Moody's Investors Services produces an *Industry Review* showing comparative statistics and financial data for firms in a particular industry. Standard & Poor's produces an "Industry Outlook" as part of its *Stock Reports.* S&P's reports are now available by ordering via automated phone system, with delivery by fax, for over 4000 companies.

Obviously, brokerage firms prepare many reports on both companies and industries. Because their research analysts typically are organized along industry lines, reports are often issued on specific industries.

The federal government also provides data on industries, primarily through the Census Bureau. These data include employment figures, number of companies, and sales. Investors who choose to do their own detailed security analysis may find such information of real value. A good source of industry accounting data is *Quarterly Financial Report for Manufacturing Corporations,* published by the Federal Trade Commission and the Securities and Exchange Commission. This report contains aggregate balance sheet and income statement data for all manufacturing corporations. Data are broken down by industry and by size (assets).

chapter 15

COMPANY ANALYSIS

Chapter 15 explains fundamental security analysis for companies, showing how this is often carried out by practicing security analysts. Investors need to have a good understanding of those factors that affect security returns. For example, while earnings per share are important in affecting security returns, the unexpected component of those earnings is critical.

After reading this chapter you will be able to:

- **Analyze companies using the techniques of fundamental analysis.**
- **Use the concepts of ROE and ROA in security analysis.**
- **Recognize the importance of earnings announcements and the impact of earnings surprises on stock prices.**
- **Understand the role of security analysts and company management in earnings forecasts.**
- **Appreciate more completely the role of the P/E ratio in security analysis.**

Once economy/market analysis has indicated a favorable time to invest in common stocks and industry analysis has been performed to find those industries that are expected to perform well in the future, it remains for the investor to choose promising companies within those industries. The last step in *top-down* fundamental analysis, therefore, is to analyze individual companies. As with the previous two steps, an investor should think in terms of the two components of fundamental value: dividends and required rate of return or, alternatively, earnings and the P/E ratio, and analyze them to the extent practical using the valuation framework presented in Chapter 10.

FUNDAMENTAL ANALYSIS

Fundamental analysis at the company level involves analyzing basic financial variables in order to estimate the company's intrinsic value. These variables include sales, profit margins, depreciation, the tax rate, sources of financing, asset utilization, and other factors. Additional analysis could involve the firm's competitive position in its industry, labor relations, technological changes, management, foreign competition, and so on. The end result of fundamental analysis at the company level is the data needed to calculate the estimated or intrinsic value of a stock using one of the valuation models.

As discussed in Chapter 10, investors can use the dividend discount model to value common stocks. Assuming that the dividend growth rate for a particular company will be approximately constant over the future, we find that the dividend discount model reduces to the constant-growth version shown as Equation 15-1 (Equation 10-5 from Chapter 10):

$$\text{Intrinsic value} = P_0 = \frac{D_1}{k - g} \qquad (15\text{-}1)$$

where

P_0 = the estimated value of the common stock today
D_1 = the expected dollar dividend to be paid next period
k = the required rate of return
g = the estimated future growth rate of dividends

In fundamental analysis, the intrinsic or estimated value of a stock is its justified price, the price justified by a company's fundamental financial variables.

Alternatively, for a short-run estimate of intrinsic value the earnings multiplier model could be used. Intrinsic value is the product of the estimated earnings per share (EPS) for next year and the multiplier or P/E ratio, as shown in Equation 15-2.[1]

$$\begin{aligned}\text{Intrinsic value} &= P_0 = \text{Estimated EPS} \times \text{estimated P/E ratio} \\ &= E_1 \times P_0/E_1\end{aligned} \qquad (15\text{-}2)$$

Using either Equation 15-1 or Equation 15-2, we can compare a stock's calculated intrinsic value to its current market price. If the intrinsic value is larger than the current market price, the stock can be considered undervalued—a buy. If intrinsic value is less than

[1] Technically, to calculate the intrinsic value of a stock using the multiplier method, analysts often determine what is called the normalized EPS, defined as the normal earnings for a company under typical operating conditions. Thus, unusual impacts on earnings such as nonrecurring earnings or extraordinary earnings are adjusted for.

FIGURE 15-1

Median change in earnings and stock price: five-year horizon.

SOURCE: V. Niederhoffer and P. J. Regan, "Earnings Changes, Analysts' Forecasts and Stock Prices," *Financial Analysts Journal*, 28 (May–June 1972), p. 71. Reprinted by permission.

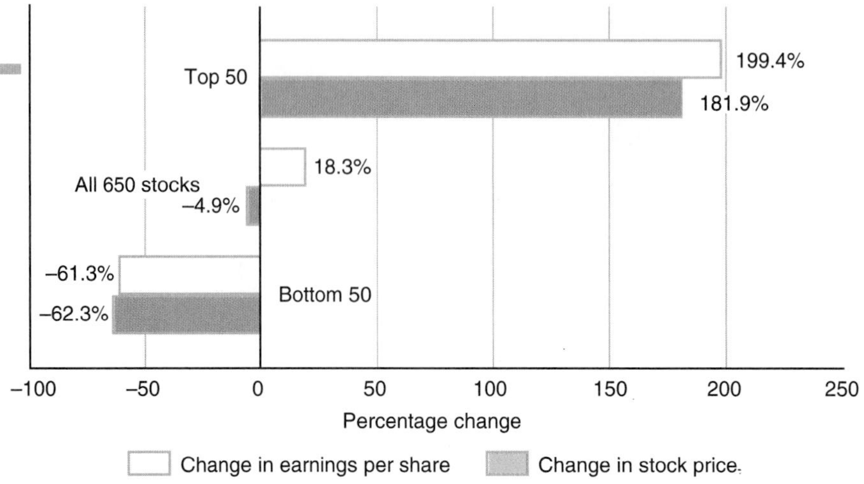

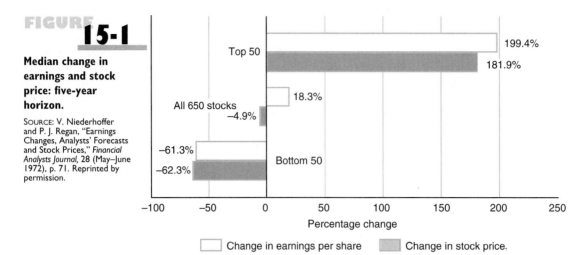

the market price, the stock is considered overvalued and should be avoided or possibly sold if owned. Alternatively, an overvalued security could be sold short.

For purposes of discussion, we concentrate on earnings and P/E ratios for several reasons. First, dividends are paid from earnings. Although the two series are not perfectly correlated, future dividend growth typically must come from future earnings growth. Second, the close correlation between earnings changes and stock-price changes is well documented and can be demonstrated graphically.

To see why investors and security analysts focus so much attention on earnings, consider Figure 15-1, which shows the 50 best and worst stocks over a five-year period. The top 50 stocks from the sample of 650 companies studied showed a five-year price appreciation of 182 percent, with a change in EPS of 199 percent; for the bottom 50 performers, with a price depreciation of −62 percent, the change in EPS was −61 percent. This figure dramatically illustrates the importance of EPS in common stock analysis. Although other comparisons of earnings and stock prices may not be as striking as those in Figure 15-1, EPS and price changes typically are very closely related both for the best-performing and worst-performing stocks and for stocks in general.

Alternatively, consider the relationship between earnings growth and price performance. A study by Elton, Gruber, and Gultekin examined the risk-adjusted excess returns available from buying stocks on the basis of next year's growth in earnings. They found that those stocks with the highest future growth in EPS showed the highest risk-adjusted returns. For the 30 percent of the companies with the highest growth in EPS, the risk-adjusted excess return was 7.48 percent; for the 30 percent with the lowest growth, the risk-adjusted excess return was −4.93 percent. Clearly, therefore, growth in reported earnings affects stock prices in a highly significant manner.

THE ACCOUNTING ASPECTS OF EARNINGS

If investors are to focus on a company's earnings per share (EPS), a critical variable in security analysis, they should understand how EPS is derived and what it represents. For investors, an EPS figure is often the bottom line—the item of major interest—in a company's financial statements. Furthermore, they must understand the components of EPS before they can attempt to forecast it.

THE FINANCIAL STATEMENTS

Financial Statements The principal published financial data about a company, primarily the balance sheet and income statement

Investors rely heavily on the **financial statements** of a corporation, which provide the major financial data about companies. To illustrate the use of financial statements in doing company analysis, we examine the 1998 financial statements for the Coca-Cola Company, a famous company with a brand name known worldwide and a company that epitomizes the global nature of business in today's world. Coca-Cola, the soft drink, is available in more than 195 countries.

The Balance Sheet The balance sheet shows the portfolio of assets for a corporation, as well as its liabilities and owner's equity, at one point in time. The amounts at which items are carried on the balance sheet are dictated by accounting conventions. Cash is the actual dollar amount, whereas marketable securities could be at cost or market value. Stockholders' equity and the fixed assets are on a book value basis.

The balance sheet for Coca-Cola, shown in Table 15-1, is for the year 1998 and also includes data for 1997. The asset side is divided into *Current Assets, Investments and Other Assets,* and *Long-term Assets* (labeled by Coke as *Property, Plant, and Equipment*) plus, in Coca-Cola's case, *Goodwill and Other Intangible Assets.* Coca-Cola's net property, plant, and equipment is less than the current assets, whereas in the case of General Motors, for example, the fixed assets exceed the current assets. Coca-Cola is also unusual in the large amount of investments and other assets carried.

The right-hand side of the balance sheet is divided between *Current Liabilities* (payable within one year), *Long-Term Debt, Other Liabilities, Deferred Income Taxes, and Shareholders' Equity.* For 1998 Coca-Cola had $8.6 billion of current liabilities, $687 million in long-term debt, and $8.4 billion in shareholders' equity, plus *Other Liabilities and Deferred Income Taxes.*

The shareholders' equity includes 3.5 billion shares of stock issued as of 1998 (out of 5.6 billion authorized), with a par value of $0.25, $2.2 billion of capital surplus, and a substantial amount of retained earnings ($19.9 billion). The retained earnings item does not represent "spendable" funds for a company; rather, it designates that part of previous earnings not paid out as dividends. Note the large amount of *treasury stock* held, representing shares of Coca-Cola being held by the company itself. This amount reduces the original stockholders' equity by more than half.

Several financial ratios that can be calculated from balance sheet data are useful in assessing the company's financial strength (e.g., the current ratio, a measure of liquidity, or the debt-to-total-assets ratio, a measure of leverage). These ratios are part of the standard ratio analysis which is often performed by managers, creditors, stockholders, and other interested groups, and are covered in most financial management texts and courses. Some of these ratios are demonstrated later in the analysis.

The Income Statement This statement is used more frequently by investors, not only to assess current management performance but also as a guide to the company's future profitability. The income statement represents flows for a particular period, usually one year. Table 15-2 shows the Consolidated Statements of Income for Coca-Cola covering the years 1998, 1997, and 1996.

The key item for investors on the income statement is the after-tax net income, which, divided by the number of common shares outstanding, produces earnings per share. Earnings from continuing operations typically are used to judge the company's success and are almost always the earnings reported in the financial press. Nonrecurring earnings, such as net extraordinary items that arise from unusual and infrequently occurring transactions, are separated from income from continuing operations.

TABLE 15-1 CONSOLIDATED BALANCE SHEETS, THE COCA-COLA COMPANY

December 31,	1998	1997
(In millions except share data)		
ASSETS		
CURRENT		
Cash and cash equivalents	$ 1,648	$ 1,737
Marketable securities	159	106
	1,807	1,843
Trade accounts receivable, less allowances of $10 in 1998 and $23 in 1997	1,666	1,639
Inventories	890	959
Prepaid expenses and other assets	2,017	1,528
TOTAL CURRENT ASSETS	**6,380**	**5,969**
INVESTMENTS AND OTHER ASSETS		
Equity method investments		
Coca-Cola Enterprises Inc.	584	184
Coca-Cola Amatil Limited	1,255	1,204
Coca-Cola Beverages plc	879	—
Other, principally bottling companies	3,573	3,049
Cost method investments, principally bottling companies	395	
Marketable securities and other assets	1,863	1,607
	8,549	6,501
PROPERTY, PLANT AND EQUIPMENT		
Land	199	183
Buildings and improvements	1,507	1,535
Machinery and equipment	3,855	3,896
Containers	124	157
	5,685	5,771
Less allowances for depreciation	2,016	2,028
	3,669	3,743
GOODWILL AND OTHER INTANGIBLE ASSETS	**547**	**668**
TOTAL ASSETS	**$19,145**	**$16,881**
LIABILITIES AND SHARE-OWNERS' EQUITY		
CURRENT		
Accounts payable and accrued expenses	$ 3,141	$ 3,249
Loans and notes payable	4,459	2,677
Current maturities of long-term debt	3	397
Accrued income taxes	1,037	1,056
TOTAL CURRENT LIABILITIES	**8,640**	**7,379**
LONG-TERM DEBT	**687**	**801**
OTHER LIABILITIES	**991**	**1,001**
DEFERRED INCOME TAXES	**424**	**426**

TABLE 15-1 (continued)

December 31,	1998	1997
(In millions except share data)		
SHARE-OWNERS' EQUITY		
Common stock, $.25 par value— Authorized: 5,600,000,000 shares Issued: 3,460,083,686 shares in 1998; 3,443,441,902 shares in 1997	865	861
Capital surplus	2,195	1,527
Reinvested earnings	19,922	17,869
Accumulated other comprehensive income and unearned compensation on restricted stock	(1,434)	(1,401)
	21,548	18,856
Less treasury stock, at cost (994,566,196 shares in 1998; 972,812,731 shares in 1997)	13,145	11,582
	8,403	7,274
	$19,145	**$16,881**

See Notes to Consolidated Financial Statements.

SOURCE: 1998 Annual Report, the Coca-Cola Company, pp. 40–41.

TABLE 15-2 CONSOLIDATED STATEMENTS OF INCOME, THE COCA-COLA COMPANY

Year Ended December 31,	1998	1997	1996
(In millions except per share data)			
NET OPERATING REVENUES	**$18,813**	**$18,868**	**$18,673**
Cost of goods sold	5,562	6,015	6,738
GROSS PROFIT	**13,251**	**12,853**	**11,935**
Selling, administrative and general expenses	8,284	7,852	8,020
OPERATING INCOME	**4,967**	**5,001**	**3,915**
Interest income	219	211	238
Interest expense	277	258	286
Equity income	32	155	211
Other income-net	230	583	87
Gain on issuance of stock by Equity investees	27	363	—
INCOME BEFORE INCOME TAXES	**5,198**	**6,055**	**4,596**
Income taxes	1,665	1,926	1,104
NET INCOME	**3,533**	**4,129**	**3,492**
NET INCOME	**1.43**	**1.67**	**1.40**
Diluted Net Income Per Share	1.42	1.64	1.38
Average Shares Outstanding	2,467	2,477	2,494
Dilutive effect of stock options	29	38	29
Average Shares Outstanding Assuming Dilution	2,496	2,515	2,523

See Notes to Consolidated Financial Statements.

SOURCE: 1998 Annual Report, the Coca-Cola Company, p. 42.

Table 15-2 clearly illustrates the "flow" in an income statement. Starting with revenues (total net sales), the cost of goods sold is deducted to obtain Gross Profit. Subtraction of selling, administrative, and general expenses results in "Operating Income," which for Coca-Cola in 1998 was $4.97 billion.

Operating income is adjusted by subtracting the interest expense, which generally is an important item for large companies because interest is tax-deductible. Note, however, that Coca-Cola earned interest and equity income and had gains on investments, all of which must be added back.

Adjustments to operating income produce "Income before Income Taxes." Subtracting out income taxes results in "Basic Net Income Per Share." A small adjustment of one cent produces "Diluted Net Income Per Share." Dividing by the *average* number of shares outstanding produces EPS for 1998 of $1.43, and adjusting for the dilution of stock options, diluted EPS of $1.42.

The charge to earnings because of an accounting change is important to investors in trying to understand earnings. What investors seek to determine is the "true" earning power of a company because ultimately they will be attempting to forecast future earnings. Although there was no impact on Coca-Cola in 1998, the difference caused by accounting adjustments can be quite large for other companies at various times. In general, investors should rely on income before changes in accounting principles.

Generally Accepted Accounting Principles (GAAP) Financial reporting requirements establishing the rules for producing financial statements

Certifying the Statements The earnings shown on an income statement are derived on the basis of **generally accepted accounting principles (GAAP).** The company adheres to a standard set of rules developed by the accounting profession on the basis of historical costs, which can be measured objectively. An auditor from an independent accounting firm certifies that the earnings have been derived according to accounting standards in a statement labeled the "auditor's report."

EXAMPLE 15-1

In certifying Coca-Cola's financial statements, Ernst & Young stated that, "In our opinion, the financial statements referred to above present fairly, in all material respects, the consolidated financial position of the Coca-Cola Company and subsidiaries."

Note that the auditor's report does *not* guarantee the accuracy or the quality of the earnings in an absolute sense; rather, it only attests that the statements are a *fair presentation* of the company's financial position for a particular period. The auditors are certifying, in effect, that generally accepted accounting principles were applied on a consistent basis. The Financial Accounting Standards Board (FASB), which succeeded the Accounting Principles Board of the American Institute of Certified Public Accountants in 1972, currently formulates accounting standards.

THE PROBLEM WITH REPORTED EARNINGS

Although earnings in particular, and financial statements in general, are derived on the basis of GAAPs and are certified in an auditor's report, problems exist with earnings. The basic problem, simply stated, is that reported EPS for a company (i.e., accounting EPS) is not a precise figure that is readily comparable over time, and the EPS figures for different companies often are not comparable to each other.

The problem with earnings is that alternative accounting principles can be, and are, used to prepare the financial statements. Many of the items in the balance sheet and income statement can be accounted for in at least two ways, resulting in what one might call the "conservative" treatment and the "liberal" treatment of EPS. Given the number of items that constitutes the financial statements, the possible number of acceptable (i.e., that conform to GAAPs) combinations that could be used is large. Holding everything else constant, such as sales, products, and operating ability, a company could produce several legal and permissible EPS figures, depending solely on the accounting principles used. The question that investors must try to answer is, "Which EPS best represents the 'true' position of a company?"

Because reported EPS is a function of the many alternative GAAPs in use, it is extremely difficult, if not impossible, for the "true" performance of a company to be reflected consistently in one figure. Since each company is different, is it reasonable to expect one accounting system to capture the true performance of all companies? With the business world so complex, one can make a case for the necessity of alternative treatments of the same item or process, such as inventories or depreciation.

Consider some of the current problem areas in GAAPs.

1. Many of the best assets today are intangible, as opposed to yesterday's plant and equipment. What makes Amazon.com or eBay such hot concepts are their ideas and software development. AOL's stock performance directly depends upon subscribers. These companies typically have to expense costs involved in their success rather than to capitalize them.
2. Research and development costs can be substantial and contribute heavily to a firm's success, but the balance sheet does not reflect it because research and development is not treated as an asset.
3. The treatment of mergers and acquisitions can cause confusion. If a company acquires a great product by buying another company, the cost is not expensed, and an asset is created. If the company develops its own great product, expenses must be written off as they occur. Does this make sense?

Accountants are caught in the middle—between investors, who want a clean, clear-cut EPS figure, and company management, which wants to present the financial statements in the most favorable light. After all, management hires the accounting firm, and, subject to certain guidelines, management can change accounting firms. As long as the company follows GAAPs, the accountant may find it difficult to resist management pressure to use particular principles. At some point, an accounting firm may resign as a company's auditor as a result of the problems and pressures that can arise.

The FASB faces conflicting demands when it formulates or changes accounting principles because various interest groups want items accounted for in specific ways. The end result is that the "standards" issued by the FASB are often compromises that do not fully resolve the particular issue; in some cases, they may create additional complications. Since its formation, the FASB has issued numerous standards and exposure drafts and has tackled some very difficult issues such as inflation accounting and foreign currency translations. Much remains to be done, however, and this will probably remain true for a long time.

Should the FASB falter in its job, or investors actively demand more action in the way of "tighter" accounting rules, the government could intervene and issue its own rulings. The Securities and Exchange Commission has the authority to do so because corporations must file detailed financial data with it. The SEC has issued some definitions of acceptable accounting practices over the years, thereby acting as a prod to the accounting groups to continue their progress. On the other hand, the SEC may feel it is unable to insist on more conformity, preferring instead to have the accounting profession take the responsibility.

INVESTMENTS INTUITION Given the difficulties involved, and the alternative accounting treatments, investors must remember that reported EPS is not the precise figure that it first appears to be. Unless adjustments are made, the EPS of different companies may not be comparable on either a time series or a cross-sectional basis.

Some EPS figures are better than others in the sense that they have been derived using more conservative principles. In other words, they are of higher quality. In an article on the quality of earnings, Bernstein and Seigel stated:[2]

> *a company's reported earnings figure is often taken by the unsophisticated user of financial statements as the quantitative measure of the firm's well-being. Of course, any professional knows that earnings numbers are in large part the product of conscious and often subjective choices between various accounting treatments and business options, as well as of various external economic factors. If he wants to assess the true earning power of each company, the financial statement user must make some determination of the "quality of its earnings" [emphasis added].*

Quality assessments are typically difficult to make and require considerable expertise in accounting and financial analysis. However, as *Forbes* magazine recently noted, "Really smart investors must go back to the original data and reinterpret it. 'Right now,' says former SEC commissioner Steven Wallman, 'we take disaggregated data and have accountants aggregate it, only to have investors disaggregate it again.' "[3]

The best advice for most investors is to go ahead and use the reported EPS because it is all that is normally available, and the majority of investors will also have to rely on this figure. Investors should, however, be aware of the potential problems involved in EPS and should constantly keep in mind its nature and derivation. For example, as the economy approaches a recession, many analysts believe that companies use aggressive accounting techniques in order to report larger earnings. Such techniques include recognizing revenues before they are actually received or delaying the recording of expenses.

International Accounting Investors who find U.S. accounting comparisons difficult will be even more troubled by international accounting practices. Practices can vary widely among countries, and differ sharply from what U.S. investors may expect to find. Some examples:

- In Japan, many companies have not expensed enough for underfunded pension liabilities.
- Because of high tax rates, some European firms often "hide" earnings.
- In Latin America, inflation accounting means that companies whose local currency debts fall as a result of inflation can flow the gain through to the income statement.
- In Korea, accounting may hide certain items, even going so far as not being in the footnotes, such as the losses of subsidiaries.

As *Forbes* magazine noted in detailing some of these practices, "Foreign companies have a lot to learn when it comes to transparency."[4]

---

[2] See Leopold Bernstein and Joel Seigel, "The Concept of Earnings Quality," *Financial Analysts Journal* (July–August 1979).
[3] See Bernard Condon, "Gaps in GAAP," *Forbes*, January 25, 1999, p. 76.
[4] This quote and the items mentioned come from Bernard Condon, "Donde esta earnings?" *Forbes*, June 15, 1998, p. 234.

ANALYZING A COMPANY'S PROFITABILITY

Return on Equity The accounting rate of return on stockholders equity

On a company level, EPS is the culmination of several important factors. Accounting variables can be used to examine these determining factors by analyzing key financial ratios. Analysts examine the components of profitability in order to try to determine whether a company's profitability is increasing or decreasing, and why. Primary emphasis is on **Return on Equity (ROE)** because it is the key component in determining earnings growth and dividend growth.

Also note the following accounting identity, which establishes the relationship between EPS and ROE:

$$\text{EPS} = \text{ROE} \times \text{Book value per share} \qquad (15\text{-}3)$$

where ROE is the return on equity and book value per share is the accounting value of the stockholders' equity on a per share basis. Book value typically changes rather slowly, making ROE the primary variable on which to concentrate. Using Coca-Cola's data from Tables 15-1 and 15-2, we would calculate EPS for 1998 as follows:

	For Coca-Cola	$	*% Return*
EPS	$= \dfrac{\text{Net income after taxes}}{\text{Shares outstanding}} = \dfrac{\$3{,}533{,}000{,}000}{2{,}467{,}000{,}000}$	= $1.43	—
ROE	$= \dfrac{\text{Net income after taxes}}{\text{Stockholders' equity}} = \dfrac{\$3{,}533{,}000{,}000}{\$8{,}403{,}000{,}000}$	= —	0.420
Book value per share	$= \dfrac{\text{Stockholders' equity}}{\text{Shares outstanding}} = \dfrac{\$8{,}403{,}000{,}000}{2{,}467{,}000{,}000}$	= $3.41	—

From an accounting standpoint, mechanically, EPS is the product of two factors, ROE and book value per share. The ROE is the accounting rate of return that stockholders earn on their portion of the total capital used to finance the company; in other words, it is the return on equity. Book value per share measures the accounting value of the stockholders' equity.

EXAMPLE 15-2

In Coca-Cola's case in 1998 the ROE was 42 percent, and the book value was $3.41 per share. Therefore:[5]

$$\text{EPS} = 0.42 \times \$3.41 = \$1.43$$

ANALYZING RETURN ON EQUITY (ROE)

The return on equity (ROE) is the end result of several important variables. These variables typically are analyzed by what is referred to as the duPont system of analysis because it originated at the duPont Corporation. The idea is to decompose the ROE into its critical components in order both to identify adverse impacts on ROE and to help analysts predict future trends in ROE.

Return on Assets The accounting rate of return on a firm's assets

Different combinations of financial ratios can be used to decompose ROE. We will use a multiplicative relationship that consists of five financial ratios, all multiplied together to produce ROE. The first four can be multiplied together to determine **Return on Assets (ROA)**, an important measure of a company's profitability. ROA measures the return on assets,

[5] This is based on EPS before the adjustment for dilution.

while ROE measures the return to the stockholders, who finance only part of the assets (the bondholders finance the other part).

1. A key component of a company's profitability is its operating efficiency, which is unaffected by interest charges, taxes, or the amount of debt financing used by a company to finance its assets (that is, the leverage). To determine operating efficiency, we analyze its components—Earnings before Interest and Taxes (EBIT)—also called Operating Income—and asset turnover.

The EBIT/sales ratio is a measure of the firm's ability to operate efficiently. EBIT reflects the earnings before the financing decision is accounted for as a result of subtracting the interest expense and before the provision for income taxes. The larger the EBIT per dollar of sales, the better in terms of operational efficiency. In effect, the EBIT reflects the gross margin on sales.

EBIT/Sales = Pretax, preinterest profit margin

2. Asset turnover is a measure of efficiency. Given some amount of total assets, how much in sales can be generated? The more sales per dollar of assets, where each dollar of assets has to be financed with a source of funds bearing a cost, the better it is for a firm. The firm may have some assets that are unproductive, thereby adversely affecting its efficiency.

Sales/Total assets = Asset turnover

3. Next, we consider the impact of interest charges. Interest expense for most companies is an important tax-deductible item. The "interest burden" can be calculated as the ratio of pretax income to EBIT:

Interest burden = Pretax income/EBIT

4. The last variable that must be considered as part of the analysis of a company's *return on assets* is the "tax burden." To calculate this amount, we divide net income by pretax income.

Tax burden = Net income/Pretax income

Return on assets (ROA) can now be calculated from these four variables that have important impacts on a company's return on assets:

$$\text{ROA} = \frac{\text{EBIT}}{\text{Sales}} \times \frac{\text{Sales}}{\text{Total assets}} \times \frac{\text{Pretax income}}{\text{EBIT}} \frac{\text{Net income}}{\text{Pretax income}} \qquad (15\text{-}4)$$

EXAMPLE 15-3

Using the data for Coca-Cola for 1998 from Tables 15-1 and 15-2:

EBIT/Sales = $4,967,000,000/$18,813,000,000 = 0.2640

Sales/Total assets = $18,813,000/$19,145,000,000 = .9827

Pretax income/EBIT = $5,198,000,000/$4,967,000,000 = 1.0465

Net income/Pretax income = $3,533,000,000/$5,198,000,000 = .6797

ROA = 0.2271 × 1.1979 × 1.0577 × .6899 = 0.184536 = 18.4536%

Return on assets (ROA) is a fundamental measure of firm profitability, reflecting how effectively and efficiently the firm's assets are used. Obviously, the higher the net income for a given amount of assets, the better the return. For Coca-Cola, the return on assets is 18.45

percent. The ROA can be improved by increasing the net income more than the assets (in percentage terms) or by using the existing assets even more efficiently.

5. Finally, the effects of leverage must be considered. The leverage ratio measures how the firm finances its assets.[6] Basically, firms can finance with either debt or equity. Debt, though a cheaper source of financing, is a riskier method, because of the fixed interest payments that must be systematically repaid on time to avoid bankruptcy. Leverage can magnify the returns to the stockholders (favorable leverage) or diminish them (unfavorable leverage). Thus, any given ROA can be magnified into a higher ROE by the judicious use of debt financing. The converse, however, applies; injudicious use of debt can lower the ROE below the ROA.

INVESTMENTS INTUITION What this analysis does not show is the impact of leverage on the risk of the firm. Remember that in this analysis we are examining only the determinants of EPS. However, as we know from our discussion of valuation, two factors, EPS and a multiplier, are required to determine value. An increase in leverage may increase the riskiness of the company more than enough to offset the increased EPS, thereby lowering the company's value. *Investors must always consider both dimensions of the value of a stock, the return side and the risk side.*

To more easily capture the effects of leverage we use an equity multiplier rather than a debt percentage.

Leverage = Total assets/Stockholders' equity

EXAMPLE 15-4 In 1998, for Coca-Cola, dividing total assets by equity produces an equity multiplier of 2.2784, which is used as the measure of leverage. In effect, $1 of stockholders' equity was financing $2.27 of assets.

The last step in the ROE analysis is to relate ROA and leverage:

$$\text{ROE} = \text{ROA} \times \text{Leverage} \tag{15-5}$$

EXAMPLE 15-5 Combining these two factors, ROA and leverage, for Coca-Cola produces the following ROE:

$$\text{ROE} = 0.1845 \times 2.2784 = 0.4204 = 42.04\%$$

A standard formulation of the ROE analysis often used in the CFA curriculum combines all factors considered above into one multiplicative equation based on these ratios or variations to accommodate the multiplication:

$$\text{ROE} = \text{EBIT efficiency} \times \text{Asset turnover} \times \text{Interest burden} \times \text{Tax burden} \times \text{Leverage} \tag{15-6}$$

$$\text{ROE} = \frac{\text{EBIT}}{\text{Sales}} \times \frac{\text{Sales}}{\text{Assets}} \times \frac{\text{Pretax income}}{\text{EBIT}} \times \frac{\text{Net income}}{\text{Pretax income}} \times \frac{\text{Assets}}{\text{Equity}}$$

[6] Leverage can be measured in several ways, such as the ratio of total debt to total assets or the ratio of debt to equity.

EXAMPLE 15-6

For Coca-Cola, using 1998 data:

$$\text{ROE} = \frac{\$4{,}967{,}000{,}000}{\$18{,}813{,}000{,}000} \times \frac{\$18{,}813{,}000{,}000}{\$19{,}145{,}000{,}000} \times \frac{\$5{,}198{,}000{,}000}{\$4{,}967{,}000{,}000}$$

$$\times \frac{\$3{,}533{,}000{,}000}{\$5{,}198{,}000{,}000} \times \frac{\$19{,}145{,}000{,}000}{\$8{,}403{,}000{,}000}$$

$$= 0.264 \times .9827 \times 1.0465 \times 0.6797 \times 2.2784 = 0.4204 \text{ or } 42\%$$

ESTIMATING THE INTERNAL (SUSTAINABLE) GROWTH RATE

An important part of company analysis is the determination of a sustainable growth rate in earnings and dividends. Such a growth rate estimate is used in the Dividend Discount Model.

Internal (Sustainable) Growth Rate (g) The estimated earnings growth rate, calculated as the product of ROE and the retention rate

What determines the sustainable growth rate? The **internal or sustainable growth rate** of earnings or dividends, g, is the product of the ROE and the retention rate—which is calculated as 1.0 minus the dividend payout ratio—as shown in Equation 15-7:

$$g = \text{ROE} \times (1 - \text{Payout ratio}) \tag{15-7}$$

Equation 15-7 is one of the principal calculations in fundamental security analysis and is often used by security analysts. We can calculate g by using data for a particular year.[7]

EXAMPLE 15-7

For 1998 Coca-Cola's ROE is 0.420 and the dividend payout ratio is 0.488. The internal growth rate estimate based on 1998 data is, therefore, .42 × .512 = 21.5 percent.

The earnings growth rate, or persistence in the earnings trend, is not always easily predicted. Investors cannot simply use the current or past internal growth rate for EPS to predict the future rate of growth.

The internal growth rate estimate produced by Equation 15-7 is reliable only if a company's profitability as measured by ROE remains in balance. If, for example, the ROE for a company grows significantly in the future or declines significantly, the actual EPS growth rate will turn out to be quite different than the internal growth rate estimate produced by Equation 15-7.

Another problem associated with using a particular year to estimate the internal growth rate is that the year used may not be a "normal" year. Basing a projection on one year's results can result in a faulty estimate; this is particularly true for companies in cyclical industries.

What matters is the future expected growth rate, not the actual historical growth rate. If investors expect the growth rate to be different in the future, they should use the expected growth rate and not simply the calculation based on current data.

Payout ratios for most companies vary over time, but reasonable estimates can often be obtained for a particular company using an average of recent years. Estimating future ROE is

[7] Technically, g is defined as the expected growth rate in dividends. However, the dividend growth rate is clearly influenced by the earnings growth rate. Although dividend and earnings growth rates can diverge in the short run, such differences would not be expected to continue for long periods of time. The standard assumption in security analysis is that g represents the growth rate for both dividends and earnings.

more challenging. The previous analysis is useful in analyzing the factors that affect ROE. The challenge is trying to determine how these factors will change in the future.

EARNINGS ESTIMATES

The EPS that investors use to value stocks is the future (expected) EPS. Current stock price is a function of future earnings estimates and the P/E ratio, not the past. If investors knew what the EPS for a particular company would be next year, they could achieve good results in the market. See Box 15-1 for a good discussion of the importance of earnings forecasts and the role that security analysts play in this process.

Box 15-1

ESTIMATING THE FUTURE

A company's earnings are key to determining its stock price. But stocks don't trade just on the money a company actually carries to the bank. Stock prices are based on expected earnings—what Wall Street calls earnings estimates—and can move up or down rapidly depending on how real earnings compare with expectations. Consider the electronics retailer Tandy: When the company's third-quarter earnings per share came in one penny short of analysts' expectations, the stock plunged 24 percent.

Earnings estimates are educated guesses made by securities analysts about the future profitability of the companies they follow. The best estimates result from careful modeling of a company's costs, the mix of products the company sells, and the demand for these products. Good analysts get out of their offices to listen to what customers say about a company's product and talk on the phone to suppliers and competitors. Large companies may be followed by 30 to 40 analysts, while small companies may be followed by only a few, or sometimes none at all.

Research firms such as Zacks Investment Research in Chicago, I/B/E/S International in New York, and First Call in Boston compile estimates from the analysts who follow a stock to calculate an average expectation for a company's future earnings. (Individual investors can check research from I/B/E/S, Zacks, and First Call through such services as CompuServe, Prodigy, and America Online.)

Such research can offer important clues to future changes in stock prices. Analysts update their estimates continually, and savvy investors look for patterns in the changes. Is the estimate of a company's earnings for the next quarter slipping? Have a few analysts raised their estimates? Investors also want to know if the spread between the high and low estimates is getting wider or narrower. A widening spread indicates analysts are increasingly divided in their opinions on a stock. "The dynamics of how the earnings estimates change tell you a lot," says Ed Keon, senior vice president of I/B/E/S.

Interpreting changes in earnings estimates requires knowledge of both a company and its industry. When expectations for a company are already low, a disappointing earnings report will not have much impact on the stock price. Take the beleaguered chemical industry, says Ben Zacks, executive vice president of Zacks Investment Research. "If a company comes in ten cents below the estimate, no one cares." But when expectations are high, a stock can get trounced if it falls short by even a few cents. That's one reason technology shares are so volatile.

Four times a year analysts get to check their best guesses against reality when companies issue their quarterly financial reports. Afterward, analysts often change their future estimates. Following Tandy's report, 15 of the 16 analysts who covered the company lowered their estimates.

But "revision fever" can strike in the days just before a company reports, as one analyst after another produces a new estimate. Many of these word-of-mouth revisions aren't picked up by the large research firms. That's why a stock that meets the published estimates can still rise or fall rapidly after earnings have been anounced.

SOURCE: Pamela J. Black, "Estimating the Future," *Worth*, February 1996, p. 119. Originally published in *Worth* magazine, February 1996. Reprinted by permission of *Worth* magazine.

In doing fundamental security analysis using EPS, an investor needs to (1) know how to obtain an earnings estimate; (2) consider the accuracy of any earnings estimate obtained; and (3) understand the role of earnings surprises in impacting stock prices. We consider each of these topics in turn.

A FORECAST OF EPS

Security Analysts' Estimates of Earnings Among the most obvious sources of earnings estimates are security analysts, who make such forecasts as a part of their job. This type of earnings information is widely available. *The Value Line Investment Survey,* for example, forecasts quarterly earnings for several quarters ahead for each company covered. I/B/E/S/ International is a well-known New York firm that tracks earnings estimates by analysts and makes them available.

Several studies suggest that individual analysts are by and large undistinguishable in their ability to predict EPS. The practical implication of these findings is that the consensus forecast is likely to be superior to the forecasts of individual analysts.

Mechanical Estimates of Earnings An alternative method of obtaining earnings forecasts is the use of mechanical procedures such as time series models. In deciding what type of model to use, some of the evidence on the behavior of earnings over time should be considered.

Time series analysis involves the use of historical data to make earnings forecasts. The model used assumes that the future will be similar to the past. The series being forecast, EPS, is assumed to have trend elements, an average value, seasonal factors, and error. The moving average technique is a simple example of the time series model for forecasting EPS. Exponential smoothing, which assigns differing weights to past values, is an example of a more sophisticated technique. A regression equation would represent another technique for making forecasts; the regression equation could handle several variables, such as trend and seasonal factors. More sophisticated models could also be used.

Studies of the behavior of the time path of earnings have produced mixed results. Most of the early studies indicated randomness in the growth rates of annual earnings. Other studies found some evidence of nonrandomness. More recent studies, particularly those of quarterly earnings, have indicated that the time series behavior of earnings is not random.

THE ACCURACY OF EARNINGS FORECASTS

A study by Brown and Rozeff found results that "overwhelmingly" favored the analysts.[8] Specifically, the study found that earnings forecasts made by *The Value Line Investment Survey* (described in Appendix 15-A) were consistently superior to those produced by well-known time series models, including the sophisticated Box–Jenkins method. Such a finding is reassuring from an economic theory standpoint because analysts' forecasts cost more than time series forecasts. On balance, the weight of the evidence tends to favor analysts over statistical models in predicting what the *actual* reported earnings will be.

Even if investors accept the relative superiority of analysts' estimates, the fact remains that analysts often over- or underestimate the earnings that are actually realized. Analysts are typically far off target on their estimates. According to one study of almost 400 companies, analysts' estimates averaged 57 percent too high in the first month of a fiscal year, and the error was still an average 12 percent by year-end.

[8] See L. Brown and M. Rozeff, "The Superiority of Analyst Forecasts as Measures of Expectations. Evidence from Earnings," *Journal of Finance,* 33 (March 1978): 1–16.

Another study by Dreman and Berry covered 66,100 analysts' consensus forecasts for the period 1974–1990. Analysts were given every advantage in the study—for example, forecasts could be made in the same quarter as earnings were reported, and the forecasts could be changed up to two weeks before the end of the quarter. Nevertheless, the average annual error was 44 percent, and only 25 percent of consensus estimates came within plus or minus 5 percent of reported earnings. Looking at the estimates on the basis of the 61 industries involved, only one industry had forecast errors averaging under 10 percent for the entire time period and, overall, the average forecast error grouped by industries was 50 percent (the median error was 43 percent).[9]

Inaccurate earnings estimates can provide opportunities for investors. Analysts are frequently wrong, and if investors can make better estimates of earnings, they can expect to profit from their astuteness.

EARNINGS SURPRISES

We have established that changes in earnings and stock prices are highly correlated. We have also discussed the necessity of estimating EPS and how such estimates can be obtained. What remains is to examine the role of expectations about earnings in selecting common stocks.

The association between earnings and stock prices is more complicated than simply demonstrating a correlation (association) between earnings growth and stock-price changes. Elton, Gruber, and Gultekin found that investors could not earn excess returns by buying and selling stocks on the basis of the consensus estimate of earnings growth. (The consensus estimate was defined as the average estimate of security analysts at major brokerage houses.) They also found that analysts tended to overestimate earnings for companies they expected would perform well and to underestimate for companies they expected would perform poorly.

Investors must form expectations about EPS, and these expectations will be incorporated into stock prices if markets are efficient. Although these expectations are often inaccurate, they play an important role in affecting stock prices. Malkiel and Cragg concluded that in making accurate one-year predictions, "It is far more important to know what the market will think the growth rate of earnings will be next year rather than to know the (actual) realized long-term growth rate."[10]

As Latane' and Jones pointed out, new information about a stock is unexpected information.[11] The important point about EPS in terms of stock prices is the difference between what the market (i.e., investors in general) was expecting the EPS to be and what the company actually reported. Unexpected information about earnings calls for a revision in investor probability beliefs about the future and therefore an adjustment in the price of the stock.

Earnings Surprises The difference between a firm's actual earnings and its expected earnings

To assess the impact of the surprise factor in EPS, Latane' and Jones developed a model to express and use the **earnings surprise** factor in the quarterly EPS of companies. This standardized unexpected earnings (SUE) model was discussed in Chapter 12 as part of the market anomalies associated with the evidence concerning market efficiency.[12] Repeating from Chapter 12,

$$\text{SUE} = \frac{\text{Actual quarterly EPS} - \text{Forecast quarterly EPS}}{\text{Standardization variable}} \qquad (15\text{-}8)$$

[9] See David Dreman, "Cloudy Crystal Balls," *Forbes,* October 10, 1994.

[10] Malkiel and Cragg, "Expectations and the Structure of Share Prices," p. 616.

[11] See H. Latane' and C. Jones, "Standardized Unexpected Earnings—A Progress Report," *Journal of Finance,* 32 (December 1977): 1457–1465.

[12] This model is explained in Latane' and Jones, "Standardized Unexpected Earnings," p. 1457. The standardization variable is the standard error of estimate for the estimating regression equation.

The SUE concept is designed to capture the surprise element in the earnings just mentioned—in other words, the difference between what the market expects the company to earn and what it actually does earn. A favorable earnings surprise, in which the actual earnings exceed the market's expectation, should bring about an adjustment to the price of the stock as investors revise their probability beliefs about the company's earnings. Conversely, an unfavorable earnings surprise should lead to a downward adjustment in price; in effect, the market has been disappointed in its expectations.[13]

In conclusion, stock prices are affected not only by the level of and growth in earnings, but also by the market's expectations of earnings. Investors should be concerned with both the forecast for earnings and the difference between the actual earnings and the forecast—that is, the surprise. Therefore, fundamental analysis of earnings should include more than a forecast, which is difficult enough; it should involve the role of the market's expectations about earnings.

What happens when the quarterly earnings are reported and the figures are below analysts' estimates? Obviously, the price is likely to drop quickly, and in some cases sharply. In a number of cases, the stock market is very unforgiving about disappointments in negative earnings surprises.

If the price does drop sharply following such an announcement, should an investor interested in owning the stock react quickly to take advantage of the price drop? According to one study of 2000 large companies that experienced single-day price drops of over 10 percent during the past 12 months, the average decline was 17 percent the first day the stock traded after the bad news.[14] However, on average these stocks were 25 percent cheaper 30 days after the report of bad news, with 90 percent of the stocks lower at that time. Sixty days after the bad news these stocks were still down an average of 23 percent, and down almost 20 percent after 90 days. Why? The initial shock is often followed by additional shocks.

The Earnings Game Investors need to realize that the process of estimating earnings, announcing earnings and determining earnings surprises has become much more of a game, or managed process, over time. The current "game" plays out as follows:

Consensus Estimate Most likely EPS value expected by analysts

1. Analysts attempt to guess what a particular company will earn each quarter.
2. The company simultaneously provides "guidance" as to what it thinks earnings will be. According to one survey, about 80 percent of companies provide guidance, as compared to 10 percent only a few years earlier.
3. The "guidance number" plays a major role in the **consensus estimate** among analysts as to the expected earnings.
4. The variance of the actual reported earnings from the consensus estimate has typically constituted the earnings surprise. However, investors must now contend with "whisper forecasts," which are unofficial earnings estimates that circulate among traders and investors before earnings are announced. A recent study suggests that these estimates are more accurate than are the consensus estimates.
5. The earnings surprises are increasingly guided by companies in the form of earnings preannouncements, which have increased sharply.

[13] Stocks can be categorized by SUEs that are divided into increments of 1.0. Thus, SUE classifications can range from all stocks with a SUE < -4.0 (category 1), all between -4.0 and -3.0 (category 2), and so on, up to the most positive category, all stocks with SUEs > 4.0 (category 10). The larger the SUE (either positive or negative), the greater the unexpected earnings, and, therefore, other things being equal, the larger the adjustment in the stock's return should be. Stocks with small SUEs (between $+1.0$ and -1.0) have little or no unexpected earnings and, therefore, should show little or no subsequent adjustment in stock return.

[14] See David Dreman, "Let the Dust Clear," *Forbes*, October 12, 1992, p. 166.

Obviously, investors must try to understand the earnings game and the likely impact it will have on stock prices as a result of earnings surprises.

USEFUL INFORMATION FOR INVESTORS ABOUT EARNINGS ESTIMATES

Summarizing our discussion about earnings forecasts, we can note the following useful information about the role, and use, of earnings forecasts in selecting common stocks:

1. Earnings reports are a key factor affecting stock prices. However, it is the surprise element in the reports that really matters—the difference between the actual results reported and the results expected by the market.
2. Surprises occur because analyst estimates are considerably off target. Surprises have typically involved the difference between the consensus forecast and the actual earnings, although "whisper forecasts," which are unofficial forecasts circulating among investors, may be more important in determining if there really is a surprise.
3. There appears to be a lag in the adjustment of stock prices to earnings surprises.
4. One earnings surprise tends to lead to another, with a 45 percent chance of repeating an earnings surprise.
5. The best guidelines to surprises are revisions in analyst estimates. If estimates are steadily being adjusted upward, a buy signal is indicated, and if the adjustments are downward, a sell signal is indicated. Individual investors can obtain information on analyst revisions from:
   a. *Analyst Watch,* a biweekly listing of regular earnings estimates as well as analysts' recommendations, published by Zacks Investment Research of Chicago.
   b. *The Value Line Earnings Forecasts,* published by *Value Line* (discussed below). Published every two weeks, this guide covers quarterly earnings estimates for the 1600 most frequently traded U.S. stocks. These estimates are based on *Value Line*'s Research Division rather than Wall Street analysts.
6. Stocks with significant revisions of 5 percent or more—up or down—often show above or below average performance.
7. Investors interested in buying stocks which report bad news and suffer a sharp decline should wait awhile. Chances are the stock will be cheaper 30 and 60 days after the initial sharp decline.
8. Increasingly, earnings are being guided by companies, both as a result of significantly influencing the consensus estimate as well as by making earnings preannouncements. Some companies report earnings that are very close to the estimates time after time—General Electric and Coca-Cola (traditionally) being good examples. Some companies provide conservative guidance, which results in positive earnings surprises. Other companies are overly optimistic.

USING THE INTERNET A number of sites have information about earnings estimates and surprises. At http://quote.yahoo.com/, under "Research," is a section on earnings surprises, showing both positive and negative. Entering the symbol for a stock will allow you to access research on the company, which provides detailed information on earnings estimates—consensus estimates, number of analysts following the company, surprises, and so forth. At http://cbs.marketwatch.com, investors can reference "Earnings Headlines" as well as "Earnings Surprises." For earnings information as well as other detailed information of all types about any company, try http://justquotes.com

THE P/E RATIO

The other half of the valuation framework in fundamental analysis is the price/earnings (P/E) ratio, or multiplier. The P/E ratio (reported in *The Wall Street Journal* and other newspapers) indicates how much per dollar of earnings investors currently are willing to pay for a stock, that is, the price for each dollar of earnings. In a sense, it represents the market's summary evaluation of a company's prospects.

EXAMPLE 15-8 In March 1999 Coca-Cola was selling for about 49 times the latest 12-month earnings. In mid-1993, on the other hand, Coca-Cola sold for about 9 times earnings.

In effect, the P/E ratio is a measure of the relative price of a stock. In one recent year, for example, investors were willing to pay about 50 times earnings for Centel but only six times earnings for Asarco. What are the reasons for such a large difference? To answer this question, it is necessary to consider the determinants of the P/E ratio.

Box 15-2 contains a discussion of P/E ratios from a recent issue of a personal finance magazine. This article discusses how P/E ratios are calculated, how they can be used in valuation analysis, how comparisons can be misleading, and some general guidelines for interpreting P/Es.

DETERMINANTS OF THE P/E RATIO

Reviewing our earlier discussion, we recall that the expected P/E ratio is conceptually a function of three factors:

$$P/E = \frac{D_1/E_1}{k - g} \tag{15-9}$$

where

D_1/E_1 = the expected dividend payout ratio
k = the required rate of return for the stock
g = expected growth rate in dividends

Investors attempting to determine the P/E ratio that will prevail for a particular stock should think in terms of these three factors and their likely changes. Each of these is considered next, in turn.

The Dividend Payout Ratio Dividends are clearly a function of earnings (although accounting earnings and cash, out of which dividends are paid, are not necessarily closely related). The relationship between these two variables, however, is more complex than current dividends being a function of current earnings. Dividends paid by corporations reflect established practices (i.e., previous earnings level) as well as prospects for the future (i.e., expected future earnings).

The majority of corporations listed on the NYSE and AMEX pay dividends, and many of the actively traded over-the-counter stocks act as if dividends matter significantly to investors. Consequently, dividends, once established at a certain level, are maintained at that level, if at all possible. Dividends are not reduced until and unless there is no alternative. In

Box 15-2

WHEN "P" AND "E" SPELL PROFITS

When do you think the *Wall Street Journal*—that bastion of daily business reporting—began publishing price-earnings ratios in its stock tables? In 1950? How about 1932, after the stock-market crash? As long ago as 1912?

The fact of the matter is, P/E ratios first made their appearance in the *Journal*'s stock listings on October 3, 1972. Less than a quarter-century later, the P/E ratio is the most used—and abused—measuring stick in the investment world.

A little knowledge can be a dangerous thing, especially if investors rely solely on P/E when deciding whether to buy a stock. A P/E ratio can mean many things, and if you don't understand the variations, you may be seriously handicapped.

A P/E ratio indicates how much you pay per dollar of a stock's earnings. It's an easy way to compare, for example, the relative value of a share of AT&T selling for $50 with a share of MCI selling for $18. You calculate a P/E ratio by dividing the price of a single share of stock by the company's per-share earnings. A stock selling at $20 per share that earned $1 per share would have a P/E of 20 to 1, or just 20.

After that, things get complicated. Most newspapers carry so-called trailing P/Es based on stocks' previous 12 months of earnings. But just as with the market as a whole, past performance does not always accurately predict future prospects. That's why Wall Street analysts spend a lot of time trying to estimate future earnings per share—and therefore future P/E ratios, too. So when someone says that Merck shares trade at "just 16 times earnings," you need to know whether that P/E is for the past 12 months, the current calendar year or the coming year. The further into the future, the less you can rely on a P/E, because forecast earnings have a way of not fully materializing.

P/E ratios vary widely among companies and industries over time. That's because they're influenced by business cycles and interest rates. Not surprisingly, there's a strong correlation between P/E ratios of individual stocks and the stock market as a whole; P/Es tend to rise during bull markets and shrink when bears are on the prowl.

It's easy to make the mistake of comparing apples with oranges when using P/Es. For example, Scientific Atlanta's current P/E of 38 makes the stock appear outrageously expensive—unless you know that lofty P/Es are common to fast-growing, high-tech companies. By contrast, Citicorp's P/E of 7 looks cheap—unless you know that financial institutions rarely command high P/Es.

You can also value an entire stock market by its P/E ratio. The chart shown below of the P/E of Standard & Poor's 500-stock index over more than 20 years.

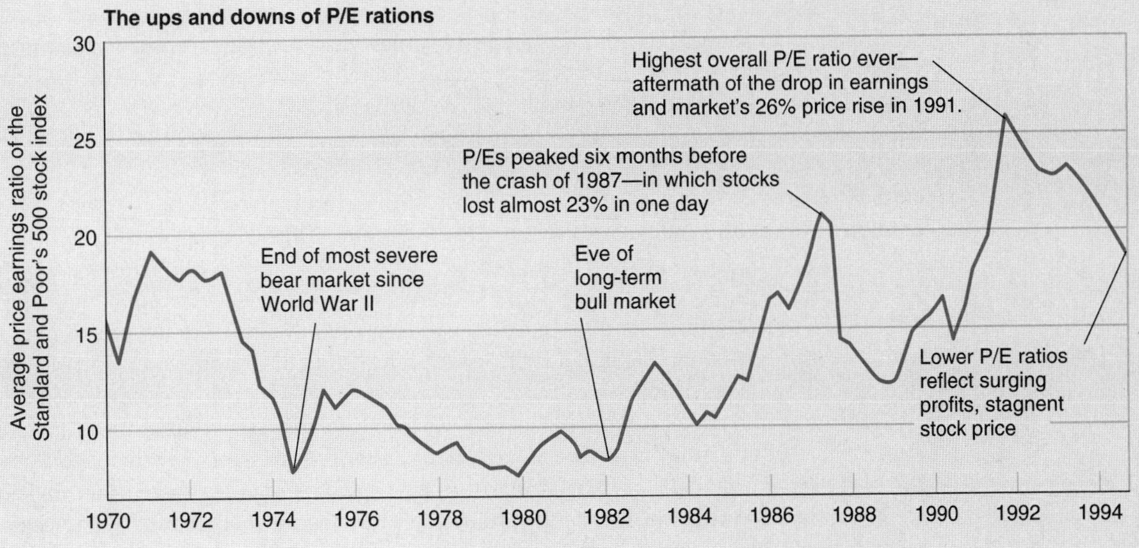
The ups and downs of P/E rations
Average price earnings ratio of the Standard and Poor's 500 stock index
30
25
20
15
10
Highest overall P/E ratio ever—aftermath of the drop in earnings and market's 26% price rise in 1991.
P/Es peaked six months before the crash of 1987—in which stocks lost almost 23% in one day
End of most severe bear market since World War II
Eve of long-term bull market
Lower P/E ratios reflect surging profits, stagnent stock price
1970
1972
1974
1976
1978
1980
1982
1984
1986
1988
1990
1992
1994

(The S&P's P/E is also reported each month in "Mutual Fund Monitor.") While you can tell from such a chart that stocks appear either richly valued or undervalued, it's difficult to use the stock market's P/E ratio to predict future market moves. The P/E ratio topped off just before the big market downturns of 1981 and 1987, but two years before the even bigger bear market of 1973–74. And not all peaks in P/E ratio are followed by bear markets.

There are, however, some general guidelines for interpreting P/Es. As a rule, high-P/E stocks—those with ratios over 20—are associated with young, fast-growing companies and considered riskier than low-P/E stocks because they rarely maintain the pace of their earnings growth. Low-P/E stocks are concentrated in mature, low-growth industries and in stocks that have fallen on hard times. So-called cyclical stocks, those that wax and wane along with the national economy, tend to rise and fall accordingly. When the trailing P/E ratio of a cyclical stock drops to single digits, it's probably time to sell, because earnings are at or near the peak.

Competing Theories The use of P/Es has spawned several competing investment theories. A number of academic studies conclude that investing in low-P/E stocks is not only less risky but also more rewarding than buying high-P/E stocks. Those who buy low-P/E stocks are called value investors. One practitioner, David Dreman, a Jersey City, N.J., money manager, admits that P/E screening is merely an easy first step in identifying prospects that fits his criteria—companies that are undervalued but possess excellent growth prospects and other unrecognized or unappreciated attributes. So-called growth investors, on the other hand, are willing to accept higher P/Es because they believe that future earnings will rapidly drive up share price.

While volumes have been written about the P/E ratio, its origin is hazy. Roger Murray, professor emeritus of Columbia University's Graduate School of Business, believes the use of P/Es evolved in the 1920s, when Arthur Stone Dewing of Harvard University and investor Edgar Lawrence Smith independently promoted the unusual notion that stocks are investments rather than speculative vehicles. They reasoned that stocks could outperform bonds if you considered both dividend yields and growth in share price. Until then, Murray says, only dividends were used to evaluate stock prices. "Growth was secondary, although you might consider stocks with lower dividends if you believed they would grow," he adds.

SOURCE: Ken Sheets, "When 'P' and 'E' Spell Profits," *Kiplinger's Personal Finance Magazine*, March 1995, pp. 129–130. Reprinted by permission.

addition, they are not increased until it is clear that the new, higher level of dividends can be supported. As a result of these policies, dividends adjust with a lag to earnings.

The P/E ratio can be expected to change as the expected dividend payout ratio changes. The higher the expected payout ratio, other things being equal, the higher the P/E ratio. However, "other things" are seldom equal. If the payout rises, the expected growth rate in earnings and dividends, g, will probably decline, thereby adversely affecting the P/E ratio. This decline occurs because less funds will be available for reinvestment in the business, thereby leading to a decline in the expected growth rate, g.

The Required Rate of Return As we know, the required rate of return, k, is a function of the riskless rate of return and a risk premium. Thus, k is equal to

$$k = \text{RF} + \text{RP} \qquad (15\text{-}10)$$

The riskless rate of return can be proxied by the Treasury bill rate. The risk premium is the additional compensation demanded by risk-averse investors before purchasing a risky asset such as a common stock.

Discounted cash flow models, discussed in Chapter 10, can be used to estimate the required rate of return for a company. We learned that the constant-growth version of the dividend discount model can be rearranged to state that k is equal to the current dividend yield plus the expected growth rate in earnings. Harris suggests that a consensus forecast of earnings growth by analysts can be used successfully as a proxy for the dividend growth rate in solving for k.[15] Since analysts' growth forecasts are readily available on a large number of stocks, this approach may offer a straightforward method of estimating required rates of return.

At the company level, the risk premium for a stock can be regarded as a composite of business risk, financial risk, and other risks which could include the liquidity, or marketability, of a particular stock. As a general rule, large NYSE companies are more liquid than small Nasdaq stocks.

Based on Equation 15-10, the following statements can be made about a company's required rate of return:

1. Other things being equal, if the risk-free rate, RF, rises, k will rise. Thus, in periods of high interest rates such as 1980–1981, k typically will be higher than in periods such as 1982–1983, when interest rates had declined from the high levels of 1980–1981.
2. Other things being equal, if the risk premium rises (falls), as a result of an increase (decrease) in business risk, financial risk, or other risks, k will rise (fall).

As we learned in Chapter 10, the relationship between k and the P/E ratio is inverse: Other things being equal, as k rises, the P/E ratio declines; as k declines, the P/E ratio rises. Because the required rate of return is a discount rate, P/E ratios and discount rates move inversely to each other.

E/P Ratio The reciprocal of the P/E ratio

To understand this relationship, consider the simplest case in valuation—*no growth*. (In other words, EPS will remain at a fixed dollar amount forever.) Rather than using an earnings multiplier, think of capitalizing the earnings. To do so, analysts use the **E/P ratio**, which is the reciprocal of the P/E ratio (i.e., E/P = [1/(P/E)]).

$$\text{Intrinsic value} = \frac{E_0}{E/P} \tag{15-11}$$

Rather than use a multiplier of, say, 10, an E/P ratio or a capitalization rate of 0.10 can be used. Obviously, if this capitalization rate increased, intrinsic value would decline.

The Expected Growth Rate The third variable affecting the P/E ratio is the expected growth rate of dividends, g. We know that $g = br$, making the expected growth rate a function of the return on equity (r) and the retention rate (b). The higher either of these variables are, the higher g will be. What about the relationship between g and P/E? P/E and g are directly related; the higher the g, other things being equal, the higher the P/E ratio.

Investors should be willing to pay more for a company with expected rapid growth in earnings than for a company with expected slower growth in earnings. A basic problem in fundamental analysis, however, is determining how much more investors should be willing to pay for growth. In other words, how high should the P/E ratio be? There is no precise answer to this question. It depends on such factors as the following:

1. The confidence that investors have in the expected growth. In the case of Cisco, for example, investors may be well justified in expecting a rapid rate of growth for the next few years because of previous performance, management's ability, and the high estimates of growth described in investment advisory services. This may not be the case for another company, where, because of competitive inroads and other factors, the high growth prospects are at great risk. Consider IBM, for example, which con-

[15] See Robert S. Harris, "Using Analysts' Growth Forecasts to Estimate Shareholder Required Rates of Return," *Financial Management* (Spring 1986), pp. 58–67.

Exhibit 15-1

A WEEKLY RATING BY *THE VALUE LINE INVESTMENT SURVEY* OF THE HIGHEST AND LOWEST P/E STOCKS.

LOWEST P/Es
Stocks with the lowest estimated current P/E ratios

Page No.	Stock Name	Recent Price	Current P/E Ratio	Timeliness	Safety Rank	Industry Group	Industry Rank
661	Integrated Health	3 7/8	3.8	5	4	Medical Services	43
1637	Pillowtex Corp.	12	4.6	4	3	Textile	94
664	Magellan Health Svcs.	4 1/4	4.8	4	4	Medical Services	43
871	Beazer Homes USA	21	5.3	2	3	Homebuilding	9
875	Hovnanian Enterpr. 'A'	7 3/8	5.5	3	4	Homebuilding	9
588	Armco Inc.	4 7/16	5.6	2	4	Steel (General)	76
279	Arkansas Best	7 1/8	5.9	2	4	Trucking/Transp. Leasing	10
1347	Terex Corp.	24	5.9	2	4	Machinery	71
1037	Pioneer-Standard	7	6.1	3	4	Electronics	31
817	Meritor Automotive	16	6.2	–	3	Auto Parts (OEM)	58
1681	Blair Corp.	16	6.3	3	3	Retail (Special Lines)	11
1635	Guilford Mills	9 1/16	6.3	5	3	Textile	94
946	Gibson Greetings	7 3/8	6.4	4	3	Packaging & Container	79
1309	Cascade Corp.	11	6.5	3	3	Machinery	71
2152	Loews Corp.	71	6.6	4	2	Financial Services	17
1589	Universal Corp.	25	6.6	3	2	Tobacco	48
571	Wyman-Gordon	8 1/2	6.6	3	4	Aerospace/Defense	44
1142	United Stationers	14	6.7	3	3	Office Equip & Supplies	36
587	Ampco-Pittsburgh	10	6.8	4	3	Steel (General)	76
268	Cont'l Airlines 'B'	38	6.8	4	4	Air Transport	33
1482	IBP, Inc.	18	6.8	2	3	Food Processing	61
584	TransTechnology	17	6.8	4	3	Metal Fabricating	77
1323	Gleason Corp.	17	6.9	4	3	Machinery	71
882	Toll Brothers	18	6.9	3	3	Homebuilding	9
883	Webb (Del) Corp.	21	6.9	2	3	Homebuilding	9
139	Esterline Technologies	13	7.0	3	3	Precision Instrument	38
1322	Foster Wheeler	13	7.0	3	3	Machinery	71
1017	Lamson & Sessions	5 5/16	7.0	3	4	Electrical Equipment	68
1368	Mark IV Inds.	14	7.0	4	3	Diversified Co.	64
2173	Reliance Group Holdings	8	7.0	5	3	Insurance (Diversified)	70
880	Ryland Group	23	7.0	2	3	Homebuilding	9
881	Standard Pacific Corp.	13	7.0	2	3	Homebuilding	9
652	Beverly Enterprises	4 1/2	7.1	–	3	Medical Services	43
1612	Fruit of the Loom	10	7.2	4	3	Apparel	45
598	Steel Technologies	7 5/8	7.2	3	3	Steel (General)	76
869	USG Corp.	53	7.2	2	3	Building Materials	35
874	D.R. Horton	16	7.3	–	4	Homebuilding	9
1634	Galey & Lord	4 3/8	7.3	5	4	Textile	94
671	PhyCor, Inc.	4 7/16	7.3	3	4	Medical Services	43
853	Ameron Int'l	35	7.4	3	3	Building Materials	35
885	Building Materials	9 3/4	7.4	2	4	Retail Building Supply	3
1188	Meditrust Cos.	12	7.4	–	3	R.E.I.T.	65
1558	Oakwood Homes	13	7.4	4	3	Manuf. Housing/Rec Veh	22
866	Owens Corning	31	7.4	3	3	Building Materials	35
585	Trinity Inds.	30	7.4	3	3	Metal Fabricating	77
879	Pulte Corp.	20	7.5	3	3	Homebuilding	9
821	Standard Products	17	7.5	4	3	Auto Parts (OEM)	58
123	TBC Corp.	6 1/4	7.5	3	3	Tire & Rubber	69
574	Amcast Industrial	17	7.6	3	3	Metal Fabricating	77
506	Int'l Specialty Prod.	7 1/8	7.6	5	3	Chemical (Specialty)	75

Page No.	Stock Name	Recent Price	Current P/E Ratio	Timeliness	Safety Rank	Industry Group	Industry Rank
1430	Liberty Financial	21	7.6	3	3	Financial Services	17
1617	Nautica Enterprises	11	7.6	4	3	Apparel	45
1040	Recoton Corp.	15	7.6	3	4	Electronics	31
1312	Chart Industries	6 5/8	7.7	4	3	Machinery	71
591	Cleveland-Cliffs	33	7.7	4	2	Steel (General)	76
889	Hughes Supply	21	7.7	3	3	Retail Building Supply	3
813	Intermet Corp.	14	7.7	4	3	Auto Parts (OEM)	58
876	Kaufman & Broad Home	23	7.7	2	3	Homebuilding	9
1349	Watts Inds. 'A'	14	7.7	5	3	Machinery	71
604	Amer. Financial Group	35	7.8	3	3	Insurance(Prop/Casualty)	87
1619	Oxford Inds.	25	7.8	3	3	Apparel	45
108	PACCAR Inc.	41	7.8	3	3	Auto & Truck	12
596	Quanex Corp.	18	7.8	3	3	Steel (General)	76
299	Sea Containers Ltd. 'A'	27	7.8	3	3	Maritime	86
897	Texas Inds.	24	7.8	4	3	Cement & Aggregates	24
1200	Conseco, Inc.	30	7.9	3	4	Insurance (Life)	26
1904	Cytec Inds.	21	7.9	3	3	Chemical (Diversified)	73
1909	IMC Global	18	7.9	3	3	Chemical (Diversified)	73
894	Lafarge Corp.	27	7.9	3	3	Cement & Aggregates	24
1018	MagneTek, Inc.	8 5/16	7.9	3	3	Electrical Equipment	68
911	Shelby Williams	10	7.9	3	3	Furn./Home Furnishings	25
1805	Anchor Gaming	41	8.0	4	3	Hotel/Gaming	63
877	Lennar Corp.	22	8.0	–	3	Homebuilding	9
1371	Nortek, Inc.	26	8.0	2	4	Diversified Co.	64
855	Armstrong World Inds.	46	8.1	4	2	Building Materials	35
1363	GenCorp Inc.	18	8.1	–	3	Diversified Co.	64
1334	Milacron, Inc.	17	8.1	3	3	Machinery	71
1201	Delphi Fin'l 'A'	31	8.2	3	3	Insurance (Life)	26
1692	Dress Barn	14	8.2	4	3	Retail (Special Lines)	11
575	Fansteel Inc.	5 1/16	8.2	3	3	Metal Fabricating	77
619	Old Republic	19	8.2	3	2	Insurance(Prop/Casualty)	87
1492	Pilgrim's Pride 'B'	16	8.2	2	3	Food Processing	61
2137	ADVANTA Corp. 'A'	10	8.3	–	3	Financial Services	17
266	Alaska Air Group	46	8.3	2	4	Air Transport	33
277	AMERCO	21	8.3	3	4	Trucking/Transp. Leasing	10
1772	Brunswick Corp.	19	8.3	3	3	Recreation	37
1005	Cable Design Techn.	12	8.3	3	4	Electrical Equipment	68
282	Consol. Freightways	11	8.3	2	4	Trucking/Transp. Leasing	10
498	Ethyl Corp.	4 1/4	8.3	3	4	Chemical (Specialty)	75
1313	Commercial Intertech	13	8.4	4	3	Machinery	71
1557	Fleetwood Enterprises	27	8.4	3	3	Manuf. Housing/Rec Veh	22
610	Fremont Gen'l	17	8.4	3	3	Insurance(Prop/Casualty)	87
518	Quaker Chemical	14	8.4	3	3	Chemical (Specialty)	75
1244	Solutia Inc.	17	8.4	–	3	Chemical (Basic)	93
873	Centex Corp.	33	8.5	2	3	Homebuilding	9
126	Fedders Corp.	5 1/8	8.5	3	3	Home Appliance	50
353	Modis Professional	8 3/4	8.5	3	4	Industrial Services	40
1498	Smithfield Foods	21	8.5	2	3	Food Processing	61
196	ADAC Labs.	12	8.6	3	3	Medical Supplies	16
567	Precision Castparts	38	8.6	3	3	Aerospace/Defense	44

HIGHEST P/Es
Stocks with the highest estimated current P/E ratios

Page No.	Stock Name	Recent Price	Current P/E Ratio	Timeliness	Safety Rank	Industry Group	Industry Rank
179	Green Mountain Pwr.	9 7/8	90.0	4	4	Electric Utility (East)	80
1862	Barrett Resources	25	89.3	4	3	Petroleum (Producing)	88
2148	Eaton Vance Corp.	22	88.0	4	3	Financial Services	17
774	Hughes Electronics	55	87.3	–	3	Telecom. Equipment	14
418	Phillips Petroleum	48	87.3	4	3	Petroleum (Integrated)	91
228	MiniMed Inc.	98	85.2	1	3	Medical Supplies	16
1921	Korea Electric ADR	15	83.3	3	3	Utility (Foreign)	–
1803	Viacom Inc. 'A'	45	81.8	1	3	Entertainment	39
1078	Applied Materials	65	81.3	3	3	Semiconductor Cap Equip	23
181	Niagara Mohawk	13	81.3	3	4	Electric Utility (East)	80
1749	IDT Corp.	24	80.0	3	4	Telecom. Services	29
1263	Glaxo Wellcome ADR	70	78.7	3	3	Drug	7
1844	News Corp. Ltd. ADR	35	77.8	3	3	Newspaper	59
1661	Venator Group	7	77.8	5	3	Retail Store	18
916	Champion Int'l	43	76.8	3	3	Paper & Forest Products	72
737	AirTouch Communic.	99	76.2	–	3	Telecom. Services	29
1091	Cisco Systems	119	75.3	1	3	Computer & Peripherals	8
1273	Monsanto	45	75.0	4	3	Drug	7
1568	Matsushita Elec. ADR	200	74.3	3	2	Foreign Electron/Entertn	62
1095	EMC Corp.	134	73.2	1	3	Computer & Peripherals	8
1922	Macromedia, Inc.	40	71.4	2	4	Internet	2
761	TV Guide 'A'	45	71.4	2	4	Telecom. Services	29
1094	Dell Computer	46	69.7	1	3	Computer & Peripherals	8
349	Information Resources	6 7/8	69.0	3	4	Industrial Services	40
2211	Microsoft Corp.	93	68.9	1	2	Computer Software & Svcs	5
1222	Teck Corp. 'B'	11	68.8	3	3	Gold/Silver Mining	56
1065	LSI Logic	35	68.6	3	4	Semiconductor	13
923	Int'l Paper	44	66.7	3	3	Paper & Forest Products	72
152	Summit Technology	14	66.7	2	4	Precision Instrument	38
1029	Gemstar Int'l	99	66.0	1	4	Electronics	31
245	VISX, Inc.	125	65.4	1	3	Medical Supplies	16
1032	KEMET Corp.	15	65.2	3	4	Electronics	31
1089	Ascend Communic.	98	64.9	–	3	Computer & Peripherals	8
1235	Phelps Dodge	50	64.9	4	3	Copper	85
606	Berkshire Hathaway	721	63.5	3	2	Insurance(Prop/Casualty)	87
148	Perkin-Elmer	108	63.5	–	3	Precision Instrument	38
1075	Vitesse Semiconductor	57	63.3	1	3	Semiconductor	13
1847	Thomson Corp.	49	62.8	3	3	Newspaper	59
213	Centocor	36	61.0	2	5	Medical Supplies	16
1829	Playboy Enterprises 'B'	26	60.5	3	3	Publishing	60
1878	ENSCO Int'l	12	60.0	3	4	Oilfield Services/Equip.	57
208	Biomatrix Inc.	74	59.7	2	4	Medical Supplies	16
143	KLA-Tencor	53	59.6	3	4	Precision Instrument	38
1277	Pfizer, Inc.	140	58.8	2	2	Drug	7
1260	Genentech	86	58.1	–	3	Drug	7
1139	Staples, Inc.	35	57.4	1	3	Office Equip & Supplies	36
1082	Teradyne Inc.	59	57.3	3	3	Semiconductor Cap Equip	23
771	Ciena Corp.	20	57.1	–	3	Telecom. Equipment	14
1652	Kohl's Corp.	71	56.8	1	3	Retail Store	18
759	SkyTel Communic.	18	56.3	2	5	Telecom. Services	29

Page No.	Stock Name	Recent Price	Current P/E Ratio	Timeliness	Safety Rank	Industry Group	Industry Rank
2158	Total System Svcs.	18	56.3	2	3	Financial Services	17
776	Lucent Technologies	64	55.7	1	3	Telecom. Equipment	14
924	Longview Fibre	11	55.0	3	3	Paper & Forest Products	72
1070	Motorola, Inc.	79	54.1	3	3	Semiconductor	13
1230	Cominco Ltd.	21	53.8	2	3	Metals & Mining (Div.)	51
752	MCI WorldCom	86	53.8	–	3	Telecom. Services	29
628	Vesta Insurance	4 1/4	53.8	4	5	Insurance(Prop/Casualty)	87
799	Vodafone Group ADR	194	53.2	1	3	Foreign Telecom.	15
887	Home Depot	64	52.9	1	2	Retail Building Supply	3
2217	Paychex, Inc.	47	52.8	2	3	Computer Software & Svcs	5
1593	DeVry Inc.	30	52.6	1	3	Educational Services	4
655	Express Scripts 'A'	82	51.9	1	3	Medical Services	43
332	Starbucks Corp.	31	51.7	1	3	Restaurant	21
779	Qualcomm Inc.	139	51.5	1	4	Telecom. Equipment	14
2214	Novell, Inc.	23	51.1	2	3	Computer Software & Svcs	5
1283	SmithKline Beecham	73	51.0	3	2	Drug	7
1872	Vastar Resources	47	50.5	4	3	Petroleum (Producing)	88
1679	Bed Bath & Beyond	36	50.0	1	3	Retail (Special Lines)	11
134	Cognex Co.	25	50.0	3	4	Precision Instrument	38
1079	Electro Scientific	46	48.9	3	3	Semiconductor Cap Equip	23
1116	Sun Microsystems	69	48.9	1	3	Computer & Peripherals	8
405	Atlantic Richfield	74	48.7	–	1	Petroleum (Integrated)	91
429	Unocal Corp.	37	48.7	3	3	Petroleum (Integrated)	91
1252	Biogen Inc.	116	48.5	1	3	Drug	7
219	Guidant Corp.	64	48.5	2	3	Medical Supplies	16
1680	Best Buy Co.	53	48.2	1	4	Retail (Special Lines)	11
782	Tellabs, Inc.	111	48.1	1	3	Telecom. Equipment	14
2188	Automatic Data Proc.	40	47.6	2	1	Computer Software & Svcs	5
1060	Cypress Semiconductor	10	47.6	3	4	Semiconductor	13
802	Drug Emporium	4 11/16	47.0	3	4	Drugstore	19
1045	Solectron Corp.	54	47.0	1	3	Electronics	31
1511	Ahold ADR	41	46.6	2	3	Grocery	41
840	TCA Cable TV	44	46.3	2	3	Cable TV	30
1081	Novellus Sys.	61	45.9	3	3	Semiconductor Cap Equip	23
1259	Forest Labs.	55	45.8	2	3	Drug	7
1076	Xilinx Inc.	44	45.8	1	3	Semiconductor Cap Equip	23
789	Deutsche Telekom ADR	43	45.7	–	3	Foreign Telecom.	15
1727	West Marine	8 5/8	45.3	3	4	Retail (Special Lines)	11
1688	Circuit City Group	69	45.1	1	3	Retail (Special Lines)	11
1594	Education Mgmt.	27	45.0	–	3	Educational Services	4
805	Walgreen Co.	27	45.0	1	2	Drugstore	19
211	Boston Scientific	40	44.9	2	3	Medical Supplies	16
832	Lauder (Estee)	95	44.6	1	3	Toiletries/Cosmetics	6
1042	Safeguard Scientifics	80	44.4	3	3	Electronics	31
1697	Gap (The), Inc.	68	44.2	1	3	Retail (Special Lines)	11
1067	Maxim Integrated	56	44.1	2	3	Semiconductor	13
1662	Wal-Mart Stores	98	43.9	1	2	Retail Store	18
713	Illinova Corp.	21	43.8	4	4	Electric Util. (Central)	78
1547	Coca-Cola	59	43.4	5	1	Beverage (Soft Drink)	90
1066	Linear Technology	58	43.3	2	3	Semiconductor	13

SOURCE: *The Value Line Investment Survey,* "Summary of Advice and Index," April 16, 1999, p. 35. Copyright © 1999 by Value Line Publishing Company Inc. Used by permission.

stantly faces a rapidly changing environment as well as the challenge of many other manufacturers.

2. The reasons for the earnings growth can be important. Is it a result of great demand in the marketplace or of astute financing policies that could backfire if interest rates rise sharply or the economy enters a severe recession? Is growth the result of sales expansion or cost cutting (which will be exhausted at some point)?

Analyzing the P/E Ratio In analyzing a particular P/E ratio, we first ask what model describes the expected growth rate for that company. Recent rapid growth and published estimates of strong expected future growth would lead investors not to use the constant-growth version of the dividend valuation model. Instead, we should evaluate the company by using a multiple-growth model. At some point, however, this growth can be expected to slow down to a more normal rate.

$$\frac{P}{E_{n+1}} = \frac{D_{n+1}/E_{n+1}}{k - g}$$

where n is the year that the abnormal growth ends.

Relative to the discussion above on the earnings game, investors must be increasingly concerned with the impact of managing earnings expectations on the P/E ratio. If a fast growing company is being conservative in guiding the estimates of its earnings, and it regularly reports earnings higher than the consensus, then the forward P/E ratio is actually lower than it appears to be based on the current consensus estimate of earnings. In other words, a company may appear to sell for 50 times next year's earnings, but this is based on an underestimate of next year's earnings because the consensus estimate has been guided to be below what actually occurs. For much of the 1990s Dell Computer fit this model, regularly reporting significantly larger earnings than the consensus estimate.

WHY P/E RATIOS VARY AMONG COMPANIES

Stock prices reflect market expectations about earnings. Companies that the market believes will achieve higher earnings growth rates will tend to be priced higher than companies that are expected to show low earnings growth rates. Thus, a primary factor in explaining P/E ratio differences among companies is investor expectations about the future growth of earnings. Variations in the rate of earnings growth will also influence the P/E.

It is important to remember the role of interest rates, which are inversely related to P/E ratios (see Chapter 10). When interest rates are declining, the largest impact is on the P/E ratios of reliable growth stocks. This is because most of their earnings will occur far out in the future, and can now be discounted at lower rates.

Exhibit 15-1 shows one of *The Value Line Investment Survey*'s weekly rankings of the lowest and highest P/E stocks out of the more than 1,700 companies covered. The lowest estimated current P/E ratios were close to 1.0, whereas the highest were close to 90.

FUNDAMENTAL SECURITY ANALYSIS IN PRACTICE

We have analyzed several important aspects of fundamental analysis as it is applied to individual companies. Obviously, such a process can be quite detailed, involving an analysis of a company's sales potential, competition, tax situation, cost projections, accounting practices, and so on. Nevertheless, regardless of detail and complexity, the underlying process is as described. Analysts and investors are seeking to estimate a company's earnings and P/E ratio and to determine whether the stock is undervalued (a buy) or overvalued (a sell).

Exhibit 15-2

A PAGE FROM A WEEKLY ISSUE OF "RATINGS AND REPORTS," *THE VALUE LINE INVESTMENT SURVEY.*

COCA-COLA NYSE-KO

RECENT PRICE	P/E RATIO	(Trailing: 47.2 / Median: 26.0)	RELATIVE P/E RATIO	DIV'D YLD	VALUE LINE
60	44.8	Trailing: 47.2; Median: 26.0	2.67	1.1%	1546

TIMELINESS 5 Lowered 3/5/99
SAFETY 1 New 7/27/90
TECHNICAL 4 Lowered 7/2/99
BETA 1.05 (1.00 = Market)

2002-04 PROJECTIONS

	Price	Gain	Ann'l Total Return
High	80	(+35%)	9%
Low	65	(+10%)	3%

Insider Decisions

	S	O	N	D	J	F	M	A	M
to Buy	0	0	0	1	0	0	0	0	0
Options	0	1	2	1	0	1	0	0	0
to Sell	0	0	0	2	0	1	0	1	0

Institutional Decisions

	3Q1998	4Q1998	1Q1999
to Buy	398	435	466
to Sell	478	455	451
Hld's(000)	1236154	1225717	1145400

	1988	1989	1990	1991	1992	1993	1994	1995	1996	1997	1998	1999
High:	5.7	10.1	12.3	20.4	22.7	22.5	26.7	40.2	54.3	72.6	88.9	70.9
Low:	4.4	5.4	8.2	10.7	17.8	18.8	19.4	24.4	36.1	50.0	53.6	57.6

Target Price Range 2002 | 2003 | 2004

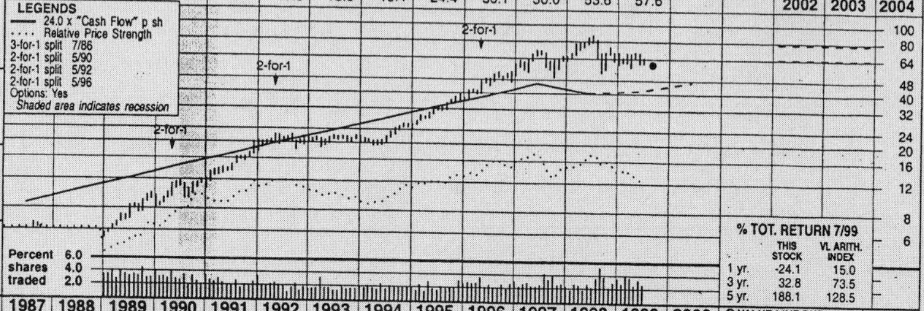

% TOT. RETURN 7/99

	THIS STOCK	VL ARITH. INDEX
1 yr.	-24.1	15.0
3 yr.	32.8	73.5
5 yr.	188.1	128.5

1983	1984	1985	1986	1987	1988	1989	1990	1991	1992	1993	1994	1995	1996	1997	1998	1999	2000	© VALUE LINE PUB., INC.	02-04
2.09	2.35	2.56	2.81	2.57	2.94	3.33	3.83	4.35	5.00	5.38	6.34	7.19	7.48	7.64	7.63	*8.00*	*8.50*	Sales per sh A	*12.00*
.22	.25	.28	.31	.36	.43	.50	.60	.71	.84	.98	1.16	1.37	1.60	1.92	1.69	*1.65*	*1.95*	"Cash Flow" per sh	*2.80*
.17	.20	.22	.26	.30	.36	.42	.51	.61	.72	.84	.99	1.19	1.40	1.64	1.42	*1.34*	*1.60*	Earnings per sh B	*2.40*
.11	.12	.12	.13	.14	.15	.17	.20	.24	.28	.34	.39	.44	.50	.56	.60	*.64*	*.68*	Div'ds Decl'd per sh C ■	*.92*
.12	.11	.16	.12	.10	.14	.17	.22	.30	.41	.31	.34	.37	.40	.44	.35	*.55*	*.60*	Cap'l Spending per sh	*.75*
.89	.88	.96	1.14	1.08	1.07	1.18	1.41	1.67	1.49	1.77	2.05	2.15	2.48	2.96	3.41	*3.50*	*3.60*	Book Value per sh D	*4.75*
3272.5	3139.8	3087.9	3080.1	2978.8	2838.3	2696.1	2673.0	2657.9	2613.7	2594.9	2551.9	2504.6	2481.0	2470.6	2465.5	*2420*	*2390*	Common Shs Outst'g E	*2300*
12.6	12.2	13.6	17.3	18.0	13.9	17.8	20.4	24.4	28.7	25.1	22.5	26.8	32.8	38.1	51.3	*Bold figures are*		Avg Ann'l P/E Ratio	*30.0*
1.07	1.14	1.10	1.17	1.20	1.15	1.35	1.52	1.56	1.74	1.48	1.48	1.79	2.05	2.20	2.70	*Value Line*		Relative P/E Ratio	*2.00*
5.2%	4.8%	4.2%	2.9%	2.6%	3.0%	2.3%	1.9%	1.6%	1.4%	1.6%	1.7%	1.4%	1.1%	.9%	.8%	*estimates*		Avg Ann'l Div'd Yield	*1.3%*
						8965.8	10236	11572	13074	13957	16172	18018	18546	18868	18813	*19300*	*20400*	Sales ($mill) A	*27600*
						21.3%	21.4%	22.3%	23.7%	24.8%	25.5%	25.2%	23.7%	29.8%	29.8%	*28.0%*	*29.5%*	Operating Margin	*30.5%*
						183.8	243.9	261.4	321.9	360.0	411.0	454.0	479.0	626.0	645.0	*700*	*750*	Depreciation ($mill)	*875*
						1192.8	1381.9	1618.0	1883.8	2188.0	2554.0	2986.0	3492.0	4129.0	3533.0	*3310*	*3900*	Net Profit ($mill)	*5625*
						32.4%	31.4%	32.1%	31.4%	31.3%	31.5%	31.0%	24.0%	31.8%	32.0%	*31.5%*	*31.5%*	Income Tax Rate	*31.5%*
						13.3%	13.5%	14.0%	14.4%	15.7%	15.8%	16.6%	18.8%	21.9%	18.8%	*17.2%*	*19.1%*	Net Profit Margin	*20.5%*
						d54.4	d153.7	26.6	d1056	d737.0	d972.0	d1898	d1496	d1410	d2260	*d2700*	*d3200*	Working Cap'l ($mill)	*d3750*
						548.7	535.9	985.3	1120.1	1428.0	1426.0	1141.0	1116.0	801.0	687.0	*785*	*875*	Long-Term Debt ($mill)	*1085*
						3485.5	3849.2	4425.8	3888.4	4584.0	5235.0	5392.0	6156.0	7311.0	8403.0	*8500*	*8630*	Shr. Equity ($mill)	*10950*
						30.2%	32.2%	30.6%	38.4%	37.7%	39.3%	46.5%	48.5%	51.2%	39.1%	*37.0%*	*42.0%*	Return on Total Cap'l	*47.5%*
						34.2%	35.9%	36.6%	48.4%	47.7%	48.8%	55.4%	56.7%	56.5%	42.0%	*39.0%*	*45.0%*	Return on Shr. Equity	*51.3%*
						22.0%	22.0%	22.1%	29.5%	28.5%	29.6%	34.8%	36.5%	37.5%	24.4%	*20.8%*	*26.0%*	Retained to Com Eq	*32.0%*
						41%	40%	40%	39%	40%	39%	37%	36%	34%	42%	*47%*	*42%*	All Div'ds to Net Prof	*38%*

CAPITAL STRUCTURE as of 3/31/99
Total Debt $5653.0 mill.
LT Debt $694.0 mill. **LT Interest** $40.0 mill.
(Total interest coverage: 20x)
(8% of Cap'l)

Pension Liability None

Pfd Stock None

Common Stock 2,467,300,000 shs.
(92% of Cap'l)

MARKET CAP: $150 billion (Large Cap)

CURRENT POSITION ($MILL.)	1997	1998	3/31/99
Cash Assets	1843.0	1807.0	1754.0
Receivables	1639.0	1666.0	1601.0
Inventory (Avg Cst)	959.0	890.0	931.0
Other	1528.0	2017.0	1966.0
Current Assets	5969.0	6380.0	6252.0
Accts Payable	3249.0	3141.0	2932.0
Debt Due	3074.0	4462.0	4959.0
Other	1056.0	1037.0	942.0
Current Liab.	7379.0	8640.0	8833.0

ANNUAL RATES of change (per sh)	Past 10 Yrs.	Past 5 Yrs.	Est'd '96-'98 to '02-'04
Sales	10.5%	9.0%	*8.0%*
"Cash Flow"	17.0%	15.5%	*8.5%*
Earnings	17.0%	15.5%	*8.0%*
Dividends	14.5%	14.0%	*9.0%*
Book Value	10.5%	12.5%	*8.5%*

Cal-endar	QUARTERLY SALES ($ mill.) Mar.31	Jun.30	Sep.30	Dec.31	Full Year
1996	4194	5253	4656	4443	18546
1997	4138	5075	4954	4701	18868
1998	4457	5151	4747	4458	18813
1999	4428	5379	*4900*	*4593*	*19300*
2000	*4700*	*5700*	*5175*	*4825*	*20400*

Cal-endar	EARNINGS PER SHARE B Mar.31	Jun.30	Sep.30	Dec.31	Full Year
1996	.28	.42	.39	.31	1.40
1997	.39	.52	.40	.33	1.64
1998	.34	.48	.36	.24	1.42
1999	.30	.38	*.35*	*.31*	*1.34*
2000	*.33*	*.49*	*.43*	*.35*	*1.60*

Cal-endar	QUARTERLY DIVIDENDS PAID C ■ Mar.31	Jun.30	Sep.30	Dec.31	Full Year
1995	--	.11	.11	.22	.44
1996	--	.125	.125	.25	.50
1997	--	.14	.14	.28	.56
1998	--	.15	.15	.30	.60
1999	--	.16	.16		

BUSINESS: The Coca-Cola Company is the world's largest soft drink company. Distributes major brands (*Coca-Cola, Sprite, Fanta, TAB*, etc.) through bottlers throughout the world. Business outside North America accounted for 63% of net sales and 73% of profits in 1998. Food division, world's largest distributor of juice products (*Minute Maid, Five Alive, Hi-C*, etc.). Coca-Cola Enterprises, 45%-owned soft drink bottler. Advertising costs, 8.5% of sales. Has approximately 29,500 employees; 366,000 stockholders. Berkshire Hathaway owns 8.1% of stock (3/99 Proxy). 1998 depr. rate: 11.3%. Chrmn. and Chief Exec. Officer: M. Douglas Ivester. Inc.: Delaware. Address: One Coca-Cola Plaza, Atlanta, Georgia 30313. Tel.: 404-676-2121. Internet: www.thecoca-colacompany.com.

Coca-Cola, long considered one of the world's outstanding growth companies, has stumbled in the past 18 months. Earnings were down in 1998 and will undoubtedly be down again this year. The primary cause for the decline last year was a steep reduction ($0.20 a share) in capital gains related to the sale of bottling subsidiaries. This year's results are being hurt by the weak economic situation in much of the world (unit case sales of Coca-Cola's products were down in both the first and second quarters), by the continuing strength of the dollar against many currencies, and by quality control problems and related adverse publicity in Europe.

In June, the company's Belgian bottler recalled products after receiving reports that people had become sick from drinking Coca-Cola soft drinks. No one was reported to be severely ill, but quality control problems were discovered at two plants. Efforts to maintain quality have since been considerably strengthened, and it is not very likely that more problems will occur, but the costs of the recall and subsequent marketing efforts were high, and consumer confidence obviously suffered. It is impossible to say when confidence may be restored, but our assumption is that it will take at least three to six months.

Nonetheless, we are still optimistic about Coke's long-term prospects. There are still vast untapped markets in much of the world, and Coke has the experience, financial strength, and marketing capabilities to develop those markets. We are also impressed by Coke's geographical diversification, which normally serves it very well. We continue to think that Coke can achieve 8%-10% volume growth outside the U.S., with markets such as China and India accounting for well above-average gains. Growth domestically is more likely to be 3%-4%. The proposed purchase of many of Cadbury Schweppes' brands outside the U.S. would strengthen the depth of the product line. With steady volume gains, moderate price increases, and a continuing stock buyback program, annual share earnings should rise 15%, or more. The stock's Timeliness rank remains low, however, because of the recent earnings shortfalls.

Stephen Sanborn, CFA *August 13, 1999*

(A) Includes Columbia Pictures: 1/83-12/86. (B) Based on primary shs. thru '96, diluted shs. thereafter. Next earnings report due mid-Oct. Excludes special gain: '86, 8¢; disc. op. gains (loss): '83, (1¢); '85, 2¢; '89, 2¢; nonrec. gain (loss): '89, 36¢; '92, (8¢). (C) Next div'd meeting about Oct. 14. Goes ex about Nov. 24. Div'd payment dates: April 1, July 1, Oct. 1, Dec. 15. ■ Div'd reinvestment plan avail. (D) Incl. intangibles. In '98: $547.0 mill., 22¢/sh. (E) In millions, adj. for stock splits.

Company's Financial Strength	A++
Stock's Price Stability	80
Price Growth Persistence	95
Earnings Predictability	80

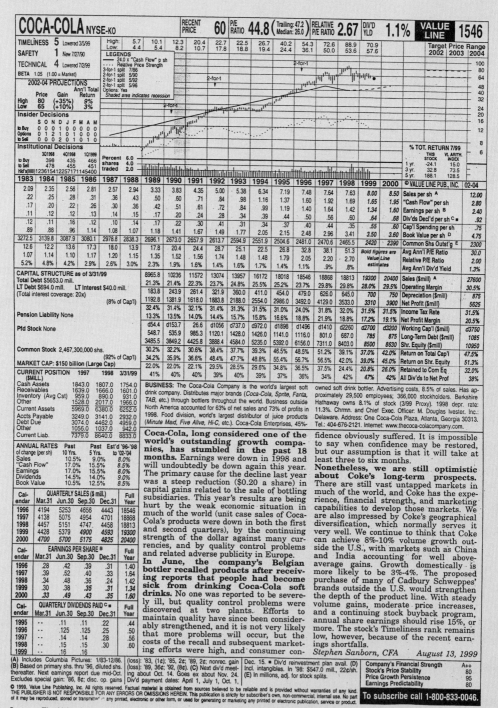

SOURCE: *The Value Line Investment Survey*, "Ratings and Reports," August 13, 1999, p. 1546. Copyright © 1999 by Value Line Publishing Company Inc. Used by permission.

In doing fundamental security analysis, investors need to use published and computerized data sources both to gather information and to provide calculations and estimates of future variables such as EPS. Appendix 15-A briefly discusses some of the major published information sources that investors have traditionally used. Exhibit 15-2 shows an excerpt from *The Value Line Investment Survey* for Coca-Cola.

The Value Line Investment Survey, as explained in the Appendix, is the largest investment advisory service in the United States and is available in many libraries. As shown in Exhibit 15-2, a significant amount of information about a particular company can be reported on one page. This information can be very helpful in terms of estimates for EPS and in terms of a prediction (by *Value Line*) as to the timeliness of each stock for the coming year (see Appendix 15-A for a more detailed discussion of this coverage).

In modern investment analysis, the risk for a stock is related to its beta coefficient, as explained in Chapter 7. Beta reflects the relative systematic risk for a stock, or the risk that cannot be diversified away. The higher the beta coefficient, the higher the risk for an individual stock, and the higher the required rate of return. Beta measures the volatility of a stock's returns—its fluctuations in relation to the market.

EXAMPLE 15-9

Refer to *The Value Line Investment Survey* (see Exhibit 15-2) for the beta for Coca-Cola. Assume it is around 1.10. Therefore, we know that Coca-Cola has slightly more relative systematic risk than the market as a whole. That is, on average, its price fluctuates more than the market. If, for example, the market is expected to rise 10 percent over the next year, investors could, on average, expect Coca-Cola to rise 11 percent based on its beta of 1.10. In a market decline, Coca-Cola would be expected to decline more, on average, than the market. If the market declined 10 percent, for example, Coca-Cola would be expected, on average, to decline in price by 11 percent.

INVESTMENTS INTUITION

It is extremely important in analyses such as these to remember that beta is a measure of volatility, indicating what can be expected to happen, on average, to a stock when the overall market rises or falls. In fact, Coca-Cola, or any other stock, will not perform in the predicted way every time. If it did, the risk would disappear. Investors can always find examples of stocks that, over some specific period of time, did not move as their beta indicated they would. This is not an indictment of the usefulness of beta as a measure of volatility; rather, it suggests that the beta relationship can only be expected to hold on the average.

In trying to understand and predict a company's return and risk, we need to remember that both are a function of two components. The systematic component is related to the return on the overall market. The other component is the unique part attributable to the company itself and not to the overall market. It is a function of the specific positive or negative factors that affect a company independent of the market.

It should come as no surprise that because security analysis always involves the uncertain future, mistakes will be made, and analysts will differ in their outlooks for a particular company. Box 15-3 illustrates two different opinions on Kellogg at the same point in time, with one analyst predicting good price appreciation and the other suggesting that the stock be sold.

As we might expect, security analysis in the 1990s is often done differently than it was in the past. The reason for this change is not so much that we have a better understanding of the basis of security analysis because the models we have discussed earlier—value as a

Box 15-3

KELLOGG (NYSE: K)

Declining sales, stagnant earnings and a recent unseating as the country's undisputed No. 1–ranked cereal maker have each taken a bite out of Kellogg's stock. Will a new CEO help these soggy shares?

"Kellogg's sure to recapture [its] lost luster." —TIMOTHY RAMEY, DEUTSCHE BANK SECURITIES

"Sell the stock. Earnings are eroding." —DAVID NELSON, CREDIT SUISSE FIRST BOSTON

YES Under new CEO Carlos Gutierrez, Kellogg has ramped up its spending on marketing to levels not seen since 1991. This is a significant catalyst that will drive future sales growth.

YES Kellogg has a slew of new products. One group offers tangible health benefits, protecting against cancer and heart disease. These products can't easily be knocked off by rival private-label cereal makers.

YES Kellogg will report quarterly sales growth of as much as 9 percent by the third quarter of 1999 and an overall earnings-growth rate in the mid-teens by 2000. With a P/E of just 22, Kellogg is trading at a discount to the market and the industry.

NO Kellogg's sharp increase in selling, advertising and promotional spending, to over $100 million a quarter, hasn't yet created growth in a food category that continues to be in decline at a rate of 2 percent a year.

NO Even though the FDA has granted Kellogg the first use of health claims for its cholesterol-lowering cereal, it's likely that others will get to use similar claims. The active ingredient in its new cereal is not a new or unique compound.

NO Kellogg's share is declining, and pricing will be flat in 1999. Earnings will decline to $1.30 in 1999, from $1.36 in 1998, as costs rise faster than sales.

SOURCE: David Geracioti, "Face Off," *SmartMoney*, March, 1999, p. 42.

function of expected return and risk—remain the basis of security analysis today. Rather, the differences now have to do with the increasingly sophisticated use of personal computers to perform many calculations quickly and objectively.

One of the new approaches to stock-picking is the use of "neural networks," whereby a computer program attempts to imitate the brain in doing security analysis and choosing stocks. One such program examines 11 different variables for 2,000 companies, searching for patterns that might be profitable to exploit and that are too subtle for humans to detect. In effect, this program searches for undervalued stocks, which is the basis of security analysis.

SUMMARY

- The analysis of individual companies, the last of three steps in fundamental security analysis, encompasses all the basic financial variables of the company, such as sales, management, and competition. It involves applying the valuation procedures explained in earlier chapters.
- Intrinsic value (a company's justified price) can be estimated using either a dividend valuation model or an earnings multiplier model. It is then compared to the current market price in order to determine whether the stock is undervalued or overvalued.
- An important first step in fundamental analysis is to understand the earnings per share (EPS) of companies. The financial statements can be used to understand the accounting basis of EPS.

- The balance sheet shows the assets and liabilities of a specific date, whereas the income statement shows the flows during a period for the items that determine net income.
- Although these statements are certified by the accounting profession, alternative accounting principles result in EPS figures that are not precise, readily comparable figures. EPS is the result of the interaction of several variables.
- Changes in earnings are directly related to changes in stock prices. To assess expected earnings, investors often consider the earnings growth rate, which is the product of ROE and the earnings retention rate.
- The lack of persistence in these growth rates may lead investors to consider EPS forecasts, which are available mechanically or from analysts. Both are subject to error. The evidence is mixed on which method is better, although a recent study favors analysts' forecasts.
- The difference between actual and forecast EPS is important because of the role of the market's expectations about earnings. Standardized unexpected earnings (SUE) attempts to evaluate the unexpected portion of quarterly earnings.
- The price/earnings (P/E) ratio is the other half of the earnings multiplier model, indicating the amount per dollar of earnings investors are willing to pay for a stock. It represents the relative price of a stock, with some companies carrying high P/E ratios and others having low ones.
- The P/E ratio is influenced directly by investors' expectations of the future growth of earnings and the payout ratio, and inversely by the required rate of return.
- P/E ratios vary among companies primarily because of investors' expectations about the future growth of earnings. If investors lower their expectations, the price of the stock may drop while earnings remain constant or even rise.
- The beta coefficient, the measure of volatility for a stock, indicates the average responsiveness of the stock's price to the overall market, with high- (low-) beta stocks exhibiting larger (smaller) changes than the overall market.

KEY WORDS

Consensus estimate
E/P ratio
Earnings per share (EPS)
Earnings surprise
Financial statements
Generally accepted accounting principles (GAAP)
Internal (sustainable) growth rate
Return on assets (ROA)
Return on equity (ROE)

QUESTIONS

15-1. What is the intrinsic value of a stock?

15-2. How can a stock's intrinsic value be determined?

15-3. What are the limitations of using Equation 15-1 to determine intrinsic value?

15-4. What is meant by GAAP?

15-5. What problems do estimating accounting earnings present?

15-6. What does the auditor's report signify about the financial statements?

15-7. How do auditors and management relate to each other in determining the financial statements?

15-8. What is the concept of earnings quality?

15-9. Outline, in words, the determination process for EPS.

15-10. Explain the role of financing in a company's EPS.

15-11. Assuming that a firm's return on assets exceeds its interest costs, why would it not boost ROE to the maximum through the use of debt financing since higher ROE leads to higher EPS?

15-12. How can the earnings growth rate be determined?

15-13. How well do earnings growth rates for individual companies persist across time?

15-14. How can investors obtain EPS forecasts? Which source is better?

15-15. What role do earnings expectations play in selecting stocks?

15-16. How can the unexpected component of EPS be used to select stocks?

15-17. Explain the relationship between SUE and fundamental security analysis.

15-18. Describe at least two variations in calculating a P/E ratio.

15-19. Using *The Value Line Investment Survey,* list the average annual P/E ratio for the following companies for the last five years: Apple Computer, Coca-Cola, Caterpillar, and Philadelphia Electric. What conclusions can you draw from this analysis?

15-20. What are the variables that affect the P/E ratio? Is the effect direct or inverse for each component?

15-21. Holding everything else constant, what effect would the following have on a company's P/E ratio?

a. An increase in the expected growth rate of earnings
b. A decrease in the expected dividend payout
c. An increase in the risk-free rate of return
d. An increase in the risk premium
e. A decrease in the required rate of return.

15-22. Why would an investor want to know the beta coefficient for a particular company? How could this information be used?

15-23. Is beta the only determinant of a company's return?

15-24. Using Exhibit 15-1, update from *Value Line* the P/E ratios for the first 10 companies in both the lowest and highest set. What does this tell you about the stability of the P/E ratio over time?

CFA

15-25. In Statement of Financial Accounting Concepts 2, the Financial Accounting Standards Board distinguishes three decision-specific primary qualities of accounting information:

- relevance
- reliability
- comparability

Describe each of these three qualities and explain why each is important to the financial analyst.

CFA

15-26. Using book value to measure profitability and to value a company's stock has limitations. Discuss five such limitations from an accounting perspective. Be specific.

PROBLEMS

15-1. GF is a large producer of food products. In 19X5, the percentage breakdown of revenues and profits was as follows:

	Revenues(%)	Profits(%)
Packaged foods	41	62
Coffee	28	19
Processed meat	19	13
Food service-other	12	6
	100	100

International operations account for about 22 percent of sales and 17 percent of operating profit.

For the 19X1–19X5 fiscal years, ending March 31, the number of shares outstanding (in millions) and selected income statement data were (in millions of dollars) as follows:

				Int.			—Net Income—	
Shares Outst.	Year	Oper. Revenues	Cap. Inc.	Exp.	Deprec.	Exp.	Before Tax	After Tax
49.93	19X1	$5472	$524	$121	$77	$31	$452	$232
49.97	19X2	5960	534	262	78	39	470	256
49.43	19X3	6601	565	187	89	50	473	255
49.45	19X4	8351	694	283	131	152	418	221
51.92	19X5	8256	721	266	133	139	535	289

a. For each year calculate operating income as a percentage of revenues.
b. Net profits after tax as a percentage of revenues.
c. After-tax profits per share outstanding (EPS). The balance sheet data for the same fiscal years (in millions of dollars) were as follows:

	Current					
Year	Cash	Assets	Total Liabilities	Long-Term Assets	Debt	Common Equity
19X1	$291	$1736	$845	$2565	$251	$1321
19X2	178	1951	1047	2978	255	1480
19X3	309	2019	929	3103	391	1610
19X4	163	2254	1215	3861	731	1626
19X5	285	2315	1342	4310	736	1872

d. Calculate the ratio of current assets to current liabilities for each year.
e. Calculate the long-term debt as a percentage of common equity.
f. For each year calculate the book value per share as the common equity divided by the number of shares outstanding.
g. Calculate ROE.
h. Calculate ROA.
i. Calculate leverage.

j. Calculate the net income margin.
k. Calculate turnover.
l. Calculate the EBIT.
m. Calculate the income ratio.
n. Calculate operating efficiency.
o. On the basis of these calculations evaluate the current status of the health of GF and the changes over the period.

15-2. Combining information from the S&P reports and some estimated data for 19X7, the following calendar-year data, on a per-share basis, are provided:

Year	Price Range Low High	Earnings	Dividends	Book Value	(D/E) 100(%)	Annual Avg. P/E	ROE = E/Book TR%
19X1	\$26.5–\$35.3	\$4.56	\$1.72	\$25.98	37.7	7.0	17.6%
19X2	28.3–37.0	5.02	1.95	29.15	38.8	6.2	17.3
19X3	23.5–34.3	5.14	2.20	32.11	42.8	5.8	16.0
19X4	27.8–35.0	4.47	2.20	30.86		7.7	
19X5	29.0–47.8	5.73	2.30	30.30		6.8	
19X6	36.6–53.5	6.75	2.40	39.85			
19X7		6.75	2.60	44.00			

a. Calculate the D/E, ROE, and TR for 19X4, 19X5, and 19X6. (Use the average of the low and high prices to calculate TRs.)
b. Show that from 19X2 through 19X6 the per annum growth rate in dividends was 6.9 percent and for earnings was 8.2 percent.
c. Using the current price of \$47, with estimated earnings for 19X7 of \$6.75, show that the P/E would be evaluated as 6.96.
d. On the basis of the annual average P/E ratios shown above and your estimate in Problem c, assume an expected P/E of 7. If an investor expected the earnings of GF for 19X7 to be \$7.50, show that the intrinsic value would be \$52.50.
e. What factors are important in explaining the difference in the P/E ratios of Coca-Cola and GF?
f. From your calculation of the growth rate of dividends in Problem b, assume that the annual rate is 7 percent. If the required rate of return for the stock is 12 percent and the expected dividend payout ratio is 0.4, show that P/E = 8.
g. If the dividend payout ratio is 0.4 and the return on equity is 15 percent, evaluate Equation 15-7 and show that $g = 0.09$.
h. Using $k = 0.14$ and $g = 0.09$, with expected 19X7 dividends of \$2.60, show that the intrinsic value is \$52.
i. Assume the "beta" for GF is 0.8 relative to Coke's beta of 1.3. Is this information of any help in explaining the different P/E ratios of these two companies?

The following question was asked on the 1991 CFA Level I examination:

CFA 15-3. The value of the components affecting the ROE of Merck & Co., Inc. for 1985 are indicated in Table 1 on the facing page. Selected 1990 income statement and balance sheet information for Merck can be found in Table 2 on the facing page.

A. Calculate each of the five ROE components for Merck in 1990. Using the five components, calculate ROE for Merck in 1990. Show all calculations.

TABLE 1 MERCK & CO., INC. 1985 ROE

Tax burden (net income/pretax income)	.628
Interest burden (pretax income/EBIT)	.989
Operating (or profit) margin	.245
Asset turnover	.724
Financial leverage	1.877

TABLE 2 MERCK & CO., INC. 1990 SELECTED FINANCIAL DATA ($ MILLIONS)

Income Statement Data	
Sales revenue	$7,120
Depreciation	230
Interest expense	10
Pretax income	2,550
Income taxes	900
Net income	1,650
Balance Sheet Data	
Current assets	$4,850
Net fixed assets	2,400
Total assets	7,250
Current liabilities	3,290
Long-term debt	100
Shareholders' equity	3,860
Total liabilities & shareholders' equity	7,250

B. Based on your calculations, describe how each ROE component contributed to the change in Merck's ROE between 1985 and 1990. Identify the major underlying reasons for the change in Merck's ROE.

The following question was asked on the 1993 CFA Level I examination:

CFA

15-4. In attempting to forecast the internal growth rate of BK Industries, you develop the following probability distributions:

ROE	Probability	Retention Rate	Probability
15%	0.4	40%	0.7
20%	0.6	60%	0.3

A. Assuming that ROE and retention rate are statistically independent, compute the probability distribution for the growth rate of BK.

B. Compute the expected value of the growth rate.

The following information applies to Problems 15-5 through 15-8:
The following questions were asked on the 1992 CFA Level I examination:

INTRODUCTION

Eastover Company (EO) is a large, diversified forest products company. Approximately 75 percent of its sales are from paper and forest products, with the remainder from financial services and real estate. The company owns 5.6 million acres of timberland, which is carried at very low historical cost on the balance sheet.

Peggy Mulroney, CFA, is an analyst at the investment counseling firm of Centurion Investments. She is assigned the task of assessing the outlook for Eastover, which is being considered for purchase and comparing it to another forest products company in Centurion's portfolios, Southampton Corporation (SHC). SHC is a major producer of lumber products in the United States. Building products, primarily lumber and plywood, account for 89 percent of SHC's sales, with pulp accounting for the remainder. SHC owns 1.4 million acres of timberland, which is also carried at historical cost on the balance sheet. In SHC's case, however, that cost is not as far below current market as Eastover's.

TABLE 1 EASTOVER COMPANY (EO) ($ MILLIONS, EXCEPT SHARES OUTSTANDING)

Income Statement Summary	1986	1987	1988	1989	1990
Sales	$5,652	$6,990	$7,863	$8,281	$7,406
Earnings before interest & taxes (EBIT)	$ 568	$ 901	$1,037	$ 708	$ 795
Interest expense (net)	(147)	(188)	(186)	(194)	(195)
Income before taxes	$ 421	$ 713	$ 851	$ 514	$ 600
Income taxes	(144)	(266)	(286)	(173)	(206)
Tax rate	34%	37%	33%	34%	34%
Net income	$ 277	$ 447	$ 565	$ 341	$ 394
Preferred dividends	(28)	(17)	(17)	(17)	(0)
Net income to common	$ 249	$ 430	$ 548	$ 324	$ 394
Common shares outstanding (millions)	196	204	204	205	201
Balance Sheet Summary	**1986**	**1987**	**1988**	**1989**	**1990**
Current assets	$1,235	$1,491	$1,702	$1,585	$1,367
Timberland assets	649	625	621	612	615
Property, plant & equipment	4,370	4,571	5,056	5,430	5,854
Other assets	360	555	473	472	429
Total assets	$6,614	$7,242	$7,852	$8,099	$8,265
Current liabilities	$1,226	$1,186	$1,206	$1,606	$1,816
Long-term debt	1,120	1,340	1,585	1,346	1,585
Deferred taxes & other	1,000	1,000	1,016	1,000	1,000
Equity-preferred	364	350	350	400	0
Equity-common	2,904	3,366	3,695	3,747	3,864
Total liabilities & equity	$6,614	$7,242	$7,852	$8,099	$8,265

TABLE 2 SOUTHAMPTON CORPORATION (SHC) ($ MILLIONS, EXCEPT SHARES OUTSTANDING)

Income Statement Summary	1986	1987	1988	1989	1990
Sales	$1,306	$1,654	$1,799	$2,010	$1,793
Earnings before interest & taxes (EBIT)	$ 120	$ 230	$ 221	$ 304	$ 145
Interest expense (net)	(13)	(36)	(7)	(12)	(8)
Income before taxes	$ 107	$ 194	$ 214	$ 292	$ 137
Income taxes	(44)	(75)	(79)	(99)	(46)
Tax rate	41%	39%	37%	34%	34%
Net income	$ 63	$ 119	$ 135	$ 193	$ 91
Common shares outstanding (millions)	38	38	38	38	38
Balance Sheet Summary	**1986**	**1987**	**1988**	**1989**	**1990**
Current assets	$ 487	$ 504	$ 536	$ 654	$ 509
Timberland assets	512	513	508	513	518
Property, plant & equipment	648	681	718	827	1,037
Other assets	141	151	34	38	40
Total assets	$1,788	$1,849	$1,796	$2,032	$2,104
Current liabilities	$ 185	$ 176	$ 162	$ 180	$ 195
Long-term debt	536	493	370	530	589
Deferred taxes & other	123	136	127	146	153
Equity	944	1,044	1,137	1,176	1,167
Total liabilities & equity	$1,788	$1,849	$1,796	$2,032	$2,104

TABLE 3 CURRENT INFORMATION

	Current Share Price	Current Dividends	1992 EPS Estimate	Current Book Value per share
Eastover	$28	$1.20	$1.60	$17.32
Southampton	48	1.08	3.00	32.21
S&P 500	415	12	20.54	159.83

TABLE 4 PROJECTED GROWTH RATES

	Next 3 Years (1992, 1993, 1994)	Growth Beyond 1994
Eastover	12%	8%
Southampton	13%	7%

CFA
15-5. Mulroney's supervisor asks her to first explore the relationship between industry lumber production and lumber production at EO and SHC. As part of this analysis, Mulroney runs two regressions, using industry lumber production as the independent variable and each company's lumber production as the dependent variable.

The results are indicated below:

	intercept (t-ratio)	slope coefficient (t-ratio)	R^2
Eastover	2.79 (6.08)	−0.03 (−0.25)	.63
Southampton	1.28 (5.25)	0.10 (13.07)	.90

The *t*-ratio critical value at the 5 percent level is 1.83.

A. The regressions produce the two intercepts and two slope coefficients shown above. Define the terms intercept and slope coefficient. State whether each of the two intercepts and each of the two slope coefficients are statistically significant.
B. Based on these regressions, identify the statistic that expresses the percentage of Eastover's and Southampton's lumber production that is explained by the independent variable (industry lumber production). State the percentage explained by the regression.
C. Based on your answer to Parts A and B above, discuss the reliability of forecasts from each of the two regressions.

CFA

15-6. Mulroney continued her examination of Eastover and Southampton by looking at the five components of return on equity (ROE) for each company. For her analysis, Mulroney elected to define equity as total shareholders' equity, including preferred stock. She also elected to use year-end data rather than averages for the balance sheet items.

A. Based on the data shown in Tables 1 and 2, calculate each of the five ROE components for Eastover and Southampton in 1990. Using the five components, calculate ROE for both companies in 1990. Show all calculations.
B. Referring to the components calculated in Part A, explain the difference in ROE for Eastover and Southampton in 1990.
C. Using 1990 data, calculate an internal (i.e., sustainable) growth rate for both Eastover and Southampton. Discuss the appropriateness of using these calculations as a basis for estimating future growth.

CFA

15-7. Mulroney recalled from her CFA studies that the constant-growth discounted dividend model (DDM) was one way to arrive at a valuation for a company's common stock. She collected current dividend and stock price data for Eastover and Southampton, shown in Table 3.

A. Using 11 percent as the required rate of return (i.e., discount rate) and a projected growth rate of 8 percent, compute a constant-growth DDM value for Eastover's stock and compare the computed value for Eastover to its stock price indicated in Table 3. Show calculations.

   Mulroney's supervisor commented that a two-stage DDM may be more appropriate for companies such as Eastover and Southampton. Mulroney believes that Eastover and Southampton could grow more rapidly over the next three years and then settle in at a lower but sustainable rate of growth beyond 1994. Her estimates are indicated in Table 4.
B. Using 11 percent as the required rate of return, compute the two-stage DDM value of Eastover's stock and compare that value to its stock price indicated in Table 3. Show calculations.
C. Discuss two advantages and three disadvantages of using a constant-growth DDM. Briefly discuss how the two-stage DDM improves upon the constant-growth DDM.

CFA
15-8. Mulroney previously calculated a valuation for Southampton for both the constant growth and two-stage DDM as shown below:

	Discounted Dividend Model Using	
	Constant Growth Approach	Two-Stage Approach
Southampton	$29	$35.50

Using only the information provided and your answers to Questions CFA 5, 6, and 7, select the stock (EO or SHC) that Mulroney should recommend as the better value, and justify your selection.

SELECTED REFERENCES

The practitioner's side of stock valuation is discussed in:

Chugh, Lal C., and Meador, Joseph W. "The Stock Valuation Process: The Analysts' View." *Financial Analysts Journal* (November/December 1984), pp. 41–44.

A more complete analysis of the SUE concept can be found in:

Jones, Charles P., Rendleman, Richard J., and Latane, Henry A. "Stock Returns and SUEs During the 1970s." *Journal of Portfolio Management* (Winter 1984), pp. 18–22.

www.wiley.com/college/jones7
This chapter focuses on fundamental security analysis. Accordingly, we will look at companies' financial statements and at earnings forecasts to see how they affect stock returns.

APPENDIX 15-A

SOURCES OF INFORMATION FOR COMMON STOCKS

THE FINANCIAL PRESS

NEWSPAPERS

Perhaps the most popular and best known source of daily financial information is *The Wall Street Journal (WSJ)*.[16] It provides detailed coverage of financial and business-related news on both a national and world level. Daily quotations from the principal bond, option, and stock markets are a well-known feature of the *WSJ*. Of particular interest to many investors is

[16] An alternative source is *The New York Times*, a daily newspaper known for its large business and financial coverage. Much of this information parallels that contained in the *WSJ*.

earnings information on various corporations—on both a reported basis, in the form of quarterly and annual earnings reports, and a prospective basis, in the form of news reports concerning expected earnings. The *WSJ* carries several columns that may be of interest to investors, including "Heard on the Street," "Abreast of the Market," "Bond Markets," and "Dividend News."

Barron's, like the *WSJ,* is published by Dow Jones; it is a weekly newspaper with more detailed articles on general business topics and particular companies. It carries weekly price and volume quotations for all financial markets as well as a large amount and variety of statistics on assets, markets, economic variables, indicators, and so forth.[17] *Barron's* also includes regular columns on weekly activities in the stock market, the bond market, the options market, commodities, the real estate market, the international situation, and dividend news.

The Wall Street Transcript is a weekly paper specializing in detailed reports on individual companies. It also features interviews with market professionals.

MAGAZINES

A wide variety of financial magazines exist. In the area of general magazines or "popular press," *Forbes* is a biweekly magazine offering articles on various companies and topics of interest to investors, as well as columnists with opinions on particular market segments and activities. *Forbes* publishes an index that measures U.S. economic activity, including graphs of its eight components (industrial production, manufacturers' new orders, housing starts, retail sales, etc.). It also features "The *Forbes* Wall Street Review," showing a graph of the overall market; "Closeup of the Market," which indicates the short-run changes in several market indexes or investment alternatives; and other selected information, such as the best and worst performing stocks.

The first issue of *Forbes* each January contains the "Annual Report on American Industry," which shows how the 1000 largest U.S. public companies compare in profitability, growth, and stock market performance for five-year periods and the latest 12 months. *Forbes* also evaluates the performance of mutual funds during the year.

Business Week covers the major developments in business during the week. It contains articles about specific companies and industries, and regular features include "Finance," "Industries," "International," "Economic Analysis," and other subjects. The "Business Week Index" page features production indicators, leading indicators, foreign exchange information, prices, monthly economic indicators, monetary indicators, and money market rates.

Fortune is a biweekly magazine with articles on general business trends, written with an emphasis on the perspective of corporate managers. A well-known regular feature of *Fortune* is "Personal Investing."[18]

Money magazine is a monthly publication intended for anyone interested in personal financial matters. It regularly publishes features such as "key economic data," "Money Update," and "Wall Street." *Money* reports detailed rankings on mutual funds. It also features a variety of articles on the financial situations of specific individuals.

CORPORATE REPORTS

An important source of information is the corporation itself. Owners of a company's common stock receive its annual report; non-shareholders can obtain the annual report from the company or their broker.

[17] Another weekly, *The Commercial and Financial Chronicle,* has daily prices for the leading exchanges and weekly prices for regional exchanges and the OTC market.

[18] Additional publications similar to the three discussed here include *Dun's Review* and *Financial World.* These publications typically carry more detailed articles.

Annual reports highlight the most recent fiscal year. Extended discussions of activities, problems, and prospects are often part of the report. In addition, the annual report contains audited financial information. The balance sheet, income statement, and statement of changes in financial position are shown, usually for at least the current and preceding year. A summary of accounting policies may be included, as well as detailed notes to the financial statements. Such information can aid diligent investors in better assessing the company's current and future condition.

BROKERAGE FIRMS

Most investors have access to investment information in the form of oral and written information from their brokers. The typical full-service brokerage house has a research department that provides a steady flow of reports for consumption by all investors, whether individuals or institutions. In addition, these firms subscribe to well-known investment information sources that can be used by their customers.

Brokerage houses, with their own research staffs of economists and analysts, make recommendations to buy, hold, or sell securities. Some brokerage houses deal primarily with institutional investors, whereas others, known as "retail" brokerage houses, work mainly with individuals. Major retail brokerage houses include Merrill Lynch; Charles Schwab; Morgan Stanley; Dean Witter; Prudential-Bache; and A. G. Edwards. Each brokerage house puts out a number of pamphlets for investors.

The traditional full-service brokerage firms provide most of this information "free" to their customers; however, the cost of providing this service is presumably built into the commissions paid by their customers. Discount brokers may or may not provide information. They are selling execution capability, and the investor makes his or her own decisions. Thus, investors have a choice and should choose brokers according to the types of services needed (and the ability of brokerage houses to deliver cost-effective services).

Brokerage houses are a source of both information and recommendations. The emphasis, however, is on recommendations because brokers earn commissions based on the amount of trading that investors do. Furthermore, most recommendations are "buy" as opposed to "sell" recommendations.

INVESTMENT INFORMATION SERVICES

A large amount of information is available to investors from companies that specialize in providing investment information and advice. Investors can subscribe to these services, several of which offer a variety of products, or they can read at least some of them free of charge at their library or at the offices of their broker. Although some of these services offer both information and investment advice, for organizational purposes they will be separated into information services (this section), and advisory (recommendation) services (next section). Remember, however, that the same service can provide both information and recommendations.

Investors can access financial information and data from a variety of investment information services, including Dun & Bradstreet, Inc., the widely known credit-reporting company. But the two best known sources of a wide variety of investment information are Standard & Poor's Corporation (S&P) (a subsidiary of McGraw-Hill) and Moody's Investor Services, Inc. (owned by Dun & Bradstreet). Both are New York based. These two services issue a systematic, continuous flow of reports on a daily, weekly, and monthly basis. Investors can subscribe to only those parts that are of interest to them, such as the common stock service or the bond service. Both sources are commonly available in larger public and college libraries.

Both services issue basic reference volumes covering corporations in some detail. For example, Moody's *Industrial Manual* devotes several pages, in very small print, to each company covered. Moody's also issues the *OTC Industrial Manual*, the *OTC Unlisted Manual, The Public Utility Manual*, the *Bank & Finance Manual*, the *Transportation Manual*, the *Municipal & Government Manual*, and the *International Manual*. All these manuals are updated in separate binders weekly.

The comparable series for Standard & Poor's is their six-volume *Corporation Records*. These are in alphabetical order and are issued regularly, with daily updates in a seventh volume called *Daily News*. Unlike Moody's, this coverage is not separated by areas such as transportation or public utilities.

Standard & Poor's also issues the two-volume *Industry Surveys*, with very detailed discussions of various industries as organized and reported on by S&P. It also issues *Statistical Services: Current Statistics*, which carries a wide variety of statistics of all types: economic production and consumption, data by industry, price data, and so forth.

Often of special interest to investors seeking information about a particular company are the short reports (two pages) on companies put out by each service. Standard and Poor's *Stock Reports* are divided into New York Stock Exchange, American Stock Exchange, and over-the-counter and regional exchanges, each in four volumes. The comparable Moody's service, *Investors Fact Sheets*, is also separated by exchanges. Although these sources are less detailed than those discussed previously, they offer the investor both a compact source of current information and a historical balance sheet, income statement, and market data (10 years for Standard & Poor's, 7 for Moody's).

Investors can use an even briefer source of information on stocks of interest from Moody's *Handbook of Common Stocks* or Standard & Poor's *Stock Guide*. The *Handbook* is issued in spring, summer, fall, and winter editions and contains one page of write-up and data for each covered stock. The *Stock Guide*, issued monthly, contains very brief information on several thousand listed and unlisted stocks. These data consist of high and low prices for selected years, sales, and yield information.

Data for small OTC firms are available in Standard & Poor's *OTC Profiles*.

Investors seeking information on the dividends paid on most securities have a wealth of information at their disposal. Standard & Poor's issues a *Quarterly Dividend Record*, with detailed information on the timing and amount of dividends by company. Moody's issues an *Annual Dividend Report* with similar detailed information.

INVESTMENT ADVISORY SERVICES AND INVESTMENT NEWSLETTERS

Investors have access to a wide variety of investment advisory services and investment newsletters, many of which offer a combination of analyses and projections along with stock recommendations. Investment advisory services may specialize in particular selection techniques or in particular assets (e.g., options) or areas (e.g., new issues). The larger services may offer several different products for investors. Most investment advisory services and investment newsletters offer trial subscriptions, allowing investors to sample what is available. Because of the wide variety of services and letters available to investors, we will describe only one in detail. We will then briefly mention others that are well known among many investors.

VALUE LINE

The Value Line Investment Survey (VL) is the largest (by number of subscribers) and probably best known investment advisory service in the United States. The *VL* covers over 1,700 stocks (including NYSE, AMEX, and some OTC) organized into 90-plus industries on a regular basis, reviewing each once every three months. Specifically, each weekly issue covers several industry groupings, completing the cycle every quarter. In addition to this "Ratings and Reports," every week subscribers also receive a "Summary and Index" and a "Selection and Opinion" section containing an overall review of the market, a highlighted stock, a record of insider transactions, and numerous other data.

The *VL* is both a reference service and a recommendation service. Essential information is presented for each industry grouping as a whole as well as for each individual company. For example, 23 series of financial and operating statistics are provided for each company for the previous 15 years and estimated for the next one or two years. These statistics can be seen in the middle of Exhibit 15-2, which shows a typical page of coverage for a company, in this case Coca-Cola. Each company report shows both historical and estimated data.

With regard to recommendations, the *VL* ranks each company from 1 (top) to 5 (bottom) on the basis of its "probable safety in the future" and its timeliness ("probable price performance in the next 12 months") in relation to the other 1700-plus stocks. The top 100 and bottom 100 stocks are in Group I and Group V, respectively; the next 300 top and 300 bottom, respectively, are in Groups II and IV; and the middle 900 are in Group III. *Value Line* recommends that investors choose stocks out of the top 400 (Groups I and II) that meet their standards for safety and current yield. If any of the selected stocks falls below the investor's standards, a switch is made into those that currently conform. This is convenient for investors because the weekly "Summary and Index" section shows the current performance and safety ratings for each of the 1700 stocks as well as their estimated yields and latest earnings.

VL's stock rankings are based on a computer model developed and modified over many years. The model includes price history over both a short and long period, earnings changes, and an earnings surprise factor to account for actual earnings significantly above or below those predicted by their analysts. The *VL* discloses the methodology for computing the ranks and regularly reports on how well the ranks have done in practice.

As Exhibit 15-2 shows, the *VL* coverage also provides such information as the beta and the P/E ratio. Additional information includes the company's financial strength, the price stability of the stock, the price growth persistence, and the earnings predictability. Quarterly sales, earnings, and dividends are shown on both a historical and an estimated basis. Note (in the upper left corner) that both institutional and insider decisions are shown. As part of its company coverage, *Value Line* issues an industry report for each of the 90 plus industries it covers. This is typically a two-page report preceding the companies assigned to that industry by *Value Line*. This discussion analyzes the current and prospective situation for the industry and has a table of composite statistics, including both historical and estimated figures.

OTHER ADVISORY SERVICES AND LETTERS

There are many other investment advisory services and letters, one of which is the well-known weekly service, Standard & Poor's *The Outlook*. It discusses general market conditions and offers portfolio advice. It also features recommended industries and stocks, with the stocks based on a "star" rating system. Five stars indicates a buy and one star indicates a sell, with three shadings in between. Available in many libraries, it is well worth reading.

Some of the well-known investment newsletters include *The Zweig Forecast, Dow Theory Forecasts, The Professional Tape Reader,* and *The Prudent Speculator. Forbes* magazine now carries Mark Hulbert as a columnist; Hulbert publishes *Hulbert Financial Digest,* which monitors investment letters.

chapter 16

TECHNICAL ANALYSIS

Chapter 16 presents the other approach to security analysis, which is technical analysis. This approach is very different from fundamental analysis and is directly affected by the Efficient Market Hypothesis discussed in Chapter 12.

After reading this chapter you will be able to:

- **Understand how technical analysis differs from fundamental analysis.**
- **Critically evaluate most of the techniques used in technical analysis as well as the claims made for these techniques.**
- **Decide what role, if any, technical analysis might play in your own investing program.**

As discussed in Chapter 11, technical analysis is the other traditional approach for selecting stocks. It is entirely different from the fundamental approach to security analysis discussed in the last three chapters.

Although the technical approach to common stock selection is the oldest approach (dating back to the late 1800s), it remains controversial.[1] The techniques discussed in this chapter appear at first glance to have considerable merit, because they seem intuitive and plausible, but they have been severely challenged in the last two decades by evidence supporting the Efficient Market Hypothesis discussed in Chapter 12.

Those learning about investments will in all likelihood be exposed to technical analysis, because numerous investors, investment advisory firms, and the popular press talk about it and use it. Furthermore, it may produce some insights into the psychological dimension of the market. In fact, technical analysis is becoming increasingly interrelated with behavioral finance, a popular field of study today. In effect, technical indicators are being used to measure investor emotions.

Even if this approach is incorrect, many investors act as if it is correct. Nevertheless, despite Burton Malkiel's (a well-known proponent of efficient markets) admission that "the market is not a perfect random walk," extensive evidence has challenged the validity of technical analysis and the likelihood of its success. Therefore, the prudent course of action is to study this topic, or indeed any other recommended approach to making investing decisions, and try to make an objective evaluation of its validity and usefulness.

Although technical analysis can be applied to bonds, currencies, and commodities as well as to common stocks, technical analysis typically involves either the aggregate stock market, industry sectors or individual common stocks. Therefore, we restrict our discussion in this chapter to common stocks.

WHAT IS TECHNICAL ANALYSIS?

Technical Analysis The use of specific market data for the analysis of both aggregate stock prices and individual stock prices

Technical analysis can be defined as the use of specific market-generated data for the analysis of both aggregate stock prices (market indices or industry averages) and individual stocks. Martin J. Pring, in his book *Technical Analysis,* states: "The technical approach to investing is essentially a reflection of the idea that prices move in trends which are determined by the changing attitudes of investors toward a variety of economic, monetary, political and psychological forces. The art of technical analysis—*for it is an art* (emphasis added)—is to identify trend changes at an early stage and to maintain an investment posture until the weight of the evidence indicates that the trend is reversed."[2]

Technical analysis is sometimes called market or internal analysis, because it utilizes the record of the market itself to attempt to assess the demand for, and supply of, shares of a stock or the entire market. Thus, technical analysts believe that the market itself is its own best source of data—as they say, "let the market tell its own story."

Economics teaches us that prices are determined by the interaction of demand and supply. Technicians do not disagree, but argue that it is extremely difficult to assess all the factors that influence demand and supply. Since not all investors are in agreement on price, the determining factor at any point in time is the net demand (or lack thereof) for a stock based on how many investors are optimistic or pessimistic. Furthermore, once the balance of investors becomes optimistic (pessimistic), this mood is likely to continue for the near term

[1] Technical analysis itself can be traced back to the rice markets in seventeenth century Japan.

[2] See Martin J. Pring, *Technical Analysis Explained* (New York: McGraw Hill Publishers), 1991.

and can be detected by various technical indicators. As the chief market technician of one New York firm says, "All I care about is how people feel about those particular stocks as shown by their putting money in and taking their money out."[3]

Technical analysis is based on published market data as opposed to fundamental data, such as earnings, sales, growth rates, or government regulations. **Market data** include the price of a stock or the level of a market index, volume (number of shares traded), and technical indicators (explained later), such as the short interest ratio. Many technical analysts believe that only such market data, as opposed to fundamental data, are relevant. For example, Joseph Granville, a well-known market forecaster who has experienced great ups and downs in terms of his own success in forecasting the market, says of fundamental analysis, "The dumb money is particularly attracted to improving earnings."

Market Data Price and volume information for stocks or indexes

Recall that in fundamental analysis the dividend discount model produces an estimate of a stock's intrinsic value, which is then compared to the market price. Fundamentalists believe that their data, properly evaluated, indicate the worth or intrinsic value of a stock. Technicians, on the other hand, believe that it is extremely difficult to estimate intrinsic value and virtually impossible to obtain and analyze good information consistently. In particular, they are dubious about the value to be derived from an analysis of published financial statements. Instead, they focus on market data as an indication of the forces of supply and demand for a stock or the market.

Technicians believe that the process by which prices adjust to new information is one of a gradual adjustment toward a new (equilibrium) price. As the stock adjusts from its old equilibrium level to its new level, the price tends to move in a trend. The central concern is not why the change is taking place, but rather the very fact that it is taking place at all. Technical analysts believe that stock prices show identifiable trends that can be exploited by investors. They seek to identify changes in the direction of a stock and take a position in the stock to take advantage of the trend.

The following points summarize technical analysis:

1. Technical analysis is based on published market data and focuses on internal factors by analyzing movements in the aggregate market, industry average, or stock. In contrast, fundamental analysis focuses on economic and political factors, which are external to the market itself.
2. The focus of technical analysis is identifying changes in the direction of stock prices which tend to move in trends as the stock price adjusts to a new equilibrium level. These trends can be analyzed, and changes in trends detected, by studying the action of price movements and trading volume across time. The emphasis is on likely price changes.
3. Technicians attempt to assess the overall situation concerning stocks by analyzing breadth indicators, market sentiment, momentum, and other indicators.

A FRAMEWORK FOR TECHNICAL ANALYSIS

Technical analysis can be applied to both an aggregate of prices (the market as a whole or industry averages) and individual stocks. Technical analysis includes the use of graphs (charts) and technical trading rules and indicators. Figure 16-1 depicts the technical analysis approach to investing.

Price and volume are the primary tools of the pure technical analyst, and the chart is the most important mechanism for displaying this information. Technicians believe that the

[3] See Jonathan Butler, "Technical Analysis: A Primer," *Worth,* October 1995, p. 128.

FIGURE 16-1

The technical analysis approach to common stock selection.

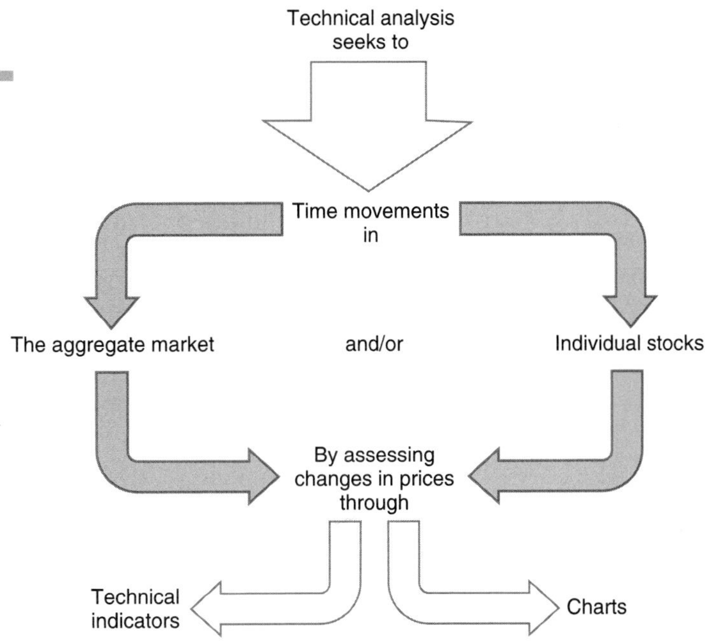

forces of supply and demand result in particular patterns of price behavior, the most important of which is the trend or overall direction in price. Using a chart, the technician hopes to identify trends and patterns in stock prices that provide trading signals.

Volume data are used to gauge the general condition in the market and to help assess its trend. The evidence seems to suggest that rising (falling) stock prices are usually associated with rising (falling) volume. If stock prices rose but volume activity did not keep pace, technicians would be skeptical about the upward trend. An upward surge on contracting volume would be particularly suspect. A downside movement from some pattern or holding point, accompanied by heavy volume, would be taken as a bearish sign.

We first consider stock price and volume techniques, often referred to as charting. However, technical analysis has evolved over time, so that today it is much more than the charting of individual stocks or the market. In particular, technical indicators are used to assess market conditions (breadth) and investor sentiment. It also includes "contrary analysis," which is an intellectual process more than a technique. The idea here is to go against the crowd when the crowd starts thinking alike.

STOCK PRICE AND VOLUME TECHNIQUES

THE DOW THEORY

Dow Theory A technique for detecting long-term trends in the aggregate stock market

The oldest and best known theory of technical analysis is the **Dow theory**, originally developed in the late 1800s by the editor of *The Wall Street Journal*, Charles H. Dow, who many regard as the father of technical analysis. Although Dow developed the theory to describe past price movements, William Hamilton followed up by using it to predict movements in the market. (It is not concerned with individual securities.) The Dow theory was very popular in the 1920s and 1930s, and articles offering support for it still appear periodically in the literature. Several investment advisory services are based on the Dow Theory.

The theory is based on the existence of three types of price movements:

1. Primary moves, a broad market movement that lasts several years.
2. Secondary (intermediate) moves, occurring within the primary moves, which represent interruptions lasting several weeks or months.
3. Day-to-day moves, occurring randomly around the primary and secondary moves.

Bull Market An upward trend in the stock market

Bear Market A downward trend in the stock market

The term **bull market** refers to an upward primary move, whereas **bear market** refers to a downward primary move. A major upward move is said to occur when successive rallies penetrate previous highs, whereas declines remain above previous lows. A major downward move is expected when successive rallies fail to penetrate previous highs, whereas declines penetrate previous lows.

The secondary or intermediate moves give rise to the so-called technical corrections, which are often mentioned in the popular press. These corrections supposedly adjust for excesses that have occurred. These movements are of considerable importance in applying the Dow theory.

Finally, the day-to-day "ripples" occur often and are of minor importance. Even ardent technical analysts do not usually try to predict day-to-day movements in the market.

Figure 16-2 illustrates the basic concept of the Dow theory, although numerous variations exist. The primary trend, represented by the dotted line, is up through time Period 1. Although several downward (secondary) reactions occur, these "corrections" do not reach the previous low. Each of these reactions is followed by an upward movement that exceeds the previously obtained high. Trading volume continues to build over this period.

Although prices again decline after time Period 1 as another correction occurs, the price recovery fails to surpass the last peak reached. (This process is referred to as an abortive recovery.) When the next downward reaction occurs, it penetrates the previous low. This movement could suggest that a primary downturn or new bear market has begun, although it is subject to confirmation. As originally conceived, the Dow Jones Industrial and Rail average (which was later replaced by the Transportation Average) must confirm each other for the movement to be validated.

The Dow theory is intended to forecast the start of a primary movement, but it does not tell us how long the movement will last. Another important consideration is that the confirmation referred to above is up to each user of the Dow theory. The trend will continue as long as the averages confirm each other. Only these averages matter; extensive records are not required, chart patterns are not studied, and so on.

The Dow theory is subject to a number of criticisms, and investors continue today

FIGURE 16-2

The basic concept of the Dow theory.

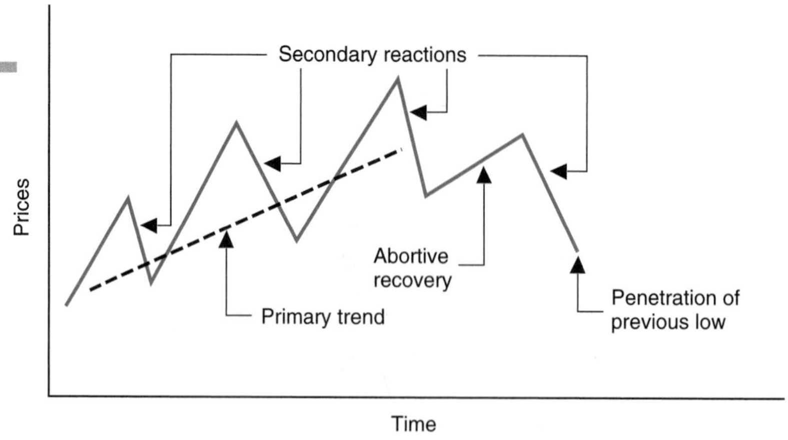

debating its merits. Studies of its success rate have been disappointing; for example, over periods of as much as 25 years, investors would have been more successful with a buy-and-hold policy in the same stocks. It is obvious that today's economy is vastly different from the one that existed when the theory was developed. In addition, confirmations are slow to arrive and are often unclear when they do. The amount of price movement needed for a confirmation is ambiguous.

One problem associated with the Dow theory is that many versions are available, including several investment letters based on the Dow theory. Its users interpret the theory in various ways, and so it may predict different (and conflicting) movements at the same time.

CHARTS OF PRICE PATTERNS

To assess individual stock-price movements, technicians generally rely on charts or graphs of price movements and on relative strength analysis. The charting of price patterns is one of the classic technical analysis techniques. Technicians believe that stock prices move in trends, with price changes forming patterns that can be recognized and categorized. By visually assessing the forces of supply and demand, technicians hope to be able to predict the likely direction of future movements.

Support Level A price range at which a technician expects a significant increase in the demand for a stock

Resistance Level A price range at which a technician expects a significant increase in the supply of a stock

Technicians seek to identify certain signals in a chart of stock prices, and use certain terminology to describe the events. A **support level** is the level of price (or, more correctly, a price range) at which a technician expects a significant increase in the demand for a stock—in other words, a lower bound on price where it is expected that buyers will act, supporting the price and preventing additional price declines. A **resistance level,** on the other hand, is the level of price (range) at which a technician expects a significant increase in the supply of a stock—in other words, an upper bound on price where sellers are expected to act, providing a resistance to any further rise in price.

Support levels tend to develop when profit taking causes a reversal in a stock's price following an increase. Investors who did not purchase earlier are now willing to buy at this price, which becomes a support level. Resistance levels tend to develop after a stock declines from a higher level. Investors are waiting to sell the stocks at a certain recovery point. At certain price levels, therefore, a significant increase in supply occurs, and the price will encounter resistance moving beyond this level.

A trendline is a line drawn on a chart to identify a trend. If a trend exhibits support and resistance levels simultaneously that appear to be well defined, the trend lines are referred to as channel lines, and price is said to move between the upper channel line and the lower channel line. Momentum is used to indicate the speed with which prices are changing, and a number of measures of momentum exist, referred to as momentum indicators. When a change in direction occurs in a short-term trend, technicians say that a reversal has occurred. A correction occurs when the reversal involves only a partial retracing of the prior movement. Corrections may be followed by periods of consolidation, with the initial trend resuming following the consolidation.

Technical analysts rely primarily on bar charts and point-and-figure charts, although other types of charts are also used.[4]

Bar Chart A plot of daily stock price plotted against time

Bar Charts

Probably the most popular chart in technical analysis, and clearly the simplest, **bar charts** are plotted with price on the vertical axis and time on the horizontal axis. Each day's price movement is represented by a vertical bar whose top (bottom) represents the high

[4] Technicians also use a basic line chart, which uses only one number—usually the closing price for the day—to reflect the price movement. Another type of chart gaining some popularity in the United States is the candlestick chart. Developed in Japan, the candlestick is similar to the bar chart, although it shows the opening price as well as the high, low and closing prices.

FIGURE 16-3

A bar chart for Unfloppy Disk, Inc.

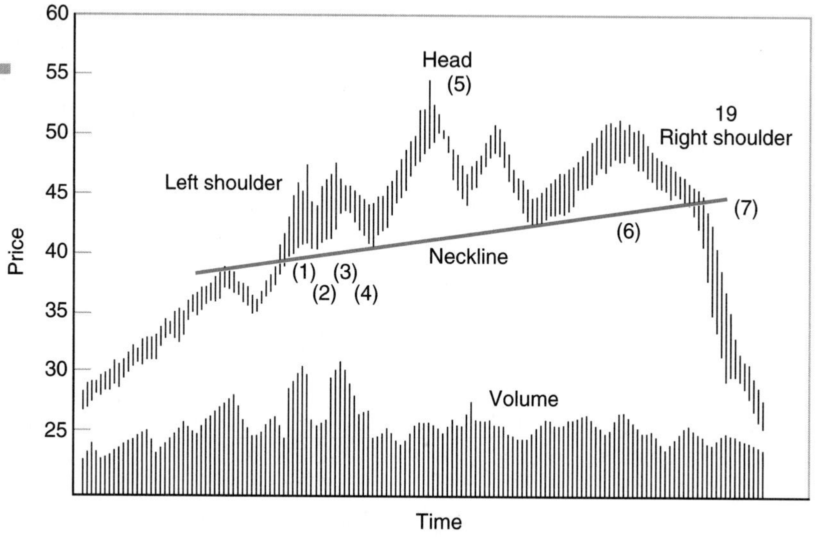

(low) price for the day. (A small, horizontal tick is often used to designate the closing price for the day.) The bottom of a bar chart usually shows the trading volume for each day, permitting the simultaneous observation of both price and volume activity.[5] *The Wall Street Journal* carries a bar chart of the Dow Jones Averages each day on the page with NYSE quotations.

Figure 16-3 shows a daily bar chart for Unfloppy Disks, Inc. The technician using charts will search for patterns in the chart that can be used to predict future price moves. Note in Figure 16-3 the strong uptrend occurring over a period of months. This trend ended with a rally on high volume (at point 1 in the figure) that forms part of the left shoulder of a famous chart pattern called a *head-and-shoulders pattern.*

The left shoulder shows initially strong demand followed by a reaction on lower volume (2), and then a second rally, with strong volume, carrying prices still higher (3). Profit taking again causes prices to fall to the so-called neckline (4), thus completing the left shoulder. (The neckline is formed by connecting previous low points.) A rally occurs, but this time on low volume, and again prices sink back to the neckline. This is the head (5). The last step is the formation of the right shoulder, which occurs with light volume (6). Growing weakness can be identified as the price approaches the neckline. As can be seen in Figure 16-3, a downside breakout occurs on heavy volume, which technicians consider to be a sell signal.

What about other patterns? Technicians have considered a very large number of such patterns. Some of the possible patterns include flags, pennants, gaps (of more than one type), triangles of various types (e.g., symmetrical, ascending, descending, and inverted), the inverted saucer or dome, the triple top, the compound fulcrum, the rising (and falling) wedge, the broadening bottom, the duplex horizontal, rectangles, and the inverted V. Figure 16-4 shows one set of price patterns said to be the most important for investors to recognize when reading charts of stock prices.

Obviously, numerous patterns are possible and can usually be found on a chart of stock prices. It is also obvious that most, if not all, of these patterns are much easier to identify in hindsight than at the time they are actually occurring.

Point-and-Figure Chart A plot of stock prices showing only significant price changes

Point-and-Figure Charts Technicians also use **point-and-figure charts.** This type of chart is more complex in that it shows only significant price changes, and volume is not

[5] The time intervals do not have to be days but could be weeks, months, or anything else a particular preparer might choose.

FIGURE 16-4

Important price patterns for investors using charts.

SOURCE: Jonathan Butler, "Technical Analysis: A Primer," *Worth*, October 1995, p. 133. Reprinted by permission of *Worth* magazine.

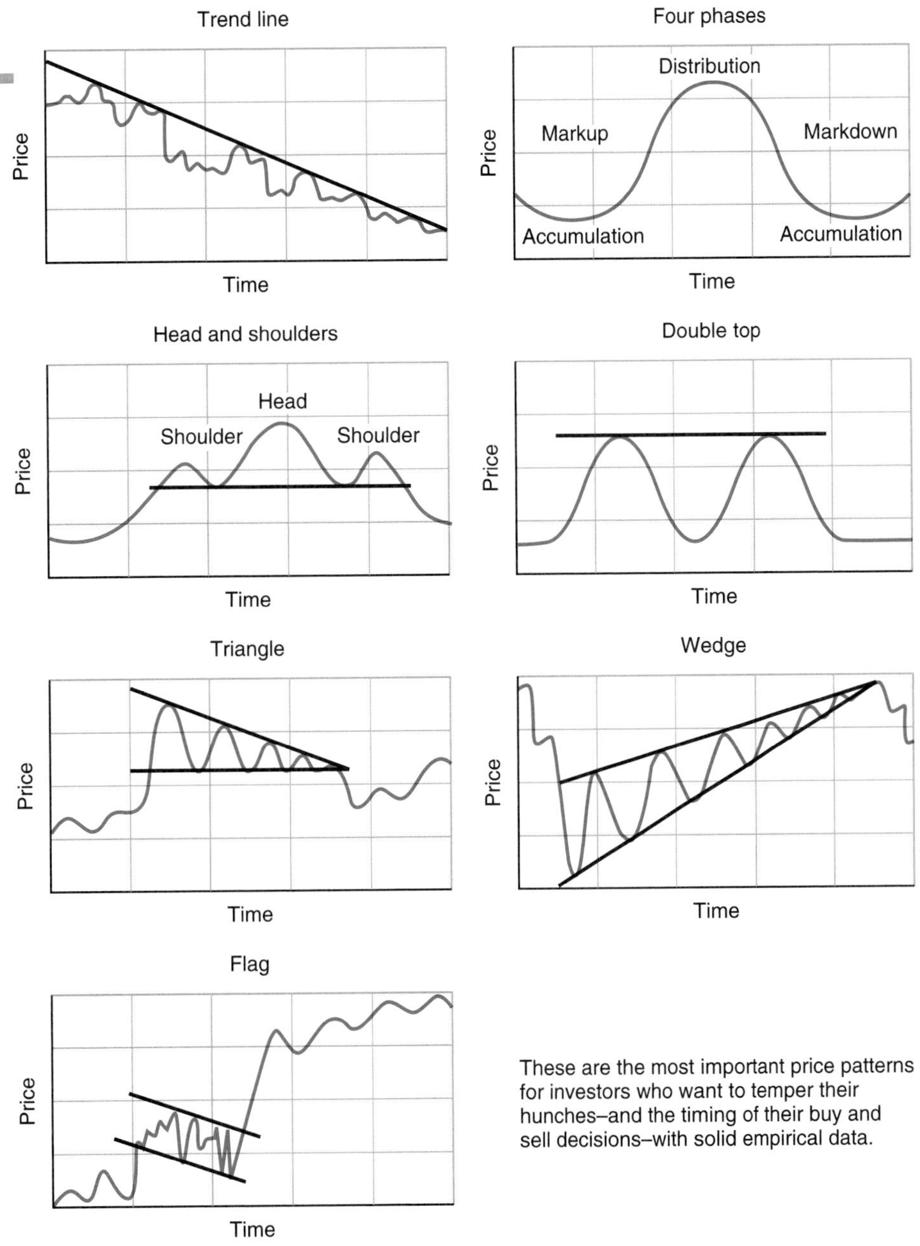

shown at all. The user determines what is a significant price change ($1, $2, etc.) and what constitutes a price reversal ($2, $3, $4, etc.). Although the horizontal axis still depicts time, specific calendar time is not particularly important. (Some chartists do show the month in which changes occur.)

An X is typically used to show upward movements, whereas an O is used for downward movements. Each X or O on a particular chart may represent $1 movements, $2 movements, $5 movements, and so on, depending on how much movement is considered significant for that stock. An X or O is recorded only when the price moves by the specified amount. Figure 16-5 illustrates the point-and-figure chart.

A point-and-figure chart is designed to compress many price changes into a small space. By doing so, areas of "congestion" can be identified. A congestion area is a compacted area

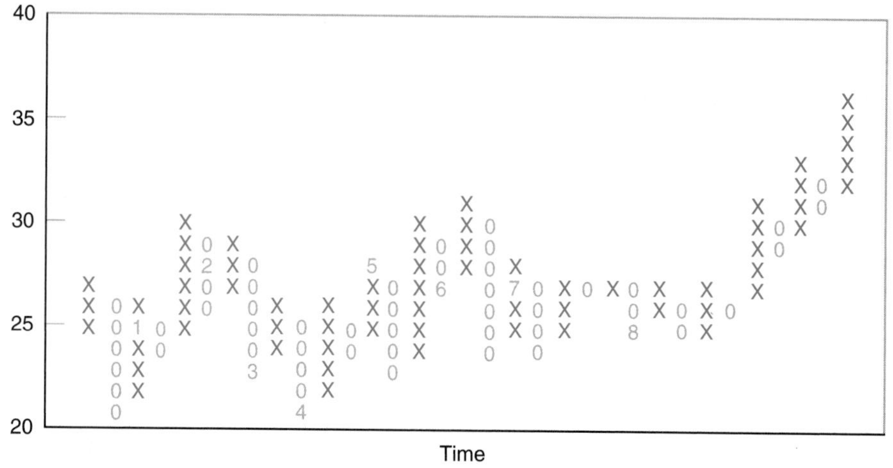

FIGURE 16-5

A point-and-figure chart for Gigantic Computers. X = $1 upward price change, 0 = $1 downward price change (numbers indicate months).

of price fluctuations (i.e., a closely compacted horizontal band of Xs and Os). The technician studies a congestion area in search of a "breakout," which will indicate an expected upward or downward movement in stock price.

Some Evidence on Price Charts There are many chart patterns, some of which were mentioned earlier, and numerous technicians analyze and interpret these patterns. It is impossible to demonstrate conclusively the lack of predictive significance in charting. Very few scientific studies of the ability of chart patterns to predict the future direction of price movements have been conducted.

Levy studied the predictive significance of "five-point" chart patterns. A five-point chart pattern is one with two highs and three lows, or two lows and three highs. As Levy noted, "The avid chartist will recognize, among the 32 patterns, several variations of channels, wedges, diamonds, symmetrical triangles, head and shoulders, reverse head and shoulders, triple tops, and triple bottoms. Each of these formations allegedly reflects underlying supply/demand and support/resistance conditions that have implications as to future price behavior. A common belief among chartists is that the appearance of certain patterns followed by a "breakout" gives a profitable buy or sell signal."[6]

The results indicated that, although some patterns did produce better results than others, none performed very differently from the market.[7] When brokerage commissions were deducted, none of the 32 patterns was found to have any "profitable forecasting ability in either [bullish or bearish] direction." The really surprising conclusion of this study, however, was that "the best performing patterns would probably be characterized as bearish by most technicians, and conversely, the worst performing patterns would, in two of the three cases, be characterized as bullish."

Opinions about charting vary widely. Since the evidence is not conclusive—at least to everyone's satisfaction—the controversy will continue.

MOVING AVERAGES

A moving average of prices is a popular technique for analyzing both the overall market and individual stocks and is used specifically to detect both the direction and the rate of change.

[6] See R. Levy, "The Predictive Significance of Five-Point Chart Patterns," *The Journal of Business*, 44 (July 1971): 316–323.

[7] Using daily prices for 548 NYSE stocks over a five-year period (1964–1969), Levy found 19,077 five-point patterns. Of these, 9,383 were followed by a breakout and were therefore studied.

Some number of days of closing prices is chosen to calculate a moving average. A well-known average for identifying major trends is the 200-day moving average (alternatively, a 10-week [50 day] average is used to identify intermediate trends). After initially calculating the average price, the new value for the moving average is calculated by dropping the earliest observation and adding the latest one. This process is repeated daily (or weekly). The resulting moving average line supposedly represents the basic trend of stock prices.

A comparison of the current market price to the moving average produces a buy or sell signal. The general buy signal is generated when actual prices rise through the moving average on high volume, with the opposite applying to a sell signal. Specific signals of an upper turning point (a sell signal) are the following:

1. Actual price is below the moving average, advances toward it, does not penetrate the average, and starts to turn down again.
2. Following a rise, the moving average flattens out or declines, and the price of the stock or index penetrates it from the top.
3. The stock price rises above the moving average line while the line is still falling.

Buy signals would be generated if these situations were turned upside down.

Figure 16-6 shows Coca-Cola plotted daily for one year, with both a 200-day moving average and a 50-day moving average included. Volume is shown at the bottom of the chart. Various publications offer plots of a 200-day moving average for some index plotted against the index itself. Numerous websites also offer free charts for personal use.

RELATIVE STRENGTH

Relative Strength The ratio of a stock's price to some market or industry index, usually plotted as a graph

A well-known technique used for individual stocks (or industries) is relative strength analysis. The **relative strength** for a given stock is calculated as the ratio of the stock's price to a market index, or an industry index, or the average price of the stock itself over some previous period. Relative strength could also be calculated as the ratio of an industry average relative to the market. These ratios can be plotted to form a graph of relative prices across time. In effect, the graph shows the strength of the stock relative to its industry, the market, or whatever. According to the chief market analyst at Merrill Lynch in New York, "Very often changes in trend, from good to bad or from bad to good, will be preceded by a change in the stock's relative performance."[8]

The relative strength of a stock over time may be of use in forecasting.[9] Because trends are assumed to continue for some time, a rising ratio (an upward-sloping line when relative strength is plotted) indicates relative strength. That is, it indicates a stock that is outperforming the market and that may continue to do so. A declining ratio would have the same implications for the downside. One rule of thumb is that a stock is attractive when the relative strength has improved for at least four months, but as with most technical indicators, technicians interpret some of these signals in different ways.

Figure 16-7 shows relative performance for Coca-Cola in recent years by plotting the ratio of closing monthly prices for Coke to closing monthly prices for the S&P 500. Coca-Cola stock during this period exhibited an upward movement, although it hit a high in June, 1998 and drifted down afterward. However, the market was in a strong upward trend during this time period, hitting a new high in the last month shown in Figure 16-7. Therefore, Coca-Cola has shown decreasing relative strength.

Relative strength is often used by technicians to identify industry sectors that look

[8] See Butler, p. 133.

[9] Some evidence supporting relative strength can be found in Narasimhan Jegadeesh and Sheridan Titman, "Returns to Buying Winners and Selling Losers: Implications for Stock Market Efficiency," *The Journal of Finance,* 48 (March 1993): 65–91.

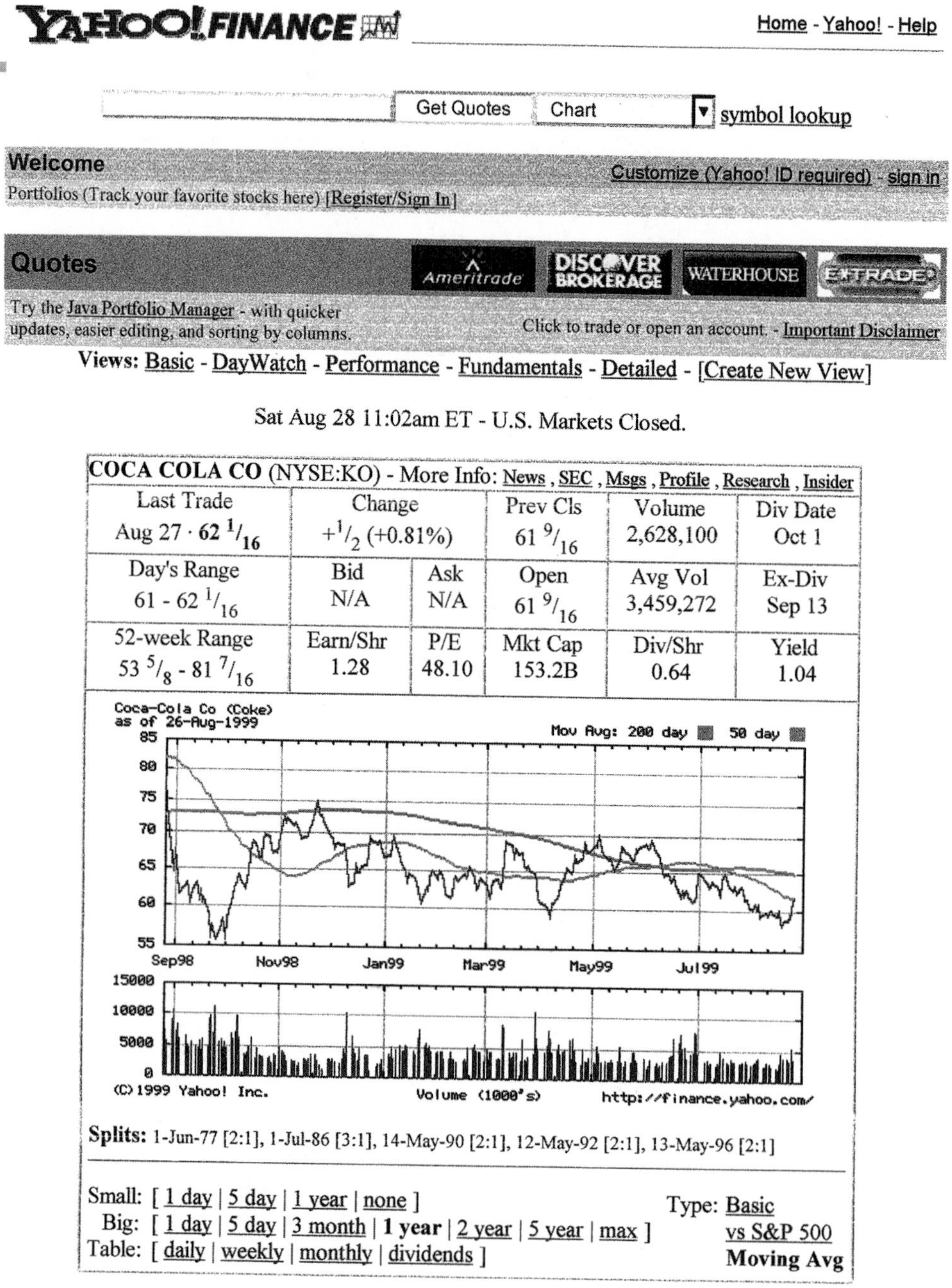
YAHOO! FINANCE

Home - Yahoo! - Help

Get Quotes | Chart | symbol lookup

Welcome

Customize (Yahoo! ID required) - sign in

Portfolios (Track your favorite stocks here) [Register/Sign In]

Quotes

Ameritrade | DISCOVER BROKERAGE | WATERHOUSE | E*TRADE

Try the Java Portfolio Manager - with quicker updates, easier editing, and sorting by columns.

Click to trade or open an account. - Important Disclaimer

Views: Basic - DayWatch - Performance - Fundamentals - Detailed - [Create New View]

Sat Aug 28 11:02am ET - U.S. Markets Closed.

COCA COLA CO (NYSE:KO) - More Info: News, SEC, Msgs, Profile, Research, Insider

Last Trade	Change		Prev Cls	Volume	Div Date
Aug 27 · **62 1/16**	+1/2 (+0.81%)		61 9/16	2,628,100	Oct 1
Day's Range	Bid	Ask	Open	Avg Vol	Ex-Div
61 - 62 1/16	N/A	N/A	61 9/16	3,459,272	Sep 13
52-week Range	Earn/Shr	P/E	Mkt Cap	Div/Shr	Yield
53 5/8 - 81 7/16	1.28	48.10	153.2B	0.64	1.04

Splits: 1-Jun-77 [2:1], 1-Jul-86 [3:1], 14-May-90 [2:1], 12-May-92 [2:1], 13-May-96 [2:1]

Small: [1 day | 5 day | 1 year | none]
Big: [1 day | 5 day | 3 month | **1 year** | 2 year | 5 year | max]
Table: [daily | weekly | monthly | dividends]

Type: Basic
vs S&P 500
Moving Avg

FIGURE 16-6

A full screen shot from Yahoo! Finance showing a bar chart of Coca-Cola.

SOURCE: *Yahoo! Finance* website, August 27, 1999. Reprinted by permission of Yahoo! Finance.

attractive, prior to selecting individual stocks.[10] This is in line with our analysis in Part V which supports a top-down approach to security analysis, with industry analysis preceding company analysis. By focusing on the selection of promising industries, investors narrow the number of possibilities to be considered.

This group selection approach may be helpful in supporting the proposition that an individual stock showing relative strength is not an anomaly, but the technique does not protect an investor against the chance that the overall market is weak, and that one or more groups which currently appear strong are next in line to show weakness. Such a possibility

[10] Such information appears on Mondays in *Investor's Business Daily*.

FIGURE 16-7

Coca-Cola price and relative performance, March 1997–February 1999.

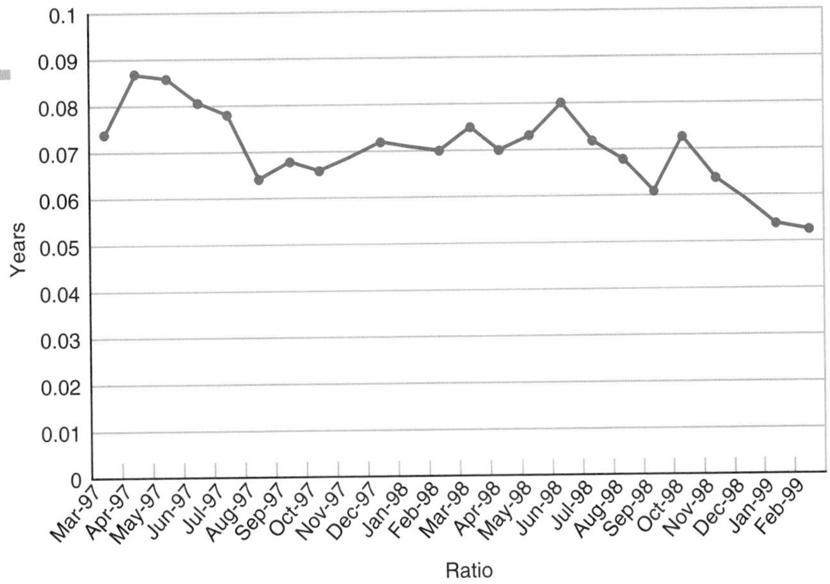

once again supports the case for a top-down approach that begins with market analysis in order to assess the likelihood that now is a good time to be investing in stocks.

One of the problems with relative strength is that a stock or group could show increasing relative strength because it is declining less quickly than the market, not because it is, in fact, increasing. This suggests that relative strength is not a technique to be used in isolation.

Numerous investment information services provide information on relative strength. For example, *The Value Line Investment Survey,* discussed in Chapter 15, divides a stock's price by the Value Line Composite Average and plots this relative strength ratio for each company it covers at the top of the page. Relative strength analysis lends itself well to computerized stock analysis. This probably accounts for its popularity among institutional investors who own highly automated and sophisticated data analysis systems. The extent to which a number of institutional investors use relative strength techniques and have the means to observe changes at about the same time can affect the volatility of a stock.

OBTAINING CHARTS TO USE IN TECHNICAL ANALYSIS

Barron's carries a regular feature entitled "Charting the Market," which shows charts for selected stocks each week. Advertisements in *Barron's* and other financial press magazines contain offers from companies for charts of various degrees of complexity for thousands of companies, updatable in a variety of ways and time frequencies.

USING THE INTERNET In today's computerized world, and with the proliferation of Internet sources of information, investors have many choices for obtaining charts and related information. Most well-known websites, such as www.quicken.com, http://yahoo.quote.com, and http://cbs.marketwatch.com provide simple charts of most stocks easily and quickly. Investors seeking more detail, such as interactive charts where comparisons can be made to indexes, and various types of indicators can be chosen, should try www.bigcharts.com. A particularly comprehensive site is www.clearstation.com, which tracks all NYSE, AMEX, and Nasdaq stocks. These charts concentrate on moving averages, which are popular with many investors, and on stochastic oscillators, which forecast change by comparing a stock's closing price to its daily price range.

TECHNICAL INDICATORS

The chart remains the technician's most important tool for making buy and sell decisions. However, in addition to looking at the plot of stock prices, technicians also like to examine the overall situation by analyzing such factors as breadth and market sentiment indicators.

BREADTH INDICATORS

The Advance–Decline Line (Breadth of the Market) The advance–decline line measures, on a cumulative daily basis, the net difference between the number of stocks advancing in price and those declining in price for a group of stocks such as those on the NYSE. Subtracting the number of declines from the number of advances produces the net advance for a given day (which, of course, can be negative). This measure may include thousands of stocks.

The advance–decline line, often referred to as the breadth of the market, results from plotting a running total of these numbers across time. The line can be based on daily or weekly figures, which are readily available from daily newspapers such as *The Wall Street Journal*.

The advance–decline line is compared to a stock average, in particular the Dow Jones Industrial Average, in order to analyze any divergence—that is, to determine whether movements in the market indicator have also occurred in the market as a whole. Technicians believe that divergences signal that the trend is about to change.

The advance–decline line and the market averages normally move together. If both are rising (declining), the overall market is said to be technically strong (weak). If the advance–decline line is rising while the average is declining, the decline in the average should reverse itself. Particular attention is paid to a divergence between the two during a bull market. If the average rises while the line weakens or declines, this indicates a weakening in the market; the average would therefore be expected to reverse itself and start declining.

New Highs and Lows Part of the information reported for the NYSE and other stocks is the 52-week high and low prices for each stock. Technicians regard the market as bullish when a significant number of stocks each day hit 52-week highs. On the other hand, technicians see rising market indexes and few stocks hitting new highs as a troublesome sign.

Volume Volume is an accepted part of technical analysis. High trading volume on the NYSE, other things being equal, is generally regarded as a bullish sign. Heavy volume combined with rising prices is even more bullish.

SENTIMENT INDICATORS

Short-Interest Ratio The ratio of total shares sold short to average daily trading volume

Short-Interest Ratio The **short interest** for a security is the number of shares that have been sold short but not yet bought back. The short-interest ratio is defined as:

$$\text{Short-interest ratio} = \text{Total shares sold short/Average daily trading volume} \quad (16\text{-}1)$$

The NYSE, AMEX, and Nasdaq report the short interest monthly for each stock. The NYSE and AMEX indicate those securities where arbitrage or hedging may be important, but the significance of these activities cannot be determined. For investors interested in the short interest, each month *The Wall Street Journal* reports NYSE and AMEX issues for which a short-interest position of at least 100,000 shares existed or for which a short-position change of 50,000 shares occurred from the previous month.

In effect, the ratio indicates the number of days necessary to "work off" the current short interest.[11] It is considered to be a measure of investor sentiment, and many investors continue to refer to it.

Investors sell short when they expect prices to decline; therefore, it would appear, the higher the short interest, the more investors are expecting a decline. A large short-interest position for an individual stock should indicate heavy speculation by investors that the price will drop. However, many technical analysts interpret this ratio in the opposite manner: a high short-interest ratio is taken as a bullish sign because the large number of shares sold short represents a large number of shares that must be repurchased in order to close out the short sales. (If the ratio is low, the required purchases are not present.) In effect, the short seller must repurchase, regardless of whether or not his or her expectations were correct. The larger the short-interest ratio, the larger the potential demand that is indicated. Therefore, an increase in the ratio indicates more "pent-up" demand for the shares that have been shorted.

The short-interest ratio for a given month should be interpreted in relation to historical boundaries, which historically were in the range of 1.0 to 2.0 for the NYSE. The problem is that the boundaries keep changing. In the 1960s, 1970s, and 1980s, a ratio of 2.0 was bullish. More recently, the ratio has been in the 3.0 to 6.0 range regardless of the market.

Short-interest figures have been distorted by hedging and arbitrage techniques that have become more popular. For example, if a fund buys Delta and shorts American Airlines, how does this affect the interpretation of the short interest? Hedged short sellers are not likely to panic if their short position moves adversely, which otherwise might lead them to buy and push the price up.

Contrary Opinion The theory that it pays to trade contrary to most investors

Mutual Fund Liquidity Several indicators are based on the theory of **contrary opinion.** The idea is to trade contrary to most investors, who supposedly almost always lose—in other words, to go against the crowd. This is an old idea on Wall Street, and over the years technicians have developed several measures designed to capitalize on this concept.

Mutual fund liquidity can be used as a contrary opinion technique. Under this scenario, mutual funds are viewed in a manner similar to odd-lotters; that is, they are presumed to act incorrectly before a market turning point.[12] Therefore, when mutual fund liquidity is low because the funds are fully invested, contrarians believe that the market is at, or near, a peak. The funds should be building up cash (liquidity); instead, they are extremely bullish and are fully invested. Conversely, when funds hold large liquid reserves, it suggests that they are bearish. Contrarians would consider this a good time to buy because the market may be at, or near, its low point.

The Opinions of Investment Advisory Newsletters *Investors Intelligence,* an investment advisory service, samples weekly the opinions of about 150 investment advisory services and calculates an index of investment service opinions. It has found that, on average, these services are most bearish at the market bottom and least bearish at the market top. This index, published since 1963, is now available weekly and is widely quoted in the investing community.

The "bearish sentiment index" is calculated as the ratio of advisory services that are bearish to the total number with an opinion. When this index approaches 55 or 60 percent, the Dow Jones Industrial Average supposedly tends to go from bearish to bullish. As it ap-

[11] For example, a ratio of 1.0 means that the outstanding short interest approximates a day's trading volume.

[12] According to the odd-lot theory, small investors who often buy or sell odd lots (less than 100 shares of stock) are usually wrong in their actions at market peaks and troughs. Supposedly, such investors typically buy (sell) when the market is at or close to a peak (bottom). In particular, small investors do not get involved with short sales unless they are particularly bearish.

proaches 15 percent, the opposite occurs. Thus, a contrarian should react in the opposite direction of the sentiment these services are exhibiting.

The reason for this seeming contradiction to logic—that investment advisory services are wrong at the extremes—is attributed to the fact that these services tend to follow trends rather than forecast them. Thus, they are reporting and reacting to what has happened rather than concentrating on anticipating what is likely to happen.

How well does this sentiment index work? According to the editor of *Investors Intelligence,* it caused the newsletter to be completely bullish in July 1982, immediately preceding the start of the great bull market of August 1982–August 1987. It also caused the newsletter to go bearish two months before the crash of October 1987. On the other hand, in a recent study, the index was found to be wrong about 50 percent of the time. In other words, it was of no value. This study attributed the strong belief in the index partly to people seeing patterns in random data.[13]

CBOE Put/Call Ratio Some technical analysts believe that people who play the options market are, as a group, almost consistent losers. Speculators buy calls when they expect stock prices to rise, and they buy puts when they expect prices to fall. Because they are generally more optimistic than pessimistic, the put to call ratio is well below 1.0. For example, a ratio of 0.60 indicates that only six puts are purchased for every 10 calls purchased. The rise of this ratio indicates pessimism on the part of speculators in options, but this is a buy signal to a contrarian. A low ratio would be a sell signal to a contrarian because of the rampant optimism such a ratio indicates.

Small changes are considered unimportant. Extreme readings are said to convey information. According to one well-known analyst, this would be a ratio below 0.7 or above 0.9.[14]

TESTING TECHNICAL ANALYSIS STRATEGIES

What constitutes a fair test of a technical trading rule? The adjustments that should be made include at least the following:

1. *Risk.* If the risk involved in two strategies is not comparable, a fair comparison cannot be made. As we know, other things being equal, a more risky strategy would be expected to outperform a less risky strategy.
2. *Transaction and other costs (e.g., taxes).* Several technical trading rules appeared to produce excess returns before transaction costs were deducted. After such costs were deducted, however, the rules were inferior to a buy-and-hold strategy, which generates little costs.
3. *Consistency.* Can the rule outperform the alternative over a reasonable period of time, such as 5 or 10 years? Any rule may outperform an alternative for a short period, but it will not be too useful unless it holds up over some longer term.
4. *Out-of-sample validity.* Has the rule been tried on data other than that used to produce the rule? It is always possible to find a rule that works on a particular sample if enough rules are tried; that is, it is possible to torture the data until it confesses.

Filter Rule A rule for buying and selling stocks according to the stock's price movements

A well-known technical trading rule is the so-called **filter rule.** A filter rule specifies a breakpoint for an individual stock or a market average, and trades are made when the stock-

[13] This information is based on John R. Dorfman, "This Stock Market Sign Often Points the Wrong Way," *The Wall Street Journal,* January 26, 1989, p. C1.

[14] See Butler, p. 129.

price change is greater than this filter. For example, buy a stock if the price moves up 10 percent from some established base, such as a previous low, hold it until it declines 10 percent from its new high, and then sell it and possibly go short.

Several studies of filters have been conducted. Fama and Blume tested 24 filters (ranging from 0.50 percent to 50 percent) on each of the 30 Dow Jones stocks.[15] Before commissions, several of the filters were profitable, in particular the smallest (0.5 percent). After commissions, however, average returns were typically negative or very small. Brokerage commissions more than offset any gains that could be exploited. The low correlations found in the statistical tests were insufficient to provide profitable filter trading rules.

Many different variations of the relative strength technique can be tested by varying the time period over which the average price is calculated and the percentage of the top stocks selected. If we conduct enough tests, we can find a rule that produces favorable results on a particular sample. Therefore, before we conclude that a trading rule of this type is successful, we should conduct a fair test as outlined earlier. Risks must be comparable, and appropriate costs must be deducted. Finally, the rule should be tried on a different sample of stocks.

SOME CONCLUSIONS ABOUT TECHNICAL ANALYSIS

Technical analysis often appeals to those who are beginning a study of investments because it is easy to believe that stock prices form repeatable patterns over time or that certain indicators should be related to future market (or individual stock) price movements. Most people who look at a chart of a particular stock will immediately see what they believe to be patterns in the price changes and clear evidence of trends that should have been obvious to anyone studying it. How should we view this situation?

On the one hand, academicians (and numerous practitioners) are highly skeptical of technical analysis, to say the least. Most academic discussions at the college level dismiss, or seriously disparage, this concept. A primary reason is that thorough tests of technical analysis techniques have failed to confirm their value, given all costs and considering an alternative, such as a buy-and-hold strategy.

In addition to these reasons, other troubling features of technical analysis remain. First, several interpretations of each technical tool and chart pattern are not only possible but usual. One or more of the interpreters will be correct (more or less), but it is virtually impossible to know ex ante (beforehand) who these will be. Ex post (after the fact), we will know which indicator or chart, or whose interpretation, was correct, but only those investors who used that particular information will benefit. Tools such as the Dow theory are well known for their multiple interpretations by various observers who disagree over how the theory is to be interpreted.

Furthermore, consider a technical trading rule (or chart pattern) that is, in fact, successful. When it gives its signal on the basis of reaching some specified value (or forms a clear picture on a chart), it correctly predicts movements in the market or some particular stock. Such a rule or pattern, if observed by several market participants, will be self-destructive as more and more investors use it. Price will reach its equilibrium value quickly, taking away profit opportunities from all but the quickest. Some observers will start trying to act before the rest on the basis of what they expect to happen. (For example, they may act before a complete head and shoulders forms.) Price will then reach an equilibrium even more quickly, so that only those who act earliest will benefit. Eventually, the value of any such rule will be negated entirely.

[15] E. Fama and M. Blume, "Filter Rules and Stock-Market Trading," *The Journal of Business: A Supplement,* 39 (January 1969): 2–21.

INVESTMENTS INTUITION No inherent reason exists for stock-price movements to repeat themselves. For example, flipping a fair coin 100 times should, on average, result in about 50 heads and 50 tails. There is some probability that the first 10 tosses could produce 10 heads. However, the chance of such a pattern repeating itself is very small.

As we saw in Chapter 12, strong evidence exists suggesting that stock-price changes over time are weak-form efficient. In effect, any patterns formed are accidental but not surprising.

Yet, it is impossible to test all the techniques of technical analysis and their variations and interpretations. In fact, technical analysis has not been tested thoroughly. The techniques of this approach are simply too numerous, and technical analysis is broader than the use of only price information. Therefore, absolutely definitive statements about this subject cannot be made. A good example of the omissions in this area is the use of volume in technical strategies. Although volume is a recognized part of technical analysis, few tests have been conducted on its use in conjunction with the rest of technical analysis.[16]

Also, in recent years some additional evidence has been presented that tends to support the basis of technical analysis. For example, Jegadeesh found predictable patterns in stock prices based on monthly returns for the period 1934–1987, a long period of time.[17] His study showed that stocks with large losses in one month are likely to show a significant reversal in the following month and that stocks with large gains in one month are likely to show a significant loss in the next month. Brown and Jennings have presented a different way of looking at technical analysis which provides a justification for technical analysis being useful to investors.[18] They construct a scenario that shows how each investor can learn something about what other investors know by observing the price at which a security trades. In effect, prices reveal information as well as simply convey information.

What can we conclude about technical analysis? On the basis of all available evidence, it is difficult to justify technical analysis. The studies that have been done in support of this concept have produced, at best, weak arguments in its favor. Studies done in support of the efficient market hypothesis, on the other hand, are much stronger and are nearly unanimous in their conclusions that technical analysis does not work on a consistent, after-transactions-cost basis.

Regardless of the evidence, technical analysis remains popular with many investors.

SUMMARY

- Technical analysis, the other approach to selecting securities, is the oldest approach available to investors and in many respects the most controversial.
- Technical analysis relies on published market data, primarily price and volume data, to predict the short-term direction of individual stocks or the market as a whole. The emphasis is on internal factors that help to detect demand-supply conditions in the market.
- The rationale for technical analysis is that the net demand (or lack thereof) for stocks can be detected by various technical indicators and that trends in stock prices occur and continue for considerable periods of time. Stock prices require time to adjust to the change in supply and demand.

[16] For additional discussion of these points, see O. Maurice Joy and Charles P. Jones, "Should We Believe the Tests of Market Efficiency?" *The Journal of Portfolio Management* (Summer 1986): 49–54.

[17] See Narasimhan Jegadeesh, "Evidence of Predictable Behavior of Security Returns," *The Journal of Finance* (July 1990): 881–898.

[18] See David Brown and Robert Jennings, "On Technical Analysis," *Review of Financial Studies*, 1989, pp. 527–552.

- Price and volume are primary tools of the technical analyst, as are various technical indicators. Technical analysis can be applied to both the aggregate market and individual stocks.
- Aggregate market analysis originated with the Dow theory, the best known technical theory. It is designed to detect the start of major movements.
- Other technical indicators of the aggregate market include, but are not limited to, the following:
    1. Moving averages, which are used to detect both the direction and the rate of change in prices.
    2. The advance–decline line (breadth of market), which is used to assess the condition of the overall market.
    3. Mutual fund liquidity, which uses the potential buying power (liquidity) of mutual funds as a bullish or bearish indicator.
    4. Short-interest ratio, which assesses potential demand from investors who have sold short.
    5. Contrary opinion, which is designed to go against the crowd. Included here are the odd-lot theory, the odd-lot short sales theory, the put-call ratio, and the opinions of investment advisory services.
- Technical analysis also involves the use of charts of price patterns to detect trends that are believed to persist over time.
- The most frequently used charts are bar charts, which show each day's price movement as well as volume, and point-and-figure charts, which show only significant price changes as they occur.
- Numerous chart "patterns" are recognizable to a technician. However, all patterns are subject to multiple interpretations because different technicians will read the same chart differently.
- Another well-known technique for individual stocks is relative strength, which shows the strength of a particular stock in relation to its average price, its industry, or the market.

KEY WORDS

Bar chart
Bear market
Bull market
Contrary opinion
Dow theory
Filter rule
Market data
Point-and-figure chart
Relative strength
Resistance level
Short interest
Support level
Technical analysis

QUESTIONS

16-1. Describe the rationale for technical analysis.

16-2. Differentiate between fundamental analysis and technical analysis.

16-3. What do technicians assume about the adjustment of stock prices from one equilibrium position to another?

16-4. What role does volume play in technical analysis?

16-5. What is the Dow theory? What is the significance of the "confirmation" signal in this theory?

16-6. How does the Dow theory forecast how long a market movement will last?

16-7. Using a moving average, how is a sell signal generated?

16-8. Why is the advance–decline line called an indicator of breadth of the market?

16-9. Why are the opinions of investment advisory services considered a contrary opinion signal?

16-10. What is the rationale for the theory of contrary opinion?

16-11. How is the odd-lot index calculated? How is it used as a buy or sell signal?

16-12. Why is a rising short-interest ratio considered to be a bullish indicator?

16-13. Distinguish between a bar chart and a point-and-figure chart.

16-14. What is relative strength analysis?

16-15. On a rational economic basis, why is the study of chart patterns likely to be an unrewarding activity?

16-16. Is it possible to prove or disprove categorically the validity of technical analysis?

16-17. Assume that you know a technical analyst who claims success on the basis of his or her chart patterns. How might you go about scientifically testing this claim?

16-18. How do the new contrarians differ from the more traditional contrarians?

16-19. Why do stock-price movements repeat themselves?

16-20. Look at the bar chart of the Dow-Jones Averages in section C1 of *The Wall Street Journal*. Does this chart cover a sufficient time period to apply the Dow theory?

16-21. With reference to Question 16-20, why would this chart, or possibly several of these charts covering a number of months, be useful in trying to apply the Dow theory?

16-22. What new financial instruments have caused the short-interest ratio to be less reliable? Why?

16-23. Describe a bullish sign when using a moving average; a bearish sign. Do the same for the advance–decline line.

16-24. Consider the plot of stock X in the following diagram. The plot shows weekly prices for one year, based on a beginning price of $30.

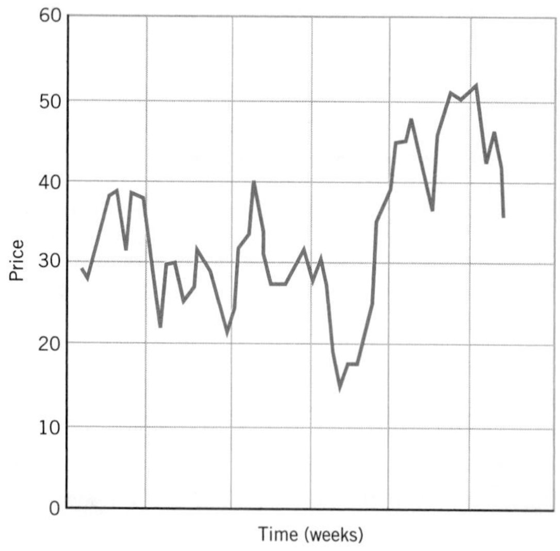

a. Do you see any chart patterns in this figure?
b. Do any patterns you see in this chart help you to predict the future price of this stock?

c. What is your forecast of this stock's price over the next three months?
d. If this price series were to be generated using random numbers, do you think it could resemble this plot?

The following questions were given on the 1990 CFA Level I examination:

CFA
16-25. Under the theory of contrary opinion, when advisory opinion is bullish it is a ______ signal, and when total outstanding short interest is abnormally high it is a ______ signal.

a. bullish, bullish
b. bearish, bullish
c. bullish, bearish
d. bearish, bearish

CFA
16-26. Under the theory of contrary opinion, the put-call ratio and the put premium are two factors in which technicians are interested. At the point where stock prices are at their lowest levels, one would expect:

a. put trading volume to increase and put premiums to increase.
b. put trading volume to decrease and put premiums to decrease.
c. call trading volume to increase and put premiums to decrease.
d. call trading volume to decrease and put premiums to remain constant.

The following question was given on the 1993 CFA Level I examination:

CFA
16-27. Two basic assumptions of technical analysis are that security prices adjust:

a. rapidly to new information, and liquidity is provided by securities dealers.
b. rapidly to new information, and market prices are determined by the interaction of supply and demand.
c. gradually to new information, and liquidity is provided by securities dealers.
d. gradually to new information, and market prices are determined by the interaction of supply and demand.

The following questions were given on the 1992 CFA Level I examination:

CFA
16-28. Which *one* of the following would be a bearish signal to a technical analyst?

a. The debit balances in brokerage accounts increase.
b. The market shows poor performance when compared to individual stocks.
c. The yield differential between high-quality and low-quality bonds increases.
d. The ratio of short sales by specialists to total short sales becomes abnormally low.

CFA
16-29. When technical analysts say a stock has a good "relative strength," they mean the:

a. ratio of the price of the stock to a market index has trended upward.
b. recent trading volume in the stock has exceeded the normal trading volume.
c. total return on the stock has exceeded the total return on other stocks in the same industry.
d. stock has performed well compared to other stocks in the same risk category as measured by beta.

SELECTED REFERENCES

Basics on technical analysis are available in the popular press, such as:

Butler, Jonathan. "Technical Analysis: A Primer," *Worth,* October, 1995, pp. 128–134.

A different view of tests of technical analysis can be found in:

Joy, O. M., and Jones, Charles P. "Should We Believe the Tests of Market Efficiency?" *The Journal of Portfolio Management* (Summer 1986): 49–54.

One of the classic commentaries on this and related subjects such as the Efficient Market Hypothesis is:

Malkiel, Burton G. *A Random Walk Down Wall Street,* 6th ed. New York: W. W. Norton, 1995.

A well-known primer on technical analysis is:

Pring, Martin J. *Technical Analysis Explained,* 3rd ed. New York: McGraw-Hill Publishers, 1991.

www.wiley.com/college/jones7

Technical analysis tries to use trends in price movements to construct winning investment strategies. The theory of market efficiency denies the validity of technical analysis. The web exercise for this chapter will evaluate different technical strategies for stock picking.

chapter 17

OPTIONS

Chapter 17 analyzes options, an important derivative security. The importance of derivative securities lies in the flexibility they provide investors in managing investment risk. Derivative instruments can also be used to speculate in these markets.

After reading this chapter you will be able to:

- **Understand why investors use options in their investment strategies.**
- **Describe the option alternatives available to investors, and how the options markets operate.**
- **Analyze basic option strategies.**
- **Understand the valuation of options.**

Rather than trade directly in common stocks, investors can purchase securities representing a claim—an option—on a particular stock or group of stocks. This option gives the holder the right to receive or deliver shares of stock under specified conditions. The option need not be exercised (and often will not be worth exercising). Instead, an investor can simply buy and sell these **equity-derivative securities,** which are securities that derive all, or part, of their value from the equity of the same corporation. Gains or losses will depend on the difference between the purchase price and the sales price.

Equity-Derivative Securities Securities that derive their value in whole or in part by having a claim on the underlying common stock

This chapter discusses put and call options. Appendix 8-A covered convertible securities, and Appendix 17-B covers warrants. All are equity-derivative securities.[1] We concentrate primarily on options on individual stocks and stock indexes, and to a much lesser extent on interest rate options. In Chapter 18 we consider futures contracts, which together with options constitutes the most commonplace derivative securities. Since we are focusing on investing instruments, we limit our discussion to *financial derivatives.*

The emphasis here is on how puts and calls work, and on their importance to portfolio managers. As derivative securities, options are innovations in *risk management,* not in risk itself, and as such should be both welcomed and used by investors and portfolio managers. Again, our emphasis is on equity securities, and our examples revolve around common stocks.

INTRODUCTION

Options Contracts giving the owner the right to buy or sell the underlying asset.

Options, which represent claims on an underlying common stock, are created by investors and sold to other investors. The corporation whose common stock underlies these claims has no direct interest in the transaction, being in no way responsible for the creating, terminating, or executing put and call contracts.

Call An option to buy stock at a stated price within a specified period of months

A **call** option gives the holder the right to buy (or "call away") 100 shares of a particular common stock at a specified price any time prior to a specified expiration date.[2] Investors purchase calls if they expect the stock price to rise because the price of the call and the common stock will move together. Therefore, calls permit investors to speculate on a rise in the price of the underlying common stock without buying the stock itself.

EXAMPLE 17-1

A Coca-Cola six-month call option at $50 per share gives the buyer the right (an option) to purchase 100 shares of Coke at $50 per share from a writer (seller) of the option anytime during the six months before the specified expiration date.

Put An option to sell a specified number of shares of stock at a specified price within a specified short period

A **put** option gives the buyer the right to sell (or "put away") 100 shares of a particular common stock at a specified price prior to a specified expiration date. If exercised, the shares are sold by the owner (buyer) of the put contract to a writer (seller) of this contract who has been designated to take delivery of the shares and pay the specified price. Investors purchase puts if they expect the stock price to fall, because the value of the put will rise as the stock

[1] Rights are another equity-derivative security. They are not discussed further because of their minor importance to most investors.

[2] It is important to remember throughout this discussion that the standard option contract on the organized exchanges is for 100 shares of the underlying common stock; therefore, when we speak of buying or selling *a* call or *a* put, we mean one contract representing an option on 100 shares of stock.

price declines. Therefore, puts allow investors to speculate on a decline in the stock price without selling the common stock short.

EXAMPLE 17-2

A writer (seller) of a Coca-Cola six-month put at $50 per share is obligated, under certain circumstances, to receive from the holder of this put 100 shares of Coke for which the writer will pay $50 per share.

WHY OPTIONS MARKETS?

An investor can always purchase shares of common stock if he or she is bullish about the company's prospects, or sell short if bearish. Why, then, should we create these indirect claims on a stock as an alternative way to invest? Several reasons have been advanced, including the following:

1. Puts and calls expand the opportunity set available to investors, making available risk-return combinations that would otherwise be impossible or that improve the risk-return characteristics of a portfolio. For example, an investor can sell the stock short and buy a call, thereby decreasing the risk on the short sale for the life of the call.[3]
2. In the case of calls, an investor can control (for a short period) a claim on the underlying common stock for a much smaller investment than required to buy the stock itself. In the case of puts, an investor can duplicate a short sale without a margin account and at a modest cost in relation to the value of the stock. The buyer's maximum loss is known in advance. If an option expires worthless, the most the buyer can lose is the cost (price) of the option.
3. Options provide leverage—magnified percentage gains in relation to buying the stock; furthermore, options can provide greater leverage than fully margined stock transactions.
4. Using options on a market index such as the S&P 500, an investor can participate in market movements with a single trading decision.

UNDERSTANDING OPTIONS

OPTIONS TERMINOLOGY

Exercise (Strike) Price The per-share price at which the common stock may be purchased from (in the case of a call) or sold to a writer (in the case of a put)

To understand puts and calls, one must understand the terminology used in connection with them. Our discussion here applies specifically to options on the organized exchanges as reported daily in such sources as *The Wall Street Journal*.[4] Important options terms include the following:

1. *Exercise (strike) price.* The **exercise (strike) price** is the per-share price at which the common stock may be purchased (in the case of a call) or sold to a writer (in the

[3] Most stocks do not have puts and calls available in the organized options markets. Several hundred stocks constitute the active options market.

[4] Puts and calls existed for many years before these organized exchanges. They could be bought or sold in the over-the-counter market through brokers who were part of the Put and Call Dealers and Brokers Association. Members of this association endeavored to satisfy investor demands for particular options on a case-by-case basis. The terms of each individual contract (price, exercise date, etc.) had to be negotiated between buyer and seller. This was clearly a cumbersome, inefficient process.

case of a put). Most stocks in the options market have options available at several different exercise prices, thereby providing investors with a choice. For stocks with prices greater than $25, the strike price changes in increments of $5, while for those under $25 the increment is $2.50. As the stock price changes, options with new exercise prices are added.[5]

Expiration Date The date an option expires

2. *Expiration date.* The **expiration date** is the last date at which an option can be exercised.[6] All puts and calls are designated by the month of expiration. The options exchanges currently offer sequential options and other shorter term patterns. The expiration dates for options contracts vary from stock to stock.

Option Premium The price paid by the option buyer to the seller of the option

3. *Option premium.* The **option premium** is the price paid by the option buyer to the writer (seller) of the option, whether put or call. The premium is stated on a per share basis for options on organized exchanges, and since the standard contract is for 100 shares, a $3 premium represents $300, a $15 premium represents $1500, and so forth. Information on options premiums can be found on *The Wall Street Journal*'s "Listed Options Quotation" page.[7] The most active contracts for the day are reported along with the individual equity options. Eleven different strike price/maturity combinations for Coke were observed on a recent day.

Long-Term Options (LEAPs) Options on individual stocks with maturities up to two years

The options page of *The Wall Street Journal* also carries the information for **long-term options (LEAPS).** These long-term options, available on a relatively few well-known stocks, have maturities ranging to two years and beyond.

EXAMPLE 17-3 In March 1999 an investor could purchase a long-term option on Coke, either put or call.

HOW OPTIONS WORK

As noted, a standard call (put) contract gives the buyer the right to purchase (sell) 100 shares of a particular stock at a specified exercise price any time before the expiration date. Both puts and calls are created by sellers who write a particular contract. Sellers (writers) are investors, either individuals or institutions, who seek to profit from their beliefs about the underlying stock's likely price performance, just as the buyer does.

The buyer and the seller have opposite expectations about the likely performance of the underlying stock, and therefore the performance of the option.

- The call writer expects the price of the stock to remain roughly steady or perhaps move down.
- The call buyer expects the price of the stock to move upward, and relatively soon.
- The put writer expects the price of the stock to remain roughly steady or perhaps move up.
- The put buyer expects the price of the stock to move down, and relatively soon.

[5] Options sold on these exchanges are protected against stock dividends and stock splits; therefore, if either is paid during the life of an option, both the exercise price and the number of shares in the contract are adjusted as necessary.

[6] American-style options can be exercised any time prior to expiration; European-style options can be exercised only at expiration.

[7] This excerpt shows only a few of the options traded, but all five markets that trade options—the Chicago Board Option Exchange, the American Stock Exchange, the Pacific Stock Exchange, the Philadelphia Stock Exchange, and the New York Stock Exchange—are carried on this page and would be read in the same manner. A composite also is reported.

EXAMPLE 17-4

Consider an individual named Carl who is optimistic about Coca-Cola's prospects. Carl instructs his broker to buy a May call option on Coca-Cola at a strike price of $65. Assume the stock price is $64½ and the premium is $6⅜ (i.e., about $637.50, since 100 shares are involved). Carl pays this premium plus brokerage commissions.

Three courses of action are possible with any option:

1. *The option may expire worthless.* Assume the price of Coke fluctuates up and down but is at $50 on the expiration date. The call gives the buyer (owner) the right to purchase Coke at $65, but this would make no sense when Coke can be purchased on the open market at $50. Therefore, the option will expire worthless.
2. *The option may be exercised.* If Coke appreciates, Carl could exercise the option by paying $6,500 (the $65 exercise price multiplied by 100 shares) and receiving 100 shares of Coke.[8]
3. *The option can be sold in the secondary market.* If Coke appreciates, the value (price) of the call will also appreciate. Carl can easily *sell the call in the secondary market* to another investor who wishes to speculate on Coke because listed options are traded continuously. Most investors trading puts and calls do not exercise those that are valuable; instead, they simply sell them on the open market, exactly as they would the common stock if they owned it.[9]

Puts work the same way as calls, except in reverse. A writer creates a particular put contract and sells it for the premium that the buyer pays. The writer believes that the underlying common stock is likely to remain flat or appreciate, while the buyer believes that the stock price is likely to decline. Unlike a buyer, a writer may have to take action in the form of taking delivery of the stock.

EXAMPLE 17-5

Assume a writer sells an August Coca-Cola put at an exercise price of $70 when the stock price is $69 7/16. The premium is 5¾, or $575, which the buyer of the put pays and the writer receives (brokerage costs would be involved in both cases). Suppose the price of Coke declines to $60 near the expiration date.

The put owner (buyer), who did not own Coke previously, could instruct the broker to purchase 100 shares of Coke in the open market for $6,000. The buyer could then exercise the put, which means that a chosen writer must accept the 100 shares of Coke and pay the put owner $70 per share, or $7,000 total (although the current market price is only $60). The put buyer grosses $425 ($7,000 received less $6,000 cost of 100 shares less the $575 paid for the put). The put writer suffers an immediate *paper* loss because the 100 shares of Coke are worth $60 per share but have a cost of $70 per share, although the premium received by the writer reduces this loss. (Brokerage costs have once again been omitted in the example.)

[8] Assume the price has appreciated to $80 before expiration. Carl now owns 100 shares of Coca-Cola worth $80 per share, for which he paid $65 per share (plus the $6⅜ per share for the call option itself). An immediate sale of the stock in the market would result in a $862 *gross profit* (brokerage costs are not included here), or [$8000 − ($6500 + $638)].

[9] One of the implications of the option pricing model to be considered later is that American calls on stocks that do not pay a cash dividend should never be exercised before the expiration date. Calls on stocks paying a cash dividend might be exercised before the expiration date.

As in the case of a call, two other courses of action are possible in addition to the exercise of the put. The put may expire worthless because the price of the common did not decline or did not decline enough to justify exercising the put. Far more likely, however, the put owner can sell the put in the secondary market for a profit (or a loss). As in the case of calls, most put investors simply buy and sell their options in the open market.

THE MECHANICS OF TRADING

The Options Exchanges Five option exchanges constitute the secondary market: the Chicago Board Options Exchange (CBOE), the American, the Philadelphia, the Pacific, and the New York. All five exchanges are continuous markets, similar to stock exchanges. Complete option prices can be found on websites.

The options markets provide liquidity to investors, which is a very important requirement for successful trading. Investors know that they can instruct their broker to buy or sell whenever they desire at a price set by the forces of supply and demand. These exchanges have made puts and calls a success by standardizing the exercise date and exercise price of contracts. One Coca-Cola May 50 call option is identical to every other Coca-Cola May 50 call option.

The same types of orders discussed in Chapter 5, in particular, market, limit, and stop orders, are used in trading puts and calls.[10] Certificates representing ownership are not used for puts and calls; instead, transactions are handled as bookkeeping entries. Option trades settle on the next business day after the trade.

The secondary markets for puts and calls have worked well in the years since the Chicago Board Options Exchange (CBOE) started operations in 1973. Trading volume has been large, and the number of puts and calls available has expanded.

Options Clearing Corporation (OCC) Stands between buyers and sellers of options to ensure fulfillment of obligations

The Clearing Corporation The **options clearing corporation (OCC)** performs a number of important functions that contribute to the success of the secondary market for options. It functions as an intermediary between the brokers representing the buyers and the writers. That is, once the brokers representing the buyer and the seller negotiate the price on the floor of the exchange, they no longer deal with each other but with the OCC.

Through their brokers, call writers contract with the OCC itself to deliver shares of the particular stock, and buyers of calls actually receive the right to purchase the shares from the OCC. Thus, the OCC becomes the buyer for every seller and the seller for every buyer, guaranteeing that all contract obligations will be met. This prevents the risk and problems that could occur as buyers attempted to force writers to honor their obligations. The net position of the OCC is zero, because the number of contracts purchased must equal the number sold.

Investors wishing to exercise their options inform their brokers, who in turn inform the OCC of the exercise. The OCC randomly selects a broker on whom it holds the same written contract, and the broker randomly selects a customer who has written these options to honor the contract. Writers chosen in this manner are said to be assigned an obligation or to have received an assignment notice. Once assigned, the writer cannot execute an offsetting transaction to eliminate the obligation; that is, a call writer who receives an assignment must sell the underlying securities, and a put writer must purchase them.

One of the great advantages of a clearinghouse is that transactors in this market can easily cancel their positions prior to assignment. Since the OCC maintains all the positions for both buyers and sellers, it can cancel out the obligations of both call and put writers

[10] Although available, the manner in which some types of orders are executed on some of the options exchanges varies from that used on the stock exchanges.

wishing to terminate their position.[11] With regard to puts and calls, margin refers to the collateral that option *writers* provide their brokers to ensure fulfillment of the contract in case of exercise. Options cannot be purchased on margin. Buyers must pay 100 percent of the purchase price.[12]

PAYOFFS AND PROFITS FROM BASIC OPTION POSITIONS

We can better understand the characteristics of options by examining their potential payoffs and profits. The simplest way to do this is to examine their value at expiration. At the expiration date, an option has an *investment value,* or *payoff,* that can be easily determined. At the expiration date, the investment value is equal to the price of the option as determined in the marketplace. In addition, we can also examine the net *profit,* which takes into account the price of the stock, the exercise price of the option, and the cost of the option. We consider both variables because option traders are interested in their net profits, but option valuation is perhaps better understood by focusing on payoffs.

As part of this analysis, we use letters to designate the key variables:

S_T = the value of the stock at expiration

E = the exercise price of the option

CALLS

Buying a Call Consider first the buyer of a call option. At expiration, the investment value or *payoff* to the call holder is:

Payoff to call buyer at expiration:

$= S_T - E$ if $S_T > E$

$= 0$ if $S_T \leq E$

This payoff to a call buyer is illustrated in Figure 17-1. The payoff is $0 until the exercise price is reached, at which point the payoff rises as the stock price rises.

EXAMPLE 17-6

Assume an investor buys a Coca-Cola three-month call with an exercise price of $50. The payoff for the call at expiration is a function of the stock price at that time. For example, at expiration the value of the call relative to various possible stock prices would be calculated as in the following partial set of prices:

Coca-Cola stock price at expiration	$40	45	50	55	60
Coca-Cola call price at expiration	$ 0	0	0	5	10

Notice that the payoff is not the same as the net profit to the option holder or writer. For example, if Coca-Cola is at $60 per share, the payoff to the option buyer is $10, but the net profit must reflect the cost of the call. In general, the profit to an option holder is the value of the option less the price paid for it.

[11] For example, a call writer can terminate the obligation to deliver the stock any time before the expiration date (or assignment) by making a "closing purchase transaction" at the current market-determined price of the option. The OCC offsets the outstanding call written with the call purchased in the closing transaction. A put writer can also close out a position at any time by making an offsetting transaction.

[12] To protect itself, the OCC requires that its member firms whose customers have written options provide collateral to it in order to protect the OCC against defaults by writers. The member firms, in turn, require its customers who have *written* options to provide collateral for their written positions.

FIGURE 17-1

Payoff profiles for call and put options at expiration.

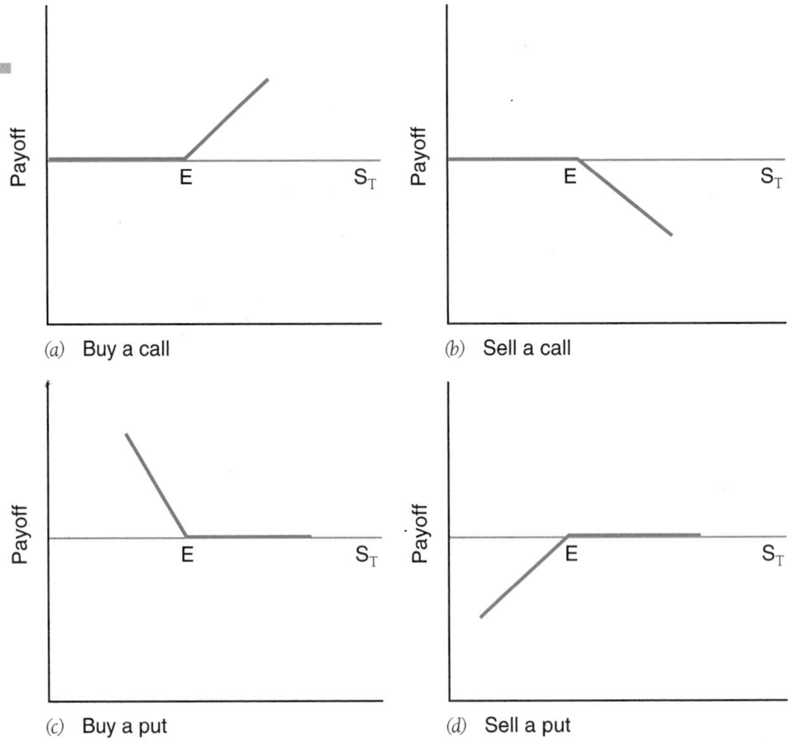

EXAMPLE 17-7

Figure 17-2 illustrates the *profit* situation for a call buyer. The price of the stock is assumed to be \$48, and a six-month call is available with an exercise price of \$50 for a premium of \$4 (i.e., \$400). If this call expires worthless, the maximum loss is the \$400 premium. Up to the exercise price of \$50, the loss is \$4. The breakeven point for the investor is the sum of the exercise price and the premium, or \$50 + \$4 = \$54. Therefore, the profit-loss line for the call buyer crosses the breakeven line at \$54. If the price of the stock rises above \$54, the value of the call will increase with it, at least point for point, as shown by the two parallel lines above the \$0 profit-loss line.

FIGURE 17-2

Profit and loss to the buyer of a call option.

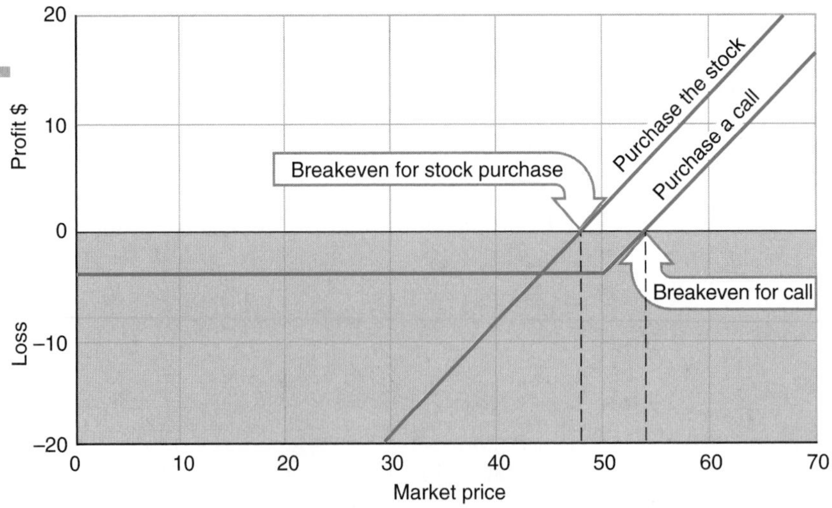

FIGURE 17-3

Profit and loss to the writer of a call option.

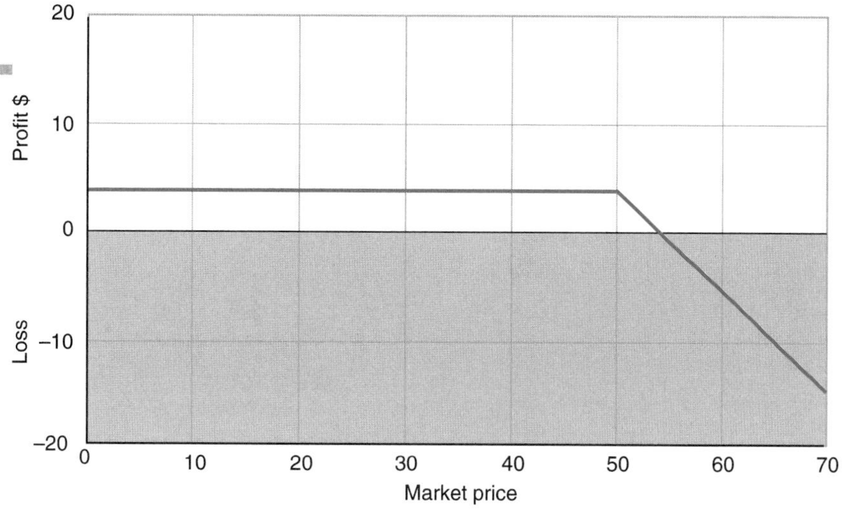

Selling (Writing) a Call A call writer incurs losses if the stock's price increases, as shown by the payoff profile in part (b) of Figure 17-1. The payoff is flat at the amount of the premium until the exercise price is reached, at which point it declines as the stock price rises. The call writer loses if the stock price rises, exactly as the call buyer gains if the stock price rises.

Payoff to call writer at expiration:

$$= -(S_T - E) \text{ if } S_T > E$$
$$= 0 \qquad \text{if } S_T \leq E$$

The net *profit* line in Figure 17-3 shows a similar pattern to that of the call buyer, except now the profit is positive up to the exercise price because the call writer is receiving the premium. The horizontal axis intercept in Figure 17-3 occurs at the breakeven point for the option writer—the sum of the exercise price and the option premium received (note that the breakeven point is identical to that of the call buyer). As the stock price exceeds the breakeven point, the call writer loses.

The mirror images of the payoff and net profit profiles for the call buyer (Figure 17-2) and the call writer (Figure 17-3) illustrate an important point. Options trading is *a zero-sum gain.* What the option buyer (writer) gains, the option writer (buyer) loses. With commissions, options trading could be unprofitable for both buyers and sellers and must be unprofitable for both taken together since it is a zero sum game.

PUTS

Buying a Put A put buyer makes money if the price of the stock declines. Therefore, as part (c) of Figure 17-1 illustrates, the payoff pattern is flat at the $0 axis to the right of the exercise price; that is, stock prices greater than the exercise price result in a $0 payoff for the put buyer. As the stock declines below the exercise price, the payoff for the put option increases. The larger the decline in the stock price, the larger the payoff.

Payoff to put buyer at expiration:

$$= 0 \qquad \text{if } S_T \geq E$$
$$= E - S_T \text{ if } S_T < E$$

Once again, the profit line parallels the payoff pattern for the put option at expiration. As Figure 17-4 illustrates, the investor breaks even (no net profit) at the point where the stock

FIGURE 17-4

Profit and loss to the buyer of a put option.

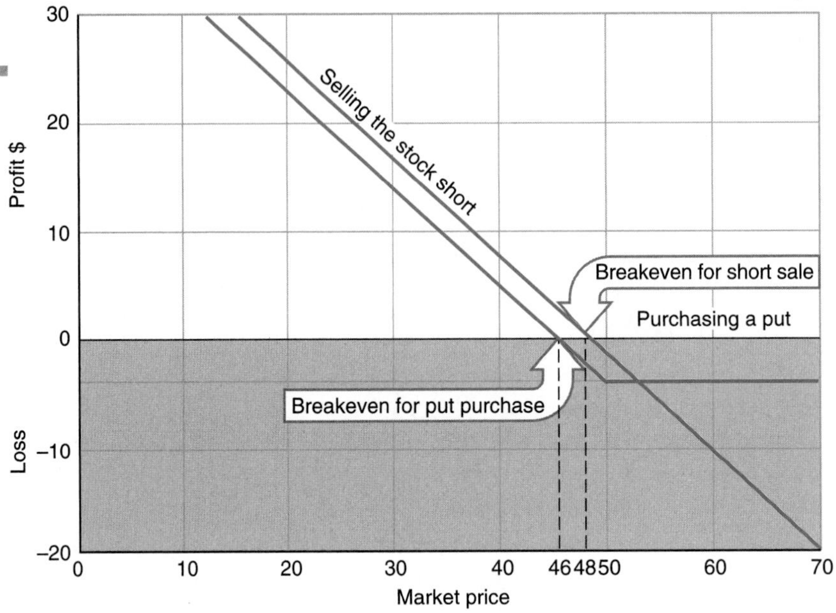

price is equal to the exercise price minus the premium paid for the put. Beyond that point, the net profit line parallels the payoff line representing the investment value of the put.

Selling (Writing) a Put The payoff pattern for the put writer is the mirror image of that for the put buyer as shown in part (d) of Figure 17-1. The put writer retains the premium if the stock price rises, and loses if the stock price declines. The put writer exchanges a fixed payoff for unknown losses.

Payoff to put writer at expiration:

$= 0 \quad \text{if } S_T \geq E$

$= -(E - S_T) \text{ if } S_T < E$

Writers (sellers) of puts are seeking the premium income exactly as call writers are. The writer obligates him- or herself to purchase a stock at the specified exercise price during the life of the put contract. If stock prices decline, the put buyer may purchase the stock and exercise the put by delivering the stock to the writer, who must pay the specified price.

Note that the put writer may be obligated to purchase a stock for, say, $50 a share when it is selling in the market for $40 a share. This represents an immediate paper loss (less the premium received for selling the put). Also note that the put writer can cancel the obligation by purchasing an identical contract in the market.[13]

EXAMPLE 17-8

Figure 17-5 illustrates the profit-loss position for the seller of a put. Using the previous figures, we see that a six-month put is sold at an exercise price of $50 for a premium of $4. The seller of a naked put receives the premium and hopes that the stock price remains at or above the exercise price. As the price of the stock falls, the seller's position declines. The seller begins to lose money below the breakeven point, which in this case is $50 − $4 = $46. Losses could be substantial if the price of the stock declined sharply. The price of the put will increase point for point as the stock price declines.

[13] Of course, if the price of the stock has declined since the put was written, the price of the put will have increased and the writer will have to repurchase at a price higher than the premium received when the put was written.

FIGURE 17-5

Profit and loss to the writer of a put option.

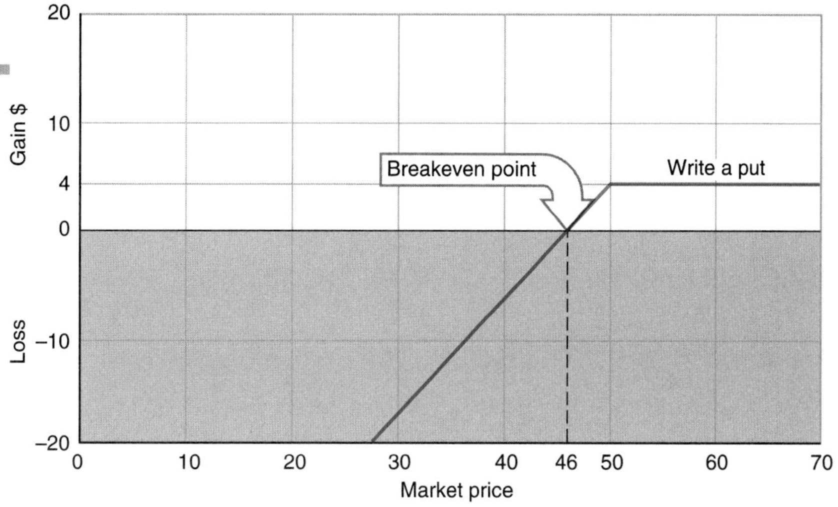

SOME BASIC OPTIONS STRATEGIES

In the previous section we examined the payoffs, and profit/losses, for basic "uncovered" positions involving options (and their underlying stocks). The six uncovered positions are: long stock, short stock, buy call, write call, buy put, and write put. In this section we analyze "covered" positions involving hedges. Spreads and combinations, which are also covered positions, are discussed in Appendix 17-A.

Hedge A strategy using derivatives to offset or reduce the risk resulting from exposure to an underlying asset

A **hedge** is a combination of an option and its underlying stock designed such that the option protects the stock against loss or the stock protects the option against loss. We consider below the more popular hedges.

COVERED CALLS

Covered Call A strategy involving the sale of a call option to supplement a long position in an underlying asset

A **covered call** involves the purchase of stock and the simultaneous sale of a call on that stock; that is, it is a long position in the stock and a short position in a call. The position is "covered" because the writer owns the stock and could deliver it if called to do so as a result of the exercise of the call option by the holder. In effect, the investor is willing to sell the stock at a fixed price, limiting the gains if the stock rises in exchange for cushioning the loss, by the amount of the call premium, if the stock declines.

Using our previous notation, the payoff profile at expiration is:

	$S_T < E$	$S_T > E$
Payoff of stock	S_T	S_T
− Payoff of call	-0	$-(S_T - E)$
Total payoff	S_T	E

Figure 17-6 illustrates the *payoffs* on the covered call hedge by showing all three situations: purchase of the stock, writing a call, and the combined position. The sale of the call truncates the combined position if the stock price rises above the exercise price. In effect, the writer has sold the claim to this gain for the call premium. At expiration, the position is worth, at most, the exercise price and the profit is the call premium received by selling the call.

As Figure 17-6 shows, if the stock price declines, the position is protected by the amount of the call premium received. Therefore, the breakeven point is lower compared to simply

FIGURE 17-6

Payoff profiles for a covered call position.

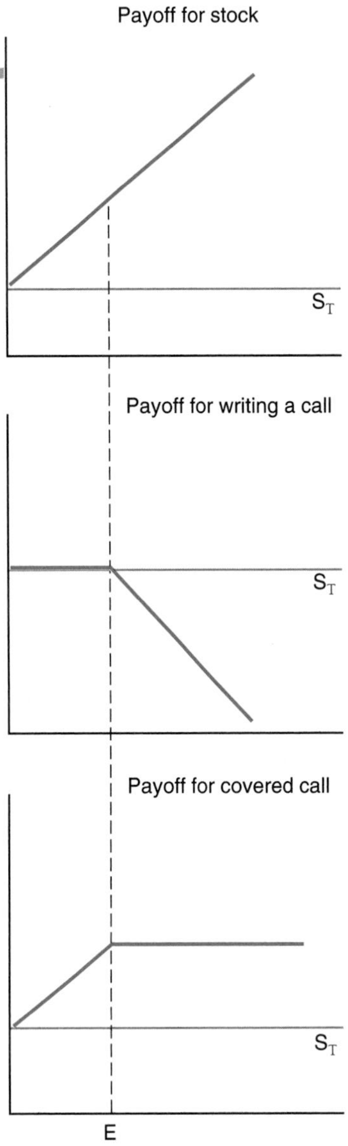

owning the stock, and the loss incurred as the stock price drops will be less with the covered call position by the amount of the call premium.

EXAMPLE 17-9

Assume that an investor purchased 100 shares of Coca-Cola last year for $40 per share and this year, with the stock price at $48, writes a (covered) six-month call with an exercise price of $50. The writer receives a premium of $4. This situation is illustrated in Figure 17-7.

If called on to deliver his or her 100 shares, the investor will receive $50 per share, plus the $4 premium, for a gross profit of $14 per share (since the stock was purchased at $40 per share). However, the investor gives up the additional potential gain if the price of this stock rises above $50—shown by the flat line to the right of $50 for the covered call

FIGURE 17-7

Profit and loss for a covered call position.

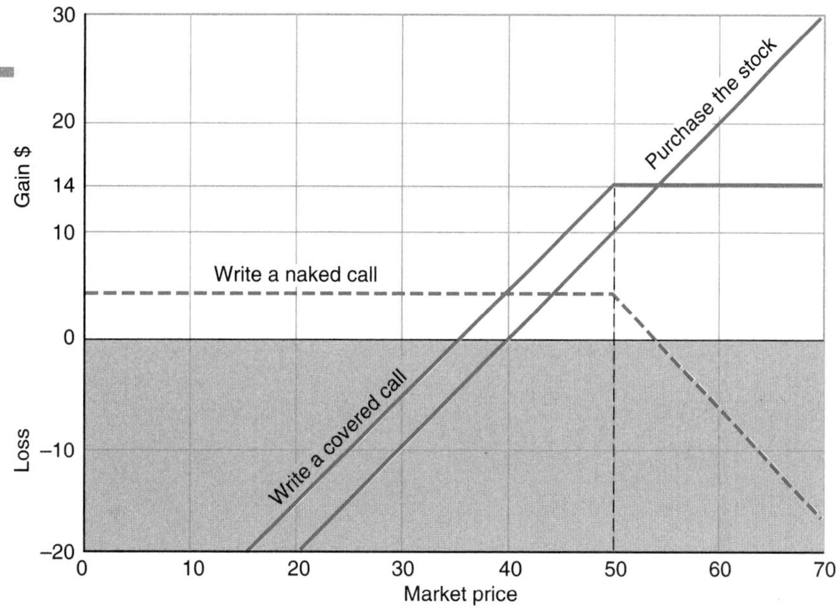

position in Figure 17-7. If the price rises to \$60 after the call is sold, for example, the investor will gross \$14 per share but could have grossed \$20 per share if no call had been written.

Writing a naked call is also illustrated (by the broken line) in Figure 17-7. If the call is not exercised, the writer profits by the amount of the premium, \$4. The naked writer's breakeven point is \$54. This position will be profitable if the price of the stock does not rise above the breakeven point. Notice that the potential gain for the naked writer is limited to \$4. The potential loss, however, is large. If the price of the stock were to rise sharply, the writer could easily lose an amount in excess of what was received in premium income.

PROTECTIVE PUTS

Protective Put A strategy involving the purchase of a put option as a supplement to a long position in an underlying asset

A **protective put** involves buying a stock (or owning it already) and a put for the same stock; that is, it is a long position in both the stock and a put. The put acts as insurance against a decline in the underlying stock, guaranteeing an investor a minimum price at which the stock can be sold. In effect, the insurance acts to limit losses or unfavorable outcomes. The largest profit possible is infinite.

The payoff profile is:

		$S_T < E$	$S_T > E$
	Payoff of stock	S_T	S_T
+	Payoff of put	$E - S_T$	0
	Total payoff	E	S_T

Above the exercise price, the payoff reflects the increase in the stock price. Below the exercise price, the payoff is worth the exercise price at expiration.

Figure 17-8 shows the protective put versus an investment in the underlying stock. As always, the payoff for the stock is a straight line, and the payoff for the option strategy is an asymmetrical line consisting of two segments. The payoff for the protective put clearly illus-

FIGURE 17-8

Payoff profile and profit/losses for a protected put position.

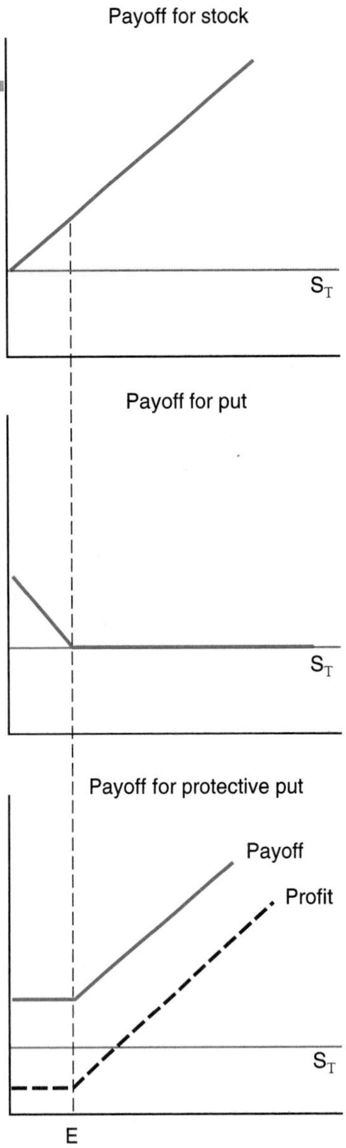

trates what is meant by the term *truncating* the distribution of returns. Below a certain stock price (the exercise price), the payoff line is flat or horizontal. Therefore, the loss is limited to the cost of the put. Above the breakeven point, the protective put strategy shares in the gains as the stock price rises. This is the true benefit of derivative securities and the reason for their phenomenal growth—derivatives provide a quick and inexpensive way to alter the risk of a portfolio.

Figure 17-8 illustrates how a protective put offers some insurance against a decline in the stock price. This insurance feature limits losses, but at a cost if the insurance turns out not to be needed—the cost of the put. Above the exercise price, the profit is less than the payoff profile for the investment because of the cost of the put. Below the exercise price, losses in the stock price are partially offset by gains from the put, resulting in a constant loss equal to the cost of the put.

This position is identical to purchasing a call except for a different intercept on the vertical axis.

The protective put illustrates a well-known concept called portfolio insurance, which is explained below.

PORTFOLIO INSURANCE

Portfolio Insurance An asset management technique designed to provide a portfolio with a lower limit on value while permitting it to benefit from rising security prices

The potential return-risk modification properties of options, and particularly the insurance aspects discussed above, are well illustrated by the technique known as **portfolio insurance.** This term refers to investment strategies designed to hedge portfolio positions by providing a minimum return on the portfolio while simultaneously providing an opportunity for the portfolio to participate in rising security prices. This asset management technique became very popular in the 1980s, with many billions of dollars of assets insured.

There are several methods of insuring a portfolio, including options, futures, and the creation of *synthetic options.* In practice, it is common to use futures contracts on market indexes (as discussed in Chapter 18). However, in principle options can be used in portfolio insurance strategies, and their use illustrates the basic nature of a hedge.

The idea behind portfolio insurance as regards options is simple. A protective put can be purchased that allows the portfolio to be sold for an amount sufficient to provide the minimum return. The remaining portfolio funds are invested in the usual manner. The protective put provides insurance for the portfolio by limiting losses in the event stock prices decline. The portfolio's value at the end of the period must equal or exceed the exercise price of the put.

EXAMPLE 17-10

An investor wishes to ensure a minimum return of 5 percent. For simplicity, we assume the investor starts with $1.[14]

- One unit of a stock market index sells for $0.9097
- A European put on this index can be bought for $0.0903.
- The put has a strike price of $1.05.

The investor has used portfolio insurance to ensure a 5 percent minimum return. If the value of the stock index exceeds $1.05 by the end of the investing period, the investor is ahead that much and allows the put to expire worthless. If the value of the index is less then $1.05 by the end of the period, the investor can exercise the option and sell the stock index for $1.05, thereby earning the required 5 percent minimum return on the initial investment of $1.00. Portfolio insurance has provided protection against the downside while allowing the investor to participate in stock price advances.

This example illustrates the conceptual use of puts in portfolio insurance strategies. In practice, however, puts and calls are not used to insure portfolios because those typically available to investors are American and not European. The exercise-at-any-time feature of American options makes them not only more valuable than corresponding European options but also much more costly for portfolio insurance purposes. Furthermore, it generally is not possible to find puts and calls with the exact time to expiration, exercise price, and so on that matches a particular portfolio.

[14] This example is based on Richard J. Rendleman and Richard W. McEnally, "Assessing the Costs of Portfolio Insurance," *Financial Analysts Journal* (May–June 1987): 27–37.

It should also be noted that portfolio insurance is not costless. The costs include:

- The *cost of the option* itself, in our example, the put cost \$0.0903. Obviously, if stocks advance and the put expires worthless, the cost of the put has been lost relative to an uninsured strategy. This can be thought of as the insurance premium.
- An *opportunity cost.* An investor who places 100 percent of investment funds in the stock index would participate fully in any market rise. In our example, the insured investor would participate in only 90.97 percent of any market rise.

OPTION VALUATION

A GENERAL FRAMEWORK

In this section we examine the determinants of the value of a put or call. Special terminology is used to describe the relationship between the exercise price of the option and the current stock price. If the price of the common stock, S, exceeds the exercise price of a call, E, the call is said to be *in the money* and has an immediate exercisable value. On the other hand, if the price of the common is less than the exercise price of a call, it is said to be *out of the money*. Finally, calls that are *near the money* are those with exercise prices slightly greater than current market price, whereas calls that are *at the money* are those with exercise prices equal to the stock price.

These same definitions also apply to puts, but in reverse. In summary,

If $S > E$, a call is in the money and a put is out of the money.
If $S < E$, a call is out of the money and a put is in the money.
If $S = E$, an option is at the money.

INTRINSIC VALUES AND TIME VALUES

The price of a call option can be dichotomized in the following manner. If a call is in the money (the market price of the stock exceeds the exercise price for the call option), it has an *immediate* value equal to the difference in the two prices. This value will be designated as the *intrinsic value* of the call; it could also be referred to as the option's minimum value, which in this case is positive. If the call is out of the money (the stock price is less than the exercise price), the intrinsic value is zero; in this case, the price of the option is based on its speculative appeal. Summarizing, where S_0 = current stock price:

$$\text{Intrinsic value of a call} = \text{Maximum } (S_0 - E), 0 \qquad (17\text{-}1)$$

EXAMPLE 17-11

Assume that on October 1 Compaq Computer closes at \$27⅝ and that a December call option with a strike price of 25 is available. This option is in the money because the stock price is greater than the exercise price.

Intrinsic value of Dec. 25 call = \$27⅝ − \$25 = \$2⅝

Puts work in reverse. If the market price of the stock is less than the exercise price of the put, the put is in the money and has an intrinsic value. Otherwise, it is out of the money and has a zero intrinsic value. Thus:

$$\text{Intrinsic value of a put} = \text{Maximum } (E - S_0), 0 \qquad (17\text{-}2)$$

EXAMPLE 17-12

Assume there is a Compaq Computer December put available on October 1 with a strike price of \$30. The current market price is \$27⅝.

$$\text{Intrinsic value of Compaq Computer Dec. 30 put} = \$30 - \$27\tfrac{5}{8} = \$2\tfrac{3}{8}$$

Arbitrageurs Investors who seek discrepancies in security prices in an attempt to earn riskless returns

An option's premium almost never declines below its intrinsic value. The reason is that market arbitrageurs, who constantly monitor option prices for discrepancies, would purchase the options and exercise them, thus earning riskless returns. **Arbitrageurs** are speculators who seek to earn a return without assuming risk by constructing riskless hedges. Short-lived deviations are possible, but they will quickly be exploited.

Option prices almost always exceed intrinsic values, with the difference reflecting the option's potential appreciation typically referred to as the *time value*. This is somewhat of a misnomer because the actual source of value is volatility in price. However, price volatility decreases with a shortening of the time to expiration—hence the term time value.

Because buyers are willing to pay a price for potential future stock-price movements, time has a positive value—the longer the time to expiration for the option, the more chance it has to appreciate in value. However, when the stock price is held constant, options are seen as a *wasting asset* whose value approaches intrinsic value as expiration approaches. In other words, as expiration approaches, the time value of the option declines to zero.[15]

The time value can be calculated as the difference between the option price and the intrinsic value:

$$\text{Time value} = \text{Option price} - \text{Intrinsic value} \tag{17-3}$$

EXAMPLE 17-13

For the Compaq Computer options referred to earlier:

$$\text{Time value of Dec. 25 call} = \$3\tfrac{1}{2} - \$2\tfrac{5}{8} = \$\tfrac{7}{8}$$

$$\text{Time value of Dec. 30 put} = \$3 - \$2\tfrac{3}{8} = \$\tfrac{5}{8}$$

We can now understand the premium for an option as the sum of its intrinsic value and its time value, or

$$\text{Premium or Option price} = \text{Intrinsic value} + \text{Time value} \tag{17-4}$$

EXAMPLE 17-14

For the Compaq Computer options:

$$\text{Premium for Dec. 25 call} = \$2\tfrac{5}{8} + \$\tfrac{7}{8} = \$3\tfrac{1}{2}$$

$$\text{Premium for Dec. 30 put} = \$2\tfrac{3}{8} + \$\tfrac{5}{8} = \$3$$

Notice an important point about options based on the preceding discussion. An investor who owns a call option and wishes to acquire the underlying common stock will always find it preferable to sell the option and purchase the stock in the open market rather than exercise

[15] For an American option, time value cannot be zero because the option can be exercised at any time.

the option (at least if the stock pays no dividends). Why? Because otherwise, he or she will lose the speculative premium on the option.

EXAMPLE 17-15

Consider the Compaq December 25 call option, with the market price of the common at \$27⅝. An investor who owned the call and wanted to own the common would be better off to sell the option at \$3½ and purchase the common for \$27⅝, for a net investment of \$24⅛. Exercising the call option, the investor would have to pay \$25 per share for shares of stock worth \$27⅝ in the market, but at a cost of 3½ per share. (Brokerage commissions are ignored in this example.)

On the other hand, it can be optimal to exercise an American put early (on a nondividend paying stock). A put sufficiently deep in the money should be exercised early because the payment received at exercise can be invested to earn a return.

BOUNDARIES ON OPTION PRICES

In the previous section we learned what the premium, or price, of a put or call consists of, but we do not know why options trade at the prices they do and the range of values they can assume. In this section we learn about the boundaries for option prices, and in the next section we discuss the exact determinants of options prices.

The value of an option must be related to the value of the underlying security. The basic relationship is most easy to understand by considering an option immediately prior to expiration, when there is no time premium. If the option is not exercised, it will expire immediately, leaving the option with no value. Obviously, investors will exercise it only if it is worth exercising (if it is in the money).

Figure 17-9A shows the values of call options at expiration, assuming a strike price of \$50. At expiration, a call must have a value that is the maximum of 0 or its intrinsic value. Therefore, the line representing the value of a call option must be horizontal at \$0 up to the exercise price and then rise as the stock price exceeds the exercise price. Above \$50 the call price must equal the difference between the stock price and the exercise price, or its intrinsic value.

For puts the situation is reversed. At expiration, a put must have a value that is the maximum of 0 or its intrinsic value. Therefore, the line in Figure 17-9B representing the value of a put option must be horizontal beyond the exercise price. Below \$50 the put price must equal the difference between the exercise price and the stock price. Note that a put option has a strict upper limit on intrinsic value, whereas the call has no upper limit. A put's strike price is its maximum intrinsic value.

What is the maximum price an option can assume? To see this think of a call. Since the call's value is derived from its ability to be converted into the underlying stock, it can never sell for more than the stock itself. It would not make sense to pay more for a call on one share of stock than the price of the stock itself. Therefore, the maximum price for a call is the price of the underlying stock.

Based on the preceding, we can establish the absolute upper and lower boundaries for the price of a call option as shown in Figure 17-9C. The upper boundary is a 45 degree line from the origin representing a call price equal to the stock price.[16] The lower boundary is the

[16] Think of this as a call with a zero exercise price and an infinite maturity.

FIGURE 17-9

Determining the boundaries on option prices.

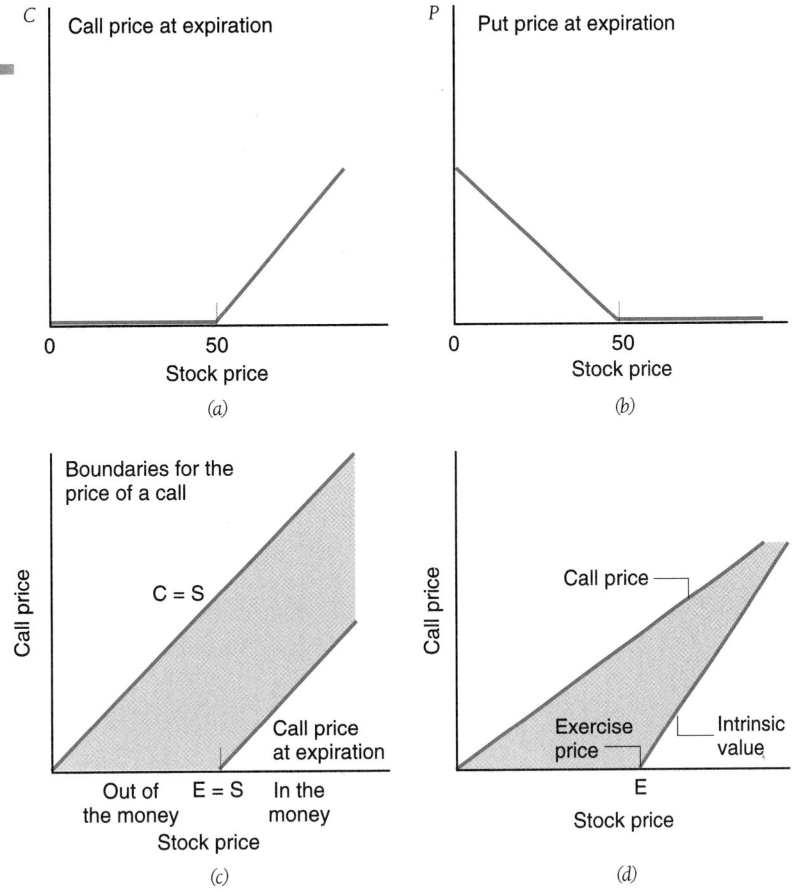

price of the option at expiration, which must be either zero or its in-the-money value. This is represented by the 45 degree line starting at the exercise price. Once again, the lower boundary can be interpreted as the value of the call at the moment the call is exercised, or its intrinsic value.

Finally, Figure 17-9(d) illustrates more precisely and realistically the variation in price for a call option by illustrating how the price of a call varies with the stock price and the exercise price. The call price is always above intrinsic value and rises as the stock price increases beyond the exercise price. The time value, represented by the shaded area in Figure 17-9(d), decreases beyond the exercise price.

To understand fully the price of a call option, we must use a formal model of call prices, the Black-Scholes model. The price of a put can also be found from this model because of a parity relationship between puts and calls.

THE BLACK-SCHOLES MODEL

Fischer Black and Myron Scholes have developed a model for the valuation of call options that is widely accepted and used in the investments community.[17] The formula itself is math-

[17] F. Black and M. Scholes, "The Pricing of Options and Corporate Liabilities," *The Journal of Political Economy,* 81 (May–June 1973): 637–654.

Black-Scholes Model A widely used model for the valuation of call options

ematical and appears to be very complex; however, it is widely available on calculators and computers. Numerous investors estimate the value of calls using the **Black-Scholes model.**

The Black-Scholes model uses five variables to value the call option of a *nondividend-paying stock.*[18] These five variables, all but the last of which are directly observable in the market, are as follows:

1. The price of the underlying stock
2. The exercise price of the option
3. The time remaining to the expiration of the option
4. The interest rate
5. The volatility of the underlying stock

The first two variables are of obvious importance in valuing an option, because, as noted before, they determine the option's intrinsic value—whether it is in the money or not. If it is out of the money, it has only a time value based on the speculative interest in the stock.

Time to expiration (measured as a fraction of a year) is also an important factor in the value of an option because value generally increases with maturity. The relationship between time and value is not proportional, however. The time value of an option is greatest when the market price and the exercise price are equal.[19]

The interest rate affects option values because of the opportunity cost involved. Buying an option is a substitute to some degree for buying on margin, on which interest must be paid. The higher interest rates are, therefore, the more interest cost is saved by the use of options. This adds to the value of the option and results in a direct relationship between the value of a call option and interest rates in the market.

The last factor, and the only one not directly observable in the marketplace, is the stock's volatility. The greater the volatility, the *higher* the price of a call option because of the increased potential for the stock to move up. Therefore, a positive relation exists between the volatility of the stock and the value of the call option.[20]

The Black-Scholes option pricing formula can be expressed as[21]

$$\text{CP} = \text{CMP}[\text{N}(d_1)] - \frac{\text{EP}}{e^{rt}}[\text{N}(d_2)] \tag{17-5}$$

where

CP = the price of the call option
CMP = current market price of the underlying common stock
$\text{N}(d_1)$ = the cumulative density function of d_1
EP = the exercise price of the option
e = the base of natural logarithms = approximately 2.71828
r = the continuously compounded riskless rate of interest on an annual basis
t = the time remaining before the expiration date of the option, expressed as a fraction of a year
$\text{N}(d_2)$ = the cumulative density function of d_2

[18] Options traded on organized exchanges are not protected against cash dividends, and this can have significant effects on option values. When a cash dividend is paid, the stock price should decline to reflect this payment. Any event that reduces the stock price reduces the value of a call and increases the value of a put.

[19] If the option is already in the money, a rise in the stock price will not result in the same percentage gain in the option price that would occur in the previous situation. For out-of-the-money options, part of the time remaining will be used for the price of the stock to reach the exercise price.

[20] "Volatility" as used in the options model is not the same concept as a stock's beta as used in Chapter 7. Volatility is used here as a measure of the variability in the stock price as opposed to sensitivity to market movements.

[21] This version of the model applies to nondividend-paying stocks. Adjustments can be made for stocks that pay dividends.

To find d_1 and d_2, it is necessary to solve these equations:

$$d_1 = \frac{\ln (\text{CMP/EP}) + (r + 0.5\sigma^2)t}{(\sigma[(t)^{1/2}])} \tag{17-6}$$

$$d_2 = d_1 - (\sigma[(t)^{1/2}]) \tag{17-7}$$

where

ln (CMP/EP) = the natural log of (CMP/EP)

σ = the standard deviation of the annual rate of return on the underlying common stock

The five variables previously listed are needed as inputs. Variables 1–4 are immediately available. Variable 5 is not, however, because what is needed is the variability expected to occur in the stock's rate of return. Although historical data on stock returns are typically used to estimate this standard deviation, variability does change over time. A formula user should try to incorporate expected changes in the variability when using historical data. To do so, the user should examine any likely changes in either the market's or the individual stock's variability.

Variables 1–3 should be identical for a given stock for everyone using the Black-Scholes model. Variable 4 should be identical or very close among formula users, depending on the exact proxy used for the riskless rate of interest. Variable 5 will vary among users, providing different option values. Empirical studies have shown that estimates of the variance obtained from other than historical data are more valuable than the estimates based on historical data. Since the price of an option can be observed at any time, it is possible to solve the Black-Scholes formula for the implied standard deviation of the stock's return. Henry Latane' and Richard Rendleman found that better forecasts of the actual standard deviation could be obtained by preparing forecasts from the model itself.[22]

EXAMPLE 17-16

The following is an example of the use of the Black-Scholes option pricing formula:

Assume

CMP = \$40

EP = \$45

$r = 0.10$

$t = 0.5$ (6 months)

$\sigma = 0.45$

Step 1: Solve for d_1.

$$d_1 = \frac{\ln (40/45) + [(0.10 + 0.5(0.45)^2]0.5}{0.45\ [(0.5)^{1/2}]}$$

$$= \frac{-0.1178 + 0.1006}{0.3182}$$

$$= -0.054$$

[22] H. Latane' and R. Rendleman, Jr., "Standard Deviations of Stock Price Ratios Implied in Option Prices," *The Journal of Finance* (May 1976): 369–382.

Step 2: Use a cumulative probability distribution table to find the value of $N(d_1)$.

$N(d_1) = 0.4801$

where $d_1 = -0.054$

Step 3: Find d_2.

$d_2 = -0.054 - [0.45((0.5)^{1/2})]$

$= -0.372$

Step 4: Find $N(d_2)$.

$N(d_2) \approx 0.3557$

Step 5: Solve for CP.

$CP = CMP[0.4801] - EP[\text{antilog} - (0.1)(0.5)][0.3557]$

$= 19.20 - 45(0.9512)(0.3557)$

$= 19.20 - 15.23$

$= \$3.97$

The theoretical (fair) value of the option, according to the Black-Scholes formula, is \$3.97. If the current market price of the option is greater than the theoretical value, it is overpriced; if less, it is underpriced.

Investors can use knowledge gained from understanding the Black-Scholes valuation model in their trading activities.

PUT OPTION VALUATION

To establish put prices, we can take advantage of the principle of put-call parity.

Put-Call Parity The formal relationship between a call and a put on the same item which must hold if no arbitrage is to occur

The **put-call parity** principle expresses the relationship between the prices of puts and calls on the same stock that must hold if arbitrage is to be ruled out. In other words, unless the price of the put and the call bear a certain relationship to each other, there will be opportunities for earning riskless profits (arbitrage). The put-call parity can be expressed as

$$\text{Price of put} = EP/(e^{rt}) - CMP + CP \qquad (17\text{-}8)$$

where all terms are as defined before.

EXAMPLE 17-17

Use the information for the call given earlier. Since the Black-Scholes model uses continuous interest, the discount factor is expressed in continuous form.[23] It is equal to e^{rt}, or $e^{.10(.5)}$. Using a calculator, this value is 1.051. Therefore,

$$\text{Price of put} = 45/1.051 - 40 + 3.96 = \$6.78$$

SUMMARIZING THE FACTORS AFFECTING OPTIONS PRICES

If we allow for stocks that pay dividends, we can summarize the factors affecting options prices into a table with six elements, as shown in Table 17-1. The + sign indicates a direct

[23] The value e^k is the equivalent of $(1 + r)$ in continuous compounding. If r is 5 percent, the value of e^k is $e^{.05}$, or 1.051.

TABLE 17-1 EFFECTS OF VARIOUS VARIABLES ON OPTIONS PRICES

Variable	Calls	Puts
Stock price	+	−
Exercise price	−	+
Time to expiration	+	+
Stock volatility	+	+
Interest rates	+	−
Cash dividends	−	+

relation, and a negative sign a negative relation. The assumption behind Table 17-1 is that all other variables remain fixed as we consider any of the six variables individually.

HEDGE RATIOS

A key concept with options is their use as a hedging device. Although risky assets themselves, options can be used to control risk. In particular, options can be used to control the riskiness inherent in common stocks.

To hedge a long stock position with options, an investor would write one call option while simultaneously buying a certain number of shares of common. This number is given by the **hedge ratio,** which is $N(d_1)$ from the Black-Scholes model.[24] The hedge ratio for an option, commonly referred to as the option's *delta,* indicates the change in the price of the option for a $1 change in the price of the common. Since the hedge ratio with a call option is $N(d_1)$, for a put option it is $N(d_1) - 1$.

Hedge Ratio The ratio of options written to shares of stock held long in a riskless portfolio

EXAMPLE 17-18

In the preceding example, $N(d_1)$ was 0.48; therefore, for every call option written, 0.48 share of the common would be required to hedge the position. For a standard 100-share option contract, 48 shares of stock would be required. A $1 increase in the price of the stock should produce a $0.48 change in the price of the option. The loss on the call options written is 100 × $0.48, or $48, which is offset by the gain on the 48 shares of stock of $48. A perfectly hedged position leaves total wealth unchanged.

The fact that hedge ratios are less than 1.0 indicates that option values change with stock prices on less than a one-for-one basis. That is, dollar movements in options prices are smaller than dollar movements in the underlying stock. However, *percentage* price changes on the option generally will be greater than percentage price changes on the stock.

USING THE BLACK-SCHOLES MODEL

What does it mean if we calculate an intrinsic value for an option that is significantly different from the market price? Although this may represent an investment opportunity, we must remember that the original Black-Scholes model is based on some simplifying assumptions, such as the payment of no dividends, a constant variance, and continuous stock prices. The standard deviation cannot be observed and must be estimated. Therefore, any observed discrepancies could reflect errors in the estimation of the stock's volatility.

Development of the Black-Scholes model was a significant event and has had a major impact on all options investors, both directly and indirectly. This model has been the basis

[24] Technically, the hedge ratio is the slope of the functional relationship between the value of the option (vertical axis) and the value of the stock (horizontal axis), evaluated at the current stock price.

of extensive empirical investigations into how options are priced. How well does this model work?

The numerous studies that have been conducted offer general support for the Black-Scholes model and the proposition that options are efficiently priced by the market. Some deficiencies have been noted.[25] The deviations and biases that appear to remain in option pricing models may derive from several sources. For example, the true stock-price volatility is unobservable. Despite any statistically significant biases that may exist in the prices generated by the option pricing models, however, the validity of these models remains intact. What are the implications of this for market efficiency?

USING THE INTERNET The Chicago Board Options Exchange has an extensive website at www.cboe.com. It includes educational materials, investment strategies, quotes, and other information. The theoretical value of an option can be calculated with user-supplied data. For those seeking a good understanding of how traders use options, try the website of the Investment Research Institute at www.options-iri.com. The Options Clearing Corporation can be found at www.optionscentral.com. It has a "Strategy of the Month" for trading options, free software as well as videos, and links to exchanges.

AN INVESTOR'S PERSPECTIVE ON PUTS AND CALLS

WHAT PUTS AND CALLS MEAN TO INVESTORS

Earlier we examined some simple strategies using puts and calls and briefly considered some more sophisticated strategies. It is important for investors to have an overall perspective on puts and calls and consider what they really add to the investment process.

Options contracts are important to investors in terms of the two dimensions of every investment decision that we have emphasized throughout this book—the return and risk from an asset or portfolio. Options can be used for various types of hedging, which involves the management of risk. Options also offer speculators a way to leverage their investment with a strict limit on downside risk.

The return-risk modification properties of puts and calls vary significantly from other derivative instruments such as futures contracts, which we consider in Chapter 18. The important point about options and portfolio return and risk is that the impact of options is not symmetrical. As discussed earlier, the distribution of payoffs is *truncated,* because in the case of buying a call the most the investor can lose is the premium, regardless of what happens to the stock price. The same is true when purchasing a put—relative to the profit-loss line when selling short—the distribution of possible profits and losses from purchasing a put is truncated. If the stock price continues to rise, adversely affecting the investor, the most that can be lost from the put purchase is the premium.

THE EVOLUTIONARY USE OF OPTIONS

Puts and calls on organized options exchanges have been available to investors since 1973, although financial derivatives were being used long before then. Puts and calls have been popular with individual investors since the beginning of CBOE trading, although the manner in which they are viewed has changed somewhat. At first, options were viewed more or less

[25] See Dan Galai, "A Survey of Empirical Tests of Option-Pricing Models," in Menachem Brenner, ed., *Option Pricing: Theory and Applications* (Lexington, Mass.: Lexington Books, 1983), pp. 45–80.

as speculative instruments and were often purchased for their leverage possibilities. Covered option writing was used to enhance portfolio yields. During the 1980s many investors were selling puts in order to capitalize on the rising trend in stock prices. This strategy worked well until the famous market crash in October 1987. As a result of the losses, many investors once again viewed options as speculative instruments and options volume did not return to the level reached in 1987 for several years.

The current emphasis by the brokerage industry is on educating investors as to how options can be used efficiently as part of their portfolio. Investor desire to hedge their portfolios against a market decline (often predicted in the mid-1990s by market observers because of the strong upward movement in the market) as well as the introduction of new products—for example, options on new indexes, country funds, ADRs, and the new LEAPs—seems to be drawing the public back into the market.

By the 1980s options had proved a respectable investment alternative and had begun to attract institutional attention.[26] Changes in regulations occurred that, in effect, encouraged institutional interest in options. Pension funds, insurance companies, and banks began to receive clearance for the trading of options, provided that such trading met the guidelines under which they normally operate.

Thus, in the 1990s options are increasingly valued for their use in strategic portfolio management. Options allow investors to create strategies that expand the set of outcomes beyond what could be achieved in the absence of options. In other words, investors and investment managers sometimes need the nonsymmetric distributions of returns that options can provide. Options strategies increase the set of contingencies that can be provided for.[27]

STOCK-INDEX OPTIONS AND INTEREST RATE OPTIONS

Stock-Index Options Option contracts on a stock market index such as the S&P 500

Interest Rate Options Option contracts on fixed-income securities such as Treasury bonds

Newer innovations in the options market include **stock-index options** and **interest rate options.** Because most investors are interested in the stock-index options, we confine our discussion to them after noting the interest options that are available. Primary interest options traded on the Chicago Board Options Exchange include 5 Year, 10 Year, and 30 Year Treasury Yield Options.

THE BASICS OF STOCK-INDEX OPTIONS

As of the beginning of 1999, stock-index options were available on a variety of market indexes, including (but not limited to) the S&P 100 Index, the S&P 500 Index, the DJIA Index, the Russell 2000 Index, the Major Market Index, the Value Line Index, the S&P Midcap Index, the Japan Index, and the Nasdaq-100 Index. Index options were also available on some industry subindexes, including Pharmaceuticals, Computer Technology, and Semiconductors. In addition, long-term index options (LEAPS) were available for the S&P 100 and 500 indexes and for the DJIA Index.[28]

Stock-index options enable investors to trade on general stock market movements or industries in the same way that they can trade on individual stocks. Thus, an investor who

[26] This discussion is based on "Money Management Begins to Accept Options As a Prudent Investment," *The Wall Street Journal,* September 22, 1980, p. 27.

[27] This discussion is based on Richard Bookstaber, "The Use of Options in Performance Structuring," *Journal of Portfolio Management* (Summer 1985): 36–37.

[28] In 1986 the S&P 500 Index option was converted to a European-style contract, meaning it cannot be exercised until the contract expires. The predictable exercise date appeals to institutional investors when they attempt to hedge their portfolios against losses in volatile markets. Hedgers using standard index options may find their hedges exercised before the contracts expire, thereby giving an edge to the European-style contracts. The Institutional Index is also European-style.

is bullish on the market can buy a call on a market index, and an investor who is bearish on the overall market can buy a put. The investor need only make a market decision, not an industry or an individual stock decision.

Overall, stock-index options are similar to the options listed on the options exchanges. As usual, the exercise price and the expiration date are uniformly established. Investors buy and sell them through their broker in the normal manner. Index option information is read in the same manner as that for stock options.

Unlike stock options which require the actual delivery of the stock upon exercise, buyers of index options receive cash from the seller upon exercise of the contract. The amount of cash settlement is equal to the difference between the closing price of the index and the strike price of the option multiplied by a specified dollar amount.

EXAMPLE 17-19

Assume an investor holds a NYSE Index option with a strike price of 135 and decides to exercise the option on a day that the NYSE Composite Index closes at 139.5. The investor will receive a cash payment from the assigned writer equal to $100 multiplied by the difference between the option's strike price and the closing value of the index, or

NYSE Composite Index close = 139.5
NYSE Index option strike price = 135.0
4.5 × $100 = $450

Note the use of the $100 multiplier for the NYSE Index Option. The multiplier performs a function similar to the unit of trading (100 shares) for a stock option in that it determines the total dollar value of the cash settlement. Since options on different indexes may have different multipliers, it is important to know the multiplier for the stock index being used.

STRATEGIES WITH STOCK-INDEX OPTIONS

The strategies with index options are similar to those for individual stock options. Investors expecting a market rise buy calls, and investors expecting a market decline buy puts. The maximum losses from these two strategies—the premiums—are known at the outset of the transaction. The potential gains can be large because of the leverage involved with options.

EXAMPLE 17-20

In September, an investor expects the stock market to rise strongly over the next two to three months. This investor decides to purchase a NYSE Index November 130 call, currently selling for 3½, on a day when the NYSE Index closed at 129.5.

Assume that the market rises, as the investor expected, to a mid-November level of 139.86 (an 8 percent increase). The investor could exercise the option and receive a cash settlement equal to the difference between the index close (139.86) and the exercise price of 130, multiplied by $100, or[29]

139.86 NYSE Index close
−130.00 Call exercise price
9.86 × $100 = $986

The leverage offered by index options is illustrated in this example by the fact that an 8 percent rise in the index leads to a 182 percent profit on the option position [($986 −

[29] Before exercising, the investor should determine if a better price could be obtained by selling the option.

$350)/$350] = 181.7%]. Obviously, leverage can, and often does, work against an investor. If the market declined or remained flat, the entire option premium of $350 could be lost. As with any option, however, the investor has a limited loss of known amount—the premium paid.

Investors can use stock-index options to hedge their positions. For example, an investor who owns a diversified portfolio of stocks may be unwilling to liquidate his or her portfolio but is concerned about a near-term market decline. Buying a put on a market index will provide some protection to the investor in the event of a market decline. In effect, the investor is purchasing a form of market insurance. The losses on the portfolio holdings will be partially offset by the gains on the put. If the market rises, the investor loses the premium paid but gains with the portfolio holdings. A problem arises, however, in that the portfolio holdings and the market index are unlikely to be a perfect match. The effectiveness of this hedge will depend on the similarity between the two.

EXAMPLE 17-21

Assume an investor has a portfolio of NYSE common stocks currently worth $39,000. It is October and this investor is concerned about a market decline over the next couple of months. The NYSE Index is currently at 130, and a NYSE Index December 130 put is available for 3. In an attempt to protect the portfolio's profits against a market decline, the investor purchases three of these puts, which represent an aggregate exercise price of $39,000, calculated as (130 × 100 × 3 = $39,000).[30]

Assume that the market declines 10 percent by mid-December. If the NYSE Index is 117 at that point,

Put exercise price = 130

NYSE Index price = 117

13 × $100 × 3 (puts) = $3,900

If the value of the investor's portfolio declines exactly 10 percent, the loss on the portfolio of $3,900 will be exactly offset by the total gain on the three put contracts of $3,900. It is important to note, however, that a particular portfolio's value may decline more or less than the overall market as represented by one of the market indexes such as the NYSE Composite Index. The value of a particular portfolio may decline less or more than the change in the index.

As before, if the option is held to expiration and a market decline (of a significant amount) does not occur, the investor will lose the entire premium paid for the put(s). In our example, the investor could lose the entire $900 paid for the three puts. This could be viewed as the cost of obtaining "market insurance."

Stock index options can be useful to institutional investors (or individuals) who do not have funds available immediately for investment but anticipate a market rise. Buying calls will allow such investors to take advantage of the rise in prices if it does occur. Of course, the premium could be lost if the anticipations are incorrect.

Investors can sell (write) index options, either to speculate or to hedge their positions. As we saw in the case of individual options, however, the risk can be large. If the seller is correct in his or her beliefs, the profit is limited to the amount of the premium; if incorrect, the seller faces potential losses far in excess of the premiums received from selling the options. It is impractical (or impossible) to write a completely covered stock-index option because of the difficulty of owning a portfolio that exactly matches the index at all points in time. Although the writer of an individual stock call option can deliver the stock if the option is

[30] The exercise value of an index option, like any stock option, is equal to 100 (shares) multiplied by the exercise price.

exercised, the writer of a stock-index call option that is exercised must settle in cash and cannot be certain that gains in the stock portfolio will *fully* offset losses on the index option.[31]

THE POPULARITY OF STOCK-INDEX OPTIONS

Stock-index options appeal to speculators because of the leverage they offer. A change in the underlying index of less than 1 percent can result in a change in the value of the contract of 15 percent or more. Given the increased volatility in the financial markets in recent years, investors can experience rapid changes in the value of their positions.

Introduced in 1983, stock index options quickly became the fastest growing investment in the United States. Much of the initial volume was accounted for by professional speculators and trading firms. As familiarity with index options increased, individual investors assumed a larger role in this market.

SUMMARY

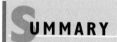

- Equity-derivative securities consist of puts and calls, created by investors, and warrants and convertible securities, created by corporations.
- A call (put) is an option to buy (sell) 100 shares of a particular stock at a stated price any time before a specified expiration date. The seller receives a premium for selling either of these options, and the buyer pays the premium.
- Advantages of options include a smaller investment than transacting in the stock itself, knowing the maximum loss in advance, leverage, and an expansion of the opportunity set available to investors.
- Buyers of calls expect the underlying stock to perform in the opposite direction from the expectations of put buyers. Writers of each instrument have opposite expectations from the buyers.
- The basic strategies for options involve a call writer and a put buyer expecting the underlying stock price to decline, whereas the call buyer and the put writer expect it to rise. Options may also be used to hedge against a portfolio position by establishing an opposite position in options on that stock.
- More sophisticated options strategies include combinations of options, such as strips, straps, and straddles and spreads, which include money spreads and time spreads.
- Options have an intrinsic value ranging from $0 to the "in the money" value. Most sell for more than this, representing a speculative premium.
- According to the Black-Scholes option valuation model, value is a function of the price of the stock, the exercise price of the option, time to maturity, the interest rate, and the volatility of the underlying stock.
- The available empirical evidence seems to suggest that the options market is efficient, with trading rules unable to exploit any biases that exist in the Black-Scholes or other options pricing models.
- Interest rate options and stock index options are also available to investors.
- Stock-index options are a popular innovation in the options area that allows investors to buy puts and calls on broad stock market indexes and industry subindexes.
- The major distinction with these option contracts is that settlement is in cash.

[31] Writers of index options are notified of their obligation to make a cash settlement on the business day following the day of exercise.

- In effect, stock-index options allow investors to make only a market decision and to purchase a form of market insurance.
- The strategies with index options are similar to those for individual stock options. Investors can both hedge and speculate.

KEY WORDS

Arbitrageurs
Black-Scholes model
Call
Covered call
Equity-derivative securities
Expiration date
Exercise (strike) price
Hedge
Hedge ratio
Interest rate options
Long-term options (LEAPS)
Margin
Option premium
Options
Options clearing corporation (OCC)
Portfolio insurance
Protective put
Put
Put-call parity
Stock-index options

QUESTIONS

17-1. Distinguish between a put and a call and a warrant.

17-2. What are the potential advantages of puts and calls?

17-3. Explain the following terms used with puts and calls:

a. Strike price
b. Naked option
c. Premium
d. Out-of-the-money option

17-4. Who writes puts and calls? Why?

17-5. What role does the options clearing corporation play in the options market?

17-6. What is the relationship between option prices and their intrinsic values? Why?

17-7. What is meant by the time premium of an option?

17-8. Explain the factors used in the Black-Scholes option valuation model. What is the relationship between each factor and the value of the option?

17-9. Give three reasons why an investor might purchase a call.

17-10. Why do investors write calls? What are their obligations?

17-11. What is a straddle? When would an investor buy one?

17-12. What is a spread? What is its purpose?

17-13. Explain two types of spreads.

17-14. Why is the call or put writer's position considerably different from the buyer's position?

17-15. What is an index option? What index options are available?

17-16. What are the major differences between a stock option and an index option?

17-17. How can a put be used to protect a particular position? a call?

17-18. How does writing a covered call differ from writing a naked call?

17-19. Which is greater for an option relative to the underlying common, dollar movements or return volatility? Why?

17-20. What is the significance of the industry subindex stock index options?

17-21. Assume that you own a diversified portfolio of 50 stocks and fear a market decline over the next six months.

a. How could you protect your portfolio during this period using stock-index options?
b. How effective would this hedge be?
c. Other things being equal, if your portfolio consisted of 150 stocks, would the protection be more effective?

17-22. Assume that you expect interest rates to rise and that you wish to speculate on this expectation. How could interest rate options be used to do this?

17-23. What does it mean to say that an option is worth more alive than dead?

The following questions were asked on the 1993 CFA Level I examination:

CFA

17-24. In the options markets, the purpose of the clearinghouse is to:

I. issue certificates of ownership.
II. ensure contract performance.
III. match up the option buyer who exercises with the original option writer.

a. II only
b. II and III only
c. III only
d. I, II, and III

CFA

17-25. Which is the *most risky* transaction to undertake in the stock-index option markets if the stock market is expected to increase substantially after the transaction is completed?

a. Write an uncovered call option
b. Write an uncovered put option
c. Buy a call option
d. Buy a put option

CFA

17-26. Which *one* of the following comparative statements about common stock call options and warrants is *correct?*

	Call option	Warrant
a. Issued by the company	No	Yes
b. Sometimes attached to bonds	Yes	Yes
c. Maturity greater than one year	Yes	No
d. Convertible into the stock	Yes	No

The following questions were asked on the 1989 CFA Level I examination:

CFA

17-27. All of the following factors influence the market price of options on a common stock *except* the:

a. expected return on the underlying stock.
b. volatility of the underlying stock.
c. relationship between the strike price of the options and the market price of the underlying stock.
d. option's expiration date.

CFA
17-28. The major difference between a warrant and a call option on a common stock is that:

a. call options are typically written by investors on existing shares, whereas warrants are issued directly by companies as a means of selling new shares.
b. call options trade on various options exchanges, whereas warrants trade only on the New York and American Stock Exchanges.
c. call option valuation models such as Black-Scholes cannot be used to value common stock warrants.
d. none of the above.

The following questions were asked on the 1990 CFA Level I examination:

CFA
17-29. Investor A uses options for defensive and income reasons. Investor B uses options as an aggressive investment strategy. An appropriate use of options for Investors A and B respectively would be:

a. writing covered calls/buying puts on stock not owned.
b. buying out-of-the-money calls/buying puts on stock owned.
c. writing naked calls/buying in-the-money calls.
d. selling puts on stock owned/buying puts on stock not owned.

CFA
17-30. To preserve capital in a declining stock market, a portfolio manager should:

a. buy stock index futures.
b. sell stock index futures.
c. buy call options.
d. sell put options.

PROBLEMS

17-1. The common stock of Teledyne trades on the NYSE. Teledyne has never paid a cash dividend. The stock is relatively risky. Assume that the beta for Teledyne is 1.3 and that Teledyne closed at a price of $162. Hypothetical option quotes on Teledyne are as follows:

Strike		Call			Put	
Price	Apr	Jul	Oct	Apr	Jul	Oct
140	23½	s	s	⅜	s	s
150	16	21	25	1	3¾	r
160	8⅞	14	20	3	7	9
170	3	9	13¼	9	10	11
180	1¼	5¼	9	r	20	r

r = not traded; *s* = no option offered.

Based on the Teledyne data, answer the following questions:
a. Which calls are in the money?
b. Which puts are in the money?
c. Why are investors willing to pay 1¼ for the 180 call but only 1 for the 150 put, which is closer to the current market price?

17-2. Based on the Teledyne data answer the following:
a. Calculate the intrinsic value of the April 140 and the October 170 calls.
b. Calculate the intrinsic value of the April 140 and the October 170 puts.
c. Explain the reasons for the differences in intrinsic values between a and b.

17-3. Using the Teledyne data, answer the following:
a. What is the cost of 10 October 150 call contracts in total dollars? From the text, what is the commission? Total cost?
b. What is the cost of 20 October 160 put contracts in total dollars? What is the commission? Total cost?
c. On the following day, Teledyne closed at $164. Which of the options would you have expected to increase? Decrease?
d. The new quote on the October 150 call was 26. What would have been your one-day profit on the 10 contracts?
e. The new quote on the October 160 put was 7½. What would have been your one-day profit on the 20 contracts?
f. What is the most you could lose on these 20 contracts?

17-4. You are considering some put and call options and have available the following data:

	Call ABC	Call DEF	Put ABC
Time to expiration (months)	3	6	3
Annual risk—Free rate	8%	8%	8%
Exercise price	$50	$50	$50
Option price	$ 3		$ 4
Stock price	$45	$45	$45

a. Comparing the two calls, should DEF sell for more or less than ABC? Why?
b. What is the time value for ABC?
c. Based on the information for the call and the put for ABC, determine if put-call parity is working.

17-5. Assume that the value of a call option using the Black-Scholes model is $8.94. The interest rate is 8 percent and the time to maturity is 90 days. The price of the underlying stock is $47.375, and the exercise price is $45. Calculate the price of a put using the put-call parity relationship.

17-6. Calculate, using the Black-Scholes formula, the value of a call option given the following information:

Stock price = $50
Exercise price = $45
Interest rate = 7%
Time to expiration = 90 days
Standard deviation = 0.4

What is the price of the put using the same information?

17-7. Using the information in Problem 17-6, determine the sensitivity of the call value to a change in inputs by recalculating the call value if
a. the interest rate doubles to 14 percent but all other values remain the same.
b. the standard deviation doubles to 0.8 but all other values remain the same.
Which change causes the greatest change in the value of the call? What can you infer from this?

17-8. Given the following information, determine the number of shares of stock that must be purchased to form a hedged position if one option contract (covering 100 shares of stock) is to be written.

Stock price = \$100
Exercise price = \$95
Interest rate = 8%
Time to expiration = 180 days
Standard deviation = 0.6

17-9. Given the information in Problem 17-8, determine how the value of the call would change if

a. the exercise price is \$100
b. the time to expiration is 80 days (use the original exercise price of \$95)
c. the time to expiration is 8 days

17-10. Determine the value of Ribex call options if the exercise price is \$40, the stock is currently selling for \$2 out of the money, the time to expiration is 90 days, the interest rate is 0.10, and the variance of return on the stock for the past few months has been 0.81.

17-11. Using the information in Problem 17-10, decide intuitively whether the put or the call will sell at a higher price and verify your answer.

SELECTED REFERENCES

A useful discussion of financial derivatives can be found in:

Federal Reserve Bank of Atlanta, *Financial Derivatives: New Instruments and Their Uses,* Federal Reserve Bank of Atlanta Research Division, Atlanta, Georgia, 1993.

A good tutorial on financial futures is available through AIMR as part of the CFA curriculum by contacting PBD, Inc., P. O. Box 6996, Alpharetta, Georgia, 30239-6996 (800/789-AIMR):

Clarke, Roger G. *Options and Futures: A Tutorial,* The Research Foundation of The Institute of Chartered Financial Analysts, P. O. Box 3668, Charlottesville, Virginia, 1992.

www.wiley.com/college/jones7
This chapter discusses the pricing and use of options. The web exercises will aid in the understanding of the different factors that affect option pricing. We will also look at how their use can transform portfolio return distributions.

APPENDIX 17-A

SPREADS AND COMBINATIONS

Puts and calls offer investors a number of opportunities beyond the simple strategies discussed in the previous section. We will briefly examine some combinations of options that can be written or purchased, and consider the use of spreads.

COMBINATIONS OF OPTIONS

Options can be mixed together in numerous ways. The typical combinations are a straddle, a strip, and a strap. A **straddle** is a combination of a put and a call on the same stock with the same exercise date and exercise price. A purchaser of a straddle believes that the underlying stock price is highly volatile and may go either up or down. Buying the straddle eliminates the need to call the market correctly. The buyer of the straddle can exercise each part separately, and therefore can profit from a large enough move either way. However, the price of the stock must rise or fall enough to equal the premium on both a put and a call; therefore, the straddle buyer must be confident that the underlying stock has a good chance of moving sharply in at least one direction.

Straddles can also be sold (written). As is always true about the two sides in an option contract, the seller believes that the underlying stock price will exhibit small volatility but could go up or down. Like the purchaser, the writer does not forecast a likely movement in one direction rather than the other.

EXAMPLE 17A-1 Consider a stock selling at $75 with a six-month straddle available with an exercise price of $75 and, for simplicity, call and put prices of $5 each. The seller of such a straddle is protected in the range of $65–85 (ignoring commissions). The buyers hope that the price exceeds one of these boundaries before expiration.

A *strip* is a combination of two puts and a call on the same security, again with the same expiration date and exercise price. In this case, the purchaser believes the probability of a price decline exceeds the probability of a price rise and therefore wants two puts (but also wants some protection in the opposite direction). The seller obviously believes the opposite.

A *strap* is similar to a strip but combines two calls with a put. Here, of course, the purchaser believes the probability of a price increase exceeds that for a price decrease, and again, the writer expects the opposite.

SPREADS

Rather than being only the buyer or the seller of various combinations of puts and calls, an investor can be both simultaneously by means of a spread. A **spread** is defined as the purchase and sale of an equivalent option varying in only one respect. Its purpose is to reduce risk in an option position, and it is a popular practice.

The two basic spreads are the *money spread* and the *time spread.* A money spread involves the purchase of a call option at one exercise price and the sale of the same-maturity option, but with a different exercise price. For example, an investor could buy an IBM January 80 call and sell an IBM January 90 call.

A time spread involves the purchase and sale of options that are identical except for expiration dates. For example, an investor could buy an IBM January 90 call and sell an IBM April 90 call.

Investors use particular spread strategies, depending on whether they are bullish or bearish.

EXAMPLE 17A-2 Assume you are bullish about IBM but wish to reduce the risk involved in options. IBM is selling for $84, with four-month call options available at exercise prices of $90 and $80 for $3 and $8, respectively. A bullish money spread consists of buying the $80 call and selling the $90 call. Your net cost is now $5, which is the maximum you could lose if the calls expire worthless because IBM's price dropped sharply. If IBM rises, you purchase the $90 call to offset the $90 call sold, resulting in a loss. However, your $80 call will be worth at least the price of the stock minus the exercise price of $80, and when this is netted against your loss on the $90 transaction, you will have a net gain. In effect, you give up some potential profit (what could have been earned on the $80 call alone) to reduce your risk (by reducing your net cost) if the stock price declines.

APPENDIX 17-B

WARRANTS

The definition of a warrant is very similar to that of the call option. A **warrant** is an option to purchase, within a specified time period, a stated number of shares of common stock at a specified price. The following are important differences between calls and warrants:

1. Warrants are issued by corporations, whereas puts and calls are created by investors (whether individuals or institutions).
2. Warrants typically have maturities of at least several years, whereas listed calls expire within nine months.
3. Warrant terms are not standardized—each warrant is unique.

Warrants are most often issued attached to bonds as a "sweetener," allowing the corporate issuer to obtain a lower interest rate (i.e., financing cost).[32] The warrants can be detached and sold separately. In effect, a purchaser of bonds with detachable warrants is buying a package of securities.

Warrants are sometimes issued in conjunction with an acquisition or reorganization. They may also be issued during a new stock sale as partial compensation to the underwriters or as part of a common stock offering to investors.

The attractiveness of warrants to investors declined with the proliferation of alternative equity-derivative securities, including not only puts and calls but also financial futures and futures options (both of which are explained in Chapter 18). By the early 1980s, however, the popularity of warrants was once again increasing, primarily in connection with bond issues. Larger and better capitalized companies, such as American Express and MCI Communications, began issuing warrants.

CHARACTERISTICS OF WARRANTS

A warrant provides the owner with an exercisable option on the underlying common stock of the issuer—that is, a claim on the equity. However, the warrant holder receives no dividends and has no voting rights.

All conditions of a warrant are specified at issuance. Although the issuer may set any expiration date, typically it is 3 to 10 years.[33] In a number of cases, the expiration date can be extended. Warrants often provide for a one-to-one ratio in conversion, allowing the holder

[32] This is particularly true of companies with small capitalizations.
[33] A few warrants are perpetual (i.e., they never expire).

to purchase a number of common shares equal to the number of warrants converted. However, any conversion rate can be specified by the company, and fractional shares may be involved.[34] The *exercise price,* defined as the per-share amount to be paid by the warrant holder on exercise, is also specified at issuance. It always exceeds the market price of the stock at the time the warrant is issued.

EXAMPLE 17B-1

Pier 1 Imports, Inc., a specialty retailer of imported home furnishings and related items, issued a warrant as part of a 20-year debenture offering (a good example of a sweetener).[35] Each $1000 11.5 percent debenture carried 42 warrants with it, exercisable at $22 cash per share on a one-to-one basis.

Some warrants contain provisions under which the corporate issuer can call the warrant or alter the expiration date if certain conditions transpire.

EXAMPLE 17B-2

The Pier 1 warrants were callable anytime for $18. The expiration date could be accelerated by up to two years if the common closed at or above $40 for 10 consecutive trading days.

WHY BUY WARRANTS?

Warrants offer investors a cheaper way to speculate on a particular common stock because the purchase of a given number of warrants is always cheaper than the purchase of a corresponding number of common stock shares. Therefore, investors can establish a given equity position for a considerably smaller capital investment through the use of warrants.

Investors trade warrants on the exchanges and over the counter exactly as they would common stock. They call their broker, usually trade in round lots, and pay normal brokerage commissions.[36] Most investors never exercise warrants but simply buy and sell them in pursuit of capital gains.

Investors are interested in warrants primarily because of their speculative appeal. Warrants provide *leverage* opportunities. Leverage produces larger percentage gains (and also losses) than the underlying common stock for given fluctuations in the price of the common.

EXAMPLE 17B-3

On one observation date, the Pier 1 common stock traded at $18.25 and the warrant traded at $5.75. Since an investor would have to pay $22 to exercise this warrant and receive a share of stock, no one would be willing to do so at that time. Nevertheless, investors were willing to pay $5.75 per warrant to speculate on future price movements. Assume, for example, the stock doubled in price to $36.50 per share (100 percent appreciation). The warrant at that point would be worth a minimum of $14.50 ($36.50 minus the $22 exercise price). This would represent a gain of $8.75 per warrant, or 152 percent appreciation. In fact, this warrant would probably sell for more than $14.50, because of increased investor interest, resulting in an even larger appreciation percentage relative to the common.

[34] Warrant conversions are usually adjusted automatically for any stock dividends or splits.

[35] *The Value Line Convertible Survey,* which is separate from the *Investment Survey,* is an excellent source of information on warrants, convertibles, and puts and calls.

[36] Prior to 1970, the NYSE had not permitted the trading of warrants for many years.

This example demonstrates the leverage potential possible from a warrant. Other things being equal, the warrant price will appreciate more *percentage-wise* than the common stock price for a given increase in the common. (Accordingly, if the stock price declines, the percentage decline of the warrant price will often be greater.)

The primary disadvantage of warrants is that, like puts and calls, they are *wasting assets.* Unless the price of the stock rises enough to make exercise worthwhile, the price of the warrant will decline over time and the warrant eventually will expire worthless.

VALUING WARRANTS

As is true for every financial asset, a warrant has value because of an expected future return of some type. In the case of warrants, since no dividends are paid, the expected return must be realized in the form of capital appreciation, or price change. Warrant valuation, therefore, involves an understanding of the price range in which a warrant may trade.

INVESTMENTS INTUITION Because warrants, like options, are equity-derivative securities, warrant prices must fluctuate within certain boundaries because the warrant price must bear a relationship with the price of the underlying stock. Otherwise, arbitrageurs would buy one security while simultaneously selling the other and earn a profit. For example, if a warrant could be exercised for one share of stock at $10 per share and the stock was selling for $20 per share, the warrant could not sell for less than $10. If it did, it would pay arbitrageurs to purchase the warrant and exercise it, in effect buying the stock for less than $20 per share.

Warrants fluctuate in price between a minimum and maximum value, similar to options.[37] The *maximum value of a warrant* is the price of the underlying common stock. The price of a warrant, which is a claim on the common stock, can never exceed the price of the stock itself because no return beyond the value of the stock is possible. In fact, most warrant prices never reach their maximum value because warrants are an expiring asset—their time value decreases as they approach maturity.

The *minimum value of a warrant* is the difference between the market price of the common and the warrant's exercise price, *if this spread is positive.* This difference must hold, at least approximately, or arbitrageurs could purchase the warrant, exercise it immediately, and sell the common stock received, thereby earning a profit. If the spread is negative (the exercise price exceeds the market price), the minimum price (MP) of the warrant is zero. Thus,

$$\text{MP} = \$0, \text{ if CMP} < \text{EP}$$

$$\text{MP} = (\text{CMP} - \text{EP}) \times \text{N}, \text{ if CMP} > \text{EP} \qquad (17\text{B-1})$$

where

MP = minimum price of a warrant
CMP = current market price of the stock
EP = the exercise price of the warrant
N = number of common shares received per warrant exercised

Equation 17B-1 is often referred to as the **theoretical (calculated) value of a warrant** because it produces the *intrinsic value* of a warrant. In actuality, warrants typically sell above

[37] For simplicity, this discussion assumes a one-to-one purchase ratio between the warrant and the common.

this calculated value. The amount in excess of the formula value is referred to as the *premium*. The premium can be calculated by rearranging Equation 17B-1 into 17B-2.

$$\text{Premium} = \begin{array}{c}\text{Market price}\\ \text{of the warrant}\end{array} - \begin{array}{c}\text{Minimum price}\\ \text{of the warrant}\end{array} \tag{17B-2}$$

EXAMPLE 17B-4

Returning to the Pier 1 Imports warrants, we find that the following calculations can be made, using the prices previously cited as an example.

Minimum price for Pier 1 warrants = \$0 because CMP < EP

The minimum price would have to be considered zero because the current market price was less than the exercise price (obviously, the price cannot be negative).

The premium would be calculated as

Premium for Pier 1 warrants = \$5.75 − \$0 = \$5.75

On the observation date, the Pier 1 Imports warrant was selling for a premium of \$5.75 above its minimum price. Investors were willing to pay this because the warrant was selling at slightly less than one-third the price of the common and the maximum loss was relatively small (i.e., \$5.75 per warrant). As shown earlier, the potential return could be large because of the leverage involved.

Some warrants, of course, are in the money—the stock price exceeds the exercise price.

EXAMPLE 17B-5

Tyco Toys issued a warrant with an exercise price of \$16.50. On one observation date, the price of the common was \$20.25, and the price of the warrant was \$7.88. Therefore, the minimum price of the warrant was \$3.75, and it was selling for a premium of \$7.88 - \$3.50, or \$4.38.

Figure 17B-1 shows the relationships that exist among the market price of the warrant, the warrant, the minimum (theoretical) price as given by Equation 17B-1, the maximum price of the warrant, and the premium. The minimum price line starts at EP, the exercise price of the warrant. The minimum price of the warrant rises (becomes positive) as the price of the stock exceeds the exercise price. Notice that as the price of the common stock continues to

FIGURE 17B-1

Relationships between the value of a warrant and the underlying common stock (EP = exercise price of the warrant).

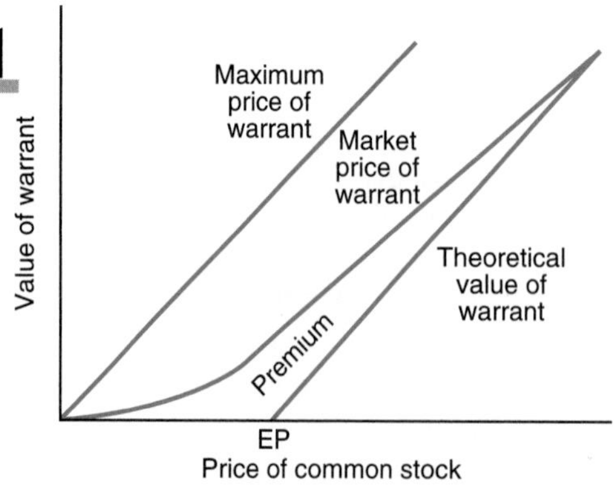

increase, the size of the premium decreases, a phenomenon illustrated in Figure 17B-1. Finally, note the line representing the maximum price for the warrant. Why is this drawn at a 45-degree angle?

THE SPECULATIVE VALUE OF A WARRANT

What determines the premium investors will pay for a warrant, that is, its speculative value? Since investors typically purchase warrants to speculate on the underlying common stock, some obvious factors will affect the premium, or speculative potential, of the warrant. These include the following:

1. *Remaining warrant life.* Clearly, other things being equal, the longer the remaining life of a warrant, the more valuable it is. A warrant that currently is unattractive to exercise may become attractive six months, two years, or eight years from now as a result of appreciation in the common. Most investors are well advised not to purchase a warrant with less than three years remaining to maturity.
2. *Price volatility of the common.* Other things being equal, the more volatile the price of the underlying common, the more likely the warrant is to appreciate during a given time period. Investors are willing to pay larger premiums for such a warrant.
3. *The dividend on the underlying common.* Since warrant holders receive no dividends, an inverse relationship exists between the warrant premium and the expected dividend on the common.
4. *The potential leverage of the warrant.* As previously explained, warrant prices rise (and decline) faster, in percentage terms, than the price of the stock. Some warrants have greater leverage possibilities than others and therefore command larger premiums.

In connection with the leverage potential of the warrant, notice in Figure 17B-1 that the premium becomes smaller as the price of the stock rises. Why? As the stock price increases, the leverage potential decreases. In other words, the ability of the warrant to magnify percentage gains on the amount invested decreases as the price of the stock rises.

EXAMPLE 17B-6

Consider the following examples for the Pier 1 Imports warrant, assuming the same stock price of $18.25 and the same warrant price of $5.75 as previously used.

Stock price doubles from $18.25 to $36.50.	100% gain
Theoretical value of warrant rises $5.75 to $14.50.	152% gain
Stock price rises an additional 50% from $36.50 to $54.75.	50% gain
Theoretical value of warrant rises from $14.50 to $32.75.[38]	126% gain
Stock price rises an additional 25% from $54.75 to $68.44.	25% gain
Theoretical value of warrant rises from $32.75 to $46.44.	42% gain

[38] $54.75 − 22 = $32.75 theoretical value; $32.75 − 14.50/14.50 = 126% gain.

chapter 18

FUTURES

Chapter 18 covers financial futures, the other derivative security of importance to investors. As with options, futures allow investors to manage investment risk and to speculate in the equity, fixed-income, and currency markets.

After reading this chapter you will be able to:

- **Understand why financial futures have been developed for use by investors.**
- **Describe the alternatives available to investors in the futures markets as well as how futures markets operate.**
- **Analyze basic strategies involving futures contracts.**

Futures markets play an important role in today's investments world. New instruments in this area have proliferated, and techniques involving the use of futures, such as program trading, have captured wide media attention. Of particular importance to many investors is the array of financial futures now available. Anyone studying investments should understand what futures contracts are, the wide variety of choices now available, and how financial futures can be used both to hedge portfolio positions and to speculate in fixed-income and equity areas. Futures contracts are an important component of derivative securities and, like options, are a major innovation in *risk management.*

UNDERSTANDING FUTURES MARKETS

WHY FUTURES MARKETS?

Forward Contract A commitment today to transact in the future. Both parties have agreed to a deferred delivery at a sales price that is currently determined, with no funds having been exchanged

Physical commodities and financial instruments typically are traded in *cash markets.* A cash contract calls for immediate delivery and is used by those who need a commodity now (e.g., food processors). Cash contracts cannot be canceled unless both parties agree. The current cash prices of commodities and financial instruments can be found daily in such sources as *The Wall Street Journal.*

There are two types of cash markets, spot markets and forward markets. Spot markets are markets for immediate delivery.[1] The spot price refers to the current market price of an item available for immediate delivery.

Forward markets are markets for deferred delivery. The forward price is the price of an item for deferred delivery.

EXAMPLE 18-1

Suppose that a manufacturer of high school and college class rings is gathering orders to fill for this school year and wishes to ensure an established price today for gold to be delivered six months from now, when the rings will actually be manufactured. The spot price of gold is not the manufacturer's primary concern, because the gold will not be purchased until it is needed for the manufacturing process. However, to reduce its risk the manufacturer is interested in contracting for gold to be delivered in six months at a price established today. This will allow the manufacturer to price its rings more accurately.

Our manufacturer could find a gold supplier who was willing to enter into a **forward contract,** which is simply a commitment today to transact in the future. The other party to the contract, such as a mining company, agrees to deliver the gold six months from now at a price negotiated today. Both parties have agreed to a deferred delivery at a sales price that is currently determined. No funds have been exchanged. Both parties have reduced their risk in the sense that the mining company knows what it will receive for the gold when it is sold six months from now and the ring manufacturer knows what it will pay for the gold when it actually needs to take delivery six months from now.

INVESTMENTS INTUITION Obviously, one of the parties may be disappointed six months later when the price of gold has changed, but that is the advantage of hindsight. If investors could foresee the future, they would know what to do to start with and would not have to worry about risk. The forward and futures markets were developed to allow individuals to deal with the risks they face because the future is uncertain.

[1] "Immediate" means in the normal course of business. For example, it may normally take two days for an item to be delivered after being ordered.

Forward contracts are centuries old, traceable to at least the ancient Romans and Greeks. Organized futures markets, on the other hand, only go back to the mid-nineteenth century in Chicago. Futures markets are, in effect, organized and standardized forward markets. An organized futures exchange standardizes the nonstandard forward contracts, establishing such features as contract size, delivery dates, and condition of the items that can be delivered. Only the price and number of contracts are left for futures traders to negotiate. Individuals can trade without personal contact with each other because of the centralized marketplace. Performance is guaranteed by a clearinghouse, relieving one party to the transaction from worry that the other party will fail to honor its commitment.

The futures markets serve a valuable economic purpose by allowing hedgers to shift price risk to speculators. The risk of price fluctuations is shifted from participants unwilling to assume such risk to those who are. Another economic function performed by futures markets is price discovery. Because the price of a futures contract reflects current expectations about values at some future date, transactors can establish current prices against later transactions.

CURRENT U.S. FUTURES MARKETS

To most people, futures trading traditionally has meant trading in commodities such as gold, wheat, and oil. However, money can be thought of simply as another commodity, and financial futures have become a particularly viable investment alternative for numerous investors. Therefore, futures contracts currently traded on U.S. futures exchanges can be divided into two broad categories:

1. Commodities—agricultural, metals, and energy-related
2. Financials—foreign currencies and debt and equity instruments

Each category can be further subdivided as shown in Exhibit 18-1. As we can see, the futures markets involve trading in a variety of both commodities and financials.

EXHIBIT 18-1 FUTURES CONTRACTS TRADED IN THE UNITED STATES, BY CATEGORY

The major commodities traded in the United States can be classified into the following categories (as shown in *The Wall Street Journal*):

I. **Commodities**	
Grains and oilseeds	Wheat, corn, oats, soybeans, soybean oils, soybean meal, flaxseed, rapeseed, rye, and canola
Livestock and meats	Cattle (both live and feeders), pork bellies, and hogs
Foods	Cocoa, coffee, orange juice, and sugar
Fibers	Cotton
Metals	Copper, gold, platinum, silver, and palladium
Oil	Gasoline, heating oil, crude oil, gas oil, propane
Wood	Lumber
II. **Financials**	
Interest rates	Treasury bills, Treasury notes, Treasury bonds, municipal bond index, 30-day federal funds, Eurodollar, 1-month Libor, Sterling, Long Gilt, Euromark, EuroSwiss, EuroLira, German Government Bond, Italian Government Bond, French Government Bond, Canadian Government Bond
Stock indexes	S&P 500 Index, S&P MidCap 400, NYSE Composite Index, Major Market Index, KR-CRB Index, KC Value Line Index, Russell 2000, CAC 40, Nikkei 225 Index, GSCI, FT-SE 100 Index, Toronto 35 Index
Foreign currencies	Japanese yen, German mark, Canadian dollar, British pound, Swiss franc, Australian dollar, and U.S. Dollar Index.

For each type of contract, such as corn or silver, different delivery dates are available. Each contract will specify the trading unit involved and, where applicable, the deliverable grade necessary to satisfy the contract. Investors can also purchase options on futures contracts. Appendix 18-A explains futures options.

One of the striking features of Exhibit 18-1 is the proliferation of foreign-based futures contracts on U.S. futures exchanges. This is true for interest rate futures and stock-index futures, and is good evidence of the move toward globalization that is occurring throughout the investing world.

FOREIGN FUTURES MARKETS

European futures exchanges are quite competitive. Most of these systems are now fully automated order-matching systems.

Japan, which banned financial futures until 1985, is now very active in developing futures exchanges. With regard to stock-index futures, the Nikkei 225 contract, the most active Japanese index futures contract, trades on the Osaka Securities Exchange.

FUTURES CONTRACTS

Futures Contract A commitment to buy or sell at a specified future settlement date a designated amount of a commodity or asset

A **futures contract** is a standardized, transferable agreement providing for the deferred delivery of either a specified grade and quantity of a designated commodity within a specified geographical area or of a financial instrument (or its cash value). The futures price at which this exchange will occur at contract maturity is determined today. The trading of futures contracts means only that commitments have been made by buyers and sellers; therefore, "buying" and "selling" do not have the same meaning in futures transactions as they do in stock and bond transactions. Although these commitments are binding because futures contracts are legal contracts, a buyer or seller can eliminate the commitment simply by taking an opposite position in the same commodity or financial instrument for the same futures month.

Futures contracts are not securities and are not regulated by the Securities and Exchange Commission. The Commodity Futures Trading Commission (CFTC), a federal regulatory agency, is responsible for regulating trading in all domestic futures markets. In practice, the National Futures Association, a self-regulating body, has assumed some of the duties previously performed by the CFTC. In addition, each futures exchange has a supervisory body to oversee its members.

THE STRUCTURE OF FUTURES MARKETS

FUTURES EXCHANGES

As noted, futures contracts are traded on designated futures exchanges, which are voluntary, nonprofit associations, typically unincorporated. There are several major U.S. exchanges.[2] The exchange provides an organized marketplace where established rules govern the conduct of the members. The exchange is financed by both membership dues and fees charged for services rendered.

All memberships must be owned by individuals, although they may be controlled by firms. The limited number of memberships, like stock exchange seats, can be traded at market-

[2] Major U.S. futures exchanges include the following: Chicago Board of Trade (CBT), Chicago Mercantile Exchange (CME), Commodity Exchange, New York (COMEX), Kansas City Board of Trade (KCBT), Mid-America Commodity Exchange (MCE), Coffee Sugar & Cocoa Exchange (CSCE), New York Cotton Exchange (CTN), New York Futures Exchange (NYFE), New York Mercantile Exchange (NYM), the International Petroleum Exchange (PE), the Philadelphia Board of Trade (PBT), and the Twin Cities Board of Trade (TCBT).

determined prices. Members can trade for their own accounts or as agents for others. For example, floor traders trade for their own accounts, whereas floor brokers (or commission brokers) often act as agents for others. Futures commission merchants (FCMs) act as agents for the general public, for which they receive commissions. Thus, a customer can establish an account with an FCM, who, in turn may work through a floor broker at the exchange.

THE CLEARINGHOUSE

The clearinghouse, a corporation separate from, but associated with, each exchange, plays an important role in every futures transaction. Since all futures trades are cleared through the clearinghouse each business day, exchange members must either be members of the clearinghouse or pay a member for this service. From a financial requirement basis, being a member of the clearinghouse is more demanding than being a member of the associated exchange.

Essentially, the clearinghouse for futures markets operates in the same way as the clearinghouse for options, which was discussed in some detail in Chapter 17. Buyers and sellers settle with the clearinghouse, not each other. Thus, the clearinghouse, and not another investor, is actually on the other side of every transaction and ensures that all payments are made as specified. It stands ready to fulfill a contract if either buyer or seller defaults, thereby helping to facilitate an orderly market in futures. The clearinghouse makes the futures market impersonal, which is the key to its success because any buyer or seller can always close out a position and be assured of payment. The first failure of a clearing member in modern times occurred in the 1980s, and the system worked perfectly in preventing any customer from losing money. Finally, as explained below, the clearinghouse allows participants to easily reverse a position before maturity because the clearinghouse keeps track of each participant's obligations.

THE MECHANICS OF TRADING

BASIC PROCEDURES

Because the futures contract is a commitment to buy or sell at a specified future settlement date, a contract is not really being sold or bought, as in the case of Treasury bills, stocks, or CDs, because no money is exchanged at the time the contract is negotiated. Instead, the seller and the buyer simply are agreeing to make and take delivery, respectively, at some future time for a price agreed upon today. As noted above, the terms *buy* and *sell* do not have the same meanings here. It is more accurate to think in terms of

Short Position An agreement to sell an asset at a specified future date at a specified price

Long Position An agreement to purchase an asset at a specified future date at a specified price

- A **short position** (seller), which commits a trader to deliver an item at contract maturity.
- A **long position** (buyer), which commits a trader to purchase an item at contract maturity.

Selling short in futures trading means only that a contract not previously purchased is sold. For every futures contract, someone sold it short and someone else holds it long. Like options, futures trading is a zero-sum game.

Whereas an options contract involves the right to make or take delivery, a futures contract involves an obligation to take or make delivery. However, futures contracts can be settled by delivery or by offset. Delivery, or settlement of the contract, occurs in months that are designated by the various exchanges for each of the items traded. Delivery occurs in less than 2 percent of all transactions.

Offset Liquidation of a futures position by an offsetting transaction

Offset is the typical method of settling a contract. Holders liquidate a position by arranging an offsetting transaction. This means that buyers sell their positions, and sellers buy in their positions sometime prior to delivery. Thus, to eliminate a futures market position, the investor simply does the reverse of what was done originally. As explained above, the clearinghouse makes this easy to accomplish. It is essential to remember that if a futures contract is not offset, it must be closed out by delivery.

Each exchange establishes price fluctuation limits on the various types of contracts. Typically, a minimum price change is specified. In the case of corn, for example, it is 0.25 cents per bushel, or $12.50 per contract. A daily price limit is in effect for all futures contracts except stock-index futures. For corn it is 10 cents per bushel ($500 per contract) above and below the previous day's settlement price.

With stocks, shortselling can be done only on an uptick, but futures have no such restriction. Stock positions, short or long, can literally be held forever. However, futures positions must be closed out within a specified time, either by offsetting the position or by making or taking delivery.

Unlike stocks, there are no specialists on futures exchanges. Each futures contract is traded in a specific "pit," in an auction market process in which every bid and offer competes without priority as to time or size. A system of "open outcry" is used, whereby any offer to buy or sell must be made to all traders in the pit.

Brokerage commissions on commodities contracts are paid on the basis of a completed contract (purchase and sale), rather than each purchase and sale, as in the case of stocks. As with options, no certificates exist for futures contracts.

The *open interest* indicates contracts that are not offset by opposite transactions or delivery. That is, it measures the number of unliquidated contracts at any point in time, on a cumulative basis.[3] The open interest increases when an investor goes long on a contract and is reduced when the contract is liquidated.

MARGIN

Futures Margin The earnest money deposit made by a transactor to ensure the completion of a contract

Recall that in the case of stock transactions the term margin refers to the down payment in a transaction in which money is borrowed from the broker to finance the total cost. **Futures margin,** on the other hand, is not a down payment because ownership of the underlying item is not being transferred at the time of the transaction.[4] Instead, it refers to the "good faith" (or earnest money) deposit made by both buyer and seller to ensure the completion of the contract. In effect, margin is a performance bond. In futures trading, unlike stock trading, margin is the norm.

Each clearinghouse sets its own minimum initial margin requirements (in dollars). Furthermore, brokerage houses can require a higher margin and typically do so. The margin required for futures contracts, which is small in relation to the value of the contract itself, represents the equity of the transactor (either buyer or seller). It is not unusual for the initial margin to be in the range of $1500 to $2500 per contract, representing some 2 to 10 percent of the value of the contract. Since the equity is small, the risk is magnified.

EXAMPLE 18-2

Assume the initial margin is equal to 5 percent of the total value and an investor holds one contract in an account. If the price of the contract changes by 5 percent because the price of the underlying commodity changes by 5 percent, this is equivalent to a 100 percent change in the investor's equity. This example shows why futures trading can be so risky!

[3] The open interest can be measured using either the open long positions or the open short positions, but not both.

[4] Because no credit is being extended, no interest expense is incurred on that part of the contract not covered by the margin as is the case when stocks are purchased on margin. With futures, customers often receive interest on margin money deposited. A customer with a large enough requirement (roughly, $15,000 and over) can use Treasury bills as part of the margin.

In addition to the initial margin requirement, each contract requires a maintenance margin or *variation margin,* below which the investor's equity cannot drop. If the market price of a futures contract moves adversely to the owner's position, the equity declines. Margin calls occur when the price goes against the investor, requiring the transactor to deposit additional cash or to close out the account. To understand precisely how this works, we must first understand how profits and losses from futures contracts are debited and credited daily to an investor's account.

Marked to the Market
The daily posting of all profits and losses on a contract to each account

All futures contracts are **marked to the market** daily, which means that all profits and losses on a contract are credited and debited to each investor's account every trading day.[5] Those contract holders with a profit can withdraw the gains, whereas those with a loss will receive a margin call when the equity falls below the specified variation margin. This process is referred to as daily resettlement, and the price used is the contract's settlement price.[6]

EXAMPLE 18-3

Table 18-1 illustrates how accounts are marked to the market daily and how a margin call can occur. Consider an investor who buys a stock-index futures contract for 75 and a second investor who sells (shorts) the same contract at the same price. Assume these contracts are on the NYSE Composite Index, where each point in the price is divided into 20 "ticks" worth \$25 each.[7] For example, a price advance from 75 to 76, or one point, represents an advance of 20 ticks worth \$25 each, or \$500. Each investor puts up an initial margin of \$3500.

Table 18-1 traces each investor's account as it is marked to the market daily.[8] At the end of day 1, the price of the contract has dropped to a settlement price of 74.5, a decrease of 10 ticks with a total value of \$250. This amount is credited to the seller's account because the seller is short and the price has dropped. Conversely, \$250 is debited to the buyer's account because the buyer is long, and the price moved adversely to this position. Table 18-1 shows that the current equity at the end of day 1 is \$3,250 for the buyer and \$3,750 for the seller.

Now assume that two weeks have passed, during which time each account has been marked to the market daily. The settlement price on this contract has reached 79.25. The aggregate change in market value for each investor is the difference between the current price and the initial price multiplied by \$500, the value of one point in price, which in this example is

$$79.25 - 75 = 4.25 \times \$500 = \$2{,}125$$

As shown in Table 18-1, this amount is currently credited to the buyer because the price moved in the direction the buyer expected. Conversely, this same amount is currently debited to the seller, who is now on the wrong side of the price movement. Therefore, starting with an initial equity of \$3,500, after two weeks the cumulative mark to the market is \$2,125. This results in a current equity of \$5,625 for the buyer and \$1,375 for the seller. The buyer has a withdrawable excess equity of \$2,125, because of the favorable price movement, whereas the seller has a margin call of \$2,125.[9]

[5] This is not true of forward contracts, where no funds are transferred until the maturity date.

[6] The settlement price does not always reflect the final trade of the day. The clearinghouse establishes the settlement price at the close of trading.

[7] The NYSE Composite Index Futures Contract is quoted in the same manner as the index itself. For trading purposes, however, the contract is quoted in units called "ticks," each worth 0.05 of one point.

[8] This example is similar to an illustration in *Introducing New York Stock Exchange Index Futures* (New York Futures Exchange), p. 8. The level of the index used here is for illustrative purposes only.

[9] If the investor's current equity drops below the maintenance level required (which in this case is \$1,500), he or she receives a margin call and must add enough money to restore the account to the initial margin level.

TABLE 18-1 AN EXAMPLE OF INVESTOR ACCOUNTS, USING STOCK-INDEX FUTURES, MARKED TO THE MARKET

	Buyer (Long)	Seller (Short)
Account after one day		
Original equity (initial margin)	$3,500	$3,500
Day 1 mark to the market	(250)	250
Current equity	$3,250	$3,750
Account after two weeks		
Original equity (initial margin)	$3,500	$3,500
Cumulative mark to the market	2,125	(2,125)
Current equity	$5,625	$1,375
Withdrawable excess equity	$2,125	
Margin call		$2,125

SOURCE: Based on *Introducing New York Stock Exchange Index Futures* (New York Futures Exchange), p. 8. Reprinted by permission of the New York Futures Exchange, Inc. Copyright ©, 1984.

INVESTMENTS INTUITION This example illustrates what is meant by the expression that futures trading, like options trading, is a zero-sum game. The aggregate gains and losses net to zero. The aggregate profits enjoyed by the winners must be equal to the aggregate losses suffered by the losers. This also means that the net exposure to changes in the commodity's price must be zero.

USING FUTURES CONTRACTS

Who uses futures, and for what purpose? Traditionally, participants in the futures market have been classified as either hedgers or speculators. Because both groups are important in understanding the role and functioning of futures markets, we will consider each in turn. The distinctions between these two groups apply to financial futures as well as to the more traditional commodity futures.

HEDGERS

Hedgers are parties at risk with a commodity or an asset, which means they are exposed to price changes. They buy or sell futures contracts in order to offset their risk. In other words, hedgers actually deal in the commodity or financial instrument specified in the futures contract.[10] By taking a position opposite to that of one already held, at a price set today, hedgers plan to reduce the risk of adverse price fluctuations—that is, to hedge the risk of unexpected price changes. In effect, this is a form of insurance.

In a sense, the real motivation for all futures trading is to reduce price risk. With futures, risk is reduced by having the gain (loss) in the futures position offset the loss (gain) on the cash position. A hedger is willing to forego some profit potential in exchange for having someone else assume part of the risk. Figure 18-1 illustrates the hedging process as it affects the return-risk distribution. Notice that the unhedged position not only has a greater chance of a larger loss, but also a greater chance of a larger gain. The hedged position has a smaller chance of a low return but also a smaller chance of a high return.

[10] The cash position may currently exist (a cash hedge) or may be expected to exist in the future (an anticipatory hedge).

FIGURE 18-1

Return distributions for hedged and unhedged positions.

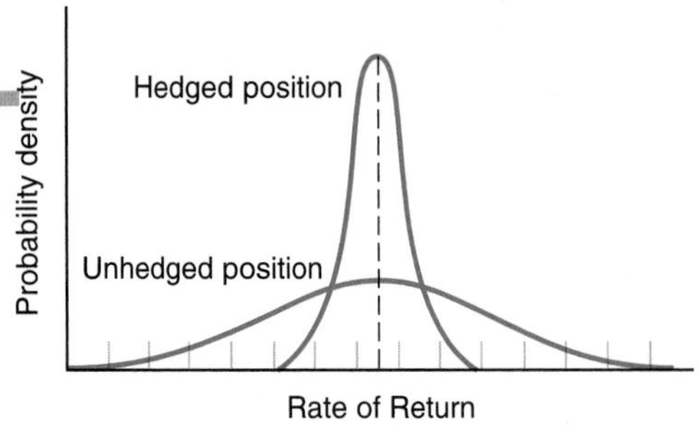

INVESTMENTS INTUITION The use of hedging techniques illustrates the tradeoff that underlies all investing decisions: Hedging reduces the risk of loss, but it also reduces the return possibilities relative to the unhedged position. Thus, hedging is used by people who are uncertain of future price movements and who are willing to protect themselves against adverse price movements at the expense of possible gains. There is no free lunch!

HOW TO HEDGE WITH FUTURES

The key to any hedge is that a futures position is taken opposite to the position in the cash market. That is, the nature of the cash market position determines the hedge in the futures market. A commodity or financial instrument held (in effect, in inventory) represents a long position because these items could be sold in the cash market. On the other hand, an investor who sells a futures position not owned has created a short position. Since investors can assume two basic positions with futures contracts, long and short, there are two basic hedge positions.

1. The short (sell) hedge. A cash market inventory holder must sell (short) the futures. Investors should think of short hedges as a means of protecting the value of their portfolios. Since they are holding securities, they are long on the cash position and need to protect themselves against a decline in prices. A **short hedge** reduces, or possibly eliminates, the risk taken in a long position.
2. The long (buy) hedge. An investor who currently holds no cash inventory (holds no commodities or financial instruments) is, in effect, short on the cash market; therefore, to hedge with futures requires a long position. Someone who is not currently in the cash market but who expects to be in the future and who wants to lock in current prices and yields until cash is available to make the investment can use a **long hedge** which reduces the risk of a short position.

Short Hedge A transaction involving the sale of futures (a short position) while holding the asset (a long position)

Long Hedge A transaction where the asset is currently not held but futures are purchased to lock in current prices

Hedging is not an automatic process. It requires more than simply taking a position. Hedgers must make timing decisions as to when to initiate and end the process. As conditions change, hedgers must adjust their hedge strategy.

One aspect of hedging that must be considered is "basis" risk. The **basis** for financial futures often is defined as the difference between the cash price and the futures price of the item being hedged:[11]

Basis The difference between the futures price of an item and the spot price of the item

Basis = Cash price − Futures price

The basis must be zero on the maturity date of the contract. In the interim, the basis fluctuates in an unpredictable manner and is not constant during a hedge period. Basis risk,

[11] The typical definition for basis is the cash price minus the futures price. For financial futures, the definition is often reversed.

therefore, is the risk hedgers face as a result of unexpected changes in basis. Although changes in the basis will affect the hedge position during its life, a hedge will reduce risk as long as the variability in the basis is less than the variability in the price of the asset being hedged. At maturity, the futures price and the cash price must be equal, resulting in a zero basis. (Transaction costs can cause discrepancies.)

The significance of basis risk to investors is that risk cannot be entirely eliminated. Hedging a cash position will involve basis risk.

SPECULATORS

In contrast to hedgers, speculators buy or sell futures contracts in an attempt to earn a return. They are willing to assume the risk of price fluctuations, hoping to profit from them. Unlike hedgers, speculators typically do not transact in the physical commodity or financial instrument underlying the futures contract. In other words, they have no prior market position. Some speculators are professionals who do this for a living; others are amateurs, ranging from the very sophisticated to the novice. Although most speculators are not actually present at the futures markets, floor traders (or locals) trade for their own accounts as well as others and often take very short-term (minutes or hours) positions in an attempt to exploit any short-lived market anomalies.

Speculators are essential to the proper functioning of the futures market, absorbing the excess demand or supply generated by hedgers and assuming the risk of price fluctuations that hedgers wish to avoid. Speculators contribute to the liquidity of the market and reduce the variability in prices over time.

Why speculate in futures markets? After all, one could speculate in the underlying instruments. For example, an investor who believed interest rates were going to decline could buy Treasury bonds directly and avoid the Treasury bond futures market. The potential advantages of speculating in futures markets include:

1. Leverage. The magnification of gains (and losses) can easily be 10 to 1.
2. Ease of transacting. An investor who thinks interest rates will rise will have difficulty selling bonds short, but it is very easy to take a short position in a Treasury bond futures contract.
3. Transaction costs. These are often significantly smaller in futures markets.

By all accounts, an investor's likelihood of success when speculating in futures is not very good. The small investor is up against stiff odds when it comes to *speculating* with futures contracts. Futures should be used for hedging purposes.

FINANCIAL FUTURES

Financial Futures Futures contracts on financial assets

Financial futures are futures contracts on equity indexes, fixed-income securities, and currencies. They give investors greater opportunity to fine-tune the risk-return characteristics of their portfolios. In recent years, this flexibility has become increasingly important as interest rates have become much more volatile and as investors have sought new techniques to reduce the risk of equity positions. The drastic changes that have occurred in the financial markets in the last 15 to 20 years could be said to have generated a genuine need for new financial instruments that allow market participants to deal with these changes.

The procedures for trading financial futures are the same as those for any other commodity, with few exceptions. At maturity, stock-index futures settle in cash because it would be impossible or impractical to deliver all the stocks in a particular index.[12] Unlike traditional futures contracts, stock-index futures typically have no daily price limits (although they can be imposed).

We will divide the subsequent discussion of financial futures into the two major categories of contracts, interest rate futures and stock-index futures. Hedging and speculative activities within each category are discussed separately.

USING THE INTERNET The Chicago Mercantile Exchange has an extensive website at www.cme.com. Included are price quotes, on-line courses, on-line simulated trading, and other educational resources. The Chicago Board of Trade has similar information at www.cbot.com. At www.futuresmag.com, investors can find daily technical information on the markets as well as links to a large number of sites involving futures. Waldemar's List, at www.netservers.comwaldemar/wl.html, is a comprehensive guide to links to numerous futures-related websites, covering a very wide range of activities.

INTEREST RATE FUTURES

Bond prices are highly volatile, and investors are exposed to adverse price movements. Financial futures, in effect, allow bondholders and others who are affected by volatile interest rates to transfer the risk. One of the primary reasons for the growth in financial futures is that portfolio managers and investors are trying to protect themselves against adverse movements in interest rates. An investor concerned with protecting the value of fixed-income securities must consider the possible impact of interest rates on the value of these securities.

Today's investors have the opportunity to consider several different interest rate futures contracts that are traded on various exchanges.[13] The Chicago Mercantile Exchange trades contracts on Treasury bills and the one-month LIBOR rate as well as Eurodollars. The Chicago Board of Trade (CBT) specializes in longer-maturity instruments, including Treasury notes (of various maturities, such as two-year and five-year) and Treasury bonds (of different contract sizes).

Exhibit 18-2 describes some futures contracts (not an exhaustive list) on fixed-income securities. Contracts are available on various maturities of U.S. Treasury notes in trading units of $100,000 and $200,000, on Treasury bonds in units of both $50,000 and $100,000, and

EXHIBIT 18-2 CHARACTERISTICS OF INTEREST RATE FUTURES CONTRACTS

Contract	Where Traded[a]	Contract Size or Trading Unit	Minimum Fluctuations
Treasury bonds	CBT	$100,000 par value 8% coupon[b]	1/32 or $31.25
10-Year Treasury notes	CBT	$100,000 par value	1/32 or $31.25
Treasury bills	CME	$1 million face value	1 basis point or $25
5-Year & 2-Year Treasury notes	CBT	$100,000 & $200,000 par value	1/32 or $31.25

[a]CBT = Chicago Board of Trade; CME = Chicago Mercantile Exchange.
[b]Bonds with other coupons are usable with price adjustments.

[12] Gains and losses on the last day of trading are credited and debited to the long and short positions in the same way—marked to the market—as was done for every other trading day of the contract. Therefore, not only is there no physical delivery of securities, but also the buyer does not pay the full value of the contract at settlement.

[13] The Chicago Board of Trade launched financial futures trading in 1975 by opening trading in Government National Mortgage Association (GNMA or Ginnie Mae) bonds. The concept accelerated in 1976, when the International Monetary Market started trading in Treasury bills. Treasury bond futures appeared in 1977.

EXHIBIT 18-3 HYPOTHETICAL QUOTES FOR ONE DAY FOR THE VARIOUS MATURITIES OF THE TREASURY BOND FUTURES CONTRACTS

	Open	High	Low	Settle	Change	Yield Settle Change	Open Interest
December 19X0	74–20	74–30	74–20	74–25	+8	11.816–0.042	100,845
March 19X1	74–06	74–13	74–03	74–07	+8	11.911–0.041	24,566
June	73–28	73–31	73–21	73–25	+8	11.985–0.042	16,548
September	73–13	73–16	73–09	73–13	+8	12.049–0.042	12,563
December	72–32	73–06	72–30	73–03	+8	12.103–0.043	8,576
March 19X2	72–22	72–30	72–23	72–27	+8	12.146–0.042	7,283
June	72–15	72–23	72–16	72–20	+8	12.184–0.042	4,801
September	72–12	72–17	72–10	72–14	+8	12.217–0.042	702

on Treasury bills in trading units of $1 million. The contracts for U.S. Treasury bonds are by far the most important.

Reading Quotes As an illustration of the quotation (reporting) system for interest rate futures, Exhibit 18-3 shows some hypothetical quotations for the Treasury bond contract on the CBT. These hypothetical quotations are intended only to illustrate relationships that typically exist. The value of the contract is $100,000, and the price quotations are percentages of par, with 32nds shown. Since one point is $1,000, 1⁄32 is worth $31.25. Thus, a price of 75 16⁄32 is equal to $75,500. Exhibit 18-3 indicates that there were eight different contract months for the Treasury bond contract, covering a period of approximately two years—since the first contract, December, could have been purchased prior to that month.

In this illustration, the December futures contract opened at 74 20⁄32 of par, traded in a range of 74 30⁄32 to 74 20⁄32, and settled at 74 25⁄32, which translates into a yield of 11.816.[14] Notice that the change in price, +8⁄32, is opposite the change in yields, −0.042. In both cases, changes are measured from the previous day's respective variables.

Hedging with Interest Rate Futures We now consider an example of using interest rate futures to hedge an investment position. Obviously, other examples could be constructed involving various transactors, such as a corporation or financial institution; various financial instruments, such as a portfolio of GNMAs or Treasury bills; and various scenarios under which the particular hedger is operating. Our objective is simply to illustrate the basic concepts. Here we concentrate on the short hedge since it is by far the more common; we discuss the concept of the long hedge below.

Short Hedge Suppose an investor has a bond portfolio and wishes to protect the value of his or her position.[15] This type of hedge is sometimes referred to as *inventory hedge.*

EXAMPLE 18-4

A pension fund manager holds $1 million of 11.75 percent Treasury bonds due 2005–10. The manager plans to sell the bonds three months from now (June 1) but wishes to protect the value of the bonds against a rise in interest rates. Since assets are owned (a long position), a short hedge is used.

[14] Futures prices on Treasury bonds are quoted with reference to an 8 percent, 20-year bond. Settlement prices are translated into a settlement yield to provide a reference point for interest rates.

[15] This example is taken from *U.S. Treasury Bond Futures* (Chicago: Chicago Board of Trade), p. 10.

EXHIBIT 18-4 ILLUSTRATION OF HEDGES USING INTEREST RATE FUTURES: A SHORT HEDGE

Cash Market	Futures Market
Short Hedge	
June 1 Holds $1 million 11¾% Treasury bonds due 2005–10. Current market price: 117–23 (yields 9.89%)	June 1 Sells 10 T-bond futures contracts at a price of 83–06
September 1 Sells $1 million of 11¾ bonds at 104–12 (yields 11.25%)	September 1 Buys 10 T-bond futures contracts at 74–09
Loss: $133,437.50	Gain: $89,062.50

To protect the position, the manager hedges by going short (selling) in the futures market. As illustrated in Exhibit 18-4, the manager sells 10 September contracts (since each contract is worth $100,000) at a current price of 83–06. In this example, interest rates rise, producing a loss on the cash side (i.e., in the prices of the bonds held in the cash market) and a gain on the futures side (i.e., the manager can cover the short position at a lower price, which produces a profit). The futures position thus offsets 67 percent of the cash market loss.[16]

The manager in this example could offset only 67 percent of the cash market loss because the T-bond contract is based on 8 percent coupon bonds, whereas the manager was holding 11.75 percent bonds. The dollar value of higher coupon bonds changes by a larger dollar amount than the dollar value of lower coupon bonds for any change in yields. One way to overcome this difference is to execute a "weighted" short hedge, adjusting the number of futures contracts used to hedge the cash position. With the example data in Exhibit 18-4, selling 14 September contracts would offset 93.4 percent of the cash market loss.[17]

Other Hedges An alternative hedge is the *anticipatory hedge,* whereby an investor purchases a futures contract as an alternative to buying the underlying security. At some designated time in the future, the investor will purchase the security and sell the futures contract. This results in a net price for the security position at the future point in time which is equal to the price paid for the security minus the gain or loss on the futures position.

Consider an investor who would like to purchase an interest rate asset now but will not have the cash for three months. If rates drop, the asset will cost more at that point in time. By purchasing a futures contract on the asset now, as a hedge, the investor can lock in the interest rate implied by the interest rate futures contract. This may be a good substitute for not being able to lock in the current interest rate because of the lack of funds now to do so. At the conclusion of this transaction, the investor will pay a *net* price that reflects the ending cash price minus the gain on the futures contract. In effect, the gain on the futures increases the rate of return earned on the interest rate asset.

[16] The $89,062.50 gain is calculated as follows: The gain per contract is $83\frac{6}{32} - 74\frac{9}{32} = 8\frac{29}{32}$, or 8.90625 percent of par value. Multiplying the gain of 8.90625 percent by par value = $8906.25 per contract, and for 10 contracts the total gain is $89,062.50.

[17] The market value of the 14 futures contracts changes from $1,164,625 to $1,039,937.50. The cash market values change from $1,177,187.50 to $1,043,750. Different Treasury bonds are related to the nominal 8 percent coupon, 20-year-maturity bond used in the contract by means of a set of conversion factors that represent the relative values of the various deliverable bonds. The conversion factor for the 11.75 percent coupon bond used in this example, rounded off, is 1.40.

Speculating with Interest Rate Futures Investors may wish to speculate with interest rate futures as well as to hedge with them. To do so, investors make assessments of likely movements in interest rates and assume a futures position that corresponds with this assessment. If the investor anticipates a rise in interest rates, he or she will sell one (or more) interest rate futures, because a rise in interest rates will drive down the prices of bonds and therefore the price of the futures contract. The investor sells a contract with the expectation of buying it back later at a lower price. Of course, a decline in interest rates will result in a loss for this investor, since the price will rise.

EXAMPLE 18-5

Assume that in November a speculator thinks interest rates will rise over the next two weeks and wishes to profit from this expectation. The investor can sell one December Treasury bond futures contract at a price of, say, 90–20. Two weeks later the price of this contract has declined to 88–24 because of rising interest rates. This investor would have a gain of 1 28/32, or $1875 (each 1/32 is worth $31.25), and could close out this position by buying an identical contract.

The usefulness of interest rate futures for pursuing such a strategy is significant. A speculator who wishes to assume a short position in bonds cannot do so readily in the cash market (either financially or mechanically). Interest rate futures provide the means to short bonds easily.

In a similar manner, investors can speculate on a decline in interest rates by purchasing interest rate futures. If the decline materializes, bond prices and the value of the futures contract will rise. Because of the leverage involved, the gains can be large; however, the losses can also be large if interest rates move in the wrong direction.

STOCK-INDEX FUTURES

Stock-index futures trading was initiated in 1982 with several contracts quickly being created. Although stock-index futures are unavailable on individual stocks as in the case of options, investors can trade futures contracts on major market indexes such as the NYSE Composite Index and the S&P 500 Index. The contract size for each of these indexes is $500 times the index level. Contracts are also available on the Major Market Index, consisting of 20 blue-chip stocks designed to track the Dow-Jones Industrial Average, and on the Nikkei 225 Stock Average (Japanese market). Other indexes also are available.[18] The S&P 500 contract is the most popular stock-index futures contract.

Delivery is not permitted in stock-index futures because of its impracticality. Instead, each remaining contract is settled by cash on the settlement day by taking an offsetting position using the price of the underlying index.[19]

Stock-index futures offer investors the opportunity to act on their investment opinions concerning the future direction of the market. They need not select individual stocks, and it is easy to short the market. Furthermore, investors who are concerned about unfavorable short-term market prospects but remain bullish for the longer run can protect themselves in the interim by selling stock-index futures.

Hedging With Stock-Index Futures Common stock investors hedge with financial futures for the same reasons that fixed-income investors use them. Investors, whether individuals or institutions, may hold a substantial stock portfolio that is subject to the risk of the

[18] There is also a futures contract on the S&P Midcap 400 Index. It has a value of $500 times the index.

[19] The final settlement price is set equal to the closing index on the maturity date.

FIGURE 18-2

The value of a well-diversified stock portfolio versus the price of the S&P 500 Index futures.

SOURCE: Charles S. Morris, "Managing Stock Market Risk with Stock Index Futures," *Economic Review* (June 1989): 9.

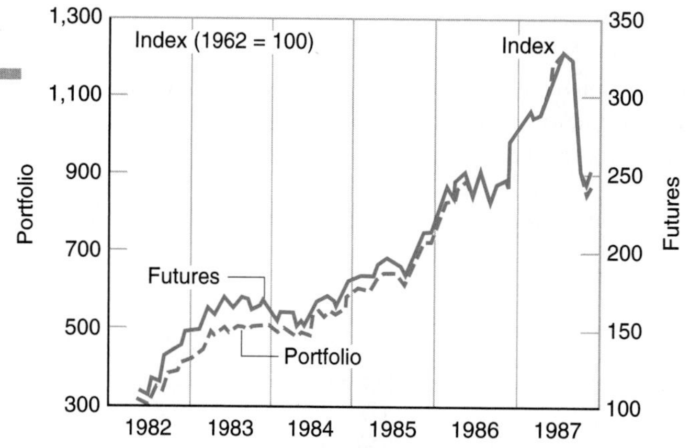

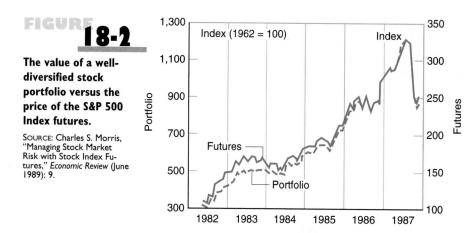

overall market, that is, systematic risk. A futures contract enables the investor to transfer part or all of the risk to those willing to assume it. Stock-index futures have opened up new, and relatively inexpensive, opportunities for investors to manage market risk through hedging.

Chapter 7 pointed out the two types of risk inherent in common stocks: systematic risk and nonsystematic risk. Diversification will eliminate most or all of the nonsystematic risk in a portfolio, but not the systematic risk. Although an investor could adjust the beta of the portfolio in anticipation of a market rise or fall, this is not an ideal solution because of the changes in portfolio composition that might be required.

Investors can use financial futures on stock market indexes to hedge against an overall market decline. That is, investors can hedge against systematic or market risk by selling the appropriate number of contracts against a stock portfolio. In effect, stock-index futures contracts give an investor the opportunity to protect his or her portfolio against market fluctuations.

To hedge market risk, investors must be able to take a position in the hedging asset (in this case, stock-index futures), such that profits or losses on the hedging asset offset changes in the value of the stock portfolio. Stock-index futures permit this action because changes in the futures prices themselves generally are highly correlated with changes in the value of the stock portfolios that are caused by marketwide events. The more diversified the portfolio, and therefore the lower the nonsystematic risk, the greater the correlation between the futures contract and the stock positions.

Figure 18-2 shows the price of the S&P 500 Index futures plotted against the value of a portfolio that is 99 percent diversified. That is, market risk accounts for 99 percent of its total risk.[20] The two track each other very closely, which demonstrates that stock-index futures can be very effective in hedging the market risk of a portfolio.

Short Hedges Since so much common stock is held by investors, the short hedge is the natural type of contract for most investors. Investors who hold stock portfolios hedge market risk by selling stock-index futures, which means they assume a short position.

A short hedge can be implemented by selling a forward maturity of the contract. The purpose of this hedge is to offset (in total or in part) any losses on the stock portfolio with gains on the futures position. To implement this defensive strategy, an investor would sell one or more index futures contracts. Ideally, the value of these contracts would equal the value of the stock portfolio. If the market falls, leading to a loss on the cash (the stock portfolio) position, stock-index futures prices will also fall, leading to a profit for sellers of futures.

[20] This example is taken from Charles S. Morris, "Managing Stock Market Risk with Stock Index Futures," *Economic Review* (June 1989): 3–16.

FIGURE 18-3

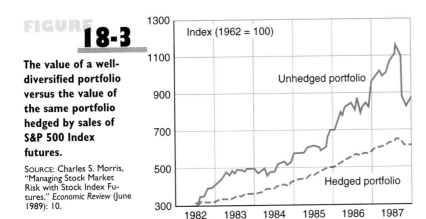

The value of a well-diversified portfolio versus the value of the same portfolio hedged by sales of S&P 500 Index futures.

SOURCE: Charles S. Morris, "Managing Stock Market Risk with Stock Index Futures," *Economic Review* (June 1989): 10.

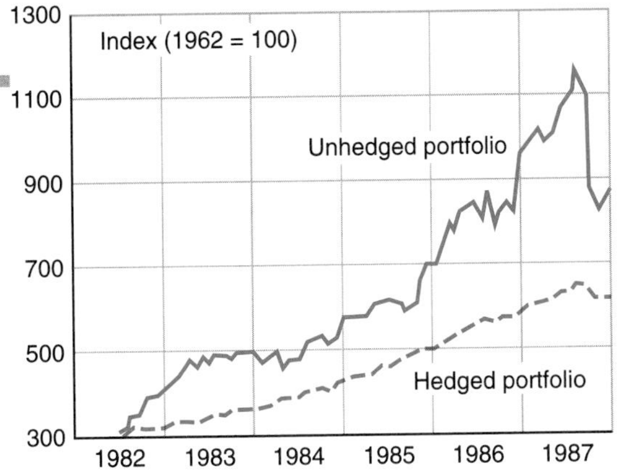

The reduction in price volatility that can be accomplished by hedging is shown in Figure 18-3, which compares the performance of a well-diversified portfolio (the unhedged portfolio) with the same portfolio hedged by sales of the S&P 500 Index futures. Clearly, there is much less variability in the value of the hedged portfolio as compared to the value of the unhedged portfolio. In fact, the volatility of the returns is 91 percent lower.[21] Notice in particular what happened in the great market crash of October 1987. The value of the unhedged portfolio fell some 19 percent, whereas the value of the hedged portfolio fell only 6 percent.

Table 18-2 (top) illustrates the concept of a short hedge using the Standard & Poor's Index when it was at 173. Assume that an investor has a portfolio of stocks valued at $90,000 that he or she would like to protect against an anticipated market decline. By selling one S&P stock index future at 173, the investor has a short position of $86,500, because the value of the contract is $500 times the index quote. As the table illustrates, a decline in the stock market of 10 percent results in a loss on the stock portfolio of $9,000 and a gain on the futures position of $8,650 (ignoring commissions). Thus, the investor almost makes up on the short side what is lost on the long side.

TABLE 18-2 EXAMPLES OF SHORT AND LONG HEDGES USING STOCK-INDEX FUTURES

	Current Position	Position after a 10% Market Drop	Change in Position
	Short Hedge		
(Long position) dollar value of portfolio	$250,000	$225,000	$(25,000)
(Short position) sell one S&P 500 futures[a] contract at 473	236,500	212,850	23,650
Gain or loss from hedging			(1,350)

	Current Position	Position or Cost Following a 10% Market Rise	Change in Position or Cost of Position
	Long Hedge		
Buy one S&P 500 futures contract at 473	$236,500	$260,150	$23,650
Amount of money to be invested in stocks (cost of stock position)	225,000	247,500	(22,500)
Gain or loss from hedging			1150

[a]Value of the futures contracts is $500 × index.

[21] See ibid.

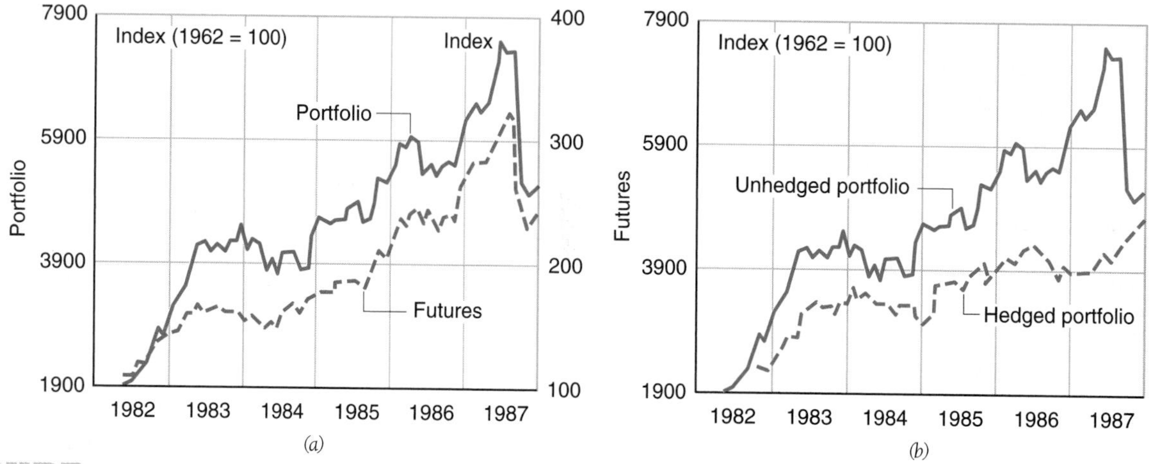

FIGURE 18-4

(a) The value of a relatively undiversified stock portfolio and the price of the S&P 500 index futures contract. (b) The value of the unhedged portfolio and the same portfolio hedged by sales of S&P 500 futures contracts.

SOURCE: Charles S. Morris, "Managing Stock Market Risk with Stock Index Futures," *Economic Review* (June 1989): 12, 13.

Long Hedges The long hedger, while awaiting funds to invest, generally wishes to reduce the risk of having to pay more for an equity position when prices rise. Potential users of a long hedge include the following:

1. Institutions with a regular cash flow who use long hedges to improve the timing of their positions.
2. Institutions switching large positions who wish to hedge during the time it takes to complete the process. (This could also be a short hedge.)

Assume an investor with $75,000 to invest believes that the stock market will advance but has been unable to select the stocks he or she wishes to hold. By purchasing one S&P 500 Index future, the investor will gain if the market advances. As shown in Table 18-2, a 10 percent market advance will increase the value of the futures contract $8,650. Even if the investor has to pay 10 percent more (on average) for stocks purchased after the advance, he or she still gains because the net hedge result is positive.

Limitations of Hedging with Stock-Index Futures Although hedging with stock-index futures can reduce an investor's risk, typically risk cannot be eliminated completely. As with interest rate futures, basis risk is present with stock-index futures. It represents the difference between the price of the stock-index futures contract and the value of the underlying stock index. A daily examination of the "Futures Prices" page of *The Wall Street Journal* will show that each of the indexes quoted under the respective futures contracts differs from the closing price of the contracts.[22]

Basis risk as it applies to common stock portfolios can be defined as the risk that remains after a stock portfolio has been hedged.[23] Note here that stock-index futures hedge only systematic (market) risk. That is, when we consider a stock portfolio hedged with stock-index futures, the basis risk is attributable to unsystematic (nonmarket or firm-specific) risk.

Figure 18-4A illustrates the effects of basis risk by comparing the value of a relatively undiversified portfolio with the price of the S&P 500 futures contract. In contrast to Figure 18-2, where the portfolio was 99 percent diversified, this portfolio is only 66 percent diver-

[22] Futures prices are generally more volatile than the underlying indexes and therefore diverge from them. The index futures tend to lead the actual market indexes. If investors are bullish, the futures are priced at a premium, with greater maturities usually associated with greater premiums. If investors are bearish, the futures are normally priced at a discount, which may widen as maturity increases.

[23] This discussion is based heavily on Morris, "Managing Stock Market Risk with Stock Index Futures," pp. 11–13.

sified. Although the two series are related, the relationship is in no way as close as that illustrated in Figure 18-2. Therefore, stock-index futures will be less effective at hedging the total risk of the portfolio, as shown in Figure 18-4B. In this situation, the variance of returns on the hedged portfolio is only 27 percent lower than the unhedged position. Note that in the crash of October 1987 both portfolios fell sharply, demonstrating that the hedge was relatively ineffective. (It did better than the unhedged position but not by much.)

From this analysis we can conclude that stock-index futures generally do not provide a good hedge for relatively undiversified portfolios.

Program Trading The use of computer-generated buy and sell orders for entire portfolios based on arbitrage opportunities

Index Arbitrage Exploitation of price differences between stock-index futures and the index of stocks underlying the futures contract

Index Arbitrage and Program Trading A force of considerable magnitude hit Wall Street in the 1980s. It is called **program trading,** and it has captured much attention and generated considerable controversy. It leads to headlines attributing market plunges at least in part to program trading, as happened on October 19, 1987, when the Dow Jones Industrial Average fell over 500 points. Because program trading typically involves positions in both stocks and stock-index futures contracts, we consider the topic within the general discussion of hedging.

The terms *program trading* and **index arbitrage** often are used together. In general terms, index arbitrage refers to attempts to exploit the differences between the prices of the stock-index futures and the prices of the index of stocks underlying the futures contract. For example, if the S&P 500 futures price is too high relative to the S&P 500 Index, investors could short the futures contract and buy the stocks in the index. In theory, arbitrageurs should be able to build a hedged portfolio that earns arbitrage profits equaling the difference between the two positions. If the price of the S&P 500 futures is deemed too low, investors could purchase the futures and short the stocks, again exploiting the differences between the two prices.

If investors are to be able to take advantage of discrepancies between the futures price and the underlying stock-index price, they must be able to act quickly. Program trading involves the use of computer-generated orders to coordinate buy and sell orders for entire portfolios based on arbitrage opportunities. The arbitrage occurs between portfolios of common stocks, on the one hand, and index futures and options, on the other. Large institutional investors seek to exploit differences between the two sides. Specifically, when stock-index futures prices rise substantially above the current value of the stock-index itself (e.g., the S&P 500), they sell the futures and buy the underlying stocks, typically in "baskets" of several million dollars. Because the futures price and the stock-index value must be equal when the futures contract expires, these investors are seeking to "capture the premium" between the two, thereby earning an arbitrage profit. That is, they seek high risk-free returns by arbitraging the difference between the cash value of the underlying securities and the prices of the futures contracts on these securities. In effect, they have a hedged position and should profit regardless of what happens to stock prices.

Normally, program traders and other speculators "unwind" their positions during the last trading hour of the day the futures expire. At this time, the futures premium goes to zero, because, as noted, the futures price at expiration must equal the stock-index value.

The headlines about program trading often reflect the results of rapid selling by the program traders. For whatever reason, traders decide to sell the futures. As the price falls, stock prices also fall. When the futures price drops below the price of the stock index, tremendous selling orders can be unleashed. These volume sell orders in stocks drive the futures prices even lower.

Speculating With Stock-Index Futures In addition to the previous hedging strategies (and others not described), investors can speculate with stock-index futures if they wish to profit from stock market volatility by judging and acting on the likely market trends. Stock-index futures are effective instruments for speculating on movements in the stock market because

1. Minimal costs are involved in establishing a futures position.
2. Stock-index futures mirror the market, offering just as much risk.

We can refer to one group of speculators as "active traders." These individuals are willing to risk their capital on price changes they expect to occur in the futures contracts. Such individuals are often sophisticated investors who are seeking the opportunity for large gains and who understand the risk they are assuming.

The strategies of active traders basically include long and short positions. Traders who expect the market to rise buy index futures. Because of the high leverage, the profit opportunities are great; however, the loss opportunities are equally great. The same is true for traders expecting a market decline who assume a short position by selling a stock-index futures contract. Selling a contract is a convenient way to go short the entire market. It can be done at any time. (No wait for an uptick is required, as with stock short sales.)

Another form of speculation involves spreaders, who establish both long and short positions at the same time. Their objective is to profit from changes in price relationships between two futures contracts. Spreads include the following:

1. The intramarket spread, also known as a calendar or time spread. This spread involves contracts for two different settlement months, such as buying a March contract and selling a June contract.
2. The intermarket spread, also known as a quality spread. This spread involves two different markets, such as buying a NYSE contract and selling a S&P contract (both for the same month).

Spreaders are interested in relative price as opposed to absolute price changes. If two different contracts appear to be out of line, the spreader hopes to profit by buying one contract and selling the other and waiting for the price difference to adjust. This adjustment may require the spread between the two contracts to widen in some cases and narrow in others.

SUMMARY

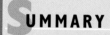

- Futures markets play an important role in risk management.
- Spot markets are markets for immediate delivery. Forward markets are markets for deferred delivery.
- An organized futures exchange standardizes the nonstandard forward contracts, with only the price and number of contracts left for futures traders to negotiate.
- A futures contract designates a specific amount of a particular item to be delivered at a specified date in the future at a currently determined market price.
- Buyers assume long positions and sellers assume short positions. A short position indicates only that a contract not previously purchased is sold.
- Most contracts are settled by offset, whereby a position is liquidated by an offsetting transaction. The clearinghouse is on the other side of every transaction and ensures that all payments are made as specified.
- Contracts are traded on designated futures exchanges, which set minimum price changes and may establish daily price limits.

- Futures positions must be closed out within a specified time. There are no certificates and no specialists to handle the trading. Each futures contract is traded in an auction market process by a system of "open outcry."
- Margin, the norm in futures trading, is the "good faith" deposit made to ensure completion of the contract.
- All futures contracts are marked to the market daily; that is, all profits and losses are credited and debited to each investor's account daily.
- Hedgers buy or sell futures contracts to offset the risk in some other position.
- Speculators buy or sell futures contracts in an attempt to earn a return and are valuable to the proper functioning of the market.
- Interest rate futures, one of the two principal types of financial futures, allow investors to hedge against, and speculate on, interest rate movements. Numerous contracts are available on both domestic instruments and foreign instruments.
- Investors can, among other transactions, execute short hedges to protect their long positions in bonds.
- Stock-index futures are available on the NYSE Composite Index, the S&P 500 Index, and numerous other indexes, both domestic and foreign.
- Investors can use stock-index futures to hedge the systematic risk of common stocks, that is, broad market movements.
- Short hedges protect a stock position against a market decline, and long hedges protect against having to pay more for an equity position because prices rise before the investment can be made.
- Index arbitrage refers to attempts to exploit the differences between the prices of the stock-index futures and the prices of the index of stocks underlying the futures contract.

KEY WORDS

Basis
Financial futures
Forward contract
Futures contract
Futures margin
Index arbitrage
Long hedge
Long position
Marked to the market
Offset
Program trading
Short hedge
Short position

QUESTIONS

18-1. Carefully describe a futures contract.

18-2. Explain how futures contracts are valued daily and how most contracts are settled.

18-3. Describe the role of the clearinghouses in futures trading.

18-4. What determines if an investor receives a margin call?

18-5. Describe the differences between trading in stocks and trading in futures contracts.

18-6. How do financial futures differ from other futures contracts?

18-7. Explain the differences between a hedger and a speculator.

18-8. What is meant by basis? When is the basis positive?

18-9. Given a futures contract on Treasury bonds, determine the dollar price of a contract quoted at 80–5, 90–24, and 69–2.

18-10. When might a portfolio manager with a bond position use a short hedge involving interest rate futures?

18-11. Is it possible to construct a perfect hedge? Why or why not?

18-12. What is the difference between a short hedge and a weighted short hedge using interest rate futures?

18-13. Why would an investor have preferences among the different stock-index futures?

18-14. Which type of risk does stock-index futures allow investors to hedge? Why would this be desirable?

18-15. Explain how a pension fund might use a long hedge with stock-index futures.

18-16. When would an investor likely do the following?

a. Buy a call on a stock index.
b. Buy a put on interest rate futures.

18-17. What is program trading? How does it work?

The following question was asked on the 1993 CFA Level II examination:

CFA

18-18. Michelle Industries issued a Swiss Franc-denominated five-year discount note for SFr 200 million. The proceeds were converted to U.S. dollars to purchase capital equipment in the U.S. The company wants to hedge this currency exposure and is considering the following alternatives:

(i) At-the-money Swiss Franc call options
(ii) Swiss Franc forwards
(iii) Swiss Franc futures

Contrast the essential characteristics of *each* of these *three* derivative instruments. **Evaluate** the suitability of *each* in relation to Michelle's hedging objective, including *both* advantages and disadvantages.

The following questions were asked on the 1993 CFA Level I examination:

CFA

18-19. Futures contracts *differ* from forward contracts in the following ways:

I. Futures contracts are standardized.
II. For Futures, performance of each party is guaranteed by a clearinghouse.
III. Futures contracts require a daily settling of any gains or losses.

a. I and II only
b. I and III only
c. II and III only
d. I, II, and III

CFA

18-20. On the maturity date, stock index futures contracts require delivery of:

a. common stock.
b. common stock plus accrued dividends.
c. Treasury bills.
d. cash.

The following question was asked on the 1990 CFA Level I examination:

CFA

18-21. To preserve capital in a declining stock market, a portfolio manager should:

a. buy stock index futures.
b. sell stock index futures.
c. buy call options.
d. sell put options.

The following questions were asked on the 1996 CFA Level I sample examinations:

CFA

18-22. An investor in the common stock of companies in a foreign country may wish to hedge against the ______ of the investor's home currency and can do so by ______ the foreign currency in the forward market.

a. depreciation; selling
b. appreciation; purchasing
c. appreciation; selling
d. depreciation; purchasing

CFA

18-23. In forward stock markets such as London and Paris:

a. investors buy and sell contracts for future delivery of shares, but the shares themselves do not change ownership.
b. settlement of transactions takes place infrequently, such as one day each month.
c. even after a transaction has been consummated, the price is not determined until a specified date in the future.
d. change of ownership of a stock takes place on the day of the transaction, although money is not exchanged until five business days later.

CFA

18-24. Which of the following best describes a stock-index arbitrage strategy?

a. taking a long or short position in the cash (spot) market represented by a market basket of stocks
b. trading in stock-index futures contracts and in individual stocks when a divergence occurs between the cash (stock) price of the market and the futures price
c. trading call and put stock options in each stock represented in a market index
d. selling stock-index futures contracts when the stock market falls

PROBLEMS

18-1. Assume that an investor buys one March NYSE Composite Index futures contract on February 1 at 67.5. The position is closed out after five days. The prices on the four days after purchase were 67.8, 68.1, 68, and 68.5. The initial margin is $3500.

a. Calculate the current equity on each of the next four days.
b. Calculate the excess equity for these four days.
c. Calculate the final gain or loss for the week.
d. Recalculate (a), (b), and (c) assuming that the investor had been short over this same period.

18-2. Given the information in Problem 18-1, assume that the investor holds until the contract expires. Ignore the four days after purchase and assume that on the next to last day of trading in March the investor was long and the final settlement price on that date was 70.5. Calculate the cumulative profit.

18-3. Calculate the dollar gain or loss on Treasury bond futures contracts ($100,000) per contract for the following transactions. In each case the position is held six months before closing it out.

a. Sell 10 T-bond contracts at a price of 82–80 and buy 10 at 76–12.
b. Sell 10 T-bond contracts at a price of 80–14 and buy 10 at 77.
c. Buy 15 T-bond contracts at 62–10 and sell 15 at 64–24.
d. Sell one T-bond contract at 70–14 and buy one at 78–08.

18-4. Assume a portfolio manager holds $1 million of 8.5 percent Treasury bonds due 1994–1999. The current market price is 76–2, for a yield of 11.95 percent. The manager fears a rise in interest rates in the next three months and wishes to protect this position against such a rise by hedging in futures.

a. Ignoring weighted hedges, what should the manager do?
b. Assume T-bond futures contracts are available at 68, and the price three months later is 59–12. If the manager constructs the correct hedge, what is the gain or loss on this position?
c. The price of the Treasury bonds three months later is 67–8. What is the gain or loss on this cash position?
d. What is the net effect of this hedge?

The following question was asked on the 1993 CFA Level I examination:

CFA
18-5. Chris Smith of XYZ Pension Plan has historically invested in the stocks of only U.S. domiciled companies. Recently, he has decided to add international exposure to the plan portfolio.

A. **Identify** and **briefly discuss** *three* potential problems that Smith may confront in selecting international stocks that he did not face in choosing U.S. stocks. Rather than select individual stocks, Smith decides to use Nikkei futures to obtain his Japanese portfolio exposure. The Nikkei index is now at 15,000 with a 2 percent dividend yield and the Japanese risk-free interest rate is 5 percent.
B. **Calculate** the price at which Smith can expect a six-month Nikkei futures contract to trade. **Show** all work.

SELECTED REFERENCES

An excellent discussion of futures, as well as options, can be found in:

Chance, Don M. *An Introduction to Derivatives.* The Dryden Press, Third Edition, 1995.

A good tutorial on financial futures is available through AIMR as part of the CFA curriculum by contacting PBD, Inc., P. O. Box 6996, Alpharetta, Georgia, 30239-6996 (800/789-AIMR):

Clarke, Roger G. *Options and Futures: A Tutorial,* Research Foundation of the Institute of Chartered Financial Analysts, P. O. Box 3668, Charlottesville, Virginia, 1992.

A useful discussion of financial derivatives can be found in:

Federal Reserve Bank of Atlanta, *Financial Derivatives: New Instruments and Their Uses,* Federal Reserve Bank of Atlanta Research Division, Atlanta, Georgia, 1993.

www.wiley.com/college/jones7
The web exercises for this chapter parallel the treatment in the text; in particular, we will address the use of futures for hedging.

APPENDIX 18-A

FUTURES OPTIONS

In Chapter 17 we discussed options (puts and calls) on common stocks. In this chapter we discussed two types of futures contracts, interest rate futures and stock-index futures. The latest innovation in financial instruments is a combination of the two, futures options. The development of this instrument is a good example of the ever-changing financial markets in the United States, where new instruments are developed to provide investors with opportunities that did not previously exist.

Options, both puts and calls, are offered on both interest rate futures and stock-index futures. Examples include the following financial futures options as reported in the popular press:[24]

Options on foreign exchange: Pound, mark, Swiss franc, yen, Canadian dollar, and a U.S. dollar index

Options on interest rate futures: U.S. Treasury bills, notes, and bonds and municipal bonds

Options on stock-index futures: The S&P 500 Index (traded on the Chicago Mercantile Exchange), the NYSE Composite Index (traded on the New York Futures Exchange), and the Nikkei 225 Stock Average (CME)

Options on commodities: Agricultural, oil, livestock, metals, and lumber

Recall from Chapter 17 that an option provides the purchaser with the right, but not the obligation, to exercise the claim provided by the contract. An option on a futures contract gives its owner the right to assume a long or short position in the respective futures contract. If this right is exercised, the holder's position will be at the exercise (strike) price of the option that was purchased. For example, the exerciser of a call option buys the futures contract at the exercise price stated in the call option.

[24] Futures options are available on various items, and this is a nonexhaustive list. Consult *The Wall Street Journal.*

FIGURE 18A-1

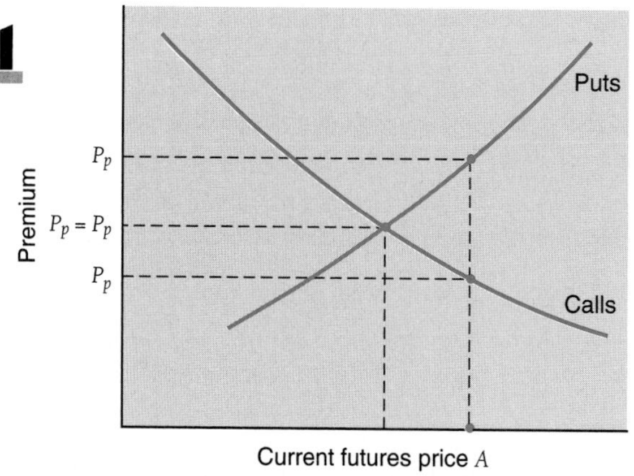

P_p = premium on a put option with strike price = A
P_p = premium on a call option with strike price = A

The key elements of an option contract on a particular futures contract are the exercise price and the premium. As in the case of stock options, premiums are determined in competitive markets. Each put and call option is either in the money or out of the money. With an in-the-money call option, the exercise price is less than the current price of the underlying futures contract. (If the exercise price is greater than the current price, it is out of the money.) For put options, the reverse is true.

Figure 18A-1 shows the relationships between premiums on put and call futures options. The exercise (strike) price is on the horizontal axis. As the strike price rises above the current futures price, the premiums on calls decline, whereas the premiums on puts rise. If the strike price were below the current futures price, the reverse would be true.

Options on futures contracts can serve some of the same purposes as the futures contracts themselves. Specifically, both futures contracts and options can be used to transfer the risk of adverse price movements from hedgers to speculators. For example, a portfolio manager with bond holdings (a long position) who expects a rise in interest rates can hedge against the risk of the capital losses resulting from such a rise by selling futures contracts on Treasury bonds. Alternatively, futures options on Treasury bonds can be used to hedge against this risk because the option's price will change in response to a change in the price of the underlying commodity.

A rise in interest rates is bearish (bond prices will fall); therefore, the portfolio manager would either buy a put or sell a call. The value of these options would rise as the price of the futures contract declined. On the other hand, an investor bullish on bond prices (i.e., one who expects interest rates to decline) would either buy a call or sell a put. In addition to these simple strategies, a number of spreading techniques can be used with options on Treasury bond futures.

The general appeal of options on futures contracts is the limited liability assumed by the purchaser. Unlike a futures contract, which has to be settled by some means (typically, by offset), the purchaser, once the contract is bought, has no additional obligation. Moreover, unlike futures, the purchaser is not subject to margin calls. Even if a speculator in futures is ultimately correct in his or her expectations, margin calls in the interim can wipe out all the equity. A writer (seller) of an option on a futures contract, however, does have an obligation to assume a position (long or short) in the futures market at the strike price if the option is exercised.[25] Sellers must deposit margin when opening a position.

[25] This discussion is based on Stanley W. Angrist, "It's Your Option," *Forbes*, February 28, 1983, p. 138.

QUESTIONS

18A-1. With regard to futures options, fill in the following blanks with either "less than" or "greater than." The current futures price is 75.

a. Put options with strike prices ________ 75 are in the money.
b. Call options with strike prices ________ 75 are out of the money.
c. Put options with strike prices ________ 75 are out of the money.
d. Call options with strike prices ________ 75 are in the money.

chapter 19

PORTFOLIO SELECTION

Chapter 19 concentrates on portfolio selection. The Markowitz portfolio selection model, involving the important concept of efficient portfolios, is considered first. This is followed by an analysis of the impact of a risk-free asset on the Markowitz efficient frontier. The separation theorem is also discussed.

After reading this chapter you will be able to:

- **Understand what the efficient frontier is and its importance to investment analysis.**
- **Select an optimal portfolio of risky assets.**
- **Describe what happens to the efficient frontier with the introduction of borrowing and lending.**
- **Understand the separation theorem and its importance to modern investment theory.**

In Chapter 7 we learned that risky assets should be evaluated on the basis of their expected returns and risk, as measured by the standard deviation, and that portfolio expected return and risk can be calculated based on these inputs and the covariances involved. Calculation of portfolio risk is the key issue. The complete Markowitz variance-covariance analysis can be used to calculate portfolio risk, or the single-index model, explained in this chapter, can be used to simplify the calculations, subject to the assumptions of the model.

We analyzed basic portfolio principles such as diversification and determined that investors should hold portfolios of financial assets in order to reduce their risk when investing. Clearly, risk reduction through diversification is a very important concept. In fact, diversification is the number one rule of portfolio management and the key to optimal risk management. Every intelligent investor will diversify his or her portfolio of risky assets.

Despite the importance of the diversification principle, our analysis is incomplete because an infinite number of potential portfolios of risky assets exist. Furthermore, investors can invest in both risky assets and riskless assets, and buy assets on margin or with borrowed funds. This chapter completes our portfolio analysis by analyzing how investors select optimal risky portfolios and how the use of a risk-free asset changes the investor's ultimate portfolio position. In effect, we are analyzing the optimal trade-off that exists between risk and expected return. This will allow us in the next chapter to analyze asset pricing and market equilibrium, following up on the CAPM model discussed in Chapter 7.

BUILDING A PORTFOLIO

To build a portfolio of financial assets, investors follow certain steps. Specifically, they

1. Identify optimal risk-return combinations available from the set of risky assets being considered by using the Markowitz efficient frontier analysis. This step uses the inputs from Chapter 7, the expected returns, variances and covariances for a set of securities.
2. Consider the impact of a risk-free asset on the Markowitz efficient frontier. The introduction of borrowing and lending possibilities leads to an optimal portfolio of risky assets and has a significant impact on the way investors think about the investment process.
3. Choose the final portfolio, consisting of the risk-free asset and the optimal portfolio of risky assets, based on an investor's preferences.

In this chapter we follow these steps, first considering the Markowitz analysis which is used to identify the efficient set of portfolios, and then discussing the impact of a risk-free asset on this analysis. We will learn how investors end up with a final portfolio consisting of the risk-free asset and a portfolio of risky assets that is optimal for them.

STEP 1: USE THE MARKOWITZ PORTFOLIO SELECTION MODEL

As we saw in Chapter 7, even if portfolios are selected arbitrarily, some diversification benefits are gained. This results in a reduction of portfolio risk. However, random diversification does not use the information set available to investors and does not, in general, lead to optimal diversification.

To take the full information set into account, we use an alternative approach based on portfolio theory as developed by Markowitz. Portfolio theory is normative, meaning that it tells investors how they should act to diversify optimally. It is based on a small set of assumptions, including

1. A single investment period; for example, one year.
2. Liquidity of positions; for example, there are no transaction costs.
3. Investor preferences based only on a portfolio's expected return and risk, as measured by variance or standard deviation.

EFFICIENT PORTFOLIOS

Efficient Portfolio A portfolio with the highest level of expected return for a given level of risk or a portfolio with the lowest risk for a given level of expected return

Markowitz's approach to portfolio selection is that an investor should evaluate portfolios on the basis of their expected returns and risk as measured by the standard deviation. He was the first to derive the concept of an **efficient portfolio** (discussed in Chapter 7), defined as one that has the smallest portfolio risk for a given level of expected return or the largest expected return for a given level of risk. Rational investors will seek efficient portfolios because these portfolios are optimized on the two dimensions of most importance to investors, expected return and risk.

Chapter 7 explained the basic details of how to derive efficient portfolios. We will assume that efficient portfolios have been calculated using the Markowitz analysis described in Chapter 7.

SELECTING AN OPTIMAL PORTFOLIO OF RISKY ASSETS

Efficient Set (Frontier) The set of portfolios generated by the Markowitz portfolio model

Once the efficient set of portfolios is determined using the Markowitz model, investors must select from this set the portfolio most appropriate for them. The Markowitz model does not specify one optimum portfolio. It generates the efficient set of portfolios, all of which, by definition, are optimal portfolios (for a given level of expected return or risk).

In economics in general, and finance in particular, we assume investors are risk averse. This means that investors, if given a choice, will not take a "fair gamble," defined as one with an expected payoff of zero and equal probabilities of a gain or a loss. In effect, with a fair gamble, the disutility from the potential loss is greater than the utility from the potential gain. The greater the risk aversion, the greater the disutility from the potential loss.

Indifference Curves Curves describing investor preferences for risk and return

To select the expected return-risk combination that will satisfy an individual investor's personal preferences, **indifference curves** (which are assumed to be known for an investor) are used. These curves, shown in Figure 19-1 for a risk-averse investor, describe investor

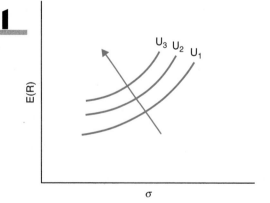

FIGURE 19-1

Indifference curves.

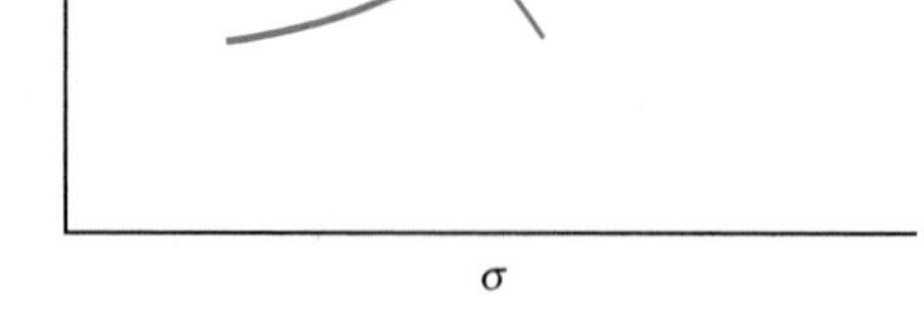

FIGURE 19-2

Selecting a portfolio on the efficient frontier.

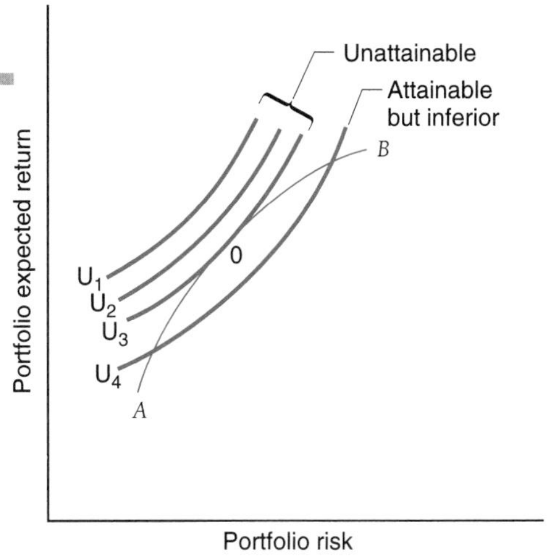

preferences for risk and return.[1] Each indifference curve represents all combinations of portfolios that are equally desirable to a particular investor.

A few important points about indifference curves should be noted. Indifference curves cannot intersect since they represent different levels of desirability. Investors have an infinite number of indifference curves. The curves for all risk-averse investors will be upward-sloping, but the shapes of the curves can vary depending on risk preferences. Higher indifference curves are more desirable than lower indifference curves. The greater the slope of the indifference curves, the greater the risk aversion of investors.

The optimal portfolio for a risk-averse investor occurs at the point of tangency between the investor's highest indifference curve and the efficient set of portfolios. In Figure 19-2 this occurs at point 0.[2] This portfolio maximizes investor utility because the indifference curves reflect *investor preferences,* while the efficient set represents *portfolio possibilities.* Notice that curves U2 and U1 are unattainable and that U3 is the highest indifference curve for this investor that is tangent to the efficient frontier. On the other hand, U4, though attainable, is inferior to U3, which offers a higher expected return for the same risk (and therefore more utility).

INVESTMENTS INTUITION Stated on a practical basis, conservative investors would select portfolios on the left end of the efficient set AB in Figure 19-2 because these portfolios have less risk (and, of course, less expected return). Conversely, aggressive investors would choose portfolios toward point B because these portfolios offer higher expected returns (along with higher levels of risk).

Three important points must be noted about the Markowitz portfolio selection model:

1. The Markowitz analysis generates an entire set, or frontier, of efficient portfolios, all of which are equally "good." No portfolio on the efficient frontier, as generated, dominates any other portfolio.

[1] Although not shown, investors could also be risk-neutral (the risk is unimportant in evaluating portfolios) or risk-seekers. A risk-seeking investor, given a fair gamble, will want to take the fair gamble, and larger gambles are preferable to smaller gambles.

[2] The investor is selecting the portfolio with the indifference curve furthest northwest.

2. The Markowitz model does not address the issue of investors using borrowed money along with their own portfolio funds to purchase a portfolio of risky assets; that is, investors are not allowed to use leverage. As we will see later in the chapter, allowing investors to purchase a risk-free asset increases investor utility and leads to a different efficient set.
3. In practice, different investors, or portfolio managers, will estimate the inputs to the Markowitz model differently. This will produce different efficient frontiers. This results from the uncertainty inherent in the security analysis part of investments as described in Chapter 1.

ALTERNATIVE METHODS OF OBTAINING THE EFFICIENT FRONTIER

The single-index model provides an alternative expression for portfolio variance, which is easier to calculate than in the case of the Markowitz analysis. This alternative approach can be used to solve the portfolio problem as formulated by Markowitz—determining the efficient set of portfolios. It requires considerably fewer calculations. In the case of the Markowitz analysis, 250 stocks require 31,125 covariances and 250 variances. Using the single-index model, we would need 250 estimates of beta, 250 estimates of residual variance, and one estimate for the variance of the market portfolio.[3]

Single-Index Model A model that relates returns on a security to the returns on a market index

William Sharpe, following Markowitz, developed the **single-index model,** which relates returns on each security to the returns on a common index.[4] A broad market index of common stock returns is generally used for this purpose.[5] Think of the S&P 500 as this index.

The single-index model can be expressed by the following equation:

$$R_i = a_i + \beta_i R_M + e_i \tag{19-1}$$

where

R_i = the return (TR) on security i

R_M = the return (TR) on the market index

a_i = that part of security i's return independent of market performance

β_i = a constant measuring the expected change in the dependent variable, R_i, given a change in the independent variable, R_M

e_i = the random residual error

The single-index model divides a security's return into two components: a unique part, represented by a_i, and a market-related part represented by $\beta_i R_M$. The unique part is a *micro*

[3] The single-index model requires $3n + 2$ total pieces of data to implement, where n is the number of securities being considered.

Example The 250 securities mentioned earlier would require $3n + 2 = 3\,(250) + 2 = 752$ estimates, consisting of 250 estimates of a_i, 250 estimates of b_i, 250 variances of the residual errors s^2_{ei}, an estimate of the expected return on the market index, and an estimate of the expected variance on the market index.

In contrast, the full variance-covariance model of Markowitz requires $[n(n + 3)]/2$ estimates for n securities.

Example In the case of the 250 securities, $[250(253)]/2 = 31{,}625$ total pieces of data, or

250 expected returns
\+ 250 variances
\+ [250(249)]/2 unique covariances
= 31,625 total pieces of data

[4] W. Sharpe, "A Simplified Model for Portfolio Analysis," *Management Science,* 9 (January 1963): 277–293.

[5] There is no requirement that the index be a stock index. It could be any variable thought to be the dominant influence on stock returns. This means that the model cannot be based on a consistent theoretical set of assumptions.

event, affecting an individual company but not all companies in general. Examples include the discovery of new ore reserves, a fire, a strike, or the resignation of a key company figure. The market-related part, on the other hand, is a *macro* event that is broad-based and affects all (or most) firms. Examples include a Federal Reserve announcement about the discount rate, a change in the prime rate, or an unexpected announcement about the money supply.

Given these values, the error term is the difference between the left-hand side of the equation, the return on security i, and the right-hand side of the equation, the sum of the two components of return. Since the single-index model is, by definition, an equality, the two sides must be the same.

EXAMPLE 19-1

Assume the return for the market index for period t is 12 percent, the $a_i = 3$ percent, and the $b_i = 1.5$. The single-index model estimate for stock i is

$$R_i = 3\% + 1.5\ R_M + e_i$$

$$R_i = 3\% + (1.5)(12\%) = 21\%$$

If the market index return is 12 percent, the likely return for stock i is 21 percent.

However, no model is going to explain security returns perfectly. The error term, e_i, captures the difference between the return that actually occurs and the return expected to occur given a particular market index return.

EXAMPLE 19-2

Assume in Example 19-1 that the actual return on stock i for period t is 19 percent. The error term in this case is $19\% - 21\% = -2\%$.

This illustrates what we said earlier about the error term. For any period, it represents the difference between the actual return and the return predicted by the parameters of the model on the right-hand side of the equation. Figure 19-3, which depicts the SIM, illustrates the difference between the actual return of Example 19-2, 19 percent, and the predicted return of 21 percent—the error term is −2 percent.

The b term, or beta, is important. As explained in Chapter 7, it measures the sensitivity of a stock to market movements. To use the single- index model, we need estimates of the beta for each stock we are considering. Subjective estimates could be obtained from analysts, or the future beta could be estimated from historical data. We consider the estimation of beta in more detail in Chapter 20.

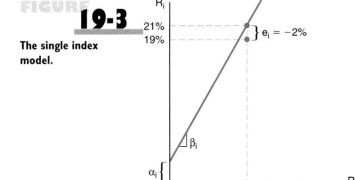

FIGURE 19-3

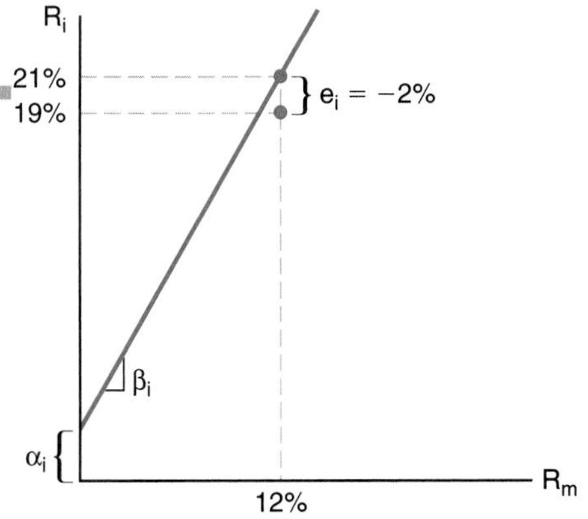

The single index model.

R_M and e_i are random variables. The single-index model assumes that the market index is unrelated to the residual error. One way to estimate the parameters of this model is with a time series regression. Use of this technique ensures that these two variables are uncorrelated.

We will use σ_{ei} to denote the standard deviation of the error term for stock i. The mean of the probability distribution of this error term is zero.

The single-index model also assumes that securities are related only in their common response to the return on the market. That is, the residual errors for security i are uncorrelated with those of security j; this can be expressed as COV $(e_i,e_j) = 0$. *This is the key assumption of the single-index model because it implies that stocks covary together only because of their common relationship to the market index.* In other words, there are no influences on stocks beyond the market, such as industry effects. Therefore

$$R_i = a_i + \beta_i R_M + e_i \text{ for stock } i$$

and

$$R_j = a_j + \beta_j R_M + e_j \text{ for stock } j$$

It is critical to recognize that this is a simplifying assumption. If this assumption is not a good description of reality, the model will be inaccurate.[6]

In the single-index model, all the covariance terms can be accounted for by stocks being related only in their common responses to the market index; that is, the covariance depends only on market risk. Therefore, the covariance between any two securities can be written as

$$\sigma_{ij} = \beta_i \, \beta_j \, \sigma^2_M \tag{19-2}$$

Once again, this simplification rests on the assumption about the error terms being uncorrelated. An alternative is to consider more than one index.

In the Markowitz model, we need to consider all of the covariance terms in the variance-covariance matrix. The single- index model splits the risk of an individual security into two components, similar to its division of security return into two components. This simplifies the covariance and greatly simplifies the calculation of total risk for a security and for a portfolio. The total risk of a security, as measured by its variance, consists of two components: market risk and unique risk.

$$\begin{aligned} \sigma^2_i &= \beta^2_i[\sigma^2_M] + \sigma^2_{ei} \\ &= \text{Market risk} + \text{Unique risk} \end{aligned} \tag{19-3}$$

The market risk accounts for that part of a security's variance that cannot be diversified away. This part of the variability occurs when the security responds to the market moving up and down. The second term is the security's residual variance and accounts for that part of the variability due to deviations from the fitted relationship between security return and market return.

This simplification also holds for portfolios, providing an alternative expression to use in finding the minimum variance set of portfolios.

$$\begin{array}{ccccc} \sigma^2_p & = & \beta^2_p[\sigma^2_M] & + & \sigma^2_{ep} \\ \text{Total} & & \text{Portfolio} & + & \text{Portfolio} \\ \text{portfolio} & = & \text{market} & & \text{residual} \\ \text{variance} & & \text{risk} & & \text{variance} \end{array} \tag{19-4}$$

Multi-Index Models As noted in the previous section, the single-index model assumes that stock prices covary only because of common movement with one index, specifically that

[6] The use of regression analysis does not guarantee that this will be true. Instead, it is a specific simplifying assumption that, in fact, may or may not be true.

of the market. Some researchers have attempted to capture some nonmarket influences by constructing multi-index models. Probably the most obvious example of these potential nonmarket influences is the industry factor.[7]

A multi-index model is of the form

$$E(R_i) = a_i + b_i R_M + c_i NF + e_i \tag{19-5}$$

where NF is the nonmarket factor, and all other variables are as previously defined. Equation 19-19 could be expanded to include three, four, or more indexes.

It seems logical that a multi-index model should perform better than a single-index model because it uses more information about the interrelationships between stock returns. In effect, the multi-index model falls between the full variance-covariance method of Markowitz and Sharpe's single-index model.

How well do these models perform? Given the large number of possible multi-index models, no conclusive statement is possible. However, one well-known study, by Cohen and Pogue, found that the single-index model outperformed a multi-index model in that it produced more efficient portfolios.[8] This study, using industry classifications, found the single-index model not only was simpler but also led to lower expected risks.

It is worth noting that the multi-index model tested by Cohen and Pogue (and by Elton and Gruber as well) actually reproduced the *historical* correlations better than the single-index model.[9] However, it did not perform better *ex ante,* which is the more important consideration, because portfolios are built to be held for a future period of time.

Some Conclusions About the Single Index Model The single-index model greatly simplifies the calculation of the portfolio variance. However, this model makes a specific assumption about the process that generates portfolio returns—the residuals for different securities are uncorrelated. Thus, the accuracy of the estimate of the portfolio variance depends on the accuracy of the key assumption being made by the model. For example, if the covariance between the residuals for different securities is positive, not zero as assumed, the true residual variance of the portfolio will be underestimated.

The end objective of the single index model is the same as that of the Markowitz analysis, tracing the efficient frontier (set) of portfolios from which an investor would choose an optimal portfolio. Its purpose is to simplify the calculations necessary to do this.

The single-index model is a valuable simplification of the full variance-covariance matrix needed for the Markowitz model. As discussed above, this model reduces by a large amount the number of estimates needed for a portfolio of securities.[10]

An obvious question to ask is how it performs in relation to the Markowitz model. In his original paper developing the single-index model, Sharpe found that two sets of efficient portfolios—one using the full Markowitz model and one using his simplification—generated from a sample of stocks were very much alike.[11] A later study also found that the Sharpe model did no worse than the Markowitz model in all tests conducted, and in tests using shorter time periods it performed better.[12]

[7] In a well-known study, Benjamin King found a common movement between securities, beyond the market effect, associated with industries. See B. King. "Market and Industry Factors in Stock Price Behavior," *Journal of Business* 39 (January 1966): 139–190.

[8] K. Cohen and J. Pogue, "An Empirical Evaluation of Alternative Portfolio Selection Models," *Journal of Business,* 46 (April 1967): 166–193.

[9] E. Elton and M. Gruber, "Estimating the Dependence Structure of Share Prices—Implications for Portfolio Selection," *Journal of Finance,* 5 (December 1973): 1203–1232.

[10] The single-index model can be used to directly estimate the expected return and risk for a portfolio.

[11] Sharpe, "A Simplified Model."

[12] G. Frankfurter, H. Phillips, and J. Seagle, "Performance of the Sharpe Portfolio Selection Model: A Comparison," *Journal of Financial and Quantitative Analysis* (June 1976): 195–204.

SELECTING OPTIMAL ASSET CLASSES

The Markowitz model is typically thought of in terms of selecting portfolios of individual securities; indeed, that is how Markowitz expected his model to be used. As we know, however, it is a cumbersome model to employ because of the number of covariance estimates needed when dealing with a large number of individual securities.

An alternative way to use the Markowitz model as a selection technique is to think in terms of asset classes, such as domestic stocks, foreign stocks of industrialized countries, the stocks of emerging markets, bonds, and so forth. Using the model in this manner, investors decide what asset classes to own and what proportions of the asset classes to hold.

Asset Allocation Decision The allocation of a portfolio's funds to classes of assets, such as cash equivalents, bonds, and equities

The **asset allocation decision** refers to the allocation of portfolio assets to broad asset markets; in other words, how much of the portfolio's funds is to be invested in stocks, how much in bonds, money market assets, and so forth. Each weight can range from zero percent to 100 percent. Examining the asset allocation decision globally leads us to ask the following questions:

1. What percentage of portfolio funds is to be invested in each of the countries for which financial markets are available to investors?
2. Within each country, what percentage of portfolio funds is to be invested in stocks, bonds, bills, and other assets?
3. Within each of the major asset classes, what percentage of portfolio funds is to go to various types of bonds, exchange stocks versus over-the-counter stocks, and so forth?

Many knowledgeable market observers agree that the asset allocation decision is the most important decision made by an investor. According to some studies, for example, asset allocation decision accounts for more than 90 percent of the variance in quarterly returns for a typical large pension fund.[13]

The rationale behind this approach is that different asset classes offer various potential returns and various levels of risk, and the correlation coefficients may be quite low. As with the Markowitz analysis applied to individual securities, inputs remain a problem because they must be estimated. However, this will always be a problem in investing because we are selecting assets to be held over the uncertain future.

Programs exist to calculate efficient frontiers using asset classes. These programs allow for a variety of constraints, such as minimum yield and no short selling.

As an indication of what can be accomplished using asset classes for an investment program, consider Box 19-1 which suggests that investors can diversify across mutual funds to create a bearproof portfolio. Portfolio funds are spread across seven asset classes: blue-chip stocks, small-cap stocks, international equities, domestic bonds, international bonds, gold, and money markets. Such a portfolio is said to have outperformed the S&P 500 Index over a 22-year period by more than two percentage points annually while avoiding every bear market during the period. The analysis in Box 19-1 does not employ the Markowitz efficient frontier technique because it simply uses equal portfolio weights for each of the seven asset classes. Presumably, Markowitz analysis could improve the results obtained from this strategy.

Whether we use the Markowitz analysis for asset classes or individual securities, the end result is an efficient frontier of risky portfolios and the choice of an optimal risky portfolio based on investor preferences. We must now consider the situation when we combine risk-free assets with the optimal portfolio of risky assets. The efficient frontier changes dramatically.

[13] See Gary P. Brinson, L. Randolph Hood, and Gilbert L. Beebower, "Determinants of Portfolio Performance," *Financial Analysts Review* (July/August 1986).

Box 19-1

DIVERSIFY IT YOURSELF

Were you one of the investors who threw in the towel during the recent market downturn? Facing down what looks like a bear market can be frightening indeed, even though we all know the virtues of being a long-term investor.

How can you keep your head when investors around you are losing theirs? Assemble a portfolio with modest volatility so you can stand pat during the severest of bear markets. For example, a portfolio split equally between common stocks and money market funds is only half as volatile as the stock market. Should stock prices tumble by 40 percent, the value of your portfolio will fall by only 20 percent.

The problem with allocating your assets this way is you reduce potential returns significantly. In this instance, your long-run annual average return potential is only about 7.5 percent. You trade return for reduced volatility.

It may seem impossible to trim volatility and earn double-digit returns. But by building a diversified mutual fund portfolio containing many different categories of assets, you can reduce volatility without sacrificing a lot of potential return. Call it the All-Weather Portfolio.

It works by spreading capital equally across seven categories of assets: blue-chip stocks, small-cap stocks, international equities, domestic bonds, international bonds, gold, and money markets. The chart illustrates the annual returns this portfolio would have earned during the past 22 years as well as those of the S&P 500 index. After more than two decades, an investor's $10,000 initial investment would have grown to $174,700, a 13.9 percent annual return, while an equivalent investment in the S&P 500 would have grown to $112,300, or 11.6 percent annually. Even more important, you would have dodged every bear market along the way. Although stocks declined by as much as 26.5 percent in 1974, the largest annual decline in the All-Weather Portfolio was a modest 3.7 percent.

Remember: Accelerating inflation drives interest rates up and bond prices down. But runaway inflation also drives the price of gold higher. Thus, losses in the bond market are offset by gains in gold. Similarly, returns among the other categories of assets in the portfolio are less than perfectly correlated with one another. That levels the peaks and valleys in the portfolio's value.

But shouldn't lower-risk portfolios provide diminished returns? Capital-market theory says portfolio risk and return are inextricably linked—the higher the risk, the higher the returns. Does our strategy fly in the face of modern investment theory? Nope. Because the All-Weather Portfolio is more efficiently diversified than a portfolio containing a handful of domestic large-cap stocks—such as the S&P 500 index—it comes much closer to the portfolio described by efficient-market theory. In short, the All-Weather Portfolio contains

ALL-WEATHER PORTFOLIO

Mutual Fund	Allocation	Expense Ratio	Yield	'93 Return
Vanguard Index Small Cap 800-662-7447	15%	0.18%	1.1%	18.7%
Vanguard Index 500 800-662-7447	15	0.20	2.7	9.9
T. Towe Price Int'l Stock 800-638-5660	15	1.05	1.6	40.1
Scudder Int'l Bond 800-225-2470	15	1.26	6.3	15.8
Benham Treasury Note 800-321-8321	15	0.75	5.4	7.9
Lexington Gold Fund 800-526-0056	10	1.89	0.2	6.0
United Services Gov't Securities 800-873-8637	15	0.20	3.5	3.3
Average		0.73	3.1	32.0

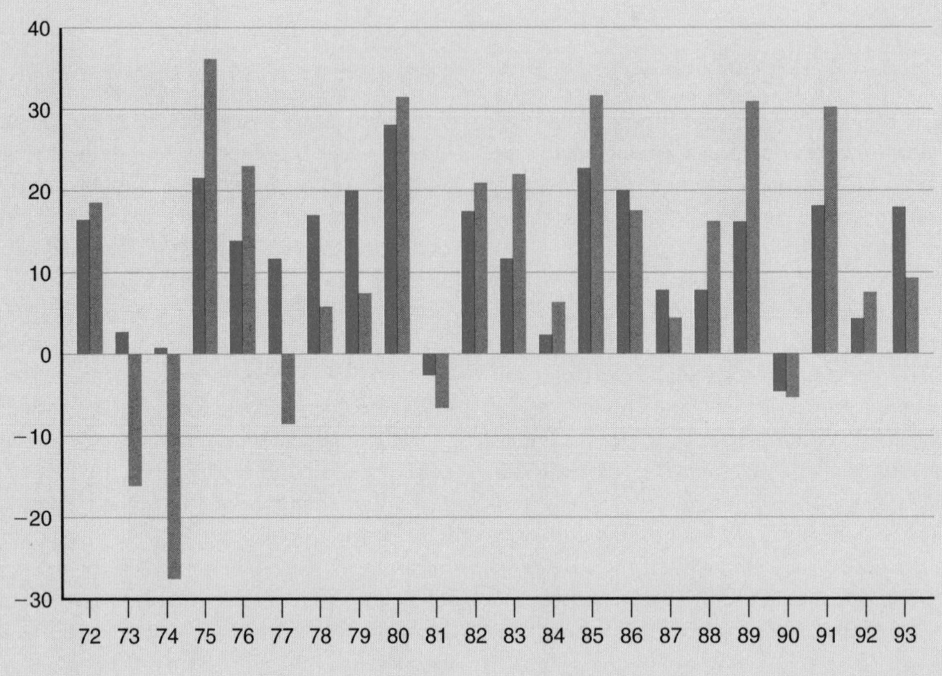

a better balance between investment return and nondiversifiable risk. It works because it conforms more closely to modern capital-market and portfolio-management theory.

How can you assemble your own version of this portfolio? Buy no-load mutual funds that invest in each category of asset contained in the All-Weather Portfolio. With mutual funds' relatively low minimum investment requirements, an investor can create a portfolio with around $20,000 (or $4,000 in an IRA). Choose mutual funds that stay fully invested at all times and those that have low expense ratios. Use index funds whenever possible.

The same portfolio shown above has a beta of 0.38, versus the market's beta of 1.00; this means your funds' volatility is 62 percent below the overall market's. The portfolio has a current yield of 3.1 percent, annual expenses are 0.7 percent, and annual returns should run 11 percent to 12 percent on average over the longer run.

Managing the portfolio shouldn't be onerous. Set initial allocations, then rebalance them one to four times a year. Rebalancing keeps the portfolio highly diversified; it also forces you to sell funds in categories that have appreciated and add to those in categories that have fallen. In other words, you buy low and sell high.

This portfolio combines all the elements required for long-term investment success: Its holdings are diversified, are oriented toward the long term, and strike a reasonable balance between risk and return. It automatically requires that you buy low and sell high. Its costs are moderate and it's simple to maintain. So if you're afraid of the stock market, are constantly losing on brokers' tips, and are always buying at market tops and selling at market bottoms, the All-Weather Portfolio is just what the doctor ordered.

SOURCE: Gerald Perritt, "Diversify It Yourself," *Worth* (June 1994), pp. 130–131. Reprinted by permission.

STEP 2: CONSIDER BORROWING AND LENDING POSSIBILITIES

As we saw above, investors can use the Markowitz analysis as a portfolio optimizer. This analysis determines the best combinations of expected return and risk for a given set of inputs for risky assets. However, investors always have the option of buying a risk-free asset such as Treasury bills. The portfolio selection question remains the same: What is the best portfolio of assets, given any set of assets under consideration, to hold? To answer this question, we will do as before—we will determine the possibilities and then match them with investor preferences.

A risk-free asset can be defined as one with a certain-to-be-earned expected return and a variance of return of zero. (Note, however, that this is a nominal return and not a real return, which is uncertain because inflation is uncertain.) Since variance = 0, the nominal risk-free rate in each period will be equal to its expected value. Furthermore, the covariance between the risk-free asset and any risky asset i will be zero, because

$$\begin{aligned}\sigma_{RF,i} &= r_{RF,i}\sigma_i\sigma_{RF} \\ &= r_{RF,i}\sigma_i(0) \\ &= 0\end{aligned}$$

where r denotes the correlation coefficient, and s denotes the respective standard deviation of asset i or the risk-free asset. Therefore, the risk-free asset will have no correlation with risky assets.

The true risk-free asset is best thought of as a Treasury security, which has no risk of default, with a maturity matching the holding period of the investor. In this case, the amount of money to be received at the end of the holding period is known with certainty at the beginning of the period.[14] The Treasury bill typically is taken to be the risk-free asset, and its rate of return is referred to here as RF.

Although the introduction of a risk-free asset appears to be a simple step to take in the evolution of portfolio and capital market theory, it is a very significant step. Investors can now invest part of their wealth in this asset and the remainder in any of the risky portfolios in the Markowitz efficient set. It allows Markowitz portfolio theory to be extended in such a way that the efficient frontier is completely changed, which in turn leads to a general theory for pricing assets under uncertainty, as discussed in the next chapter.

RISK-FREE BORROWING AND LENDING

Assume that the efficient frontier, as shown by the arc AB in Figure 19-4, has been derived by an investor. The arc AB delineates the efficient set of portfolios of risky assets. (For simplicity, assume these are portfolios of common stocks.) We now introduce a risk-free asset with return RF and $\sigma = 0$.

As shown in Figure 19-4, the return on the risk-free asset (RF) will plot on the vertical axis because the risk is zero. Investors can combine this riskless asset with the efficient set of portfolios on the efficient frontier. By drawing a line between RF and various risky portfolios on the efficient frontier, we can examine combinations of risk-return possibilities that did not exist previously.

Risk-Free Lending Consider an arbitrary point on the efficient frontier, risky portfolio X. An investor who combines the risk-free asset with portfolio X of risky assets would have a portfolio somewhere on the line RF–X (e.g., point Z). Assume this investor places w_{RF} of investable funds in the risk-free asset and the remainder $(1 - w_{RF})$ in portfolio X. The expected return on this combined portfolio p would be

$$E(R_p) = w_{RF} + (1 - w_{RF})\,E(R_X) \qquad (19\text{-}6)$$

As always, the expected return of a portfolio is a weighted average of the expected returns of the individual assets. Since portfolio X, consisting of risky assets, would always be assumed to have a larger expected return than the return on the risk-free asset (RF), the greater the

[14] If there is no uncertainty about the terminal value of the asset, the standard deviation must be zero and the asset must, therefore, be riskless.

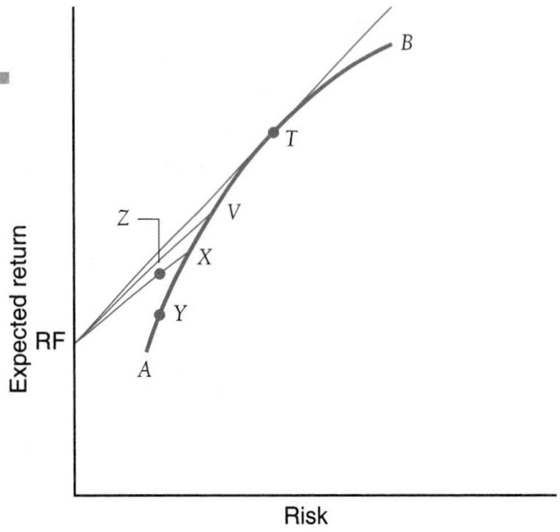

FIGURE 19-4

The Markowitz efficient frontier and the possibilities resulting from introducing a risk-free asset.

percentage of an investor's funds committed to X, $(1 - w_{RF})$, the larger the expected return on the portfolio.

The standard deviation of this portfolio is

$$\sigma_p = (1 - w_{RF})\sigma_X \tag{19-7}$$

because $\sigma_{RF} = 0$ and the correlation between RF and any risky portfolio is zero, eliminating the covariation term. Thus, the standard deviation of a portfolio combining the risk-free asset with a risky asset (portfolio) is simply the weighted standard deviation of the risky portfolio.

EXAMPLE 19-3

Assume that portfolio X has an expected return of 15 percent, with a standard deviation of 10 percent, and that the risk-free security has an expected return of 7 percent. If half of investable funds is placed in each (i.e., $w_{RF} = 0.5$ and $1 - w_{RF} = 0.5$), then

$$E(R_p) = 0.5(7\%) + 0.5(15\%) = 11\%$$

and

$$\sigma_p = (1.0 - 0.5)10\% = 5\%$$

An investor could change positions on the line RF–X by varying w_{RF}, and hence $1 - w_{RF}$. As more of the investable funds are placed in the risk-free asset, both the expected return and the risk of the portfolio decline.

INVESTMENTS INTUITION It should be apparent that the segment of the efficient frontier below X (i.e., A to X) in Figure 19-4 is now dominated by the line RF–X. For example, at point Z on the straight line, the investor has the same risk as portfolio Y on the Markowitz efficient frontier, but Z has a larger expected return.

In Figure 19-4 a new line could be drawn between RF and the Markowitz efficient frontier above point X, for example, connecting RF to point V. Each successively higher line will dominate the preceding set of portfolios. This process ends when a line is drawn tangent to the efficient set of risky portfolios, given a vertical intercept of RF. In Figure 19-4 we will call this tangency point T. The set of portfolio opportunities on this line (RF to T) dominates all portfolios below it.

Portfolio T is important in this analysis. The Markowitz efficient set consists of portfolios of risky assets. In Figure 19-4 no other portfolio connected to the risk-free rate, RF, lies northwest of the straight line connecting RF and portfolio T. This line has the greatest slope.

The straight line from RF to the efficient frontier at point T, RF–T, dominates all straight lines below it and contains the superior *lending portfolios* given the Markowitz efficient set depicted in Figure 19-4. Lending refers to the purchase of a riskless asset such as Treasury bills, because by making such a purchase, the investor is lending money to the issuer of the securities, the U.S. government. We can think of this risk-free lending simply as *risk-free investing*.

Through a combination of risk-free investing (investing funds at a rate of RF) and investing in a risky portfolio of securities, T, an investor has changed the opportunity set available from the Markowitz efficient frontier which consists only of portfolios of risky assets. With the introduction of the possibility of risk-free investing (i.e., purchasing a risk-free asset), investors have several alternatives:

1. To invest 100 percent of investable funds in the risk-free asset, providing an expected return of RF and zero risk.
2. To invest 100 percent of investable funds in risky-asset portfolio T, offering $E(R_T)$, with its risk $\sigma(R_T)$.
3. To invest in any combination of return and risk between these two points, obtained by varying the proportion w_{RF} invested in the risk-free asset.

Borrowing Possibilities What if we extend this analysis to allow investors to borrow money? The investor is no longer restricted to his or her wealth when investing in risky assets. Technically, we are short-selling the riskless asset. One way to accomplish this borrowing is to buy stocks on margin, which has a current initial margin requirement of 50 percent.

Of course, investors must pay interest on borrowed money. We will assume initially that investors can also borrow at the risk-free rate RF. We will remove this assumption later.

Borrowing additional investable funds and investing them together with the investor's own wealth allows investors to seek higher expected returns while assuming greater risk. These borrowed funds can be used to lever the portfolio position beyond point T, the point of tangency between the straight line emanating from RF and the efficient frontier AB. As in the lending discussion, point T represents 100 percent of an investor's wealth in the risky asset portfolio T. The straight line RF–T is now extended upward, as shown in Figure 19-5, and can be designated RF–T–L.

What effect does borrowing have on the expected return and risk for a portfolio? These parameters can be calculated in the usual manner. However, the proportions to be invested are now stated differently. Since the proportions to be invested in the alternatives are stated as percentages of an investor's total investable funds, various combinations must add up to 1.0 (i.e., 100 percent, representing an investor's total wealth). Therefore, the proportion to be borrowed at RF is stated as a negative figure, so that

$$w_{RF} + (1 - w_{RF}) = 1.0 = 100\% \text{ of investor wealth}$$

Assume an investor can borrow 100 percent of his or her investable wealth, which, together with the investable wealth itself, will be invested in risky-asset portfolio T (i.e., 200 percent of investable wealth is invested in portfolio T). The $1 - w_{RF}$ weight must now equal 2.0 to represent the sum of original wealth plus borrowed funds. To obtain this result, the proportion of investable funds associated with w_{RF} is negative; specifically, it is -1.0, representing borrowed funds at the rate RF. Therefore, the proportion to be invested in portfolio T is $[1 - (-1)] = 2$.

Overall, the combined weights are still equal to 1.0, since

$$w_{RF} + (1 - w_{RF}) = 1.0$$
$$-1 + [1 - (-1)] = 1.0$$

The expected return on the investor's portfolio *p*, consisting of investable wealth plus borrowed funds invested in portfolio T, is now

$$\begin{aligned} E(R_p) &= w_{RF}\ RF + (1 - w_{RF})E(R_T) \\ &= -1(RF) + 2\ E(R_T) \end{aligned}$$

The expected return increases linearly as the borrowing increases. The standard deviation of this portfolio is

$$\begin{aligned} \sigma_p &= (1 - w_{RF})\sigma_T \\ &= 2\sigma_T \end{aligned}$$

Risk will increase as the amount of borrowing increases.

Borrowing possibilities (i.e., leverage) are illustrated by the following example.

EXAMPLE 19-4

Assume that the expected return on portfolio T is 20 percent, with $\sigma_T = 13$ percent. The expected risk-free rate, RF, is still 7 percent, as earlier. However, it now represents the borrowing rate, or the rate at which the investor must pay interest on funds borrowed and invested in the risky asset T. The expected return on this portfolio would be

$$\begin{aligned} E(R_p) &= -1(7\%) + 2(20\%) \\ &= -7\% + 40\% \\ &= 33\% \end{aligned}$$

The standard deviation of this leveraged portfolio would be

$$\begin{aligned} \sigma_p &= (1.0 - w_{RF})\sigma_T \\ &= [1.0 - (-1.0)]\sigma_T \\ &= 2\sigma_T \\ &= 26\% \end{aligned}$$

THE NEW EFFICIENT SET

The end result of introducing risk-free investing and borrowing into the analysis is to create lending and borrowing possibilities and a set of expected return-risk possibilities that did not exist previously. As shown in Figure 19-5, the new risk-return trade-off is a straight line tangent to the efficient frontier at point T and with a vertical intercept RF.

The introduction of the risk-free asset significantly changes the Markowitz efficient set of portfolios. Specifically, the following points emerge:

1. The new efficient set is no longer a curve, or arc, as in the Markowitz analysis. It is now linear.
2. Borrowing and lending possibilities, combined with one portfolio of risky assets, T, offer an investor whatever risk-expected return combination he or she seeks; that is, investors can be anywhere they choose on this line, depending on their risk-return preferences.

FIGURE 19-5

The efficient frontier when lending and borrowing possibilities are allowed.

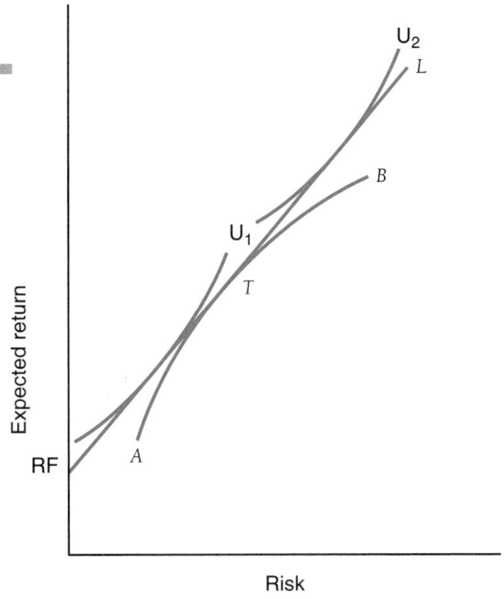

STEP 3: CHOOSE THE FINAL PORTFOLIO BASED ON PREFERENCES

Each investor would choose a point on the efficient-set line that corresponds to his or her risk preferences. Formally, this would be where the investor's highest indifference curve is tangent to the straight line in Figure 19-5. In practical terms this means that the more conservative investors would be closer to the risk-free asset designated by the vertical intercept RF. More aggressive investors would be closer to, or on, point T, representing full investment in a portfolio of risky assets. Even more aggressive investors could go beyond point T by using leverage to move up the line.

THE SEPARATION THEOREM

We have established that each investor will hold combinations of the risk-free asset (either lending or borrowing) and the tangency portfolio from the efficient frontier. By combining these two assets into various portfolios, an investor can form efficient portfolios along line RF–T–L in Figure 19-5 because portfolio T is from the Markowitz efficient set. Given the assets under consideration, investors cannot reach a higher risk-return trade-off.

Consider now the case of an investment firm with multiple clients. (Alternatively, we could assume that all investors have identical forecasts of expected returns, standard deviations, and covariances and select the same optimal portfolio of risky assets.) The investment firm, having determined the Markowitz efficient frontier from the set of securities it analyzes for investment purposes, will offer the same portfolio of risky assets to each of its clients. This portfolio is determined as above, where the ray from RF is tangent to the efficient frontier as its highest point.

Unlike the Markowitz analysis, it is not necessary to match each client's indifference curves with a particular efficient portfolio, because only one efficient portfolio is held by all investors. Rather, each client will use his or her indifference curves to determine where along the new efficient frontier RF–T–L he or she should be. In effect, each client must determine how much of investable funds should be lent or borrowed at RF and how much should be invested in portfolio T. This result is referred to as a separation property.

Separation Theorem The idea that the decision of which portfolio of risky assets to hold is separate from the decision of how to allocate investable funds between the risk-free asset and the risky asset

The **separation theorem** states that the investment decision (which portfolio of risky assets to hold) is separate from the financing decision (how to allocate investable funds between the risk-free asset and the risky asset). The risky portfolio T is optimal for every investor regardless of that investor's utility function; that is, T's optimality is determined separately from knowledge of any investor's risk-return preferences and is not affected by investor risk preferences. All investors, by investing in the same portfolio of risky assets (T) and either borrowing or lending at the rate RF, can achieve any point on the straight line RF–T–L in Figure 19-5. Each point on that line represents a different expected return-risk tradeoff. An investor with utility curve U1 will be at the lower end of the line, representing a combination of lending and investment in T. On the other hand, utility curve U2 represents an investor borrowing at the rate RF to invest in risky assets—specifically, portfolio T.

The concept of the riskless asset–risky-asset (portfolio) dichotomy is an important one in investments, with several different applications. As we have seen, using the two in combination allows investors to achieve any point on the expected return-risk trade-off that all investors face. This is in sharp contrast to the traditional investing approach where investment firms and money managers "tailored" a portfolio of stocks to each individual client because of their unique preferences. For example, a retiree living off the income from a stock portfolio would be guided to a portfolio of relatively conservative stocks with an emphasis on their dividend yields. A 35-year-old investor doing well in his or her profession, on the other hand, might be guided to a portfolio with considerably more risk and expected return.

The separation theorem, given multiple clients or complete agreement by all concerned about the future prospects of securities, argues that this "tailoring" process is inappropriate. All investors should hold the same portfolio of risky assets and achieve their own position on the risk-return trade-off through borrowing and lending. The opportunity set is the same—investors with different preferences can be accommodated with this same opportunity set.

Furthermore, some of the new techniques in investments utilize the same two assets. For example, portfolio insurance (see Chapter 17) can be regarded as an *asset allocation strategy* that seeks to rebalance a portfolio between a risky component and a riskless component in order to keep the portfolio return from declining below some specified minimum return.

THE IMPLICATIONS OF PORTFOLIO SELECTION

The construction of optimal portfolios and the selection of the best portfolio for an investor has implications for the pricing of financial assets. As discussed in Chapter 7, approximately half of the riskiness of the average stock can be eliminated by holding a well-diversified portfolio. This means that part of the risk of the average stock can be eliminated and part cannot. Investors need to focus on that part of the risk that cannot be eliminated by diversification because this is the risk that should be priced in the financial markets. Chapter 20 discusses asset pricing models.

SUMMARY

- Markowitz portfolio theory provides the way to select optimal portfolios based on using the full information set about securities.
- An efficient portfolio has the highest expected return for a given level of risk, or the lowest level of risk for a given level of expected return.
- The Markowitz analysis determines the efficient set of portfolios, all of which are equally desirable. The efficient set is an arc in expected return—standard deviation space.

- The efficient frontier captures the possibilities that exist from a given set of securities. Indifference curves express investor preferences.
- The optimal portfolio for a risk-averse investor occurs at the point of tangency between the investor's highest indifference curve and the efficient set of portfolios.
- In addition to owning risky assets, investors can also buy risk-free assets, earning the riskless rate RF. We can assume that they can borrow at the same rate.
- Risk-free borrowing and lending changes the efficient set to a straight line.
- The separation theorem states that the investment decision (what portfolio of risky assets to buy) can be separated from the financing decision (how much of investable funds should be put in risky assets and how much in the risk-free asset).
- Under the separation theorem, all investors should hold the same portfolio of risky assets and achieve their own position on the return–risk trade-off through borrowing and lending.
- Investors need to focus on that part of portfolio risk that cannot be eliminated by diversification because this is the risk that should be priced in financial markets.
- Total risk can be divided into systematic risk and nonsystematic risk. Nonsystematic risk, also called diversifiable risk, can be eliminated by diversification.
- Market risk cannot be eliminated by diversification and is the relevant risk for the pricing of financial assets in the market.

KEY WORDS

Asset allocation decision
Efficient set
Efficient portfolio
Indifference curves
Separation theorem
Single-index model

QUESTIONS

19-1. Calculate the number of covariances needed for an evaluation of 500 securities using the Markowitz model. Also, calculate the total number of pieces of information needed.

19-2. Using the Sharpe model, how many covariances would be needed to evaluate 500 securities? How many total pieces of information?

19-3. The Markowitz approach is often referred to as a mean-variance approach. Why?

19-4. When, if ever, would a stock with a large risk (standard deviation) be desirable in building a portfolio?

19-5. Using the Markowitz analysis, how does an investor select an optimal portfolio?

19-6. Why do rational investors seek efficient portfolios?

19-7. Given a set of inputs, explain conceptually how efficient portfolios are determined.

19-8. How is an investor's risk aversion indicated in an indifference curve? Are all indifference curves upward-sloping?

19-9. How does the introduction of a risk-free asset change the Markowitz efficient frontier?

19-10. What is meant by the term *lending portfolios?*

19-11. Explain the separation theorem.

19-12. What does the separation theorem imply about the "tailored" approach to portfolio selection?

The following questions were asked on the 1992 CFA Level I examination:

CFA

19-13. Which *one* of the following portfolios cannot lie on the efficient frontier as described by Markowitz?

	Portfolio	Expected Return	Standard Deviation
a.	W	9%	21%
b.	X	5%	7%
c.	Y	15%	36%
d.	Z	12%	15%

CFA

19-14. Portfolio theory as described by Markowitz is most concerned with
a. The elimination of systematic risk
b. The effect of diversification on portfolio risk
c. The identification of unsystematic risk
d. Active portfolio management to enhance return

19-15. Select the correct statement concerning the Markowitz model:
a. The Markowitz model determines the optimal portfolio for each investor.
b. The efficient frontier expresses preferences while indifference curves express possibilities.
c. All conservative investors would have the same optimal portfolio.
d. An investor's optimal portfolio can be found where his or her highest indifference curve is tangent to the efficient frontier.

19-16. Choose the portfolio from the following set that is not on the efficient frontier.
a. Portfolio A: expected return of 10 percent and standard deviation of 8 percent.
b. Portfolio B: expected return of 18 percent and standard deviation of 13 percent.
c. Portfolio C: expected return of 38 percent and standard deviation of 32 percent.
d. Portfolio D: expected return of 15 percent and standard deviation of 14 percent.
e. Portfolio E: expected return of 26 percent and standard deviation of 20 percent.

19-17. Select the correct statement from among the following:
a. Knowing the covariance between two securities and the standard deviation of each, the correlation coefficient can be calculated.
b. When the total returns for a security are plotted against the total returns for a market index and a regression line is fitted, this line is referred to as the capital market line.
c. With perfect negative correlation, two securities' returns have a perfect direct linear relationship to each other.
d. The optimal portfolio for any investor occurs at the point of tangency between the investor's lowest indifference curve and the efficient frontier.

19-18. Choose the statement below that is most closely associated with the work of Markowitz.
a. Risk-free borrowing and lending can change the efficient frontier.
b. Nonsystematic risk can be identified and assessed.
c. The efficient frontier can be changed from an arc to a straight line.
d. Efficient portfolios can be calculated and chosen.

PROBLEMS

19-1. Given the following information for four securities:

Security	1	2	3	4
E(R) %	10	12	14	18
s^2	300	350	400	450

$r(1,2) = 0.2$; $r(1,3) = 0.4$; $r(1,4) = 0.6$; $r(2,3) = 0.1$; $r(3,4) = 0.9$; $r(2,4) = 0.5$.
Calculate five efficient portfolios using the Markowitz analysis, an upper boundary of 25 percent, and a lower boundary of 10 percent.

a. What is the highest expected return from these five portfolios?
b. What is the lowest standard deviation from these five portfolios?
c. Which portfolios involve short sales?
d. Which portfolio should be preferred by an investor?

19-2. Using the information in Problem 19-1, determine the effects of changing the correlation coefficient between securities 1 and 2 from 0.20 to −0.20.

a. What is the effect on the expected return of the portfolios?
b. What is the effect on the variance of the portfolios?

19-3. Based on the information in the table below, determine which of these portfolio(s) would constitute the efficient set.

Portfolio	Expected Return (%)	Standard Deviation (5)
1	10	20
2	12	24
3	8	16
4	6	12
5	9	21
6	20	40
7	18	36
8	8	15
9	11	19
10	12	22
11	14	26

19-4. Given the following information:

Standard deviation for stock X = 12%
Standard deviation for stock Y = 20%
Expected return for stock X = 16%
Expected return for stock Y = 22%
Correlation coefficient between X and Y = 0.30

The covariance between stock X and Y is

a. .048
b. 72.00
c. 3.60
d. 105.6

19-5. Given the information in Problem 19-4 regarding risk, the expected return for a portfolio consisting of 50 percent invested in X and 50 percent invested in Y can be seen to be

a. 19%
b. 16%
c. less than 16%
d. more than 22%

19-6. Given the information in Problem 19-4, assume now that the correlation coefficient between stocks X and Y is +1.0. Choose the investment below that represents the minimum-risk portfolio.

a. 100% investment in stock Y
b. 100% investment in stock X
c. 50% investment in stock X and 50% investment in stock Y
d. 80% investment in stock Y and 20% investment in stock X

SELECTED REFERENCE

A good discussion of the intricacies of portfolio theory can be found in:

Elton, Edwin J., and Gruber, Martin J. *Modern Portfolio Theory and Investment Analysis*, 5th ed. New York: John Wiley, 1995.

www.wiley.com/college/jones7

This chapter discusses how one should go about constructing a portfolio, using the concepts learned in the previous chapter. The exercises for Chapter Nineteen on the Jones Investments website address the following topics:

- Using Mutual Funds versus individual stocks as portfolio components
- Diversifiable and Nondiversifiable risk
- The use of riskfree securities to manage risk exposure

chapter 20

CAPITAL MARKET THEORY

Chapter 20 analyzes the two best-known capital market theories, the Capital Asset Pricing Model and Arbitrage Pricing Theory. The implications of these theories to investors are considered, as are the shortcomings of these models. This chapter provides a solid basis for understanding and estimating the required rate of return, an important concept to all investors.

After reading this chapter you will be able to:

- **Understand capital market theory as an extension of portfolio theory.**
- **Recognize the capital market line, which applies to efficient portfolios, and the security market line, which applies to all portfolios as well as individual securities.**
- **Understand and use the Capital Asset Pricing Model (CAPM), a cornerstone of modern finance.**
- **Describe how betas are estimated, and how beta is used.**
- **Recognize an alternative theory of how assets are priced, Arbitrage Pricing Theory.**

In the last chapter we discussed elements of Portfolio Theory, which is normative, describing how investors should act in selecting an optimal portfolio of risky securities. We also considered how this optimal portfolio can be combined with risk-free lending or borrowing at the rate RF to achieve a preferred risk-return trade-off.

Capital Market Theory Describes the pricing of capital assets in financial markets

In this chapter we consider **capital market theory.** What happens if all investors seek portfolios of risky securities using the Markowitz framework under idealized conditions? How will this affect equilibrium security prices and returns? In other words, how does optimal diversification affect the market prices of securities? Under these idealized conditions, what is the risk-return trade-off that investors face? In effect, we wish to examine models that explain security prices under conditions of market equilibrium.

One equilibrium model discussed in this chapter is known as the Capital Asset Pricing Model, typically referred to as the CAPM. It allows us to measure the relevant risk of an individual security as well as to assess the relationship between risk and the returns expected from investing.

The CAPM is attractive as an equilibrium model because of its simplicity and its implications. Because of serious challenges to the model, however, alternatives have been developed. The primary alternative to the CAPM is Arbitrage Pricing Theory, or APT, which allows for multiple sources of risk. Therefore, we conclude the chapter by examining APT.

THE ASSUMPTIONS OF THE CAPM

Capital Asset Pricing Model (CAPM) Relates the required rate of return for any security with the risk for that security as measured by beta

The **Capital Asset Pricing Model (CAPM)** is concerned with the equilibrium relationship between the risk and the expected return on risky assets. The traditional CAPM was derived independently by Sharpe, Lintner, and Mossin in the mid-1960s.[1] Although several extensions of this model have been proposed, the original CAPM remains a central tenet of modern financial economics.

The CAPM involves a set of predictions concerning equilibrium expected returns on risky assets. It typically is derived by making some simplifying assumptions in order to facilitate the analysis and help us to understand the arguments without fundamentally changing the predictions of asset pricing theory.

Capital market theory builds on Markowitz portfolio theory. Each investor is assumed to diversify his or her portfolio according to the Markowitz model, choosing a location on the efficient frontier that matches his or her return-risk preferences. Because of the complexity of the real world, additional assumptions are made to make individuals more alike:

1. All investors have identical probability distributions for future rates of return; they have identical (or homogeneous) expectations with respect to the three inputs of the portfolio model explained in Chapter 7: expected returns, the variance of returns, and the correlation matrix. Therefore, given a set of security prices and a risk-free rate, all investors use the same information to generate an efficient frontier.
2. All investors have the same one-period time horizon.
3. All investors can borrow or lend money at the risk-free rate of return (designated RF in this text).
4. There are no transaction costs.

[1] Much of this analysis is attributable to the work of Sharpe. See W. Sharpe, "Capital Asset Prices: A Theory of Market Equilibrium under Conditions of Risk," *The Journal of Finance,* 19 (September 1964): 425–442. Lintner and Mossin developed a similar analysis.

5. There are no personal income taxes—investors are indifferent between capital gains and dividends.
6. There is no inflation.
7. There are many investors, and no single investor can affect the price of a stock through his or her buying and selling decisions. Investors are price-takers and act as if prices are unaffected by their own trades.
8. Capital markets are in equilibrium.

These assumptions appear unrealistic and often disturb individuals encountering capital market theory for the first time. However, the important issue is how well the theory predicts or describes reality, and not the realism of its assumptions. If capital market theory does a good job of explaining the returns on risky assets, it is very useful and the assumptions made in deriving the theory are of less importance.

Most of these assumptions can be relaxed without significant effects on the capital pricing asset model or its implications; in other words, the CAPM is robust.[2] Although the results from such a relaxation of the assumptions may be less clear-cut and precise, no significant damage is done. Many conclusions of the basic model still hold.

Finally, most investors recognize that all of the assumptions of the CAPM are not unrealistic. For example, some institutional investors are tax-exempt, and their brokerage costs, as a percentage of the transaction, are quite small. Nor is it too unreasonable to assume that for the one-period horizon of the model, inflation may be fully (or mostly) anticipated and, therefore, not a major factor.

EQUILIBRIUM IN THE CAPITAL MARKETS

If the assumptions listed above hold, what is the equilibrium situation that will prevail in the capital markets? Market equilibrium exists when prices are at levels that provide no incentive for speculative trading. In other words, what are the implications of these assumptions?

1. All investors will choose to hold the aggregate market portfolio, which includes all assets in existence.
2. This market portfolio will be on the Markowitz efficient frontier and will be the optimal risky portfolio to hold.
3. All efficient portfolios will plot on the trade-off between the standard deviation and the expected return for efficient portfolios, and all securities and inefficient portfolios will plot on the trade-off between systematic risk and expected return.

We will consider these implications below.

THE MARKET PORTFOLIO

We start with the assumptions discussed above and the analysis of Chapters 7 and 19. We use the mean-variance criteria from Chapters 7 and 19 to identify preferred investments. As before, the *feasible set* contains all potential portfolios. The mean-variance *efficient set* contains *portfolios* of risky assets (no individual securities) not dominated by any others. Rational investors eliminate all inefficient portfolios from consideration.

[2] For a discussion of changing these assumptions, see E. Elton and M. Gruber, *Modern Portfolio Theory and Investment Analysis,* Fifth Edition (New York: John Wiley & Sons, 1995), Chapter 11.

FIGURE 20-1

The efficient frontier with borrowing and lending.

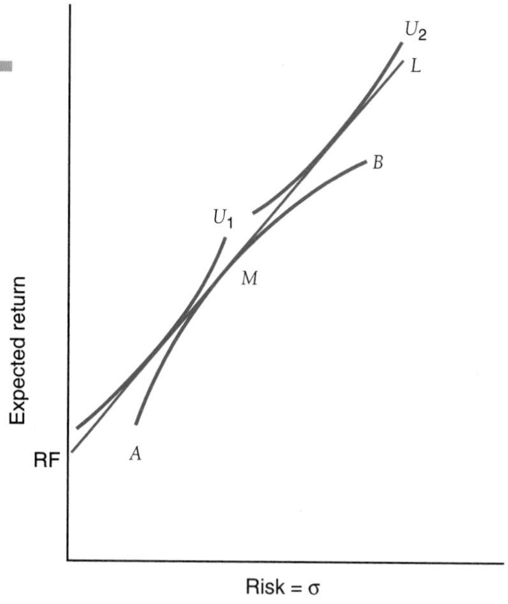

In addition to the efficient frontier, we learned in Chapter 19 that investors combine risk-free assets with risky portfolios. The potential risk-return combinations are now given by a straight line tangent to the efficient set at the steepest point.

Market Portfolio The portfolio of all risky assets, with each asset weighted by the ratio of its market value to the market value of all risky assets

Figure 20-1 is the same as Figure 19-5 except the point of tangency has been changed from T to M. Portfolio M in Figure 20-1 is called the **market portfolio** of risky securities. It is the highest point of tangency between RF and the efficient frontier and is *the* optimal risky portfolio. This optimal risky portfolio from the Markowitz efficient set is found by determining which efficient portfolio offers the highest risk premium, given the existence of a risk-free asset. Because this line produces the highest attainable return for any given risk level, all rational investors will seek to be on this line.

THE IMPORTANCE OF THE MARKET PORTFOLIO

All investors would want to be on the optimal line RF–M–L, and, unless they invested 100 percent of their wealth in the risk-free asset, they would own portfolio M with some portion of their investable wealth or they would invest their own wealth plus borrowed funds in portfolio M.[3] This portfolio is the optimal portfolio of risky assets.

Why do all investors hold identical risky portfolios? Based on our assumptions above, all investors use the same Markowitz analysis on the same set of securities, have the same expected returns and covariances, and have an identical time horizon. Therefore, they will arrive at the same optimal risky portfolio, and it will be the market portfolio, designated M.

It is critical to note that although investors take different positions on the straight-line efficient set in Figure 20-1, all investors are investing in portfolio M, the same portfolio of risky assets. This portfolio will always consist of all risky assets in existence. The emergence of the market portfolio as the optimal efficient portfolio is the most important implication of the CAPM. In effect, the CAPM states that portfolio M is the optimal risky portfolio.

[3] Keep in mind that with lending the investor earns a rate RF, whereas with borrowing the investor pays the rate RF on the borrowed funds.

COMPOSITION OF THE MARKET PORTFOLIO

In equilibrium, all risky assets must be in portfolio M because all investors are assumed to arrive at, and hold, the same risky portfolio. If the optimal portfolio did not include a particular asset, the price of this asset would decline dramatically until it became an attractive investment opportunity. At some point investors will purchase it, and it will be included in the market portfolio. Because the market portfolio includes all risky assets, *portfolio M is completely diversified.* Portfolio M contains only systematic risk which, even with perfect diversification, cannot be eliminated because it is the result of macroeconomic factors that effect the value of all securities.

All assets are included in portfolio M in proportion to their market value. For example, if the market value of IBM constitutes 2 percent of the market value of all risky assets, IBM will constitute 2 percent of the market value of portfolio M and, therefore, 2 percent of the market value of each investor's portfolio of risky assets. Therefore, we can state that security *i*'s percentage in the risky portfolio M is equal to the total market value of security *i* relative to the total market value of all securities.

In theory, the market portfolio should include all risky assets worldwide, both financial (bonds, options, futures, etc.) and real (gold, real estate, etc.), in their proper proportions. The global aspects of such a portfolio are important to note. By one estimate, the value of non-U.S. assets exceeds 60 percent of the world total. U.S. equities make up only about 10 percent of total world assets. Therefore, international diversification is clearly important.

A worldwide portfolio, if it could be constructed, would be completely diversified. Of course, the market portfolio is unobservable.[4] In practice, the market portfolio is often proxied by the portfolio of all common stocks, which, in turn, is proxied by a market index such as the Standard & Poor's 500 Composite Index, which has been used throughout the text. Therefore, to facilitate this discussion, think of portfolio M as a broad market index such as the S&P 500 Index. The market portfolio is, of course, a risky portfolio, and its risk will be designated σ_M.

THE EQUILIBRIUM RISK-RETURN TRADE-OFF

Given the analysis above, we can now derive some predictions concerning equilibrium expected returns and risk. The CAPM is an equilibrium model that encompasses two important relationships. The first, the Capital Market Line, specifies the equilibrium relationship between expected return and *total risk* for efficiently diversified portfolios. The second, the Security Market Line, specifies the equilibrium relationship between expected return and *systematic risk.* It applies to individual securities as well as portfolios.

THE CAPITAL MARKET LINE

The straight line shown in Figure 20-1, which traces out the risk-return trade-off for efficient portfolios, is tangent to the Markowitz efficient frontier at point M and has a vertical intercept RF. We now know that portfolio M is the tangency point to a straight line drawn from RF to the efficient frontier, and that this straight line is the best obtainable efficient-set line. All investors will hold portfolio M as their optimal risky portfolio, and all investors will be somewhere on this steepest trade-off line between expected return and risk because it rep-

[4] Market values and returns have been computed for a "world market wealth portfolio" consisting of stocks, bonds, cash, real estate, and metals. See Roger G. Ibbotson, Laurence B. Siegel, and Kathryn S. Love, "World Wealth: Market Values and Returns," *Journal of Portfolio Management* (Fall 1985): 4–23.

FIGURE 20-2

The capital market line and the components of its slope.

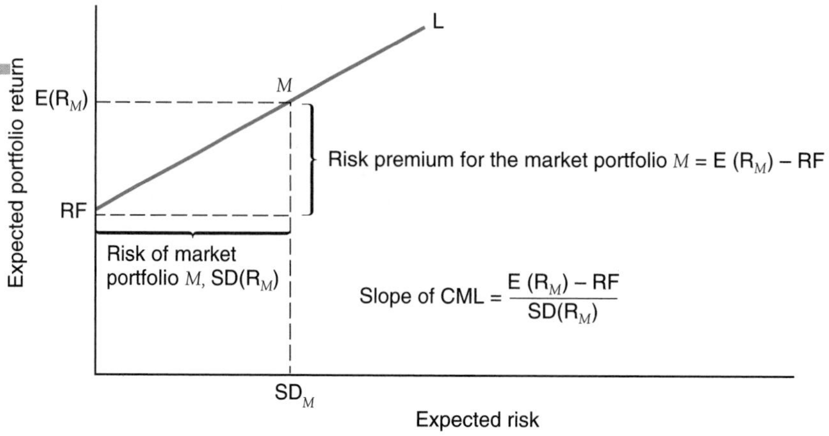

resents those combinations of risk-free investing/borrowing and portfolio M that yield the highest return obtainable for a given pool of risk. Investors will differ only in the amount of their funds invested in RF versus portfolio M.

Capital Market Line (CML) The tradeoff between expected return and risk for efficient portfolios

This straight line, usually referred to as the **capital market line** (CML), depicts the equilibrium conditions that prevail in the market for *efficient portfolios* consisting of the optimal portfolio of risky assets and the risk-free asset. All combinations of risky and risk-free portfolios are bounded by the CML, and, in equilibrium, all investors will end up with portfolios somewhere on the CML.

Consider the equation for the CML, which is shown as a straight line in Figure 20-2 without the now-dominated Markowitz frontier. We know that this line has an intercept of RF. If investors are to invest in risky assets, they must be compensated for this additional risk with a risk premium. The vertical distance between the risk-free rate and the CML at point M in Figure 20-2 is the amount of return expected for bearing the risk of the market portfolio, that is, the excess return above the risk-free rate. At that point, the amount of risk for the market portfolio is given by the horizontal dotted line between RF and σ_M. Therefore,

$$\frac{E(R_M) - RF}{\sigma_M} = \text{Slope of the CML}$$

$$= \text{Expected return-risk trade-off for efficient portfolios}$$

The slope of the CML is the *market price of risk* for efficient portfolios or the equilibrium price of risk in the market.[5] It indicates the additional return that the market demands for each percentage increase in a portfolio's risk, that is, in its standard deviation of return.

EXAMPLE 20-1

Assume that the expected return on portfolio M is 13 percent, with a standard deviation of 25 percent, and that RF is 7 percent. The slope of the CML would be

$$(0.13 - 0.07)/0.25 = 0.24$$

In our example a risk premium of 0.24 indicates that the market demands this amount of return for each percentage increase in a portfolio's risk.

[5] The assumption throughout this discussion is that $E(R_M)$ is greater than RF. This is the only reasonable assumption to make, because the CAPM is concerned with expected returns (i.e., ex ante returns). After the fact, this assumption may not hold for particular periods, that is, over historical periods such as a year RF has exceeded the return on the market, which is sometimes negative.

We now know the intercept and slope of the CML. Since the CML is the trade-off between expected return and risk for efficient portfolios, and risk is being measured by the standard deviation, the equation for the CML is

$$E(R_p) = RF + \frac{E(R_M) - RF}{\sigma_M}\sigma_p \qquad (20\text{-}1)$$

where

$E(R_p)$ = the expected return on any efficient portfolio on the CML
RF = the rate of return on the risk-free asset
$E(R_M)$ = the expected return on the market portfolio M
σ_M = the standard deviation of the returns on the market portfolio
σ_p = the standard deviation of the efficient portfolio being considered

In words, the expected return for any portfolio on the CML is equal to the price necessary to induce investors to forego consumption plus the product of the market price of risk and the amount of risk on the portfolio being considered. Note that:

RF is the price of foregone consumption.

$$\frac{E(R_M) - RF}{\sigma_p} = \text{Market price of risk}$$

$$\sigma_p = \text{Amount of risk taken on a particular portfolio}$$

The following points should be noted about the CML:

1. Only efficient portfolios consisting of the risk-free asset and portfolio M lie on the CML. Portfolio M, the market portfolio of risky securities, contains all securities weighted by their respective market values—it is the optimum combination of risky securities. The risk-free asset has no risk. Therefore, all combinations of these two assets on the CML are efficient portfolios.
2. As a statement of equilibrium, the CML must always be upward sloping because the price of risk must always be positive. Remember that the CML is formulated in a world of expected return, and risk-averse investors will not invest unless they expect to be compensated for the risk. The greater the risk, the greater the expected return.
3. On a historical basis, for some particular period of time such as a year or two, or four consecutive quarters, the CML can be downward sloping; that is, the return on RF exceeds the return on the market portfolio. This does not negate the validity of the CML; it merely indicates that returns actually realized differ from those that were expected. Obviously, investor expectations are not always realized. (If they were, there would be no risk.) Thus, although the CML must be upward sloping ex ante (before the fact), it can be, and sometimes is, downward sloping ex post (after the fact).
4. The CML can be used to determine the optimal expected returns associated with different portfolio risk levels.[6] Therefore, the CML indicates the required return for each portfolio risk level.

THE SECURITY MARKET LINE

The capital market line depicts the risk-return trade-off in the financial markets in equilibrium. However, it applies only to efficient portfolios and cannot be used to assess the equi-

[6] This assumes that we can readily compute a portfolio's standard deviation, which in practice is difficult to do.

librium expected return on a single security. What about individual securities or inefficient portfolios?

Under the CAPM all investors will hold the market portfolio, which is the benchmark portfolio against which other portfolios are measured. How does an individual security contribute to the risk of the market portfolio?

We know from Chapter 7 that the equation for portfolio standard deviation consists of many variance and covariance terms. Now consider the equation for the standard deviation of the market portfolio. Each security in the market portfolio consisting of n securities will have a variance term and $n - 1$ covariance terms multiplied by two (for securities 1 and 2, for example, there is COV 1,2 and COV 2,1). These complex variance and covariance terms can be simplified to the following equation for the standard deviation of the market portfolio:

$$\begin{aligned}\sigma_M &= [X_1 COV(R_1, R_M) + X_2\ COV(R_2, R_M) + \cdots +]^{1/2} \\ &= [\text{security's 1's contribution to portfolio variance} \\ &\quad + \text{security's 2's contribution to portfolio variance} + \cdots \cdots]^{1/2}\end{aligned} \tag{20-2}$$

We can see from Equation 20-2 that the contribution of each security to the standard deviation of the market portfolio depends on the size of its covariance with the market portfolio. Therefore, investors consider the relevant measure of risk for a security to be its covariance with the market portfolio.

We can evaluate how each security affects the standard deviation of the market portfolio by evaluating the way it would change if the proportion invested in a particular security changes. (In effect, we take the partial derivative of the standard deviation of the market portfolio with respect to the proportion of portfolio funds invested in that particular security.) The result is that a security's contribution to the risk of the market portfolio is given by:

$$\frac{\sigma_{i,M}}{\sigma_M}$$

where $\sigma_{i,M}$ = the covariance between stock i and the market portfolio.

Now consider the CML equation again (Equation 20-3):

$$E(R_p) = RF + \frac{E(R_M) - RF}{\sigma_M}\sigma_p \tag{20-3}$$

We can write the expected return for an individual security as:

$$E(R_i) = RF + \frac{E(R_M) - RF}{\sigma_M}\frac{\sigma_{i,M}}{\sigma_M} \tag{20-4}$$

or

$$E(R_i) = RF + \frac{E(R_M) - RF}{\sigma_M^2}\sigma_{i,M} \tag{20-5}$$

We could relate each individual security to the risk of the portfolio through its covariance with the market portfolio, $COV_{i,M}$. However, it is more convenient to use a standardized measure of systematic risk, the beta coefficient, by taking advantage of the following relationship:

$$\sigma_i = \frac{\sigma_{i,M}}{\sigma_M} \tag{20-6}$$

To derive the expected return-risk relationship for one security, recognizing that the contribution of a security to the total risk of a diversified portfolio is its systematic risk, we

FIGURE 20-3

The security market line (SML).

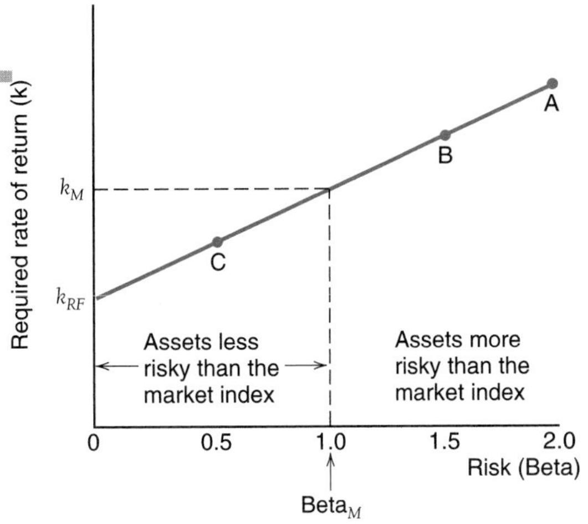

Beta A measure of volatility, or relative systematic risk, for stock or portfolio returns

Security Market Line (SML) The graphical depiction of the CAPM

simply reformulate the expected return-risk trade-off with beta (the measure of relative systematic risk) on the horizontal axis, as shown in Figure 20-3. Beta is discussed in Chapter 7, and should be reviewed there. The vertical axis is now the expected return, and the intercept of the trade-off on this vertical axis remains the risk-free rate of return, RF.

The line RF–Z in Figure 20-3 is called the **security market line (SML).** It depicts the trade-off between risk and expected return for all assets, whether individual securities, inefficient portfolios, or efficient portfolios. The SML was discussed in Chapter 7.

INVESTMENTS INTUITION As we could (and should) expect, Figure 20-3 again demonstrates that if investors are to seek higher expected returns, they must assume a larger risk as measured by beta, the relative measure of systematic risk. The trade-off between expected return and risk must always be positive. In Figure 20-3 the vertical axis can be thought of as the expected return for an asset. In equilibrium, investors require a minimum expected return before they will invest in a particular security. That is, given its risk, a security must offer some minimum expected return before a given investor can be persuaded to purchase it. Thus, in discussing the SML concept, we are simultaneously talking about the required and expected rate of return.

Required Rate of Return The minimum expected rate of return on an asset required by an investor to invest in that asset

As discussed in Chapter 7, the CAPM in its expected return–beta relationship form is a simple but elegant statement. It says that the expected rate of return on an asset is a function of the two components of the **required rate of return**—the risk-free rate and the risk premium. Thus,

$$k_i = \text{Risk-free rate} + \text{Risk premium} \qquad (20\text{-}7)$$
$$= RF + \beta_i[E(R_M) - RF]$$

where

k_i = the required rate of return on asset i
$E(R_M)$ = the expected rate of return on the market portfolio
β_i = the beta coefficient for asset i

The CAPM's expected return–beta relationship is a simple but elegant statement about expected (required) return and risk for any security or portfolio. It formalizes the basis of investments, which is that the greater the risk assumed, the greater the expected (required) return should be. This relationship states that an investor requires (expects) a return on a risky asset equal to the return on a risk-free asset plus a risk premium, and the greater the risk assumed, the greater the risk premium.

Over-and-Undervalued Securities The SML has important implications for security prices. In equilibrium, each security should lie on the SML because the expected return on the security should be that needed to compensate investors for the systematic risk.

What happens if investors determine that a security does not lie on the SML? To make this determination, they must employ a separate methodology to estimate the expected returns for securities. In other words, a SML can be fitted to a sample of securities to determine the expected (required) return-risk tradeoff that exists. Knowing the beta for any stock, we can determine the required return from the SML. Then, estimating the expected return from, say, fundamental analysis, an investor can assess a security in relation to the SML and determine whether it is under- or overvalued.

EXAMPLE 20-2

In Figure 20-4, two securities are plotted around the SML. Security X has a high expected return derived from fundamental analysis and plots above the SML; security Y has a low expected return and plots below the SML. Which is undervalued?

Security X, plotting above the SML, is undervalued because it offers more expected return than investors require, given its level of systematic risk. Investors require a minimum expected return of $E(R_X)$, but security X, according to fundamental analysis, is offering $E(R_X')$. If investors recognize this, they will do the following:

> Purchase security X, because it offers more return than required. This demand will drive up the price of X, as more of it is purchased. The return will be driven down, until it is at the level indicated by the SML.

Now consider security Y. This security, according to investors' fundamental analysis, does not offer enough expected return given its level of systematic risk. Investors require $E(R_Y)$ for security Y, based on the SML, but Y offers only $E(R_Y')$. As investors recognize this, they will do the following:

> Sell security Y (or perhaps sell Y short), because it offers less than the required return. This increase in the supply of Y will drive down its price. The return will be driven up for new buyers because any dividends paid are now relative to a lower price, as is any expected price appreciation. The price will fall until the expected return rises enough to reach the SML and the security is once again in equilibrium.

FIGURE 20-4

Overvalued and undervalued securities using the SML.

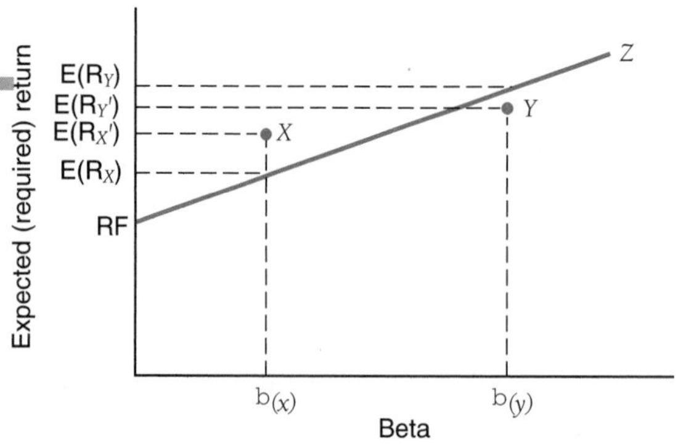

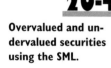

ESTIMATING THE SML

To implement the SML approach described here, an investor needs estimates of the return on the risk-free asset, the expected return on the market index, and the beta for an individual security. How difficult are these to obtain?

The return on a risk-free asset, RF, should be the easiest of the three variables to obtain. In estimating RF, the investor can use the return on Treasury bills for the coming period (e.g., a year).

Estimating the market return is more difficult because the expected return for the market index is not observable. Furthermore, several different market indexes could be used. Estimates of the market return could be derived from a study of previous market returns (such as the Standard & Poor's data in Table 5-1). Alternatively, probability estimates of market returns could be made, and the expected value calculated. This would provide an estimate of both the expected return and the standard deviation for the market.

Finally, it is necessary to estimate the betas for individual securities. This is a crucial part of the CAPM estimation process. The estimates of RF and the expected return on the market are the same for each security being evaluated. Only beta is unique, bringing together the investor's expectations of returns for the stock with those for the market. Beta is the only company-specific factor in the CAPM; therefore, risk is the only asset-specific forecast that must be made in the CAPM.

ESTIMATING BETA

Market Model Relates the return on each stock to the return on the market, using a linear relationship with intercept and slope

A less restrictive form of the Single Index Model is known as the **Market Model.** This model is identical to the Single Index Model except that the assumption of the error terms for different securities being uncorrelated is not made.

The Market Model equation is the same as Equation 19-15 for the Single Index Model (again, without the restrictive assumption):

$$R_i = \alpha_i + \beta_i R_M + e_i \qquad (20\text{-}8)$$

where

R_i = the return (TR) on security *i*
R_M = the return (TR) on the market index
α_i = the intercept term
β_i = the slope term
e_i = the random residual error

The Market Model produces an estimate of return for any stock.

To estimate the Market Model, the TRs for stock *i* can be regressed on the corresponding TRs for the market index. Estimates will be obtained of α_i (the constant return on security *i* that is earned regardless of the level of market returns) and β_i (the slope coefficient that indicates the expected increase in a security's return for a 1 percent increase in market return). This is how the estimate of a stock's beta is often derived.

EXAMPLE 20-3

To illustrate the calculation of the Market Model, we use Total Return (TR) data for the Coca-Cola company (ticker symbol "KO"). Fitting a regression equation to 60 months of return data along with corresponding TRs for the S&P 500, the estimated equation is:

$$R_{KO} = 1.06 + 1.149\ R_{S\&P500}$$

FIGURE 20-5

The characteristic line for Coca-Cola, monthly data.

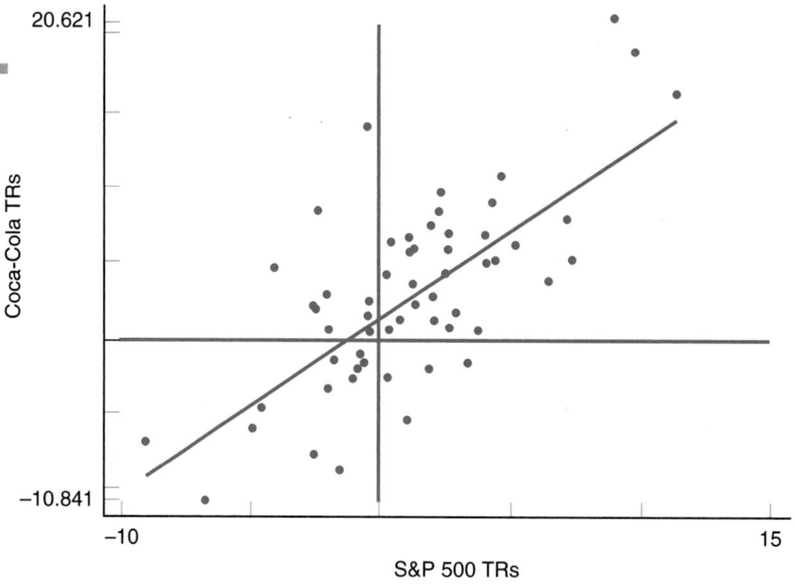

Characteristic Line A regression equation used to estimate beta by regressing stock returns on market returns

When the TRs for a stock are plotted against the market index TRs, the regression line fitted to these points is referred to as the **characteristic line.** Coca-Cola's characteristic line is shown in Figure 20-5.

The characteristic line is often fitted using *excess returns*. The excess return is calculated by subtracting out the risk-free rate, RF, from both the return on the stock and the return on the market.

In excess return form, the same analysis as before applies. The alpha is the intercept of the characteristic line on the vertical axis and, in theory, should be zero for any stock. It measures the excess return for a stock when the excess return for the market portfolio is zero.

In excess return form, the beta coefficient remains the slope of the characteristic line. It measures the sensitivity of a stock's excess return to that of the market portfolio.

The variance of the error term measures the variability of a stock's excess return not associated with movements in the market's excess return. Diversification can reduce this variability.

Many brokerage houses and investment advisory services report Betas as part of the total information given for individual stocks. For example, *The Value Line Investment Survey* reports the Beta for each stock covered, as do such brokerage firms as Merrill Lynch. Both measures of risk discussed above, standard deviation and beta, are widely known and discussed by investors.

Whether we use the Single Index Model or the Market Model, Beta can be estimated using regression analysis. However, the values of α_i and β_i obtained in this manner are estimates of the true parameters and are subject to error. Furthermore, beta can shift over time as a company's situation changes. A legitimate question, therefore, is how accurate are the estimates of beta?

As noted, beta is usually estimated by fitting a characteristic line to the data. However, this is an estimate of the beta called for in the CAPM. The market proxy used in the equations for estimating beta may not fully reflect the market portfolio specified in the CAPM. Furthermore, several points should be kept in mind:

1. We are trying to estimate the future beta for a security, which may differ from the historical beta.

2. In theory, the independent variable RM represents the total of all marketable assets in the economy. This is typically approximated with a stock market index, which, in turn, is an approximation of the return on all common stocks.
3. The characteristic line can be fitted over varying numbers of observations and time periods. There is no one correct period or number of observations for calculating beta. As a result, estimates of Beta will vary. For example, *The Value Line Investment Survey* calculates betas from weekly rates of return for five years, whereas other analysts often use monthly rates of return over a comparable period.
4. The regression estimates of α and β from the characteristic line are only estimates of the true α and β, and are subject to error. Thus, these estimates may not be equal to the true α and β.
5. As the fundamental variables (e.g., earnings, cash flow) of a company change, beta should change; that is, the beta is not perfectly stationary over time. This issue is important enough to be considered separately.

Blume found that in comparing nonoverlapping seven-year periods for 1, 2, 4, 7, 10, 21, and so on, stocks in a portfolio, the following observations could be made:[7]

1. Betas estimated for individual securities are unstable; that is, they contain relatively little information about future betas.
2. Betas estimated for large portfolios are stable; that is, they contain much information about future betas.

In effect, a large portfolio (e.g., 50 stocks) provides stability because of the averaging effect. Although the betas of some stocks in the portfolio go up from period to period, others go down, and these two movements tend to cancel each other. Furthermore, the errors involved in estimating betas tend to cancel out in a portfolio. Therefore, estimates of portfolio betas show less change from period to period and are much more reliable than are the estimates for individual securities.

Researchers have found that betas in the forecast period are, on average, closer to 1.0 than the estimate obtained using historical data. This would imply that we can improve the estimates of beta by measuring the adjustment in one period and using it as an estimate of the adjustment in the next period. For example we could adjust each beta toward the average beta by taking half the historical beta and adding it to half of the average beta. Merrill Lynch, the largest brokerage firm, reports adjusted betas based on a technique such as this. Other methods have also been proposed, including a Bayesian estimation technique.

TESTS OF THE CAPM

The conclusions of the CAPM are entirely sensible:

1. Return and risk are positively related—greater risk should carry greater return.
2. The relevant risk for a security is a measure of its effect on portfolio risk.

The question, therefore, is how well the theory works. After all, the assumptions on which capital market theory rest are, for the most part, unrealistic. To assess the validity of

[7] See M. Blume, "Betas and Their Regression Tendencies," *The Journal of Finance,* 10 (June 1975): 785–795; and R. Levy, "On the Short-Term Stationarity of Beta Coefficients," *Financial Analysts Journal,* 27 (December 1971): 55–62.

this or any other theory, empirical tests must be performed. If the CAPM is valid, and the market tends to balance out so that realized security returns average out to equal expected returns, equations of the following type can be estimated:

$$R_i = a_1 + a_2\beta_i \tag{20-9}$$

where

R_i = the average return on security i over some number of periods
β_i = the estimated beta for security i

Market Risk Premium The difference between the expected return for the equities market and the risk-free rate of return

When Equation 20-9 is estimated, a_1 should approximate the average risk-free rate during the periods studied, and a_2 should approximate the average market risk premium during the periods studied.

An extensive literature exists involving tests of capital market theory, in particular, the CAPM. Although it is not possible to summarize the scope of this literature entirely and to reconcile findings from different studies that seem to be in disagreement, the following points represent a reasonable consensus of the empirical results:[8]

1. The SML appears to be linear; that is, the trade-off between expected (required) return and risk is an upward-sloping straight line.
2. The intercept term, a_1, is generally found to be higher than RF.
3. The slope of the CAPM, a_2, is generally found to be less steep than posited by the theory.
4. Although the evidence is mixed, no persuasive case has been made that unsystematic risk commands a risk premium. In other words, investors are rewarded only for assuming systematic risk.

The major problem in testing capital market theory is that it is formulated on an ex ante basis but can be tested only on an ex post basis. We can never know investor expectations with certainty. Therefore, it should come as no surprise that tests of the model have produced conflicting results in some cases and that the empirical results diverge from the predictions of the model. In fact, it is amazing that the empirical results support the basic CAPM as well as they do. Based on studies of many years of data, it appears that the stock market prices securities on the basis of a linear relationship between systematic risk and return, with diversifiable (unsystematic) risk playing little or no part in the pricing mechanism.

The CAPM has not been proved empirically, nor will it be. In fact, Roll has argued that the CAPM is untestable because the market portfolio, which consists of all risky assets, is unobservable.[9] In effect, Roll argues that tests of the CAPM are actually tests of the mean-variance efficiency of the market portfolio. Nevertheless, the CAPM remains a logical way to view the expected return-risk trade-off.

ARBITRAGE PRICING THEORY

Arbitrage Pricing Model (APM) An equilibrium theory of expected returns for securities involving few assumptions about investor preferences

The CAPM is not the only model of security pricing. Another model that has received attention is based on **Arbitrage Pricing Theory (APT)** as developed by Ross and enhanced by others. In recent years APT has emerged as an alternative theory of asset pricing to the CAPM. Its appeal is that it is more general than the CAPM, with less restrictive assumptions. However, like the CAPM, it has limitations, and like the CAPM, it is not the final word in asset pricing.

[8] For a discussion of empirical tests of the CAPM, see Elton and Gruber, *Modern Portfolio Theory*.

[9] See R. Roll, "A Critique of the Asset Pricing Theory's Tests; Part I: On Past and Potential Testability of the Theory," *Journal of Financial Economics*, 4 (March 1977): 129–176.

Similar to the CAPM, or any other asset pricing model, APT posits a relationship between expected return and risk. It does so, however, using different assumptions and procedures. Very importantly, APT is not critically dependent on an underlying market portfolio as is the CAPM, which predicts that only market risk influences expected returns. Instead, APT recognizes that several types of risk may affect security returns.

APT is based on the *law of one price,* which states that two otherwise identical assets cannot sell at different prices. APT assumes that asset returns are linearly related to a set of indexes, where each index represents a factor that influences the return on an asset. Market participants develop expectations about the sensitivities of assets to the factors. They buy and sell securities so that, given the law of one price, securities affected equally by the same factors will have equal expected returns. This buying and selling is the arbitrage process, which determines the prices of securities.

APT states that equilibrium market prices will adjust to eliminate any arbitrage opportunities, which refer to situations where a *zero investment portfolio* can be constructed that will yield a risk-free profit. If arbitrage opportunities arise, a relatively few investors can act to restore equilibrium.

Unlike the CAPM, APT does not assume:

1. A single-period investment horizon
2. The absence of taxes
3. Borrowing and lending at the rate RF
4. Investors select portfolios on the basis of expected return and variance

APT, like the CAPM, does assume:

1. Investors have homogeneous beliefs
2. Investors are risk-averse utility maximizers
3. Markets are perfect
4. Returns are generated by a factor model.

Factor Model Used to depict the behavior of security prices by identifying major factors in the economy that affect large numbers of securities

A **factor model** is based on the view that there are underlying *risk factors* that affect realized and expected security returns. These risk factors represent broad economic forces and not company-specific characteristics and, by definition, they represent the element of surprise in the risk factor—the difference between the actual value for the factor and its expected value.

The factors must possess three characteristics:[10]

1. Each risk factor must have a pervasive influence on stock returns. Firm-specific events are not APT risk factors.
2. These risk factors must influence expected return, which means they must have nonzero prices. This issue must be determined empirically, by statistically analyzing stock returns to see which factors pervasively affect returns.
3. At the beginning of each period, the risk factors must be unpredictable to the market as a whole. This raises an important point. In our example above, we used inflation and the economy's output as the two factors affecting portfolio returns. The rate of inflation is *not* an APT risk factor because it is at least partially predictable. In an economy with reasonable growth where the quarterly rate of inflation has averaged 3 percent on an annual basis, we can reasonably assume that next quarter's inflation

[10] See Michael A. Berry, Edwin Burmeister, and Marjorie B. McElroy, "Sorting Out Risks Using Known APT Factors," *Financial Analysts Journal* (March–April 1988): 29–42.

rate is not going to be 10 percent. On the other hand, unexpected inflation—the difference between actual inflation and expected inflation—is an APT risk factor. By definition, it cannot be predicted since it is unexpected.

What really matters are the *deviations* of the factors from their expected values. For example, if the expected value of inflation is 5 percent and the actual rate of inflation for a period is only 4 percent, this 1 percent deviation will affect the actual return for the period.

EXAMPLE 20-4

An investor holds a portfolio of stocks that she thinks is influenced by only two basic economic factors, inflation and the economy's output. Diversification once again plays a role because the portfolio's sensitivity to all other factors can be eliminated by diversification.

Portfolio return varies directly with output, and inversely with inflation. Each of these factors has an expected value, and the portfolio has an expected return when the factors are at their expected values. If either or both of the factors deviates from expected value, the portfolio return will be affected.

We must measure the sensitivity of each stock in our investor's portfolio to changes in each of the two factors. Each stock will have its own sensitivity to each of the factors. For example, stock #1 (a mortgage company) may be particularly sensitive to inflation and have a sensitivity of 2.0, while stock #2 (a food manufacturer) may have a sensitivity to inflation of only 1.0.

Based on this analysis, we can now understand the APT model. It assumes that investors believe that asset returns are randomly generated according to a *n*-factor model, which, for security *i*, can be formally stated as:

$$R_i = E(R_i) + \beta_{i1}f_1 + \beta_{i2}f_2 + \cdots + \beta_{in}f_n + e_i \qquad (20\text{-}10)$$

where

R_i = the actual (random) rate of return on security *i* in any given period *t*
$E(R_i)$ = the expected return on security *i*
f = the deviation of a systematic factor F from its expected value
β_i = sensitivity of security *i* to a factor
e_i = random error term, unique to security *i*[11]

It is important to note that the expected value of each factor, F, is zero. Therefore, the *f*s in Equation 20-10 are measuring the deviation of each factor from its expected value. Notice in Equation 20-10 that the actual return for a security in a given period will be at the expected or required rate of return if the factors are at expected levels [e.g., $F_1 - E(F_1) = 0$, $F_2 - E(F_2) = 0$, and so forth] and if the chance element represented by the error term is at zero.

A factor model makes no statement about equilibrium. If we transform Equation 20-10 into an equilibrium model, we are saying something about *expected* returns across securities. APT is an equilibrium theory of expected returns that requires a factor model such as Equation 20-10. The equation for expected return on a security is given by Equation 20-11.

$$E(R_i) = a_0 + b_{i1}\bar{F}_1 + b_{i2}\bar{F}_2 + \cdots + b_{in}\bar{F}_n \qquad (20\text{-}11)$$

[11] It is assumed that all covariances between returns on securities are attributable to the effects of the factors; therefore, the error terms are uncorrelated.

where

$E(R_i)$ = the expected return on security i

a_0 = the expected return on a security with zero systematic risk

$\overline{F}$ = the risk premium for a factor (for example, the risk premium for F_1 is equal to $E(F_1) - a_0$)

With APT, risk is defined in terms of a stock's sensitivity to basic economic factors, while expected return is directly related to sensitivity. As always, expected return increases with risk.

The expected return-risk relationship for the CAPM is:

$$E(R_i) = RF + \beta_i[\text{market risk premium}]$$

The CAPM assumes that the only required measure of risk is the sensitivity to the market. The risk premium for a stock depends on this sensitivity and the market risk premium (the difference between the expected return on the market and the risk-free rate).

The expected return-risk relationship for the APT can be described as:

$$E(R_i) = RF + b_{i1}\text{ (risk premium for factor 1} + b_{i2}\text{ (risk premium for factor 2)} + \cdots + b_{in}\text{ (risk premium for factor n)}$$

Note that the sensitivity measures (β_i and b_i) have similar interpretations. They are measures of the relative sensitivity of a security's return to a particular risk premium. Also notice that we are dealing with risk premiums in both cases. Finally, notice that the CAPM relationship is the same as would be provided by APT if there were only one pervasive factor influencing returns. APT is more general than CAPM.

The problem with APT is that the factors are not well specified, at least ex ante. To implement the APT model, we need to know the factors that account for the differences among security returns. The APT makes no statements about the size or the sign of the F_i's. Both the factor model and these values must be identified empirically. In contrast, with the CAPM the factor that matters is the market portfolio, a concept that is well understood conceptually; however, as noted earlier, Roll has argued that the market portfolio is unobservable.

Most empirical work suggests that three to five factors influence security returns and are priced in the market. For example, Roll and Ross identify five systematic factors:

1. Changes in expected inflation
2. Unanticipated changes in inflation
3. Unanticipated changes in industrial production
4. Unanticipated changes in the default-risk premium
5. Unanticipated changes in the term structure of interest rates

These factors are related to the components of a valuation model. The first three affect the cash flows of a company while the last two affect the discount rate.

According to this model, different securities have different sensitivities to these systematic factors, and investor risk preferences are characterized by these dimensions. Each investor has different risk attitudes. Investors could construct a portfolio depending upon desired risk exposure to each of these factors. Knowing the market prices of these risk factors and the sensitivities of securities to changes in the factors, the expected returns for various stocks could be estimated.

Another study has suggested that an APT model that incorporates unanticipated changes in five macroeconomic variables is superior to the CAPM. These five variables are:[12]

1. Default risk
2. The term structure of interest rates
3. Inflation or deflation
4. The long-run expected growth rate of profits for the economy
5. Residual market risk

USING APT IN INVESTMENT DECISIONS

Roll and Ross have argued that APT offers an approach to strategic portfolio planning. The idea is to recognize that a few systematic factors affect long-term average returns. Investors should seek to identify the few factors affecting most assets in order to appreciate their influence on portfolio returns. Based on this knowledge, they should seek to structure the portfolio in such a way as to improve its design and performance.

Some researchers have identified and measured, for both economic sectors and industries, the risk exposures associated with APT risk factors such as the five identified previously in the work of Berry, Burmeister, and McElroy. These "risk exposure profiles" vary widely. For example, the financial, growth, and transportation sectors were found to be particularly sensitive to default risk, while the utility sector was relatively insensitive to both unexpected inflation and the unexpected change in the growth rate of profits.

An analysis of 82 different industry classifications showed the same result—exposure to different types of risk varies widely. For example, some industries were particularly sensitive to unexpected inflation risk, such as the mobile home building industry, retailers, hotels and motels, toys, and eating places. The industries least sensitive to this risk factor included foods, tire and rubber goods, shoes, and breweries. Several industries showed no significant sensitivity to unexpected inflation risk, such as corn and soybean refiners and sugar refiners.

A portfolio manager could design strategies that would expose them to one or more types of these risk factors, or "sterilize" a portfolio such that its exposure to the unexpected change in the growth rate of profits matched that of the market as a whole. Taking an active approach, a portfolio manager who believes that he or she can forecast a factor realization can build a portfolio that emphasizes or deemphasized that factor. In doing this, the manager would select stocks that have exposures to the remaining risk factors that are exactly proportional to the market. If the manager is accurate with the forecast—and remember that such a manager must forecast the unexpected component of the risk factor—he or she can outperform the market for that period.

SOME CONCLUSIONS ABOUT ASSET PRICING

The question of how security prices and equilibrium returns are established—whether as described by the CAPM or APT or some other model—remains open. Some researchers are convinced that the APT model is superior to the CAPM. For example, based on their research using the five factors discussed above, the authors concluded that "The APT model with these five risk factors is vastly superior to both the market model and the CAPM for explaining stock returns." The CAPM relies on the observation of the market portfolio which, in actuality, cannot be observed. On the other hand, APT offers no clues as to the identity of the factors that are priced in the factor structure.

[12] These factors are based on Berry et al.

In the final analysis, neither model has been proven superior. Both rely on expectations which are not directly observable. Additional testing is needed.

SUMMARY

- Capital market theory, based on the concept of efficient diversification, describes the pricing of capital assets in the marketplace.
- Capital market theory is derived from several assumptions that appear unrealistic; however, the important issue is the ability of the theory to predict. Relaxation of most of the assumptions does not change the major implications of capital market theory.
- Given risk-free borrowing and lending, the new efficient frontier has a vertical intercept of RF and is tangent to the old efficient frontier at point M, the market portfolio.
- In theory, the market-value-weighted market portfolio, M, should include all risky assets, although in practice it is typically proxied by a stock market index such as the Standard & Poor's 500.
- All investors can achieve an optimal point on the new efficient frontier by investing in portfolio M and either borrowing or lending at the risk-free rate RF.
- The new efficient frontier is called the capital market line, and its slope indicates the equilibrium price of risk in the market. In effect, it is the expected return-risk trade-off for efficient portfolios.
- Ex ante, the CML must always be positive, although ex post it may be negative for certain periods.
- Based on the separation of risk into its systematic and nonsystematic components, the security market line (CAPM) can be constructed for individual securities (and portfolios). What is important is each security's contribution to the total risk of the portfolio, as measured by beta.
- Using beta as the measure of risk, the SML depicts the trade-off between required return and risk for securities.
- The Market Model can be used to estimate the alpha and beta for a security by regressing total returns for a security against total returns for a market index.
- The Characteristic Line is a graph of the regression involved in the Market Model.
- Beta, the slope of the Characteristic Line, is a relative measure of risk. It indicates the volatility of a stock.
- Betas for individual stocks are unstable while betas for large portfolios are quite stable.
- If the expected returns for securities can be estimated from security analysis, and plotted against the SML, undervalued and overvalued securities can be identified.
- Problems exist in estimating the SML, in particular, estimating the betas for securities. The stability of beta is a concern, especially for individual securities; however, portfolio betas tend to be more stable across time.
- Tests of the CAPM are inconclusive. An ex ante model is being tested with ex post data. It has not been proved empirically, nor is it likely to be, but its basic implications seem to be supported.
- Alternative theories of asset pricing, such as the arbitrage pricing theory, also exist but are unproved.
- APT is not critically dependent on an underlying market portfolio as is the CAPM, which predicts that only market risk influences expected returns. Instead, APT recognizes that several types of risk may affect security returns.

- A factor model recognizes risk factors that affect realized and expected security returns. These risk factors represent broad economic forces and not company-specific characteristics and, by definition, they represent the element of surprise in the risk factor.
- APT is more general than the CAPM. If only one factor exists, the two models can be shown to be identical.
- The problem with APT is that the factors are not well specified, at least ex ante.
- Most empirical work suggests that three to five factors influence security returns and are priced in the market.

KEY WORDS

Arbitrage pricing theory (APT)
Capital asset pricing model (CAPM)
Capital market line (CML)
Capital market theory
Characteristic line
Factor model
Market model
Market portfolio
Required rate of return
Security market line (SML)

QUESTIONS

20-1. How do lending possibilities change the Markowitz model? borrowing possibilities?

20-2. Why, under the CAPM, do all investors hold identical risky portfolios?

20-3. In terms of their appearance as a graph, what is the difference between the CML and the SML?

20-4. What is the market portfolio?

20-5. What is the slope of the CML? What does it measure?

20-6. Why does the CML contain only efficient portfolios?

20-7. How can we measure a security's contribution to the risk of the market portfolio?

20-8. How can the SML be used to identify over- and undervalued securities?

20-9. What happens to the price and return of a security when investors recognize it as undervalued?

20-10. What are the difficulties involved in estimating a security's beta?

20-11. What is the major problem in testing capital market theory?

20-12. How can the CAPM be tested empirically? What are the expected results of regressing average returns on betas?

20-13. What is "the law of one price"?

20-14. Why does Roll argue that the CAPM is untestable?

20-15. The CAPM provides required returns for individual securities or portfolios. What uses can you see for such a model?

20-16. What is the relationship between the CML and the Markowitz efficient frontier?

20-17. How does an investor decide where to be on the new efficient frontier represented by the CML?

20-18. The CML can be described as representing a trade-off. What is this trade-off? Be specific.

20-19. Draw a diagram of the SML. Label the axes and the intercept.

a. Assume the risk-free rate shifts upward. Draw the new SML.
b. Assume that the risk-free rate remains the same as before the change in (a) but that investors become more pessimistic about the stock market. Draw the new SML.

20-20. What common assumptions do the CAPM and APT share? How do they differ in assumptions?

20-21. What is a factor model?

20-22. What characteristics must the factors in a factor model possess?

20-23. Based on empirical work, how many factors are thought to influence security returns? Name some of these likely factors.

20-24. What does a factor model say about equilibrium in the marketplace?

20-25. How can APT be used in investment decisions?

20-26. What role does the market portfolio play in the APT model?

20-27. What is meant by an "arbitrage profit"? What ensures that investors could act quickly to take advantage of such opportunities?

20-28. Why is the standard deviation of a security's returns an inadequate measure of the contribution of that security to the risk of a portfolio that is well diversified?

The following questions were asked on the 1993 CFA Level I examination:

CFA

20-29. **Identify** and **briefly discuss** three criticisms of beta as used in the Capital Asset Pricing Model (CAPM).

CFA

20-30. **Briefly explain** whether investors should expect a higher return from holding Portfolio A versus Portfolio B under Capital Asset Pricing Theory (CAPM). Assume that both portfolios are fully diversified.

	Portfolio A	Portfolio B
Systematic risk (beta)	1.0	1.0
Specific risk for each individual security	High	Low

The following questions were asked on the 1993 CFA Level I examination:

CFA

20-31. Capital Asset Pricing Theory asserts that portfolio returns are best explained by:

a. diversification.
b. systematic risk.
c. economic factors.
d. specific risk.

CFA

20-32. The security Market Line depicts:

a. a security's expected return as a function of its systematic risk.
b. the market portfolio as the optimal portfolio of risky securities.
c. the relationship between a security's return and the return on an index.
d. the complete portfolio as a combination of the market portfolio and the risk-free asset.

CFA
20-33. What is the expected return of a zero-beta security?

a. Market rate of return
b. Zero rate of return
c. Negative rate of return
d. Risk-free rate of return

CFA
20-34. Assume that both X and Y are well-diversified portfolios and the risk-free rate is 8 percent.

Portfolio	Expected Return	Beta
X	16%	1.00
Y	12%	0.25

In this situation, you would conclude that portfolios X and Y:

a. are in equilibrium.
b. offer an arbitrage opportunity.
c. are both underpriced.
d. are both fairly priced.

CFA
20-35. The Arbitrage Pricing Theory (APT) differs from the Capital Asset Pricing Model (CAPM) because the APT:

a. places more emphasis on market risk.
b. minimizes the importance of diversification.
c. recognizes multiple unsystematic risk factors.
d. recognizes multiple systematic risk factors.

CFA
20-36. You ask John Statdud, your research assistant, to analyze the relationship between the return on Coca-Cola Enterprises (CCE) common stock and the return on the market using the Standard & Poor's 500 Stock Index as a proxy for the market. The data include monthly returns for both CCE and the S&P 500 over a recent five-year period. The results of the regression are:

$$R_{CCE} = .59 + .94\ R_{S\&P500}$$
$$(3.10)$$

The numbers in parentheses are the t-statistics (the 0.1 critical value is 2.66). The coefficient of determination (R^2) for the regression is .215.

Statdud wrote the following summary of the regression results:

1. The regression statistics indicate that during the five-year period under study, when the annual return on the S&P 500 was zero, CCE had an average annual return of 0.59 percent.
2. The alpha value of .59 is a measure of the variability of the return on the market.
3. The coefficient of .94 indicates CCE's sensitivity to the return on the S&P 500 and suggests that the return on CCE's common stock is less sensitive to market movements than the average stock.

4. The t-statistic of 3.10 for the slope coefficient indicates the coefficient is not statistically significant at the .01 level.
5. The R^2 for the regression of .215 indicates the average estimate deviates from the actual observation by an average of 21.5 percent.
6. There is no concern that the slope coefficient lacks statistical significance since beta values tend to be less stable (and therefore less useful) than alpha values.
7. The regression should be rerun using 10 years of data. This would improve the reliability of the estimated coefficients while not sacrificing anything.

Identify which of the seven statements made by Statdud are incorrect and justify your answer(s).

DEMONSTRATION PROBLEMS

20-1. CALCULATION OF THE CHARACTERISTIC LINE: Calculate the characteristic line for EG&G by letting Y be the annual TRs for EG&G and X be the TRs for the S&P 500 Index. The summary statistics are as follows:

$$n = 10$$
$$\Sigma Y = 264.5$$
$$\Sigma Y^2 = 19{,}503.65$$
$$\Sigma X = 84.5$$
$$\Sigma X^2 = 4{,}660.31$$
$$\Sigma XY = 6{,}995.76$$
$$SS_y = \Sigma(Y - \bar{Y})^2 = \Sigma Y^2 - \frac{(\Sigma Y)^2}{n} = 12{,}507.625$$
$$SS_x = \Sigma(X - \bar{X})^2 = \Sigma X^2 - \frac{(\Sigma X)^2}{n} = 3{,}946.285$$
$$SS_{xy} = \Sigma(X - \bar{X})(Y - \bar{Y})^2 = \Sigma XY - \bar{Z}XY - \frac{(\Sigma X)(\Sigma Y)}{n} = \frac{(\Sigma X)(\Sigma Y)}{n} = 4{,}760.735$$
$$\hat{\beta} = \frac{SS_{xy}}{SS_x} = 1.206384$$
$$\hat{a} = \bar{Y} - \hat{\beta}\bar{X} = 16.256$$
$$\hat{Y} = 16.256 + 1.206X$$

Analysis of Variance Source (Risk)		Sum of Squares	No. of Observations	Variance
Total SS_y	=	12,507.625	$n - 1 = 9$	1,389.736 = Total variance
Systematic $\beta^2 SS_x$	=	5,743.275	$n - 1 = 9$	638.142 = Systematic variance
Nonsystematic	=	6,764.350	$n - 1 = 9$	751.594 = Nonsystematic variance

PROBLEMS

20-1. Given the following information show that the characteristic line for this company is

$$\hat{Y} = 5.055 + 0.776X$$
$$\Sigma X = 264.5$$
$$\Sigma X^2 = 4{,}660.31$$
$$\Sigma Y = 116.1$$
$$\Sigma Y^2 = 6{,}217.13$$
$$\Sigma XY = 4{,}042.23$$
$$SS_x = 3{,}946.285$$
$$SS_y = 4{,}869.209$$
$$SS_{xy} = 3{,}061.185$$

20-2. The expected return for the market is 12 percent, with a standard deviation of 21 percent. The expected risk free rate is 8 percent. Information is available for five mutual funds, all assumed to be efficient, as follows:

Mutual Funds	SD (%)
Affiliated	14
Omega	16
Ivy	21
Value Line Fund	25
New Horizons	30

a. Calculate the slope of the CML.
b. Calculate the expected return for each portfolio.
c. Rank the portfolios in increasing order of expected.
d. Do any of the portfolios have the same expected return as the market? Why?

20-3. Given the market data in Problem 20-2, and the following information for each of five stocks.

Stock	Beta	R_i
1	0.9	12
2	1.3	13
3	0.5	11
4	1.1	12.5
5	1.0	12

a. Calculate the expected return for each stock.
b. With these expected returns and betas, think of a line connecting them—what is this line?
c. Assume that an investor, using fundamental analysis, develops the estimates labeled R_i for these stocks. Determine which are undervalued and which are overvalued.
d. What is the market's risk premium?

20-4. Given the following information:
Expected return for the market, 12 percent
Standard deviation of market return, 21 percent
Risk-free rate, 8 percent

Correlation coefficient between
Stock A and the market, 0.8
Stock B and the market, 0.6
Standard deviation for stock A, 25 percent
Standard deviation for stock B, 30 percent

a. Calculate the beta for stock A and stock B.
b. Calculate the required return for each stock.

20-5. Assume that RF is 7 percent, the estimated return on the market is 12 percent, and the standard deviation of the market's expected return is 21 percent. Calculate the expected return and risk (standard deviation) for the following portfolios:

a. 60 percent of investable wealth in riskless assets, 40 percent in the market portfolio
b. 150 percent of investable wealth in the market portfolio
c. 100 percent of investable wealth in the market portfolio

20-6. Assume that the risk-free rate is 7 percent and the expected market return is 13 percent. Show that the security market line is

$$E(R_i) = 7.0 + 6.0\beta$$

Assume that an investor has estimated the following values for six different corporations:

Corporation	β_i	R_i(%)
GF	0.8	12
PepsiCo	0.9	13
IBM	1.0	14
NCNB	1.2	11
EG&G	1.2	21
EAL	1.5	10

Calculate the ER_i for each corporation using the SML, and evaluate which securities are over-valued and which are undervalued.

20-7. Assume that Exxon is priced in equilibrium. Its expected return next year is 14 percent, and its beta is 1.1. The risk-free rate is 6 percent.

a. Calculate the slope of the SML.
b. Calculate the expected return on the market.

The following question was asked on the 1993 CFA Level I examination.

CFA
20-8. Within the context of the Capital Asset Pricing Model (CAPM), assume:

- Expected return on the market = 15 percent
- Risk free rate = 8 percent
- Expected rate of return on XYZ security = 17 percent
- Beta of XYZ security = 1.25

Which *one* of the following is *correct?*

a. XYZ is overpriced.
b. XYZ if fairly priced.
c. XYZ's alpha is −0.25%.
d. XYZ's alpha is 0.25%.

SELECTED REFERENCE

A good discussion of capital market theory can be found in:

Edwin Elton and Martin Gruber. *Modern Portfolio Theory and Portfolio Analysis,* Fifth Edition. New York: John Wiley & Sons, 1995.

www.wiley.com/college/jones7

This chapter looks at the Capital Asset Pricing Model and the Arbitrage Pricing Theory. The web exercises ask you to compute stock betas and to look at the relationship between expected returns and beta risk.

chapter 21

PORTFOLIO MANAGEMENT

Chapter 21 concerns why and how portfolio management should be thought of as a process. An understanding of the process allows any portfolio manager to apply a consistent framework to the management of a portfolio for any investor, whether individual or institution. It also allows us to consider some topics of importance to all investors, such as taxes, protection against inflation, how expectations about future market returns are formed, the life cycle of investors, and other related issues.

After reading this chapter you will be able to:

- **Discuss why portfolio management should be considered, and implemented as, a process.**
- **Describe the steps involved in the portfolio management process.**
- **Apply the process to any type of investment situation.**
- **Assess related issues of importance, such as asset allocation.**

Portfolio management involves a series of decisions and actions that must be made by every investor, whether individual or institution. Portfolios must be managed whether investors follow a passive approach or an active approach to selecting and holding their financial assets. As we saw when we examined portfolio theory, the relationships among the various investment alternatives that are held as a portfolio must be considered if an investor is to hold an optimal portfolio and achieve his or her investment objectives.

Portfolio management can be thought of as a process. Having the process clearly in mind is very important, allowing investors to proceed in an orderly manner.

In this chapter we outline the investment management process, making it clear that a logical and orderly flow does exist. This process can be applied to each investor, and by any investment manager. Details may vary from client to client, but the process remains the same.

PORTFOLIO MANAGEMENT AS A PROCESS

The portfolio management process has been described by Maginn and Tuttle in a book that forms the basis for portfolio management as envisioned by AIMR, and advocated in its curriculum for the CFA designation.[1] This is an important development because of its contrast with the past, where portfolio management was treated on an ad hoc basis, matching investors with portfolios on an individual basis. Portfolio management should be structured so that any investment organization can carry it out in an effective and timely manner without serious omissions.

Maginn and Tuttle emphasize that portfolio management is a *process,* integrating a set of activities in a logical and orderly manner. Given the feedback loops and monitoring that is included, the process is both continuous and systematic. It is a dynamic and flexible concept, and extends to all portfolio investments, including real estate, gold, and other real assets.

The portfolio management process extends to all types of investment organizations and investment styles. In fact, Maginn and Tuttle specifically avoid advocating how the process should be organized, who should make the decisions, and so forth. Each investment management organization should decide for itself how best to carry out its activities, consistent with viewing portfolio management as a process.

Having structured portfolio management as a process, any portfolio manager can execute the necessary decisions for an investor. The process provides a framework and a control over the diverse activities involved, and allows every investor, individual or institution, to be accommodated in a systematic, orderly manner.

As outlined by Maginn and Tuttle, portfolio management is an ongoing process by which:

1. Objectives, constraints, and preferences are identified for each investor. This leads to the development of explicit investment policies.
2. Strategies are developed and implemented through the choice of optimal combinations of assets. This step relates to our discussion of portfolio theory in Part II.
3. Market conditions, relative asset mix, and the investor's circumstances are monitored.
4. Portfolio adjustments are made as necessary to reflect significant changes that have occurred.

[1] See John L. Maginn, CFA, and Donald L. Tuttle, CFA, eds., *Managing Investment Portfolios,* 2nd. ed. (Charlottesville, Va: Association for Investment Management and Research, 1990). This chapter follows the format advocated in this book and is indebted to it for much of the discussion.

FIGURE 21-1

The portfolio construction, monitoring, and revision process.

SOURCE: John L. Maginn and Donald L. Tuttle, "The Portfolio Management Process and Its Dynamics, in John L. Maginn, CFA, and Donald L. Tuttle, CFA, eds., *Managing Investment Portfolios,* 2nd. ed. (Charlottesville, Va: Association for Investment Management and Research, 1990), pp. 1–4.

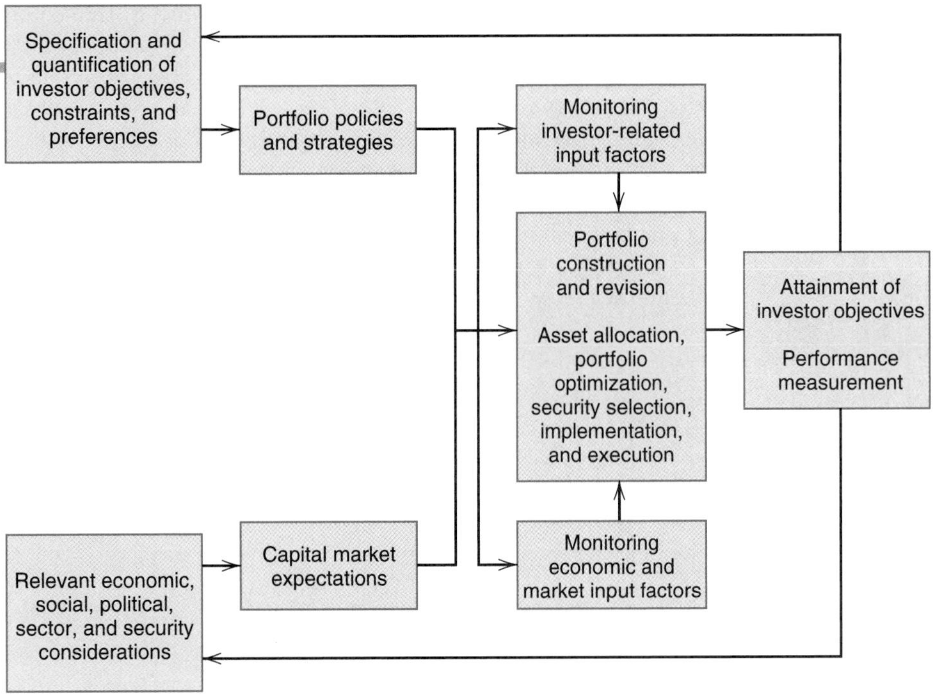

Figure 21-1 explains the portfolio construction, monitoring, and revision process. Notice that we begin with the specification of investor objectives, constraints and preferences. This specification leads to a statement of portfolio policies and strategies. Next, capital market expectations for the economy as well as individual assets must be determined and quantified.

The combination of portfolio policies/strategies and capital market expectations provides the investment manager with the basis for portfolio construction and revision. This includes the asset allocation decision (discussed in Chapter 19), a very important determinant of the success of the investment program. Also included here are the portfolio optimization and security selection stages of portfolio management; that is, we must determine appropriate portfolio strategies and techniques for each asset class and the selection of individual securities.

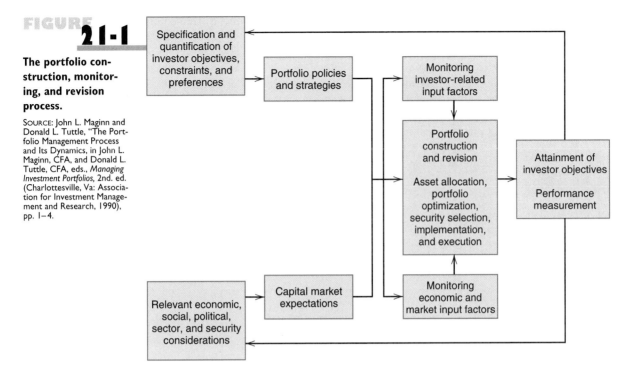

Monitoring is an important part of the process. As indicated in Figure 21-1, the portfolio manager should monitor both investor-related input factors as well as economic and market input factors and rebalance as necessary. For example, the manager may need to respond to any changes in investor objectives and constraints and/or capital market expectations. Finally, the process concludes with the attainment of investor objectives. In order to assess how successful this is, we must measure and evaluate portfolio performance, which is discussed in Chapter 22. We will discuss these steps in more detail below, but first we consider the differences between individual investors and institutional investors. As we noted in Chapter 2, investors can invest directly and indirectly through institutional investors, and an understanding of both types of investment decision making is important.

INDIVIDUAL INVESTORS VS. INSTITUTIONAL INVESTORS

Significant differences exist among investors as to objectives, constraints and preferences. We are primarily interested in the viewpoint of the individual investor but the basic investment management process applies to all investors, individuals, and institutions. Furthermore, individuals are often the beneficiaries of the activities of institutional investors, and an understanding of how institutional investors fit into the investment management process is desirable.

A major difference between the two occurs with regard to time horizon because institutional investors are often thought of on a perpetual basis, but this concept has no meaning when applied to individual investors. As explained below, for individual investors it is often useful to think of a life-cycle approach, as people go from the beginning of their careers to retirement. This approach is less useful for institutional investors because they typically maintain a relatively constant profile across time.

Kaiser has summarized the differences between individual investors and institutional investors as follows:[2]

1. Individuals define risk as "losing money" while institutionals use a quantitative approach, typically defining risk in terms of standard deviation (as in the case of the returns data presented in Chapter 6).
2. Individuals can be characterized by their personalities, while for institutions we consider the investment characteristics of those with a beneficial interest in the portfolios managed by the institutions.
3. Goals are a key part of what individual investing is all about, along with their assets, while for institutions we can be more precise as to their total package of assets and liabilities.
4. Individuals have great freedom in what they can do with regard to investing, while institutions are subject to numerous legal and regulatory constraints.
5. Taxes often are a very important consideration for individual investors, whereas many institutions, such as pension funds, are free of such considerations.

The implications of all of this for the investment management process are as follows:

- **For individual investors:** Because each individual's financial profile is different, an investment policy for an individual investor must incorporate that investor's unique factors. In effect, preferences are self-imposed constraints.
- **For institutional investors:** Given the increased complexity in managing institutional portfolios, it is critical to establish a well-defined and effective policy. Such a policy must clearly delineate the objectives being sought, the institutional investor's risk tolerance, and the investment constraints and preferences under which it must operate.

The primary reason for establishing a long-term investment policy for institutional investors is twofold:

1. It prevents arbitrary revisions of a soundly designed investment policy.
2. It helps the portfolio manager to plan and execute on a long-term basis and resist short-term pressures that could derail the plan.[3]

FORMULATE AN APPROPRIATE INVESTMENT POLICY

Investment Policy The determination of portfolio policies

The determination of portfolio policies—referred to as the **investment policy**—is the first step in the investment process. It summarizes the objectives, constraints and preferences for

[2] See Ronald W. Kaiser, "Individual Investors," in *Managing Investment Portfolios,* 2nd. ed., John L. Maginn, CFA and Donald L. Tuttle, CFA, eds. (Charlottesville, Va.: Association for Investment Management and Research, 1990), p. 3–2.

[3] See "Portfolio Management: The Portfolio Construction Process," in *1997 CFA Level I Candidate Readings,* AIMR, Charlottesville, VA, 1997, p. 177.

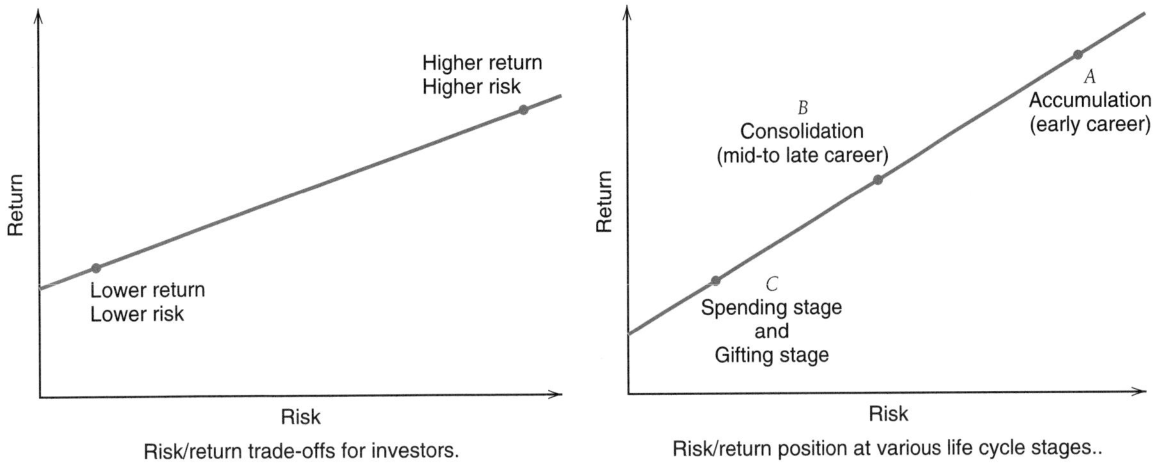

FIGURE 21-2

Risk/return position at various life cycle stages.

SOURCE: Ronald W. Kaiser, "Individual Investors," in John L. Maginn, CFA, and Donald L. Tuttle, CFA, eds., *Managing Investment Portfolios,* 2nd. ed. (Charlottesville, Va: Association for Investment Management and Research, 1990), pp. 1–4.

the investor. A recommended approach in formulating an investment policy is simply to provide information, in the following order, for any investor—individual or institutional. They should state the:

- OBJECTIVES: **return requirements** and **risk tolerance**

followed by the:

- CONSTRAINTS AND PREFERENCES: **liquidity, time horizon, laws and regulations, taxes,** and **unique preferences and circumstances**

We discuss each of these in turn below.

OBJECTIVES

Portfolio objectives are always going to center on return and risk because these are the two aspects of most interest to investors. Investors seek returns, but must assume risk in order to have an opportunity to earn the returns. The best way to describe the objectives is to think in terms of the return-risk trade-off developed in Chapter 1 and emphasized throughout the text. Expected return and risk are related by an upward sloping tradeoff.

We know from Chapter 7 that investors must think in terms of expected returns, which implicitly or explicitly involves probability distributions. The future is uncertain, and the best that investors can do is to make probabilistic estimates of likely returns over some holding period, such as one year. Because the future is uncertain, mistakes are inevitable, but this is simply the nature of investing decisions. Estimates of expected returns must be made regardless of the uncertainties, using the best information and investment processes available.

The issue of the life cycle of investors fits in to this discussion because of its impact on individual investors' risk and return preferences. The conventional approach is to think in terms of the risk-return trade-off as discussed throughout this text. This is shown in part (a) of Figure 21-2.

Alternatively, the life-cycle approach can be depicted as shown in part (b) of Figure 21-2. Here we see four different phases in which individual investors view their wealth, although it is important to note that the boundaries between the stages are not necessarily clear-cut and can require years to complete. Furthermore, an individual can be a composite of these stages at the same time. The four stages are:

1. *Accumulation Phase* In the early stage of the life cycle, net worth is typically small, but the time horizon is long. Investors can afford to assume large risks.
2. *Consolidation Phase* In this phase, involving the mid-to-late career stage of the life cycle when income exceeds expenses, an investment portfolio can be accumulated. A portfolio balance is sought to provide a moderate trade-off between risk and return.
3. *Spending Phase* In this phase, living expenses are covered from accumulated assets rather than earned income. While some risk-taking is still preferable, the emphasis is on safety, resulting in a relatively low position on the risk-return trade-off.
4. *Gifting Phase* In this phase, the attitudes about the purpose of investments changes. The basic position on the trade-off remains about the same as in stage 3.

Investment Policy Statement A statement of a few sentences describing policies to be followed for a client

Inflation Considerations An **investment policy statement** often will contain some statement about inflation-adjusted returns because of the impact of inflation on investor results over long periods of time. For example, a wealthy individual's policy statement may be stated in terms of maximum after-tax, *inflation-adjusted* total return consistent with the investor's risk profile, while another investor's primary return objective may be stated as *inflation-adjusted capital preservation,* perhaps with a growth-oriented mix to reflect the need for capital growth over time.

Inflation is clearly a problem for investors. The inflation rate of 13 percent in 1979–1980 speaks for itself in terms of the awful impact it had on investors' real wealth. But even with a much lower inflation—say, 3 percent—the damage is substantial. It can persist steadily, eroding values. At a 3 percent inflation rate, for example, the purchasing power of a dollar is cut in half in less than 25 years. Therefore, someone retiring at age 60 who lives to approximately 85 and does not protect his or herself from inflation will suffer a drastic decline in purchasing power over the years.

Contrary to some people's beliefs, common stocks are not always an inflationary hedge. In the 1970s, for example, inflation more than doubled to an average annual rate of about 7.5 percent, and the average stock showed a return of slightly less than 6 percent. On the other hand, one of the primary reasons for the strong stock market in 1995 and 1996 was the low (by historical standards) and steady rate of inflation of approximately 3 percent.

CONSTRAINTS AND PREFERENCES

To complete the investment policy statement, these items are described for a particular investor as the circumstances warrant. Since investors vary widely in their constraints and preferences, these details may vary widely also.

Time Horizon Investors need to think about the time period involved in their investment plans. The objectives being pursued may require a policy statement that speaks to specific planning horizons. In the case of an individual investor, for example, this could well be the investor's expected lifetime. In the case of an institutional investor, the time horizon can be quite long. For example, for a company with a defined-benefit retirement plan whose employees are young, and which has no short-term liquidity needs, the time horizon can be quite long.

Liquidity Needs As noted in Chapter 2, liquidity is the ease with which an asset can be sold without a sharp change in price as the result of selling. Obviously, cash equivalents (money market securities) have high liquidity, and are easily sold at close to face value. Many stocks also have great liquidity, but the price at which they are sold will reflect their current market valuations.

Investors must decide how likely they are to sell some part of their portfolio in the short run. As part of the asset allocation decision, they must decide how much of their funds to keep in cash equivalents.

Tax Considerations Individual investors, unlike some institutional investors, must consider the impact of taxes on their investment programs. The treatment of ordinary income as opposed to capital gains is an important issue because typically there is a differential tax rate. Furthermore, the tax laws in the United States have been changed several times, making it difficult for investors to forecast the tax rate that will apply in the future.

In addition to the differential tax rates and their changes over time, the capital gains component of security returns benefits from the fact that the tax is not payable until the gain is realized. This tax deferral is, in effect, a tax-free loan that remains invested for the benefit of the taxpayer.

Retirement programs offer tax sheltering whereby any income and/or capital gains taxes are avoided until such time as the funds are withdrawn. Investors with various retirement and taxable accounts must grapple with the issue of which type of account should hold stocks as opposed to bonds (given that bonds generate higher current income).

Legal and Regulatory Requirements Investors must obviously deal with regulatory requirements growing out of both common law and the rulings and regulations of state and federal agencies. Individuals are subject to relatively few such requirements, while a particular institutional portfolio, such as an endowment fund or a pension fund, is subject to several legal and regulatory requirements.

With regard to fiduciary responsibilities, one of the most famous concepts is the Prudent Man Rule.[4] This rule, which concerns fiduciaries, goes back to 1830, although it was not formally stated until more than 100 years later. Basically, the rule states that a fiduciary, in managing assets for another party, shall act like people of "prudence, discretion and intelligence" act in governing their own affairs.

The important aspect of the Prudent Man Rule is its flexibility because interpretations of the rule can change with time and circumstances. Unfortunately, some judicial rulings have specified a very strict interpretation, negating the value of flexibility for the time period and circumstances involved. Also unfortunately, in the case of state laws governing private trusts, the standard continues to be applied to individual investments rather than the portfolio as a whole, which violates all of the portfolio-building principles we learned earlier.

One of the important pieces of federal legislation governing institutional investors is the Employment Retirement Income Security Act, referred to as ERISA. This act, administered by the Department of Labor, regulates employer-sponsored retirement plans. It requires that plan assets be diversified and that the standards being applied under the act be applied to *management of the portfolio as a whole.*

The investment policy thus formulated is an operational statement. It clearly specifies the actions to be taken to try to achieve the investor's goals, or objectives, given the preferences of the investor and any constraints imposed. While portfolio investment considerations are often of a qualitative nature, they help to determine a quantitative statement of return and risk requirements that are specific to the needs of any particular investor.

Unique Needs and Circumstances Investors often face a variety of unique circumstances. For example, a trust established on their behalf may specify that investment activities

[4] This discussion is indebted to "Portfolio Management: The Portfolio Construction Process," in John L. Maginn, CFA, and Donald L. Tuttle, CFA, eds., *Managing Investment Portfolios,* 2nd ed. (Charlottesville, Va: Association for Investment Management and Research, 1990).

be limited to particular asset classes, or even specified assets. Or an individual may feel that their life span is threatened by illness, and wish to benefit within a certain period of time.

EXAMPLE 21-1

To illustrate the application of the investment management process, consider a question from the Level I CFA Examination.[5] The answer is contained in a succinct but sufficient form.

A. **Outline** a generalized framework that could be used to establish investment policies applicable to all investors.
B. **List** and **briefly discuss** *five* differences in investment policy that might result from the application of your Part A framework to:

(1) the pension plan of a young, fast-growing consumer products company; and
(2) the modest life insurance proceeds received by a 60-year-old widow with two grown children.

Answers:

A. FRAMEWORK

Objectives	*Constraints*
Return	Time Horizon
Risk	Liquidity Needs
	Tax Considerations
	Legal/Regulatory Issues
	Unique Needs and Circumstances

B. APPLICATION DIFFERENCES

	Pension Fund	*Widow's Portfolio*
Return	Total Return Objective	Income-Oriented Objective with Some Inflation Protection
Risk	Above-Average Capacity; Company Bears Risk	Somewhat Below-Average Capacity Indicated; Widow Bears Risk; Safety Important
Time Horizon	Long Term; Infinite	Medium Term; Infinite Life
Liquidity	Low; Cash Flow Accrues	Probably Medium to High; No Reinvestment Likely
Tax	U.S. Tax-Exempt	Federal (and Probably State) Income Taxes Paid On Most Investment Receipts
Legal/Regulatory	Governed by ERISA	"Prudent Man" Rule Applies (State)
Unique Needs and Circumstances	Cash Flow Reinvested; Opportunity for Compounding	Widow's Needs Are Immediate and Govern Now; Children's Needs Should Be Considered in Planning for the Future

[5] This question and answer are taken from Question 8 of the 1989 Level I Examination. Reprinted in I: *The CFA Study Guide*, 1991, The Institute of Chartered Financial Analysts, Charlottesville, Virginia, pp. 165 and 173.

DETERMINE AND QUANTIFY CAPITAL MARKET EXPECTATIONS

Having considered their objectives and constraints, the next step is to determine a set of investment strategies based on the policy statement. Included here are such issues as asset allocation, portfolio diversification, and the impact of taxes. Once the portfolio strategies are developed, they are used along with the investment manager's expectations for the capital market and for individual assets to choose a portfolio of assets. Most importantly, the asset allocation decision must be made.

Forming Expectations The forming of expectations involves two steps:

1. *Macroexpectational factors* These factors influence the market for bonds, stocks, and other assets on both a domestic and international basis. These are expectations about the capital markets.
2. *Microexpectational influences* These factors involve the cause agents that underlie the desired return and risk estimates and influence the selection of a particular asset for a particular portfolio.

RATE OF RETURN ASSUMPTIONS

Most investors base their actions on some assumptions about the rate of return expected from various assets. Obviously, it is important for investors to plan their investing activities on realistic rate of return assumptions.

As a starting point, investors should study carefully the historical rates of return available in such sources as the data provided by Ibbotson Associates or the comparable data discussed in Chapter 6. We know the historical mean returns, both arithmetic and geometric, and the standard deviation of the returns for major asset classes such as stocks, bonds, and bills.

Having analyzed the historical series of returns, there are several difficulties in forming expectations about future returns. For example, how much should investors be influenced by recent stock market returns, particularly when they are unusually good returns?

EXAMPLE 21-2

The cumulative gain on the S&P 500 Index for 1995 and 1996 was 69.2 percent, the best two-year period in a generation and one of the best in the history of stock market returns for this index (only four other consecutive two-year periods were better as measured by the S&P 500). The average gain of more than 30 percent a year for the years 1995 and 1996 was three times the annual average gain for common stocks over many years.

Do investors form unrealistic expectations about future returns as a result of such activity? Over the past four decades, bear markets have occurred on average about once every four years. In the four previous cases of two-year cumulative returns averaging 30 percent per year or more (comparable to 1995–1996), the average annual return for the next five years was negative in two cases (−7.5 percent and −11.2 percent), and less than 9 percent in two cases of positive returns. Moreover, most observers believe that stock returns tend to "revert toward the mean" over time—that is, periods of unusually high returns tend to be followed by periods of lower returns (although not necessarily losses), and the opposite is also true.

Following the bottom that was reached in the stock market in August 1982, the S&P 500 Composite Index has shown a compound annual average return of approximately 17.5

percent a year. This is 60 percent larger than the long-run average return of about 10.7 percent a year. And the return was negative in only one year, 1990, and this was relatively small. Therefore, it is valid to ask how investor expectations about stock returns are influenced by this now substantial, but unusual by historical standards, time period. How are investors, particularly relatively new investors, affected by this history as they form expectations about future returns?

Investors should recognize some key points about future rates of return. In estimating the expected return on stocks (as proxied by the S&P 500), Ibbotson Associates combines the riskless rate and expected risk premium of large company stocks over riskless bonds. The expected equity risk premium to be used in this calculation is based on the *arithmetic mean* of equity risk premiums and not the geometric mean because this is an additive relationship. As stated in the Ibbotson Associates *Yearbook*, ". . . the arithmetic mean is correct because an investment with uncertain returns will have a higher expected ending wealth value than an investment that earns, with certainty, its compound or geometric rate of return each year."[6]

A second key point that investors should recognize in thinking about expected rates of return, and the returns they can realistically expect to achieve, is that common stock returns involve considerable risk. While we know that the annual average compound rate of return on common stocks for the period 1926–1998, according to Table 6-5, was 10.9 percent, that does not mean that all investors can realistically expect to achieve this historical rate of return. To see this, we can analyze the probabilities of actually realizing various compound rate of returns over time.

Jones and Wilson have analyzed data for the S&P 500 index for the period 1926–1993 using "authentic" S&P observations.[7] The annual geometric mean of this data for that time period was 9.98766 percent, or almost 10 percent. The differences in this mean and that provided by Ibbotson Associates (10.3 percent for the period 1926–1993) stems from a difference in the data used for the earlier years of the S&P 500, which results in a slightly lower mean in the Jones and Wilson study.

Jones and Wilson determined from a statistical analysis of the data that the historical returns on the S&P 500 Index are lognormally distributed, which means that we can use compound rates of return to estimate probabilities based on the mean and standard deviation of the logs of annual total returns. These probabilities are calculated and reported as the probabilities of achieving any specified *compound* annual average rate of return over any specified holding period. It is important to note that these are probabilities of achieving *at least* the stated compound rate of return or more.

Table 21-1 shows the probabilities of achieving at least a specified compound rate of return, or *more*, based on the history of the S&P 500 Index over the period 1926–1993. In analyzing this table, remember that the approximate geometric mean for the revised S&P 500 for this period was 10 percent. These probabilities should be interpreted in the following manner: "Based *solely* on the entire history of annual returns on the S&P Index for the period 1926–1993, where the geometric mean was approximately 10 percent, what are the probabilities of achieving *at least* a specified *compound* rate of return over various holding periods?"

As Table 21-1 shows, the probability of achieving approximately 10 percent or more on a compound basis is (essentially) 50 percent, regardless of the holding period. Note that for rates of return of 10 percent or more, the probabilities of achieving that rate of return *decrease* over time, contrary to assertions of many market observers that the risk of owning common stocks decreases over time. On the other hand, the probabilities of achieving at least

[6] See Roger G. Ibbotson and Rex A. Sinquefield, *Stocks, Bonds, Bills, and Inflation (SBBI)*, updated in *Stocks, Bonds, Bills, and Inflation 1996 Yearbook*, p. 155. Chicago: Ibbotson Associates. All rights reserved.

[7] See Charles P. Jones and Jack W. Wilson, "Probabilities Associated with Common Stock Returns," *The Journal of Portfolio Management* (Fall 1995): 21–32.

TABLE 21-1 PROBABILITIES OF ACHIEVING, AT LEAST, A GIVEN ANNUAL NOMINAL GEOMETRIC MEAN RATE OF RETURN OVER VARIOUS INVESTMENT HORIZONS, BASED ON THE S&P RETURNS FOR 1926–1993

Geometric Mean—R%—for the period was 9.98766%
The Corresponding Standard Deviation was 21.38195%

Per annum	Investment Horizon								
R%	1 yr	3 yr	5 yr	10 yr	15 yr	20 yr	25 yr	30 yr	40 yr
60	.0265	.0004	.0000	.0000	.0000	.0000	.0000	.0000	.0000
55	.0383	.0011	.0000	.0000	.0000	.0000	.0000	.0000	.0000
50	.0547	.0028	.0002	.0000	.0000	.0000	.0000	.0000	.0000
45	.0769	.0067	.0007	.0000	.0000	.0000	.0000	.0000	.0000
40	.1065	.0155	.0027	.0000	.0000	.0000	.0000	.0000	.0000
35	.1452	.0335	.0090	.0004	.0000	.0000	.0000	.0000	.0000
30	.1942	.0676	.0269	.0032	.0004	.0001	.0000	.0000	.0000
25	.2545	.1264	.0699	.0184	.0053	.0016	.0005	.0001	.0000
20	.3265	.2181	.1574	.0775	.0408	.0222	.0123	.0069	.0022
19	.3422	.2407	.1817	.0994	.0577	.0346	.0211	.0130	.0051
18	.3583	.2648	.2086	.1256	.0799	.0523	.0348	.0234	.0109
17	.3749	.2903	.2379	.1566	.1084	.0769	.0554	.0403	.0218
16	.3918	.3171	.2696	.1925	.1437	.1097	.0848	.0662	.0412
15	.4091	.3452	.3035	.2335	.1865	.1519	.1251	.1039	.0729
14	.4267	.3744	.3396	.2794	.2369	.2041	.1776	.1556	.1211
13	.4446	.4046	.3776	.3296	.2946	.2664	.2428	.2225	.1889
12	.4627	.4356	.4171	.3837	.3585	.3378	.3200	.3042	.2770
11	.4811	.4674	.4579	.4406	.4274	.4163	.4066	.3978	.3825
10	.4998	.4996	.4995	.4993	.4991	.4990	.4988	.4987	.4985
9	.5186	.5321	.5415	.5585	.5715	.5825	.5920	.6006	.6158
8	.5375	.5647	.5833	.6170	.6423	.6631	.6810	.6969	.7242
7	.5565	.5972	.6247	.6734	.7090	.7375	.7613	.7818	.8156
6	.5756	.6293	.6650	.7266	.7698	.8030	.8297	.8517	.8860
5	.5946	.6609	.7039	.7756	.8232	.8579	.8844	.9052	.9351
4	.6137	.6916	.7408	.8195	.8684	.9018	.9257	.9432	.9662
3	.6326	.7213	.7756	.8580	.9052	.9351	.9548	.9682	.9839
2	.6514	.7498	.8079	.8907	.9341	.9591	.9741	.9835	.9931
1	.6700	.7770	.8374	.9179	.9558	.9754	.9861	.9920	.9973
0	.6884	.8026	.8640	.9399	.9715	.9860	.9930	.9964	.9991
−1	.7065	.8266	.8877	.9571	.9823	.9924	.9967	.9985	.9997
−2	.7243	.8489	.9085	.9702	.9895	.9961	.9985	.9994	.9999
−3	.7417	.8693	.9265	.9799	.9940	.9981	.9994	.9998	1.0000
−4	.7586	.8880	.9417	.9868	.9967	.9992	.9998	.9999	1.0000
−5	.7752	.9048	.9545	.9916	.9983	.9996	.9999	1.0000	1.0000
−6	.7912	.9198	.9651	.9948	.9992	.9999	1.0000	1.0000	1.0000
−7	.8067	.9331	.9736	.9969	.9996	.9999	1.0000	1.0000	1.0000
−8	.8216	.9448	.9803	.9982	.9998	1.0000	1.0000	1.0000	1.0000
−9	.8360	.9549	.9856	.9990	.9999	1.0000	1.0000	1.0000	1.0000
−10	.8497	.9635	.9897	.9995	1.0000	1.0000	1.0000	1.0000	1.0000
−11	.8627	.9708	.9927	.9997	1.0000	1.0000	1.0000	1.0000	1.0000
−12	.8751	.9769	.9950	.9999	1.0000	1.0000	1.0000	1.0000	1.0000
−13	.8869	.9819	.9966	.9999	1.0000	1.0000	1.0000	1.0000	1.0000
−14	.8979	.9861	.9977	1.0000	1.0000	1.0000	1.0000	1.0000	1.0000
−15	.9082	.9894	.9985	1.0000	1.0000	1.0000	1.0000	1.0000	1.0000
−16	.9179	.9920	.9991	1.0000	1.0000	1.0000	1.0000	1.0000	1.0000
−17	.9269	.9941	.9994	1.0000	1.0000	1.0000	1.0000	1.0000	1.0000
−18	.9352	.9957	.9996	1.0000	1.0000	1.0000	1.0000	1.0000	1.0000
−19	.9428	.9969	.9998	1.0000	1.0000	1.0000	1.0000	1.0000	1.0000
−20	.9498	.9997	.9999	1.0000	1.0000	1.0000	1.0000	1.0000	1.0000
−25	.9759	.9997	1.0000	1.0000	1.0000	1.0000	1.0000	1.0000	1.0000
−30	.9901	1.0000	1.0000	1.0000	1.0000	1.0000	1.0000	1.0000	1.0000
−35	.9967	1.0000	1.0000	1.0000	1.0000	1.0000	1.0000	1.0000	1.0000
−40	.9991	1.0000	1.0000	1.0000	1.0000	1.0000	1.0000	1.0000	1.0000
−45	.9998	1.0000	1.0000	1.0000	1.0000	1.0000	1.0000	1.0000	1.0000
−50	1.0000	1.0000	1.0000	1.0000	1.0000	1.0000	1.0000	1.0000	1.0000

SOURCE: Charles P. Jones and Jack W. Wilson, "Probabilities Associated with Common Stock Returns," *The Journal of Portfolio Management*, Fall 1995, pp. 21–32.

9 percent rate of return, or an 8 percent rate of return, or any lower return, increase over time.

The message from Table 21-1 is important. Based on the known history of stock returns, the chance that an investor will actually achieve some compound rate of return over time from owning common stocks may not be as high as he or she believes. Common stocks are risky, and expected returns are not guaranteed.

CONSTRUCTING THE PORTFOLIO

Having considered the objectives and constraints, and formed capital market expectations, the next step is portfolio construction and revision based on the policy statement and capital market expectations. Included here are such issues as asset allocation, portfolio optimization, and security selection. In summary, once the portfolio strategies are developed, they are used along with the investment manager's expectations for the capital market and for individual assets to choose a portfolio of assets.

The portfolio construction process can be viewed from a broad perspective as consisting of the following steps (again, given the development of the investment policy statement and the formulation of capital market expectations):

1. Define the universe of securities eligible for inclusion in a particular portfolio. For institutional investors, this traditionally meant asset classes, in particular stocks, bonds, and cash equivalents. More recently, institutional investors have broadened their investment alternatives to include foreign securities, small stocks, real estate, venture capital, and so forth. This step is really the asset allocation decision, probably the key decision made by investment managers.
2. Utilize an optimization procedure to select securities and determine the proper portfolio weights for these securities.

Both of these steps are discussed in more detail as follows.

ASSET ALLOCATION

The asset allocation decision involves deciding the percentage of investable funds to be placed in stocks, bonds, and cash equivalents. It is the most important investment decision made by investors because it is the basic determinant of the return and risk taken. This is a result of holding a well-diversified portfolio, which we know from Part II is the primary lesson of portfolio management.

The returns of a well-diversified portfolio within a given asset class are highly correlated with the returns of the asset class itself. Within an asset class, diversified portfolios will tend to produce similar returns over time. However, different asset classes are likely to produce results that are quite dissimilar. Therefore, differences in asset allocation will be the key factor over time causing differences in portfolio performance.

The Asset Allocation Decision Factors to consider in making the asset allocation decision include the investor's return requirements (current income versus future income), the investor's risk tolerance, and the time horizon. This is done in conjunction with the investment manager's expectations about the capital markets and about individual assets, as described above.

How asset allocation decisions are made by investors remains a subject that is not fully understood. It is known that actual allocation decisions often differ widely from how investors say they will allocate assets.

According to some analyses, asset allocation is closely related to the age of an investor. This involves the so-called life-cycle theory of asset allocation. This makes intuitive sense because the needs and financial positions of workers in their 50s will differ on average from those who are starting out in their 20s. According to the life-cycle theory, for example, as individuals approach retirement they become more risk-averse.

Table 21-1 illustrates the asset allocation decision by presenting two examples to show how major changes during life can affect asset allocation. One investor is "conservative," and one "aggressive." They begin their investment programs with different allocations and end with different allocations, but their responses to major changes over the life cycle are similar. Both investors have a minimum of 50 percent allocated to stocks at all stages of the life cycle because of the need for growth.

Table 21-1, published in *AAII Journal,* a magazine for average investors, is illustrative only. Different investors will choose different allocations. Lifestyle changes could cause investors to move from one stage to the other, or changes in life may not cause a change in the allocation percentages. Moreover, even among similar age groups, goals can vary substantially. Overall, asset allocation decisions may depend more upon goals than age. The important point is that all investors must make the asset allocation decision, and this decision will have a major impact on the investment results achieved.

It seems reasonable to assert that the level of risk aversion affects the asset allocation decision. One study examined the risk preferences of households using financial data for a large random sample of U.S. households. The definition of risk used was relative risk aversion, defined as investors' tolerance for risk as measured relative to his or her wealth level. This study found differences in relative risk aversion across three distinct categories of individuals—those 65 and older, those with very high levels of wealth, and those with incomes below the poverty level. The study also found clear patterns for asset allocation over wealth and income levels, with the proportion allocated to risky assets rising consistently with both income and wealth.

Types of Asset Allocation William Sharpe has outlined several types of asset allocation.[8] If all major aspects of the process have been considered, the process is referred to as *integrated asset allocation.* These include issues specific to an investor, particularly the investor's risk tolerance, and issues pertaining to the capital markets, such as predictions concerning expected returns, risks, and correlations. If some of these steps are omitted, the asset allocation approaches are more specialized. Such approaches include:

1. *Strategic asset allocation* This type of allocation is usually done once every few years, using simulation procedures to determine the likely range of outcomes associated with each mix. The investor considers the range of outcomes for each mix, and chooses the preferred one, thereby establishing a long-run, or strategic asset mix.
2. *Tactical asset allocation* This type of allocation is performed routinely, as part of the ongoing process of asset management. Changes in asset mixes are driven by changes in predictions concerning asset returns. As predictions of the expected returns on stocks, bonds and other assets change, the percentages of these assets held in the portfolio changes. In effect, tactical asset allocation is a market timing approach to portfolio management intended to increase exposure to a particular market when its performance is expected to be good, and decrease exposure when performance is expected to be poor.

[8] See William F. Sharpe, "Asset Allocation," in *Managing Investment Portfolios,* 2nd. ed., John L. Maginn, CFA and Donald L. Tuttle, CFA, eds. (Charlottesville, Va.: Association for Investment Management and Research, 1990), p. 7-21–7-27.

PORTFOLIO OPTIMIZATION

Stated at its simplest, portfolio construction involves the selection of securities to be included in the portfolio and the determination of portfolio funds (the weights) to be placed in each security. As we know from Chapter 7, the Markowitz model provides the basis for a scientific portfolio construction that results in efficient portfolios. An efficient portfolio, as discussed in Chapter 19, is one with the highest level of expected return for a given level of risk, or the lowest risk for a given level of expected return.

On a formal basis, the Markowitz model provides a formal model of optimization, which allows investors to construct portfolios that are efficient.

MONITOR MARKET CONDITIONS AND INVESTOR CIRCUMSTANCES

MONITORING MARKET CONDITIONS

The need to monitor market conditions is obvious. Investment decisions are made in a dynamic marketplace where change occurs on a continuing basis. Key macro variables, such as inflation and interest rates, should be tracked on a regular basis. Information about the prospects for corporate earnings is obviously important because of the impact of earnings on stock prices.

CHANGES IN INVESTOR'S CIRCUMSTANCES

An investor's circumstances can change for several reasons. These can be easily organized on the basis of the framework for determining portfolio policies outlined above.

- *Change in Wealth* A change in wealth may cause an investor to behave differently, possibly accepting more risk in the case of an increase in wealth, or becoming more risk-averse in the case of a decline in wealth.
- *Change in Time Horizon* Traditionally, we think of investors aging and becoming more conservative in their investment approach.
- *Change in Liquidity Requirements* A need for more current income could increase the emphasis on dividend-paying stocks, while a decrease in current income requirements could lead to greater investment in small stocks whose potential payoff may be years in the future.
- *Change in Tax Circumstances* An investor who moves to a higher tax bracket may find municipal bonds more attractive. Also, the timing of the realization of capital gains can become more important.
- *Change in Legal/Regulatory Considerations* Laws affecting investors change regularly, whether tax laws or laws governing retirement accounts, annuities, and so forth.
- *Change in Unique Needs and Circumstances* Investors face a number of possible changes during their life, depending on many economic, social, political, health, and work-related factors.

MAKE PORTFOLIO ADJUSTMENTS AS NECESSARY

Even the most carefully constructed portfolio is not intended to remain intact without change. Portfolio managers spend much of their time monitoring and rebalancing existing portfolios.

The key is to know when and how to do such rebalancing because a trade-off is involved: the cost of trading versus the cost of not trading.[9]

The cost of trading involves commissions, possible impact on market price, and the time involved in deciding to trade. The cost of not trading involves holding positions that are not best suited for the portfolio's owner, holding positions that violate the asset allocation plan, holding a portfolio that is no longer adequately diversified, and so forth.

PERFORMANCE MEASUREMENT

The portfolio management process is designed to facilitate making investment decisions in an organized, systematic manner. Clearly, it is important to evaluate the effectiveness of the overall decision-making process. The measurement of portfolio performance allows investors to determine the success of the portfolio management process, and of the portfolio manager. It is a key part of monitoring the investment strategy that was based on investor objectives, constraints, and preferences.

Performance measurement is important to both those who employ a professional portfolio manager on their behalf as well as to those who invest personal funds. It allows investors to evaluate the risks that are being taken, the reasons for the success or failure of the investing program, and the costs of any restrictions that may have been placed on the investment manager. This, in turn, could lead to revisions in the process.

Unresolved issues remain in performance measurement despite the development of an entire industry to provide data and analyses of ex-post performance. Nevertheless, it is a critical part of the investment management process, and the logical capstone in its own right of the entire study of investments. We therefore consider this issue next as a separate and concluding chapter of the text.

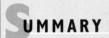

SUMMARY

- Portfolio management should be thought of as a process that can be applied to each investor. It is continuous, systematic, dynamic, and flexible.
- The portfolio management process can be applied to each investor to produce a set of strategy recommendations for accomplishing a given end result.
- The entire process consists of:
  developing explicit investment policies, consisting of objectives, constraints, and preferences
  determining and quantifying capital market expectations
  constructing the portfolio
  monitoring portfolio factors and responding to changes
  rebalancing the portfolio when necessary
  measuring and evaluating portfolio performance
- The first step is to develop an investment policy for the investor, consisting of carefully stated objectives, constraints, and preferences.
- The portfolio construction process can be thought of in terms of the asset allocation decision and the portfolio optimization decision.
- Asset allocation is the most important investment decision made by investors. Types of asset allocation include strategic and tactical.

[9] This discussion is indebted to Robert D. Arnott and Robert M. Lovell, Jr., "Monitoring and Rebalancing the Portfolio," in *Managing Investment Portfolios,* Second Edition, edited by John L. Maginn and Donald L. Tuttle. New York: Warren, Gorham and Lamont, 1990.

KEY WORD

Investment policy
Investment policy statement

QUESTIONS

21-1. What is meant by the portfolio management process?

21-2. Must each investment management firm be organized the same way in order to carry out the investment process?

21-3. What are some of the differences between individual investors and institutional investors?

21-4. What is meant by *the investment policy?*

21-5. How can the investment policy be thought of as an operational statement for investment managers to follow?

21-6. Why is the asset allocation decision the most important decision made by investors?

21-7. Explain the difference between tactical asset allocation and strategic asset allocation.

21-8. How does a well-specified investment policy help institutional investors?

21-9. In forming expectations about future returns from stocks, to what extent should investors be influenced by the more recent past (e.g., the previous 15 years) versus the history of stock market returns starting in 1926?

The following question was asked on the 1989 CFA Level I examination:

CFA
21-10. a. **Outline** a generalized framework that could be used to establish investment policies applicable to all investors.

b. **List** and **briefly discuss** *five* differences in investment policy that might result from the application of your Part A framework to:
1. the pension plan of a young, fast-growing consumer products company, and
2. the modest life insurance proceeds received by a 60-year-old widow with two grown children. (Note: you may find a matrix format helpful in organizing your answers to Part B.)

The following question was asked on the 1991 CFA Level I examination:

CFA
21-11. a. **List** the objectives and constraints that must be considered in developing an investment policy statement.

b. **Explain** why the asset allocation decision is the primary determinant of total portfolio performance over time.

c. **Describe** *three* reasons why successful implementation of asset allocation decisions is even more difficult in practice than in theory.

The following question was asked on the 1990 CFA Level I examination:

CFA

21-12. You are being interviewed for a junior portfolio manager's job at Progressive Counselors, Inc., and are eager to demonstrate your grasp of portfolio management basics.

a. Portfolio management is a process whose *four* key steps are applicable in all investment management situations. **List** these *four* key steps.

An endowment fund has a conservative Board of Trustees. The Board establishes an annual budget that relies on gifts as well as investment income. Gift income is unpredictable, having represented from 10 to 50 percent (averaging 30 percent) of annual spending over the past 10 years. If the gift component of any year's total income falls short of this average level, the shortfall is met from liquidity reserves.

b. **List** and **briefly discuss** the objectives and constraints that must be considered in developing an Investment Policy Statement for this endowment fund.

The following two questions were asked on the 1996 CFA Level II examination:

CFA

21-13.

INTRODUCTION

The following information is available on two U.S.-based accounts managed by Omega Trust Company.

ACCOUNT 1: THE FOOTE FAMILY

Dr. and Mrs. Sheraton Foote are both 35 years old and have a combined annual income of \$250,000. They are both professionals and intend to remain childless. They pay a marginal income tax rate of 40 percent on dividends, interest, and realized capital gains, and dislike paying taxes. Their managed account, which Mrs. Foote inherited, is just over \$1,000,000 in value. The Footes do not expect to use the principal in or the income from their managed account until their planned retirement at age 65. Any funds remaining at their death will be left to Hope Ministries.

ACCOUNT 2: HOPE MINISTRIES

Hope Ministries is a tax exempt charitable organization which was established to provide financial assistance to homeless people. The Foundation's charter requires that all income earned from its endowment fund must be used in operations; any increase in the value of the principal of the endowment fund, whether realized or not, must be retained in the endowment fund. Hope currently requires \$90,000 annual income from its \$1,500,000 endowment fund.

The Omega Trust Company uses the CAPM in managing investment portfolios, combining U.S. Treasury bills (as a proxy for the risk-free rate) and co-mingled funds having differing characteristics. A summary of prevailing expectations for selected capital markets and for each of Omega's co-mingled funds are outlined in Table VIII:

TABLE VIII OMEGA TRUST COMPANY INVESTMENT CHOICES

Investment	Expected Return	Beta
U.S. Treasury Bills (risk-free rate)	40%	0.0
S&P 500 (the equity market portfolio)	12.0%	1.0
Fund A (aggressive equity)	16.5% (including 1.0% from dividends)	1.7
Fund B (diversified equity)	13.0% (including 3.0% from dividends)	1.1
Fund C (global bond)	8.0% (including 8.0% from interest)	0.5

Use the Introduction and Table VIII to answer the following questions about the Foote Family.

(a) **Create** and **justify** an investment policy statement for *the Foote Family* based solely on the information provided. Be specific and complete as to the objectives and constraints.
(b) **Create** and **justify** an asset allocation for *the Foote Family* portfolio, considering both the requirements of the policy statement created in Part A and the returns that are required by the prevailing security market line. Use only the co-mingled funds (A, B, C) shown in Table VIII.

Assume the Footes have received an additional \$350,000 from a new inheritance and invested in a broadly-diversified portfolio and small-capitalization stocks having a 12 percent expected return and a beta of 1.4. They are considering borrowing an additional \$150,000 at an interest rate of 8 percent to increase this investment to \$500,000.

(c) **Explain** the effect of the borrowing on the expected return on the \$350,000 inheritance. **Show** any calculations.
(d) **State** whether the borrowing is appropriate for the Footes. **Justify** your statement with reference to the investment policy statement you created in Part A.

CFA

21-14. Use the Introduction from above and Table VIII to answer the following questions about Hope Ministries.

a. **Create** and **justify** an investment policy statement for *Hope Ministries* based solely on the information provided. Be specific and complete as to the objectives and constraints.
b. **Create** and **justify** an asset allocation for the *Hope Ministries* portfolio, considering both the requirements of the policy statement created in Part A and the returns which are required by the prevailing security market line. Use only the three co-mingled funds (A, B, C) shown in Table VIII.

www.wiley.com/college/jones7
The web exercises for this chapter explore asset allocation from the viewpoint of the goals of individual investors.

chapter 22

EVALUATION OF INVESTMENT PERFORMANCE

Chapter 22 explains what is involved in the evaluation of investment performance. While it might seem like a straightforward process to determine how well an investor's portfolio has performed, such is not the case. Chapter 22 emphasizes the so-called composite measures of portfolio performance and includes a discussion of AIMR's Performance Presentation Standards as well as a brief consideration of some other issues such as performance attribution.

After reading this chapter you will be able to:

- **Understand the issues involved in evaluating portfolio performance.**
- **Evaluate critically popular press claims about the performance of various portfolios, such as mutual funds, available to investors.**
- **Analyze the performance of portfolios using the well-known measures of Sharpe, Treynor, and Jensen.**

We have now discussed, in an organized and systematic manner, the major components of the investing process. One important issue that remains is the "bottom line" of the investing process: evaluating the performance of a portfolio. The question to be answered is: Is the return on a portfolio, less all expenses, adequate to compensate for the risk that was taken? Every investor should be concerned with this issue because, after all, the objective of investing is to increase or at least protect financial wealth. Unsatisfactory results must be detected so that changes can be made.

Evaluating portfolio performance is important regardless of whether an individual investor manages his or her own funds or invests indirectly through investment companies. Direct investing can be time consuming and has high opportunity costs. If the results are inadequate, why do it (unless the investor simply enjoys it)? On the other hand, if professional portfolio managers (such as mutual fund managers) are employed, it is necessary to know how well they perform. If manager A consistently outperforms manager B, other things being equal, investors will prefer manager A. Alternatively, if neither A nor B outperforms an index fund, other things being equal, investors may prefer neither. The obvious point is that performance has to be evaluated before intelligent decisions can be made about existing portfolios.

Portfolio evaluation has changed significantly over time. Prior to the mid-1960s, evaluation was not a major issue, even for investment firms, but it is in today's highly competitive money-management environment. Currently, thousands of mutual funds are operating, with roughly $6 trillion under management. The pension fund universe is even larger, with many employing multiple managers. The majority of all U.S. pension plans with assets greater than $2 billion employ multiple managers. In addition to these money managers, trusts, discretionary accounts, and endowment funds have portfolios that must be evaluated.

Evaluation techniques have become more sophisticated, and the demands by portfolio clients more intense. The broad acceptance of modern portfolio theory has changed the evaluation process and how it is viewed.

In this chapter we discuss the evaluation of portfolio performance, with an eye to understanding the critical issues involved and the overall framework within which evaluation should be conducted. We also review the well-known measures of composite portfolio performance and the problems associated with them.

FRAMEWORK FOR EVALUATING PORTFOLIO PERFORMANCE

When evaluating a portfolio's performance, certain factors must be considered. We discuss below some of the obvious factors that investors should consider and outline the performance presentation standards recently recommended by the Association for Investment Management and Research, which will play a prominent role in performance evaluation in the future.

To illustrate our discussion about comparisons, assume that in 1999 the GoGrowth mutual fund earned a total return of 20 percent for its shareholders. It claims in an advertisement that it is the #1 performing mutual fund in its category. As a shareholder, you are trying to assess GoGrowth's performance. What can you say?

SOME OBVIOUS FACTORS TO CONSIDER

Differential Risk Levels Based on our discussion throughout this text of the risk-return trade-off that underlies all investment actions, we can legitimately say relatively little about GoGrowth's performance. The primary reason is that investing is always a two-dimensional process based on return and risk. These two factors are opposite sides of the same coin, and both must be evaluated if intelligent decisions are to be made. Therefore, if we know nothing about the risk of this fund, there is little we can say about its performance. After all, its managers may have taken twice the risk of comparable portfolios to achieve this 20 percent return.

Given the risk that all investors face, it is totally inadequate to consider only the returns from various investment alternatives. Although all investors prefer higher returns, they are also risk averse. To evaluate portfolio performance properly, we must determine whether the returns are large enough given the risk involved. If we are to assess performance carefully, we must evaluate performance on a risk-adjusted basis.

Differential Time Periods It is not unusual to pick up a publication from the popular press and see two different mutual funds of the same type—for example, aggressive equity funds or balanced funds—advertise themselves as the #1 performer. How can this occur?

The answer is simple. Each of these funds is using a different time period over which to measure performance. For example, one fund could use the 10 years ending December 31, 1999, while another fund uses the five years ending December 31, 1999. GoGrowth could be using a one year period ending on the same date, or some other combination of years. Mutual fund sponsors can choose any time period they wish in promoting their performance. Funds can also define the group to which comparisons are made.

Although it seems obvious when one thinks about it, investors tend not to be careful when making comparisons of portfolios over various time periods. As with the case of differential risk, the time element must be adjusted for if valid performance of portfolio results is to be obtained.

Appropriate Benchmarks A third reason why we can say little about the performance of GoGrowth is that its 20 percent return, given its risk, is meaningful only when compared to a legimitate alternative. Obviously, if the average-risk fund or the market returned 25 percent in 1997, and GoGrowth is average, we would find its performance unfavorable. Therefore, we must make *relative* comparisons in performance measurement, and an important related issue is the benchmark to be used in evaluating the performance of a portfolio.

The essence of performance evaluation in investments is to compare the returns obtained on some portfolio with the returns that could have been obtained from a comparable alternative. The measurement process must involve relevant and obtainable alternatives; that is, the **benchmark portfolio** must be a legitimate alternative that accurately reflects the objectives of the portfolio owners.[1]

Benchmark Portfolio An alternative portfolio against which to measure a portfolio's performance

An equity portfolio consisting of S&P 500 stocks should be evaluated relative to the S&P 500 Index or other equity portfolios that could be constructed from the Index, after adjusting for the risk involved. On the other hand, a portfolio of small capitalization stocks should not be judged against the benchmark of the S&P 500. Or, if a bond portfolio manager's objective is to invest in bonds rated A or higher, it would be inappropriate to compare his or her performance with that of a junk bond manager.

Even more difficult to evaluate are equity funds that hold some mid-cap and small stocks while holding many S&P 500 stocks. Comparisons for this group can be quite difficult.

EXAMPLE 22-1

Most of the largest equity funds underperformed the S&P 500 Composite Index for the years 1994, 1995, and 1996. Why? These funds held more small and mid-cap stocks than are in the S&P 500 Index, and such stocks underperformed the large capitalization stocks in those years.

[1] For a discussion of benchmarks, see Jeffrey V. Bailey, "Evaluating Benchmark Quality," *Financial Analysts Journal* (May–June 1992): 33–39.

The S&P 500 has been the most frequently used benchmark for evaluating the performance of institutional portfolios such as those of pension funds and mutual funds. However, many observers now agree that multiple benchmarks are more appropriate to use when evaluating portfolio returns for reasons such as those described in Example 22-1. Customized benchmarks also can be constructed to evaluate a manager's style that is unusual.

Constraints on Portfolio Managers In evaluating the portfolio manager rather than the portfolio itself, an investor should consider the objectives set by (or for) the manager and any constraints under which he or she must operate. For example, if a mutual fund's objective is to invest in small, speculative stocks, investors must expect the risk to be larger than that of a fund invested in S&P 500 stocks, with substantial swings in the annual realized returns.

It is imperative to recognize the importance of the *investment policy* pursued by a portfolio manager in determining the portfolio's results. In many cases, the investment policy determines the return and risk of the portfolio. For example, Brinson, Hood, and Beebower found that for a sample of pension plans the investment policy accounted for approximately 94 percent of the total variation in the returns to these funds.[2] This obviously leaves little variation to be accounted for by the manager's skills.

If a portfolio manager is obligated to operate under certain constraints, these must be taken into account. For example, if a portfolio manager of an equity fund is prohibited from selling short, it is unreasonable to expect the manager to protect the portfolio in this manner in a bear market. If the manager is further prohibited from trading in options and futures, nearly the only protection left in a bear market is to reduce the equity exposure.

Other Considerations Of course, other important issues are involved in measuring the portfolio's performance, including evaluating the manager as opposed to the portfolio itself if the manager does not have full control over the portfolio's cash flows. It is essential to determine how well diversified the portfolio was during the evaluation period, because, as we know, diversification can reduce portfolio risk. If a manager assumes nonsystematic risk, we want to know if he or she earned an adequate return for doing so.

All investors should understand that even in today's investment world of computers and databases, exact, precise universally agreed-upon methods of portfolio evaluation remain an elusive goal. One popular press article summarized the extent of the problem by noting that "most investors . . . don't have the slightest idea how well their portfolios are actually performing." This article suggests some do-it-yourself techniques as well as some "store-bought solutions" and discusses some new trends in the money management industry to provide investors with better information.

As we will see below, investors can use several well-known techniques to assess the actual performance of a portfolio relative to one or more alternatives. In the final analysis, when investors are selecting money managers to turn their money over to, they evaluate these managers only on the basis of their published performance statistics. If the published "track record" looks good, that is typically enough to convince many investors to invest in a particular mutual fund. However, the past is no guarantee of an investment manager's future. Short-term results may be particularly misleading.

AIMR'S PRESENTATION STANDARDS

The Association for Investment Management and Research (see Appendix 1-A), based on years of discussion, has now issued *minimum* standards for presenting investment perfor-

[2] See Gary P. Brinson, Randolph Hood, and Gilbert L. Beebower, "Determinants of Portfolio Performance," *Financial Analysts Journal* (July/August 1986): 39–44.

TABLE 22-1 AIMR'S PERFORMANCE PRESENTATION STANDARDS

Requirements

1. **Total return**—must be used to calculate performance
2. **Accrual accounting**—use accrual, not cash, accounting except for dividends and for periods before 1993
3. **Time-weighted rates of return**—to be used on at least a quarterly basis and geometric linking of period returns
4. **Cash and cash equivalents**—to be included in composite returns
5. **All portfolios included**—all actual discretionary portfolios are to be included in at least one composite
6. **No linkage of simulated portfolios with actual performance**
7. **Asset-weighting of composites**—beginning-of-period values to be used
8. **Addition of new portfolios**—to be added to a composite after the start of the next measurement period
9. **Exclusion of terminated portfolios**—excluded from all periods after the period in place
10. **No restatement of composite results**—after a firm's reorganization
11. **No portability of portfolio results**
12. **All costs deducted**—subtracted from gross performance
13. **10-year performance record**—minimum period to be presented
14. **Present annual returns for all years**

There are additional requirements for international portfolios and for real estate. In addition, performance presentations must disclose several items of information, such as a complete list of a firm's composites, whether performance results are gross or net of investment management fees, and so on.

SOURCE: *Performance Presentation Standards 1993,* Association for Investment Management and Research, Charlottesville, Va., 1993.

Performance Presentation Standards (PPS) Minimum standards for presenting investment performance as formulated by AIMR

mance.[3] These **Performance Presentation Standards (PPS)** are a set of guiding ethical principles with two objectives:

1. To promote full disclosure and fair representation by investment managers in reporting their investment results.
2. To ensure uniformity in reporting in order to enhance comparability among investment managers.

Some aspects of the standards are mandatory, and others are recommended. Table 22-1 summarizes many of the key points of most relevance to this discussion. We will encounter some of these points as we consider how to go about evaluating portfolios.

RETURN AND RISK CONSIDERATIONS

Performance measurement begins with portfolio valuations and transactions translated into rate of return. Prior to 1965, returns were seldom related to measures of risk. In evaluating portfolio performance, however, investors must consider both the realized return and the risk that was assumed. Therefore, whatever measures or techniques are used, these parameters must be incorporated into the analysis.

MEASURES OF RETURN

When portfolio performance is evaluated, the investor should be concerned with the total change in wealth. As discussed throughout this text, a proper measure of this return is the total return (TR), which captures both the income component and the capital gains (or losses) component of return. Note that the Performance Presentation Standards require the use of total return to calculate performance.

[3] Association for Investment Management and Research, *Performance Presentation Standards 1993,* Charlottesville, Va. 1993.

In the simplest case, the market value of a portfolio can be measured at the beginning and ending of a period, and the rate of return can be calculated as

$$R_p = \frac{V_E - V_B}{V_B} \tag{22-1}$$

where V_E is the ending value of the portfolio and V_B is its beginning value.

This calculation assumes that no funds were added to or withdrawn from the portfolio by the client during the measurement period. If such transactions occur, the portfolio return as calculated, R_p, may not be an accurate measure of the portfolio's performance. For example, if the client adds funds close to the end of the measurement period, use of Equation 22-1 would produce inaccurate results because the ending value was not determined by the actions of the portfolio manager. Although a close approximation of portfolio performance might be obtained by simply adding any withdrawals or subtracting any contributions that are made very close to the end of the measurement period, timing issues are a problem.

Dollar-Weighted Rate of Return (DWR) Equates all cash flows, including ending market value, with the beginning market value of the portfolio

Dollar-Weighted Returns Traditionally, portfolio measurement consisted of calculating the **dollar-weighted rate of return (DWR),** which is equivalent to the internal rate of return (IRR) used in several financial calculations. The IRR measures the actual return earned on a beginning portfolio value and on any net contributions made during the period.

The DWR equates all cash flows, including ending market value, with the beginning market value of the portfolio. Because the DWR is affected by cash flows to the portfolio, it measures the rate of return to the portfolio owner. However, because the DRW is heavily affected by cash flows, it is inappropriate to use when making comparisons to other portfolios or to market indexes, a key factor in performance measurement.

Time-Weighted Rate of Return (TWR) Measures the actual rate of return earned by the portfolio manager

Time-Weighted Returns Since 1966, the **time-weighted rate of return (TWR)** typically is calculated for comparative purposes when cash flows occur between the beginning and the end of a period. TWRs are unaffected by any cash flows to the portfolio; therefore, they measure the actual rate of return earned by the portfolio manager.

Calculating the TWR requires information about the value of the portfolio's cash inflows and outflows. To compute the TWR, we calculate the return to the portfolio immediately prior to a cash flow occurring. We then calculate the return to the portfolio from that cash flow to the next, or to the end of the period. Finally, we link these rates of return together by computing the compound rate of return over time. In other words, we calculate the rate of return for each time period defined by a cash inflow or outflow, and then calculate a compound rate of return for the entire period. If frequent cash flows are involved, substantial calculations are necessary.

Which Measure to Use? The two methods described previously, the dollar-weighted return and the time-weighted return, can produce different results, and at times these differences are substantial. The time-weighted return captures the rate of return actually earned by the portfolio *manager,* while the dollar-weighted return captures the rate of return earned by the portfolio *owner.*

For evaluating the performance of the portfolio manager, the time-weighted return should be used because he or she generally has no control over the deposits and withdrawals made by the clients. The objective is to measure the performance of the portfolio manager independent of the actions of the client, and this is better accomplished by using the time-weighted return. As we can see in Table 22-1, the Performance Presentation Standards require that returns be computed using the TWR approach.

RISK MEASURES

Why can we not measure investment performance on the basis of a properly calculated rate of return measure? After all, rankings of mutual funds are often done this way in the popular press, with one-year, three-year, and sometimes, five-year returns shown. Are rates of return, or averages, good indicators of performance?

As stated in Chapter 1 and restated above, we must consider risk when making judgments about performance. Differences in risk will cause portfolios to respond differently to changes in the overall market and should be accounted for in evaluating performance.

We now know that the two prevalent measures of risk used in investment analysis are total risk and nondiversifiable risk. The standard deviation for a portfolio's set of returns can be calculated easily with a calculator or computer and is a measure of total risk.

Beta can be calculated with any number of software programs. However, we must remember that betas are only estimates of systematic risk. Betas can be calculated using weekly, monthly, quarterly, or annual data, and each will produce a different estimate. Such variations in this calculation could produce differences in rankings which use beta as a measure of risk. Furthermore, betas can be unstable, and they change over time.

RISK-ADJUSTED MEASURES OF PERFORMANCE

Composite (Risk-Adjusted) Measures of Portfolio Performance Portfolio performance measures combining return and risk into one calculation

Based on the concepts of capital market theory, and recognizing the necessity to incorporate both return and risk into the analysis, three researchers—William Sharpe, Jack Treynor, and Michael Jensen—developed measures of portfolio performance in the 1960s. These measures are often referred to as the **composite (risk-adjusted) measures of portfolio performance,** meaning that they incorporate both realized return and risk into the evaluation. These measures are often still used, as evidenced by Morningstar, perhaps the best-known source of mutual fund information, reporting the Sharpe ratio explained below.

THE SHARPE PERFORMANCE MEASURE

Reward-to-Variability Ratio (RVAR) Sharpe's measure of portfolio performance calculated as the ratio of excess portfolio return to the standard deviation

William Sharpe, whose contributions to portfolio theory have been previously encountered, introduced a risk-adjusted measure of portfolio performance called the **reward-to-variability ratio (RVAR)** based on his work in capital market theory.[4] This measure uses a benchmark based on the ex post capital market line.[5] This measure can be defined as

$$
\begin{aligned}
\text{RVAR} &= [\overline{\text{TR}}_p - \overline{\text{RF}}]/\text{SD}_p \\
&= \text{Excess return/Risk} \\
\overline{\text{TR}}_p &= \text{the average TR for portfolio } p \text{ during some period of time (we will use annual data)} \\
\overline{\text{RF}} &= \text{the average risk-free rate of return during the period} \\
\text{SD}_p &= \text{the standard deviation of return for portfolio } p \text{ during the period} \\
\overline{\text{TR}}_p - \overline{\text{RF}} &= \text{the excess return (risk premium) on portfolio } p
\end{aligned}
\qquad (22\text{-}2)
$$

The numerator of Equation 22-2 measures the portfolio's excess return, or the return above the risk-free rate. (RF could have been earned without assuming risk.) This is also referred

[4] W. Sharpe, "Mutual Fund Performance," *Journal of Business* (January 1966): 119–138.

[5] Sharpe used it to rank the performance of 34 mutual funds over the period 1954–1963.

TABLE 22-2 RETURN AND RISK DATA FOR FIVE EQUITY MUTUAL FUNDS, 1979–1993

Mutual Fund	Average Return	Standard Deviation	Beta	R^2
Dreyfus Growth	15.86	22.85	1.46	.64
Ivy Growth	18.10	13.44	.96	.79
Kemper Growth	18.59	21.68	1.45	.69
Magellan (Fidelity)	22.09	17.27	1.24	.79
Windsor (Vanguard)	18.39	11.82	.60	.39
S&P 500	16.35	12.44		
RF	7.96			

to as the risk premium. The denominator uses the standard deviation, which is a measure of the total risk or variability in the return of the portfolio. Note the following about RVAR:

1. It measures the excess return per unit of total risk (standard deviation).
2. The higher the RVAR, the better the portfolio performance.
3. Portfolios can be ranked by RVAR.

As an example of calculating the Sharpe ratio, consider the data for five equity mutual funds for the years 1979 through 1993 chosen randomly for illustrative purposes only: Dreyfus (D), Ivy (I), Kemper (K), Magellan (M), and Windsor (W). Table 22-2 shows annual shareholder returns, the standard deviation of these returns, the beta for the fund, the average return for the S&P 500 Index for those years, and the average yield on Treasury bills as a proxy for RF. On the basis of these data, Sharpe's RVAR can be calculated using Equation 22-2, with results as reported in Table 22-3.

Based on these calculations, we see that three of these five funds—I, W, and M—outperformed the S&P 500 Index on an excess return-risk basis during this period, although the average return exceeded that for the S&P 500 for four of the funds. Since this is an ordinal (relative) measure of portfolio performance, different portfolios can easily be ranked on this variable. Using only the Sharpe measure of portfolio performance, we would judge the portfolio with the highest RVAR best in terms of ex post performance. A RVAR value for the appropriate market index can also be calculated and used for comparison purposes.

As we can see, W, I, and M have RVAR ratios that exceed the RVAR of 0.67 for the S&P 500 for the period. The average return for three of these funds—I, K, and W—were very close together—18.10 percent, 18.59 percent, and 18.39, respectively. However, their standard deviations were very different—13.44 percent, 21.68 percent, and 11.82 percent, respectively. Therefore, their RVAR ratios differed significantly. In effect, Kemper's risk was

TABLE 22-3 RISK-ADJUSTED MEASURES FOR FIVE EQUITY MUTUAL FUNDS, 1979–1993

Mutual Fund	RVAR	RVOL	Jensen's Alpha
Dreyfus	.35	5.40	−3.95
Ivy	.75	10.54	2.67
Kemper	.49	7.33	−1.04
Magellan	.82	11.42	4.21
Windsor	.88	17.38	5.35
S&P 500	.67		

FIGURE 22-1

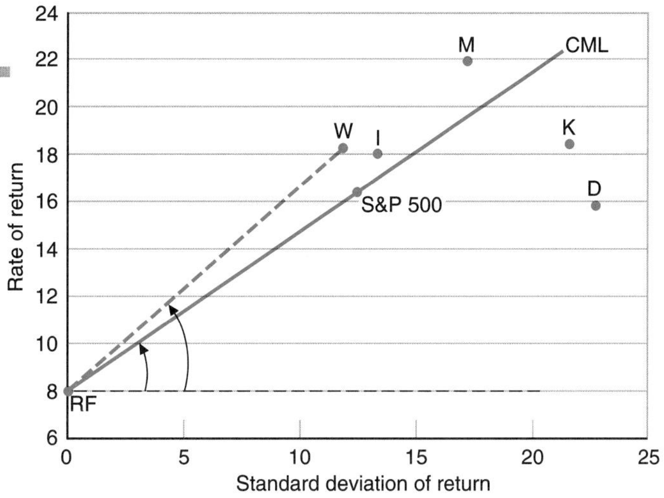

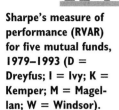

Sharpe's measure of performance (RVAR) for five mutual funds, 1979–1993 (D = Dreyfus; I = Ivy; K = Kemper; M = Magellan; W = Windsor).

very high in relation to its average return as compared in particular to Windsor, which showed slightly less average return but with a much lower standard deviation.

Sharpe's measure for these funds is illustrated graphically in Figure 22-1. The vertical axis is rate of return, and the horizontal axis is standard deviation of returns. The vertical intercept is RF. As Figure 22-1 shows, RVAR measures the slope of the line from RF to the portfolio being evaluated. The steeper the line, the higher the slope (RVAR) and the better the performance. The arrow indicates the slope for the S&P 500 and for Windsor, the fund with the greatest slope.

Because of their better performance, Windsor, Magellan, and Ivy have the higher slopes, whereas Kemper's and Dreyfus's slopes are lower than that of the S&P 500. Because the RVAR for these three portfolios is greater than the RVAR for the market measure (in this case the S&P 500), these portfolios lie above the CML, indicating superior risk-adjusted performance. The other two lie below the CML, indicating inferior risk-adjusted performance.

INVESTMENTS INTUITION In Figure 22-1 we are drawing the capital market line (CML) when we plot the market's return against its standard deviation and use RF as the vertical intercept. Based on the discussion in Chapter 20, all efficient portfolios should plot on this line, and an investor with the ability to borrow and lend at the rate RF should be able to attain any point on this line. Of course, this is the ex post and not the ex ante CML.

THE TREYNOR PERFORMANCE MEASURE

Reward-to-Volatility Ratio (RVOL) Treynor's measure of portfolio performance calculated as the ratio of excess portfolio return to beta

At approximately the same time as Sharpe's measure was developed (the mid-1960s), Jack Treynor presented a similar measure called the **reward-to-volatility ratio (RVOL).**[6] Like Sharpe, Treynor sought to relate the return on a portfolio to its risk. Treynor, however, distinguished between total risk and systematic risk, implicitly assuming that portfolios are well diversified; that is, he ignored any diversifiable risk. He used as a benchmark the ex post security market line.

In measuring portfolio performance, Treynor introduced the concept of the characteristic line, used in earlier chapters to partition a security's return into its systematic and non-

[6] J. Treynor, "How to Rate Management of Investment Funds," *Harvard Business Review* (January–February 1965), pp. 63–75.

systematic components. It is used in a similar manner with portfolios, depicting the relationship between the returns on a portfolio and those of the market. The slope of the characteristic line measures the relative volatility of the fund's returns. As we know, the slope of this line is the beta coefficient, which is a measure of the volatility (or responsiveness) of the portfolio's returns in relation to those of the market index.

Characteristic lines can be estimated by regressing each portfolio's returns on the market proxy returns using either raw returns for the portfolios and raw proxy returns or excess portfolio returns and excess market proxy returns where the risk-free rate has been subtracted out. The latter method is theoretically better and is used here.

Treynor's measure relates the average excess return on the portfolio during some period (exactly the same variable as in the Sharpe measure) to its systematic risk as measured by the portfolio's beta. The reward-to-volatility ratio is

$$\begin{aligned} \text{RVOL} &= [\overline{\text{TR}_p} - \overline{\text{RF}}]/\beta_p \\ &= \text{Average excess return on portfolio } p \qquad (22\text{-}3) \\ \beta_p &= \text{the beta for portfolio } p \end{aligned}$$

In this case we are calculating the excess return per unit of systematic risk. As with RVAR, higher values of RVOL indicate better portfolio performance. Portfolios can be ranked on their RVOL, and assuming that the Treynor measure is a correct measure of portfolio performance, the best performing portfolio can be determined.

Using the data in Table 22-1, we can calculate RVOL for the same five portfolios illustrated and for the S&P 500, which has a beta of 1.0. These calculations indicate that three funds outperformed the market on the basis of their excess return/systematic risk ratio—I, M, and W. The two funds with the highest betas, D and K, had RVOL ratios lower than the beta for the S&P 500. Although the beta for Magellan was higher than those for the other two top performers, I and W, its higher return was sufficient to compensate for this larger risk (at least in these comparisons).

Figure 22-2 illustrates the graph of the Treynor measure in a manner similar to Figure 22-1 for the Sharpe measure. In this graph we are viewing the *ex post* SML. Again, three funds plot above the line—I, M, and W—and two funds plot below—D and K. Once again, if we were to draw lines to each fund's return—risk point, the steepest line would have the largest slope and represent the best performance.

FIGURE 22-2

Treynor's measure of performance (RVOL) for five mutual funds, 1979–1993 (D = Dreyfus; I = Ivy; K = Kemper; M = Magellan; W = Windsor).

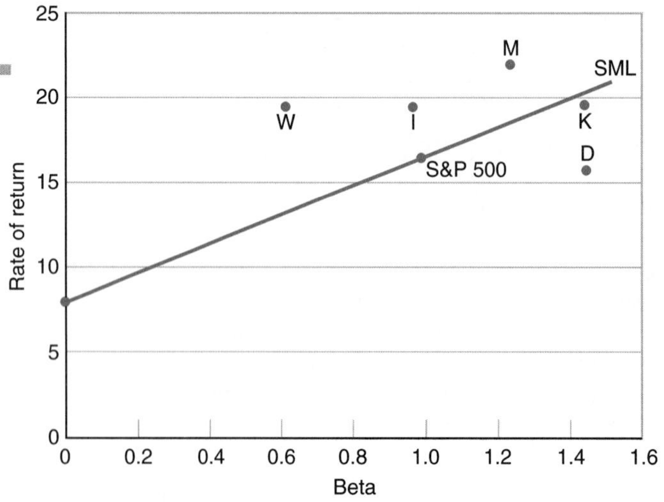

The use of RVOL, of course, implies that systematic risk is the proper measure of risk to use when evaluating portfolio performance; therefore, it implicitly assumes a completely diversified portfolio. (Similarly, the use of RVAR implies that total risk is the proper measure to use when evaluating portfolios.) As we now know, systematic risk is a proper measure of risk to use when portfolios are perfectly diversified so that no nonsystematic risk remains. (A procedure for measuring the degree of diversification is discussed below.)

Comparing the Sharpe and Treynor Measures Given their similarity, when should RVAR or RVOL be used, and why? Actually, given the assumptions underlying each measure, both can be said to be correct. Therefore, it is usually desirable to calculate both measures for the set of portfolios being evaluated.

The choice of which to use could depend on the definition of risk. If an investor thinks it correct to use total risk, RVAR is appropriate; however, if the investor thinks that it is correct to use systematic risk, RVOL is appropriate.

What about the rankings of a set of portfolios using the two measures? If the portfolios are perfectly diversified—that is, the correlation coefficient between the portfolio return and the market return is 1.0—the rankings will be identical. For typical large, professionally managed portfolios, such as broad-based equity mutual funds, the two measures often provide identical, or almost identical, rankings.

As the portfolios become less well diversified, the possibility of differences in rankings increases. This leads to the following conclusion about these two measures: RVAR takes into account how well diversified a portfolio was during the measurement period. Differences in rankings between the two measures can result from substantial differences in diversification in the portfolio. If a portfolio is inadequately diversified, its RVOL ranking can be higher than its RVAR ranking. The nonsystematic risk would not affect the RVOL calculation. Therefore, a portfolio with a low amount of systematic risk and a large amount of total risk could show a high RVOL value and a low RVAR value. Such a difference in ranking results from the substantial difference in the amount of diversification of the portfolio.

This analysis leads to an important observation about the Sharpe and Treynor measures. Investors who have all (or substantially all) of their assets in a portfolio of securities should rely more on the Sharpe measure because it assesses the portfolio's total return in relation to total risk, which includes any unsystematic risk assumed by the investor. However, for those investors whose portfolio constitutes only one (relatively) small part of their total assets—that is, they have numerous other assets—systematic risk may well be the relevant risk. In these circumstances, RVOL is appropriate because it considers only systematic or nondiversifiable risk.

Measuring Diversification Portfolio diversification is typically measured by correlating the returns on the portfolio with the returns on the market index. This is accomplished as part of the process of fitting a characteristic line whereby the portfolio's returns are regressed against the market's returns. The square of the correlation coefficient produced as a part of the analysis, called the **coefficient of determination**, or R^2, is used to denote the degree of diversification. The coefficient of determination indicates the percentage of the variance in the portfolio's returns that is explained by the market's returns. If the fund is totally diversified, the R^2 will approach 1.0, indicating that the fund's returns are completely explained by the market's returns. The lower the coefficient of determination, the less the portfolio's returns are attributable to the market's returns. This indicates that other factors, which could have been diversified away, are being allowed to influence the portfolio's returns.

Coefficient of Determination The square of the correlation coefficient, measuring the percentage of the variance in the dependent variable that is explained by the independent variable

The R^2 figures in Table 22-2 indicate that four of the funds had R^2 in the range of 0.64 to 0.79. The R^2 for Windsor was only 0.39, indicating that it was exposed to more nonsystematic risk than the other funds, presumably because the portfolio managers expected to earn adequate returns to compensate for this risk.

JENSEN'S DIFFERENTIAL RETURN MEASURE

Differential Return Measure (Alpha) Jensen's measure of portfolio performance calculated as the difference between what the portfolio actually earned and what it was expected to earn given its level of systematic risk

A measure related to Treynor's RVOL is Jensen's **differential return measure** (or **alpha**). Jensen's measure of performance, like Treynor's measure, is based on the CAPM. The expected return for any security (i) or, in this case, portfolio (p) is given as

$$E(R_{pt}) = RF_t + \beta_p(E(R_{Mt}) - RF_t) \tag{22-4}$$

with all terms as previously defined.

Notice that Equation 22-4, which covers any ex ante period t, can be applied to ex post periods if the investor's expectations are, on the average, fulfilled. Empirically, Equation 22-4 can be approximated as Equation 22-5.

$$R_{pt} = RF_t + \beta_p[R_{Mt} - RF_t] + E_{pt} \tag{22-5}$$

where

R_{pt} = the return on portfolio p in period t
RF_t = the risk-free rate in period t
R_{Mt} = the return on the market in period t
E_{pt} = a random error term for portfolio p in period t
$[R_{Mt} - RF_t]$ = the market risk premium during period t

Equation 22-5 relates the realized return on portfolio p during any period t to the sum of the risk-free rate and the portfolio's risk premium plus an error term. Given the market risk premium, the risk premium on portfolio p is a function of portfolio p's systematic risk—the larger its systematic risk, the larger the risk premium.

Equation 22-5 can be written in what is called the risk premium (or, alternatively, the excess return) form by moving RF to the left side and subtracting it from R_{pt}, as in Equation 22-6:

$$R_{pt} - RF_t = \beta_p[R_{Mt} - RF_t] + E_{pt} \tag{22-6}$$

where

$R_{pt} - RF_t$ = the risk premium on portfolio p

Equation 22-6 indicates that the risk premium on portfolio p is equal to the product of its beta and the market risk premium plus an error term. In other words, the risk premium on portfolio p should be proportional to the risk premium on the market portfolio if the CAPM model is correct and investor expectations were generally realized (in effect, if all assets and portfolios were in equilibrium).

A return proportional to the risk assumed is illustrated by Fund Y in Figure 22-3. This diagram shows the characteristic line in excess return form, where the risk-free rate each period, RF_t, is subtracted from both the portfolio's return and the market's return.[7]

Equation 22-6 can be empirically tested by fitting a regression for some number of periods. Portfolio excess returns (risk premiums) are regressed against the excess returns (risk premiums) for the market. If managers earn a return proportional to the risk assumed, this relationship should hold. That is, there should be no intercept term (alpha) in the regression, which should go through the origin, as in the case of Fund Y in Figure 22-3.

[7] This version is usually referred to as a characteristic line in risk premium or excess return form.

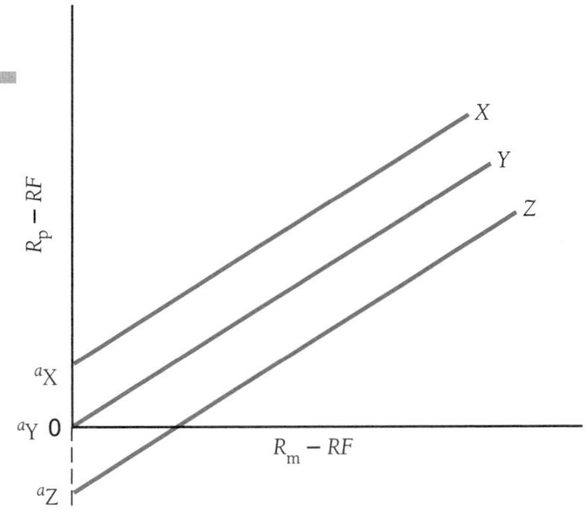

FIGURE 22-3

Jensen's measure of performance for three hypothetical funds.

Given these expected findings, Jensen argued that an intercept term, alpha, could be added to Equation 22-6 as a means of identifying superior or inferior portfolio performance. Therefore, Equation 22-6 becomes Equation 22-7 where α_p is the alpha or intercept term:

$$R_{pt} - RF_t = \alpha_p + \beta_p[R_{Mt} - RF_t] + E_{pt} \tag{22-7}$$

The CAPM asserts that equilibrium conditions should result in a zero intercept term. Therefore, the alpha should measure the contribution of the portfolio manager since it represents the average incremental rate of return per period beyond the return attributable to the level of risk assumed. Specifically,

1. If alpha is significantly positive, this is evidence of superior performance (illustrated in Figure 22-3 with portfolio X, which has a positive intercept).
2. If alpha is significantly negative, this is evidence of inferior performance (illustrated in Figure 22-3 with portfolio Z, which has a negative intercept).
3. If alpha is insignificantly different from zero, this is evidence that the portfolio manager matched the market on a risk-adjusted basis (as in the case of portfolio Y).

Note that Equation 22-7 can be rearranged to better demonstrate what α_p really is. Rearranging terms, Equation 22-7 becomes

$$\alpha_p = (R_p - RF) - [\beta_p(R_M - RF)] \tag{22-8}$$

where the bars above the variables indicate averages for the period measured.

Equation 22-8 states that α_p is the difference between the actual excess return on portfolio p during some period and the risk premium on that portfolio that should have been earned, given its level of systematic risk and the use of the CAPM. It measures the constant return that the portfolio manager earned above, or below, the return of an unmanaged portfolio with the same (market) risk.

As noted, this difference can be positive, negative, or zero. It is important to recognize the role of statistical significance in the interpretation of Jensen's measure. Although the estimated alpha may be positive or negative, it may not be significantly different (statistically) from zero. If it is not, we would conclude that the manager of the portfolio being evaluated performed as expected. That is, the manager earned an average risk-adjusted return, neither more nor less than would be expected given the risk assumed.

Jensen's performance measure can be estimated by regressing excess returns for the portfolio being evaluated against excess returns for the market (in effect, producing a characteristic line in excess return form). When this was done for the five mutual funds evaluated earlier, the results are as shown in Table 22-2.

Three of the funds showed positive alphas, and reasonably high ones given the alphas typically observed for mutual funds. If significant, the 5.35 for Windsor would indicate that this fund, on the average, earned an annual risk-adjusted rate of return that was more than 5 percent above the market average. In other words, Windsor earned a positive return attributable to factors other than the market, presumably because of the ability of its managers. However, the standard errors for each fund indicate that the alphas are not significantly different from zero.[8] Therefore, we cannot conclude that these funds exhibited superior performance. As in any regression equation, the coefficients must be statistically significant for any conclusions to be drawn.

Portfolios often fail to meet this statistical significance test because of the variability in security returns. This means that although the manager may actually add value, it cannot be detected statistically. The larger the number of observations, the more likely we are to find statistical significance.

Superior and inferior portfolio performance can result from at least two sources. First, the portfolio manager may be able to select undervalued securities consistently enough to affect portfolio performance. Second, the manager may be able to time market turns, varying the portfolio's composition in accordance with the rise and fall of the market. Obviously, a manager with enough ability may be able to do both.

A computational advantage of the Jensen measure is that it permits the performance measure to be estimated simultaneously with the beta for a portfolio. That is, by estimating a characteristic line in risk premium form, estimates of both alpha and beta are obtained at the same time. However, unlike the Sharpe and Treynor measures, each period's returns must be used in the estimating process, rather than an average return for the entire period. Thus, if performance is being measured on an annual basis, the annual returns on RF, RM, and R_p must be obtained.

A Comparison of the Three Composite Measures The Sharpe measure, which uses the standard deviation, evaluates portfolio performance on the basis of both the portfolio's return and its diversification. Treynor's measure considers only the systematic risk of the portfolio and, like the Sharpe measure, can be used to rank portfolios on the basis of realized performance. Although the Sharpe and Treynor measures rank portfolios, they do not tell us in percentage terms how much a fund outperformed (or underperformed) some benchmark.

Like the Treynor measure, Jensen's alpha uses beta as the measure of risk. Jensen's measure is not suitable for ranking portfolio performance, but it can be modified to do so. The Jensen and Treynor measures can produce, with proper adjustments, identical relative rankings of portfolio performance.[9]

If a portfolio is completely diversified, all three measures will agree on a ranking of portfolios. The reason for this is that with complete diversification, total variance is equal to systematic variance. When portfolios are not completely diversified, the Treynor and Jensen measures can rank relatively undiversified portfolios much higher than the Sharpe measure does. Since the Sharpe measure uses total risk, both systematic and nonsystematic components are included.

Another difference in the measures is that the Sharpe and Treynor measures use average

---

[8] A general rule of thumb is that a coefficient should be twice its standard error in order to be significant at the 5 percent level. Alternatively, t values can be examined in order to test the significance of the coefficients. For a reasonably large number of observations, and therefore degrees of freedom, t values of approximately 2.0 would indicate significance at the 5 percent level.

[9] Jensen's alpha divided by beta is equivalent to Treynor's measure minus the average risk premium for the market portfolio for the period.

returns over the measurement period, including the average risk-free rate. The Jensen measure uses the period-by-period returns and risk-free rate.

PROBLEMS WITH PORTFOLIO MEASUREMENT

Using the three risk-adjusted performance measures just discussed to evaluate portfolios is not without problems. Investors should understand their limitations and be guided accordingly.

First, these measures are derived from capital market theory and the CAPM and are therefore dependent on the assumptions involved with this theory, as discussed in Chapter 20. For example, if the Treasury bill rate is not a satisfactory proxy for the risk-free rate, or if investors cannot borrow and lend at the risk-free rate, this will have an impact on these measures of performance.

An important assumption of capital market theory that directly affects the use of these performance measures is the assumption of a market portfolio that can be proxied by a market index. We have used the S&P 500 Index as a market proxy, as is often done. However, there are potential problems.

Richard Roll has argued that beta is not a clear-cut measure of risk.[10] If the definition of the market portfolio is changed, for example, by using the New York Stock Exchange Index instead of the S&P 500, the beta can change. This could, in turn, change the rankings of portfolios. In addition, if the proxy for the market portfolio is not efficient, the SML used may not be the true SML. Errors can occur when portfolios are plotted against an incorrect SML. This is referred to as *benchmark error.*

Although a high correlation exists among most of the commonly used market proxies, this does not eliminate the problem—that some may be efficient but others are not. This relates to Roll's major point, mentioned in Chapter 20, that using a market portfolio other than the "true" market portfolio does not constitute a test of the CAPM. Rather, it is a test only of whether or not the chosen market proxy is efficient. According to Roll, no unambiguous test of the CAPM has yet been conducted. This point should be kept in mind when we consider performance measures based on the CAPM, such as the Treynor and Jensen measures.

The movement to global investing increases the problem of benchmark error. The efficient frontier changes when foreign securities are added to the portfolio. The measurement of beta will be affected by adding foreign securities. Given that a world portfolio is likely to have a smaller variance than the S&P 500 Index, any measure of systematic risk is likely to be smaller.

A long evaluation period is needed to successfully determine performance that is truly superior. Over short periods, luck can overshadow all else, but luck cannot be expected to continue. According to some estimates, the number of years needed to make such an accurate determination is quite large. As we saw in Table 22-1, the Performance Presentation Standards stipulate the presentation of at least a 10-year performance record.

Theoretically, each of the three performance measures discussed should be independent of its respective risk measure. However, over the years some researchers have found a relationship between them. In some cases the relationship was negative, and in others it was positive. It can be shown that a fundamental relationship does exist between the composite performance measures and their associated risk measure.[11] Given an empirical CML, the

---

[10] See R. Roll, "Ambiguity When Performance Is Measured by the Securities Market Line," *The Journal of Finance,* 33 (September 1978): 1051–1069; "Performance Evaluation and Benchmark Error, Part I," *The Journal of Portfolio Management,* 6 (Summer 1980): 5–12, and Part II (Winter 1981): 17–22.

[11] See J. Wilson and C. Jones, "The Relationship Between Performance and Risk: Whence the Bias?" *The Journal of Financial Research,* 4 (Summer 1981): 109–117.

relation between Sharpe's measure and the standard deviation can be instantly derived. Similarly, given an empirical SML, the relationship between Jensen's and Treynor's performance measures and beta can be derived instantly. The only other variable needed to do these calculations is the mean market return for the period.

OTHER ISSUES IN PERFORMANCE EVALUATION

MONITORING PERFORMANCE

Portfolio evaluation of managed portfolios should be a continuing process. The results of the portfolio must be calculated using some of the techniques discussed above. In addition, a monitoring process should evaluate the success of the portfolio relative to the objectives and constraints of the portfolio's owners.

PERFORMANCE ATTRIBUTION

Most of this chapter has considered how to measure a portfolio manager's performance. However, portfolio evaluation also is concerned with the reasons why a manager did better or worse than a properly constructed benchmark with complete risk adjustment. This part of portfolio evaluation is called **performance attribution,** which seeks to determine, after the fact, why a particular portfolio had a given return over some specified time period and, therefore, why success or failure occurred.

Performance Attribution A part of portfolio evaluation that seeks to determine why success or failure occurred

Typically, performance attribution is a top-down approach; it looks first at the broad issues and progresses by narrowing the investigation. Its purpose is to decompose the total performance of a portfolio into specific components that can be associated with specific decisions made by the portfolio manager.

Performance attribution often begins with the policy statement that guides the management of the portfolio. The portfolio normally would have a set of portfolio weights to be used. If the manager uses a different set, this will account for some of the results. In effect, we are looking at the *asset allocation decision* referred to in Chapter 21. If the manager chooses to allocate portfolio funds differently than the weights that occur in the benchmark portfolio, what are the results?

After this analysis, performance attribution might analyze sector (industry) selection and security selection. Did the manager concentrate on, or avoid, certain sectors, and if so what were the results? Security selection speaks for itself.

Part of this process involves identifying a benchmark of performance to use in comparing the portfolio's results. This bogey is designed to measure passive results, ruling out both asset allocation and security selection decisions. Any differences between the portfolio's results and the bogey must be attributable to one or more of these decisions made by the portfolio manager.

Another way to think about performance attribution is to recognize that performance different from a properly constructed benchmark comes from one of two sources, or both:

1. Market timing
2. Security selection

Techniques are available to decompose the performance of a portfolio into these two components.[12]

[12] See R. Henriksson, "Market Timing and Mutual Fund Performance: An Empirical Investigation," *Journal of Business* (1984): 73–96.

CAN PERFORMANCE BE PREDICTED?

The objective of performance evaluation is to measure the performance of a portfolio and its manager over the same time period. Having assessed how well a portfolio manager has performed over the past, is such information valuable in predicting future portfolio performance? After all, in choosing a mutual fund or closed-end fund, won't investors rely heavily on both the absolute and relative results reported by the fund?

Most studies suggest the correlation between past relative performance and future performance is weak. For example, if average returns for a five- or ten-year period are correlated with average returns for the subsequent five- or ten-year period, the correlations are quite low, typically less than 0.20. Therefore, past relative returns do not successfully predict future relative returns, but may provide some help (see Box 3-1).

SUMMARY

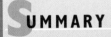

- Evaluation of portfolio performance, the bottom line of the investing process, is an important aspect of interest to all investors and money managers.
- The framework for evaluating portfolio performance consists of measuring both the realized return and the differential risk of the portfolio being evaluated, determining an appropriate benchmark portfolio to use to compare a portfolio's performance, and recognizing any constraints that the portfolio manager may face.
- AIMR has issued a set of Performance Presentation Standards designed to promote full disclosure by investment managers in reporting their investment results and help ensure uniformity in reporting.
- The time-weighted, as opposed to the dollar-weighted, return captures the rate of return actually earned by the portfolio manager. Total returns are used in the calculations.
- The two prevalent measures of risk are total risk (standard deviation) and systematic risk (beta).
- The most often used measures of portfolio performance are the composite measures of Sharpe, Treynor, and Jensen, which bring return and risk together in one calculation.
- The Sharpe and Treynor measures can be used to rank portfolio performance and indicate the relative positions of the portfolios being evaluated. Jensen's measure is an absolute measure of performance.
- Both the Sharpe and Treynor measures relate the excess return on a portfolio to a measure of its risk. Sharpe's RVAR uses standard deviation, whereas Treynor's RVOL uses beta.
- Since RVAR implicitly measures the lack of complete diversification in a portfolio and RVOL assumes complete diversification, portfolio rankings from the two measures can differ if portfolios are not well diversified.
- The coefficient of determination can be used to measure the degree of diversification in a portfolio.
- The Sharpe measure is more appropriate when the portfolio constitutes a significant portion of an investor's wealth, whereas the Treynor measure is more appropriate when the portfolio constitutes only a small part of that wealth.
- Jensen's differential return measures the difference between what the portfolio was expected to earn, given its systematic risk, and what it actually did earn. By regressing the portfolio's excess return against that of the market index, alpha can be used to capture the superior or inferior performance of the portfolio manager.
- Based on capital market theory, alphas are expected to be zero. Significantly positive or negative alphas are used to indicate corresponding performance.

- The composite measures are not without their limitations and problems. If there are problems with capital market theory and the CAPM, such problems carry over to performance measurement.
- One problem in particular is the market portfolio, which can be measured only imprecisely. Failure to use the true ex ante market portfolio may result in different betas and different rankings for portfolios because of benchmark error.
- Performance attribution is concerned with why a portfolio manager did better or worse than an expected benchmark. It involves decomposing performance to determine why the particular results occurred.

KEY WORDS

Benchmark portfolio
Coefficient of determination
Composite (risk-adjusted) measures of portfolio performance
Differential return measure (Alpha)
Dollar-weighted rate of return (DWR)
Performance attribution
Performance Presentation Standards (PPS)
Reward-to-variability ratio (RVAR)
Reward-to-volatility ratio (RVOL)
Time-weighted rate of return (TWR)

QUESTIONS

22-1. Outline the framework for evaluating portfolio performance.

22-2. Why can the evaluation of a portfolio be different from the evaluation of a portfolio manager?

22-3. Explain how the three composite measures of performance are related to capital market theory and the CAPM.

22-4. What role does diversification play in the Sharpe and Treynor measures?

22-5. How can one construct a characteristic line for a portfolio? What does it show?

22-6. How can portfolio diversification be measured? On the average, what degree of diversification would you expect to find for a typical mutual fund?

22-7. For what type of mutual fund discussed in Chapter 3 could you expect to find complete diversification?

22-8. In general, when may an investor prefer to rely on the Sharpe measure? the Treynor measure?

22-9. Explain how Jensen's differential return measure is derived from the CAPM.

22-10. Why is the Jensen measure computationally efficient?

22-11. What role does statistical significance play in the Jensen measure?

22-12. How does Roll's questioning of the testing of the CAPM relate to the issue of performance measurement?

22-13. Illustrate how the choice of the wrong market index could affect the rankings of portfolios.

22-14. In theory, what would be the proper market index to use?

22-15. Explain why the steeper the angle, the better the performance in Figures 22-1 and 22-2.

22-16. Do the Sharpe and Jensen measures produce the same rankings of portfolio performance?

The following questions were asked on the CFA Level I 1990 Examination:

CFA

22-17. A plan sponsor with a portfolio manager who invests in small capitalization, high growth stocks should have the plan sponsor's performance measured against which *one* of the following?

a. S&P 500 Index
b. Wilshire 5000 Index
c. Dow Jones Industrial Average
d. S&P 400 Index

CFA

22-18. In measuring the comparative performance of different fund managers, the preferred method of calculating rate of return is:

a. internal
b. time weighted
c. dollar weighted
d. income

CFA

22-19. Which *one* of the following is a valid benchmark against which a portfolio's performance can be measured over a given time period?

a. The portfolio's dollar-weighted rate of return
b. The portfolio's time-weighted rate of return
c. The portfolio manager's "normal" portfolio
d. The average beta of the portfolio

PROBLEMS

22-1. The following data are available for five portfolios and the market for a recent 10-year period:

	Annual Return (%)	Standard Deviation (%)	Average β_p	R^2
1	14	21	1.15	0.70
2	16	24	1.1	0.98
3	26	30	1.3	0.96
4	17	25	0.9	0.92
5	10	18	0.45	0.60
S&P 500	12	20		
RF	6			

a. Rank these portfolios using the Sharpe measure.
b. Rank these portfolios using the Treynor measure.
c. Compare the rankings of portfolios 1 and 2. Are there any differences? How can you explain these differences?
d. Which of these portfolios outperformed the market?

22-2. Consider the five funds shown below:

	α	β	R^2
1	2.0	1.0	0.98
2	1.6[a]	1.1	0.95
3	3.5	0.9	0.90
4	1.2	0.8	0.80
5	0.9[a]	1.20	0.60

[a]Significant at 5 percent level.

a. Which fund's returns are best explained by the market's returns?
b. Which fund had the largest total risk?
c. Which fund had the lowest market risk? The highest?
d. Which fund(s), according to Jensen's alpha, outperformed the market?

22-3. The following diagram shows characteristic lines in risk premium form for two portfolios. Assume that the alphas for each portfolio are statistically significant.
a. Label each axis.
b. Which fund has the larger beta?
c. Based on a visual inspection, which fund has the larger alpha?
d. Which fund outperformed the market?

22-4. Annual total returns for nine years are shown below for eight mutual funds. Characteristic lines are calculated using annual market returns. The *ex post* values are as follows:

Fund	(1) R_p (%)	(2) σ_p (%)	(3) α_p	(4) β_p	(5) R^2
A	17.0	20.0	7.53	0.88	0.82
B	19.0	17.8	11.70	0.65	0.57
C	12.3	25.0	3.12	0.83	0.47
D	20.0	24.5	9.00	1.00	0.72
E	15.0	17.4	6.15	0.79	0.88
F	19.0	18.0	10.11	0.83	0.89
G	8.6	19.0	−1.37	0.91	0.95
H	20.0	21.5	9.52	0.93	0.78

where

R_p = mean annual total return for each fund
σ_p = standard deviation of the annual yields
α_p = the constant of the characteristic line
β_p = the slope

Using an 8.6 percent risk-free return:

a. Calculate Sharpe's RVAR for each of these eight funds and rank the eight funds from high to low performance.
b. Calculate Treynor's RVOL for each fund and perform the same ranking as in part a.
c. Use the R^2 in column 5 to comment on the degree of diversification of the eight mutual funds. Which fund appears to be the most highly diversified? Which fund appears to be the least diversified?

d. The returns, standard deviations, and characteristic lines were recalculated using the annual Treasury bill rate. The results are shown in the following table in excess yield form:

Fund	R_p	σ_p	α_p	SE(α)	β_p	t Values
2.15	A	8.60	20.00	6.57	(3.53)	0.87
2.23	B	10.30	16.90	8.81	(4.78)	0.61
0.24	C	3.70	25.50	1.58	(7.37)	0.86
1.96	D	11.50	25.00	8.98	(5.23)	1.03
1.91	E	6.30	18.09	4.34	(2.51)	0.81
4.21	F	10.80	18.20	8.69	(2.40)	0.83
−1.49	G	−0.02	19.80	−2.22	(1.65)	0.92
2.40	H	11.30	23.40	8.88	(4.20)	0.95

In the column to the right of the α_p is the calculated standard error of alpha [SE(α)]. The critical value of t for 7 degrees of freedom (number of observations minus 2) for a two-tailed test at the 5 percent level is 2.365. With a large number of degrees of freedom (more observations), the critical value of t is close to 2.00. The calculated t values are shown in the last column of the table (t for α_p). If the absolute value in that column exceeds 2.365, that fund's alpha is significantly different from zero. On the basis of this test, which funds exhibit above, or below, average performance?

e. Compare the values of α and β calculated in excess yield form with those calculated initially. Can you suggest any generalizations about the relative magnitudes of these values?

22-5. Given the following information:

Period	Market Return	RF	Portfolio 1	Portfolio 2
1	0.12	.07	0.14	0.16
2	0.10	.07	0.18	0.20
3	0.02	.08	0.06	0.04
4	0.20	.08	0.30	0.26
5	0.16	.07	0.21	0.21
6	−0.03	.08	−0.04	−0.06
7	−0.05	.07	−0.04	−0.01
8	0.13	.07	0.14	0.12
9	0.30	.08	0.28	0.32
10	−0.15	.09	−0.20	−0.25

a. Rank the portfolios on RVAR
b. Rank the portfolios on RVOL
c. Rank the portfolios on alpha
d. Which portfolio had the smaller nonsystematic risk?
e. Which portfolio had the larger beta?
f. Which portfolio had the larger standard deviation?
g. Which portfolio had the larger average return?
h. How are the answers to (f) and (g) related to the results for the composite performance measures?

22-6. Given the following information for three portfolios for a six-year period:

Period	Market Return	RF	Portfolio 1	Portfolio 2	Portfolio 3
1	0.10	.05	0.15	0.16	0.17
2	0.02	.06	0.09	0.11	0.13
3	0.20	.08	0.26	0.28	0.18
4	0.30	.09	0.34	0.36	0.42
5	−0.04	.08	−0.02	−0.03	−0.16
6	0.16	.07	0.16	0.17	0.17

Answer (a) through (d) without doing the calculations.

a. Which portfolio would you expect to have the largest beta?
b. Which portfolio would you expect to have the largest standard deviation?
c. Which portfolio would you expect to have the largest R^2?
d. Which portfolio would you expect to rank first on the basis of RVAR?
e. Determine the rankings of the three portfolios on RVAR and RVOL.
f. How did the portfolios rank in terms of R^2?
g. Which portfolio had the largest alpha?
h. Which portfolio exhibited the best performance based on the composite measures of performance?

22-7. The following information is available for two portfolios, a market index, and the risk-free rate:

Period	Market Return	RF	Portfolio 1	Portfolio 2
1	0.10	.06	0.10	0.20
2	0.12	.08	0.12	0.24
3	0.20	.08	0.20	0.40
4	0.04	.08	0.04	0.08
5	0.12	.08	0.12	0.24

a. Without doing calculations, determine the portfolio with a beta of 1.0.
b. Without doing calculations, determine the beta of portfolio 2.
c. Without doing calculations, determine the R^2 for each portfolio.
d. Without doing calculations, what would you expect the alpha of portfolio 1 to be?
e. What would you expect the RVAR and RVOL to be for portfolio 1 relative to the market?

The following questions were asked on the CFA Level I 1994 examination:

The administrator of a large pension fund wants to evaluate the performance of four portfolio managers. Each portfolio manager invests only in U.S. common stocks. Assume that during the most recent 5-year period, the average annual total rate of return including dividends on the S&P 500 was 14 percent, and the average nominal rate of return on government Treasury bills was 8 percent. The following table shows risk and return measures for each portfolio.

RISK AND RETURN DATA

Portfolio	Average Annual Rate of Return	Standard Deviation	Beta
P	0.17	0.20	1.1
Q	0.24	0.18	2.1
R	0.11	0.10	0.5
S	0.16	0.14	1.5
S&P 500	0.14	0.12	1.0

CFA
22-8. The Treynor portfolio performance measure for Portfolio P is:

a. 0.082
b. 0.099
c. 0.155
d. 0.450

CFA
22-9. The Sharpe portfolio performance measure for Portfolio Q is:

a. 0.076
b. 0.126
c. 0.336
d. 0.880

CFA
22-10. When plotting Portfolio R relative to the Security Market Line (SML), Portfolio R lies:

a. on the SML.
b. below the SML.
c. above the SML.
d. insufficient data given.

CFA
22-11. When plotting Portfolio S relative to the Capital Market Line (CML), Portfolio S lies:

a. on the CML.
b. below the CML.
c. above the CML.
d. insufficient data given.

CFA
22-12. An analyst wants to evaluate Portfolio X, consisting entirely of U.S. common stocks, using both the Treynor and Sharpe measures of portfolio performance. Table 3 provides the average annual rate of return for Portfolio X, the market portfolio (as measured by the Standard & Poor's 500 Index), and U.S. Treasury bills (T-bills) during the past 8 years.

	Average Annual Rate of Return	Standard Deviation of Return	Beta
Portfolio X	10%	18%	0.60
S&P 500	12	13	1.00
T-bills	6	n/a	n/a

n/a = not applicable

A. **Calculate** *both* the Treynor measure and the Sharpe measure for *both* Portfolio X *and* the S&P 500. **Briefly explain** whether Portfolio X underperformed, equaled, or outperformed the S&P 500 on a risk-adjusted basis using *both* the Treynor measure and the Sharpe measure.
B. Based on the performance of Portfolio X relative to the S&P 500 calculated in Part A, **briefly explain** the reason for the conflicting results when using the Treynor measure versus the Sharpe measure.

SELECTED REFERENCES

Some of the problems in performance measurement are discussed in:

Ferguson, Robert. "The Trouble with Performance Measurement" *The Journal of Portfolio Management* (Spring 1986): 4–9.

A short discussion of performance measurement can be found in:

Good, Walter. "Measuring Performance" *The Financial Analysts Journal* (May–June 1983), 19–23.

The relationships among the composite measures are explained in:

Wilson, Jack, and Jones, Charles. "The Relationship Between Performance and Risk: Whence the Bias?" *Journal of Financial Research* (Summer 1981): 109–117.

www.wiley.com/college/jones7

In this chapter, the exercises will ask you to compute measures of portfolio performance. We will also explore performance attribution.

Glossary

A

Abnormal Return Return on a security beyond that expected on the basis of its risk.

Active Management Strategy A strategy designed to provide additional returns by trading activities.

American Depository Receipts (ADRs) Securities representing an ownership interest in the equities of foreign companies.

Arbitrageurs Investors who seek discrepancies in security prices in an attempt to earn riskless returns.

Arbitrage Pricing Model (APM) An equilibrium theory of expected returns for securities involving few assumptions about investor preferences.

Asked Price The price at which the specialist or dealer offers to sell shares.

Asset Allocation Decision The allocation of a portfolio's funds to classes of assets, such as cash equivalents, bonds, and equities.

Asset-Backed Securities (ABS) Securities issued against some type of asset-linked debts bundled together, such as credit card receivables or mortgages.

Asset Management Account Brokerage accounts involving various services for investors, such as investment of cash balances and check-writing privileges.

Auction Market A securities market with a physical location, such as the New York Stock Exchange, where the prices of securities are determined by the actions of buyers and sellers.

B

Bar Chart A plot of daily stock price plotted against time.

Basis The difference between the futures price of an item and the spot price of the item.

Basis Points 100 basis points is equal to one percentage point.

Bear Market A downward trend in the stock market.

Behavioral Finance The study of investment behavior, based on the belief that investors do not always act rationally.

Benchmark Portfolio An alternative portfolio against which to measure a portfolio's performance.

Beta A measure of volatility, or relative systematic risk, for stock or portfolio returns.

Bid Price The price at which the specialist or dealer offers to buy shares.

Black-Scholes Model A widely used model for the valuation of call options.

Blocks Transactions involving at least 10,000 shares.

Blue Chip Stocks Stocks with long records of earnings and dividends—well known, stable, mature companies.

Bonds Long-term debt instruments representing the issuer's contractual obligation.

Bond-Equivalent Yield Yield on annual basis, derived by doubling the semiannual yield.

Bond Ratings Letters assigned to bonds by rating agencies to express the relative probability of default.

Bond Swaps An active bond management strategy involving the purchase and sale of bonds in an attempt to improve the rate of return on the bond portfolio.

Book Value The accounting value of the equity as shown on the balance sheet.

Broker An intermediary who represents buyers and sellers in securities transactions and receives a commission.

Bottom-Up Approach Approach to fundamental analysis that focuses directly on a company's fundamentals.

Bubble When speculation pushes asset prices to unsustainable highs.

Bull Market An upward trend in the stock market.

Business Cycle The recurring patterns of expansion, boom, contraction, and recession in the economy.

C

Call An option to buy a specified number of shares of stock at a stated price within a specified period.

Call Provision Gives the issuer the right to call in a security and retire it by paying off the obligation.

Capital Asset Pricing Model (CAPM) Relates the required rate of return for any security with the risk for that security as measured by beta.

Capital Gain (Loss) The change in price on a security over some period of time.

Capital Market The market for long-term securities such as bonds and stocks.

Capital Market Line (CML) The tradeoff between expected return and risk for efficient portfolios.

Capital Market Theory Describes the pricing of capital assets in financial markets.

Cash Account The most common type of brokerage account in which a customer may make only cash transactions.

Characteristic Line A regression equation used to estimate beta by regressing stock returns on market returns.

Chartered Financial Analyst (CFA) A professional designation for people in the investments field.

Closed-End Investment Company An investment company with a fixed capitalization whose shares trade on exchanges and OTC.

Coefficient of Determination The square of the correlation coefficient, measuring the percentage of the variance in the dependent variable that is explained by the independent variable.

Common Stock An equity security representing the ownership interest in a corporation.

Composite Indexes of General Economic Activity Leading, coincident, and lagging indicators of economic activity.

Composite (Risk-Adjusted) Measures of Portfolio Performance Portfolio performance measures combining return and risk into one calculation.

Consensus Estimate Most likely EPS value expected by analysts.

Contrary Opinion The theory that it pays to trade contrary to most investors.

Convertible Bonds Bonds that are convertible, at the holder's option, into shares of common stock of the same corporation.

Corporate Bonds Long-term debt securities of various types sold by corporations.

Correlation Coefficient A statistical measure of the extent to which two variables are associated.

Conversion Premium With convertible securities, the dollar difference between the market price of the security and its conversion value.

Conversion Price Par value divided by the conversions ratio.

Conversion Ratio The number of shares of common stock that the owner of a convertible security receives upon conversion.

Conversion Value A convertible security's value based on the current price of the common stock.

Convertible Securities Bonds or preferred stock convertible into common stock.

Convexity A measure of the degree to which the relationship between a bond's price and yield departs from a straight line.

Covariance An absolute measure of the extent to which two variables tend to covary, or move together.

Covered Call A strategy involving the sale of a call option to supplement a long position in an underlying asset.

Cumulative Abnormal Return (CAR) The sum of the individual abnormal returns over the time period under examination.

Cumulative Wealth Index Cumulative wealth over time, given an initial wealth and a series of returns on some asset.

Current Yield A bond's annual coupon divided by the current market price.

Cyclical Industries Industries most affected, both up and down, by the business cycle.

D

Dealer An individual (firm) who makes a market in a stock by buying from and selling to investors.

Debenture An unsecured bond backed by the general worthiness of the firm.

Defensive Industries Industries least affected by recessions and economic adversity.

Derivative Securities Securities that derive their value in whole or in part by having a claim on some underlying security.

Differential Return Measure (Alpha) Jensen's measure of portfolio performance calculated as the difference between what the portfolio actually earned and what it was expected to earn given its level of systematic risk.

Direct Investing Investors buy and sell securities themselves, typically through brokerage accounts.

Discount Broker Brokerage firms offering execution services at prices typically significantly less than full-line brokerage firms.

Diversifiable Risk Unique risk related to a particular security that can be diversifed away; nonsystematic risk.

Dividend Discount Model (DDM) A model for determining the estimated price of a stock by discounting all future dividends.

Dividend Reinvestment Plan (DRIPs) A plan offered by a company whereby stockholders can reinvest dividends in additional shares of stock at no cost.

Dividends Cash payments declared and paid quarterly by corporations to stockholders.

Dividend Yield Dividends divided by current stock price.

Dollar-Weighted Rate of Return (DWR) Equates all cash flows, including ending market value, with the beginning market value of the portfolio.

Dow Jones Industrial Average (DJIA) A price-weighted series of 30 leading industrial stocks, used as a measure of stock market activity.

Dow Theory A technique for detecting long-term trends in the aggregate stock market.

Duration A measure of a bond's lifetime that accounts for the entire pattern of cash flows over the life of the bond.

E

EAFE Index The Europe, Australia, and Far East Index, a value-weighted index of the equity performance of major foreign markets.

Earnings Multiplier The P/E ratio for a stock.

Earnings Surprises The difference between a firm's actual earnings and its expected earnings.

Economic Value Added (EVA) A technique for focusing on a firm's return on capital in order to determine if stockholders are being rewarded.

Efficient Market A market in which prices of securities quickly and fully reflect all available information.

Efficient Market Hypothesis (EMH) The proposition that securities markets are efficient, with the prices of securities reflecting their economic value.

Efficient Portfolio A portfolio with the highest level of expected return for a given level of risk or a portfolio with the lowest risk for a given level of expected return.

Efficient Set (Frontier) The set of portfolios generated by the Markowitz portfolio model.

Electronic Communications Networks (ECNs) A computerized trading network for buying and selling securities electronically.

Emerging Markets Markets of less developed countries, characterized by high risks and potentially large returns.

Equity-Derivative Securities Securities that derive their value in whole or in part by having a claim on the underlying common stock.

Equity Risk Premium The difference between stocks and the risk-free rate.

E/P Ratio The reciprocal of the P/E ratio.

Event Study An empirical analysis of stock price behavior surrounding a particular event.

Exchange Rate Risk The variability in returns on securities caused by currency fluctations.

Expectations Theory States that the long-term rate of interest is equal to an average of the short-term rates that are expected to prevail over the long-term period.

Expected Return The ex ante return expected by investors over some future holding period.

Exercise (Strike) Price The per-share price at which the common stock may be purchased from (in the case of a call) or sold to a writer (in the case of a put).

Expiration Date The date an option expires.

F

Factor Model Used to depict the behavior of security prices by identifying major factors in the economy that affect large numbers of securities.

Filter Rule A rule for buying and selling stocks according to the stock's price movements.

Financial Assets Pieces of paper evidencing a claim on some issuer.

Financial Futures Futures contracts on financial assets.

Financial Statements The principal published financial data about a company, primarily the balance sheet and income statement.

Fixed-Income Securities Securities with specified payment dates and amounts, primarily bonds.

Forward Contract A commitment today to transact in the future at a price that is currently determined, with no funds having been exchanged.

Forward Rates Unobservable rates expected to prevail in the future.

Fourth Market A communications network linking large institutional investors.

Full Service Broker A brokerage firm offering a full range of services, including information and advice.

Fundamental Analysis The stock of a stock's value using basic data such as its earnings, sales, risk, and so forth.

Futures Contract Agreement providing for the future exchange of a particular asset at a currently determined market price.

Futures Margin The earnest money deposit made by a transactor to ensure the completion of a contract.

G

Generally Accepted Accounting Principles (GAAP) Financial reporting requirements establishing the rules for producing financial statements.

Geometric Mean The compound rate of return over time.

Global Funds Mutual funds that keep a minimum of 25 percent of their assets in U.S. securities.

Government Agency Securities Securities issued by federal credit agencies (fully guaranteed) or by government-sponsored agencies (not guaranteed).

Growth Industries Industries with expected earnings growth significantly above the average of all industries.

H

Hedge A strategy using derivatives to offset or reduce the risk resulting from exposure to an underlying asset.

Hedge Ratio The ratio of options written to shares of stock held long in a riskless portfolio.

Horizon Return Bond returns to be earned based on assumptions about reinvestment rates.

I

Immunization The strategy of immunizing (protecting) a portfolio against interest rate risk by canceling out its two components, price risk and reinvestment rate risk.

Index Arbitrage Exploitation of price differences between stock-index futures and the index of stocks underlying the futures contract.

Index Funds Mutual funds holding a bond or stock portfolio designed to match a particular market index.

Indifference Curves Curves describing investor preferences for risk and return.

Indirect Investing The buying and selling of the shares of investment companies which, in turn, hold portfolios of securities.

Industry Life Cycle The stages of an industry's evolution from pioneering to stabilization and decline.

Initial Margin That part of a transaction's value a customer must pay to initiate the transaction, with the remainder borrowed.

Initial Public Offering (IPO) Common stock shares of a company being sold for the first time.

Instinet An electronic trading network, part of the fourth market.

Institutional Investors Pension funds, investment companies, bank trust departments, life insurance companies, and so forth, all of whom manage large portfolios of securities.

Interest on Interest The process by which bond coupons are reinvested to earn interest.

Interest Rate Options Option contracts on fixed-income securities such as Treasury bonds.

Interest Rate Risk The variability in a security's returns resulting from changes in interest rates.

Interest Rate Swaps A contract between two parties to exchange a series of cash flows based on fixed-income securities.

Interest-Sensitive Industries Industries particularly sensitive to expectations about changes in interest rates.

Intermarket Trading System (ITS) A form of a central routing system, consisting of a network of terminals linking together several stock exchanges.

Internal (Sustainable) Growth Rate (g) The estimated earnings growth rate, calculated as the product of ROE and the retention rate.

International Funds Mutual funds that concentrate primarily on international stocks.

Intrinsic Value The estimated value of a security.

Investment The commitment of funds to one or more assets that will be held over some future time period.

Investment Banker Firm specializing in the sale of new securities to the public, typically by underwriting the issue.

Investment Company A financial company that sells shares in itself to the public and uses these funds to invest in a portfolio of securities.

Investment Policy The first step in the portfolio management process, involving investor objectives, constraints and preferences.

Investment Policy Statement A statement of a few sentences describing policies to be followed for a client.

Investments The study of the investment process.

J

January Effect The observed tendency to be higher in January than in other months.

Junk Bonds Bonds that carry ratings of BB or lower, with correspondingly higher yields.

L

LEAPS Puts and calls with longer maturity dates, up to two years.

Limit Order An order to buy or sell at a specified (or better) price.

Liquidity The ease with which an asset can be bought or sold quickly with relatively small price changes.

Liquidity Preference Theory States that interest rates reflect the sum of current and expected short rates, as in the expectations theory, plus liquidity (risk) premiums.

Long Hedge A transaction where the asset is currently not held but futures are purchased to lock in current prices.

Long Position An agreement to purchase an asset at a specified future date at a specified price.

Long-Term Options (LEAPs) Options on individual stocks with maturities up to two years.

M

Maintenance Margin The percentage of a security's value that must be on hand at all times as equity.

Margin The investor's equity in a transaction, with the remainder borrowed from a brokerage firm.

Margin Account An account that permits margin trading, requiring $2000 to open.

Margin Call A demand from the broker for additional cash or securities as a result of the actual margin declining below the maintenance margin.

Marked to the Market The daily posting of all profits and losses on a contract to each account.

Marketable Securities Financial assets that are easily and cheaply traded in organized markets.

Market Anomalies Techniques or strategies that appear to be contrary to an efficient market.

Market Data Primarily stock price and volume information.

Market Maker A broker/dealer who is registered to trade in a particular security in the OTC market.

Market Model Relates the return on each stock to the return on the market, using a linear relationship with intercept and slope.

Market Order An order to buy or sell at the best price when the order reaches the trading floor.

Market Portfolio The portfolio of all risky assets, with each asset weighted by the ratio of its market value to the market value of all risky assets.

Market Risk The variability in a security's returns resulting from fluctuations in the aggregate market.

Market Risk Premium The difference between the expected return for the equities market and the risk-free rate of return.

Market Segmentation Theory States that investors confine their activities to specific maturity sectors and are unwilling to shift from one sector to another to take advantage of opportunities.

Modified Duration Divided by 1 + yield to maturity.

Momentum Investing Investing on the basis of recent movements in the price of a stock.

Money Market The market for short-term, highly liquid, low-risk assets such as Treasury bills and negotiable CDs.

Money Market Fund (MMFs) A mutual fund that invests in money market instruments.

Municipal Bonds Securities issued by political entities other than the federal government and its agencies, such as states and cities.

Mutual Funds The popular name for open-end-investment companies.

N

Nasdaq National Market System (Nasdaq/NMS) A combination of the competing market markers in OTC stocks and the up-to-the-minute reporting of trades using data almost identical to that shown for the NYSE and AMEX.

Nasdaq Stock Market (Nasdaq) The automated quotation system for the OTC market, showing current bid-ask prices for thousands of stocks.

National Association of Securities Dealers (NASD) A self-regulating body of brokers and dealers overseeing OTC practices.

National Market System (NMS) The market system for U.S. securities called for, but left undefined, by the Securities Acts Amendments of 1975.

Negotiated Market A market involving dealers, such as the OTC.

Net Asset Value (NAV) The total market value of the securities in an investment company's portfolio divided by the number of investment company fund shares currently outstanding.

New York Stock Exchange (NYSE) The major secondary market for the trading of equity securities.

Nondiversifiable Risk Variability in a security's return directly associated with overall movements in the general market; systematic risk.

Nonsystematic (Nonmarket) Risk Risk attributable to factors unique to a security.

O

Offset Liquidation of a futures position by an offsetting transaction.

Open-End Investment Company An investment company whose capitalization constantly changes as new shares are sold and outstanding shares are redeemed.

Option Premium The price paid by the option buyer to the seller of the option.

Options Rights to buy or sell a stated number of shares of a security within a specified period at a specified price.

Options Clearing Corporation (OCC) Stands between buyers and sellers of options to ensure fulfillment of obligations.

Over-the-Counter (OTC) Market A network of securities dealers linked together to make markets in securities.

P

Par Value (Face Value) The redemption value of a bond paid at maturity, typically $1,000.

Passive Management Strategy A strategy whereby investors do not actively seek out trading possibilities in an attempt to outperform the market.

Payout Ratio Dividends divided by earnings.

Performance Attribution A part of portfolio evaluation that seeks to determine why success or failure occurred.

Performance Presentation Standards (PPS) Minimum standards for presenting investment performance as formulated by AIMR.

Perpetuity A security without a maturity date.

P/E Ratio (Earnings Multiplier) The ratio of stock price to earnings, using historical, current or estimated data.

Point-and-Figure Chart A plot of stock prices showing only significant price changes.

Portfolio The securities held by an investor taken as a unit.

Portfolio Insurance An asset management technique designed to provide a portfolio with a lower limit on value while permitting it to benefit from rising security prices.

Portfolio Management The second step in the investment decision process, involving the management of a group of assets (i.e., a portfolio) as a unit.

Portfolio Weights Percentages of portfolio funds invested in each security, summing to 1.0.

Preferred Habitat Theory States that investors have preferred maturity sectors in which they seek to invest but are willing to shift to other maturities if they can expect to be adequately compensated.

Preferred Stock An equity security with an intermediate claim (between the bondholders and the stockholders) on a firm's assets and earnings.

Price to Book Value The ratio of stock price to per share stockholders' equity.

Price/Sales Ratio A company's total market value divided by its sales.

Primary Market The market for new issues of securities, typically involving investment bankers.

Program Trading Involves the use of computer-generated orders to buy and sell securities based on arbitrage opportunities between common stocks and index futures and options.

Prospectus Provides information about an initial public offering of securities to potential buyers.

Protective Put A strategy involving the purchase of a put option as a supplement to a long position in an underlying asset.

Put An option to sell a specified number of shares of stock at a stated price within a specified period.

Put-Call Parity The formal relationship between a call and a put on the same item which must hold if no arbitrage is to occur.

R

Real Assets Physical assets, such as gold or real estate.

Real Risk-Free Rate of Interest The opportunity cost of foregoing consumption, given no inflation.

Realized Compound Yield (RCY) Yield earned based on actual reinvestment rates.

Realized Return Actual return on an investment for some previous period of time.

Reinvestment Rate Risk That part of interest rate risk resulting from uncertainty about the rate at which future interest coupons can be reinvested.

Relative Strength The ratio of a stock's price to some market or industry index, usually plotted as a graph.

Required Rate of Return The minimum expected rate of return necessary to induce an investor to purchase a security.

Resistance Level A price range at which a technician expects a significant increase in the supply of a stock.

Return on Assets The accounting rate of return on a firm's assets.

Return on Equity The accounting rate of return on stockholders equity.

Return Relative The total return for an investment for a given time period stated on the basis of 1.0.

Reward-to-Variability Ratio (RVAR) Sharpe's measure of portfolio performance calculated as the ratio of excess portfolio return to the standard deviation.

Reward-to-Volatility Ratio (RVOL) Treynor's measure of portfolio performance calculated as the ratio of excess portfolio return to beta.

Risk The chance that the actual return on an investment will be different from the expected return.

Risk-Averse Investor An investor who will not assume a given level of risk unless there is an expectation of adequate compensation for having done so.

Risk-Free Rate of Return The return on a riskless asset, often proxied by the rate of return on Treasury securities.

Risk Premium That part of a security's return above the risk-free rate of return.

S

S&P 500 Composite Index (S&P 500) Market value index of stock market activity covering 500 stocks.

Secondary Markets Markets where existing securities are traded among investors.

Securities and Exchange Commission (SEC) A federal government agency established by the Securities Exchange Act of 1934 to protect investors.

Security Analysis The first part of the investment decision process, involving the valuation and analysis of individual securities.

Security Market Line (SML) The graphical depiction of the CAPM.

Semistrong Form That part of the Efficient Market Hypothesis stating that prices reflect all publicly available information.

Senior Securities Securities, typically debt securities, ahead of common stock in terms of payment or in case of liquidation.

Separation Theorem The idea that the decision of which portfolio of risky assets to hold is separate from the decision of how to allocate investable funds between the risk-free asset and the risky asset.

Shelf Rule Permits qualified companies to file a short form registration and "place on the shelf" securities to be sold over time under favorable conditions.

Short Hedge A transaction involving the sale of futures (a short position) while holding the asset (a long position).

Short-Interest Ratio The ratio of total shares sold short to average daily trading volume.

Short Position An agreement to sell an asset at a specified future date at a specified price.

Short Sale The sale of a stock not owned in order to take advantage of an expected decline in the price of the stock.

Single-Country Fund Investment companies, primarily closed-end funds, concentrating on the securities of a single country.

Single Index Model A model that relates returns on each security to the returns on a market index.

Size Effect The observed tendency for smaller firms to have higher stock returns than large firms.

SPDRs Tradable securities representing a claim on an equity market index.

Specialist A member of an organized exchange who is charged with maintaining an orderly market in one or more stocks by buying or selling for his or her own account.

Standard Deviation A measure of the dispersion in outcomes around the expected value.

Standard Industrial Classification (SIC) system A classification of firms on the basis of what they produce using Census data.

Standardized Unexpected Earnings (SUE) A variable used in the selection of common stocks, calculated as the ratio of unexpected earnings to a standardization factor.

Stock Dividend A payment by the corporation in shares of stock rather than cash.

Stock Index Options Option contracts on a stock market index such as the S&P 500.

Stock Split The issuance by a corporation of shares of common stock in proportion to the existing shares outstanding.

Stop Order An order specifying a certain price at which a market order takes effect.

Street Name When customers' securities are held by a brokerage firm in its name.

Strong Form That part of the Efficient Market Hypothesis stating that prices reflect all information, public and private.

SuperDOT An electronic order-routing system for NYSE-listed securities.

Support Level A price range at which a technician expects a significant increase in the demand for a stock.

Systematic (Market) Risk Risk attributable to broad macro factors affecting all securities.

T

Technical Analysis The use of specific market data for the analysis of both aggregate stock prices and individual stock prices.

Term Structure of Interest Rates The relationship between time to maturity and yields for a particular category of bonds.

Theoretical Spot Rate Curve A graph depicting the relationship between spot rates and maturities, based on theoretical considerations.

Third Market An OTC market for exchange-listed securities.

Time-Weighted Rate of Return (TWR) Measures the actual rate of return earned by the portfolio manager.

Top-Down Approach Approach to fundamental analysis that proceeds from market/economy to industries to companies.

Total Return Percentage measure relating all cash flows on a security for a given time period to its purchase price.

Treasury Bill A short-term money market instrument sold at discount by the U.S. government.

Treasury Bond Long-term bonds sold by the U.S. government.

U

Underwriting The process by which investment bankers purchase an issue of securities from a firm and resell it to the public.

Unit Investment Trust An unmanaged form of investment company, typically holding fixed-income securities, offering investors diversification and minimum operating costs.

W

Warrant A corporate-created option to purchase a stated number of common shares at a specified price within a specified time (typically several years).

Weak Form That part of the Efficient Market Hypothesis stating that prices reflect all price and volume data.

Wrap Account A new type of brokerage account where all costs are wrapped in one fee.

Y

Yield The income component of a security's return.

Yield Curve A graphical depiction of the relationship between between yields and time for bonds that are identical except for maturity.

Yield Spreads The relationship between bond yields and the particular features on various bonds such as quality, callability, and taxes.

Yield to Call The promised return on a bond from the present to the date that the bond is likely to be called.

Yield to Maturity The promised compounded rate of return on a bond purchased as the current market price and held to maturity.

Z

Zero Coupon Bond A bond sold with no coupons at a discount and redeemed for face value at maturity.

Interest Tables

TABLE A-1 COMPOUND (FUTURE) VALUE FACTORS FOR $1 COMPOUNDED AT R PERCENT FOR N PERIODS

	R =												
N	1%	2%	3%	4%	5%	6%	7%	8%	9%	10%	11%	12%	13%
1	1.01	1.02	1.03	1.04	1.05	1.06	1.07	1.08	1.09	1.1	1.11	1.12	1.13
2	1.02	1.04	1.061	1.082	1.103	1.124	1.145	1.166	1.188	1.21	1.232	1.254	1.277
3	1.03	1.061	1.093	1.125	1.158	1.191	1.225	1.26	1.295	1.331	1.368	1.405	1.443
4	1.041	1.082	1.126	1.17	1.216	1.262	1.311	1.36	1.412	1.464	1.518	1.574	1.53
5	1.051	1.104	1.159	1.217	1.276	1.338	1.403	1.469	1.539	1.611	1.685	1.762	1.842
6	1.062	1.126	1.194	1.265	1.34	1.419	1.501	1.587	1.677	1.772	1.87	1.974	2.082
7	1.072	1.149	1.23	1.316	1.407	1.504	1.606	1.714	1.828	1.949	2.076	2.211	2.353
8	1.083	1.172	1.267	1.369	1.477	1.594	1.718	1.851	1.993	2.144	2.305	2.476	2.658
9	1.094	1.195	1.305	1.423	1.551	1.689	1.838	1.999	2.172	2.358	2.558	2.773	3.004
10	1.105	1.219	1.344	1.48	1.629	1.791	1.967	2.159	2.367	2.594	2.839	3.106	3.395
11	1.116	1.243	1.384	1.539	1.71	1.898	2.105	2.332	2.58	2.853	3.152	3.479	3.836
12	1.127	1.268	1.426	1.601	1.796	2.012	2.252	2.518	2.813	3.138	3.498	3.896	4.335
13	1.138	1.294	1.469	1.665	1.886	2.133	2.41	2.72	3.066	3.452	3.883	4.363	4.898
14	1.149	1.319	1.513	1.732	1.98	2.261	2.579	2.937	3.342	3.797	4.31	4.887	5.535
15	1.161	1.346	1.558	1.801	2.079	2.397	2.759	3.172	3.642	4.177	4.785	5.474	6.254
16	1.173	1.373	1.605	1.873	2.183	2.54	2.952	3.426	3.97	4.595	5.311	6.13	7.067
17	1.184	1.4	1.653	1.948	2.292	2.693	3.159	3.7	4.328	5.054	5.895	6.866	7.986
18	1.196	1.428	1.702	2.026	2.407	2.854	3.38	3.996	4.717	5.56	6.544	7.69	9.024
19	1.208	1.457	1.754	2.107	2.527	3.026	3.617	4.316	5.142	6.116	7.263	8.613	10.197
20	1.22	1.486	1.806	2.191	2.653	3.207	3.87	4.661	5.604	6.727	8.062	9.646	11.523
21	1.232	1.516	1.86	2.279	2.786	3.4	4.141	5.034	6.109	7.4	8.949	10.804	13.021
22	1.245	1.546	1.916	2.37	2.925	3.604	4.43	5.437	6.659	8.14	9.934	12.1	14.714
23	1.257	1.577	1.974	2.465	3.072	3.82	4.741	5.871	7.258	8.954	10.026	13.552	16.627
24	1.27	1.608	2.033	2.563	3.225	4.049	5.072	6.341	7.911	9.85	12.239	15.179	18.788
25	1.282	1.641	2.094	2.666	3.386	4.292	5.427	6.848	8.623	10.835	13.585	17	21.231
30	1.348	1.811	2.427	3.243	4.322	5.743	7.612	10.063	13.268	17.449	22.892	29.96	39.116
35	1.417	2	2.814	3.946	5.516	7.686	10.677	14.785	20.414	28.102	38.575	52.8	72.069
40	1.489	2.208	3.262	4.801	7.04	10.286	14.974	21.725	31.409	45.259	65.001	93.051	132.782
45	1.565	2.438	3.782	5.841	8.985	13.765	21.002	31.92	48.327	72.89	109.53	163.98	244.641
50	1.645	2.692	4.384	7.107	11.467	18.42	29.457	46.902	74.358	117.39	184.56	289.00	450.735

TABLE A-1 COMPOUND (FUTURE) VALUE FACTORS FOR $1 COMPOUNDED AT R PERCENT FOR N PERIODS (Continued)

	R =												
N	14%	15%	16%	18%	20%	22%	24%	25%	30%	35%	40%	45%	50%
1	1.14	1.15	1.16	1.18	1.2	1.22	1.25	1.25	1.3	1.35	1.4	1.45	1.5
2	1.3	1.323	1.346	1.392	1.44	1.488	1.538	1.563	1.69	1.823	1.96	2.103	2.25
3	1.482	1.521	1.561	1.643	1.728	1.816	1.907	1.953	2.197	2.46	2.744	3.049	3.375
4	1.689	1.749	1.811	1.939	2.074	2.215	2.364	2.441	2.856	3.322	3.842	4.421	5.063
5	1.925	2.011	2.1	2.288	2.488	2.703	2.932	3.052	3.713	4.484	5.378	6.41	7.594
6	2.195	2.313	2.436	2.7	2.986	3.297	3.635	3.815	4.827	6.053	7.53	9.294	11.391
7	2.502	2.66	2.826	3.185	3.583	4.023	4.508	4.768	6.275	8.172	10.541	13.476	17.086
8	2.853	3.059	3.278	3.759	4.3	4.908	5.59	5.96	8.157	11.032	14.758	19.541	25.629
9	3.252	3.518	3.803	4.435	5.16	5.987	6.931	7.451	10.604	14.894	20.661	28.334	38.443
10	3.707	4.046	4.411	5.234	6.192	7.305	8.594	9.313	13.786	20.107	28.925	41.085	57.665
11	4.226	4.652	5.117	6.176	7.43	8.912	10.657	11.642	17.922	27.144	40.496	59.573	86.498
12	4.818	5.35	5.936	7.288	8.916	10.872	13.215	14.552	23.298	36.644	56.694	86.381	129.746
13	5.492	6.153	6.886	8.599	10.699	13.264	16.386	18.19	30.288	49.47	79.371	125.25	194.62
14	6.261	7.076	7.988	10.147	12.839	16.182	20.319	22.737	39.374	66.784	111.12	181.61	291.929
15	7.138	8.137	9.266	11.974	15.407	19.742	25.196	28.422	51.186	90.158	155.56	263.34	437.894
16	8.137	9.358	10.748	14.129	18.488	24.086	31.243	35.527	66.542	121.71	217.79	381.84	656.841
17	9.276	10.761	12.468	16.672	22.186	29.384	38.741	44.409	86.504	164.31	304.91	553.67	985.261
18	10.575	12.375	14.463	19.673	26.623	35.849	48.039	55.511	112.45	221.82	426.87	802.83	1477.892
19	12.056	14.232	16.777	23.214	31.948	43.736	59.568	69.389	146.19	299.46	597.63	1164.1	2216.838
20	13.743	16.367	19.461	27.393	38.338	53.358	73.864	86.736	190.05	404.27	836.68	1687.9	3325.257
21	15.668	18.822	22.574	32.324	46.005	65.096	91.592	108.42	247.06	545.76	1171.3	2447.5	4987.885
22	17.861	21.645	26.186	38.142	55.206	79.418	113.57	135.52	321.18	716.78	1639.8	3548.9	7481.828
23	20.362	24.891	30.376	45.008	66.247	96.889	140.83	169.40	417.53	994.66	2297.8	5145.9	11222.74
24	23.212	28.625	35.236	53.109	79.497	118.20	174.63	211.75	542.80	1342.7	3214.2	7461.6	16834.11
25	26.462	32.919	40.874	62.669	95.396	144.21	216.54	264.69	705.64	1812.7	4499.8	10819.	25251.17
30	50.95	66.212	85.85	143.37	237.37	389.75	634.82	807.79	2619.9	8128.5	24201.	69348.	191751.1
35	98.1	133.17	180.31	327.99	590.66	1053.4	1861.0	2465.1	9727.8	36448.	130161.	444508.	
40	188.88	267.86	378.72	750.37	1469.7	2847.0	5455.9	7523.1	36118.	163437	700037		
45	363.67	538.76	795.44	1716.6	3657.2	7694.7	15994.	22958.	134106.	732857.			
50	700.23	1083.6	1670.7	3927.3	9100.4	20796.	46890.	70064.	497929.				

TABLE A-2 PRESENT VALUE FACTORS (AT R PERCENT) FOR $1 RECEIVED AT THE END OF N PERIODS

	R =												
N	1%	2%	3%	4%	5%	6%	7%	8%	9%	10%	11%	12%	13%
1	.990	.980	.971	.962	.952	.943	.935	.926	.917	.909	.901	.893	.885
2	.980	.961	.943	.925	.907	.890	.873	.857	.842	.826	.812	.797	.783
3	.971	.942	.915	.889	.864	.840	.816	.794	.772	.751	.731	.712	.693
4	.961	.924	.888	.855	.823	.792	.763	.735	.708	.683	.659	.636	.613
5	.951	.906	.863	.822	.784	.747	.713	.681	.650	.621	.593	.567	.543
6	.942	.888	.837	.790	.746	.705	.666	.630	.596	.564	.535	.507	.480
7	.932	.871	.813	.760	.711	.665	.623	.583	.547	.513	.482	.452	.425
8	.923	.853	.789	.731	.677	.627	.582	.540	.502	.467	.434	.404	.376
9	.914	.837	.766	.703	.645	.592	.544	.500	.460	.424	.391	.361	.333
10	.905	.820	.744	.676	.614	.558	.508	.463	.422	.386	.352	.322	.295
11	.896	.804	.722	.650	.585	.527	.475	.429	.388	.350	.317	.287	.261
12	.887	.788	.701	.625	.557	.497	.444	.397	.356	.319	.286	.257	.231
13	.879	.773	.681	.601	.530	.469	.415	.368	.326	.290	.258	.229	.204
14	.870	.758	.661	.577	.505	.442	.388	.340	.299	.263	.232	.205	.181
15	.861	.743	.642	.555	.481	.417	.362	.315	.275	.239	.209	.183	.160
16	.853	.728	.623	.534	.458	.394	.339	.292	.252	.218	.188	.163	.141
17	.844	.714	.605	.513	.436	.371	.317	.270	.231	.198	.170	.146	.125
18	.836	.700	.587	.494	.416	.350	.296	.250	.212	.180	.153	.130	.111
19	.828	.686	.570	.475	.396	.331	.277	.232	.194	.164	.138	.116	.098
20	.820	.673	.554	.456	.377	.312	.258	.215	.178	.149	.124	.104	.087
21	.811	.660	.538	.439	.359	.294	.242	.199	.164	.135	.112	.093	.077
22	.803	.647	.522	.422	.342	.278	.226	.184	.150	.123	.101	.083	.068
23	.795	.634	.507	.406	.326	.262	.211	.170	.133	.112	.091	.074	.060
24	.788	.622	.492	.390	.310	.247	.197	.158	.126	.102	.082	.066	.053
25	.780	.610	.478	.375	.295	.233	.184	.146	.116	.092	.074	.059	.047
30	.742	.552	.412	.308	.231	.174	.131	.099	.075	.057	.044	.033	.026
35	.706	.500	.355	.253	.181	.130	.094	.068	.049	.036	.026	.019	.014
40	.672	.453	.307	.208	.142	.097	.067	.046	.032	.022	.015	.011	.008
45	.639	.410	.264	.171	.111	.073	.048	.031	.021	.014	.009	.006	.004
50	.608	.372	.228	.141	.087	.054	.034	.021	.013	.009	.005	.003	.002

TABLE A-2 PRESENT VALUE FACTORS (AT R PERCENT) FOR $1 RECEIVED AT THE END OF N PERIODS (Continued)

	R =												
N	14%	15%	16%	18%	20%	22%	24%	25%	30%	35%	40%	45%	50%
1	.877	.870	.862	.847	.833	.820	.806	.800	.769	.741	.714	.690	.667
2	.769	.756	.743	.718	.694	.672	.650	.640	.592	.449	.510	.476	.444
3	.675	.658	.641	.609	.579	.551	.524	.512	.455	.406	.364	.328	.296
4	.592	.572	.552	.516	.482	.451	.423	.410	.350	.301	.260	.226	.198
5	.519	.497	.476	.437	.402	.370	.341	.328	.269	.223	.186	.156	.132
6	.456	.432	.410	.370	.335	.303	.275	.262	.207	.165	.133	.108	.088
7	.400	.376	.354	.314	.279	.249	.222	.210	.159	.122	.095	.074	.059
8	.351	.327	.305	.266	.233	.204	.179	.168	.123	.091	.068	.051	.039
9	.308	.284	.263	.225	.194	.167	.144	.134	.094	.067	.048	.035	.026
10	.270	.247	.227	.191	.162	.137	.116	.107	.073	.050	.035	.024	.017
11	.237	.215	.195	.162	.135	.112	.094	.086	.056	.037	.025	.017	.012
12	.208	.187	.168	.137	.112	.092	.076	.069	.043	.027	.018	.012	.008
13	.182	.163	.145	.116	.093	.075	.061	.055	.033	.020	.013	.008	.005
14	.160	.141	.125	.099	.078	.062	.049	.044	.025	.015	.009	.006	.003
15	.140	.123	.108	.084	.065	.051	.040	.035	.020	.011	.006	.004	.002
16	.123	.107	.093	.071	.054	.042	.032	.028	.015	.008	.005	.003	.002
17	.108	.093	.080	.060	.045	.034	.026	.023	.012	.006	.003	.002	.001
18	.095	.081	.069	.051	.038	.028	.021	.018	.009	.005	.002	.001	.001
19	.083	.070	.060	.043	.031	.023	.017	.014	.007	.003	.002	.001	
20	.073	.061	.051	.037	.026	.019	.014	.012	.005	.002	.001	.001	
21	.064	.053	.044	.031	.022	.015	.011	.009	.004	.002	.001		
22	.056	.046	.038	.026	.018	.013	.009	.007	.003	.001	.001		
23	.049	.040	.033	.022	.015	.010	.007	.006	.002	.001			
24	.043	.035	.028	.019	.013	.008	.006	.005	.002	.001			
25	.038	.030	.024	.016	.010	.007	.005	.004	.001	.001			
30	.020	.015	.012	.007	.004	.003	.002	.001					
35	.010	.008	.006	.003	.002	.001	.001						
40	.005	.004	.003	.001	.001								
45	.003	.002	.001	.001									
50	.001	.001	.001										

TABLE A-3 COMPOUND SUM ANNUITY FACTORS FOR $1 COMPOUNDED AT R PERCENT FOR N PERIODS

	R =												
N	1%	2%	3%	4%	5%	6%	7%	8%	9%	10%	11%	12%	13%
1	1	1	1	1	1	1	1	1	1	1	1	1	1
2	2.01	2.02	2.03	2.04	2.05	2.06	2.07	2.08	2.09	2.1	2.11	2.12	2.13
3	3.03	3.06	3.091	3.122	3.152	3.184	3.215	3.246	3.278	3.31	3.342	3.374	3.407
4	4.06	4.122	4.184	4.246	4.31	4.375	4.44	4.506	4.573	4.641	4.71	4.779	4.85
5	5.101	5.204	5.309	5.416	5.526	5.637	5.751	5.867	5.985	6.105	6.228	6.353	6.48
6	6.152	6.308	6.468	6.633	6.802	6.975	7.153	7.336	7.523	7.716	7.913	8.115	8.232
7	7.214	7.434	7.662	7.898	8.142	8.394	8.654	8.923	9.2	9.487	9.783	10.089	10.405
8	8.286	8.583	8.892	9.214	9.549	0.897	10.26	10.637	11.028	11.436	11.859	12.3	12.757
9	9.369	9.755	10.159	10.583	11.027	11.491	11.978	12.488	13.021	13.579	14.164	14.776	15.416
10	10.462	10.95	11.464	12.006	12.578	13.181	13.816	14.487	15.193	15.937	16.722	17.549	18.42
11	11.567	12.169	12.808	13.486	14.207	14.972	15.784	16.645	17.56	18.531	19.561	20.655	21.814
12	12.683	13.412	14.192	15.026	15.917	16.87	17.888	18.977	20.141	21.384	22.713	24.133	25.65
13	13.809	14.68	15.618	16.627	17.713	18.882	20.141	21.495	22.953	24.523	26.212	28.029	29.985
14	14.947	15.971	17.086	18.292	19.599	21.015	22.55	24.215	26.019	27.975	30.095	32.393	34.883
15	16.097	17.291	18.599	20.024	21.579	23.276	25.129	27.152	29.361	31.772	34.405	37.28	40.417
16	17.258	18.639	20.157	21.825	23.657	25.673	27.888	30.324	33.003	35.95	39.19	42.753	46.672
17	18.43	20.012	21.762	23.698	25.84	28.213	30.84	33.75	36.974	40.545	44.501	48.884	53.739
18	19.615	21.412	23.414	25.645	28.132	30.906	33.999	37.45	41.301	45.599	50.396	55.75	61.725
19	20.811	22.841	25.117	27.671	30.539	33.76	37.379	41.446	46.018	51.159	56.939	63.44	70.749
20	22.019	24.297	26.87	29.778	33.066	36.786	40.995	45.762	51.16	57.275	64.203	72.052	80.947
21	23.239	25.783	28.676	31.969	35.719	39.993	44.865	50.423	56.765	64.002	72.265	81.699	92.47
22	24.472	27.299	30.537	34.248	38.505	43.392	49.006	55.457	62.873	71.403	81.214	92.503	105.491
23	25.716	28.845	32.453	36.618	41.43	46.996	53.436	60.893	69.532	79.543	91.148	104.60	120.205
24	26.973	30.422	34.426	39.083	44.502	50.816	58.177	66.765	76.79	88.497	102.17	118.15	136.831
25	28.243	32.03	36.459	41.646	47.727	54.865	63.249	73.106	84.701	98.347	114.41	133.33	155.62
30	34.785	40.568	47.575	56.085	66.439	79.058	94.461	113.28	136.30	164.49	199.02	241.33	293.199
35	41.66	49.994	60.462	73.652	90.32	111.43	138.23	172.31	215.71	271.02	341.59	431.66	546.681
40	48.886	60.402	75.401	95.026	120.8	154.76	199.63	259.05	337.88	442.59	581.82	767.09	1013.704
45	56.481	71.893	92.72	121.02	159.7	212.74	285.74	386.50	525.85	718.90	986.63	1358.2	1874.165
50	64.463	84.579	112.79	152.66	209.34	290.33	406.52	573.77	815.08	1163.9	1668.7	2400.0	3459.507

TABLE A-3 COMPOUND SUM ANNUITY FACTORS FOR $1 COMPOUNDED AT R PERCENT FOR N PERIODS (Continued)

	R =												
N	14%	15%	16%	18%	20%	22%	24%	25%	30%	35%	40%	45%	50%
1	1	1	1	1	1	1	1	1	1	1	1	1	1
2	2.14	2.15	2.16	2.18	2.2	2.22	2.24	2.25	2.3	2.35	2.4	2.45	2.5
3	3.44	3.472	3.506	3.572	3.64	3.708	3.778	3.813	3.99	4.172	4.36	4.552	4.75
4	4.921	4.993	5.066	5.215	5.368	5.524	5.684	5.766	6.187	6.633	7.104	7.601	8.125
5	6.61	6.742	6.877	7.154	7.442	7.74	8.048	8.207	9.043	9.954	10.916	12.022	13.188
6	8.536	8.754	8.977	9.442	9.93	10.442	10.98	11.259	12.756	14.438	16.324	18.431	20.781
7	10.73	11.067	11.414	12.142	12.916	13.74	14.615	15.073	17.583	20.492	23.853	27.726	32.172
8	13.233	13.727	14.24	15.327	16.499	17.762	19.123	19.842	23.858	28.664	34.395	11.202	49.258
9	16.085	16.786	17.519	19.086	20.799	22.67	24.712	25.802	32.015	39.696	49.153	60.743	74.887
10	19.337	20.304	21.321	23.521	25.959	28.657	31.643	33.253	42.619	54.59	69.814	89.077	113.33
11	23.045	24.349	25.733	28.755	32.15	35.962	40.238	42.566	56.405	74.697	98.739	130.16	170.995
12	27.271	29.002	30.85	34.931	39.581	44.874	50.895	54.208	74.327	101.84	139.23	189.73	257.493
13	32.089	34.352	36.786	42.219	48.497	55.746	64.11	68.76	97.625	138.48	195.92	276.11	387.239
14	37.581	40.505	43.672	50.818	59.196	69.01	80.496	86.949	127.91	187.95	275.3	401.36	581.859
15	43.842	47.58	51.66	60.965	72.035	85.192	100.81	109.68	167.28	254.73	386.42	582.98	873.788
16	50.98	55.717	60.925	72.939	87.442	104.93	126.01	138.10	218.47	344.89	541.98	846.32	1311.682
17	59.118	65.075	71.673	87.068	105.93	129.02	157.25	173.63	285.01	466.61	759.78	1228.1	1968.523
18	68.394	75.836	84.141	103.74	128.11	158.40	195.99	218.04	371.51	630.92	1064.6	1781.3	2953.784
19	78.969	88.212	98.603	123.41	154.74	194.25	244.03	273.55	483.97	852.74	1491.5	2584.6	4431.676
20	91.025	102.44	115.38	146.62	186.68	237.98	303.60	342.94	630.16	1152.2	2089.2	3748.7	6648.513
21	104.76	118.81	134.84	174.02	225.02	291.34	377.46	429.68	820.21	1556.4	2925.8	5436.7	9973.77
22	120.43	137.63	157.41	206.34	271.03	356.44	469.05	538.10	1067.2	2102.2	4097.2	7884.2	14961.65
23	138.29	159.27	183.60	244.48	326.23	435.86	582.63	673.62	1388.4	2839.0	5737.1	11433.	22443.48
24	158.65	184.16	213.97	289.49	392.48	532.75	723.46	843.03	1806.0	3833.7	8032.9	16579.	33666.22
25	181.87	212.79	249.21	342.60	471.98	650.95	898.09	1054.7	2348.8	5176.5	11247.	24040.	50500.34
30	356.78	434.74	530.31	790.94	1181.8	1767.0	2640.9	3227.1	8729.9	23221.	60501.	154106.	383500.1
35	693.57	881.17	1120.7	1816.6	2948.3	4783.6	7750.2	9856.7	32422.	104136.	325400.	987794.	
40	1342.0	1779.0	2360.7	4163.2	7343.8	12936.	22728.	30088.	120392.	466960.			
45	2490.5	3585.1	4965.2	9531.5	18281.	34971.	66640.	91831.	447019.				
50	4994.5	7217.7	10435.	21813.	45497.	94525.	195372.	280255.					

TABLE A-4 PRESENT VALUE ANNUITY FACTORS (AT R PERCENT PER PERIOD) FOR $1 RECEIVED PER PERIOD FOR EACH OF N PERIODS

	R =												
N	1%	2%	3%	4%	5%	6%	7%	8%	9%	10%	11%	12%	13%
1	0.990	0.980	0.971	0.962	0.952	0.943	0.935	0.926	0.917	0.909	0.901	0.893	0.885
2	1.970	1.942	1.913	1.886	1.859	1.833	1.808	1.783	1.759	1.736	1.713	1.690	1.668
3	2.941	2.884	2.829	2.775	2.723	2.673	2.624	2.577	2.531	2.487	2.444	2.402	2.361
4	3.902	3.808	3.717	3.630	3.546	3.465	3.387	3.312	3.240	3.170	3.102	3.037	2.974
5	4.853	4.713	4.580	4.452	4.329	4.212	4.100	3.993	3.890	3.791	3.696	3.605	3.517
6	5.795	5.601	5.417	5.242	5.076	4.917	4.767	4.623	4.486	4.355	4.231	4.111	3.998
7	6.728	6.472	6.230	6.002	5.786	5.582	5.389	5.206	5.033	4.868	4.712	4.564	4.423
8	7.652	7.325	7.020	6.733	6.463	6.210	5.971	5.747	5.535	5.335	5.146	4.968	4.799
9	8.566	8.162	7.786	7.435	7.108	6.802	6.515	6.247	5.995	5.759	5.537	5.328	5.132
10	9.471	8.983	8.530	8.111	7.722	7.360	7.024	6.710	6.418	6.145	5.889	5.650	5.426
11	10.368	9.787	9.253	8.760	8.306	7.887	7.499	7.139	6.805	6.495	6.207	5.938	5.687
12	11.255	10.575	9.954	9.385	8.863	8.384	7.943	7.536	7.161	6.814	6.492	6.194	5.918
13	12.134	11.348	10.635	9.986	9.394	8.853	8.358	7.904	7.487	7.103	6.750	6.424	6.122
14	13.004	12.106	11.296	10.563	9.899	9.295	8.745	8.244	7.786	7.367	6.982	6.628	6.302
15	13.865	12.849	11.938	11.118	10.380	9.712	9.108	8.559	8.061	7.606	7.191	6.811	6.462
16	14.718	13.578	12.561	11.652	10.838	10.106	9.447	8.851	8.313	7.824	7.379	6.974	6.604
17	15.562	14.292	13.166	12.166	11.274	10.477	9.763	9.122	8.544	8.022	7.549	7.120	6.729
18	16.398	14.992	13.754	12.659	11.690	10.828	10.059	9.372	8.756	8.201	7.702	7.250	6.840
19	17.226	15.678	14.324	13.134	12.085	11.158	10.336	9.604	8.950	8.365	7.839	7.366	6.938
20	18.046	16.351	14.877	13.590	12.462	11.470	10.594	9.818	9.129	8.514	7.963	7.469	7.025
21	18.857	17.011	15.415	14.029	12.821	11.764	10.836	10.017	9.292	8.649	8.075	7.562	7.102
22	19.660	17.658	15.937	14.451	13.163	12.042	11.061	10.201	9.442	8.772	8.176	7.654	7.170
23	20.456	18.292	16.444	14.857	13.489	12.303	11.272	10.371	9.580	8.883	8.266	7.718	7.230
24	21.243	18.914	16.936	15.247	13.799	12.550	11.469	10.529	9.707	8.985	8.348	7.784	7.283
25	22.023	19.523	17.413	15.622	14.094	12.783	11.654	10.675	9.823	9.077	8.422	7.843	7.330
30	25.808	22.396	19.600	17.292	15.372	13.765	12.409	11.258	10.274	9.427	8.694	8.055	7.496
35	29.409	24.999	21.487	18.665	16.374	14.498	12.948	11.655	10.567	9.644	8.855	8.176	7.586
40	32.835	27.355	23.115	19.793	17.159	15.046	13.332	11.925	10.757	9.779	8.951	8.244	7.634
45	36.095	29.490	24.519	20.720	17.774	15.456	13.606	12.108	10.881	9.863	9.008	8.283	7.661
50	39.196	31.424	25.730	21.482	18.256	15.762	13.801	12.233	10.962	9.915	9.042	8.304	7.675

TABLE A-4 PRESENT VALUE ANNUITY FACTORS (AT R PERCENT PER PERIOD) FOR $1 RECEIVED PER PERIOD FOR EACH OF N PERIODS (Continued)

	R =												
N	14%	15%	16%	18%	20%	22%	24%	25%	30%	35%	40%	45%	50%
1	0.877	0.870	0.862	0.847	0.833	0.820	0.806	0.800	0.769	0.741	0.714	0.690	0.667
2	1.647	1.626	1.605	1.566	1.528	1.492	1.457	1.440	1.361	1.289	1.224	1.165	1.111
3	2.322	2.283	2.246	2.174	2.106	2.042	1.981	1.952	1.816	1.696	1.589	1.493	1.407
4	2.914	2.855	2.798	2.690	2.589	2.494	2.404	2.362	2.166	1.997	1.849	1.720	1.605
5	3.433	3.352	3.274	3.127	2.991	2.864	2.745	2.689	2.436	2.220	2.035	1.876	1.737
6	3.889	3.784	3.685	3.498	3.326	3.167	3.020	2.951	2.643	2.385	2.168	1.983	1.824
7	4.288	4.160	4.039	3.812	3.605	3.416	3.242	3.161	2.802	2.508	2.263	2.057	1.883
8	4.639	4.487	4.344	4.078	3.837	3.619	3.421	3.329	2.925	2.598	2.331	2.109	1.922
9	4.946	4.772	4.607	4.303	4.031	3.786	3.566	3.463	3.019	2.665	2.379	2.144	1.948
10	5.216	5.019	4.833	4.494	4.192	3.923	3.682	3.571	3.092	2.715	2.414	2.168	1.965
11	5.453	5.234	5.029	4.656	4.327	4.035	3.776	3.656	3.147	2.752	2.438	2.185	1.977
12	5.660	5.421	5.197	4.793	4.439	4.127	3.851	3.725	3.190	2.779	2.456	2.196	1.985
13	5.842	5.583	5.342	4.910	4.533	4.203	3.912	3.780	3.223	2.799	2.469	2.204	1.990
14	6.002	5.724	5.468	5.008	4.611	4.265	3.962	3.824	3.249	2.814	2.478	2.210	1.993
15	6.142	5.847	5.575	5.092	4.675	4.315	4.001	3.859	3.268	2.825	2.484	2.214	1.995
16	6.265	5.954	5.668	5.162	4.730	4.357	4.033	3.887	3.283	2.834	2.489	2.216	1.997
17	6.373	6.047	5.749	5.222	4.775	4.391	4.059	3.910	3.295	2.840	2.492	2.218	1.998
18	6.467	6.128	5.818	5.273	4.812	4.419	4.080	3.928	3.304	2.844	2.494	2.219	1.999
19	6.550	6.198	5.877	5.316	4.843	4.442	4.097	3.942	3.311	2.848	2.496	2.220	1.999
20	6.623	6.259	5.929	5.353	4.870	4.460	4.110	3.954	3.316	2.850	2.497	2.221	1.999
21	6.687	6.312	5.973	5.384	4.891	4.476	4.121	3.963	3.320	2.852	2.498	2.221	2.000
22	6.743	6.359	6.011	5.410	4.909	4.488	4.130	3.970	3.323	2.853	2.498	2.222	2000
23	6.792	6.399	6.044	5.432	4.925	4.499	4.137	3.976	3.325	2.854	2.499	2.222	2000
24	6.835	6.434	6.073	5.451	4.937	4.507	4.143	3.981	3.327	2.855	2.499	2.222	2000
25	6.873	6.464	6.097	5.467	4.948	4.514	4.147	3.985	3.329	2.856	2.499	2.222	2000
30	7.003	6.566	6.177	5.517	4.979	4.534	4.160	3.995	3.332	2.857	2500	2.222	2000
35	7.070	6.617	6.215	5.539	4.992	4.541	4.164	3.998	3.333	2.857	2500	2.222	2000
40	7.105	6.642	6.233	5.548	4.997	4.544	4.166	3.999	3.333	2.857	2500	2.222	2000
45	7.123	6.654	6.242	5.552	4.999	4.545	4.166	4.000	3.333	2.857	2500	2.222	2000
50	7.133	6.661	6.246	5.554	4.999	4.545	4.167	4.000	3.333	2.857	2.500	2.222	2.000

Index